The Development of Western Music
A HISTORY

The Development of Western Music
A HISTORY

K Marie Stolba

Professor of Music
Indiana University-Purdue University at Fort Wayne

 Wm. C. Brown Publishers

Book Team

Editor *Meredith M. Morgan*
Developmental Editor *Raphael Kadushin*
Production Editor *Kennie Harris*
Designer *David C. Lansdon*
Art Editor *Barbara J. Grantham*
Photo Research Editor *Michelle Oberhoffer*
Permissions Editor *Vicki Krug*
Visuals Processor *Joyce E. Watters*

 Wm. C. Brown Publishers

President *G. Franklin Lewis*
Vice President, Editor-in-Chief *George Wm. Bergquist*
Vice President, Director of Production *Beverly Kolz*
Vice President, National Sales Manager *Bob McLaughlin*
Director of Marketing *Thomas E. Doran*
Marketing Communications Manager *Edward Bartell*
Marketing Manager *Kathleen Nietzke*
Production Editorial Manager *Colleen A. Yonda*
Production Editorial Manager *Julie A. Kennedy*
Publishing Services Manager *Karen J. Slaght*
Manager of Visuals and Design *Faye M. Schilling*

Cover illustration by Alex Boies.

Library of Congress Catalog Card Number: 88–71254

ISBN 0–697–00182–2

Printed in the United States of America by Wm. C. Brown Publishers, 2460 Kerper Boulevard, Dubuque, IA 52001

10 9 8 7 6 5 4 3 2 1

S. D. G.

Contents

Contents

Eminent Composers of the Early Eighteenth Century 387

Eighteenth-Century Pre-Classical Music 429

The Classic Era 475

From Classicism to Romanticism 535

Contents

Insights

Preface

Since the time of Pierre Michon, known as Abbé Bourdelot (1610–85), interested persons have gathered information preparatory to writing the history of music "from the earliest times down to the present day." And from 1690, when Wolfgang Printz brought out his *Historische Beschreibung der edelen Sing-und-Klingkunst. . . ,* histories of music have been written and published. Over the centuries the quality of this kind of publication has improved a great deal; some histories on the market today are quite good. Why, then, write another? There are several reasons. Historians, musicologists, and even archaeologists continue to delve into the past in a seemingly insatiable quest for knowledge. Their research broadens the spectrum; their finds cast new light on persons, places, and productions. This necessitates repainting the panorama to include new features, alter shadings to conform to facts, and remove details no longer pertinent. The result is a historical picture more meaningful, more enlightening, and, it is hoped, more comprehensible to the observer. This new account— *The Development of Western Music: A History*— incorporates data from recent research in a number of areas.

As a student, I noticed that most music history texts lacked certain features that seemed to be normal components of general histories; as an educator, I can still make the same observation. Maps are vital to any historical study, and chronologies and comparative charts that summarize concisely the main developments of an era should be included in specialized histories as well as in generalized ones. Such items are features of this music history text.

Music is not a cloistered art. It reflects and is directly affected by contemporary conditions and world affairs. Therefore, a music history must take into account important events in areas other than music. In this book, most of the chapters commence with a general historical overview, and each chapter concludes with a summary of the developments in music discussed therein. Chronologies, in the form of charts, place musical developments in proper perspective with world events and thus help present a true picture of the relationship between music and government, politics, economics, science, literature, art, etc. Thirty-two color plates correlate artworks with specific compositions and/or historical developments in music.

A history text should be interesting to read, as well as accurate and informative. As history was being made, the participants were interested in and probably excited about what they were doing; the same kind of interest and enthusiasm should pervade the study of the history they made. Music history is not an account of dead people in a dull past, but a recounting of the endeavors and accomplishments of persons going about their daily affairs, coping with the demands of earning a living, composing and performing to meet contemporary needs, whether those needs were their own or those of others. Moreover, music history is not merely a study of the arrangement of symbols on staff paper, but a consideration of all that went into making musical compositions that were performed and enjoyed when they were created, and that can be re-created for the same kind of enjoyment in modern performances. Biographies provide glimpses of the conditions under which composers worked and the particular circumstances that prompted them to create specific compositions.

The Development of Western Music: A History traces the development of Western art music from antiquity to the present—from c. 18,000 B.C. into the late 1980s. Throughout the book, the contributions made by women—as authors, composers, copyists, engravers, performers, and patrons—are duly considered. Music in the Americas is introduced in chapter

16, in connection with seventeenth-century instrumental music, and is a regular part of the discussion thereafter. Two and one-half chapters are devoted to twentieth-century music. Included is an account of the technological discoveries, inventions, and advances that enabled avant-garde musicians to create the variety of styles that have colored this century. An abundance of figures and music examples illustrate the text, and thirty-three "Insights" present interesting and enlightening material closely related to the text.

The historical coverage is full, with headings clearly designating topics under discussion. Instructors who wish to omit certain sections, e.g., Scandinavian music, Canadian music, or the music of Latin America, should find it relatively easy to do so.

Analyses of a sufficient number of compositions are included in the text to represent a composer's output and style characteristics, and to permit the instructor to select those he or she wishes to emphasize.

Titles of compositions are stated in the original language with English translation in parentheses, except for Cyrillic Slavic and Russian titles, which are given only in English. The date of composition and, where appropriate, the instrumentation of the work are stated when the composition is first mentioned. A few abbreviations are used: LU for *Liber Usualis,* KJV for King James Version of *The Bible,* and standard abbreviations for voices and instruments.

Auxiliary to the history text is *The Development of Western Music: An Anthology,* in two volumes, whose selections are recorded and are obtainable in LP, CD, or cassette form. In the text, the letters DWMA followed by a number indicate the presence and location of a composition in the Anthology.

Instead of a separate glossary, terms, when introduced, are presented in boldfaced type, then defined. A Guide to the Correct Pronunciation of Church Latin is in the Appendix. The Select Bibliography is designed to provide for students' further reading and research on the subject matter presented in the text.

Available ancillaries include a set of transparencies, an Instructor's Manual with Test Item File, and a computerized TestPak for use with Apple, McIntosh, IBM, and IBM 3.5 computers.

Particular thanks are due to Robert P. Roubos, formerly my department chairman at Indiana University–Purdue University at Fort Wayne (IPFW) and currently Director of the School of Music at Southern Illinois University, Carbondale, IL, who insisted that I write this text; to the late Ruth Harrod, who constantly encouraged me during the first stages of the writing; and to Karen Speerstra, who was quick to recognize the worth of the project and to further its publication. Thanks are due also to the many students in my music history classes who urged me to put in writing the interesting details that made music history live for them.

It is impossible to name all of those who contributed to this project. From time to time, several of my colleagues have given me the benefit of their specialized knowledge and have loaned me music from their personal libraries. Many librarians assisted in procuring materials for my research. Great demands have been made upon the Music Library at Indiana University, Bloomington, and thanks are due especially to R. Michael Fling, Music Librarian, who responded promptly to my numerous requests for materials. Reference librarians at Helmke Library, IPFW, and at Allen County Public Library were helpful, efficient, and generous with their time. I wish to express my gratitude to Kenneth Balthaser, who made available the services of the technicians at the IPFW Learning Resource Center for the preparation of specialized illustrations, particularly, cartographer and graphics artist Melvin E. Stewart, graphics artist Roberta Shadle, and photographers James Whitcraft and Elmer Denman.

I wish to express my appreciation to my editors at Wm. C. Brown Publishers, who carefully considered my requests, and to Alex Boies, who produced a collage that incorporated all of the items I requested in a cover design. I am cognizant of and greatly appreciate the work of the many reviewers who read these chapters in their various stages, offered valuable suggestions, and occasionally made pertinent comments that sent my thoughts in new directions, sometimes in ways they probably had not intended.

K Marie Stolba
Fort Wayne, Indiana

Reviewers

Hermione Abbey

James R. Anthony
University of Arizona–Tucson

Raymond Barr
University of Miami

J. Peter Burkholder
University of Wisconsin–Madison

W. C. Greckel
Indiana University S.E.

Doreen Grimes
Angelo State University

Paul Hilbrich
University of Wisconsin–Eau Claire

Dale Monson
University of Michigan–Ann Arbor

Robert D. Reynolds
Arizona State University at Tempe

Edward R. Rutschman
Western Washington University

Edwin Schatkowski
Kutztown University

Charles H. Sherman
University of Missouri–Columbia

Robert Stewart
California State University–Fullerton

Thomas F. Taylor
University of Michigan–Ann Arbor

The Development
of Western Music
A HISTORY

The system of pitch identification used throughout this book is:

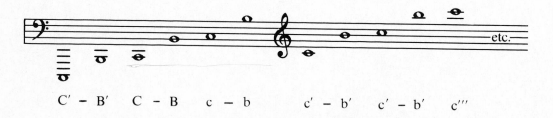

C′ – B′   C – B   c – b   c′ – b′   c′ – b′   c′′′

Prelude

Music has existed from time immemorial. Archaeologists have unearthed traces of music in the most ancient civilizations, ethnomusicologists have found it in even the most primitive tribal cultures, and scientists have claimed it is present in space. Yet no one has been able to establish precisely when, where, why, or how music originated.

In both Oriental and Occidental cultures there are numerous assertions and inferences that music is of divine origin. Plato placed the origin of music in creation, and numerous legends present music as the gift of the gods or the invention of one of them. Some peoples, for example, the Hebrews and the Hindus, firmly root music's origin in their sacred scriptures. The Hindus believe Brahma, the creator, placed music in the Vedas, their four sacred writings, to be interpreted and revealed to man by an ascetic brotherhood called Munis. Vedic psalmody, a type of sung recitation, was an essential element in the worship of the Aryans in India approximately 1500 years before the Christian era. The Hebrews account for the origin of music by tracing in the scrolls of the Torah the genealogy from Cain, son of Adam and Eve, through the seventh generation to Jubal, who was "the father of all such as handle the lyre and pipe [flute]" (Genesis 4:17–21). The Hebrew words used for those instruments account for both serene and sensuous music, and the instrument types are comparable with those of the ancient Greeks.

Our noun "music" was originally an adjective derived from *Muse*, a Greek term denoting any one of nine goddesses who collectively presided over song and prompted the memory and who individually governed a particular realm of literature, art, or science. Apollo, guardian of the Muses, was god of "music." He played the lyre, which Hermes (Mercury) supposedly invented by boring nine holes into each end of a tortoise shell and threading cords through them, one cord rep-

A relief of a musician discovered in Khafajah, Mesopotamia; dated c. 2000 B.C. *(From John J. Davis,* Paradise to Prison. *Copyright © 1975 Baker Book House, Ada, MI. Reprinted by permission.)*

resenting each Muse. It was natural, then, that the representative instrument of the Greek cult of Apollo was the lyre.

According to Greek mythology, Athena (Minerva), patroness of arts and trades, invented the *aulos,* which she threw to earth when Eros (Cupid) taunted her because she made faces when playing it. This was the instrument associated with the orgiastic cult of Dionysus (Bacchus), god of wine in all its aspects—social, benevolent, and intoxicating.

A more recent theory proposes that in all cultures music originated in a similar manner, from a universal source (**monogenesis**). The investigations of these theorists are comparable with linguists' search for a universal source of language through a study of features common to all tongues. Certainly, the fact that ethnomusicologists report finding basic similarities in the musical beginnings of various cultures in widely separated parts of the globe lends credence to such a theory. There is also the possibility that music originated from the desire of primitive people to communicate, vocally or instrumentally, with their neighbors; or, that primitive people first sang because they wanted to imitate the sound of a bird or other creature; or, that in exultation or sorrow a primitive person produced sounds that relieved emotions and that were pleasurable to repeat.

Each of the theories concerning the origin of music—whether fact, fiction, or still unproven scientific investigation—has its place in the history of Western music. Mythology, legends, and the musics of ancient cultures have influenced Western art music significantly. Therefore, this historical account of the development of Western music shall commence with a consideration of our musical heritage from ancient peoples.

Chapter

1

Heritage from Antiquity

Our heritage of written music from antiquity is meager, and much of this **primary source** material is fragmentary and undecipherable. The few pieces to be located were fairly recent finds and consist mainly of vocal music. Archaeologists are constantly turning up evidence of music in very ancient civilizations—several different instruments made from mammoth bones c. 18,000 B.C. were discovered in the Ukraine—but rarely is actual music found.

Near Eastern Music

In 1975 archaeologists working at Tell Mardikh in Mesopotamia unearthed more than 15,000 clay tablets covered with cuneiform writing in Sumerian and Eblaite script. The city-state Ebla was thriving in 2400 B.C., but c. 2000 B.C. it was destroyed by a holocaust that preserved the city's history by baking the script-covered clay tablets. Scholars have deciphered a good deal of the writing and have found that one tablet contains a list of professions. From another tablet it has been learned that garments were furnished to "great" and "small" singers, but no actual music has been located. In Paris, Suzanne Haïk-Vantoura has transcribed the curious little marks that appear both above and below the words in some scrolls containing the Hebrew Old Testament of the Bible. These marks resemble the letters V and S lying sidewise, horseshoes, slanting lines, and clusters of dots, and correspond to melodic formulas or symbols known as *ta'amim* (fig. 1.1). The Bible verses Mme Vantoura sang and recorded may be more than 3,000 years old. Probably, Hebrew *ta'amim* symbols served as a model for some of the earliest notation of Christian church chants.

Psalm 137

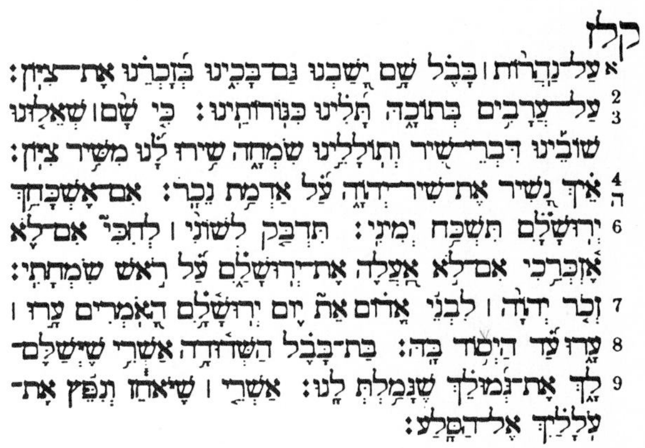
קלז
א עַל נַהֲרוֹת ׀ בָּבֶל שָׁם יָשַׁבְנוּ גַּם־בָּכִינוּ בְּזָכְרֵנוּ אֶת־צִיּוֹן׃
2 3 עַל־עֲרָבִים בְּתוֹכָהּ תָּלִינוּ כִּנֹּרוֹתֵינוּ׃ כִּי שָׁם ׀ שְׁאֵלוּנוּ
שׁוֹבֵינוּ דִּבְרֵי־שִׁיר וְתוֹלָלֵינוּ שִׂמְחָה שִׁירוּ לָנוּ מִשִּׁיר צִיּוֹן׃
4 ה אֵיךְ נָשִׁיר אֶת־שִׁיר־יְהוָה עַל אַדְמַת נֵכָר׃ אִם־אֶשְׁכָּחֵךְ
6 יְרוּשָׁלָם תִּשְׁכַּח יְמִינִי׃ תִּדְבַּק לְשׁוֹנִי ׀ לְחִכִּי אִם־לֹא
אֶזְכְּרֵכִי אִם־לֹא אַעֲלֶה אֶת־יְרוּשָׁלַם עַל רֹאשׁ שִׂמְחָתִי׃
7 זְכֹר יְהוָה ׀ לִבְנֵי אֱדוֹם אֵת יוֹם יְרוּשָׁלָם הָאֹמְרִים עָרוּ ׀
8 עָרוּ עַד הַיְסוֹד בָּהּ׃ בַּת־בָּבֶל הַשְּׁדוּדָה אַשְׁרֵי שֶׁיְשַׁלֶּם־
9 לָךְ אֶת־גְּמוּלֵךְ שֶׁגָּמַלְתְּ לָנוּ׃ אַשְׁרֵי ׀ שֶׁיֹּאחֵז וְנִפֵּץ אֶת־
עֹלָלַיִךְ אֶל־הַסָּלַע׃

Figure 1.1 Psalm 137, from Hebrew Scriptures, with *ta'amim* markings. *(Source: Psalm 137, "By the Waters of Babylon," Hebrew Scriptures.)*

B.C. 2500	2000	1500	1000	B.C. 500
Sumerian City-states	c. 1790–1750 Babylon: Hammurabi	c. 1330 Egypt: Tutankhamen Pharaoh	c. 1000 Israel: King David *Psalms*	753 Rome founded / 660 Byzantium founded
c. 2300 Ebla: singers	c. 1760 Code of Laws	c. 1500 India: Vedic psalmody		700———510 Etruscan domination of north-central Italy
		c. 1400 Ugarit: "Hymn to Nikal" harps	c. 790 Homer *Iliad*	586 Sakadas programmatic aulos solo at Pythian games

B.C. 500	400	300	200	100	A.D. 1
480————————323 Greek Classic Period					4 Birth of Jesus
515–497 Pythagoras fl. pitch proportions	400————280 Etruscan power declines in Italy		200————30 Rome conquers Hellenistic lands		
c. 500 Pindar fl. Odes			c. 150 Delphic Hymns		44 Julius Caesar assassinated
			Epitaph of Seikilos		27 Vergil *Aeneid*
	460————406 Euripides fl. plays with choral music		190——159 Terence plays with music		
	448————385 Aristophanes				
		380 Plato *Republic*			
		350 Aristotle *Politics*			
		330 Aristoxenus *Harmonic Elements*			

The music considered the most ancient preserved example is a song in the Hurrian language, inscribed in wedge-shaped cuneiform characters on both sides of a clay tablet unearthed in Syria in the early 1950s (fig. 1.2). Musicologists and Assyriologists have determined that the tablet survives from the ancient civilization of Ugarit (modern Ras-Shamra; fig. 1.3) in the Near East. The cuneiform writing contains the text of a hymn to Nikal, wife of the moon god, and instructions for performing it (DWMA1). Unfortunately, cracks in the tablet have obliterated a small portion of the text. The singer is accompanied by harp, and the harmony includes many thirds and sixths, as well as a few fourths and one fifth. Another tablet provides instruction for tuning a harp.

(a)

(b)

Figure 1.2 Hurrian hymn to Nikal, in cuneiform notation on (*a*) front and (*b*) back of clay tablet from Ugarit dated c. 1400 B.C. *(National Museum, Damascus, Syria.)*

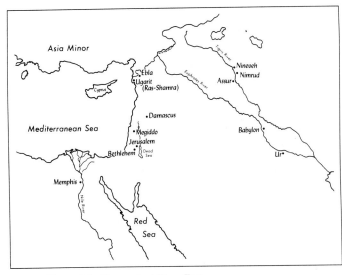

Figure 1.3 The ancient Near East.

Greek Music

Approximately 15 examples of ancient Greek music survive, all from comparatively late periods in Greek history. The most important of these are:

1. Two *Delphic Hymns to Apollo* (c. 130 B.C.). Both hymns are incomplete because the stones on which they are incised have been damaged. The *First Delphic Hymn* is the most extensive example of Greek music we have and is written in the "vocal" notation of that era (fig. 1.4; DWMA2). The *Second Delphic Hymn*, ascribed to Limenius of Athens, is in "instrumental" notation. Both notation types use Greek characters as symbols in a kind of tablature. Probably, these hymns were sung by a priestess at the Delphic oracle of Apollo.

Heritage from Antiquity

Figure 1.4 *First Delphic Hymn,* in ancient Greek notation incised in stone dated c. 130 B.C. *(National Archaeological Museum, Delphi, Greece.)*

Figure 1.5 *Epitaph of Seikilos,* in ancient Greek notation incised in tomb stele. *(Copenhagen, Danish National Museum.)*

2. *Epitaph of Seikilos* (second century B.C. or later). This *skolion,* or drinking song, carved into a tombstone, was discovered near Tralles in Asia Minor in 1883. The short song is complete, with every syllable of text set to music, and rhythmic signs chiseled above pitches (fig. 1.5; DWMA3).

3. *Hymn to the Muse* (actually two poems), *Hymn to the Sun* (DWMA4), and *Hymn to Nemesis* (fig. 1.6). The latter is attributed to Mesomedes (d. A.D. 138) of Crete. These hymns were located by Girolamo Mei among ancient Greek writings in archives at the Vatican and were sent by him in a letter written to Vincenzo Galilei, who published them untranscribed in his *Dialogo della musica antica et moderna* (Dialogue about ancient and modern music; 1581), along with several of Mei's letters.

Papyrus fragments in Greek notation, probably written down in the third century A.D., were located at Oxyrhynchos, Egypt, in the nineteenth century (fig. 1.7). One of them contains the earliest notated example of a Christian hymn.

Included among other extant papyrus fragments are some lines from Euripides's tragedy *Orestes* with music from a choral antistrophe (the second of two paired verses) written down sometime between 250 and 150 B.C.; a portion of a paean to Apollo; some lines, presumably from a tragedy, concerning the suicide of Ajax the elder; and some bits of instrumental music. Also, Friedrich Bellermann included in *Anonymi scriptio de musica* (Anonymous writings about music; 1841) some Greek instrumental music by an unidentified composer.

These items constitute the stockpile of primary resource material available for a study of Greek music—items that were all located after 1575. Fortunately, our knowledge of Greek music is not limited to these few extant pieces of music. **Secondary sources** are available for consultation: surviving artifacts such as vases decorated with paintings of persons holding instruments or performing on them, actual musical instruments, literary writings, and treatises. Scholars have diligently studied these materials and have pieced together a picture of the Greek view of music, its place in society, and a little about the theoretical processes to which it was subjected. Admittedly, this collage is neither complete nor definitive.

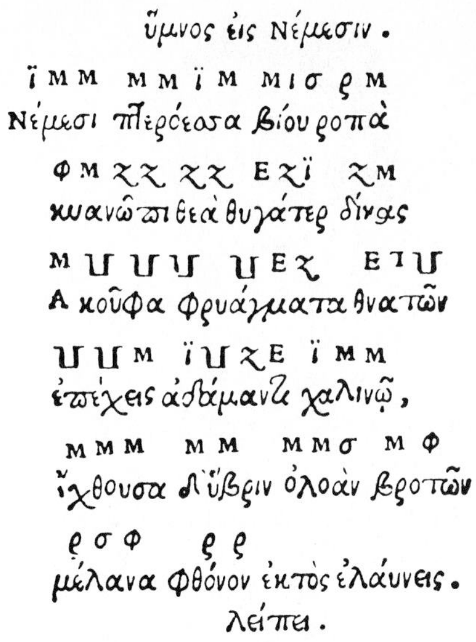

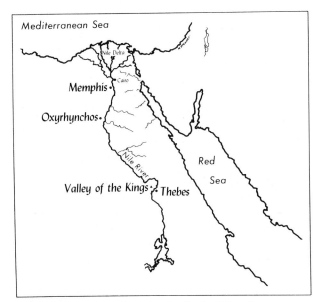

ὕμνος εἰς Νέμεσιν.

ῗ Μ Μ   Μ Μ ῗ Μ   Μ ῗ σ ϱ Μ

Νέμεσι πτερόεσσα βίου ῥοπὰ

Φ Μ ᗱᗱ ᗱᗱ Ε ᗱῗ ᗱ Μ

κυανῶπι θεὰ θυγάτερ δίκας

Μ ᑌ ᑌ ᑌ ᑌ Ε ᗱ   Ε ῗ ᑌ

Α κοῦφα φρυάγματα θνατῶν

ᑌ ᑌ Μ ῗ ᑌ ᗱ Ε ῗ Μ Μ

ἐπέχεις ἀδάμαντι χαλινῷ,

Μ Μ Μ   Μ Μ   Μ Μ σ Μ Φ

ἔχθουσα δ᾽ ὕβριν ὀλοὰν βροτῶν

ϱ σ Φ   ϱ ϱ

μέλανα φθόνον ἐκτὸς ἐλαύνεις.

λείπει.

Figure 1.6 *Hymn to Nemesis,* attributed to Mesomedes, as printed in V. Galilei's *Dialogo. (Source: Vincenzo Galilei, Dialogo della musica antico et della moderna, 1581.)*

Figure 1.8 Interior of a white kylix: Apollo holding lyra and pouring libations. *(National Archaeological Museum, Delphi, Greece.)*

Figure 1.7 Location of Oxyrhynchos in the Nile valley.

Musical Instruments

In ancient Greece, vocal music was preferred and musical virtuosity was discouraged. Though instrumental solos were comparatively rare, instrumental music was functional, and several types of instruments were in use.

The main string instruments were the *lyra* (fig. 1.8), used by amateurs, and the *kithara* (fig. 1.9), favored by professionals. Basically, the two instruments were of similar construction, each having a resonator from which projected two curved arms connected by a crossbar. A variable number of gut strings (from 3 to 11 on the kithara) were stretched from the resonator across a bridge to the crossbar. The soundbox of the lyra was a tortoise-shell bowl topped with a skin belly; the kithara's resonator was a square, rather flat, wooden box. The strings were plucked with either the fingers or a plectrum. In performance, the lyra was held tilted, but the larger and more cumbersome kithara remained more or less upright. It is believed that the player probably used "gapped" tuning (not strictly pentatonic) determined by the requirements of the music, and made whatever adjustments or adaptations were necessary by stopping the strings.

Figure 1.9 Greek youth playing kithara and singing. *(Detail from vase in Metropolitan Museum of Art, New York City.)*

Figure 1.10 *Aulos* player wearing *phorbeia.*

The most important wind instrument was the *aulos,* a double-reed instrument composed of a pair of even pipes with (usually) four finger holes each. The player held one pipe in each hand and inserted the reeds into his mouth through slits in a wide leather band (*phorbeia*) that covered his mouth and was fastened at the back of his head (fig. 1.10). The *phorbeia* provided support both for steadying the pipes and for the inflated cheeks of the performer. The aulos-player probably controlled pitches in much the same manner as a modern oboist—by the devices of "lipping" and over- or under-blowing the pitches (colorplate 1).

The *syrinx* was a shepherd's pipe formed by fastening together reed pipes of equal length to form a raftlike shape. These reeds were closed at one end and were stopped with wax at graduated intervals so that different pitches might be produced from the individual reeds. From 3 to 13 reeds might be included; generally, 7 were used.

Brass instruments served military purposes but were considered secondary to the aulos. They included the *salpinx,* a straight trumpet, and the *keras,* a curved brass horn. Both had mouthpieces of horn.

Around the third century B.C. the *hydraulos* (*hydōr,* water; *aulos,* pipe) was invented. In this early type of organ, the wind supply was regulated by the weight of the water in a reservoir partially filled with water.

Percussion instruments included the *tympanon,* a two-headed frame drum; *kymbala,* cymbals approximately 12 inches in diameter, played in pairs, especially used in orgiastic rites; and *krotala,* clappers constructed in pairs. The *kroupalon* was not so much an instrument as a conductor's device. It consisted of a wooden clapper attached to a sandal that was worn on the player's right foot; it served percussively to beat time.

The Greek View of Music

The Greeks regarded music from three different aspects: (1) as an abstract science, a branch of mathematics whose elements could be computed; (2) as a power, a shaping force that could influence both the individual and the state; and (3) as an art, to be understood, enjoyed, and practiced by the citizens as intelligent amateurs but not as professionals. Music was associated with melody, words, and rhythm including dancing; instrumental accompaniment to song was duplication of the melodic line with occasional heterophony but without counterpoint to or chordal accompaniment of the melody. This view of music and these features of the music itself seem to have remained constant through the ages. However, it would be erroneous to assert that musical conditions were identical in all periods of ancient Greek history. A brief résumé of music in ancient Greece is, therefore, apropos.

From the eighth century B.C. poets associated their lines with music, called the sections of their epics "cantos," included in their verses various references to music, and doubtless presented their poems (wholly or partially) in song. Homer, in the *Iliad,* treated music as an accomplishment of both gods and men; in the *Odyssey,* the power of song was invoked to staunch the bleeding of a wound. Even Vergil, writing in Latin some centuries later, commenced his *Aeneid* with the words *Arma virumque canō . . .*—"I sing of arms and the man. . . ." There is no reason to doubt that Vergil sang his epic, even though no actual music survives. Music was created anew for each performance, so preservation of notation for any single rendition was unnecessary.

At Pythia (Delphi) in the sixth century B.C. games were designed for competition in music and poetry. Records indicate that at the Pythian Games held in 586 B.C. a person named Sakadas was awarded a prize for playing on the *aulos* a *nome* (an instrumental solo) describing the fight between Apollo and the dragon. Also, the **strophic dithyramb** stems from the sixth century B.C., when it was used by a circular chorus of 50 males to commemorate in song and dance the birth of Dionysus. (A strophic dithyramb is a wildly emotional poem constructed in verses, according to a special formal pattern.) This poetic form, combined with song and the sounds of the aulos, remained a part of the cult of Dionysus from that time; in combination with choric dance it gave rise to that drama known as tragedy.

Skolia (singular, *skolion*) were sung by men at drinking parties, each man in turn contributing a line as he quaffed a goblet of wine, then passed the responsibility zigzag (hence the name, *skolion,* zigzag) across the table to a colleague.

In Aeolia, where Athens was important as city-state, Pindar created odes that were performed with kithara accompaniment. He used the terms "Aeolian" and "Dorian" interchangeably when describing music. By the end of the fifth century B.C. the term "Aeolian" had virtually disappeared from musical use, and the prevalent types of tunings were Dorian and Phrygian. The Dorian was diatonic, stable, and classic; associated with the ode and the kithara (or lyra), the Dorian mode was used to create lyric music for the worship of Apollo. The Phrygian, described as "chromatic" and considerably less stable, was combined with the somewhat wavering and more pliable tones of the aulos to present through the dithyramb the ecstatic music of Dionysian rites.

The Athenians frequented the theater to witness or to participate in performances of tragedy and comedy. These dramas incorporated a citizen chorus composed of amateurs whose knowledge of music and choreography was limited to training received as a part of the three years of such education required by the state. The tones of a single aulos played by a professional supported such a chorus, which performed a melodic line either in unison or in octaves. Euripides, in his later plays, and Aristophanes reduced the size of the chorus and inserted pieces of lyric **monody** (solo song) to be sung by an actor. From time to time, in composing lyrics for these songs both Euripides and Aristophanes deviated from the classic norm by writing **through-composed** rather than **strophic** monodies. (A through-composed setting has new music for each line of a poem; in a strophic song all stanzas are sung to the same music.) No music for these survives; doubtless the actor-singer improvised the melodies. Classic Greek comedy served also as a vehicle for music criticism. Directly and in parody Aristophanes inserted into some of his plays (in *Peace; Wasps; Birds;* and *Frogs*) lines that voiced his displeasure with the music being presented by some of his contemporaries. For example, in *Frogs,* he parodied Euripides's manner of repeating syllables of a word, a kind of musical stuttering.

In the fourth century B.C., the virtuoso performer rose to prominence, but, though admired, he was not accorded high social standing. The aristocratic Greek was careful not to pursue music to the extent that he was considered a professional. Choral singing was still taught to boys, who at that time received only two

11

years of required music education, but adult participation in music declined so much that it became necessary to import professionals to serve in the "citizen" chorus.

Philosophy and the Doctrine of *Ethos*

Greek philosophers writing in the fourth century B.C. said a great deal about music—what it had been, what it was in their time, and what they wished it to be. Plato, in *Laws,* wrote about the changes that had occurred in music: (1) The classic purity of former times had succumbed to popular taste; (2) professional virtuosi who adhered to traditional practices were scorned by the public who preferred the vulgarity of "modern" music; and (3) musical forms—prayers (*hymnia*), dirges, paeans, dithyrambs, and others— once held inviolate had been carelessly intermingled. For Plato, the "sung poem" was the important part of music, not the strumming of the lyra or kithara that duplicated the melodic line.

In *The Republic,* Plato discoursed on the organization of a utopia in which music would build harmonious personalities and calm human passions, and gymnastics would build healthy bodies. Music and gymnastics were divine gifts to mankind for the express purpose of providing the proper degree of tension and relaxation to adjust the soul and the body harmoniously. Music without gymnastics would completely dissolve a man's spirit; gymnastics untempered by contact with the Muse would foster in man a beastly nature—violence and savagery. And what constituted musicianship? According to Plato, the most perfect and most harmonious musician was the man who could best blend gymnastics with music and apply them to the soul, not the person who played the kithara well. In Plato's utopia, music and gymnastics would form an important part of the education of boys—an education carefully regulated by the government.

Aristotle discussed in *The Politics* the branches of study to be included in education in the ideal state and justified music as one of these not only because of its value as a leisure pastime, but because it had the power to produce a certain effect on the moral character of the soul. All men should be educated in music, but only the young should take part in it as performers, since professional musicians were considered vulgar people. Older persons should not make music; they should merely listen and judge what they heard.

Athenaeus recorded in *Deipnosophists* daily conversations of the Sophists concerning music, mentioning and commenting upon treatises written by more ancient Greek authors. *Deipnosophists* is especially valuable because Athenaeus specified those treatises by title and author and sometimes quoted from writings that have not survived. The matter of the mysterious power of music to influence and shape character (*ethos*) entered into the Sophists' discussions.

The doctrine of *ethos* received considerable attention from the Greek philosophers. For the Greeks the term *ethos* had a dual meaning: (a) the morals and character of the people, and thus it was related to ethics, and (b) the specific character of a musical mode or tuning that affected the morals and character of the people. The morals and character (*ethos*) of the people were important, for the welfare of the state was determined by the ethics of her people. Music, through its influential power, was a shaping force in determining the nature of the moral character of the populace; therefore, music should be included in education and should be regulated carefully by the state. Music's power to affect persons favorably or adversely was derived from its structure— music was constructed according to the same mathematical principles by which the universe had been formed. Thus, music stood in direct relationship to the universe as microcosm to macrocosm. The so-called golden equations written down by Plato in *Timaeus* support the philosophy that God created the universe musico-mathematically, using the same proportions that determine the intervals of the musical scale.

Athenaeus wrote that each mode possessed a specific character (*ethos*) or feeling (*pathos*). Any philosopher who devoted any space whatsoever to music gave some consideration to the peculiar attributes that each of the different modes possessed and that each was capable of passing on to listeners. The various rhythms affected persons in a similar manner, and instrumental timbres could depress, stabilize, or excite performers and auditors. For example, it was thought that the Mixolydian mode produced mournful and restrained reactions; the Lydian was considered effeminate; the Dorian was sober yet intense and fostered composure, bravery, and virility, while, according to Aristotle, the Phrygian and the aulos were both violently exciting and emotional, and were especially suited for Bacchic versification, the dithyramb, and choric dance. Aristotle stated also that it was not easy to explain precisely what potency music expressed, but it was clear that the various kinds of melodies, rhythms, and tunings affected persons in dramatically different ways. Music was peculiar among the arts in that it alone had the ability to influence character, and exposure to certain modal tunings over long periods of time brought about the characteristics of that mode in the nature of the listener. Because of its stabilizing and virile attributes, the Dorian was the preferred tuning and the one thought to produce in citizens the most desirable character. Inasmuch as the factors of music are melody and rhythm, Aristotle wrote, music with a "good" rhythm and a "good" melody was to be preferred. Incidentally, music could help in defeating an enemy, for by exposing the enemy to music with weakening attributes one could weaken his defenses. (No one mentioned what might happen to the performers.)

Music of the Spheres

The association of music with astronomy and the relationship of certain modes with certain heavenly bodies was a natural outgrowth of the classification of music as one of the mathematical sciences: arithmetic, geometry, astronomy, and music—the four sciences that later became the *quadrivium* of the university curriculum. In *The Republic,* Plato wrote about the "music of the spheres"—a phrase and a topic that would be taken up in later centuries by several authors, including Boethius and Shakespeare. Nor would the idea be lost in the twentieth century—Paul Hindemith's *Die Harmonie der Welt* (The harmony of the world) expressed it symphonically in three movements whose titles were derived from classifications of music in Boethius's treatise. Claudius Ptolemy (second century A.D.), in his *Harmonics,* presented first the theoretical principles of music, then applied the same ratios and proportions to a consideration of astronomic features of the cosmos.

Figure 1.11 Guido d'Arezzo, *seated at left,* demonstrates use of monochord marked with pitches of the scale from Γ through a (modern G – a'), including both square and round b. Miniature in twelfth-century MS Wn 51, fol.35v. *(Osterreichische Nationalbibliothek, Vienna.)*

Greek Music Theory

Much remains to be learned about Greek music theory. There is still confusion and disagreement concerning what has been uncovered so far, but a core of data is regarded as factual.

From the time of Pythagoras of Samos (sixth century B.C.), the Greeks regarded music as a branch of mathematics. Intervals computed mathematically were visibly demonstrated by means of the monochord, a device consisting of a single string stretched, over a movable bridge, across the calibrated upper surface of a long rectangular box (fig. 1.11). Claudius Ptolemy's *Harmonics,* written in the second century A.D., has been called the best scientific and the best arranged treatise on the theory of musical scales that we possess in Greek. Ptolemy was an astronomer and mathematician who, like Pythagoras and Plato, explained the universe as being bound together by mathematico-musical principles.

Rhythm

The rhythm of Greek music was that of its poetry. Quantitative rather than qualitative, it is comparable with the long and short patterns known as "iambic," "trochaic," etc. The matter of stress or accent seems to have been of little importance. For compositions in free verse, such as the skolion of Seikilos, the temporal unit (*chronos*) might be stated above the notation (fig. 1.5). No marking indicated the *chronos protos,* or one beat; a single line ⏤ designated two beats; ⏌ or ⎣ meant three beats; ⎣⏌ four beats; and ⎣⎦ five beats. A complete or partial *lambda* (λ, \) designated a rest.

Tetrachords and Systems

The portions of Aristoxenus's (born c. 360 B.C.) *Harmonics* and *Elements* that survive are the oldest theoretical writings on Greek scales. Aristoxenus systematically presented the theoretical principles of his era, which probably were based to a considerable extent on the teaching of his predecessors. To Aristoxenus, the range of sound was a line like a monochord string, containing pitches, and the distance from one pitch to another was an interval. He divided the octave into six equal tones, the tone into two equal semitones, and the semitone into two equal quarter tones. However, in contrast with the Pythagoreans, who calculated and expressed musical intervals as mathematical ratios, Aristoxenus believed that musical intervals should be measured by the trained ear.

The basis of practical Greek music theory was the **tetrachord,** a descending succession of four tones the highest and lowest of which were a perfect fourth apart. The outer limits of this fundamental four-tone unit, its highest and lowest pitches, remained constant, but the location of the two pitches within these confines was variable. The two inner tones might be arranged in any one of three different patterns to form three different *genera,* or types, of tetrachord: diatonic, chromatic, or enharmonic. The diatonic *genus* exhibited the normal (natural) arrangement of the four tones, the first or highest interval containing two semitones (a whole tone), followed by another whole tone and a semitone (ex. 1.1a). This tone-tone-semitone (T T S) pattern corresponded with the first segment of the characteristic octave of the Greater Perfect System (ex. 1.2).

In the chromatic genus the first interval was expanded to contain three semitones, and the space remaining was divided into two semitones (ex. 1.1b). In the enharmonic genus the first interval was widened

Example 1.1 The three Greek tetrachords: (*a*) diatonic, (*b*) chromatic, and (*c*) enharmonic.

still further to contain four semitones, and the division of the remaining space produced two quarter tones (ex. 1.1c). It is quite possible that in performance this remaining space was sometimes divided unequally, producing microtones of varying proportions rather than two actual quarter tones. Tones such as b♯ and c′ were not identical in Greek theory. The modern piano produces such tones as identical pitches, but wind and brass players can "lip" the tones to differentiate them, and string players can adjust fingers to achieve this.

Tetrachords were combined to form scale patterns. This joining might be disjunct, with the lowest note of one tetrachord being placed just above the highest note of the other, or conjunct, with the lowest note of the upper tetrachord being identical with the highest note of the lower tetrachord. Two diatonic tetrachords joined disjunctly formed a diatonic octave, or diatonic scale (ex. 1.2, central octave e′–e).

Two scale systems were formed: the Greater Perfect System and the Lesser Perfect System (ex. 1.2). The Greater consisted of a two-octave scale formed from two pairs of conjunct tetrachords joined disjunctly, with the neighboring tone A, called *Proslambanomenos,* added as the last pitch. At the center of the system was the note a, called *Mese* ("middle"). Greek nomenclature was a practical terminology. Each tetrachord in the scale system was named in accordance with its position within the system, and each of the pitches within each tetrachord bore a double name indicating the tetrachord to which it belonged and its position within that tetrachord. It should be stressed that these names did *not* designate actual pitch but served merely as terms of reference for locations within the System. The fact that the names were assigned on the basis of the position of the kithara when played, the lowest pitches being at the top of the instrument when held in playing position, explains the peculiarity of the Greek scale patterns seeming to proceed downward from highest pitch to lowest—just the opposite of our modern scales.

Plate 1 Wooden votive tablet, c. 540 B.C., found in cave of Pitsa near Corinth. Among the worshipers in this sacrificial scene are a lyra player and an aulos player wearing a *phorbeia*. *(National Archaeological Museum, Athens.)*

(a)

Plate 2 Hagia Sophia (Church of Holy Wisdom),
Constantinople, c. 1850. (*a*) View of the church from the
southwest. (*b*) Interior of the church. Polychrome lithographs
made by Gaspare Fossati, c. 1850.

(b)

Plate 4 *Sumer is icumen in,* English rota, c. 1250. *(MS Harley 978, folio 11v. British Library, Reference Division, London.)*

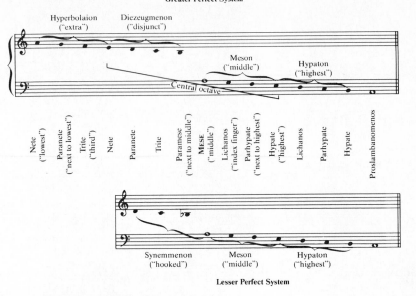

Example 1.2 The Greater Perfect and the Lesser Perfect Systems.

Central within the Greater Perfect System was the octave e′–e, called the Dorian octave or mode, and frequently referred to by modern theorists as the "characteristic octave." Its central location may explain the preference of Plato, Aristotle, and other Greek writers for this particular series of pitches, or arrangement of tones.

The Lesser Perfect System was formed from three conjunct tetrachords plus the *Proslambanomenos.* The top tetrachord (*synnemnon,* "hooked") may be represented by the pitches d′–c′–b♭–a.

Modes or *Tonoi*

No discussion of Greek music theory can be considered complete without some discussion of the matter of modes or *tonoi.* Yet, it must be realized that this is the area of least established fact—the area of greatest confusion and most disagreement. Several theories have been proposed, but all remain suppositions.

One theory presents a mode as a definite pattern of tones and semitones within the compass of an octave and having a definite tonal center. Each mode was individual, i.e., distinctive. Thus, the Dorian scale or

mode proceeded from e′ down to e, the Phrygia[n] d′ down to d, etc., in scale patterns using n[o] matically altered tones (ex. 1.3, column 3[)] Dorian scale presented the sequence of tones [and] semitones (S): T T S T T T S; the Phrygia[n] sented the succession: T S T T T S T; and other[s] had particular successions. This older theory i[s based] on Ptolemy's description of the scale patt[ern] functional position within the Greater Perfect S[ystem,] e.g., the Dorian proceeding from *Nete Diezeu[gmenon]* to *Hypate Meson,* and the Phrygian from [*Nete*] *Diezeugmenon* to *Lichanos Hypaton.* (Ex. 1[.3 gives] the functional names.) It is believed that the [Greeks] did not confine themselves to the tones in th[e sys-] tems or scales as absolute pitches, but that the[se] were relative, thus adjustable to fit the vocal [range of] the singer. However, the arrangement of t[ones and] semitones within a mode was carefully obse[rved.]

A more recent theory, also based on P[tolemy's] *Harmonics,* states that (1) only one octave s[eries was in] practical use, e′–e, the central octave of the [Greater] Perfect System; (2) this served as a char[acteristic] pattern of tones and semitones that was tr[ansposed] upwards and downwards along the pitch[es]

Example 1.3 Comparison: The two interpretations of the Greeks' use of the seven species of *tonoi*.

(a)

Greater Perfect System; and (3) those tones that overflowed the range of the e'–e octave were transferred from the top to the bottom of the scale (or vice versa), so that they would fit within the central octave. This would create a different arrangement of the tones and semitones within that central octave for each adjusted transposed scale. For example, it was stated that the Phrygian sequence was T S T T T S T. According to the newer theory, this pattern was obtained by first transposing the scale pattern of the central (Dorian) octave to the pitches

f♯'–e'–d'–c♯'–b–a–g–f♯
T T S T T T S

and then fitting those pitches within the e'–e octave. This transposition process chromatically altered some

pitches within the e'–e octave and changed the tone-semitone pattern to T S T T T S T or Phrygian:

e'–d'–c♯'–b–a–g–f♯–e
T S T T T S T

The same kind of thing happens in modern music theory when the major scale pattern is transposed round the circle of fifths and the pitches are lowered to usable range. (The *Epitaph of Seikilos* was written in Phrygian mode.)

Ptolemy stated that transposition of the Dorian scale (which he called modulation) was practiced to produce an impression of an altered ethos, by shifting the position of the *Mese* to a higher or lower position within the scale. Transposition of the Dorian scale pattern makes no changes in the melodic scale form;

(b)

Plate 3 Mosaic murals in the apse of the Church of San Vitale, Ravenna, Italy, depicting (*a*) Emperor Justinian I flanked by court officials, military, and priests, and (*b*) Empress Theodora and her attendants, all in Offertory procession of Mass. (© *Art Resource.*)

it is only when the scale is adjusted to fit within the boundaries of the central octave that the Mese shifts to a high or a low position within the e′–e octave. This, according to Ptolemy, is the primary reason for transposing the scale pattern. One can see in the choice of the Dorian octave as the pattern the importance attached to the ethical character (the ethos) of this particular mode. Ptolemy indicated that the term Mese was assigned to the fifth pitch in the octave scale, whatever that pitch might be. (This is at variance with the older belief that the pitch a in the middle of the Greater Perfect System was always designated Mese.) When the transposed scale was adjusted to fit within the central octave, the position of the Mese shifted; it would not always *remain* as fifth pitch. If the Mese were in a low location within the central octave, the ethos of that Mode would be considered "low"; if the Mese happened to be in a high position, the ethos would be considered "high."

The first two columns of example 1.3 illustrate the transposition process and the relocation of the pitches within the central octave. Comparison of columns 2 and 3 reveals that the scales produced by the transposition theory exhibit the same tone-semitone patterns set forth in the older theory. Moreover, whether the pitch of the Mese is considered to change, as in the newer interpretation, or whether it remains constant as the pitch a according to the older theory, its location within the individual scales is identical. The matter of high or low ethos is achieved by either of the two interpretations, and *the end results do not differ.*

It should be noted that the Greek principle of transposition corresponds with a similar practice in modern music theory. Thus, a mode would be comparable to a key, with different modes being created by transposition of the basic octave pattern of tones and semitones (T T S T T T S) to different pitch levels. An even closer similarity is recognizable—the T T S T T T S Dorian (central) octave pattern of the Greeks, if employed to proceed upward in pitch rather than downward as it is believed they used it, is exactly the same as the pattern of our major scale:

e′ d′ c′ b a g f e	c′ d′ e′ f′ g′ a′ b′ c″
T T S T T T S	T T S T T T S
Greek Dorian pattern	**17th–20th c. Major pattern**

Was the central octave in practical use in Greek music? Or was it only theoretical? We are not certain. When one realizes that vocal music was of prime import to the Greeks—that instrumental music was serviceable mainly as accompaniment (i.e., accessory) to the voice or to drama—the matter of vocal range certainly would be of utmost consideration in establishing a practical system of music. Greek music was monophonic, and those melodies and fragments of melodies that have survived seem to lie within the range of an octave (if modern transcriptions of them are correct). Instrumentalists accompanying singers did not merely duplicate the pitches being sung; rather, it is believed they improvised heterophonically. Most of the instruments then in use had a compass of about one octave. Instrument tunings were adjustable, to some degree, and, as more strings were added to the kithara, certainly by stopping strings the player could produce all of the notes in the Greater Perfect System plus chromatically altered pitches and microtones.

It is certain that this transposition (or "modulation") was not done merely to transpose a melody to a range more in accord with a singer's vocal range. Ptolemy made this clear in *Harmonics.* That kind of adjustment was done automatically because the singer merely sang where he could and the instrumentalist retuned his instrument to match the singer's range. Remember that for the Greeks all pitch was relative, not absolute.

Singing by Syllables

The Greeks practiced a very limited manner of singing by syllables. The four syllables τη, τω, τε, τα (pronounced *tay, toh, teh, tah*), in descending order, were used to symbolize the relative position of the tones in the Dorian tetrachord, with *teh-tah* being comparable to our *fa-mi* as representing a semitone. To what extent singing by syllable was used has not been determined.

Music in Ancient Rome

Present knowledge of Rome's early music is based entirely on secondary sources, for no ancient Roman music has been located. Undoubtedly, some indigenous Roman music was produced—there must have been folk music at some time—but nothing seems to have survived. What music the Romans played or sang, how they performed it, and what techniques were employed in its production are unknown to us, but play and sing they did! Literary accounts describe instruments and performances; cues for music (without actual music notation) are included in the prefaces of some of Terence's plays; statutes are of record regulating the number and kinds of musicians permitted to perform on certain occasions, e.g., the number of pipers who might be employed to provide music at a funeral; artists depicted in fresco, relief, and mosaic, various types of musical instruments as well as performers playing instruments; and some actual instruments have been found. It seems likely that when performing the musicians either improvised or relied on memory, as none of the artistic depictions or literary accounts indicate the presence of notated music at a performance. Nor do any of the writings divulge information concerning the techniques used in playing the instruments.

Rome was a conqueror, and as the Romans subdued nations they borrowed from those cultures items of value, many of which were renamed, adapted, and developed so that they became, in a sense, Roman. Musically, Rome was indebted to the Etruscans, the Greeks, and peoples of Near Eastern lands; borrowings from them are apparent in the instruments Romans used.

Musical Instruments

Though vocal music reigned supreme, a variety of instruments existed in ancient Rome. Aerophones included the animal-horn *bucina,* and several instruments made from bronze: the *tuba,* a type of long, straight trumpet (made in sections that fit together) equipped with a conical mouthpiece; the large G-shaped *cornu,* also with conical mouthpiece; and the J-shaped *lituus* (fig. 1.12). Both cornu and lituus were of Etruscan origin.

Graduated lengths of true reeds bound together formed the Pan pipes, or *syrinx.* Double reeds comprised the *tibia,* as the Romans called the Greek aulos, and the Phrygian pipes. The latter consisted of a pair of uneven pipes, the right instrument being straight, and the left instrument being longer and J-shaped, terminating in an upturned bell made from horn.

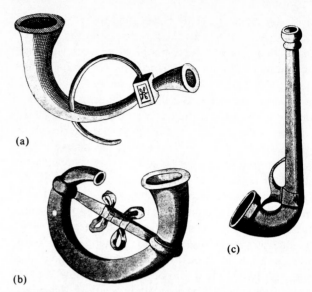

Figure 1.12 Roman instruments: (*a*) *bucina,* (*b*) *cornu,* and (*c*) *lituus. (From Romain Goldron,* Ancient and Oriental Music. *Copyright © 1968 H. S. Stuttman Co., Inc., New York, NY.)*

Both *hydraulos* and pneumatic organs were used. Harps of various kinds and sizes existed, including the Greek lyra and kithara; the latter was the instrument soloists preferred. However, at the hands of the Romans the kithara assumed much larger proportions than the original Greek instrument bearing the same name.

Numerous percussion instruments were employed, including cymbals, tambourine, drums, and rattles of various kinds. The *scabellum,* like the Greek kroupalon a kind of wooden clapper attached to the player's foot, percussively served to beat time.

Music in Roman Life

Music was a part of everyday life in Rome, where musicians seem to have enjoyed a rather high social status. Trade guilds established during the reign of Numa, second king of Rome, placed pipers first in the hierarchy, with tuba and cornu players ranking second. Pipers participated in sacred rites; tuba players supplied ceremonial music for imperial festivities, occasions of honor, and gladiatorial games; the bronze cornu and tuba were assigned definite military functions. Although, as mentioned previously, pipers provided music at funerals, it would seem that trumpeters also assumed some function at such affairs. The colloquialism *ad tubicines mittas* (send for the trumpeters) was indicative of an impending funeral.

The Capitoline Games, founded by Domitian around the end of the first century, provided competitions every fourth year and attracted virtuosi from far and near. Rome imported professional artists to concertize; Mesomedes of Crete enjoyed an active career at Hadrian's court. The Roman populace accorded considerable adulation to virtuoso performers, who commanded large fees, which even greedy Vespasian is said to have paid.

Music in the theater varied from a simple stage play with musical accompaniment, to lengthy dramas with musical interludes between scenes and acts. Pantomimes, extremely popular but of low quality, favored choreography over music.

Musical entertainment was provided at private dinner parties, whether a large gathering or a simple *tête-à-tête*. Sometimes guests at a large dinner party would be provided a choice of entertainment: music, choreography, or a reading by an author. Ensemble music, both vocal and instrumental, was frequently enjoyed, especially at homes of the wealthy; a duet between aulos and kithara was not uncommon.

Many of society's élite were musical amateurs; talented slaves served as both teachers and performers. Lucian reports that many women participated in music, as did several rulers. Nero's musical aspirations were sincere. Contrary to legend, his "fiddle" was probably a kithara, but he received singing and instrumental lessons, practiced diligently, performed (frequently before a captive audience), and participated in contests—always with the fear of infringing upon the rules and always with the hope of winning first prize. Had Nero been content to remain a dilettante, Rome would not have been outraged; it was not the degree of his musical talent but his desire to achieve professional status that shocked society.

Ancient Romans seem to have been interested primarily in secular music, but sacred music was not neglected. Music was an important part of the religious cults of the time. In succeeding centuries, Rome's concentration would be on the sacred, particularly, the music of the Christian church. With the rise of Christianity and the establishment of the papacy near Rome, it is quite possible that the zeal of the church to remove all traces of paganism was a great factor in the successful eradication of all evidence of notated music that might have been indigenous to Roman culture.

Summary

Archaeologists have unearthed musical instruments dating from c. 18,000 B.C., but very little written music survives from antiquity, and much of that is fragmentary. The oldest extant music consists of the *ta'amim* inscribed in scrolls of Hebrew Scripture, and a Hurrian cult hymn from c. 1400 B.C. *Ta'amim* symbols probably served as a notation model for the earliest written chant music of the Christian church. Approximately 15 pieces of ancient Greek music survive, all from comparatively late periods in Greek history, and all located after c. 1575. Through treatises, musical instruments, and artifacts, the ancient Greeks left a considerable legacy to posterity: (1) an acoustical theory established by Pythagoras, stated in mathematical terms and demonstrated both audibly and visibly via the monochord; (2) the concept of the scale, together with a theory of transposition of a scale pattern; (3) the doctrine of *ethos,* a belief that music is a powerful force capable of affecting character, thought, and conduct; and (4) constructional principles for several types of musical instruments. Unfortunately, a rudimentary system of singing by syllables seems to have been soon forgotten. Certain features and views were transmitted by the ancients that cannot be assigned to any particular ethnic group: (1) the idea of music as monophony, associated with words and rhythm (including dance); (2) a practical view of music in performance as a commodity to be created anew for each use, thus placing value on improvisation; and (3) a philosophy that regarded music as a microcosm closely related to the universe as macrocosm, since music was structured according to the same mathematical principles as the cosmos.

No examples of Roman music have been located. The Romans were conquerors who borrowed from the cultures of the peoples they subdued, and adapted, renamed, and developed those cultural items to the extent that they seemed Roman. Conquered Greeks became slaves who taught their Roman masters the features and philosophical views of Greek music. In antiquity, Romans seem to have been interested mainly in secular music, though music was important in religious rites of pagan cults. In succeeding centuries, Rome seems to have concentrated on sacred music, particularly, the music of the Christian church.

2

The Early Christian Era

Christianity grew from its humble beginnings largely as a result of the work of Saul of Tarsus, who, converted and transformed into Paul, preached this faith as a universal brotherhood of mankind without national or racial limitations. Paul maintained contact with small Christian communities and kept them in communication with each other by means of his letters, some of which became the Bible Epistles. Paul personally carried the gospel message to Rome, where he was joined by other evangelists and Peter. Traditionally, the Roman government considered religious beliefs a matter of private concern as long as citizens remained loyal to the state. However, Christians found the expected loyalty to the state incompatible with allegiance to God and refused to burn incense before the imperial image or to serve as soldiers. The classical world had difficulty understanding the Christians' attitude and their regard for God as the supreme authority of heaven and earth.

The degree of oppression Christians suffered varied with the times, but not even the severe persecution that occurred under Diocletian (r. 303–305) could wipe out this faith; rather, oppression unified and strengthened the church. Christianity was practiced in the household of Emperor Constantine I (r. 306–337), who, by the Edict of Milan (313), provided religious toleration throughout his empire and recognized the church as an institution with the right to own property. However, that Edict established the political ruler as head of the church. Julian (r. 361–363) was anti-Christian, but Theodosius I (r. 379–395), by

the Edict of Thessalonica (380), established Christianity as the state religion to be practiced by all Roman citizens except Jews. Thereafter, all Roman emperors were Christians.

After the death of Theodosius I, the Roman empire split apart. In the face of Visigoth invasions, the Western emperor, Honorius I (r. 395–422), who was little more than a puppet ruler, fled north to Ravenna for refuge; in 410 the Visigoths, led by Alaric, sacked Rome and moved westward through Gaul to settle in Spain. More and more, Romans were confronted with the necessity of defending their lands and repelling barbarian invaders. For a time, mercenaries were procured to augment Roman military forces, but often these hired soldiers turned situations to their own advantage, making Romans the losers. Honorius's successors were even weaker than he and honored Germanic chieftains with impressive but meaningless titles. In 476, one of those chieftains, Odovacar, deposed the last Roman emperor, 12-year-old Romulus Augustus. The Western empire had collapsed, for reasons both internal and external.

In general, the literacy level of the Roman people declined. The invasions, which resulted in destruction or desolation of urban centers, eradicated cultural advantages, and the once prosperous economic pattern was gradually replaced by subsistence agriculture. The Germanic chieftains who ruled, with recognition by the Eastern emperor, favored Germanic customs. If any indigenous Roman secular music was extant at that time, it would have had difficulty surviving longer in its pristine state.

The Early Christian Era

A.D. 1	100	200	300	400	500

c. 30
Crucifixion
of Jesus

54–68 Nero

68–79 Vespasian

67 d. of Peter

306–337 Constantine I

379–395 Theodosius I

313 Edict of Milan

380 Edict of Thessalonica

476
Fall
of Rome

G r a d u a l   d e v e l o p m e n t   o f   t h e   C h r i s t i a n   L i t u r g y -

325 Council of Nicaea

374 Ambrose, Bishop of Milan

c. 150 Ptolemy:
Harmonics

340 *Vulgate*

413 Augustine:
Confessions

c. 285
Oxyrhynchos
fragment

425 Founding of
U. of Constantinople

Monastic communities
arose

500	600	700	800	900	1000

Boethius fl.

Cassiodorus fl.

590 Gregory I,
elected Pope
d. 604

751 Pepin
King of Franks

800 Charlemagne
crowned Holy Roman Emperor

987
Hugh Capet
King of France

527 Benedictine
Order founded - - - - R i s e   o f   m o n a s t e r i e s - - - - - - - - - - - - - - - - Music cultivated in monasteries

756 Donation of Pepin

c. 612 Hermitage established at Saint Gall

c. 622–632 Mohammed fl.

Notker Balbulus 840————————912

Hucbald c. 840————————930

527–565
Justinian I, Byzantium

778 Battle of Roncevaux
(Roland)

848 Abbey founded, St. Martial

T h e   M a s s   c o n t i n u e s   t o   d e v e l o p - f o r m a t   s e t t l e d   c.   1 0 1 4

Byzantine *kanon*
John Damascene
d. 760

Carolingian reform of Roman chant
Church modes
Troping - - - Sequences - - - - - - - Liturgical drama

c. 850 { *Musica enchiriadis* / *Scolica enchiriadis* }

Various liturgies and chants in use, with ultimate dominance of "Gregorian" type -

Ambrosian chant -

601 See of Canterbury
Sarum chant -

Mozarabic chant -

The Established Christian Church

During the second century, the sacred writings comprising the New Testament were identified and assembled, a body of dogma was established, and the central organization of the church was expanded. The spiritual and physical welfare of a Christian community was supervised by a bishop (*episkopos*) with authority superior to that of the teaching elders and deacons. By the fourth century, a definite hierarchy existed within the church: There were approximately 250 bishops. The bishop of the leading city in each political province was a *metropolitan* with jurisdiction over his colleagues. The metropolitans of the most important cities—Rome, Constantinople, Antioch, and Alexandria—were called *patriarchs*. Later, the bishop of Jerusalem also held this title because that city was the site of Jesus's death and resurrection. Both the patriarch of Alexandria and the patriarch of Rome were entitled *pope*. The fact that the bishop of Rome was the only patriarch in the Western provinces enhanced his position; his prestige was further increased by his location in the ancient capital of the empire and the belief that his authority was a legacy from St. Peter, who was considered the first bishop of Rome. However, not until the reign of Pope Gregory I (590–604) did the four Eastern patriarchs acknowledge the supremacy of their Roman colleague.

The First Ecumenical Council, held at Nicaea in 325, was a gathering of all the bishops to resolve a doctrinal controversy between followers of the Alexandrian priest Arius and the supporters of St. Athanasius concerning Christ's consubstantiality and coeternity with God. The decision of the council resulted in the formulation and adoption of a Creed that, as modified by the Council of Constantinople (381) and the Council of Chalcedon (451), ultimately became the so-called Nicene Creed, used as *Credo* of the Mass. Though the matters under consideration were doctrinal, the Council of Nicaea was called by Constantine I and presided over by him, for Constantine considered himself Christ's representative on earth and God's vice-regent, as well as head of the Roman empire. This idea survived, and for at least the next five centuries the emperors were able to maintain supervision over the church. Although Christianity divided mankind's allegiance between the political and heavenly kingdoms, there was cooperation between church and state.

The Church Fathers and Music

It was indicated previously that the lack of extant primary source material for Roman music was presumed to be in some measure due to the activities of the early Christian church in its zeal to exterminate all that it considered pagan. But to state that the early Christians were against music would be to give a false impression. Certainly, the church fathers appreciated music; they wished merely to channel its use in the proper direction and to guard the Christian church against the intrusion of any semblance of the orgiastic rites and music of the pagan cults. The writings of great theologians such as St. Basil of Caesarea (c. 330–378), St. John Chrysostom (345–407), and Aurelius Augustinus (St. Augustine, 345–430) reveal that they assigned to music a special place in the life of the church. Like Pythagoras of Samos and other ancient Greeks, these church fathers expressed a belief in the existence of a music of the universe, created by the Holy Spirit and imbued with certain supernatural powers that enabled it to rout demons, summon angelic aid, heal the sick, strengthen moral character, and in numerous other ways contribute to the harmonious order of the world.

Psalms were especially favored for they were inspired by God and singing them provided both pleasure and help. Religious chant, too, fulfilled the special purpose of uplifting the mind as well as offering praise to God. St. John Chrysostom, patriarch of Constantinople, wrote that he considered as churches those assemblies at which there were prayers, psalms, dances of prophets, and singers with pious intentions. St. Jerome (340–420), who spent most of his life in Jerusalem, also advocated singing psalms, for they affected "the seat of the *ethos*" and determined a person's moral conscience. The Latin version of the Bible (the *Vulgate*) prepared by St. Jerome in the fourth century became the authorized version of the Scriptures used in the Roman Catholic Church.

Nor did these saints reject all musical instruments. According to St. Basil, the psaltery, a kind of plucked stringed instrument with a resonator at the top, was particularly acceptable because it alone, of all musical instruments, has the source of its sound above. This, he wrote, was an indication that persons should seek those things which are on high and not be led by pleasant melody to pursue carnal passions.

St. Augustine, bishop of Hippo, confessed that he so enjoyed church music that sometimes he felt he sinned, and that occasionally he wished music banished from the church. However, he recognized and affirmed the usefulness of music in the worship Service. Realizing that actually he was moved by the sung words and not by the music itself, St. Augustine stated that he approved the use of singing in the church as a means of strengthening weak minds and developing greater religious devotion.

Monasticism

Monasticism existed in the third century in Egypt and the Syrian desert, where hermits lived in solitude. By the fourth century, more regulated monastic communities had arisen, such as that of St. Basil of Caesarea. The most important monastic system was that established by Benedict of Nursia (480–543), an Italian nobleman, who founded the monastery at Monte Cassino, south of Rome, in 529. The code of regulations (Rule of St. Benedict) prepared for this monastery spread throughout western Europe. Requirements of the Benedictine Order included prayer, meditation, and physical and intellectual work. Much of that intellectual work was done in the *scriptoria* (writing rooms), where monks copied and prepared books and manuscripts. The sixth-century Rule of St. Benedict lists among the items considered essential for each monk certain wax-filled bone tablets upon which he could write or draw with a stylus (fig. 2.1). Such tablets were common personal possessions throughout the Middle Ages and may have been used as an aid in preparing music manuscripts, also.

Monasteries became depositories of knowledge, and the schools connected with them constituted the salvation of learning in times of sacking and burning, war and famine. Because materials for books and manuscripts were costly, only the most important and valuable items were copied. Certainly, where music was concerned, the secular and vernacular would have had the lowest priority.

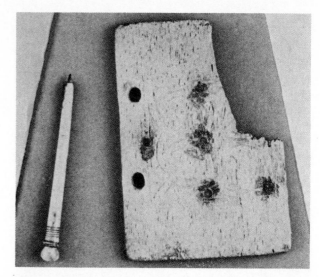

Figure 2.1 Stylus and carved bone tablet, the other side of which was hollowed and filled with a wax writing surface, essential items for Benedictine monks in the sixth century. *(The Lindisfarne Gospels, Oxford: Phaidon Press, Ltd., 1981; Department of Medieval and Later Antiquities, British Museum.)*

Great Latin Writers: Cassiodorus, Boethius

Perhaps the greatest of the Ostrogothic barbarian kings was Theodoric (r. 489–526), who appreciated education and encouraged arts and letters at Ravenna, his capital. His successors seem not to have shared his interests, however. Among the educated Romans at Theodoric's court were Boethius and Cassiodorus, the greatest Latin writers of the time.

Magnus Aurelius Cassiodorus (c. 485–c. 580), a historian, statesman, and monk, founded monasteries at Castellum and Vivarium, and held various offices at the courts of Theodoric and Athalaric. After retiring to Vivarium (c. 540), Cassiodorus wrote *De artibus ac disciplinis liberalium litterarum* (The Liberal Arts), which contains a section entitled *Institutiones musicae* (Principles of Music) based on ancient Greek writings. Cassiodorus knew Augustine's *De musica* and the works of Euclid, Ptolemy, and Alypius.

Anicius M. T. S. Boethius (b. 480), Roman philosopher and mathematician, became Consul in 510 and served as counselor to Theodoric until accused of treason and executed in 524. Boethius's treatise *De institutione musica* (Principles of Music, or Concerning the Arrangement of Music) was considered the most authoritative source on music in the Middle Ages and was used as a text in universities for many centuries. Boethius analyzed, discussed, and sought to explain the theories of Pythagoras, Nicomachus, Aristoxenus, and Ptolemy. In Book V, devoted to Ptolemy's explanation of the Greek tonal system, Boethius used the Latin term *modus* as translation for the Greek word *tonos* (key). This error led medieval musicians into designating the modal scale patterns by the names of the Greek keys. Boethius stressed the importance of music in shaping morals and character (*ethos*), in the education of youth, and as a basis for philosophical studies. Moreover, he seems to have agreed with Aristotle in regarding the philosopher-critic, rather than the performer, as the true musician.

As did the ancient Greek theorists, Boethius emphasized the mathematical side of music and the macrocosmic-microcosmic relationship between the universe and music. Music was divided into three categories: (1) *musica mundana,* the macrocosm, the inaudible music of the spheres discernible in the orderly movement of the planets and the stars; (2) *musica humana,* the inaudible harmonious relationship between soul and body influenced by the order of the cosmos and comparable with musical consonance; and (3) *musica instrumentalis,* the microcosm, the audible sounds called "music" that are produced by instruments (including the human voice) by means of the orderly application of acoustical principles.

The medieval educational system comprised studies in the seven liberal arts. Because of music's relationship with mathematics and the cosmos, it was grouped with arithmetic, geometry, and astronomy in the *quadrivium* of higher studies. The *trivium* of lower studies consisted of grammar, rhetoric, and logic.

Pope Gregory I, "the Great"

In 590 the emperor still exercised much of the ultimate authority within the church. For instance, he called church councils, presided over them, and even confirmed papal elections. However, when Gregory became Pope (r. 590–604), he assumed a position of effective leadership that was temporal as well as spiritual. Gregory (b. 540) was a Roman nobleman trained for a political career; he had been prefect of Rome and had served for six years as papal ambassador to the imperial court at Constantinople. Therefore, he was well acquainted with imperial administration. He returned to Rome c. 586 to become an adviser to Pope Pelagius II, whom he succeeded in 590. Gregory I headed a real papal court, which he managed efficiently. He was able to assert and maintain the supremacy of the Western papacy and to consolidate the church under his leadership. An important facet of this consolidation was reuniting the church at Milan with Rome. He was concerned with the spread of Christianity through missionary activity. In 596, St. Augustine was sent to England, and Christianity was established among the Anglo-Saxons; centuries later, Anglo-Saxons were continental missionaries to the Franks. Aethelbert, King of Kent, was converted and baptized by Augustine, and in 601 the See of Canterbury was founded. On the Continent, conversions of rulers included the Arian king of the Visigoths in Spain and the Arian heir to the Lombard throne.

Gregory was interested in music as an adjunct to worship. There is no certainty that he composed any "Gregorian" chants, but his desire for standardization and codification of the Roman chants has given them his name. A papal choir had been in existence for more than a century, and Gregory fully realized the choir's importance in relieving officiating priests and deacons of the responsibility for much musical performance. Therefore, he instructed Roman seminaries to train choir singers, and he founded orphanages with a similar aim. Gregory helped standardize the liturgy somewhat by assigning certain antiphons, offertories, responses, and other chants to designated Services and feast days. The distribution of specific chants throughout the church year had been begun by Gregory's predecessors and was completed by his immediate successors in the papacy.

Establishment of Papal States

For the territory known as the Papal States, the Roman Catholic Church is indebted to the Franks, a confederation of northern tribes that gradually gained strength and power during the fourth century. Under their chieftain, Meroveus, the Franks allied with the Romans in their fight against Attila. Meroveus's

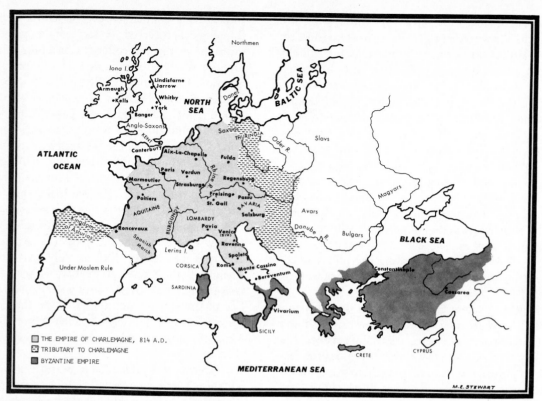

Figure 2.2 The extent of Charlemagne's empire and the Byzantine Empire in A.D. 814.

grandson, Clovis (r. 481–511), extended the Franks' kingdom until almost all of Gaul had been gained, but after Clovis's death, the Merovingian dynasty weakened. Strength lay in the nobility and in the hands of the king's chief minister, the mayor of the palace. In the early eighth century, the mayor was Charles Martel, who earned considerable prestige through military prowess and was the real power behind the Frankish throne. Charles's son Pepin (r. 741–768) inherited the mayoralty but desired the title of king and petitioned Pope Zacharias (r. 741–751) for it. The request was granted. The Merovingian heir was placed in a monastery, and Pepin was anointed king in 751.

In 754, Pope Stephen III (r. 752–757) reanointed Pepin, along with his sons Carloman and Charles, and bestowed upon all three the title "Roman Patrician." Thus, the Carolingian dynasty was established. In return for this recognition, Pepin agreed to defend the Pope against the Lombards, who were threatening. All of the Lombard territories that Pepin con-

quered—the city of Rome and most of the lands of Ravenna—were given to the Pope. These lands, the "Donation of Pepin," were the basis of the Papal States. Moreover, by the agreement and gift an alliance was formed whereby the Carolingians became the Pope's temporal protectors.

According to custom, Charles and Carloman jointly inherited the throne at Pepin's death and were expected to divide the kingdom. Carloman soon died, however, and Charles I (Charlemagne) ruled alone. In 774, he confirmed the Donation of Pepin and went to Italy to battle the Lombards on the Pope's behalf. While there, Charlemagne acquired the Lombard crown.

In 778, an army commanded by Charlemagne's nephew Roland was annihilated at Roncevaux in the Pyrenees. This disaster was memorialized in the medieval epic, *Le Chanson de Roland* (The Song of Roland). By 796 Charlemagne's kingdom extended from the Atlantic Ocean and the Pyrenees Mountains over to the Elbe and Danube Rivers and down into the center of Italy (fig. 2.2). In 800, Charlemagne

Figure 2.3 The extent of the Byzantine Empire during the reign of Justinian I (r. 527–65).

went to Rome to help Pope Leo III (r. 795–816) quell a disturbance, and while there, at Mass on Christmas Day, the Pope crowned him Emperor of the Romans.

The Byzantine Church

As Rome's power faded, Constantinople grew to urban splendor, with a brilliant cultural life. The University of Constantinople, founded in 425, prospered and during the reign of Justinian I (r. 527–65) supported chairs of philosophy, law, Greek and Latin grammar and rhetoric. In many ways, Constantinople maintained the cosmopolitan tradition Rome had once acquired from the Hellenes.

Justinian I sought to strengthen religious life throughout his extensive Byzantine Empire and wanted Constantinople to be recognized as an ecclesiastical center (fig. 2.3). With that in mind, he ordered the construction of Hagia Sophia, which was dedicated on 27 December 537 (colorplate 2). That edifice, once considered the world's largest church, is now a museum. St. Sophia and other churches were decorated richly with icons and mosaics; their leather-bound and jewel-encrusted liturgical books contain beautifully illumined pages.

The church of San Vitale, in Ravenna, Italy, dedicated by Bishop Maximianus in 547, typifies Byzantine art and architecture. A pair of mosaic murals in the apse of the church convey the view then prevalent that the emperor was God's vice-regent on earth. The murals depict the Offertory procession of the Mass (colorplate 3). In the left mural, Justinian I holds a golden vessel containing the bread. He is flanked on his left by Bishop Maximianus and other clergy and on his right by court and military personnel. The jeweled cross and jewel-encrusted liturgical book are typical. In the right mural, Empress Theodora extends in offering a golden cup containing the wine. The empress and her attendants portray the luxury of the Byzantine court.

Byzantine Hymns

In the Byzantine church, Mass was celebrated often, but not daily. By decree in 528 Justinian made daily singing of Matins, Lauds, and Vespers compulsory. Hymn singing was an important part of the liturgy. Byzantine hymns are of three types: *troparia, kontakia,* and *kanones.* The *troparion,* used in the fourth

The Early Christian Era

and fifth centuries, developed from responses sung between psalm verses; *troparia* were poetic interpolations sung between the last several verses of a psalm. *Kontakia* flourished during the sixth and seventh centuries. At Matins, or Morning Service, there was no homily (sermon). Instead, the reading of the Gospel for the day was followed by the singing of the appropriate *kontakion,* a musical homily explaining or interpreting that Gospel. The kontakion was strophic and consisted of from 24 to 30 poetic stanzas sung to the same melody.

The *kanon* came into existence when the Council of Trullo decreed in 692 that daily preaching of the Word was obligatory for the higher clergy. To use both a kontakion and a homily would be duplication, so the kontakion was deleted and a new form, the kanon, was created to serve as meditative commentary upon the Scripture passages and the coordinating sermon. Originally, a kanon consisted of nine main sections called *odes,* each with its own melody; each ode normally had nine stanzas. The text of each ode corresponded with one of the nine Biblical **canticles** used in the liturgy. (Canticles are special lyrical portions of the Bible.) Later, the second ode, based on the Song of Moses (*Attendite, coeli*; Give ear, heavens; Deut. 32), was considered too somber and reproachful and was omitted except during Lent. At first, the melodies of the kanones were simple syllabic settings of the text. Gradually, the melodies became longer and more complex, so that when a kanon was sung in slow tempo much time was consumed by the singing of eight odes. This was especially problematic during Lent and Holy Week when the Services themselves were longer. The obvious remedy was to shorten the kanon; the number of stanzas per ode was reduced to three.

The first known writer of kanones was Andrew of Crete (c. 660–c. 740). During the second quarter of the eighth century, an important school of kanon poet-composers flourished at the monastery of Mar Saba near the Dead Sea (fig. 2.3, St. Sabas). The most notable of these men were John of Damascus (c. 700–c. 760) and his foster brother Kosmas of Jerusalem (died c. 760). Among surviving hymns by Kosmas are nineteen kanones for the great feasts of the church year, including the penitential "Great Kanon" based on Psalm 51, which is sung at Lauds on Thursday of Passion Week.

John of Damascus (John Damascene) is credited with introducing into the Byzantine liturgy the *oktō-echos*—eight-week cycles of hymns, with the hymns for each week composed in a different *echos* or "mode." These *echoi* were not scale patterns but collections of melody patterns. Commencing at Easter, the most important festival of the church year, for the first week a group of hymns in the First Mode (First Echos) was sung; the following week a group of hymns in the Second Mode was used, and so on. John played a significant role in the development of kanon literature. In manuscripts containing model stanzas for kanones, the first melody in each group is attributed to him. Among extant hymns by John is the Easter kanon, known as the Golden Kanon or Queen of Kanones (*Anastaseos imera*). J. M. Neale's English translation of that hymn text, "The Day of Resurrection," is sung in many churches on Easter Sunday.

The Jewish Synagogue

It was the Service of the Jewish synagogue, not the Temple, upon which the Christian community patterned its divine worship Service. The Jewish synagogue was an institution for the layperson. In the first century A.D., three daily prayer Services were observed in the synagogue: in the morning at some time between 7 and 10 A.M., in the afternoon between 3 and 4 P.M., and in the evening "at dusk." At these services, there were prayers of praise, thanksgiving, supplication and personal petition, and benediction, as well as professions of faith through doxology and the *Sh'ma',* the creed prayer commencing "Hear, O Israel, The Lord our God, The Lord is one." The two doxologies in use were the *Kaddish,* whose opening phrases have much in common with the Christians' The Lord's Prayer, and the *Kedusha,* or Thrice-Holy.

The weekday morning and evening Services were similar in content, opening with an exhortation to prayer in praise of the Lord, and including praise prayers, the *Kedusha,* the *Sh'ma',* a required set of silent prayers offered standing, and concluding with the *Kaddish.* The afternoon Service was simpler, with one or two psalms chanted, and the *Kaddish.* Observation of the Sabbath began with the Service at dusk on Friday and continued through Service at sunset on Saturday. The morning worship was more elaborate than that on weekdays and included the singing of more than a dozen psalms (including the Hallelujah Psalms 146–50) and Miriam's Song (Exod. 15:1–19). Central to the Service were readings from the Scriptures, one Lesson from the Pentateuch and one from the Prophetic Books, followed by appropriate prayers. The afternoon Service, too, was expanded by additional psalms and portions of the Song of Songs. The evening Service was characterized by prayers and psalm singing, and concluded with the ceremony of *Habdala* (Separation).

Many of the practices in synagogue Services became part of the worship Services of the early Christians and carried over into the **liturgy** of the Catholic Church. (The liturgy is the prescribed ritual or format for worship in the church.) Common elements of the Services of both faiths were recitation or musical intonation of passages from Scriptures, singing of psalms and hymns, affirmation of a creed, praise through doxologies and a Thrice-Holy, congregational and priestly prayers, giving of offerings, and benediction. Grace and blessing over bread and wine, together with psalm singing, were ancient Jewish customs observed in worship in the home. Both Jewish and Christian faiths established a liturgical calendar with similar organizational details.

As used around the first century A.D., the term **psalmody** referred to the musical intonation or chanting of any Scriptural or liturgical texts. Passages from Scriptures were recited or chanted by one person in a kind of musical intonation that could be termed speech-song. Such a rendition, done from beginning to end by one person, is **direct psalmody.** Not all Scriptural texts were chanted or intoned in the same manner. The type of musical inflection varied with the text, the season of the liturgical year, and the specific occasion. The belief was prevalent among the Jews, as it was among the Greeks, that each type of music had a special character to which listeners (in this case, worshipers) responded in a certain way.

The Book of Psalms was especially important in both Jewish and Christian Services. Much Scriptural poetry is structured in bipartite verses, designed for or conducive to **antiphonal rendition.** Antiphonal rendition means performance in alternation, and in **antiphonal psalmody** the first half of the verse is chanted by one group or choir of singers and the second half by another group or choir. Another form of antiph-

onal psalmody is the singing of psalm verses in alternation by two choirs, each choir singing a complete verse of the psalm. **Responsorial psalmody** was used, too, in which the cantor or precentor sang a verse of psalm or Scripture and the congregation answered with a certain response. Psalm 136 provides an example, for the second half of each of its 26 verses is "For his loving kindness endureth for ever."

Summary

Christianity survived various degrees of persecution before Constantine I advocated religious toleration in 313 and Theodosius I formally established it as the state religion in 380. Imperial espousal of Christianity brought also imperial guardianship that at times amounted to control. The church fathers supported music as an adjunct to worship; music's function was to enhance the Service.

After the death of Theodosius, the Roman empire split apart. For reasons both internal and external, the Western segment declined and ultimately collapsed in 476. Theodoric was the greatest of the barbarians who ruled the Western kingdom, and at Ravenna, his capital, arts and letters were encouraged. There, in the early sixth century, Cassiodorus and Boethius wrote treatises on music. Boethius's *De institutione musica,* considered the most authoritative source on music in the Middle Ages, explained the macrocosmic-microcosmic relationship between the universe and music and divided music into three categories: cosmic music, human music, and instrumental music. Boethius stressed also the ethical and mathematical aspects of music.

Monasticism began in the third century as desert hermitages, and flourished. Monasteries became depositories of culture and learning in the darkest ages, and housed copyists whose work made ancient treatises more available. In 529 Benedict of Nursia established at Monte Cassino the Order that bears his name.

Gregory the Great (r. 590–604) elevated the papacy to a position of temporal and spiritual leadership. He reunited the Christian church, encouraged *scholae cantorum,* and continued the standardization and codification of liturgical chants that his immediate predecessors began and his immediate successors continued.

In the middle of the fourth century, the Franks, under Merovius's leadership, began to strengthen considerably. After Clovis's death, the Merovingian dynasty weakened, and the real governing power lay in the hands of the mayor of the palace. In mid-eighth century Mayor Pepin successfully petitioned Pope Zacharias for the title of king and, in return, donated to the Pope the Italian lands that formed the basis of the Papal States. Charlemagne, Pepin's son, expanded the Frankish kingdom considerably and became so militarily invaluable to the Pope that on Christmas Day, 800, Pope Leo III crowned him Emperor of the Romans.

The Eastern empire, centered at Constantinople, enjoyed a brilliant cultural life and maintained the cosmopolitan tradition Rome had once inherited from the Hellenes. Justinian I (r. 527–565) fostered monasticism and strongly supported Christianity. By his decree in 528, daily singing of Matins, Lauds, and Vespers became compulsory. Hymn singing was an important part of the liturgy and included three types of Byzantine hymns: *troparia,* poetic interpolations used in the fourth and fifth centuries; *kontakia,* musical homilies that flourished in the fifth and sixth centuries; and *kanones,* meditative commentaries used after the Council of Trullo in 692. Notable composers of *kanones* were Kosmas of Jerusalem and John Damascene, who is credited with introducing the *oktō-ēchos* into the Byzantine liturgy.

The Jewish synagogue provided the model for the worship Services and for the liturgical calendar of the Christian community. Psalmody was an important feature of worship Services of both faiths. Three types of psalmody were used: direct, antiphonal, and responsorial. Over the years, the expansion of antiphonal psalmody led to the creation of new forms of Christian church music.

Ecclesiastical Chant

The development of Western music is inseparably linked with the music of the Roman Catholic Church. Not only was the church vital in preserving music through the so-called Dark Ages, it was the center of activity of the community. The music of the church was an integral part of lay life; chants of the church were sung outside its walls and frequently served as the basis for secular songs. From the ninth century on, composers have written music based upon or incorporating chant melodies. In some centuries, settings of certain parts of the liturgy (specifically, motet and Mass) were the most significant forms of music. It is important, therefore, to understand the nature of ecclesiastical chant and the historically settled format of the Roman liturgy.

Ecclesiastical chant forms the largest body of monophonic music in existence, and a major portion of that body is Gregorian chant. Yet, opportunities to hear Gregorian chant performed in the traditional manner are rare. Until the early 1960s one might hear the liturgy sung in Latin in Gregorian chant in Roman Catholic Churches throughout the world. However, in accordance with decisions and recommendations made by Vatican Council II (1962–65), Services in the vernacular have superseded the Latin. Traditional Gregorian chant has been displaced by other music or supplied with vernacular translations of the text that the music does not accommodate. A considerable amount of new music, of all degrees of quality, has found its way into ecclesiastical use.

Gregorian Chant

Gregorian chant is purely functional music designed to enhance the worship service and is objective and impersonal. It consists of a single unaccompanied melodic line constructed according to tonal patterns different from those forming the major and minor scales, it traditionally used Latin words, and it was originally intended to be sung by men, and, from the fourth century, by women in cloistered religious communities. In other words, chant is monophonic and modal. It is usually sung in a flexible rhythm without regular accentuation or beat because, as written, no fixed temporal values are specified for the notes.

Chant Rhythm

To date no manuscript or treatise has been located that gives explicit instructions for authentic performance of the rhythm of Gregorian chant, though there is evidence that there was some rhythmic variation in performance. For instance, in some late ninth-century manuscripts the letters *t* and *c* appear above some note symbols. The *t* is interpreted as *trahere* (to prolong or lengthen) and the *c* as *celeriter* (quickly). Sometimes a straight line is attached to a note symbol, and this is interpreted as a prolongation sign. (Fig. 3.1.)

Surviving treatises by eminent medieval theorists indicate that they were not in agreement concerning the rhythm of chant. In the twentieth century several differing views exist: (1) One group, known as mensuralists, believe that basically there were two note

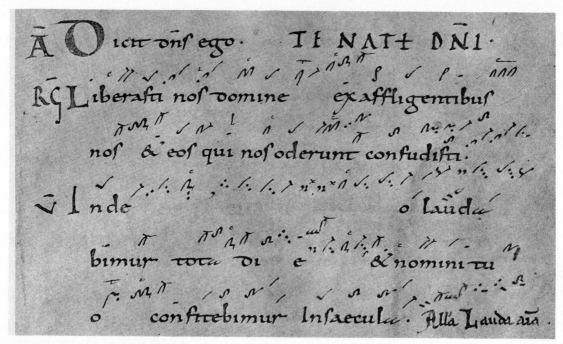

Figure 3.1 Portion of ninth-century manuscript showing chant with small letters *t* and *c* written above some notation symbols. *(Source: Ninth-century manuscript, Codex 359, fol. 125, Stiftsbibliothek, St. Gall, Switzerland.)*

values, a long and a short, with the long having twice the value of the short. Mensuralists have proposed several different systems by which these note values may have been arranged. (2) Another group, called accentualists, contend that rhythm was governed by the accentuation (or stress) normally given the Latin words when spoken. In syllabic and neumatic chants (i.e., chants with one syllable of text per note shape or neume), the primary accent of the Latin word is stressed. In melismatic chants (i.e., chants with many neumes per syllable), the stress falls on the first note of each neume. (3) Still another opinion is held by the Benedictine monks of Solesmes, France, who, for well over a century, have been officially designated by the Vatican to edit and publish the liturgical books used in the Roman Catholic Church. They use as fundamental rhythmic unit a single beat or pulse that is indivisible. Binary and ternary groupings of these pulses are freely interlaced and may form larger rhythmic units. The first note of the group, which they

term the *ictus,* is most important rhythmically. In their rules for interpretation of chant, the Solesmes editors state that the natural rhythm of Latin prose is the vital determinant of chant rhythm. They use three rhythmic indications: a vertical *episema* (') to indicate the *ictus*; a horizontal *episema* (–) to indicate a slight lengthening of a note; and a dot placed after a note (▪ ·) to double the value of that note.

Gregorian Chant Notation

In modern liturgical books, Gregorian chant music is printed on a four-line staff in plainsong ("square") notation that indicates relative rather than absolute pitches (fig. 3.2; DWMA5).

For each chant, one of two movable clefs is used: or , indicating, respectively, the position of c′ ("middle c") or f (the f below "middle c"). Clef mobility keeps the chant notation on the staff and eliminates the necessity for ledger lines. Notation is by means of **neumes** (note symbols), which may appear

Figure 3.2 *Kyrie* from Easter Mass (*a*) in Gregorian chant notation (LU,16), and (*b*) transcribed in modern notation. *(Figure a from* The Liber Usualis, *edited by The Benedictines of Solesmes. Copyright © 1956 Desclée Company, Tournai, Belgium.)*

as single square notes —▪— or in a grouping of two or more squares in a composite neume ▪▪ . Each square indicates one note. The notes are read from left to right, with one exception—in a *podatus,* or *pes* ▪ , the lower note is sung first. Compound neumes (groupings of more than three notes) may include oblique bars and diamond shapes, such as ◆ or ▪♦ . An oblique bar contains only two notes, one marked by each end of the bar; each diamond shape constitutes one note. The jagged note known as *quilisma* ≡ has the same value as other notes in a

neume group but is sung lightly. The small note in the neume ♪ is a liquescent neume and is sung lightly. A liquescent neume usually occurs on a diphthong, as the *au* in *lauda,* or where two consonants occur in succession, as the *ng* in *angelus.* Only one syllable is sung per neume, regardless of the number of notes involved. However, in melismatic chants many neumes may be notated to be vocalized to a single syllable of text. (Guide to correct pronunciation of ecclesiastical Latin in Appendix.)

Only one chromatic alteration is used in Gregorian chant: B♭. Infrequently, the flat symbol ♭ appears immediately after the clef at the beginning of the chant, in which case it is in effect for the entire chant. More often, the flat indication occurs within a chant and is valid for only the word in which the symbol is involved, or until the next phrase marking.

Chant music is not divided into measures by bar lines. Phrasing is indicated by vertical slashes intersecting one or more of the staff lines, depending on the importance of the phrase. A vertical slash through the top line of the staff (a quarter-bar) marks the end of the smallest melodic division of the chant; a vertical line intersecting the center two lines of the staff (a half-bar) marks the end of a section of a phrase; a full-bar through all four staff lines marks the end of a complete phrase; and a double-bar through all four lines indicates either the end of the chant or a change of performers of the chant. An asterisk (*) placed in the text of a chant marks the point at which the choir commences after a solo portion of chant, and vice versa. The letters *ij* and *iij* indicate, respectively, that the preceding phrase is to be repeated either once or twice.

The *custos* is a small guide symbol resembling half a note that is placed at the end of a line of music to designate the first pitch at the beginning of the next line. Such a guide was necessary in ages past when an entire choir might be required to read from a single huge page of vellum in a book chained to a lectern, and there might not be sufficient time for one's eye to travel back the width of the manuscript page to see the next neume and sing it without disrupting the rhythmic flow of the chant.

The symbol ℟ designates a Response. ℣ indicates that the words are a Verse, as a verse of Scripture; Ps. signifies that a portion of a psalm follows. The letters *e u o u a e* printed under neumes at the conclusion of a chant constitute an abbreviation derived from the last six vowels of the words *in saecula saeculorum Amen* ("through ages of ages. Amen," or, "for ever. Amen") found at the conclusion of the *Gloria Patri,* the usual termination of a psalm or a canticle in the Roman rite. This abbreviation, known as the *evovae,* serves as a formula to indicate the particular variant ending of the psalm tone to be sung.

An Arabic or Roman numeral appearing at the beginning of a chant melody indicates the ecclesiastical mode of that chant. There are eight of these modes, each designated by number and not by name. This labeling of the chants was a later addition and probably occurred at some time during codification when some person(s) analyzed the chants and classified them modally. Many of the chants, especially the early ones, give every indication of having been created by the assembling of melodic formulas, a process known as **centonization.** Centonization was common practice in the East, as evidenced by the use of melodic patterns called *maqām* by the Arabs, *rāga* by the Hindus, *ta'amim* by the Hebrews, and *echoi* by the Byzantines.

The Church Modes

The modes originally assigned to Gregorian chants are not identical with those used later in other medieval Western music. Rather, the church modes were a combination of Eastern practice and Western terminology.

Medieval Western music theory employed a set of eight abstract scale patterns also called modes. In the Eastern Christian church, chants were grouped according to the types of melodic motives they contained; these groups of melody types were divided into eight categories, arranged in four pairs, with finals on the pitches d, e, f, and g. Each category was an *echos* (pl., *echoi*); collectively, the eight categories formed the *oktōēchos.*

At some time between the late sixth and late eighth centuries, the Carolingian clergy acquired a working knowledge of the Byzantine system. When Alcuin and his co-workers carried out Charlemagne's directives to write down the liturgy, the Eastern system was borrowed and adapted. Chants were grouped into eight basic categories arranged in pairs, but the term *echos* was not used. Instead, the pairs were numbered, and the categories designated according to their **tessitura** (the average compass or general "lie" of the music) as being either authentic or plagal (derived). The authentic-plagal designation is used in the medieval Western modes. Antiphons and psalms were labeled with mode numbers. Conceivably, the Carolingian clergy assigned mode classifications to chants in order to avoid harmonic clashes when antiphons and psalm verses were combined to form Introits, Offertories, and Communions. The first verified classification of psalms according to a system of eight modal divisions is found in a fragment of a *Tonary* in Charlemagne's *Psalter.* (Fig. 3.3.) (A *Tonary* was a medieval eight-mode scheme that stated distinct preferences for using certain modes for specific types of chants.)

In modern liturgical books, the modes are referred to by numbers (from I to VIII, or 1 to 8), and the mode of each chant is designated.

Classes and Forms of Chant

Ecclesiastical chant may be classified according to the source and literary nature of the text, the number of notes per syllable of text in the musical setting, and the manner in which it is performed. Texts may be Biblical or non-Biblical, prose or poetry. For example, psalms and canticles are Biblical poetry; Epistles are Biblical prose. The *Te Deum laudamus* (We praise Thee, God) is non-Biblical prose; hymns are non-Biblical poetry.

Text settings may be **syllabic,** with one note of music per syllable of text; **neumatic,** with one neume (either simple or composite) per text syllable; or **melismatic,** with several neumes per syllable of text (fig. 3.4). Chants with lengthy texts were often given syllabic settings, as were Credo II (*Liber Usualis,* 66) and Credo IV (LU,77). Alleluias, which are jubilant, usually exhibit melismatic settings (LU,409; LU,779). *Kyrie (clemens rector)* (LU,79) is also melismatic. Examples of neumatic settings are the Easter Introit, *Resurrexi* (LU,778); the antiphon *Asperges me* (LU,13); and the hymn sung at Lauds on Epiphany, *O sola magnarum urbium* (LU,456).

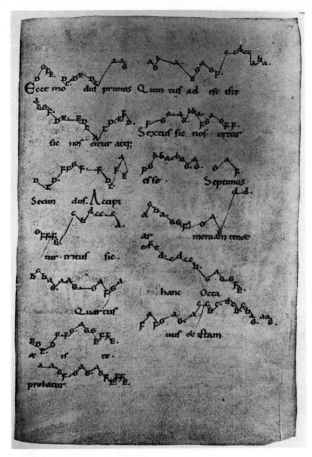

Figure 3.3 A Tonary from the late eleventh century. *(Fol. 128, MS Lat. 7211, Bibliothèque nationale, Paris.)*

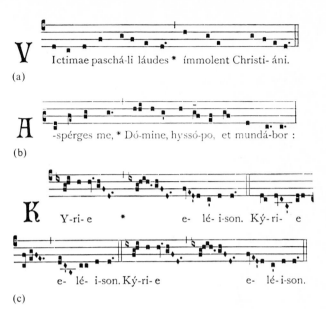

(a)

(b)

(c)

Figure 3.4 Chant text settings: (*a*) syllabic (LU,780); (*b*) neumatic (LU,13); (*c*) melismatic (LU,79). *(From* The Liber Usualis, *edited by The Benedictines of Solesmes. Copyright © 1956 Desclée Company, Tournai, Belgium.)*

In performance, some chants are **antiphonal,** with sections or phrases being sung by alternating choirs; some are **responsorial,** being sung by soloist with response by choir; some are **direct,** being sung from beginning to end without alternation. The Psalms provide examples of all three types.

Psalm Tones

In the liturgical Services called Offices, the Psalms are chanted antiphonally according to certain melodic patterns called **psalm tones.** Just as a psalm verse is constructed in two parts, so the psalm tone has a binary division. The major portion of each psalm verse is chanted in a kind of monotone on a pitch called variously the *tuba, tenor, dominant,* or *reciting note.* There are nine psalm tones: one for each of the eight ecclesiastical modes and the *Tonus Peregrinus* (Migratory Tone), which is distinctive in its use of two different reciting notes, one for each half of the psalm verse. The earliest verified use of the system of eight psalm tones is in the previously mentioned *Tonary* of Charlemagne's *Psalter.*

Psalms are sung as inflected recitative. The psalm tone commences with an *initio,* a two- or three-note *intonation* leading into the reciting note upon which the verse is chanted. At the binary division of the psalm verse, a mediant cadence, the *mediatio,* occurs. The reciting note is resumed for the second half of the verse, which concludes with the *terminatio,* or final cadence (fig. 3.5). When the first part of the psalm verse is quite long, it is subdivided by a *flex*—a bending or lowering of the pitch by the interval of a second or a third for two notes; this is marked in the text by a small cross (†).

De pro-fúndis clamávi *ad te* Dómine : * Dómine exáu*di vócem* mé- **am.**

Figure 3.5 Portion of Psalm 129 as intoned on Psalm Tone 4.

Reciting Notes

Certain portions of the liturgy, such as prayers and readings from Scripture, are chanted in a kind of liturgical recitative that is very similar to but simpler than psalm tones. The chanting is done rather rapidly on a reciting note that usually approximates either the pitch a or c′. A short intonation precedes the reciting note, and brief melodic cadences punctuate verse endings.

Regional Liturgies

Several different regional liturgies were in existence by the fourth century. All have basic similarities in text, format, and musical chant, yet each possesses unique features that probably resulted from regional peculiarities infiltrating the chants and liturgies that missionaries originally brought into the areas (fig. 3.6). The principal liturgies and chants were Byzantine in the East, and Roman, Gregorian, Ambrosian, Gallican, Celtic, and Mozarabic in the West.

Mozarabic chant functioned in the liturgy of the Iberian peninsula, where Christians living under Moslem rule were called "Mozarabs." In 1085 this liturgy was banned officially in favor of Roman, but upon petition of six churches in Toledo permission was granted for continued use of Mozarabic in those specific places. In 1988, Mozarabic liturgy was still used (in the form established and printed by Cardinal Ximenes in 1500) in a chapel of the Cathedral of Toledo. A sizable repertory of Mozarabic chant is extant, but the music has not been transcribed because much of the notation is illegible.

The Celtic liturgy and its chant originated in monastic communities founded in Ireland by St. Patrick (d. 461); it had use also in Scotland and some parts

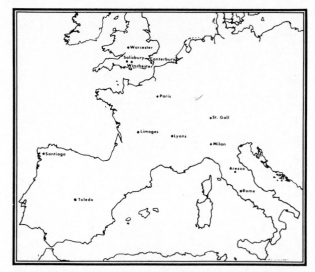

Figure 3.6 Location of principal monasteries, centers of the various chant types, centers of troping, and centers of early polyphony.

of England. Celtic communities were important centers of civilization and produced significant illuminated manuscripts such as *The Lindisfarne Gospels* and *The Book of Kells*. During the sixth and seventh centuries Celtic monks migrated to Europe where they established hermitages and monasteries. The most influential of these was located at Sankt Gallen (St. Gall) in what is now Switzerland but was then northern Italy. No pure Celtic chant seems to have survived.

Ambrosian chant is still used in the archdiocese of Milan. The chant was named for St. Ambrose, who was bishop of Milan from 374 to 397. A comparison of Gregorian and Ambrosian chants reveals that (a) if the text was set simply, the Ambrosian chant is simpler than Gregorian, and (b) if the text was set ornately, the Ambrosian is more ornate than Gregorian. According to St. Augustine, Ambrose brought into the Western church the Eastern customs of antiphonal psalmody and hymn singing. Many hymn texts have been attributed to Ambrose, but only four are considered authentic.

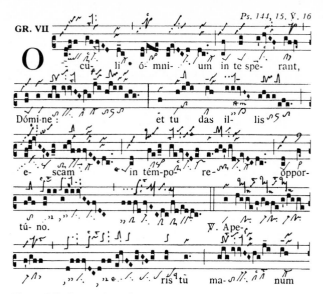

Figure 3.7 Comparison of chant notation: square notation used in twentieth-century *Graduale Romanum* printed on the staff; neumes in the ninth-century MS (Codex 359, St. Gall) written below the square notation; and neumes of tenth-century MS (Codex 239, Laon) written above the square notation. *(From Graduale Triplex, copyright © 1979, Abbaye S. Pierre de Solesmes, F-72300 Sablé-Sur-Sarthe, France.)*

Gallican chant and liturgy, used by the Franks, flourished from the fifth to the eighth century. Supposedly, it was suppressed during the reigns of Pepin (r. 752–768) and Charlemagne (r. 768–814), who preferred Roman chant and imported liturgical books from Rome. Probably, those rulers' desire to unify their Empire was a greater factor in their liturgical reforms than personal preference. The imported *Sacramentaries* were sketchy, at best, containing only the variable texts used for feasts that changed from day to day. In 786, Pope Hadrian I (r. 772–795) sent Charlemagne a Roman *Sacramentary,* which the king directed Alcuin to supplement and complete. Undoubtedly, Alcuin incorporated local materials, and Gallican elements began to infiltrate the Roman liturgy. Since Alcuin had been head of York Cathedral school before Charlemagne brought him to Aix-la-Chapelle to direct the palace school, Celtic characteristics probably crept in, too. No examples of pure Gallican chant are known to exist, but some of the Gallican liturgy that was absorbed into the Roman can be identified, e.g., the verse *Crux fidelis* (Faithful cross), which is sung antiphonally with stanzas of the Gallican hymn *Pange, lingua, gloriosi . . .* (Sing, tongue, the glorious . . . ; LU,709) in the Good Friday Service.

Old Roman chant, as scholars believe it existed prior to c. 800, survives in two *Antiphoners* and three *Graduales* written in the eleventh, twelfth, and thirteenth centuries. The chants in these five manuscripts differ from Gregorian in specific minute details only, such as the length of melismas and the number of times a short melodic formula is repeated before the melody moves on. Both types of chant are modal, but Gregorian seems more consciously related to the eight ecclesiastical modes. This conscious relationship may be a Frankish contribution.

The modifications of the Old Roman chant made during the Carolingian era created the Romano-Frankish type that ultimately became known as Gregorian chant (fig. 3.7). Though the chant remained impersonal and objective, it became more expressive, less dependent upon melodic formulas, and melodic intervals of thirds and fifths were included more often. The greater use of the third may have been a Celtic influence—the people of Britain seem always to have had a predilection for thirds and a "major" sound. Chants were further modified through the practice of troping, and new forms of chant were developed.

In many places, the basic Roman Catholic ritual was altered by the incorporation of local variations and customs that, after a time, became distinctive. Such variant rituals are referred to as the "Use" of that particular church or region, for example, the Use of Sarum (fig. 3.8). Sarum Use was employed at Salisbury Cathedral and throughout much of England in the Middle Ages and early Renaissance; it was formally abolished by decree in 1547, after Henry VIII broke away from the Catholic Church. During the Renaissance, continental composers frequently based polyphonic compositions on Sarum chant melodies.

Figure 3.8 Manuscript page from Use of Sarum, Easter liturgy. (*From* Antiphonale Sarisburiense.)

Summary

The development of Western music is inseparably linked with the music of the Roman Catholic Church. Ecclesiastical chant is the largest body of monophonic music in existence, and the major portion of it is Gregorian chant. Chant is modal, functional music, written in a distinctive notation. No manuscript or treatise has been located that gives explicit instructions for authentic performance of the rhythm of Gregorian chant, and several differing views exist concerning chant rhythm. The modes originally assigned to Gregorian chants were a combination of Eastern practice and Western terminology and are not identical with those used later in other medieval Western music. The first verified classification of psalms according to a system of eight modal divisions is found in a fragment of a *Tonary* in Charlemagne's *Psalter*.

Ecclesiastical chant may be classified according to the source and literary nature of the text (Biblical or non-Biblical, poetry or prose), the number of notes per syllable of text in the musical setting (syllabic, neumatic, melismatic), and the manner in which it is performed (direct, responsorial, antiphonal). In the liturgical Offices, psalms are chanted as inflected recitative, according to psalm tone patterns. A simpler type of liturgical recitative, done on a reciting note, is used for prayers and readings from Scripture.

Several types of liturgies and chants were in existence by the fourth century: Byzantine in the East, and Roman, Gregorian, Ambrosian, Gallican, Celtic, and Mozarabic in the West. Ambrosian chant is still used in Milan, but the Franko-Roman type known as Gregorian chant supplanted the other Western varieties in most places.

The Roman Liturgy

Meetings of the early Christian communities commonly featured either (a) reenactment of the Lord's Supper or (b) psalm singing, Scripture reading, and prayer. These two types of religious observances developed into the two principal Services of the Roman Catholic Church, respectively, the Mass and the Offices, or Canonical Hours. The prescribed ritual (liturgy) for the Services developed gradually and became settled, insofar as essentials are concerned, by about the ninth century. Important changes occurred later: the Vatican's formal acceptance of the Credo into the Ordinary of the Mass, in 1014; recommendations of the Councils of Trent (1545–63) that caused the deletion of numerous Sequences from the Mass; advocations and directives of Vatican Council II (1962–65) that permitted use of the vernacular and that instigated reform of the liturgy and its music. Though Vatican Council II directed that congregations learn and be able to sing the Mass Ordinary in Latin, in many countries that directive has not been observed. The use of Latin in the Service has almost become obsolete.

Liturgical Year

The calendar for the liturgical year traditionally comprised two concurrent cycles: the Proper of the Time and the Proper of the Saints. The Proper of the Time consists of the liturgical observance of all Sundays of the year and the commemoration of the principal events in Christ's life. Some of these events are fixed dates, as is Christmas; others are movable, as is Easter. The Proper of the Saints concerns the honoring of certain Saints on certain specified dates, in accordance with the church's system of ranking feasts. The liturgical year may be outlined as follows:

Advent, a penitential season, commencing the fourth Sunday before Christmas;

Christmas, the twelve days from Christmas Eve to Epiphany (January 6);

From January 7 until the Pre-Lenten season, the time called "after Epiphany";

Pre-Lent, a period of preparation, commencing nine weeks before Easter;

Lent, a penitential season, from Ash Wednesday to Easter;

Eastertide, from Easter to Pentecost (including Ascension Thursday);

Pentecost, or Whit Sunday, which is seven weeks after Easter;

Trinity, from the first Sunday after Pentecost to the beginning of Advent.

Liturgical Books

The contents of the liturgical books are arranged according to the liturgical calendar. Early liturgical books, such as those used in the seventh century, contained only the texts for the great festival Services as celebrated by the Pope; those Services were modified when used in smaller churches. The *Sacramentary,* used by a celebrant bishop or priest, contained only the texts that varied in accordance with the feast being celebrated. Presumably, invariable texts were memorized. The *Ordo* (pl., *Ordines*) was a book of directions detailing procedural order of the ceremony and the actions accompanying the ritual.

Modern liturgical books containing the Services of the Mass and the Offices, both music and rubrics, have been edited by the Benedictine monks of the Abbey at Solesmes, France. Texts for the Offices are in the *Breviarium* (Breviary); texts for the Masses, in the *Missale* (Missal). The *Antiphonale pro Diurnis Horis* (Antiphonal for the Daily Hours) holds text and music for the Offices; the *Kyriale seu Ordinarium Missae* (Kyrial or Ordinary of the Mass) is a slim volume containing music and texts for the Ordinary, that part of the Mass whose texts do not change; the *Graduale Romanum* (Roman Gradual) has in it the variable chants for the Proper of the Time and Proper of the Saints and includes in an appendix chants of the Ordinary and the Requiem Mass. *The Liber Usualis* (Common Book) contains the most frequently used chants (texts and music) for both Mass and Offices.

In accordance with provisions of the Constitution *De sacra liturgia* (On sacred liturgy) adopted by Vatican Council II in November 1963, Pope Paul VI (r. 1963–78) directed that new editions of the liturgical books be prepared. The Benedictines of the Abbey of Saint Peter, at Solesmes, France, and the Consociety of International Sacred Music accepted that assignment. The revised *Missale romanum* was published in Rome in 1970, and revised editions of other liturgical books followed. A new volume, the *Liber cantualis* (Book of Chants; 1978) is Part I of a selected repertory of Gregorian chants, with Latin texts, suitable for international use.

The Offices

The Offices, or Canonical Hours, constitute the prescribed daily round of worship and prayer in monastic communities, whether recited privately or sung in public. The Hours began as Vigils first held as night watches on Easter eve. Late in the fourth century the worship services in Jerusalem included Vigils, Lauds, Terce, None, and Vespers; in Bethlehem, Prime was observed, and in Chalcedon, Compline. Early in the fifth century, the Offices observed were almost identical in all of the church provinces, though the actual ritual differed in various areas.

The fixed order for the Offices was set by the Rule of St. Benedict in the sixth century as: Matins, during the night but after midnight; Lauds, before dawn; Prime (*ad primam horam,* literally, "at the first hour"), 6 A.M.; Terce, 9 A.M.; Sext, noon; None, 3 P.M.; Vespers, at sunset; and Compline, before retiring. At one time the Offices were intended to mark three-hour intervals commencing with Matins just after midnight and concluding with Compline at 9 P.M., but practice altered this considerably. It was not unusual to find Matins, Lauds, and Prime being celebrated together, though in proper order, at about 6 A.M. or sunrise, and Compline, which grew out of the practice of saying prayers before retiring, occurring immediately after Vespers. Vatican Council II directed that the traditional sequence of the Hours be restored so that as far as possible they are again genuinely related to the time of day at which they are prayed.

Musically, the most important Offices are Vespers, Matins and Lauds, and Compline, in that order. All of the Hours contain Scripture readings with Responses, hymn singing, and Psalms verses chanted in alternation with their **antiphons.** An antiphon is a chant sung in alternation with verses of a psalm and its concluding doxology. Originally, this alternate singing was between two choirs or two half-choirs, and, for this reason, the early antiphons are simple, syllabic or neumatic settings in a rather limited range, e.g., *Confitemini Domino* (LU,295) or *Lumen ad revelationem* (LU,1357; fig. 4.1). Later, when soloists assumed responsibility for much of the liturgical singing, antiphons became more ornate. Antiphons are the most numerous type of chant.

Some Offices contain canticles, which, like psalms, are sung in alternation with antiphons. Figure 4.1 illustrates the procedure when the antiphon *Lumen* is sung with the canticle *Nunc dimittis.* Old Testament canticles are included in both Matins and Lauds. New Testament canticles are sung in Lauds (*Benedictus Dominus Deus Israel,* "Blessed is the Lord God of Israel," the words of Zacharias, Luke 1:68–79); Vespers (*Magnificat anima mea Dominum,* "My soul doth magnify the Lord," the words of Mary, Luke 1:46–55); and Compline (*Nunc dimittis servum tuum*

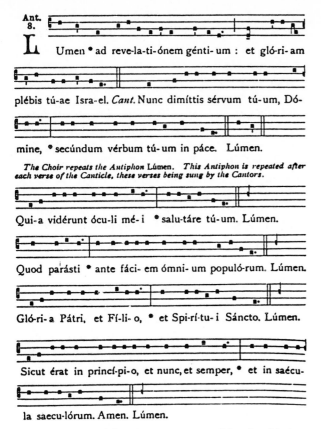

Figure 4.1 The Antiphon *Lumen* as sung traditionally with the Canticle *Nunc dimittis*. (*From* The Liber Usualis, *edited by The Benedictines of Solesmes. Copyright © 1956 Desclée Company, Tournai, Belgium.*)

Figure 4.2 The Marian Antiphon *Regina caeli laetare*. (*From* The Liber Usualis, *edited by The Benedictines of Solesmes. Copyright © 1956 Desclée Company, Tournai, Belgium.*)

Domine, "Now lettest Thou Thy servant depart, Lord," the words of the aged Simeon, Luke 2:29–32). Polyphony was sung in Vespers from medieval times, and was admitted in Matins and Lauds during *Tenebrae,* the last three days of Holy Week, but was excluded from the other Offices.

Compline uses also a **votive** antiphon to the Blessed Virgin Mary. (A votive chant or Service is one honoring a particular saint.) There are four so-called Marian antiphons, one assigned to each of the principal divisions of the church year: *Alma Redemptoris Mater* (Gracious Mother of the Redeemer), used from the Saturday before Advent to and including February 1; *Ave Regina caelorum* (Hail, Queen of Heaven), from February 2 through Wednesday of Holy Week; *Regina caeli laetare* (Rejoice, Queen of Heaven), from Easter Sunday to and including Friday after Pentecost (fig. 4.2); and *Salve, Regina* (Hail, Queen) from Trinity to the Saturday before Advent. These chants were eleventh- and twelfth-century additions to the Offices. In spite of the designation, they are not true antiphons and are not used with a psalm or canticle in the manner of antiphons (DWMA5).

The Mass

Early History

The early Christians observed Jesus's directive to remember Him through symbolic breaking of bread and drinking from the wine cup (I Cor. 11:24). At first, this commemoration of the Lord's Supper occurred in connection with the breaking of unleavened bread and concluded with sharing the wine cup. Prayers and singing of psalms figured prominently at these gatherings. As Christian communities increased in size, special religious services were held on Sabbath morning for this commemoration; later, in recognition of the first day of the week as "the Lord's Day," the Service was moved to Sunday morning. By the second century, the commemorative rite had become

The Roman Liturgy

known as the Eucharist, from the Greek word ευχαριστω (*eucharisto*), meaning "I give thanks." Portions of the synagogue service, e.g., reading Scripture passages and singing psalms, became part of the Christian ritual.

In addition to recognized members of the Christian community, persons who had not yet embraced the Christian faith were present at the Services. These persons, called catechumens, were not permitted to remain for the Eucharist but were dismissed at the conclusion of the instructional portion of the Service.

During the first four centuries of the Christian church, the structured religious service commenced with a greeting and continued with what might be termed Liturgy of the Word: three Scripture readings (from the Old Testament, an Epistle, and a Gospel) interspersed with psalms singing; a homily, followed by a prayer. When this instructional liturgy was completed, the catechumens were dismissed. The second half of the Service, the Eucharist or Communion observance, began with the offering of gifts, including the bread and wine, and the consecration of these items. Special prayers were offered, including a prayer of thanksgiving and a prayer of the faithful. Some of these prayers developed into the Preface and Canon and included the Sanctus (the Thrice-Holy, from Isaiah 6:3) but not the Benedictus that is now part of that chant. After the congregation partook of the bread and wine in the Communion ritual, another prayer was offered, and the congregation was dismissed.

Eventually, probably because the congregation consisted primarily of professed believers and few catechumens were in attendance, all present were permitted to remain for the Communion portion of the Service. The early dismissal chant, no longer needed, was eliminated. When required, a profession of faith was inserted. In the sixth century, the number of Scripture readings was reduced from three to two. Other changes occurred gradually.

By the time Ambrose was bishop of Milan (374–397) the Service was being called *Missa*. This name is derived from the chant with which the Service concludes, *Ite, missa est,* signifying that the congregation is dismissed (*Ite,* Go) and that the message has been sent forth (*missa est,* it [the message] has been sent forth). Inherent is a directive in accordance with Matthew 28:19 and Mark 16:15, "Go into all the world and proclaim the gospel to all creation." The response *Deo gratias* (Thanks be to God) is, therefore, appropriate.

Jesus taught in Aramaic, but the apostles adopted Greek for dissemination of the gospel message; Greek was the language used in worship for about three hundred years. After Christianity was proclaimed state religion of the Roman empire, vernacular replaced Greek in some areas, and Latin (which had been used in Christian churches in Africa for some time) became the official liturgical language of the Roman Catholic Church. In 1963, Vatican Council II permitted use of vernacular languages in Services throughout Christendom.

The Mass Liturgy

The Roman Catholic Mass liturgy attained its historically settled form by c. 1014. The early division of the Mass into an instructional Liturgy of the Word and a commemorative Eucharistic Liturgy is apparent when the Mass is outlined as in figure 4.3. The numbering of the items in that outline indicates the order of performance and illustrates the interweaving of Proper and Ordinary (DWMA6). Recommendations and directives of Vatican Council II have effected some changes in the Mass liturgy since 1965 (Insight, "Reforms of Vatican Council II").

The chants used in the Mass are classified as belonging to either the **Ordinary** or the **Proper** of the Mass according to whether or not their texts change. Chants of the Ordinary have texts that are invariable; the words remain the same for each rendition of the chant though the music to which they are set may differ. Chants of the Proper have variable texts that are appropriate to the season of the liturgical year or the particular commemoration or feast being celebrated. Thus, the Ordinary, with its unchanging texts, forms a core of the Mass liturgy around which are placed the Scripture readings, Psalm settings, and other texts (including the Homily) that are appropriate, or Proper, to the specific religious occasion.

Mass may be sung or said at any hour from dawn until noon; on Christmas Eve, Mass is sung at midnight. A *Missa Solemnis* (High Mass) includes chanting by a celebrant, a deacon, and a subdeacon, and singing by choir with possibly soloist(s) and/or

Ordinary of the Mass	Proper of the Mass	Proper / Ordinary (P)　　(O)
Text invariable	Text variable	
Sung in plainsong or composed music	Sung in plainsong; sometimes composed music used (e.g., motets)	Sung or recited in simple plainsong
Forms normal composed "Mass"		

	Liturgy of the Word, for Instruction:	
	1) Introit	
2) Kyrie eleison		
3) Gloria in excelsis Deo		
		4) Collect (P)
		5) Epistle (P)
	6) Gradual	
	7) Alleluia or Tract	
	8) Sequence used at Easter, Whit Sunday, Corpus Christi, Seven Dolours (and in Requiem Mass)	
		9) Gospel (P)

At this point, the Sermon (Homily) occurs, if one is presented.

10) Credo		
	Liturgy of the Eucharist:	
	11) Offertory	
		12) Secret (P)
		13) Preface (P)
14) Sanctus, Benedictus		
		15) Canon (O) Pater noster
16) Agnus Dei		
	17) Communion	
		18) Postcommunion Prayer(s) (P)
		19) Ite, missa est or Benedicamus Domino Response (O)

Figure 4.3 Outline of historically settled Mass liturgy used after c. 1014.

the congregation. In a *Missa Lecta* (Low Mass) all texts are said or recited by one celebrant priest, assisted by a server; no music is sung or chanted. An intermediate type of Mass, the *Missa Cantata* (Sung Mass), is celebrated by one priest with musical assistance from choir and/or congregation.

Introit

The Introit seems to have developed from the sixth-century custom of having processionals on important feast days, especially on those days when the Pope visited one of the several churches in Rome. The music accompanying the procession from its entrance into

Continued on page 46

Reforms of Vatican Council II

On 25 January 1959, ninety days after being crowned Pope, John XXIII (r. 1958–63) announced his plans to convoke the Twenty-first Ecumenical Council of the Roman Catholic Church. After nearly four years of preparation, that body, which became known as Vatican Council II, began its deliberations. It met in four sessions: (1) 11 October to 8 December 1962; (2) 29 September to 4 December 1963; (3) 14 September to 21 November 1964; and (4) 14 September to 3 December 1965. The 16 documents prepared and approved by the Council were promulgated by Pope Paul VI (r. 1963–78), and an English translation of them was published in 1966 under the title *The Documents of Vatican II*. Of those documents, the Constitution *De sacra liturgia* (On sacred liturgy) has special relevance for music history because it contains directives and recommendations that, either directly or indirectly, affect the liturgical music.

Vatican Council II sought to reform, simplify, and purify the liturgy and chant, and, insofar as possible, restore them to their original form and condition. To this end, it provided that research be done and that new editions of the liturgical books be prepared. Pope Paul VI carried out that directive, and the Benedictines of Abbaye Sainte-Pierre, Solesmes, France, and the Congress of International Sacred Music prepared revisions and published new editions of the liturgical books. In addition, they prepared a new book, *Liber cantualis* (Book of chants), containing a selected repertory of Gregorian chants, with Latin texts, suitable for international use. The *Liber cantualis* was specifically designed to comply with the Council's directive that, though it is permissible to celebrate the Mass in the vernacular, steps should be taken to ensure that the congregation is able to sing or to say together in Latin those parts of the Ordinary of the Mass that pertain to them (Art. 54, *De sacra liturgia*).

The liturgical calendar has been altered slightly with regard to nomenclature, and the designation "Ordinary Time" assigned to the following periods: (1) from the Monday after the Sunday following January 6, up to and including the Tuesday before Ash Wednesday; (2) from the Monday after Pentecost up to, but not including, the first evening prayer of the first Sunday of Advent.

Vatican Council II directed that the traditional sequence of the Canonical Hours (the Offices) be restored so that as far as possible they are again genuinely related to the time of day at which they are prayed. However, the Hour of Prime is to be suppressed; Lauds and Vespers are to be considered the chief Hours and celebrated accordingly (Art. 89).

The Mass liturgy has been altered in several respects (fig. 4.4). The Council recommended that in the liturgy greater use be made of psalms and other Scripture passages and directed that "elements which have suffered injury through accidents of history are now to be restored to the earlier norm of the holy Fathers" (Art. 50). Therefore, the third Scripture reading has been restored to the Mass, and a new doxology has been added after the *Pater noster* (Lord's Prayer): "For the kingdom and the power and the glory are Yours for ever. Amen." In many churches, the psalms are being accorded more use; for example, several verses (instead of just one) are sung in the Introit. Since 1965, *Benedicamus Domino,* once serving as an alternate dismissal chant, has fallen into disuse.

Some alterations have been made in the use and form of the Sequences. Before 1963, five Sequences were in use and a particular one of them was incorporated in the Mass at certain specified feasts. By directive of Vatican Council II, "Except on Easter Sunday and Pentecost the Sequences are optional." Moreover, simplified versions of two of the Sequences have been provided. Only the last four strophes of *Lauda Sion* (optional for Corpus Christi Mass) are printed in the *Liber cantualis* of 1978, under the title *Ecce panis (Lauda Sion)*. These strophes have been renumbered 1 to 4, signifying that the Sequence has been shortened for congregational singing. Rubrics in the *Graduale Romanum* of 1974 state that, if *Lauda Sion* is sung, either the complete or the abbreviated form may be used. The *Stabat Mater* appears as a Sequence in *Liber cantualis* in a strophic setting, but the three-phrase sentence of chant music is that used for the hymn (LU,1424) and provides a syllabic setting for the 21 strophes. However, the traditional setting of the *Stabat Mater* Sequence is printed in the *Graduale Romanum* of 1974.

The general atmosphere as well as the structure of the Requiem Mass has changed. In accordance with the statement adopted by Vatican Council II that "the rite for the burial of the dead should evidence more clearly the paschal character of Christian death," the Requiem Mass has been altered to correspond with the twentieth-century view of death as a glorious home-going rather than dreaded judgment. Most often, clergy wear white vestments for the rite. Three Scripture readings are used in the Service: Old Testament, New Testament other than Gospel, and Gospel; an Alleluia may be used before the Gospel reading. The Sequence is optional, and the judgmental text of *Dies irae* is seldom chanted. A homily is presented, but no eulogy. The altered format of the Requiem Mass is given in figure 4.5.

THE MASS

Ordinary	Proper	Prayers and Lessons
	Introductory Rites:	
	1) Introit	
2) Kyrie eleison		
3) Gloria in excelsis Deo		
		4) Collect
	Liturgy of the Word:	
		5) First Reading: Old Testament
	6) Gradual	
		7) Second Reading: from Epistles, or Acts, or Revelation
	8) Alleluia or Tract	
	9) Sequence, used at Easter and Pentecost (optional at Corpus Christi, Seven Dolours, and Requiem)	
		10) Gospel
	11) Homily (Exegesis and Application of Scriptures)	
12) Credo		
		13) Intercessory Prayers
	Liturgy of the Eucharist:	
	14) Offertory	
		15) Secret
		16) Preface
17) Sanctus, Benedictus		
		18) Canon
	Communion Rite:	
		19) Pater noster Doxology Sign of Peace
20) Agnus Dei		
	21) Communion	
		22) Postcommunion Prayers
	Concluding Rite:	
		(Any brief announcements may be made)
		23) Benediction
24) Dismissal, Ite, missa est		

Figure 4.4 Outline of Mass liturgy in use after Vatican Council II.

Insight continued

Figure 4.5 Outline of Requiem Mass in use after Vatican Council II.

Ordinary	Proper	Proper / Ordinary
	1) Introit: *Requiem aeternam dona eis Domine*	
2) Kyrie		
		3) Collect
		4) First Scripture Reading: from Old Testament
	5) Gradual (Responsorial Psalm)	
		6) Second Reading: Epistle
	7) Alleluia	
		8) Third Reading: Gospel
	9) Brief Homily	
	10) Offertory	
		11) Eucharistic Prayer: *Sursum corda*
		12) Preface of the Dead
13) Sanctus, Benedictus		
		14) Canon
		15) *Pater noster* Doxology Sign of Peace
16) Agnus Dei		
	17) Communion: *Lux aeterna*	
		18) Postcommunion Prayer(s)
		19) *Requiescat in pace. Amen*

the church and up to the altar had to be expandable or contractible in accordance with the degree of pomp and the size of the procession. Originally, this music—the Introit—consisted of an antiphon, a complete psalm, the Lesser Doxology (the *Gloria Patri*), and a repetition of the antiphon. The Introit could be shortened by eliminating psalm verses. In some churches the antiphon was chanted after each verse of the psalm and in the middle and at the end of the doxology. The music was sung antiphonally, as an alternating chant between two choirs or between two half-choirs. At some time during the late eighth or early ninth century, the Introit was reduced to antiphon, one psalm verse, doxology, and antiphon and was performed after the celebrant reached the foot of the altar. Thus, the Introit became a prelude to the Service rather than processional or entrance music.

An Introit is known by the first word of its antiphon's text. Some examples of Introits are: *Resurrexi* (LU,777), for Easter Mass; *Puer natus est nobis* (LU,408), for Mass on Christmas Day; *Requiem aeternam* (LU,1807), for Requiem Mass. The antiphon *Resurrexi* (DWMA6) is mainly neumatic but contains some short melismas; thus, it contrasts with the simple intonation of Psalm 139:1,2 and the doxology.

Kyrie eleison

The *Kyrie eleison* and *Agnus Dei* were Eastern imports that entered the Mass via the litany, where each of them frames solemn supplications and responses addressed to God, to the Virgin Mary, or to a particular saint. The Kyrie appeared in the litany in Milan in the fourth century and was in use in Rome by the sixth century. To the phrase *Kyrie eleison* (Lord, have mercy), used in pagan rites, the Christian church added *Christe eleison* (Christ, have mercy).

Figure 4.6 Manuscript page from Use of Sarum showing *Kyrieleison* elision.

The Kyrie of the Requiem Mass (LU,1807) uses the same music for all but the final phrase, which is slightly varied: AAA,AAA,AAA′. This pattern is especially suitable for congregational singing; probably this Kyrie is one of the oldest chants. Other formal patterns include overall ABA with all exclamations of the same text having the same music (LU,28); ABC, with all utterances within a section using basically the same music (LU,25); or more sophisticated versions of those patterns, with the musical phrases being expanded upon repetition, or even with different music for some of the repeated texts (LU,22).

In medieval times, the words *Kyrie eleison* were frequently elided in performance: *Kyrieleison* (fig. 4.6).

Gloria

The Gloria, whose opening lines are the song of the heavenly host on the night of the Nativity (Luke 2:14), is sometimes called the Song of the Angels, or the Greater Doxology. At first, the Gloria was included in the Mass only on those special occasions when a bishop was celebrant. Gradually, its use was extended to other festal days and Sundays, but the Gloria is excluded on penitential days, during Advent and Lent, and from ferial and Requiem Masses. (A ferial day is a weekday on which no Roman Catholic feast occurs.)

In performance the opening phrase, *Gloria in excelsis Deo* (Glory to God in the highest), is always chanted by the bishop or celebrant priest. Originally, the remainder of the chant was sung by the congregation, but little by little portions were assumed by assisting clergy, and ultimately all but the opening phrase was assumed by full choir who chanted the Gloria antiphonally. There are no textual repetitions in this chant, and no overall formal pattern is apparent. Frequently, the musical setting of the Gloria is neumatic (DWMA6).

Gradual

Designated *responsorium graduale* in early manuscripts, the Gradual is very melismatic psalmody. The Gradual followed the First Lesson (first Scripture reading), and in performance the soloist stood on the *gradus,* the step leading to the raised pulpit. From this performance practice came the name Gradual.

In its simplest form, the Kyrie consisted of the nine phrases that constitute the invocation in modern use in the Mass: *Kyrie eleison* chanted three times, *Christe eleison* chanted three times, *Kyrie eleison* chanted three times (DWMA6). The Greek text was retained in the Roman liturgy until after Vatican Council II. The triple rendition of each phrase of text permits a variety of musical settings, as well as a kind of musical cadence rhyme in which all cadences employ a common phrase as a unifying feature. This may be seen in *Kyrie Rex Genitor* (LU,31).

Analysis of Graduals indicates that many of them were created by centonization technique. In each mode there were a number of standard melodic motives and phrases, which, with their extensions and variations, were combined to form a Gradual. Occasionally, newly composed phrases or motives were inserted.

Until the thirteenth century, the Gradual had ternary (ABA) form: a choral respond, a solo verse, and repetition of the choral respond. Like some other chants, the Gradual was reduced and consists of a choral respond followed by a solo verse. In modern performance, the Gradual commences with a solo intonation, but the choir sings most of the respond; a soloist sings the verse as far as its last phrase, at which point the choir joins for conclusion of the chant.

Some historically significant Graduals are: *Viderunt omnes* (LU,409), used in Christmas Mass; *Haec dies* (LU,778), the Easter Gradual (DWMA6); and *Sederunt principes* (LU,416), sung in Mass on St. Stephen's Day, December 26.

Alleluia

The Alleluia came to the Christian church from the Hebrew synagogue; the Hebrew words *Hallelu Jah* mean "Praise ye Jehovah." In earliest times, this chant was sung throughout the year in both Eastern and Western churches as responsorial psalmody, with a soloist singing a verse and the congregation (later, the choir) responding with "Alleluia." However, certain Roman popes placed restrictions on its performance: Damasus (r. 366–384) limited its use in Rome to the Easter season; Gregory I prohibited it during Lent.

In modern liturgical practice, from Easter to Pentecost the word Alleluia is sung at the end of every important chant of the Proper in both Offices and Mass, but the Alleluia has been excluded from the Service when its joyous text is deemed inappropriate to the occasion—during penitential seasons, and, until c. 1965, the Requiem. At those times, a Tract is substituted. As a general rule, when a Mass contains no Gloria, it contains no Alleluia.

In performance, a soloist sings the first Alleluia, which is repeated by the choir and concludes with the textless melismatic coda known as the *jubilus*; most of the ensuing verse is sung by cantors, and the choir joins them for the last phrase. Finally, a soloist sings

the Alleluia as at the beginning, and the choir performs the *jubilus* (DWMA6). The Alleluia is one of the most melodious and artistic chants of the Mass. Although it is considered a very melismatic chant in the Roman rite, it is even more florid in Eastern, Mozarabic, and Ambrosian liturgies.

Tract

Called *cantus tractus* because the chant was designed to be sung from beginning to end without interruption, the Tract consists of a series of psalm verses, all taken from the same psalm, performed by a soloist. Rarely is a complete psalm used. The Tract is the most ancient solo chant of the Mass, having its roots in Hebrew synagogue solo psalmody. The ornate melodies, created by centonization technique, were constructed in the second and eighth modes only. Although included in the Mass at times when the joyous Alleluia is prohibited, the Tract is not particularly sorrowful or solemn. Even the Tract used in the Requiem Mass, *Absolve, Domine* (LU,1809), is well supplied with melismas (DWMA7).

Sequence

The Sequence, which came into existence during the ninth century as a result of the practice of troping (discussed on p. 52), was sung in the Mass immediately following the Alleluia, from whose *jubilus* it seems to have sprung. If two Alleluias are included in the Mass, the Sequence follows the second one. Thousands of Sequences were composed during the Middle Ages and early Renaissance. These chants varied from region to region, diocese to diocese, according to the particular customs and requirements of the churches in which they were used. As a result of the deliberations of the Council of Trent, all but four Sequences were eliminated from liturgical use: *Dies irae* (Day of wrath), *Victimae paschali laudes* (Praises to the Paschal Victim), *Lauda Sion* (Zion, praise), and *Veni Sancte Spiritus* (Come, Holy Spirit).

Until c. 1965, *Dies irae* (LU,1810), attributed to St. Thomas of Celano (d. 1520), was sung after the Tract in the Requiem Mass. Its poetic text consists of 18 strophes and a short requiem prayer. Most of the strophes are paired in the musical setting. Analysis of *Dies irae* by strophes gives the following pattern: a a b b c c a a b b c c a a b b c d e f.

Victimae paschali laudes (LU,780) is sung in the Easter Mass (DWMA6). The setting is syllabic, and the pairing of strophes typical of Sequences is apparent in the music: a b b c c d. Originally, this Sequence had seven strophes, but during the reign of Pope Pius V (1566–72) the sixth strophe, using "d" music, was deleted.

Lauda Sion (LU,945), used in Mass at Corpus Christi, was composed in 1263 by St. Thomas Aquinas (1227–74) as part of a Communion Service commissioned by Pope Urban IV (r. 1261–64). Its long poetic text (24 strophes) is set syllabically in paired strophes.

Veni Sancte Spiritus (LU,880), written in the late twelfth century by an anonymous composer, is sung on Whit Sunday (Pentecost) and for six days thereafter. Its ten rhymed strophes are set neumatically and paired: a a b b c c d d e e.

In 1727 Pope Benedict XIII (r. 1724–30) readmitted to the liturgy the Sequence *Stabat Mater dolorosa* (The sorrowful Mother stood), for use at the Feast of the Seven Dolours of the Blessed Virgin Mary, on September 15. This Sequence (LU,1634v) is attributed to Jacopone da Todi (d. 1306). The *Stabat Mater* text is used in the Offices also, as a hymn, at Vespers on Friday after Passion Sunday (see LU,1424).

Credo

The Credo was first used liturgically as an individual profession of faith made at baptism; this accounts for the singular verb *Credo* (I believe). The text is the so-called Nicene Creed, basically formulated by the Council of Nicaea in 325 and altered by the Councils of Constantinople in 381 and Chalcedon in 451.

In Eastern and Mozarabic churches the Credo was used in the Mass liturgy in the sixth century, but not until 798 was the Credo regularly included in the Mass in Gallic or Roman churches. Then, in conjunction with Charlemagne's reforms, the Council of Aix-la-Chapelle decreed that the Credo be sung at Mass between the Gospel reading and Communion. Charlemagne's adviser, Alcuin (c. 735–804), advocated use of a Latin translation instead of Greek. Alcuin lived in York prior to 780 and undoubtedly was familiar with the use of a sung Credo in Celtic liturgy. Though Pope Leo III (r. 795–816) sanctioned the use of the Credo in Frankish churches, that chant did not

officially enter the Roman Mass until Pope Benedict VIII required it in 1014, at the insistence of Emperor Henry II (r. 1002–24).

Originally, the Credo was deemed appropriate for Sundays and important feasts only; it is not included in ferial or Requiem Masses. In modern performance, the celebrant priest chants the first phrase, *Credo in unum Deo* (I believe in one God), and the choir or congregation continues from *Patrem omnipotentem* (the Father Almighty). Credo I (LU,64) is considered the oldest Credo; its setting is almost completely syllabic, and recurrent use of melodic formulas is apparent (DWMA6).

Offertory

St. Augustine (d. 430) is credited with introducing into the liturgy at Carthage the custom of singing an Offertory chant while the gifts of bread and wine were brought forward to be consecrated. It is believed that this chant consisted originally of a psalm, sung antiphonally by the two halves of the choir. However, the earliest Offertory chants in existence are elaborate melodies for antiphons and verses, which would indicate solo performance. In these eighth- and ninth-century manuscripts, the Offertory consists of an antiphon, two or three verses, and a respond or refrain that most often is an exact repetition of the conclusion of the antiphon. In Gregorian liturgy, the verses were gradually deleted until only the antiphon remained; perhaps the deletions were concurrent with changes in the character of the offering and the manner of its collection. In Ambrosian and Mozarabic liturgies Offertory verses are still present.

In modern performance, the first phrase of the Offertory is sung by cantor(s), and the remainder of the antiphon is performed by choir (DWMA6). The Offertory is highly melismatic. Frequently, the expressive character of the melismas suggests an early use of text painting, for example, melismas rising in pitch on the words *ascendit* (ascends) or *caelo* (heaven) and lowering in pitch on *descendit* (descends).

Communion

From early Christian times, the singing of a psalm or a hymn during Communion was common practice. Use of a hymn may have derived from Gospel accounts of events at the Lord's Supper: "And having sung a hymn, they went forth to the Mount of Olives" (Matt. 26:30; Mark 14:26). Several of the Church Fathers cited the use of Psalm 33 (34, King James Version) in which verse 8 was considered especially appropriate: "O taste and see that the Lord is good: blessed is the man that trusteth in Him."

The use of psalms and hymns was not identical in all liturgies, however. In Byzantine and Celtic rites, both hymns and psalms were used during Communion, on different occasions. In the Ambrosian rite, two antiphons (without psalms) were sung: one during fraction of the Host, the other during distribution of the elements. In the Roman ritual, Communion music consisted of an antiphon and a psalm, performed antiphonally, with embellished psalm tones being used for the verses. Originally, in the Roman Mass, Introit and Communion were similar; frequently, both used the same psalm, with different antiphons. Some eighth-century *Ordines* detail explicitly the manner of performance, instructing the choir to commence singing the antiphon as soon as the priest began administering the sacrament, and to follow the antiphon with the psalm. When all communicants had partaken of the elements, the priest signaled the choir to sing the *Gloria Patri,* followed by repetition of the antiphon.

During the eleventh century, psalm verses were gradually deleted from the Communion; a century later, only the antiphon remained. At that time, the congregation received Communion infrequently.

Communion settings do not exhibit uniformity of style. Most Communions are rather short; the music possesses a serenity appropriate to the sacrament. Though many Communions contain melismas, the floridity is restrained rather than exuberant.

Sanctus/Benedictus

The text of this acclamation is a combination of portions of verses from both Old and New Testaments, the Sanctus taken from Isaiah 6:3 and the Hosanna and Benedictus from Matthew 21:9. Both Scripture verses were modified slightly. The Sanctus was used in the Hebrew synagogue; Hosanna and Benedictus were Christian additions.

Originally, congregation and clergy together sang the Sanctus. This is obvious from the concluding words

of the Preface, which suggest that the people join the heavenly host in singing a hymn of praise, saying *Sanctus, sanctus, sanctus* (Holy, holy, holy). Gradual transference of the chant from congregation to assisting clergy to trained choir began in the eighth century, occurring at different times in different areas. In most churches, by the end of the twelfth century the choir had assumed full responsibility for the Sanctus. In the Service, there is a pause after the Sanctus, during which time the Elevation of the Host occurs; then the Benedictus is sung (DWMA6).

No standard pattern is apparent in the musical settings of the Sanctus. Some are syllabic; others are neumatic except for melismas on the first three words. Frequently, these three melismatic pronouncements of the word *Sanctus* are set musically as a b a; often the two Hosanna sections are given identical or very similar music. For example, in Sanctus II (LU,21), the first three words of the chant have a b a melismas; the two Hosanna sections are identical; and the Benedictus music varies only slightly from that of the *Pleni sunt caeli* section of the Sanctus. It would seem natural to assume that syllabic settings of the Sanctus are the oldest. Yet, if the dating in *The Liber usualis* is accurate, the reverse might be true, for Sanctus XVII (LU,63), from the thirteenth-century, is far simpler than others with earlier dating.

Agnus Dei

Introduction of the Agnus Dei into the Mass in the late seventh century is credited to the Greek Pope Sergius I (r. 687–701). Like the Kyrie, the Agnus Dei is an acclamation, a petition for mercy. Part of the text is a modification of the words of John the Baptist, recorded in John 1:29: "Behold the Lamb of God, who takes away the sin of the world." Originally, in the chant, only a single line of text was used: *Agnus Dei, qui tollis peccata mundi, miserere nobis* (Lamb of God, who takes away the sins of the world, have mercy upon us). At first this was sung by the congregation, as were the other chants of the Ordinary, but by the end of the eighth century the Agnus Dei was being sung by the trained choir in many churches.

At the time of its introduction into the Mass, the Agnus Dei was sung during Fraction. Breaking the loaves of leavened bread consumed a considerable amount of time; therefore, the chant was repeated an indefinite number of times. During the tenth and eleventh centuries, it became customary to use small pieces of unleavened bread instead of leavened loaves, and actual fraction was no longer necessary. Fewer repetitions of the chant were required. From time to time, the Agnus Dei was assigned other functions, but ultimately was used to fill the time between Consecration of the Host and distribution of the Communion elements. The number of acclamations in the chant was finalized at three, and the third petition was revised, substituting the words *dona nobis pacem* (give us peace) for *miserere nobis* (have mercy upon us). This exchange of text caused no musical problems; each of the two phrases contains six syllables and the grammatical accentuation is identical (DWMA6). At the same time, an adjustment was made in the Agnus Dei of the Requiem Mass (LU,1815); the word *sempiternam* was added to the last phrase to make the chant conclude *dona eis requiem sempiternam* (give them eternal rest).

Various formal patterns are found in the musical settings of the Agnus Dei, such as ABA (Agnus Dei XV, LU,58); AAA (Agnus Dei XVIII, LU,63); and AA'A (Agnus Dei IX, LU,42). Sometimes, within an overall ABA setting of the three petitions, the musical setting of the words *qui tollis* is identical (Agnus Dei X, LU,45). Musical cadence rhyme occurs often, e.g., in Agnus Dei II, IV, VIII, and others.

Dismissal

The dismissal *Ite, missa est* has always been chanted by the celebrant priest or a deacon. Originally, the congregation responded with *Deo gratias* (Thanks be to God). Eventually, the choir assumed this response, along with other congregational functions, and it became more elaborate.

In the eleventh century, the alternate dismissal chant *Benedicamus Domino* (Let us bless the Lord) came into use as replacement for *Ite, missa est* when the Mass did not contain a Gloria. Both dismissal chants and the response are sung to the same music.

Although the Mass attained its settled liturgical format through a process of gradual growth and development, a remarkable symmetry is apparent, especially with regard to the Ordinary. The affirmation of faith, Credo, is centrally located. The texts of both Gloria and Sanctus include songs of the heavenly host, and the Kyrie and Agnus Dei parallel each other in many respects: both were Eastern imports; both are textually tripartite; both were used in the litany in a manner similar to their employment in the Mass—the Kyrie at or near the beginning and the Agnus Dei at or near the end. The location of these chants in the Mass was balanced by similar antiphonal psalmody: the Introit preceding the Kyrie, and the Communion following the Agnus Dei. Moreover, the texts of these two acclamations contain some of the same phrases—the Greek *eleison* and the Latin *miserere nobis* both mean "have mercy upon us." Perhaps this was one reason the Kyrie remained in Greek when the other chants were translated into Latin.

Requiem Mass

The Requiem Mass (Mass for the Dead) received its name from the first word of the antiphon to its Introit and its Gradual, which commences *Requiem aeternam dona eis Domine* (Give them eternal rest, Lord). Though the Collect, Scripture reading, Secret, and Postcommunion may vary on certain occasions, the remainder of the Proper and the Ordinary texts are invariable. Neither Gloria nor Credo are used in the Requiem; the Tract *Absolve, Domine* (Lord, absolve . . .) traditionally replaced the Alleluia and was followed by the Sequence *Dies irae* (Day of wrath; DWMA8). On very solemn occasions, the Responsory *Libera me, Domine* (Free me, Lord) is sung after the Communion.

In the development of the Requiem Mass, the Sequence was the last item to be added; the essential features of the Mass were settled by the fourteenth century. Prior to the Councils of Trent, the Gradual *Si ambulem in medio umbrae mortis* (If I walk in the midst of the shadow of death) and the Tract *Sicut cervus desiderat ad fontes aquarum* (As the hart longs for springs of water) might be used as alternatives; these derive from Sarum Use.

The traditional Requiem Mass, in the format used prior to reforms of Vatican Council II, is outlined in figure 4.7.

Ordinary	Proper	Proper / Ordinary
Text invariable	Text invariable	
Sung: Plainsong or composed music	Plainsong, sometimes composed	Plainsong

Ordinary	Proper	Proper / Ordinary
	1) Introit: *Requiem aeternam dona eis Domine*	
2) Kyrie		
		3) Collect
		4) Epistle: I Thess. 4:13–18
	5) Gradual: *Requiem aeternam* ℣. *In memoria aeterna erit*	
	6) Tract: *Absolve, Domine*	
	7) Sequence: *Dies irae, dies illa*	
		8) Gospel: John 11:21–27
	9) Offertory: *Domine Jesu Christe*	
		10) Secret
		11) Preface for the Dead
12) Sanctus, Benedictus		
13) Agnus Dei		
	14) Communion: *Lux aeterna* (Sometimes, Responsory *Libera me, Domine* is included)	
		15) Postcommunion
		16) *Requiescant in pace. Amen.*

Figure 4.7 Outline of the Requiem Mass as sung prior to Vatican Council II.

Tropes

Troping is the expansion of a chant by means of: (a) words added to an existing chant melisma, (b) music added to extend an existing melisma or to create a new one, or (c) new music and text added before, within, or at the end of an existing chant (fig. 4.8). Usually, textual interpolations complement, elaborate, or clarify the original words of the chant; the interpolations themselves, when considered apart from the original text, are coherent. It is not known precisely when and where troping began, for tropes are present in the earliest extant manuscripts of liturgical chant music, which date from the late eighth or early ninth century, but it is believed the practice started in Frankish lands. It is certain that troping did not originate at St. Gall, though that monastery and St. Martial at Limoges became important centers of troping.

The troping of chants flourished during the tenth through twelfth centuries. Virtually every kind of chant except the Credo was troped, and the practice gave rise to new forms of liturgical music. In accordance with recommendations for reform made by the Councils of Trent, textual tropes were deleted from liturgical chants. Vestiges of tropes remain, however, in some textless melismas and in the titles of Kyries, e.g., Kyrie *orbis factor* (Lord, creator of the world). Moreover, the practice of troping gave rise to several new forms of church music, including the Sequence, liturgical drama, and motet (discussed on p. 94).

Notker Balbulus, "the Stammerer" (c. 840–912), famed poet and author of many tropes, related in the Preface to his *Liber Ymnorum* (Book of Hymns) the circumstances that first acquainted him with textual tropes. As a youth, he experienced difficulty remembering very long melismas and sought some device to help him retain them. About that time (c. 852), a priest came to St. Gall from Jumièges (near Rouen)

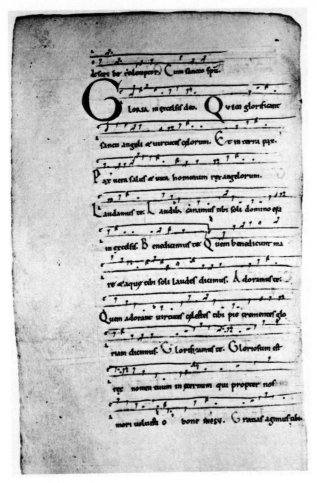

Figure 4.8 A troped *Gloria. (From twelfth-century MS Lat. 10.508, fol. 32v, Bibliothèque nationale, Paris.)*

because his monastery had been devastated by Normans. Notker noticed in the refugee's *Antiphoner* that words had been written beneath certain melismas called *sequentiae* (Sequences). Though the supplemental texts were distasteful to Notker, the idea fascinated him. He troped an Alleluia, then showed the trope to his teacher, Iso, who emended it and instructed, "Each neume of the melody should have one syllable." Notker continued to write tropes, and, following the suggestion of Marcellus, choirmaster at St. Gall, assembled these in *Liber Ymnorum* c. 880.

Liber Ymnorum is significant for several reasons. Its Preface establishes an approximate time when troping was introduced at St. Gall. The book contains no music, and not all of its texts are related to Alleluias. However, in the early repertory a certain text fits only one melody. Scholars have been able to match Notker's texts with specific chants, to place certain chants definitely in the ninth century, and to determine that the most important melodies in the West Frankish liturgy were used at St. Gall also.

Notker wrote in his Preface that he showed his tropes to other monks, and that Marcellus had his choirboys sing some of them. Tuotilo (d. 915), a pupil of Iso and Marcellus and a contemporary of Notker at St. Gall, was also a talented poet and composer of tropes.

Sequences

As described by Amalar of Metz (c. 775–c. 850) in *Liber officialis,* written c. 823, the *sequentia* was an extensive melisma substituted for the *jubilus* at the repetition of the Alleluia section after the Verse. (The *jubilus* is the long melisma vocalized on the syllable -*ia* between the Alleluia and the Verse.) Thus, in the early ninth century a definite relationship existed between the *sequentia* and the Alleluia—a relationship that later undoubtedly influenced placement of the independent Sequence after the Alleluia in the Mass.

In many manuscripts, the same *sequentiae* appear in different contexts: (a) melodies alone, grouped in a section titled *Sequentarium;* (b) melodies with syllabically set texts, grouped in a section called *Prosarium;* and (c) melodies with or without texts, notated with the chants for which they are interpolations. Often, in both *Sequentarium* and *Prosarium* sections, a melody is preceded by the designation *Alleluia I,* implying that the notated melody was used as Amalar stated.

Sequentiae soon became detached from Alleluias and were written as independent chants—Sequences—each complete in itself musically and textually. Many Sequences cannot be linked with known Alleluias and may have been created without reference to any particular Alleluia. Yet, when the Sequence entered the Mass, the early association of Sequence with Alleluia was reflected in the location of the two chants in the liturgy.

The earliest Sequences are prose; even when end-rhyme is present, the lines cannot be scanned poetically. Most of the Sequences written after A.D. 1000 are poetry, with recognizable rhyme scheme and regular accentuation that permits poetic scansion. By the twelfth century, Sequences contain poetic stanzas. The mature Sequence may be defined as a syllabic setting of a Latin text written mainly as a series of couplets that are isosyllabic lines; both lines of a couplet are sung to the same melody, but successive couplets use different melodies and usually differ in length.

The manner of performance of early Sequences is not known. Probably, they were sung antiphonally, as was much medieval music. Both Notker's mention of an *Antiphoner* and the association of Sequence with Alleluia lend credence to this. Although some Sequence texts mention instruments, it does not necessarily follow that those instruments were used in the church Service. Such references may be only symbolic. At least one eleventh-century manuscript containing Sequences is illustrated by miniatures of instrumentalists, and in some regions legislation prohibited performance on certain instruments during church Services. Edict and practice do not always coincide, however. Probably, the only musical instrument authorized for church use was the organ, but whether its tones supported the singing of Sequences is not known.

Liturgical Drama

Introductions to chants form an important part of trope repertory. These introductions vary considerably. Some are quite short and serve merely to set the scene or to identify a character or characters whose words form the ensuing chant. Notker included in *Liber Ymnorum* a cycle of eleven four-line introductory tropes to Introits of the Mass for the most important commemorations in the liturgical year. Some authors constructed introductions as dialogues, the performance of which varied in accordance with the ingenuity of the performers and the artistic indulgence of the local church authorities. Dialogue tropes to the Introit of the Mass are the simplest forms of liturgical drama.

Important centers of liturgical drama were Winchester Cathedral in England and the Abbeys of St. Gall and St. Martial. Tenth-century *Tropers* from these centers survive.

The most important and most numerous of the early liturgical dramas are the *Quem quaeritis* dialogue tropes to Introits of the Masses for Easter and Christmas (fig. 4.9). Some of these are quite simple, but more than 400 are expanded versions—even tropes were troped. In its simplest form, the Easter dialogue consists of three sentences:

Quem quaeritis in sepulchro, o Christicolae?
Jesum Nazarenum crucifixum, o caelicolae.
Non est hic, surrexit sicut praedixerat;
ite, nuntiate quia surrexit de sepulchro.

Translated:

Whom seek ye in the tomb, O Christians?
The crucified Jesus of Nazareth, O heavenly ones.
He is not here, he is risen as he predicted;
go, announce that he is risen from the tomb.

This version is in tenth-century manuscripts from both St. Martial and St. Gall (DWMA9). Manuscripts from the tenth to the sixteenth century contain enlarged versions, called *Visitatio sepulchri,* which are assigned various liturgical locations, including the Offices. In Sarum Use, the Easter drama appears in two fourteenth-century *Processionals* used at the Church of St. John the Evangelist, in Dublin; there, the drama was performed after the last Respond at Easter Matins. In a fourteenth-century manuscript used at the collegiate church at Essen, where both canons and canonesses served, the rubrics for *Visitatio sepulchri* show that the lines of the three Marys were sung by women, and those of the angels by men. The participants in the drama wore normal ecclesiastical robes and were permitted to sing from a book if they had not memorized the music.

In addition to *Quem quaeritis* dialogues, surviving liturgical dramas include an early thirteenth-century *Play of Daniel* created by students at the cathedral school at Beauvais, the *Conversion of Saint Paul* and the *Raising of Lazarus* from Fleury, the *Play of Herod,* and several dramas honoring the Virgin Mary and other saints. All of the plays were intended to convey a mood of joyful celebration. The primary purpose of the *Play of Daniel* is to celebrate Christmas—the drama presents the Biblical story of Daniel, prophet of Christ's coming, but the play's conclusion leaps ahead in time when an angel suddenly cries out, "*Natus est Christus!*" ("Christ is born!")

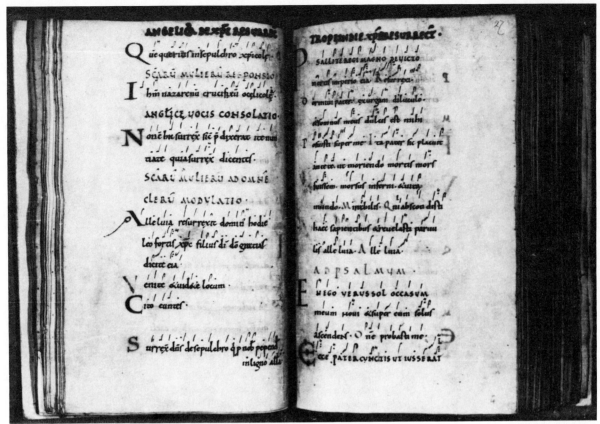

Figure 4.9 *Winchester Troper* manuscript book open to page showing *Quem quaeritis* trope. *(MS 473, Parker Library, Corpus Christi College, Cambridge, England.)*

Summary

The Mass and the Offices, the two principal Services of the Roman Catholic Church, evolved from the religious observances of the early Christian communities. Practices of the Hebrew synagogue figured prominently in these observances; as the Mass developed, Hebrew synagogue practices were retained and some items were transferred from the Byzantine church, also. The Mass liturgy attained its historically settled format in 1014 when Pope Benedict VIII formally added the Credo to the Ordinary. Troping was an innovation of the ninth century; the Abbeys at St. Gall and St. Martial became important centers of troping. The production of tropes led to new liturgical forms, among them the Sequence, the liturgical drama, and later the motet.

Liturgical reforms advocated by the Councils of Trent (1545–63) resulted in the deletion of trope texts from the liturgy, and all but four Sequences were removed from the Mass repertory. However, the *Stabat Mater* Sequence was readmitted in 1727. Further reforms occurred after Vatican Council II (1962–65). In addition to permitting use of the vernacular in the Mass Service, Vatican Council II advocated reform that would restore the chant and the liturgy as nearly as possible to the old Roman type. By 1987, new editions of the official liturgical books had been prepared by the Benedictine monks of Abbaye Saint-Pierre, Solesmes.

5

Early Middle Ages

In the ninth through eleventh centuries, the political pattern in Europe exhibited increasing fragmentation and complexity. The Carolingian empire of the Franks was divided and subdivided more than once as rulers died and their kingdoms were partitioned to satisfy heirs. Marauders invaded Europe from north, south, and east, conquering and plundering, but not always bringing only destruction. For example, the Arabs, who had learned much from the populations they conquered, contributed much to Western culture. Oriental science and Greek philosophy had been absorbed into Arab culture. The writings of Aristotle and other ancients had been translated into Arabic and were given back to the Western world in Latin; the decimal system was accepted as the basis of mathematics; and the first medical school established at Salerno, in southern Italy, was in an area with Muslim associations.

The tenth and eleventh centuries witnessed the rise of the feudal system and the growth of a monarchial system that used the church to its own ends by replacing insubordinate vassals with clergy to achieve political stability. These centuries saw also an increase in population, the growth of towns and a revival of urban life, and the rise of a middle-class populace. Commerce and trade, which were at a low ebb after the dissolution of the Carolingian empire, now began their comeback.

Feudalism, begun under the Merovingians, was widespread in Europe by the twelfth century. Feudalism was a system of land tenure and personal relationships in which a lord gave land to vassals in return for specific services and pledged loyalty. The system, which embraced both clergy and laity, filled the need for protection for self, family, and property. Contractual agreements between lord and vassal created a hierarchy that extended from the king to the lowest peasant. Linked with feudalism was the manorial system under which landlords exercised financial, judicial, and other rights over peasants bound to their land. Widespread belief that the king provided security contributed to the rise of monarchies. Those in England and France were well established by the end of the twelfth century.

In Byzantium, art and scholarship flourished, with free education available at the University of Constantinople. In spite of the apparent well-being of the empire, strained relations existed between Eastern and Western branches of the Church. Triggered by the incompatibility of the papal envoy and the Eastern patriarch, a complete break between Eastern and Western churches occurred in 1054. On the heels of that came the onslaught of the Seljuk Turks.

In 1095 Pope Urban II (r. 1088–99) called the First Crusade; others ensued, until the middle of the fifteenth century. Regardless of the success or failure of the individual Crusades, collectively they had a significant effect on contemporary society. Among other things, they strengthened the position of the papacy, stimulated commerce by creating a demand for luxury goods from the East, and invigorated intellectual activity through the making of new contacts.

Early Middle Ages

850	900	950	1000	1050	1100	1150	1200	1250
Russia founded	911 Normans estab. Normandy	987–96 Hugh Capet (Fr.)		1066 Battle of Hastings		1154–1189 Henry II of England and Anjou		
		936–Otto I–973 German Emperor		1054 Schism: East. & West. Churches		1154—1190 Frederick I, Emperor (Barbarossa)		
					1096 First Crusade			

O r g a n u m -

850	900	950	1000	1050	1100	1150	1200	1250
Strict, simple Strict, composite Modified	Free				Melismatic	Discant-style Clausula	Triplum standard Occasional quadruplum Substitute clausulae	

c. 930–1130 School of poet-composers at St. Martial, rise of polyphony in twelfth century

- Santiago de Compostela - - - - - -

Parisian (Notre Dame) School - - - - - - - - - - - -

Léonin fl. 1163–1190
Magnus liber organi

850	900	950	1000	1050	1100	1150	1200	1250
Musica enchiriadis *Scolica enchiriadis*								
St. Gall: Notker Balbulus Tropes Sequence		Liturgical drama	*The Winchester Tropers*			Pérotin fl. c. 1190———1225		

Versus

- - - - - - Conductus -
(monophonic)   (polyphonic)

850	900	950	1000	1050	1100	1150	1200	1250
			995———1050 Guido d'Arezzo staff notation hexachord system mutation; "hand"			Rhythmic modes - - - - - - Modal notation - - - - - - -		
				Chanson de Roland				

Jongleurs - - Minstrels - - Guilds -

Troubadours -

Trouvères -

c. 1145———Trobairitz fl.———c. 1225

850	900	950	1000	1050	1100	1150	1200	1250
		Spielleute - - - - - - - - - - - - - -			Minnesänger -			
		Scops, Gleemen - - - - - Minstrels						

During the ninth through eleventh centuries France, England, and several other nations of modern Europe emerged and began to develop (Insight, "Europe's National Beginnings"). Music flourished in their churches and in their courts and undoubtedly had a place in secular life elsewhere. Part-music was improvised and eventually composed, principles were established governing the improvisation and composition of melodies, a system of music notation gradually developed, and theoretical treatises appeared.

Europe's National Beginnings

During the ninth through eleventh centuries, several of Europe's nations emerged and began to develop. After the death of Louis I, the Pious (r. 814–40), the Carolingian empire was divided among his three sons, creating three separate dynasties. By the Treaty of Verdun (843), Lothar became emperor and received Italy and a middle portion of the empire called Lorraine, a territory that would be controversial even in the twentieth century; Charles II (the Bald) was given the western portion, which became "France"; the eastern part went to Louis I ("the German") and eventually became "Germany." The Treaty of Verdun was the first document written in French and German languages; use of both vernaculars indicates that eastern and western parts of the empire were already pulling apart. When Lothar I died (855), his empire was divided among his three sons: Louis II received Italy and the imperial crown; Charles was given Provence and southern Burgundy; and Lothar II received Lorraine. In 870 Lorraine was again partitioned, between Charles the Bald and Louis II.

In "Germany," the last Carolingian ruler, Louis the Child, died in 911. Thereafter, rulership became elective. Louis's successor, King Conrad I (r. 911–19) had to withstand five powerful military leaders—the dukes of Lorraine, Saxony, Franconia, Swabia, and Bavaria—as well as combat Magyar invasions. Otto I the Great (r. 936–73) dispensed with both problems (fig. 5.1). Whereas Conrad had created a monarchial administration excluding the dukes, Otto achieved political stability by choosing clergy as royal administrators. Otto's solution strengthened the power of the church, as well as his own. Nevertheless, churchmen became the ruler's vassals.

Northmen came to Europe by sea in annual incursions that were especially disastrous to monasteries and churches. In 911 the Vikings invaded Frankish land and captured a large district on the lower Seine River. This territory, called Normandy, served as a base for expeditions that, in the eleventh century, extended Viking rule considerably. The Northmen moved across the English Channel, and after the decisive Battle of Hastings (1066) England became Norman territory ruled by William I, the Conqueror. By this time, the Vikings were moving into southern Italy and Sicily. The last Arab base in Sicily was conquered by Normans in 1091. The Norman kingdom established there was not fused with the Germans until 1194, when Emperor Henry VI, husband of the Norman heiress, became King of Sicily, Apulia, and Calabria.

In France, Hugh Capet (r. 987–996) ruled only in Île de France, a small area between the Seine and Loire Rivers. Most of Hugh's successors in the eleventh century were deemed "helpless" rulers. Louis VI, the Fat (r. 1108–37), manipulated the machinery of feudal law effectively, using it to suppress vassal uprisings by awarding churchmen governmental positions, a procedure that increased the support given him by the French church. His successor, Louis VII (r. 1137–80), was ineffectual. When Louis's marriage to Eleanor of Aquitaine ended in divorce, she wed Henry, Duke of Normandy and Count of Anjou and Maine, who became Henry II of England (r. 1154–89). Henry was never willing to learn the English language. His political policies created friction on two fronts: between England and France and between church and state. England's control of territories on the continent was one cause of the Hundred Years' War (fig. 5.2). Henry, the first great Plantagenet king of England, tried to limit the authority of the church in England, and in 1170 had the Archbishop of Canterbury, Thomas à Becket, slain in his own cathedral. The pope excommunicated the ruler. Ultimately, Henry capitulated and did humbling penance.

In southwestern Europe, the Franks had managed to keep invading Arabs south of the Pyrenees, but the Arab kingdom established at Cordova, Spain, in 756 survived until 1031.

Vikings invaded Eastern Europe, too, and conquered the scattered Slavic tribes in Russia. In many areas, Slavic and Viking cultures merged. Gradually, a rather loosely organized confederacy of principalities came into being under leadership of the senior prince at Kiev. A strong Kievan state existed under the rule of Oleg (r. c. 880–912); he may be considered the real founder of that Russian state. The territory came within Constantinople's cultural sphere after the marriage of Princess Anna, sister of Emperor Basil II, to Prince Vladimir of Kiev, in 988.

The spread of Christianity into Kiev and other Slavic regions resulted also in creation of the Cyrillic Russian-Slavic languages. In the ninth century, the Slavs established Great Moravia, a powerful principality in central Europe. In 863, at the request of Rotislav, ruler of Moravia, Pope Nicholas I sent St. Cyril and St. Methodius to them from Constantinople for purposes of conversion. These missionaries created the Slavic language, using Greek characters for the alphabet. Great Moravia was short-lived; it succumbed to the Magyars at the beginning of the tenth century. The marauding Magyars were defeated by German

Continued

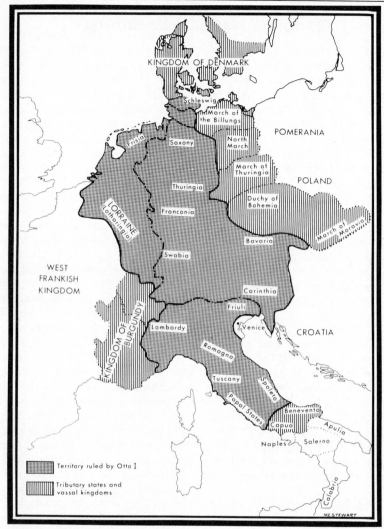

Figure 5.1 Territory ruled by Otto I the Great c. 937.

Emperor Otto I in 955 and were forced back to the Hungarian plains, where they settled. As time passed, this Slavic-Asiatic region in central Europe formed a barrier separating the two halves of Europe. The invasions of Asiatic tribes contributed to the separation of East and West in Europe and strengthened the Slavic wedge between the two; constant invasions provided distraction, which increased the chaos.

In the eleventh century, the church supported rulers only to the extent that its own independence was not threatened.

In 1059 the power rulers exercised over the church was curbed somewhat when Pope Nicholas II (r. 1059–61) decreed that papal election would be accomplished by a college of cardinals, and expressly excluded secular intervention. Further rupturing of church-state relations occurred in 1073, when Pope Gregory VII (r. 1073–85) clearly outlined papal authority and declared papal supremacy in his *Dictatus papae.*

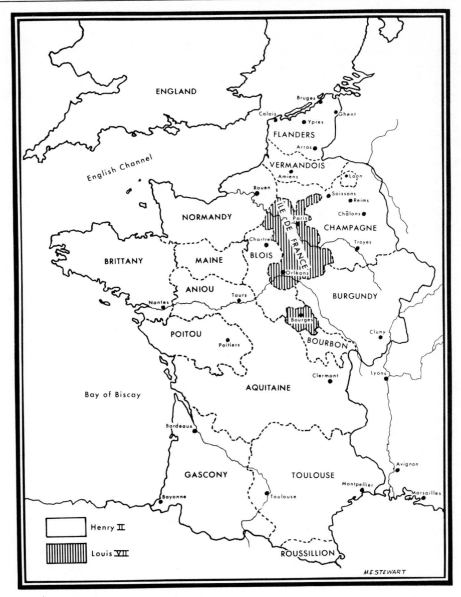

Figure 5.2 Territories ruled by Henry II of England and Louis VII of France.

Medieval Music Theory

Modal Scales

Medieval treatises were either philosophical and speculative, like Boethius's *De institutione musica,* or practical and theoretical, like the *De harmonica institutione* (Harmonic principles) attributed to Hucbald (c. 840–930), a monk of the Abbey of St. Amand at Tournai. Hucbald's treatise was intended to provide a method for speedily and efficiently instructing the monastic choir to sing chants accurately. Hucbald did not claim to have originated the system; he merely explained it and illustrated each principle with a chant. The method described is an extension of the system used by the Carolingians to classify chants according to melody types, and the presentation achieves a synthesis of Byzantine *oktōēchos,* liturgical (Gregorian) chant, and ancient Greek theory as interpreted by Boethius. What emerged was a system of eight diatonic scale patterns, arranged as four authentic-plagal pairs, with **finals** on the pitches d, e, f, and g. These scale patterns were called **modes.**

Each pair of modes had the same pitch as **final** (ex. 5.1). An authentic modal scale began on its final, but a plagal scale began a perfect fourth below its final. The **reciting notes** (also called **dominants,** or **tenors**) of paired modes differed, however. The dominant of an authentic mode was a perfect fifth above its final, unless that fifth was b; the dominant of a plagal mode was a third below the dominant of its related authentic mode, unless that pitch was b. In that case, the pitch c became the dominant. Next in importance to the final, the dominant functioned at times as a secondary tonal center. The pitch b could not serve as dominant because two b pitches were in use—b-natural and b-flat. At that time, no other pitches were chromatically altered; b♭ is still the only chromatically altered pitch that appears in Gregorian chant. Moreover, the pitch b was unstable—in performance of nonliturgical music, to avoid the tritone f–b the performer(s) consistently lowered b to b♭.

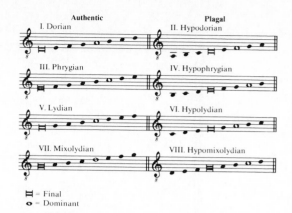

Example 5.1 The medieval modes.

The medieval modal scales were numbered individually, from I to VIII. However, at some time during the late tenth century, the names of the ancient Greek *tonoi* became attached to the medieval modes, fallaciously. This error was probably caused by Boethius's incorrect translation of the Greek word *tonos* (key) as "mode." Greek and medieval scale patterns assigned the same name differ in pitch content, direction, and internal intervallic structure (ex. 5.2). Modern liturgical books refer to modes by number, but most textbooks use the Greek names for the medieval modes.

Identification of a mode was by range, dominant, and final. Two scales comprising identical pitches were differentiated by their finals and dominants. (Compare Dorian and Hypomixolydian patterns in ex. 5.1.) Modal classification of a melody is not always easy. Not all medieval melodies end on the final of a mode. Sometimes modal classification must be determined by tessitura and the frequency with which certain pitches occur. Usually, the dominant figures prominently in a melody. Chants do not always use the entire octave range—some melodies have a range of only a fifth; others use more than an octave. As notated, the modal scales contain no chromatically altered tones, but under certain circumstances b♭ might be used in modes I and II, V and VI. Two things should be remembered: (1) In the Roman Catholic liturgical books

Ancient Greek Dorian Mode

T T S T T T S

Medieval Dorian Mode

T S T T T S T

Example 5.2 Comparison of Ancient Greek Dorian mode with Medieval Dorian mode.

the mode of each chant is stated. (2) Chant melodies were not notated as absolute pitches; in performance, melodies were transposed to fit vocal ranges.

Notation

The ancient Greeks notated pitches by letter names, and Boethius used the letters from A to P to designate pitches on the monochord. A kind of alphabetic letter notation was in use in some places in Europe as late as the eleventh century (see fig. 3.3). In the ninth and tenth centuries, the authors of some treatises used a different kind of letter notation, called Daseian, which was based on the symbol used for the aspirate sound ("h") in ancient Greek. Modified versions of this F-like symbol were assigned to the pitches d-e-f-g ( ) and were used in different postures for the rest of the scale.

The earliest surviving manuscripts containing notated Western music that had practical use date from the ninth century. In these manuscripts, produced at St. Gall, the chant music is written in **accent neumes**— thinly drawn lines, hooks, and upward and downward curves intended to represent graphically the rise and fall of the melodic line. The ekphonetic notation employed in ninth-century Byzantine music was very similar. Use of the word "neume" for this kind of notation symbol may imply that the symbols were inspired by cheironomy, for the Greek word *neuma* means "gesture." It is known that in the Western church hand movements were used to indicate melodic movements. In the Middle Ages, the word *neuma* denoted a short melodic passage, and a single written symbol was a *nota*. Infrequently, the word *neume* was used with its modern connotation; Guido used it that way.

In the ninth century, at some places in Frankish territory, e.g., in Aquitaine and Lorraine, **point neumes** were used to represent pitches. These dotlike neumes were placed above the words of the text without any point of reference to indicate a definite pitch. Scholars

sometimes refer to them as *neumae in campo aperto*— staffless neumes in an open field. By the eleventh century, some scribes regularly drew a dry-point line across the page and heighted the neumes with reference to that line. Later, the line was inked, sometimes in color, and occasionally a letter was placed at the beginning of the line to designate a definite pitch (fig. 4.8). Such designation and coloration became customary; commonly, a red line was used for F and a yellow line for c'. These lines were forerunners of the staff.

Guido d'Arezzo (c. 990–1050) seems to have been the first person to recognize the value of using a staff notation to designate definite pitches.

Guido d'Arezzo

Guido was educated at the Benedictine abbey at Pomposa, Italy. While there, he acquired a reputation for teaching singers to learn new chants quickly. Around 1025, Bishop Theodaldus summoned Guido to Arezzo, where he was assigned to train singers in the cathedral school. Pope John XIX heard of Guido's effective teaching and invited him to Rome (c. 1028) to explain his pedagogical methods and the new system of notation used in an Antiphoner he had prepared. The hot, damp climate of Rome affected Guido's health adversely; he stayed there only a short time, then entered a monastery near Arezzo.

Guido's writings reveal his methods. In *Aliae regulae* (Some Rules), the Prologue to his Antiphoner, Guido advocated learning chants by reading music rather than by rote, and he explained his use of a notation system of lines and spaces to designate pitch heights. Certain lines in this system were drawn with different colored inks and labeled with pitch letters. In his four-line staff Guido used a yellow line for c' and a red line for f; he preferred to identify those pitches because they were associated with semitones. (In modern liturgical books, a four-line staff is still used for notation of Gregorian chant, with versions of the letters C and F identifying those pitch lines of the staff. The identification of certain staff lines by pitch letters became standard and survives in modern notation in the use of modified G and F letter shapes called **clefs.**)

In a letter addressed to Brother Michael at Pomposa, Guido explained the method he used in teaching boys to learn quickly to sing chants previously unknown to them. Guido required the boys to memorize the chant shown in figure 5.3.

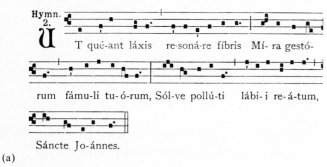

(a)

(b)

Figure 5.3 Hymn *Ut queant laxis* (*a*) in chant notation (LU,1504) and (*b*) in modern notation. *(Figure a from* The Liber Usualis, *edited by The Benedictines of Solesmes. Copyright © 1956 Desclée Company, Tournai, Belgium.)*

Each of the first six phrases of this chant begins with a different pitch and a different syllable of text; successively the six initial pitches form the C hexachord. The singers were expected to relate these six syllable-pitch combinations to the notes in an unfamiliar chant and to sing the chant correctly. Guido acknowledged that singers could determine precise pitches by using the monochord. However, his sight-singing method was faster.

Ut queant laxis (DWMA10), written during the Carolingian era, is an enigmatic Sapphic poem containing an encoded esoteric message. The poem entered the liturgy in the form of a hymn to St. John the Baptist, but was divided, half being sung at Lauds and the other half at Vespers on the feast day honoring St. John (LU,1497, 1504). In the early eleventh century, the hymn was relatively unknown except in northern Italy, and Guido stated in a letter that he composed this chant melody to serve his specific pedagogical purposes. As his method of sight-singing became known, use of his setting became widespread.

The pitch-syllable combinations Guido used for sight-singing have become standard but have been extended to include a seventh scale-step called *ti*. In the modern European fixed-*ut* system, *ut* always means C, *re* always means D, etc. In America, the syllable *do* has replaced *ut*, and the system is movable (transposable). The term **solmization** is now applied to the practice of singing by syllables.

Guido's *Micrologus* (Short Discourse) is the earliest extant comprehensive treatise that discusses both plainchant and polyphonic music. *Micrologus* was a standard textbook in monasteries throughout the Middle Ages; in the thirteenth century it was used as a textbook in universities. The treatise, addressed to singers, was designed primarily to improve skills in sight-singing and use of the new notation system. Guido included also a discussion of his method for teaching choirboys to improvise melodies. He stressed the importance of ear training and the value of letting the ear be the final judge when selecting melodic intervals, especially when forming cadences. The creation of a beautiful melody was not merely the mechanical application of rules but a matter of ear training and musical taste. (For Guido's views on diaphony, see p. 72.)

Guido recognized a scale of pitches covering two octaves and a fifth, the combined ranges of men's and boy's voices. The scale proceeded upward from G, which was written as Greek *gamma* (Γ), and included both b-natural and b-flat in its upper two octaves. The shape of the printed letter b indicated whether that pitch was *durum* (hard, harsh to the ear; b-natural) or *molle* (soft, pleasant; b-flat): The letter used for b-natural was a squared shape called *b quadrum* (♮); that used for b-flat was a rounded shape called *b rotundum* (♭). A few centuries later, scribal variants of these different shapes for b became the modern symbols used to indicate chromatic alterations: ♭, ♯, and ♮.

Example 5.3 Guido's hexachord system.

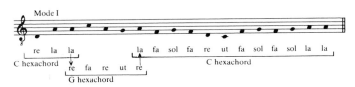

Example 5.4 Mutation is necessary when the eleventh-century chant *Kyrie Summe Deus* is sung by syllables. Using syllables, this chant would be vocalized as "re la la-re fa re ut re-la fa," moving from C hexachord into G hexachord temporarily and returning to C hexachord.

Guido divided the scale into seven overlapping hexachords (ex. 5.3) that do not coincide with medieval modes and that he did not in any way relate to modes. Hexachords that contain no b pitches were "natural"; those containing b-flat were *molle* (soft) and those containing b-natural were *durum* (hard). In other words, C hexachords were natural, G hexachords were hard, and F hexachords were soft. In conjunction with his sight-singing method, Guido added a syllable name to each pitch letter. That letter-syllable name located the pitch within the scale system and indicated the hexachord(s) in which the pitch resided. The lowest pitch in the scale system became *gamma ut* (from this came our word "gamut"); middle c (c') was *c sol fa ut,* and e'', Guido's highest note, was *e la.* (Guido's nomenclature endured far beyond his own time—some eighteenth-century composers still used it.) Guido's hexachords were transposable and represented relative rather than absolute pitches. The idea of absolute pitch was not established until the Renaissance.

When a singer encountered a melody whose range exceeded six notes, the requisite additional range was acquired through **mutation**—the singer selected a chant note that was resident in more than one hexachord and used that pitch as pivot. The singer entered the pivot note by using its syllable name in one hexachord, but exited the note by using its syllable name in another hexachord. This process, as applied to *Kyrie Summe Deus,* is illustrated in example 5.4. Mutation was not permitted where it would disrupt the *mi-fa* semitone. Mutation was usually accomplished at *re* of the new hexachord when ascending and at *la* of the new hexachord when descending. Guido's process of moving from one hexachord to another by mutation is comparable with the modern process of modulating from one key to another via a pivot chord.

For modal classification of chants, Guido used the older system of four paired authentic-plagal modes, rather than the eight individually numbered modes being used by some of his contemporaries. He regarded the last note of a chant melody as the final determinant of its modality.

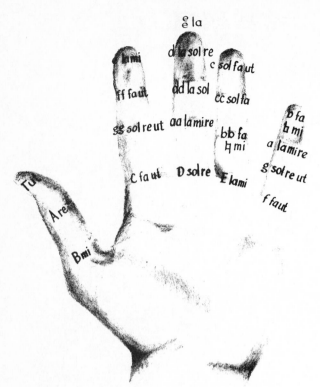

e la
d la sol re
c sol fa ut
a mi
cc sol fa
ff fa ut
dd la sol
gg sol re ut aa la mi re
bb fa
h mi
b fa
h mi
a la mi re
g sol re ut
C fa ut   D sol re   E la mi
f fa ut
Tu
A re
B mi

Figure 5.4 A "Guidonian" hand, its joints labeled according to Guido's hexachord system solmization.

Another pedagogical device was employed during the Middle Ages and Renaissance to help singers learn music. Each of the pitches in the scale recognized by Guido, from *gamma ut* to *e la,* was assigned to one of the joints of the left hand (fig. 5.4). The teacher pointed to one of the joints of his open left hand, and the pupils were expected to respond by singing the proper pitch. The hand was used for teaching both scales and intervals. Some twelfth-century music manuscripts and most late medieval and Renaissance textbooks contained a sketch of the hand with the joints appropriately labeled, using the composite solmization names in Guido's system. The device, known as the Guidonian hand, was probably so-named because of its use of Guido's terminology. There is no evidence that Guido invented it, and it is not present in any of his extant writings. However, it was extremely significant. As late as the sixteenth century, strong objections to chromaticism were based on the fact that it was "not in the hand."

Medieval Instruments

Organ

In the early Christian era, few organs seem to have been in use. The organ was known in Byzantium but was not used liturgically, and it was not a church instrument in western Europe until c. 900.

At Constantinople, an obelisk erected during the reign of Theodosius I (d. 395) depicted a small organ whose wind supply was generated by bellows that were trodden. In the early sixth century, Cassiodorus described an organ in his commentary on Psalm 150. But it was not until after the middle of the eighth century that the arrival of an organ in western Europe created a stir. In 757 the Byzantine Emperor, Constantine V Copronymus, sent an organ as a gift to Pepin, King of the Franks. That organ was placed at Compiegne. In 814 there was an organ in the church of Cluain-Cremha, Ireland; that seems to be the earliest date at which an organ is known to have been located in a church. There was neither organ builder nor organist available in Rome in 872, so Pope John VIII sent to Bavaria for a person with those talents. Customarily, organs came into western Europe from Byzantium or Greece via Bavaria or Hungary.

In *Schedula diversarum artium* (Treatise on Various Trades), written c. 1100 by a monk named Theophilus, several chapters deal with practical organ building. At that time, pitch selection was by means of hand-operated slider keys, which formed the "keyboard"; these sliders were pulled out, then pushed back manually (fig. 5.5).

Small positive organs were in use from the tenth to the seventeenth century (fig. 5.6). Keys might be either T-shaped or slider variety; one person used both hands to operate the "keyboard" while another person worked the bellows. Early church organs were of this type. Even when larger organs became available in the thirteenth century, many churches retained positives.

Not until the twelfth century was the portative organ used (fig. 5.7). These small monophonic treble instruments usually had a range of about two octaves and were sometimes equipped with one or two drones. The single rank of pipes was occasionally arranged in two rows. The instrument, held at right angles to the body, was suspended from a strap placed across the

(a)

Figure 5.6 A positive organ, placed on a table for use. *(Source: Michael Praetorius,* Theatrum Instrumentorum, *1620.)*

(b)

Figure 5.5 (*a*) Miniature from folio 13v of Stephen Harding's Bible, from early twelfth century, depicts King David playing harp and musicians playing bells, some kind of horn (possibly an oliphant), a vielle, and an organ with slider keys, whose pitches are marked above the keys. (*b*) Miniature from MS 13096, folio 46, in Bibliothèque nationale, Paris, depicts musicians playing harps, vielle, slider organ, and psaltery. *(Figure* a—*Bibliothèque Municipale, Dijon, France. Figure* b—*Bibliothèque nationale, Paris.)*

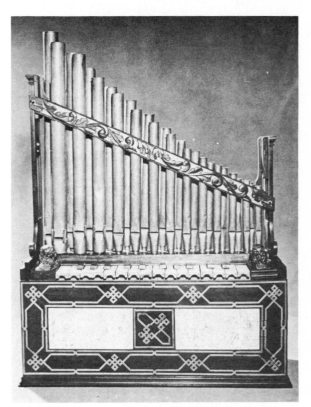

Figure 5.7 A portative organ of Italian make, now in Conservatoire Royal de Musique, Brussels. The organ was carried by the performer, who operated the bellows (not visible in picture) with one hand and the keys with the other hand.

Figure 5.8 Portion of the carving on the Portico de la Gloria of the Cathedral of Santiago de Compostela, Spain. The second and third persons from the left are playing an organistrum.

Strings

The *organistrum* (hurdy-gurdy) was used in medieval churches from the tenth century. Odo of Cluny (c. 878–942) described the instrument in his treatise *Quomodo organistrum construature* (How to Construct an Organistrum). The organistrum was five to six feet long. Its fiddle-shaped body was equipped with three strings that sounded simultaneously when set in vibration by a hand-cranked rosined wooden wheel located at the lower end of the body. The strings were stopped by a set of rods in a short pegbox at the upper end of the body. The instrument had a one-octave range, including both B♮ and B♭. In performance, the instrument was placed across the laps of two persons, one of whom cranked the wheel while the other operated the pitch rods (fig. 5.8). When large church organs came into use in the thirteenth century, the

back of the player's neck. For performance, the right hand operated buttonlike or T-shaped keys while the left hand worked the bellows.

organistrum was employed less frequently; from that time, the instrument was made in a smaller size. The *vièle à roue* (viele with a wheel) was a small hurdy-gurdy similar to the organistrum (fig. 5.9).

Vielle, fiedel, and *fiddle* are only a few of the names used to designate any medieval bowed stringed instrument having a **pegdisc.** (A pegdisc is the continuation of the neck of a stringed instrument into which tuning pegs are inserted from front or rear. If pegs are inserted from the sides, the extension is called a **pegbox.**) These instruments existed in a variety of shapes and sizes (fig. 5.10). Bowed string instruments were first used in the tenth century.

The Roman *lyre* survived, and by the year 1000 its use extended over much of Europe, as far north as Scandinavia and into the British Isles. The *harp* was played in Ireland early in the Middle Ages and was introduced to continental Europe before the ninth century. Medieval harps were not standard in size or in number of strings. In epics such as *Beowulf* harpers are referred to as historians, chroniclers, and

Figure 5.9 Georges de La Tour (1593–1652): *Le jouer de vièle* (The vièle player). The man is playing a *vièle à roue,* or hurdy-gurdy. Note the crank that rotates the wheel, the keys, and the pegdisc with tuning pegs protruding from the top. *(Musée des Beaux-Arts, Nantes.)*

Figure 5.10 Central portion of miniature in *L'Apocalypse de Jean Audrez,* depicting vielle and rebec players surrounding the Lamb of God. *(Bibliothèque nationale, Paris.)*

entertainers. The *psaltery* was described by the Church Fathers and by Cassiodorus as a delta-shaped (Δ) instrument whose resonator was on top. In the late Middle Ages, the word *psaltery* meant a zitherlike instrument that existed in various shapes and that was plucked with either bare fingers or a plectrum (fig. 5.11).

The *lute* was brought to Spain by Islamic Arabs. It was first used in France c. 1270.

Winds and Percussion

The transverse flute, or *cross-flute,* entered Europe from the East via Byzantium and Slavic countries, and its use spread into Germanic lands. In the late Middle Ages this flute was primarily a military instrument. The vertical flute, or *flageolet,* was of Asiatic origin. Usually made from wood or reed, it seems to have been first used in Europe in the eleventh century. A beaked flute, sometimes played in pairs, was used in Europe from c. 1180 until the middle of the seventeenth century. The beaked flute, played vertically, has its upper end shaped like a beak to facilitate blowing.

The *shawm,* a double-reed instrument introduced to western Europe from the Near East, was in use from the twelfth to the seventeenth century. The *musa* (bagpipe) was known to Romans in the first century, but is not mentioned in other parts of Europe until the ninth century. Chaucer was the first writer to use the word *bagpipe* for this instrument. The bagpipe may have been used a great deal as a folk instrument.

Early medieval *horns* made of wood or metal were used by Europeans for military purposes or by watchmen. From the eleventh century, carved ivory horns were used by nobility as hunting horns. One such horn was the *oliphant,* a short, thick, richly carved ivory horn that was end-blown. The Hebrew *shofar,* a ram's horn, is the only horn that has retained its original form from antiquity to the present (fig. 5.12).

The Church Fathers referred to the short straight trumpet by its Greek and Roman names—*salpinx* and *tuba.* After the fall of Rome, the trumpet seems to have fallen into disuse. It reappeared at the time of

(a)

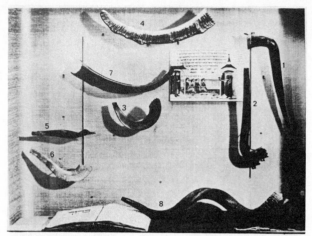

Figure 5.12 Display of shofars in Israel Museum, Jerusalem:
(1) Hungary, early nineteenth century; (2) Germany, eighteenth
century; (3) Algeria, nineteenth century; (4) Yemen, nineteenth
century; (5) Tripoli, early nineteenth century; (6) Morocco, c.
nineteenth century; (7) Central Europe, early nineteenth
century; (8) Yemen, eighteenth century.

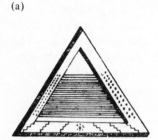

(b)

Figure 5.11 (a) Early thirteenth-century wire-strung O'Brien
Harp, or Clarsech, at Trinity College, University of Dublin,
Ireland. (b) Two of several psalteries shown in Michael
Praetorius's *Syntagma Musicum* (Wolfenbüttel, 1620). *(Source:
Figure a photo by R. B. Armstrong,* English and Irish
Instruments, *Edinburgh, 1908. Figure b Michael Praetorius,*
Syntagma Musicum, *1620.)*

the Crusades—the long straight trumpet was war
booty taken from the Saracens. Though some wandering musicians carried trumpets with them, the instrument was used primarily as a signal instrument
and by watchmen. The tones produced were in the

low register. Performers puffed their cheeks when
blowing the trumpet, and the sound generated was airy
and tremulous.

Drums, which were introduced from Asia, were
struck with sticks and served to beat time for dancing
and singing.

Early Polyphony

Polyphony is the term given to that kind of music that
results from the simultaneous combination of two or
more independent melodic lines. Polyphony should not
be confused with **heterophony,** which is the simultaneous performance of two different versions of the
same melody, e.g., the performance of a simple melody
along with an ornamented version of the same tune.
Nor is polyphony identical with **magadizing,** that kind
of singing in octaves resultant from the simultaneous
singing of the same melody by changed (men's) and
unchanged (boys') voices, or by male and female
voices.

Organum

The polyphony used in liturgical music from the late ninth century to around 1250 was called **organum,** meaning "organized" or "planned" music. The earliest surviving writings that clearly describe and give detailed directions for the production of organum are two anonymous treatises written c. 850–c. 900: *Musica enchiriadis* (Music Manual) and *Scolica enchiriadis* (Commentary Manual). (*Scolica* was the Latin term used to denote the marginal entries scholars penned in textbooks and treatises as explanatory comments on the subject matter presented.) Though earlier treatises mention the simultaneous singing of concords, and even use the word organum, the language used by the authors of those writings is ambiguous, and no music examples are presented.

As explained and illustrated by music examples in *Musica enchiriadis* and *Scolica enchiriadis,* the diaphony called organum consisted of a chant melody, named the *vox principalis* (principal voice), and one, two, or three additional voice parts derived by duplicating the chant melody in parallel motion at a specified harmonic interval that was regarded as a consonance. The duplicate voice was called *vox organalis* (organal voice). Creation of an organal voice was permitted at three levels of consonance—the octave, the fifth, and the fourth. Three types of organum are considered in these treatises: simple, composite, and modified parallel organum (DWMA11).

Simple organum was produced by singing an exact duplicate of the chant melody in strict parallel motion at the interval of an octave, a fifth, or a fourth below the original chant. Strict simple organum at the fifth is shown in example 5.5. Actually, strict simple organum at the octave was merely contrived magadizing.

Composite organum was produced by doubling at the octave either or both of the voice parts of a simple organum (ex. 5.6). Octave doubling of one or both melodic lines of a strict simple organum at the fifth, or a strict simple organum at the fourth, brought all of the three available consonant intervals into simultaneous use. There were two ways of doing this: Both lines of a strict simple organum might be duplicated at the octave, or the principal voice could be duplicated an octave lower and the organal voice duplicated an octave higher.

Example 5.5 Example of strict simple organum.

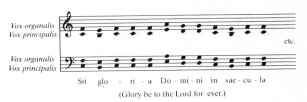

Example 5.6 Example of strict composite organum.

Example 5.7 Transcription of the first two strophes of the Sequence *Rex coeli Domine,* an example of modified parallel organum. *Vox principalis* is top voice; *vox organalis* is bottom voice.

Parallel organum at the fourth was the only type of early organum modified, so that the voices were not in parallel fourths throughout the chant. The necessity for modification seems to have been occasioned originally by the peculiar disjunct-tetrachord scale structure used in *Musica enchiriadis,* though it was implied that modification was desirable in order to avoid the tritone. In the examples presented, the *vox principalis* lies above the *vox organalis,* and most of the phrases begin and end on the unison. In one example (ex. 5.7), the voices begin in unison, then diverge in oblique motion—the principal voice proceeds with the chant melody, while the organal voice reiterates its original pitch until the two voices are a fourth apart; from that point the voices sing in parallel fourths up to the penultimate interval; the last two intervals are unisons. This convergence on the unison at the end of a phrase was called *occursus* (meeting).

All early organum was improvised. It was based on chant and was sung in a slow tempo, using the rhythm of the chant text.

Guido disliked strict parallel organum and preferred modified parallel organum at the fourth. He established rules for using oblique motion to avoid the tritone, which was considered *diabolus in musica* (the devil in music). In concluding a piece of modified parallel organum, Guido advocated achieving *occursus* (convergence to unison) by moving through the interval of a major third or a major second. His rules permitted *vox principalis* and *vox organalis* parts to cross for a brief time.

The significance of modified organum at the fourth is twofold: (1) It was a forerunner of late eleventh- and twelfth-century free organum that admitted various intervals but placed restrictions on the kind of interval that could be used at the beginning and end of a phrase. (2) The care given the *occursus* foreshadowed the attention that would be focused on cadences and cadential preparation in future centuries.

When, where, and why was organum created? The definite date and place of origin and the reasons for the creation of this diaphony are not known. Since the earliest examples of Western polyphony are vocal part-music in which one voice is chant, it might be conjectured that polyphony originated when men and choirboys singing together could not find common pitches that were comfortable for the unison singing of chants for a Service, and duplication of the chant melody at a comfortable consonant interval was the solution for them. Or, choirboys and monks may have unintentionally magadized, and, finding those octave sounds pleasant, may have consciously sought other harmonies. It is equally probable that this kind of parallelism existed in secular vocal or instrumental music that has not survived, and that secular practices were borrowed for liturgical use. It is noteworthy that ethnomusicologists report finding among tribes of primitive peoples musical structures similar to those used in medieval Western music—part-singing in parallel motion and the playing of instruments with drone bass. Such likenesses cannot be anything other than similar stages of development occurring in different ethnic cultures in different eras. Still another conjecture is plausible: The creation of

Western polyphony may have been a conscious endeavor as an extension of troping, and the placement of the added (organal) voice determined logically by the application of Pythagorean proportional mathematics. *Scolica enchiriadis* devotes space to a discussion of those Pythagorean principles. It is significant that organum flourished in those abbeys that were centers of troping, e.g., St. Gall, and St. Martial.

Practical use of organum is documented by a repertory of approximately 160 two-voice organa in a supplemental section of the later of two manuscripts known as *The Winchester Tropers* (fig. 5.13). As the title indicates, the manuscripts contain troped chants. The later manuscript, which was copied in the early eleventh century, is primarily a revised version of the early manuscript. The manuscripts were copied in England, but the music they contain was probably used in western France. The music is notated in staffless neumes that are only partially heighted. (**Heighted** neumes are those written with vertical placement in staffless space on the page, thus making pitch differences discernible.) Two-thirds of the note-against-note organa in the supplement are settings of Alleluias and Responds.

A treatise entitled *De musica* (Concerning Music), dated c. 1100, is attributed to John Cotton or to Johannes de Afflighem. The writing is concerned mainly with monophonic music but contains one chapter on organum. The author favored using a variety of motions, but especially contrary motion; voice crossing was desirable.

The anonymous treatise *Ad organum faciendum* (How to Make Organum), written c. 1100, reveals that by the end of the eleventh century composition had begun to replace improvisation. The formation of organum was actually the creation of a new melodic line designed to enhance the chant, rather than improvised duplication of the chant melody. Choice was a factor in creating the *vox organalis*; this is indicated by music examples showing dissimilar organal lines constructed above the same chant melody. Parallel, oblique, and contrary motion were intermingled; a limited amount of voice crossing was permitted. The various consonant intervals—unison, octave, fifth, and fourth—were mixed freely. At times a dissonant third was included, followed by its appropriate resolution to the unison (DWMA12).

(a)

(b)

Figure 5.13 *The Winchester Troper* (MS 473), open to
(*a*) folios 55v and 56r, showing monophonic troped chants; and
(*b*) folios 135v and 136r from supplement at the back of the
bound manuscript, showing the *vox organalis* part for those
same chants. (*Corpus Christi College, Cambridge, England.*)

73

Early Middle Ages

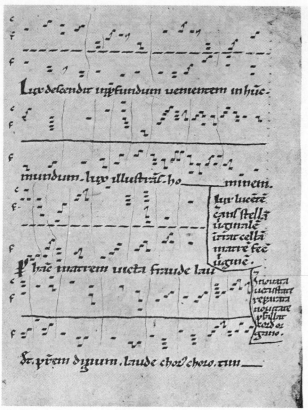

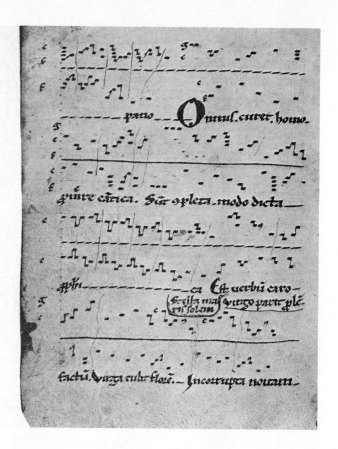

Figure 5.14 The organum *Lux descendit* as notated on folios 2–2v of British Museum MS Add. 36.881, a twelfth-century manuscript. The manuscript shown in figure 5.15 also dates from the twelfth century. *(Source: London, British Museum.)*

Twelfth-century Polyphony

In manuscripts compiled in the twelfth century, the notation indicates clearly the pitches of the notes (fig. 5.14). Though the rhythm is not obviously indicated in the notation, a consensus of rhythmic knowledge must have existed at that time, so that singers knew how to perform polyphonic music that was more complex than note-against-note. The manuscripts contain no instructional rubrics. There are three rhythmic possibilities: (a) rhythm was free; (b) musical rhythm was based on the accentual or poetic rhythm of the text; or (c) musical rhythm was indicated in a way not obvious to musicians of later generations.

St. Martial (Aquitanian) School

The Abbey of St. Martial de Limoges was founded in 848 at the site of the tomb of St. Martial, the first Bishop of Limoges, in the province of Aquitaine. As legends about the Saint grew up and spread, the Abbey became more prestigious, and many persons made pilgrimages to it. From c. 930 to 1130 a school of poets and composers flourished in Aquitaine, and the twelfth century was marked by the rise of Aquitanian polyphony. The Abbey became a repository of liturgical manuscripts that originated in southern France. These manuscripts form the richest surviving collection of west Frankish tropes, sequences, and *versus* (versesongs). The notation used in them ranges from early **point** and **accent** neumes to the incipient square notation used in the twelfth century. (Point neumes are heighted neumes that, for the most part, resemble dots and clearly indicate pitch differences. Accent neumes indicate the direction a melody moves but do not have

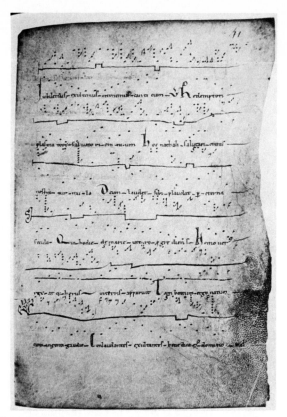

Figure 5.15 The organum *Jubilemus exultemus,* a *Benedicamus* trope for the Nativity, notated in Aquitanian point neumes on folio 41 of MS Lat. 1139, the oldest of the extant St. Martial manuscripts. *(Bibliothèque nationale, Paris.)*

Figure 5.16 *Benedicamus domino* in melismatic organum. *(MS Pluteus 29.1, folio 86v, Biblioteca Medicea-Laurenziana, Florence.)*

placement that indicates discernible pitch differences.) Among the manuscripts are four that contain a total of 69 pieces of twelfth-century polyphony, along with other items (fig. 5.15).

The music from St. Martial Abbey exhibits two basic styles of polyphonic writing: **melismatic (florid) organum,** and **discant.** Both styles are notated **in score**—the parts are arranged one below the other on different staves. The chant melody, placed in the bottom voice, is written on the lower of the two staves.

In **melismatic** (florid) organum, more notes than one—usually several or many notes—are written in the organal voice opposite one note of the original chant (fig. 5.16). Presumably, in performance each note of the chant melody was sustained by the choir (or a small group of singers) for a sufficient length of time to permit a soloist to sing the melisma written

above that note of chant. It is believed that as polyphony developed, the improvised organal line gradually became more elaborate, and the notes of the chant became more sustained. Ultimately, the chant lost its melodic character and became a series of pedal points or drones, each of which served as support for a new melodic phrase. Eventually, this kind of organum was notated instead of being improvised in each performance. Because of the sustained character of the chant, melismatic organum is sometimes referred to as "sustained-note" style (DWMA13).

The voice parts were now given new names. This two-part polyphony was known as **organum duplum,** and the organal voice was called the **duplum** (fig. 5.17). The principal voice was renamed **tenor** (Latin, *tenere,* to hold), probably because it held the original chant melody and sustained its tones. For several centuries,

Early Middle Ages

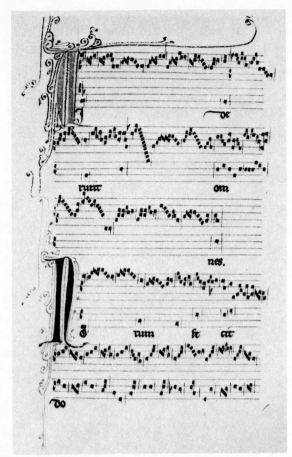

Figure 5.17 *Viderunt omnes* notated as organum duplum. *(MS W₂, fol. 53r, Wolfenbüttel, Herzog August-Bibliothek: Cod. Guelf. 628 Helmst.)*

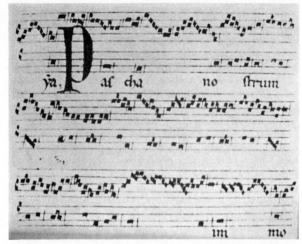

Figure 5.18 On folio 109r (old numbering cix) of MS Pluteus 29.1, in the verse *Pascha nostrum,* the word *Pascha* is notated as organum duplum, and the word *nostrum* is notated in discant-style organum. *(Biblioteca Medicea-Laurenziana, Florence.)*

the melody upon which a polyphonic composition was based (the *cantus firmus,* firm or fixed song) was placed in the tenor voice, and until four-part polyphony became standard the tenor was the lowest voice part.

Text was indicated only for the chant, in the tenor. Whether the soloist performed the duplum as textless vowel sound or sang the syllables of the chant words is not definitely known. Vertical lines sketchily drawn through the staves at the ends of phrases aid in establishing congruence. Though phrases commence and end on the accepted consonances, dissonances occur as passing tones and sometimes produce interesting tonal clashes against the tenor pitches.

Discant is that style of writing in which a text was set syllabically in note-against-note polyphony (fig. 5.18). Lines of congruence seem to mark off measures in the music. Both voices use the same text, which is laid under the tenor. Later in the twelfth century, this style of polyphony admitted neume-against-neume writing, thus producing a text setting that was not purely syllabic (DWMA14). Although one syllable of text was set per neume, each neume did not contain the same number of notes, so the two voices were not necessarily balanced note-against-note. Historians refer to this type of polyphony as "developed" discant. In some instances, discant style was further modified at important cadences to include a kind of neume-against-neume writing in which the syllables of text were set melismatically but the melismas of the two voice parts were balanced note-against-note.

A *versus* is a newly composed setting of a Latin sacred poem of scannable rhymed verse (DWMA15). This kind of song was used primarily as an extra-liturgical addition to a Service on an important feast day. Most of the Aquitanian versus have texts that relate to the Incarnation and the Virgin birth. The musical setting of versus is discant, developed discant, or a mixture of those two styles. The two parts are in the same vocal range. All kinds of motion are used, but contrary motion predominates. When parallel motion occurs, the voice parts usually move in streams of parallel thirds or sixths. Phrases begin and end on accepted consonances—octaves, unisons, fifths.

Thirds and sixths are used freely; seconds and sevenths occur briefly as dissonant ornaments or passing tones. The lower of the voice parts was probably composed first, and the upper line was written later to enhance the first melody. Versus and conductus seem to be the earliest polyphonic music not based on chant.

The oldest of the surviving manuscripts containing Aquitanian polyphony dates from the beginning of the twelfth century; in it melismatic organum predominates. The other manuscripts date from the end of that century and show a preference for discant and developed-discant style. The St. Martial (Aquitanian) school was contemporary with that centered at Notre Dame de Paris (see p. 86), but in the thirteenth century the Aquitanian school declined and the center of activity shifted to Paris.

Santiago de Compostela

Santiago de Compostela is located in the northwest corner of Spain, in an area that was never conquered by the Moors and that has always been intensely Christian. The Cathedral, begun in 1078, was constructed over the grave of St. James the Apostle, patron saint of Spain. Because the bones of St. James were thought to be interred there, the Cathedral was a shrine of such importance in the Middle Ages that pilgrimages to it were comparable with those made to Rome and Canterbury. According to the *Liber Sancti Jacobi* (Book of Saint James), "choirs of pilgrims" from all parts of Europe kept perpetual vigil at the altar of the Cathedral; they brought with them and performed on all kinds of instruments—citterns, lyres, drums, flutes, flageolets, trumpets, harps, crwths, and others.

The Cathedral is important musically; the *Liber Sancti Jacobi,* housed in the Cathedral Library, contains in manuscript both texts and music for the complete Services of the Vigil and Feast of St. James as they were performed early in the twelfth century. *Liber Sancti Jacobi,* known also as *Codex Calixtinus,* contains both monophonic and polyphonic music and is an important source of performance practices of that time. The Codex, written c. 1137–39, shows that all sections of the Ordinary except the Credo were troped, as well as some portions of the Proper of the Mass, and the Offices. The polyphonic settings of sacred rhymed Latin poems used for processionals and

as introductions to the Offices were labeled *conductus.* The texts of the versus and conductus indicate clearly that these compositions are related to the religious celebrations.

All but 1 of the 21 polyphonic compositions are in a section at the end of the manuscript. These pieces comprise (a) settings of conductus and *Benedicamus Domino* tropes written in discant style and (b) settings of untroped *Benedicamus* chants and Responsories written in melismatic (sustained-note) organum. Only those portions of the chants that were performed by soloists were given polyphonic settings; poetic texts were given discant-style settings. The polyphonic music appears in score notation, on four-line staves, with vertical lines drawn through and connecting both staves to indicate textual or musical congruence, either at harmonic consonances or at the beginning or end of a syllable.

One of the compositions on the first folio of the polyphonic section of the manuscript has three voice parts notated on two staves; two colors of ink (red and black) were used on the lower staff to differentiate the two parts notated there. Notating these two parts on the same staff was probably a space-saving device. This composition, *Congaudeant catholici* (Let Catholics rejoice together; fig. 5.19; DWMA16) is a *Benedicamus* trope with the refrain *Die ista* (This day). There are seven stanzas, each consisting of two lines. The text was set strophically. Words of the first strophe and the refrain appear under the bottom staff; the remainder of the text is printed after the music notation. The two lower voices are in note-against-note counterpoint; the top voice was given from one to five notes to sing against each note in the lower voices. The three parts move in the same vocal range, and voice crossing occurs. It would seem that the three voice parts were created successively, with the top voice being composed last. *Congaudeant catholici* seems to be the earliest three-part polyphonic composition that has survived.

Liber Sancti Jacobi was not compiled at Santiago de Compostela, and the music it contains was not written by Spanish composers. Though the pieces were used in Services honoring St. James, they may have been used at a church other than the Santiago de Compostela Cathedral. Remarks written on pages

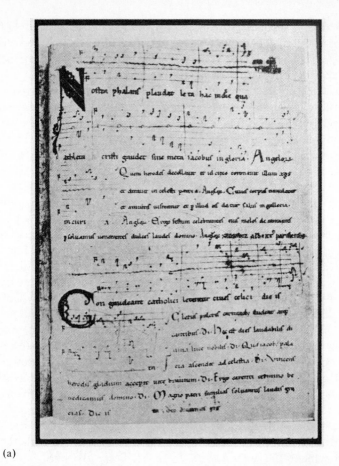

(a)

(b)

Figure 5.19 The conductus *Congaudeant catholici* (*a*) in manuscript and (*b*) in modern notation.

of the manuscript attribute the compositions to several French authors; some of those attributions are probably false. It is generally agreed, however, that *Liber Sancti Jacobi* was written somewhere in France, perhaps at the Abbey at Cluny. Portions of the *Liber Sancti Jacobi* contain a plethora of inaccuracies—grammatical errors and incorrect Latin words that create humorous and sometimes obscene *faux pas*. It is thought that these sections of the manuscript were intended for the instruction of young students in Latin and other subjects taught in cathedral schools and monasteries at that time. It has been suggested also that a portion of the manuscript was intended to encourage pilgrimages to the shrine at Santiago.

Britain

English interest and participation in polyphony are attested by surviving manuscript sources. The polyphonic contents of the second *Winchester Troper* have been mentioned (p. 72). The next complete manuscript of solely English polyphonic music that has survived is the fifteenth-century Old Hall Manuscript. Significant pieces of English polyphony are extant in fragments of manuscripts and in handwritten collections of continental music. In Britain, the most active centers of polyphony were the important Benedictine abbeys; some pieces of thirteenth-century polyphony survive from Reading Abbey, Bury St. Edmunds, and Worcester.

A Cornish manuscript in the Bodleian Library, Oxford, contains the only example of part-music written in letter notation preserved outside of treatises. The music is in Boethian letter notation, which used the letters A to P to designate the pitches of the two octaves from A to a'. In this setting, the lower (principal) voice is the Sarum chant *Ut tuo propitiatus* (That, appeased by your [intercession]), a verse of the respond *Sancte Dei pretiose* used in the Office on St. Stephen's Day, December 26. The fact that the organal voice has an unusually wide compass—an octave and a fourth—may indicate that this was experimental polyphony or that the upper voice was intended to be performed on an organ. This example of late eleventh-century note-against-note polyphony was probably written for St. Augustine's monastery, Canterbury.

The Old Saint Andrews Manuscript, otherwise known as Wolfenbüttel 677, or W_1, has long been considered one of the principal manuscript sources of Notre Dame polyphonic repertoire. Some later research disputes this, however, and professes that the manuscript contains a Sarum repertory that was strongly influenced by the Parisian school. Some items included in W_1 are not found in the Notre Dame repertoire. The manuscript was probably compiled for and used in the Augustinian priory of St. Andrews, in Scotland. There are eleven fascicles in the manuscript, most of which was copied around the middle of the thirteenth century. (A fascicle is a series of manuscript pages fastened together forming a section of a complete manuscript.) The last fascicle of this manuscript differs in style and content from the other sections of the manuscript and may be older. It contains a repertory of both Ordinary and Proper sections for a cycle of votive Masses of the Blessed Virgin Mary (Lady Masses). The music is principally two-part polyphony in discant style, often note-against-note. In some of the Alleluias a third (middle) voice part has been supplied in some cadences.

The performance of polyphonic music in the liturgy is specifically detailed in some of the Customaries of the Use of Sarum (books of Rules and Regulations for practice of Sarum liturgy). For example, on Christmas Day and the following four days—the days of the feasts of St. Stephen, St. John the Apostle, the Holy Innocents, and St. Thomas—the *Benedicamus* was to be sung in two-part polyphony. This polyphony was to be based on the *Benedicamus* plainsong. At Westminster Abbey and St. Augustine's in Canterbury, the Benedictus, Magnificat, Sequences, and some processionals were sung in two-part polyphony on all principal feast days. Records indicate that the soloists who performed the polyphonic music received extra pay. In the Exeter Ordinal, the Latin words *discantare, organizare,* and *jubilare* were used to designate the type of polyphony that was to be performed.

Summary

During the ninth through twelfth centuries, the nations of modern Europe began to emerge and develop.

Feudalism, widespread by the twelfth century, contributed to the rise of monarchies and was manipulated by governmental authorities to achieve political stability. Incompatibility between the papal envoy to Byzantium and the Eastern patriarch triggered a complete break between Eastern and Western churches in 1054. In reaction to invasions of the Seljuk Turks, Pope Urban II called the First Crusade in 1095; other Crusades followed, until the middle of the fifteenth century.

Music flourished in churches and in courts, and, undoubtedly, in the secular life of the common people as well. Medieval treatises were written concerning performance practices and detailing theoretical principles by which chants and other melodies were to classified or composed. Hucbald described a system of eight diatonic scale patterns that became known as modes. At some time during the late tenth century, the names of the ancient Greek *tonoi* were attached to these medieval modes, erroneously.

Gradually, a system was developed for legibly and intelligibly notating music. Various kinds of letter notation systems were in use from the time of the ancient Greeks until the eleventh century. However, in manuscripts written at St. Gall in the ninth century music was written in accent neumes—symbols that graphically represented the rise and fall of the melodic line. In Aquitaine and Lorraine, point neumes were used to represent relative pitches. By the eleventh century, dry-point lines and heighted neumes were used; then colored lines labeled with pitch names appeared—forerunners of the staff. Guido d'Arezzo seems to have been the first person to recognize the value of using staff notation to designate definite pitches.

Guido made several important contributions to the development of music: (1) a workable system of sight-singing by syllables, based on his setting of the Sapphic poem *Ut queant laxis*; (2) a hexachord system with a process of mutating from one hexachord to another via a pivot note; and (3) a pedagogical method that assigned the syllable names of pitches to the joints of a hand, later named the Guidonian hand. Moreover, though he may not have invented it, his consistent use of a four-line staff with the letters F and C identifying those pitch levels certainly was influential in promoting that kind of staff notation.

The various kinds of medieval instruments in use include organs, organistrum and other hurdy-gurdy types, bowed and plucked stringed instruments, flutes, double-reed wind instruments, horns, trumpets, and percussion instruments.

The polyphony used in liturgical music from the late ninth century to c. 1250 was called organum. Ninth-century treatises discuss three types: simple, composite, and modified parallel organum. All early organum was improvised, was based on chant, and was sung in slow tempo using the rhythm of the chant text. Modified organum at the fourth has twofold significance—it was a forerunner of late eleventh- and twelfth-century free organum, and it foreshadowed the attention that would be focused on cadences and cadential preparation in future centuries. The definite date and place of origin and the reasons for the creation of organum are not known, but practical use of it is documented by the contents of *The Winchester Tropers*. Treatises written c. 1100 indicate that by the end of the eleventh century composition had begun to replace improvisation. Choice was a factor in creating the organal voice; parallel, oblique, and contrary motion were intermingled, and some voice crossing was permitted.

In manuscripts compiled in the twelfth century, the notation indicates clearly the pitches of the notes, but the rhythm is not obvious. Important centers of polyphony were the Abbey of St. Martial de Limoges in Aquitaine and Santiago de Compostela in northwest Spain. St. Martial became a repository for liturgical manuscripts that originated in southern France, the richest surviving collection of west Frankish tropes, sequences, and versus. The music from St. Martial Abbey exhibits two basic styles of polyphonic writing: melismatic (florid) organum, and discant. In melismatic organum many notes are written in the organal voice opposite one note of the original chant. As the organal line became more elaborate, the notes of the chant became more sustained; eventually, the chant became a series of pedal points, each serving as support for a new melodic phrase. This two-part polyphony was called organum duplum; the organal voice was called the duplum, and the principal voice was renamed the tenor. Discant is that style of writing in which a text was set syllabically in note-against-note polyphony, both voices using the same text. Later in the twelfth century, this style admitted neume-against-neume writing, known as "developed" discant. Versus were also written at St. Martial. The versus is a newly composed setting of a Latin sacred poem of scannable rhymed verse. It was used primarily as an extra-liturgical addition to a Service on an important feast day.

Santiago de Compostela Cathedral is important musically. Its library houses manuscripts of both text and music for the complete Services of the Vigil and Feast of St. James as they were performed early in the twelfth century. Much of the liturgical music used there was troped. Texts of the polyphonic settings of sacred rhymed Latin poems used for processionals (labeled *conductus*) and versus indicate clearly that these compositions are related to religious celebrations. The *Benedicamus* trope *Congaudeant catholici* seems to be the earliest three-part polyphonic composition that has survived.

English interest and participation in polyphony are attested by surviving manuscript sources, including the second *Winchester Troper,* a Cornish manuscript in Bodleian Library at Oxford, and the Old Saint Andrews Manuscript. Moreover, the performance of polyphonic music in the liturgy is specifically detailed in some of the Customaries of the Use of Sarum.

Early Middle Ages

6

The Middle Ages—*Ars Antiqua*

Historians commonly refer to the period from c. 1160 to c. 1320 as the Age of *Ars Antiqua* (old art). Some historians perceive the era as being divided into two stages: Early Gothic, c. 1160–c. 1250; and High Gothic, c. 1250–c. 1320.

History of Paris

When Roman soldiers were conquering Gaul c. 53 B.C., they found the small islands in the Seine River settled by Celtic fishermen and boatmen. The Roman settlement established on one island was named Lutetia and was developed extensively. The Romans built two wooden bridges, supported by piles, to join the island to the mainland, and the 30-foot-wide stone-paved road the Romans constructed across the island became an important link on the main route between Soissons and Orléans. The community church was a Gallo-Roman temple, Temple de Jupiter (fig. 6.1). By the fourth century, Lutetia had become "Paris," a name derived from the Celtic tribe called "the Parisii." For a few centuries, there was relative peace. Occasionally, barbarian invaders had to be repelled. Between 845 and 885, five Norman attacks brought hardship, followed by some years of famine, flood, and disease, with consequent decrease in population. After 987, when Capetian rule began, prosperity gradually returned.

In the twelfth century, Paris and its environs assumed intellectual and cultural leadership of Europe. The original island settlement was now the Île de la Cité and was at the heart of the city. The Gallo-Roman

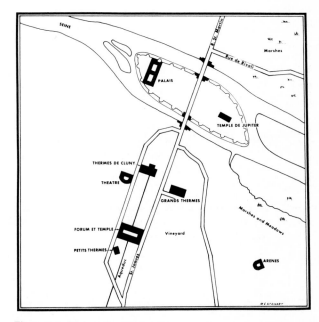

Figure 6.1 Paris in the third century.

temple had been replaced successively by a Christian basilica and a Romanesque church. The latter, constructed in Carolingian times, was a bishopric, the Cathedral of Notre Dame. The north or Right Bank of the Seine had become a trade center; the south or Left Bank was dominated by the newly formed university and was known as the Latin Quarter. Though vernacular tongues were in use in Europe, Latin was the official language of the church, the cathedral schools and universities, and the French government.

83

Notre Dame Cathedral

Construction of the cathedral of Notre Dame de Paris, authorized by Bishop Maurice de Sully in 1160, was not completed during his 36 years as bishop; his five successors also witnessed the continuing construction (fig. 6.2). Pope Alexander III laid the cornerstone of Notre Dame Cathedral in 1163. The Gothic structure rose in three stages. The choir

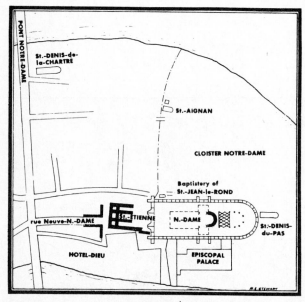

Figure 6.2 Location of church of St. Étienne and the Cathedral of Notre Dame de Paris on the Île de la Cité c. 1217.

was constructed between 1163 and 1182, and the high altar was consecrated on 19 May 1182 (Pentecost). After the main altar was dedicated, old Notre Dame could be torn down to make way for the transept and nave of the new cathedral. However, the nave was already under way by 1178. Transept and nave were completed in 1200, and the façade, on the west, was begun in 1190 and finished in 1250. As the cathedral was being built, Bishop de Sully ordered all buildings in the periphery demolished. On 4 December 1218, the relics were transferred from the neighboring church of St. Étienne to the new cathedral, and the church of St. Étienne was torn down.

Notre Dame Cathedral was distinctive in many respects. The ribbed vault of the cathedral was exceptionally high— over 108 feet. The flying buttress was invented in the 1180s, and Notre Dame was the first structure to employ true flying buttresses. A buttress is an architectural support built against and projecting from a wall to resist the thrusts from within, e.g., sidewise pressure and weight of the vaulting. A flying buttress arches away from the wall and consists basically of an inclined bar connected to an upper wall and grounded in a masonry mass some distance from that wall (fig. 6.3). Large stained glass windows were used to increase the amount of light admitted and to transform it. The interior of the edifice was cruciform, with double aisles, but without chapels along the ambulatory. Portals were designed with three-dimensional jamb statues integrated with the architecture. Typically, all three portals are different. The statues were painted and stood out against the golden background of the façade. The rose window, 32 feet in diameter, appears as a gigantic halo for the sculpture of the Virgin and Child at its base (fig. 6.4).

The University of Paris began in the early twelfth century, when students gathered in the streets to sit at the feet of the philosopher-theologian Pierre Abélard (1079–1142). Students came from all over Europe to study the seven liberal arts and to hear renowned scholars like Peter Lombard expound upon special topics. A *universitas* had formed at Paris by c. 1200. Freedom of inquiry existed, but all learning was under the jurisdiction of the papacy; in 1215, Pope Innocent III formally authorized the corporation of the University of Paris.

Religion and the supernatural dominated medieval life. In government, kings and prelates worked together to increase the prestige and wealth of both church and state. Suger, Abbot of Saint-Denis (1122–51), was legal, political, and spiritual adviser to both Louis VI and Louis VII. For many years, Saint-Denis was the church used by the king and royal family.

In the university, study of the seven liberal arts provided knowledge of the divine and the power to express that knowledge; many master teachers were theologians. The great cathedrals constructed in the

Notre Dame Cathedral towered above and dominated its medieval surroundings. The parks that are now to the east and south of the structure did not exist then, and the square in front of the entrance was small.

Figure 6.3 Apse of Notre Dame Cathedral, showing flying buttresses.

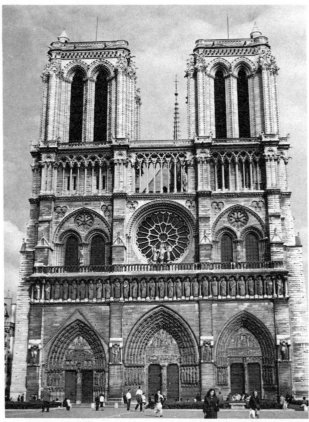

Figure 6.4 West façade of Notre Dame Cathedral. Consider the rose window as halo for the statue of the Virgin. *(Museum of Notre Dame de Paris.)*

twelfth and thirteenth centuries were considered physical representations of the heavenly kingdom on earth. The physical light admitted to the sanctuary through the windows was analogous to divine light; as stained glass helped create mysticism by transforming natural light, so polyphonic music was intended to intensify the aura of otherworldliness created by Gregorian chant.

When Maurice de Sully succeeded Peter Lombard as Bishop of Paris in 1160, the cathedral chapter owned half of the land of Île de la Cité and all of the

neighboring Île de Notre Dame. One of de Sully's first official acts as bishop was to arrange for replacement of the Carolingian church of Notre Dame with a great cathedral that would embody the new Gothic style of architecture, painting, and sculpture that had emerged in the Royal Domain (Île de France) c. 1140. The edifice was actually begun in 1163 and was not completed until 1250; Services were held in St. Étienne until December 1218.

Age of Ars Antiqua

1163 - - Notre Dame Cathedral, Paris, constructed - - - - - - - - - - - - - - -

Organum flourished -diminishes

Conductus -diminishes as composed piece, survives as style

Clausulae   Substitute clausulae
                   Substitute clausula troped, becomes Motet

Rise of Motet -

Léonin fl.   Pérotin fl.   Franco of Cologne fl. c. 1250–80
Magnus liber   Organum triplum   *Ars cantus mensurabilis*
Organum duplum   & quadruplum

                                                   Petrus de Cruce
                                                   fl. c. 1270–1300

Mensural notation -

Rhythmic modes; Modal notation -

Some use of five-line staff -

Hocket used -

Technique of Voice Exchange (*Stimmtausch;* Rondellus) used -

English rondellus motets

c. 1250, *Sumer is icumen in*

Troubadours ⎱ - Adam de la Halle
Trouvères ⎰   b. 1245, d. 1288 or 1306
                                                   Le Jeu de Robin et Marion, 1285

Minnesänger -

Trobairitz - - - - - - - - - - - - - - - - - - -

Laude, and   *Cantigas de*   c. 1325
Laude spirituali   *Santa Maria*   Robertsbridge
                                                   Codex

The Parisian (Notre Dame) School

At the time the new Cathedral of Notre Dame was being constructed, there was active in and around Paris a school of composers who were producing polyphonic liturgical music. An anonymous treatise written c. 1275 by someone familiar with the music of England and France—possibly a student—provides tangible information concerning music at Paris during the century before his stay in Paris. That author, whom historians commonly refer to as Anonymous IV, named two composers—Léonin and Pérotin—who made important contributions to the early polyphonic liturgical repertoire used there. Anonymous IV wrote: "And note that Master Leoninus, according to what was said, was the best composer (or singer) of organum [*optimus organista*], who made the great book of organum from the gradual and antiphonal for amplifying the divine service." This *Magnus liber organi* (Great Book of Organum) was in use until the time of Pérotin the Great, who abbreviated it and composed many sections (called *clausulae*, discussed on p. 89) that were much better. Pérotin was considered the best composer (or singer) of discant (*optimus discantor*). He composed three- and four-voice organa also, and monophonic and polyphonic conductus. Anonymous IV cited Pérotin's "excellent" four-voice settings of *Viderunt* and *Sederunt* (fig. 6.5) and his "renowned" three-voice settings of Alleluias with the verses *Posui adiutorium* and *Nativitas*. Books of music composed by Pérotin were still in use at "the great Church of the Blessed Virgin"—presumably the Cathedral of Notre Dame—in Paris at the time Anonymous IV wrote his treatise.

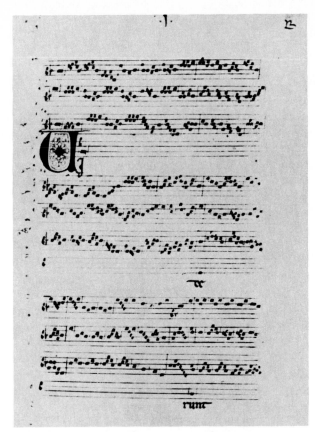

Figure 6.5 Beginning of organum quadruplum *Viderunt* attributed to Pérotin. MS Pluteus 29.1, fol. 1r. *(Biblioteca Medicea-Laurenziana, Florence.)*

Example 6.1 The rhythmic modes with comparable poetic metric patterns.

One of the significant contributions made by the Parisian school of composers was the use of rhythm and meter—the employment of rhythmic modes and modal notation—in the creation of polyphonic settings of chant.

Rhythmic Modes

Concerning rhythm, Anonymous IV wrote: "The notes . . . in the old books were excessively ambiguous, because the simple materials were all equal, and they [singers] were occupied solely with the intellect saying, 'I understand this to be a long note, I understand this to be a short one.' "

By the thirteenth century, the need for some means of notating rhythms had become increasingly apparent and had been met. In much the same manner as musician-scribes of the late eighth century classified liturgical chants modally according to melodic patterns, thirteenth-century composers notated and classified rhythms according to patterns that they called **modes**. There were six rhythmic modes, identified by number. Modal rhythm was based on two values, long and short, arranged in stereotyped patterns markedly similar to the metrical patterns used for scansion of Latin and French poetry. For example, the long-short scheme of Mode I is the same as poetic *trochaic;* the short-long pattern of Mode II is identical with poetic *iambic* (ex. 6.1). Theorists called the threefold unit of measure for each mode a *perfectio* (perfection). In the medieval science of numbers, three was a perfect number—it was the smallest cardinal number to have a beginning, a middle, and an ending. Moreover, in speculative thought, the perfection of the number three was related theologically to the Holy Trinity.

In the last quarter of the twelfth century, Aquitanian neumes were given more definite shapes and were written in square forms. The neumes and square notation used for chant were adapted to meet the need for a notation that defined rhythms. Pitches and rhythmic pattern were united in specially devised neumes called **ligatures**. The form of the ligature—especially the first ligature of a phrase—indicated the rhythmic mode to be used (fig. 6.6). Modal notation was quantitative and was based on two note values: a *longa* (long), and a *brevis* (short), which might be altered. (These alterations and other complexities of the notational system need not concern us here.) Notational signs for rests were devised also. Mode V was

Figure 6.6 Notation of rhythmic Mode I (*a*) in ligatures, with (*b*) transcription. A phrase in rhythmic Mode I was notated as a three-note ligature that is followed by one or more two-note ligatures.

(a)   (b)

Mode I, First ordo

Mode I, Second ordo

Mode I, Third ordo

Example 6.2 Rhythmic Mode I in First, Second, and Third ordo patterns.

usually written with a rest after each pattern, thus forming the equivalent of what is in modern music two complete measures.

The rhythmic patterns were grouped in *ordines*. The number of times a rhythmic pattern was repeated without interruption constituted its *ordo* (ex. 6.2).

Rhythmic modes were discussed in treatises written by many thirteenth-century theorists. In *De musica mensurabili* (Concerning Mensural Music), written c. 1240, Johannes de Garlandia (fl. c. 1240) considered both organum and discant. He introduced the use of strokes of different lengths to indicate rests of different durations; his signs were adopted by others. Garlandia seems to have been the first medieval theorist to give a thorough explanation of rhythmic notation; in general, he laid the groundwork for the system of mensural notation presented in treatises written by Franco of Cologne and others.

Léonin

It is presumed that Léonin flourished in Paris between c. 1163 and 1190, and that Pérotin, who emended Léonin's work, belonged to the next generation of Parisian composers and flourished between c. 1190 and c. 1225. The complete *Magnus liber organi* created by Léonin no longer exists in its original form. However, there survive three manuscripts that are considered the main sources of polyphonic settings of the Parisian school: MS Pluteus 29.1, in Biblioteca Laurenziana, Florence; MS Wolfenbüttel 677 (W₁);

and MS Wolfenbüttel 1206 (W₂). From a study of these manuscripts, historians have been able to reconstruct the probable format of the original *Magnus liber organi* and to determine that the repertoire was used in a secular (not a monastic) church, probably Notre Dame Cathedral. This conclusion is reenforced by Anonymous IV's statement that the music was used at the great cathedral of the Blessed Virgin in his own time.

Creation of the *Magnus liber organi* was a significant achievement in the development of early polyphonic music. *Magnus liber organi* contained two-part settings of the solo portions of responsorial chants for the great feast days of the liturgical year, commencing with Christmas Day—a cycle of the solo portions of Graduals and Alleluias for Mass and of the solo portions of the Great Responsories for Vespers. In all of the extant manuscript sources, the settings are arranged in two groups, in the following order: (a) an Antiphonary section containing the Vespers Responsories, which were the most elaborate chants used for this Office during the Middle Ages; and (b) a Graduale section containing the chants for Mass. The book was designed to be used by soloists; chants sung by the choir were in the regular chant-book.

Although the probable contents of the original *Magnus liber organi* have been determined, the *exact* nature of the music itself has not been established. It is presumed that the two-voice settings were melismatic organum in which the tenor voice consisted of the solo portions of the original chant written in sustained note values, and that the duplum was a free-flowing melismatic line that incorporated some recurrent use of short melodic motifs. Léonin may have used modal rhythmic patterns in some portions of the duplum, for rhythmic modes and modal notation had limited use in northern France in Léonin's time. Possibly, Léonin was one of the composer-performers in northern France who were instrumental in creating modal rhythms and meters, but this has not been proven.

Figure 6.7 MS Pluteus 29.1, folios 87v–88r. The *Benedicamus domino* organum commencing at the end of the second pair of staves on folio 87v has the word *Benedicamus* set as melismatic organum (organum duplum) and the word *dominus* set in discant style, as a clausula. The *Benedicamus domino* commencing at the top of folio 88r is a clausula.

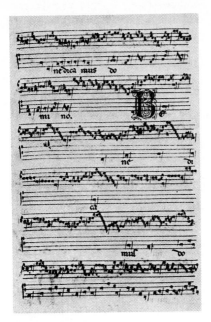

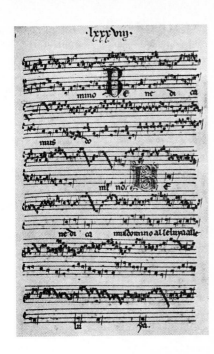

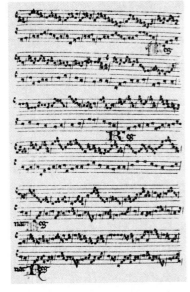

Figure 6.8 Independent (i.e., substitute) clausulae on *Regnat* melisma. MS Pluteus 29.1, fol. 166v. *(Biblioteca Medicea-Laurenziana, Florence.)*

Because Anonymous IV referred to "better *clausulae*" created by Pérotin, it must be presumed that Léonin's *Magnus liber organi* contained *clausulae*. A *clausula* was a polyphonic section of chant in which both voices were written in discant style counterpoint with both voices proceeding at approximately the same rate. The clausula was a distinct section, with a final cadence; all kinds of motion were used, and the rules of consonance were respected. The basis of the section—the tenor voice—was a melismatic portion of solo chant. Both tenor and duplum were organized in measured modal rhythms (fig. 6.7). As was the custom at St. Martial, where the original chant was syllabic, composers used sustained-note style and wrote "organum"; where the chant was melismatic, a setting in discant style (at first, note-against-note; later, with all voices rhythmically modal) was written (DWMA17). The solo portions of the great responsorial chants used at Notre Dame contained long melismas that were especially suitable for clausulae.

In Pérotin's time, several different clausulae were constructed from the same chant melismas. These clausulae were of various lengths, and, because the tenor melody was identical in all of the settings, one clausula could be substituted for another without disturbing the basic structure of the Service (fig. 6.8; DWMA18). *Substitute clausulae* were valuable because of their ability to alter the amount of time consumed by a Service. The amount of time allotted to a certain chant varied in accordance with the number of dignitaries present at the Service and the amount of time required for completion of the liturgical actions performed during the singing of that particular chant. If only a short amount of time was needed, a short clausula was used; if a longer period of time was required, a longer clausula was substituted.

Considerable variety was present in performance of a Service in the churches and cathedrals of northern France in the late twelfth and early thirteenth centuries. Soloist(s) and choir alternated when monophonic chants were sung, and polyphony was used for some solo portions of the liturgy. Those polyphonic sections themselves provided variety, for melismatic organum (now called *organum purum,* or pure organum) could be alternated with sections written in discant style, and clausulae could be used. Moreover, the substitution of different clausulae provided variety while fulfilling a liturgical function.

During the last decades of the twelfth century composers began to write polyphony for more than two voices. Organum written for three voices is called *organum triplum* (DWMA19); that for four voices is *organum quadruplum* (DWMA20). In the first quarter of the thirteenth century, use of organum triplum became standard in northern France; organum quadruplum was written for special occasions. Organum was notated in score arrangement. Commencing with the lowest voice, and reading from bottom of the score to the top, the parts are named tenor, duplum, triplum, and quadruplum. Theoretical treatises indicate that the parts were composed successively, in that order. The tenor held the section of the original chant upon which the polyphony was based. The rhythm of the chant was altered; some portions were written in sustained-note style and others in modal rhythmic patterns. Some sections of organum triplum and quadruplum were in discant style. The upper voices were notated in modal rhythms, with the first mode being the predominant choice. In writing the two or three upper voices of an organum, the composer might choose to employ a different rhythmic mode in each of the voices or might elect to write all but one of three upper voices in the same modal rhythmic pattern. The measured discant style used in the composition of the upper voices of organum was not necessarily strict note-against-note counterpoint.

Each of the upper voice parts was written to be consonant with the tenor; agreement with the other polyphonic voices was not expected. Contrary, oblique,

and parallel motion were all used, and attention was paid to achieving consonance with the tenor. Although the unison, fourth, fifth, and octave were still considered perfect consonances, the fourth appeared less frequently, and the third was sometimes used within a phrase. At the beginnings and ends of phrases, the normal chord-structure comprised an octave and a fifth above the tenor. Perfect consonances were expected at the beginning and end of each of the ordinal patterns of the rhythmic mode being used. In the chord successions that were created, harsh dissonances sometimes occurred. Complete triads occasionally appeared. However, stability lay in the hollow sound of the octave with the open fifth; for a conclusive cadence, the composer of organum relied on a chord structure from which the third was absent.

Only the tenor was supplied with text—the word or words of the chant upon which the organum was based; the upper voices were textless. It is not known whether the singers sang the same syllable of text or voiced the same vowel sound as that being sung by the tenor, or whether a single vowel sound, such as "ah," was intoned throughout the piece. If changing vowel sounds were used rather than syllables, this would provide another element of contrast in performance. The vocal sound produced seems to have been a straight-line, vibratoless intonation of pitches, which probably resounded effectively in the Gothic cathedrals and stone churches of the Middle Ages. Organum was intended to be sung by men in liturgical Services; therefore, all of the voice parts are at approximately the same pitch level. The melodies are narrow in range, and the voices frequently cross. In many passages, the modern listener is more aware of chord successions than of linear polyphonic melodies (fig. 6.9).

Many organa were quite lengthy, and Parisian composers employed various structural devices to organize their compositions. Melodic motives were used frequently as unifying devices. Short motives were transferred from part to part, sometimes in reiteration, sometimes in inversion; at other times, motives appeared in melodic sequences or were repeated in the same voice part. Occasionally, composers wrote a few notes of incidental imitation at the beginning of a section, or included a bit of canon. Voice exchange was employed frequently (ex. 6.3). The practice may

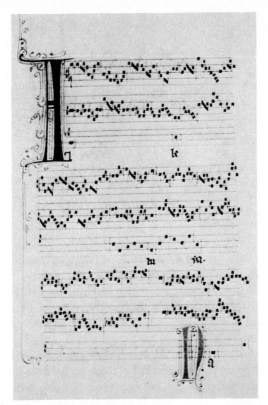

Figure 6.9 Organum triplum *Alleluya Nativitas*, attributed to Pérotin. MS Helmstedt 1099 (W₂), fol. 16r. *(Herzog August-Bibliothek, Wolfenbüttel.)*

Example 6.3 Two instances of Pérotin's use of *Stimmtausch* in the organum quadruplum *Sederunt*. Transcribed from MS Pluteus 29.1: (*a*) fol. 4v; (*b*) fol. 6r.

have been imported from England, for the English used it extensively; they referred to it as *rondellus* technique. The German term for voice exchange is *Stimmtausch*. The practice entails the exchange of two- or three-measure motives or phrases between voices; sometimes all three of the upper voices of organum quadruplum might be involved in this interchange of motivic or melodic material.

Pérotin

That Pérotin was working in Paris during the last decade of the twelfth century seems to be substantiated by two data: (a) Anonymous IV's citation of Pérotin's excellent four-voice polyphonic settings of *Viderunt omnes* and *Sederunt principes,* and (b) two decrees issued in 1198 and 1199 by the Bishop of Paris, Eudes de Sully, permitting the use of triple or quadruple organum in certain specified Services in which

those chants were sung. The Bishop's decrees were designed to eliminate frivolous and sometimes rather sacrilegious behavior of subdeacons, deacons, and priests when they took charge of the Services celebrating the traditional medieval "Feasts of Fools" on the several days after Christmas. At Christmas 1198, the Bishop's decree stated the format for celebration of First Vespers on the Vigil of the Feast of Circumcision (January 1) and permitted the singing of the Respond and the *Benedicamus Domino* in triple or quadruple organum by four subdeacons. (The specification of four subdeacons indicates that the Bishop expected performance of four-voice organum.) Also, at Matins the third and sixth Responds might be sung in triple or quadruple organum, and at Mass the Gradual and Alleluia might be sung in either triple or quadruple organum by "four men walking in procession." By a similar decree issued at Christmas 1199, Bishop Eudes de Sully established the format for the observance of the Feasts on St. Stephen's Day (December 26) and Circumcision (January 1); that decree also permitted the singing of the Gradual or Alleluia of the Mass in triple or quadruple organum.

Figure 6.10 Organum quadruplum attributed to Pérotin: conclusion of *Sederunt* verse and beginning of *Mors.* MS Helmstedt 628 (W₁, Heinemann 677), fol. 4v. *(Herzog August-Bibliothek, Wolfenbüttel.)*

[su]-um   an - - - - - - - - - - - -

Example 6.4 Excerpt from organum quadruplum *Notum fecit dominus,* from *Viderunt,* showing canon between duplum and triplum. Transcribed from MS Pluteus 29.1, fol. 3v.

chants survive, as does also a quadruplum setting of *Mors,* a clausula from the Easter Alleluia verse *Christus resurgens* (fig. 6.10). All of these three surviving quadrupla have been attributed to Pérotin, though he did not sign his name to his work. (DWMA20.)

Many of Pérotin's organa were quite long. In them he used various unification devices such as recurrent melodic motives, melodic sequences, voice exchange, and, occasionally, a few notes of incidental imitation at the beginning of a section, or a bit of canon. A lengthy passage in canon was unusual; however, Pérotin included a twelve-measure canon at the fifth in the quadruplum *Viderunt* (ex. 6.4).

The performance of a lengthy organum quadruplum such as Pérotin's *Viderunt omnes,* with the changing colors of the vowel sounds and chord successions and the patterns of the modal rhythms and melodic motives, must have had a kaleidoscopic effect that rivaled that of the light filtering through the large stained glass windows of Notre Dame Cathedral.

Composers of the Parisian (Notre Dame) school continued to write organum until c. 1250; after that date their interest in the form waned. Traces of organum are found in some Germanic lands in the fourteenth through sixteenth centuries. In Iceland, strict parallel organum was used in the fourteenth century; in the twentieth century, Icelanders still sing the *Tvi-söngur* (two-part song), which is constructed in strict parallel fifths.

Later, a similar provision was made for St. John's Day (December 27), when the priests took charge of the Services. The Bishop's provision of additional money for those who sang the polyphony on those days was an incentive to use quadruplum.

The Gradual used on January 1 was *Viderunt omnes*—the same one used at High Mass on Christmas Day; the Gradual used on St. Stephen's Day was *Sederunt principes.* Because Anonymous IV credited Pérotin with composition of organum quadruplum settings of these chants, it has been assumed that Pérotin was living in Paris and working at Notre Dame Cathedral in late December 1198 and the ensuing years. Organum quadruplum settings of these

Conductus

The composers of the Parisian school did not confine their polyphonic writing to organum. All three of the manuscript sources of Notre Dame music previously mentioned—Pluteus 29.1, W_1, and W_2—contain compositions that medieval theorists commonly called *conductus*. The largest collection of conductus is in Pluteus 29.1: approximately 185 two- and three-voice settings, 3 four-voice settings, and more than 140 monophonic conductus. Some texts received both monophonic and polyphonic settings. That Pérotin composed conductus is attested by Anonymous IV, who cited a three-voice *Salvatoris hodie* and a two-voice *Dum sigillum summi patris*.

The texts of conductus are metrical Latin poems that deal with a variety of subject matter. Some of the texts are sacred but nonliturgical; some are devout and pious but not sacred; others are serious and secular and often concern morals or political and historical topics. Some conductus had quasi-liturgical use and probably found their way into Services without official sanction. In such instances, a conductus might serve as a processional or as an introduction to a liturgical chant. Some conductus may have been used for instruction; others seem to have been designed purely for entertainment.

In the treatise *Ars cantus mensurabilis* (The Art of Mensurable Song), written c. 1260, the theorist Franco of Cologne described the process of composing a "conduct." The conductus was not based on chant but, according to Franco, used for its tenor a newly composed melody. Against this melody, a duplum was written in discant style. If additional voices were desired, they were composed successively with care being taken that any discordant notes in the triplum and quadruplum were concordant with one of the other voices. The English theorist Walter Odington disagreed slightly with Franco. In *Summa de speculatione musicae* (Comprehensive Observations about Music), written c. 1300, Odington stated that conductus tenors might be either newly composed or preexistent melodies. In fact, some tenors were newly composed, but others exhibit a combination of newly composed and borrowed materials.

In the history of Western music, the conductus and the versus (see p. 76) provide the earliest examples of completely original polyphonic compositions.

The conductus was less complex musically than organum. All voice parts moved within the same vocal range, which was rather narrow. Voice crossing occurred frequently; often the voices exchanged melodic fragments (*Stimmtausch*). The discant style of writing was organized to produce basically the harmonic intervals that were regarded as perfect consonances (octaves, fifths, and fourths). Thirds, though considered dissonant, occur frequently in some compositions. Rhythmically, a triple division of the beat was used, and all voices moved in nearly the same rhythm. The music was written in score notation. The text was set syllabically or neumatically and was written under the tenor melody. The same music was used for each stanza of text; in other words, the setting was **strophic.**

When performed, the conductus produced a sound that had, in effect, a chordal or pseudo-chordal texture. The kind of writing used for conductus was sometimes employed in other polyphonic compositions and is often referred to by historians as "conductus style."

A distinguishing feature of some conductus is the presence of *caudae*. Caudae are rather long textless melismas, which usually occur at the beginning, in the middle, and at the end of a conductus. However, a cauda may be present only at the end of a conductus. The word *cauda* (tail) is related to the Italian word *coda,* which is used to designate the passage or section that brings a composition to a satisfactory conclusion. Some historians classify conductus without caudae as *conductus simplex* (simple conductus) and conductus with caudae as *embellished conductus*.

It is generally presumed that the conductus was performed vocally, with all parts being sung and all voices singing the same text. However, it is possible that instrumentalists performed the upper parts, or that vocal lines were doubled by instruments. If the parts were doubled, the caudae may have been performed instrumentally.

(a)

(b)

Figure 6.11 Conductus with cauda: (*a*) *Hac in anni janua,* MS W₁, fol. 78r. (*b*) *Roma gaudens iubila,* MS W₁, fol. 107r. *(Herzog August-Bibliothek, Wolfenbüttel.)*

The conductus *Veri floris* (Of the true flower) exists in both two- and three-voice polyphonic settings, as well as in a monophonic version, and is found in nine different manuscripts. This short piece is a characteristic example of simple conductus (DWMA21). An example of a two-voice conductus with caudae interspersed throughout is *Roma gaudens iubila* (Rome rejoicing; fig. 6.11a). The only cauda in the three-voice conductus *Hac in anni ianua* (In this new year) occurs at the end of the piece (fig. 16.11b; DWMA22).

As was the case with organum, after 1250 composers gradually ceased writing conductus and turned their attention to the **motet.**

Motet

In two pieces of St. Martial organa the melismatic upper voice was supplied with words that troped those of the chant tenor. In their bitextuality, these pieces and a few similarly troped organa in the Notre Dame repertoire are forerunners of the thirteenth-century motet. However, the musical style of these textually troped organa bears little resemblance to that of the motet.

When a single textual trope was sung by all of the discant-style upper voices of organum triplum or organum quadruplum, the sound produced by the upper voices was similar to that of conductus. In fact, two of Pérotin's quadrupla, *Viderunt* and *Sederunt,* were supplied with tropes of this kind (DWMA23). This style of writing survived in the **conductus motet** (see p. 98).

The motet as an independent form of music originated when a text—in essence, a literary trope—was added to the duplum of an independent or substitute clausula. The texted duplum was called *motetus,* a Latinized noun formed from the French word *mot* (word). The independent clausula with added words and the entire species it generated became known as *motetus* (motet). A motet might have two, three, or four voice parts. As in organum, the third part was called the triplum, and the fourth part was the quadruplum. A motet with two additional texts is called a **double motet;** one with three additional texts, a **triple motet.** Motets were not given titles. They are identified by the opening word(s)—the **incipit**—of each line of text, commencing with the highest voice, e.g., *En non diu—Quant voi—Eius in Oriente* (Now in truth—When I see—His [star] in the East) (fig. 6.12; DWMA24).

Because some independent clausulae with troped Latin texts in the duplum are found in Wolfenbüttel MS 677 (W$_1$), the date of origin of the motet is usually given as c. 1200. The most important extant manuscripts containing thirteenth-century motets are: (a) Montpellier Codex (MS H196), whose 336 polyphonic compositions include 325 motets; (b) Bamberg Codex (MS Ed.IV.6), which contains 100 double motets, a conductus, and 7 clausulae; and (c) Las Huelgas Codex, containing 58 motets, some organa, some polyphonic conductus, and 45 monophonic pieces.

Most of the surviving motets are anonymous. Many motets exist in several versions, with variant versions appearing in different manuscripts. For example, the same duplum or triplum melody may have sacred words in one manuscript and secular words in another. Yet, the tenor melody and its incipit remained constant. Music was used and reused. It was common for the same tenor to be used with different melodies and texts in the upper voices. Nor was it unusual for a two-voice motet to be supplied with a triplum and appear in another manuscript as a double motet.

A motet was written in layers. A preexistent melody was selected to serve as the tenor, the foundation of the composition. The preexistent melody used as the basis for another composition is called

cantus firmus (fixed song). The tenor melody was given rhythmic organization, and another melody was composed to serve as its duplum. If a chant melisma chosen to serve as tenor was not long enough to balance the melody written as duplum, the chant melody was repeated until the proper length was attained. A third melodic layer became the triplum.

A majority of thirteenth-century motets were based on sacred Latin tenors derived from chant. The portion of chant used was clearly identified by its text incipit. Until c. 1250, composers most often selected their motet tenors from the Latin clausulae tenors in the *Magnus liber organi.* After c. 1250, composers began to use portions of other liturgical chants—Kyries, Alleluias, antiphons, and verses of the latter two—as motet tenors. When used for a motet, the borrowed tenor was written in a regular pattern in one of the rhythmic modes. Only the incipit of the Latin tenor text was written in the motet music. Perhaps this was because the composer believed that performers would (or should) know the chant melody and its text. Possibly, the tenor melody was performed instrumentally rather than vocally. As the century progressed, motet tenors—and motets in general—became increasingly more secular. Melodies of monophonic secular songs sometimes served as motet tenors. Even street cries of vendors were used, as in *On parole—À Paris—Frese nouvele* (They say—In Paris—Fresh strawberries) (fig. 6.13).

In the earliest motets, the duplum was supplied with Latin words; by c. 1250, however, words for the upper voice(s) might be in either Latin or French. Usually, both duplum and triplum were in the same language. All texts were related in meaning, though sometimes the relationship was remote and tenuous. When the texts of the upper voices were in French, the poetry usually concerned love. Combining sacred and secular texts and music was not considered sacrilegious, for the church was at the center of secular life.

During the second half of the thirteenth century, the three-voice polytextual motet became standard. Composers made no attempt to achieve a homogeneous sound; the voices enjoyed linear independence. Texts for the upper voices were set syllabically, and phrases of different lengths were used. Because of this,

(a)

(b)

Figure 6.12 Motet *En non diu—Quant voi—Eius in Oriente*:
(*a*) in Montpellier MS H196, fol. 145v–146r; (*b*) in modern
notation. *(Source: Figure a—Bibliothèque Interuniversitaire,
Section Medecine, Montpellier MS H196, folios 145v–146r.)*

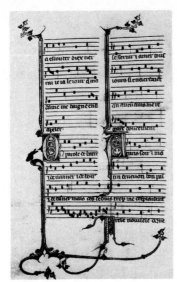

Figure 6.13 Beginning of motet *On parole—'A Paris—Frèse nouvele* notated on lower half of MS H196, fol. 368v. *(Bibliothèque Interuniversitaire, Section Medecine, Montpellier.)*

Example 6.5 Cadence patterns.

Figure 6.14 Melisma on *eius* in Alleluia verse *Vidimus stellam eius in Oriente*, LU,460: (*a*) in Gregorian chant notation; (*b*) transcription of pitches; (*c*) rhythmic organization of those pitches for use as tenor of motet (cf. fig. 6.12*b*). *(Figure a from The Liber Usualis, edited by The Benedictines of Solesmes. Copyright © 1956 Desclée Company, Tournai, Belgium.)*

musical phrase endings overlapped, and often all voices did not cadence simultaneously until the end of the motet. At the final cadence all voices were in perfect consonance, forming a final chord that consisted of either (a) an octave with an open fifth (and thus included a perfect fourth also), (b) an octave, (c) a fifth, or (d) a unison.

During the last half of the thirteenth century three basic cadence patterns evolved (ex. 6.5). These became standard and formed the basis for cadences that were used during the next two centuries. In forming these cadences, each of the voices moved by step from the penultimate to the final note of its melody, the tenor proceeding down and the duplum and triplum moving up. This produced a final consonance that was the summation of three perfect consonances: the octave, the fifth, and the fourth.

Each melodic line was consonant with the tenor; all voices were not necessarily consonant with each other. The upper voice(s) formed perfect consonances with the tenor at the beginning and end of each rhythmic pattern (and sometimes in between), and dissonances occurred as passing tones. Each melodic line lay within the scope of an octave. Because all voices moved within the same narrow range, voice crossing was common.

En non diu—Quant voi—Eius in Oriente may be considered a typical thirteenth-century motet of the Notre Dame school (DWMA24). The tenor was derived from the chant *Vidimus stellam eius in Oriente* (We have seen His star in the East), the Verse of the Alleluia for Epiphany. The pitches of the chant were retained in the motet tenor, but the rhythm was restructured in the pattern of the first ordo of rhythmic mode I (fig. 6.14). Duplum and triplum employ a basically similar rhythm. The melodies create perfect consonances on the first and last notes of each rhythmic pattern of the tenor. The motet concludes on the consonance of a perfect fifth. Voice crossing occurs frequently; the two upper voices exchange texts and some melodic fragments in measures 1–4 and 21–24. The opening words of the triplum, sung by the duplum at the end of the motet, were borrowed from the refrain of a trouvère song. Such quotations were common in thirteenth-century motet texts. Though canon was rarely used, it occurs briefly in measures 5–6, with the triplum imitating the duplum. The secular French texts of the two upper voices speak of love, but they have a tenuous relationship with the chant text through their reference to the budding rose, which is symbolic of the Christ-child. The tenor

melody is repeated, commencing with the second note of measure 7. This treatment of the tenor fore-shadows the fourteenth-century technique of iso-rhythm (see p. 128).

One type of motet was strongly influenced by conductus and is known as **conductus motet,** or **conductus-style motet** (fig. 6.15; DWMA25). In this type, the two or three upper voices strongly resemble the conductus. They move in basically the same rhythm and sing the same text simultaneously. The tenor is derived from chant and uses one of the rhythmic modes. The upper voices of conductus motets were notated in score, with the text written beneath the duplum. The conductus motet differs from conductus in that the motet tenor is a preexistent melody, has a different text incipit, and is notated in a rhythm different from that used by the upper voices. Although the production of conductus decreased considerably in the last half of the thirteenth century, some conductus-style motets were still being composed.

In the early motets the rhythm of the upper voices is structured similarly; no doubt the practice of writing the upper voices of clausulae in discant style influenced this. As more motets were produced, greater rhythmic variety was employed; it was not uncommon for a different rhythmic mode to be used

for each voice. Before the century ended, composers were writing motets that were bilingual (if the tenor text was sung), polytextual, polyphonic, and poly-rhythmic.

The earliest motets appear in manuscripts in score notation. It soon became evident, however, that valuable manuscript space was wasted when the voice parts were aligned, for the rhythmic modal notation of the tenor required much less space than the upper voices. Scribes began to place the voice parts successively on the manuscript page(s): the triplum first, the duplum next, and the tenor last (fig. 6.16). Later, motets appear in manuscripts with the triplum and duplum notation in parallel columns, and the tenor ligatures written beneath these columns, on a staff the width of the page (fig. 6.17). This latter kind of notation is called **choirbook notation.**

The original function of motets is not known. A motet whose duplum troped the text of the chant-based tenor may have had liturgical use. Possibly, the earliest motets were substituted, as were clausulae, in the performance of a complete organum; thus, they functioned liturgically. If all texts of a motet were sacred and in Latin, perhaps the motet occupied a special place as an independent piece used quasi-liturgically in celebration of a certain feast. Certainly, with the increased use of French vernacular in

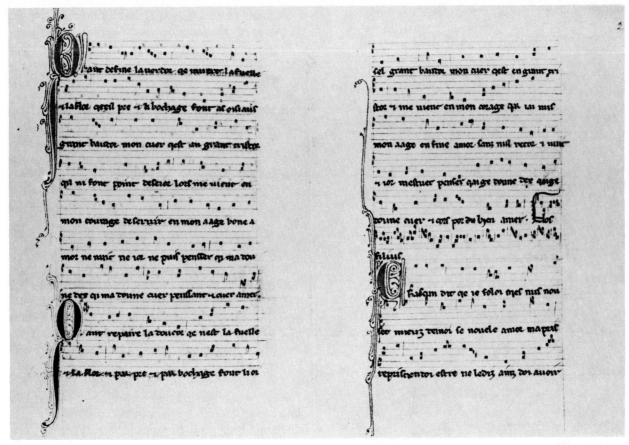

Figure 6.16 Successive notation of motet voice parts. Triplum is at top of left-hand page; duplum follows; tenor (*Flos filius*) commences at end of fifth staff, right-hand page. MS

Helmstedt 1099 (W₂), fol. 214v–215r. *(Herzog August-Bibliothek, Wolfenbüttel.)*

the upper voices, the concentration of the poetry on love, and the secularization of the tenor, the motet moved out of the realm of the church and into secular entertainment.

Franco of Cologne

The theorist Franco of Cologne (fl. c. 1250–after 1280) may or may not have been a composer. No compositions have been located that can be definitely attributed to him. However, thirteenth-century motets in which triplum, duplum, and tenor are distinctive rhythmically and melodically have come to be known as "Franconian" motets (fig. 6.18). In those motets,

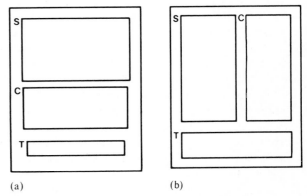

(a)   (b)

Figure 6.17 Diagrams of manuscript pages written in (*a*) successive notation and (*b*) choirbook notation. The manuscript page shown in figure 6.20 is in choirbook notation.

Figure 6.18 The motet *Ave Maria gratia plena—Ave lux luminum—Neuma* in Franconian notation. MS Pluteus 29.1, fol. 94r. *(Biblioteca Medicea-Laurenziana, Florence.)*

Anonymous IV wrote that Franco of Cologne began to notate some things differently in his books. Franco explained his notation system in his treatise *Ars cantus mensurabilis* (The Art of Mensurable Music), written c. 1260. The principles he established in that treatise formed the basis of the system of notation that, with some modification and amplification, was used for the next two centuries.

Franco believed different note shapes should be used to signify the various note values. However, he did not introduce new note shapes. By formulating a set of rules for the correct notation of rhythms, he simply created a system that freed the existing symbols from ambiguity. He recognized four single-note shapes: *double long* ▜ , *long* ▜ , *breve* ▪ , and *semibreve* ♦ . The relationship between these notes was founded upon the principle of ternary grouping. The basic unit of time, the *tempus* (pl., *tempora*), was the breve.

The value of the double long remained constant; as its name implies, it always had the value of two longs. The long and the breve might be either perfect or imperfect, depending on whether they were subdivided into three or two smaller note values. A perfect long contained three *tempora*; an imperfect long had two. Although a breve normally had the value of one *tempus,* certain circumstances might cause it to be worth two *tempora*; then, it was called an *altered breve*. In Franco's system, a breve normally comprised three semibreves; this was an innovation. Under certain conditions, however, a breve might have only two semibreves, one of which was worth twice as much as the other. Note that, with the exception of the double long, equal binary division of a note was impossible. The durational value of the long, the breve, and the semibreve was determined not only by the shape of the note itself, but also by the kinds of notes placed within a *perfectio* (perfection). A perfection was the equivalent of the modern "measure" or "bar" and contained three *tempora,* i.e., three lengths of time or three beats. Franco stressed that the same rules that governed the relation between the long and the breve governed the relation between the breve and the semibreve. The equivalence between note values in the Franconian system and those used in modern notation is shown in figure 6.19.

the triplum was given the longest text, which was set in shorter note values than those used for duplum and tenor. Frequently, each melodic line was written in a different rhythmic mode. An oft-cited example of this is the motet *Pucelete—Je languis—Domino* (Maiden—I languish—Lord; DWMA26), in which the triplum uses Mode VI, the duplum Mode II, and the tenor Mode V. Typically, musical phrases in the triplum were short, or appeared to be short because the text was set syllabically to fast-moving notes. Phrase endings in the two lower voices might coincide, or the duplum might have longer phrases than those of the tenor. Sometimes the chant-based tenor was cast in a rigid rhythmic pattern; at other times, phrases of varying lengths were used.

Translation:
Triplum: Love can protest, seeing itself now weakened,
for faith and constancy have begun to diminish. (etc.)

Duplum: Faith and constancy follow after and accompany love,
for [love] is founded on them. (etc.)

Tenor: (No text.)

Translation:
Triplum: Hail, joy of the world, light of the errant faithful,
voice of the [ones] rejoicing, sacrifice for paradise . . .

Duplum: Hail, salvation of mankind, royal queen
who bore the Lord, you [His] daughter . . .

(b) Tenor: It is fitting . . .

Figure 6.19 Two Franconian motets (*a*) in manuscript (Montpellier Codex,
MS H196, folios 378v–379r) and (*b*) in modern transcription. *Amor potest—
Ad amorem—Tenor* has an ostinato Tenor; the tenor of *Ave mundi—Ave
salus—Aptatur* is based on a chant melisma. (*Bibliothèque Interuniversitaire,
Section Medecine, Montpellier.*)

(a)

Barlines were not used. When clarification was needed, Franco placed a small stroke between notes to indicate a division between two perfections.

Notes might be grouped and written as ligatures. Directions were given so that notes in ligatures would be recognized as semibreves, breves, or longs. The following signs were used for rests:

Perfect long	Imperfect long	Perfect breve	Major semibreve	Minor semibreve	
= 3	2	1	2/3	1/3	Breve(s)

Petrus de Cruce (Pierre de la Croix)

The smallest note value in the Franconian system was the semibreve, and the breve could be divided into no more than three semibreves. By c. 1280, the need had arisen for a reliable way to notate the division of the breve into four or more semibreves, or, preferably, for note values shorter than a semibreve. Composers were writing motets in which the triplum moved rapidly, in a speechlike rhythm, above a much slower duplum; usually, the chant-based tenor was written in a strict rhythmic pattern and was probably performed instrumentally. Triple meter prevailed. Motets exhibiting these stylistic traits are often referred to as "Petronian," regardless of whether Petrus de Cruce (fl. c. 1270–1300) composed them. The triplum of the motet *Aucuns vont souvent—Amor qui cor—Kyrie* (Some often go—Love that [wounds] the [human] heart—Lord have mercy; DWMA27) exhibits Petronian features (fig. 6.20).

Petrus de Cruce wrote motets whose tripla contained groupings of from four to seven semibreves per breve. This was no mere whim—he used the number of semibreves required to set the syllables of the text. Sometimes Petrus placed dots in the music to group semibreves. These **dots of division** were his innovation. In Petronian motets, the style of the triplum differed considerably from that of the two lower voice parts; often, the triplum assumed the character of a solo.

By c. 1300, composers were writing tripla that contained as many as nine semibreves per breve. This use of an abundance of semibreves caused a deceleration of the beat, for it was impossible to achieve

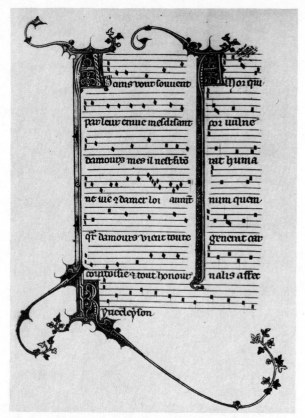

Figure 6.20 Beginning of bilingual motet *Aucuns vont souvent—Amor qui cor—Kyrie eleyson* (Some often go—Love that [wounds] the [human] heart—Lord have mercy). MS H196, fol. 290v. *(Bibliothèque Interuniversitaire, Section Medecine, Montpellier.)*

rhythmic uniformity of the semibreve. In performance, the breve received twice its previous temporal value, and the duration of the semibreve equaled that of the Franconian breve. In other words, the semibreve actually became the unit of the beat.

Polyphony in Britain

The amount of British polyphonic music that has survived from the twelfth and thirteenth centuries is meager. The English had close political, territorial, and cultural ties with France, and some French music was known and used in the British Isles. The thirteenth-century English polyphony that has survived consists mainly of (1) chant settings; (2) troped chant settings; (3) sequences, conductus, and *rondelli* (sing., *rondellus*); and (4) motets. No large collection of purely English motets has survived, but traces of collections are found in incomplete extant manuscripts. The purely secular motet seems not to have been used in England.

As defined by English theorist and scientist Walter Odington (fl. 1298–1316) in *Summa de speculatione musicae*, **rondellus** is duple or triple voice exchange, i.e., phrase exchange. The word *rondellus* denotes either (a) the compositional technique or (b) a piece of music written entirely by means of that technique. Thirteenth-century English composers used rondellus extensively.

Hocket is another polyphonic technique described in Odington's treatise. By using hocket, a composer created two voice parts from one melodic line in this way: The melody was truncated, and individual notes or small groups of notes were parceled out in alternation with rests to two voices, so that in performance one voice was always silent when the other was singing. The sound effect produced was jerky, in keeping with the meaning of the Latin word *oquetus* (hiccup). Passages in hocket appear in some late thirteenth- and fourteenth-century motets; Petrus de Cruce used hocket occasionally. A composition in which hocket technique was used consistently was called a hocket.

It was stated previously that Wolfenbüttel MS 677 (W$_1$), written for and used at the Augustinian priory of St. Andrews in Scotland, contained a repertory of Notre Dame music. There are no complete motets in that manuscript. However, at least six compositions that appear to be conductus have been identified as the upper voices of conductus-style motets whose tenors were omitted from the manuscript.

Motets comprise the major portion of the music in the surviving manuscript pages known as The Worcester Fragments. Some of these motets are conductus style. In others, the tenor is in a rigid rhythmic pattern, and the two upper voices have basically note-against-note counterpoint. Phrases of varying lengths create overlapping cadences. In some of the pieces, the lowest voice part is labeled *Pes* (foot, or foundation) instead of Tenor.

The Verses of several Alleluias in The Worcester Fragments are supplied with tropes designed to be sung simultaneously with the liturgical text. Motetlike settings were written for these Verses. Some Alleluias were equipped with prelude tropes—motetlike settings of tropes intended to be sung as prelude to the soloistic beginning of the Alleluia. The rondellus *Alleluia psallat* (Alleluia, sings . . .) is a prelude trope. Most prelude tropes exhibit *rondellus* technique.

The manuscript catalogued Harley 978 in the British Museum contains, among other items, the index to a lost collection of 164 polyphonic pieces thought to have been used at Reading Abbey. Names of composers listed include W. de Winton, W. de Wicumbe, and R. de Burg[ate], who was Abbot at Reading from 1268 to 1290. Four of the seven sections listing music are devoted to motets, both two- and three-voice.

Sumer is icumen in

One of the items in MS Harley 978 is the famous Reading rota, *Sumer is icumen in* (colorplate 4; DWMA28). A **rota** is a canon, or round. *Sumer is icumen in* is a four-voice rota, superimposed on a duplex *Pes*. Rubrics provide instructions for performance of the composition. The *Pes* is a two-measure rondellus that is repeated until the piece concludes. This two-measure cantus firmus was derived from the first five notes of the Marian antiphon *Regina caeli laetare*; English secular words were substituted for the Latin sacred text. Two texts appear under the rota melody. Beneath the original rota text, which is in English, a later hand printed a Latin poem that commences, *Perspice christicola que dignacio* (Observe, Christian, what an honor). The relationship between texts and music is intricate: (1) The melody of the *Pes* is the Easter-season Marian antiphon, and the Latin text of the rota paraphrases a Verse of a Sarum chant Sequence used on Easter Day, *Perspice christicolas, qualiter laeti*. (2) The English text of the rota speaks of the approach of summer and of events of nature occurring around Eastertime; the Latin concerns Christ's sacrifice and refers to the "heavenly husbandman" by using the word *agricola* (farmer). (3) "Sing cuccu" in the *Pes* is echoed in the English "Lhude sing cuccu."

Sumer is icumen in is an ingenious composition. The independent character of its two melodies is apparent when one realizes that, in performance, no voice part forms parallel octaves or unisons with the lower voice of the *Pes*. It is conjectured that the composition dates from c. 1250. *Sumer is icumen in* is the only known six-voice composition prior to the fifteenth century and the only known composition that combines rondellus and rota techniques. Moreover, the composition is a motet, for it is polyphonic, is based on liturgical chant, and is bitextual. And, it is one of those rare motets in which duplum and triplum texts are in different languages.

Musica ficta

The term *musica ficta* (literally, feigned music) refers to notes that were chromatically altered in performance to produce pitches not found in Guido's hexachord system and that were outside the gamut of Gregorian chant. The theorist Johannes de Garlandia seems to have been first to use and define *musica ficta* as being "when a tone is made into a semitone and vice versa." He indicated that *musica ficta* was used to avoid "the error of the third sound," i.e., the tritone. Magister Lambertus (fl. c. 1270) used the symbols ♭ and ♮ to indicate chromatic alterations. The ♮ was used to create an F♯. With the exception of Marchetto of Padua, who first used the ♯ symbol c. 1318, the only chromatic symbols admitted by thirteenth- and fourteenth-century theorists were ♭ and ♮.

Summary

During the Age of *Ars Antiqua,* the Parisian school dominated Western music. Organum and conductus were developed to their fullest extent; these types began to wane c. 1250, when composers focused their attention on motets. Three-voice writing became standard; occasionally, four-part compositions were written. The motet, which began c. 1200 as a literarily troped clausula, became the dominant form of composition. This new form of music stimulated codification of the rhythmic modes and the production of a system of mensural notation. Triple meter was favored. Sound was confined within a narrow vocal range. Most compositions were based on liturgical chant; melodic lines, composed successively, were superimposed on a rhythmically structured liturgical cantus firmus. As was chant, the music was objective in spirit. Few chromatic alterations other than B♭ were notated; after c. 1260, some were created in performance, as *musica ficta.*

A survey of the extant polyphonic music from the Age of *Ars Antiqua* indicates that at the beginning of the Age composed music was primarily sacred. As time passed, composers combined sacred and secular, Latin and vernacular, texts in their works; by the end of the thirteenth century, purely secular motets were being composed. A new "art" of composition was encroaching upon the old; in the fourteenth century, *ars antiqua* would be superseded by *ars nova.*

Medieval Monophony

Although attention has been focused on the development of polyphony, it must be remembered that throughout the Middle Ages monophonic music was being created and performed. It is possible to identify by name a good many of the composers of that monophony.

Latin Songs

Venantius Fortunatus (c. 530–609) is the oldest known medieval poet of France. He was born near Treviso, Italy, and was educated at Ravenna, which was then under Byzantine rule. After a visit to the tomb of St. Martin at Tours, he traveled to Poitiers, where he entered the priesthood and eventually became Bishop. Fortunatus wrote both secular and sacred Latin poetry. Many of his works were written for specific persons and events. Several of his hymns are used liturgically during Holy Week and Easter: (a) *Vexilla Regis prodeunt* (The banners of the King go forth), used at Vespers on Passion Sunday (LU,545); (b) *Crux fidelis, inter omnes* (Faithful cross, of all . . . ; fig. 7.1) and *Pange, lingua, gloriosi praelium* (Sing, tongue, the glorious battle), for the Veneration of the Cross ceremony on Good Friday (*Graduale Romanum*, 1974, p. 182); and (c) *Salve, festa dies* (Hail, festive day), for the procession of those newly baptized at Easter. *Vexilla Regis* and *Pange, lingua* were written in 569 to celebrate the arrival in Poitiers of the fragment of the true cross that Emperor Justinian II sent to Radegunde, widow of Chlothar, king of the Franks.

Figure 7.1 The chant *Crux fidelis* as used with *Pange, lingua*. (*From* Graduale Romanum, *copyright © 1974, Abbaye S. Pierre de Solesmes, F-72300 Sablé-Sur-Sarthe, France.*)

Some isolated examples of the *epitaphium* (Greek, *epitaphion*, epitaph) and *planctus*, written in staffless neumes, survive in manuscripts from the seventh to eleventh centuries. An *epitaphium* is not a

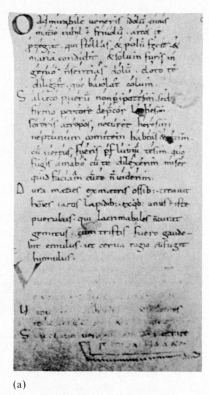

(a)

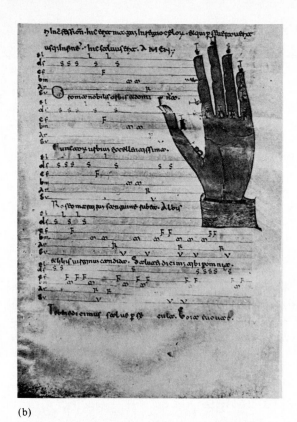

(b)

Figure 7.2 (*a*) The staffless neumes written above the first strophe of poetry for *O admirabile veneris* in MS Gg.5.35 (The Cambridge Songs), fol. 441v, present the same melody as the letter notation in (*b*) *O Roma nobilis*, MS q.318, fol. 291. *(Figure a by permission of the Syndics of Cambridge University Library; figure b from Abbazia, Monte Cassino, Italy.)*

tombstone engraving but a poem or song performed at a funeral. A *planctus* is a lament. *Planctus Karoli*, a lament for Charlemagne, was probably written in 814; *Planctus cygni* (Lament of the swan) melody was in existence in the late ninth century.

The Cambridge Songs

An eleventh-century manuscript owned by Cambridge University Library contains a collection of 47 Latin songs on a variety of sacred and secular subjects (MS Gg. 5.35, folios 432–41). Historical data in some poems indicate that the manuscript was compiled after 1028. The collection appears to be a repertory from which a wandering entertainer might select a program. One of the poems is a portion of Venantius's *Salve, festa dies.* Two of the so-called Cambridge Songs have staffless neumes written above two stanzas of their poetry (fig. 7.2a). One of these poems is *O admirabile Veneris idolum* (O lovely image of Venus), a love song. The melody is the same as that written in letter notation in another manuscript for the pilgrim song *O Roma nobilis* (O noble Rome; fig. 7.2b).

Even after polyphony was cultivated, the great majority of the liturgical music was still monophonic chant. Polyphony was used for solo portions of the liturgy, but the main body of Service music was chant. In medieval times, the two most important varieties of chant, as far as the history of Western music is concerned, were Franko-Roman (Gregorian) and Sarum; composers writing polyphony selected from those chant repertoires the melodies they used as cantus firmus bases for their polyphonic works. New chants were still being composed for both Ordinary and

Proper of the Mass and for the Offices. The monophonic Sequences written by Wipo of Burgundy, St. Thomas of Celano, and St. Thomas Aquinas were mentioned previously (pp. 48–49).

Hildegard von Bingen

Hildegard von Bingen (1098–1179), a Benedictine who became Abbess of Rupertsberg, is known for her diplomatic activities in religious and political situations, her poetry and other literary writings, and her musical compositions. Hildegard was consulted by and had correspondence with persons in all walks of life, including popes, emperors, kings, archbishops, lower clergy, and laypersons. Her literary works deal with both religious and secular topics; two writings on natural history and medicine are entitled *Physica* and *Cause et cure.*

Hildegard began writing musical settings of lyrical poetry in the 1140s. Ten years later, she assembled some of her works under the title *Symphonie armonie celestium revelationum* (Harmonic symphonies of heavenly revelation). Two extant manuscripts contain 77 poems with music. These comprise antiphons, responds, sequences, hymns, a Kyrie, an Alleluia, and three miscellaneous items. The responds are complete with verse; the antiphons close with *evovae*; the hymns conclude with *Amen.* The compositions form a liturgical cycle; most of the works have designations that link them with feasts or classes of feasts. The music notation is in early German neumes, written on four-line staves with f and/or c letter-clef identification (fig. 7.3). The texts are visionary with brilliant imagery. Some of Hildegard's poems are similar to those of Notker Balbulus; others exhibit the richness and imaginativeness found in the poetry of Pierre Abélard.

Hildegard's music is original composition, not based on chant formulas. The music relies on melodic patterns or formulas she composed. These patterns are part of Hildegard's compositional stockpile, but her music does not degenerate to patchwork-quilt status or mere centonization. In style, the music sometimes sounds more akin to Lieder written by a medieval Minnesinger than to chants designed for use in an abbey or church Service. Hildegard's compositions vary from syllabic settings to ones that are highly melismatic. Sometimes the range is very wide and the

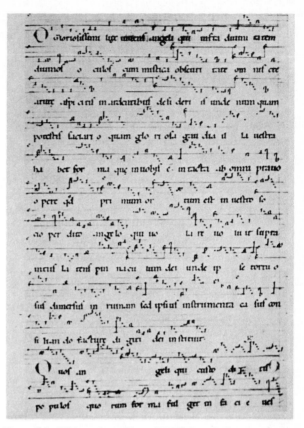

Figure 7.3 Hildegard von Bingen's Antiphon *O gloriosissimi* in manuscript, Cod. 9, fol. 159r. (*Benedictine Abbey of St. Peter and St. Paul, Dendermonde, Belgium.*)

melody verges on being improvisatory in its freedom. For example, the antiphon *In Evangelium,* to be used in Vespers before Benedictus or Magnificat on the feast day honoring St. Ursula, has a range of an octave and a fourth, from c to f'; the respond *O vos, felices radices* covers a range of an octave and a seventh, from A to g'. And, unless there has been a scribal error, the respond *O vos angeli* employs a range of two octaves and a seventh, from G to f''.

The *Kyrie* composed by Hildegard makes frequent use of two melodic patterns, both of which incorporate scalar passages. The form of the movement is ABC. The *Christe* section has the widest range of pitches, covering an octave and a fifth, from c to g'. Each section of the modal music begins and ends on f and incorporates b♭ (DWMA29).

Hildegard's play, *Ordo virtutum,* is considered the earliest morality play (fig. 7.4; DWMA30). The plot concerns the battle for the Soul (*Anima*) waged between the Sixteen Virtues and the Devil (*Diabolus*). The play is written in dramatic verse and contains 82 melodies that are neumatic (or nearly so) settings of the text. Hildegard provided no music for *Diabolus*; all of his lines are spoken.

Anonymous Latin Songs

Many of the Latin songs of the late Middle Ages are anonymous. Some of them were written by wandering clerics who had no permanent positions but worked at whatever jobs they could obtain. Others were written and performed by persons known as *goliards,* who were rejects or dropouts from religious life. The so-called Bishop Goliard who was their mentor and the Order of Goliards to which they supposedly belonged never existed. Goliards had low social status. Their songs were of the "eat, drink, and be merry" type, appropriate to the wanton kind of life the goliards lived.

The largest surviving manuscript of secular Latin songs is Codex latinus 4660 in the Bavarian State Library, Munich. Until 1803, the manuscript was in the library of the Benedictine monastery at Benediktbeurn. The manuscript contains more than 200 poems. Some are supplied with melodies written in staffless neumes; space was provided for music notation for others. In 1847, J. A. Schmelker edited and published the poems under the title *Carmina Burana* (Secular Songs of Benediktbeurn); Carl Orff (1895–1982) composed musical settings for some of the poems, using the same title. A majority of the poems in the manuscript are love songs, notorious for their obscenity. Others parody religious songs and services, irreverently and sometimes blasphemously. Included also are some gambling and drinking songs, a few serious satirical poems, and six liturgical plays. Not all of the poems are in Latin; approximately one-fourth of them are in a Bavarian dialect.

The monophonic type of *conductus* was written in the eleventh to thirteenth centuries. As the name implies, these nonliturgical, metrical Latin songs were probably used, originally, as processionals or for

Figure 7.4 Beginning of Hildegard's morality play *Ordo virtutum. (From Hildegard von Bingen:* Lieder, *ed. Pudentiana Barth, M. Immaculata Ritscher, and Joseph Schmidt-Görg. Salzburg: Otto Muller Verlag, 1969. Used by permission.)*

background music when a person was being conducted from one place to another in a Service. A conductus melody was newly composed. By the end of the twelfth century, the term *conductus* might be applied to any nonliturgical serious song, sacred or secular, with a metrical Latin text.

Vernacular Songs

An early type of French vernacular song was the *chanson de geste* (song of heroic deeds). Long narrative epics of this kind were intended to be sung, but they were not supplied with music notation in manuscripts. The national epic of France, *Chanson de Roland* (Song of Roland), narrates the heroism of Charlemagne's nephew, Roland, who lost his life when ambushed by Basques at Saragosse in 778. The poem can be traced to the first half of the eleventh century; it is mentioned in the *Roman du Mont-Saint-Michel*

(Story of Mont-Saint-Michel), written c. 1160 by William of Saint-Pair. The *Song of Roland* comprises 3998 ten-syllable lines, arranged in 291 stanzas of uneven length. It was probably performed by a *jongleur,* who improvised the melody as he sang the words, and accompanied his singing by strumming a stringed instrument, perhaps a kind of harp. This kind of performance is described in the English epic *Beowulf* (lines 88–99, 867–74, 2104–17), which originated in the eighth century.

Jongleurs (jugglers), or *joculatores,* and *ménestrels* (minstrels) were at the bottom of the social scale. They were social outcasts personally but were acceptable as entertainers capable of providing all kinds of amusements. They were performers, not creators of music, and are important historically because their wanderings contributed to the spread and survival of medieval monophonic song. Names of some early jongleurs are known; Taillefer was jongleur to Duke William of Normandy (William the Conqueror). Sometime around 1120, Parisian jongleurs formed a guild, the Confrèrie de Notre Dame des Ardents, which remained active until abolished by law in the eighteenth century.

Troubadours, Trouvères

In the eleventh through thirteenth centuries, the poet-composers working in the south and north of France were known, respectively, as *troubadours* and *trouvères*. Both names are translated literally as "finders" or "inventors." In Provence, the region that is now southern France, the poets used the Provençal vernacular—the *langue d'oc*; in northern France, the *langue d'oïl* was used. In the respective dialects, *oc* and *oïl* mean "yes." Medieval *langue d'oïl* evolved into modern French.

Many of the troubadours and trouvères were from the nobility; however, a nonaristocrat might enjoy high social status because of his exceptional talent. Marcabru (fl. 1128–50), Bernart de Ventadorn (c. 1130–c. 1190), and Guiraut de Bornelh (c. 1140–c. 1200) were some who did. Many troubadours and trouvères could and did sing their own songs. Minstrels also performed them, and, as they traveled from place to place, taught them by rote to other performers. In the process, variant versions arose. Thus,

some of the surviving manuscripts may contain different versions of the same songs. In fact, none of the surviving thirteenth- and fourteenth-century manuscripts of troubadour-trouvère songs is an exact duplicate of the music in any other manuscript. The manuscript collections of French songs are called *chansonniers* (songbooks), from the French word *chanson* (song).

Not all troubadour and trouvère songs were written down, and of those that were notated many have been lost. Extant poems by troubadours number approximately 2600; those by trouvères, about 4000. Surviving melodies are fewer: about 265 by troubadours and 1400 by trouvères. Generally, the poetry is not profound, and the music, particularly that of the trouvères, may be quite simple. The poems cover a variety of subjects; the musical and poetical forms are equally varied. Most texts are set syllabically, with an occasional short melisma near the end of a poetic line. The melismas in any one song are similar, if not identical, which seems to indicate that they were standard melodic formulas. Phrases are short; melodies are modal and narrow in range—sometimes as narrow as a fifth and seldom greater than an octave. The rhythm is conjectural because the notation used for these monophonic songs is nonmensural, and relative note values are not indicated. Modern transcription in triple meter seems suitable for many of the songs, but the rhythm used may have been at the discretion of the performer and regular rhythmic patterns may not have been followed.

In the first part of the eleventh century, the troubadours called their sung poems *vers*. Later, distinctive terms were applied to specific types of sung poems. Several of the poetic and musical forms employed by the troubadours were paralleled by those of the trouvères and had similar names. The troubadour *canso* (trouvère *chanson*) was a song about courtly or chivalric love. The troubadour *pastorela* (trouvère *pastourelle*), a narrative poem, depicts a pastoral scene in which a knight meets a shepherdess whom he seeks to seduce. Sometimes he succeeds; more often, the shepherdess's lover or a relative appears at the appropriate "saving" moment.

Example 7.1 Guiraut de Bornelh's *Reis glorios,* an *alba.* Transcribed from MS *fr.*22543, fol. 8, Bibliothèque nationale, Paris.

Translation: Glorious king, true light and clarity,
God Almighty, Lord, if it pleases Thee,
To my companion be a faithful aide,
For I have not seen him since night fell,
And soon it will be dawn.

The troubadour *alba* (trouvère *aube*), a morning or dawn song, usually concerns either the parting of lovers at daybreak or a warning given to lovers that dawn is approaching. A warning of this kind is given in the medieval play *Tristan et Iseut,* and Richard Wagner composed an *aube* (in German, *Wächterlied*) for that scene in Act II of his opera *Tristan und Isolde.* (Of course, Wagner's music is in nineteenth-century operatic style.) Some albas express concern for a companion who has been gone through the night. Such an alba is *Reis glorios* (Glorious King) by Guiraut de Bornelh (ex. 7.1; DWMA31).

Songs written in dialogue include the troubadour *tenso* (dispute) and *joc parti* (literally, "shared game," a debate), comparable respectively to the trouvère *descort* and *jeu parti* (pl., *jeux partis*). Participants in the debates were addressed by name; usually, the poet-composer participated.

The *sirventes* was originally a song of service. The word service had a dual meaning: A borrowed secular melody served as music for a poem a troubadour wrote for the lord he served. Sirventes were not necessarily complimentary, however; frequently, they were moral or political satires. Bertran de Born (c. 1145–c. 1215) was famous for his satirical sirventes. Bertran has been immortalized in Dante's *Divine Comedy* (Canto xxviii, lines 118–42). Dante depicted Bertran as decapitated, carrying his severed head in his hands as he wandered through Hell; this was Bertran's punishment for the discord he created between Henry II and his sons.

The *chanson de toile* (picture song), written by trouvères in the twelfth century, has a narrative text related by a lady who commences by describing the scene in which she finds herself at the moment. Generally, the song continues with a tale of the lady's woes and the reasons therefor. (The French word *toile* was used to refer to either a piece of woven cloth or a picture such as that woven into the tapestries for which Arras was famous.)

The *lai* (lay), of Celtic origin, was a long narrative poem in the vernacular, written in rhymed couplets. One of the first French poets to write *lais* was Marie de France, who spent some time at the court of Henry II and Eleanor of Aquitaine; her *lais* were on historical or legendary subjects and were not intended for singing. Later, the trouvères used the same kind of couplet format for *lais* that were intended for singing, but their lyrics concerned love.

The troubadour *balada* or *dansa,* a dance song, usually has a text that mentions spring or a spring festival, such as May Day, and refers to love. *Kalenda*

Translation: I find her much too difficult, indeed!
Because she is so simple.
Much too presumptuous did I act,
Though I felt positively sure
Of what I shall not have for months, alas!
'Tis that which hurts me most of all.
I find her much too difficult, indeed!
Because she is so simple.

Maya (The first of May), by Raimbaut de Vaqueiras (d. 1207), is a love poem set to music that has the character of an *estampie,* a stomping dance (DWMA32). However, *Kalenda Maya* uses aab structure rather than the typical *estampie* form (see p. 119). The trouvères composed dance songs called *carole, ronde, rondel, rondelet,* and other diminutives of *ronde.* These were performed with round dances. Musical structure of the songs was strophic with refrain; a soloist—perhaps the leader of the dance—sang the strophe, and the entire group sang the refrain.

Musical Forms

Typically, the troubadour-trouvère songs are strophic, and many of them have refrains. Sometimes the refrain is a repetition of the opening phrase of the piece; at other times, only the closing strain of the first strophe recurs as refrain in the ensuing stanzas. The refrain may belong solely to the song in which it appears, or it may have been borrowed from another

song; use of quotations as refrains was common practice in the late Middle Ages. The dance songs previously mentioned were forerunners of late thirteenth-century literary forms that became known as the *formes fixes* (fixed forms) of French poetry: *ballade, rondeau,* and *virelai.*

Both capital and lower-case letters are used in the analysis of formal structures of vocal music. Each distinctive melody is identified by a letter, alphabetically. For example, in the formal pattern AbbaA, two different melodies occur: a music and b music. A capital letter is used to indicate that a phrase of text set to a particular musical phrase recurs. Thus, the capital A in the formal pattern given indicates that the composition commences and concludes with the same words and the same music. In this particular formal pattern, the A music and words constitute a refrain. Use of the lower-case letter b twice indicates that the b music is used two times but the words differ. Similarly, the lower-case a indicates use of the same melody as A but with different words (ex. 7.2).

Example 7.3 *Prendés i garde,* a *rondeau,* by Guillaume d'Amiens, with formal pattern ABaAabAB marked. Transcribed from MS Reg. Christ. 1490, Biblioteca Vaticana, Rome.

Translation: *Take care that no one looks at me! If anyone looks at me, tell me.* It is all down there in those woods. *Take care that no one looks at me!* The country girl tends the cows: Pretty brunette, I am yours. *Take care that no one looks at me! If anyone looks at me, tell me.*

The trouvère *ronde* or *rondel* eventually came to be known by the name *rondeau* (pl., *rondeaux*). As a *forme fixe,* the literary *rondeau,* which incorporates a refrain, consists of a single eight-line stanza with only two rhymes; the musical setting comprises only two melodic phrases. All poetic lines having the same rhyme are sung to the same melodic phrase. The poetic and musical forms of the *rondeau* may be indicated by the same pattern of letters: ABaAabAB. However, some thirteenth-century *rondeaux* consisted of only six lines; they did not commence with a refrain but followed the formal pattern aAabAB. The anonymous *C'est la jus* (It is the right) is a six-line rondeau, and *Prendés i garde* (Take care) by Guillaume d'Amiens has eight lines (ex. 7.3; DWMA33). Most thirteenth-century monophonic rondeaux appear without musical notation in literary works, such as *romans* (long narrative poems in the vernacular). The music for some of these rondeaux can be reconstructed because their refrains have been quoted in motets.

From the troubadour *balada* came both the French *ballade* and *virelai* and the Italian *ballata.* Virelai and ballata use the same formal structure. Originally, both ballade and virelai commenced and concluded with a refrain; soon, however, the opening refrain was omitted from the ballade, with a resultant difference in formal structure. Adam de la Halle's *Dieus soit* (The gods be . . .) is a ballade with a refrain at both beginning and end of the stanzas (DWMA34).

The late thirteenth-century *ballade* text has three short stanzas that use the same meter and rhyme scheme and end with the same refrain. The musical setting for each stanza forms the pattern aab. Only a few Provençal dance songs using this form are extant. One is the anonymous *A l'entrada del tens clar* (At the coming of spring; ex. 7.4; DWMA35). As the musical setting of a *forme fixe,* the ballade frequently followed the pattern aabC, with C being the refrain. In other words, three sections of music were used, with the first section being repeated. The court poet and

Example 7.4 *A l'entrada del tens clar,* with aab formal pattern marked. Transcribed from MS *fr.*20050, fol. 82v, Bibliothèque nationale, Paris.

a *Solo:* A l'en-tra-da del tens clar, *Chorus:* E - y - a,

Solo: Pir joi-e re-co-men-çar *Chorus:* E - y - a,

a *Solo:* E pir ja-lous ir-ri-tar, *Chorus:* E - y - a,

Solo: Vol la re-gi-ne mo-strar K'ele est si a-mo-rou-se.

b *Chorus:* A-la-vi', A-la-vi-e, Ja-lous, las-saz nos, las-saz nos bal-lar en-tre nos en-tre nos.

Translation: When the good weather comes, Eya, to bring back joy, Eya, and to annoy jealous ones, Eya, I wish to show the queen for she is so much in love. On your way, on your way, jealous ones, leave us, leave us to dance among ourselves, among ourselves.

composer Machaut (c. 1300–1366) used this formal structure for the musical setting of some of his ballades (see p. 135).

The French *virelai* and Italian *ballata* use AbbaA formal structure. Virelais having more than one stanza use the refrain only once between stanzas: AbbaA bbaA bbaA. Two examples of the virelai, both anonymous, are *C'est la fin* (It is the end) and *Or la truix* (Now I find . . . ; ex. 7.2; DWMA36). *Or la truix* appears in Montpellier MS H196 as the Tenor of the motet *Toutes voies—Trop ai grieté—Je la truis* (All voices—Too many have suffered—I find her).

The first troubadours whose names are known are Eblon (or Ebles), Viscount of Ventadour, and his contemporary, William IX (1071–1127), Count of Poitiers and Duke of Aquitaine. Duke William IX is the only known troubadour in the first quarter of the twelfth century whose poems have survived and are documented. His son, William X, supported but did not participate in the troubadour art; Marcabru (fl. 1128–50) worked at his court. The granddaughter of William IX, Eleanor of Aquitaine (1122–1202), was

both patroness of troubadours and ancestress of trouvères. In 1137, Eleanor married King Louis VII of France (r. 1137–80); they had two daughters, Marie and Alix. Eleanor and Louis were divorced in 1152; soon thereafter Eleanor married Henry, Duke of Normandy and Count of Anjou and Maine, who became Henry II of England (r. 1154–89). One of Eleanor's eight children by Henry was Richard Coeur-de-Lion (1157–99), a talented trouvère. The best known of Richard's songs is *Ja nus hons pris* (Indeed, no prisoner; ex. 7.5; DWMA37), written when he was captured and held for ransom by the Germanic emperor, Henry VI, during the Crusades. (Henry was also a poet-musician.) Richard's lyrics are set to **aab**-type music. According to legend, Richard's friend, the trouvère Blondel de Nesle (fl. 1180–1200) was able to locate the imprisoned Richard by means of a song the two had coauthored.

Marie and Alix, in their respective positions as Countesses of Champagne and Chartres, actively supported poets and composers. Poesy and music flourished at the court of Champagne during the last

Example 7.5 Richard Coeur-de-Lion's *Ja nus hons pris*. Transcribed from *Chansonnier Cangé*, MS *fr*.846, fol. 62v, Bibliothèque nationale, Paris.

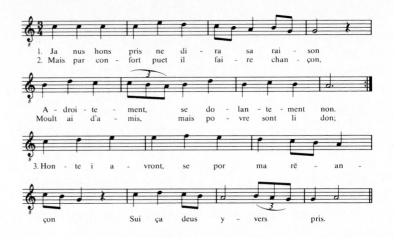

1. Ja nus hons pris ne di — ra sa rai — son
2. Mais par con — fort puet il fai — re chan — çon,

A — droi — te — ment, se do — lan — te — ment non.
Moult ai d'a — mis, mais po — vre sont li don;

3. Hon te i a — vront, se por ma rë — an —

çon Sui ça deus y — vers pris.

Translation: Indeed, no prisoner can tell his story Honestly, without sadness. But for comfort he can make a song. I have many friends, but poor are their gifts; They will be ashamed, if for my ransom I am held for two winters.

30 years of the twelfth century. Among those whom Marie encouraged were Chrétien de Troyes, Gace Brulé, and Conon de Béthune. Marie (d. 1198) herself possessed some poetic talent. Her grandson, Count Thibaut of Champagne (1201–53), who later became King Thibaut IV of Navarre (in modern Spain), was one of the best of the trouvères. Two of Thibaut's love songs, *Pour ce se d'amer me dueil* (Love brings me grief) and *Por conforter ma pesance faz un son* (To ease my thoughts I compose a song), use aab form. Of the 491 songs notated in MS n.a.fr.1050, at Bibliothèque nationale, Paris, 62 are by Thibaut, 48 by Gace Brulé, and 14 by Blondel de Nesle.

The troubadours and trouvères flourished from c. 1086 to c. 1300. Among those active during the time of Léonin and Pérotin were troubadours Bernart de Ventadorn, Guiraut de Bornelh, Bertran de Born, Raimbaut de Vaqueiras, Raimon de Miraval, and trouvères Richard Coeur-de-Lion and Blondel de Nesle.

Adam de la Halle

Adam de la Halle, who is considered greatest of the trouvères, was born at Arras in Picardie c. 1245; it is not certain whether his death occurred in Naples c. 1288 or in England c. 1306. Adam was prolific and versatile. He is one of three thirteenth-century poets who wrote *congés* (farewell poems) to the community

of Arras. Adam wrote literary and musical works in almost every genre used in the late thirteenth century; he is one of the few medieval composers to have both monophonic and polyphonic compositions to his credit. All of his music is secular. His compositions survive in more than two dozen manuscripts, one of which (Paris Bibl. nat. MS fr.25566) contains all of his known works. Included are 36 monophonic chansons, 18 monophonic *jeux-partis,* 16 three-voice *rondeaux* (songs with refrains), 5 three-voice motets, and 3 plays that contain some music. The *rondeaux,* grouped in the manuscript under the heading *Li Rondel Adan,* are some of the earliest polyphonic settings of dance songs. The most famous of the plays, and the one containing the most music, is *Le Jeu de Robin et de Marion* (The Play about Robin and Marion), a dramatic *pastourelle* in which spoken dialogue is interspersed with songs. The music is monophonic, but certain specified instruments accompany the singing. The play was first performed at the Naples court where Adam was working in 1285 (DWMA38).

Fourteen of Adam's *jeux-partis* were debates with Jehan Bretel (c. 1210–72), another noted poet of Arras, who was himself the author of numerous *jeux-partis.* Arras was an important center of trouvère activity in the last half of the thirteenth century. The guild of musicians and poets to which the trouvères of Arras belonged, the *Puy d'Arras,* was headed by an elected "Prince." Bretel held that office for several years. In its endeavors to promote a high quality of musicianship, the Puy d'Arras held annual contests, also called *puys,* with prizes given for the best songs.

Trobairitz

Trobairitz (woman troubadours) were active in southern France from c. 1145 to c. 1225. Their poems (*trobar*), written in Provençal, survive in several manuscripts, including MSS fr.844, fr.854, fr.856 at Bibliothèque nationale, Paris; MSS 5232 and 3207 at Biblioteca Vaticana, Rome; MS α.R.4.4 at Biblioteca estense, Modena. At least 18 trobairitz are known by name, but *vidas* (biographies in manuscripts) exist for less than half of them.

The trobairitz were in a unique social position. They were aristocratic ladies, the *Midons* (Miladies) and "adored things" (*res*) to and about whom troubadours wrote poems of courtly love. Several trobairitz were patrons of troubadours, yet as poets these ladies and men met as equals. The trobairitz, too, produced love poems, but their lines discussed love realistically and candidly. Trobairitz verses were not visionary but were intimate in expression; at times the ladies frankly stated their feelings about physical love, both pro and con. In their poetry, the trobairitz expressed pride, joy, admiration, love, rejection, hurt, distaste, and injury; sometimes the verses question, doubt, or inquire. Some poems divest the knight of his chivalric armor and reveal the human character of the man. Trobairitz poems vary in rhyme scheme, number of strophes, and number of lines per strophe.

The trobairitz also wrote *tensos* (debates, discussions) in which the participants were clearly identified. In the poem *Gui d'Ussel, be.m pesa de vos* (Gui d'Ussel, I am distraught because of you), Maria de Ventadorn was distressed because Gui had given up composing. In 1209 a papal legate had directed Gui to cease writing poems about courtly love. Maria urged Gui to resume composition, then discussed with him the matter of the true social status of a man and a woman in love. Who outranked whom? Or, were they equal? This *tenso* is one of the few trobairitz poems for which a *razo* survives. A *razo* is a prose paraphrase of a song, used by a *joglar* as introduction to his performance of the song.

Maria de Ventadorn (1165–after 1221) was the daughter of Raimon II, Viscount of Turenne, in Limousin. She and her two sisters were praised in poetry by Bertan de Born, c. 1182. In 1183 Maria married Ebles V of Poitou, whose great-grandfather was troubadour Ebles II (Eblon), a contemporary of William of Poitou and Aquitaine. Maria was a patron of troubadours, including Gui. (She was not related to Bernhart de Ventadorn.)

All of the trobairitz were aristocrats; *joglars* would have been available to perform their songs. The musical setting of only one trobairitz poem has been located—*A chantar mes al cor que n̄ deurie* (My heart must sing. . . ; DWMA39) by the Countess of Dia (MS fr.844, fol. 204r). Another version of the poem begins *A chantar m'er de so qu'ieu non volria.* Three other poems by the Countess (c. 1140–63) are extant. It is thought that Beatritz, Countess of Dia, was one of the twin daughters of Marguérite of Bourgogne Comté (d. 1163) and Guigues IV, dauphin of Viennois and Count of Alban (d. in battle 1142). Beatritz married Guillem of Poitiers; their son was Count of Dia, and Beatritz chose to be known as Countess of Dia. The Countess was a friend of troubadour Raimbaut d'Orange (c. 1146–73).

Raimbaut's older sister, Tibors (c. 1130–82), was one of the trobairitz. In her early teens, she married Bertrand des Baux; the couple had three sons. According to her *vida,* Tibors wrote many *trobar,* but only a fragment of one of them survives.

Garsenda de Forcalquier (c. 1170–after 1257), wife of Alphonse II of Provence, held the highest social rank of all the trobairitz. She was regent of Provence from 1209–c. 1220. Around 1225 she retired to the Abbey of La Celle and was still living there in 1257. She is mentioned in the *vidas* of troubadours Gui de Cavaillon and Elias de Barjols.

Among other known trobairitz are Almucs de Castelnau, Iseut de Capio, Guillelma de Rosers, Clara d'Anduza, and Bieiris de Romans.

Spanish Monophony

French and Provençal rulers and nobles frequently visited Spanish and Portuguese shrines and courts and took their musicians and poets with them. The Christian kings of Spain made similar visits to France and

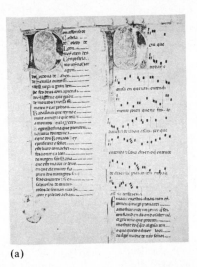

(a)
(b)

Provence. Troubadours and jongleurs traveled independently, too. Spanish musicians and rulers were quite aware of cultural developments north of the Pyrenees, and until the thirteenth century much of the poetry created in the Iberian peninsula was in the Provençal language. After c. 1225, however, the Galician dialect of Portugal and the Spanish vernacular were employed more frequently.

The oldest surviving Galician-Portuguese songs are seven monophonic *canciones de amor* (love songs) by Martin Codax (fl. c. 1230), six of which have notated melodies. They are modal, move within the compass of a sixth, and follow aab form.

The most extensive and most important manuscript of Galician-Portuguese medieval music that has survived is the *Cantigas de Santa Maria* (Ballads about Saint Mary; fig. 7.5). The manuscript (El Escorial, MS b.I.2) was prepared c. 1250–80 at the direction of Alfonso X the Wise, King of Castile and Léon (r. 1252–84). The parchment leaves contain a Prologue (intended to be sung; DWMA40a) and 400 songs honoring the Virgin Mary. Most of these 400 *cantigas* recount miracles attributed to the Virgin, but every tenth *cantiga* is a song praising her (DWMA40b). (The Galician word *cantiga* is pronounced with stress on the first syllable: *cántiga*.) The manuscript is beautifully illuminated with miniatures

that provide valuable information concerning medieval instruments and musical performance (fig. 7.6). The Galician poems are set to music written in mensural notation on five-line staves. Both duple and triple meter were used. The songs have refrains and use the AbbaA formal structure that later became the fixed form of the French virelai and Italian ballata.

Italian Monophony

The proximity of northern Italy to Provence tended to promote the use of Provençal as well as Italian for poetry. The southern third of Italy, which with the island of Sicily formed the Kingdom of Sicily, was ruled from 1197 to 1250 by Holy Roman Emperor Frederick II, a respected statesman and a patron of arts and learning. Frederick was a scholar and authored treatises and poetry. Refugees from the cruelties of the "Albigensian Crusade" and the Spanish Inquisition sought and found protection at his Sicilian court.

Extant manuscripts contain little Italian secular monophony that was produced during the Middle Ages. No doubt a great deal of the monophonic music that was composed was never notated but was transmitted orally. There survive less than 200 thirteenth-century Italian nonliturgical religious songs called *laude* (praises; sing., *lauda*) or *laude spirituali* (spiritual praises). These are songs of wandering penitents

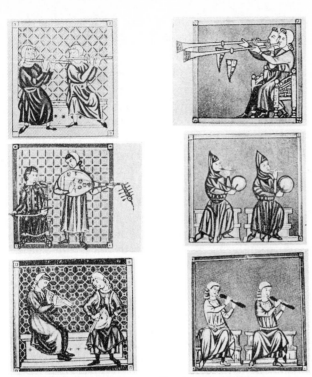

Figure 7.6 Several of the many illuminations in MS b.I.2 depicting instrumentalists performing. *(El Escorial, Barcelona.)*

who sought to achieve atonement for their sins by self-inflicted whippings and by singing songs of praise at wayside shrines. The *laude* are strophic and commence with a *ripresa* (refrain) that recurs after each strophe (DWMA41). The music reflects the influence of Gregorian chant, folk song, and troubadour songs. In their turn, the *laude* and the Italian flagellants influenced the fourteenth-century German penitents who created songs called *Geisslerleider*.

Germanic Monophony

The Germanic counterparts of the jongleurs were called *Spielleute* (entertainers). No specific *Spielleute* repertory has survived; it is possible that none was ever written down. Presumably, these wandering entertainers recited or sang epics and other poetry, told folk tales, and performed Latin and vernacular songs.

The art of the troubadours and trouvères strongly influenced the development of lyric poetry and song among the Germans. Frederick I Barbarossa, who was elected King of the Germans in 1152 and ruled as Holy Roman Emperor from 1154 to 1190, was married in 1156 to Beatrice of Upper Burgundy. Frederick and Beatrice are credited with promoting French and Provençal song in the lands they ruled. The Emperor sponsored an international festival at Mainz in 1184.

The twelfth- and thirteenth-century poet-musicians called *Minnesänger* (sing., *Minnesinger,* one who sings about courtly love) were the German counterparts of troubadours and trouvères. The types of songs created by the *Minnesänger* are similar to those produced by the troubadours and trouvères: (a) *Frauenstrophe* (ladies' songs) parallel the chanson de toile. (b) The *Tagelied* (song of day) heralds approaching dawn, as do alba and aube; and (c) the *Wächterlied* (watcher's song) is closely akin to these. (d) The *Streitgedicht* (dispute poem) is comparable to the jeu parti and tenso. (e) The *Minnelied* (pl., *Minnelieder;* love song) concerns courtly love (*Minne*), as do the canzo and early French chanson. (f) The *Kreuzlied* (song of the cross) finds its counterpart in the Crusaders' songs composed by trouvères. (g) The *Leich* is similar to the lai sung by the trouvères. (h) The German *Sprüche* (proverbs) are moralistic songs, but are not satirical as are the troubadour sirventes.

The Germanic poet-composers used a variety of formal patterns for their song settings, but the structure most preferred was aab, or *Bar* form. The medieval German poem called *Bar* was constructed in three or more stanzas, each having aab structure. In both the poem and the songs using that form, the b section is usually much longer than the a. In extant manuscripts, the notation does not indicate relative note values or ends of phrases. Moreover, in some manuscripts, scribes wrote the music above the poem, and, to save manuscript space, music that was used for the repeated a section was written down only once.

Though the *Minnesänger* were active from c. 1150 to c. 1320, the period between c. 1180 and 1230 is considered their "golden age." Among the best of the German poet-composers were Wolfram von Eschenbach (c. 1170–1220) of Bavaria, Walther von der Vogelweide (c. 1170–1228), Neidhardt von Reuenthal (c. 1190–c. 1237), Der Tannhäuser (c. 1205–70), and Heinrich von Meissen (c. 1250–1318).

Walther von der Vogelweide is credited with perfecting the Minnelied and Spruch and making them original compositions rather than relying upon melodic formulas; in his poetry, too, Walther achieved a higher degree of refinement and originality than his predecessors and contemporaries. One of his best-known compositions, and one of the few of his poems for which the complete melody is extant, is *Palästinalied* (Palestine Song; DWMA42).

Niedhart von Ruenthal tended to use realism and satirical wit in his poetry and particularly directed the satire toward rustic life and manners. Most of his lyrics commence with a description of either the winter or summer season; hence, his poems are sometimes classified as being either "summer" or "winter" songs.

Der Tannhäuser was considered by later German poet-composers as one of the twelve *alte Meister* (old masters). His surviving poems—six Leich and ten Lieder—are important for the autobiographical data they provide. Both Tannhäuser and Wolfram von Eschenbach participated in a song contest held at the Wartburg in 1207, an event Richard Wagner depicted in his music drama *Tannhäuser.* Wagner based his music drama *Parsifal* on Wolfram's epic *Parzival.*

Heinrich von Meissen is better known as Frauenlob (praise of ladies), a name he acquired because he regarded women highly and preferred use of the word *frouwe* (*Frau,* lady) rather than *wip* (*Weib,* woman). So strong were his feelings on the matter that he publicly debated the issue with a colleague. One of Frauenlob's songs begins: *"Ey ich sach in dem trone/Ein jungfraw . . ."* (I saw on the throne/A virgin . . .). Frauenlob was also named one of the *alte Meister* by the Meistersinger.

Meistersinger

The *Meistersinger* were citizens of German cities who belonged to guilds that regulated and promoted the composition and performance of songs (*Meisterlieder*). Meistersinger came primarily from lower and middle classes of society, but talented upper-class citizens were not excluded from the guilds. In contrast with the Minnesinger, who was a professional poet-composer, the Meistersinger regarded composing and singing as a serious avocation. Exactly when or where the first Meistersinger guild was formed is not known.

The guilds were most active from the fourteenth through the seventeenth centuries, though a few still existed in the nineteenth century, and the last Meistersinger (a member of the Memmingen guild) died in 1922. One of the most important of the Meistersinger guilds, and the only one about which specific information is available, was that at Nuremberg. Hans Vogel (died c. 1550) and the shoemaker Hans Sachs (1494–1576) were influential members of the Nuremberg guild, which Richard Wagner depicted in his opera *Die Meistersinger von Nürnberg.* (However, Wagner treated medieval stories, ideas, and forms of music in a nineteenth-century manner.)

Surviving manuscripts of Meisterleider date from the fifteenth century; they contain words and music for approximately 16,000 songs. All of the surviving Meisterlieder are monophonic. These songs, which the Meistersinger called *Bare* (sing., *Bar*), are constructed in the aab pattern now known as **Bar form.** The composers called the a sections *Stollen* and the b section *Abgesang.* Often the *Abgesang* was considerably longer than the *Stollen*; frequently, the last two lines of *Abgesang* melody were identical with the last two lines of the *Stollen* music. It is believed that Meistersinger melodies were intended to be performed as unaccompanied vocal monody, sung by soloists or, rarely, by a chorus.

English Monophony

In medieval England before the Norman Conquest, the professional musician was either a *scop,* who enjoyed a more or less permanent position as resident entertainer at the hall of an *atheling* (petty king), or a *gleeman,* who traveled from place to place and performed wherever and whenever he could find work. After the Norman Conquest, both scops and gleemen vanished, though their functions did not. *Minstrels* appeared and assumed the functions of both scop and gleeman, entertaining by singing songs or by reciting long narrative poems while strumming a harp. No examples of scop or gleeman music are extant.

The paucity of English music in surviving manuscripts may be attributed to the use of Norman-French at British courts after the Norman Conquest. French was the official language of the English court until the latter part of the fourteenth century. Henry II, first of the Angevin kings, and his wife, Eleanor of Aquitaine, spent little time in England. The greater part of the territory Henry controlled was on the European continent. Henry was never willing to learn the English language. Though troubadours and trouvères visited the English court, and Richard I Coeur-de-Lion was himself a trouvère, the French poet-musicians never established a "school" in Britain.

The earliest surviving vernacular English songs are those by a visionary Saxon hermit, St. Godric (died c. 1170). One of his nonliturgical religious songs, "Crist and Sainte Marie," uses portions of a Kyrie, both words and music, as framework at the beginning and end of the English lyrics. This seems to be an example of an English *farse*—a liturgical chant, in this case a Kyrie, with a single long vernacular trope inserted between the opening phrase and the remainder of the chant. Only three songs by St. Godric are extant; the other two are prayers.

Only a few thirteenth-century English secular songs exist today. Among them are: *Worldes blis ne last* (The world's bliss does not last); *Man mei longe him lives wene* (Long may man want his life to be); *Mirie it is while sumer ilast* (Merry it is while summer lasts), written c. 1225; and *Byrd one brere* (Bird on a briar), a love song written in mensural notation on the back of a twelfth-century papal bull.

Instrumental Music

Only a few pieces of purely instrumental music from the Middle Ages have survived. Yet, literary writers and authors of theoretical and practical treatises mentioned instruments and instrumental performances; miniatures illuminating manuscripts picture instrumentalists performing; church and cathedral sculptures depict musical instruments. Each jongleur and minstrel was required to be proficient on a number of instruments. After guilds were formed, these professional musicians were subjected to proficiency examinations regularly. But the instrumental music that was performed has not survived. Perhaps it was never written down. Undoubtedly, melodies were passed on by rote; also, musicians may have improvised upon basic tunes or used the melodies of vocal music in their performances.

In the Middle Ages, some leisure time was occupied by dancing, and the presence of dance songs in surviving manuscripts indicates that singing accompanied dancing. The oldest form of choral dance is the circle or round dance, accompanied by the playing and singing of *dansas, baladas,* and other dance songs. Wolfram wrote in *Parzival* about knights and ladies dancing, and Neidhart mentioned *Tanz* (dance) and instrumentalists in several of his lyrics. Some of Niedhart's descriptions are quite informative; in one of his poems, he wrote that for the Tanz *muosten drîe vor ihm gîgen und der vierde pheif* (three must fiddle in front and the fourth [person] pipe). The thirteenth-century poet Meier Helmbrecht also mentioned fiddling (*videlaere*) in connection with *Tanz.* Poet-historian Jean Froissart (c. 1333–1400) wrote of minstrels playing pipes while youths and maidens danced: First came the *estampies;* then, with scarcely a pause, the dancers joined hands and began a *carole* (round dance).

The estampie existed as both a poetic and a musical form. Only one of the medieval poems designated as estampies has music notation with it. This, the earliest extant musical composition called an estampie, is *Kalenda Maya* by Raimbaut de Vaquieras (see p. 111). According to the composer, the music was based on a melody he heard two "fiddlers" play at the court of the Marquis de Montferrat.

Similar terms in different languages—French *estampie,* Provençal *estampida,* and Italian *istampida*—indicate that this dance was widely known. Music for an estampie is constructed in sections, or periods, called *puncta.* Each *punctum* is repeated and is equipped with open and closed (first and second) endings. The music for each of the puncta is not always individualistic; although each punctum begins with new music, after the first few "measures" the melody is much the same as that in all of the other puncta. Most of the extant estampies have from four to six puncta; a dance with only two or three is referred to as a *ductia.*

The manuscript of trouvère songs known as *Le Chansonnier du Roy* (The King's Songbook; Paris, Bibl. nat. MS fr.844), contains monophonic music in mensural notation for 11 instrumental dances: Eight are numbered and identified by the words *estampie real* (royal estampie); one is named *Dansse Real*; one is called *Danse*; and one is unidentified. These are the earliest known instrumental estampies.

Thirteenth-century English manuscripts contain a total of four instrumental dances. All of the dances are sectional, but none of them conforms completely to estampie form. Three of the dances are two-part polyphony. The other consists of eleven puncta, ten of which are monophonic; the concluding section is three-part polyphony in which parallel thirds figure prominently.

The earliest known notated music for a keyboard instrument, probably an organ, is preserved in the Robertsbridge Codex, fragments of a British manuscript written c. 1325–50. Three of the six keyboard pieces in that manuscript are transcriptions of vocal motets (one incomplete) and three are estampies (one incomplete). (Fig. 7.7; DWMA43.)

An Italian manuscript of fourteenth-century polyphonic music contains also 15 medieval monophonic dances, 8 of them estampies. These 8 are structurally similar to other estampies but with much longer, more complex puncta, a fact that seems to indicate that they were performed for listeners rather than for dancers. The other 7 dance pieces include 1 *trotto*, 4 *saltarelli*, and 2 compositions entitled *Lamento di Tristano* and *La Manfredina*, respectively. All of these dances are constructed of short puncta. The *saltarello* dance is characterized by leaping, and the *trotto* by high stepping. *Lamento di Tristano* and *La Manfredina* are not single dances but contain pairs of related dances. Although paired dances are referred to in some trouvère poems, these two Italian instrumental pieces are the earliest surviving paired dance music.

Summary

Throughout the Middle Ages, even after the discovery and adoption of polyphony, monophonic music of all kinds continued to be created: instrumental and vocal, secular and sacred, liturgical and nonliturgical. Much of what was produced was never notated and was eventually lost; medieval monophony in extant manuscripts was inscribed decades and sometimes a century or two after it originated, and the variant versions that survive attest to years of oral transmission,

Figure 7.7 An estampie, one of six pieces of keyboard music in the Robertsbridge Codex. MS Brit. Mus. Add. 28850, fol. 43v. *(The British Museum.)*

alteration, and rote learning of the melodies. Traveling professional entertainers—jongleurs, minstrels, *Spielleute,* and others, most of whom remain anonymous—are significant historically because they widely disseminated vernacular monophony. Court patronage and the merging of lands and customs through marriages of nobility contributed also to the spread of these secular songs.

Members of early twelfth-century Provençal nobility are the first known poet-composers of secular vernacular songs. Women were not only patrons but *trobairitz* as well. The art of the Provençal *troubadours* was paralleled and surpassed by the French *trouvères* who, in their turn, influenced the Germanic *Minnesänger.* Songs created by French, German, and Provençal poet-composers were counterparts in subject matter and type. French and Provençal dance songs with refrains followed formal patterns that later became the three *formes fixes* of French court poetry and song. Instrumentalists not only accompanied the dance songs but performed independent dance music such as the estampie.

Trouvères and their songs were known in England but engendered no school there. Extant English monophony is sparse but provides the earliest surviving keyboard music. Surviving Italian medieval monophony consists mainly of *laude* sung by flagellants, and the extant Galician-Portuguese songs are primarily *cantigas* honoring the Virgin Mary.

Late Medieval Music

Before the end of the thirteenth century, the people of Britain had been consolidated into one well-defined race under a limited monarchy. Edward I (r. 1272–1307) conquered Wales and bestowed on his eldest son the title Prince of Wales but was unsuccessful in his attempts to gain Scotland. Perhaps Edward's greatest achievement was the establishment of Parliament (1295). Both Lords and Commons were represented, but clear distinction between them and separation into House of Lords and House of Commons came later, in the fourteenth century. France had had a *Parlement*, but in 1302 Philip IV called a parliamentary assembly with middle-class representation—an *Estates General*, composed of the Nobility, the Clergy, and the Third Estate (middle class). The expansion of middle-class power evident in these developments was accompanied by a decline in feudal aristocracy. Chivalry degenerated to mere formality and became ceremonial display and a code of manners.

Feudalism never had a firm grip in Italy. Though France and England were developing as monarchies, Italy was a decentralized aggregation of rival states, competitors in commerce, trade, and crafts. The leading states were known by their principal cities—Florence, Milan, Naples, and Venice—with central Italy comprising the Papal States (fig. 8.1). Heads of courts in all of these states were patrons of the arts.

Shortly before 1300, Pope Boniface VIII (r. 1294–1303) became involved in a heated dispute with King Philip IV (r. 1285–1314) of France concerning Philip's taxation of clergy. A war of words culminated in

Figure 8.1 Italy c. 1365.

Late Medieval Period

1300	1325	1350	1375	1400	1425	1450

1309 ◄ - - - - - - - - - - - Papacy at Avignon - - - - - - - - - - - ►1377◄ - - - - Great Schism - - - ►1417

1338 - - - - - - - - - - - - The Hundred Years' War -

Plague   Plague   Plague

- - - Giotto - - - - - - - - - - - - - - - - -   - - - - - -the van Eycks - - - - - -

Dante   Petrarch   Boccaccio   Wycliffe   Chaucer
Divine Comedy   poetry   *Decameron*   Eng. *Bible*   *Canterbury Tales*

FRANCE: Leadership in music - *ENGLAND:* Leadership in music - - - - - - - -

c. 1315◄- *Ars nova Era* - - - - - - - - - - - - - ► c. 1377◄ - - *Ars subtilior* - ► c. 1420
mensural notation - - red, black notation   manneristic music
- - - - - i s o r h y t h m -

de Vitry - - *Ars nova* c. 1318 - - - - - - - - - - - - - - - - - d. 1361

1315 *Le Roman de Fauvel*

1300 - - - - - - - - - - - - - Guillaume de Machaut - - - - - - - - - - - - 1377   B. Cordier fl.
          formes fixes   *Messe de Nostre Dame*   c. 1400 Chantilly Codex

cantilena style -

ENGLAND: c. 1325 Robertsbridge Codex   - - - music of Old Hall MS - - -

1375 - - Leonel Power - - (liturgical Latin music) - - - - 1445

c. 1390 - - - - John Dunstable - - - - - - - - - - - - - - 1453
          (Masses, Magnificats, motets)

- - - - C a r o l -

ITALY: Marchetto:
      Pomerium c. 1318
      - - - music of Rossi Codex   - - music of Squarcialupi Codex - - - - - -
      m a d r i g a l s , c a c c e , b a l l a t e -

1325 - - - - - - - - - - Francesco Landini (ballate) - - - - - - - - 1397
        "Landini cadence"
      Jacopo da Bologna fl. 1340–60
      (mainly madrigals)

SPAIN: - - *Llibre Vermell* - - - - -   Fourteenth-century folk songs
      caça, Pilgrim songs   collected by de Salinas

GERMANY: - - - continuation of Meistersinger tradition - - - - - - - - - - - - - - - -

---

Philip taking legal action against the pope; the shock and humiliation hastened Boniface's death. His successor, Benedict XI (r. 1303–4), let Philip have his way. When the French bishop of Bordeaux was elected pope and became Clement V (r. 1305–13), he decided in 1309 to move the papal residency from Rome to Avignon, in Provence, where it remained until 1377. The poet Petrarch (1304–74) called those years the "Babylonian captivity of the church." Thus, he equated the period the papacy operated from Avignon with the Israelites' years of captivity in Babylon. The French popes who ruled at Avignon were able administrators of that opulent court and were liberal patrons of the arts. In 1377, Gregory XI (r. 1370–78) conceded to heavy Italian pressure and moved the papal residency back to Rome. After his death, the college of cardinals split into two factions, and each elected a pope. One ruled at Avignon, the other at Rome. Thus began the Great Schism that lasted until 1417. During that time there were two and ultimately three rival claimants to the papal throne.

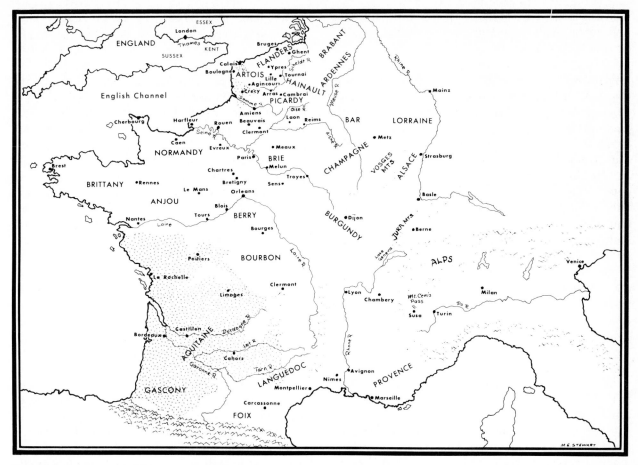

Figure 8.2 France c. 1367. Shaded areas in Gascony, Aquitaine, Artois, and Flanders are territories owned by England.

From 1338 to 1453 England and France were intermittently at war, and at times the fighting was fierce. The immediate cause of this so-called Hundred Years' War was the claim of England's King Edward III (r. 1327–77) to the French throne when Charles IV (r. 1322–28) died without a male heir. Underlying causes were more complex. Britain's control of important trade centers on the continent—especially, the wine-producing district around Bordeaux and the wool cloth and tapestry weaving industries at Ghent and Bruges, in Flanders (fig. 8.2)—had long been a thorn-in-the-flesh to the French, who sought to drive the "foreigner" out of those areas, and eventually succeeded. In 1453 the only territory England held on the continent was the port of Calais.

The war was still young when the Pestilence came. Trading ships from the East that docked at Italian ports late in 1347 left not only cargo but rats infected with fleas that carried bubonic plague, for which there was no known cure. The epidemic spread through Italy, then northward through Germany and France and outward to England in 1348, and into Spain in 1350. Between 1347 and 1351 the Black Death killed approximately 75 million people in Europe; one-third of the population of England died of it. The disease ravaged Europe again in the mid-1360s and still again around 1375.

There were also urban revolts, peasant insurrections, and heresies to be dealt with from time to time, such as the uprisings of the *Jacquerie* in France, the Lollards in England, the Hussites in Moravia, and the citizens of Anagni in Italy.

The Hundred Years' War was barely over when England was torn by civil war—the Wars of the Roses (1455–85) between the House of Lancaster and the House of York, rival claimants to the throne. Rivalry ceased when Henry VII (Tudor), a descendant of the House of Lancaster, became ruler in 1485; his wife was Elizabeth of York.

As cities and towns grew and the middle-class populace became larger and more influential, secular interests increased and vernacular languages became more important. Increased use of the vernacular in literature reflects this. Several literary masterpieces written in the vernacular contain references to music: Dante Alighieri's *Divine Comedy* (1307); Boccaccio's *Decameron* (1353), which relates how several persons spent their days of isolation while trying to avoid the plague; and Geoffrey Chaucer's *Canterbury Tales* (1386), stories from all levels of society. In 1362, legislation was enacted in England requiring use of English language instead of Latin in law courts. Around 1380, the followers of John Wycliffe (c. 1320–84) translated the Bible into English and distributed copies. Morality plays became popular.

There was renewed interest in the study of Greek and Latin classical literature. The beginnings of *humanism* were apparent, with its emphasis on human beings, their practical ethics and moral virtues, and their potentials in their earthly lives. Humanism was an intellectual movement in that it stressed study of the classics and sought answers to questions in treatises of the ancient writers. In fourteenth-century philosophical thinking, divine revelation and human reason operated in separate spheres, as should Church and State, and religion and science. Francesco Petrarch, who spent some years at the Avignon court, is considered the first important Italian humanist.

Medieval scholars, artists, authors, and composers hid essential meanings behind layers of secondary meanings and clothed thought in allegory so that truth lay behind natural appearances. This is exemplified in du Bus's *Roman de Fauvel,* Machaut's motets, and, more visibly, in the van Eycks' large *Ghent Altarpiece,* which, when unfolded, reveals new subjects depicted in sequence (colorplate 5; fig. 8.3a,b).

Changes were occurring in architecture, art, and sculpture. Sculpture was no longer viewed as part of the architecture of a building; individual pieces of free-standing sculpture were created for individual patrons. Artists often identified themselves by signing their creations. The work of the architect and painter Giotto di Bondone (1267–1337) is representative of some changes taking place in art. His paintings express naturalness and convey a feeling of solid three-dimensionality (colorplate 6). Perspective is apparent—sometimes created by haziness and variation of color, at other times by line—in the paintings of Huybrecht van Eyck (d. 1426) and Jan van Eyck (d. 1441) and the three Limbourg brothers who worked at the court of Jean, Duke of Berry.

The word *chapel* was used during the reigns of Pepin and Charlemagne to designate a reliquary, a repository for relics of saints and articles associated with the life of Christ. The most revered of the relics was the cape (*cappa*) of St. Martin. Persons who guarded the cape were *cappelani* (chaplains). Periodically, the *cappelani* sang *laudes* (praises) in honor of the relics and sometimes for high church officials and royalty. Gradually, the *cappella* (chapel) developed into a special staff of chaplains and clerics who officiated at Services at a specified location. Kings kept royal chapels; princes and nobles had household chapels. Having a personal chapel was a symbol of prestige.

In the fourteenth century, chapels of royalty and nobility came into prominence musically. By this time the chapel included a salaried group of vocalists and some instrumentalists. In 1334, Pope Benedict XII had at Avignon a Grand Chapelle of 30 to 40 members, plus a private chapel of 16 singers. In performance, singers clustered about a lectern that held a single huge choirbook of manuscript music. No more than 20 to 25 persons were able to see the music (colorplate 7).

(a)

(b)

Figure 8.3 Details from panels of The Ghent Altarpiece: (a) singers; (b) instrumentalists. *(St. Bavo, Ghent.)*

France — *Ars nova*

The period of French *Ars nova* (New Art) extends from c. 1315 to c. 1375. During those years the production of secular music far exceeded that of sacred. Perhaps it only seems that way because more secular music was written down and has survived, but even that fact reflects the general increase in secular interests in the fourteenth century. Music was written in accord with new notational practices, some of which were codified c. 1318–20 by Philippe de Vitry in his treatise *Ars nova*. The name given the era derives from the title of that treatise.

Philippe de Vitry

Philippe de Vitry (1291–1361), poet, theorist, and composer, spent much of his life in and around Paris. Although he received income from several **prebends** that he held simultaneously, he worked mainly at the French court as secretary and adviser to Charles IV (r. 1314–28), Philippe VI (r. 1328–50), and Jean II (r. 1350–64). (A prebend is an endowment or monetary allowance provided by a cathedral or large church as living expenses for a clergyman, though the recipient may not actually work at that church.) De Vitry was sent on several diplomatic missions to the papal court at Avignon, where he met and became a friend of Petrarch. In 1351 de Vitry was appointed Bishop of Meaux, a position he held until his death. He was acclaimed as an outstanding scholar, especially in the mathematical disciplines, which included music.

In his *Ars nova*, de Vitry codified the new aspects of rhythm and notation, especially with regard to imperfect mensuration and the minim. He recognized five note values: duplex long ▜ , long ▐ , breve ■ , semibreve ◆ , and minim ♩ . The term "minim" did not originate with de Vitry; it was used earlier in Navarre.

The Franconian system of notation was based on perfect mensuration. De Vitry extended that system to include equal duple division of all note values down to and including the semibreve. The division of the long into breves was called *modus* (mood); the division of the breve into semibreves was *tempus* (time);

and the division of the semibreve into minims produced *prolationis species* (prolation). Precise symbols designated the various mensurations (fig. 8.4a). The mensuration signs actually constitute time signatures and can be related to modern time signatures (fig. 8.4b).

The dot placed within the complete or broken circle as indication of perfection became known as *punctum perfectionis* (point of perfection) and was sometimes referred to as "the prick of perfection." The broken circle has been retained in modern notation where it represents $\frac{4}{4}$ meter, often referred to as "common time." (The symbol ₡ , with its designation "alla breve," which has also survived in modern notation, was not used by de Vitry but was an early Renaissance notation symbol used to shift the beat from the semibreve to the breve.)

In de Vitry's system, the semibreve might be subdivided in three ways: (a) *tempus perfect maius* (perfect major time) resulted when three semibreves were divided into three minims each; (b) *tempus perfectum medium* resulted when three semibreves were divided into two minims each; and (c) *tempus perfectum minimum* resulted when each semibreve contained three minims but minims followed each other

so closely that further subdivision was impossible. This might be interpreted to mean that the tempo was quite rapid, or that many minims were used in succession.

De Vitry is credited with the invention of red notes, which functioned: (a) to temporarily alter note values from perfect (ternary) to imperfect (binary), or vice versa; (b) to designate any deviations from the original in a melody used as cantus firmus; and (c) to indicate transposition an octave higher. The earliest known motet with mensural red notation is *Garrit gallus—In nova fert—N[euma]* (The cock babbles—Changed into new—N . . . ; DWMA44), which is cited by de Vitry as an example of that technique. Use of red notes is called **coloration** (colorplate 8).

Thirteenth-century music was written mainly in perfect mood, i.e., in longs and triple groupings of breves. In the fourteenth century, mood and time were used primarily in the lower voice(s) of motets. With the availability of shorter note values, the upper voice(s) usually were written in one or more of the prolations. The chief characteristic of French fourteenth-century music is its rhythmic organization, which was truly a "new art." Composers used with considerable freedom and ingenuity the variety of rhythmic possibilities at their disposal.

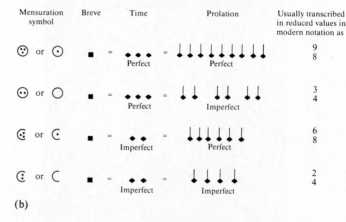

Figure 8.4 Interpretation of the mensuration symbols used by De Vitry to indicate (*a*) modus and tempus and (*b*) the four prolations.

Much of de Vitry's music has been lost. Only 12 of his motets have survived, and some of those are attributed to him through citations in other writings. Five are in *Le Roman de Fauvel;* five others are in the Ivrea Codex. Of the extant motets only one has a French text; all others use Latin. The tenor is patterned (isorhythmic; discussed on p. 128) and proceeds at a slower tempo than the two upper voices, which are written primarily in semibreves and minims. Phrases in the upper voices are constructed to bridge rather than coincide with the rhythmic patterns of the tenor. In structure, each of de Vitry's motets is individualistic, poetically and musically.

Other Theorists

Johannes de Muris (c. 1300–c. 1350) was a highly respected music theorist and author whose several treatises were regarded as authoritative and were used in universities for at least two centuries. In *Ars nove musice* (The art of the new music), written c. 1321, de Muris agreed, in tactfully worded statements, with the principles of notation and mensuration set forth by de Vitry.

There were those, however, who did not accept the changes without protest. One such person was Jacobus de Liège (c. 1260–c. 1331). His treatise, *Speculum musice* (Mirror of music), is an encyclopedic dissertation on music from Greek antiquity to his own time. In Book 7 of that treatise, Jacobus attempted to refute de Muris's supportive statements about imperfect tempus and championed the traditional music notation. Jacobus reported the division of the breve into as many as nine semibreves. His statement that the Franconian semibreve equaled the minim of the "moderns" confirms that the tempo of music had slowed.

The term **counterpoint** originated during this era. First use of the expression *punctus contra punctum* (note-against-note) was by theorist Petrus frater in his *Compendium de discantu mensurabili* (Summary of mensurable discant), written in 1336. The term *contrapunctus* (counterpoint) was first used and explained in anonymous treatises c. 1350, but throughout the fourteenth century the word *contrapunctus* meant note-against-note style of writing.

Le Roman de Fauvel

The earliest and one of the most important fourteenth-century French manuscripts containing music is MS fr.146 at Bibliothèque nationale, Paris. The major portion of this illuminated document is *Le Roman de Fauvel* (Narrative about Fauvel), a long satirical poem written in two sections by Gervais du Bus, who was a notary at the French royal chancery c. 1313–36 (fig. 8.5). According to the poem itself, du Bus completed the *roman* 6 December 1314. Popularity of this poem is attested by its inclusion in eleven other manuscripts. The copy in MS fr.146 is unique, however, because it contains musical interpolations, both monophonic and polyphonic, that were added to the *roman* by Chaillou de Pesstain shortly after the poem was completed. The music was selected carefully to enhance the moralistic satire of the narrative, an allegory on the social corruption then rampant in both Church and State. In the manuscript, the music is anonymous.

Figure 8.5 Folio from *Le Roman de Fauvel* manuscript, MS fr.146. *(Bibliothèque nationale, Paris.)*

Late Medieval Music

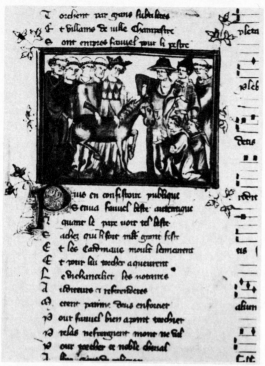

Figure 8.6 Miniature in *Le Roman de Fauvel*, MS *fr.*146, depicts persons rubbing Fauvel, i.e., currying favor. *(Bibliothèque nationale, Paris.)*

The name of the main character, *Fauvel,* has several hidden meanings: (a) *fauve* denotes an unlovely brownish-yellow color, or an animal that color; (b) *fauve* may also mean horse or ass; (c) *fau + vel* = veiled falsehood, or hypocrisy; and (d) the six letters of the name *Fauvel* represent six vices: *Flaterie, Avarice, Vilanie, Variété, Envie,* and *Lascheté* (Flattery, Greed, Villany, Inconstancy, Envy, and Lasciviousness). In the allegory, persons of all social strata come to rub down or curry the ass, Fauvel (fig. 8.6). This action gave rise to the French expression *étriller Fauvel* (to curry Fauvel, or to flatter deceitfully); in modern English the saying is, "to curry favor."

The music comprises more than 50 monophonic pieces and 34 motets. The monophony includes types of liturgical chant and conductus in Latin, as well as lais, ballades, rondeaux, and virelais. The motets form a collection that exemplifies the various stages of motet development up to c. 1315, the time the manuscript was inscribed. Early thirteenth-century, Franconian,

Petronian, and early fourteenth-century motets are represented. One motet is four-voice; 10 are two-voice; and 23 are three-voice. Five motets have been identified as de Vitry's.

The mensural notation often conveys duple rhythm. A mixture of prolations was employed within a motet, so that in modern transcription barlines do not always coincide in all voices. The lack of physical alignment of notated parts was of no concern to fourteenth-century French musicians, whose music used neither barlines nor score notation. A new feature of fourteenth-century notation is **coloration,** the use of red notes to designate certain deviations from normal values, which were then written as solid black notes. When written in red ink instead of in black, a perfect note loses one-third of its value; therefore, it becomes imperfect. Another fourteenth-century feature of the motets is **isorhythm.**

Isorhythm

The word isorhythm (same rhythm) is not found in late medieval treatises, nor is the compositional procedure described in detail in those writings, though the Latin terms *talea* and *color* (pronounced cōlor) were used. Isorhythm is a twentieth-century term coined by musicologist Friedrich Ludwig to indicate a special kind of structural organization frequently used by fourteenth-century composers in the tenors (and sometimes other voices) of their motets. The procedure involves the establishment of a rhythmic pattern, called *talea* (cutting; pl., *taleae*), that is reiterated one or more times in the tenor (the cantus firmus) of a composition. The melody of the isorhythmic voice part is called *color* (pl., *colores,* color or hue). The *color* may consist of a melodic segment that is repeated one or more times, or the entire tenor line may consist of only one statement of the melody. If melodic segments are used, their length may or may not match that of the *talea,* and their presentation may or may not coincide with statements of the *talea.* Isorhythm may appear in more than one voice of a polyphonic composition and may be combined with other compositional techniques, such as voice exchange or hocket.

In the isorhythmic motet *Detractor est—Qui secuntur—Verbum iniquum* (A disparager is—Those who follow—Iniquitous words; DWMA45) from

(a)

Verbum iniquum et dolorosum abhominabitur Dominus

Translation:
Triplum: The slanderer is the most worthless fox.
   By his slander he harms others and himself worse.
Duplum: [Those] who follow camps are wretched because
   poorly [are their services rewarded].
Tenor: The Lord will despise an unjust and painful word.

(b)

Figure 8.7 (*a*) The isorhythmic motet *Detractor est—Qui secuntur—Verbum iniquum* in manuscript, MS *fr.*146. (*b*) Transcription of the first two phrases of that motet; the first six measures of the Tenor state the talea. *(Bibliothèque nationale, Paris.)*

Roman de Fauvel, the *talea* comprises six modern measures and is stated seven times in the tenor, whose text and melody are chant (fig. 8.7). Actually, the *talea* is a rhythmic ostinato. In the tenor of Machaut's motet *S'il estoit nulz—S'amours—Et gaudebit* (If there is anyone—If love—And [the heart] will rejoice), the *color* is stated twice, and three statements of *talea* appear within each statement of *color.*

Isorhythm did not occur as the result of any one composer's sudden inspiration. Rather, its roots can be traced to thirteenth-century motet tenors structured in rhythmic modes and notated in a series of identical ligatures. The next stage in the development of isorhythm involved couching a liturgical cantus firmus in a certain *ordo* as a kind of rhythmic ostinato punctuated by rests and then combining repetition of the melody with that ostinato. This occurs in the thirteenth-century motet *En non diu—Quant voi—Eius in Oriente* (DWMA24). Full-fledged isorhythm emerged when composers devised tenors that reiterated individually designed rhythmic schemes (*taleae*). Melodic repetition was combined with this kind of rhythmic pattern also, most often in a manner that

was not obvious. These procedures indicate that, though composers still based compositions on chant, they were constructing their works according to purely musical considerations, rather than liturgical or textual ones. As the fourteenth century advanced, *taleae* became longer and more involved, and isorhythm invaded all voices of the motet and entered the Mass.

Composers organized tenors isorhythmically in three basic ways: (a) using several reiterations of *talea* but no melodic repetition; (b) combining one or more repetitions of *color* with reiterations of *talea;* and (c) using (*b*) plus a final statement of *talea* (with or without *color*) in diminution. All three of these plans were used by de Vitry and Guillaume de Machaut (p. 132).

Jehannot de l'Escurel

The manuscript holding the musical version of *Roman de Fauvel* concludes with six folios containing 34 works by Jehannot de l'Escurel (d. 1304). This manuscript section appears to be an incomplete collection of de l'Escurel's works; these are his only extant works.

Figure 8.8 Jehannot de l'Escurel's polyphonic rondeau *A vous, douce debonaire* appears in score notation in the left column of fol. 57, MS fr.146. *(Bibliothèque nationale, Paris.)*

Included are virelais, ballades, rondeaux, and rondeau refrains. The music and texts are arranged alphabetically; the last ones inscribed commence with the letter G.

The section opens with de l'Escurel's only surviving polyphonic piece, *A vous, douce debonaire* (To you, sweet good-natured lady), a three-voice conductus-style rondeau with the main melody placed in the middle voice (fig. 8.8). The piece appears later in the manuscript as a monophonic rondeau. The notation does not include minims, and groups of two to five semibreves occur in the lyrical monophonic pieces, in Petronian style. The monophonic pieces indicate that de l'Escurel was adept at text painting, the technique of describing musically the words being set. For example, he used curving musical lines to set *Bien se lace,* which speaks of "embracing."

Guillaume de Machaut

Guillaume de Machaut (c. 1300–77), renowned poet and leading French composer of the fourteenth century, held responsible positions at various royal courts and several important churches, including Reims Cathedral. (Insight, "Guillaume de Machaut".) Machaut spent much of his time at court, which probably accounts for the fact that most of his music is secular. However, in his few sacred compositions he made significant contributions to the development of music. Machaut composed both monophonic and polyphonic pieces and used both conservative and avant-garde forms, styles, and techniques. His versatility as a composer and the high quality of his music were unparalleled in his time.

Motets

The motet was an established form of secular music, but Machaut's treatment of that form was avant-garde in many respects. Of his 23 motets, 4 (Nos. 5, 21, 22, 23) are for four voices; the remainder are for three. Three motets use French secular tenors; incipits of the Latin tenors of the others imply chant derivation. (Sources of all the Latin tenors have not been identified.) Six of the motets have Latin texts; two are furnished with Latin duplum and French triplum; upper voices of the rest are in French. In the four-voice motets the contratenor is textless. Tenors and textless contratenors were probably performed instrumentally.

In the fourteenth century, the voice parts above the tenor were usually named **motetus** and **triplum.** In four-voice polyphony, the additional voice part was placed below the tenor and was called **contratenor** or **contratenor bassus** (low [voice] opposite the tenor). Contratenor bassus was predecessor of the modern **bass** voice part.

The Latin motets exhibit some of Machaut's finest work. They may have been used liturgically in the Offices. The motet *Felix virgo—Inviolata—Ad te suspiramus* (No. 23; Fortunate virgin—Inviolate—To you we breathe) is clearly a Marian motet. Not only is the tenor derived from the Marian Antiphon *Salve, Regina,* but the words of the two upper parts are addressed to the Virgin. Possibly, choirboys sang these upper parts, while instrumentalists played tenor and contratenor on organs or sackbuts (ancestors of the trombone).

Guillaume de Machaut

Guillaume de Machaut was born in the province of Champagne in the diocese of Reims. Little is known of his early life and education except that he took holy orders. Sometime around 1323, he obtained a clerical position at the court of John of Luxembourg, who was also King of Bohemia (r. 1310–46); various promotions elevated Guillaume to the position of king's secretary. Jean de Machaut, Guillaume's brother, was also employed at that court. King John traveled widely, and Guillaume was included in the king's large retinue. Details of some of those journeys appear in Guillaume's poetry. With King John's assistance, both Guillaume and Jean received from Pope John XXII (r. 1316–34) several grants that provided income and promised a position as canon when a vacancy occurred; Guillaume received grant income from Verdun (1330), Arras (1332), and Reims (1333) Cathedrals. When Pope Benedict XII (r. 1334–42) confirmed the Reims appointment in 1335, Guillaume relinquished the others. He served King John until 1346, then actually became one of the 72 canons at Reims. He was not required to reside with other churchmen but had a house of his own and was at liberty to work at the court of John's daughter Bonne, wife of Jean, Duke of Normandy (who became King Jean II of France, r. 1350–64). Machaut seems to have moved among nobility with ease. After Bonne's death in 1349, Machaut's various patrons included Charles of Navarre; Jean, Duc de Berry; and King Charles V of France (r. 1364–80).

In his poetry Guillaume recorded important historical data and interesting particulars of his personal life but said very little about his church work. He revealed that he was short of stature, blind in one eye, and suffered from gout; he enjoyed horseback riding and falconry and appreciated the beauty of nature; he related his experiences during the great pestilence that ravaged Europe (1348–50) and the seige of Reims (1359–60) during The Hundred Years' War. And, in *Livre du Voir Dit* (Book of the True Story), written c. 1365 at the request of teen-aged Péronne d'Armentières, he revealed "the true story" of his involvement with her—a series of platonic episodes that generated a good deal of correspondence and inspired some romantic love poetry and songs.

During the last years of his life, Guillaume prepared some manuscripts of his works for nobility and book collectors. One of these manuscripts (Paris, Bibl. nat. MS fr.1584) constitutes his own catalogue of his works. However, five extant works are not included in that listing. The catalogue begins with a poetic Prologue (believed to have been written last), then lists seventeen items of poetry, followed by seven categories of musical compositions: Lais, Motets, Mass, Hocket, Ballades, Rondeaux, Virelais. Two works catalogued as poetry contain music: No. 5, *Remède de Fortune* (Fortune's Remedy), in which seven songs are incorporated; and No. 15, *Livre du Voir Dit,* which has eight. In *Remède de Fortune,* Guillaume recounted the events of an entire day at a court. Musical performances are described, and, in connection with the minstrels' entrance into the great hall, more than 30 instruments are listed. *La Prise d'Alexandrie* (The Capture of Alexandria) contains an even longer list of musical instruments.

Both Guillaume and Jean de Machaut were interred in Reims's Cathedral of Notre Dame (fig. 8.9). Evidence of the two men's devotion to Our Lady is their endowment of a weekly performance (on Saturday) of a Mass of the Virgin, a commemoration that was still being observed, with its donors recognized, in the eighteenth century.

Figure 8.9 Reims Cathedral. Façade, begun in 1230s.

Machaut's notation employs the fourteenth-century mensurations explained by de Muris and de Vitry in their treatises. In the upper voices of 15 motets Machaut used imperfect tempus with major prolation—the equivalent of modern $\frac{6}{8}$ meter; this is typical of French fourteenth-century polyphony. A majority of the tenors use the longer note values of perfect mood.

With Machaut, the isorhythmic motet became an established form—one that interested composers through the fifteenth century. All of Machaut's motets with Latin tenors are isorhythmic. In some motets, isorhythmic passages occur in the upper voices as well as in the tenor, along with one or more other compositional techniques, such as hocket and syncopation. Machaut's *taleae* are remarkable for their symmetry and balance. Sometimes voice parts exchange *taleae,* and occasionally a *talea* is retrograde, thus creating a **rhythmic palindrome**. A palindrome reads the same backwards and forwards, as do the words "Anna" and "madam" and the rhythm in example 8.1. Frequently, Machaut alternated units of three breves and six breves in devising his patterns. In approximately half of his motets, he wrote the concluding statement of *talea* in diminution, sometimes one-half and sometimes one-third of the original note values. His isorhythmic tenors do not always contain melodic repetition. In those that do, most often *talea* and *color* do not coincide. Certainly, Machaut imposed a high degree of structural rigidity upon his isorhythmic compositions; however, he manipulated the intricate details of his music so skillfully that the restrictions are not apparent to the listener. One thing Machaut required of his music was that it be pleasing to the ear.

Even his non-isorhythmic motets have tenors that are strictly structured. For example, the French motet *Trop plus—Biauté—Je ne suis* (Too much more—Beauty—I am not) is not isorhythmic but its tenor is a rondeau pattern (abaaabab) formed from two very similar melodies with rhythms that are almost identical. Only the first statement of the a and the b melody have text underlaid. This tenor may have been a well-known monophonic rondeau; if so, the tenor of the motet may have been sung, with the complete rondeau text, or even with appropriate repetition of the two phrases of text given. More likely, instrumental performance was intended, as for the Latin tenors. The two upper voices are in the same vocal range and experience some voice crossing; some passages are in hocket. This vernacular motet concludes with a brief entreaty for God's grace, and an Amen.

Mass

La Messe de Nostre Dame (Our Lady's Mass) is Machaut's longest composition—730 modern measures including requisite repeats. This may be the longest single medieval composition extant. The work is significant historically because it is the earliest known unified polyphonic setting of the complete Mass Ordinary by one identified composer. The Mass is modal, but all movements are not in the same mode. The first three movements are in Dorian (final on d); the last three, Lydian (final on f). The music is four-voice polyphony, which was seldom written in that era. Machaut's setting includes the dismissal *Ite, missa est* and its Response, *Deo gratias,* which normally uses the same music as the dismissal. Composers of polyphonic Masses rarely set the dismissal.

In writing the Mass, Machaut was no doubt influenced to some extent by the several papal bulls that admonished composers and singers of liturgical polyphony that the musical setting must not obscure the text. He seems to have paid particular attention to correct declamation and to ensuring that the words of the text would be heard clearly. Also, he must have been aware of the fact that Pope John XXII (r. 1316–34) had expressly forbidden the use of hocket in liturgical music, and he did not use much of it. Instead, he achieved the effect of hocket in some phrases by the judicious placement of rests and the use of syncopation.

Example 8.1 Rhythmic palindromes.

Those sections of the Ordinary with the longest texts, the Gloria and Credo, were given nearly syllabic settings in note-against-note counterpoint so that the four voices almost always pronounce the text syllables simultaneously. Melismas occur in the Amen sections of these movements, however, and the Amen of the Credo is isorhythmic. The Gloria and Credo settings appear sectional, almost strophic, and in the Gloria very short textless passages occur between some phrases. No doubt these episodes were performed instrumentally; perhaps instruments doubled all voices. For emphasis, Machaut set certain words of these two movements—*Et in terra pax* and *Jesu Christe* in the Gloria, and *Ex Maria Virgine* in the Credo—in duplex longs; in performance, the note-against-note counterpoint produced sustained chordal harmony. Many later composers gave these words similar emphasis. Machaut further emphasized the words *Ex Maria Virgine* by preceding them with a general pause (ex. 8.2).

The entire Mass exhibits profound rhythmic complexity, especially in those movements that are wholly or partly isorhythmic: Kyrie, Sanctus, Agnus Dei, and *Ite, missa est*. Some of the rhythmic intricacies involve (a) interlocking and overlapping *taleae* and (b) the exchange of *taleae* among voices. Rhythmic symmetry pervades each movement—as a whole, in sections, and in individual *taleae*. For example, each section of the Kyrie is organized symmetrically, as is each acclamation within each section.

The cantus firmus tenors of the isorhythmic movements use chant melodies. The Kyrie is based on the tenth-century *Kyrie cunctipotens genitor Deus* from Gregorian Mass IV (LU,25); Sanctus and Agnus

Dei use eleventh- and thirteenth-century versions of those respective chants from Gregorian Mass XVII (LU,61); and the dismissal is based on the eleventh-century Sanctus from Gregorian Mass VIII (LU,38). The isorhythmic sections are balanced and move outward from the center in rhythmic symmetry. In other words, they are palindromic. In the Agnus Dei, only the *qui tollis* sections are isorhythmic; isorhythm appears in all four voices of that section of Agnus Dei II.

Analysis of the *qui tollis* section of Agnus Dei II (DWMA46) will give some idea of the restrictions and rhythmic complexities involved in Machaut's isorhythmic compositions. Each voice has a *talea* that is rhythmically distinctive. Tenor and contratenor each present three statements of *talea*, arranged so that the rhythmic statements in the two voices do not coincide. Combination of tenor and contratenor produce, in performance, a hocket effect. The two top voices each state a *talea* six times; the rhythmic patterns do not coincide. Combination of these two voices produces syncopation, rather than pseudo-hocket. The section is 19 modern measures long; the fourth measure, and every third measure thereafter, comprises a single sustained chord containing medieval perfect consonances. The melody of the top voice (Cantus I) is constructed of alternating groups of three and six breves, which create the following symmetrical pattern:

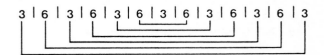

Example 8.2 Machaut's setting of the words *ex Maria virgine* in the Credo of his Mass (mm. 69–76 in modern notation). *(Source: Machaut, Credo of Messe de Nostre Dame.)*

Late Medieval Music

Some sections of the Mass movements are much more complicated rhythmically than Agnus Dei II. Transcription into modern notation does injustice to Machaut's compositional genius, for barlines impose artificial restraints upon the music and often split ligatures, thus obscuring the full import of the rhythmic patterns Machaut created. It must be remembered that these complexities are not audibly perceived, and that the quality of the music in no way suffers because of them.

In his compositions Machaut sometimes used small melodic motives. Two motives appear frequently in the Mass:

Example 8.3 Melodic motives that appear frequently in Machaut's Mass.

Whether these motives were intended as unifying devices is not known, but the fact that they recur frequently is significant. They may be standard figures in Machaut's repertoire—they appear frequently in his other compositions.

Hocket

Like the Mass and Motet 23, *Hoquetus David* is Marian-related. Its isorhythmic tenor is derived from the long melisma on the word *David* that concludes the Alleluia Verse *Nativitas gloriosae virginis* (Nativity of the glorious Virgin). *Hoquetus David* is unique in fourteenth-century music literature. Machaut's reason for composing it, and the intended place and manner of its performance, are unknown. Since the *Hoquetus* is textless, instrumental rendition is presumed. Pérotin composed organal settings of part of the *Nativitas* verse, but the *David* melisma was performed as chant. Perhaps Machaut composed this hocket for use with Pérotin's organum as a substitute for the monophonic chant melisma. Pérotin, too, used hocket. The means of unification in this piece is, of course, the isorhythmic tenor, which is written in two sections, each with its own *taleae*. The first section presents three *colores* in eight *taleae;* the second section has one statement of the melody presented through four *taleae*.

Lais

In writing *lais* Machaut was following in trouvère footsteps. Moreover, 15 of his 19 lais are monophonic. No musical lais have been located after Machaut, though poetic ones exist. Machaut's writing does not support the theory that the lai was always composed in couplets; his poetry is more complex structurally. He usually constructed his lai texts in 12 stanzas that collectively use a musical pattern of abcdefghijka. Each stanza is divided into equal halves, both set to the same melody. The modal melodies move mainly by step, with rests punctuating the musical phrases; the text setting is almost syllabic. Though first and twelfth stanzas use the same melody, Machaut usually transposed it up a fifth (or down a fourth) for the final strophe.

Lais 11, 12, 17, and 18 are polyphonic; Nos. 11 and 12 are canonic. In No. 11, *Je ne cesse de prier* (I do not cease to entreat), each even-numbered stanza is labeled *chace* with the direction that the last half of the stanza succeeds the first half without pause. Because the French *chace* is a canon at the unison for three voices, it is generally presumed that Machaut's use of the word *chace* implies three-voice canon. If this was his intent, the monophonic first stanza of Lai No. 11, with its melody transposed a fifth degree, becomes a three-voice canon at the unison for the final strophe. No. 12, *Le lay de confort* (The lai of comfort), is in its entirety a canon at the unison.

Ballades

Machaut referred to the voice parts of his three-voice secular songs as *cantus* (melody), *tenor,* and *contratenor.* In *Livre du Voir Dit,* he stated that he composed the *cantus* first, then added the remainder of the musical setting. His terminology is appropriate, for his polyphonic settings place the lyrical melody of the *cantus* in a soloistic position, supported by textless tenor and contratenor designed for instrumental performance. This kind of musical setting is known as **cantilena style.**

Machaut wrote many of his secular songs in the *formes fixes* of fourteenth-century court poetry: ballade, rondeau, and virelai. In his hands, these types of music were not always dance songs but were informal entertainment to be enjoyed by a nonparticipating court audience. The social function of music

Example 8.4 Machaut's use of cadence rhyme (musical rhyme) in the ballade *Biauté qui toutes autre.*

was changing. It was still a utilitarian art, serving primarily as an adjunct to worship and other activities and occupations, but one of those activities was court entertainment.

Machaut wrote 42 ballades with music: 1 monophonic, 16 two-voice, and the remainder three-voice. Two of the latter are triple ballades: No. 17 is a three-voice canon with a different text in each voice, and in No. 29 the three voices have individual melodies and texts. Only ballade No. 1, *S' amours ne fait* (If love does not), is isorhythmic. Apparently, Machaut decided the technique was not suitable for secular polyphony; he did not use isorhythm in any other secular songs.

The texts of the ballades resemble trouvère poetry and are constructed in three strophes with a refrain. Musically, the formal pattern of most of them is aabC. The a sections are provided with open and closed endings. Machaut often used musical rhyme, making the end of the second section of a piece musically identical with or a transposition of that of the first. He employed this technique increasingly. In some early works only the cadences are alike (cadence rhyme), but gradually the rhyme was extended backwards and eventually six or even eight measures rhyme musically (ex. 8.4).

Syncopation is a prominent feature of many of Machaut's songs and sometimes creates harsh dissonances that are suitably resolved. At cadences syncopation is frequently combined with an escape note, thus forming a so-called *Landini cadence*—a cadence pattern named for Machaut's Italian contemporary, Francesco Landini (ex. 8.5).

Example 8.5 The "Landini" cadence pattern.

Rondeaux

Machaut composed 21 musical rondeaux, using the standard ABaAabAB pattern: 7 two-voice, 12 three-voice, and 2 four-voice. All of them are cantilena style—only the *cantus* is furnished with text. Machaut's most unusual rondeau, *Ma fin est mon commencement* (DWMA47), is the one most widely known. Machaut's penchant for symmetry and balance is well demonstrated in this piece. The music interprets the text: "My end is my beginning and my beginning my end. . . ." The composition is symmetrical; a and b sections each consist of 20 modern measures. Machaut constructed the music in this fashion: (1) Cantus and tenor are the reverse of each other. Moreover, the b music of the tenor is the retrograde of the a melody of the cantus, and the b melody of the cantus is the retrograde of the a music of the tenor. (2) The contratenor melody is half as long as the other voice parts, and the a music is used retrograde to form the b section. Machaut seems to have been the first composer to use the word **retrograde** in connection with a musical composition.

	A Section	**B Section**
Cantus:	Cantus **a** melody	Tenor **a** melody retrograde
Tenor:	Tenor **a** melody	Cantus **a** melody retrograde
Contratenor:	Contratenor **a** melody	Contratenor **a** melody retrograde

A more typical three-voice rondeau is *Se vous n'estes* (If you are not). Written in cantilena style, its first section concludes with a complete triad on the final of the mode, but the final chord of the second section is the traditional open-sounding octave and fifth (DWMA48).

Virelais

Machaut preferred to call his songs in this form *chansons balladées* rather than virelais; perhaps his pieces were in some way still associated with dancing. Nevertheless, all of them use the standard AbbaA form and are virelais. There are 33 of them: 25 monophonic, 7 two-voice, and 1 three-voice. Each of them has three stanzas. In general, the musical style of these pieces is quite simple, with some use of melodic motives and musical rhyme. In more than half of the virelais, Machaut supplied the b section with open and closed endings, a feature that would become standard with later composers.

Machaut was a transitional composer. Some of his works are linked to the past; some demonstrate clearly the advanced techniques and styles of his own day; others predict future trends. Like Adam de la Halle, Machaut was a poet-composer of both monophonic and polyphonic works. In some respects Machaut, too, was a trouvère. In his monophonic pieces, he followed trouvère tradition, but his cantilena settings of polyphonic ballades and rondeaux moved these forms out of the dance-song category and into the realm of art song. These pieces are accompanied vocal solos. Machaut broadened the thirteenth-century motet by the intricacies of his isorhythm and the new prolations. His three four-voice Latin motets point toward the Latin sacred motets of Renaissance composers, in musical style, number of voices, and liturgical purpose. Their texts are entirely sacred, and each of them is related to a specific feast, event, or person. Machaut was writing four-part polyphony when most composers were writing for three voices. His greatest single achievement, *La Messe de Nostre Dame,* was the first of many unified polyphonic settings of the complete Mass Ordinary. Customarily, isolated movements were assembled to form a polyphonic Mass Ordinary. However, in the late fourteenth century the situation began to change. The next generation of composers would regard composition of a Mass as a proving ground for their talents.

Other Mass Compositions

In the fourteenth century, composers began to think of the *Mass* as being the five sections of the Ordinary that were sung: Kyrie, Gloria in excelsis Deo, Credo, Sanctus, and Agnus Dei. Machaut was not the only composer to set those texts. Nor did the papal bulls condemning certain kinds of polyphony and the state of polyphonic singing in the liturgy deter composers from writing liturgical polyphony. Apparently, they were not very interested in setting Proper texts, and they seem to have preferred setting individual Mass movements rather than the complete Ordinary. A good many independent movements survive, grouped together in manuscripts according to text, i.e., Kyries in one section, Glorias in another, and so on. The *Ivrea Codex* contains a collection of Mass movements grouped in that manner. Unless a composer signed his work (and many did not) or some unifying feature is obvious in several movements, there is no way of knowing which of the movements, if any, were intended to form a certain complete Mass Ordinary.

Movements of Masses were written in four styles of polyphony: (a) motet style, with the same text in two upper voices and a textless tenor; (b) cantilena style, with text in the top voice only; (c) conductus style, with all voices texted and simultaneous (or nearly so) pronunciation of text indicated; and (d) hybrid settings involving all of the foregoing styles. A word of caution—absence of a text in a manuscript does not mean a text never existed for that voice part. A scribe may have inadvertently omitted the text for that line. The music was sectional, corresponding with the sections of text in the movement being set; usually, the voices cadenced simultaneously at the ends of sections.

Several complete, or almost complete, fourteenth-century Mass settings are extant:

1. The Mass of Tournai, a three-voice Mass in a manuscript in the library of the Cathedral of Tournai, is considered oldest of the surviving settings. It consists of conductus-style setting of the five movements of the Ordinary and motet-style setting of *Ite, missa est*. The movements were assembled to form a complete Mass; probably all movements were not written by the same composer.
2. The Mass of Toulouse, in a mid-fourteenth-century manuscript at the municipal library of Toulouse, is incomplete. There is no Gloria, and only a small portion of the Credo exists. Kyrie, Sanctus, and Agnus Dei are cantilena style, for three voices; *Ite, missa est* is a motet. The movements were not copied as a unit, but c. 1400 they were individually placed within the manuscript wherever space was available.
3. The Mass of Barcelona contains no setting of the dismissal. The five movements of the Ordinary were copied as a unit, but the movements are in miscellaneous styles. Some movements are for three and others are for four voices.
4. The Sorbonne Mass is incomplete—there is no Credo, and Gloria and Sanctus are incomplete—but there is a two-voice setting of the *Benedicamus Domino* dismissal. The surviving movements are related. The Mass is attributed to Johannes Lambuleti, whose name appears near the end of the Kyrie.

Ars subtilior

Ars subtilior (more subtle art) is the twentieth-century name given to the **manneristic style** of music composed c. 1375–c. 1420, a period almost coinciding with the Great Schism. Music written in manneristic style is characterized by extremely complex rhythms and notation. Composers writing in this style worked in a geographical area in southern France and near the Pyrenees Mountains. Principal centers of *Ars subtilior* were the courts of the French popes at Avignon, the King of Aragon, and the Count of Béarn and Foix. The chief manuscript sources of *Ars subtilior* music contain both sacred and secular polyphonic compositions: Credos, Glorias, religious motets, secular motets, ballades, rondeaux, and virelais. Almost 50 composers are represented, including Baude Cordier, Solage, Philippe de Caserta, Jacob Senleches, and Guillaume de Machaut.

The three-voice secular songs written in manneristic style use a newly composed tenor with rhythmic stability designed to support the upper voices. The basic intervals of the contrapuntal lines are consonances, but embellishments and rhythmic irregularities in the upper voice(s) produce a dissonant effect. The *cantus* (top voice) appears to have been created for a professional singer of virtuoso caliber. Rhythms are extremely complex, as is also the notation. Cohesion is achieved by the convergence of all contrapuntal lines for cadences at the ends of phrases.

Manneristic music developed gradually from the cantilena style of Machaut's ballades. The tenor became more independent and supportive in character, and the solo line was made more intriguing by minim displacements and melodic and rhythmic sequences. At the height of its development, manneristic music was characterized by extreme rhythmic flexibility and intricacy that included elaborate rhythmic subdivisions, displacement syncopation, alternate proportions, and split- or half-colorations. The notes may be black, red, or white (hollow notes with black outlines). *Ars subtilior* music attained a degree of rhythmic complexity that was not matched until the twentieth century.

Displacement syncopation was achieved when the notes comprising a perfection were separated, and the unity of that perfection was disrupted by the insertion of one or more complete perfections. A simple example in modern notation without barlines is shown in example 8.6:

Example 8.6 Displacement syncopation is created when the notes (marked with *) comprising a perfection are separated by the insertion of other perfections.

The notes marked with asterisks form the disrupted perfection; the last note completes the perfection begun by the first note. Barlines were not used when this music was written, nor were notated parts aligned in the manuscript. Syncopation is enhanced visibly by the presence of barlines of modern notation. When barlines are inserted, the modern notation becomes:

Example 8.7 The displacement syncopation of example 8.6 in modern notation with barlines.

In some modern transcriptions, the displacement syncopation is avoided on paper by changing the meter signature, using alternative barring, and then readjusting the meter signature so that barlines coincide at cadence points (ex. 8.8). This kind of modern notation does not accurately convey what the composer intended.

Example 8.8 Displacement syncopation is avoided (or disregarded) if the rhythm presented in example 8.7 is notated with several changes of meter signature.

Alternation of proportions provided another rhythmic variable. A simple example of this technique is the consistent alternation of a measure in $\frac{3}{4}$ with a measure in $\frac{6}{8}$ time, while keeping the basic beat constant.

Another innovation of manneristic composition was clothing the musical composition in an appropriate artistic shape. Examples of this are:

1. Baude Cordier's *Toute par compas suy composée* (Entirely by compass I have been composed), is a puzzle canon that is both a virelai and a chace. The notation is on circular staves placed as a circle within a circle. Performance instructions and lyrics are placed in circles at the four corners of the page.
2. *Belle bonne* (Beautiful [lady], good . . .), also by Cordier, is a rondeau notated on staves shaped and arranged to form a heart. In the text, the red outline of a heart is substituted for the word *coeur* (heart). (Colorplate 9; Chantilly, MS 564.)
3. Jacob Senleches notated *La harpe de melodie* (The harp of melody) on staff lines that form the harp's strings. Rubrics are encoded in a rondeau printed on the ribbon wound around part of the harp frame (colorplate 10).

England

English medieval polyphony in extant manuscripts is almost exclusively liturgical and Latin. Surviving music with English texts is rare. These statements paint a false picture, however. Undoubtedly, secular English music existed, but the constant wandering of many professional performers and their want of permanent patronage at some court prevented the inscription of their songs in manuscripts. Much music has been lost. It was natural for monastic communities and cathedral chapters with *scriptoria* to place priority on copying liturgical music.

Until almost the end of the fourteenth century English royalty and nobility used the French language. French music of all kinds, and especially the Notre Dame repertoire, was known and used in England. Organum and conductus had continued use in Britain well into the fourteenth century, after those forms had gradually disappeared from continental service.

Surviving music indicates an English predilection for troping, rondellus technique, an emphasis on thirds and sixths, and some use of streams of parallel intervals. This parallelism sometimes produced discant-style two-voice pieces called *gymel* (twin voices).

Exactly what is meant by the term **English discant** is debatable. The term is frequently used in reference to the homorhythmic passages of smooth successions of $\frac{6}{3}$ chords (sounding like first-inversion triads) that appear in English music. According to some late medieval theorists, the English practiced *discantus supra librum* (discanting over the book)—improvising *around* a notated cantus firmus melody (called the *meane,* middle) to produce a parallel line a fourth above the cantus firmus and another a third below it. A stream of $\frac{6}{3}$ chords resulted. Some twentieth-century theorists interpret those theoretical writings as describing a process of transposition that was used to avoid writing ledger lines.

Other medieval English theorists describe **discanting** as singing an unnotated part against a notated chant or cantus firmus in note-against-note counterpoint. In this practice of discanting, consecutive perfect fifths and consecutive octaves were forbidden, and contrary motion was preferred, but occasionally passages of parallel thirds and sixths might be sung. The passages of parallel $\frac{6}{3}$ chord successions that appear quite often in notated English music of the late fourteenth and fifteenth centuries reflect the English predilection for thirds and sixths, and the harmonious blend of these intervals contributes to the "sweet sound" of English music (ex. 8.9).

Example 8.9 Burden II from the carol *Salve, sancte parens* contains streams of parallel $\frac{6}{3}$ chords. *(Source: Salve, sancte parens, mm. 17–19, in John Stevens,* Musica Brittanica, *Vol. 4,* Mediaeval Carols, *Stainer & Bell, Ltd., London, England.)*

Old Hall Manuscript

The Old Hall Manuscript (London, Brit. Lib. Add.57950) is an important collection of English sacred music composed in the late fourteenth and early fifteenth centuries. Until July 1973, it was owned by the College of St. Edmund, Old Hall (near Ware). Unfortunately, the manuscript is incomplete and has been mutilated; vandals or souvenir gatherers have cut out some of the illuminated initials.

The main part of the manuscript was copied c. 1410; some additional pieces were entered c. 1420. The manuscript was carefully planned. Compositions are arranged by liturgical category, with movements of the Mass (Ordinary and some of the Proper) grouped in sections in the order of their appearance in the Service, and with compositions notated in score or pseudo-score (i.e., with notes seemingly but not actually aligned) preceding compositions in choirbook notation. Isorhythmic motets and *Deo gratias* Responses are last. There is no Kyrie in the Old Hall Manuscript. Possibly, a section containing Kyries has been lost. However, customarily, in England the Kyrie of the Mass was sung in chant and most often was troped. Polyphonic Kyries by English late medieval composers are almost nonexistent. Even later, some English composers wrote "complete" Mass settings without a Kyrie. Another peculiarity is apparent in English settings of the Credo—certain clauses were consistently omitted or phrases telescoped.

In the manuscript, the name of the composer is inscribed either at the top of the folio or at the beginning of the first line of his composition. The original compilation includes compositions by Leonel (Power), Pycard, Typp, Byttering, Chirbury, Excetre, Roy Henry, and others. Presumably, Roy Henry is King Henry V (r. 1413–22); his two works are a Gloria and a Sanctus. Leonel (c. 1375–1445) is represented by 23 compositions. Persons represented by the added pieces include Damett and Dunstable (c. 1390–1453).

The mensural notation used for some of the compositions is highly sophisticated. Colorations are indicated by black, red, blue, and half-colored notes, and reversed and colored signatures appear. In most of the pieces, the tenor or *cantus firmus* is not the bottom voice but is placed just above the bottom voice.

In some of the Mass movements, specific instructions are given for certain passages to be performed by a chorus (not an ensemble of soloists). This does not necessarily imply that the chorus was large. And, at times, passages of duets alternate with passages for chorus; centuries later, that procedure characterizes post-Reformation Anglican verse anthems.

Various musical styles and techniques are represented:

1. Some three-voice pieces notated in score (or pseudo-score) display English discant; the chant cantus firmus is in the middle voice, which is labeled *meane*.
2. More than 30 of the works are treble-dominated musically. In most of these, the text is shared by all voices. The top voice moves in a range slightly higher than the tenor and contratenor, which are in the same range and frequently cross.
3. The isorhythmic compositions display that technique in various stages of its development. In one work, a short *talea* is imposed upon a long tenor. In the isorhythmic Gloria and Credo by Leonel, *color* and *talea* are treated more flexibly, and they do not always coincide. Isorhythm pervades all parts of a motet by Dunstable, and the *color* is presented in successive diminutions.
4. Seven of the compositions are canonic: a Gloria by Byttering, two anonymous Credos, and three Glorias and a Sanctus by Pycard. None of the seven canons are structurally alike. A five-voice Gloria by Pycard may be the earliest extant example of a double canon. In it, the two top voices are in canon, as are also the tenor and contratenor; the other voice is free. One of the anonymous Credos is for five voices, with the three upper voices written as a mensuration canon. This means that each of those three voices sings the same melody in a different mensuration. The notation for all voices of this Credo is extremely involved.
5. Leonel sometimes placed a paraphrase of the chant cantus firmus in the top voice. Later, this paraphrase technique is used increasingly on the continent.

The Old Hall Manuscript is historically significant for several reasons. It is one of few extant manuscripts containing an extensive repertory of English medieval music. That repertory not only confirms the existence and character of specifically English musical traits, it also reveals the extent of the development of English music, the influence of continental practices in that development, and suggests influences English composers may have had upon continental music.

Leonel Power

Leonel Power (c. 1375–1445) was one of the two leading composers of English music between 1410 and 1445. The other was John Dunstable. Little is known about Power's early life; in documents he is referred to as "a Kent man." He served for some time as clerk and instructor of choristers in the household chapel of Thomas, Duke of Clarence (d. 1421), brother of Henry V. In 1423, Leonel became associated with the fraternity of Christ Church, Canterbury. That he was a layman is evidenced by the listing of his name among esquires (gentlemen) rather than among clergy. By 1439, he had become master of the choir that sang Services in the Lady Chapel.

Extant works known to be Power's number 40. All are liturgical—either settings of Marian texts or Mass movements. Approximately 17 other works have been tentatively attributed to him. Like Machaut and Dunstable, Power was a pioneer in composing Mass cycles. He was interested in creating paired movements of the Ordinary; four pairs are in the Old Hall Manuscript. He achieved unification by means of: (a) motives, including **head-motive** technique (using the identical motive at the opening of each movement or each section of a movement); (b) the same or related chants as tenor cantus firmus or placed in the top voice; and (c) parallel style and structure. He used some isorhythm.

Only one complete Mass has been definitely ascribed to him, the Mass *Alma redemptoris mater*. In its four movements—there is no Kyrie—the tenor presents the first half of the chant *Alma redemptoris mater* simply and unornamented, so that it is clearly identifiable. Attribution of two other complete Masses (Mass *Rex seculorum* and Mass *Sine nomine*) wavers between Leonel and Dunstable. In Mass *Rex seculorum* the same chant melody serves as cantus firmus for all movements, though the cantus firmus is treated flexibly. Power and Dunstable composed the earliest complete Masses based on a single cantus firmus, a practice that became standard procedure for the next generation of composers.

Power's compositions in Old Hall Manuscript far outnumber those of any other composer, and the variety of styles represented by those compositions indicates that by c. 1410 he had mastered all the compositional techniques and styles of his generation. He demonstrated capably his knowledge of French *Ars nova* and *Ars subtilior;* he combined with that a gift for creating melody and for using the full sonorities of English music. He composed skillfully for as many as five voices and was original and even daring in his combination of conflicting rhythms, yet he constructed contrapuntal lines so that each was basically consonant with all the others. His high level of musical craftsmanship is marred only by some lack of attention to correct declamation of text. (Of course, it is possible that this is scribal error.)

John Dunstable

Few biographical data relative to John Dunstable (c. 1390–1453) are available. His earliest works date from c. 1410–20; on this basis, his birth year is presumed to be c. 1390 or earlier. A Latin epitaph gives his death date as 24 December 1453. Another epitaph calls him mathematician and astronomer as well as musician. Dunstable was employed as a chapel singer by the Duke of Bedford, a brother of King Henry V; Bedford was Regent of France (1422–29) and Governor of Normandy (1429–35). Doubtless, Dunstable was a member of Bedford's continental retinue. Bedford's wife was sister to Philip the Good, Duke of Burgundy, a noted patron of music and art, and personnel of the two courts exchanged visits. Thus, Dunstable was well aware of musical developments at the Burgundian court; he may have known Du Fay and Binchois personally. Dunstable's work was well known in continental Europe; most of his compositions are preserved in continental manuscripts. His influence on later French composers, especially Du Fay and Binchois, was attested by Martin le Franc, who wrote in *Le Champion des dames* (c. 1441) that Du Fay and Binchois were superior to their French predecessors because they were influenced by Dunstable and the *contenance angloise,* the English style of music. The theorist Tinctoris, writing in 1477,

credited the accomplishments of continental composers to the fact that they had learned their art from Dunstable, Du Fay, and Binchois.

The *contenance angloise* to which le Franc referred is audibly sweeter and fuller than the continental music of the era. Technical features producing that sound are: (a) chords that regularly include the third (except final cadence chords), (b) passages in block chords or of lightly ornamented homorhythmic texture, and (c) polyphonic lines primarily consonant with all other lines, constructed with carefully prepared and resolved dissonances placed on weak beats. Textural contrast was provided by duets strategically placed in three-, four-, or five-voice compositions.

Approximately 51 compositions have been definitely credited to Dunstable. Authorship of 7 others has been attributed to either Dunstable or Power; distinguishing between these two composers' music is not always easy. Most of Dunstable's works are sacred, with Latin texts: Masses and Mass movements, antiphons, Sequences, hymns, Magnificats and other music for Offices. Much of Dunstable's sacred music is **votive,** that is, honoring a particular saint or the Virgin Mary. Seven of Dunstable's works are for three voices, 7 are four-voice, and the carol *I pray you all* is for two. In addition to the carol, only 4 other secular works by Dunstable survive: 2 rondeaux, a ballade, and the modified ballata *O rosa bella* (O lovely rose).

Dunstable's compositions are of various styles: (1) isorhythmic; (2) non-isorhythmic, with chant cantus firmus in the tenor; (3) with melody (either freely composed or a paraphrase of a chant) in the top voice, and two supporting lower voices moving at a slower pace; or (4) freely composed, without cantus firmus. Dunstable's melodies are typically English in their use of short note values in basically conjunct motion; any melodic skips present are usually thirds. There is no rhythmic redundancy or unnecessary repetition. Often the melody begins with a rising triad or an ornamented one.

In two isorhythmic motets written for Whit Sunday, Dunstable combined hymn and Sequence texts for Pentecost: (a) *Veni Sancte Spiritus et emitte—Veni Sancte Spiritus et infunde—Veni Creator Spiritus—Mentes tuorum* (Come, Holy Spirit, and send forth—Come, Holy Spirit, and pour—Come,

Creator Spirit—[Visit] the minds of your [people]), and (b) *Veni Sancte Spiritus et emitte—Consolator optime—Sancti Spiritus assit* (Come, Holy Spirit, and send forth—Best consoler—Holy Spirit breathe [on us]).

A majority of Dunstable's 14 isorhythmic motets exhibit a subtle propulsion (a drive) toward the cadence. In the tenor, the *color* is presented three times in note values that become proportionally progressively faster, i.e., in the ratio of 3:2:1. A drive to the cadence is a regular feature of much Renaissance music.

The non-isorhythmic motet *Quam pulchra es* (How fair thou art; DWMA49) is the most carefully set of all Dunstable's works. It is freely composed, without cantus firmus. Several verses from *Song of Solomon,* as used in an antiphon in Sarum Rite, form the text. The conductus-style setting was made with careful attention to correct declamation. A short string of parallel $\frac{6}{3}$ chords occurs in measures 12–14. Cadences are the standard medieval types or a slightly ornamented version of such. The closing Alleluia exhibits a drive to the cadence as well as the English preference for closing a motet with a long melisma.

English Carol

In the late Middle Ages, the English *carol* was no longer associated with dancing—it was a polyphonic song with Latin, English, or mixed Latin-English text. However, the carol retained the form of a dance song. It was composed of uniform stanzas and had a **burden** (a kind of refrain) that was sung at the beginning and end of each stanza—a structure closely resembling the French virelai. In some carols, the stanzas conclude with a recurring line, called **refrain,** as distinct from the **burden.** The famous Agincourt carol *Deo gratias Anglia* (Thanks be to God, England) has such a refrain line. Carols deal with all kinds of sacred and secular subjects; some praise the Virgin or celebrate the birth of Christ (DWMA50). Occasionally, a carol was used as an optional part of the liturgy, such as the *Benedicamus,* at certain festivals. Often carols served as processional songs in civic, court, and church functions.

Italy

In Italy, a gradual development of polyphonic music cannot be traced through notated compositions in manuscripts. In his *Micrologus,* Guido discussed organum and referred to it as being practiced. A half-dozen thirteenth-century liturgical dramas containing some music for two equal voices have been located at Padua, and thirteenth-century *Ordines* of churches at Siena and Lucca designate organal singing of many melodies. Liturgical polyphony seems to have been improvised, even as late as the fourteenth century. If organum and motets were composed and notated, they have not survived. Seemingly, Italian secular polyphony appeared suddenly in the fourteenth century and flourished. Its roots may be in solo song with improvised polyphonic accompaniment. When French troubadours, jongleurs, and minstrels fled to Italy and Spain during the Albigensian Crusade (1209–29), undoubtedly they brought with them information concerning polyphonic music in southern France, especially at St. Martial. Italian *trovatori* (troubadours) were active to some extent in the thirteenth century, but only monophonic *laude* survive in manuscripts.

Italian Notation

The earliest Italian treatise dealing with polyphony is the metaphorically titled *Pomerium artis musicae mensuratae* (Orchard of the art of measured music), written c. 1318–26 by Marchetto da Padua (c. 1274–after 1326). The first section of *Pomerium . . .* deals with the functions of stems, dots, and rests; the central portion considers note shapes and divisions of time; the last section concerns discant, ligatures, and rhythmic modes. Four imperfect rhythmic modes were added to the traditional perfect modes. Marchetto knew the French notation system and cited parts of it, but the Italian system included mensural combinations not used in French notation. These combinations produced a distinct rhythmic style different from that of the French. The *dot of division,* an essential feature of the Italian system, was used to separate groupings of notes and had a definitive and restrictive function similar to that of modern barlines.

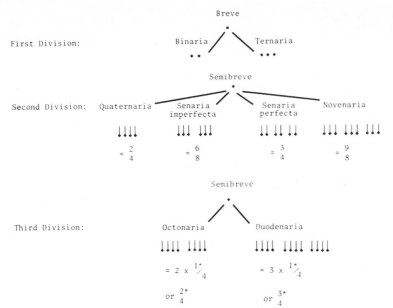

Figure 8.10 The three divisions of Italian notation.

The breve was the unit of measure. Three "divisions" (*divisiones*) of note values existed, each of them admitting both binary and ternary groupings. These divisions are diagrammed in figure 8.10. Both second and third divisions used minims. Note, however, that the third division was not a subdivision of the second, but stood in direct relationship to the first division, and had proportional relationship to the second division that produced a kind of hemiola effect. In both second and third divisions, the breve is equivalent to a full modern measure. However, a *senaria imperfecta* measure contains six minims and an *octonaria* measure contains eight minims; both measures move at the same tempo. Modern editors differentiate the tempos by placing an asterisk after the upper digit of the meter signature in third division.

Throughout the fourteenth century, Marchetto was considered an authority where mensural theory was concerned, but by c. 1360 use of the Italian notational procedures had begun to decline. More and more, composers favored the French system.

Manuscript Sources

The oldest surviving manuscript containing Italian polyphony is the fragmentary Rossi Codex at The Vatican Library. This document, prepared before c. 1350, contains approximately three dozen anonymous pieces written in the Italian notation described by Marchetto. The Rossi Codex provides the earliest notated examples of the three most-used forms of Italian *trecento* secular polyphony: madrigal, *caccia*, and ballata.

The most abundant manuscript source of fourteenth-century Italian secular polyphony is the Squarcialupi Codex. The manuscript was named for its former owner, Antonio Squarcialupi (1416–80). Squarcialupi did not compile the manuscript; how, why, or when he acquired it is not known. Squarcialupi was the most famous Italian organist of his time. In Florence, he served as organist at Orsanmichele (1431–33) and at Cathedral S. Maria del Fiore (1432–80). He worked closely with both Lorenzo de' Medici (the Magnificent) and Guillaume Du Fay. It is believed that Squarcialupi was also a composer, but none of his works have been located.

The Squarcialupi Codex, copied sometime between 1415 and 1440, contains 354 pieces: 115 madrigals, 12 *cacce,* and 227 ballatas. The music is arranged in sections according to composer, in chronological order. The first folio of each section is beautifully illuminated with floral, instrumental, or scenic

Figure 8.11 Folio 122v of the Squarcialupi Codex (MS Med. Palat. 87) portrays Landini playing a portative organ. The composition is his madrigal *Musica son. (Biblioteca Medicea-Laurenziana, Florence.)*

borders, and a miniature portrait of the composer (fig. 8.11). Included are works by Giovanni da Cascia, Jacopo da Bologna, Gherardello da Firenze, Vincenzo da Rimini, Lorenzo da Firenze, Donato da Cascia, Niccolò da Perugia, Bartolino da Padova, Franciscus da Florentia (Francesco Landini), Egidius and Giulielmo da Francia, Zacar, and Andreas da Florentia. The manuscript was never completed; 39 folios headed with composers' names contain only blank staves. Landini is represented by 146 compositions; Bartolino by 37; Jacopo da Bologna by 28.

Biographical data on Jacopo da Bologna (fl. 1340–60) are meager. He worked at the Visconti court in Milan during the reign of Luchino (r. 1339–49), then moved to the court of Mastino II della Scala at Verona. Of Jacopo's 34 surviving works, 25 are two-voice madrigals and 7 are three-voice madrigals. The remaining 2 are a ballata and a motet.

Madrigal

The madrigal was one of the earliest forms of Italian secular polyphony. Probably, the name *madrigal* derives from the composition's use of poetry in the vernacular or mother tongue (*matricalis,* belonging to the womb). Some early madrigals were called *matrigale.*

Madrigal poems were constructed in two or three three-line stanzas with an additional two-line *ritornello* (refrain). The subject matter is amatory, idyllic, or pastoral; sometimes the tone is satirical. Most fourteenth-century madrigals were composed for two voices. The musical setting is strophic (i.e., all stanzas are set to the same music), with different music for the ritornello. Both voices sing the same text but do not always sing the words simultaneously.

Jacopo da Bologna's setting of Petrarch's *Non al suo amante* (Not to her lover; DWMA51) is typical. The composition, written c. 1350, is the only known contemporary setting of a Petrarch poem. The upper voice is more florid than the lower, with long melismas occurring on (or immediately after) the first and last accented syllables of each poetic line. The melismas resemble the *caudae* of conductus; composers probably were influenced by that form. Both voices sing the same text, but the lower voice enters three measures later than the upper voice. Music for the stanzas is in duple meter; that for the ritornello is triple. A feature of Italian music is the sequential use of short melodic figures (ex. 8.10).

Jacopo's madrigals are fully texted in all voices, and there is no voice crossing. He seems to have been the first to write three-voice noncanonic madrigals. For him, the essence of music was a smooth, sweet melody.

Example 8.10 Melodic sequential figure used in the opening melisma of the third poetic line of Jacopo da Bologna's *Non al suo amante. (Transcribed from MS Med. Palat. 87.)*

That he planned the modal tonality of his pieces is apparent; over half of his madrigals begin and end on the same pitch. In his madrigals, change of meter occurs only at the ritornello. One of Jacopo's best-known madrigals is *Fenice fu'* (I was a phoenix), written c. 1360 (DWMA52).

Caccia

The *caccia* (pl., *cacce;* chase, hunt) is a three-voice composition that flourished c. 1345–70. It comprises a canon at the unison for two equal voices supported harmonically by an untexted (instrumental) lower line that commences when the first voice begins the melody. Frequently, a *caccia* concludes with a ritornello that may or may not be canonic. The *caccia* is a kind of pun, for one voice (the *dux,* leader) is "chased" by another (the *comes,* companion, fellow traveler) in strict imitation. The poetic text may describe a hunt or some sort of outdoor activity; hunting calls, bird songs, or other appropriate sounds usually appear in the music.

One of the *cacce* in the Squarcialupi Codex is *Tosto che l'alba* (As soon as the dawn; DWMA53) by Gherardello da Firenze. The two upper voices form a canon at the unison at the distance of ten measures, with a free supporting line commencing at the same time the first upper voice enters. The *dux* sings a long melisma on the last syllable of text while the *comes* completes the last phrase of text. In this piece, the ritornello is canonic; the *comes* follows the *dux* at the sixth measure. Otherwise, the design of the ritornello parallels that of the verse.

Ballata

Undoubtedly, composers of the Italian *ballata* were influenced by the French *virelai*—the ballata is cast in a more elaborate version of virelai form. A two-line *ripresa* (refrain) frames a six-line poetic stanza containing three pairs of lines in bba rhyme scheme. The formal structure created is, therefore, AbbaA. The musical setting matches the poetic form. When the poetic text is longer than one stanza, the form becomes Abba Abba A, etc.

Francesco Landini

Like de Vitry and Machaut, Francesco Landini (1325–97) was a poet-composer. He was the most important fourteenth-century Italian composer and the leading composer of Italian *ballate*. His compositions represent approximately one-fourth of the entire extant Italian fourteenth-century secular repertoire. Giovanni da Prato, in *Il Paradiso degli Alberti,* written c. 1425, related the use of instrumental and vocal music in Italian life c. 1389 and described Landini's organ playing as attracting gatherings of birds that added their songs to his music. Da Prato specifically mentioned Landini's ballata *Or su, gentili spiriti.*

In no music manuscript is Francesco named "Landini," nor does that name appear on his tombstone in the church of San Lorenzo. The name Landini was probably derived from his grandfather, Landino de Manno. Francesco's father, Jacopo del Casentino, was a painter of the Giotto school and co-founder of the Florentine guild of painters. Francesco, who was blind from early childhood as a result of smallpox, mastered several instruments and worked as organ builder, tuner, and instrument maker, as well as church organist, singer, and composer. He was involved with building the organs at the church of Ss. Annunziata and the Cathedral at Florence.

Of the 154 compositions definitely known to be Landini's, 90 are two-voice and 42 are three-voice ballatas. In addition, he composed 10 madrigals, 1 being a three-voice canonic madrigal, 1 caccia, and 1 French virelai. If he composed any sacred music, it has not survived. Landini possessed a gift for expressive melody. His style varies from pure Italian to a synthesis of French and Italian. His three-voice madrigals indicate his knowledge of French techniques: *Si dolce non sonò* (Did not [Orpheus] sound so sweetly; DWMA54) uses isorhythmic tenor, and in *De, dimmi tu* the tenor and contratenor display canon at the fifth.

Landini was a pioneer in composition of ballatas. In 82 of his two-voice ballatas, both voices have text. Many of the three-voice pieces are late works and use only one text, which is placed in the top voice

Example 8.11 Examples of Landini's use of 7-6-8 melodic succession in cadences: (*a*) *Ara' tu pietà*, mm. 24–26 (final cadence of Ritornello); (*b*) *Sy dolce non sonò*, mm. 80–93 (final cadence).

(a)

(b)

(DWMA55). In the late works, he paid more attention to modality (beginning and ending a section on the same pitch), and at times phrases rhyme musically. Some syncopations are present. Frequently, phrases end with a 7-6-8 melodic succession, forming the ornament of the so-called Landini cadence (ex. 8.11).

An overall survey of Landini's compositions seems to indicate that he used the older Italian style until c. 1370; from c. 1370–85 there is infiltration of French stylistic characteristics; and from c. 1385–97 a synthesis of French and Italian is apparent, with greater consideration for vertical harmony.

Spain

Music flourished at the fourteenth-century court of Catalonia-Aragon, in northern Spain (fig. 8.12). Court records reveal the names of approximately 600 singers, minstrels, and *joglars* (jongleurs) who served there between c. 1290 and 1400. King John I of Aragon (r. 1350–96) was a lover of books, an enthusiastic patron of music, and an avid collector of musical instruments. He actively sought fine musicians for his court. According to Juan Ruiz, the king wrote poetry and composed lais, virelais, and rondeaux.

The *Llibre Vermell* (Red Book), a fourteenth-century manuscript owned by Monasterio de S. Maria, Montserrat (near Barcelona), contains three *caças* and some short polyphonic *Cants dels Romeus* (Pilgrim Songs). The caça resembles the French *chace* in having no free instrumental tenor; directions indicate these caças may be performed as either two- or three-voice canons. Melodies of several of the Pilgrim Songs are folk songs; some tunes remained popular for more than a century after *Llibre Vermell* was compiled.

A valuable source of Spanish fourteenth-century music is the collection of folk songs made by Francisco de Salinas (1513–90) during the middle half of the sixteenth century. The songs were used as music examples in his treatise *De Musica Libri Septem* (Seven Books of Music), published in 1577. This is the oldest known collection of such folk songs. Salinas, blind from the age of ten, was an excellent organist and teacher. He held an abbacy in Naples, and while visiting Rome in 1538 he became intrigued with folk songs and began collecting them. He filled several important positions as cathedral organist, and from 1567 until his death he taught music at the University of Salamanca. Salinas was an advocate of equal temperament for fretted string instruments, but at the same time he sought to revive the chromatic and enharmonic genera of the Greeks and used a specially tuned keyboard instrument designed with 19 subdivisions of the octave.

Performance Practices — *Musica ficta*

Chromatic alterations other than B♭—the only chromatic alteration used in Guido's system and in Gregorian chant—were still considered *musica ficta*.

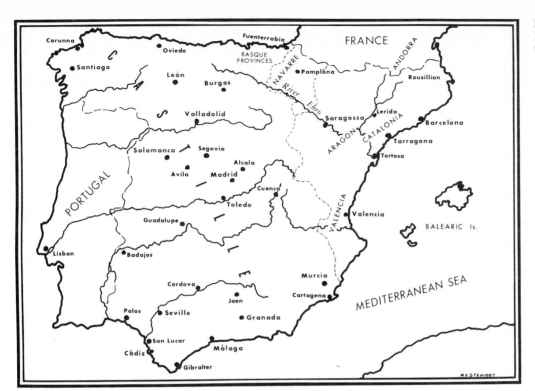

Figure 8.12 The Iberian peninsula in the fourteenth century.

Though the ♯ symbol was used more frequently before an f or a c pitch, especially by Italian composers, there were many instances where the application of a chromatic alteration was left to the performer. Unnotated chromatic alterations continued to be applied to music for various reasons, all of which could be reduced to either *causa necessitatis* (reason of necessity) or *causa pulchritudinis* (reason of beauty). A set of rules was gradually formulated to regulate the chromatic alteration of pitches under certain specified conditions. For example, a b between two a's was "soft" (♭), but a b between two c's was "hard" (♮). Similarly, a c between two d's was chromatically raised, as was an f between two g's.

Chromatic alteration commonly occurred at cadences to reduce the whole-step between the seventh degree of the modal scale and its final. Rules applicable here were: (a) When the interval of a sixth proceeds to an octave, the sixth must be major (ex. 8.12a). (b) When the interval of a third proceeds to a fifth, the third must be major. (c) When the interval of a third moves to a unison, the third must be minor (ex.

Example 8.12 Chromatic alteration by application of *musica ficta* at cadences to comply with rules governing: (*a*) a sixth (here, in outer voices) progressing to an octave, and (*b*) a third moving to a unison.

8.12b). Application of these rules created cadences wherein the penultimate chord contained either a single or a double leading tone. No chromatic alteration was used at cadences with a final on e because normal use of the Phrygian modal scale provided the proper intervals (ex. 8.13).

Example 8.13 Phrygian cadences.

The tritone (f–b♮) was to be avoided, both melodically and harmonically. In general, any augmented fourth or diminished fifth interval was chromatically altered in performance. Occasionally, chromatic alterations were made where no rules necessitated them but simply because the adjusted musical sound was more pleasant.

In some late fourteenth-century music, particularly in works by Italian composers such as Landini, partial signatures were used. For example, a ♭ might be placed at the beginning of the tenor line of a piece, as a kind of "key signature," but this did not appear at the beginning of the music for the other voice parts. Presumably, the singer(s) would apply the appropriate chromatic alteration(s) where needed in the upper part(s). In many instances, however, the tenor is the only part needing the chromaticism.

The application of *musica ficta* was not a problem for persons living in the Middle Ages and Renaissance. For those musicians and composers, it was common practice. The music they created was practical—to meet the needs of their own age; they cared not whether it would be preserved for use after their lifetimes. In fact, they probably never gave that any thought. It is only for later generations who wish to perform this early music properly that problems arise because of unwritten or inconsistently notated chromatic alterations. In music written after 1450, the absence of chromatic alterations is even more apparent—they virtually disappear from the notation! Conscientious modern editors of early music do not add chromatic alterations to the music found in original sources; instead, they indicate in small symbols either above or below the staff the chromatic alterations that most likely were applied when the music was originally performed. In this way, modern performers may benefit from editorial advice and still see the music as it originally existed.

Instruments

Most music manuscripts do not indicate the medium of performance for the music they contain. The presence or absence of text is not a reliable indication that the music is vocal or instrumental. Literary and pictorial sources indicate that in the fourteenth and early fifteenth centuries music was most often performed by small vocal and instrumental ensembles, usually with one musician to a part. No doubt they used whatever was available that produced the desired result, a procedure this writer calls "the theory of availability." Sometimes instrumentalists doubled vocal lines or substituted for voices. Facts indicate that in cantilena-style music the cantus was often performed by both a vocal soloist and an instrumentalist who appropriately embellished the line. Isorhythmic and textless tenors were probably intended for instrumental performance.

Literary sources—da Prato, John Lydgate, and others—mention a great variety of instruments and cite specific uses of them. Lydgate (c. 1373–c. 1450), in *Reson and Sensuallyte,* wrote of "Instrumentys high and lowe/Wel mo than I koude knowe" and of "lowde" instruments being used for dancing. French authors mentioned *haut* and *bas* instruments. The words "high" (*haut*) and "low" (*bas*) refer to volume, not pitch. High instruments were loud; low ones, soft. Loud instruments and larger ensembles were used on festive occasions, for especially solemn ceremonies, and out-of-doors; small ensembles of loud instruments provided music for dancing. There is no indication of crescendo and/or diminuendo in the music or that instruments were capable of any appreciable amount of variation in the volume of the sound they produced. Literary descriptions and artists' depictions indicate that the ensembles grouped instruments of heterogeneous rather than homogeneous timbre. In general, the tones produced were clear and bright, even shrill and strained. Artists' and sculptors' portrayal of singers indicate this was true of vocal music, also. Observe carefully the head position, formation of mouth and lips, and strained throat muscles of singers in paintings and sculpture (fig. 8.3). Some instructions for use of vibrato in specified instances indicate that, ordinarily, tone production was straight-line, without vibrato.

Low instruments included flute, harp, lute, psaltery, portative organ, and vielle. High instruments included chalumeau or shawm, various kinds of horns, sackbut (ancestor of the trombone), and trumpet. Percussion instruments, depending on their size, might fit into either category.

Three types of organs were in use: portative, positive, and the large organs installed in cathedrals and large churches. By the late fourteenth century some organs (e.g., Rouen Cathedral, 1386) had a small second (or tenor) keyboard. This eventually became the organ's pedal keyboard. Most organ keyboards had C as the lowest note; both b♭ and b♮ were "white" keys. Keyboard instruments of the clavichord-harpsichord type appeared in the fourteenth century but seem to have been used infrequently.

Summary

Literary accounts and pictorial representations indicate that in the fourteenth century music was enjoyed by all classes of society on all kinds of occasions. Undoubtedly, folk music was created, and both instrumental and vocal music were improvised. Much of the music that has survived seems to have been composed for aristocratic patrons or inscribed in manuscripts compiled for them.

Traces of trouvère tradition are found in the monophonic songs of late medieval poet-composers and in the poetic forms used for their verses. However, fourteenth-century composers concentrated on writing three-voice polyphonic settings of secular vernacular texts. Most of the *chansons* followed the formal patterns of the *formes fixes* of court poetry; Italian madrigals seem to exhibit closer ties with the common people. The presence of refrains in many secular vocal forms is to some extent a vestige of thirteenth-century dance songs.

Rhythmic diversity, freedom, and intricacy constituted perhaps the most outstanding feature of fourteenth-century music, especially in France. Rhythmic freedom was aided by recodification and extension of notational principles (a) to recognize equal binary as well as equal ternary division of notes and (b) to introduce smaller note values. During the *Ars nova* era, the highly structured patterns of isorhythm provided an unobtrusive unifying device, but they became more and more complex as they were designed to express nonmusical as well as musical dimensions. Motets were written to mark special events and were deemed especially appropriate for ceremonial or political occasions. For this reason, motets were suitable vehicles for isorhythm and symbolism. In France, a majority of the motets composed were secular and vernacular; the tenors were derived from either sacred or secular sources. Late in the century, however, composers resumed using sacred Latin texts for some of their motets. In England, the motet retained its Latin liturgical character; many motets were votive.

Increased rhythmic freedom generated additional intricacies. The degree of rhythmic complexity attained by composers of *Ars subtilior* music was unparalleled until the twentieth century.

Latin was, of course, used for settings of movements of the Mass Ordinary, some of which were composed as musically related pairs. Several complete, or almost complete, fourteenth-century settings of the Mass Ordinary are extant. However, Machaut's four-voice, unified, polyphonic setting of the complete Mass Ordinary is the earliest known such composition by one identified composer. Its four-voice structure was exceptional for that time. Yet it was not long before English composers were producing four-voice polyphonic settings of complete Masses, Mass movements, and sacred Latin motets, in which the tenor was the next-to-bottom voice. Some English liturgical compositions call for choral singing of certain phrases of composed polyphonic Service music.

As the fourteenth century advanced, more attention was paid to modal tonality and its organization, both melodic and harmonic. Linear polyphony was still being written with melodic lines of equal interest, but now the melodic lines were constructed so that all of them were in agreement. In addition, cantilena-style settings were composed, with the lower polyphonic voice(s) providing harmonic support for the solo melody. As this treble-dominated polyphony grew in favor, a corresponding proficiency in organizing harmonies around modal tonal centers is apparent. Rules governed the progression or succession of intervals (not chords), especially at cadence points, where the application of *musica ficta* created in the penultimate chord the equivalent of a leading tone. The concluding chord of principal cadences, and especially the final chord of a piece, comprised only perfect consonances (unison, octave, fifth). The sound of the music was important; chromatic alterations might be applied according to the rules of *musica ficta* for no other reason than to create a lovelier and more flexible melodic line. Thirds and sixths, considered imperfect consonances, appeared more frequently on strong beats, and short strings of parallel $^6_3$ chord successions added sweetness to English music.

When the fourteenth century opened, French composers held musical leadership. During the first half of the century, French and Italian composers used differing notational systems and produced different styles of music, but by 1400, many Italian composers were notating their songs according to French principles, and the styles were beginning to coalesce. French domination of the musical scene lasted for most of the fourteenth century, but c. 1400 leadership passed to the English for a few decades. Through Dunstable and other British composers who visited Europe, English musical practices were transmitted to continental composers, and the way was partially paved for the eventual emergence of a single international style of music.

and the division of the semibreve into minims produced *prolationis species* (prolation). Precise symbols designated the various mensurations (fig. 8.4a). The mensuration signs actually constitute time signatures and can be related to modern time signatures (fig. 8.4b).

The dot placed within the complete or broken circle as indication of perfection became known as *punctum perfectionis* (point of perfection) and was sometimes referred to as "the prick of perfection." The broken circle has been retained in modern notation where it represents $\frac{4}{4}$ meter, often referred to as "common time." (The symbol ₵ , with its designation "alla breve," which has also survived in modern notation, was not used by de Vitry but was an early Renaissance notation symbol used to shift the beat from the semibreve to the breve.)

In de Vitry's system, the semibreve might be subdivided in three ways: (a) *tempus perfect maius* (perfect major time) resulted when three semibreves were divided into three minims each; (b) *tempus perfectum medium* resulted when three semibreves were divided into two minims each; and (c) *tempus perfectum minimum* resulted when each semibreve contained three minims but minims followed each other

so closely that further subdivision was impossible. This might be interpreted to mean that the tempo was quite rapid, or that many minims were used in succession.

De Vitry is credited with the invention of red notes, which functioned: (a) to temporarily alter note values from perfect (ternary) to imperfect (binary), or vice versa; (b) to designate any deviations from the original in a melody used as cantus firmus; and (c) to indicate transposition an octave higher. The earliest known motet with mensural red notation is *Garrit gallus—In nova fert—N[euma]* (The cock babbles—Changed into new—N . . . ; DWMA44), which is cited by de Vitry as an example of that technique. Use of red notes is called **coloration** (colorplate 8).

Thirteenth-century music was written mainly in perfect mood, i.e., in longs and triple groupings of breves. In the fourteenth century, mood and time were used primarily in the lower voice(s) of motets. With the availability of shorter note values, the upper voice(s) usually were written in one or more of the prolations. The chief characteristic of French fourteenth-century music is its rhythmic organization, which was truly a "new art." Composers used with considerable freedom and ingenuity the variety of rhythmic possibilities at their disposal.

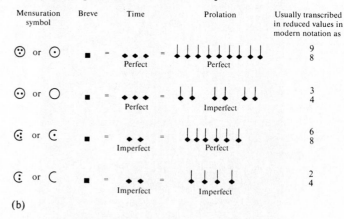

(b)

Figure 8.4 Interpretation of the mensuration symbols used by De Vitry to indicate (*a*) modus and tempus and (*b*) the four prolations.

Perfect modus :   longa   =   3 breves

Imperfect modus :   longa   =   2 breves

Perfect tempus :   breve   =   3 semibreves

Imperfect tempus :   breve   =   2 semibreves

Perfect modus, perfect tempus: longa   =   3 breves   ;   breve   =   3 semibreves

Imperfect modus, imperfect tempus: longa   =   2 breves   ;   breve   =   2 semibreves

(a)

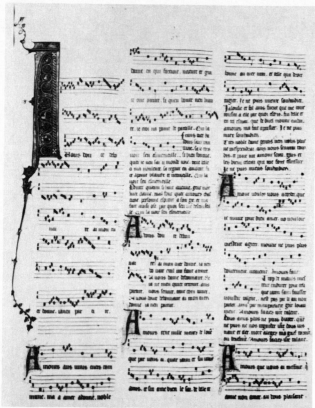

Figure 8.8 Jehannot de l'Escurel's polyphonic rondeau *A vous, douce debonaire* appears in score notation in the left column of fol. 57, MS fr.146. *(Bibliothèque nationale, Paris.)*

Included are virelais, ballades, rondeaux, and rondeau refrains. The music and texts are arranged alphabetically; the last ones inscribed commence with the letter G.

The section opens with de l'Escurel's only surviving polyphonic piece, *A vous, douce debonaire* (To you, sweet good-natured lady), a three-voice conductus-style rondeau with the main melody placed in the middle voice (fig. 8.8). The piece appears later in the manuscript as a monophonic rondeau. The notation does not include minims, and groups of two to five semibreves occur in the lyrical monophonic pieces, in Petronian style. The monophonic pieces indicate that de l'Escurel was adept at text painting, the technique of describing musically the words being set. For example, he used curving musical lines to set *Bien se lace,* which speaks of "embracing."

Guillaume de Machaut

Guillaume de Machaut (c. 1300–77), renowned poet and leading French composer of the fourteenth century, held responsible positions at various royal courts and several important churches, including Reims Cathedral. (Insight, "Guillaume de Machaut".) Machaut spent much of his time at court, which probably accounts for the fact that most of his music is secular. However, in his few sacred compositions he made significant contributions to the development of music. Machaut composed both monophonic and polyphonic pieces and used both conservative and avant-garde forms, styles, and techniques. His versatility as a composer and the high quality of his music were unparalleled in his time.

Motets

The motet was an established form of secular music, but Machaut's treatment of that form was avant-garde in many respects. Of his 23 motets, 4 (Nos. 5, 21, 22, 23) are for four voices; the remainder are for three. Three motets use French secular tenors; incipits of the Latin tenors of the others imply chant derivation. (Sources of all the Latin tenors have not been identified.) Six of the motets have Latin texts; two are furnished with Latin duplum and French triplum; upper voices of the rest are in French. In the four-voice motets the contratenor is textless. Tenors and textless contratenors were probably performed instrumentally.

In the fourteenth century, the voice parts above the tenor were usually named **motetus** and **triplum.** In four-voice polyphony, the additional voice part was placed below the tenor and was called **contratenor** or **contratenor bassus** (low [voice] opposite the tenor). Contratenor bassus was predecessor of the modern **bass** voice part.

The Latin motets exhibit some of Machaut's finest work. They may have been used liturgically in the Offices. The motet *Felix virgo—Inviolata—Ad te suspiramus* (No. 23; Fortunate virgin—Inviolate—To you we breathe) is clearly a Marian motet. Not only is the tenor derived from the Marian Antiphon *Salve, Regina,* but the words of the two upper parts are addressed to the Virgin. Possibly, choirboys sang these upper parts, while instrumentalists played tenor and contratenor on organs or sackbuts (ancestors of the trombone).

with musical form treated freely. By the end of the century, the motet had become a setting of a Latin religious text other than the Mass Ordinary. (Settings of the Ordinary would, of course, be Mass movements.)

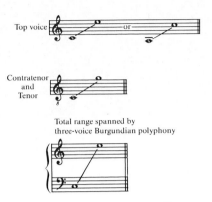

Example 9.7 Vocal ranges for which Burgundian composers usually wrote.

Among Burgundian composers, treble-dominated (cantilena-style) three-voice polyphony predominated; imitation was used sparingly. *Faux bourdon* was sometimes employed in sacred music, principally for variety in settings of strophic chants. Most compositions were in triple meter; in long, sectional works, duple meter provided contrast. Cross-rhythms, principally **hemiola** (three against two) occurred in the lower voices. Lyrical simplicity characterized the principal polyphonic melody; melismas were included near cadences. Undoubtedly, the vocal range a composer used for a composition was determined by that of the singer(s) available to perform the work. In most compositions, vocal range remained within Guido's gamut (ex. 9.7); occasionally, it extended beyond (see Binchois, p. 169). Cadential formulas were those shown in example 9.8 and ornamented versions of them. Though the tonality was modal, a sense of dominant-tonic relationship was becoming apparent, primarily at cadences.

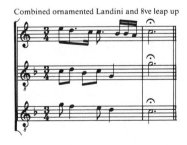

Example 9.8 Types of cadences written by Burgundian composers.

Basse danse

The *basse danse* was the favorite court dance in the fifteenth and early sixteenth centuries. It was at its height at the Burgundian court during the reigns of Philip the Good and Charles the Bold. When performing the *basse danse,* couples moved quietly and gracefully, with a gliding or walking movement of the feet (fig. 9.10). Costumes worn at court would have favored a slow dance. Gentlemen wore short doublets and tight-fitting hose; shoes were extremely pointed, the tips often projecting as much as two feet beyond the wearer's toes. (Broad-toed shoes became fashionable c. 1500.) Swords and hats were worn during dancing. Women's gowns, fashioned of heavy fabric, had full skirts with trains; sometimes five yards of fabric trailed behind a lady. Women's hats (called *hennins*) were very tall, often heart-shaped or pointed, with long veils extending down the back as far as a lady's knees, or even to the floor.

Primary sources of *basse danse* music are: MS 9085 in Bibliothèque de Bourgogne, Brussels, a beautiful manuscript with gold and silver notation (colorplate 12); and *L'art et instruction de bien dancer,* printed by Michel de Toulouze c. 1496. *Basse danse* music appears to be monophonic and is notated in uniform breves, which are augmented to longs when performed. The notation is merely a tenor cantus firmus the length of the choreography, with each note corresponding to a complete dance step. A letter symbolizing the dance step to be performed appears below the appropriate note of the cantus firmus. In performance, an ensemble of three or four instrumentalists—usually a slide-trumpet and two or three shawms—improvised polyphony based on the cantus firmus. *Basse danse* tenors were derived from tenors of favorite chansons. Binchois's rondeaux *Tristre plaisir* (Sad pleasure), *Mon doulx espoir* (My sweet hope), and *La merchi* (Pity) furnished *basse danse* tenors.

Gilles de Binche (Binchois)

Gilles de Binche (Binchois; (c. 1400–1460) was born in the province of Hainaut, near Mons. He probably grew up at court, for his father (Jean) was court councillor, but nothing definite is known about Gilles's early life or education. Ockeghem stated in his *Déploration* (Lament) that Binchois was a soldier in his

Figure 9.10 In *The Dance at the Court of Herod,* an engraving made c. 1500, Israhel van Meckenhem mixed historical eras and depicted the Biblical event in a setting typical of his own time. *(National Gallery of Art, Washington, D.C.)*

youth and then went into the service of the church. The earliest mention of Binchois in church records is at the Mons Church of Ste Waudru where, from 8 December 1419 to 28 July 1423, he was organist. Then he moved to Lille, where he may have obtained employment with the English Earl of Suffolk.

There is no proof that Binchois was an ordained priest. Priesthood was not required for chaplaincy at the Burgundian court, where he served from c. 1427 until his retirement in February 1453. Nor was priesthood requisite for obtaining benefices; for much of his lifetime, Binchois received income from benefices he held *in absentia* at five churches. He did not have a university degree, yet in 1452 was appointed provost of the collegiate church of St. Vincent at Soignies. He spent the last several years of his life at Soignies. At the time of his death, he was eulogized in laments by Du Fay, Ockeghem, and others. Du Fay's lament, a rondeau, contains the titles of two Binchois songs: *Dueil angoisseux* (Anguished mourning) and *Tristre plaisir* (Sad pleasure).

Binchois is ranked third (after Dunstable and Du Fay) among the great masters of the first half of the fifteenth century. Though the major portion of his music is secular and courtly, in accordance with his position at the Burgundian court of Philip the Good, Binchois composed a considerable amount of sacred music. His chansons provided material for works by others, including Masses by Ockeghem and Bedyngham, a motet by Senfl, and three *basse danses.*

Binchois's music was included in more than 50 manuscripts compiled in the fifteenth century. His surviving works comprise 12 single and 8 pairs of Mass Ordinary movements; 6 Magnificats; a *Te Deum; In exitu Israel* (When Israel left [Egypt], Ps. 113; KJV,114); 28 short motets and settings of various hymns, antiphons, and a Sequence; 60 three-voice chansons (7 are ballades); and the four-voice chanson *Filles à marier* (Girls to be married, [never marry]).

Chansons

For chanson lyrics, Binchois chose writings of favorite court poets, such as Christine de Pisan's *Dueil angoisseux* and Charles d'Orléans's *Mon cuer chante* (My heart sings). Binchois preferred poetry with four- or five-line strophes. In setting that poetry, he avoided the sectioning that would be created by following fixed poetic formal patterns; in other words, he did not write musical settings to obviously match the strophic sectioning or the poetic rhyme scheme. For example, in *De plus en plus* (More and more), he set some poetic aabba-patterned strophes as ab musically. The entire poem, of several strophes, was given the standard pattern of the rondeau, ABaAabAB. In the fifteenth century, rondeau was the dominant form of chanson; the favorite subject was *fin' amours* (courtly love). Most of Binchois's chansons comply with court preferences; *Filles à marier* is an exception.

All but one of Binchois's chansons are for three voices, with the principal melody usually placed in the top voice. The tonality is modal. Rhythm is usually ternary, and the two lower voices move more slowly than the superius. In most of the chansons, only the superius is supplied with text. However, some chansons have words in two voices; in a few songs all voices are texted, e.g., the May song *Vostre alée* (Your journey). That chanson provides an early example of **pervading imitation** (imitation in all voices). *Filles à marier* contains a good deal of imitation, but it is confined to the two upper voices. The untexted lines were intended for instrumental performance, and the presence of textless interludes between phrases of text in some songs suggests that an instrumentalist may have doubled the vocal line.

Binchois's melodies tend to be simple, graceful, and without rhythmic intricacies. There is in his music a kind of joyous melancholy, in keeping with the *Tristre plaisir et douloureuse joie* (Sad pleasure and dolorous joy) about which he wrote. He used musical material economically. Each musical phrase rises to a high point, then proceeds to a cadence. In many songs, the final cadence employs the octave leap to avoid successive parallel fifths (which actually are audible); the final chord is an octave with an open fifth. Occasionally, Binchois used an extremely wide range or an unusual range. In *De plus en plus* (DWMA61), the superius range is low, extending from g to c″. The superius of *Jamais tant que je vous revoye* encompasses a ninth but extends beyond Guido's gamut. The pitch f″, used twice in the chanson, is marked with a ♭ each time to indicate that it is *fa ficta*—outside Guido's hand.

Sacred Works

Binchois seems to have been the only major composer in the fifteenth century who did not write a cyclic Mass, though he wrote individual and/or paired settings of all movements of the Mass Ordinary. In his sacred music, he was conservative rather than innovative. Sections within Mass movements are contrasted in texture, range, and mensuration. Compositions based on liturgical chant present the chant elaborated and melodically paraphrased, rather than as tenor cantus firmus in long note values. The chant is meant to be recognized. Frequently, the paraphrased chant melody is placed in the top voice. That is the case in *Gloria, laus et honor* (Glory, praise and honor), based on a chant from Sarum Use. The first three notes of the chant are presented unornamented, in sustained notes of equal value; thereafter, the chant is designed rhythmically and its melody slightly elaborated. *Gloria, laus et honor* is set for three low voices. The lowest voice frequently descends to D, a fourth below Guido's lowest pitch; the two lower voices sometimes cross, and in some of those instances the middle voice contains a D pitch.

The Kyrie based on Gregorian Kyrie VIII (*De Angelis*; LU,37) presents the chant, slightly paraphrased, in both superius and contratenor. As seen in example 9.9, the original pitches of the chant were retained for the superius paraphrase but placed an octave higher. For the contratenor the chant was transposed and set a fourth below the superius. From

Example 9.9 Excerpt from the Kyrie Binchois based on Gregorian chant Kyrie VIII (*De Angelis*).

time to time, successions of $\frac{6}{3}$ chords appear in the harmonic structure; usually, they are preceded or followed by $\frac{8}{5}$ chords. The influence of English discant is apparent. Some of Binchois's sacred works in Italian manuscripts have sections that are clearly marked to be sung by chorus. It should be remembered that some English Mass movements in the Old Hall manuscript contained sections similarly marked.

Binchois used *faux bourdon* in his sacred music only. It is found in the Magnificats, and his setting of Psalm 113 (KJV,114) resembles *faux bourdon,* with free counterpoint used near the end of the piece. The *Te Deum laudamus* is a harmonization of that chant for three voices (fig. 9.11). Two of the parts are notated, in parallel sixths, in triple meter. The rubric *a faulx bourdon* indicates that the entire middle voice is created through *faux bourdon.* Where recitative occurs in the liturgical chant, the harmonization becomes chordal recitative.

Only one of Binchois's motets is isorhythmic, a four-voice piece with three Latin texts and a textless tenor, composed for the baptism of Antoine, son of Philip the Good. In the text, Binchois names all of his colleagues in the Burgundian ducal chapel. In the three-voice motet *Ave Regina celorum* (LU,1864), the chant appears in the superius with elaboration at or near cadence points. The first two phrases commence with the tenor imitating the superius and presenting the chant an octave lower with the elaboration deleted.

Two of Binchois's sacred works are *contrafacta.* A *contrafactum* is a vocal piece in which the original secular text has been replaced by a sacred one. *Rerum conditor respice* is *contrafactum* of the ballade *Dueil angoisseux*; *Virgo rosa venustatis* (Virgin, lovely rose) is *contrafactum* of the rondeau *C'est assez* (It is enough).

Binchois is the foremost representative of the Burgundian style of musical composition. Tinctoris (c. 1435–c. 1511) and other authors of theoretical treatises cited portions of Binchois's works as examples; Binchois's name was consistently included in various differing lists of the ten most skillful composers of polyphonic music. His chansons supplied material for major works by at least a dozen other composers; six of his songs were intabulated for keyboard and included in the *Buxheimer Orgelbuch.* His *Te Deum* was copied into choirbooks and used in Milan and in Spain.

Antoine de Busne (Busnois)

Nothing is known about the early life of Antoine de Busne (Busnois; c. 1430–92), though his name indicates that he was born at or lived in the small town of Busne in northeastern France. Very little biographical data can be gleaned from the texts of his works. Hacqueville and Jacqueline d'Hacqueville are mentioned in four of his chansons. The motet *In hydraulis* (On the organ) reveals that at some time prior to 1467 Busnois was an "unworthy musician" at the court of

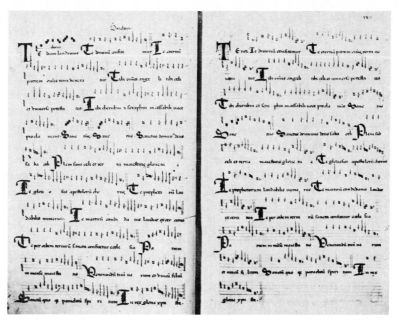

Figure 9.11 Portion of Binchois's *Te Deum laudamus*, MS
α.X.1.11, fol. 21v–22r. *(Biblioteca estense, Modena, Italy.)*

Charles, Count of Chaulois; in 1467, Charles became
Duke of Burgundy, and Busnois is listed as a singer
in the ducal chapel. From time to time, Busnois obtained special benefices through Charles the Bold.
After Charles's death (1477), Busnois served as priest-
chaplain to Mary of Burgundy (d. 1482); his whereabouts between 1482 and c. 1491 are unknown. At
the time of his death, he was *rector cantoriae* at the
Church of St. Sauveur, Bruges.

Busnois was a talented poet as well as musician
and composer; his chanson texts appear in contemporary collections of poetry. His secular songs were
very popular, and his capable handling of Burgundian
style caused his contemporaries to regard him second
only to Ockeghem between c. 1465–92. Busnois was
mentioned in numerous poems; in addition to being
cited in praise, his name was fragmented and hidden
in the rhyme and sometimes appeared acrostically.
Tinctoris dedicated a treatise jointly to Ockeghem and
Busnois and listed the four leading composers of the
era as Ockeghem, Busnois, Caron, and Fauges. Other
authors similarly acclaimed Busnois, and several
composers borrowed from his works for theirs.

In addition to 64 secular polyphonic songs, Busnois's surviving compositions comprise 2 Masses, 6
motets, and settings of 2 hymns, 2 Marian antiphons,
the Easter Sequence, and the Magnificat. The chief
source of Busnois's sacred music is MS 5557 in Bibliothèque Royale, Brussels. Among the many manuscripts containing his chansons is the unusual
Chansonnier Cordiforme, a heart-shaped manuscript
bound in red velvet covers, in Bibliothèque nationale,
Paris (colorplate 13). The form of some of Busnois's
songs cannot be determined because portions of texts
are missing. However, a majority of the chansons are
rondeaux; 13 are *bergerettes* (one-stanza virelais).

Busnois excelled in the composition of small
forms. His chansons are typical of Burgundian style
in the third quarter of the fifteenth century; most of
these pieces are for three voices. The melodies are
characterized by simplicity and clear phrasing; often
all voices cadence simultaneously, thus establishing a
feeling for the modality of the piece. Superius and
tenor have smooth melodic lines with some bits of imitation; much of the time the contratenor is instrumental filler, but sometimes all three voices partake
of motives imitatively. Busnois used a good deal of
imitation, most often at the octave, unison, or the fifth
scale degree.

As Busnois's imitative use of small motives increased, the vocal range he covered in his three-voice writing expanded. The pitch F occurs frequently; sometimes a vocal line descends to D. Nor are these low pitches confined to the bottom part; they appear in the middle voice also, and sometimes the voices cross. In the four-voice rondeau *Je ne demande* (I do not ask), both contratenor lines are in the "bass" register. This chanson served as basis for Masses by Alexander Agricola and Jacob Obrecht, and the chanson tenor was used as cantus firmus by Ludwig Senfl and Heinrich Isaac.

In most of his *bergerettes* Busnois achieved contrast by using triple rhythm for the refrain and duple for the verse. He tended to avoid the harmonic interval of a fourth but frequently used parallel thirds, sixths, and tenths. This was a firm departure from late medieval harmonic practice.

Si placet (optional) parts for a fourth voice exist for some of the chansons; these optional parts may or may not have been composed by Busnois, but their presence is indicative of a growing demand for four-voice secular polyphony in the late fifteenth century. When a fourth voice was added, it was usually another contratenor, which necessitated a clear differentiation of the two contratenor parts. This was accomplished by labeling one *contratenor altus* (high contratenor) and the other *contratenor bassus* (low contratenor.) Eventually, the word "contratenor" was dropped, and the parts became simply "contraltus" or "altus" and "bassus." Often, the top voice was not labeled; sometimes it was identified as either *cantus* or *superius*. From this terminology came the modern designation of voice parts:

Name	Meaning	Became
Superius	"uppermost" or "top"	Soprano
Contratenor altus	"high against tenor" or "above tenor"	Contralto and Alto
Tenor	"holds melody"	Tenor
Contratenor bassus	"low against tenor" or "below tenor"	Bassus or Bass

Busnois's two extant Masses—*Missa O crux lignum* (O wooden cross) and *Missa L'Homme armé*—are four-voice cantus firmus Tenor Masses. The cantus firmus is unornamented and serves as skeletal framework for the Mass structure. As such, it contrasts with the other parts. In his *Missa L'Homme armé,* Busnois used a head motive and some canon. Busnois was probably the second composer to write a Mass based on the *L'Homme armé* tune—Du Fay was the first; Busnois's Mass served as model for that by Obrecht. Thereafter, almost every well-known composer up to and including Palestrina wrote a Mass based on the *L'Homme armé* melody.

For his four-voice motet *In hydraulis,* which praises Ockeghem, Busnois designed a cantus firmus from a three-note ostinato. The three notes are stated in various transpositions and in proportional diminutions. The three-voice motet *Anima mea liquifacta est—Stirps Jesse* (My soul is weakened—The root of Jesse), composed c. 1475, uses the Responsory chant, slightly elaborated, as tenor cantus firmus. Busnois used the sequences in the chant to advantage, as motives to be imitated, sometimes in stretto, and on occasion created a short sequence of his own (ex. 9.10).

In his sacred music, Busnois was not experimental, though occasionally he did unusual things. For example, in the motet *Anthoni usque lumina* the tenor is given by verbal canon only and consists of the single pitch d', whose bell-like intonations may have been instrumental rather than vocal. Unfortunately, the rubric does not state clearly where those intonations are to occur, but the d' pitch would fit into most of the harmonies.

Busnois used orderly procedures to achieve desired goals. For him, imitation was an integrative device; also, it could provide contrast or direct attention to either the climax of a piece or the beginning of a phrase. At times, he created rhythmic interplay between voices by commencing the imitation of a motive on the third beat of a ternary rhythm but retained the same rhythmic accent previously used (i.e., on the first beat). Textual imitation adds subtlety. The interplay is more noticeable in modern transcriptions because barlines are present (ex. 9.10). Short sequences and repeated rhythmic patterns serve Busnois as organizational devices.

Busnois occupies an important place in the development of contrapuntal music from Du Fay to Desprez. Busnois's style is a mixture of the old and the new. In his chansons he epitomizes the Burgundian style but includes more motivic imitation; in his

Example 9.10 Busnois used the sequences in the chant *Stirps Jesse* to advantage in his motet *Anima mea liquefacta est—Stirps Jesse.* In this excerpt he used sequences in imitation at the climax of the phrase. (*Transcribed from MS α.X.1.11, fol. 83v–84r; Biblioteca estense, Modena, Italy.*)

sacred works, the sense of form, sense of harmony, and greater homogeneity of contrapuntal lines point ahead to the achievements of Jacob Obrecht and Josquin Desprez.

Franco-Netherlands Composers

Alexander Agricola

Singer-composer Alexander Agricola (c. 1446–1506) was highly regarded at Galeazzo Maria Sforza's Milan court, where he was employed from 1471–74. In 1476 Agricola worked at Cambrai Cathedral. His whereabouts during the years 1477–91 are not completely known; for part of that time he was a member of the French royal chapel. In 1491–92 he was in Italy; he died of plague while traveling in Spain in 1506.

Extant compositions by Agricola include 8 Masses, 4 Credos, 18 motets, 3 bilingual (French-Latin) chanson-motets, 47 chansons (mainly rondeaux and bergerettes), 25 instrumental pieces, and some settings of hymns, Magnificats, and Lamenta-

tions. Other works of dubious attribution exist. The instrumental pieces are based on tenors from or are arrangements of chansons by Binchois, Frye, Hayne van Ghizeghem, and Ockeghem, as well as popular tunes.

Agricola's musical style is closely allied with that of late medieval Franco-Flemish composers; though he worked in Italy for a time, no Italian early-Renaissance influence is apparent in his music. He wrote long, rhythmically complex, melismatic melodies that were constructed by linking rather small decorative motives. The devices of repetition, sequence, and imitation appear in his counterpoint.

Johannes Tinctoris

Johannes Tinctoris (c. 1435–1511) was esteemed in his own time as a writer and music theorist; he was highly regarded also as composer, poet, lawyer, and mathematician. He worked as instructor of choirboys at the Cathedral of Orléans and at Chartres Cathedral, then, c. 1472, entered the service of King Ferdinand I of Naples as tutor to Beatrice, Ferdinand's daughter. Though residing in Italy, Tinctoris held a canonicate at the church at Nivelles, near Brussels.

Tinctoris's surviving compositions include 9 chansons, most of them based on tenors of chansons by his contemporaries Frye, Binchois, Ockeghem, Morton, and Hayne van Ghizeghem; 6 Masses, one based on the *L'Homme armé* tune; and a few motets and hymn settings. His compositional style is eclectic and transitional, reflecting some elements of both late medieval and early Renaissance music.

In his 12 extant treatises, Tinctoris considered all aspects of music from antiquity up to and including his own time. Only two of these writings were published during his lifetime. His three most significant treatises are *Terminorum musicae diffinitorium* (Dictionary of Musical Terms), *Liber de arte contrapuncti* (Book on the Art of Counterpoint), and *De inventione et usu musicae* (Concerning the composition and performance of music). *Terminorum musicae diffinitorium,* the earliest printed music dictionary, was printed in 1495 at Treviso, Italy, by Gerardus de Lisa, who, c. 1470, set up one of the first printing presses in Italy.

In *Liber de arte contrapuncti,* written in 1477, Tinctoris devoted considerable space to improvisation; in Book III he set down eight rules, with detailed explanation, for correct and effective improvisation and cited music examples from Du Fay, Busnois, Ockeghem, and Caron. Variety was desirable; repetition of any kind was to be shunned. Successive cadences should be dissimilar. In improvisation, both linear (melodic) and vertical (harmonic) aspects of the music must be taken into consideration. Certainly, the emphasis Tinctoris placed upon correct improvisation is indicative of its importance in the fifteenth century.

De inventione et usu musicae was printed c. 1486 by del Tuppo at Naples. In this writing Tinctoris discussed, among other matters, the qualifications for being a good singer and singled out Ockeghem as the finest bass he knew. Several chapters of the treatise are devoted to instruments and instrumental performance practices. Instruments discussed include shawm or *celimela*; cromorne or *dulcina*; bombarda;

brass *tuba*; Italian *trompone* and French *sacque-boute* (early trombone types); lyra or *leute* (lute); viol; rebec; guitar; citole; and *tambura* (an oriental lute). In range, the shawm, cromorne, and bombarda were comparable with soprano, tenor, and contratenor voices; a low contratenor part might be played on the brass *tuba*. Wind instruments were played at church festivals, weddings, banquets, in processions, and on various civic occasions, as well as for private entertainments at court. Invention of the guitar was credited to the Catalans; in Catalonia, women played guitar accompaniments when they sang love songs. Accomplished lutenists were able to perform two-, three-, and four-part music. Moreover, Jean and Charles Fernand, instrumentalists to Charles VIII of France, could skillfully perform two-part music on the *viola cum arculo* (bowed viol)—a difficult feat.

(a)

(b)

Figure 9.12 Two of the several engravings Israhel van Meckenhem made depicting musicians: (*a*) *The Lute Player and the Harpist;* (*b*) *The Organ Player and His Wife. (National Gallery of Art, Washington, D.C.)*

Plate 5 H. and J. van Eyck. The Ghent Altarpiece, completed 1432. (a) Altarpiece closed, approximately 11'3" × 7'3"; (b) altarpiece open, approximately 11'3" × 14'6". (Original in Cathedral of St. Bavo, Ghent.)

(a)

(b)

Plate 6 Giotto di Bondone. *Lamentation,* fresco, 7'7'' × 7'9'',
painted c. 1305. Original in Arena Chapel, Padua, Italy.
(© Fratelli Alinari/Art Resource.)

Plate 7 Miniature depicting Johannes Ockeghem (wearing glasses) with his chapel singers. *(MS fr. 1537, folio 58v, in Bibliothèque nationale, Paris.)*

Plate 8 Philippe de Vitry's isorhythmic motet *Garrit gallus—In nova fert—Neuma. (MS fr. 146, folio 44v, Bibliothèque nationale, Paris.)*

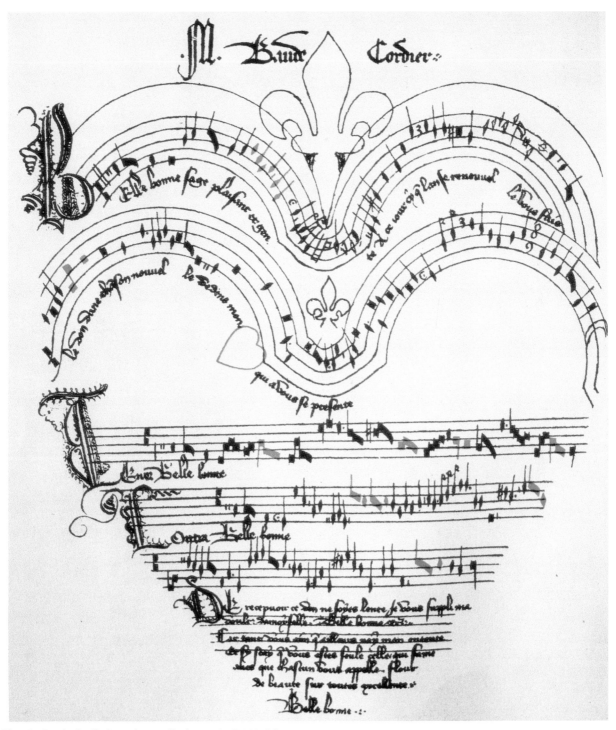

Plate 9 Baude Cordier's rondeau *Belle, bonne. (MS 564, folio 11v, Musée Condé, Chantilly.)*

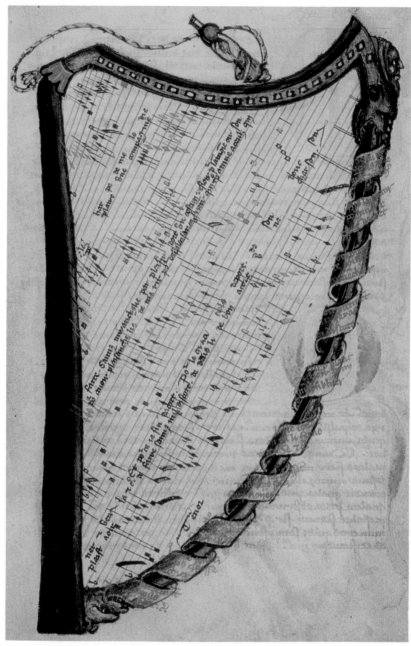

Plate 10 Jacob Senleches's virelai *La harpe de melodie. (MS 54.1, folio 10. Courtesy of The Newberry Library, Chicago.)*

Plate 11 Miniature depicting *The Annunciation*, folio 30, *The Belles Heures of Jean, Duke of Berry. (Original manuscript in* *The Cloisters Collection, Metropolitan Museum of Art, New York City.)*

Plate 12 Two *basse danses*, notated in gold and silver on black page. *(MS 9085, Bibliothèque de Bourgogne, Brussels.)*

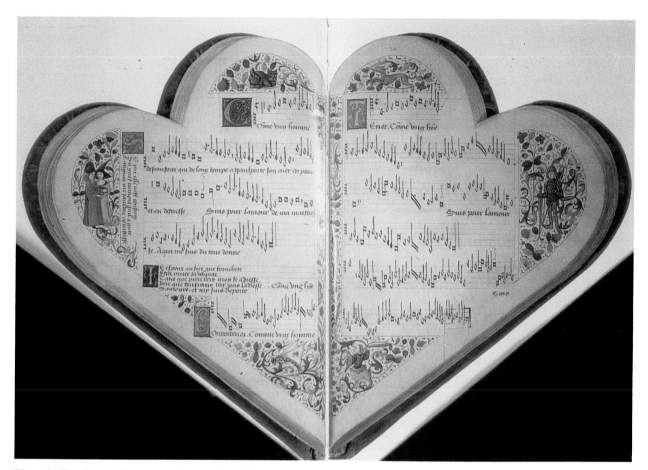

Plate 13 The chanson *Comme ung homme desconforte.*
(Chansonnier Cordiforme, MS Rothschild 2973, folios 19v–20r,
Bibliothèque nationale, Paris.)

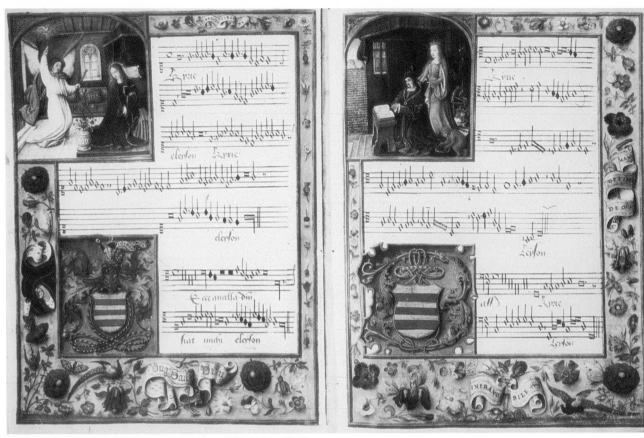

Plate 14 Kyrie of Ockeghem's *Missa Ecce ancilla Domini. (MS Chigi C.VIII.234, folios 19v–20r, Biblioteca Apostolica Vaticana, Rome.)*

Plate 15 Raphael Sanzio. *The School of Athens,* 1509–11, fresco approx. 26′ × 18′. In Stanza della Segnatura, Vatican Palace, Rome. *(© Art Resource.)*

Plate 16 The Master of Female Half-Lengths. *Three Musicians,* also known as *The Concert.* The trio of voice, lute, and transverse unkeyed flute are performing Sermisy's chanson *Joyssance vous donneray. (The Harrach Collection, Schloss Rohrau, Vienna.)*

Spain

Spanish composer Johannes Cornago (fl. 1455–85), a member of the Franciscan Order, worked primarily at the Neapolitan courts of Alfonso I (r. 1442–58) and Ferdinand I (r. 1458–94). Both Tinctoris and Ockeghem were acquainted with Cornago's music; Tinctoris, who also was employed by Ferdinand at Naples, probably knew Cornago personally. Ockeghem made a four-voice setting of Cornago's three-voice chanson *Qu'es mi vida preguntays* (What is my life, you ask).

Only a few of Cornago's works are extant: 11 secular songs (5 with Italian texts, the rest Spanish); 2 Masses; and the four-voice *Patres nostri peccaverunt* (Our fathers sinned), one of the earliest polyphonic settings of a passage from Lamentations. The Spanish and Italian interest in exploration is reflected in Cornago's three-voice *Missa Ayo visto lo mappa mundi* (I have seen the map of the world), which is based on an Italian popular song. *Missa de nostra donna S. Maria* (Mass of Our Lady Saint Mary) is for four voices.

Cornago's compositions indicate that he was acquainted with the Franco-Flemish musical style, but he is credited with developing a distinctly Spanish style of polyphonic courtly love song. All of his solo songs follow the form of the *canción* (contemporary Spanish lyric poetry), set musically as abba. His secular songs are three-part polyphony, with expressive melancholy melodies and long textless passages designed for instrumental performance. Frequently, he included passages in parallel thirds and sixths, and usually he included all components of the triad in chords.

England

No complete manuscripts of English music from the middle and late fifteenth century have survived. Important extant partial manuscripts include MS Egerton 3307 and the Eton College Choirbook. The latter holds polyphonic votive antiphons honoring the Virgin Mary, and Magnificat settings. The Egerton manuscript has two sections, the first comprising a repertory of Sarum liturgical music, principally for Holy Week, and the second containing carols. In the liturgical section are two three-voice polyphonic settings of Passion music (St. Matthew and St. Luke);

these seem to be the earliest surviving examples of polyphonic settings of the Passion. The music is in score notation. Stylistically, the liturgical settings in the manuscript resemble the antiphons and hymns of Binchois and some early works of Du Fay, thus indicating English influence on their works. But there is some evidence of Burgundian influence on English music, too. The harmonies reflect the English preference for sixth-chords and continental use of *faux bourdon*, but the directive *a faux bourdon* never appears in the Egerton manuscript. In other words, there was a transformation of *faux bourdon* from improvisation to stylistic polyphonic writing.

Among the English composers active in continental Europe were Robert Morton and Walter Frye. Little biographical data is available concerning either of them. Morton (c. 1430–c. 1478) was a priest and served as clerk and chaplain—he is listed as *chappellain angloix* (English chaplain)—at the Burgundian court from 1457 to 1476. Only 8 of his secular works survive; all are for three voices. Two of his songs, *Le souvenir de vous* (The memory of you) and *N'aray je jamais mieulx que j'ay* (I shall never have better than I have), appear in at least 14 European manuscripts and served as bases for works by other composers, including Tinctoris and Desprez.

Walter Frye (fl. c. 1450–1475) worked for almost a decade at Ely Cathedral and c. 1453 went to London as a cantor; he may have been in Burgundy for a time. His Masses, motets, and secular songs circulated widely in continental Europe during c. 1450–80 and survive in several manuscripts copied in Europe. Frye's extant works comprise 3 Masses, the rondeau *Tout a par moy* (Everything has through me), the English ballade *Alas, alas,* 5 motets, and a few secular pieces also attributed to others. The ballade *Alas, alas* exists also as *O sacrum convivium* (O sacred guest), a *contrafactum*. Josquin Desprez based his *Missa Faisans regres* (Having regrets) on this four-note motive from the second section of Frye's rondeau:

Fai - sans   re - gres

Frye's Masses are *Missa Summe Trinitati* (Highly, to the Trinity) and *Missa Nobilis et pulchra* (Noble and beautiful), both for three voices, and *Missa Flos regalis* (Royal flower), for four voices. All are cyclic, with unornamented cantus firmus placed in the tenor. Masses *Summe Trinitati* and *Nobilis et pulchra* are based on Sarum Responsories. Motto beginnings appear consistently, and duos provide contrast; the duo sections exhibit the English characteristic of commencing with a short simultaneous rest. The musical style reflects discant in that superius and tenor are paired to provide the basic framework, while the contratenor supplies harmonic filler. Harmonies are primarily consonant, with many complete triads; most of the dissonances are suspensions, which are properly resolved. Frye's melodies are often triadic and are characterized also by a figure containing an octave leap after a short rest:

In accordance with English custom, *Missa Summe Trinitati* and *Missa Flos regalis* have no composed Kyries; a troped Kyrie was chanted. However, *Missa Nobilis et pulchra* is provided with a polyphonic setting of the troped *Kyrie (Deus creator)* text; the Kyrie is the longest movement of that Mass.

Three of Frye's motets are without cantus firmus: *Ave Regina* (Hail, Queen); *O florens rosa* (O flowering rose); *Trinitatis dies* (Day of Trinity). The motet *Salve virgo mater* (Hail, Virgin Mother) exhibits parody relationship with *Missa Summe Trinitati*— the motet music parodies the Mass, which is unusual. The first four lines of the motet *Sospitati dedit* (He gave for the welfare...) are set for three voices; thereafter, the lines are set in alternate two- and three-voice sections. In the two-voice sections, the contratenor is silent.

Germany

In Germany, middle-class citizens of the towns were interested in all kinds of music. Instrumental music was accorded a special place, and the *Stadtpfeifer* (town pipers) were professional musicians who had their own guilds, as did the *Meistersinger*. The *Meistergesang* tradition was strong and tended to exclude polyphonic song. However, in the last half of the fifteenth century, the *Tenorlied* was developing among the middle classes as a distinctly German type of polyphonic song with the main melody in the tenor. The *Tenorlied,* a solo song, used the melody of a preexistent *Lied* as "tenor" or *cantus firmus,* with two or three contrapuntal lines accompanying it. The accompaniment parts are more active rhythmically than the solo voice. In manuscripts, only the cantus firmus has the complete text underlaid. The *Tenorlied* soon spread into the courts at Munich and Torgau, and became the principal type of German polyphonic *Lied* between c. 1450 and c. 1550.

Several important German manuscript collections survive, including the *Lochamer Liederbuch* (Locham Songbook, copied 1452–60) and the *Glogauer Liederbuch* (Glogau Songbook, copied c. 1480). The *Glogauer Liederbuch* comprises three paper partbooks, rather than a single manuscript. Partbook notation came into existence c. 1460; the earliest known example of partbook notation is the *Glogauer Liederbuch.* This manuscript holds 294 items. Among them are liturgical music for Mass and Offices, 120 motets, 63 German secular songs, and 59 textless pieces. Fifteen of the latter are instrumental. In the manuscript all items are anonymous; some of the motets are *contrafacta* of French secular songs, and a few of the textless pieces have been identified as French chansons. French composers represented include Busnois, Du Fay, Caron, and Tinctoris.

Bound with the *Lochamer Liederbuch* is a manuscript of Conrad Paumann's *Fundamentum organisandi* (Fundamentals of Organ-playing). Paumann's treatise appears also in another manuscript, the *Buxheimer Orgelbuch* (Buxheim Organ Book, copied c. 1470), which contains a large collection of organ pieces. The instrumental compositions in the *Buxheimer Orgelbuch* are creations of the Paumann school.

Conrad Paumann

Conrad Paumann (c. 1410–1473) was born blind. Despite heavy handicaps, he became Germany's foremost organist and was a lutenist and composer as well. In 1446 he was organist at St. Sebald in Nuremberg and in 1447 was named official town organist there. In 1450 he was appointed court organist to Duke Albrecht III of Bavaria and moved to Munich, where he resided for the remainder of his life. From time to time Paumann visited other courts and performed on various instruments there; he became famous internationally as organist and composer. However, besides the organ method, only one vocal piece by Paumann—a *Tenorlied*—and a few instrumental pieces survive. Presumably, because of his blindness he improvised most of his works rather than dictating them to a scribe. Sebastian Virdung, in *Musica getutscht* (German music, 1511), credited Paumann with the invention of German lute tablature; certainly, lute tablature would have been a dictational aid.

Paumann's extant organ works are three-voice treble-dominated settings of secular cantus firmi, and indicate his knowledge of and ability to compose in the Burgundian style.

---

insight

Music Printing

Throughout the fifteenth century, much of the music was circulated in manuscript copies. It was possible to print music by means of woodblocks, and some was printed that way, but carving the blocks took infinite pains, and the inking had to be done very carefully to avoid fuzzing and blobs at the junctures of notes and stems and at staff intersections. Hollow note heads with a staff line running through them were particularly troublesome. However, woodblock printing survived for several centuries. It was used for the first music printed in America, in the ninth edition of the so-called *Bay Psalm Book* (1698), and for some small books printed in the nineteenth century.

At some time during the 1440s, Johann Gutenberg (c. 1396–1468), who was working in the Mainz River valley, invented the technique of printing from movable type. Using that technique, c. 1450 he printed a book of liturgical texts for use at Constance, and between 1453 and 1455 he printed a copy of the Bible. Until c. 1473 the printing of books containing music was makeshift—usually, the texts were printed and space was left for insertion of the notation and illuminated letters by hand. However, there survive a Constance *Graduale* with text and chant music printed by two typographical impressions somewhere in southern Germany c. 1473 (fig. 9.13), and a *Missale* with text and music printed typographically in red and black ink by Ulrich Hahn in Rome in October 1476. Both books are of excellent quality. Between 1476 and 1500, at least 65 craftsmen were typographically printing liturgical books containing music, the principal centers of such printing being Augsburg, Bamberg, Basle, and Venice. Not until 1500 was a *Missale* with music printed in London. When music was printed typographically, the double impression method was used, i.e., separate printing of text and of notation.

In 1480, mensural music was first printed from type; it consisted of a few lines of notes, properly spaced, but without staff lines. The next extant examples were printed c. 1496 by Michel de Toulouze, in Paris. One of the books is a treatise by Guerson; the other is *L'art et instruction de bien danser* (see p. 168), which contains 18 pages of music. Two pages are in mensural notation; the other pages have music in chantlike notation, with black notes printed on red four-line staves.

Around 1490, Ottaviano dei Petrucci went to Venice to study printing techniques so that he might be able to print polyphonic music from movable type. His endeavors bore fruit early in the sixteenth century (see p. 210). Though he used a triple impression method, Petrucci consistently produced printed music and lute tablatures that were not only accurate but cleanly printed and well spaced.

Figure 9.13 Folio 1r from the Constance *Graduale,* the earliest known typographically printed music, c. 1473. Notation is Germanic style often referred to as *Hufnagelschrift* (horseshoe nail writing). The music, used on the first Sunday of Advent, is the Introit *Ad te levavi animam meam* (Unto Thee do I lift up my soul; Ps. 25:1–3) and the Verse *Vias tuas domine demonstra mihi* (Show me Thy ways, Lord; Ps. 25:4). *(British Library, London.)*

Summary

The work of some fifteenth-century composers may be classified as late Medieval, while that of others was clearly transitional, exhibiting some late-Medieval traits but with features that pointed toward or became characteristic of Renaissance music. Until about mid-century, musical leadership was held by the English, many of whom worked in continental Europe. After Dunstable's death, French composers were the recognized leaders, particularly those who were trained in or who worked in northern France and the Low Countries. The mobility of Franco-Netherlands composers and the fame of the Burgundian court did much to promote an international musical style; Maximilian I's fascination with the music he experienced at Mary of Burgundy's court helped disseminate that style within the Holy Roman Empire. However, English practices had been absorbed, and English influence was apparent in the work of continental composers—in the increased use of thirds and sixths (imperfect consonances), the sixth-chord sound produced by *faux bourdon,* the use of a head motive (motto), the drive to the cadence, the paraphrasing of a cantus firmus, and cyclic settings of the Mass Ordinary. (Probably, the drive to the cadence was influenced equally by concluding melismas in English works and by conductus *caudae.*)

The composition of a cyclic polyphonic Mass—the first large-scale multimovement form in music history—was a challenge accepted by almost all important fifteenth-century composers. Continental composers set all five movements of the Ordinary, whereas English composers normally set only the last four. A majority of the Masses were written for four voices—four-voice writing first became standard in polyphonic settings of the Mass Ordinary. Most polyphonic Mass settings were unified by a cantus firmus, placed in the tenor; both sacred and secular melodies were borrowed for that purpose. By the last third of the century, canon, head motive, and imitation also served as integrative devices; at times, the cantus firmus permeated the other voices.

By c. 1450, the isorhythmic motet had virtually disappeared. The rigid structural basis isorhythm had provided was supplanted by a cantus firmus usually chosen from chant and placed in the tenor voice. The character of the motet gradually changed—usually a single Latin poetic text was set, and most often that text was sacred or was associated with a religious occasion. At times, a motet resembled a Mass movement in miniature; in fact, some motets were parodied in Masses. In both motets and Masses there was an increased tendency towards greater equality of voices.

Burgundian composers wrote motets, Masses, and settings of other liturgical texts but were encouraged to concentrate compositional endeavors on chansons for court entertainment. Most chansons were three-voice cantilena-style polyphony in rondeau, virelai, or bergerette form; the ballade was used infrequently and by c. 1470 had become obsolete. Some chansons were supplied with optional parts for a fourth voice. Tenors of popular chansons provided cantus firmi for Masses and *basse danses.*

The range of most compositions remained within the limitations of Guido's gamut; occasionally a superius extended upwards to g″ and a contratenor bassus descended as low as E. Music was modal; an increased awareness of harmonies and harmonic successions was evident. Sonorities were predominantly consonant, with dissonance carefully controlled. Sixth chords resulted from the application of *faux bourdon* as well as being notated. The drive to the final cadence usually included the seventh degree of the modal scale; chromatic raising of this pitch through the application of *musica ficta* created a "leading tone" tendency. Rarely did the final chord of a piece contain the third, but the last two cadential chords frequently formed a modal harmonic succession comparable with the dominant-to-tonic progression in key tonality.

Instruments were available in wide variety. Instrumentalists provided music for dancing, performed chansons with vocal soloists, and probably doubled vocal lines of motets and Masses, especially on highly festive occasions. Not all churches had organs; some—very few—cathedrals banned instrumental music. In Germanic lands, town musicians performed at the Town Hall regularly and participated in civic ceremonies. Some popular chansons and *Lieder* were arranged for keyboard.

The first music manuscripts in partbook format were copied in Germany c. 1450. At about the same time, Johannes Gutenberg invented a method of printing with movable metal type. By the end of the century, a few books containing music had been printed by multiple impression.

The Renaissance:
Franco-Netherlands Composers

The *Renaissance* (French, rebirth) was an age of innovation and invention, an era that witnessed expansion through sea and land explorations and through astronomical, medical, and other scientific discoveries. The period was colored by *humanism,* which placed a high value on the individual. Many authors, artists, and scholars evidenced great interest in the classicism of ancient Greece and Rome. Artists drew on those ancient cultures for subject matter and patterned their works after classical models; scholars were interested in Greek and Roman literature. Both secular and religious topics provided themes for creative endeavors in all the arts.

A spirit of optimism prevailed. The attitude prevailed that it was the best of times, and that the quality of the masterworks being produced would never be surpassed. In a sense, that was true. The Renaissance in art and literature began in the fourteenth century with the frescoes of Giotto and the poetry of Petrarch. Over the next two hundred years, many persons created masterpieces, including visual artists Sandro Botticelli, Michelangelo Buonarotti, Benvenuto Cellini, Raphael Sanzio, and Leonardo da Vinci; authors Dante Alighieri, Giovanni Boccaccio, Baldassare Castiglione, Desiderius Erasmus, Niccolò Machiavelli, Thomas More, and William Shakespeare; and composers Johannes Ockeghem, Jacob Obrecht, Josquin Desprez, Claudio Monteverdi, and Giovanni Pierluigi da Palestrina.

Figure 10.1 The head of Michelangelo's statue of David has been used as basis for depicting the many interests that filled the mind of the Renaissance man. *(Mainliner, Cover, July 1977.)*

During the Renaissance it was common for a person to evidence interest and talent in many arts and sciences, not in just one (fig. 10.1). Many artists were sculptors and/or architects as well as painters;

The Renaissance: Diffusion of Franco-Netherlands Polyphonic Style

1400	1425	1450	1475	1500	1525	1550	1575

Hundred Years' War - - - - - - - - - - 1453

- - - - - - Greek treatises available in W. Europe - - - - - - - -
Mei located Greek hymns c. 1564

1501 Petrucci: *Odhecaton*

1547 Loris: *Dodecachordon*

1504 Michelangelo: *David*

1511 Raphael: *School of Athens*

1514 Machiavelli: *The Prince*

1516 More: *Utopia*

Diffusion of Franco-Netherlands polyphonic style - Rise of Venetian School - - - - -

c. 1410 - - - - - - - - - - - - Johannes Ockeghem - - - - - - - - - - - 1497

c. 1450 - - - - - - Jacob Obrecht - - - - - 1505

c. 1440 - - - - - - - - - - - Josquin Desprez - - - - - - - - - - 1521

c. 1450 - - - - - - - - Heinrich Isaac - - - - - - - - 1517

c. 1459 - - - - - - - - - - Jean Mouton - - - - - - - - - - 1522

c. 1460 - - - - - - Pierre de La Rue - - - - - 1518

c. 1490 - - - - - - - - - - Adrian Willaert - - - - - - - - - - c. 1562

c. 1495 - - - - - - - - Nicolas Gombert - - - - - - c. 1560

c. 1515 - - - - - Jacob Clement - - - - - c. 1556

c. 1465 - - - - - - - - - Pedro de Escobar - - - - - - - - - - c. 1536

c. 1470 - - - - - - - - F. de Peñalosa - - - - - - - - 1528

c. 1500 - - Cristóbal de Morales - - 1553

---

a number of musicians wrote the texts for their compositions. Leonardo da Vinci was not unusual in being poet, musician, inventor, and scientist, as well as master of several visual arts. Renaissance authors voiced clear admiration for the talents of their contemporaries. Boccaccio wrote in *Decameron* that Giotto had brought art out of the shadows; Villani had high regard for Dante's poetry; and Tinctoris believed that no music written more than 40 years before his own time was worth hearing. To Heinrich Loris, Desprez was the greatest of all composers. According to Castiglione, in *Il Libro del cortegiano* (The Book of the courtier; written 1508–16), a courtier required a well-rounded set of musical accomplishments: the ability to sing, to read and understand music notation, and to play diverse instruments; though the ability to sing polyphony was good, to be able to sing solos with lute accompaniment was much better.

In music history, the era known as the Renaissance is generally considered to encompass the years from c. 1450 to c. 1600. Where music was concerned, there was no true rebirth or literal revival of ancient Greek and Roman classicism, for musicians and composers had no ancient music to use as models. It was not until c. 1564 that Girolamo Mei (1519–94) found in the library of Ranuccio Farnese the three Greek hymns attributed to Mesomedes and sent them to Vincenzo Galilei (c. 1525–91), who published them in 1581.

Greek treatises and philosophic writings had been virtually inaccessible to Europeans for centuries, though they were known to Byzantine scholars and had been translated into Arabic. When Turkish invaders captured Constantinople in 1453, and the Eastern half of the Holy Roman Empire collapsed, many of the scholars who fled Byzantium sought refuge in Italy. Among the valuable possessions they brought with them were manuscript copies of treatises—the writings of Plato, Aristotle, Aristoxenus, and ancient authors—in Greek and in Arabic translations from Greek. In Italy these writings were translated into Latin and most of them were available to Europeans by c. 1500. Mei, who worked at the Vatican, read the Greek plays and prepared editions of some of them, thoroughly studied the writings of Greek philosophers and theorists, and in his *De modis* (written 1567–73) comprehensively discussed the principles of Greek music theory, music education, and the doctrine of *ethos*. Mei's work was of fundamental importance in the development of monody and early opera in Florence during the last decades of the sixteenth century.

Heinrich Loris investigated Greek *tonoi* and medieval modes, then wrote *Dodecachordon* (1547), in which he recognized 12 modes—the 8 medieval modes plus Aeolian and Ionian and their related plagal modes. The Aeolian and Ionian correspond, respectively, to the modern A minor and C major scales. (Loris, who was born in the canton of Glarus, in modern Switzerland, is known also as Glareanus.)

Johannes Gutenberg's invention of printing from movable metal type in the 1440s, and Petrucci's adaptation of that process to the printing of polyphonic music (1501), not only made the preservation of music more practical but made notated music more accessible. Some printers issued editions in lots of 500, 1000, or more copies; the fact that many volumes were reprinted indicates that the music was salable. Both secular and sacred music were printed. The fact that more music survives from the Renaissance than from previous eras may not indicate that more music was composed but, rather, that more copies were available and that more secular music was preserved.

The major composers of the early Renaissance devoted their energies to writing Masses, motets, and chansons, with the amount of sacred music produced considerably outweighing that of secular. By the end of the fifteenth century, it had become customary, in many churches with proficient choirs, to sing the five movements of the Ordinary of the Mass in polyphony instead of chant. Most major composers wrote at least one unified Mass cycle; many composers wrote a dozen

or even more. During the sixteenth century, the production of motets increased considerably. Also, there was growing interest in the composition of secular songs reflecting regional or national interests and customs; the texts of such songs were, of course, in the vernacular.

Some three-voice, treble-dominated polyphony was still being produced, but the majority of the music composed during the Renaissance was written in from four to six polyphonic lines of generally equal importance, for voices homogeneous in timbre. The presentation of musical phrases in imitative counterpoint shared by all voice parts contributed to a feeling of linear equivalence, especially in those instances where a paraphrased cantus firmus was entrusted to the superius, or a bassus clearly defined the modal harmonies. Though the tonality is modal, and pitch and chord successions were determined by contrapuntal rules governing linear melodic movement and harmonic consonance among the lines, often the modal chords produced resemble triads or first-inversion triads of key tonality.

Only a small minority of Renaissance vocal music is polytextual. Composers became increasingly aware of the importance of setting texts so that listeners could clearly understand the words and comprehend their meaning. A single text set imitatively was more comprehensible than multiple texts set homorhythmically. Even more comprehensible was a homorhythmic syllabic setting of a single text, all voices singing the same syllable at the same time. Such homorhythmic syllabic writing is termed **familiar-style counterpoint.** Composers used it to emphasize certain portions of a text and also to provide contrast within a movement or section of a work. Josquin Desprez was especially careful to set words in accordance with correct declamation. Not only were composers concerned with textual clarity, they became increasingly interested in word (or text) painting.

In compositions characterized by free-flowing imitative counterpoint, composers wrote homorhythmic passages (pseudo-chordal linear counterpoint) for contrast or to emphasize certain portions of the text. Some secular songs are almost entirely homorhythmic. Instrumental pieces intended for dancing have recognizable rhythmic patterns that are strongly marked; other instrumental works were written in rhythms designed to sound improvisatory.

The total vocal range encompassed was gradually expanded beyond Guido's gamut, only slightly at the top, but considerably at the bottom where a true bass range was produced. By c. 1500, the total range extended from BB♭ to g″.

Compositions were notated in the old mensural symbols, but the tempo had accelerated to the extent that the minim was now the unit of the beat. The notated music appears to be for unaccompanied voices, and some of the sacred music may have been performed in that manner. It is highly probable, however, that in performance instruments may have supported or substituted for one or more of the voice parts. Any chromatic alterations not notated but deemed necessary were made by the performers through the application of *musica ficta,* rules for which were printed in many theoretical treatises. For the most part, these regulations concern adjustments to be made to ensure the proper size of melodic and harmonic intervals. For example, if a third is included in the final chord of a composition, that third must be major—a rule that often produces the type of concluding chord modern theorists term *Picardian.*

The prevailing style of music internationally during the early Renaissance was that of the Franco-Netherlands composers, many of whom were employed in important secular and religious courts throughout Europe. Acknowledged masters of that style were Johannes Ockeghem, Jacob Obrecht, and Josquin Desprez.

Compositions by early Renaissance conservative composers are characterized by nonimitative (free) linear counterpoint with overlapping phrases and without internal cadences to interrupt the polyphonic flow; final cadences follow the forms favored by Du Fay and his contemporaries. The work of Johannes Ockeghem may be considered representative of the conservative early Renaissance composers. Progressive composers, such as Jacob Obrecht and Josquin Desprez, consistently used imitative counterpoint structured in **points of imitation,** and they used new cadential patterns that forecast the authentic and plagal cadences of key tonality and frequently included the third in the final chord of a work. The term point of imitation denotes a portion of a polyphonic

Example 10.1 Measures 1–18 of Josquin's four-voice motet *Ave Maria* show the first two phrases (and the beginning of the third) each set as a point of imitation. *(From* Josquin Desprez: Werken, *edited by A. Smijers, et al., 1921.)*

composition in which a single musical subject, used to set a phrase (sometimes less) of text, is treated imitatively. The beginning of one point of imitation overlaps the conclusion of another, so that, in analysis, a diagonal rather than a vertical aspect of the composition becomes apparent (ex. 10.1).

Johannes Ockeghem

It is generally presumed that Johannes Ockeghem (c. 1410–1497) spent his early life in East Flanders. For a year (24 June 1443 to 24 June 1444), he was a singer at the Cathedral of Notre Dame in Antwerp; from 1446 until c. 1450 he was a member of the chapel of Charles, Duke of Bourbon, at Moulins. From 1451 until his death, Ockeghem served as singer, composer, first chaplain, and ultimately (from 1465) *maître de chapelle* to the kings of France: Charles VII (r. 1422–61), Louis XI (r. 1461–83), and Charles VIII (r. 1483–98). Records indicate that Ockeghem was not a priest when he joined the royal chapel of Charles VII.

The king of France was nominal abbot of St. Martin de Tours monastery, and in 1459 Charles VII appointed Ockeghem treasurer of that abbey, an office the composer held until his death. Being treasurer of St. Martin's was one of the most lucrative and responsible positions in the country. The treasurer was charged with guarding the jewels, ornaments, and relics of the church, and the important letters, treaties, and maps of France, as well as protecting the sepulchre of St. Martin; no doubt Ockeghem had some

Figure 10.2 On these manuscript pages of Ockeghem's *Missa Fors seulement* Kyrie, the modern bass clef symbol appears at the beginning of the last staff on the left-hand page but the Gamma clef sign was used on the first staff of that Bassus part in order to keep the notation on the staff. MS Chigi C.VIII.234. *(Biblioteca Vaticana, Rome.)*

responsibility for music at the abbey, too. Religious ceremonies at St. Martin's were magnificent—at times their splendor rivaled those at Rome. Documents at Bibliothèque nationale (Paris) record expenditures in 1465 for a long robe of scarlet with grey fur so that Ockeghem would be better attired for Services there (colorplate 7).

Ockeghem enjoyed other benefices, also: a canonicate at Notre Dame Cathedral, Paris (1463–70) and a chaplaincy at St. Benoît. In addition to journeys made as part of the king's retinue, he traveled within France on ecclesiastical business and at least once was sent on a royal diplomatic mission to Spain. He visited Cambrai several times and enjoyed Du Fay's hospitality while there.

Ockeghem was widely known and highly respected as a person as well as a composer and musician. His death was lamented by many distinguished poets and composers. Among these were Guillaume Crétin, who wrote a long *Déploration* (Lament); Erasmus, whose Latin dirge, *Joanni Okego, Musico Summo* (To Johannes Ockeghem, Greatest Musician), was set to music by Johannes Lupi; and Jean Molinet, who wrote several epitaphs, including *Nymphes du boys* (Wood nymphs) for which Josquin Desprez composed music. In 1476 Tinctoris considered Ockeghem the leading composer at that time. Other authors commented upon Ockeghem's contrapuntal achievements and included excerpts from his compositions in their treatises; they wrote nothing concerning the musicality of his works. For centuries Ockeghem was remembered primarily for his contrapuntal mastery and ingenuity rather than for the high artistic quality of his music. Only in the twentieth century has he been accorded acclaim on both counts.

The most important manuscript source of Ockeghem's Masses is Chigi Codex C.VIII.234 at Biblioteca apostolica vaticana, Rome. This is a lavish manuscript, beautifully illuminated, and bound in red velvet. Its 289 large folios contain 40 compositions of sacred music notated in choirbook format; 15 of those pieces were composed by Ockeghem. His Masses occupy the first part of the manuscript; several of the Kyries are decorated with miniatures. The floral border and miniature on the first folio of *Missa Ecce ancilla Domini* (Mass Behold the handmaid of the Lord) closely resemble the work of the celebrated Netherlands illuminator known only as "The Master of Mary of Burgundy" (fl. 1470–90), whose artwork adorns Books of Hours created for Mary, Maximilian I, and their son Philip. The music in Chigi Codex was meticulously copied on fine parchment in the white notation (black-outlined hollow notes) then in use (colorplate 14). Although most of the clef signs are in medieval shapes, occasionally the scribe used the modern bass clef sign (𝄢) in Ockeghem's Masses (fig. 10.2).

Ockeghem's surviving works comprise 10 complete Masses (2 for three voices, 8 for four voices); several Mass movements and incomplete Masses; a Requiem Mass; 9 motets; the Lament for Binchois; 21 chansons; and arrangements of 2 chansons (of Bedyngham and Cornago). To arrange Ockeghem's works in chronological order is impossible; he dated none of his works, and only one piece—the Lament—can be associated with a particular event.

Secular Music

Ockeghem's chansons, like those of Du Fay and Binchois, are three-voice, treble-dominated polyphony but with the range expanded downward; thus, there was less necessity for voice crossing. Occasionally, imitation was used. In most of the chansons, only the superius was supplied with text. Undoubtedly, these songs were performed as vocal solos with instrumental accompaniment.

The chansons *Ma bouche rit* (My mouth laughs) and *Ma maistresse* (My mistress) were popular favorites. Both are virelais. *Ma bouche rit* is in duple meter throughout; in *Ma maistresse* the a section of the music is in triple meter and the b section in duple. In both chansons, the only simultaneous cadences occur at the ends of sections.

Prenez sur moi vostre exemple (Clothe me with your example) was a favorite of Isabella d'Este, who had it worked in marquetry in her study in the palace at Mantua. Marquetry is decorative inlaid work of wood and other materials. In the Renaissance, marquetry was frequently used on walls and in corners of rooms to create an illusion of cabinetry and shelving (fig. 10.3). For *Prenez sur moi* Ockeghem notated a single melodic line that, when performed in accordance with directions, generates a three-voice canon at the fourth above. Theorists cited this work under the title *Fuga trium vocum in epidiatessaron* (Canon at the fourth above, for three voices). The piece is a **catholicon.** The word catholicon means "universal"; in music, a catholicon is a composition that can be sung in more than one mode. (DWMA62.)

Sacred Music

As was the case with many Renaissance composers, Ockeghem's style of writing secular music differed in several respects from that used for his sacred works.

Figure 10.3 Marquetry creates the illusion of a wall cabinet containing a spinet. In reality, neither cabinet nor instrument exist. *(Genoa, San Lorenzo. Photo Cresta.)*

It is in the sacred works, particularly the Masses, that his contrapuntal genius, his ingenuity, and the development of his style may be seen to best advantage. Ockeghem's music is modally diatonic—chromatic alteration seldom appears. Melodies were constructed in long, flowing polyphonic lines, in long-breathed phrases with seemingly infrequent cadences. Cadences within a movement were handled so skillfully that they never interfere with the onward flow of the linear polyphony. Downward expansion of the gamut produced a true bass range; in five-voice compositions the two lowest parts were labeled *Bassus*. It was not unusual for Ockeghem to include C in those vocal lines. Occasionally, the two *Bassus* lines were written in the same range, and some voice crossing occurred (ex. 10.2). When a bass part remained in a very low register for some time, Ockeghem used the Gamma clef to keep the notation on the staff (see fig. 10.2).

In Ockeghem's writing, all voice parts are very nearly equivalent. No voice part can be singled out as being the sole determinant of both phrase structure and harmonization; no vocal line can be eliminated without impairing the whole. It is evident that, although Ockeghem was writing linear polyphony, he conceived all voices simultaneously. He was keenly aware of vocal timbres and used them effectively. Frequently, he enhanced one pitch in a chord by doubling it and blending timbres. He achieved contrast by (a) pairing voices and setting one pair against another; (b) writing sections of a movement as duos or

Example 10.2 (*a*) Total range encompassed and (*b*) ranges of voice parts in Ockeghem's music.

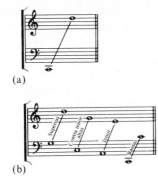

(a)

(b)

Example 10.3 In *Agnus Dei* III of Ockeghem's *Missa Caput*, the drive to the final cadence commences as the cantus firmus is concluding; note the increased use of smaller note values, dotted rhythms, and the abundance of tritones and seventh scale steps. *Musica ficta* would have been applied to only the penultimate pitches in superius and contratenor altus—pitches pointed up by suspensions—to create a double leading-tone cadence. *(From Missae Caput, edited by Alejandro Enrique Planchart. © 1964 Yale University, New Haven, CT. Reprinted by permission.)*

trios and other sections with the full complement of voices, and (c) writing homorhythmic, chordal-sounding passages (familiar-style counterpoint) to emphasize certain portions of a text, a technique Machaut used in his Mass. Occasionally, Ockeghem added extra notes to the final chord of a movement by writing *divisi* parts in some voices; usually these *divisi* parts doubled or sounded the octave of pitches sung by other voices. At times, the final chord contained the third.

Ockeghem's treatment of melody and harmony is sometimes unpredictable but always purposeful. He seemed to delight in doing the unexpected, but he did not violate rules or disregard accepted procedures. In an era when imitation was being used increasingly, he preferred to use canon, yet he never allowed the stricter device to impede the spontaneity or the melodic flow of the music. He did not shun imitation but used it incidentally.

A drive to the cadence is an important feature of Ockeghem's compositions. In cadential approaches, the rhythmic pace of all voices was accelerated, and dotted rhythms were included. Tension was increased by the presence of the tritone, and the seventh degree of the modal scale was used prominently. Probably, in performance, tritones in a cadential drive were not chromatically altered, and *musica ficta* was applied only where it would create a "leading tone" effect—just before the final chord (ex. 10.3).

Masses

Ockeghem based most of his Masses on melodies borrowed from secular songs or from chant, but the cantus firmus melodies are not always easily identified because he usually altered and adapted the original

source material to serve the purposes of his composition. Moreover, his treatment of the cantus firmus varied considerably in each of those Masses. He did not always adhere strictly to the cantus firmus melody, nor did he always place that melody in the tenor voice to serve as scaffolding for the composition. Sometimes he (a) used a migrant cantus firmus; (b) changed the order of the phrases of the original melody; (c) placed the cantus firmus in two voices at the same time, but without using canon or imitation or doubling the melody; (d) simplified the original melody; (e) freely paraphrased the cantus firmus; or (f) concluded a statement of the cantus firmus with newly composed material. For example, in *Missa De plus en plus* (Mass More and more), based on the tenor of Binchois's chanson, the borrowed melody was ornamented and treated freely. In *Missa Ecce ancilla Domini,* whose cantus firmus was derived from the second half of the antiphon *Missus est Gabrieli* (Gabriel was sent), Ockeghem freely paraphrased the borrowed melody, sometimes changed the order of the chant's musical phrases, and in the Credo transposed the melody a fifth lower. But, in *Missa L'Homme armé* the secular melody is clearly recognizable; it was placed in the tenor and handled in accordance with traditional cantus firmus technique.

Ockeghem seems to have patterned his *Missa Caput* after that attributed to Du Fay. The chant melisma that provides the cantus firmus is not disguised; however, Ockeghem placed the cantus firmus in the lowest voice part rather than within the polyphonic texture—perhaps he was making symbolic reference to the word "feet" in the text of the Sarum chant from which the melisma was borrowed. All movements but the Kyrie commence with the two upper voices presenting a paired head motive. Another unifying device is Ockeghem's systematic conclusion of each movement (and some sections within movements)—the cantus firmus melody ends while the drive to the cadence is beginning or while it is still gaining momentum; the lowest voice is given an extended rest, then reenters with one or two statements of the final of the mode (d) at the very end of the cadence. The conclusion of the Agnus Dei of *Missa Caput* is given in example 10.3. Note the increased use of smaller note values, the frequent occurrences of the tritone, the dotted rhythms, the extended rest following conclusion of the statement of the cantus firmus, and the single utterance of the mode final by the lowest voice in the last chord. In setting the Credo of *Missa Caput,* Ockeghem followed the English custom of telescoping some portions of the text.

Missa Au travail suis (Mass With labor I am . . .) has for cantus firmus the tenor of the chanson *Au travail suis,* variously attributed to Barbingant and Ockeghem. The cantus firmus, slightly altered, serves as the tenor of the Kyrie of the Mass; in the other movements only the first ten notes of the borrowed melody appear in the tenor, and newly composed material completes the line. The head of the cantus firmus

is used imitatively at the commencement of all movements, but the distance between imitative entries and the number of voice parts involved varies. Ockeghem segmented the borrowed melody, and at times a segment migrates from voice to voice, e.g., in the *Et incarnatus est* section of the Credo.

Some of Ockeghem's Masses are unified by means other than cantus firmus, e.g., *Missa Quinti toni* (Mass in Mode V), a three-voice Mass written in the fifth mode. *Missa Mi-mi* has two unifying features, one of which probably explains its name. The movements are unified by a head motive—the pitches e-A-A-e or e-A-e—stated in the Bass voice (ex. 10.4). According to Guido's gamut and hexachord system, the pitch e is labeled *e-la-mi*—it bears the syllable *mi* in the natural hexachord—but the pitch A, which is in the hard hexachord, is given *only* the syllable *re.* Therefore, the e-A descending fifth in the head motive of the Mass represents the syllables *mi-re* and does not explain the title. The other unifying feature of the Mass does. In every movement each of the four voices commences on a pitch that may be sung to the syllable *mi,* but, because two of the four voice parts commence on the same pitch, only three different *mi* pitches are sounded in each opening chord (see ex. 10.4). Also, all five movements end on *mi* chords. *Mi* pitches seem to be featured in the Mass; e.g., notice especially the contratenor at the beginning of the Gloria.

The Masses for which Ockeghem was most acclaimed by succeeding generations are *Missa Cuiusvis toni* (Mass in any mode; fig. 10.4) and *Missa Prolationum* (Prolation Mass). Both compositions have structural features that demonstrate Ockeghem's contrapuntal genius; moreover, both Masses are excellent music. *Missa Cuiusvis toni* (Mass in any mode) is an extended catholicon that, with appropriate alteration by the performers, may be sung in any of the four authentic modes: I, III, V, or VII. The music is notated without clefs; instead, Ockeghem placed the symbol ☰ on each staff in the position of the final of the mode. Singers must supply the clefs appropriate to the desired mode and apply *musica ficta* in the proper places. This Mass could have been used to test the ability of singers to transmutate

Example 10.4 Beginnings of the five movements of Ockeghem's *Missa Mi Mi* (*My My*). Note use of head motive and many "mi" pitches.

Figure 10.4 Kyrie of Ockeghem's *Missa cuiusvis toni. (MS Chigi C.VIII.234, Biblioteca Vaticana, Rome.)*

(transpose) music. *Missa cuiusvis toni* is unified by a head motive that appears frequently within the body of the composition also.

The unification of a Mass by an abstract idea involving a constructional procedure was a new technique. When used by a composer less talented than Ockeghem, such a technique could cause a composition to be mere pedantry. It cannot be stressed too strongly that in Ockeghem's hands techniques enhance rather than detract from the musical artistry. His *Missa Prolationum* is proof of this. The Mass is without cantus firmus and without head motive. It is

Figure 10.5 Credo of Ockeghem's *Missa Prolationum*. The aligned clef and mensuration symbols indicate that two voice parts are derived from each notated part. *(MS Chigi C.VIII.234, Biblioteca Vaticana, Rome.)*

unified by the fact that the movements form a cycle of double canons, proceeding from double canon at the unison through double canon at the octave (for Kyrie through Osanna), and concluding with two double canons at the fourth (for Benedictus and Agnus Dei I) and two at the fifth (for Agnus Dei II and III). Double canon occurs when two canons are performed simultaneously. *Missa Prolationum* seems to be the earliest composition written as a cycle of canons. Later composers wrote works unified by this principle: Palestrina's *Missa Repleatur os meum* presents a cycle of canons (see p. 257), as does also J. S. Bach's *"Goldberg" Variations* (see p. 412).

The name *Missa Prolationum* derives from Ockeghem's use of the four prolation signs to indicate not only the mensurations of the various voice parts but also the intervals of the canons. For each section of the Mass, only two lines of music were notated. Whenever possible, prolation signs were vertically aligned on the staff to indicate the interval of the canon; when this could not be done, verbal directions were supplied. Sometimes clefs were vertically aligned, too, and for a few sections all of these informational devices were used. In manuscript, one notated part bears the mensuration signs ○ and ℂ; the other part, labeled *Contra,* bears the mensuration signs ⊙ and ℂ (fig. 10.5).

In the canon performed by the upper two voices, both parts use minor prolation, but one voice is in perfect time while the other is in imperfect. Though both voices commence together, one proceeds more slowly than the other, thus producing the canonic imitation. A similar situation occurs in the lower two voices; both use major prolation, but one is in perfect time and lags behind the other, which uses imperfect time (ex. 10.5; DWMA63).

For *Missa Fors seulement,* Ockeghem borrowed the superius and tenor lines of his chanson *Fors seulement l'attente* (Except for waiting). Material from both borrowed voices was used simultaneously but was placed in lower voice parts in the Mass; occasionally, small bits of all of the chanson voices appear (ex. 10.6). This foreshadows true **parody** technique, which involves extensive borrowing from the total substance of a preexistent composition, such as a chanson or motet, as basis for a Mass or Magnificat. Another term for parody Mass is **derived** Mass. In *Missa Fors seulement,* Ockeghem seems to develop the borrowed material—he expanded and recombined portions of the melodies and increased the complexity of the musical fabric as the movements of the Mass proceed. The added (fifth) voice in this Mass is placed between the tenor and the *Bassus* and is also labeled *Bassus.* The range of the lowest voice extends down to C; that of the bass above it reaches down to A.

The *Requiem Mass* composed by Ockeghem is the earliest extant polyphonic setting of the Requiem. Crétin described it in his *Déploration* as being "exquisite and perfect" music. The order of the liturgy in Ockeghem's *Requiem* differs in several respects from that of the modern Requiem, though in the omission of the *Dies irae* Ockeghem's Mass would be in accord with post-Vatican II recommendations. In the fifteenth century, there were no firm regulations as to which chants of the Proper were to be included in the Mass for the Dead; local practices often influenced the Service. In Franco-Netherlands churches, it was customary to use the chant *Si ambulem* (If I walk; Ps. 24/KJV, 23) in place of the Gradual, and Ockeghem observed that custom in his polyphonic setting. In several sections allowance was made for the appropriate plainchant intonation to be sung by the officiating priest; then polyphony was furnished.

Example 10.5 Kyrie I of Ockeghem's *Missa Prolationum* in modern notation, showing double canon created in performance. *(From Johannes Ockeghem, Complete Works, 2d ed, Vol. 2. Copyright © 1947, 1966 American Musicological Society, Philadelphia, PA. Reprinted by permission of the American Musicological Society.)*

Example 10.6 Kyrie I, *Missa Fors seulement*, transcribed from MS Chigi C.VIII.234.

For reasons unknown to us, Ockeghem's setting concludes with the Offertory; the remainder of the Requiem was sung in chant. The tessitura used for the entire Requiem is rather low; the tone color of each movement is distinctive. Contrast was achieved by varying the number of vocal lines—some sections were set for two voices; others, for three or four. There is some text painting.

Motets

Ockeghem's motets follow no standard pattern, though most of them are Marian-related. Five motets are for four voices; three are for five voices. In general, the tessitura used for the motets is low, but *Alma redemptoris mater* (Kind mother of the Redeemer) has an unusually high tessitura. The motets *Intemerata Dei mater* (Undefiled mother of God) and *Ave Maria* (Hail, Mary) were not based on borrowed melodic material but were written in freely composed counterpoint. *Intemerata Dei mater* closely resembles a Mass movement in miniature, with sections written in different mensurations and with duos and trios interspersed with full five-voice sonority. Ockeghem's other motets were based on chant, and the cantus firmus was usually ornamented or paraphrased. In one *Salve regina* the paraphrased chant was placed in the top voice; in the other *Salve regina,* the cantus firmus became a bass melody. The liturgical chant borrowed for *Alma redemptoris mater* (LU,273) was paraphrased and placed in the contratenor altus. Not only did it provide basic support but seems to have generated much of the composition.

Mort, tu as navré—Miserere (Death, you have grieved—Have mercy), the lament for Binchois, is a **song motet,** a work of rather small proportions that combines treble-dominated (cantilena) style with a tenor cantus firmus. Both in its style and its use of two texts, the work is archaic.

Ut heremita solus (Alone, like a hermit) is a long motetlike work that may have been intended for instrumental performance. Its tenor line consists of a series of sustained pitches derived by solving a complicated riddle that is stated in three verbal canons. The other three voices move much more rapidly.

Jacob Obrecht

Jacob Obrecht (c. 1450–1505) was probably born in Bergen op Zoom, in northwest Brabant (now a part of Belgium). Nothing is known concerning his early life, his general education, or his musical training. He became a priest and said his first Mass on 23 April 1480. Between c. 1476 and 1478, he served as *zangmeester* (singing master) at Utrecht, where Erasmus was a choirboy. In 1479, Obrecht became choirmaster for the Corporation of Notre Dame at St. Gertrude in Bergen op Zoom; he remained there five years, then spent a year at Cambrai as singing master to the choirboys. He served less than a year (October 1486 to August 1487) as *succentor* at St. Donatien, in Bruges, before requesting leave to accept the invitation of Duke Ercole I d'Este to visit Ferrara. Obrecht resumed his duties at Bruges a year later. In 1494, he was a chaplain at Notre Dame in Antwerp. For the next several years, he seems to have changed jobs annually, moving from Antwerp to Bergen op Zoom, back to Antwerp, then to Bruges, and finally, in 1500, retiring because of poor health. Except for occasional trips to Antwerp, Obrecht remained in Bergen op Zoom until 1504, when he returned to the ducal court at Ferrara. In Italy he contracted plague and died.

Obrecht was highly respected as a composer and seems to have earned that respect at an early age; in Tinctoris's *Complexus effectuum musices* (written c. 1473–74), Obrecht was included in a list of outstanding composers, along with Dunstable, Du Fay, Ockeghem, Busnois, and Desprez. An invitation to visit the Este court at Ferrara was an honor—Obrecht visited there twice. His work was well known in Italy. At the time of Obrecht's death, Italian poet Gaspari Sardi wrote an epitaph in which he praised the composer as a "most learned musician, an artist second to none." Sardi's use of the word "learned" was appropriate, as will be seen later.

Both manuscripts and printed books from the Renaissance preserve Obrecht's compositions. Petrucci included some of Obrecht's chansons in *Harmonice musices odhecaton A* (One hundred polyphonic pieces, [Volume] A; 1501; fig. 10.6) and *Canti B* (Songs, [Volume] B; 1501); printed some of his motets in *Motetti a cinque, Libro primo* (Five-voice motets,

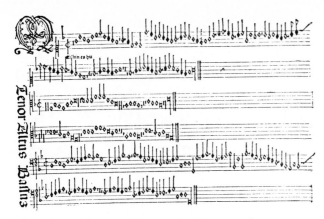

Figure 10.6 Obrecht's *Meskin es hu*, from Petrucci's *Odhecaton. (Source:* Harmonica musices odhecaton A, *published 1501 by Ottaviano Petrucci, Venice, Italy.)*

Book One; 1505); and published *Messe Obreht* [sic] (Obrecht Masses; 1503), a volume comprising five of Obrecht's four-voice Masses (fig. 10.6). The Basle music printer Gregorius Mewes published four of Obrecht's Masses in four partbooks entitled *Concentus harmonici quattuor Missarum peritissimi m[u]sicorum Jacobi Obrecht* (Four-part polyphonic Masses by the most experienced composer Jacob Obrecht); the copy of this publication in the Basle University Library seems to be the only surviving one, and it is the only known source of *Missa Maria zart* (Mass Mary tender). Obrecht's other Masses and his motets may be found in several extant manuscripts in Italian and German libraries.

Obrecht's surviving works include 26 Masses, 26 motets, and 27 chansons. Some of his compositions have been lost, and the attribution of other works to him has been contested. The almost equal number of compositions in each category is deceptive, for some of the motets are quite long, and most of them have two sections; in comparison, the chansons are generally rather short. The preponderance of sacred works is an indication of the interests of early Renaissance composers.

Secular Music

Most of Obrecht's chansons were written for four voices; only six of the pieces are three-voice. Three of those three-voice compositions are textless, as is also a four-voice canon in which three voices are in canon at the unison, and the fourth voice is an augmentation of the melody. Another textless two-voice canon exists, which is the same music as the *Qui cum patre* (To whom with the Father) of *Missa Salve diva parens* (Mass Hail, divine parent). More than half of the chansons are supplied with only an incipit of the text. Two of the chansons have Italian texts; six are supplied with French texts or text incipits; the remainder have Dutch texts or incipits. In Obrecht's time, Italian was being used more frequently for secular songs, thus his use of Dutch for a majority of the secular pieces is most unusual. The absence of text does not always imply that a work was intended for instrumental performance; the piece may have been so well known that the publisher or scribe considered it unnecessary to underlay the text. Because of the absence of texts, specific statements cannot be made concerning formal structure of many of the chansons. However, it appears that Obrecht, like his progressive contemporaries, was abandoning the *formes fixes* for freer forms. He set some texts that previously had been treated by others, e.g., *Fors seulement,* which Ockeghem had set, and *J'ay pris amours.* For both new settings, rondeau form was retained. In general, the texture of Obrecht's four-voice chansons approximates that of his motets; the voices are more nearly equal rather than being treble-dominated, and sometimes phrases commence imitatively. These features may be seen in *T'saat een meskin* (There sat a maiden), a textless piece that seems to be instrumental. Obrecht's secular pieces are colored by melodic sequences and by frequent use of parallel thirds or tenths; both traits are characteristic of the secular works of Busnois, too. Some chansons survive under two titles and in both three- and four-voice versions, as does *Meskin es hu* (You are a maiden; also *Adiu, adiu,* Goodbye, goodbye; DWMA64).

Sacred Music

The characteristics of Obrecht's style are clearly visible in his sacred music. For the most part, melodies are constructed in smooth, singable phrases of moderate length. Obrecht's phrases are gently curved or slightly arched, rather than winding as do Ockeghem's. It is apparent that Obrecht envisioned and composed each of his works as a complete harmonic entity rather than building line upon line. (Composers had at their disposal composing sheets called *cartelle,* which might be used when planning a phrase or a series of harmonies and then erased. A *cartella* has been described as a blank sheet of parchment incised with sets of staff lines. No *cartella* is known to exist in 1988; apparently, all of them were worn out.) Often, the polyphonic lines of Obrecht's pieces blend in modal harmonies that produce what modern theorists term "root-position" chords. Internal cadences are unobtrusive and often are elided; final cadences frequently end with modal chord successions resembling the dominant-tonic chord progressions of key tonality. Imitation is used sparingly; sections of a work may commence with points of imitation, but an entire section or movement is not constructed through continuous use of that technique. None of Obrecht's compositions is integrated by continuous imitation; that further step was left for Desprez to take.

Motets

Fourteen of Obrecht's motets are for four voices; seven are five-voice; six, three-voice; and one, six-voice. *Salve regina misericordiae* (Hail, merciful queen) exists in three- and six-voice versions; the upper three voices of the latter version are designated *puer* (for boys' voices). Many of the motets are large works, constructed in two or more sections. Nearly all of the motets are based on one or more borrowed melodies, with the cantus firmus manipulated in various ways. In many of the motets, the cantus firmus is placed in the tenor, and portions of the borrowed material appear in other voices.

Some motets are polytextual. *Beata es, Maria* (Blessed art thou, Mary), based on the chant of the same name, becomes polytextual in its second section, when the contratenor altus adds melody and text of the Sequence *Ave Maria . . . Virgo serena* (Hail, Mary . . . Serene Virgin). Texts of Ps. 133, vs. 9, and Ps. 23, vs. 4, are incorporated in *Si sumpsero* (If I take [the wings of the morning]). The five-voice *Factor orbis* (Creator of the world) may be considered somewhat like a *quodlibet* both musically and textually since it incorporates texted musical phrases from several antiphons. A *quodlibet* (Latin, whatso-

Figure 10.7 Portion of Obrecht's *Parce, Domine* printed in Glareanus: *Dodecachordon,* 1547.

ever you please) is a composition formed by combining phrases of well-known melodies and/or texts either successively or simultaneously.

Three of the five voices of *Haec Deum coeli* (This is the God of heaven) present the melody of Guido's hymn *Ut queant laxis* in a not-quite-strict canon against the counterpoint of the other two parts.

The short three-voice *Parce, Domine* (Have mercy, Lord) was used by Glareanus in *Dodecachordon* (Twelve-stringed instrument) to illustrate use of Aeolian mode (fig. 10.7; DWMA65). In this motet, the sustained notes of the cantus firmus appear in the tenor in rather short segments separated by rests, in contrast with the flowing, expressive counterpoint of the two upper voices. Several passages of parallel sixths occur. Dissonance was carefully controlled; suspensions were used frequently, especially at cadence points. The final cadence illustrates Obrecht's use of parallel sixths interspersed with suspensions, and the descent of a fifth in the sustained pitches in the tenor create modal harmonies resembling the V–I chord progressions of key tonality (ex. 10.7).

Example 10.7 Conclusion of Obrecht's *Parce, Domine*, transcribed from *Dodecachordon*, pp. 260–61.

Masses

Most of Obrecht's Masses were written for four voices; *Missa De tous biens plaine* and *Missa Fors seulement* are for three, and *Missa Sub tuum praesidium* is cumulative, moving from three to seven voices. All of Obrecht's Masses were based on borrowed melodies. Obrecht did not abandon the idea of using a single borrowed melody as scaffolding, but frequently he used some of the cantus firmus material in more than one voice; often he borrowed from more than one vocal line of a chanson and, on occasion, used some of the quoted material simultaneously. Usually, he placed the main cantus firmus in the tenor. The borrowed material might be paraphrased, segmented, or combined with one or more other borrowed melodies. Schematic manipulation of the cantus firmus is an important feature of Obrecht's Masses. Obrecht was rational in his compositional procedures—he selected the cantus firmus material, planned in detail the treatment of it, and adhered to his plan.

Most of the major fifteenth- and sixteenth-century composers wrote *Caput* and *L'Homme armé* Masses; Obrecht was no exception. He modeled his *Missa L'Homme armé* on that composed by Busnois. Obrecht borrowed Busnois's cantus firmus but changed the mode; at times, Obrecht subjected the melody to augmentation and retrograde inversion, and he gave each voice an opportunity to sing the borrowed melody. Despite Obrecht's manipulations, the direct relationship between his Mass and in its model is apparent—in overall length, similarity of sections and of movements, manner of polyphonic treatment of material, and location of modal transpositions. One way in which Obrecht's *Missa Caput* differs from those composed by his predecessors and contemporaries is that Obrecht relocated the cantus firmus in each movement. It is in the tenor of the Kyrie and Credo, the superius of the Gloria, the contratenor altus of the Sanctus, and the bassus of the Agnus Dei.

Sometimes Obrecht's methods of presenting borrowed material were unusual. In the Credo of *Missa Graecorum* (Greek Mass), the pitches of the cantus firmus were used in the order of their mensural value. First, all the longs were extracted, then all the semibreves, etc.; after being thus segregated, the pitches were used in the order of their appearance in the original melody, but their durational values were augmented.

For some Masses based on nonmensural melodies, Obrecht prepared paraphrased versions of the original chants, then treated the cantus firmus material freely. This method was used in Masses *Beata viscera* (Blessed viscera), *Petrus apostolus* (Apostle Peter), *O quam suavis* (O, how sweet), *Sicut spinam rosam* (As the rose thorn), and *Libenter gloriabor* (I shall willingly glorify).

Obrecht did not write a true parody Mass. He used parody technique often but not as the prime constructional basis for a Mass. For *Missa Rosa playsante* (Mass Pleasant rose), Obrecht borrowed all three voices of the chanson attributed to Caron and used portions of those voices simultaneously in some places of each movement of the Mass. The tenor of the chanson serves as cantus firmus for the Mass.

Obrecht's contrapuntal genius rivaled—perhaps surpassed—that of Ockeghem. The measure of Obrecht's talent becomes apparent through analysis of a group of Masses in which the cantus firmus material is segmented, e.g., in *Missa Maria zart* and *Missa Sub tuum praesidium* (Mass Under Thy protection). These Masses have both an intellectual and an aesthetic basis. Obrecht created them according to a threefold rational schematic: (a) segmented cantus firmus, placed in the tenor, as scaffolding; (b) subsidiary use of borrowed material in those sections of movements where the tenor is silent; and (c) cabalistic numerological symbolism carefully concealed in the mensuration notation and overall plan. Subsidiary use of borrowed material in Masses unified by segmented cantus firmus scaffolding is the direct quotation of an entire vocal line from the original source; this is presented in a section of the Mass not supported by a segment of the cantus firmus. **Cabalistic numerological symbolism** means that through a code of numbers hidden in the musical notation—the kinds of notes, their arrangement, the manner of their subdivision, the number of temporal units used, etc.—the composer made symbolic reference(s) to specific persons, places, things, and/or events in some way associated with the composition. Only through analysis of the music in the original mensural notation can this symbolism be interpreted; it is completely obliterated by transcription into modern notation.

It is evident that Obrecht spent considerable time in mathematical computation before notating the music for a Mass employing a segmented cantus firmus. He precisely computed the number of *taktus* (temporal units) to be used per section, per movement, and per Mass in order to incorporate the desired numerological symbolism. For example, the number of *taktus* Obrecht notated for *Missa Sub tuum praesidium* totals 888, the cabalistic number representing Christ. Obrecht's use of symbolism was not unique. Many scholars were expressing in their work the principles of Pythagorean proportions, the philosophies of Plato, Aristotle, and Boethius, mystic numerology, and *Gematrian* cabalism. (*Gematria* was a branch of cabala that interpreted Scripture by interchanging words whose letters have the same numerical value when added.) This kind of scholarly thinking and planning is inherent in many literary works, in theoretical diagrams and treatises, such as those by Gaffurius, and in works of art, such as Raphael's *School of Athens* (colorplate 15). To analyze in detail Obrecht's compositional procedures is beyond the scope of this writing. A thorough discussion of the principles and philosophies involved, as well as a scientific-mathematical analysis of Obrecht's use of cabalistic symbology, are included in musicologist Van Crevel's editions of *Missa Sub tuum praesidium* and *Missa Maria zart.*

Missa Sub tuum praesidium is made still more complex by its cumulative voicing, which also has numerological significance. The Mass commences with three voices in the Kyrie, adds another voice for each successive movement, and concludes with seven voices in the Agnus Dei. Moreover, several additional Gregorian chants and their texts were borrowed and incorporated in the musical fabric.

Obrecht selected a melody to serve as cantus firmus, segmented it, and organized the segments with a rigidity comparable with that of isorhythm. Usually, a segment was used several times per movement, first appearing in long note values, then with values proportionately reduced. The segments are separated by rests; each segment is stated several times before the next segment is presented. The mensural notation is economical; directives to the singers are given by means of prolation signs placed on several lines of a single staff, repeat signs after the rests at the end of a segment of cantus firmus, and verbal canons (fig. 10.8). When segmenting the borrowed material for cantus firmus use, Obrecht disregarded the original phrasing of the melody.

Typically, Obrecht changed mensuration during the course of the tenor within a Mass section. In *Missa Rosa playsante,* three shifts of mensuration occur in each Agnus Dei—a total of nine shifts in the entire movement. This is part of the concealed numerological plan underlying the structure of the Mass.

In *Missa Si dedero* (Mass If I give up), there are sufficient segments to support all movements of the Mass, but this is not always the case. When all segments of the cantus firmus had been used prior to conclusion of the Mass, Obrecht presented the borrowed melody in a subsidiary manner in the remaining section(s) of the Mass. For example, in *Missa Malheur me bat* (Mass Misfortune strikes me), based on Ockeghem's chanson, the last segment of the cantus firmus was used in Agnus Dei I. In Agnus Dei II, the complete chanson tenor is stated by the bass, and in Agnus Dei III the top voice presents the entire superius of the chanson. *Missa Si didero* is based on Agricola's three-voice song motet; to base a Mass on preexistent sacred polyphony was rare.

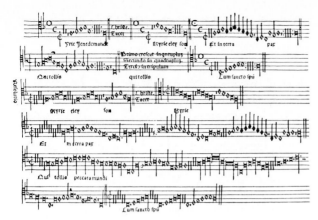

Figure 10.8 Page from Petrucci's printed volume of Obrecht's Masses showing Tenor of Kyrie and Gloria of *Missa Je ne demande*. Petrucci printed the *Resolutio* of the Tenor beneath Obrecht's abbreviated notation.

Josquin Desprez. *(Woodcut from Petrus Opmeer:* Opus chronographicum, *1611.)*

It must be stressed, strongly, that all of these machinations were skillfully concealed in the music. In no way did they detract from the serious function of the Mass, its aesthetic intent and content, or the overall effectiveness and beauty of the music when performed.

Josquin Desprez

It is believed that Josquin Desprez (c. 1440–1521) was born somewhere in northern France, but data concerning his life prior to July 1459 are not available. At that time he was employed as an adult singer at Milan Cathedral, a position he occupied until December 1472. At some time in 1473, he received a benefice from Duke Galeazzo Maria Sforza; Josquin served as singer in that duke's chapel from July 1474 until Galeazzo's assassination in December 1476. Then Josquin's services as singer were transferred to the chapel of Cardinal Ascanio Sforza. Josquin accompanied Ascanio when he went into exile because of family disputes and when he was on diplomatic missions made on behalf of the Pope to settle a conflict between the Pope and the King of Naples. Thus, the Pope was apprised of Josquin's talents, and he entered the papal chapel in 1486. How long he remained there is not known; possibly, he divided his time to spend some months in Ascanio's chapel and some months in the Pope's.

Josquin spent the years 1501–03 in France, where, reportedly, he was foremost among the singers at the court of Louis XII. In April 1503, Josquin was chosen in preference to Isaac to become *maestro da cappella* at the court of Ercole I d'Este at Ferrara, a position he occupied for only one year. No doubt Josquin's decision to leave Ferrara was prompted to some extent by the outbreak of plague there in 1503. Obrecht succeeded him at the Ferrara court, contracted the plague, and perished.

Josquin went directly from Ferrara to Condé-sur-l'Escaut, in Hainaut, where he was one of four canons admitted to the Cathedral of Notre Dame. He remained there for the rest of his life. He bequeathed his real estate to the cathedral as endowment for certain Services in his memory and for the performance of two of his six-voice polyphonic motets (*Pater noster* and *Ave Maria*) in front of his house during processions.

Many literary and musical tributes to Josquin were written at the time of his death. Jheronimus Vinders set the epitaph *O mors inevitabilis* (O, unavoidable death); Nicholas Gombert and Benedictus Appenzeller composed elegies, both setting Avidius's text *Musae Jovis* (Muses of Jove). Also, there survives an anonymous six-voice elegiac motet, *Absolve, quaesumus, Domine* (Absolve, we ask, Lord), which some persons believe was composed by Josquin himself. Heinrich Loris (Glareanus) considered Josquin the greatest composer; Rabelais and Castiglione praised him; and Martin Luther said Josquin was "Master of the notes" whereas other composers were mastered by them. Josquin's influence was felt throughout the sixteenth century. Coclico, who claimed to have been Josquin's pupil, described him as a master teacher who required that his students sing well, with good enunciation; after he was assured of those capabilities, he taught, successively (1) how to embellish melodies, (2) how to set text, and (3) counterpoint.

Many musicologists consider Josquin the greatest of all Renaissance composers. He was the foremost composer of secular music of his time and an acknowledged master of Mass and motet composition—his motets are his finest music. Josquin's works were well known throughout Europe. Several of his compositions were cited as examples in theoretical treatises and were used as models by other composers. While Josquin was still living, Petrucci devoted three volumes solely to his Masses (publ. 1501, 1505, 1514), and he included some of his motets, Mass movements, and secular songs in several books containing each of those specific types of music. Petrucci's books were reprinted several times, and throughout the sixteenth century other printers included some of Josquin's music in their publications. In 1545, Antwerp composer and music publisher Tylman Susato issued *Septiesme livre des chansons* (Seventh book of songs) as a memorial to Josquin; in addition to pieces by Josquin, the book contains some elegies honoring him. Four years later, Attaignant (in Paris) reprinted that volume but replaced the elegies with pieces that he believed Josquin had written.

Divergent features of the compositional styles of Ockeghem and Obrecht are found in the work of Josquin and were used compatibly by him. Josquin's style is related to that of Ockeghem in the extensive use of canon, the paraphrasing or embellishment of borrowed melodies, the drive to the final cadence, and the unification of some multi-sectional or multi-movement works purely by compositional procedures.

Josquin's style is an extension of Obrecht's in the use of imitation, the singable nature of the melodies and their phrasing, the literal quotation of material as cantus firmus, and the rational schematic manipulation of basic material. A feature of Josquin's late motets is **pervading imitation,** a technique the next generation of composers would use often. He wrote a new musical phrase for each phrase of text and treated each phrase as a point of imitation, skillfully overlapping the definitive cadences at the conclusion of each phrase so that melodic flow was uninterrupted. Careful attention to correct declamation is characteristic of all of Josquin's writing.

Josquin's extant works include 18 Masses, 6 independent Mass movements, 95 motets, and 68 secular songs. In addition, there are many compositions whose attribution to Josquin is doubtful or disputed. Some works by lesser-known composers were printed under Josquin's name in the hope that this would make them salable. None of Josquin's compositions are dated, and few contain references to events or persons so that dates can be assigned to them. (He composed a Lament for Ockeghem in 1497 and wrote three special works for Ercole I d'Este.) It is believed that the great majority of works by which Josquin is best known were written after he reached the age of 50. Undoubtedly, many of his early works have been lost.

The distribution of works in a list of Josquin's compositions indicates not only his personal interests and the nature of his employment but also the general trend of musical composition in the late fifteenth and the sixteenth centuries. The overwhelming majority of Josquin's extant compositions are sacred music, and most of those sacred works are motets. His personal interest in Marian music, especially liturgical texts and Services related to the Annunciation, is apparent.

In the early Renaissance, the successful composition of a Mass cycle was the accepted mark of a master composer. To apply some measure of originality to the traditional ways of unifying the five movements presented a decided challenge, for the unvarying text of the Ordinary and the liturgical conventions and objective nature of the Service were in themselves restrictive. Room for experimentation was extremely limited. On the other hand, motet composition offered almost unlimited opportunity for experimentation. There were many texts from which to choose; length was not restricted; few precedents had been set; and, because motets were sung on special occasions, there was greater opportunity for expression and originality. More and more, in the early sixteenth century, composers chose to compose motets, and, as the century progressed, the motet became the vehicle for new ideas and the most progressive form of sacred composition.

Secular Music

Most of Josquin's secular works are chansons, but he wrote a few *frottole*. Regardless of its sacred title, *In te Domine speravi* (In Thee, Lord, I shall hope) is a *frottola* (see p. 215), as is *El grillo è buon cantore* (The cricket is a good singer). Possibly *El grillo* refers to Carlo Grillo, a singer Josquin knew at the Sforza court; however, the chirp of the cricket is imitated in the song. Approximately two-thirds of Josquin's chansons are for three or four voices; the remainder are for five and six. The chansons exhibit a variety of forms. Only a few follow the *formes fixes*; those that do are believed to be early works. *Une musque de Biscaye* and *Bergerette savoyenne,* new settings of borrowed melodies, are ballades. Often, Josquin set long poems strophically; however, some of his songs are quite short and are through-composed. He soon abandoned treble-dominated (cantilena) style in favor of polyphonic settings in which the voices are of equal importance, or nearly so, with all parts meant to be sung. Frequently, in his four-voice settings, the voices are paired and are used imitatively, in dialogue fashion. Canon figures prominently in Josquin's chanson writing; imitation and repetition are characteristic. Double canon occurs in the four-voice chansons *En l'ombre d'un buissonet au matinet* (In the shade of a little bush in the morning) and *Baisez moy* (Kiss me). Canon and imitation intermingle in the five-voice *Faulte d'argent* (Lack of money), which is basically ternary in form. Quite often Josquin based chansons on preexistent material, especially popular tunes, which he elaborated or paraphrased. A few of his chansons are light in texture and in a style that anticipates the one used by Clément Janequin (see p. 229). Some of Josquin's chansons have been supplied with German texts; *Comment peult haver joye* (How can I have joy) became the Lutheran motet *O*

Jesu fili David (Oh, Jesus, son of David), a *contrafactum*. Other chansons survive without texts and may have been written for instruments. One such is the canonic *Vive le roy* (Long live the king).

Sacred Music

Masses

All but two of Josquin's 18 Masses (*De beata Virgine* and *Pange lingua*) were composed before 1505. He based a majority of his Masses on borrowed material: five on chansons by other composers, four on popular songs, four on chant melodies, and one on a motet. Of the remaining four, two are canonic, and two are unified by motives created from solmization syllables. All but one of the Masses were written basically for four voices, though in some sections of some Masses one or two additional voices are generated by canon. *Missa De beata Virgine* commences as a four-voice Mass, but a fifth voice is added in the Credo and is retained for all but one section of the remainder of the Mass; the Agnus Dei II is a duo.

In the composition of Masses, Josquin was at his most conservative. He demonstrated his ability to handle all of the methods used by his predecessors and contemporaries, as well as some advanced procedures. Brief analyses of some of Deprez's Masses reveal the extent to which Du Fay, Ockeghem, and Obrecht influenced his work.

Missa L'Ami Baudechon is unified by a head motive, as well as by its cantus firmus, borrowed from a popular song. Josquin's treatment of the material reflects Du Fay's compositional techniques.

Josquin used canon extensively, as did Ockeghem. *Missa ad fugam* (Canon Mass) is unified by a head motive, canonic technique (usually between superius and tenor), and a melody that, if borrowed, has not been identified. In *Missa Sine nomine* (Unnamed Mass), there is canon at the octave, fifth, fourth, and second. Canon is present in *Missa Hercules Dux Ferrarie* (Mass Hercules Duke of Ferrara), also. The contrived motive unifying this Mass was described by the theorist Zarlino as *soggetto cavato dalle vocali di queste parole* (subject carved from the vowels of the words). From the words "Hercules Dux Ferrarie" Josquin extracted the vowels and translated them into solmization syllables and pitches: *re-ut-re-ut-re-fa-mi-re* became the pitches d-c-d-c-d-f-e-d:

re ut re ut re fa mi re
Her- cu- les dux Fer- ra - ri - e

The motive thus created was treated as cantus firmus, but was used in the superius as well as in the tenor. In Agnus Dei III, the number of vocal lines was increased from four to six; three pairs of voices present melodies in canon.

Josquin based two Masses on the *L'Homme armé* tune. In *Missa L'Homme armé super voces musicales* (Mass The Soldier, on the musical syllables) he carried out a rational plan and achieved variety by schematic manipulation. The cantus firmus is presented successively on each pitch of the natural hexachord, commencing with c in the tenor of the Kyrie and ascending one pitch per movement until the Agnus Dei, where the borrowed melody is stated on g in Agnus Dei I and on a in Agnus Dei III. Despite the transposition, there is modal unity, for all movements end on d; in Agnus Dei III, the modal a concluding the transposed melody becomes the consonant fifth of the final d chord. In addition to straightforward presentation, the secular tune appears in retrograde, in diminution, in augmentation, and with all rests deleted (according to the directive *clama ne cesses,* cry aloud without stopping). When the cantus firmus is stated in small note values, it moves at the same speed as the other voices and blends into the fabric. Sections of the Mass in which the cantus firmus does not appear were organized in other ways. For example, the Benedictus and Agnus Dei II are mensuration canons. In most sections of the Mass, the voice bearing the cantus firmus ends before the conclusion of the section—a procedure used by Ockeghem.

Missa L'Homme armé sexti toni (Mass The Soldier, in sixth mode) was rationally planned and reflects Josquin's knowledge of compositional techniques used by Machaut, Du Fay, Ockeghem, and Obrecht.

The borrowed melody is richly ornamented, but the embellishments differ in some presentations of it. Sometimes the cantus firmus is treated as scaffolding; at other times it blends into the texture. Statement of the cantus firmus is not restricted to the tenor. The *Et resurrexit* section of the Credo is isorhythmic, with both *colores* and *taleae* obvious in the long notes of the superius. In Agnus Dei III, the superius and contratenor altus voices, both *divisi,* sing a complex double canon above double scaffolding in tenor and bass; the sustained notes of the tenor state the b section of the borrowed melody in normal motion as far as the center of the section, then, after a rest, reverses to state its notes retrograde, while the bass has the a section of the secular melody. In the four upper voices, the drive to the final cadence is imitative and features dotted rhythms; the bass sustains modal dominant and modal final pedal tones. The movement concludes on a chord that is a well-balanced F-f-a-c′ triad.

Missa Pange lingua (Mass Sing, tongue) is based on the plainsong hymn of Fortunatus (LU,957; see also p. 105). The chant, slightly embellished, is woven into the contrapuntal fabric. The initial phrase of the chant is treated as a head motive and presented in imitation at the beginning of most sections of the Mass. Only in Agnus Dei III were these notes extended in value, and placed in the superius, as recognizable cantus firmus. Frequently, Josquin included chant melodies in his Masses, particularly in Credos. *Missa De beata Virgine* (Mass Of the Blessed Virgin) is unified liturgically by the inclusion of chants from the appropriate movements of various Gregorian Masses sung for feasts of the Virgin. Appropriate chant melodies were included in the Kyrie, Gloria, and Credo of *Missa Faysant regretz,* whose title and tenor derive from the opening four-note motive of the second part of Frye's chanson *Tout a par moy.*

For *Missa Fortuna desperata,* Josquin borrowed all three voices of the chanson *Fortuna desperata* and began his Mass as a parody of the chanson (ex. 10.9). Portions of the chanson are quoted in block elsewhere in the Mass, and each of the chanson voices serves as cantus firmus in some Mass section. Josquin used parody technique to some extent in *Missa Malheur me bat* and *Missa Mater patris,* also. For the latter, he borrowed Brumel's motet and in most sections of

Example 10.9 (*a*) Opening of Busnois's chanson *Fortuna desperata* compared with opening of (*b*) Kyrie, (*c*) Gloria, and (*d*) Credo of Josquin's *Missa Fortuna desperata*. (*Source:* Josquin Desprez: Werken, edited by A. Smijers, et al., 1921.)

the Mass used two voices from the motet simultaneously. In the Agnus Dei, however, he increased the number of voices to five and included the entire three-voice motet. Josquin may have been the first composer to unify a Mass by means of parody; his *Missa Mater patris* seems to be the earliest Mass unified by parodying a motet.

Missa D'ung aultre amer (Mass To love another), based on the tenor of Ockeghem's chanson, is a *Missa Brevis* (Short Mass). The Sanctus and Agnus Dei use the corresponding chants from Gregorian Mass XVIII. Josquin did not compose a Benedictus for *Missa D'ung aultre amer,* but he indicated that the *Prima Pars* of his motet *Tu solus qui facis mirabilia* (You alone who do miracles) was to substitute for the Benedictus of the Mass. The *Secunda Pars* of that four-voice motet—the part not included in the substitution—quotes from both superius and tenor of Ockeghem's chanson. Substitution of motets for sections of the Mass was common practice at Milan cathedral in the late fifteenth century.

Motets

Josquin's finest compositions are his motets. Here, his choice of text was virtually unrestricted, and he was free to be innovative in his treatment of the musical material. His motets are principally of two types: (1) four-voice settings of Biblical texts, mainly Psalms, and (2) large-scale five- or six-voice cantus firmus type compositions, usually based on melodies borrowed from chant. Many of the motets are Marian-related. In composing motets, he applied the same techniques used in Masses but used paraphrase and points of imitation more frequently.

Josquin seems to have been the first to compose motet-style psalm settings. The four-voice motet *Dominus regnavit* (The Lord shall reign; Ps. 92/ KJV,93) was freely composed. Paired voices were set antiphonally, in keeping with the ancient manner of performing psalms; homorhythmic passages (familiar style counterpoint) were used for emphasis. The double-texted *Ave Redemptoris mater—Ave Regina coelorum* pairs the two upper against the two lower voices, with each pair singing both texts (ex. 10.10). Triple rhythms include short passages in hemiola; perfect and *alla breve* duple rhythms occur simultaneously in paired voices.

Josquin's mastery of pervading imitation is apparent in his late motets. The polyphony is presented in a continuous flow, in singable phrases structured as points of imitation, each point concluding with a clear cadence but the cadencing concealed by the overlapping of the points of imitation. The music is expressive of the text, not only through Josquin's choices of melody and harmony but through his manipulation of both to depict the meaning of the words. For example, a rising scale might be used for "ascend" and a descending scale for "descend"; as "heaven" is higher than "earth" and "hell" is still lower, so might their representative pitches be. Terms commonly used to indicate this kind of musical depiction are **word painting** and **text painting.** One aspect of text painting is *augenmusik* (eye music), music in which the depiction is visible to the singers but not necessarily audible. Josquin's Lament on the death of Ockeghem is an extreme example of *augenmusik*—the piece was written entirely in black notes.

Ave Maria . . . virgo serena (Hail, Mary . . . serene Virgin) exists in two settings: *Discantus secundus* and *tenor secundus* parts were inserted in the

Example 10.10 Josquin's use of duple and triple rhythms in his motet *Ave Redemptoris mater—Ave Regina coelorum*, mm. 127–39. (*Source:* Josquin Desprez: Werken, *edited by A. Smijers, et al., 1921.*)

four-voice motet to form the six-voice version. The structure of the motet was designed to interpret and enhance the text being set. Basically, the music is in duple meter. In the four-voice version (DWMA66), the first four phrases are in points of imitation, with the first two points structured so the voices enter successively from highest to lowest, in canon at the octave or unison. The rhymed couplets of the votive chant (a Sequence) that follows are also set imitatively but as duets or trios interspersed with a point of imitation shared by all four voices. Triple rhythm is used for the two rhymed couplets forming the fourth strophe

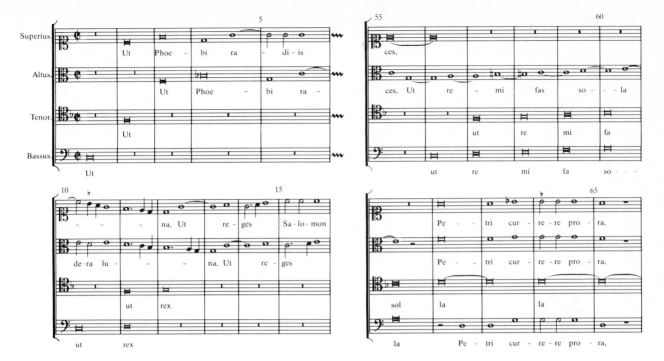

Example 10.11 Excerpts from Josquin's motet *Ut Phoebi radiis* (mm. 1–5, 10–15, 55–65) illustrating use of solmization syllables. Note partial key signature. *(Source:* Josquin Desprez: Werken, *edited by A. Smijers, et al., 1921.)*

of the liturgical text, commencing with the words *Ave vera virginitas* (Hail, true virginity); all four voices participate, the tenor entering one semibreve later than the others and in canon at the interval of a fifth below the superius, which creates some interesting syncopation in the chordal writing. Duple meter resumes with the last notes of this strophe and continues to the end of the motet. After several points of imitation, all voices rest for the space of a full modern measure. Chordal declamation of the line *O Mater Dei, memento mei* (Oh, Mother of God, remember me) concludes with *Amen* sung as a sustained c-c'-g'-c'' chord. All of the main cadences in this motet are on c.

The four-voice *Ave Maria, . . . benedicta tu* (Hail, Mary, . . . blessed art Thou) is based on the *Ave Maria* from a Gregorian votive Mass (LU,1861). Josquin transposed the chant up a fourth, paraphrased it, and treated it imitatively much of the time. The cantus firmus permeates all voices of the motet, but the music is well under way before all four voices sing a phrase as an ensemble. The last phrase is an

Ockeghem-like drive to the cadence, filled with tritones and dotted rhythms and concluding on a g-g-d'-g' chord. Though this work exhibits mature Renaissance style of motet composition, Josquin wrote an ornamented Landini cadence at the words *gratia plena* (full of grace), and he concluded the motet with a chord that lacks the third.

In the five-voice *Salve Regina,* Josquin used the first five notes of the Marian antiphon as a motive, in rigid ostinato scaffolding. Each of the five notes has the value of a breve; each statement of the motive is separated by three-breve rests. The antiphon melody, freely paraphrased, is presented above the ostinato, principally in the top voice.

Both canon and solmization characterize the four-voice motet *Ut Phoebi radiis* (ex. 10.11). Solmization syllables are incorporated in the text as well as represented musically. Bassus and tenor present the natural hexachord in canon, commencing with the single utterance of the syllable *ut* on the pitch c and continuing in scales that expand one note and one syllable

The Renaissance: Franco-Netherlands Composers

at a time, until the complete hexachord has been voiced. Short scalar passages are used sequentially in the upper voices. The tenor sustains g as pedal while bassus completes the *Prima pars* in free counterpoint. In the *Secunda pars* of the motet, descending scales are used, but the procedure is the same.

The lament of David for his son Absalom, *Absalon fili mi* (Absalom, my son; II Sam. 18:33) may have been composed at the time of death of either the son of Pope Alexander VI (1497) or the son of Maximilian I (1506). The tessitura of the motet is low—the bass descends to BBb at the conclusion of the setting of the words *sed descendam in infernum plorans* (but weeping, descend into hell). In setting those words, Josquin wrote in all four voices melodies whose pitches spell out descending triads and also produce chord successions whose harmonies might be analyzed in modern terminology as harmonic progressions along the circle of fifths. The final chord is a hollow-sounding BBb-Bb-f-bb. (DWMA67.)

In *Victimae paschali laudes* Josquin combined the chant melody of the Easter Sequence with the superius of two chansons, Ockeghem's *D'ung aultre amer* and Hayne van Ghizeghem's *De tous bien playne*. The two motets *Ave nobilissima creatura* (Hail, noblest creature) and *Huc me sydereo* (If I lower myself to this degree) have cantus firmi that are identical in pitch and rhythm for the reason that they are based on two musically identical antiphons, *Benedicta tu inter mulieribus* (Blessed art thou among women; LU,1541) and *Plangeant eum quasi unigenitum* (They mourn for him as for an only child; LU,735). Texts of the two motets differ, however; the first concerns the Annunciation, and the latter represents Christ speaking from the cross.

Analysis of Josquin's works reveals that he applied the compositional techniques of all who preceded him—from anonymous thirteenth-century composers to Obrecht—as well as those used by his contemporaries. He dared to try new procedures and succeeded, and in several instances he charted paths other Renaissance composers would travel.

Josquin's Contemporaries

Perhaps the two most illustrious Franco-Netherlands contemporaries of Obrecht and Josquin were Heinrich Isaac and Pierre de La Rue.

Heinrich Isaac

Heinrich Isaac (c. 1450–1517) was born in Flanders; biographical data are not available concerning his activities prior to autumn 1484, when he visited Innsbruck. He was then on his way to Florence where he was employed by Lorenzo de' Medici to sing at the Cathedral, the Baptistry, and St. Annunziata. Isaac was under Lorenzo's patronage until the latter's death in 1492 and was closely associated with the Medici family; he set some of Lorenzo's carnival songs and his religious drama *San Giovanni e San Paolo* (St. John and St. Paul) and probably was music teacher to Lorenzo's children. After the Medici were driven from Florence, and while Savonarola was influential, Isaac had no court position but remained in Italy.

In 1497 he became court composer to Emperor Maximilian I. Since Isaac was hired only as composer, he was not required to remain at court but was free to travel about, even outside the boundaries of the empire; that fact accounts for the music he composed for other courts. For short periods of time he lived in Florence, Innsbruck, and Constance. The Church at Constance commissioned him to compose some liturgical settings appropriate to their Use; in 1508–09 he wrote the cycles of Mass Propers that form the second volume of *Choralis constantinus*. Isaac spent most of his remaining years in Italy, where the emperor had given him some land. In May 1514, Pope Leo X, son of Lorenzo de' Medici (and probably former pupil of Isaac), secured for him a pension with an annuity equivalent to the salary he had earned while in Lorenzo's employ. Though Isaac was no longer active as singer or court composer, occasionally he served Maximilian as diplomat.

In both quantity and quality, Isaac's music compares favorably with that of Josquin. Talent scouts for rulers compared the capabilities of the two composers; surviving records indicate that Isaac sometimes received the more favorable report. Isaac's importance in music history is based equally on the uniformly high quality of his music and the fact that he was the first Franco-Netherlands master to disseminate that style in Germanic lands. He excelled as teacher, also; perhaps his most famous pupil was Ludwig Senfl (c. 1486–1543), outstanding composer of *Lieder* (German art songs).

Three distinct compositional styles, and a mixture of those styles, are apparent in Isaac's works. His chansons, motets, and some of his Masses exhibit traditional Netherlands techniques; the *frottole,* written while he was in Italy, are Italian; settings of Mass Propers, some of the Mass Ordinary cycles, and *Lieder* are German. When Isaac worked in Germanic lands, he adopted the performance practices and liturgical customs of the Germans; in Isaac's hands, technical elements of Franco-Netherlands style infiltrated Germanic forms. His secular pieces exhibit a variety of styles, varying from late Burgundian cantilena type (e.g., *J'ay pris amours*) to a kind of chanson approximating those by Josquin, with four almost-equal voices, and some imitation.

Isaac composed approximately 40 settings of the Mass Ordinary. About half of the Masses are Germanic and are based on appropriate liturgical chants; the other half are in Netherlands style and use as cantus firmi nonrelated chants or secular melodies. Some of the Germanic Masses are **alternatim** settings based on chant Ordinaries; *alternatim* settings have polyphonic sections interspersed with sections in plainchant or with sections to be performed on organ. Most of the Masses were written for four voices; some of the Germanic settings are five- or six-voice. The Mass cycles were unified by various traditional means. In the late fifteenth and early sixteenth centuries, it was customary in Germanic lands to sing composed polyphonic settings of Propers in the Service. Isaac composed approximately 100 cycles of Mass Propers; he is credited with writing the first polyphonic settings of Propers for the entire church year that can be attributed to a single composer. Of the three volumes of liturgical music entitled *Choralis constantinus,* only volume two was composed for the church at Constance; the other two volumes were written for the Habsburg Hofkapelle. All volumes were published posthumously; the third one, left unfinished at the time of Isaac's death, was completed by Ludwig Senfl. At that time, many Germanic Mass settings contained no polyphonic Credo. Isaac composed 13 independent Credos suitable for insertion in that kind of Mass. In addition, he wrote more than 50 motets that are unrelated to his Ordinary or Proper settings. (DWMA68.)

Isaac made significant contributions to the German Tenorlied. In these songs, the principal melody lies in the tenor, with the superius melody being only slightly less significant. The tenor and superius lines of *Isbruck, ich muss dich lassen* (Innsbruck, I must leave thee) are both so melodious that for some time there was a dispute about which voice bore the main melody. This very popular song became the *contrafactum O welt, ich muss dich lassen* (O world, I must leave thee); Isaac's melody, harmonized by J. S. Bach, appears in several twentieth-century hymnals. Isaac handled canon capably and frequently combined two canonic voices with two imitative voices. This may be seen in *Zwischen Berg und tiefem Tal* (Between mountain and deep valley; DWMA69).

Pierre de La Rue

Little information is available concerning the life of Flemish composer Pierre de La Rue (c. 1460–1518) prior to 1482, when he sang tenor at Siena (Italy) Cathedral. Between 1485 and 1516, his career as singer included employment at 's-Hertogenbosch Cathedral (1489–92); in the Burgundian court chapel of Maximilian until Maximilian became emperor in 1493; in the chapel of Philip the Fair, Maximilian's son, until Philip's death in Spain in 1506, and thereafter for Philip's widow; at the Mechelen court of Marguerite of Austria; and in Archduke Karl's private chapel (1514–16). In 1516 La Rue retired.

It is believed that all of La Rue's extant compositions were written during the last 20 years of his life. These works include approximately 30 complete Masses, 2 Kyries, 5 Credos, about 30 motets, around 30 chansons, a cycle of Magnificats, and *Lamentationes Hieremiae* (Lamentations of Jeremiah). The numerous two- and three-voice Lutheran motets attributed to La Rue are *contrafacta*; they are sections of his Masses supplied with new texts.

La Rue's contemporaries regarded his music highly; theorists cited his works in their treatises. Most of his compositions are for four voices; he wrote five five-voice Masses, and a few chansons for three, five, or six voices. Though he spent some years in Italy and in Spain, his music exhibits only Burgundian and Netherlands characteristics. He wrote canon and pervading imitation skillfully and used a variety of techniques to unify Masses. He preferred to use chants rather than secular melodies as cantus firmi for Masses and motets; he liked to write passages for pairs of voices, and he had a predilection for canon. Several of his Masses are completely canonic; e.g., in *Missa O salutaris hostia* (Mass O healing sacrifice) the four vocal lines are created canonically from one melody. La Rue used parody technique infrequently. *Missa Ave sanctissima Maria* (Mass Hail, most holy Mary) is a parody Mass based on a three-voice motet with the same title; in the Mass, three polyphonic lines yield six voice parts, through canon at the fourth above. The melodic flow of La Rue's polyphonic lines is in no way impeded by the rigidity of canonic technique. Some of his chansons are typically Burgundian in style— treble dominated, with only the superius texted, and using one of the *formes fixes*. In other chansons, the polyphonic lines are more nearly equal, with some imitation, and with passages for paired voices. In this type of chanson and in some of the motets, La Rue's writing displays some similarity to Josquin's compositional style.

Jean Mouton

Another excellent composer was Jean Mouton (c. 1459–1522), who served in the royal chapels of Anne of Brittany, Louis XII, and François I of France. Mouton's compositions include 15 Masses, about 20 chansons, and more than 100 motets. In his Masses may be seen clearly the transition from cantus firmus technique to **paraphrase** and **parody.** Paraphrase is the free elaboration of an existing melody, with original and added notes subtly blended to form a seemingly new melody. Parody involves borrowing all lines of another polyphonic composition and supplementing and modifying them to create a new work. During the sixteenth century, parody supplanted the use of a single borrowed melody as cantus firmus and became the favored technique for Mass composition. Mouton was among the first to write full-fledged parody Masses. He was a talented contrapuntist, especially skilled in writing totally canonic compositions, such as the eight-voice motet *Nesciens mater virgo virum* (The Virgin mother knew no man), which is a quadruple canon based on chant. Though Mouton was highly regarded internationally as a composer, he is best known historically as the teacher of Adrian Willaert (see p. 206).

The Next Generation of Franco-Netherlands Composers

The three most important Franco-Netherlands composers in the generation after Josquin were Nicolas Gombert, Jacob Clement, and Adrian Willaert.

Jacob Clement

Jacob Clement (c. 1515–c. 1556) was known after 1545 as Clement non Papa, perhaps for clear identification from Netherlands composer Jacob Papa. Details of Clement's biography are sketchy. He was a presbyter and from March 1544 to June 1545 served as succentor at Bruges Cathedral; from 1545–49, he was choirmaster to Charles V's great general, Philippe de Croy, and for the last three months of 1550 was employed by the Marian Brotherhood in 's-Hertogenbosch. Clement's seven-voice motet, *Ego flos campi* (I am a flower of the field) incorporates symbolisms of that Order. Some of his published works indicate that he worked in Dordrecht, in Ieper, and in Leiden. Six choirbooks used at St. Pieterskerk, Leiden, contain 2 Masses, a Magnificat cycle, and 52 motets by Clement.

Clement was a prolific composer; it is believed his surviving works were created within about 12 years. His extant sacred works include 14 Masses, a four-voice Requiem, 2 four-voice Magnificat cycles, 230 motets, and 159 *Souterliedekens* (little Psalter songs) and *Lofzangen* (praise songs). Thirteen of the Masses are parody settings; no source has been located for the other Mass. One Mass is for six voices, 6 are five-voice, and 7 are four-voice. Clement's surviving secular compositions comprise 79 chansons, 8 Dutch songs, 2 instrumental arrangements of chansons, 8 textless pieces, and 3 secular motets in praise of music. A majority of the secular pieces are four-voice.

Clement's polyphony is, for the most part, note-against-note, with texts set syllabically. Sometimes he wrote short melismas on the penultimate or antepenultimate syllable of a phrase, e.g., *Vox in Rama audita est* (A voice was heard in Rama). His melodies were skillfully shaped, with careful attention paid to phrasing; canon was used sparingly but imitation persistently. The notation contains very few chromatic alterations. Musicologist Edward Lowinsky (1908–1985) advanced the controversial theory that in their motets Netherlands composers relied on a

Example 10.12 Measures 56–63 of Clemens's motet *Vox in Rama* showing how the "secret chromatic art" could create a chain of tritones requiring chromatic alteration through application of *musica ficta* in performance.

"secret chromatic art" whereby numerous requisite unnotated chromatic alterations were supplied in performance through application of rules of *musica ficta*. The theory is complicated but, in short, amounts to this: When a singer chromatically altered a pitch to avoid a tritone, the alteration created another tritone that required alteration, which in its turn created another; this kind of chain reaction filled a motet with unnotated chromaticisms (ex. 10.12).

The *Souterliedekens* and *Lofzangen* were printed by T. Susato in 1556–57 in four volumes, each comprising three partbooks—superius, tenor, bassus (fig. 10.9). These were the first polyphonic settings of the 150 Psalms in the Dutch language. The metrical texts, prepared by Willem van Zuylen van Nijevelt, were first published in Antwerp in 1540, set monophonically to melodies borrowed from all kinds of popular songs. Clement, assisted by Susato, made simple three-voice polyphonic settings of those melodies, with the borrowed tune placed in either the tenor or superius. (Susato's settings are clearly identified.) Each voice is supplied with text, set syllabically. The *Souterliedekens* are strophic and predominantly homorhythmic; they were intended for use in home devotions.

SOVTER LIEDEKENS .I.

Het vierde mufyck boexken mit dry

PARTHIEN, VVAER INNE BEGREPEN
fyn die Ierfte xlı pfalmen van Dauid, Gecomponeert by Iacobus Clement non papa, den Tenor altyt houdende die voife van gemeyne bekende liedekens, Seer luftich om fingen ter eeren Gods, Gedruckt Tantwerpen by Tielman Sufato wonende voer die Nyeuwe waghe Inden Cromhorn.

SVPERIVS.

Cum gratia & priuilegio Re. Ma.
Anno. M. CCCCC. LVI.
Ondertekent. Strick.

(a)

(b)

Figure 10.9 *Souterliedekens,* Volume I: (*a*) title page; (*b*) Psalm I as printed in Superius part book.

Nicolas Gombert

Nicolas Gombert (c. 1495–c. 1560) may have been a pupil of Josquin; he knew Josquin and lamented his death in the motet *Musae Jovis* (Muses of Jove) based on *Circumdederunt me* (They surrounded me), a chant Josquin especially liked. Details of Gombert's early life are lacking. From 1526 to c. 1540, he served Emperor Charles V (r. 1519–56) as singer in the court chapel and as *maître des enfants*; unofficially, he was also court composer. Gombert was a cleric and held benefices at various French and Belgian churches, including Notre Dame de Tournai. Because of an offense at court c. 1540, he was dismissed by the Emperor and sentenced to exile on the high seas. While exiled, Gombert composed some music for the Emperor that secured his pardon; Gombert was granted a benefice and by 1547 was again in Tournai.

Surviving music by Gombert includes 11 Masses, a Magnificat cycle, more than 160 motets, and over 70 chansons. His compositional style is seen at its best in his motets, about 40 of which are Marian-related. The motets are for four, five, or six voices generally equal in importance, although at cadences the bass assumes a harmonic function. When writing for five or six voices, Gombert favored low tessitura. He consistently used pervading points of imitation; thus, clear phrase divisions and simultaneous cadencing were avoided. Frequently, final cadences are characterized by plagal extensions and pedal notes in the superius. Usually, dissonances were carefully prepared and resolved. At times, however, the polyphony seems to require the application of *musica ficta* to the extent that true modality is strained. One of Gombert's best-known motets is *Super flumina Babilonis* (By the waters of Babylon; DWMA70), a setting of Ps. 137, vs. 1–4. Agnus Dei II of the five-voice *Missa Media vita* also exemplifies his style of writing.

Most of Gombert's chansons are similar in texture and style to the Netherlands motets but are more animated. Some chansons are lighter in texture, with syllabic text settings and marked rhythm. Gombert seldom used text painting; however, he composed two very descriptive chansons: *Resveillez vous* (Awaken), containing many bird calls, and *Or escoutez* (Now listen), which depicts the chase of a hare. Descriptive chansons of this type, filled with text painting, often

Adrian Willaert. *(Woodcut from his* Musica nova, *1559.)*

are called program chansons though they are not true program music. Chansons of this kind were quite popular in the early sixteenth century.

Many of Gombert's compositions served as basis for instrumental works by other composers. His consistent use of pervading points of imitation was thus transferred to instrumental composition and became a factor in the evolution of the *ricercar* and basically imitative instrumental forms. (A *ricercar* is the instrumental counterpart of the motet.)

Adrian Willaert

Adrian Willaert (c. 1490–1562) was studying law in Paris when he decided to embark upon a career in music and became a pupil of Jean Mouton, a member of the royal chapel. In 1515, Willaert entered the service of Ippolito I d'Este at Ferrara as singer. When Ippolito became Cardinal and later Archbishop of Esztergom (Hungary), Willaert went along; after Ippolito's death, Alfonso d'Este became Willaert's patron. Willaert's setting of Horace's *Quid non ebrietas* (What is not drunkenness . . . ; c. 1519) is a puzzle quartet and is one of the earliest compositions to modulate, via hexachords, completely around the circle of fifths.

In December 1527, Willaert was appointed *maestro da cappella* at the church of San Marco (St. Mark's), Venice, a position he held until his death. He was the first major Netherlands composer to obtain a permanent position in Venice. Under Willaert's leadership, St. Mark's became the most prestigious chapel in Europe, and Venice became an important center for music. Willaert was influential in the formation of the "Venetian school" of composers and a major figure in the development of polyphonic music in Italy. He maintained high standards, requiring among other things that all singers employed at St. Mark's have thorough contrapuntal training. He was careful to set texts according to correct declamation and insisted that printers underlay texts accurately. Willaert was one of the most important composers and teachers of the sixteenth century. Among his pupils were Cipriano de Rore (who succeeded him as *maestro da cappella* in 1563), Nicolo Vicentino, Andrea Gabrieli, and Gioseffo Zarlino.

As was the case in several Italian churches, St. Mark's had two fine organs, and excellent composers were employed as organists, including Annibale Padovano, Andrea and Giovanni Gabrieli, and Claudio Merulo. The acoustical and physical properties of St. Mark's, which was structured with two opposing choir lofts and with many alcoves and balconies, were conducive to *cori spezzati* ("broken" or divided choirs)— small choral ensembles spatially separated for antiphonal singing and physically positioned for special effects (fig. 10.10). Later in the century, these features were used to full advantage by Giovanni Gabrieli. Antiphonal choral singing of polyphony had been done in Italy for at least a century. The polyphonic settings of hymns and psalms that Willaert composed for use at important liturgical festivals included *salmi spezzati,* settings of psalm verses for antiphonal singing by a divided choir; psalm verses with their responses; and psalm verses without responses. In the *salmi spezzati,* two four-voice choirs sang alternate verses of psalms, then sang the concluding doxology together in eight-voice polyphony.

Willaert was a versatile composer, producing Masses, motets, Magnificats, hymns, settings of psalms, chansons, madrigals, other Italian secular vocal pieces, and three-voice *ricercars.* His sacred music—the major portion of his writing—was published in collections devoted solely to his own works; most of his secular pieces appeared in anthologies containing principally works by other composers. Three collections of motets—two books for four voices and one book for five—were published in 1539; these are among the earliest published collections of motets by a single composer.

Willaert's nine Masses are early works. They are based on motets, principally by Mouton, and display compositional techniques used at the French court chapel where Mouton was employed.

The 173 motets represent some of Willaert's finest work. In them, the polyphony is designed to accommodate and complement the text in every respect. Textual phrases determine musical ones; rests do not interrupt words, phrases, or thoughts, and the rhythm enhances the correct Latin accentuation. Willaert skillfully evaded frequent complete cadences; often he wrote vocal lines as if leading into a complete cadence, then by a turn of phrase continued the polyphony. Complete cadences were deferred until the conclusion of a section. (*Victimae paschali laudes*; DWMA71.)

Five of the motets are for seven voices, 38 for six, 51 for five, 78 for four, and 1 for three. The four-voice motets set a variety of Latin texts; a few are secular, and the sacred ones are both liturgical and quasi-liturgical. One of Willaert's important secular motets is Queen Dido's lament, *Dulces exuviae* (Sweet mementos; from Vergil's *Aeneid,* Book IV, lines 650ff). Contrapuntal techniques used in the four-voice motets include chordal declamation, free imitation, canon, paired voices, and the combination of two lower voices in canon with two upper voices in free counterpoint.

Most of the five-voice motets were written for special occasions or to honor patrons. This type of motet is frequently bitextual; Willaert selected an appropriate cantus firmus and usually retained its text in one voice. Many of the six-voice motets are purely contrapuntal (without cantus firmus). In *Victimae paschali laudes,* the cantus firmus is shared by Sextus

Figure 10.10 Interior of St. Mark's, Venice. View from west where one organ is located in the balcony, looking east to the small chancel with the other organ and space for a small choir. *(© Art Resource.)*

and Quintus voices. Triads are an important feature of the harmony, and the third (major) is usually included in the final chord.

Musica nova (New music; publ. 1559), is a collection of four- to seven-voice motets and serious madrigals that Willaert had written earlier but had not published; it is one of the few sixteenth-century publications to contain both sacred and secular works. The volume contains 25 secular Italian pieces, most of them settings of Petrarch's sonnets, and 33 large motets. *Musica nova* is especially significant because Willaert's sonnet settings, as madrigal cycle, are among the earliest large-scale vocal compositions.

Willaert is counted among the first generation of madrigal composers and was closely associated with Verdelot, who was one of the originators of the madrigal. Several of Verdelot's madrigals were arranged by Willaert for voice and lute. A number of Willaert's Italian secular songs are *villanesche,* light, pastoral, strophic songs with refrain. Willaert's chansons were relatively unknown in France but were circulated widely in Italy, were copied into Italian manuscripts, and were included in collections printed by Antico. Many of the chansons were written for the Ferrara court; Duke Ercole II d'Este's wife was Princess Renée of France.

Spain

From time to time, Ockeghem and other Franco-Netherlands composers visited the Iberian peninsula, and the Franco-Netherlands style of polyphony was known and practiced there. Spain became politically linked with the House of Habsburg when Philip the Handsome, son of Mary of Burgundy and Maximilian, married Juana la Loca, daughter of Isabella and Ferdinand of Spain. Chapels of Spanish Habsburg rulers were led or influenced by Netherlanders until well into the seventeenth century, and throughout the sixteenth century Spain's musical achievement increased. The hundred years from 1559 to 1659 are regarded by the Spanish as the *siglo de oro* (the golden century) of Spanish literature, art, and music. During the first 50 years of that golden century, Spain was the political leader of Europe, under Philip II (r. 1556–98).

Pedro de Escobar (c. 1465–c. 1536), a Portuguese composer and singer, served for several years as *maestro de capilla* of Seville Cathedral and as music teacher to the choirboys. Among Escobar's few surviving compositions are a four-voice Mass, a Requiem, 7 motets, several hymns and antiphons, and 18 secular songs (*villancicos*). His Masses and motets indicate that he was a skilled contrapuntist. One of his finest works is the four-voice motet *Clamabat autem mulier Cananea* (The Canaanite woman was shouting).

Francisco de Peñalosa (c. 1470–1528), a singer in the chapel choir of Ferdinand V and in the Papal choir of Leo X and a canon of Seville Cathedral, was regarded as the finest Spanish composer of his time. The fact that his motet *Sancta Mater, istud agas* (vs. 11 of *Stabat Mater*) was erroneously attributed to Josquin attests his contrapuntal skill and describes his compositional style. Peñalosa's surviving sacred works comprise 7 Masses, 10 motets, 4 hymns, several Magnificat settings, and 10 secular pieces. One of the latter is a six-voice *quodlibet, Por las sierras de Madrid* (In the mountains of Madrid).

Cristóbal de Morales (c. 1500–1553) is considered the first major Spanish composer of early sixteenth-century sacred music. Morales was born at Seville and was fiercely proud of his Sevillian heritage. He knew and possibly studied with both Escobar and Peñalosa at Seville Cathedral. Morales served as *maestro de capilla* at Avila Cathedral (1526–28), worked at Plasencia Cathedral (1529–30), then moved to Italy where, from 1535 to 1545, he sang baritone in the papal choir. His compositional talents were soon recognized, and he was provided with numerous opportunities to compose music for special ecclesiastical and governmental occasions. His six-voice motet *Jubilate Deo omnis terra* (Let all the earth praise God) was composed for the celebration at Nice in June 1538 commemorating the peace treaty signed by Holy Roman Emperor Charles V (r. 1519–1556; r. as King Charles I of Spain 1516–56) and Francis I of France (r. 1515–47). In 1539, Morales's six-voice motet *Gaude et laetare ferrariensis civitas* (Praise and rejoice, citizens of Ferrara) was performed at ceremonies in Ferrara honoring Ippolito II d'Este's elevation to Cardinal. In both of these motets Morales used ostinato construction: throughout each composition one voice reiterates a word or phrase of text set to a figure or phrase of Gregorian chant, while the other five polyphonic voices sing words appropriate to the occasion.

In 1545 Morales returned to Spain where he worked as *maestro de capilla*: at Toledo Cathedral (1545–47); at Marchena, for the Duke of Alva (1548–51); and at Málaga Cathedral (1551–53). The sacred music composed for performance at these Spanish churches appears to be *a cappella*; however, at Toledo Cathedral two organs were used at most Services. Two of Morales's pupils became reputable composers: Francisco Guerrero and Juan Navarro.

Only 5 of Morales's surviving works are secular. Extant are more than 20 Masses, 2 Requiem Masses, 2 Magnificat cycles, over 100 motets, and several Lamentations settings. Morales's style is comparable with that of Josquin and Willaert and evidences a firm foundation in Franco-Netherlands techniques prevalent during the first half of the sixteenth century. Morales set texts expressively, with due regard for correct declamation. His motets were usually based on fragments of liturgical melodies rather than complete chants; frequently, a chant fragment was used as ostinato in one voice of a motet. Important words of a text were set homorhythmically, sometimes in longer note values, for emphasis. Many of Morales's motets are bitextual, with one voice being given a text different from that set for the other voices. An example of this is *Emendemus in melius* (Let us make amends), in which the middle voice (of five) sings *Memento, homo, quia pulvis es* (Remember, man, that you are dust; Genesis 3:19; DWMA72). Compositional techniques used in the Masses include cantus firmus (*Missa L'Homme armé*), canon (*Missa Caça*), ostinato, paraphrase, and parody. Six Masses are based on motets or chansons by Josquin, Févin, Gombert, Mouton, Richefort, and Verdelot; several Masses are Marian-related.

Morales was accorded international reputation. Jacques Moderne of Lyons printed some of Morales's motets in 1539; for the next two decades, music printers throughout Europe included Morales's sacred compositions in their publications, and for almost a century after his death, his works were cited as models in theoretical treatises. Morales composed two books of Masses especially for the papal choir to which he belonged; these books were published in Rome in 1544. In the same year, a manuscript copy of *Missarum liber primus* (First book of Masses) arrived at Puebla Cathedral in Mexico, and in 1553 a printed copy of that book was in use at Cuzco Cathedral in Peru. Morales's music was performed at the memorial services for Charles V that were held at Mexico City Cathedral in 1559. Ecclesiastical appointments to Spanish and Portuguese cathedrals and missions in the New World were the province of the crown, and appointees enjoyed royal patronage. Cathedrals at Mexico City, Puebla, Cuzco, and other principal settlements were modeled after those in Europe. In 1553, Cuzco Cathedral had two organs, situated at opposite sides of the choir. Iberian musicians were appointed to the important positions of chapelmaster and organist(s) in these cathedrals; through these musicians, European sacred polyphony quickly found its way to the New World.

Advances in Printing

Ottaviano dei Petrucci (1466–1539), an Italian printer working in Fossombrone, moved to Venice c. 1490 to study the technique of printing polyphonic music from movable metal type. By 1498 he had devised a workable method, and he obtained from the Venetian government the exclusive privilege of printing lute and organ tablatures and polyphonic music in Venice for a period of 20 years. No other printer published music in Venetian territory until 1520.

The first book of music Petrucci printed under that privilege was issued in May 1501. Although it was entitled *Harmonice musices odhecaton A* (One hundred polyphonic songs, [vol.] A), the volume contained 96 three- and four-voice secular songs by well-known composers, such as A. Agricola, Busnois, Compère, Josquin, and Isaac. *Canti B* (1501) and *Canti C* (1503) continued the series. Petrucci printed by a triple-impression process: the staff lines were printed first, then the notation symbols, and finally, any words. The compositions in *Odhecaton* and its sequels were supplied with text incipits only. All volumes of music issued by Petrucci had oblong shape: ☐. His first three publications (*Odhecaton A, Canti B,* and *Motetti A*) were in choirbook format; commencing with *Josquin Desprez: Misse* (1502), partbook format was used for volumes of Masses and motets.

Petrucci was the first to print tablatures of any kind; in 1507, he issued a book of lute tablatures—original compositions and transcriptions by Francesco Spinacino. Between 1501 and 1509, Petrucci printed the 3 *Odhecaton* books, 5 books of *Motetti,* 16 volumes of Masses, 6 lutebooks, and 11 collections of frottolas (fig. 10.11).

Early in 1511, Petrucci left his Venetian business in charge of a partner and returned to Fossombrone, where he continued to print Masses, motets, and secular songs until c. 1521. Fossombrone was situated within the Papal States; therefore, Petrucci requested and obtained from Pope Leo X a 15-year privilege for printing polyphonic music and organ tablature. He failed to print any keyboard music, however, and in 1516 the Pope revoked that portion of the permit. In that year, Andrea Antico, of Rome, secured a privilege for printing organ tablature and choirbooks. Antico was primarily a woodcarver and engraver and used a different method—woodblock for the music and metal type for the text.

From 1516 to 1519, Petrucci was inactive as a music printer but participated in civic affairs. In 1520, he built a paper mill near Fossombrone and derived his income from operating that business. At the request of the Senate, he returned to Venice in 1536 to

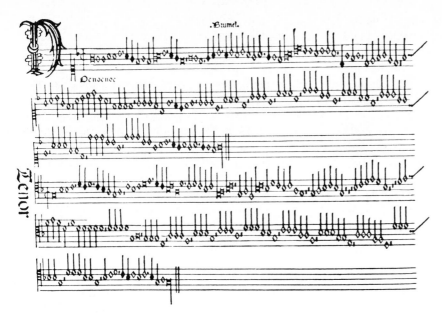

Figure 10.11 Brumel's *Noe,* from Petrucci's *Canti B,* Venice, 1501.

assist in printing Italian and Latin classical texts. That same year, the Senate granted Francesco Marcolini a privilege for printing music from movable metal type.

The 61 editions of music issued by Petrucci were carefully prepared and clearly printed. Many of the books were reprinted several times. The volumes printed in Venice consisted primarily of works by Franco-Netherlanders and Italians; the books printed at Fossombrone contain Italian and French music. Petrucci's publications form the most important body of printed music issued during the first 20 years of the sixteenth century. More importantly, his development of a successful method of printing polyphonic music from movable metal type by multiple impression was a vital factor in the dissemination of polyphonic music during the early sixteenth century.

Summary

The reliance on ancient Greek and Roman models that characterized literature and the visual arts during the Renaissance was not a prime factor in Renaissance musical developments; no examples of ancient Greek and Roman music were discovered until after 1560. However, theoretical and philosophical treatises on ancient Greek music became available in western Europe by c. 1500.

By 1475, Gutenberg's method of printing from movable metal type was being used for books containing monophonic music. The rise of printed music began c. 1500, when Petrucci adapted Gutenberg's method to the printing of polyphonic music.

In the early Renaissance, Ockeghem, Obrecht, Isaac, and Josquin Desprez were the acknowledged masters of the Franco-Netherlands polyphonic style that prevailed internationally. Isaac helped diffuse that style in Germanic lands; it was the foundation of the music of Peñalosa and Morales in Spain, and Iberian musicians transmitted it to Central and South America. The most prestigious positions in European secular and ecclesiastical courts were awarded to Netherlanders until after c. 1555; then the Venetian school, under the leadership of Willaert, began its rise to prominence.

Masses, motets, and chansons were the principal types of compositions. Composers demonstrated their capabilities by writing Mass cycles, but motet texts offered greater opportunity for experimentation and attracted interest increasingly; by the beginning of the sixteenth century the motet was the favored form of sacred music. Both sacred and secular works provided source material for Masses. A melody chosen for use as cantus firmus might be set in the tenor or be migrant; often, borrowed material was embellished and paraphrased. Occasionally, a Mass parodied a chanson. Parody and paraphrase became the leading kinds of Masses written in the sixteenth century. Masses were unified by abstract ideas, numerological symbolism, canon, and other technical devices.

Canon, preferred by Ockeghem, was gradually superseded (but never eradicated) by less rigid imitation; early in the sixteenth century points of imitation began to pervade the musical fabric.

Contrast was achieved within a composition by voice pairings, by setting some phrases homorhythmically, or by writing some sections of a Mass movement as duos or trios. In sacred music, four-voice writing was common; five voices were used frequently; compositions for six or more voices were written occasionally. All vocal lines were equivalent, or nearly so. Vocal range was expanded downward considerably, producing a true bass sound, but was extended upward only slightly. By c. 1500, the vocal range extended from BB♭ to g″.

Much of the secular music was three-voice, treble-dominated polyphony, performed by a soloist with instrumental accompaniment. By the beginning of the sixteenth century, four-voice chansons were being written, with vocal equivalency strengthened by the incorporation of imitative counterpoint.

A drive to the final cadence is an important feature of Masses and motets. Though Renaissance music is modal, the last chord successions of many compositions approximate the dominant-to-tonic progressions of key tonality. Obrecht's frequent use of Aeolian mode and careful attention to modal chord successions often created harmonies closely akin to those of key tonality, especially at final cadences, where chromatic alterations made through application of *musica ficta* produced a leading tone or a Picardian chord. Recodification of the modal system to include Aeolian and Ionian and their plagal counterparts signaled the approach of key tonality.

The Rise of Regional Styles

Franco-Netherlands counterpoint formed a common international musical language during the fifteenth and sixteenth centuries; Franco-Netherlands composers worked in churches and courts throughout Europe. Yet in every region there was some vernacular vocal music with regional characteristics. During the sixteenth century these regional styles achieved greater prominence. The styles were national in the sense that each was representative of a people with common culture and language, but they were not national in the sense that each represented a people united under a single government; e.g., the regions now known as Italy and Germany did not become unified nations until 1871.

Italy

Lauda

Monophonic *laude* continued to be sung throughout the fifteenth century; polyphonic *laude* were composed also. From c. 1480 to 1530 laude were very popular, especially in Florence; they form the largest body of Italian sacred music written c. 1500. These nonliturgical hymns of praise and devotion were intended for performance by laypersons and by semiprofessional *Compagnie de Laudesi* (companies of *lauda* singers) who met regularly for devotional purposes, and especially for singing praises to the Virgin Mary. In some Italian churches and cathedrals, e.g., Florence cathedral c. 1501, professional members of the choir were instructed to sing laude in certain chapels at specific times. Laude were sung by monks

and nuns in monasteries and convents and were included in some religious plays (*rappresentazioni sacre*). Savonarola condemned all polyphonic music except laude; he even wrote some laude texts.

Most polyphonic laude are two- or three-voice pieces; a few four-voice laude survive. The vast majority of laude have Italian texts; a few are in Latin. The text is usually underlaid for the main melody only, which is in the top voice; for the most part settings are simple, syllabic, and basically homorhythmic. The bass line may have been performed instrumentally. Each poetic line is given its own melodic phrase; all voices begin and conclude phrases together.

The chief sources of laude are MS Grey 3.b.12, in South African Public Library, Capetown, and two books published by Petrucci in 1507 and 1508. His *Laude, libro primo* consists entirely of pieces by Innocentius Dammonis, about whom virtually nothing is known. *Laude, libro secondo* contains works by Marchetto Cara (e.g., *Sancta Maria ora pro nobis,* Holy Mary, pray for us), Bartolomeo Tromboncino, Josquin Desprez, and other musicians who composed *frottole* also.

After the Council of Trent, there was a surge of laude production. Among principal contributors to laude repertory in the last half of the sixteenth century were Giovanni Razzi (1531–1611) who assembled six collections of them (two published, four in manuscript), and Giovanni Animuccia (c. 1500–1571), whose 12 books of laude were written primarily for Filippo Neri's Congregazione dell'Oratorio in Rome. Some of Animuccia's laude had narrative

The Rise of Regional Styles

1450	1475	1500	1525	1550	1575	1600	1625

ITALY:

- - - - - - - monophonic *lauda* - - - - - - - -

1480 - - polyphonic *lauda* - - - - - - - - - 1530

1498 - *canti* - 1520
carnascialeschi

1500 - - - - - - - - - 1525
frottola

1530 - - - - - - - - - - - - *villanella* - - - - - - - - - - - -

1525 - *madrigal* - - - - - - - - - - - - - - - -

1560 - - - - *canzonetta* - - - - - - - 1605

1560 - - - *balletto* - - - 1590
(lute)

1591 - - - *balletto* - - 1620
(vocal)

FRANCE:

- - - treble-dominated *chanson* - - - 1500   imitative contrapuntal
chanson

1530 - Parisian - - 1560
chanson

- - - - - - Franco-Netherlands style *chanson*

- - *voix de ville* - -

air de cour -
solo - - - - polyphonic - - - - solo - - - - -
1570-80   1580-1600   after 1608

- - - - - - - - *musique mesurée* - - - - - - - - -

ENGLAND:

- - secular part songs - -

1580 - - *madrigal* - - 1605
and *ballett*

1560 - - - consort song -

1597 - - - ayre - -
lute song

**GERMANIC
LANDS:**

- - - improvised *Meisterlied* -

1530 - - - *Tenorlied* - - - begins to decline in importance
after c. 1550

1490 - - - - - - - ode - - - - - - - 1540

1544 - - *quodlibet* - - - - - -

IBERIA:

- - - romance -

1490 - - - *villancico* -

---

or dramatic texts; thus, they were influential in the beginnings of the *oratorio volgare* (vernacular oratorios) presented by Neri's Congregation c. 1600 (see p. 331).

Canti carnascialeschi

Canti carnascialeschi (carnival songs) are uniquely Florentine. During the late fifteenth and early sixteenth centuries festivals were held in Florence in conjunction with the pre-Lenten Carnival and Calendimaggio (a celebration of spring observed from

May 1 to June 24). A feature of these festivals was the singing of several kinds of Italian part songs, known generically as *canti carnascialeschi*. Some of the songs—*mascherate* (masquerades)—were performed by groups of masked men and boys on foot; *trionfi* (triumph songs) were performed by costumed singers on carts. Song texts were written by both aristocrats and commoners and were set to music by well-known composers, such as Alexander Agricola and Henrich Isaac. Carnival songs reached a high level of artistic quality during the time of Lorenzo de' Medici, who wrote some texts. Over 300 texts and approximately 70 complete settings of carnival songs survive. A majority of the songs are strophic with a refrain, similar in formal structure to the *ballata*. Musically, the songs are three- or four-part settings in homorhythmic chordal style, usually in duple meter, with concern for clear enunciation and correct declamation. Harmonic progressions are apparent. In many of the songs, each line of a strophe's text has a new musical phrase; each musical phrase has a clearly defined cadence, often on tonic or dominant. Presumably, the songs were performed with some kind of instrumental accompaniment, but only one manuscript mentions use of a lute. While Savonarola held sway (1494–97) all secular aspects of festivals were supplanted by religious processions, and laude replaced *canti carnascialeschi*. The collections of laude compiled by Giovanni Razzi (1531–1611) are important in the history of *canti carnascialeschi* for they preserve settings that might otherwise have been lost, e.g., Lorenzo de' Medici's *Trionfo di Bacco e d'Arianna* (Triumph of Bacchus and Ariadne). After Savonarola's death, secularity again colored the festivals; carnival songs flourished between 1498 and 1520. Thereafter, carnival songs merged with other types of Italian secular music; e.g., the *mascherata* became a type of *villanella* (see p. 217).

Frottola

Petrucci began his music publishing business in Venice (1501) by printing anthologies of polyphonic chansons designed for instrumental performance; next came collections of motets and Masses. In 1504 he printed a book of Italian secular songs entitled *Frottole* (Frottolas); additional volumes ensued, and in 1514 Petrucci issued his eleventh collection of *frottole*. Some books were reprinted several times. Petrucci's ten extant collections (most of Book X is lost) are the major sources of *frottole*. Between 1510 and 1531, other Italian printers issued 15 collections of *frottole*.

The word *frottola* is a generic term covering various types of Italian secular song current in the late fifteenth and early sixteenth centuries. *Frottola* is used also to denote a specific type of Italian secular song, the *barzelletta*, sometimes called the "frottola proper." In general, frottole are three- or four-part polyphonic songs that are predominately homorhythmic, with simple harmonies, and the main melody in the top voice. Duple meter prevails. In four-voice frottole usually all members of a triad are present in a chord; frequently the tenor sings in thirds with the superius. Movement in the bass line is principally by the interval of a fourth or a fifth, and at times a succession of modal harmonies approximates chord progressions of key tonality. For the most part, the text is set syllabically, each poetic line having its own melodic phrase. Frottole seem to fall into two compositional types: those in which all voices begin and conclude all phrases together, and those in which one voice—usually, but not always, the superius—enters one note later than the other three voices but all voices conclude the phrase together (ex. 11.1). Settings are strophic or strophic with a refrain, those with refrain bearing formal resemblance to the fourteenth-century *ballata*. In many publications all voices have text for the refrain but only the top voice is supplied with text for the verse(s), which would indicate that a soloist sang the verses to lute (or possibly harpsichord) accompaniment, and other vocalists joined in the refrain (fig. 11.1).

The frottola is rooted in the custom of reciting poetry to musical accompaniment, a practice that was widespread during the fifteenth century. The courts of the Este family provided fertile ground for the frottola; it flourished at Ferrara, Urbino, and especially at Mantua, where Isabella d'Este (1474–1539), daughter of Ercole I of Ferrara, and her husband, Marchese Francesco Gonzaga, were patrons of all the arts and maintained an especially fine musical establishment. Isabella had studied instrumental and vocal

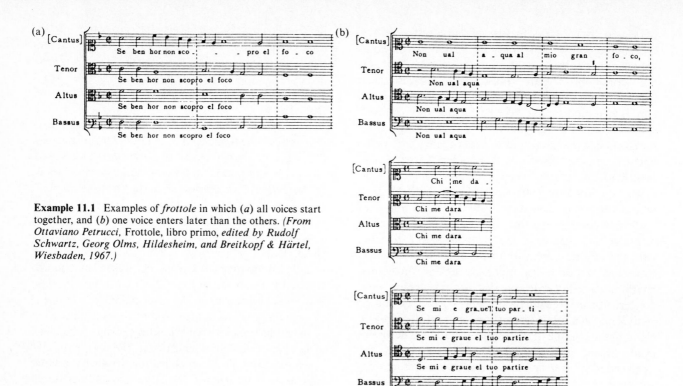

(a)

(b)

Example 11.1 Examples of *frottole* in which (*a*) all voices start together, and (*b*) one voice enters later than the others. *(From Ottaviano Petrucci,* Frottole, libro primo, *edited by Rudolf Schwartz, Georg Olms, Hildesheim, and Breitkopf & Härtel, Wiesbaden, 1967.)*

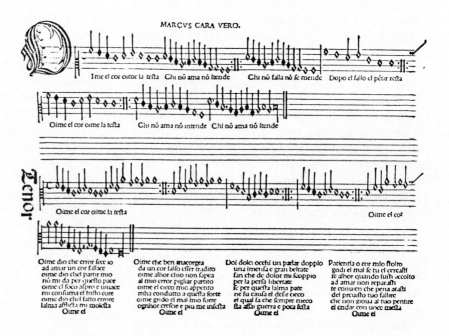

Figure 11.1 Portion of Marchetto Cara's *Oimè el cor* as printed in Petrucci's *Frottole, libro primo* (Venice, 1504). This *frottola* is strophic with refrain.

music; she was an accomplished performer on several instruments and understood the technical aspects of musical composition. Two of the leading composers of frottole were at Mantua: Marchetto Cara (c. 1470–c. 1525) and Bartolomeo Tromboncino (c. 1470–c. 1535). Both gentlemen were from Verona. Cara was *maestro di cappella* at Mantua in 1511–25; he was renowned chiefly as a composer but was acclaimed also as singer and lutenist. He set verses by noble amateurs as well as noted Italian poets such as Castiglione, Michelangelo, and Petrarch. Cara composed music for more than 100 frottole, in addition to setting odes, sonnets, and other types of Italian poetry. A characteristic of his frottole is subtle variation of the repetition scheme within the stereotyped *ballata* pattern. (See *Oimè el cor,* Alas! the heart; DWMA73.)

Bartolomeo Tromboncino grew up in Mantua; his name appears in documents of the Gonzaga court from 1494 to 1501. He was frequently in difficulty because of his stormy emotional temperament, but his musical talent was so valued at Mantua that he was pardoned even for murdering his unfaithful wife in 1499. When troubles occurred again in April 1501, Tromboncino left Mantua without the Duke's permission; he returned very briefly in 1504 to fulfill a commission for Isabella d'Este. In February 1502, Tromboncino sang at the wedding of Lucrezia Borgia and Alfonso d'Este at Ferrara; he served at their court from 1502 to 1513. He petitioned for repatriation as a Venetian citizen in 1521 and can be traced in that republic until his death. He requested also a composer's patent prohibiting others from printing any of his works; apparently his request was granted, for no composition by him was published in Venice after 1521.

Tromboncino was one of the most prolific of the early frottolists. His known works include a cycle of Lamentations, the motet *Benedictus Dominus Deus,* 17 laude, and 168 frottole; 12 additional frottole are of doubtful attribution. He is especially important for his choice of more serious and better quality poetry early in the century when most composers of frottole were setting mediocre or trivial verses. Although he did not name the authors of the lyrics he set, many of the texts have been identified as the work of "classical" and Renaissance poets—Petrarch, Galeotto,

Dall'Aquila, Castiglione, Michelangelo, and others. For his settings, Tromboncino preferred nonimitative polyphony rather than the usual simple homorhythmic style used by many of his contemporaries.

The frottola spread throughout Italy, from north to south, eventually reaching Naples, and is historically significant in three respects: (1) Its chordal style and simple harmonies probably had some bearing on the homorhythmic (quasi-chordal) counterpoint written by contemporary Franco-Netherlands composers working in Italy. (2) The frottola setting more serious poetry, especially that type Petrarch termed *canzona,* was forerunner of the madrigal. (3) In Naples the lighter variety of frottola influenced the development of the *villanella* (or *villanesca*), which flourished from the 1530s to the early seventeenth century.

Villanella

Villanella is a generic term used to denote a type of light music, often witty and sophisticated, designed for aristocratic audiences. Many *villanelle* satirize peasant life or the madrigal. Prominent musical features of the villanella are simple homorhythmic (chordal) texture with the melody in the top voice, and regular rhythms with some syncopation. Subtypes of villanella are differentiated by dialect, type of text, or social function. For example, the *mascherata* was used for masked entertainments and carnival activities; *moresca* texts concern Moors; the *giustiniana* usually relate amorous fantasies of three old men. One of the harmonic devices frequently appearing in villanelle is a chord stream of triads containing a series of parallel fifths—progressions forbidden by contrapuntal (and harmonic) rules.

Madrigal

In the early sixteenth century there was renewed interest in Petrarch's poetry. Pietro Bembo (1470–1547), poet, literary theorist, papal secretary from 1512 to 1520, and cardinal from 1539 to 1547, was the leading Petrarch advocate of the time; his edition of Petrarch's works was published in 1501. Bembo eulogized Petrarch and Boccaccio for their literary use of Tuscan language and cited their work as embodying every desirable characteristic of literary style.

Petrarch provided the model of poetic perfection. Many sixteenth-century writers emulated his poetic style, usually with results that fell short of the mark. There was much admiration for the free alternation of 7- and 11-syllable lines, but frequently the sound of the words received more attention than their content. The quality of the poems produced varied considerably, and, as was mentioned in connection with the frottola, composers set mediocre and trivial verse as well as fine poetry.

Around 1530 the word *madrigal* was used generically in Italy to denote musical setting of various types of Italian verse—sonnets, *canzoni, ballate,* and others, one of which was called the *madrigale*. Actually, the poetic *madrigale* is a single-stanza *canzone*. The sixteenth-century madrigal and that of the fourteenth century (see p. 144) have only the name in common. The fourteenth-century madrigal is strophic with a *ritornello* (refrain). The sixteenth-century madrigal comprises a single stanza with a varying number of 7- and 11-syllable lines in a free rhyme scheme. The number of lines in a madrigal varies from 6 to 16; most madrigals contain 10. The sixteenth-century madrigal has no refrain, but often the last line is repeated. Some madrigals conclude with a rhymed couplet that occasionally is moralistic, e.g., Arcadelt's four-voice *Il bianco e dolce cigno* (The white and gentle swan) or Gibbons's five-voice setting of that poem as *The Silver Swan*.

Musically, the sixteenth-century madrigal is a through-composed setting of a one-stanza poem or a single stanza from a multi-stanza poem, treated phrase by phrase. The music is usually quasi-sectional, constructed as a series of overlapping or interlocking phrases, some in imitative counterpoint, some in familiar style (homorhythmic and chordal). In this respect, a madrigal setting resembles that of a motet or the *canzone*-type frottola. However, in performance the three varieties of vocal music differ: The frottola is soloist music, presumably instrumentally accompanied; the motet is polyphonic choral music; the madrigal is ensemble polyphony for from 3 to 12 voices, one person per part—vocal chamber music.

The musical setting of a madrigal was designed to enhance the poetry. Composers of early madrigals seemed content to express the mood of a poem or to convey the meaning of its most significant lines; as the madrigal developed, considerable word painting or text painting was used. Sometimes composers included depictions for the visual enjoyment of the performers and wrote *Augenmusik* (eye music), such as black notation (*nota nere*) to portray blindness, darkness, death, sorrow, or moonless night. Thus, in its mature form the madrigal became an amalgamation of art, literature, and music—a miniature *Gesamtkunstwerk*.

Madrigal development can be viewed in three phases: (1) early madrigals, written c. 1525–c. 1545; (2) mature, or "classical," madrigals, composed c. 1545–1580; and (3) late madrigals, produced c. 1580–1620.

Centers of early madrigal production were Rome and Florence, two cities that were culturally close during the reigns of Medici Popes Leo X (r. 1513–21) and Clement VII (r. 1523–34). Some early madrigals by Bernardo Pisano (1490–1548) appear in Petrucci's *Musica de meser Bernardo Pisano sopra la canzone del Petrarcha* (Bernardo Pisano's settings of *canzoni* by Petrarch; 1520). Pisano was trained at the cathedral school in Florence and was chapelmaster at the cathedral from 1512 to 1514; he was a singer in the papal chapel from 1514 until his death. Philippe Verdelot (c. 1475–c. 1535), a Franco-Netherlander working in Florence and Rome in the 1520s, was another pioneer madrigal composer; two publications issued in Rome c. 1526 contain individual madrigals by him. However, the first collection of pieces published as madrigals is *Madrigali de diversi musici: libro primo* (Madrigals by various composers: book I; 1530). The collection contains eight madrigals by Verdelot, two by Costanzo Festa, two by Sebastiano Festa, one by Maistre Jhan of Ferrara, some light Italian songs, and some chansons. The inclusion of chansons is not surprising since many composers of madrigals wrote them, also.

Verdelot, Costanzo Festa (c. 1480–1545), and Jacob Arcadelt (c. 1505–68) were the leading early composers of madrigals. Pisano may have had some influence on all of them, for he worked with each of them at some time. Two books of Verdelot's four-voice madrigals were published c. 1533; the books were reprinted several times, then issued as a single-volume edition in 1540, and that had numerous reprintings. Verdelot's *Madrigali a cinque voci, libro primo* appeared in 1535.

In the early madrigals, which are for three or four voices, some imitation is present, but the music is predominantly chordal, with clear cadences separating poetic phrases; expression is rather subdued. Frequent skips of a fourth or a fifth in the bass line create an interesting mixture of modality and key tonality. Festa's *Quando ritrova la mia pastorella* (When I find my shepherdess; DWMA74) provides an example.

In the 1540s madrigals became quite popular; almost all composers working in Italy wrote some. They were sung regularly at court and were commissioned by aristocrats for special celebrations, by noblemen to honor their ladies, and by literary academies for their own entertainment; sometimes madrigals served as incidental music or *intermedi* for plays, e.g., Arcadelt's settings of canzoni for Machiavelli's *La Clizia* and *La Mandragola*. More than 200 of Arcadelt's madrigals survive. Five books of his four-voice madrigals were published between 1539 and 1544; a book of his three-voice madrigals appeared in 1542. Arcadelt's madrigals were extremely popular; his books were reprinted many times. His madrigals contain a considerable amount of imitative counterpoint, with declamatory chordal writing being reserved for important phrases. This may be seen in *Quando col dolce suono* (When with sweet sound), or in *Voi ve n'andat' al cielo, occhi* (You look heavenward, eyes), which exhibits motetlike features as well as the expressiveness of the madrigal.

In the 1540s, the center of madrigal composition shifted to Venice. Adrian Willaert, working at St. Mark's, occupies an intermediate position as a composer writing in both early and classical madrigal styles. Although he was writing madrigals, canzoni, and *villanesche* in the 1540s, his madrigals were not printed as collections until after mid-century, e.g., *Musica nova* appeared in 1559. All but 1 of the 25 madrigals in that volume are settings of Petrarch's sonnets (see p. 208). Willaert's mature madrigals display a subtle mixture of imitative and chordal texture and precise declamation of text.

After 1540 some composers began to write some of their pieces in smaller note values (i.e., note heads filled in or black) with a C mensuration sign, rather than in the usual white notation (i.e., note heads unfilled) with an *alla breve* (₵) signature. Madrigals written in this newer notation are referred to variously as *madrigali a nota nere* (madrigals in black notes), *madrigali a misura di breve* (madrigals in *breve* measure), or *madrigali cromatici* (madrigals in colored, i.e., black, notation and using *crome* or flagged semi-minims). Cipriano de Rore (1516–65), a Netherlander working in Italy, used some of this newly fashionable notation in *I madrigali,* a book of five-voice madrigals (1542); an enlarged edition of that volume is entitled *Il primo libro de madregali* [sic] *cromatici* (The first book of chromatic madrigals; 1544). In his later books of madrigals, he used this new notation sparingly.

Details of Rore's early life are lacking. In the early 1540s, he was in Venice and may have studied with Willaert. From 1547 to 1559 Rore was *maestro di cappella* at Ferrara; he spent the next two years at the Farnese court in Parma. In 1563 he succeeded Willaert as *maestro di cappella* at St. Mark's, Venice, but resigned in 1564 and returned to Parma. Though he composed Masses, motets, and chansons, Rore is remembered chiefly for his madrigals, approximately 120 of which survive. He was the leading madrigalist of his generation. Like Willaert, Rore preferred to set serious poetry of high literary quality, especially that of Petrarch. Rore's *Il terzo libro di madrigali a cinque voci* (1548) opens with a cycle of 11 *madrigali spirituali* (madrigals setting devotional texts)—a setting of Petrarch's *canzone, Vergine bella* (Beautiful Virgin), stanzas of invocation to the Virgin Mary that conclude Petrarch's *Canzoniere, o Rime in vita e morte di Madonna Laura* (Songs, or Poems on the Life and Death of Madonna Laura). Other composers writing *madrigali spirituali* include Palestrina and Willaert.

All of Rore's madrigals are four- or five-voice settings. His writing is firmly rooted in traditional Franco-Flemish counterpoint; his five-voice madrigals are polyphonic, motetlike, and serious in tone. There is a good deal of imitation, and the bass line fulfills the dual role of providing harmonic support while supplying a melodic contrapuntal line. Rore exercised concern for expressing the meaning of the poetry and used chromatic alterations and text painting effectively but not idly or indiscriminately. *Da le belle contrade d'oriente* (From the fair regions

The Rise of Regional Styles

of the east; DWMA75) is representative of his five-voice madrigals. His four-voice madrigals have a more transparent texture, and some are comparatively simple, though contrapuntal, e.g., *Anchor che col partire* (Even while departing), which is probably his most famous madrigal.

The usual publication format for madrigals was partbooks. Yet, in 1577 an edition of Rore's collected four-voice madrigals was printed in score, which indicates that the collection was prepared for study purposes, and that Rore's four-voice madrigals were considered models of the form. This is one of the earliest books of printed scores in existence.

Other composers producing madrigals of the classical type were Andrea Gabrieli, Lassus, Palestrina, Giaches de Wert, and Philippe de Monte. Monte (1521–1603), Flemish by birth, went to Italy at an early age. He italianized his name, and as Filippo di Monte he worked as singer, teacher, and composer. During 1542–51 he served the Pinelli family in Naples; in 1554 he went to Antwerp, then moved to England, where he worked for about a year in the private chapel of Philip II of Spain, husband of Mary Tudor. Monte's exact whereabouts for the next dozen years are unknown; in 1567, he was in Rome. When Palestrina rejected the offer to become court Kapellmeister to Emperor Maximillian II, the position was tendered Monte. He accepted the appointment and served as Kapellmeister to Habsburg rulers from May 1568 until his death.

Monte was a prolific composer—he wrote 40 Masses, about 260 other sacred works, approximately 50 chansons, 5 books of *madrigali spirituali,* and more than 1100 madrigals published in 34 books issued between 1554 and 1603. Most of the madrigals Monte composed before 1576 set texts by Petrarch or sixteenth-century poets writing in the style of Petrarch; for later madrigals Monte chose contemporary pastoral poetry, especially G. B. Guarini's *Il pastor fido* (The faithful shepherd). Monte's last two books of madrigals comprise seven-voice settings of texts from that play and are Monte's only books with delineative titles: *La fiammetta . . . libro primo* (The little flame . . . book I; 1599) and *Musica sopra Il pastor fido . . . libro secondo* (Music on *The faithful shepherd . . .* book II; 1600).

Translation: So from one clear living fountain
Pour forth the sweet and the bitter...

Example 11.2 Monte's expressive use of chromaticism is apparent in this excerpt from the *Seconda parte* of his six-voice madrigal setting Petrarch's *Hor che 'l ciel.* Quinto and Bassus are tacet here. From *Il terzo libro de madrigali a sei voci, 1576. (From* New Grove Dictionary of Music and Musicians, *6th ed., vol. 12. Copyright © 1980* The New Grove Dictionary of Music and Musicians. *Reprinted by permission.)*

Monte's madrigals, most of which are five- and six-voice pieces, demonstrate his mastery of counterpoint. However, he was not averse to violating contrapuntal rules in order to achieve an expressive effect. Characteristics of his style include frequent use of cross-relations (ex. 11.2), melismas in connection with text painting, and pairing or grouping of voices for special effects.

Little is known concerning the early life of Flemish composer Giaches de Wert (1535–96) save that, as a child, he was a choirboy in an Italian court chapel. By 1558 he was in the service of Alfonso Gonzaga at Novellara and may have been there as early as 1553. Details of Wert's activities during 1558–65 are unclear; in 1561 he may have been a chapel singer at the Farnese court in Parma where Rore was *maestro di cappella.* Dedications of Wert's books of madrigals indicate that he maintained connections with the Gonzaga family even when he was not in their service.

Wert's permanent employment at the Gonzaga ducal establishment in Mantua began in 1565. As *maestro di cappella,* he was in charge of music at the palatine basilica of Santa Barbara and at court, and he was directly responsible to the duke. Wert was included in the musical retinue accompanying Guglielmo on state visits and during the 1570s developed an association with the Este court at Ferrara. This association was strengthened after Margherita Gonzaga's marriage to Alfonso II d'Este in 1579 (see p. 227); Wert received commissions from Ferrara and visited there frequently, sometimes for more than a year. Some of his madrigals appear in *Il lauro secco* (The dry laurel; 1582) and *Il lauro verde* (The green laurel; 1583), two compilations of madrigals honoring Laura Peverara, of the Ferrarese *concerto delle donne* (ensemble of ladies; see p. 225). The pieces in Wert's *L'ottavo libro de madrigali* (Eighth book of madrigals; 5 vc.; 1586) may have been performed by that small ensemble at Ferrara. From c. 1584 to 1589 Wert had a secret liaison with Tarquinia Molza, accomplished poet, conductor, and musician who was a member of the second Ferrarese *concerto delle donne.* When Alfonso II learned of the affair, Tarquinia was dismissed, and Wert returned to Mantua.

Fourteen books of Wert's madrigals were published between 1558 and 1595, one for four voices (1561), the rest for five. A book of his madrigals for five to seven voices was published posthumously in 1608. A volume of five-voice *villanelle* appeared in 1589. For his madrigals he selected poetry of high literary quality; he set 60 poems of Petrarch, and Ariosto, Tansillo, Tasso, and Guarini are each represented by a dozen or more stanzas. The first three books of madrigals are stylistically much like those of Rore's—basically note-against-note counterpoint, in which textually rather than structurally induced imitation contrasts with chordal writing. Wert used unconventional melodic intervals (e.g., augmented second, leap of a seventh) more frequently than either Rore or Willaert, however.

In Books IV–VI, there is a tendency toward more homophonic writing and more lyricism. In these works Wert frequently used two opposing opening motives. Book VII contains the earliest-known settings of Tasso's *Gerusalemme liberata* (Jerusalem delivered). An interesting feature of Book VIII is the inclusion of settings of 12 stanzas from Tasso's *Gerusalemme liberata* grouped according to textual dramatic content. Actually, each group forms a secular cantata in madrigal form. In several places, the three high voices are definitely the main voices, with the lower voices having accompaniment status. *Concertante* structure is apparent in dialogues between upper and lower voices, a type of writing that is rooted in but goes beyond Josquin's method of contrasting vocal groups. (The term *concertante* signifies music that is, in a sense, soloistic but that contrasts with other music in the same piece—e.g., chamber music with contrasting sections used in dialogue fashion.) Some vocal lines in the madrigals in Book VIII exhibit very wide vocal range (ex. 11.3). Wert used chromatic alterations and text painting effectively but usually not to extremes. At times, through his skillful application of chromatic alterations, modality approaches key tonality, e.g., in *Ah dolente partita!* (Ah, sad parting!; 5 vc.; Book XI), which is ostensibly Hypodorian but frequent sharped f and flatted e pitches give the madrigal the sound of g minor. Wert's late madrigals evidence stylistic characteristics found also in works by his contemporaries and foreshadow some musical developments of the seventeenth century.

In the late sixteenth century, native Italians resumed leadership in madrigal composition, the principal composers being Luca Marenzio (c. 1553–99), Carlo Gesualdo (c. 1561–1613), and Claudio Monteverdi (1567–1643). Luzzascho Luzzaschi (c. 1545–1607) also made some important contributions.

Little information is available concerning Marenzio's early life. He grew up near Brescia, and it is generally believed that he received his early musical

The Rise of Regional Styles

Example 11.3 Measures 1–12 of Wert's *Solo e pensoso* illustrate the wide range encompassed by the vocal lines in some of his madrigals. From *Il settimo libro de madrigali,* 1581. *(Source: Wert's* Solo e pensoso *from* G. De Wert: Collected Works, *edited by C. MacClintock and M. Bernstein.)*

training from Giovanni Contino (c. 1513–74). Contino served the Gonzagas at Mantua from c. 1568 to 1574, and Marenzio may have been with him there. From c. 1574 to 1578 Marenzio was employed as a singer by Cardinal Cristoforo Madruzzo (d. 1574) in Rome; after Madruzzo's death, Cardinal Luigi d'Este (1538–86) became Marenzio's patron. Vatican politics prevented d'Este from securing for Marenzio a place in the papal choir. When Cardinal Ferdinando de' Medici became Grand Duke in 1587, he aspired to surpass the Estense musical establishment at Ferrara. To that end, he brought to Florence many musicians he had known in Rome; Marenzio was one of them. Details of the last decade of Marenzio's life are

sketchy. Late in 1589 he returned to Rome and resided with Duke Virginio Orsini until 1593; then Marenzio entered the service of Cardinal Aldobrandini, papal secretary of state. Marenzio spent 1596–97 in Poland; he died shortly after returning to Rome in 1599.

Though Marenzio composed approximately 75 motets and may have written some Masses, his reputation as a composer is based upon his secular compositions, particularly his madrigals. More than 450 of his secular works survive. Between 1580 and 1588, a book of his motets and 17 books of his secular pieces were published; no new works appeared in print until 1591; during 1591–99 six books of madrigals and a

Example 11.4 Luca Marenzio's madrigal *Solo e pensoso*, mm. 1–12. (© 1931/1959 Breitkopf & Härtel, Wiesbaden.)

book of sacred music were printed. Marenzio's immediate success in Rome was partly because his early madrigals filled Roman society's need for new music that could be sung by talented amateurs. Most of his pieces are for five voices. Characteristic of his writing are his setting of the poetry in short, concise musical phrases and his musically symbolic depiction of the text whenever possible. In addition, many of his pieces exhibit continuous polyphony, e.g., *S'io parto, i' moro* (If I leave, I shall die) and *Madonna mia gentil ringratio* (I thank you, my kind lady). The madrigals in Marenzio's last six books are more serious than the early pieces, and the settings display more unusual harmonic treatment; however, Marenzio used chromatic alterations in moderation and only to achieve expressive effects. His setting of Petrarch's *Solo e pensoso* (Alone and thoughtful) appears to be a five-part instrumentally accompanied solo madrigal (DWMA76). The opening lines of the poem—"Alone and thoughtful I walk through the deserted fields with measured, slow, and dragging steps"—are presented in long note values as a quasi-cantus firmus, via a scalar passage that ascends chromatically from g' to a'', then descends chromatically to a sustained d''. Seventh- and ninth-chords are spelled out in the other voices (ex. 11.4).

Carlo Gesualdo, Prince of Venosa and Count of Conza, was afflicted with melomania (a mad passion for music) that became increasingly obsessive and was complicated by melancholia as he grew older. He managed to keep his mania semisecret until the notoriety occasioned by his murder of his wife and her lover in October 1590. In 1594 Gesualdo visited the Este court at Ferrara for two reasons: he was fascinated by reports of the musical establishment there, and he married Leonora d'Este (1561–1637), niece of Duke Alfonso II. The marriage contract had been signed in 1593, for reasons mutually beneficial to Ferrara and Gesualdo. Alfonso arranged the marriage to secure Vatican support for the future when controversy would arise over ducal succession at Ferrara, for he had no male heir. (Actually, those precautions were useless.) Gesualdo, too, desired a male heir but wanted a marriage alliance outside the kingdom of Naples; moreover, he was attracted to Ferrara because of its reputation as a center of music.

Gesualdo remained at Ferrara for several years. In 1594 his *Madrigali libro primo* (Madrigals, book I)—actually, his second book of madrigals—was published there. Also, his first book of madrigals, originally published under the *nom de plume* Gioseppe Pilonij, was reissued in Ferrara in 1594 as *Madrigali libro secondo* (Madrigals, book II). Gesualdo found conditions at Ferrara conducive to composition; his third and fourth books of madrigals were published there in 1595 and 1596, respectively. He, too, composed some madrigals for the *concerto delle donne*. At Ferrara, Gesualdo could maintain his aristocratic status and still work professionally with Luzzaschi and

The Rise of Regional Styles

the virtuoso court musicians. Gesualdo admired Luzzaschi and was influenced by his use of chromaticism. Both Luzzaschi and Gesualdo were interested in Nicola Vicentino's (1511–c. 1576) chromatic *arcicembalo* (see p. 269). The instrument was kept at Ferrara, and Luzzaschi had played it during the Este-Gesualdo wedding festivities. Gesualdo attempted (with professional assistance) to build a similar instrument in Naples but failed.

After the death of Alfonso II in 1597, Ferrara reverted to the Papal States, and Gesualdo returned to his castle at Gesualdo in Naples. His fifth and sixth books of madrigals were published there in 1611.

Gesualdo was a skillful composer. In his madrigal settings he was primarily interested in conveying emotional expression, and he used chromaticism both harmonically and melodically for that purpose. He employed chromaticism wisely, restricting its abundant use to passages that are not complicated rhythmically. (See *Moro lasso al mio duolo,* I die from my pain; DWMA77.) Usually, Gesualdo confirmed audacious strident harmonies and unconventional chord progressions by immediately repeating them, either exactly or in sequence (ex. 11.5). He used text painting effectively in *Io pur respiro* (I yet breathe).

Luzzascho Luzzaschi, a pupil of Rore, spent his entire life at Ferrara. He entered d'Este service in 1561 as a singer; in 1564 he was appointed first organist. His duties gradually were expanded to include directing a court orchestra, training some of the court musicians, composing for the court, and performing at the keyboard. By 1570 he was in charge of Alfonso II's private *musica da camera,* including the *concerto delle donne* (see p. 227). Duke Alfonso's numerous private concerts were Luzzaschi's responsibility; he arranged the programs, composed a good deal of the music, and performed at the keyboard. After dissolution of the Este court in 1597, Luzzaschi remained in Ferrara in service of the papal governor, Cardinal Aldobrandini.

Eight books of Luzzaschi's madrigals were published during 1571–1604. *Madrigali per cantare, et sonare a uno, e doi, e tre soprani* (Madrigals to be sung and played by one, two, and three sopranos; 1601) contains madrigals composed for the secret

Example 11.5 This excerpt from Gesualdo's *Resta di darmi noia* contains sequential repetition of a strident chromaticism. *(From C. Gesualdo, Sämtliche Werke, Vol. 6, edited by W. Weismann and G. E. Watkins, Hamburg: Ugrino.)*

repertoire of the *concerto delle donne.* The pieces, which were written before 1597—some of them perhaps as early as 1590—are supplied with keyboard accompaniment. This is the earliest extant publication containing written-out keyboard accompaniments.

Claudio Monteverdi occupies a transitional position between Renaissance and Baroque eras. The first four books of his madrigals are purely Renaissance compositions; the pieces in his next two books are transitional, and the madrigals in his seventh book, which is entitled *Concerto,* are clearly Baroque in style. Detailed discussion of Monteverdi commences on p. 304.

Canzonetta

The *canzonetta* (literally, little song), an Italian light, secular song, appeared in southern Italy c. 1560 and spread northward. The texts, usually strophic, treat subjects that are amorous, erotic, pastoral, or satirical. Early *canzonette* were treble-dominated, rhythmically varied homophony for three to five voices; three-voice *canzonette* became very popular in the early 1580s. By the end of that decade, however, four- and six-voice textures were preferred and more contrapuntal elements were included. Those *canzonette* satirizing madrigals exhibit contrived simplicity and combine textural clarity with madrigalian devices such as word painting. *Canzonette* by Orazio Vecchi (1550–1605) and Marenzio were popular, both in Italy and north of the Alps. By the end of the century, *canzonette* were sung in translation in Germany and England, and composers in those areas were writing pieces in *canzonetta* style.

Balletto

The word *balletto* was used in Italy in the late sixteenth and early seventeenth centuries for a type of instrumental and vocal music that developed in connection with a specific Italian dance called the *balletto*. Traditionally, *balletti* were performed in association with dancing. The Italian instrumental *balletto* (principally for lute) flourished from c. 1560 to 1590; the vocal *balletto* appeared c. 1591 and flourished for about three decades; after c. 1620 the instrumental chamber ensemble *balletto* became popular.

Giovanni G. Gastoldi (c. 1552–c. 1622), who worked for the Gonzagas at the church of Santa Barbara and at the Mantuan court in 1572–1608, is credited with writing the earliest vocal *balletti*. His *Balletti a cinque voci con li suoi versi per cantare, sonare, e ballare* (*Balletti* for five voices, with music for singing, playing, and dancing) was published in Venice in 1591 and was reprinted a dozen times in two decades. *Balletti* are characterized as strophic, homophonic in texture, with regular rhythmic patterns, clearly delineated phrases, and diatonic harmonies of key tonality. Modality is virtually nonexistent in *balletti*. Nonsense syllables, such as *fa-la-la* or *li-rum*, are interpolated at the ends of lines, couplets, or as a refrain. (The modern Christmas carol *Deck the halls* is in essence a *balletto*.)

Balletti became popular outside of Italy. Many were written in Germany, and in England, where they were called *balletts*, those by Thomas Morley were very popular. Morley's *Balletts to Five Voyces* was published in both English and Italian (1595); the book mimics Gastoldi's collection, each piece being a parody of an existing Italian work. For example, Morley's *Sing wee and chaunt it* (DWMA78) is a parody of Gastoldi's *A lieta vita* (In merry life; DWMA79). The *Concerto di pastori* (Shepherds ensemble) concluding Morley's collection contains the seven-voice echo dialogue *Phyllis, I fain would leave thee now*, a work unique in English music literature. Morley was aware that *balletti* were dance songs, for he mentioned that fact in his *A Plaine and Easie Introduction to Practicall Musick*; however, English *balletti* evidence greater attention to musical detail and text setting than Italian ones, and it is generally presumed that English *balletti* were not intended for use with dancing.

Music at Italian Courts

Members of d'Este, Gonzaga, and Medici families patronized the arts lavishly, and activities at their courts played an important role in the development of music in Italy during the sixteenth century. Marital ties linked these ruling families, and personal visits between courts occurred frequently (fig. 11.2). Innovative cultural events at one court soon were taken up at one or more of the others.

In the last half of the sixteenth century, the excellence of the musical establishment at the Este court at Ferrara was well known. Several ensembles were permanently maintained there. The *concerto grande* (large ensemble) performed at all large entertainments; in the 1570s this group comprised about 60 vocalists and instrumentalists. Court records indicate that the last male sopranos employed at the Ferrara court came in the late 1550s; thereafter, female sopranos were recruited. In the 1570s there were at court several aristocratic ladies who sang well: Lucrezia and Isabella Bendidio and Leonora Sanvitale di Scandiano (d. 1582). These talented amateurs sang solos and performed together as a *concerto delle donne* (ladies ensemble). It must be stressed that these were prestigious noblewomen who would have been at court even if they had not been able to sing; they were not recompensed specifically for their singing. In 1577 they were joined by Signora Vittoria Cybò Bentivoglio. The four ladies performed together regularly in private concerts for a small select audience in the personal apartments of Lucrezia d'Este. Isabella and Lucrezia Bendidio sang solos and duets with harpsichord accompaniment, as well as performing in the ensemble; sometimes Giulio Cesare Brancaccio (c. 1520–d. after 1585), a professional bass, sang with Lucrezia, Leonora, and Vittoria. Court composer

Figure 11.2 Northern Italy in the sixteenth century.

Example 11.6 Excerpt from *Si com'ai freschi matutini rai,* No. 3 in *L'ottavo libro di madrigali* (1586), illustrates Wert's notation of ornaments in more than one vocal line. The ornaments are written out, not indicated by symbols. *(Source: G. de Wert: Collected Works, edited by C. MacClintock and M. Bernstein.)*

Luzzasco Luzzaschi rehearsed the small ensemble and played harpsichord accompaniments for the singers. In contemporary accounts, these private concerts of the *concerto delle donne* were referred to as *musica reservata* and *musica secreta.* (Colorplate 16.)

In 1579 Alfonso II d'Este married for the third time; his bride was 15-year-old Margherita Gonzaga of Mantua, whose lively interest in music, dancing, and the theatre had been fostered by the atmosphere of her father's court. Shortly after the marriage, Alfonso added to the Ferrara court singers a female soprano whose singing Margherita had enjoyed at Mantua. Other semiprofessional women singers were attracted to the court, and gradually the original members of the *concerto delle donne* were replaced by semiprofessional singers—the new *concerto delle donne* was a virtuoso ensemble whose members were at court only because they possessed excellent singing voices. (The ladies were paid for singing and spent considerable time cultivating their musical talents, but they had not been trained from childhood for a musical career. That was not possible for a woman in the late sixteenth century.) The original "singing ladies" remained at court but no longer performed in the select ensemble.

In 1582, the *concerto delle donne* comprised Laura Peverara (c. 1545–1601), Anna Guarini (b. after 1561–d. 1598; daughter of Taddea Bendidio and poet G. B. Guarini), and Livia d'Arco (d. 1611). Tarquinia Molza (1542–1617) joined the ensemble in 1583. The vocal talent of Laura Peverara was well known in Italy; renowned poets praised her in verses that famous composers set as madrigals. Bardi, Luzzaschi, Marenzio, Wert, and others contributed madrigals to two anthologies honoring her: *Il lauro secco* (1582) and *Il lauro verde* (1583). Often Brancaccio and a tenor sang with three of the ladies in the *musica secreta* performances given in the chambers of Duchess Margherita.

Giaches de Wert became enamored of Tarquinia Molza and visited the Ferrara court frequently. He had in mind the talents of the *musica secreta* quintet at Ferrara when he composed his *L'ottavo libro de madrigali* (Eighth book of madrigals; 5 vc.; 1586); the book is dedicated to Alfonso I and Margherita d'Este. The change in performance practices at Ferrara is significant—no longer were noble amateurs performing for their peers; semiprofessionals were performing before an audience. The virtuosi added diminutions to their solos; ornaments such as *passaggi* (passage work), *tiradi* (runs), *cadenze* (cadential ornaments), *trilli* (trills), *gruppi* (turns), and *messe di voce* (small crescendo-diminuendo on a sustained pitch) were planned and rehearsed before they were performed. Solo madrigals so ornamented became known as *madrigali ariosi.* Wert notated ornaments of these kinds in more than one vocal line in several of the pieces in *L'ottavo libro de madrigali* (ex. 11.6). From the solo singing, a new style of polyphony arose in which some characteristics of the serious madrigal and the lighter forms of Italian song were intermingled: concentration of the main melody

The Rise of Regional Styles

in the top voice, supported by uncomplicated harmonies, with little imitation. Several of the madrigals in Wert's *L'ottavo libro de madrigali* are *concertato* type, with the three upper (female) voices clearly grouped and contrasted against the two lower (male) voices, yet in agreement (in concert) with them, e.g., No.9, *Non è si denso velo* (The veil is not so thick; DWMA80).

At Ferrara there was a strong tradition of singing associated with dramatic productions—*intermedi* (interludes between acts of a play) were presented by soloists in a vocal style midway between recitation and singing. That kind of performance may have promoted the establishment of a group of semiprofessional madrigal singers and the separation between performers and audience associated with the concerts given by such a group.

Margherita Gonzaga d'Este's interest in dancing led to the formation of a *balletto delle donne* (ensemble of dancing ladies) at Ferrara. Presentations by the ladies did not interpret a story through dance but consisted of a series of dances by costumed performers. There was, of course, instrumental accompaniment, and at times madrigals were interpolated. Both *balletto delle donne* and *concerto delle donne* seem to have existed at Ferrara until that duchy reverted to the papacy in 1598. G. B. Guarini's experiences at Ferrara are reflected in his inclusion of dancing and madrigals in his play *Il pastor fido*. At Ferrara the play was performed with music by Luzzaschi; at Mantua, new music was supplied by Wert and possibly by Monteverdi.

At Mantua, Duke Guglielmo Gonzaga (1538–87) was not only genuinely interested in the arts, he was musically literate. A competent composer with published works, he could (and did) specify precisely in technical terms the style and content of the music he wanted composed. He maintained a permanent musical establishment with professional singers and music teachers. Outstanding composers, performers, artists, and authors were attracted to and found employment at Mantua. Madrigals were sung; dramatic presentations were enjoyed. Wert, who had previously been employed at the Neapolitan court of Don Francesco d'Este (son of Lucrezia Borgia and Alfonso I d'Este), was the first madrigalist permanently employed at Mantua; madrigals flourished there after his arrival.

Vincenzo Gonzaga, brother of Margherita, spent considerable time at the Ferrara court in the early 1580s. After he inherited the duchy of Mantua, he attempted to copy at Mantua the musical establishment and performances he had witnessed at Ferrara. Wert was court composer and a capable madrigalist. The regular musical establishment was enlarged, and a small ensemble of skilled professional female singers was assembled. Lucia and Isabella Pellizzari were employed by 1592; they were joined later by Lucrezia Urbana and Caterina Romana (Caterina Martinelli). By 1600 Mantua ranked with Florence as one of the leading musical centers in Italy.

A similar ensemble of "singing ladies" was formed at the Medici court in Florence in the early 1580s. Laura Bovia joined the court singers in 1581. In 1583 Giulio Caccini (c. 1545–1618) directed an ensemble of three sopranos at the Medici court; in 1584, two female singers—Vittoria Archilei and a Bolognese lady (probably Laura Bovia)—performed with other musicians at the festivities celebrating the marriage of Vincenzo Gonzaga and Leonora de' Medici. When the Florentine *concerto delle donne* was disbanded in 1589, Laura Bovia found employment in the ensemble at Mantua.

Several features of *concerto delle donne* and *balletto delle donne* performances at Italian courts in the late sixteenth century are historically significant: (1) ladies were featured as performers (singers and dancers); (2) performances were rehearsed; (3) performers and audience were separated; (4) chamber music concerts were reserved for selected court personnel or important visitors (*musica reservata*); (5) vocal music was incorporated into dance scenes; and (6) both music and dance were integrated with drama.

France

Chanson

Pierre Attaingnant (c. 1494–c. 1552) was active in Paris as printer and publisher of music from 1525 until his death; during 1537–47 his royal *privilège* to print music named him music printer and music librarian to King Francis I (r. 1515–47). Attaignant invented a method of printing music notation in a single impression; his process soon replaced the double- and triple-impression techniques used by other European printers and became the first international method of music printing. Single-impression printing reduced production time and costs considerably; more music could be printed, and it was available for public purchase at affordable prices. In April 1528, Attaingnant published *Chansons nouvelles* (New songs). (Attaingnant's publication bears date 1527, but at that time the annual calendar commenced with Easter eve.) By 1552 he had published over 50 collections of chansons—approximately 1500 songs. Those songs were distinctly French in character, and most of them had been written by composers living in and around Paris.

Chansons had always used the French language. In mid-fifteenth century, most chansons were written in the Burgundian treble-dominated style and followed one of the *formes fixes* of courtly poetry. In the hands of Ockeghem and Busnois, during the late fifteenth century, the chanson was characterized by continuous polyphony with more equality among the voices, and it contained melodic figures, turns of phrase, and cadential formulae common to the musical vocabulary of most Franco-Netherlands composers. In chansons written c. 1500, the several polyphonic lines are equal in importance but independent. The gradual increase in this style of writing in the late fifteenth and early sixteenth centuries coincides with the gradual abandonment of formal patterns of the poetic *formes fixes*. It should be remembered, however, that although the imitative chanson used the same contrapuntal techniques as the motet, the two types of vocal music differed in purpose and text and in the fact that the chanson always used quicker and more decisive rhythms than the motet. Many chansons characteristically commenced with repeated pitches in the rhythm ♩ ♩ ♩ , a feature that carried over into the instrumental canzona (see p. 274).

Among sixteenth-century Franco-Flemish composers writing imitative contrapuntal chansons were Gombert, Clement, Thomas Crecquillon (c. 1490–c. 1557), and Pierre de Manchicourt (c. 1510–64). Crecquillon's *Pour ung plaisir* (For a pleasure) was quite popular in Italy; Andrea Gabrieli made a keyboard arrangement of it.

The musical style of the chansons published in Paris by Attaingnant was markedly different. They were light in texture, strongly rhythmic, usually in duple meter, with texts set syllabically for four voices. Though the songs are predominantly homorhythmic and homophonic, with the main melody in the highest voice, short points of imitation were sometimes included. Frequently, the chansons are characterized by passages containing many repeated notes. The structure of each musical phrase corresponds with that of the poetry, but formally they were constructed in distinct short sections, some of which were repeated: aba, aabc, aba'ca'', and others. In many respects, this style of chanson—sometimes called the Parisian chanson—resembles the frottola. This type of chanson was especially popular during the 1530s and 1540s. The principal composers of Parisian chansons were Claudin de Sermisy (c. 1490–1562), Clément Janequin (c. 1485–1558), and Pierre Certon (d. 1572). All are well represented in Attaingnant's publications. Typical examples are Sermisy's *Tant que vivray* (As long as I live), *Jouissance vous donneray* (Delight I will give you), and *Vivray je tousjours en soucy* (Shall I live always in anxiety . . .). (See ex. 11.7.) In *A ce ioly moys* (In this pretty month; DWMA81), a four-voice *chanson* in abba form, Janequin combined imitative polyphony and repeated notes in a kind of light patter.

Many of Janequin's chansons are descriptive, containing bird calls, street cries, fanfares, and other similar, realistic text painting. Some examples are *L'alouette* (The Lark), *Le Chant des oiseaux* (The song of birds), and *Le Caquet des femmes* (Women's chatter). Janequin's most famous descriptive chanson is *La bataille de Marignan* (*La Guerre*; DWMA82), supposedly written about the Battle of Marignan (1515); this chanson served as model for other "battle" pieces by Janequin and by other composers.

Almost all composers of chansons wrote motets and Masses, also. Many chansons served as models for parody Masses or provided thematic material for Masses and motets.

During the last half of the sixteenth century some composers, especially those working in northern France and the Netherlands, wrote chansons in the traditional Franco-Netherlands style. Parisian composers Claude Le Jeune, Jacques Mauduit, and others

(a)

(b)

(c)

Example 11.7 Sermisy's Parisian chansons contain features typical of the genre: (*a*) the opening three-note figure and the homorhythmic, syllabic style of *Tant que vivray*; (*b*) the repeated notes in *Vivray je tousjours en soucy* (mm. 1, 4–5); and (*c*) the paired voices in the four-voice texture of *Jouissance vous donneray*. *(From Claudin de Sermisy,* Collected Works, *vol. 3, p. 138; vol. 4, pp. 99, 127–28. Corpus mensurabilis musicae 52, American Institute of Musicology.)*

who wrote *airs de cour* and *musique mesurée* composed serious polyphonic chansons, also. At the hands of versatile composers such as Arcadelt and Lassus, who were adept at writing both madrigals and chansons, expressive madrigalian devices infiltrated chansons. Arcadelt worked in France after c. 1553; his extant works include 126 chansons, most of them for four voices. His early chansons exhibit conventional Netherlands-style polyphony; his late chansons are homophonic, with simultaneous pronunciation of text by all voices. Lassus composed some of the finest chansons written during the last half of the sixteenth century. Between 1550 and c. 1585 he wrote approximately 150 of them. Most of the poems he set were authored by French writers—Ronsard, Baïf, Villon, Marot, and others. The texts are of all kinds, from bawdy (*Il estoit une religeuse,* There was a nun) to serious; some have a moral or religious theme (*Susanne un jour,* One day Susanna; Daniel, ch.13, apocryphal). Lassus's musical settings vary accordingly: there are dialogues, Parisian patter-type chansons, serious motetlike pieces, and witty, light-hearted songs. Popular chansons such as *Bon jour, mon coeur* (Good day, my love) were arranged for keyboard.

Voix de ville

Around the middle of the sixteenth century, a type of courtly poetry was written—often by some of the most famous poets of the age—that was known as *voix de ville* (city voice). Occasionally, the alternate spelling *vau de ville* was used; by c. 1580, the single word *vaudeville* was common. A *voix de ville* poem has several short stanzas that are set strophically to music in a homophonic chordal style, with the melody in the top voice. In many respects, a *voix de ville* setting resembles that used for the Parisian chanson. Adrien Le Roy's publication *Le second livre de guiterre, contenant plusieurs chansons en forme de voix de ville* (The second book for guitar, containing several songs in *voix de ville* form; 1555) presents the complete text of each *voix de ville* together with its melody and tablature for guitar accompaniment.

Air de cour

Le Roy stated in the Preface to *Livre d'air de cours miz sur le luth* (Book of court airs set for lute; 1571) that the kind of song contained in this volume was formerly called *voix de ville.* The volume contains 22 solo songs with lute accompaniment. Le Roy printed the vocal and instrumental parts on opposite pages. The vocal part is in ordinary notation without barlines; the accompaniment is in lute tablature with barlines. A solo song with lute accompaniment is known also as **lute song.**

During 1571–c. 1650, the term *air de cour,* or simply the word *air,* was used to denote a secular, strophic song sung at court for the entertainment of the king and his courtiers. *Airs de cour* were written for four or five unaccompanied voices or for solo voice with instrumental (usually lute) accompaniment. Nearly all of the *airs de cour* composed between 1580 and 1600 are polyphonic; solo *airs de cour* with lute accompaniment flourished again after 1608.

Musique mesurée

In the last third of the sixteenth century, a group of French poets known as the *Pléiade,* chief of whom was Jean-Antoine de Baïf (1532–89), wrote verses in which they attempted to apply to the French language an accentual version of the quantitative principles of Greek and Latin verse. By these principles, long was equated with accented syllables and short with unaccented syllables. In 1571, Baïf and singer-composer Thibault de Courville (d. 1581) founded the *Académie de Poésie et de Musique* (Academy of Poetry and Music), with letters patent from King Charles IX (r. 1560–74).

Baïf believed that music and poetry should be united as they were—or as he thought they were—in ancient times. To this end, he and some of his musical colleagues devised a system whereby *vers mesurées* could be set to music. Quantitative scansion of the poetry determined the musical note values—a long syllable was set to a note double the value of that used for a short syllable. The musical settings, called *musique mesurée à l'antique* (measured music in ancient style), or simply *musique mesurée,* were homophonic and almost totally homorhythmic and chordal, so that the words could be heard clearly. The artificiality of the procedure prohibited true expression of the text; as a result, *musique mesurée* was short-lived. Its principal composers were Jacques Mauduit (1557–1627) and Claude Le Jeune (c. 1530–1600). All but 3 of Le Jeune's 146 surviving *airs* are *musique mesurées,* e.g., *D'une coline* (On a hill). At times, Le

Example 11.8 Opening of Le Jeune's *Revecy venir du printans* set as *vers mesurée*. (Taken from: Claude Le Jeune, AIRS [1608] edited by D. P. Walker [Miscellanea 1, vol. 1.] © 1951/1959 by American Institute of Musicology/ Hänssler-Verlag, Neuhausen-Stuttgart, West Germany.)

Jeune included short melismas in his settings of *vers mesurées*, e.g., in *Revecy venir du printans* (ex. 11.8; DWMA83). *Airs de cour* written during the last quarter of the sixteenth century were influenced significantly by the asymmetrical rhythms and homophonic character of *musique mesurée*.

England

Music flourished in England during the sixteenth century. As a younger son of Henry VII, Henry VIII (r. 1509–47) was educated for a career in the church rather than as prospective ruler; naturally, his education included musical training. Henry possessed a fair measure of talent; he played organ, lute, and virginals and was an active composer of both sacred and secular music. Among his 34 surviving compositions are 13 instrumental pieces, the three-voice motet *Quam pulchra es* (How lovely thou art), and numerous three- and four-voice part songs. Music played an important part in court life during Henry VIII's reign. The number of musicians permanently employed at court increased; in addition to singers, court account books for 1548 list 58 instrumentalists, many of whom were foreigners.

Edward VI (r. 1547–53) and Mary (r. 1553–58) also supported music. Elizabeth I (r. 1558–1603) had received training in music, as did all noble women, and was a competent virginalist. During her reign music attained a high level of excellence rarely equaled thereafter.

In the early sixteenth century, secular part songs flourished. Essentially, these were English-language chansons presumably intended for choral singing. One

of the earliest music books printed in England is a collection of such songs: *In this boke ar cōteynyd xx sōges, ix of iiii ptes and xi of thre ptes* (In this book are contained 20 songs, 9 of 4 parts and 11 of three parts; 1530). The only other known collection of secular English part songs printed during 1530–80 is Thomas Whythorne's (1528–96) *Songs to three, fower, and five voyces* (1571). In almost all of these 76 songs, the top voice carries the main melody; the other voices provide nonimitative contrapuntal accompaniment.

Madrigal

The influence of the Italian madrigal was felt strongly in England in the last two decades of the sixteenth century. Manuscript copies of Italian madrigals, some of them in English translation, were circulating in England by mid-century. Increased interest of the English in madrigals c. 1580 inspired Nicholas Yonge (d. 1619) to edit and publish *Musica transalpina* (Music across the Alps; London, 1588), a collection of 57 Italian madrigals with texts translated into English. According to the book's Preface, the translations were made in 1583, and the songs were sung by a group of gentlemen who met at Yonge's home daily for the practice of music. Before 1598, four other collections appeared, including Yonge's second anthology, also entitled *Musica transalpina* (1597).

During the 1590s nearly all English composers wrote some madrigals. Even William Byrd, who favored other song forms, composed two madrigals. Thomas Morley (c. 1557–1602), a pupil of Byrd, was the leading composer and provided the stylistic model for the Elizabethan light madrigal that enjoyed great popularity for about a decade. Morley's first two books of light madrigals are *Canzonets or Little Short Songs to Three Voyces* (1593) and *Madrigalls to Foure Voyces* (1594). The pieces in these books are relatively simple and are clearly harmonic but contain more counterpoint than Italian light madrigals of the time. Both *The First Book of Balletts to Five Voyces* (1595) and *The First book of Canzonetts to Two Voyces* (1595) were printed in parallel English and Italian editions issued simultaneously; these books consist principally of free transcriptions of works by Gastoldi and Felice Anerio (c. 1560–1614) and are even lighter music than Morley's earlier madrigals. The strophic settings are homophonic and dancelike, often with a refrain that incorporates *fa-la* syllables. Morley's madrigals are markedly lacking in chromaticism, word painting, and dramatic effects, features found in the madrigals of his English and Italian contemporaries. Among his best-known works are *Aprill is in my mistris face* (4 vc.; 1594; DWMA84) and *Sing wee and chaunt it* (*A lieta vita*, 5 vc.; based on Gastoldi; DWMA78, DWMA79).

Morley's anthology *The Triumphes of Oriana to 5. and 6. Voices* (1601) is modeled after the Italian anthology *Il trionfo di Dori* (The Triumphs of Dori; 1592). The English publication comprises 24 madrigals by 22 different composers; Morley and Ellis Gibbons (1573–1603; older brother of Orlando Gibbons) each contributed two pieces. The publication was designed to honor Queen Elizabeth I, who was frequently referred to in contemporary pastoral poetry as "Oriana." Each of the madrigals in the anthology concludes with the lines: "Then sang the shepherds and nymphs of Diana,/'Long live fair Oriana'!" or a slight variant thereof.

Thomas Weelkes (1576–1623), John Wilbye (1574–1638), and John Bennet (fl. 1599–1614) also made significant contributions to English madrigal repertory. Bennet's writing is in many respects similar to that of Morley, but his pieces are replete with madrigalisms, e.g., the pastoral *Thyrsis, Sleepest Thou?* (DWMA85). Weelkes's and Wilbye's settings are more serious than those of Morley, their music less Italianate than his. Wilbye's three-voice *As fair as morn* contains much imitative counterpoint. In general, English composers gave greater attention to the purely musical features of their madrigal settings than to mere depiction or dramatization of textual elements. Word painting is present but is assigned a role subservient to the overall musical structure of the piece. Many of Weelkes's madrigals are saturated with counterpoint that at times seems more instrumentally than vocally conceived. This is especially true of the pieces in his *Madrigals of 5. and 6. Parts* (1600), and the designation on the title page that the pieces are "Apt for the Viols and Voices" seems to recognize this fact.

The various types of English madrigals were intended primarily for performance by unaccompanied solo voices; however, title pages of many publications state that the pieces are "apt for voices and viols," and doubtless the pieces were performed by any available combination of voices and viols. The pieces were printed in partbooks in notation devoid of barlines. English composers paid particular attention to correct declamation of text; though vocal performance of all lines might evoke a fascinating accentual counterpoint, this never interfered with the musical phraseology.

Consort Song

The **consort song** is an exclusively English type of vocal music that flourished in the late sixteenth and early seventeenth centuries. Around the middle of the sixteenth century the consort of viols became increasingly popular as a performing ensemble in England. Some English composers wrote songs for one or more solo voices with an *obbligato* (required) instrumental accompaniment that was usually intended for a consort of viols. Songs of this kind are known as **consort songs.** The compositional style of the consort song was not affected by either the Italian madrigal or the French air. Consort songs were being written in the early 1560s, but the stature of the consort song was enhanced considerably in the 1570s when William Byrd adopted it in preference to the madrigal; his earliest settings of English poems are strophic songs for one solo voice and a consort of viols. In fact, all of Byrd's consort songs are strophic settings in which the text is set syllabically, and the lines of text clearly differentiated; frequently, there is a melisma on the penultimate syllable of a line of text. Prose as well as poetic texts were used.

Sometimes the consort song was expanded by the addition of a chorus. When an ecclesiastical text was set and the accompaniment was suitable for performance on organ, the consort song became a **verse anthem,** a form Byrd is credited with inventing (see p. 247). Byrd and Orlando Gibbons (1583–1625) were the leading composers of consort songs. More than half of Gibbons's verse anthems have fully written-out accompaniments for viols and alternative accompaniments for organ. None of Gibbons's church music was published during his lifetime.

Lute Song or Ayre

The **lute song** and the solo song with viol accompaniment became popular in France early in the sixteenth century but did not flourish in England until the late 1590s. Its rise in popularity in England coincided with the decline of the English madrigal. In England the solo song with lute accompaniment was commonly known as **lute ayre,** or simply **ayre.** Its leading composers were John Dowland (1563–1626) and Thomas Campion (1567–1620).

Dowland's *The First Booke of Songes or Ayres of Foure Partes with Tableture* [sic] *for the Lute* (1597) contains 21 of his songs written for performance either by solo voice with lute accompaniment or as four-part songs with or without lute. *The Second Booke of Songs or Ayres of 2, 4 and 5 parts; with Tableture* [sic] *for the Lute or Orpherian* [sic], *with the Viol de Gamba* was published in 1600 (fig. 11.3); *The Third and Last Booke of Songs or Aires Newly Composed to Sing to the Lute, Orpharion or Viols* appeared in 1603. (The orpharion, now obsolete, was a kind of substitute lute in use during c. 1580–c. 1655. The instrument is about 40 inches long; its body is flat like a guitar, with a scalloped outline. It is fitted with six double courses of thin wire strings, and uses lute tuning. Two authentic orpharions were known to exist in 1988.) In these publications the solo ayres have the vocal and lute music printed on the same page, no doubt for the convenience of the vocalist who wanted to play his own accompaniment (fig. 11.4, left side).

Most of Dowland's songs, including the well-known "What if I never speede," from *The Third and Last Booke of Songs or Aires* . . . , are printed in two versions: for vocal ensemble and as vocal solo with

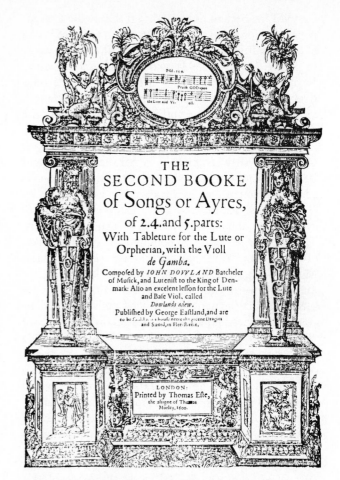

Figure 11.3 Title page of Dowland: *The Second Booke of Songs or Ayres,* published in 1600.

lute accompaniment. In the original publications, the music is printed so that all of the performers could sit around a table and read the music from the same book (fig. 11.4).

Other well-known ayres by Dowland are "Flow my tears," from *The Seconde Booke of Ayres* . . . ; "Go crystall teares" (1597); "Fine knacks for ladies" (1600); "Sweet stay a while, why will you rise?" (1612); and "In darkness let mee dwell" (1610). Many of Dowland's works are characterized by melancholy; the tragic and emotionally intense "In darkness let mee dwell" is accompanied by piercing discords (DWMA86).

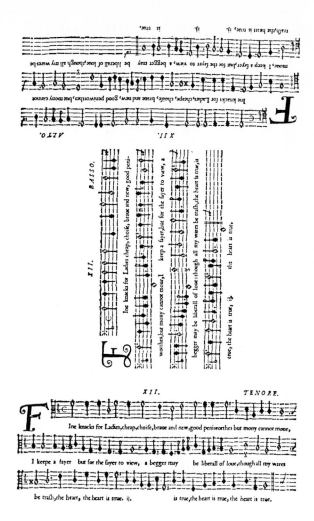

Figure 11.4 Dowland's ayre *Fine knacks for ladies,* as printed in the original edition.

Germanic Lands

Meisterlieder

The composition and performance of music was an avocation for the *Meistersinger,* each of whom worked at another trade in a German, Austrian, or Moravian city or town. *Meisterlieder,* the monophonic German songs created and performed by members of the Meistersinger guilds, flourished especially during the sixteenth century, yet relatively few *Meisterlieder* melodies have been preserved, for the art of the Meistersinger was an almost exclusively oral tradition.

After 1540, guild regulations expressly forbade the performance of printed *Lieder* at the public concerts given by Meistersinger. Sources relative to the Meistersinger and their music include records of guild meetings, posters announcing guild activities, artwork, and historical accounts written by Meistersinger, such as Cyriac Spangenberg (1528–1604). Johann Christoph Wagenseil (1633–1703) included some *Meisterlieder* in his treatise (publ. 1697) on the Meistersinger of Nuremberg, one of the most important sixteenth-century guilds, and that to which the shoemaker Hans Sachs (1494–1576) belonged. Wagenseil's treatise was Richard Wagner's (1813–83) prime source of information for the opera *Die Meistersinger von Nürnberg,* in which Hans Sachs is a character.

All *Meisterlieder* are monophonic; they were performed unaccompanied, usually by a vocal soloist, occasionally by a chorus. A *Meisterlied* comprises an odd number of stanzas—a minimum of three—constructed poetically and set musically in aab form (Bar form). The extant melodies are narrow in range and are notated without any rhythmic indications; presumably, the rhythm is declamatory and determined by the text.

Polyphonic *Lied*

In the second decade of the sixteenth century several German printers published collections of anonymous polyphonic *Lieder*. In later editions, some of the pieces are identified as the work of Adam von Fulda (c. 1445–1505), Heinrich Finck (c. 1445–1527), Paul Hofhaimer (1459–1537), and Heinrich Isaac (c. 1450–1517). Finck and Isaac are considered masters of the polyphonic *Lied*.

Both fifteenth- and early sixteenth-century polyphonic *Lieder* may properly be termed *Tenorlieder,* because the main melody lies in the tenor voice. However, in the fifteenth century the tenor was often the highest voice of the song; in the sixteenth-century pieces the tenor is the highest male voice and is surrounded by other voices whose music is more disjunct and has livelier rhythm. Isaac's Lieder do not always follow this pattern, however. *Isbruck, ich muss dich lassen* exists in two versions, one of which differs from the norm in having the main melody in the superius. In *Zwischen Perg und tieffe Tal* (*Zwischen Berg und tiefem Tal;* DWMA69), bass and tenor present the main melody in canon at the octave. Elements of Netherlands counterpoint frequently infiltrate Isaac's Lieder. This is a more outstanding characteristic of the Lieder written by Isaac's pupil Ludwig Senfl (c. 1486–1543), who brought the polyphonic Lied to artistic perfection. Through his skillful application of Netherlands contrapuntal techniques Senfl created motetlike Lieder settings of great beauty.

From c. 1530 to c. 1555, many published collections of polyphonic Lieder contained pieces in from two to eight parts, with the performance instruction *zum Singen und auf allerlei Instrumenten dienlich,* indicating that, although all voices are supplied with text, the music might be performed by any suitable combination of voices and instruments. No doubt publications of this kind were an attempt to supply the demand for Lieder for home and communal music making.

After the middle of the sixteenth century, the secular *Tenorlied* decreased in importance, though sacred music in *Tenorlied* style was still being composed for use in Lutheran churches. The polyphonic *Lied* is preserved in some of the sacred songs of Michael Praetorius. In the secular song *Ach, Schatz* (Ah, darling), Hans Leo Hassler (1562–1612) placed the main melody in the middle voice. Hassler wrote almost 60 polyphonic Lieder setting his own texts. *Ach, süsse Seel'* (Ah, sweet soul; 6 vc.) and *Mein G'müt ist mir verwirret* (see p. 243; DWMA87), both in the collection *Lustgarten neuer teutscher Gesäng, . . .* (Pleasure garden of new German songs . . . ; 4–8 vc.; 1601), exemplify his Lieder style. Hassler, who had studied with Andrea Gabrieli in Venice, incorporated Italian madrigal techniques in some of his *Lieder*. Also, he composed two- to four-voice German songs in the style of madrigals, e.g., the collection *Neue teutsche Gesäng nach Art der welschen Madrigalien und Canzonetten* (New German songs in the style of madrigals and *canzonette*; 1596). Many of the Lieder composed by Lassus (p. 264) after c. 1570 resemble motets or chansons, e.g., *Ich armer Mann* (I, poor man).

Ode

Poetic odes created in classical antiquity were intended to be sung; the word *ode* derives from the Greek word meaning "I sing." Usually, the music was improvised; however, a few medieval settings of odes by Sappho and Horace survive.

In the 1490s academic interest in the classical ode was extended to musical composition when the German humanist Celtes commissioned his pupil P. Tritonius to compose four-voice settings illustrating the poetic meters in Horace's odes. Tritonius's settings, in *Tenorlied* style, were sung by students at the end of lectures; in 1507, Tritonius's settings were published. In 1534 Ludwig Senfl made new settings of the odes, in cantional style, with Tritonius's tenor melodies as the superius, and new harmonizations. Other composers followed Senfl's lead, including Paul Hofhaimer, whose *Harmoniae poeticae* (Poetical harmonies) appeared in Nuremberg in 1539. During the sixteenth century, choral odes were included at the ends of acts in Latin plays written by German schoolmasters. These plays were on sacred or allegorical subjects and were performed by students.

Quodlibet

The *quodlibet* (literally, whatsoever you please) is a piece in which well-known melodies or fragments of melodies (with or without their original texts) are combined successively or simultaneously. Composers wrote *quodlibets* for two purposes: humorous parody or display of technical virtuosity. Though a few pieces of this kind were created in medieval times, the term *quodlibet* was first used in connection with music in 1544, when Walter Schmetzl published a collection of 25 such songs. Songs of similar structure appeared in other countries during the Renaissance: the *fricassée* in France, *messanza* or *misticanza* in Italy, *ensalada* in Spain, and *medley* in England.

Iberia

The principal types of Spanish sixteenth-century secular vocal music are the *romance* and the *villancico*. The *romance* is a ballad, i.e., its text is strophic and narrative. Musical settings of romances are for three or four voices and are strophic and homophonic, with the main melody in the top voice. The exact manner in which a *romance* was performed is not known. In manuscripts, the text is underlaid for the first strophe only, and only under the principal melody. These songs may have been performed by a soloist with instrumental accompaniment; however, it is generally believed that until c. 1550 these romantic ballads were sung at court chorally, with one or more persons per part.

The term *villancico* is a diminutive of *villano,* meaning "peasant." The *villancico* originated in a medieval Spanish dance lyric with a refrain; its formal construction resembles that of the *ballata* and *virelai*: a prefatory refrain, followed by several strophes separated by the refrain, and a concluding refrain. The refrain is called *estribillo*; the strophe, *copla.*

Important manuscript sources of early *villancicos* include the Spanish *Cancionero musical de Palacio* (Palace Songbook; compiled c. 1490–c. 1520 for the court of Ferdinand and Isabella), containing more than 300 *villancicos*; the Portuguese *Cancionero musical de la Hortênsia* (Hortênsia Songbook; compiled c. 1500), containing 65 courtly love songs for three voices. Important composers of the early *villancico* are Juan del Encina, Pedro de Escobar, and Francesco Peñalosa; 62 of the pieces in *Cancionero musical de Palacio* are by Encina.

The *Cancionero musical de Palacio* was once owned by Fernando Colón (1488–1539), Spanish bibliophile and music collector, who was the illegitimate son of Christopher Columbus. At the time of Colón's death, he owned more than 15,000 items, including many valuable manuscripts and printed books of music; he willed his library to Seville Cathedral. Unfortunately, only about 4000 items from his library were known to exist in 1988, but some of those are unique and very valuable medieval music manuscripts and Petrucci prints. Colón's precise catalogues of his holdings survive and reveal the extent of his acquisitions.

Early *villancicos* are for three or four voices. Though the music is contrapuntal, the main melody is in the superius, and the other voices provide accompaniment. Usually, the text is underlaid for the superius only and is set syllabically. Duple mensuration prevails. (DWMA88.)

Juan del Encina (1468–c. 1530), Spanish poet, dramatist, and composer, wrote almost all of his literary and musical works before he was 30. He was one of the first to write dramatic works specifically for performance, with instructions that specify singing and dancing. The earliest of these are religious plays associated with festivals such as Christmas and Easter and resemble medieval mystery plays; his later plays are secular and pastoral. Music and dancing are included in all of Encina's plays and are an integral part of the action. Encina placed a *villancico* either midway through or at the conclusion of the play; sometimes

The Rise of Regional Styles

villancicos were sung and danced in both places in the play. Texts of the *villancicos* comment on the preceding dramatic events or summarize the preceding dialogue. Some of Encina's *villancicos* are intended for solo or duet vocal performance with instrumental accompaniment; in other *villancicos* by him, all parts are to be sung. His melodies are expressive and flowing but are concise, with syllabic settings of text; the final cadence of the verse is slightly ornamented. The pieces are homorhythmic polyphony, but the rhythm, influenced by the accents of the poetry, is flexible and varied (DWMA89).

Six *romances* by Encina are extant. These melodies are simple syllabic settings, cast in four phrases; they are homorhythmic and chordal, chorale-like and serious in tone.

The next generation of sixteenth-century Spanish composers wrote polyphonic *villancicos* in which all voices share text and melody. Imitative counterpoint predominates, but homorhythmic (familiar style) counterpoint appears frequently. Often the text comprises the *estribillo* and one *copla*. Principal sources of this kind of *villancico* include the manuscript *Cancionero musical de Barcelona* (Barcelona Songbook), containing 20 *villancicos* composed c. 1520–34; and the printed *Cancionero del Duque de Calabria* (Songbook of the Duke of Calabria), containing 53 anonymous *villancicos* composed between c. 1530 and 1550.

Villancicos composed around the middle of the sixteenth century reflect the influence of the Italian madrigal. Typical *villancicos* of this time appear in two published collections of works by Juan Vasquez (c. 1510–c. 1560): *Villancicos y canciones* (*Villancicos* and canzonas; 1551) and *Recopilación de sonetos y villancicos* (Collection of sonnets and *villancicos*; Seville, 1560). The *estribillo* is expanded and often leads directly (i.e., without pause) into the single *copla,* which is through-composed; a varied form of the *estribillo* concludes the piece.

In the last quarter of the sixteenth century some devotional and liturgical *villancicos* were produced. Some of these were secular pieces with modified texts; others were new compositions, e.g., the liturgical *villancicos* in Francisco Guerrero's (1528–99) *Canciones y villanescas espirituales* (1589).

Summary

A great amount of secular music was produced during the sixteenth century; by the end of the century, the center of interest in musical composition was secular song. Much of the secular music was written for use at court. However, the emergence of a large bourgeois public for whom music was primarily a form of recreation created a body of performing amateurs who provided a ready market for printed anthologies of secular music, e.g., the books of *frottole* and *chansons* issued by Petrucci and Attaingnant. In Germanic lands tradesmen for whom music was an avocation composed and performed their own secular music and maintained high standards through guild regulations.

Though some monophonic music was produced, most of the sixteenth-century secular songs were polyphonic, with the main melody in the highest voice. Both ensemble music and instrumentally accompanied vocal solos were composed. Except for the presence of a lute tablature, or the statement on a title page that a collection was suitable for singing or playing, printed music appeared to be unaccompanied vocal music. Instrumentally accompanied solo song was not new, but the prominence, in the late sixteenth century, of the vocal solo with simple harmonic accompaniment was an important factor in musical developments in the seventeenth century. Each region had distinctive types of vernacular vocal music, but the Italian madrigal, with its expressive musical language, was the most influential. Not only did it influence the style of secular music in England, Spain, and other countries, but the manner in which madrigals were performed at several Italian courts during the last two decades of the sixteenth century (performers before an audience, planned and rehearsed performances, and the inclusion of solo and ensemble madrigals in dramatic productions), was an indication of the direction of musical developments in the seventeenth century.

Chapter

12

Reformation
and Counter-Reformation

From time to time over the centuries there had been agitation for various kinds of reform—administrative, doctrinal, political, musical—within the Roman Catholic Church. Periodically, papal complaints had been registered against polyphony, but composers and performers had managed to circumvent most papal antipolyphonic directives or recommendations.

In the main, the Church had weathered all storms. It had survived the exile in Avignon (sometimes referred to as the Babylonian Captivity of the Church) and the Great Schism; John Wyclif (1328–84) and the Lollards had been suppressed; Jan Hus (1369–1415) had been burned at the stake, but his followers had been granted small doctrinal concessions. Musically, the Hussites preferred simple, monophonic hymns; they exiled polyphony and musical instruments from their churches. Around mid-sixteenth century, however, austerity began to soften, and some note-against-note part-music crept in.

A new religious sect arose in Bohemia and Moravia c. 1450. The group, known as Bohemian Brethren, eventually established an independent church with lay priesthood. However, certain of their beliefs, e.g., the equality of all persons in a society without class distinctions, brought the Brethren persecution, imprisonment, execution, and, in 1618, expulsion from Bohemia and Moravia. Remnants of the sect survived in Saxony; in 1722 the brotherhood was reestablished in Herrnhut as *Unitas Fratrum,* or Moravian Brethren. Shortly thereafter, some Brethren emigrated to America, where they made significant contributions to the development of music (see pp. 532, 533).

For the Brethren, singing was an integral part of everyday life—at home, in school, and in the church. In the sixteenth century, they rarely used polyphony, though children were taught part-singing in school. The Brethren's preference for monophony was, no doubt, a reflection of their belief in the equality of all things. Their interest in hymns is reflected in the compilation and publication of extensive hymnbooks, most of which had several editions. The first of these books, edited by their bishop, Luke, appeared in 1505. Jan Roh's compilation, prepared in 1541, included 308 hymns; the hymnbook compiled in 1561 by Jan Blahoslav contained approximately 750. The melodies are relatively simple, with close affinity between the vernacular words and the music.

The Reformation

Martin Luther

Martin Luther (1483–1546) unintentionally created the rift that caused the Protestant Reformation. When Luther posted his 95 theses on the door of the Schlosskirche, which served as the community bulletin board at Wittenberg, he was merely announcing that he wanted to debate those controversial points with an interested party. The incident was the opening wedge that split the Catholic Church. The reforms Luther advocated were primarily doctrinal. His theological beliefs were based on Scripture, not Church traditions; practices such as the sale of indulgences were repugnant and sacrilegious to him. When the Church could not subdue Luther, he was excommunicated; when called before the Diet of Worms, he refused to recant and was condemned as a State outlaw. Nevertheless, he continued to teach and preach, and virtually all sixteenth-century Protestant reformers were influenced to some extent by his activities.

Luther's father was a prosperous Thuringian who intended his son to become a lawyer and educated him accordingly. Martin Luther attended Latin schools in Magdeburg, Mansfield, and Eisenach, earned baccalaureate and masters degrees at the University of Erfurt, then began to study law. Soon, however, his interests changed. In 1505 he became an Augustinian monk; two years later he was ordained a priest and said his first Mass. While on an Augustinian commission to Rome in 1510, Luther was appalled at the commercialism of the Church and the worldliness of the clergy. He returned to Wittenberg, earned the doctorate in theology in 1512, and became professor of Scripture at Wittenberg University. He held that position until his death.

Luther considered music a gift of God, second only to theology; the place of music in the sixteenth-century Lutheran church mirrored this view. Luther stated his position clearly in the Preface to Walter's *Geystliches gesangk Buchleyn* (Little book of sacred songs; see p. 244): "It is not my view that the Gospel

Martin Luther.

should cause all the arts to be struck down and disappear; on the contrary, I should like to see all the arts, and especially music, used in the service of Him who gave and created them." Luther's attitude toward instrumental music is inherent in a statement included in the Preface to the *German Mass:* "Whenever it was helpful I would have all the bells peal, all the organs thunder, and everything sound that could sound." Yet, in many sixteenth-century Lutheran churches the organ was used only for intonations before and interludes between unaccompanied vocal music.

Luther possessed a mastery of music beyond that of a mere enthusiast. He had received musical training in school; as a youngster, he sang in the *Kurrende,* a boys' choir that went about singing from door to door to obtain alms. As an adult, he had a fine tenor voice, was an accomplished performer on flute and lute, understood music theory, and was a skilled composer. He enjoyed Franco-Netherlands polyphony, especially that of Josquin Desprez. Luther composed some polyphonic music; two four-voice motets by him are extant: *Höre Gott meine Stimm' in meiner Klage*

Reformation — Counter-Reformation

Moravian Brethren

Rise of Lutheranism -

1483 - - - -Martin Luther - - - - - - - - - - - - - - 1546

- Chorale -
- German hymnals; German Mass

Zwingliism - - -

Calvinism -

- Genevan Psalter

- *Souterliedekens*

- English Reformation -

c. 1543 - - Byrd - (1623)

c. 1490 - - - Taverner - - - - - - - - - - - - - 1545

c. 1505 - - Tye -c. 1572

- Council
of Trent -

c. 1525 - - - Palestrina -1594

1548 - - Victoria - - - - - - - - - - - - - - - - - - (1611)

1532 - - Lassus -1594

(God, hear my voice in my complaint) and *Non moriar, sed vivam* (I shall not die, but live; Ps. 118, vs.17). The latter was reissued in 1917 by Breitkopf & Härtel. Luther believed music had educational value and ethical power; he advocated *Kantorei* and choir schools and congregational participation in the Service music. (A *Kantorei* was a choir of professional singers employed by a church.)

Luther had no desire to abolish Latin, and his *Formula missae* (Order of the Mass; 1523) was intended for use by cathedrals, collegiate churches, and other congregations that knew Latin. It consisted primarily of the five parts of the Ordinary in chant; hymns might be added after the Sanctus and Agnus Dei. The *Deudsche Messe* (German Mass; 1526) was designed for churches with congregations of "unlearned lay folk." Luther's was not the first vernacular German Mass, nor was it intended as a definitive format for the Lutheran vernacular Service; many variants were used. The *Deudsche Messe* (fig. 12.1) was an altered version of the Roman Catholic Mass. The Gloria was omitted; German hymns were substituted for some sections; other sections were omitted

```
              DEUDSCHE MESSE (1526)

Introit   (A hymn or psalm, in 1st mode)
Kyrie     (troped)
Collect
Epistle   (on 8th tone)
Nun bitten wir den Heiligen Geist  (Now let us pray to
    the Holy Spirit)    replacing the Gradual
Gospel    (on 6th tone)
Sermon    (based on the Gospel text)
Lord's Prayer
Communion sacrament, in condensed form
Communion hymn:  Jesus Christus, unser Heiland (Jesus
    Christ, our Savior)
Jesaja dem Propheten des geschah  (Isaiah the prophet saw)
    = the German Sanctus
Optional:  Christe, du Lamm Gottes  (Christ, Lamb of God)
    = the German Agnus Dei
```

Figure 12.1 Outline of Luther's German Mass.

or shortened. The portions retained were not merely textual translations from Latin into German, but adaptations, for Luther realized that in a vernacular Mass the musical and textual rhythms and accents must be compatible. When preparing materials for the church, Luther sought the advice of composers whose music he admired and musicians whose opinions he trusted: Ludwig Senfl, Conrad Rupsch, Georg Rhau, Johann Walter, Sixtus Dietrich, and others.

The Lutheran church made some use of the *Leise* (pl., *Leisen*), also. In these German folk hymns, the refrain *Kyrieleison* or *Kyrieleise* (Lord, have mercy) concluded every stanza. Luther expanded some of the older *Leisen—Nun bitten wir den heiligen Geist* (Now we ask the Holy Spirit) is one—and wrote some new hymns in *Leise* style.

Chorale

At the heart of Lutheran music is the German *Choral,* or *Kirchenlied* (church song), called in English a **chorale.** A chorale is a German hymn comprising a text and a melody and was originally sung *a cappella;* thus, a chorale is comparable to a monophonic chant. In the early Lutheran church, chorales were intended for congregational singing; most chorales were strophic. Some sixteenth-century chorales were newly composed melodies; others were *contrafacta*—chants, nonliturgical spiritual songs, secular melodies, or folk songs fitted with German sacred texts. For example, the chant *Veni Redemptor gentium* (Come, Redeemer of the people) became *Nun komm' der Heiden Heiland* (Come, Savior of the nations); the folk song *Es hat ein Meidlin sein Schuh verlorn* (A maiden has lost her shoe) was transformed to *Gottes Huld hab ich verlorn* (I have lost God's grace). In his endeavor to provide a sufficient number of suitable chorales for the church, Luther urged his composer friends and music advisers to write chorales and make *contrafacta*. Luther wrote numerous chorale texts and is credited with composing and/or arranging the music for them. His best-known chorale is *Ein' feste Burg ist unser Gott* (A mighty fortress is our God; fig. 12.2). Luther's hymns were intended to convey a message, not create a mood. He wrote the music in mensural notation, with the semibreve as basic unit of the beat. In terms of modern metronome markings, the hymns were probably sung at a tempo of approximately M.M. $\quad\text{\textquoteright} = 60$.

In early January 1524 Jobst Gutknecht of Nürnberg printed the first Lutheran hymnal, entitled *Etlich Christlich lider* (Some Christian songs) but commonly referred to as *Das Achtliederbuch* (The Book

Figure 12.2 Luther's chorale *Ein' feste Burg ist unser Gott,* in manuscript. *(Source: Concordia Theological Seminary, Fort Wayne, IN.)*

of eight songs). The volume contained four chorale melodies and eight texts: one anonymous, three by Paul Speratus (1484–1551), and four by Luther, including *Nu freut euch, lieben Christen gmeyn* (Dear Christians, let us now rejoice) and *Aus tieffer not schrey ich zu dyr* (From deep trouble I cry to Thee; Ps. 130). At least three more editions of *Das Achtliederbuch* and four other collections of chorales appeared in 1524 (fig. 12.3). In succeeding years, several similar publications ensued.

Chorales were set polyphonically for choir use. Various compositional styles were employed: (1) the melody treated as cantus firmus, written in long note values and placed in the tenor; (2) each melodic phrase written as a point of imitation, in Netherlands-motet style; (3) the melody in the tenor voice, with the other voice(s) in pseudo-chordal counterpoint; and occasionally (4) in *cantional* style, with the chorale in the top voice. As the sixteenth century advanced, use of treble-dominated style increased. In 1586 Lucas Osiander (1534–1604) published *Fünfftzig geistliche Lieder und Psalmen* (Fifty sacred songs and psalms), the first collection of chorales in four-part cantional-style settings. Frequently thereafter, chorales were set as simple chordal harmonizations of a soprano melody.

Figure 12.3 Title page of *Etlich Christlich lider* (1524), commonly called *Das Achtliederbuch. (Concordia Lutheran Seminary, Fort Wayne, IN.)*

Probably, in performance, the chorale melody was sung, and the organ (or, possibly, other instruments) doubled the melody and provided the harmony.

Chorales served as basic material for motets in much the same manner as chant was used. Polyphonic pieces of this kind, known as **chorale motets,** were composed for two or more voices. A chorale-based *bicinium* or *tricinium* (a two-voice or three-voice composition) resembles a twelfth-century organal motet in that the principal melody appears in the tenor (the bottom voice) and is supplemented and enhanced by the polyphony of the other voice(s) (ex.12.1; DWMA90). In other chorale motets, the chorale melody might be treated imitatively, or it might be retained in one voice while other voices supplemented it with imitative counterpoint. Near the end of the sixteenth century, chorale motets were written increasingly. Hans Leo Hassler (1562–1612) and Michael Praetorius (c. 1572–1621) wrote some of the finest Lutheran motets of that era. Hassler's 52 four-voice *Psalmen und christliche Gesänge* (Psalms and Christian songs; 1607) are stylistically conservative, written in imitative linear counterpoint with some canon and other techniques typical of mid-sixteenth century. Hassler composed many secular songs, also. The melody of his Lied *Mein G'müt ist mir verwirret* (My peace of mind is disturbed, [this has a maiden

(a)

(b)

Example 12.1 Opening phrases of two chorale settings by Johann Walter: (*a*) *Ein' feste Burg* . . . , as a bicinium; (*b*) *Von himmel hoch* . . . ., as a bicinium with optional third voice for a tricinium. *(From Georg Rhau:* Musikdrucke VI, *Bicinia gallica, latina, germanica. Bärenreiter Kassel, Basel, London/Concordia Publ. House/St. Louis/London.)*

done]; 1601; DWMA87) was used by Johann Crüger with Paul Gerhardt's words *O Haupt voll Blut und Wunden* (O, bloody and wounded head); that combination of text and tune was reharmonized by J. S. Bach and used five times in the *Passion according to St. Matthew*. Bach's setting appears in modern hymnals as the Passion hymn *O, sacred head, now wounded*.

Johann Walter

In a Codicil to his Will, Johannes Blankenmüller (1496–1570) stated that, as a needy schoolboy, he had been aided and later adopted by a Thuringian family; thereafter, he had used the name "Johann Walter." Few data concerning his early life can be documented. While a student at Leipzig University (1521–25), he sang bass in the *Hofkapelle* of Frederick the Wise, Elector of Saxony. Then, for approximately two decades, Walter instructed choirboys and organized the singing at the parish church at Torgau. From 1548 to 1554 he directed the Dresden *Hofkapelle*. Walter, a staunch Lutheran, became personally acquainted with Luther at some time prior to 1524. In autumn 1525, when Luther was drafting the *German Mass*, Walter and Conrad Rupsch (c. 1475–c. 1530) served as his advisers.

Walter was both poet and composer; he wrote Magnificat and Psalms settings, motets, many *Tenorlieder* and hymns, and two Passions. His *Passion according to St. Matthew* (1550) uses German text and is of the "dramatic" type, with the words of the *turba* (the crowd) set in motetlike polyphony, and the solo portions in chant. Later composers, e.g., Heinrich Schütz, followed Walter's example when writing Passion settings.

Walter's significance in music history rests primarily on his *Geystliches gesangk Buchleyn* (Little book of sacred songs; 1524), preparation of which Luther supervised and for which he wrote the Preface. This, the earliest published collection of Lutheran choral music, was intended for use by young persons. The first edition contained 5 Latin motets and 38 Lieder; texts for 23 of the German settings were by Luther. The Lieder are cantus firmus works: 36 are *Tenorlieder*; 2 are treble dominated. Walter's collection, which had several subsequent editions, served as model for other collections, many of which included some of the same material.

Georg Rhau

Georg Rhau (1488–1548), German composer and printer of music, theoretical treatises, and theological writings, became one of the most important sixteenth-century publishers of music for Reformation churches. Rhau was esteemed by his contemporaries; on several occasions, Luther consulted him about liturgical music. Rhau's extant publications reveal the high quality and accuracy of his printing and provide a representative repertory of music used in early Protestant worship and pedagogy. Church school curricula included both secular and sacred music.

From his childhood, Rhau was involved in music. He earned a baccalaureate degree at University of Wittenberg (1514), and undoubtedly he became acquainted with Luther while studying there. For the next four years, Rhau worked in his uncle's publishing house in Wittenberg. Rhau's theoretical treatise *Enchiridion . . .* (Manual . . .), dealing with chant, appeared in 1517; a second volume, *Enchiridion musices mensuralis* (Manual of mensural music; 1520), concerns polyphony.

Rhau composed Magnificat and Psalms settings, Latin motets, German hymns, and at least one Mass; these works are not extant. That Rhau was a competent composer and performer is evident—in 1518–20 he served as Kantor of the Thomasschule and Thomaskirche at Leipzig and was a member of the music theory faculty at Leipzig University. From 1523 until his death, he operated a publishing business in Wittenberg. Prefaces to the various music books he printed were written by Luther, Melanchthon, and Bergenhagen—men whose theological writings Rhau published.

Between 1538 and 1545 Rhau issued 15 major collections of polyphonic music. One of these was an enlarged edition of Walter's *Wittembergisch deudsch geistlich Gesangbüchlein* (Little book of Wittenbergian sacred songs in German; 1544). Of greater significance is *Newe deudsche geistliche Gesenge CXXIII*

. . .für die gemeinen Schulen (123 New sacred songs in German . . . for community schools; 1544). This compilation of motets and polyphonic arrangements of chorales includes compositions by leading Germanic composers of the early sixteenth century: Martin Agricola (1486–1556), Arnold von Bruck (c. 1500–54), Sixtus Dietrich (c. 1493–1548), Benedictus Ducis (c. 1490–1544), Georg Forster (c. 1510–68), Lupus Hellinck (c. 1496–1541), Heinrich Isaac (c. 1450–1517), Stephan Mahu (c. 1485–c. 1540), Balthasar Resinarius (c. 1485–1544), Ludwig Senfl (c. 1486–c. 1543), Thomas Stoltzer (c. 1475–1526), and Johann Weinmann (c. 1477–1542), plus 12 anonymous works. Stylistically, the chorale settings vary considerably; thus, the book presents an overview of early Protestant styles. Some pieces are similar to *Tenorlieder*; some resemble Franco-Flemish motets; others are homorhythmic and verge on being chordal, with the chorale melody in the superius. As the century progressed, use of this treble-dominated pseudo-chordal style increased.

Scandinavia

Denmark governed Norway and Sweden from 1379 (date of the Union of Kalmar) until 1522, when Sweden achieved independence under leadership of Gustavus Vasa. Finland had been and remained a Swedish province. Gustavus I (r. 1523–60) and subsequent Swedish rulers actively supported music; Eric XIV composed. Sacred music was an important subject in the school curriculum.

In sixteenth-century Sweden, Lutheranism coexisted with traditional Latin Gregorian Services. In 1531 Olaus Petri prepared the Swedish vernacular Mass, using Luther's *Formula missae* as basis, plus optional music. Though government control of the church provided greater liturgical uniformity than was found in many other countries, the amount of music included gradually increased. Polyphony was seldom used. Chorales occupied a central position in worship, and many German chorales were adapted for Scandinavian use, but until 1586 hymnbooks contained only texts.

A young Finnish student at the University of Rostock, Theodoricus Petri Nylandensis (c. 1560–c. 1616), compiled a song anthology that was published in 1582 as *Piae cantiones . . .* (Sacred songs . . .).

Twelve of the 74 songs in the collection are polyphonic, for from two to four voices; the other 62 are monophonic melodies. Gustav Holst (1874–1934), Jean Sibelius (1865–1957), and John M. Neale (1818–66) made settings of some of these melodies; several of Neale's harmonizations have become familiar carols, e.g., "Good King Wenceslas looked out."

France, Switzerland, Holland

In those parts of France and Switzerland affected by the Reformation, church music was restricted drastically. Ulrich Zwingli (1484–1531) and his followers regarded art and music as powers to distract the faithful rather than as beneficial adjuncts to worship. Zwingli was educated in music; he was quite talented both vocally and instrumentally. For a time, he considered pursuing a career in music. After ordination to priesthood (1506), he entered a monastery in Einseideln; there he continued his musical activities. In 1518 he applied for appointment to the office of people's priest at Grossmünster, in Zurich. He was almost rejected because of his involvement with music but did receive the appointment and served there until 1531. Within three years after his appointment, Zwingli began radical reformation at Grossmünster that reduced ritual and ceremony to a minimum and ultimately excluded all music. He permitted in church only those things expressly commanded in Scripture. In 1527 the organs in Grossmünster were dismantled; no organ music was performed in that church for almost 350 years. Though Zwingli came to be regarded as an enemy of music, he never completely relinquished his personal use of it; he composed several settings of sacred vocal texts between c. 1520 and 1529. Zwingli's reform spread through the northern cantons of Switzerland; the southern cantons remained loyal to Catholicism. Eventually, civil war erupted; Zwingli lost his life in the second Cappel War.

Jean Calvin (1509–64) studied theology in Paris and law in Orléans and Bourges. At the University of Paris in the early 1530s he became interested in reformed doctrines. When the court proscribed Lutheranism there, Calvin fled to Switzerland. In 1536 he visited the court at Ferrara. There he met poet Clément Marot (c. 1496–1544), who, at the instigation of Marie d'Angoulême, had made metrical translations of some of the Psalms to be sung to popular

Reformation and Counter-Reformation

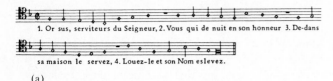

1. Or sus, serviteurs du Seigneur, 2. Vous qui de nuit en son honneur 3. De-dans

sa maison le servez, 4. Louez-le et son Nom eslevez.

(a)

Praise God from whom all bless-ings flow; Praise Him, all crea-tures here be-low;

Praise Him a-bove, ye heaven-ly host: Praise Fa-ther, Son, and Ho-ly Ghost. A-MEN.

(b)

Figure 12.4 (*a*) Loys Bourgeois's melody for Psalm 134 in *Le Psautier Huguenot*; (*b*) modern use of the same melody, harmonized by Bourgeois c. 1551, for a Doxology. *(Source: Figure b text by Bishop Thomas Ken, 1692, Old Hundredth [original rhythm] "Genevan Psalter," arr. by Louis Bourgeois, 1551, English version of last phrase.)*

French secular melodies for the enjoyment of persons at the court of King François I. Calvin was interested in Marot's texts.

Calvin spent 1537–38 in Geneva, then went to Strasbourg. There he was influenced by Martin Butzer's (1491–1551) limitation of Service music to monophonic congregational singing. Calvin supervised preparation and publication of *Aulcuns pseaulmes et cantiques mys en chant* (Some psalms and canticles set to music; 1539), an anthology of 9 of his own and 13 of Marot's translations, with some melodies from Strasbourg hymnals. Calvin returned to Geneva in 1541 and worked to establish an order of Service that included congregational unison singing of psalms and canticles in the vernacular. In 1542 he published an anthology of psalms that became the nucleus of Calvinist music. Théodore de Bèze (1519–1605), French poet, jurist, and humanist, completed the metrical translation of the Psalms begun by Marot. The complete Psalter (sometimes called the Genevan or Huguenot Psalter), was published in 1562 simultaneously in Geneva, Paris, and Lyons. It contained 125 melodies, many by Loys Bourgeois (c. 1510–60). His melody for Psalm 134, used in English-language Psalters for Psalm 100, is commonly called "Old Hundredth." It was still in use as both hymn and doxology in many Protestant churches in 1988 (fig. 12.4).

Polyphonic settings of psalms were used in home devotions. The earliest polyphonic settings were published in 1546 by Pierre Certon (d. 1572). Bourgeois's *Pseaulmes cinquante de David* (Fifty Psalms of David; Lyons, 1547) had wider circulation; his four-part settings are predominantly chordal, with melody in tenor. Claude Goudimel (c. 1515–72) began publishing small books of *pseaumes . . . en forme de*

motetz in Paris in 1551; by 1564 he had completed setting the 150 Psalms. Claude le Jeune (c. 1528–1600) wrote predominantly chordal four- and five-voice polyphonic settings of the entire Genevan Psalter; the 1601 (posthumous) edition of his Psalms was translated into several languages and circulated widely.

In Holland a Dutch metrical version of Psalms (*Souterliedekens*) made by Willem Zuylen van Nyevelt was in use c. 1540. In the seventeenth century this was gradually superseded by Dutch translations of the Genevan Psalter. Three-voice polyphonic settings of *Souterliedekens* made by Clement and Susato were published in partbooks in 1556–57 (see p. 204). Jan Pieterzoon Sweelinck (1562–1621) wrote a polyphonic setting of the entire Genevan Psalter, using the melodies as basis for pieces in various styles for four to eight voices. The first two Psalms settings appeared anonymously in a collection in 1597; his first book of (50) Psalms was published in 1604, and the final book (fourth) was issued shortly after his death. Sweelinck's settings were not intended for church use, but for private devotions in the homes of the circle of wealthy amateurs to whom they were dedicated. The collection is considered a monument of Netherlands sacred polyphony.

England

England's break with the Roman Catholic Church resulted from political conditions and the personal desires of Henry VIII (r. 1509–47) rather than from doctrinal disagreement. The formal separation occurred in 1534. In 1535 the Act of Supremacy was passed, naming Henry "Supreme Head on earth of the Church of England." Thomas Cromwell (1485–1540) was appointed vicar-general in ecclesiastical affairs; through him the king exercised power to effect dissolution of Britain's monasteries and to confiscate their wealth for the royal treasury. Many valuable manuscripts were lost or destroyed. An English translation of the Bible was used in churches commencing in 1536, and English gradually supplanted Latin but was not yet the official language in the Services. Henry opposed Lutheranism, and the English church retained a form of Catholicism without the Pope. There were no immediate liturgical changes. Music was not appreciably affected until Archbishop Cranmer indicated in 1544 that votive antiphons and votive Masses were no longer to be used, and that syllabic settings of liturgical texts were preferable. While Edward VI was king (r. 1547–53), Calvinism and Lutheranism were tolerated, and the Church of England became Protestant. On 14 April 1548 the Dean and Chapter of Lincoln Minster were ordered to sing anthems in English, using syllabic settings; the Act of Uniformity of 21 January 1549 directed that after June 9 the only liturgy to be used for public worship was that set forth in the English Book of Common Prayer.

Thus, the English Reformation consisted of six principal changes: (1) subordination of church to state; (2) separation from the papacy; (3) abolition of monasteries; (4) adoption of English for Bible readings and Services; (5) simplification of church ceremonies; and (6) adoption of Protestant doctrines.

Queen Mary (r. 1553–58) was a devout Roman Catholic; during her brief reign Catholicism returned. The pendulum swung the other way again with the accession of Elizabeth I (r. 1558–1603), who had always been opposed to Catholicism. By the Act of Settlement (1559) she abolished Sarum rite and restored the Anglican but permitted the use of Latin in specified collegiate chapels and certain churches whose congregations preferred it.

English Protestantism brought with it some changes in liturgical terminology and a new body of English church music. The principal form of Anglican music is the **Service.** As in the Roman Catholic Mass, a Service contains sections that remain constant and portions that vary in accordance with the church calendar. A complete Service comprises music for the unvarying sections of Morning Prayer, Evening Prayer, and Communion; these correspond to Matins, Vespers, and Mass in Roman Catholic liturgy. The Communion music comprises the Decalogue (Responses after the Commandments) and/or Kyrie, the Creed, Sanctus, Benedictus, Agnus Dei, and Gloria in excelsis Deo; often, however, only Kyrie and Creed were composed. In the sixteenth and seventeenth centuries, a Service using contrapuntal, melismatic music was termed a **Great Service;** one using syllabic, homorhythmic (chordal) music was a **Short Service.** There was no difference in the number of musical items Short and Great Services contained. Christopher Tye (c. 1500–c. 1572) and Thomas Tallis (c. 1505–85) were the first to compose Services in accord with Archbishop Cranmer's recommendations for syllabic settings.

The Anglican version of the motet is the **anthem.** A **full anthem** is choral throughout and is usually contrapuntal. Many appear to be *a cappella* but may actually have been accompanied when performed. A **verse anthem** alternates accompanied solo verses with choral ones; solo verses may be for one or more soloists. William Byrd (c. 1543–1623) is credited with writing the first verse anthems.

The sixteenth century was not an easy one for many English composers. The fluctuation between Roman Catholic and Anglican worship necessitated a certain amount of adaptability on their part. Several noted composers produced both Catholic and Anglican music of high quality.

Gradually, an English Psalter developed. Myles Coverdale's *Goostly psalmes and spirituall songs* (publ. c. 1539) contained the earliest metrical psalms in English that were printed with tunes. However, the book was banned because some of the melodies were Lutheran chorales. *Certayne Psalmes* (publ. c. 1548) by court poet Thomas Sternhold (d. 1549) contained 19 psalms in metrical English verse, without music; he had prepared these for court circles. In 1549 an enlarged Psalter was published, containing 37 of Sternhold's metrical psalms, plus 7 by John Hopkins; there was no music. Protestants who fled England during Queen Mary's reign took the Sternhold and Hopkins Psalter with them; some went to Geneva, others to Frankfurt and Holland. The next edition of the Psalter, published in Geneva in 1556, contained 7

Example 12.2 The long melisma on "Amen" concluding Byrd's *Christ Is Risen. (Source: Wm. Byrd,* Songs of Sundry Natures, *originally published 1589.)*

additional metrical psalm translations by William Whittingham and some melodies by Loys Bourgeois from the French Geneva Psalter. By 1562 the entire Psalter had been versified; this Sternhold and Hopkins Psalter was the most important English Psalter of the sixteenth century.

English Protestants who went to Holland were influenced by practices there. Eventually, a Psalter was produced that combined English and French-Dutch elements: *The Book of Psalmes: Englished both in Prose and Metre* published by Henry Ainsworth (Amsterdam, 1612). This was brought to America by the Pilgrims in 1620.

Much of the extant polyphonic English sacred music from the late fifteenth and early sixteenth centuries consists of votive antiphons, Magnificats, and Masses. A majority of this music is for five or six voices, displaying typical English full sonority. A characteristic of English music is the use of a long melisma in the concluding phrase or word of a piece, e.g., on the final *Alleluia* or *Amen* of a motet or anthem (ex. 12.2).

John Taverner

John Taverner (c. 1490–1545) was the most important English composer during the first part of the sixteenth century. Nothing is known about his parentage or early life. He was the first instructor of choristers at Cardinal College (now Christ Church, Oxford), which opened in October 1526. The college choir was very large, consisting of 12 chaplains, 12 lay clerks,

and 16 choristers. In 1528 he became involved in an outbreak of Lutheran heresy at the college. From 1530 to 1537 he served as a lay clerk in the large St. Mary Gild choir at Boston, England. The allegations that he participated actively in Cromwell's suppression of monasteries cannot be proved.

Taverner's most significant works are festal Masses, Magnificats, and votive antiphons. These display the traits typical of English music during this time. His Masses contain no Kyrie, which was customarily sung in plainsong, and some phrases are omitted from the Credo, another English custom. Often Taverner used a melodic fragment sequentially as a kind of ostinato in a melismatic passage or developed a melodic fragment through imitation or canon.

Three English composers—Taverner, Tye, and John Sheppard (c. 1515–c. 1559)—each composed a four-voice Mass based on the secular tune *The Western Wynde* (ex. 12.3). All three men treated the cantus firmus in the same unconventional manner—as basis for a series of variations—which suggests that they knew one another and may have been working in the same vicinity, or that there was a specific reason for their composing this Mass in that manner. Moreover, other Masses by these three composers have similarities. Taverner's Mass is a set of 36 contrapuntal variations, systematically arranged with 9 variations per movement. The arrangement of variations within the Gloria parallels that of the Credo; the plan of the Sanctus corresponds with that of the Agnus Dei.

Example 12.3 *The Western Wynde* melody.

Taverner based his six-voice *Missa Gloria tibi Trinitas* on the first antiphon sung at Vespers on Trinity Sunday, in Sarum rite. He placed the cantus firmus in the alto voice (labeled *Mean*) and used the melody as basis for both solo and full sections. This Mass is significant historically for its generation of numerous instrumental *In nomine* pieces (see p. 274).

Christopher Tye

Nothing definite is known about the life of Christopher Tye (c. 1505–c. 1572) prior to 1536 when he took the B.Mus. degree at Cambridge. The documents supporting his appointment as a lay clerk at King's College in 1537 state that he had studied music for ten years and had much experience in composition and in teaching boys. His whereabouts between 1537 and 1543 are unknown. He was *Magister choristarum* at Ely Cathedral in 1543, was unofficially associated with the royal chapel in 1544, and received the D.Mus. from University of Cambridge in 1545. He attained priesthood in July 1560; in 1561 he was appointed to serve at Doddington-cum-Marche, one of the richest areas in England.

Tye is recognized as a leading English composer around the middle of the sixteenth century, but much of his music has been lost. He composed both Latin and English sacred music and instrumental works, including 21 *In nomine* consort pieces, all given enigmatic titles. Tye was an organist, and his numerous works for viol consort suggest that he was also an accomplished viol player.

Thomas Tallis

The first recorded information concerning Thomas Tallis (c. 1505–85) is his appointment as organist at the Benedictine Priory, Dover, in 1532. He was at Waltham Abbey c. 1538; in 1541–42, he was a lay clerk at Canterbury Cathedral. From c. 1545 until his death he was a member of the Chapel Royal, serving under Henry VIII, Edward VI, Mary, and Elizabeth I. In 1575 Tallis and William Byrd were granted a 21-year monopoly for printing music and manufacturing music paper. These Letters Patent were the first of their kind in England. Tallis and Byrd jointly produced *Cantiones . . . sacrae* (Sacred songs; 1575), an anthology of Latin motets; each contributed 17 works, perhaps commemorating the 17th year of Elizabeth's reign.

A list of Tallis's music reflects ecclesiastical changes in England. He composed Masses and votive antiphons during Henry VIII's reign, Anglican Services and anthems while Edward VI ruled, Latin hymns and a Mass when Mary was Queen, and both Latin and English music after Elizabeth I was crowned. His motet *Gaude gloriosa* is addressed to Queen Mary and praises her for restoring Catholicism. Among his finest vocal compositions are his two sets of *Lamentations,* in which the melismatic setting of the letters of the Hebrew alphabet contrasts with the expressive syllabic verses. Tallis composed numerous liturgical and nonliturgical keyboard works, only a small fraction of which survive, and several pieces for viol consort.

William Byrd

William Byrd (c. 1543–1623) brought English virginal music to a high level of excellence and composed some of the finest Latin church music produced in England during the latter part of the sixteenth century. Nothing is known about Byrd's ancestry or his early life. Probably, he studied with Tallis at some time. Three motets written for Sarum liturgy indicate that Byrd was composing by the age of 16. From 1563 to 1572 he served as Organist and Master of the Choristers at Lincoln Cathedral. While there, he began to compose English virginal music. He had a habit of writing a piece and drawing on that work for other compositions, then rewriting the original work. His keyboard *Fantasia in A minor* and some *In nomine* settings for viol consort date from this period.

Byrd's earliest settings of English poems are strophic songs for one voice and a consort of viols; in other words, they are consort songs. Some of them are settings of English metrical psalms. Those psalm settings that have simple choruses at the ends of stanzas lie at the root of the **verse anthem,** which Byrd is credited with inventing. When he was at Lincoln Minster there was considerable need for new Anglican music. With the exception of Byrd's *Great Service,* his English liturgical music became a staple of the cathedral repertory.

In 1570 Byrd was admitted to the Chapel Royal, and c. 1572 he held a joint appointment with Tallis as organist. In 1575, shortly after the Queen granted them a printing monopoly, Byrd and Tallis published the collection of motets *Cantiones, quae ab argumento sacrae vocantur* (Songs which are called sacred because of their texts). After Tallis's death (1585), Byrd held the monopoly alone, but leased it to a printer; when it expired in 1596, the Queen granted Thomas Morley (c. 1557–1602) a monopoly. Morley and Thomas Tomkins (1572–1656) were Byrd's pupils.

Italian composer Alfonso Ferrabosco (1543–88) worked at the English court intermittently during 1562–1578. He and Byrd wrote and exchanged a series of canons on *Miserere* plainsong; through Ferrabosco, Byrd came to understand Netherlands-style counterpoint. Byrd seems to have been the first English composer to employ Franco-Flemish imitative contrapuntal techniques easily, effectively, and expressively.

During the 1580s Byrd renewed his commitment to Catholicism. He composed a number of motets relating to the Babylonian captivity; in these he used word painting extensively. He chose the texts for his motets carefully; the Biblical words seem to express his personal pro-Catholic feelings. In 1583–84 he exchanged Latin motets with Philippe de Monte (1521–1603) on verses from Psalm 137, *Super flumina Babilonis* (By the waters of Babylon), stressing the text *Quomodo cantabimus* (How shall we sing [the Lord's song in a strange land?]). During this same time period, Byrd composed music for the Anglican church, such as *Rejoice unto the Lord* for Accession Day 1586

and *Look and bow down* (text written by Queen Elizabeth) to mark the defeat of the Spanish Armada. At some time during the 1580s Byrd composed the *Great Service* for the Anglican church.

In 1588 Byrd published *Psalmes, Sonets and Songs,* a collection of part songs adapted from consort songs. This was only the third book of English songs that had been published; it was very popular and was reprinted twice in 1588. Two books of miscellaneous *Cantiones sacrae* (Sacred songs) were issued: Book I for five voices (1589) and Book II for five and six voices (1591). From Book I comes the verse anthem *Christ rising again.* In it Byrd effectively applied chromatic alterations to bring about cross-relations (ex. 12.4).

After 1590, Byrd resumed composition of Latin sacred music for the Catholic Church, selecting texts from appropriate sections of the liturgy. Between 1593 and 1595, three Masses were composed and published individually; they are for three, four, and five voices, respectively. The Masses are freely composed, without extensive polyphony, and there is little repetition of words. They are conservative in style and are archaic in their reliance upon head motives for unification. Yet, the four- and five-voice Masses are considered the finest Mass settings written by an English composer up to this time.

Byrd composed two books of *Gradualia,* published in 1605 and 1607, respectively. Both volumes were reprinted in 1610. Together, the books contain 100 pieces that are motet sections rather than motets, for many can serve more than one liturgical function. Complete Mass propers are provided—Introit, Gradual, Tract/Alleluia, Offertory, Communion—for the major feasts of the church year, plus Marian feasts and votive Marian Masses. If the same text was used on different occasions, only one setting of that text was composed, and instructions were given to transfer the setting from the printed position to the appropriate place in the liturgy. Some of the pieces should not be sung as printed, for they are printed in composite, and the appropriate section of that composite should be extracted for use in its proper place. Because of this mobility of pieces, a group of motet sections retains the same mode and same number of voices. The high

Example 12.4 Measures 1–16 of Byrd's verse anthem *Christ rising again.* Note the cross relations between f♯ and f′ in measures 4, 8, and 13. *(From Historical Anthology of Music, Vol. II, edited by Archibald T. Davison and Willi Apel. © 1950 by The President and Fellows of Harvard College; renewed 1978 by Alice D. Humez and Willi Apel. Reprinted by permission of Harvard University Press, Cambridge, MA.)*

quality of Byrd's contrapuntal writing and his use of Netherlands techniques may be seen in *Ego sum panis vivus* (I am the living bread; DWMA91) from *Gradualia,* Book II. Byrd was fond of concluding a motet with a coda on words such as *Alleluia* or *Amen,* as he did in this motet.

Byrd's last collection of *Psalmes, Songs and Sonnets* appeared in 1611. The book contains full anthems (English choral motets), verse anthems, six-part consort songs, and two fantasias for consort. The keyboard music Byrd composed after 1590 consists primarily of pavans and galliards, but he wrote three important variations: *Go from my window, John come kiss me now,* and *O mistress mine, I must.* Some of his pavans, galliards, and preludes were included with keyboard music by Bull and Gibbons in *Parthenia* (publ. c. 1612).

Byrd did not occupy a commanding position among his contemporaries, but his Anglican music continued to be used after his death. During the revival of Tudor and Jacobean music in the 1880s, his music attracted attention; in the twentieth century there has been renewed interest in his motets.

The Counter-Reformation

Pope Paul III (r. 1534–49) comprehended the problems caused by Protestantism and approached them through conciliation. He appointed commissions and councils to assess the condition of the Roman Catholic Church and to recommend corrective measures. At first, the Pope sought reconciliation with the Protestants. A conference at Regensburg in 1541 between some Catholic and Protestant leaders came to nought. Pope Paul abandoned the idea of compromise and turned to Reformation within the Catholic Church—in effect, a *Counter*-Reformation. One of the Catholic leaders was Cardinal Gian Pietro Caraffa, a Dominican, who became Pope Paul IV in 1555.

Another leader was Don Iñigo Lopez de Loyola (1491–1556), who became a soldier of the church when his military career was cut short by a serious leg wound in 1521. He went to Paris, studied at the Sorbonne, accepted orthodox Catholicism unquestioningly, and became imbued with religious fervor. He was convinced that he could best serve God by preaching, teaching, and supporting the Pope. Loyola (now known as Ignatius Loyola) and his followers formed a brotherhood that they called *Societas Jesu* (Company of Jesus), headed by a General; others gave them the appellation "Jesuit Society" later. Loyola developed a system of disciplined asceticism and methodical prayer called *Spiritual Exercises*; this became the manual of the Company. Members took four vows: poverty, chastity, obedience, allegiance to the Pope. After two years' consideration, Pope Paul III chartered the Company in 1540. Loyola sought to propagate the beliefs of the Company and the Catholic Church through education. In 1542 the first Jesuit College was founded in Coimbra, Portugal; on 22 February 1551 the Collegio Romano (later, Papal Gregorian University) opened its doors in Rome. By 1556 the Society had more than 1000 members, and 30 Jesuit colleges and secondary schools were operating throughout Europe. Jesuits were influential politically, serving as councillors and confessors to rulers and securing appointments on important commissions. Jesuits were present at meetings of the Council of Trent.

In May 1542 Pope Paul III issued the *bulla* convoking the first meeting of the Council of Trent. Trent is situated in the Italian Alps, on the river Etsch, about 43 miles from Venice. It is partly fortified; the walled episcopal palace where the council convened is outside the city proper. The 3 cardinals and 31 bishops comprising the Council deliberated in three sessions: December 1545–March 1547; April 1551–April 1552; January 1562–December 1563. During the course of the deliberations four popes reigned. On 26 January 1564 Pope Pius IV (r. 1559–65) issued the bull *Benedictus Deus,* proclaiming as law the Council's decrees. Under consideration were matters concerning the definition of church doctrine and problems of church reform, deemed necessary because of a multitude of abuses. Church music was only one of the areas discussed—a small part of the Council's work. Concerns voiced in that area included: (1) the intrusion of secularism, evidenced in Masses parodying chansons or using secular cantus firmi; (2) extensive multi-voiced imitative polyphony that obscured texts and made their meaning incomprehensible; (3) wide variances in liturgical music, such as innumerable different Sequences in use in various locales; (4) widespread use of musical instruments, especially "noisy" ones, in church; and (5) the irreverent attitude, carelessness, and bad habits of singers (incorrect pronunciation, poor enunciation). The last point was the subject of a reprimand given by Pope Marcellus II to the papal singers on Good Friday 1555, the third day of his reign (see p. 256). One of the delegates to the Council, Giovanni Morone of Modena, abolished polyphony at Modena Cathedral and permitted only chant. The only music known to have been composed especially for performance at a session of the Council was *Preces speciales* (Special prayers), which the Bishop of Augsburg commissioned Jacobus de Kerle

(c. 1531–91) to compose in 1561. The conservative style and devotional spirit of Kerle's music convinced the Council that polyphony need not be abolished from church music.

Where music was concerned, the only direct action taken by the Council of Trent was actually liturgical: The number of Sequences was reduced to four, specifically, *Victimae paschali laudes* (Easter); *Veni, Sancte Spiritus* (Whit Sunday); *Lauda Sion* (Corpus Christi); and *Dies irae* (Requiem). A fifth Sequence, *Stabat Mater dolorosa* (The sorrowful Mother was standing), was readmitted to the liturgy in 1727. The Council directed that impurity and lasciviousness, secularity and "unedifying language," were to be avoided so that "the House of God may truly be called a house of prayer." Actual reform was left to local authorities; in the Holy See and the Curia

it was the Pope's responsibility. The deliberations of the Council were effective in making composers conscious of the fact that church authorities were aware of their use of secular materials; for a time, those Masses with a secular relationship were entitled *Missa sine nomine* (Untitled Mass). Several composers, including Palestrina, stated or implied in prefaces to published works that the music had been composed in accordance with the reforms of the Council of Trent. Many composers aimed at a musical style that incorporated a melodic line moving primarily by step in smoothly curved phrases that were easily sung; counterpoint that was rather transparent, having imitative sections interspersed with homorhythmic passages; avoidance of chromaticism other than that occasioned by normal application of *musica ficta*; uncomplicated, regular rhythms; and intelligibility of text

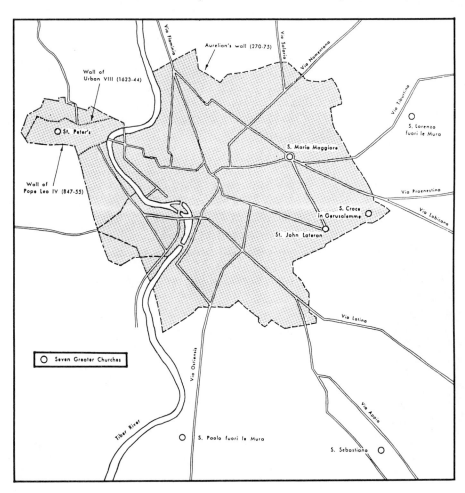

Figure 12.5 Location of important churches in Rome.

Reformation and Counter-Reformation

setting. Emphasis was placed on the function of music as an adjunct to worship rather than as an esthetic enhancement of a Service. The music of Giovanni Pierluigi da Palestrina (c. 1525–94) and that of several of his contemporaries conforms to those standards.

Giovanni Pierluigi da Palestrina

To some extent, the Counter-Reformation and the deliberations of the Council of Trent influenced Palestrina's work, but legends exaggerate his participation in those events. When the Council of Trent first convened (1545), his career was beginning; when the meetings concluded (1563), his career was well established (Insight, "Giovanni Pierluigi da Palestrina"). He did not appear before the Council, nor was any of his music performed at the meetings. In October 1577 Pope Gregory XIII (r. 1572–85) appointed Palestrina and Annibale Zoilo (1537–92) to prepare a new edition of the Roman *Graduale* in accordance with the recommendations of the Council of Trent. Zoilo, who held no full-time position then, worked on the *Antiphonale* and the *Proprium sanctorum*; Palestrina revised the other portions of the *Graduale*. Lack of funds caused the project to lapse; it had not been completed at the time of Palestrina's death. Others continued their work, and the *Editio Medicaea* (Medici Edition) was published in 1614. That edition was used until publication of the Vatican Edition in 1908.

Giovanni P. da Palestrina. *(Courtesy of Brown Brothers.)*

Palestrina has occupied a unique position in the history of music. His associations with prestigious patrons, his appointments at the papal chapel, and his numerous publications in Rome and Venice added to his prestige. The esteem accorded him during his lifetime was maintained in succeeding centuries. Legends that proclaimed him the "savior of church music" contributed greatly to this. In music pedagogy, since the early seventeenth century Palestrina has been upheld as chief exponent of the strict style of diatonic modal counterpoint used in the sixteenth century, and his music has provided the models to be followed. He is the first composer to be so consciously imitated by later generations. Palestrina was the ideal of Pietro Cerone (1566–1625), who cited his work in *El melopeo y maestro* (Melopoeia and the master; Naples, 1613). In 1725 Johann J. Fux (1660–1741) published *Gradus ad Parnassum* (Steps to Parnassus), a pedagogical treatise on sixteenth-century counterpoint; that book was still being used as a text in some universities in 1988. Fux's treatise explains Renaissance counterpoint through a dialogue between Master Aloysius (Palestrina) and pupil Joseph (Fux). Each succeeding generation of theorists has produced a pedagogical treatise based on Palestrina's contrapuntal style.

Almost all of Palestrina's life—from his early music education through most of his years of employment—was spent in association with the Roman Catholic Church; his music reflects that background. The aura of the Roman Catholic Church emanates from it, as it does from Gregorian chant. His sacred music is conservative, serious, and objective, and thus most appropriate for liturgical use, especially for the texts of the Ordinary. His compositional style may be seen clearly in his Masses. There is little secularity; most of that is confined to his madrigals. Careful attention was paid to correct declamation; the texture of the musical fabric does not obscure intelligibility of the text. The basis of Palestrina's style is Franco-Flemish imitative counterpoint, with which he was thoroughly familiar. In some Mass movements, pervading imitation occurs, each phrase of text having its own melodic motive and being set imitatively. In other movements, imitative sections are interspersed effectively with homorhythmic passages. There is

Giovanni Pierluigi da Palestrina

Giovanni Pierluigi da Palestrina (c. 1525–94) was born in the town of Palestrina (formerly Praeneste) near Rome. He was always known as Palestrina or Praenestino, rather than by his family name. He received his early education and musical training in Rome, where he served as choirboy at Santa Maria Maggiore. From 1544 to 1551 he was organist and choirmaster at St. Agapito Cathedral in his home town. Presumably, he composed Masses and other sacred music while there, but none survives. Little is known of his life during those years, except that in 1547 he married Lucrezia Gori. They had three sons, all musically talented: Rodolfo (1549–72), Angelo (1551–75), and Iginio (1557–1610).

Cardinal Giovanni Maria del Monte, Bishop of Palestrina from 1542 to 1550, was Palestrina's first patron. Shortly after the Cardinal became Pope Julius III (r. 1550–55), he appointed Palestrina *maestro* of Cappella Giulia, the musical chapel at St. Peter's (Rome) named for Pope Julius II who in 1513 reorganized it and advocated the employment of native Italian musicians there. In January 1555 Palestrina was admitted to the Pope's official musical chapel, Cappella Sistina, without examination, without consent of the other singers, and in spite of the fact that he was married.

Julius died in March 1555; his successor was Cardinal Marcello Cervini, Pope Marcellus II, who reigned only three weeks (d. April 30) and whom Palestrina honored with *Missa Papae Marcelli* (Mass for Pope Marcellus). Marcellus was succeeded by Cardinal Pietro Caraffa, as Pope Paul IV (r. 1555–59). In September 1555 Pope Paul enforced the Sistine Chapel's rule of celibacy and dismissed Palestrina and two other married singers. Palestrina's successor was Giovanni Animuccia (1500–71) who retained the position until his death.

In October 1555 Palestrina became *maestro di cappella* at the church of St. John Lateran; he left there suddenly in July 1560 after a dispute relative to funds for the musicians and took with him his son Rodolfo, a choirboy. Palestrina's whereabouts for the next several months are unknown. In March 1561 he was appointed choirmaster at Santa Maria Maggiore; he worked there five years. Apparently, his position was not time consuming, for in 1564 he accepted summer employment at Villa d'Este, at Tivoli, outside Rome. In 1566–71 he taught music at the Jesuit Seminario Romano, where his three sons were enrolled; from August 1567 to March 1571 he again served Duke Ippolite II d'Este.

Other rulers were aware of Palestrina's talents. In 1568 Emperor Maximilian II offered Palestrina the choirmaster position at his Vienna court; when Palestrina declined, Philippe de Monte was hired. Duke Guglielmo Gonzaga also offered Palestrina employment, but withdrew the offer because he could not afford to pay the high salary Palestrina requested. Palestrina's only extant correspondence is that with Gonzaga during 1568–87. For Gonzaga's chapel at Mantua Palestrina composed 11 Masses based on chants peculiar to the Mantuan liturgy.

After the death of Animuccia (April 1571), Palestrina returned to Cappella Giulia, St. Peter's, as choirmaster and worked there for the remainder of his life. From time to time he considered and declined other positions. He experienced family disasters—between 1572 and 1580 epidemics of plague struck Rome; Palestrina was seriously ill, and his wife and sons Rodolfo and Angelo died of the dread disease. (Rodolfo had just been appointed organist at the Mantua court.) For a time Palestrina contemplated entering priesthood.

In 1581 Palestrina married Virginia Dormoli, widow of a prosperous Roman fur merchant; for the next decade, Palestrina participated actively in the fur business and in real estate. He continued to compose prolifically and to have his works published. In 1584 he was instrumental in establishing an association of professional musicians, the Vertuosa Compagnia dei Musici di Roma, dedicated to St. Cecelia. The company had concern for the welfare of its members and was active in arranging for publication of their works. The members jointly composed a 12-voice Mass setting the Cecelian text *Cantantibus organis,* for which each member (including Palestrina) wrote a movement; he was represented also in their collection of madrigals, *Le gioie* (Joy; publ. 1589).

Palestrina's fame spread beyond Italy; some of his sacred music was performed in Munich, and four of his madrigals were included in *Musica Transalpina* (London, 1588). In 1592 Palestrina received a singular tribute from the leading musicians of Venetia, Lombardy, and Tuscany—they dedicated to him the published collection of their 16 five-voice settings of the Vesper Psalms. In appreciation, Palestrina composed the motet *Vos amici mei* (Ye are my friends). Late in 1593 Palestrina contemplated retirement in his home town. As he was making preparations to leave Rome in January 1594, he became ill; he died on February 2. Crowds attended his funeral services at St. Peter's; he was interred there under the pavement of Capella Nuova. That chapel was destroyed during subsequent remodeling of St. Peter's, and Palestrina's remains were lost.

almost no chromaticism; of course, rules of *musica ficta* were applied. Although Palestrina wrote modal linear polyphony, the melodic lines often converge to form triads or first-inversion triads (sixth chords). His harmonic awareness is apparent, too, in his resolution of some tensions seemingly according to harmonic rather than purely intervallic laws. Frequently, the bass line moves by leaping a fourth or a fifth. Palestrina was writing modal counterpoint, however; his music cannot be analyzed according to principles of key tonality. In many respects, Palestrina's style does not differ appreciably from that used by Arcadelt, Festa, and Morales in their sacred music. Others of the Roman school were writing similarly.

Palestrina was the first sixteenth-century composer for whom nineteenth-century musicologists attempted to prepare an *Opera omnia;* under general editorship of F. X. Haberl, 33 volumes of *G. P. da Palestrina: Werke* were published (Leipzig, 1862–1903). Another edition, *G. P. da Palestrina: Le opere complete,* was begun by R. Casimiri in 1938 and has been continued by others since his death.

Palestrina was a prolific composer. His known compositions include 104 Masses, more than 375 motets, a cycle of 68 offertories, a cycle of 65 hymns, 35 Magnificats, 5 sets of Lamentations settings, and more than 140 secular and spiritual madrigals. He seems to have composed only *a cappella* vocal music; the organ *Esercizi* and *Ricercari* once attributed to him have been deemed spurious. During his lifetime, 6 of his 12 books of Masses, 5 books of his motets, and 4 books of his madrigals were published in Rome and Venice. His books of Masses were dedicated to popes or foreign rulers; the dedications of books of motets published before 1581 were addressed to his patrons or potential Italian patrons.

Palestrina's first publications occurred in 1554—a madrigal in an anthology and *Missarum liber primus* (First book of Masses) dedicated to Pope Julius III. The Pope considered this a special honor, for Palestrina's was only the second book of Masses by a native Italian composer (Gasparo de Alberti published a book of three Masses in Venice in 1549), and the first such book published in Rome. Morales's *Liber secundus missarum* (1544) was Palestrina's model; each composer commenced his volume with a tenor Mass honoring the reigning Pope. Palestrina's *Missarum liber primus* opens with the four-voice *Missa Ecce sacerdos magnus* (Behold the great priest) based on the antiphon of the same name.

Secular Music

At various times during his career Palestrina composed madrigals; they are the least important of his compositions. One of his first published works was a madrigal (1554); a book of his four-voice madrigals was published in 1555 and another madrigal book appeared in 1586, though the pieces were probably composed earlier. Generally, Palestrina's madrigals are quite conservative in style. This may be seen in *Alla riva del Tebro* (At the bank of the Tiber). Two of his madrigals, *Io son ferito* (I am wounded; 1561) and the sonnet *Vestiva i colli* (The hills are clothed; 1566) became very popular. Palestrina wrote 8 five-voice *madrigali spirituali*, settings of 8 stanzas of Petrarch's *Vergini*. Palestrina rued having composed madrigals, and he expressed this regret to the Pope in the dedication to *Motettorum liber quartus ex Canticis canticorum* (Fourth book of motets from Song of Songs; 1584), 29 motets based on verses from Song of Solomon. However, madrigalesque word painting is a feature of those motets.

Sacred Music

Palestrina composed Masses of every type being written during the sixteenth century. Some are freely composed, as is *Missa Papae Marcelli* (1567 or earlier). The reason for its composition is unknown; possibly, it reflects Good Friday 1555, when, after the Services, Pope Marcellus admonished his chapel singers concerning their performance of Holy Week music and advised that sacred music should be sung clearly, in a suitable manner, so that the words could be heard and understood. That Palestrina's Mass was designed for intelligibility of the words is apparent. Approximately 80 percent of Palestrina's Masses are chant-based; this percentage takes into consideration the fact that many of the motets serving as basis for parody Masses are themselves chant-based. There are 53 parody Masses, 22 of them derived from his own works, the remainder parodying polyphonic compositions by French, Flemish, and Spanish composers who worked in Rome. *Missa Hodie Christus natus est* (Mass Christ is born today) is one of two parody Masses that commence homorhythmically, the block chords emphasizing the text.

In 35 Masses, chants or secular melodies are paraphrased. In accordance with tradition, Palestrina retained Gregorian chant for the Introit, Gradual, Tract, and Communion of his *Missa pro defunctis* (Requiem Mass) and paraphrased the appropriate chants in the other movements. Fifteen other Masses are based on plainsong Mass cycles, 11 of them for the Mantuan chapel.

There are seven cantus firmus Masses, including a five-voice *Missa L'homme armé,* the four-voice *Missa Ecce sacerdos magnus* in his first publication, and a six-voice *Missa Ave Maria.* These reflect the Flemish tradition, as do the canonic Masses. *Missa Ad fugam* (Canon Mass), for four voices, is in double canon throughout. In the five-voice *Missa Repleatur os meum* (Mass My mouth shall be filled; 1570), based on a motet by Jaquet, Palestrina's systematic application of canon is just the reverse of Ockeghem's procedure in *Missa prolationum.* From Kyrie through Agnus Dei I, Palestrina wrote canons in decreasing intervals of imitation from octave to unison, then constructed a double canon in the final Agnus Dei—one at the octave, the other at the fourth. Moreover, in each canon the interval and distance of imitation correspond; e.g., in the canon at the octave the *comes* enters eight semibreves after the *dux* commences. The three-voice Crucifixus and Benedictus sections have no canon.

Canons appear within Masses that are basically constructed according to other techniques. The hard hexachord serves as cantus firmus for the six-voice *Missa Ut re mi fa sol la* (Hexachord Mass). A seventh voice is added in the final Agnus Dei, to sing the cantus firmus in canon at the fifth below Superius II.

The six books of motets Palestrina published in 1563–84 contain 177 of his motets and three by others: his sons Rodolfo and Angelo and his half-brother Silla. More than one-third of Palestrina's approximately 375 motets are for 4 voices; almost as many are for 5 voices. Of the remainder, 60 are for 8 voices, and 10 are for 12 voices. Most of his motets are based on antiphons and responsory texts.

The early four-voice motets are models of Renaissance polyphonic composition, displaying correct voice leading and intervallic construction, carefully controlled dissonance, and equilibrium of part writing. Texts are set with correct declamation; usually, a text is set by complete phrases. These features may be seen in the motet *Lauda Sion* (1563), based on the Sequence for the feast of Corpus Christi (ex. 12.5; DWMA92). The motet is basically in duple meter. It commences imitatively, the four voices entering in turn from superius down to bass; each phrase of text is given its own melody, with slight overlapping of phrases at cadence points. Phrases are smoothly curved, and of suitable length to be sung easily. Short melismas occur near the ends of phrases. The words of supplication, commencing *Bone pastor, panis vere* (Good shepherd, true bread), are set homorhythmically, in triple (perfect) meter. There is a return to duple meter for the final phrase and *Amen.* Palestrina's *Missa Lauda Sion* (DWMA93) was derived from the motet.

The four-voice motet *Sicut cervus* (As the hart) exhibits typical "Palestrina curves" within its phrase structure—a gradual rise of the melodic line balanced by a gradual decline (ex. 12.6). Typical construction of a bass line is displayed in the eight-voice *Alma Redemptoris Mater,* written for double choir.

Between 1588 and 1593 Palestrina published two books of Litanies and four important collections of other liturgical compositions: settings of Lamentations, hymns, Magnificats, and offertories. The fact that he had previously written other cycles in some of these categories implies that in some Italian churches polyphony had replaced Gregorian chant for these portions of the Services. Palestrina composed five sets of *Lamentations of Jeremiah,* but only the last set was published (1588). In them there is much dissonance, always properly prepared.

Palestrina wrote several cycles of liturgical works. *Hymni totius anni . . .* (Hymns for the entire year . . . ; 1589) is a cycle of 45 hymns for the church year. He adhered to sixteenth-century practice by writing different settings for the odd-numbered stanzas of the hymns. The first verses of all hymns are four-voice settings; from three to six voices are used for other verses. *Magnificat octo tonum liber primus*

Example 12.5 Beginning of Palestrina's motet *Lauda Sion. (Source:* G. P. Palestrina: Le Opere complete, *ed. R. Casimiri et al., [Rome, 1939–], Vol. 3, 42.)*

Example 12.6 Palestrina's setting of the first phrase of Vulgate Psalm 43 (KJV,42) in the superius of his motet *Sicut cervus* shows the balanced rise and fall typical of his melodic lines.

(Magnificats in 8 Tones, Book I; 1589) comprises two series of Magnificats in the eight Tones. Two other series, composed earlier, survive. All are traditional settings, in which verses set polyphonically alternate with those intoned according to psalmodic formulas. The cycle of 68 Offertories for the entire church year, *Offertoria totius anni . . .* (1593), is historically important. It is one of the first settings to be freely composed, in motet style, without any reference to chants. The pieces are for five voices. A shorter set by Lassus is similar in style.

Tomás Luis de Victoria

One of Palestrina's contemporaries in Rome was Tomás Luis de Victoria (1548–1611), organist and composer. Victoria was the greatest Spanish composer in the Renaissance and wrote some of the finest church music produced in Europe during his time. He received his early musical training at Avila Cathedral, where he served as choirboy. When his voice changed c. 1565, he was sent to Jesuit Collegio Germanico, Rome, which had been founded in 1552. The school accepted music students as well as German seminarians; Victoria enrolled as a singer. At that time, Palestrina was teaching at the Jesuit Seminario Romano; undoubtedly, Victoria knew Palestrina and may have gone to him for some lessons. Certainly, Victoria was well acquainted with Palestrina's compositional style.

From January 1569 to January 1574 Victoria was singer and organist at Santa Maria di Montserrato, Rome. Also, in 1571 he was engaged to teach music at Collegio Germanico and ultimately served as *maestro di cappella* there (1573–77). When the German seminarians were separated from the other students in 1573, a special ceremony was held at which Victoria's newly composed eight-voice setting of Psalm 136, *Super flumina Babylonis* (By the waters of Babylon) was sung. In 1575 Victoria attained priesthood, and joined the newly formed community of lay priests led by Filippo Neri, the Congregazione dei Preti dell' Oratorio (Congregation of Priests of the Oratory). Victoria was a chaplain at St. Girolamo from 1578 to 1585 but derived most of his income from five benefices he held at Spanish churches. Five volumes of his music were published during those years: hymns, Masses, motets, Magnificat settings, and Offices for Holy Week.

Victoria wished to return to Spain as a priest and expressed this desire in the dedication of *Missarum libri duo* (Masses, Book II; 1583). King Philip II, to whom the dedication was addressed, appointed him chaplain to Dowager Empress Maria, at the Monasterio de las Descalzas de Santa Clara, Madrid. Victoria was *maestro* of the convent choir from 1587 to 1604, then served as organist until his death. That choir comprised 12 priests (3 per part) and 4 boys; instrumentalists were hired for Easter and the octave of Corpus Christi. Instrumental doubling of vocal lines was widely practiced in Spain. By royal decree in 1601, a bassoonist was employed to perform at all Services, 3 priests were replaced by 2 clergy with excellent voices, and the number of choirboys was increased to 6. Victoria taught them composition as well as singing. While at the convent, Victoria enjoyed the special privileges of travel to Rome to oversee publication of another book of Masses (7 Masses for 4, 6, 8 vcs.; 1592), to be present at performances of his works in 1593, and to attend Palestrina's funeral in 1594. At the time of the Dowager Empress's death (1605), Victoria composed *Officum defunctorum* (Office of the dead). In Madrid, Victoria lived in the chaplain's residence at the convent; he died there and was buried at the convent.

Victoria wrote only sacred music, and most of it was published during his lifetime. His works comprise 20 Masses, 52 motets, 8 psalm settings (7 for 2 four-voice choirs, 1 for 3 four-voice choirs), 38 hymns, 2 Magnificat settings (with polyphony for alternate verses only), the Offices for Holy Week, and other liturgical works including Responsories, Sequences, and the Office for the Dead.

Fifteen of Victoria's Masses parody his own works: seven are based on motets, three on Marian antiphons, one on a psalm setting; four parody works by others—Guerrero, Morales, Palestrina, and Janequin. Victoria's nine-voice *Missa pro victoria* (Mass for victory), a battle Mass based on Janequin's chanson *La guerre,* was popular in Spain. *Missa Quarti toni* (Mass in fourth mode) is freely composed; the other four Masses are paraphrase type. Victoria was one of the first composers to base a Mass on one of his own motets; the first Mass in which he did so is *Missa Dum complerentur* (Mass When [the day of Pentecost] had fully come; 1576). Palestrina and Guerrero both did this later. Victoria's *Missa Ave Regina coelorum* and *Missa Alma Redemptoris Mater,* both eight-voice Masses for double choir, were performed frequently in Bogotá, Colombia, and Mexico City in the early seventeenth century. These two Masses parody Marian antiphons composed by Victoria. A characteristic of Victoria's Masses is tonal fluctuation, seen in the use of such melodic successions as e-f-e♭ and f-g-f♯. Basically, Victoria wrote modal counterpoint. However, in the Masses his treatment of Dorian mode often becomes minor key tonality; similarly, Ionian mode is translated into major key tonality.

The motets *O magnum mysterium* (O great mystery) and *O vos omnes* (O, all ye [who pass]; DWMA94) are among his best-known compositions. *O vos omnes* is a four-voice setting of Lamentations 1:12. In it Victoria combined imitative counterpoint with dramatic, attention-getting repeated notes. The command *attendite et videte* (behold and see) is

Reformation and Counter-Reformation

Example 12.7 Victoria's expressive setting of the words *"sicut dolor meus"* concluding his motet *O vos omnes. (From Historical Anthology of Music, Vol. 1, edited by Archibald T. Davison and Willi Apel. © 1946, 1949 by The President and Fellows of Harvard College; renewed 1974 by Alice D. Humez and Willi Apel. Reprinted by permission of Harvard University Press, Cambridge, M.A.)*

emphasized by general rests. Minor seconds are plentiful. The expressive quality characteristic of Victoria's style is felt in his setting of the words *sicut dolor meus* (like unto my sorrow; ex. 12.7).

All of the psalm settings are polychoral. The cycle of hymns follows the same order as Palestrina's, but Victoria set even-numbered strophes polyphonically and avoided using canon. (Palestrina used canon in the final verses of his hymn settings.) The Offices for Holy Week (1583) include 9 Lamentations, 18 Responsories, 2 Passions (St. John; St. Matthew), and other pieces. The Lamentations settings are predominantly chordal, and the hymns homophonic, but the *St. Matthew Passion* is polyphonic.

Whereas Palestrina's music is coolly impersonal, Victoria's is expressive within the bounds of decorum. Quite a few of Victoria's compositions convey a sense of joy and well-being that may be a reflection of his optimistic attitude and joyful nature. This joyfulness is apparent in his setting of the Easter Sequence. On the other hand, sorrowful texts elicited from Victoria dolorous music, as evidenced by the Lamentations. Some of Victoria's music is mystical and intense; the Lamentations contain some definite Spanish elements.

Orlande de Lassus

Orlande de Lassus (1532–94) was one of the great composers of sacred music in the last half of the sixteenth century (Insight, "Orlande de Lassus"). Unlike Palestrina, Lassus was not ashamed of writing secular music and composed quite a lot of it. Moreover, secular works—his own and those of others—figured prominently as bases for his sacred works. Lassus wrote more than 2000 compositions. He composed music in all genres used during his era: Masses, motets, Magnificat settings, Passions, hymns, psalm settings, other liturgical music, chansons, madrigals, and Lieder. More than 100 volumes of Lassus's compositions were published between 1555 and 1619; many of those volumes were reprinted. Between 1575 and 1598 Adam Berg of Munich printed *Patrocinium musices,* a 12-volume collection of music by five composers; 7 volumes were devoted to sacred music by Lassus.

Sacred Music

Lassus's musical style is as versatile as his compositional output. He is best known for his motets; he composed approximately 525 of them for from 2 to 12 voices. *Magnum opus musicum* (Great book of music; 1604) contains 516 of his motets, edited by his sons Ferdinand and Rudolf. Lassus's motets are varied in style, but in all of them—in fact, in all of Lassus's compositions—the words generate the music and are master of it. His music is expressive and at times moody and dramatic. Harmonic clarity is apparent in all of his motets; even when much chromaticism is present, the contrapuntal lines often form triadic chords within the modal harmony. This may be seen in the first nine measures of *Carmina chromatico* (Chromatic songs), the introductory motet of the *Prophetiae Sibyllarum* (Prophecies of the Sybils) cycle (ex. 12.8). *Prophetiae Sibyllarum* comprises 13 motets, one as introduction and one invoking each of the 12 Sibyls who, in ancient times, prophesied the

Example 12.8 Lassus's chromaticism forms triadic chords in the modal harmony at many places in *Carmina chromatico*, the short introductory motet of *Prophetiae Sibyllarum*, composed c. 1560.

coming of Christ. These motets indicate Lassus's awareness of avant-garde practices and may reflect some influence of Vicentino and Rore. Lassus *chose* to write in a conservative style; he was well aware of contemporary developments.

Stylistically, Lassus's early motets exhibit a combination of Franco-Netherlands and Italian practices. Imitation is important and voice pairing occurs frequently; both techniques appear in *Tristis est anima mea* (My soul is sorrowful; 1565; DWMA95). The five voices enter imitatively, but bass and middle voice are paired, and the top voice enters at a pitch widely separated from the others. The use of antiquated chord structure (no third) in the simultaneous cadence on *mortem* (death; m.14) effectively emphasizes that word. The words *circumdabit me* (surround me) are depicted musically.

Canon is used in *Creator omnium Deus* (God, Creator of all), based on a setting by Willaert; *Fremuit spiritu Jesu* (Jesus's spirit groaned) is unified by an ostinato. In some motets Lassus employed cantus firmus or *soggetto cavato* techniques. In others, e.g., *De pacem Domine,* a prayer for peace, he alluded to the Gregorian chant but did not present it complete in any one voice. Chordal declamation appears in motets written between c. 1555 and 1570. Text painting is used but does not disrupt the balance or fluidity of the contrapuntal lines. The chromaticism of *Carmina chromatico* includes (in modern notation) all of the semitones of the tempered C chromatic scale. In Lassus's time, these pitches may have been sung in *just* (not tempered) intonation.

Most but not all of Lassus's motets are sacred. Probably, at one time he considered writing a cycle of motets for the entire church year, for among the motets in *Magnum opus musicum* are sections that fit the liturgical calendar. There are motets based on the Marian antiphons, Gospel motets, and Epistle motets, e.g., *Cum essem parvulus* (When I was little; I Cor. xiii:11). Lassus's *Psalmi Davidis poenitentialis* (Penitential Psalms of David; 1584) are well known (Ps. 6, 31, 37, 50, 101, 129, 142 in Vulgate; Ps. 6, 32, 38, 51, 102, 130, 142 in Bible, KJV); however, these motets do not adequately represent Lassus's work. At the Munich court these Psalm settings were copied into choirbooks illuminated by court painter Hans Mielich. Another member of the court, Samuel Quickelberg, who wrote about Bavarian court customs, referred to these pieces as *musica reservata*—music reserved for a special audience (see p. 227).

German and French are used, as well as Latin, in secular motets, e.g., for drinking songs; some of the humorous motets are macaronic. (Macaronic texts use a mixture of languages.) Humorous text painting occurs in the very short *Laudent Deum cythara* (Praise God [with] harp), in which characteristic music is used to set the names of five instrumental families. Musical depiction of instruments occurs also in *In hora ultima* (In the last hour; 1604).

Some of the two- and three-voice motets seem to have been written for didactic purposes. For example, the 24 *bicinia* (1577) may have been intended as demonstrative exercises for younger members of the Bavarian court choir as well as for other pupils of Lassus. These pieces present technical problems for performers and illustrate Lassus's contrapuntal practice. Certainly, two-part writing was an important part of sixteenth-century counterpoint lessons. Twelve of the *bicinia* are textless. The 24 pieces were written in

Reformation and Counter-Reformation

Orlande de Lassus

Orlande de Lassus (1532–94) was born in Mons, in the province of Hainaut, an area that produced many noted Renaissance composers. Nothing definite is known about him prior to the summer of 1544, when he was noticed by Ferrante Gonzaga, who was visiting in the Low Countries. Gonzaga took Lassus to Sicily where Gonzaga was Viceroy to Charles V (King of Spain 1516–56; Holy Roman Emperor 1519–56). Lassus spent 1547–49 in Milan. He next obtained employment as a singer in the della Torza household in Naples and may have begun to compose at that time. Then he went to Rome where for a time he served as singer in the household of Antonio Altoviti, Archbishop of Florence (but residing in Rome).

In the spring of 1553, when he was just 21, Lassus succeeded Animuccia as *maestro di cappella* at St. John Lateran. Lassus must have had an excellent reputation as a musician to secure such an important post; none of his compositions had been published yet. In 1554 he returned to Hainaut to visit his parents; when he arrived in Mons, he learned they had died. (Palestrina was appointed to the position Lassus vacated at St. John Lateran.)

Early in 1555, Lassus traveled to Antwerp. There he met printers T. Susato and Jean de Laet, and some publications resulted: a collection of four-voice madrigals, *villanesche,* French chansons, and motets (Susato, 1555); and a volume of five- and six-voice motets (Laet, 1556). In Venice, Antonio Gardane published Lassus's *First book of madrigals* (1556) for five and six voices. Apparently, Lassus had delayed publication of any works until several collections had accumulated. Several other compositions may have been written before the end of 1556 and held for publication years later.

In 1556 Duke Albrecht V of Bavaria decided to revitalize his Munich court chapel by employing Franco-Flemish singers. He engaged Lassus as *tenor secundus* and in 1557

Figure 12.6
(*a*) Woodcut portrait of Lassus. (*b*) Lassus's signature.

(a)

(b)

hired six more Netherlanders; in 1560 he sent Lassus to Flanders to recruit chapel singers. In 1562 Andrea Gabrieli was in the retinue accompanying Duke Albrecht V and his chapel on a state visit to Frankfurt am Main; Lassus and Gabrieli became friends. Years later, Giovanni Gabrieli joined the Munich chapel; he may have studied with Lassus.

Duke Albrecht V was a Roman Catholic, as was Lassus. Albrecht had been tolerant towards Protestants and had employed some in highly responsible positions at court, but, after 1555, as positions were vacated, he chose Catholics as replacements. Ludwig Daser, a Lutheran, was *maestro di cappella* when Lassus joined the chapel. When Daser was pensioned in 1563, Lassus was appointed chapelmaster; he retained that position until he died.

---

modes with finals on D, E, F, and G; modes with finals on A and C were not used. Apparently, Lassus advocated using only the traditional eight modes.

Lassus composed approximately 60 Masses; two are Requiem Masses. Lassus built only a few Masses on Gregorian chant. He used parody technique in most of his Masses, basing them primarily on motets

(mainly his own) but using secular songs as models also. Among the latter were chansons by Gombert, Monte, and Willaert and madrigals by Arcadelt, Festa, Palestrina, and Rore. In these parodies, Lassus usually made direct quotation from his model in the Kyrie, then alluded to the model at significant places (beginning, conclusion, important passages) in the other Mass movements. The relationship with the

Lassus's responsibilities as *maestro di cappella* at the Munich court included supplying requisite music for Services and all special religious feasts and for political ceremonies and private celebrations such as state visits, banquets, birthdays, and hunting parties. For Morning Service, polyphonic Masses and motets were needed; Vespers required Magnificats and motets. Obviously, he needed to compose much music. In addition, he supervised the education of choirboys, arranged for copying of manuscripts, and secured printed music for the ducal library.

Lassus became a trusted friend of the ducal family; surviving correspondence between Lassus and Duke Wilhelm, son and heir of Albrecht V, reveals the personalities of the two, as well as the warmth and sincerity of their friendship. In 1569, when Wilhelm and Renée of Lorraine were married, Lassus composed special music and also acted in the Italian comedies performed as part of the nuptial festivities.

In 1558 Lassus married Regina Wäckinger. They had six children; three of their four sons became musicians: Ferdinand (c. 1560–1609), Rudolf (c. 1563–1625), and Ernst (b. after 1565–d. after 1594). A daughter, Regina, married court artist Hans von Ach; the oil portrait of Lassus he painted c. 1580 was given to the Jesuit seminary in Munich sometime after 1600.

Lassus's reputation as composer spread throughout Europe. Enlarged editions of his 1555–56 publications were issued; a second book of madrigals and other secular songs appeared in 1557. Commencing in 1560, individual works were printed, and then volumes of his music were published by the most reputable printers in Antwerp, Venice, Rome, Frankfurt, Nuremberg, Louvain, and Paris. Lassus received honors rarely given to musicians: In 1570 Emperor Maximilian II (r. 1564–76) bestowed on him a patent of nobility; in 1574 Pope Gregory XIII named him *Cavaliere dello Sperone d'Oro* (Knight of the Golden Spur). On three occasions (1571, 1573, 1574) Lassus was invited to the French court of Charles IX (r. 1560–74 with his mother, Catherine de' Medici, as regent during his minority). In 1575 Lassus's Cecelian motet was awarded the prize at Evreux.

Duke Albrecht died in 1579. Wilhelm reduced the size of the ducal chapel considerably, but Lassus declined an invitation to work at Dresden. Albrecht had provided that Lassus would receive his salary for life, and the composer did not want to leave Munich. Lassus complained that he felt old, but he continued to compose, and in 1581–85 many of his Masses, motets, Psalms and Magnificat settings, and Lieder were published. In 1585 Lassus made a pilgrimage to Loreto and visited Ferrara and Verona. Around 1590, his son Ferdinand, who had been working elsewhere, joined the Munich court to assist his father; Rudolf de Lassus was then court organist and music instructor to the younger members of the choir, and Ernst de Lassus was a singer in the court chapel.

Orlande de Lassus was in poor health during the last decade of his life and frequently consulted the court physician about feelings of depression. However, he still accompanied Duke Wilhelm on official journeys. In 1593, they traveled to the Diet of Ratisbon where Lassus met Philippe de Monte and other well-known musicians. Lassus composed intermittently; his last volume of works, written in 1594, comprises a cycle of 20 spiritual madrigals entitled *Lagrime di San Pietro* (Tears of St. Peter) and the seven-voice motet *Vide homo quae pro te patior* (See the man who suffers for you); the volume was dedicated to Pope Clement VIII (r. 1592–1605).

Lassus died in Munich on 14 June 1594. He was buried in the Franciscan cemetery there. When the Franciscan establishment was secularized, the rectangular reddish marble monument that marked Lassus's grave was moved to the garden of the National Museum in Munich.

model is most tenuous in sections written for few voices. Lassus's handling of parody technique is not stereotyped but considerably varied; his Masses are instructive in the various ways of employing parody technique. Three of Lassus's best Masses are *Missa Dixit Joseph* (Mass, Joseph said; 6 vc.), *Missa In te Domine speravi* (Mass, In Thee, Lord, I will hope; 6 vc.), both based on his own music, and *Missa Io son ferito* (Mass, I am wounded; 5 vc.) based on Palestrina's madrigal. *Missa Jesus ist ein süsser Nam'* (Mass, Jesus is a sweet name; 6 vc.) is one of two Masses based on German music. The fact that Lassus parodied secular works in his Masses indicates that in Germanic lands there was less strict compliance with the recommendations of the Council of Trent than in Italy. Also, Lassus stubbornly resisted some of those recommendations.

Court customs caused him to write several syllabic *Missae breves* (Short Masses). For example, the very short *Missa Venatorum* (*Jäger Mass* or Hunt Mass; 4 vc.) was designed for a brief Service on days the court went hunting.

Approximately half of Lassus's 101 Magnificat settings are based on Gregorian chant; the remainder parody chansons, madrigals, and motets. Lassus was the first composer to use parody technique in Magnificat settings. For most of these parodies he preferred his own motets and chansons but used works by other sixteenth-century composers, e.g., Rore's madrigal *Ancor che col partire*. Lassus composed five Magnificat cycles, each comprising a six-verse setting for all eight Tones. In these cycles the appropriate chant Tones are used; cantus firmus technique is varied. These are traditional *alternatim* settings in which the even-numbered verses were composed and the odd-numbered verses chanted or played as organ versets.

Lassus composed at least four Passions, one according to each of the four Gospel Evangelists: St. Matthew (first publ. 1575), St. Mark (1582), St. Luke (1582), St. John (1580). The *Passion according to St. Matthew* was still performed in 1743; during the Baroque era it was supplied with a *basso continuo* (accompaniment) part. (*Basso continuo,* a technique used in the Baroque era, is discussed on p. 286.) In the *St. Matthew Passion,* the words of the *turba* (crowd) are sung by five-voice chorus; the words of Christ and the evangelist are chanted; those of other individuals are sung by soloists in polyphonic duos or trios.

Among Lassus's other Roman Catholic liturgical settings are the Offices for Christmas, Easter, and Pentecost, the Lessons for Matins on Christmas morning, a complete set of nine *Lamentations of Jeremiah* (1585), and a cycle of hymns (c. 1580).

In 1583 Caspar Ulenberg published a German Psalter that contained 50 one-line melodies. Lassus and his son Rudolf composed three-voice settings of those 50 melodies, each man writing 25; that volume of *Teutsche Psalmen* appeared in 1588.

Secular Works

Lassus composed some of the finest chansons written during the last half of the sixteenth century. Between 1550 and c. 1585 he wrote approximately 150 of them (see p. 231). He wrote no Lieder until 1567; by that time he was sufficiently familiar with the German language to set it properly. He was wise to wait, for Ludwig Senfl had worked at the Munich court, and his excellent Lieder were well known. Lassus used both sacred and secular poems for his 93 Lieder; he set the texts in various ways: some are *Tenorlieder;* others are motetlike or madrigalian. *Ich armer Mann* (I, poor man; 1576) is humorously satirical.

Lassus wrote approximately 176 Italian secular pieces: madrigals, villanellas, and morescas. The *Libro de villanelle, moresche, et altre canzoni* (Book of villanellas, morescas, and other songs; Paris, 1581) contains some of his most popular Italian songs, e.g., *Matona mia cara* (Matona, my dear), which is witty and slightly suggestive. Many of his later madrigals are more serious, especially the poetry Petrarch wrote after the death of his beloved Laura, e.g., *Nessun visse giamai* (No one ever lived; 1584).

Near the end of his life, Lassus set 21 octava stanzas of Luigi Tansillo's (1510–68) *Lagrime de San Pietro* (Tears of St. Peter; publ. 1595) as a cycle of seven-voice spiritual madrigals. Lassus's personal feelings of depression color these settings. A book of three-voice Italian songs published in Munich in 1595 is lost—*Musica nuova dove si contengono madrigali, sonnetti, stanze, canzoni, villanelle et altri compositioni* (New music which contains madrigals, sonnets, stanzas, canzonas, villanellas, and other compositions).

Summary

Several times over the centuries there had been agitation for various kinds of reforms within the Roman Catholic Church. Until the first quarter of the sixteenth century all activities papal authorities deemed heretical had been suppressed. In 1517 Martin Luther unintentionally caused the rift that created the Protestant Reformation. Luther suggested few changes in the Mass liturgy but proposed a possible format for a German Mass. He favored the arts, especially music; congregational singing was given an important place in Lutheran Services. At the heart of Lutheran music is the chorale. Under Luther's supervision new chorales were composed and preexistent melodies were adapted as chorales. Among composers working with Luther in the creation of a body of Lutheran church music were Johann Walter and Georg Rhau. Lutheranism spread through northern Germanic lands and into Scandinavian countries where it coexisted with Catholicism.

In those parts of France and Switzerland affected by the Reformation, music was restricted drastically. Zwingli ultimately excluded all music from Services; Calvin restricted church music to singing of the Psalms. Marot's and de Bèze's metrical French translations of the Psalms were set to melodies by Bourgeois and others; these formed the Genevan (Huguenot) Psalter published in 1562. In Holland, Dutch translations of that Psalter gradually superseded the *Souterliedekens*. Polyphonic settings of the Psalms were used in home devotions; Sweelinck wrote a polyphonic setting of the entire Genevan Psalter.

England's break with the Roman Catholic Church in 1534 resulted from political conditions and the personal desires of Henry VIII rather than from doctrinal disagreement. During much of the remainder of the sixteenth century, the pendulum swung between Catholicism and Anglicanism, with ultimate supremacy given the latter. The Mass was replaced by the Anglican Service; full and verse anthems replaced motets. In addition to writing Anglican Services, Byrd composed some of the finest Latin church music produced in England during the latter part of the sixteenth century. Also, he brought English virginal music to a summit of excellence.

Within the Catholic Church a Counter-Reformation occurred. Where music was concerned, the Council of Trent reduced the number of liturgical Sequences to four and directed that impurity, lasciviousness, secularity, and improper language were to be avoided; actual reform was left in the hands of local authorities. Many composers aimed at a musical style that incorporated smoothly curved melodic phrases, with little or no chromaticism, and regular rhythms; counterpoint was rather transparent, having imitative counterpoint interspersed with homorhythmic sections. Intelligibility of text was a major consideration. The Masses and motets of Palestrina and Lassus exemplify this style. The sacred music of Victoria is more expressive than that of Palestrina and is some of the finest produced during the sixteenth century. In addition to sacred works, Lassus wrote German, Italian, and French secular music; he composed some of the finest chansons of his era.

13

Renaissance Instrumental Music

The Renaissance is generally thought of as an age of vocal music, and most of the surviving music from the Renaissance is vocal polyphony. However, a wide variety of musical instruments existed, and an important musical development during the sixteenth century was the creation of a body of music literature designed especially for instruments—music that (a) had its own styles and forms, (b) was idiomatic to the specific instruments sounding it, and (c) was coherent and meaningful without relying on words. Moreover, didactic literature—both treatises and music—was written.

Instruments

Most Renaissance instruments were built in families or sets incorporating graduated sizes; a set of a particular type of instrument provided coverage of the entire vocal range then in use, in homogeneous instrumental timbre. An ensemble in which all instruments belonged to the same family was called a **whole consort;** an ensemble including various kinds of instruments was a **broken consort.** Such a mixed ensemble is the subject of the woodcut shown in figure 13.1. Instrumental ensemble music published before c. 1597 did not specify instrumentation. One of the earliest pieces to specify exact instrumentation—trombones, cornetto, and *violino*—is Giovanni Gabrieli's *Sonata pian e forte* (Sonata soft and loud; DWMA96). Music for keyboard or lute was identifiable by the peculiarities of its **tablature.** Tablature is the general term used for notational systems in

Figure 13.1 This woodcut illustrates a broken consort performing. Instruments represented include viola da gamba, cornetto, lute, transverse flute, and virginal. *(Source: Adam Berg:* Patrocinium musices, *1589.)*

which pitches are indicated by letters, numbers, or symbols other than notes on a staff (fig. 13.2). Title pages of some printed music stated that it was *per cantare e sonare* (for singing and playing), *convenable tant à la voix comme aux instruments* (suitable for voice and/or instruments), or "apt for voyces or vyols." The actual instrumentation was determined by the musician in charge of a performance, who selected appropriate instruments from those available at his place of employment.

Instruments were still classified as loud (*haut*) or soft (*bas*); in general, the sounds they produced had less volume and less intense tonal colors than those of modern instruments. However, a blanket comparative

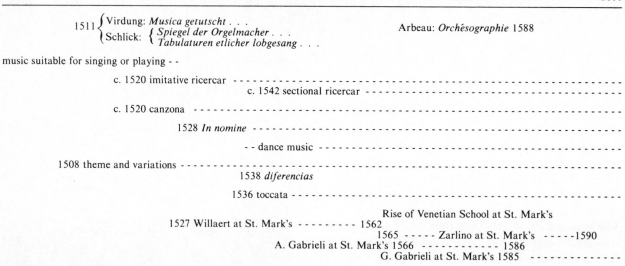

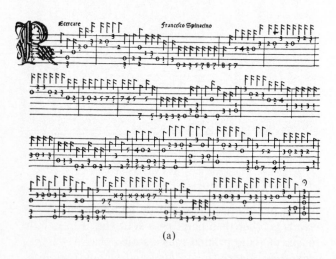

(a)

LA DEDICASSE.

(b)

Figure 13.2 (a) Italian and (b) French lute tablatures. Each line represents a course. The figure 0 or the letter *a* indicates an open string, and subsequent numbers or letters (in numerical or alphabetical order) represent frets. Each number or letter on a line indicates the point on the course, i.e., the fret, at which the finger must stop the string to produce the required pitch. (*Source: Figure a—Petrucci,* Intabolatura de lauto. Libro primo. *Venice, 1507, p. 39. Figure b—Denis Gaultier,* La Rhétorique des dieux, *Berlin, Kupferstichkabinett Ms. 142, ca. 1650, pp. 25, 26.*)

judgment should not be made to the detriment of Renaissance instrumental sonorities. Environmental effect must be given due consideration—the effect of such factors as the acoustical properties of the constructional materials of the chambers in which the music was performed, the presence or absence of tapestries or other draperies in the rooms, the degree to which the auditors' ears were (or were not) bombarded by noises created by daily living conditions, and the resultant auditory sensitivity (or lack of it) to musical nuances. Renaissance audiences may have enjoyed finer musical subtleties than many modern listeners can comprehend.

Also, tuning and temperament must be considered. Voices are capable of producing at will pure fifths and thirds (**just intonation**) in any mode, but Renaissance instruments could not do this. The **mean-tone** system in use c. 1500 is based on a fifth slightly smaller than the perfect fifth. This tuning is fairly satisfactory melodically and harmonically when only one or two flats or sharps are involved, but noticeable pitch discrepancies result when more chromatics occur, because flatted notes are higher than sharped ones, e.g., a♭ is higher than g♯. Some sixteenth-century organs were constructed with divided keys, so that flatted and sharped notes could be played more accurately in tune; however, this proved inadequate for the needs of increased chromaticism, more fully developed harmonies, and modulations. Experiments with **equal temperament**—the division of the octave into 12 equal semitones—began c. 1518, but the system was not clearly expounded until c. 1600 and was not widely accepted until after 1700.

For performance of the extremely chromatic madrigals he was interested in composing, Nicola Vicentino designed and had built c. 1560 two keyboard instruments—an *arcicembalo* and an *arciorgano*—which could sound all of the various intervals contained in the diatonic, chromatic, and enharmonic *genera* used by the ancient Greeks. Vicentino presented his interpretation of the three *genera* in his treatise *L'antica musica ridotta alla moderna prattica* (Ancient music adapted to modern practice; 1555). He explained the *arciorgano* in *Descrizione dell' arciorgano* (Description of the *arciorgano*; 1561).

The earliest printed treatise describing musical instruments is Sebastian Virdung's *Musica getutscht* (Music, [written] in German), published in Basle in 1511. The writing, structured as dialogue, is illustrated by woodcuts of instruments and tablature notation (fig. 13.3). Treatises by other authors ensued. One of the most notable Renaissance treatises on musical instruments is *De organographia* (Concerning instruments), which is Vol. II of Michael Praetorius's *Syntagma musicum* (Treatise on music), published in 1618. An appendix in that volume is entitled *Theatrum instrumentorum* (Theater of instruments); it contains 42 woodcuts of scale drawings illustrating the various instruments discussed in the volume (fig. 13.4).

Figure 13.3 Description of clavichord and virginal, with illustrations, printed in Virdung's *Musica getutscht* (1511).

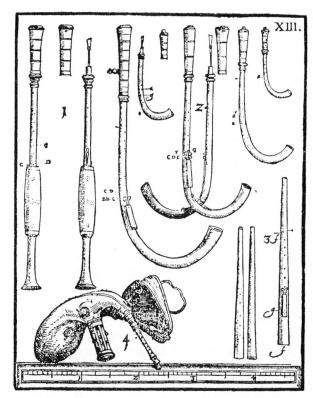

1. Nicolo Bassett 2. Krummhorns 3. Soft Cornets 4. Bagpipe with Bellows.

Figure 13.4 Woodcut illustration of wind instruments. *(Source: Plate XIII in M. Praetorius's* Syntagma musicum, *Volume II,* De Organographia, *1620.)*

Wind Instruments

The principal types of Renaissance wind instruments were recorder, *cromorne,* shawm, cornetto, trumpet, and trombone. The Renaissance recorder was intended for use as an ensemble, not a solo, instrument; usually, recorder sets comprised a trio or a quartet of instruments. The first recorder method was published in Venice in 1535; dance music was printed by Jacques Moderne (Lyons), Attaignant (Paris), Susato (Antwerp), and others.

The *cromorne* (French, crooked horn; German, *Krummhorn*) is a J-shaped woodwind whose double-reed is enclosed in a cap. A set of cromornes contained six instruments. Though used sporadically in the early fifteenth century, the cromorne was in vogue as an ensemble instrument from c. 1475–c. 1600.

The shawm is a woodwind with an exposed double reed; it was considered a loud instrument, for ensemble use. Shawms were constructed in families of six, with sizes ranging from high treble to great bass.

The cornetto (little horn), a wooden instrument with a cup-shaped mouthpiece of ivory or bone, was made in both straight and curved models and in three sizes. Mainly, the cornetto was used with trombone and organ as support for choral music. The cornetto was the nucleus of the instrumental ensembles formed by Andrea and Giovanni Gabrieli at Venice c. 1600.

The straight trumpet existed from antiquity; the trumpet with looped tubing appeared c. 1400. During most of the fifteenth century, trumpeters were employed as town musicians, principally as tower watchmen. After c. 1480, however, five-part trumpet consorts performed at many courts; ownership of a trumpet ensemble was a symbol of a ruler's importance. In 1482, there were 18 trumpeters at the Sforza court. The social prestige of trumpeters mounted considerably in 1548 when, by decree, Charles V placed them directly under the jurisdiction of the emperor.

Trombones were used at the Burgundian and Franco-Flemish courts by mid-fifteenth century. In addition to ensemble performance with cornetto and organ to double voices singing choral music in church Services, trombonists played in town and court bands.

String Instruments

The viol, a bowed string instrument with fretted fingerboard, first appeared in Spain in the last third of the fifteenth century and quickly became known in other European countries; it flourished as both solo and ensemble instrument until c. 1750. Viols were built in six sizes: treble, alto, small tenor, tenor, bass, and contrabass (*violone*). A viol consort usually consisted of treble, tenor, and bass viols; a chest of viols contained two of each of those three sizes. The viol is characterized by a wide neck, sloping shoulders, and deep ribs. Seven gut frets gird the neck and fingerboard at semitone intervals. The six strings are tuned in fourths around a central major third: bass *viola da gamba* tuning is D-G-c-e-a-d'; the treble viol is tuned an octave higher. In the sixteenth century, the tenor viol was sometimes tuned a fifth below the treble and sometimes a fifth above the bass. All viols are played in an upright, almost vertical position, with the instrument resting on the lap or the calves of the legs of the player. Thus, the viol was properly named *viola da gamba* (leg viol). Unlike the modern 'cello and string bass, the instrument had no end pin for support. (The term *viola da braccio,* meaning "arm viol," was used in the sixteenth century to designate instruments of the violin family.) To stop a string, the viol player's finger firmly depresses a string *directly behind* a fret, thus bringing that string into tight contact with the fret; when the string is bowed, the timbre of the sound produced is that of an unstopped (open) string. The viol bow stick is convex and is gripped underhand, with the palm upward; tension of the bow hair is controlled by pressure of the middle finger directly on the hair. The bow is glided over the strings, without pressure. Heavy accents cannot be produced on a viol; therefore, the instrument is ineffective for dance music. However, the viol is very responsive and resonant; its tone is quiet, with a distinctive reedy or nasal quality—characteristics ideal for the clarity of texture vital to effective performance of polyphonic music.

Instruments of the violin family—violin, viola, violoncello—were in existence in the second quarter of the sixteenth century. Philibert Jambe de Fer described them and discussed their use in his treatise *Epitome musicale des tons, . . . violes et violons* (Music treatise on tones, . . . viols and violins; Lyon, 1556). The violin differs from the viol in having four strings tuned in fifths, an unfretted fingerboard, an arched back and belly, and rounded and less-sloping shoulders. The violin bow stick is grasped primarily between the player's thumb and middle finger, with the hand held palm downward; the bow is drawn

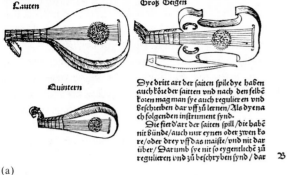

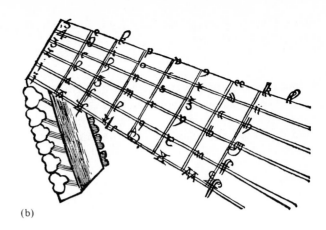

Figure 13.5 Illustrations of (*a*) lute and other string instruments and (*b*) lute neck with frets clearly lettered on the courses. *(Source: Virdung: Musica getutscht, 1511.)*

across the strings with varying degrees of pressure. Because of its capability to accent rhythmically, the violin is suitable for performing dance music—one of its principal functions in the Renaissance. No one knows who invented the violin; it seems to have originated in the Milan-Brescia-Cremona area of Italy. Founder of the Cremonese school of violin making was Andrea Amati (c. 1510 or earlier–c. 1580); his descendants crafted superb instruments until after 1675. Amati instruments were imported to the French court by Catherine de' Medici, by Charles IX, and by Henri IV. Accounts of the performance of the dramatic ballet *Circé* at court in 1581 relate that two of the five-voice dances were played by ten violins. In the first three-quarters of the sixteenth century, violins were used primarily to double vocal lines and to supply music for dancing. Prior to 1600, violinists generally held lower social status than violists—viols were played by aristocratic amateurs as an avocation, as well as by professionals, but violinists were professional musicians hired to perform at court, for municipal or church festivities, or for special celebrations at a wealthy household.

The lute was one of the most popular Renaissance instruments; most households owned at least one. Training in playing the lute was considered an essential part of the education of a cultured lady. Lutes were constructed in several sizes; performance of most of the surviving music requires treble, tenor, and bass instruments. The Spanish lute (*vihuela*) resembles a guitar; the standard lute used in other

European countries is characterized by a body shaped like a halved avocado, a wide neck with a fretted fingerboard, and a pegbox bent backwards at right angles to the neck of the instrument (fig. 13.5). The sixteenth-century lute had eleven strings arranged in six **courses,** two strings for all but the highest course. (A course is a group of strings tuned in unison or as an octave and sounded simultaneously to obtain increased volume.) The tenor lute was tuned either G-c-f-a-d′-g′ or A-d-g-b-e′-a′. The strings of the two lowest courses might be tuned in unison or in octaves, for example, G-g c-c′; those of the next three courses were always tuned in unison. Tones are produced from the six courses of strings by plucking them with the fingertips. Chords as well as single notes can be played; rapid runs and ornaments are not especially problematic. Lute tones are rather soft, more suitable for a chamber than a concert hall. The lute was used as a solo instrument, in ensembles, and to accompany singers.

Keyboard Instruments

The generic term *clavier* (French, keyboard; German, *Klavier*) was used for keyboard instruments other than the organ. Two types of claviers existed: clavichord and harpsichord (see fig. 13.3). In outward appearance, the fifteenth-century clavichord was a rectangular box with a keyboard set into one of its long sides. Depressing a key causes a brass tangent to strike a pair of strings within the box; the tangent remains in contact with the string until the key is released. Increased or decreased pressure on the key can slightly alter a pitch once it has begun sounding or create a vibrato. In the fifteenth century all strings in a clavichord were the same length and were tuned in unison; differences in the sounding length of each string (i.e., the portion of the string activated by a tangent) created the different pitches. By mid-sixteenth century, the clavichord had a four-octave range, from F to f′′′ but lacked F♯ and G♯. (In other words, the lowest octave was a "short" octave—short two pitches.)

The harpsichord was invented c. 1400. During the Renaissance, instruments of the harpsichord type were built in various shapes and sizes and were known by different names, such as clavicembalo, clavecin, spinet, and virginal. When a harpsichord key is depressed, a jack is activated and a plectrum plucks a string, thus sounding a pitch. The harpsichord was both a solo and ensemble instrument.

The portative organ disappeared from use early in the sixteenth century; positive organs remained in use until the early seventeenth century. The **regal** was a small positive organ with reed pipes only. Early in the sixteenth century, it was incorporated into the large church organ as a rank of pipes; however, some independent regals were still being used in the seventeenth century. The Renaissance church organ could cover the entire gamut in a uniform sonority, or, by means of a variety of stops, different tone colors could be produced. The slider-chest, built into the organ c. 1500, could easily isolate or combine separate ranks of pipes. Pedal keyboards, both with solo pipes and with couplers to manuals, first appeared in Germanic and Franco-Netherlands territories, then were introduced in other countries. Organ-playing techniques improved during the sixteenth century; if desired, harmonies could be played on the pedals alone. However, thumbs were almost never used in playing. Renaissance organ cases were richly ornamented and often had side cases whose doors sheltered beautiful paintings.

The treatise *Spiegel der Orgelmacher und Organisten* (Mirror of the organmaker and organ player; 1511) by Arnolt Schlick (c. 1460–c. 1522), German organist-composer, is the first German publication dealing comprehensively with organ building and playing; the book contains some organ music. Schlick's

Tabulaturen etlicher lobgesang und lidlein uff die orgeln un lauten (Tabulatures of some praise songs and little songs for organ and lute; 1511) contains the earliest printed organ tablatures. The advanced state of some German organs and Schlick's talents as organist may be seen in his *Ascendo ad Patrem meum* (I ascend unto my Father), a ten-voice organ work that, according to Schlick, could be played on the organ with four parts on the pedals and six parts on the manuals. The chorale-like cantus firmus, set in long notes in an inner voice, is surrounded by contrapuntal melodies.

The church organ was used both as a supportive and a solo instrument. Verses of some liturgical music, such as the Magnificat and various sections of the Proper of the Mass, were often performed alternately by singer(s) and organ. Similarly, certain sections of Kyrie or Gloria might be performed by organ in alternation with singers. In the sixteenth century, some complete settings of the Mass Ordinary were written according to this alternation principle—organ polyphony alternating with vocal music; such a setting is known as an *Organ Mass*. An example is Cavazzoni: *Missa Apostolorum*. Sometimes short organ solos, called *versets* or *verses*, were substituted for chant in some portions of the Proper of both Mass and Offices. Organ pieces written in the style of motets served a like purpose. Arnolt Schlick composed eight canonic versets, in from three to five voices, on the Sequence *Gaude Dei genitrix* (Rejoice, mother of God); no two versets are alike contrapuntally (DWMA97).

Percussion

A variety of percussion instruments were used during the Renaissance: anvil and hammer, bells and chimes, small cymbals, side drum, dulcimer (psaltery), tabor, tambourine, trapezoid-shaped triangle with jingling rings at its angles, nakers (like six- to ten-inch kettledrums), kettledrums (tympani), and xylophone. Percussion instruments were used mainly for religious ceremonies, civic processions, military signals and encouragement, and dancing. If notated music was used, it has not survived; presumably, percussionists learned rudiments by rote and improvised music appropriate to the occasion. In *Orchésographie* (1588), Arbeau clearly described percussion instruments, stated that the side drum—a type of snare drum—was used as a pacemaker to organize military marches, and notated the various rhythms used by French drummers. Percussion instruments had been described and depicted previously in treatises by several authors, including Sebastian Virdung (1511), Arnolt Schlick (1511), and Martin Agricola (1528), and in an anonymous encyclopedic manuscript prepared c. 1585 for Henry III of France. The *Strohfiedel,* or xylophone, was first mentioned by Schlick as "wooden percussion." Dulcimers were popular and were played by hitting the wire strings with sticks. True kettledrums—large copper tympani—were introduced to western Europe from Russia early in the fifteenth century. They were cavalry instruments, carried by horses, and associated with war, pomp, and ceremony. In 1511, Virdung wrote disparagingly about tympani, called them *Rumpelfesser* (rumbling tubs), and said they had been created by the devil. But royalty desired them and added them to their instrument collections. Almost invariably tympani were played along with trumpets; players of both kinds of instruments were highly esteemed. In Germany, the Imperial Guild of Trumpeters and Kettledrummers was established by decree in 1528; its members guarded their craft and transmitted their performance secrets by rote from generation to generation. No doubt this kind of professional secrecy was partially responsible for the lack of notated music for percussion instruments.

Instrument Collections

Increased interest in instrumental music is attested by the fact that many churches and courts owned rather large collections of instruments. This was necessary in order to have complete sets of instruments available for performance of ensemble music or to support voices with instruments of homogeneous timbre. Rosters of permanent employees at these institutions include names of instrumentalists. In the sixteenth century, it became fashionable to collect instruments; some wealthy households owned hundreds of them. For example, in 1566 the music room of Raymond Fugger's home in Augsburg contained approximately 400 instruments. Surviving inventories indicate that 70 to 80 percent of the instruments in most collections were winds. Instruments in private collections were not treated as art objects to be

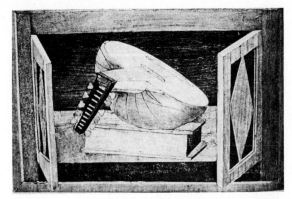

Figure 13.6 *Intarsia* from Federigo da Montefeltro's *studiolo* at Gubbio. (Intarsia *owned by The Metropolitan Museum, New York.)*

admired—they were used and might be loaned to professional musicians. Valuable decorated harpsichords usually were considered part of the decor of their respective chambers and were used only in those rooms. In most court residences and private palatial homes, a keyboard instrument was kept in every room in which music was performed. Persons who could not amass as many instruments as they desired might simulate collections by means of *intarsia* or *marquetry,* as did Federigo da Montefeltro in his homes at Urbino and Gubbio (fig. 13.6). (*Intarsia* and *marquetry* are types of surface decoration done by inlaying various colors and kinds of wood.)

Instrumental Music

Instruments were used to double vocal lines or substitute for them, to provide accompaniment for vocal solos, to work in alternation with vocalists, and to perform ensemble and solo music. Some pieces were written especially for instrumental performance. This music was of four main types: (1) pieces modeled on or derived from vocal compositions; (2) dance music; (3) variations; and (4) improvisatory works.

Music from Vocal Models

Instrumental performance of vocal music soon led to the composition of purely instrumental pieces of similar character. Motet and chanson served, respectively, as prototypes for the imitative *ricercar* (Italian, *ricercare,* to seek, to try out) and *canzona* (Italian, chanson). The contrapuntal ricercar is characterized

Example 13.1 Opening of Cavazzoni's organ canzona based on Josquin's chanson *Faulte d'argent*.

by imitative treatment of one or more themes that usually are not melodically or rhythmically individualistic; stylistically, the ricercar is very similar to the motet. Terminology was not explicit; this kind of composition might be labeled *ricercare, capriccio, fuga, verset, fantasia,* or with some other name.

The precise origin of the imitative ricercar is not known. The keyboard ricercars in Marc Antonio Cavazzoni's (c. 1490–c. 1560) *Recerchari, motetti, canzoni . . . libro primo* (Ricercars, motets, canzonas . . . book 1; 1523) and those of his son Girolamo (c. 1525–c. 1578) published in *Intavolatura cioè recercari canzoni himni magnificati . . . libro primo* (Intabulations of ricercars, canzonas, hymns, Magnificats . . . book 1; 1543) resemble the imitative motet. Likewise, the 18 pieces named *ricercari* that are printed in *Musica nova* (New music; Venice, 1540) are in motet style, with pervading imitation. Most ricercars are of short to moderate length.

Imitative ricercars were written for instrumental ensembles and for organ. Some ensemble ricercars were labeled *da cantare et sonare* (to be sung and played), and presumably they were vocalized on solmization syllables. The imitative ricercar for organ might be monothematic or might have several themes each treated rather extensively in a separate section of the piece. Some of the earliest sectional ricercars were written c. 1542 by Girolamo Cavazzoni (DWMA98). The organ monothematic ricercar and the organ canzona are ancestors of the fugue (see p. 353). An imitative ricercar by Antonio de Cabezón is entitled *Fuga al contrario* (Fugue in contrary motion).

Some nonimitative instrumental pieces of improvisatory nature were written for lute, organ, and viols and were also entitled *"ricercare."* These are not related to the motet; they are more properly classified with the toccata and free prelude.

The term *canzona* originally denoted an instrumental arrangement of a polyphonic chanson; frequently, such an arrangement was labeled *canzon francese* (French chanson), or, if for an ensemble, *canzon da sonar* (instrumental chanson). Early canzonas closely resemble the chanson. In fact, the Italian word *canzona* and the French word *chanson* have the same meaning—"song." Most canzonas commence with the 𝅝 𝅗𝅥 𝅗𝅥 (or 𝅗𝅥 𝅗𝅥 𝅗𝅥) rhythmic figure that typically opens a chanson (ex. 13.1). Lute transcriptions of polyphonic chansons were in existence early in the sixteenth century. The earliest examples of keyboard arrangements of polyphonic chansons—called *canzoni*—appear in M. A. Cavazzoni's *Recerchari motetti canzoni . . . libro primo* (1523). In Girolamo Cavazzoni's *Intavolatura cioè recercari canzoni . . .* (1543), one canzona is a condensation and complete reworking of Josquin's *Faulte d'argent*. However, by that date, original compositions entitled *canzoni* were being written for keyboard and for instrumental ensembles. Around mid-century, ensemble canzonas were written with distinct sections that had contrasting themes both melodically and rhythmically. As the canzona developed, the sections increased in length and diversity, then split apart into independent sections or "movements," and in the seventeenth century gave birth to the *sonata da chiesa* (church sonata). An example is Tarquinio Merula's canzona, *La Strada,* for two violins, violoncello, and organ (1637; DWMA99). Title is not always clear indication of the character of a piece. Andrea Gabrieli's *Ricercare del 12° tono* (Ricercar on the 12th tone) exhibits characteristics of a canzona; it is clearly sectional and employs the unifying principles of repetition and contrast, as does Merula's *La Strada.*

Among instrumental ensemble music derived from vocal models is a unique type that is exclusively English—the *In nomine* (In the name). This compositional type had a single model: that section of the

Benedictus of John Taverner's six-voice Mass *Gloria tibi Trinitas* setting the words *In nomine Domine* (In the name of the Lord). The cantus firmus for that Mass is the Sarum antiphon *Gloria tibi trinitas aequalis* (Glory to thee, equal trinity), sung at first Vespers on Trinity Sunday. Taverner used only four voices for the *In nomine* portion of the Benedictus of the Mass; the entire antiphon appears in long note values in the second-highest voice, which is labeled *Mean,* an English term for cantus firmus. That section of the Benedictus was used as an independent composition for voices, and in various arrangements: for voice(s) with instruments, and as a purely instrumental piece for keyboard or for consort. Taverner seems to have made the first instrumental arrangement of his Mass section; his contemporaries soon followed his lead (DWMA100). Approximately 65 *In nomine* pieces written in the sixteenth and seventeenth centuries are extant. Early ones are for four voices, but the majority use five; a few six- and seven-voice *In nomine* pieces survive.

In addition to canzonas and ricercars, liturgical vocal music provided models for organ compositions. There were organ Masses and versets (see p. 272), settings of Lutheran chorales, and pieces based on plainchant. Arnold Schlick's *Tabulaturen etlicher Lobgesang und Lidlein uff die Orgel und Lauten* (see also p. 272) contains 14 pieces for organ with pedals. All are based on sacred vocal music—one on the German sacred song *Maria zart,* the others on plainchant.

Dance Music

From mid-sixteenth to mid-seventeenth century, dancing was popular both as a social art and in the theater. A wealth of dance music appeared in print, and the strong rhythmic patterns of dance music permeated secular vocal music of the era. Dancing-masters abounded; both nobility and middle-class citizens sought to acquire dancing skills. Three basic kinds of dances were performed at social gatherings: stately processional types such as the *pavane*; circular dances, such as the *branle*; and progressive "long-line" dances, such as the *allemande.* Dance music was written for performance by ensemble, keyboard, or lute. Usually, two or three contrasting dances were grouped together. Favorite combinations paired a slow,

stately dance such as *pavane* (*pavan, padovana*) with a leaping dance such as the *gaillarde* (Italian, *gagliarda,* English, *galliard*), or a *passamezzo* (or *pass' e mezzo,* literally, a step and a half) with a *saltarello.* Both *pavane* and *passamezzo* are slow, stately, processional-type dances in duple meter; *gaillarde* and *saltarello* are rollicking, leaping dances in compound duple ($\frac{6}{8}$) meter interspersed with hemiola ($\frac{3}{4}$) passages. The *pavane* uses a gliding step that produces an undulating movement reminiscent of a peacock's strut; the *gaillarde* is more vigorous with higher leaps than the *saltarello,* whose steps are more like skipping. The *gaillarde* was one of the few dances men performed with their heads uncovered; when dancing the *gaillarde,* a man held his hat in his hand. In Germanic lands, a slow dance in duple meter might be followed by a *Proportz* or a *Tripla,* a fast dance in triple meter. It is not uncommon for paired dances to use the same melody or variants of it.

Other paired sixteenth-century dances include the *allemande* and *courante,* both of which became standard movements of the seventeenth-century suite. The *allemande* (French, German dance; English, *alman* or *almain*; Italian, *allemanda*) may have originated as a German version of the *basse danse*; the earliest known use of *allemande* occurs in a 1521 *basse danse* manual. By mid-sixteenth century, however, the *allemande* was a distinct genre. It is a couple dance in which a man and a woman proceed side by side, in a stately procession of couples moving to duple-meter music in moderate tempo, from one end of the hall to the other; the line then reverses and the couples return to their original starting point. The allemande is followed by a *courante* (French, running; Italian, *corrente*), a contrasting dance in triple meter. The *courante* was a kind of pantomimic wooing dance performed by couples moving in a zigzag pattern from one end of the room to the other. The *Bergomasca,* also a wooing dance, was a round dance. Near the end of *A Midsummer Night's Dream,* Shakespeare had Bottom suggest that a *Bergomask* (English spelling) be danced.

Not all Renaissance dances were paired. The *jig,* which originated in the British Isles, was danced in Scotland, Ireland, and England and apparently existed in two forms: a male solo dance and a couple dance. Both types are characterized by vigorous movement up and down. During the reign of Elizabeth I, the jig became a popular couple dance at the English court and spread across the Channel into France.

Printed dance manuals were available for purchase. Such books contained descriptions of the dances and instructions for performing them, dance music, and sometimes comments about the musical structure. Many fifteenth-century dance manuals are anonymous; typical sixteenth-century books include Fabritio Caroso's *Il ballarino* (The dancer; 1581), and *Orchésographie* by Thoinot Arbeau (the pseudonym of Jehan Tabourot), printed in 1588. Thomas Morley included a section on dances and dance music in *A Plaine and Easie Introduction to Practicall Musicke* (1597).

Dances are significant in the development of music not merely because music is an integral part of their performance, but because the pairing of contrasting dances led to larger groupings and because their music generated stylized versions that, in the seventeenth century, became the Baroque suite and *sonata da camera* (chamber sonata).

Ballet de cour (court ballet) was popular at the Burgundian and French courts. The earliest ballet in which poetry, music, scenery, and dance were combined in support of drama was *Circé ou le Balet comique de la Royne* (Circé or The Queen's dramatic ballet; performed 15 October 1581). The drama concerned the destruction of Circé's powers of enchantment in order to restore harmony and order; the ballet, commissioned by Catherine de' Medici, combined several talents, including those of dancing-master Baltasar de Beaujoyleux and composers Jacques Salmon and Lambert de Beaulieu. Not until 1609 was another dramatic ballet of comparable quality performed in France.

Variations

Sets of variations upon a theme were written principally in Spain and England. However, the earliest surviving examples appear in Petrucci's *Intabolatura de Lauto,* Vol. 4 (lute tablatures). Dance pieces were especially favored as bases for variation sets. In Spain, variation technique was highly developed by vihuelist-composer Luys de Narváez (fl. 1530–50) and organist-composer Antonio de Cabezón (1510–66).

Narváez's book *Los seys libros del delphin* (The six books of the dauphin) is believed to be the earliest publication to contain pieces clearly identified as *diferencias* (sets of variations); in these variations, tempos are indicated by symbols. Narváez's variations are of two types: (1) those in which the cantus firmus is present in each variation, e.g., variations on the hymn melody *O gloriosa Domina*; (2) variations on ostinato harmonies, e.g., *Diferencias sobra Guárdame las vacas* (Variations on *The Cowboy*). Cabezón, blind from childhood, was one of the greatest keyboard performers of his time. In his *diferencias* based on popular melodies and dance tunes, the cantus firmus is placed in a different voice in successive variations; individual variations are not sectioned off but flow into one another. (*Diferencias sobra Cavallero;* DWMA101.) Most of Cabezón's compositions were published by his son in 1578; these pieces indicate that Cabezón was ahead of his time in advocating use of the thumbs when playing organ.

An early sixteenth-century English example of continuous variation upon a short *pes* or ground is *My Lady Carey's Dompe,* found in British Museum MS Roy. App. 58, dating from c. 1530. This three-voice work, the oldest of 16 extant *domps,* is a series of variations written above ostinato tonic and dominant harmonies. The piece has been conjecturally attributed to Hugh Aston.

One of the most important manuscript sources of English sixteenth-century keyboard music is *The Mulliner Book,* a manuscript compilation made c. 1550–c. 1575 by Thomas Mulliner. The manuscript contains dance pieces, transcriptions of secular and sacred vocal works, organ versets, and cantus firmus-type variations on hymn and chant melodies. A school of English virginalist composers flourished in the late sixteenth century. (The **virginal** was a type of small harpsichord with only one set of strings and one keyboard.) Chief among this school of virginalists was William Byrd; others of importance were John Bull, Giles Farnaby, Orlando Gibbons, and Thomas Tomkins. At their hands, all known variation types attained artistic and technical maturity. Bull, Byrd, Farnaby, and Gibbons are the most important composers represented in *The Fitzwilliam Virginal Book,* a manuscript copied c. 1609–19. More than two-thirds of the approximately 300 pieces in the manuscript use some form of variation technique; most of the types of variation known in the sixteenth century are represented. John Bull's *The Spanish Paven* (DWMA102) presents the 16-measure dance theme, followed by seven variations. Works by Bull, Byrd, and other English virginalists were known in Europe and exerted an important influence on northern European composers of keyboard music, such as Jan Sweelinck.

Improvisatory Works

Improvisation was widely practiced during the Renaissance. Performers usually improvised in one of three ways: (1) by adding one or more new polyphonic lines to an existing melody selected as *cantus firmus*; (2) by embellishing or paraphrasing an existing melody; or (3) by freely improvising, without reference to a preexistent melody or harmony or predetermined formal pattern. The extemporization of one or more additional polyphonic lines was an extension of the practices of English discant (*discantus supra librum*—improvising over the book) and continental *faux bourdon* (see p. 159). Fleshing a composition from a skeletal musical line was practiced wherever and whenever the *basse danse* was performed (see p. 168). Extemporaneous embellishment or paraphrasing of a melodic line was an outgrowth of compositional practice—composers embellished and paraphrased preexistent melodies when writing Masses and motets.

Freely improvised compositions were given various titles, such as *fantasia* or *fancy, preambulum* or other designations for *prelude, ricercar, toccata* (from the Italian verb *toccare,* to touch). Vihuelists and lutenists commonly improvised introductions to popular court airs to establish the mode and create the mood of the piece.

Many compositions in improvisatory style are included in *Libro de musica de vihuela de mano. Intitulado El Maestro* (Book of vihuela music. Entitled The Master; Valencia, 1535) by Luys de Milán (c. 1500–c. 1561 or later). *El Maestro* is the earliest printed collection of guitar (vihuela) music and the earliest source of music with verbal tempo indications. The treatise is an instruction manual with music for performance; Milán supplied performance instructions for individual compositions (fig. 13.7). The book contains both vocal and instrumental music and

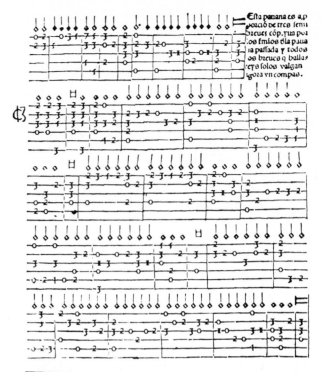

Figure 13.7 Folio VI verso of Luys de Milán's *El Maestro* (1536). The last four staves of notation contain a *pavane.*

includes *pavans, tentos,* and 40 fantasias composed in idiomatic vihuela style, with chordal passages, runs, and sequences freely interspersed. Milán advised the performer to play pieces of this kind in a free tempo, rendering the ornamented passages rapidly and the chordal harmonies slowly. *Fantasia no. 17* is an example (DWMA103).

The earliest surviving pieces of freely composed keyboard music appear in tablature in fifteenth-century German manuscripts such as the *Buxheimer Orgelbuch* (see p. 176). Two rhapsodic *ricercari* are among the keyboard music in *Recerchari, motetti, canzoni* (1523) of Marco Antonio Cavazzoni; these rambling pseudo-improvisatory pieces were intended as introductions to motet transcriptions.

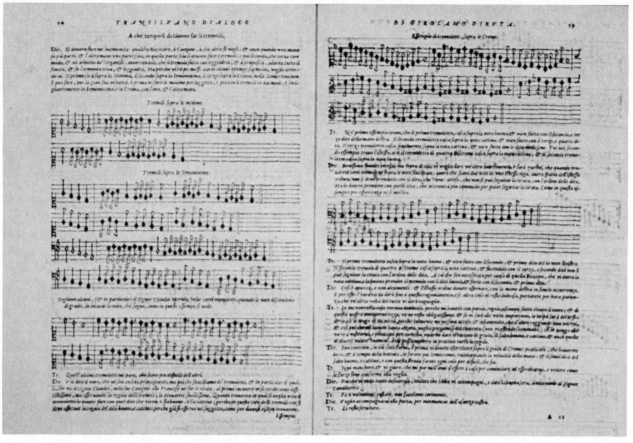

Figure 13.8 Examples of correct manner of performing *tremolo* given by Diruta in *Il Transilvano dialogo* (1593), Part I, pp. 18–19.

The first pieces designated as *toccatas* appeared in the sixteenth century. A *Tochata* by Francesco Canova da Milano is one of three toccatas printed in Casteliono's *Intabolatura de leuto de diversi autori* (Lute tablatures by various composers; 1536); keyboard toccatas by Sperindio Bertoldo were printed in 1591. More important is *Il transilvano dialogo sopra il vero modo di sonar organi, et istromenti da penna* (The Transylvanian dialogue concerning the true method of playing organs and harpsichords; Part I, 1593), the first comprehensive treatise on organ playing, by Girolamo Diruta (c. 1554–c. 1611). The treatise, written as dialogue between the inquiring Transylvanian and Diruta, summarizes keyboard practice of the time. The discussion includes rudiments of music and musical notation, basics of organ playing and harpsichord playing, transposition and modulation, and performance practices such as when and how to properly ornament a melody. Diruta provided music examples to clarify the principles; complete compositions illustrate various problems encountered in performance. The compositions are, therefore, true **études.** (An *étude* is a complete composition with both musical and pedagogical intent and content featuring at least one consistently recurring problem of physiological, technical, or musical difficulty which requires of the player not only mechanical application, but proper study and correct interpretation as well.)

Examples of *tremolo* and *groppi*—ornaments like the modern *trill* and *turn*—show clearly that in music of Diruta's time these ornaments are measured and

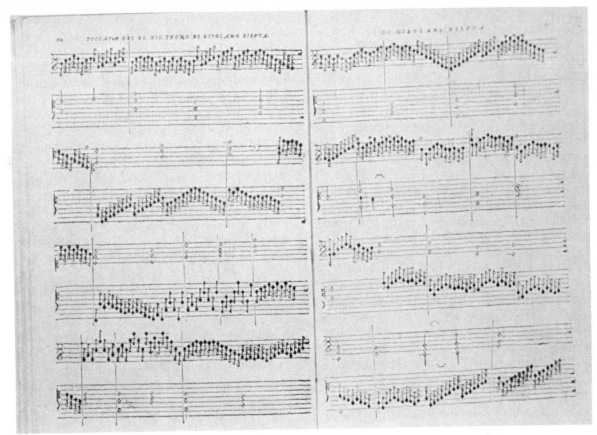

Figure 13.9 Portion of a toccata by Diruta, from *Il Transilvano dialogo*, Part I, pp. 50–51.

are begun after the notated pitch is sounded (fig. 13.8). The compass of the keyboard (*la tastatura*) is from A to a''.

Diruta, a pupil of Claudio Merulo (1533–1604), included in the *Prima parte* of his treatise toccatas by himself, Merulo, Andrea and Giovanni Gabrieli, Luzzasco Luzzaschi, and several others. Diruta's toccatas consistently use passage work in one hand against chords in the other (fig. 13.9; DWMA104), toccatas by some of his contemporaries alternate passage work with chordal and imitative phrases. Merulo's toccatas, published in two volumes entitled *Toccate d'intavolatura d'organo* (Toccatas in organ tablature; 1598, 1604), contain brilliant passage work alternated between hands, sustained chordal passages, and ricercar-like sections.

The Venetian School

Venice was an independent city-state whose public officials were elected to office; political prominence and authority did not reside in any one noble family. The city had no tradition of artistic patronage, though ceremonial music had been composed and performed when special occasions had warranted it. There is no record of any kind of formal musical establishment at the church of San Marco (St. Mark's) until the early fourteenth century, when Zuccheto was appointed organist. Not until 1408 was a *schola cantorum* founded at St. Mark's, with Marcantonio Romano as *Magister,* to provide trained singers for the choir. In 1420 the cathedral was San Pietro di Castello. (A cathedral is the principal church in a bishop's see and contains the bishop's throne, the *cathedra.*) The church

Renaissance Instrumental Music

of San Marco did not become a cathedral until 1807. The church was located next door to the ruler's palace and was in essence Il Doge's private chapel; the clergy, *magister cantus,* and musicians at San Marco were primarily responsible to Il Doge and his administration and secondarily responsible to ecclesiastical authority.

Musical activity in Venice increased during the last quarter of the fifteenth century: various religious confraternities began to employ four or six vocalists and an equal number of instrumentalists on a permanent basis; a new organ was built at St. Mark's, and in 1490 Francesco d'Ana (c. 1460–c. 1503), one of the earliest of the important *frottola* composers, was appointed second organist there; and, also in the 1490s, Petrucci set up his print shop in Venice and soon began publishing music. In 1520, the church of San Marco was elevated to basilica status. (A basilica is the designated church at which the Pope worships or conducts Services when he is in the city.) A *maestro di cappella* was appointed who, with the assistance of the two organists, was responsible for teaching the boys and young priests, as well as for directing all of the music at the church. Adrian Willaert served as *maestro di cappella* from 1527 to 1562.

Under Willaert's supervision the musical establishment at St. Mark's was enlarged and strengthened. High standards of musical excellence were established and maintained; Willaert selected new musicians carefully and insisted that they be excellent performers, well versed in counterpoint and musical style. Competition for the organist positions was highly competitive, and candidates were subjected to stringent examination. The sixteenth-century organists at St. Mark's were excellent composers as well as renowned performers, and included, in succession: as first organists, Jacques Buus, Girolamo Parabosco, Claudio Merulo, and, briefly, Andrea Gabrieli; as second organists, Giovanni Armonio, Annibale Padovano, Andrea Gabrieli, and Giovanni Gabrieli. By 1562, the position of *maestro di cappella* at St. Mark's was the most desired one in Italy. Willaert's successor was one of his pupils—another Netherlander—Cipriano de Rore. Rore was unable to cope with administrative responsibilities and left in 1564. He was

succeeded by Zarlino, who encouraged the organists and composers and further expanded the musical establishment. In 1568 a permanent instrumental ensemble (three players) was appointed; a dozen or more additional instrumentalists might be hired for special occasions. After 1575, the combined talents of choirmaster Zarlino, organists Andrea and/or Giovanni Gabrieli, 30 choir singers, and about 20 instrumentalists brought music at St. Mark's to unprecedented heights of excellence. Musical resources there were ample for division into *cori spezzati,* with small groups of performers—often, ensembles producing contrasting sonorities—placed in the various choir galleries. Performances by spatially separated choirs (*cori spezzati*), both vocal and instrumental, were a prominent feature of Venetian church music between c. 1575 and c. 1610 (DWMA105).

During the last quarter of the sixteenth century, as knowledge of musical events in Italy—particularly, developments at San Marco—spread abroad, musical leadership was assumed by the Italians. Musicians from European regions north of the Alps traveled to Italy to study and to work. Some came to Venice, and to St. Mark's, especially to study with Andrea or Giovanni Gabrieli, and the Venetian school, headed by native Venetians, flourished.

Andrea Gabrieli

Andrea Gabrieli (c. 1510–86) first came to the church of San Marco as a singer in 1536, when Willaert was chapelmaster. In 1557, Gabrieli was employed as organist at San Geremia and was an unsuccessful competitor for the position of first organist at San Marco—Merulo received the appointment. In 1562 Gabrieli traveled to Germany as a member of Duke Albrecht V's retinue. While there, Andrea met Lassus, and a lasting friendship resulted. The five-voice motets Gabrieli published as *Sacrae cantiones* (1565) reflect many aspects of Lassus's style. When the second organist position at San Marco was open in 1566, Gabrieli competed and received the appointment. He advanced to first organist on 1 January 1585.

Andrea Gabrieli was a prolific and versatile composer who made significant contributions to many musical genres. As organist, composer, and teacher, he was highly respected; through his pupils, especially Giovanni Gabrieli and H. L. Hassler, Andrea was an important influence in Italy and Germanic lands.

Andrea Gabrieli's extant vocal works include 6 Masses, over 100 motets, almost 200 madrigals, and some secular choral compositions; his instrumental pieces comprise keyboard canzonas, organ *intonationi* and toccatas, keyboard and ensemble ricercars, and 3 organ Masses. The *intonationi* are short preludes, written in an improvisatory style, with chords in one hand and figuration in the other. Some of the ricercars are contrapuntal and nonsectional and closely approach being monothematic fugues; others are actually instrumental canzonas.

For his madrigals, Gabrieli chose light pastoral verses; he tended to set the texts syllabically for verbal clarity and sometimes used word painting. Many of the motets published posthumously in *Concerti* (1587) are for eight or more voices, all texted. In writing for divided choirs, Gabrieli effected a quickly moving dialogue in phrases of varying lengths, using simple harmonies and homophonic texture. Vocal lines may have been doubled by instruments, especially those in which the tessitura is quite low. With the expanded instrumental resources at St. Mark's during the 1580s, Gabrieli was able to write vocal music wherein he reenforced the lower voices with trombones and the upper voices with cornetts, thereby achieving timbral contrasts. He was well aware of the effectiveness of such contrasts and seems to have deliberately exploited them in some of his ceremonial works for more than one choir.

Giovanni Gabrieli

Giovanni Gabrieli (c. 1553–1612) received his musical training from his uncle. For a time, Giovanni worked at the court of Duke Albrecht V in Munich. In 1584 he served as temporary organist at San Marco, and, after participating in the competition held in January 1585, received a permanent appointment there. After the death of Andrea Gabrieli in 1586, Giovanni edited many of Andrea's compositions and published them along with some of his own.

Giovanni Gabrieli's early music shows the influence of Andrea, and, through him, that of Lassus. However, the works most characteristic of Giovanni's style are those for divided choirs. The earliest of these works were published, along with compositions by Andrea, in *Concerti* (1587). This volume is an important source of ceremonial music performed in Venice. The compositions by uncle and nephew are similar in style—constrasting groups of different sonorities, high voices against low ones, and in performance supplying instrumental support for some or all of the voices, especially those in which the tessitura is low or quite high. This style is more refined in Giovanni's *Sacrae symphoniae* (Sacred symphonies) of 1597, with thematic material being developed and with dialogue between choral groups structured in a more irregular manner. Giovanni's interest in writing for divided choirs lessened after 1605, when he became interested in more modern (i.e., Baroque) compositional techniques.

There is no indication that Giovanni Gabrieli composed any complete Mass cycles or organ Masses. A catalogue of his works includes 6 twelve-voice Mass movements, 7 Magnificats, more than 100 motets and liturgical settings, about 30 madrigals, and many instrumental compositions: canzonas, sonatas, *intonationi,* ricercars, fugues, and fantasias. In fact, he is credited with being the most prolific composer of instrumental ensemble works during his era.

Many of Gabrieli's instrumental works are innovative, as are the 14 *canzoni* and 2 *sonate* in the volume of *Sacrae symphoniae* published in 1597. The term *sonata* indicates merely that the composition is instrumental. *Sonata pian e forte* (DWMA96) is one of the first compositions in which specific instrumentation is designated; it is the earliest known ensemble work in which dynamic contrasts are indicated. The eight-voice composition is for two choirs: *Coro I* comprises a cornetto and three trombones; *Coro II,* one *violino* and three trombones. The low tessitura of the *violino* part indicates that probably it was intended for a *viola da braccio*. In his instrumental works Gabrieli used only cornetto, trombone, and *violino*; his preference for these instruments may have been conditioned by the fact that skilled performers on them were readily available at St. Mark's. Gabrieli applied the compositional principle of repetition after contrast in several of the *canzoni* included in the volume entitled *Canzoni et sonate* (publ. 1615), a collection of instrumental ensemble works in from 3 to 22 voices. Some of these pieces were supplied with *basso continuo* (a continuous fundamental bass line), a fact indicating that Gabrieli was writing in the new Baroque style (see p. 286).

Summary

Significant developments in instrumental music occurred during the Renaissance. A variety of instruments existed, with winds predominating; most types of instruments were built in families or sets containing graduated sizes. Instrumental music might be performed by a whole consort to produce a homogeneous timbre; or by a mixed consort to enhance one or more of the polyphonic lines. In the late sixteenth century, spatially separated choirs or groups, frequently combining voices and instruments, performed in *concertato* style.

Some instruments, such as the portative organ, disappeared from use; many Italian churches had two permanently installed organs, one large and one small. New instruments appeared, including harpsichord, large copper tympani, and the violin family. The lute was the most popular household instrument. Most

churches and courts, many rulers, and wealthy citizens amassed large collections of instruments. Treatises were published that described and depicted instruments and discussed matters of technique and performance practice. Some contained music for performance.

Although instruments continued to be used to double, support, or substitute for voices, composers began to write music specifically for instruments; by 1600 a small but significant body of idiomatic instrumental music existed. This music was of four main types: (1) pieces modeled on or derived from vocal compositions; (2) dance music; (3) variations; and (4) freely composed and quasi-improvisatory works. Some types of instrumental music engendered Baroque forms: The organ monothematic ricercar and the organ canzona were predecessors of the fugue; the ensemble canzona was ancestor of the Baroque *sonata da chiesa*; paired dances were nuclei of the Baroque *suite*.

The work of Adrian Willaert brought international prestige to the position of *maestro di cappella* at the church of San Marco, Venice. Musicians from all over Europe came to St. Mark's to study, and a Venetian school developed. Through Willaert's pupils, colleagues, and successors working at St. Mark's as chapelmasters and organists, musical leadership was transferred from Franco-Netherlanders to native Italians. Italy retained that leadership for more than a century.

The Baroque Era

The historical period between c. 1600 and c. 1750 and the style of the music composed during that era are generally known as *Baroque*. The French word *baroque*, a derivative of Portuguese *barroco* (an irregularly shaped pearl), has been used since the sixteenth century in connection with jewelry making. The term *baroque* was first applied to music in a derogatory sense in 1746 by Noel Pluche, who contrasted *musique chantante* (smoothly flowing, songlike music) and *musique baroque* (fast, pulsating, noisy music with surprising, audacious sounds). J. J. Rousseau, in his *Dictionnaire de musique* (Paris, 1768), defined Baroque music in less than complimentary words: "A baroque music is that in which the harmony is confused, charged with modulations and dissonances, the melody is harsh and little natural, the intonation difficult, and the movement constrained." Around 1755, the word *baroque* was used in adverse criticism of architecture. In 1839, philosopher-historian Jacob Burckhardt applied the word *Barockstyl* to the kind of art produced in the decadent phase of the Renaissance. Gradually, art historians discontinued using *baroque* as connoting the bizarre, extravagant, and irregular, and advanced the idea of *Baroque* style as a legitimate expression of a historical period. Music historians were reluctant to accept this concept and preferred such designations as Thorough-bass Period, Figured-bass Era, *Concertato*-style Period, or Third Style Period. Not until c. 1940 was *Baroque* generally (though not universally) accepted as the name for this musical style period.

Changes in musical style were noticeable in Venice in the 1560s (though some of the music then being published had been composed a decade or two earlier). By 1580 elements of the new style were widespread in northern Italy; they gradually permeated continental Europe, and by the third decade of the seventeenth century had infiltrated Britain. By mid-century, the new musical language had been firmly established, and composers could use it expressively and freely.

At the outset, as composers sought more extensive and intensive means of expressing thoughts and emotions musically, they altered existing forms of Renaissance music, such as madrigals and motets. Some of the new stylistic elements appear in Willaert's *Musica nova* (compiled in 1540s, published in 1559), Giovanni Gabrieli's motets, the accompanied and concerted madrigals Luzzaschi and Wert composed for the *concerti delle donne,* and the musical entertainments staged at Estense and Gonzaga courts.

Two Practices, Three Styles

The new music did not supplant the Renaissance style of music but coexisted with it. Throughout the Baroque era—for the first time in music history—two distinct styles of music were purposely cultivated. Authors and composers used various terms to differentiate these styles, including: *stile antico* (old style) and *stile moderno* (modern style); *stylus gravis* (severe [strict] style) and *stylus luxurians* (luxuriant

The Baroque Era

1575	1600	1625	1650	1675	1700

ENGLAND:
Elizabeth I - - - - - - - - - →1603◄ - - - - James I - - →1628→Charles I→1648   1660→- Charles II - - →1685–88 ◄ William III
                                                                                                                                James II   and Mary
                                                                                                1649 Commonwealth

1588 defeat of Spanish Armada

                                    1608 - - - - - - - - - - - - - - - - - -John Milton - - - - - - - - - - - - - - - - 1674
                                                                                                                        1667 *Paradise Lost*
    Shakespeare fl. 1590–1616
            1602 *The Merry Wives of Windsor*   1652 - - - - astronomer Edmund Halley - - - (d. 1742)
            1604 *Othello*

                                                                    1642 - - - Isaac Newton - - - - - - - - - - - - - - - - - - - (d. 1727)

- - - architect Inigo Jones - 1652

            1611 King James Version, *The Bible,* published

                                                                                        1672 Banister's first public
                                                                                                concert, London

                                                                                        1675–1710 St. Paul's Cathedral
                                                                                                built—Christopher Wren

FRANCE:
Henri III - - →1589 ◄ - Henri IV - →1610◄ - Louis XIII - - - - - - →1643◄ - Louis XIV - (1715)
        1600 m. Maria de' Medici
                                        1622 - - - - - - - 1642 - - - - - - 1652   - Paris, Europe's cultural center
                                        Richelieu   Mazarin

                                        1622 - - - - - - - - - - - -Molière - - - - - - - - - - - 1673

                            1606 - Corneille - 1684

                                        1639 - - - Racine -1699

                                                LaSalle claims Louisiana for France 1682

SPAIN:
Philip II - - - - - - - →1598 ◄ Philip III - - - → 1621◄ Philip IV - - - - - - - - - - - - - - - →1665◄ - - Charles II - - - - - - - - - 1700

Netherlands revolt
        1583 Netherlands independence from Spain
        - - El Greco fl. in Spain - -

HOLY ROMAN EMPIRE:
1576◄- - Rudolf II - - - - - - - - →1612◄→1619→Ferdinand II→1637 ◄ - - - - - - →1657 ◄ - - - - - - -Leopold I - - - - - - - - (1705)
            Matthias   Ferdinand III

            1618 Thirty Years' War - - 1648
RUSSIA:
        1584 - Boris Godunov - 1605
        regent →1598→Tsar' - - - - - -

[ornamented] style). Claudio Monteverdi used the terms *prima prattica* (first practice) and *seconda prattica* (second practice)—in fact, he may have invented those terms. In the preface to *Il quinto libro de madrigali* (The fifth book of madrigals; 1605),

Monteverdi differentiated the two "practices" thusly: *Prima prattica* is the style of vocal polyphony written according to the accepted rules governing Franco-Netherlands counterpoint, as codified in Gioseffo Zarlino's (1517–90) theoretical treatise *Le istitutioni harmoniche* (The harmonic institutions; 1558). In *prima prattica*, the composer's main concern is the beauty of the contrapuntal writing; in other words, the music dominates the text. *Seconda prattica* is the new style of vocal polyphony in which the text dominates the music, in accordance with Plato's statement (in *The Republic*) that melody, relationship of sounds, and rhythm should follow the words or thought of the text. In *seconda prattica*, effective expression of the text justifies deviation from contrapuntal rules and legitimizes such things as unprepared dissonances, unorthodox resolutions, and melodic crudities. According to Monteverdi, *prima prattica* attained perfection with Willaert; *seconda prattica* was used by Rore, Gesualdo, Luzzaschi, Wert, Caccini, Monteverdi, and numerous others.

Some theorists prepared detailed and comprehensive classifications of the types of musical styles existing within each of the two basic practices. In *Breve discorso sopra la musica moderna* (Short discourse on modern music; Warsaw, 1649) Marco Scacchi (c. 1600–c. 1685) stated that Renaissance composers had only one practice and one style in which to write music, but composers of his time had the advantage of two practices and three styles. The two practices are those Monteverdi defined, though Scacchi named them differently. Scacchi wrote the oft-quoted phrases: in the first practice "harmony is mistress of the text" (*harmonia sit domina orationis*), and in the second practice "the text is mistress of the harmony" (*oratio sit domina harmoniae*). As models for *prima prattica* he chose Josquin, Lassus, and Palestrina; eventually, that type of music became known as "Palestrina style." Scacchi's three styles reflect the intended use of the music: *ecclesiasticus* (church), *cubicularis* (chamber), and *scenicus seu theatralis* (scenic or theater). Within each of these three styles were many subdivisions. Scacchi's classification had wide acceptance. It was expanded by later seventeenth-century theorists and formed a basis for the divisions of musical genres in J. J. Fux's counterpoint text, *Gradus ad Parnassum* (Steps to Parnassus; Vienna, 1725), and the classification of styles in Johann Mattheson's *Der vollkommene Kapellmeister* (The perfect Chapelmaster; Hamburg, 1739).

Idiomatic Composition

In the Baroque era, the mainstream of musical development divided. One branch continued the development of vocal music, with concentration on dramatic or quasi-dramatic music, both sacred and secular. The other branch developed idiomatic instrumental music. When emancipated from almost total dependence on vocal forms, instrumental music flourished and by the end of the era it was in a position of dominance. Idiomatic instrumental styles were developed, such as those for violin and for harpsichord; composers began to write for specific instruments, and idiomatic instrumental repertoires accumulated. In ensemble music, instruments were selected for their specific tone colors, either to blend or to contrast. Members of the violin family became favored instruments in Italy and eventually supplanted viols in France; harpsichord and organ music began to be differentiated, and the fortepiano was invented. Composers used a larger variety of words as tempo markings and began to indicate dynamics in the musical notation.

The Affections

Widespread interest in the writings of the ancient Greeks (especially Aristotle) resulted in a preoccupation with and a concern for the *affections*—rationalized emotional states, or passions—described by those authors. The fact that ancient Greek and Roman rhetoricians considered it the duty of orators to arouse the passions in their listeners engendered in composers the same sense of obligation to portray musically the emotional states expressed by the text being set. Throughout the Baroque era, composers endeavored to represent musically the various affections. This may well have been the feature of the music that first caused it to be called *baroque*, in the original sense of that word. Composers depicted anger, fear, and other affections boldly, even violently, for passions were no longer viewed as human weaknesses, and the ability to feel emotions deeply was appreciated. Critics unaware of a composer's motivation and intention could have considered a composition of this kind grotesque or bizarre.

The Baroque Era

Composers endeavored to express in their vocal music the basic affections related to the texts, not their own feelings. Musical interpretation of a text might cause some rapid shifts between radically different emotional states, expressed in the extreme. However, during much of the Baroque era, a composition—or a movement of a multimovement work—expressed only one affection, and its representation served as a means of unifying the composition. In portraying the affections, composers did not rely on their own ingenuity but drew on a common repertoire of musical devices or *figures*. A figure might be as simple and obvious as a rapid scale passage or an undulating serpentine melodic line, or it might be a complex and unobtrusive combination of melody, rhythm, harmony, and texture. Many Baroque composers—especially those working in Germanic lands—used special musical figures to depict and reenforce literal and implied meanings of texts. Commencing around the middle of the seventeenth century, many theorists devoted portions of their treatises to defining, describing, and categorizing types of the affections, and presenting ways in which the passions could be expressed musically. Representation of the affections was not limited to vocal music; composers used the same musical devices in their instrumental works.

Writers drew other analogies between rhetoric and music. One of these compares the creation of a musical composition with the preparation of an oration or a piece of writing. (The terminology was, of course, borrowed from Latin writings on rhetoric.) The creative process involved three steps: *inventio* (Latin, the inventive faculty), finding the subject; *dispositio* (Latin, a regular arrangement, order), planning or outlining the work; *elaboratio* (Latin, worked out, elaborated), fleshing out the skeletal outline by composing the music, writing the treatise, or preparing the actual wording of the oration.

Texture: *Basso continuo*

In some of the *musica secreta* performances at the Ferrara court in the 1580s, the *concerto delle donne* and a professional bass sang madrigals, accompanied at the keyboard by Luzzaschi. Sometimes one soprano and the bass sang, with harpsichord accompaniment. Contemporary accounts of some of those performances describe in detail the embellishments embroidering the treble. Accompanied solo singing was not new—the *cantilena*-style polyphony of Machaut bears witness to that. The novelty was the texture—a polarity of florid treble and firm bass with unobtrusive accompaniment—features that became characteristic of Baroque music and that were displayed prominently in the trio sonata (see p. 367).

During the last decades of the sixteenth century, some church music printed in Italy included a *bassus pro organo* (organ bass) part. Such a bass, later called *basso seguente* (following bass), was formed by notating the lowest pitch to be sung at each successive point throughout the piece. Using these pitches as foundation, the organist played above them the chordal harmonies of the piece and usually reenforced the imitative entries of the voices also. The earliest known *basso seguente* survives in manuscript copies of *Ecce beatam lucem* (Behold the blessed light), the 40-part polychoral motet (for four choirs of 8, 10, 16, and 6 voices) that the Florentine court composer Alessandro Striggio (c. 1540–92) composed for the wedding of Duke Albrecht IV of Bavaria in 1568. (Striggio's son, also named Alessandro, was librettist for Monteverdi at Mantua.)

By 1600, composers had begun to write independent bass lines rather than slavishly following the vocal pitches. Some of these basses not only provided the foundation for improvised harmonies but were melodic lines integrated with the vocal polyphony. Because the bass line was continuous throughout the composition, it came to be known as *basso continuo* (continuous bass) or *thoroughbass* (bass [played] throughout). Most often, the *basso continuo* was a *figured bass,* i.e., composers placed Arabic numerals or symbols for chromatic alterations above or below some of the *basso continuo* notes to convey their intentions with regard to the harmony (ex. 14.1). The numbers indicate the intervals at which pitches are to be supplied above the bass note. However, in the early Baroque, many *basso continuo* lines were unfigured.

The process of improvising the accompaniment outlined by the basso continuo line is called **realization.** When basso continuo was first used, a keyboard player provided the accompaniment. Soon, however, it became customary for two instrumentalists to perform this task—the continuous notated bass

Example 14.1 A few measures of figured bass.

line was played on a bass instrument capable of sustaining tones (e.g., violoncello, viola da gamba, bassoon), and the harmonies were improvised on an instrument capable of producing chords (e.g., keyboard, lute). A specialization of functions—accompanist and soloist—resulted, a division of labor wherein those instruments (and their players) realizing the basso continuo for accompaniment were classified as *fundamental,* and those providing the melody (and embellishing it) were *ornamental.* This division of labor was a factor in the creation of the instrumental concerto.

No individual composer invented basso continuo, though Ludovico Grossi da Viadana (c. 1560–1627) claimed in the preface to *Cento concerti ecclesiastici* (One hundred church concertos; Venice, 1602) that he had done so. Three works with figured basses were published in Florence and Rome in 1600; Emilio de' Cavalieri's (c. 1550–1602) *Rappresentatione di Anima, et di Corpo* (The play about Soul, and Body; Rome, February 1600) was the first of these. However, Viadana seems to have been the first to use the *term* basso continuo in print and the first to compose a basso continuo with the dual function of participating in the melodic, imitative polyphony and providing the foundation for the nonnotated chordal accompaniment.

The transition from *basso seguente* to *basso continuo* can be traced by examining several works by the same composer. For example, in Viadana's *Cento concerti ecclesiastici, Salve regina* (Hail, queen) uses *basso seguente* in all but a very few measures; *Exaudi me, Domine* (Hear me, Lord) has *basso continuo.* Monteverdi's fifth, sixth, and seventh books of madrigals also show the transition (see pp. 309–10). Some of the pieces in Book Five appear to be *a cappella,* others have *basso seguente.* In Book Six, some madrigals are supplied sporadically with measures of *basso continuo,* interspersed with the directive "*basso seguente*" and no notated bass notes. Book Seven, named *Concerto,* has *basso continuo* throughout.

The use of basso continuo did not cease when the Baroque era came to an end but continued to a diminishing extent until c. 1800.

In addition to works that exhibited a polarized texture of firm bass and florid treble, composers wrote music in *stile antico.* The homogeneous blend of equal voices in linear counterpoint was still present in *a cappella* motets and madrigals. Some instrumental ensemble music did not include basso continuo; solo keyboard and lute music did not need it. In those contrapuntal pieces equipped with a basso continuo, the flow and blend of the linear melodies was regulated by the harmonic framework the basso continuo defined. In other words, instead of being intervallically determined and regulated, as it was during the Renaissance, the linear counterpoint was harmonically based and controlled. Polyphony not only persisted throughout the Baroque era, it attained the acme of perfection in the music of J. S. Bach.

Harmonic control permitted increased use of dissonance. In the early seventeenth century, both chromaticism and dissonance were experimental and were sometimes used to extreme. Gesualdo's music is full of them. Around the middle of the century, use of dissonance was modified and controlled; its main employment was in quasi-improvisatory instrumental pieces, such as fantasias, and toccatas. Ultimately, by the last part of the Baroque, when the system of major-minor key tonality had been perfected, chromaticism and dissonance were used freely but within the boundaries of the harmonic system.

During the Renaissance, counterpoint was modal; melody was diatonic and in a rather narrow range; and harmony, created as a by-product of the part-writing, through the interaction of intervallically regulated melodic lines, amounted to a series of chordal successions. In the Baroque era, counterpoint was harmonically based; melody might be either diatonic or chromatic, and its range was rather wide; and harmony was planned and deliberately created, by means of chords that progressed according to principles of key tonality.

Key Tonality

Key tonality may be defined as a system of chordal relationships based on the attraction of a tonal center, the tonic chord, whose root gives the key its pitch name. Though each of the chords within the system is a self-contained entity, each chord has a functional relationship to the others, and, more especially, to the tonic chord.

The evolution of the system of major-minor key tonality was a slow process that began in the Renaissance and was not completed until late in the Baroque era. A vital step in that process was the recognition of the triad as a harmonic unit. The Ionian scale on C and the Aeolian scale on A, recognized by Glareanus (in *Dodecachordon*; 1547) as part of the modal system, remain modal as long as they are considered in terms of melodic patterns and intervals. They do not become C major and A natural minor scales until their pitches are viewed as roots of chordal harmonies with the functions and relationships of key tonality. Once the functions and relationships were established, the scale patterns could be transferred from modality to key tonality.

The change from *basso seguente* to *basso continuo* and the use of figured bass indicated that composers were thinking chordally (and performers whose employment required them to realize basso continuo parts were forced to do so). However, many basso continuo lines were melodic, and their harmonies were regulated by a melodic principle. The presence of certain sequences of chords in modulations or at cadence points did evidence some planned harmonic progressions. In many instances, the conflict between modality and key tonality within a composition enhanced that work. Not until composers conceived their compositions in terms of chordal-harmonic functional relationships was the evolution completed. The earliest surviving music that fully realizes key tonality with no trace of modality—the music of Corelli—was published after 1680. No theoretical explanation of the system was advanced until Rameau's *Traité de l'harmonie* (Treatise on harmony) was published in Paris in 1722.

Rhythm

At the beginning of the seventeenth century, composers writing sacred music in *stile antico* continued to use the even rhythmic flow of the *tactus* (the beat) that characterized Renaissance counterpoint. (The *tactus* remained constant, its regularity and rate of speed comparable with that of a healthy human pulse.)

However, two other types of rhythmic organization prevailed: a regular metrical rhythm derived from the definite patterns of strong and weak beats that were vital to dance music, and a flexible unmetrical rhythm that was founded on speech. Frequently, for variety and contrast in multisection or multimovement works, composers used these two kinds of rhythm successively, e.g., following a quasi-improvisatory section with a rhythmically precise one.

Notation

With changes in rhythm came changes in notational practices. Near the end of the sixteenth century, when publishers were beginning to print compositions in score form, barlines were used as a matter of convenience in coordinating the various parts. In the seventeenth century, composers used barlines to mark off—or *measure*—the definite patterns of strong and weak beats used in their music. At first the use of barlines was not consistent, for the patterns did not regularly recur. Not until the middle of the seventeenth century were barlines used systematically to mark off **measures** of regularly recurring rhythmic patterns of strong and weak beats. By this time, most of the old proportion signs had been supplanted by modern **time signatures,** such as $\frac{4}{4}$, $\frac{3}{4}$, $\frac{2}{4}$. Two proportion signs remained in use: C and ₵. The broken circle C retained its Renaissance connotation—one breve per tactus imperfectly subdivided—and in Baroque terminology denoted one measure divided into two groups of two, or $\frac{4}{4}$. The ₵, referred to in the twentieth century as "cut time," proportioned the breve to half-tactus—a tempo twice as fast as C —and is comparable to a $\frac{2}{2}$ time signature. During the seventeenth century, it became customary for the composer to

(a)

(b)

place a single time signature at the beginning of a composition (or movement) to indicate the basic rhythmic pattern used in that work.

Three movable clef signs were in use, as they had been since the fifteenth century, representing f, c′, and g′ pitches. By the Baroque era, their shapes had been stylized and somewhat resembled those in modern use. Composers placed individual or grouped flat or sharp symbols at the beginning of a composition, as a kind of key signature, but it was not until the late eighteenth century that a specific signature was definitely associated with a certain key. It was not unusual for a signature to have sharps placed on both the line and the space for f♯, or flats on both the space and the line for e♭ (fig. 14.1a). Often, Baroque composers wrote signatures with one less flat or one less sharp than the corresponding modern signature (fig.

14.1b). Moreover, during much of the Baroque era, a chromatic alteration of a pitch did not affect an entire measure but was valid for only the note it immediately preceded, unless that note was repeated, or the musical figure in which the alteration appeared was immediately and exactly repeated one or more times, an intervening barline notwithstanding. In other words, the presence of the barline was of no importance where chromatic alterations were concerned.

Music Printing

In Venice, Nuremberg, Paris, and Antwerp, music publishing reached a peak shortly before 1580. Many of the volumes of music printed in Venice after that date show a decline in quality—the music is less spacious on the page and general lack of craftsmanship

Figure 14.2 Two pages from Giovanni Maria Nanino's motet *Jesu spes penitentibus* (Jesus, hope of the penitent) in the anthology *Diletto spirituale canzonette* (Rome, 1586), printed by Verovio from engraved copper plates. The four vocal parts, printed successively, are on left page; keyboard score and lute tablature are on right page.

is apparent in many books. Printing by means of incised copper plates had been invented but was still experimental in the early sixteenth century. There were sporadic attempts to apply the process to music—often it was used for music notation in art prints. The earliest known practical music printed from engraved copper plates is a volume of lute tablatures by Franceso da Milano issued sometime before 1540. The volume is not dated and the printer did not identify himself; the work has been attributed to Marcolini da Forli.

The first publisher to be successful in printing books of music *entirely* from incised copper plates was Simone Verovio (fl. 1575–1608). A calligrapher and engraver, Verovio came to Rome from the Netherlands in 1575, set up a shop, and began editing music. In 1586, he engraved and printed two volumes of music, one of them being *Diletto spirituale* (Spiritual delights) a collection of three- and four-voice canzonettas, with accompaniment for keyboard and lute. His printed texts attest his calligraphic talent (fig. 14.2). Either because the process was too time consuming, or because it was too expensive—certainly not because of inferior workmanship—Verovio issued only about 20 editions between 1586 and 1608.

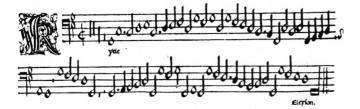

Figure 14.3 Excerpt from the Kyrie of a Mass by Carpentras that Jean de Channey printed in 1532 from music type designed by Briard. *(Source: Carpentras: Liber primus missarum, Avignon, 1532.)*

During the seventeenth century, engraved music seems to have been largely a luxury enjoyed by distinguished patrons. For example, in England in 1613, engraved plates were used for printing *Parthenia*, an anthology of virginal music by William Byrd, John Bull, and Orlando Gibbons that was a wedding gift to Princess Elizabeth (daughter of James I) and Prince Frederick V, Elector Palatine of the Rhine (r. 1610–32). Later in the century, John Walsh in London and Estienne Roger in Amsterdam realized the commercial advantages of engraving music. Some composers—e.g., Telemann and J. S. Bach—engraved some of their own music.

Despite the development of engraving, letterpress printing and manuscript copying of music were still used extensively until c. 1700. In fact, letterpress printing was the most feasible method when most of the book, e.g., a treatise, consisted of text. Some publishers issued some music in manuscript instead of in printed copies. Publishing in manuscript was favored by many eighteenth-century Italian opera companies because it gave them a greater measure of control over the production of certain works, and also because manuscript notation could be altered more easily than printed music. Undoubtedly, controlled publication in manuscript form is the reason some music is not extant.

Pear- or teardrop-shaped notes appear in some manuscripts in the early sixteenth century. Around 1530, Étienne Briard, a type designer working in Avignon, designed and cut music type with rounded note heads. His type was first used by Jean de Channey for printing Carpentras's (c. 1470–1548) *Liber primus missarum* (First book of Masses; Avignon, 1532; fig. 14.3). However, Verovio's engraved notes more nearly approximate the oval note heads of modern printed music.

Until well into the seventeenth century, many printers used note heads cut as lozenges, squares, or diamonds, with stems centered. The innovator of type with oval or roundish note heads with stems placed either to the left or right was John Heptinstall, a London printer, who first used it in 1687. After some refinement, oval or rounded note heads became standard in the eighteenth century.

Summary

Music in the Baroque era was characterized by two practices—old-style Renaissance counterpoint in which music dominated the text, and modern music in which the text was of prime import—and three styles (church, chamber, and theater). As composers began to write idiomatically for instruments, regard for instrumental music heightened, purely instrumental forms evolved, and instrumental repertoires, both solo and ensemble, accumulated. Composers attempted to portray musically the affections expressed in the texts. In texture, the new music exhibited a polarity of florid treble and firm bass; filler harmonies, not notated, were improvised as the accompanists realized the *basso continuo* line. Modality persisted through much of the seventeenth century; the system of major-minor key tonality slowly evolved. Two types of rhythmic organization prevailed: (a) the regular metrical rhythm vital to dance music and (b) a flexible unmetrical rhythm founded on speech. Notational practices reflected changes in the music: figured bass, barlines, meter and key signatures came into use. New printing methods were developed; by the eighteenth century rounded note heads appeared.

The Baroque Era

Baroque Vocal Music

Monody

Monody is the modern term for the kind of Italian accompanied solo song, especially secular song, that was in use between c. 1600 and 1640. Giulio Caccini (c. 1545–1618), who is credited with inventing of this kind of song, called his pieces **madrigal** or **aria.** Most monodies were written for high voice and had a figured bass that usually was realized by a keyboard player only; Caccini suggested that the figured bass lines for his monodies be realized on a chitarrone (an instrument he played well) or other suitable stringed instrument. Around 1620, strophic arias began to supplant solo madrigals and by c. 1630 had done so. Composition of monody was centered in northern Italy, principally in Florence before 1620. Of the more than 100 composers who wrote monodies, Caccini, Alessandro Grandi (c. 1575–1630), Jacopo Peri (1561–1633), and Sigismondo d'India (c. 1582–1629) made the most significant contributions. Monody was an important forerunner of Italian aria and chamber cantata.

Caccini's *Le nuove musiche* (The new music; Florence, 1602) was influential in establishing the popularity of monody in Italy. *Le nuove musiche* contains 12 solo madrigals and 10 arias, the latter being either strophic songs or strophic variations. In **strophic variation,** the bass line remains constant (or very nearly so) while the melody for each strophe varies. In Caccini's monodies, an expressive vocal line is projected against a harmonic background conceived as

Figure 15.1 The opening portion of the madrigal *Amarilli mia bella,* whose figured bass line indicates that harmonies include a number of dissonant 11ths resolving to 10ths and 7ths resolving to 6ths. *(Source: Caccini:* Le nuove musiche, *1602.)*

support for the voice. He sought to reflect the structure of the poem through a setting that was rather declamatory, with a flexible rhythm. According to Caccini, several of the songs—*Dovrò dunque morire?* (Must I die, then?) was one—had been composed in the 1580s. Perhaps the best-known song in the collection is *Amarilli mia bella* (Amarillis, my sweetheart; fig. 15.1; DWMA106).

The Development of Opera

1575	1600	1625	1650	1675	1700

ITALY:
madrigals - - - - pastorales - - - - madrigal comedies - - - - - - - - - -

monody -
1602 Caccini: *Le nuove musiche*

1581
Galilei: *Dialogo*

intermedi - - - opera -

FLORENCE:
Bardi's   Corsi's
Camerata   Academy

1598 *Dafne*

1600 Peri: *Euridice*

ROME: 1600 Cavalieri: *Rappresentatione di Anima, . . .*

1632 Landi: *Il Sant' Alessio*

MANTUA: 1607 Monteverdi: *L'Orfeo*
                      1608   *Arianna*

VENICE: 1637 First public opera house

1640 Monteverdi: *Il ritorno d'Ulisse . . .*
1642   *L'incoronazione di Poppea*

Venice becomes the operatic capital -

NAPLES:
                                                            1684 A. Scarlatti -

**GERMANIC
   LANDS:**   1627 Schütz: *Dafne*   1668 Cesti: *Il pomo d'oro*

1644 Staden: *Seeleweg
               Singspiel*

FRANCE:
1581 *Circé*   (1632 - - - - - -) - - Lully - 1687
dramatic ballet   ballet de cour   in France from 1652   1674 *Alceste*
                                                                         tragédies lyriques - - - - - - - - - - - - -

ENGLAND: masque -
                                                    - plays with music - -

1656 *The Siege of Rhodes*
Blow: *Venus and Adonis* 1684
Purcell: *Dido and Aeneas* 1689

SPAIN: 1629 Vega: *La selva sin amor*

1660 Calderón: *La púrpura de la rosa*

In the preface to *Le nuove musiche*, Caccini complained that singers had not embellished his songs correctly. Therefore, he included advice on how to elaborate a song, and he wrote out many of the ornaments in his monodies, as in *Sfogava con le stelle* (With the stars, he gave vent [to his grief]). In 1614, Caccini published a second collection of his monodies, *Nuove musiche e nuova maniera di scriverle* (New music and a new way of writing it). The "new way of writing it" means "exactly as it is to be sung"—the ornaments are notated instead of being left for the singer to improvise.

Caccini spent much of his career in the employ of the Medici in Florence. From 1570 to the mid-1580s, he participated in meetings of an informal Florentine academy known as the Camerata, which

Other Large Vocal Forms

1575	1600	1625	1650	1675	1700

Oratorio -

Rome: Neri's
Oratory Congregation
sings *laude*

1619 Anerio - *volgare* oratorios for Neri

oratorio latino -

- - Carissimi - - -

Jephthe

Charpentier
in France

Cantata -
L. Rossi, M. Mazzoli

c. 1650 Carissimi - - -

1670 Stradella, Steffani

- - A. Scarlatti - - - - - - - - - -

Passion -

motet passion

1641 Selle: oratorio passion

1645 Schütz: *Die sieben Worte . . .*

Schütz: 4 *Historiae*

---

met at the home of Count Giovanni de' Bardi (1534–1612). There he was exposed to the humanistic ideals of Girolamo Mei (1519–94), Vincenzo Galilei (1527–91), and Bardi. Under that strong influence, Caccini developed monody and also a style of singing that he described as being closely related to speaking in tones. That style became known as *stile recitativo* (literally, recited style).

Mei was not actually a member of the Camerata but certainly was mentor to that group. Had he not suffered intensely from severe attacks of gout after c. 1575, probably he would have attended some of their meetings. In 1572 Galilei learned of Mei's research into Greek music and contacted him by letter and in person. Galilei's *Discorso sopra la musica antica et moderna* (Discourse on ancient and modern music; 1581) was inspired by and contains (without crediting Mei) several letters Mei wrote him. Mei's ideas concerning monody were conveyed to the Camerata by Galilei. Both Mei and Galilei denounced the Renaissance type of word painting; they affirmed that the correct way to set a text was through a solo melody that approximated the natural speech inflections of a fine orator. Caccini, who was in Rome in 1592 as Bardi's secretary, may have received those same views from Mei personally at that time.

During his lifetime, Caccini's greatest renown was as tenor singer and singing teacher. He taught many famous male singers and trained all members of his own family as musicians. Both of his daughters composed music and were employed as singers at Medici courts; in 1614 his daughter Francesca was one of the highest-paid musicians at the Florentine court. Her *Il primo libro delle musiche* (First book of music; 1618) is an important contribution to monody repertoire. In her solo songs, which no doubt were composed for her personal use, she sought to exploit the brilliance of the human voice. Her opera, *La liberazione di Ruggiero* (The liberation of Ruggiero; Florence, 1625) was the first Italian opera performed outside of Italy.

Opera

One of the most important new musical developments in the seventeenth century was the origin, growth, and dissemination of opera. **Opera** (Italian, work) is drama presented musically, with all or most of the text being sung and with appropriate instrumental music, as required by the plot or for accompaniment. It is a combined-art form, an amalgamation of various aspects of art (scenery, costumes), literature (poetic or prose lines of plot), theatre (acting), and dance, with vocal and instrumental music.

Baroque Vocal Music

Precursors of Opera

The association of music with drama was not new. It can be traced back to the ancient Greeks—to the prize-winning drama of Thespis (534 B.C.), which had one actor and a chorus, and the tragedies of Aeschylus, Sophocles, and Euripides (fifth century B.C.), which used three actors and a citizens' chorus of 12 to 15 men. Mei, who edited Sophocles's dramas, found indications that the chorus leader sometimes had solo lines and participated in dialogue; the chorus sang and danced as a group. In fact, Mei believed that Greek dramas were sung throughout.

Medieval liturgical dramas, such as *Quem quaeritis, christicolae?* and *The Play of Daniel,* were sung and dramatized in church. In Hildegard von Bingen's morality play, *Ordo virtutum* (twelfth century), every character but the devil sings. Religious mystery plays, produced by medieval trade guilds, used music only incidentally; the same is true of miracle plays dramatizing incidents from the lives of saints and performed on their special feast days. Some trouvère compositions may have been acted; certainly, Adam de la Halle's *Le jeu de Robin et de Marion* is suitable for performance as drama.

Some Renaissance authors placed choral music at the beginning or conclusion of the acts of their plays. For Juan del Encina, who was musician as well as dramatist, music was an integral part of the action; he included villancicos in all of his plays.

It became customary during the sixteenth century to present allegorical, mythological, or pastoral interludes between the acts of a comedy. Such an interlude was called an *intermedio* (literally, middle). *Intermedi* were first performed at the Este court in Ferrara in the late fifteenth century, between the acts of ancient comedies by Plautus and Terence. *Intermedi* served a practical purpose—they divided the play into acts, for the curtain was opened at the beginning of the play and remained open until it concluded. During the sixteenth century, attempts were made to correlate the subject of *intermedi* with that of the drama or to unify the several *intermedi* used with a drama so that collectively they presented another plot. All *intermedi* contained music—some were elaborate musical productions, especially those performed on state occasions or in connection with weddings of members of ruling families.

Though descriptions of *intermedi* abound, few complete *intermedi* are extant. Surviving are two sets performed at nuptial festivities at the Medici court in Florence: (1) those composed by G. B. Strozzi for the wedding of Cosimo I de' Medici to Eleonora of Toledo in 1539; and (2) those performed for the wedding of Ferdinando de' Medici and Christine of Lorraine in 1589—said to be the most lavish and costly *intermedi* ever produced. For the latter, texts by Giovanni de' Bardi, Ottavio Rinuccini (1562–1621), and Laura Guidiccioni (1550–99) were set to music by several noted composers, including Marenzio, Peri, Caccini, Antonio Archilei, and Emilio de' Cavalieri. (The *intermedi* were published in Venice in 1591.) Bardi chose as theme for the musical stories the power of ancient music. One of these *intermedi,* depicting Apollo's victory over the serpent Python, is a direct ancestor of the first opera, *Dafne* (see p. 298). A good deal of the music in these *intermedi* consisted of lavishly embellished solos with simple harmonic accompaniment. Vittoria Archilei (1550–c. 1620), Italian soprano and lutenist, had a major part in the performance; for some of her solos she played her own chitarrone accompaniment.

Madrigal settings were made of dramatic scenes from lengthy poems, such as Tasso's *Gerusalemme liberata* (Jerusalem delivered) and Guarini's *Il pastor fido* (The faithful shepherd). Both Monteverdi and Wert wrote some. Also, composers wrote **madrigal cycles,** a series of madrigals presenting an uncomplicated plot through descriptive music and (sometimes) dialogue. Orazio Vecchio's (1550–1605) *L'Amfiparnaso* (The slopes of Parnassus; 1597) comprises a prologue and 13 scenes grouped into 3 acts. Vecchio's designations of this work as *comedia harmonica* and *comedia musicale* have generated the twentieth-century term **madrigal comedy** for the genre. This is humorous poetry set to light, lively music; the cycle was intended for performance at private entertainments. Adriano Banchieri (1568–1634) also composed madrigal cycles of this kind, e.g., *La pazzia senile* (Senile folly; 1598), portraying old men duped by ladies.

The *pastorale* (pastoral) is a genre in literature, drama, and music that depicts characters and scenes of rural life. Poets have written about shepherds and shepherdesses, rural deities, and rustic scenes for centuries, and composers have set those poetic depictions

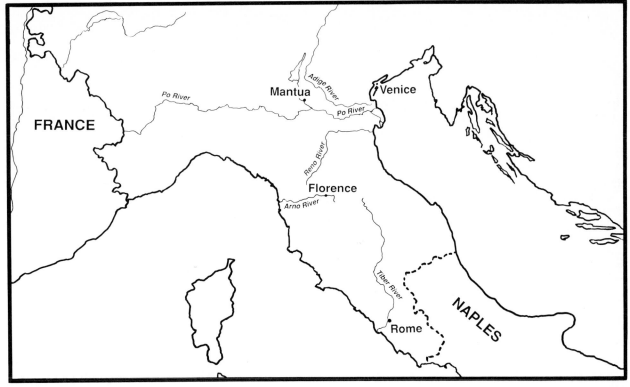

Figure 15.2 Location of centers of opera composition in Italy in the seventeenth century.

to music over an equally long time span. Pastoral poems were especially popular during the Renaissance; by the end of the sixteenth century, the predominant type of Italian poetry produced was the pastorale. Cavalieri composed settings for several of Laura Guidiccioni's pastorales, including *Il satiro* (The satyr) and *La disperazione di Fileno* (Fileno's despair), both performed at Carnival in Florence in 1590, and *Il giuoco della cieca* (The game of blindman's buff), performed at the Pitti Palace, Florence, in 1595 and again in 1599. *Il giuoco della cieca* is an adaptation of Act 3, Scene 2, of Guarini's *Il pastor fido,* wherein nymphs and shepherds play a type of blindman's buff. All of these settings are lost.

The First Operas

During the same years the Florentine Camerata met informally at the home of Bardi for humanistic and musical discussions, another group of artists and literati gathered at the home of Jacopo Corsi (1561–1602), composer and patron of the arts. It is possible

that Corsi was associated with the Camerata but highly probable that he was not; Bardi and Corsi were more rivals than friends where music and its patronage were concerned, and Florentine musicians and composers tended to group themselves in support of their patrons. Yet, there was some interaction between groups, for Bardi, Corsi, and some of their associates were members of the Accademia degli Alterati. After Bardi moved to Rome in 1592, Corsi was the recognized leader of the principal cultural group in Florence, and, after the Medici family, he was the most important patron of music in that city. Among those who were frequent guests at Corsi's home in the 1590s were Jacopo Peri and Ottavio Rinuccini. Occasionally, Monteverdi visited there. Corsi and those who met at his home were interested in finding an effective way to set stage music—a *stile rappresentativo* (theatrical style)—a manner of singing that was more expressive than ordinary speech but less melodious than song. They arrived at a style in which a declamatory melody, in flexible rhythm,

Baroque Vocal Music

with irregular phrasing, is presented over a static bass. However, they did not use that style exclusively; in dramatic productions, both dialogue and soliloquy occur, and their presentation differs.

Dafne

Late in 1594, Corsi, who had begun to compose a setting of Rinuccini's pastorale *Dafne,* requested Peri to complete the music in *stile rappresentativo.* Peri agreed. The task took him three years. *Dafne,* which is considered the first opera, was performed at Corsi's home during Carnival, 1598. It was performed twice in January 1599, and, in revised form, several times during the next decade. *Dafne* was never printed. Rinuccini's *libretto* (literally, little book, the text that is set to music) is extant, and music for six of the songs has been located—three songs in each of two different manuscripts. Single strophes of music (with additional stanzas of text) survive from the Prologue and from all scenes but 3 and 4. The style of the vocal line differs in some of the songs, but this cannot be attributed to the fact that two of the six songs are by Corsi and the others attributed to Peri. In some the metric pulse is regular; in others, rhythm is flexible and measuring irregular. Only *Qual nova meraviglia!* (What amazing news!), the messenger's song, has nonstrophic text and music that could be considered declamatory recitative (ex. 15.1). **Recitative** is the term ultimately given to the style of vocal music designed to imitate natural speech inflections. As opera developed, recitative came to be the style used for narrative prose texts and rapid passages of dialogue, to carry the action between soliloquy-type songs.

Dafne comprises a Prologue and six scenes. The thesis of the plot—to demonstrate the dangers that await those who scorn Love's power—is presented by Ovid, who sings the Prologue, *Da' fortunati campi* (From the fortunate fields). For Scene 1, Rinuccini reworked material he had written for one of the *intermedi* performed in 1589—the tale of Apollo slaying Python. In the *Dafne* scene, a chorus of nymphs and shepherds complain about the monster that has been terrorizing them and destroying their flocks. Apollo appears and slays Python. After Apollo tells the nymphs and shepherds that they are safe, the chorus sings in praise and gratitude: *Almo Dio, ch'il carr' ardente* (Almighty God, who in the fiery chariot).

Example 15.1 Beginning of *"Qual nova merviglia!"* from *Dafne. (From William V. Porter, "Peri and Corsi's* Dafne: *Some New Discoveries and Observations" in* Journal of the American Musicological Society, *Vol. XVIII, No. 2, p. 180, Summer 1965. Copyright © 1965 American Musicological Society, Philadelphia, PA. Reprinted by permission of the American Musicological Society.)*

Scene 2 is dialogue between Apollo and Cupid and between Cupid and Venus. Apollo taunts Cupid, belittling Cupid's prowess in shooting love's arrows. Cupid vows vengeance; he tells his mother, Venus, that he will gain control over Apollo by darting him. In Scene 3, Apollo, whom Cupid's arrow has hit, becomes enamored of the nymph Dafne, but she spurns him. Cupid, in Scene 4, brags to Venus about his victory over Apollo. The fifth scene is the climax. *"Qual' nova meraviglia!"* (What amazing news!) the messenger sings. He tells the people (the chorus) that Dafne, to escape Apollo's relentless pursuit, prayed for divine intervention; her prayer was answered—she was transformed into a laurel tree. The messenger describes Apollo's grief. From time to time, there are responses from the chorus. In the final scene, Apollo stands before the laurel tree, declares his continuing love for Dafne, claims the laurel as his tree, and vows to wear laurel leaves in his hair always. The scene concludes with choral commentary addressed to Dafne, *Bella ninfa fuggitiva* (Beautiful fugitive nymph; DWMA107).

In many respects, *Dafne* established a pattern that was followed by other composers of early opera. Some structural features of *Dafne* were used consistently for

LE MVSICHE
DI IACOPO PERI
NOBIL FIORENTINO
Sopra L'Euridice

DEL SIG· OTTAVIO RINVCCINI
Rappresentate Nello Sponsalizio
della Cristianissima

MARIA MEDICI
REGINA DI FRANCIA
E DI NAVARRA

IN FIORENZA
APPRESSO GIORGIO MARESCOTTI·
MDC·

(a)

(b)

Figure 15.3 (*a*) Title page and (*b*) first page of original printed score of Peri's *Euridice* (1600/1601.)

more than a century: (1) The opera commences with a Prologue in which a character not otherwise involved in the story apprises the audience of the central theme of the opera. In *Dafne,* the Prologue is sung by Ovid; in other operas, by Music, Tragedy, Time, or a similar generality. (2) The text is poetry, and the plot is based on classic mythology. (3) Pastoral characters and scenes are incorporated. (4) An emotional appeal or moving prayer is sung by the main character, and the difficulty is resolved at the crucial moment by divine intervention. (Later, this kind of resolution is referred to as *deus ex machina.*) (5) The music is mainly accompanied solo song, though some use is made of chorus. (6) Choral singing concludes the opera.

Though composers stated that they were seeking to approximate the manner in which the ancient Greeks presented their dramas, the humanists' interest in ancient Roman culture is apparent in Rinuccini's libretto. The plot is constructed and developed along lines used by the Roman poet Ovid (43 B.C.–A.D. 18) in his dramas. Therefore, Rinuccini's choice of Ovid to present the Prologue of *Dafne* is appropriate.

Euridice

Corsi was responsible, too, for the production on 6 October 1600 of the Peri-Caccini setting of Rinuccini's *Euridice.* The production was Corsi's wedding gift to Maria de' Medici and Henri IV of Navarre, King of France (r. 1589–1610); Peri dedicated his published score of *Euridice* (Florence, 1601) to Maria (fig. 15.3). The performance was given before a select audience of 200 guests in the private apartment of Don Antonio de' Medici in the Pitti Palace. Peri, who was slender, blond, and acclaimed for his beautiful tenor voice, sang the role of Orpheus; Corsi played harpsichord accompaniments behind the scenes. Caccini's contribution was small. Out of jealousy, he would not permit any of his court singers to perform Peri's music, and he rewrote their songs. These included Euridice's music, three choral pieces, and a few solo lines of nymphs and shepherds. In the preface to the published *Euridice,* Peri credited Caccini with these.

Rinuccini's libretto of *Euridice* has a Prologue and five scenes; Peri's setting of it takes approximately an hour and a half to perform. Rinuccini constructed the libretto along the same lines as that for

Dafne. However, he modified the mythological tale to give the traditional tragedy a happy ending—more appropriate for a royal wedding; this is indicated in the Prologue of the opera, sung by Tragedy. Briefly, the story is this: Euridice, Orpheus's beloved, is gathering flowers and dancing in the meadow with nymphs and shepherds. She is bitten by a snake and dies. The nymph Dafne carries the tragic news to Orpheus. Grieving, he consults Venus, who, promising him triumph over death, leads him to Hades. There, Orpheus pleads with Pluto, obtains Euridice's release, and takes her back to earth.

Each of the five scenes concludes with a strophic chorus summarizing the scene's events. Peri's music is appropriate to each happening; he had achieved sufficient mastery of the style midway between speech and song—the *stile rappresentativo*—to regulate the degree of emotional intensity expressed. Orpheus's deeply emotional monologues are colored by unexpected harmonic progressions, unprepared dissonances, suspensions, and frequent rests, as in *Non piango e non sospiro* (I do not weep and I do not sigh; Scene 2), sung after Dafne tells him of Euridice's death, and the lament *Funeste piagge* (Funereal shores; Scene 4), sung when he stands on the shores of the underworld. How different are the joyous harmonies and small graces in Orpheus's songs about love at the beginning of Scene 2! Dafne's recounting of her message is true recitative, commencing calmly, gaining momentum as she becomes more emotional; this increased agitation Peri accomplished through smaller note values, suspensions, and flexible rhythm above static harmony (fig. 15.4). (The role of Dafne was sung by a young boy soprano, Jacopo Giusti, from Lucca.)

The Prologue music in *Euridice* resembles that of *Dafne* in several respects. The two Prologues are in the same key, and there is marked similarity in both treble and bass in the opening measures. Peri composed music slowly; he may have left composition of the Prologue until last, and, pressed for time, borrowed and remodeled. There are indications, too, that composers relied on some standard melodic patterns when composing strophic monodies and arias.

Figure 15.4 Excerpt from Dafne's long recitative in Scene 3 of Peri's *Euridice.*

In performance, the solos were appropriately ornamented; both Peri and Caccini would have seen that this was done correctly. In Peri's published *Euridice,* he included an *Avvertimento* (Notice) concerning the proper realization of his figured bass lines:

AVVERTIMENTO.

Sopra la parte del basso, il diesis congiunto col 6. dimostra sesta maggiore, e la minor: senza 'l diesis; Il quale quando è solo, è contrassegno della terza, ò della decima maggiore: Et il b. molle, della terza, ò decima minore; e non si ponga mai, se non a quella sola nota, doue è segnato, quantunque più ne fussero in vna medesima Corda.

Above the bass line, a sharp in conjunction with a 6 denotes a major sixth, and a 6 without a sharp is a minor sixth. When a sharp is alone [above a note], it signifies a major third or tenth; and a flat alone, a minor third or tenth. And a chromatic alteration is never to be played except with the one note on which it is marked, although there may be several notes of the same pitch denomination.

It was one of the peculiarities of Baroque music notation that a chromatic alteration placed above or before a note affected the pitch of *only* that note, unless the note was immediately repeated, a barline notwithstanding. In the Baroque era, the barline did not have the same connotation with regard to chromatic alterations as it does in modern notation.

Caccini prepared a complete setting of Rinuccini's *Euridice* (Florence, 1601), which Caccini claimed he had written earlier. His music is more melodious than Peri's, more in the style of the monodies in *Le nuove musiche*. It should be noted that Caccini's spectacle, *Il rapimento di Cefalo* (The abduction of Cefalo), was also a part of the wedding festivities and was performed three nights after Peri's *Euridice*. Peri sang in Caccini's production.

Peri composed other dramatic works, both secular and sacred, in the ensuing years; unfortunately, all of those that he referred to as operas or oratorios are lost. An **oratorio** resembles an opera but has a narrator, places greater emphasis on chorus, and is presented without stage action, scenery, or costumes (discussed on p. 331). Most oratorios are on religious subjects; however, oratorios and operas may be sacred or secular.

Emilio de' Cavalieri

The career of Emilio de' Cavalieri (c. 1550–1602) was closely associated with the Medici. Cavalieri was talented and versatile—he was composer, organist, singing teacher, dancer and choreographer, administrator and diplomat. He served Cardinal Ferdinando de' Medici in Rome, and when the cardinal became Grand Duke of Tuscany in 1587, Cavalieri was appointed overseer of all artistic and musical activities and supervisor of all artists, craftsmen, and musicians at the Florentine court. Some of his music was performed at the nuptial festivities there in 1589. Cavalieri's music for the final *ballo* in the sixth *intermedio,* with Laura Guidiccioni's text *O che nuovo miracolo* (O, that new wonder), became known as *Aria di Fiorenza* and gave rise to approximately 130 pieces by later composers.

Cavalieri was in charge of the wedding festivities honoring Maria de' Medici and Henri IV and composed for the banquet on 5 October 1600 a setting of Guarini's *La contesa fra Giunone e Minerva* (The contest between Juno and Minerva). But somehow Caccini managed to gain control over the production of the main nuptial spectacle—his own *Il rapimento di Cefalo*—to the exclusion of Cavalieri. The latter, disappointed, disgruntled, and disillusioned over what he considered the poor quality of all of the nuptial spectacles except those presented at the banquet, left for Rome and never returned to Florence. When Caccini and Peri engaged in a controversy over which of them invented *stile rappresentatione,* Cavalieri asserted that he had. Peri, in the preface to his published *Euridice,* stated that he had first heard the style in the music of Cavalieri but claimed to be the first to use that style in opera.

From time to time during the 1590s, Cavalieri had supervised musical productions at the Oratorio del Crocifisso in the church of San Marcello, Rome. In February 1600, his *Rappresentatione di Anima, et di Corpo* (The play about Soul, and Body) was presented in Rome twice, in the Oratory of Chiesa Nuova (New Church). Reportedly, the entire Sacred College attended. This is the earliest known performance in an oratory of a large-scale musical dramatic work containing solo monodies. In fact, no other operas or staged dramas with music are known to have been performed in any oratories in Rome. *Rappresentatione di Anima, et di Corpo,* according to its dedication, was prepared for publication in September 1600 and is the earliest printed score using figured bass (fig. 15.5).

Rappresentatione di Anima, et di Corpo is in three Acts, each containing several short Scenes; there are 91 numbered pieces of vocal music in the published score. The play opens with a lengthy spoken dialogue between Avveduto (Wisdom) and Prudentio (Prudence); the music ensues and commences with a short prologue (though not so labeled) sung by Tempo (Time), *Il tempo, il tempo fugge* (Time, time flies), and concludes with two choruses. Once the music begins, there is no further spoken dialogue; Avveduto and Prudentio have no singing roles.

Rappresentatione di Anima, et di Corpo contains strophic songs, madrigals, speechlike recitative, and choral songs (labeled *ballo*) with dancelike rhythms and meters. Undoubtedly, dancing accompanied the singing of those *balli*. Instrumental *ritor-*

Figure 15.5 (*a*) Title page and (*b*) first page of music in the published score of Cavalieri's *Rappresentatione di anima, et di corpo* (1600).

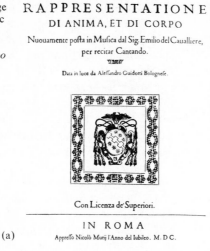

(a)

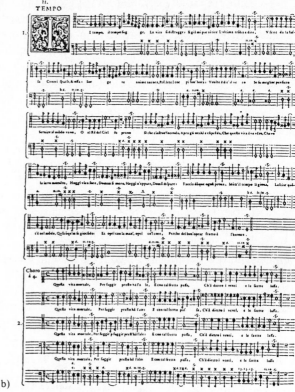

(b)

nelli (literally, little returns) serve as interludes between strophes. (A *ritornello* is a short passage of music that recurs several times, as a kind of refrain.) These *ritornelli,* some of which are segments of the choral pieces, unify the work. A five-part instrumental *Sinfonia* (unnumbered) is performed between chorus Nos. 15 and 16 and between chorus Nos. 54 and 55. *Ritornelli* and *sinfonie* were used later by other composers of early opera. Chorus No. 54 is polychoral, with solo and choral echo effects. The recitatives in *Rappresentatione . . .* contain false relations and sudden changes of harmony but lack the rhythmic flexibility and variety found in Peri's recitatives.

Rappresentatione di Anima, et di Corpo is variously referred to as opera and oratorio. It was first performed in the Oratorio of a church, and Avveduto and Prudentio are sometimes considered narrators, though they appear only in the spoken dialogue and do not present musical narration. However, when *Rappresentatione . . .* was presented in Rome it was staged, as a musical dramatic production. Cavalieri's *Rappresentatione di Anima, et di Corpo* is an allegorical opera.

Librettists

Music alone does not make an opera; an appropriate libretto is vital. Thus, Laura Guidiccioni and Ottavio Rinuccini were shaping forces in early opera—Guidiccioni wrote expressive poetic texts in lines with an irregular number of syllables, to be set to music in *pastorales* and *intermedi*; Rinuccini couched his Ovidian plots in lines of similar construction. Cavalieri set many of Guidiccioni's lines; Rinuccini provided texts for Corsi, Peri, Caccini, Monteverdi, and a host of others.

Laura Guidiccioni

Laura Guidiccioni (1550–99), daughter of Nicolò Guidiccioni and Caterina de' Benedetti, was born in Lucca. It is not known when she married Orazio Lucchesini. She was persuaded by a certain Ippolito Santini, priest at the cathedral, to pursue her literary talents, and he urged Orazio to take Laura to Florence, where cultural activities, especially at the Medici court, might provide an outlet for her poetry. There her talent flourished. She met Tasso, Guarini, and Rinuccini; she was well acquainted with Corsi, Peri, Caccini, and other noted musicians and composers who worked at the Medici court. Cavalieri set many of her lines.

Ottavio Rinuccini

Ottavio Rinuccini (1562–1621), a native of Florence, was educated as a courtier. His literary service at the Medici court began in 1579, and his association as librettist for Corsi began in 1590. Rinuccini's historical significance, musically, lies (a) in his ability to write verse suitable for setting in the *recitativo* style used by Peri, Caccini, and Monteverdi and (b) in his construction of an Ovidian plot that was tragi-comic. A prologue and a happy ending resulting from divine intervention are characteristic of his libretti. From time to time between 1600 and 1604, Rinuccini visited the French court of Maria de' Medici. There he observed court ballet, and its influence can be seen in some of his later works, e.g., *Il ballo delle ingrate* (The ingrates' dance) set by Monteverdi in 1608. He furnished the libretto for Monteverdi's opera *L'Arianna* and poetry for sonnets, canzoni, and madrigals, e.g., Monteverdi's *Zefiro torna* (The breeze returns) and *Lamento della ninfa* (The nymph's lament).

Alessandro Striggio

Among the viol players participating in the nuptial festivities for Grand Duke Ferdinando de' Medici in Florence in 1589 was Alessandro Striggio (1573–1630). A native of Mantua, Striggio studied law and chose a career as diplomat, serving the Mantuan court as ambassador to Milan. On a diplomatic mission to Venice he contracted plague and died.

Striggio's father (also named Alessandro) was a madrigalist, and the son edited and published several volumes of his father's works. However, the younger Alessandro Striggio's main contribution to the development of music is literary—he prepared several libretti for Monteverdi, including the opera *L'Orfeo* (1607), the ballet *Tirsi e Clori* (1615), and *Lamento d'Apollo* (lost). Striggio and Monteverdi were friends; after Monteverdi moved to Venice in 1613, Striggio provided a close link with the Mantuan court.

Mantua

At Mantua, the chapel singers and instrumental ensemble employed by Duke Vincenzo I Gonzaga were of virtuoso caliber. Court singers included Lucrezia Urbana, Caterina Martinelli, Adriana Basile, and Francesco Razi. In 1589, when Monteverdi joined the court musicians as violist, Giaches de Wert was court *maestro di cappella* and G. P. Gastoldi (c. 1551–c. 1622) was chapelmaster at the basilica of Santa Barbara, which was also administered by the reigning duke. High-quality church music was performed there, and Vincenzo presented weekly Friday-evening concerts at the palace and promoted theatrical entertainments. Reportedly, the court singers performed madrigals in "a theatrical manner."

A number of persons at Mantua were aware of opera's existence. Members of the Gonzaga family had attended opera performances in Florence, Alessandro Striggio had performed in them, and undoubtedly Monteverdi had discussed them with Corsi and others. In 1607, when Francesco Gonzaga and the Accademia degli Invaghiti requested Monteverdi to compose an opera for Carnival, Striggio provided the libretto for *L'Orfeo* (Orpheus). Though *Euridice* and *L'Orfeo* are based on the same legend, and Striggio's model was Rinuccini's *Euridice,* the operas differ considerably. *L'Orfeo* is more advanced musically and is more effective theater, for Monteverdi thought in terms of human drama, even though Striggio adhered more closely to the traditional Orpheus-Euridice myth. *L'Orfeo,* in its first performance, did not have a happy ending—Apollo did not descend from heaven to console Orpheus, as is the case in the revised version. The choice of conclusion may have been made from necessity, however. The production of an opera required considerable machinery—pulleys, chains, and other mechanical devices—and adequate space for the operation of that machinery. *L'Orfeo* was first performed in a "small room of apartments the duchess used," and probably that room could not accommodate the requisite machinery for a god's descent from heaven. The names of all who sang the solo roles in *L'Orfeo* are not known. Some were sung by soprano castrati (Insight, "Castrati"); one of the *concerto delle donne* may have sung the Messenger role. There was a major difference in the performance of Monteverdi's later operas—though castrati performed in some of them, women sang the leading female roles. There were excellent female sopranos at the Gonzaga court, and Monteverdi considered their talents when he composed for Mantua.

Late in 1607, Marco da Gagliano (1582–1643) composed an opera, setting Rinuccini's revised libretto *Dafne;* when it was performed at Mantua

Castrati

Castrati, male singers who had been castrated before puberty in order to preserve the high treble voice range (either soprano or alto), figured prominently in the history of music during the seventeenth and eighteenth centuries. The operation itself was never sanctioned by church authorities, but the castrato voice was almost universally admired. Most of the castrati were Italian, though there were some Spanish and a very few English.

The reason for the increased number of castrati in the late Renaissance and throughout the Baroque is not known. Undoubtedly, one factor was the belief prevalent in many lands that women were to be silent in church. I Corinthians 14:34 was interpreted literally—"Let your women keep silence in churches." Another factor may have been the multiplicity of parts in contrapuntal vocal music. Male soprano and alto voices were much more powerful than female ones, and seldom was a boy's voice strong enough to hold up a treble part in an ensemble. Falsettists (many of them from Spain) and castrati were admitted to the Sistine Choir in the second half of the sixteenth century; Lassus had six castrati in his chapel choir at Munich in the 1570s.

Castrati played important roles in opera from the time of its inception. In the Papal States, from the time of Pope Sixtus V (r. 1585–90), there was a ban on women appearing on the stage; the extent to which this was enforced varied considerably, however. In view of the relationship between the Medici, the College of Cardinals, and the Papacy, it is not surprising that the role of Euridice in Peri's opera *Euridice* (1600) was sung by a castrato and the role of Dafne by a boy soprano. Monteverdi's *L'Orfeo* (1607) had castrati in the cast; many other instances can be cited. Moreover, composers wrote heroic male roles for high voices that could be sung by either tenors or castrati. There were no castrato parts in French opera.

Castrati were at the height of their popularity between 1650 and 1750. Operatic roles were still written for them after that time, e.g., by Mozart, Gluck, and Meyerbeer (in 1824). Although Pope Pius X (r. 1903–14) formally banned castrati from the papal chapel in 1903, there were castrati in the Sistine Choir until 1913.

---

during Carnival in 1608 Caterina Martinelli sang the leading role. The success of *Dafne* prompted Vincenzo to commission another opera from Monteverdi. He composed *L'Arianna* (Ariadne; 1608), on a libretto by Rinuccini, but its performance was postponed because of the death of Caterina Martinelli, who was to have sung the title role. Only fragments of *L'Arianna* survive. Virginia Andreini, who was employed at court after Caterina's untimely death, did not have vocal talent comparable to that of Caterina; this is reflected in the simpler melodic style Monteverdi used in his next work, the full-length ballet *Il ballo delle ingrate.*

Musical activities at Mantua declined after Vincenzo's death in 1612. Later that year Monteverdi was dismissed and moved to Venice where he became *maestro di cappella* at St. Mark's church. Occasionally, he composed pieces for the Gonzaga court, including *La finta pazza Licori* (Licoris's pretended madness; 1627; music lost), which was never performed. Only the ballet *Tirsi e Clori* (Thyrsis and Chloris; 1616), on a libretto by Striggio, survives.

Claudio Monteverdi

The transition from Renaissance to Baroque may be seen in the work of Claudio Monteverdi (1567–1643; see Insight, "Claudio Monteverdi"), who, in many respects, was a Renaissance man. From 1589 to 1612 Monteverdi worked at the Gonzaga court in Mantua as violinist, viol player, and composer. He spent the last thirty years of his life as *maestro di cappella* at St. Mark's church, Venice, and composed much sacred music, but he is best known for his secular music, much of which embodies Baroque characteristics. In his first several books of madrigals and in much of his sacred music Monteverdi employed the principles of Netherlands counterpoint, which he termed *prima prattica* or *stile antico* (first practice or old style). Some of his works (both sacred and secular) are clearly in Baroque style; in other compositions he applied the affective principles of the *seconda prattica* or *stile moderno* (second practice, modern style) to music that was more Renaissance than Baroque.

Example 15.2 Excerpt from Monteverdi's *Non schivar, non parar* (mm. 30ff.) containing the measured tremolo of *stile concitato* and printed instructions for playing *pizzicato. (From* Madrigals of War and Love.*)*

Monteverdi's musical style is rooted in his understanding of Plato's ideas concerning music. He interpreted literally Plato's statement that music is composed of text, the combination of sounds, and rhythm—because Plato listed text first, it was of prime import; the music was secondary and was subservient to the text. Closely related to this is the concept of *ethos* as expressed by Plato and other ancient Greek philosophers—the ability of music to move the affections and to affect the entire person. Plato stated that all aspects of music had this power, rhythm as well as melody and *tonos;* just as there was direct correlation between certain *tonoi* and certain character traits, so there was direct correlation between certain rhythmic patterns and certain emotional states. It was Monteverdi's aim to compose music in which the text was presented clearly and in a manner that expressed its affective nature accurately. To this extent, his ideas

and those of the Florentine Camerata were in accord (see p. 295). However, Monteverdi believed his aims could be realized in polyphonic music; the Camerata turned to homophony and accompanied monody. This does not imply that Monteverdi rejected homophony; he wrote some homophonic music, but he sought to achieve new ends through traditional means. For instance, he continued to compose madrigals after others had discarded the genre.

In his application of the principles of *ethos* through rhythm, Monteverdi created *stile concitato,* the excited style. His use of measured tremolo in *Non schivar, non parar* (Not to dodge, not to parry) from *Il combattimento di Tancredi e di Clorinda* (The fight between Tancred and Clorinda) is an example of this (ex. 15.2). *Non schivar, non parar* contains also the first instructions (written in the music) for playing *pizzicato* on bowed string instruments.

Baroque Vocal Music

Claudio Monteverdi

Claudio Monteverdi (1567–1643) was born in Cremona, Italy. His father, a highly respected physician, sent Claudio and his brother Giulio Cesare (1573–1630) to Marc' Antonio Ingegneri (1547–92), *maestro di cappella* at Cremona Cathedral, for music training, but they were not choirboys. By the age of 16, Claudio had published three books of music: three-voice motets (1582), four-voice *Madrigali spirituali* (1583), and three-voice *Canzonette* (1583). Next, two books of his five-voice madrigals appeared (1587, 1590).

Before 1589 Monteverdi had no permanent position; occasionally, he secured work as a performer in string ensembles. In 1589 he was hired as violinist and viol player at the Mantua court of Duke Vincenzo I Gonzaga (r. 1587–1612). Monteverdi soon became a valued court musician and was included in the ducal retinue on journeys, even those outside Italy. On some occasions he performed with the Mantuan ensemble at the Estense court in Ferrara. When Giaches de Wert died (1596), Monteverdi hoped to succeed him as *maestro di cappella,* but Pallavicino received the appointment. Not until 1601 was Monteverdi elevated to *maestro di cappella* at the Gonzaga court. By that time, his reputation was firmly established in Italy.

In May 1599 Monteverdi married Claudia de Cattaneis, a court singer. They had three children, the eldest of whom, Francesco (1601–c. 1679), worked as singer and composer at St. Mark's, Venice, from 1623 to 1679.

Undoubtedly, Claudio Monteverdi performed in the ensemble accompanying theatrical productions at court, such as the 1598 presentation of Guarini's *Il pastor fido,* and in 1604 he wrote some ballet music. In February 1607 his first opera, *L'Orfeo,* was presented at Mantua before the Accademia degli Invaghiti. Then Claudia became ill; her death in September was a crushing blow. Monteverdi was disinclined to remain at Mantua, but his opera *L'Arianna* (Ari-

Claudio Monteverdi. Portrait by Bernardo Strozzi (1582–1644). *(Trioler Landesmuseum Ferdinandeum, Innsbruck, Austria.)*

adne) was scheduled for production at court, and he needed to be present at rehearsals. All did not go smoothly. The production was not ready for Carnival season and was rescheduled to coincide with nuptial festivities honoring Francesco Gonzaga and Margaret of Savoy, in May 1608. Caterina Martinelli, who was to sing the Ariadne role, was stricken with smallpox and died; Virginia Andreini, a member of a traveling troupe performing in Mantua, sang the role on short notice. Monteverdi wrote other music for the celebration, too, including *Il ballo delle ingrate,* a full-length ballet.

It was Monteverdi who advanced the idea of two practices: *prima prattica,* the first practice, being Renaissance polyphony based on the principles of Franco-Flemish counterpoint, with emphasis on the music; *seconda prattica,* the second practice, based on the ideas of the ancient Greeks, and being the presentation of the text through music expressing its affections. Baroque composers used Monteverdi's terminology but altered the meaning of *seconda prattica.* Monteverdi believed the Renaissance modal system was antiquated. He advocated a wider and more expressive use of dissonance. In his madrigals, he achieved this by (1) using melodic intervals expressly forbidden by Renaissance contrapuntal principles, e.g., a downward leap of a minor sixth; (2) notating embellishments commonly improvised,

After Claudia's and Caterina's deaths, Monteverdi suffered from severe depression. By the time the wedding festivities concluded, his nerves were on edge, and he sought to be released from court responsibilities, but the petition was denied. He reacted by writing an accusing letter to Vincenzo, and in 1610 Monteverdi was granted a pension but still was not released. Monteverdi actively sought a new position and went to Rome to arrange for publication of a volume of sacred music. When he returned to Mantua, he began another book of madrigals. After the death of Vincenzo I, in 1612, the duchy experienced financial difficulties that caused Francesco Gonzaga to reduce the size of the court's musical body; Monteverdi was among those dismissed.

After almost a year of idleness, Monteverdi auditioned for and obtained the *maestro di cappella* position at St. Mark's church, Venice. He retained that position until his death. The quality of musical performances at St. Mark's had declined considerably, and music was at a low ebb there when Monteverdi assumed his duties. Under his leadership, conditions improved, but music at St. Mark's never regained the heights to which it had soared during the Gabrielis' tenure. Transference of some of the compositional workload at St. Mark's to younger composers enabled Monteverdi to accept commissions from other sources: secular academies, religious confraternities, wealthy Venetian families, and Italian courts. For Mantua he composed several works, including the ballet *Tirsi e Clori* (1616). In 1620 Monteverdi declined an offer to return to the Gonzaga court but continued to compose for Mantua. His full-length opera *La finta pazza Licori* (1627) was intended as part of the succession festivities for Vincenzo II. When Vincenzo II died in 1628 without an heir, the Gonzaga line ended, and Monteverdi's connection with Mantua was severed.

In 1628 Monteverdi was granted leave of absence from St. Mark's to visit Parma and fulfill a commission for several items to be performed at the Farnese court. *Gli Amori di Diana e d'Endimione* (The Love of Diana and Endymion) was produced there in 1628; that music is lost. From time to time, Monteverdi composed stage works for performance at the Mocenigo home in Venice. Two such works were *Il combattimento di Tancredi e Clorinda* (1624) and *Proserpina rapita* (Proserpina abducted; 1630).

During the 1630s, Monteverdi seems to have written little music—a Mass of thanksgiving for deliverance from the epidemic of plague that swept through Venice in 1630–31; *Scherzi musicali* (1632), a small collection of arias and madrigals for one and two voices with *basso continuo*. *Madrigali guerrieri et amorosi* (Madrigals of war and love), published in 1638, had been written earlier. A collection of sacred music appeared in 1641.

The first public opera house, Teatro San Cassiano, opened in Venice in 1637; a second, Teatro SS Giovanni e Paolo, opened in 1639. Monteverdi's *L'Arianna* was revived in 1640; thereafter, he resumed composition of opera. *Il ritorno d'Ulisse in patria* (Ulysses's return to his homeland) was produced at San Cassiano in 1640 and again in 1641; Venetian singers performed it in Bologna in 1640, also. *Le nozze d'Enea con Lavinia* (The marriage of Aeneas and Lavinia) was presented at SS Giovanni e Paolo in 1641; only the scenario and libretto survive. Monteverdi's last opera, *L'incoronazione di Poppea* (The coronation of Poppea), was produced at SS Giovanni e Paolo in 1642.

In 1643 Monteverdi requested leave to visit Cremona. He died shortly after he returned to Venice. Dual funeral services were held in St. Mark's and Santa Maria dei Frari, with music under the direction of two of his pupils, Rovetta and Marinoni. Monteverdi's remains were interred in the chapel of St. Ambrosius in the church of Santa Maria dei Frari; a commemorative plaque marks the place.

thereby making their dissonances visible instead of fleetingly audible; (3) writing unprepared dissonances; and (4) resolving suspensions irregularly. His harmonic innovations did not go without criticism. Especially critical was theorist G. M. Artusi (1540–1613) of Bologna, who singled out for attack certain passages in *Anima mia perdona* and *Cruda Amarilli* (ex. 15.3; DWMA108). Monteverdi responded in the

Foreword to his fifth book of madrigals (1605) by referring to a "Second Practice" of modern music, and saying, "concerning consonances and dissonances, there is another way of considering them, different from the established way, which . . . defends the modern method of composing." Two years later, Giulio Cesare Monteverdi wrote a Declaration in Claudio's defense, asserting that harmony must be servant of

Example 15.3 Monteverdi: *Cruda Amarilli*, mm. 9–14. Note unprepared entrance of a″ followed by equally unprepared f″ in m. 13.

Monteverdi's Works

Much of Monteverdi's music has been lost. His works that survive intact include 3 operas, a ballet, 12 volumes containing approximately 250 madrigals and other secular songs, 5 volumes of sacred music, and approximately 20 sacred pieces published in anthologies.

Sacred Music

For the greater part of his working life, Monteverdi was employed in the service of the church, yet the amount of his sacred music that survives is minimal. Moreover, much of that music strongly reflects his secular interests and style. There is no evidence that he had any responsibility for church music prior to 1601, and his position as *maestro di cappella* at Mantua did not include furnishing music for Santa Barbara. Possibly, he wrote the 26 motets in *Sacrae cantiunculae* (Enticing sacred songs; 1572) in connection with his counterpoint lessons from Ingegneri.

The volume published in 1610, containing a Mass for the Virgin, Vespers with two Magnificat settings, and motets, was dedicated to the Pope, which suggests that Monteverdi wanted church employment. In

the text and not its master, a principle that underlies all of Monteverdi's music. Such criticism and discussion of Monteverdi's works was beneficial—it kept his name before the public and heightened circulation of his music.

the votive Mass, ten themes from Gombert's motet *In ill"e tempore* (In this time) are treated contrapuntally; canon appears often. In the publication the themes are printed separately so that they are identifiable in the Mass. Some Mass sections are homorhythmic (chordal); there is almost no word painting. In contrast to the Renaissance style of the Mass, the Vesper psalms display a mixture of styles. The chant-based melodies are subjected to various techniques, including *falsobordone* (chordal chanting), cantus firmus, and strophic variation. Some psalm settings are madrigalesque. In others, walking bass lines, ostinato or ground bass, and basso continuo are present. In the Vespers, the tenor motet *Nigra sum* (I am black) incorporates material from the Lament in *L'Arianna* (p. 311). The Magnificats, for voices and instruments, are among the earliest *concertato* settings of that canticle. The motets, which are not strictly liturgical, exhibit *seconda prattica* and probably were written for the virtuoso singers at Mantua. Much figuration embellishes the melody, and dissonance is used extensively to enhance the text.

Monteverdi's Venetian sacred music was published in two collections, one in 1641, the other posthumously in 1651. Though the collections are large, they cannot possibly contain all of the music he composed for St. Mark's during his 30 years of service there. All three compositional styles are represented: strict Renaissance counterpoint, *seconda prattica,* and mixed. *Prima prattica* was used in two four-voice Masses and several psalm settings. The imitative counterpoint is diatonic, with comparative rhythmic regularity; dissonance is carefully controlled and text painting seldom occurs.

Monteverdi's church music is unusual in its inclusion of many secular elements, especially operatic ones. During the first half of the seventeenth century most Italian churches adhered to Renaissance-style music; composers in church positions had little or no opportunity to write opera. The fact that Monteverdi was permitted to engage in secular theatrical productions while employed by a major Italian church evidences his employers' and contemporaries' high regard for his talent. In essence, he pursued two careers simultaneously. No doubt he carefully selected the items he included in the volume of sacred music published in 1641. He may have deliberately delayed publication of some of his church music because of its avant-garde character—the inclusion of operatic elements would have precluded its use in other Italian churches at that time. Many of Monteverdi's sacred compositions foreshadow the merging of sacred and secular elements that became common practice a century later.

Madrigals, Secular Songs

Monteverdi's madrigals are among the finest composed during the late Renaissance and early Baroque era. His philosophy, *prima le parole, poi la musica* (first the words, then the music), is borne out in his settings. The majority of his madrigals were written for professional singers, both women and men. Many of the poems he set were by Tasso and Guarini, both of whom spent some time at the Gonzaga court.

Of Monteverdi's youthful works, only the bass part of *Madrigali spirituali* (1583) survives. All but one of the songs in the book of three-voice canzonettas (1584) are strophic settings of light verse with uncomplicated music colored by word painting.

The first six books of madrigals are for five voices. The presence of three linked madrigals in the first book (1587) hints at Monteverdi's later interest in madrigal cycles. *Ardo, si, ma non t'amo* (I burn, but I do not love you), *Ardi o gela a tuo voglia* (Burn or freeze, as you will), and *Arsi e also a mia voglia* (Love or hate, it matters not to me) are integrated by musical motifs with similar rhythms. In the second book (1590), a collection of madrigals written over a three-

year period, most of the poems are pastoral, and the settings reveal Monteverdi's talent for imaginative imagery as well as his mastery of conventional word-painting devices. Greater prominence is given the upper voices. In a few madrigals two sopranos and an alto form an ensemble; perhaps the *concerto delle donne* from Ferrara had performed in Mantua, or Monteverdi was writing for a similar trio at the Gonzaga court.

Two cycles by Tasso and poems by Guarini dominate Monteverdi's third book of madrigals (1592). Particular attention was paid to setting the words expressively; dissonance plays a large role in this. In *Stracciami pur il core* (I will tear even the heart) harsh discords are created by double suspensions and by sounding the dissonant note and the note of resolution simultaneously. *Vattene pur, crudel, con quella pace* is not profound but is expressively passionate. Choral recitative is relieved by expressive setting of emotional words; for effective (and affective) performance three evenly matched women's voices are required. As in Book II, madrigals in cycles are linked by inconclusive endings.

The fourth and fifth books (1603, 1605) contain some of Monteverdi's best madrigals. In Book IV the words are emphasized through homophonic texture and natural accentuation and declamation; melismas are reserved for expressive purposes. Chromaticism is rare; use of dissonance is minimal, but when present it is intense. In declamatory passages, Monteverdi's notation is that used for psalmody—only the chord is written; the rhythm is left to the singers who must perform with ensemble precision. More than half of the poems in Book V are from Guarini's *Il pastor fido*. In all of his madrigals, where Monteverdi desired specific embellishments he notated them. Several of the madrigals in Book V are furnished with a *basso seguente* line (instrumental bass doubling the lowest pitch of each chord) that, at first glance, seems unnecessary in performance. Undoubtedly, Monteverdi notated that line because he wanted (a) to reenforce the bass line and (b) the instrumental sonority. The last six madrigals have a basso continuo that supplies pitches not present in the vocal harmonies; often it forms the third part in a trio. Frequently, an embellished solo voice supported by an instrumental bass effectively contrasts with the full ensemble.

Book VI (1614) is the product of a bereaved man grieving deeply; in a sense, the book is a memorial to Caterina Martinelli. Approximately half of the volume is taken up by two madrigal cycles: an arrangement of the *Lamento d'Arianna,* and a threnody (*Incenerite spoglie*) on Caterina's death. In the latter, Monteverdi integrated recitative in the madrigal structure, used highly expressive harmonies, and reserved extreme dissonance for important climaxes. This cycle is ranked among the finest of his madrigals. In the Ariadne cycle, unity is achieved through thematic links, some fragments being used in rondo fashion. Most of the single pieces in Book VI are *continuo* madrigals.

Monteverdi titled his seventh book of madrigals *Concerto* (1619). It contains pieces for one, two, three, four, and six voices, and each piece is supplied with a basso continuo line. A majority of the madrigals are instrumentally accompanied duets of three types: (1) comparable in style with solo *continuo* madrigal; (2) arias; and (3) a series of continuous variations above a ground bass such as romanesca or passacaglia. Representative of the first type is *O come sei gentile, caro angellino* (O, how gentle you are, dear little angel), a soprano duet filled with word painting and virtuosic display. *Chiome d'oro* (Golden hair; DWMA109) is a strophic aria duet for soprano and bass, with instrumental ensemble of two violins and basso continuo; each strophe is interrupted by a vocal cadenza. Monteverdi used the violin melody in his setting of the Vespers psalm *Beatus vir* (Blessed is the man). *Ohimè, dov'è il mio ben?* (Alas, where is my beloved?) is constructed as variations above a recurring bass line, a technique Monteverdi handled well.

In the Foreword to Book VIII, *Madrigals of War and Love* (1638), Monteverdi explained that the volume contains music depicting the three humors of man: (1) "stillness," reflected in a state of calmness; (2) "agitation," reflected in war; and (3) "supplication," reflected in love or passion. Music, Monteverdi wrote, must depict these humors and inspire these states in listeners. The large volume is a collection of madrigals written over the previous 30 years. It contains *Il combattimento di Tancredi e Clorinda,* a madrigal cycle presented at the Mocenigo palace in 1624; a revised form of *Il ballo delle ingrate,* originally performed at Mantua in 1608; and a ballet written for the coronation festivities of Emperor Ferdinand III in 1636. Three singers form the cast of *Il combattimento . . .* : the Crusader Thyrsis and the Muslim girl Clorinda, who sing in arioso dialogue, and a narrator. Descriptive accompaniment is provided by string orchestra, with basso continuo. Perhaps the finest of the numerous smaller pieces in the volume is *Lamento della ninfa Amor* (The lament of the nymph Love), portraying "supplication." An introduction and conclusion frame the lament, which is constructed on a four-note ground bass. The soloist is accompanied by three male voices and basso continuo. If the soloist sings in *tempo rubato* while the others keep strict time, the dissonance is enhanced and there is a heightened feeling that the emotions of lamenting Love cause separation from the world. "Agitation" is depicted in the battle cycle *Il combattimento di Tancredi e Clorinda,* where *stile concitato* and *pizzicato* are introduced (see p. 305). All three humors are represented in the setting of Petrarch's sonnet *Hor che'l ciel e la terra* (Now while the heavens and the earth [and the wind rest]); the music appropriately paints the words, contrasts the three humors, and expresses their inner meaning.

The ninth book of madrigals, issued posthumously (1651), consists entirely of music previously published.

Stage Works

As a violinist or viol player at the Gonzaga court, Monteverdi undoubtedly played for many ballet productions, for Vincenzo I was fond of them and the usual instrumentation for them was five-part string ensemble. When Guarini's *Il pastor fido* was performed in 1598, the music was probably supplied by Giaches de Wert. Monteverdi is known to have written music for a ballet in 1604, but no music or script for that production survives. From time to time, throughout his career, Monteverdi wrote ballets. The most significant of these are *Il ballo delle ingrate* (1608) and *Tirsi e Clori* (1616); madrigals figure prominently in both works. When writing music for a ballet, Monteverdi studied the choreography before writing any of the music; similarly, he became thoroughly familiar with a poem or an opera libretto before setting the text. Customarily, he opened his operas with a prologue. In several places in his operas, he wrote the words *come sta,* thus indicating that the music was to be performed exactly as notated, with no embellishments added.

The earliest surviving stage production by Monteverdi is the revised score of the opera *L'Orfeo* produced at Mantua in 1607. The plot bears some similarity to that of Peri's *Euridice,* but in *L'Orfeo* Hades claims Euridice twice. Striggio's libretto encompasses five scenes, requiring two scene changes: Scenes 1, 2, and 5 are set in the Thracian fields; Scenes 3 and 4, in Hades. The Prologue is sung by Music, who pays homage to the Gonzagas, tells of the power (*ethos*) of music and of Orfeo's singing, mentions the music of the spheres, and describes the scenery. Although Monteverdi was aware of the experiments of the Florentine Camerata, he did not follow their procedures when writing his opera. Only a small portion of *L'Orfeo* is recitative; Monteverdi included madrigal, monody, arioso, and all kinds of instrumental music. The overture is a short toccata; orchestral *ritornelli* and *sinfonie* figure prominently throughout the opera. The orchestra comprised 40 instruments, used in small ensembles for affective purposes, programmatic effects, and dramatic functions, such as covering scenery changes and dividing the opera into "acts." For scenes set in Hades, trombones, chitarrone, and regal (a small portable organ with reed pipes) are used; pastoral scenes are accompanied by recorders and harpsichord; harp and violins or viols simulate heavenly music and the sound of the lyre. Short sinfonias between scenes effect a change of mood or place. Strophic variation is used for the Prologue, sung by Music, and for *Possente spirto* (Powerful spirit), Orfeo's appeal to Charon for aid in crossing the river Styx.

Monteverdi's insight into human nature and his ability to characterize through music are apparent in this opera. Charon, the underworld ferryman who transports souls across the river Styx into Hades, is cast as a bass; his indifference to Orfeo's plea is conveyed by the unchanged melody of his reply. Hope, who travels with Orfeo to Hades' gates, is a soprano. *L'Orfeo* is Renaissance in its presentation of characters as allegorical representations; however, Monteverdi reveals through his music the human side of

Example 15.4 Opening measures of Orfeo's *Possente spirto* for which Monteverdi notated the solo line twice, once unornamented and once with the appropriate embellishments.

those characters. Orfeo, son of Apollo and Calliope, has both a human and a godly nature; allegorically, he represents the power of music, yet in the final strophe of *Possente spirto* his humanity is revealed. *Possente spirto* [DWMA110] requires vocal virtuosity; for this piece Monteverdi wrote two solo lines, one unornamented and the other with all embellishments notated, thus indicating to the singer the manner in which he wanted the solo performed (ex. 15.4). Monteverdi's notation of ornaments provides a valuable guide to vocal performance practices in Italy in the first decade of the seventeenth century. Monteverdi and Striggio seem to have been aware of the medieval mathematician Fibonacci's theory of the Golden Section, for *Possente spirto,* the climax of the opera, is positioned in Act III in accord with Fibonacci's equation (Insight, "Fibonacci").

Contemporary accounts indicate that Monteverdi's second opera, *L'Arianna* (1608), was dramatically superior to *L'Orfeo* and was more popular, but from *L'Arianna* only the libretto and *Lamento* survive. This Lament was the first of many written by Monteverdi and was greatly admired. Soon other composers began to write operatic laments and this type of piece became quite popular.

The music for *La finta pazza Licori* (Licoris's pretended insanity; 1627) has been lost. Extant correspondence indicates this was a full-length comic opera, which was unusual at that time. The characters are humans, without allegorical association. Again, Monteverdi's interest in human psychology and characterization is apparent; Licoris was to pretend insanity, and Monteverdi instructed Margherita Basile to act word by word rather than by phrase. The plot was designed so that the three virtuoso singers at the Mantua court had roles of equal importance.

Baroque Vocal Music

Fibonacci

Leonardo Pisano (c. 1170–d. after 1240), Italian mathematician known as Fibonacci, studied the various numerical systems available for use in calculation and found Hindu-Arabic numerals the most satisfactory. His treatise *Liber abaci* (Book of the abacus; 1202) appeared when very few people knew those numerals and how they could be used in arithmetical operations. Copies of *Liber abaci* circulated widely. Fibonacci's *Practica geometria* (Practice of geometry) appeared in 1220; it was followed by *Liber quadratorum* (Book of square numbers; 1225), an exposition of equations containing squares. Though *Liber quadratorum* is considered Fibonacci's masterpiece, *Liber abaci* was more influential.

Leonardo is remembered by modern mathematicians and musicians principally for the "Fibonacci numbers" sequence—[1], 1, 2, 3, 5, 8, 13, 21, 34, 55, and so on. This, the first recursive number sequence known in Europe, was derived from a problem in *Liber abaci*:

> A pair of rabbits is placed in a walled enclosure. How many pairs of rabbits will be produced from this pair in a year if it is presumed that every month each pair of rabbits produces a new pair that becomes productive in the second month? (Answer: 377 pairs.)

As the numbers in that recursive series increase in magnitude, the ratio between succeeding numbers approaches the "Golden Section" (*phi*, or $\frac{1+\sqrt{5}}{2}$), the ancient mean and extreme ratio, whose value is .6180. . . . Scientists have observed that the numbers (and the ratio) are present in nature, for instance, in pine cones, in spirals in animal horns and shells, and in flowers. This special proportional relationship (known as the "Golden Proportion" or "Golden Ratio") appears to be a natural phenomenon that can be expressed in arithmetical, algebraic, and geometric terms: the lesser is to the greater as the greater is to their sum. It is encountered in geometry quite often and is present in figure 15.6, where A + B is to A as A is to B (or, xy:A :: A:B).

Figure 15.6 Diagram of the Golden Proportion.

From ancient times architects and artists knew and used Golden Proportion in their works, and many composers, from the Middle Ages to the present, have incorporated Fibonacci numbers and Golden Proportion in their musical designs. Analysis of a number of important works by outstanding composers reveals structural relationship to recursive numbers and a structural or dynamic climax or some other highly significant event positioned 61.8 percent of the way through a composition.

Only two of Monteverdi's last three operas are extant; *Le nozze d'Enea con Lavinia* (The marriage of Aeneas and Lavinia; 1641) is lost. In both *Il ritorno d'Ulisse in patria* (Ulysses's return to his native land; 1640) and *L'incoronazione di Poppea* (The coronation of Poppea; 1642) Monteverdi's portrayal of the characters and their emotions is excellent. Penelope, Ulysses's wife, was given much expressive recitative. In *L'incoronazione . . . ,* Nero's neurotic sudden changes of mood are depicted by contrasting single phrases; that role was written for a high castrato. Nero acts predictably in every situation—cruel with Drusilla, generous with Poppea, angry with Seneca. Monteverdi composed fine arioso laments for Otho (Poppea's husband) and Octavia (the deposed empress); Octavia was played by Anna Renzi (c. 1620–60), famous Italian soprano. Another realistic depiction is the trio (Act II, Scene 3; DWMA111), in which Seneca's three friends try to dissuade him from committing suicide. Monteverdi's imitative treatment of the chromatic theme verges on being a fugal exposition. The inclusion of a trio in an opera was unusual at this time.

Iro, the beggar, does not appear in the legend about Ulysses's return; his role was created to supply comic relief in the opera. Comic interludes appear in *L'incoronazione di Poppea,* too, often given to nonessential characters, such as the page who mocks Ottone. Particularly effective is the disguise scene, where Ottone, wearing Drusilla's clothes, sneaks into Poppea's garden. Scenes like this were made easier by the fact that some of the male roles were sung by castrati. The *buffo* duet between Valletto and Damezella (Act II, Scene 5) seems to foreshadow some written by Mozart more than a century later.

Stile concitato and orchestral *ritornelli* were employed effectively in both operas. One example is the climactic test scene in which Ulysses defeats Penelope's suitors because he is the only one capable of drawing his own bow. In *L'incoronazione . . . , stile concitato* is used to depict war, anger, and cruelty.

In his last operas, Monteverdi distinguished clearly between recitative and aria and frequently wrote duets that were strophic variations or used some kind of ground bass.

Rome

The presentation of Cavalieri's *Rappresentatione di Anima, et di Corpo* in Rome did not inspire immediate sequels. In Rome, opera composition was sporadic until almost 1630. In 1606, Agostino Agazzari (1578–1640), *maestro di cappella* at the Jesuit Seminario Romano, composed the pastoral opera *Eumelio* for performance at the school. The plot, like that of *Rappresentatione . . . ,* is moralistic: A boy, Eumelio, is lured from his pastoral life by the Vices and is taken to the Underworld; Apollo and Mercury rescue him and return him to Arcadia. A Prologue sung by Poetry is followed by three short Acts, each concluding with a chorus. Short choruses are sung by the Vices and by shepherds, but *Eumelio* consists mainly of recitatives and strophic arias for solo voice accompanied by basso continuo. Agazzari's music is very similar to that of Cavalieri.

Stefano Landi (c. 1586–1639) was a student at Seminario Romano when *Eumelio* was performed there. Subsequently, he served as a singer at Oratorio del Ss Crocofisso, and by 1618 was *maestro di cappella* to the Bishop of Padua. Landi's first opera, *La morte d'Orfeo* (The death of Orpheus; 1619), was written in Padua but was performed at Borghese wedding festivities in Rome and is considered Rome's first secular opera. Its musical style more closely resembles Monteverdi's *L'Orfeo* than Peri's *Euridice*. Landi returned to Rome in 1620. On recommendation of the Barberini family, with whom he became closely associated, he was admitted to the papal choir in 1629, as an alto. He did not write another opera until 1631.

Meantime, Filippo Vitali's *Aretusa* was performed at Ottavio Corsini's palatial home in honor of Cardinal Scipione Borghese in 1620, and Domenico Mazzochi's *La catena d' Adone* (The chain of Adonis) was presented at Marquis Evandro Conti's house in 1626. Some of Mazzochi's arias are strophic variations.

Rome had no central secular formal court; opera developed mainly through the interest and patronage of wealthy churchmen. Theaters were constructed in private homes; private presentations of operas helped circumvent papal opposition to female singers and women appearing on stage. The Barberini nephews of Pope Urban VIII (r. 1623–44) became interested in opera and during 1631–44 regularly presented operas in their residences. On two occasions in 1632 Landi's sacred opera *Il Sant' Alessio* (Saint Alexis) was performed at Palazzo Barberini. The libretto was by Giulio Rospigliosi (1600–69), who later became Pope Clement IX (r. 1667–69). Rospigliosi wrote many libretti, both sacred and secular; he is credited with originating, through his libretti, both sacred opera (nonallegorical) and comic opera. Many of his serious opera libretti contain comic roles. His poetry is excellent, and he was well versed in the demands of staging and music. Rospigliosi's operas have a larger number of characters than the very early operas, and some have subplots. Composers reacted to these features by creating a kind of recitative that was less melodious, with many repeated notes over static insignificant harmonies, in order to quicken the delivery.

Il Sant' Alessio is Landi's most important work. It is the first opera on a historical subject and the first on the inner life of a human character. Briefly, the plot is this: Alexis, having renounced the world for a religious life, returns incognito to his family home where demons tempt him and pages taunt him, but he remains true to his faith; eventually, he receives his reward in Heaven. Operatic machinery was used to full advantage in scenes depicting Religion's descent to earth in a chariot of clouds and the Devil being engulfed in Hell's flames. Formally, *Il Sant' Alessio* resembles Monteverdi's *L'Orfeo*. *Il Sant' Alessio* comprises a Prologue and three Acts. The Prologue and Acts II and III are each preceded by a *sinfonia*; Acts I and III commence with a chorus, and every Act concludes with a chorus and dancing. The *sinfonie* are the earliest opera overtures that are not mere fanfares. The opening *sinfonia* is in four sections and foreshadows *sonata da chiesa* in form. The *sinfonie* preceding Acts II and III are canzonalike; each is in three sections, fast-slow-fast in tempo. That structure anticipates the **Italian overture** used later in the seventeenth century (p. 321). The third section of the *sinfonia* to Act II is itself sectional, commencing chordally and continuing in imitative counterpoint; it suggests the form that has become known as **French overture** (p. 326). Landi's recitatives contain many repeated notes with minimal accompaniment. There are some strophic arias, and there are two *ariette* whose strophes are separated by instrumental *ritornelli*. In a comic duet, the pages ridicule Alexis. The "Lament" sung *a cappella* by Alexis's wife and parents closely resembles a chromatic madrigal written in three sections separated by recitatives.

Within the next decade, Roman opera changed considerably. The composers and librettists who created the first operas viewed this kind of composition as *dramma per musica*—drama through music—with drama being of first importance. But by c. 1642, the quality of the music and the production of an entertaining spectacle had become the main concern, and the integrity of the drama was minor. The mythological stories that formed the basis for most of the operas were expanded and altered considerably.

The extent to which Roman opera changed may be seen in the work of Luigi Rossi (c. 1597–1653), who composed only two operas. For Carnival, 1642, Rossi wrote for Cardinal Antonio Barberini the opera *Il palazzo incantato* (The enchanted palace; libretto, Rospigliosi). The opera has numerous characters, in addition to chorus and dancers; the plot and subplots are filled with intrigue and lightened by comedy. Its performance was an extravagant spectacle lasting seven hours. In 1646, when the French court wanted to produce an opera similar to those presented by Barberini, Cardinal Mazarin (1602–61) invited Rossi to Paris. Mazarin, an Italian who became a naturalized French citizen in 1639, had attended a performance of Landi's *Il Sant' Alessio* at Palazzo Barberini in 1632. He wanted to produce Italian opera in France for political reasons, but the first three Italian operas he produced at court were not well received. Rossi's *Orfeo* is the first Italian opera written specifically for Paris. It is another spectacular opera—the librettist (Francesco Buti) buried the simple mythological tale

in intrigue and comedy that required many additional characters and scenes and, of course, much more music for solos, choruses, and dancing. Rossi was one of the leading Roman composers of vocal music—his chamber cantatas are excellent—and *Orfeo* contains many beautiful arias and ensembles. The performance of *Orfeo* at the French royal court in March 1647 lasted six hours and was such a success that it was repeated once before and six times after Lent.

Venice

In Venice, after political upheaval in 1582, the governing Council of Ten was actually a council of seventeen, for *Il Doge* and his six ducal councillors were voting members. During Doge Marino Grimani's reign (1597–1605), it was customary to perform a *favola pastorale* (pastoral fable) in the courtyard of the Doge's palace three times a year. Though songs and choruses were included, these pastoral presentations cannot be considered early operas. Monteverdi's madrigal cycle *Il combattimento di Tancredi e Clorinda* was performed at the Mocegino home in 1624, and his (lost) opera *Proserpina rapita* was presented as part of the nuptial festivities honoring Giuistiana Mocenigo and Lorenzo Giustiniani in 1630. There is no indication that other operas were performed in Venice at that time.

In fact, little dramatic music was performed in Venice until the first public opera house, Teatro San Cassiano, was established there in 1637. The venture was largely supported by subscription sales of boxes, but single admission tickets were available. The inaugural production was *L'Andromeda,* composed by Francesco Manelli (c. 1595–1667), a friend of Landi. For economy, roles were doubled—Manelli, a bass, sang the roles of Neptune and Astarco; Maddalena, his wife, sang the Prologue and the role of Andromeda. Manelli wrote at least four more operas for Venice.

When Teatro San Cassiano proved successful, several more opera houses were constructed, including Teatro SS Giovanni e Paolo (1639). In the seventeenth century, a Venetian theater was usually named for the parish in which it was located; a theater was built and owned by a noble family but was managed by an impresario. Francesco Manelli was both impresario and composer. Monteverdi's *Il ritorno d'Ulisse in patria* was produced at San Cassiano in 1640 and 1641 and *L'incoronazione di Poppea* at SS Giovanni e Paolo in 1642.

After Monteverdi's death (1643), Pietro Francesco Cavalli (1602–76) was the leading composer of operas in Venice. Cavalli's association with Monteverdi began in 1616 when, as an unusually gifted boy soprano, Cavalli entered the *cappella* of St. Mark's; his voice matured to tenor, and he remained in the *cappella*. In 1639, he was appointed second organist at St. Mark's. Almost simultaneously, he invested in Teatro San Cassiano and began to write operas for production there. It was profitable financially; for composing an opera and supervising its first performances he earned as much as the annual salary of the *maestro di cappella* at St. Mark's. Most of Cavalli's 33 operas were written for performance in Venice; some were composed for Florence, Naples, and Milan. *Egisto* (1643), *Giasone* (Jason; 1649), *Xerse* (Xerxes; 1655), and *Erismena* (1656) became part of standard opera repertoire in Italy during the 1660s and 1670s. *Giasone* was Cavalli's most popular opera.

After much hesitation, Cavalli accepted Mazarin's commission to compose an opera for the marriage of Louis XIV to Maria Theresia of Spain in 1660. Cavalli spent almost two years in Paris, but little music survives from that visit. *Ercole amante* (Hercules in love; 1662) was not completed in time for the wedding festivities and a revised version of *Xerse* was substituted. Noticeable alterations were the transposition of Xerxes's role down an octave, to place it in bass-baritone range, and the insertion of ballet scenes by Lully.

For the approximately 25 years that Cavalli composed operas, his style of writing remained fairly stable. Free verse is usually set as recitative accompanied only by basso continuo; in almost all of the rare instances when strings provide recitative accompaniment, viols are used instead of violins. *Ercole amante* is exceptional in using violins in the five-part string ensemble accompanying recitative; Cavalli may have included them for contrast because Ercole was a bass, or because the opera was for Paris and Lully used that instrumentation in his ballets (see p. 325). Cavalli's arias are strophic, usually in triple meter, with text set syllabically except for occasional small flourishes to beautify the vocal line. Almost all of his operas contain at least one lament; these are either modeled on Monteverdi's *Lament d'Arianna* or use an ostinato bass based on a descending tetrachord (sometimes labeled "passacaglia"). Cavalli wrote orchestral *sinfonie* and *ritornelli* and made some use of *stile concitato,* the excited style featuring measured tremolo. Dance music indicated in the libretti is rarely found in his scores; when present, only the basso continuo line for it is notated.

Cavalli's main competitor in the area of opera was Antonio Cesti (1623–69), whose opera *Orontea* (perf. Venice, 1649) enjoyed popularity in Italy equal to that of Cavalli's *Giasone*. Cesti, a Franciscan monk, was assigned variously to the monastery at Arezzo, to San Croce in Florence, and to the Franciscan seminary at Volterra. (When Pietro Cesti became a monk, he chose to use the name "Antonio." His given name was Pietro. He has often been referred to, erroneously, as "Marc' Antonio.") At Volterra, where he enjoyed Medici patronage, he sang in some operas. Conflict between his religious duties and his secular interests was finally resolved in 1659 when, with the Pope's assistance, he secured release from his monastic vows but remained a secular priest. Cesti spent considerable time at the imperial court in Innsbruck, where 5 of his 15 operas were produced; 5 of the others were written for Vienna. He wrote at least 68 secular cantatas and 5 sacred vocal pieces.

Il pomo d'oro (The golden apple; composed 1666–68; perf. Vienna, 13–14 July 1668) is more spectacular than most of Cesti's operas because it was created for and performed as part of the wedding festivities of Emperor Leopold I (r. 1657–1705) and Princess Margherita of Spain, and funds available for its production were unlimited. Leopold I (1640–1705) was not only a major patron of music, he was a composer. He was especially interested in dramatic works and composed several; some of the arias in *Il pomo d'oro* are by him. That opera, a lavish court production, is in five acts, with many choruses, and a cast and orchestra larger than those in most of Cesti's operas. Its overture is in three sections: the first two, considered together, resemble French overture; the third section is contrapuntal and imitative. Instruments double the chorus parts, accompany, and provide *ritornelli* in *Di bellezza e di valore* (For beauty and for valor), which is largely contrapuntal and imitative.

Baroque Vocal Music

(a)

(b)

Example 15.5 Opening measures of (*a*) Sinfonia and (*b*) trumpet aria *Vitrici schiere trombe guerriere,* from Act I, Scene 1 of Sartorio's opera *Adelaide* (Venice, 1672).

Orontea is typical of Cesti's operatic writing. Usually, his arias are strophic; some use is made of *arioso,* accompanied solo in a style midway between recitative and aria. A majority of Cesti's arias have only basso continuo accompaniment; for *ritornelli* he used two violins with basso continuo. In general, his music is not as vigorous and forceful as that of Cavalli. Cesti's best writing is found in comic scenes, and in lyrical arias and duets. For example, in *Orontea* the servant Gelone has some solo comic scenes and sings some of the finest arias in the entire opera.

Between the time of its inception and the time of Cesti's death, opera changed considerably. After 1650, music was no longer the accessory vehicle through which drama was effectively presented, in the manner of the ancient Greeks, but had become the prime factor in opera, and drama was accessory to the presentation of music, which was concentrated in solo singing. Recitative and aria were two distinct types of solo song, with arioso midway between the two. Vocal ensembles were seldom used, and instrumental music consisted of overtures, introductions, and *ritornelli.* The view of opera prevalent in the late 1660s and the general formal outline then in use remained fairly constant for approximately the next two centuries.

Venetian opera was spread throughout Italy by a number of opera troupes that traveled from city to city, obtaining patronage in cities they visited, using the services of local musicians when necessary, and giving performances for paid admission. A troupe of this kind, called the Febi Armonici, was instrumental in establishing opera in Naples. Opera was disseminated also by aristocratic patrons (e.g., the Barberini) who, for various reasons, went into exile in other countries; by foreign rulers or officials (e.g., Mazarin) who experienced opera at other courts and commissioned similar works for special occasions at their own; by Italian composers (e.g., Cesti) who secured appointments in other countries; and by foreign composers (e.g., Heinrich Schütz) who studied or worked in Italy for a time and then returned to their own lands. Opera, which originated in the experiments of a handful of humanists, literati, and musicians in Florence in 1600, was to be one of the major forms of Western music.

During the second half of the seventeenth century, Venice remained the principal Italian center of opera. Among the principal composers there in the 1660s and 1670s were Antonio Sartorio (1630–80) and Giovanni Legrenzi (1626–90). In 1675–85 operas by Carlo Pallavicino (d. 1688) were successful.

Sartorio's operas contain a large number of arias of many different kinds; some of his best pieces are laments and trumpet arias. *L'Adelaide* (Adelaide; 1672) seems to be the first of many Venetian operas specifying trumpets in the orchestration, mentioning trumpets in the texts, and incorporating trumpetlike figures in the vocal line (ex. 15.5). Sartorio's operas

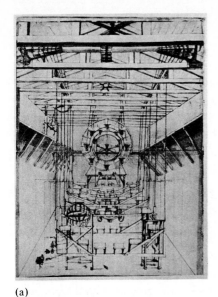
(a)

(b)

Figure 15.7 (*a*) Machinery used for (*b*) cloud scene in Legrenzi's opera *Germanico sul Reno* (Venice, 1676).

are on heroic subjects, both mythological and historical. He was especially adept at expressing deep passions musically. An example is the scene in *Antonino e Pompeiano* (Antonino and Pompei; 1677) where Antonino's assassination by the liberators of Rome is depicted on stage. Another aspect of Sartorio's talent in portraying affections is his juxtaposition of the heroic and the banal for comic relief.

Legrenzi, an organist, was active in many areas of composition. His operas are heroic-comic, with complicated plots requiring large casts and much machinery (fig. 15.7). Often in arias he combined two or more formal aspects; for example, **motto**, ostinato bass, and da capo (ABA) form may appear in the same aria. A motto aria is one in which the opening phrase of the vocal solo is presented, is followed by a rest or two, then is restated and the aria proceeds. In the aria *Vanne ingrata crudel e spietata* from *Il Giustino* (1683), Legrenzi used a motto beginning and a bass line of constantly moving eighth and sixteenth notes; both features were used frequently by other composers in the late seventeenth and early eighteenth centuries (ex. 15.6).

Pallavicino's first two operas, *Demetrio* and *Aureliano,* were produced in Venice in 1666, when he was organist at the church of San Antonio, in Padua. From 1667 to 1673, he served as a vice-Kapellmeister at the Dresden court, where the aged Schütz (1585–1672) was Kapellmeister. (Schütz is credited with

Example 15.6 Beginning of aria *Vanne ingrata crudel e spietata* from Legrenzi's opera *Il Giustino.* Note the motto opening and the running bass line.

composing the first German opera in 1627, a setting of Rinuccini's *Dafne* as adapted by Martin Opitz. See p. 328.) Pallavicino returned to Padua for six months, then became music director of Ospedale degli Incurabili, Venice. For the next ten years, he was one of the leading opera composers in Venice. All but 2 of his 24 operas were produced there. In his early operas, the arias are simple songs with basso continuo accompaniment; after 1674 he increasingly used *da capo* aria and orchestral accompaniment.

Baroque Vocal Music

Johann Georg III, Elector of Saxony, wanted to establish Italian opera at the Dresden court and persuaded Pallavicino to return there as Kapellmeister in 1685. However, all of the six operas Pallavicino completed during the next three years were produced in Venice. *Antiope,* unfinished at the time of his death, was completed by N. A. Strungk and was performed at Dresden in 1689.

Naples

In the first half of the seventeenth century, the main centers of musical activity in Naples were the viceregal chapel and important churches and other religious institutions. Theatrical presentations and musical entertainments such as *ballo* and *mascherata* formed a part of special celebrations, but opera was not introduced to Naples until c. 1652 when a traveling troupe, Febi Armonici, presented some Venetian operas there. A Neapolitan, Francesco Provenzale (c. 1626–1704), became associated with that troupe; in 1653 Febi Armonici presented his first opera, *Il Ciro,* at Teatro SS. Giovanni e Paolo. Also, Provenzale arranged some of Cavalli's operas for performance by the troupe. In 1658 Provenzale's *Il Theseo* (Theseus; libretto extant) was performed at Teatro S. Bartolomeo. Only two operas by Provenzale survive: *Il schiavo di sua moglie* (The servant of his wife; 1671) and *La Stellidaura vendicata* (Stellidaura avenged; 1674). In both operas there is free alternation of recitatives, ariosos, and arias, and some use of ensembles. Very few of the arias are in the *da capo* form that became a feature of Neapolitan opera at the end of the century. In 1663 Provenzale was appointed *maestro* at Conservatorio S. Maria di Loreto. There, he included in his teaching the performance of sacred opera and in 1672 composed two such works: *La fenice d'Avila* (The phoenix of Avila) and *La colomba ferita* (The wounded dove).

In 1676 Filippo Coppola, *maestro di cappella* at the viceregal court, established the custom of chapel musicians producing operas for royal name days and anniversaries. On other occasions, itinerant companies performed operas at the palace. When Coppola died in 1680, Provenzale sought the viceregal chapelmaster position, but it was awarded to P. A. Ziani, and after his death (1684), Alessandro Scarlatti was appointed to the post.

More than half of the operas produced in Naples were by Scarlatti, but Teatro San Bartolomeo offered also fine works by north-Italian opera composers such as Legrenzi, Sartorio, Pallavicino, Bononcini, and Pasquini. During the rule of the Duke of Medinacelli (r. 1695–1702), a generous patron of music, Teatro San Bartolomeo was enlarged, and Neapolitan opera rose to unprecedented heights of splendor. The Duke's departure may have induced Scarlatti to leave. As a result of the Spanish war of succession, the Kingdom of Naples became Habsburg property in 1707. When Scarlatti returned, at the invitation of the Austrian Viceroy, Grimani, sacred opera and comic opera assumed greater prominence.

By the end of the seventeenth century, operas composed at Naples exhibited features that became standard in eighteenth-century Italian opera. Two distinct types of recitative emerged: (1) *recitativo secco* (dry recitative), in which the solo voice was accompanied by basso continuo only (harpsichord and sustaining bass instrument), used for lengthy dialogue and monologue, to proceed quickly through the narrative; and (2) *recitativo accompagnato* (accompanied recitative), in which the solo voice was orchestrally accompanied, used for extremely emotional or dramatically tense situations. *Recitativo accompagnato* was not always orchestrally accompanied throughout; short portions of it might be sung unaccompanied, or with basso continuo, and the orchestra used to reenforce the high points or to punctuate emotional outbursts in the solo line.

Commentary and soliloquy were set as aria, for which a variety of forms were used. Simple ternary form (ABA) was lengthened considerably. Often composers did not write out the repeat of the A section, but simply indicated it by the words *da capo* (from the beginning) placed at the end of the B section, and designated the conclusion of the aria by the word *Fine* (end) placed at the end of the A section. If the aria begins with an orchestral introduction that is not to be repeated when the A section is returned, the words *dal segno al fine* (from the sign to *fine*) appear at the end of the B section of the aria, and the appropriate sign of congruence indicates the place to which the performers return.

Composers continued to use the term *arioso* (arialike) to denote that a melody is neither as rhythmically free as in recitative nor as regular and lyrical as in aria. Actually, *arioso* was in use before speechlike *recitativo secco* came into existence.

The transition from the style of Baroque opera prevalent in the last decades of the seventeenth century to the newer style used in the eighteenth century is evident in the operas of Alessandro Scarlatti, who is no longer considered the founder of the Neapolitan school but the composer who brought it into prominence.

Alessandro Scarlatti

Alessandro Scarlatti (1660–1725) was born in Palermo and, presumably, received his early education there. At the age of 12, he was sent to Rome with his two sisters, Anna Maria (1661–1703) and Melchiorra Brigida (1663–1736). Both girls were singers. Nothing further is recorded concerning Alessandro until 12 April 1678, when he married Antonia Anzalone. Two of their ten children, Pietro (1679–1750) and Domenico (1685–1757), had careers in music.

Anna Maria Scarlatti enjoyed a singing career. She appeared in Pietro Agostini's (c. 1635–80) *Il ratto delle sabine* (The rape of the Sabines; Venice, 1680). She married twice; her second husband, shipowner Nicolo Barbapiccola, became impresario of Teatro San Bartolomeo in Naples in 1703, and he staged Domenico Scarlatti's first operas. Melchiorra eventually settled in Naples. Allegedly, she was influential in 1684 in securing Alessandro's appointment as *maestro di cappella* at the Viceroy's chapel there.

In 1679, Alessandro Scarlatti's first oratorio and his first opera were performed in Rome. Queen Christina of Sweden and Cardinals Benedetto Pamphili and Pietro Ottoboni became his patrons. All of them maintained theaters in their palaces, and Scarlatti composed at least four more operas, six more oratorios, and many cantatas under their auspices before moving to Naples in 1684. At that time there was no activity in public theaters in Rome because of the opposition of Pope Innocent XI (r. 1676–89).

Naples was not a center of opera when Scarlatti went there. That it became one is largely due to his endeavors—he composed over half of the new operas presented in Naples between 1684 and 1702. More than 40 of his operas from those years survive, and many of his works are lost if, as he claimed, *Lucio Manlio* (1705) is his 88th stage work. The main patrons of opera were the viceroys, who had theaters in

Alessandro Scarlatti. Artist is unknown. *(Civico Museo Bibliografico Musicale, Bologna.)*

the palace and summer residence and promoted the public theaters. The principal public theater was San Bartolomeo; it had a permanent opera company, and Scarlatti became its director. It was customary in Naples for the first performance of a cantata or opera to be presented at the palace; thereafter, the production was transferred to Teatro San Bartolomeo for public enjoyment.

In 1702, Alessandro Scarlatti and his son Domenico visited the Medici court in Florence, where Alessandro endeavored, unsuccessfully, to secure appointments for both of them. Next, he went to Rome (1703). There he found that public theaters had been closed since 1700, and there were few performances of opera in private theaters. With little opportunity for performance of new operas, Scarlatti turned to composition of cantatas, serenatas, and oratorios and produced them in profusion. He was elected a member of the Arcadian Academy and was initiated at the same time as Pasquini and Corelli. Scarlatti supervised the production of some of his operas in Venice, but the Venetians were extremely critical of *Il Mitridate Eupatore* (1707), one of his best operas.

Example 15.7 Scarlatti used *stile concitato* effectively in Griselda's aria *Figlio! Tiranno!* from Act II, Scene 4 of *La Griselda*, as this excerpt (mm. 1–6) shows. *(From* The Operas of Alessandro Scarlatti, *edited by Donald Grout and Joscelyn Godwin. © 1975 by The President and Fellows of Harvard College. Reprinted by permission of Harvard University Press, Cambridge, MA.)*

In 1708, at the invitation of the new Austrian Viceroy of Naples, Cardinal Grimani, Scarlatti resumed his former position at that court. Under Grimani's patronage, he composed 11 operas, including *Il Tigrane* (1715). Around 1706, Neapolitans had become interested in comic opera in vernacular dialect with popular style music, and works of that kind flourished in small theaters there. Scarlatti wrote comic *intermezzi* for three of his operas, and composed one comic opera, *Il trionfo dell' onore* (The triumph of honor; 1718). Also, c. 1715, he began to compose instrumental works, such as *concerti grossi* (see p. 367).

From 1718 to 1722 Scarlatti lived in Rome. There, he composed the operas *Telemaco* (1718), *Marco Attilio Regolo* (Marco Attilio, ruler; 1719), and *La Griselda* (1721). The latter is his last surviving opera. With the exception of a minor part for tenor, all roles in *La Griselda* were written for castrati. Its performance marked the professional debut of Giovanni Carestini (c. 1705–59), one of the most

talented sopranos of his day, as Griselda. In 1722 Scarlatti returned to Naples and spent his remaining years in comparative retirement there.

Scarlatti labeled most of his operas *dramma per musica*. He preferred serious plots with happy endings; most of them concern rulers' love affairs and their complications. Consequently, the characters are rulers, their confidants, and their servants and most often are presented in pairs. Rarely are the characters mythological; Scarlatti preferred historical or imaginary personages, stylized, with no inner life revealed. His musical settings contain many arias, usually quite short, set off by recitatives in which the musical interest is minimal. Recitative-aria pairing became standard. However, he wrote many scenes of dialogue in which no aria occurs, e.g., *La Griselda*, Act I, Scenes 10 and 16. Act II, Scene 4 of *La Griselda* (DWMA112), consists of a long *secco* recitative dialogue between Griselda and Ottone, followed by Griselda's *da capo* aria *Figlio! Tiranno!* (Son! Tyrant!). In that aria, the *stile concitato* of the string orchestra mirrors Griselda's agitation (ex. 15.7). In Scarlatti's

Example 15.8 Measures 1–6 of the *siciliana* aria *Colomba innamorata* sung by Ottone in Act II, Scene 2 of *La Griselda. (From* The Operas of Alessandro Scarlatti, *edited by Donald Grout and Joscelyn Godwin.* © *1975 by The President and Fellows of Harvard College. Reprinted by permission of Harvard University Press, Cambridge, MA.)*

early operas, arias in ABA form are common; after c. 1698, full *da capo* arias predominate. Rarely do his aria melodies exceed a tenth in range. Most of the arias in his early operas have only basso continuo accompaniment; for the longer *da capo* arias, orchestral accompaniment is provided. Customarily, Scarlatti concluded an act with an important aria sung by a major character.

Since *La Griselda* concerns the King and Queen of Sicily, it was natural for Scarlatti to include some *siciliana* arias. Derived from folk song, a *siciliana* melody is simple, *cantabile,* in slow $\frac{6}{8}$ or $\frac{12}{8}$ meter (ex. 15.8). Usually associated with pastoral scenes, it sometimes is rather melancholy. Frequently, Scarlatti used the Neapolitan sixth chord in sicilianas and placed the flat supertonic in the upper part.

The orchestral *sinfonie* Scarlatti composed for overtures to his operas usually have no musical connection with the operas they introduce. The *sinfonia* that opens *La Griselda* is an **Italian overture,** written in three distinct sections, in Presto-Adagio-Presto order of tempo. The last Presto has a gigue-like rhythm.

Near the end of Scarlatti's career, his contemporaries considered his music out-of-date. Nevertheless, the era of Italian Baroque opera composition that began with Monteverdi and proceeded through Cavalli and Cesti achieved consummation in Scarlatti's work.

France

When Maria de' Medici was married to Henri IV of France in Florence in 1600, Peri's *Euridice* was part of the nuptial festivities. Opera was favored in Medici courts in Italy, but it was some time before it caught a foothold in France. There were several reasons for its failure to do so: a long-standing tradition of theater in Paris, the French love of staged dance (ballet), and the fact that the French language is difficult to sing. The Confrérie de la Passion, a theatrical association, was organized in Paris in 1402 and by 1420 had established itself in a permanent indoor theater; in 1518 the Confrérie obtained a monopoly on theatrical production in Paris. Professional theater was strong enough in Paris in 1608 that one prestigious

Baroque Vocal Music

troupe was permitted to call itself The King's Players (*Les Comédiens du roi*), and it was not long before a theater was constructed in the palace. In the early seventeenth century, the principal French playwright was Alexandre Hardy (c. 1575–c. 1630), who supplied The King's Players with several hundred tragicomedies. He was followed by three outstanding dramatists: Pierre Corneille (1606–84) and Jean Racine (1639–99), noted for their tragedies, and J.-B. Molière (1622–73), who is remembered principally for his comedies.

Ballet de cour (court ballet) had been a featured form of entertainment at the French court since the performance of *Circé ou le Balet comique de la Royne* (Circe or the Queen's dramatic ballet) at the palace on 15 October 1581. In *Circé*, poetry, music, decor, and dance were combined to support a central dramatic action—destruction of the power of the enchantress Circé and the reestablishment of order and harmony. Baltasar de Beaujoyleux (c. 1535–c. 1587), who planned and created *Circé*, stated in his preface to the published score (Paris, 1582) that he used the word *comique* in the title to indicate that the work had dramatic unity. *Circé* is musical drama; as such, it is precursor to opera in France.

Louis, son of Maria de' Medici and Henri IV, was born in 1601. After Henri was assassinated in 1610, Maria served as regent for her son, Louis XIII (r. 1610–43), but soon sought political power for herself. For a time, Richelieu (1585–1642), minister at court, was able to reconcile mother, son, and the French nobility. In 1622 Richelieu was created Cardinal. Eventually, Louis believed Richelieu alone could maintain order in France, and in 1624 named him first minister; Richelieu gained almost complete control of the French government. Among those whom Richelieu brought into government office was Cardinal Jules Mazarin (1602–61), an Italian who had served Cardinal Antonio Barberini in Rome. After Richelieu's death, Mazarin became principal minister of France. He had experienced opera in Italy and saw it as a means of political intrigue in France. More importantly, it could divert attention from his own political maneuvers. To that end, he introduced Italian opera at court and invited Italian opera companies and Italian composers to Paris. Because of the French penchant for ballet, the Italian operas that Mazarin brought to Paris were adapted to include ballet scenes.

Louis XIII died in 1643 and was succeeded by his five-year-old son, Louis XIV (r. 1643–1715), with Anne of Austria as matriarchal regent and Mazarin as minister. When plans were made for Louis XIV's marriage to Maria Teresia of Spain in 1660, Mazarin invited Cavalli to compose an opera for performance at the nuptial festivities. Cavalli did not complete *Ercole amante* in time, and a revised version of his *Xerse* was substituted. (A Spanish opera was also written for that wedding; see p. 329.)

When Mazarin died (1661), Louis XIV determined to assume complete personal control of the government. His attitude is understandable, in view of the fact that, though king, his affairs had been dominated by his mother and the chief minister for 18 years. He had a palace constructed at Versailles for three reasons: to get away from the noise of Paris, to create an appropriate setting for a king and his court, and to provide residences under his watchful eye for the most important nobles. *Privilèges* (permits) to establish theaters and to print music and books had to be obtained from the office of the king's minister of finance, J. B. Colbert. Louis XIV was interested in music, dance, and the theater. At the age of 13, he danced on stage for the first time in *Ballet de Casandre* (1651). Two years later, in *Ballet de la nuit* (Ballet of the night), a young Florentine named Giovanni Battista Lulli danced on stage alongside the king.

Jean-Baptiste Lully

Giovanni Battista Lulli (1632–87), a Florentine miller's son, was brought to France in 1646 by Roger de Lorraine (Chevalier de Guise) to help his niece, Mlle de Montpensier, learn the Italian language. Lulli stayed at the Montpensier establishment six years. There, he became an accomplished dancer, learned to play guitar and violin, and heard *airs* and dialogues composed by Michel Lambert (1610–96), who became music master to the king in 1661. Lulli retained the Italian spelling of his name until 1661, when he became a naturalized French citizen. In 1662, he

Jean-Baptiste Lully.

Pierre Perrin (c. 1620–75), a poet and librettist of mediocre talent, was influential in convincing Colbert, the king's minister of finance, that France should have its own opera. In June 1669 Perrin obtained a 12-year *privilège* to establish academies for the performance of opera anywhere in the French realm. He wanted to produce French-language operas that were Italian in style. Earlier, Perrin had collaborated with composer Robert Cambert (c. 1627–77) in writing two *pastorales*: *Pastoral d'Issy* and *Ariane ou Le mariage de Bacchus* (Ariadne, or Bacchus's marriage). Both are lost. In March 1671 the academy in Paris opened with Cambert's and Perrin's opera *Pomone*; they enjoyed the success of 146 performances. Only a portion of *Pomone* is extant—the overture, prologue, and a few pages of music from Act II. Perrin had hired two business managers whose methods were somewhat unscrupulous; as a result, he found himself in debtors' prison. Lully, who was aware of Perrin's predicament and also of the success of *Pomone,* purchased Perrin's *privilège* for a sum sufficient to settle Perrin's debts and to provide him with an adequate pension.

Next, Lully contracted with architect-machinist Carlo Vigrane to construct an acceptable opera theater and selected Philippe Quinault (1635–88) as librettist. During 1673–83 Lully composed 13 operas—a new opera each year except 1681. Quinault provided the libretti for 11 of them, and Louis XIV supplied the subject matter for several, including *Persée, Amadis, Roland,* and *Armide.*

Lully's principal contribution to the development of music was in the field of opera. However, after 1683 he composed a considerable amount of religious music for Louis XIV's royal chapel. On 8 January 1687, to celebrate the king's recovery from an operation, Lully conducted more than 150 musicians in a performance of his *Te Deum* (written in 1677). It was Lully's custom to beat time by striking the floor with a cane—in French, a *baton,* or stick. During this performance, he inadvertently hit one of his toes with the sharp point of that cane. Despite medical treatment, gangrene set in. Lully stubbornly refused to permit the physician to amputate the toe. His condition deteriorated, and he died on 22 March 1687.

married Lambert's daughter Madeleine. During the next three years, Lambert and Lully collaborated in composing music for three court ballets.

In 1652, when Mlle de Montpensier was exiled for political reasons, Lully went to Paris. In February 1653, he and the king danced in the *Ballet de la nuit.* In March, Lully was appointed *compositeur de la musique instrumentale du Roi* (composer of instrumental music to the king). He was responsible for composing instrumental music for court ballets, and he sang and danced in some of them, also. By 1656 he had received permission to conduct the 16 *petits violons,* whose performance practices he disciplined—he regulated bowings and forbade excessive ornamentation and unorthodox improvisation techniques; by 1666 the *petits violons* and the *24 violons du Roi* were combined under his direction for court ballet performances. Lully furnished some ballet *entrées* for Corneille's *Oedipe* (Oedipus) in 1664, and from 1664 to 1670 collaborated with Molière in writing *comédies-ballets.* In 1671, Lully terminated his collaboration with Molière, who then used Marc-Antoine Charpentier's music.

Lully's Works

Lully's stage works may be grouped by genres into three temporal periods: (1) 1653–63, *ballets de cour;* (2) 1663–72, *pastorales, comédies-ballets,* and *tragédies-ballets;* and (3) 1672–87, large stage works. The latter group includes the *pastorale Les fêtes de l'Amour et de Bacchus* (The festivals of Love and of Bacchus; 1672), the 13 operas termed *tragédies lyriques,* the 2 ballets *Le triomphe de l'amour* (Love's triumph; 1681) and *Le temple de la paix* (The temple of peace; 1685), and *Acis et Galatée,* a *pastorale héroïque* (1686). At the time of his death, Lully had completed only the overture and Act I of *Achille et Polyxène;* Acts II–V were composed by Colasse.

During his first decade at the French royal court, Lully learned to differentiate between Italian and French musical styles. Until 1661, most of the music he contributed to the court ballets was Italianate. The ballet *L'amour malade* (Sick love; 1657), for which he composed all of the music, is a short Italian *opera buffa* (comic opera) within a French ballet. By 1661, he distinguished clearly between French and Italian styles of music and reserved songs in the Italian language for comic scenes or laments. He became especially adept at setting comedy and had a special talent for using comic scenes to inject social satire. From time to time, Lully's operas drew adverse criticism from clergy and from some Sorbonne professors who interpreted certain passages in the texts as veiled criticism of political conditions in France. Their criticism was not unjustified. For example, in Act IV, Scene 1 of *Alceste,* when Charon exacts tribute from the shades crossing the River Styx, the comment is made, "It is not enough to pay while alive, one must still pay after death."

Lully introduced new dances into the *ballet de cour*—bourrées and minuets supplanted courantes and gaillardes. Gradually, he transformed *ballet de cour* from a collection of dances and autonomous scenes into a dramatic spectacle with a prologue and choral finales.

In the *comédies-ballets* composed during 1663–72, Lully began to write passages of recitative and wrote short *airs* with words set syllabically in short phrases; frequently, he used anapestic rhythms (short-short-long). Lully and Molière introduced pastoral scenes into some of the *comédies-ballets. Les amants magnifiques* (The magnificent lovers; 1670) contains some features of the operas Lully composed later: a prologue sung throughout, *ritournelles* for winds, use of the orchestra to dramatize entrances (e.g., trumpets and drums at Apollo's entrance). Louis XIV danced the role of Apollo in *Les amants magnifiques,* which actually combines *ballet de cour* and *comédie-ballet.* In *comédie-ballet,* part of the text is sung and part of it is spoken. In some of the Lully-Molière *comédies-ballets,* e.g., *Le bourgeois gentilhomme* (The middle-class gentleman; 1670), there is a merging of music, dance, and poetry that foreshadows *opéra comique. Psyché* (1671), whose libretto resulted from the collaboration of Molière, Pierre Corneille, and Quinault, was called a *tragédie-ballet* when performed in January 1671. In 1678 Lully and Thomas Corneille transformed it into a *tragédie lyrique* (i.e., an opera) by adding recitatives and making some minor alterations.

Example 15.9 These recitatives sung by Céphise and Straton in *Alceste* exemplify Lully's careful attention to correct declamation when setting text.

The *tragédies lyriques* are on a larger scale than Lully's earlier works and have continuous music. Their subjects are drawn from Greek mythology or Latin and Spanish chivalric romances. In most of Lully's operas, the drama deals with the conflict between glory and duty, or glory and love. The main plot concerns a pair of lovers and one or more rivals—usually a deity is involved—and in the subplot persons of lesser importance are implicated in parallel intrigue. All of Lully's *tragédies lyriques* are constructed with a prologue and five acts; this became standard in French opera. A typical Lully opera opens with an overture, is followed by a prologue that has little connection with the drama that ensues, and then, usually, the overture is repeated. In *Amadis* (1684), however, the two main characters in the prologue have roles in the tragedy.

In composing *tragédie lyrique,* Lully considered the poetry of prime importance and insisted that the music be appropriate for correct declamation of the text (see example 15.9). The drama was developed through simple recitative, which Lully insisted be sung exactly as notated, with no added embellishments and no alteration in the rhythm other than the fluctuations specifically notated. An example is the monologue from Act II, Scene 5 of *Armide.* Armide, knife in hand, stands by the sleeping warrior Renaud, her captive. It is in her power to kill him, but her love for him prevents her from doing so. In this monologue, rests and short phrases enhance the drama.

In many recitative-air combinations, Lully used orchestra for introductory *ritournelle* and to accompany the air but only basso continuo for the recitative portion. An example is *Le ciel protège les héros* (Heaven protects the heroes) from *Alceste.* After 1679 Lully used accompanied recitative more often. In *Amadis* (1684) and *Roland* (1685), those leading roles are written principally in accompanied recitative. In the French opera of Lully's time, the distinction between accompanied recitative and air is not as great as that between recitative and aria in Italian opera. Lully's favorite small ensemble was the duo. Often, he involved the chorus in the action by writing short choral utterances of encouragement or supplication. The chorus was used also in **divertissements.** A divertissement (literally, diversion) is a section (or scene) within an act of a large stage work, such as opera, that consists of dances, vocal solos, and ensembles and may or may not be essential to the plot. At times, a divertissement is a spectacle, such as the wedding scene in *Roland.*

Lully's basic orchestration was for five-part strings, with occasional doubling by oboes and bassoons, plus basso continuo. A trio of two oboes and bassoon was frequently used in contrast with strings or in pastoral scenes. The funeral scene in *Alceste* (*Pompe funèbre,* Act III, Scene 5) opens with music by five-part string orchestra with *basso continuo*; two flutes (or recorders) are added when the choral singing commences, and for *ritournelles* only flutes (or recorders) and basso continuo are retained for the soft, plaintive (*doux et plaintif*) mood. When other instruments, such as trumpets or drums, were required for special effects, Lully added them, as he did in the Prologue to *Alceste* before and during the appearance

Figure 15.8 A contemporary (1676) engraving of a scene from a performance of Lully's *Alceste* at Versailles.

Baroque Vocal Music

of *La Gloire* (Glory), who, befitting her divinity, descends from on high with martial harmonies. (The lengthy prologue to *Alceste* contains numerous examples of Lully's effective orchestration.)

Lully had used **French overtures** in his *ballets de cour*; he continued to use that formal pattern for the overtures to his *tragédies lyriques*. A French overture is in two sections, each of them marked to be repeated. The overture commences with a slow section that is homophonic and features dotted rhythms. The second section, in a fast tempo, is fugal or quasi-fugal and concludes with a brief return to the slow tempo and dotted rhythms of the beginning (see overture to *Alceste*, DWMA113). The overall mood of a French overture is serious, dignified, and festive.

Lully's *tragédies lyriques* set the standard for French opera for the eighteenth century. Succeeding composers made few alterations in his basic plan, other than to expand the *divertissement* scenes containing ballets and choruses. Increased emphasis on ballet is reflected also in the creation of *opéra-ballet* by André Campra (1660–1744). In *opéra-ballet* there is an overall idea but each act is independent, with its action only loosely related to the main plot, and each act contains a divertissement. Campra's first *opéra-ballet* was *L'Europe galante* (1697), whose four *entrées* are set in different countries: France, Spain, Italy, and Turkey.

The precision of Lully's orchestra was much admired, especially by foreign visitors at court. Georg Muffat (1653–1704), who studied with Lully, explained (in four languages) Lully's style and orchestral techniques in the Foreword to *Florilegium primum* (First flower garden; 1695). In the Foreword to *Florilegium secundum* (Second flower garden; 1698) Muffat discussed Lully's performance practices at greater length. Johann G. Conradi (d. 1699) is credited with introducing the French operatic style in Hamburg in the 1690s. Conradi and Johann S. Kusser (1660–1727), who studied with Lully for six years, used the French overture as an introductory movement in orchestral suites.

England

In England, opera was influenced by both French and Italian musical presentations. During the seventeenth century, there flourished in England a kind of aristocratic entertainment known as **masque,** so-named because in some portions of the performance participants wore masks. Based on an allegorical or mythological theme, a masque is a blend of lyric and dramatic poetry, song, dance, and instrumental music presented in elaborate settings.

Some of the finest court masques were written between 1605 and 1631 by poet laureate Ben Jonson (1573–1637) and were presented in settings created by stage architect Inigo Jones (1573–1652). Jonson's *Masque of Blackness* (1605) was the first masque to use a stage and curtain (instead of dispersed scenery in a room); at this point, masque moved out of the realm of court entertainment and into the realm of theater. *Masque of Blackness* is the first masque from which specific music survives—one song by Alfonso Ferrabosco (1578–1628) is extant. Ferrabosco composed music for several of Jonson's masques. Jonson structured the masque in five or six "entries"—the word "act" was not used—commencing with a prologue. Dance was considered the most important element in a masque; next, came the staging, with machinery and sets; then, the text, with music as a mere accessory to the total presentation. Usually, the plot was developed in spoken dialogue. An exception is Jonson's *Lovers Made Men* (1617), which, according to its preface, was sung throughout "after the Italian manner, *stylo recitativo,* by Master Nicholas Lanier." None of that music survives. Lanier (1588–1666) is credited with being the first to set English words in the style of Italian recitative in "Bring away this sacred tree," from *The Masque of Squires* (1617). That song is extant.

Masques were given privately during the period of Civil War (1642–49), the Commonwealth (1649–60), and the Restoration of Charles II (c. 1660–85). In 1653, Christopher Gibbons (1615–76) and Matthew Locke (c. 1621–77) were commissioned to compose the music for James Shirley's (1596–1666) *Cupid and Death,* which was given on March 26 to welcome the Portuguese ambassador. The music includes recitatives, airs, choruses, dances, and other instrumental pieces. *Cupid and Death* was revised in 1659 and given at the military grounds, Leicester Fields. Commencing in 1656, Locke composed music for several of Sir William Davenant's (1606–68) masques and "moral representations" and for theater productions of other authors.

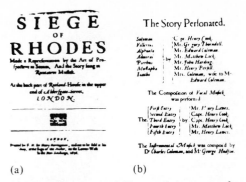

(a)   (b)

Figure 15.9 (a) Title page and (b) cast of characters of Davenant's *The Siege of Rhodes.*

Davenant's *The Siege of Rhodes* (1656) is often referred to as the first English opera. It was sung throughout, and reportedly most of the music was recitative; each of the five entries concludes with a chorus. Though the music is lost, copies of the published libretto survive (fig. 15.9). Five composers supplied the music for *The Siege of Rhodes,* the most significant being Henry Lawes and Matthew Locke. Locke wrote the music for the Fourth Entry and sang the role of the Admiral of Rhodes. *The Siege of Rhodes* differs from masque in having a unified dramatic plot; moreover, the plot concerns a contemporary heroic subject, rather than being mythological or allegorical as in early Italian opera.

John Blow's (1649–1708) setting of *Venus and Adonis* (1684) is variously regarded as masque and miniature opera. The work is sung throughout and contains elements of French and Italian opera, but it is not of the same stature as Purcell's *Dido and Aeneas. Venus and Adonis* is Blow's only dramatic work; he composed it at the king's request, as a vehicle for the king's mistress and her daughter.

During the Commonwealth period, Oliver Cromwell banned theater productions but permitted concerts, stage performances of plays with music, and "moral representations" that included music and dance. Henry Purcell (1659–95) expanded plays by inserting incidental music and lengthy *divertissements* of the type used in French opera; usually, a French overture preceded the play. In fact, the plays contained so much music that they virtually became semioperas.

Purcell's only true opera is *Dido and Aeneas* (1689), composed for performance at dancing master Josias Priest's School for Young Ladies, in Chelsea. The libretto is by Nahum Tate, who became England's poet laureate in 1692. (In 1696, Tate collaborated with Nicholas Brady in producing metrical versions of the Psalms. That Psalter was used in the American colonies during the eighteenth century.) *Dido and Aeneas* is based on the tragedy of Dido, Queen of Carthage, as related in Book IV of Vergil's *Aeneid.* The three-act opera has only four principal roles and takes a little over an hour to perform. The orchestra consists of strings and basso continuo. A French overture opens the opera. In addition to recitatives and arias, there are choruses and dances. Dido's lament ("When I am laid in earth") and the recitative preceding it ("Thy hand, Belinda") constitute one of the finest recitative-aria combinations in opera literature (DWMA114). Purcell cast Dido's lament as a binary over a bass line that is an extended chromatic passacaglia ground. The aria concludes with an orchestral passage in which melodic sighs lead directly into the final chorus, "With drooping wings." Other arias in this opera, and many of the arias Purcell composed for inclusion in plays, were constructed as binary over ostinato bass.

John Eccles's (c. 1668–1735) full-length opera *Semele* (1707) was never performed. This is regrettable, for performance of it might have inspired other English operas and laid the foundation for national English opera. Eccles's music is a fusion of English and Italian styles. His *secco* recitative is sensitive and well suited to the English language, and his arias are comparable in quality with those by Purcell.

During the eighteenth century, no English composer achieved lasting success in the field of opera. Though the vast majority of English people could not understand the Italian language, they favored Italian opera. They appreciated the beauty of Italian song and the excellent voices of famous Italian singers. Besides, printed program booklets contained both the Italian libretto and its English translation so the audience could comprehend the plot. The Haymarket theater, which opened in 1705 for the presentation of plays, was soon devoted to the production of Italian opera. In 1711 Handel's *Rinaldo* was presented there, and its favorable reception caused him to pursue a career as opera composer in England (see p. 420).

Germanic Lands

Many leading Italian composers worked at German and Austrian courts, but attempts to establish German (i.e., vernacular) opera met with limited success in many places. Italian opera fared better. In 1627 Martin Opitz adapted Rinuccini's libretto *Dafne* for Heinrich Schütz to set to music. This, the first opera created in Germany, was performed at Hartenfels castle in Torgau as part of the nuptial festivities for the Elector's daughter Sophia Eleonora and Landgrave Georg II of Hessen-Darmstadt. Unfortunately, all of Schütz's stage works are lost (see also p. 338).

Emperor Leopold I (1640–1705) was interested in music—especially dramatic music—and composed some operas, oratorios, arias, Masses, and other vocal works. His music is Venetian in style, but the language of the texts varies, Latin being used for the liturgical music, Italian for oratorios, and Italian and German for individual arias and stage works. As second son of Emperor Ferdinand III, Leopold had received a humanistic education rather than being trained as future emperor; when his elder brother died, Leopold became King of Hungary (1655) and Bohemia (1656), and he succeeded his father as Holy Roman Emperor (r. 1657–1705). During Leopold's reign, the Hofkapelle was expanded considerably, and many Italian composers and musicians were employed (see Cesti, p. 315).

Agostino Steffani (1654–1728) was taken to the Munich court as a singer in 1667 and at court expense was trained as organist and composer; he served the emperor for 21 years. While at Munich, Steffani composed six operas, including *Marco Aurelio* (1681) and *Alarico* (1687). Disappointed at not being named imperial Kapellmeister in 1688, Steffani sought employment at the court of Duke Ernst August at Hanover. The Duke had built a new theater, and in 1688 the first permanent Italian opera company was established there and was maintained for a decade. Steffani was appointed Kapellmeister and supervised the theater. For the first half of his 15 years at Hanover, he had ample time for music; he composed many chamber duets and at least six operas, including *Henrico Leone* (1689). Then his diplomatic talents were recognized, and various political and ecclesiastical responsibilities left little time for composing music. In April 1709 he was appointed Apostolic Vicar in

Agostino Steffani. Lithograph by Heinrich von Winter. *(Original in Österreichische Nationalbibliothek, Vienna.)*

northern Germany and chose to make Hanover the base for his ecclesiastical work. In 1727 he was elected president of the Academy of Vocal Music in London and composed three works for them: a madrigal, a motet, and *Stabat Mater*.

Steffani's finest compositions are his chamber duets; these secular pieces are typical of the Italian solo cantatas of that time. In his operas, he incorporated elements of French music, such as ballet, French overture, and arias in minuet and gavotte rhythms. Most of his arias are in *da capo* form; some use motto. Two of his operas are based on events in German history: *Alarico* (Munich, 1687) and *Henrico Leone* (Hanover, 1689). The operas Steffani composed for Hanover provided stimulus for opera composition in northern Germany; in the late 1690s they were translated into German and were staged in Hamburg.

Until well into the eighteenth century, at the Dresden and Vienna courts only Italian operas were performed. Because few people in the audiences were familiar with the Italian language, it was customary to print programs with the opera libretto in both Italian and German, in parallel columns.

German opera was slow in getting started. Among its influential predecessors are church and secular school plays that contained songs; traveling troupes whose dramatic presentations contained vocal and instrumental pieces; musico-dramatic performances presented by the leading religious orders, especially Jesuits; and various forms of court entertainment, such as pastorales, ballets, and comic intermezzos. During 1642–49, German poet and librettist Georg Harsdörffer published in Nuremberg eight volumes of a journal entitled *Frauenzimmer Gesprächspiele* (Women's dialogues), containing various literary works and texts for or with music. One of the selections in Volume IV (1644) is *Das geistliche Waldegedicht oder Freudenspiel genant Seelewig* (Sacred sylvan poem or Joyful play named Seelewig); it is designated *Singspiel* (play with music), written "in the Italian manner." The pastoral poem is by Harsdörffer; its through-composed musical setting is by Sigmund Theophil Staden (1607–55), Nuremberg organist. *Seelewig* contains both recitatives and strophic songs. Many historians consider it the earliest surviving German opera.

Singspiel was the usual German term for opera in the late seventeenth century. The term was accurate, for many of the early operas in German consist of spoken dialogue and strophic songs.

In Hamburg, despite violent opposition from church authorities, a group of musicians founded the first German opera company in 1678, and German-language operas were performed at the Theater am Gänsemarkt until c. 1750. At the outset, local poets provided the librettos. No outstanding virtuoso singers were employed, and castrati were not used. The most important composer of German operas for Hamburg was Reinhard Keiser (1674–1739), who wrote approximately 75 stage works for performance there between 1696 and 1734. He wrote Italian as well as German operas and occasionally inserted an Italian aria in a German opera. Keiser seems to have been the first to write German comic operas. One of his greatest successes was *Der Carneval von Venedig* (The Carnival of Venice; 1707); for some of its arias and comic scenes he used Plattdeutsch, the Lower Saxon dialect traditional in Hamburg. The subjects of Keiser's operas are varied and cosmopolitan; so are his musical models. He used accompanied recitative, with effective harmonic changes, to highlight emotion; aria

forms include binary, strophic variation, *basso ostinato,* and *da capo.* His dramatic use of arioso foreshadows Bach's treatment of it in his Passions. Keiser's musical depiction of pastoral scenes is excellent. A notable feature of his operas is his inventive instrumentation; folk as well as traditional instruments were used to achieve proper sound effect. For example, Act II of *Croesus* (1710) calls for a zuffolo, a boxwood whistle capable of producing birdlike sounds. Zuffolo is used in the comic opera *Prinz Jodelet* (1726), also. Sometimes Keiser wrote for whole consorts of instruments, e.g., five flutes or five bassoons; at other times, broken (mixed) consort is specified. Or, articulations are contrasted, as in *Arsinoe* (1710), where legato oboe and solo violin are combined with stringed instruments playing pizzicato.

Telemann, Handel, and Mattheson were among the eighteenth-century composers writing operas for Hamburg audiences. Handel's first operas—*Almira* (1705), *Nero* (1705), and *Florindo* (1708)—were written for performance at Hamburg's Theater am Gänsemarkt (see p. 419).

Spain

The earliest Spanish drama completely set to music was Lope de Vega's *La selva sin amor* (The forest without love; 1629). When it was performed, the instrumentalists were hidden from the spectators' view, as was the case in early Italian opera.

Pedro Calderón de la Barca (1600–81) wrote plays for secular public theater until he became a priest in 1651; thereafter, he became Spain's leading exponent of Christian drama. He wrote *autos sacramentales* (short allegorical plays for the feast of Corpus Christi) and spectacular court plays and used music in them increasingly. Through his use of a semispoken style of recitative, Calderón was instrumental in bringing opera to the Spanish court. In the *loa* (complimentary ode sung as preface) to his one-act opera *La púrpura de la rosa* (The purple of the rose; Madrid, 1660) he voiced his opinion that the Spanish would not readily accept pure opera, yet, to the end of his life, he and the leading Spanish composers, especially Juan Hidalgo (c. 1613–85), persisted in writing it. Calderón and Hidalgo created *La púrpura de la rosa* to celebrate the marriage of Louis XIV and Spanish Infanta Maria Teresia. The plot presents the mythological story of Venus and Adonis; however, for comic relief Calderón added to the main characters a soldier, a peasant, and the peasant's wife. The music for *La púrpura de la rosa* is lost. Hidalgo's *Celos aun del aire matan* (Jealousy, even of the air, kills; 1660), on a libretto by Calderón concerning the jealousy of Diana's nymphs, is the earliest Spanish opera whose music survives. It consists of recitatives, strophic arias, and choruses. When these operas were performed, women sang most of the male roles.

Calderón is credited with inventing the *zarzuela,* a Spanish dramatic form that combines singing and dancing with spoken dialogue. He wrote his first *zarzuela* in 1648. That he patterned the mature *zarzuela* after Italian opera is apparent in *El laurel de Apolo* (Apollo's laurel; 1657), though the Spanish popular element is not lacking. During the last decades of the seventeenth century, Spanish composers devoted their energies to *zarzuela* rather than to serious opera. However, after Philip V married Elisabeth Farnese (1714) Italian opera was favored at court.

In Spanish colonies in America, opera was composed early in the eighteenth century. In 1701 the Viceroy of Peru commissioned Tomás de Torrejón y Velasco (1644–1728) to write an opera to honor Philip V (r. 1700–46) on his eighteenth birthday and the first year of his reign. Torrejón set Calderón's *La púrpura de la rosa,* an appropriate choice, for Philip V was grandson of Louis XIV and Maria Teresia. The opera was performed at the viceregal palace, Lima, on 19 October 1701. Torrejón, born in Spain, went to Peru c. 1658; from 1676 until his death, he was *maestro di capilla* of Lima Cathedral. *La púrpura de la rosa* is his only opera (fig. 15.10).

Torrejón wrote a new *loa* text for his opera and set the *loa* for solo, duet, and four-part chorus. The opera is in one long act, with several scenes. Torrejón assigned to each of the main characters (Adonis, Venus, Mars) a distinctive refrainlike theme that identifies that character throughout a scene. Only a basso continuo line of accompaniment is notated in the score, and the instruments used to realize it are not specified; it is believed that strings and harpsichord were used. The approach of Mars is heralded by trumpets and drums offstage.

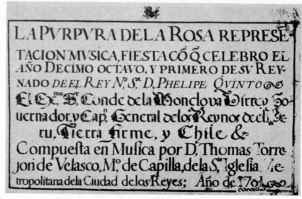

Figure 15.10   Title page of Torrejón's *La púrpura de la rosa.*

The second opera produced in the New World was composed by Mexican-born Manuel de Zumaya (c. 1678–1756), chapelmaster at Mexico City Cathedral. Zumaya entered service of the cathedral as a choirboy and received all of his musical training there. He attained priesthood in 1700 and became *maestro di capilla* in 1711. His three-act opera *La Parténope*—the first full-length opera composed in North America—was performed at the viceregal palace, Mexico City, on 1 May 1711.

Russia, Bohemia

Russia was relatively isolated from western European musical developments until the time of Tsar' Peter I, the Great (r. 1672–1725). Peter had viewed operatic performances when he traveled in western Europe and wanted Russia to have some, but not until his daughter Anne's reign (r. 1730–40) was an Italian opera company permanently established at the Russian court. Francesco Araia (1709–after 1762), who was *maestro di capella,* wrote many Italian operas for court performance. Only once did he set a Russian libretto—*Tzéfal i Procris* (Cephalus and Procris; 1755); Russian singers performed it.

While Bohemia and Moravia were under Habsburg rule, Italian opera flourished at their courts. The earliest opera based on a Bohemian subject is *Primislao, primo re di Boemia* (Primislao, first king of Bohemia; 1698). Its composer is unknown. Bartolomeo Bernardi's (c. 1660–1732) *Libussa,* on the same legend, was performed at Prague in 1703. When Emperor Charles VI decided in 1723 to establish his imperial court permanently at Vienna, the importance of Prague declined considerably, and there were few lavish musical entertainments in Bohemian castles.

Oratorio

An **oratorio** is a large-scale musical composition that resembles an opera but has a narrator, places greater emphasis on chorus, and is presented without stage action, scenery, or costumes. In an oratorio, the chorus may be used for narrative and dramatic purposes, as well as for commentary or summation of the plot. Although an oratorio may be secular, the vast majority have sacred subjects. The name "oratorio" derives from the place in which this kind of composition was first performed, the Oratorio (oratory, or prayer room) of a church.

Forerunners of oratorio include liturgical drama, certain of the Offices for special saints' feasts, early presentations of Passion liturgy in dialogue, and dialogue *laude*. Immediate antecedents of oratorio are motets with narrative texts (such as Lassus's settings of Bible stories), dramatic renditions of the Passion, and *laude spirituale*.

Filippo Neri

Filippo Neri (1515–95), Italian religious leader canonized in 1622, was educated at the Dominican friary of San Marco in Florence. By 1534 he was studying in Rome but soon abandoned formal studies to devote his life to charitable works and prayer. In 1551 he became a priest. A small group of laymen met regularly in his living quarters at San Girolamo della Carità for purposes of prayer and religious discussions. Within three years, the group had increased to such an extent that meetings were held in a special prayer room (Oratorio) of the church. Neri included the singing of *laude spirituale* in the group's spiritual exercises. In 1575, Pope Gregory XIII (r. 1572–85) recognized Neri's group as a religious order, Congregazione dell' Oratorio (Oratory Congregation) and assigned them a church, a new building called simply Chiesa Nova (New Church). Neri's significance in music history lies in his emphasis on congregational singing of *laude,* his use of music as a means of attracting people to the Oratory Services, and his association with composers who wrote music specifically for those Services.

Giovanni Animuccia

Giovanni Animuccia (1500–71), who came to Rome from Florence in 1550 to enter service of Cardinal Ascanio Sforza, met Neri in 1551 and a close friendship developed. Animuccia succeeded Palestrina as *magister cantorum* (singing master) at Cappella Giulia, St. Peter's, in 1555 and served there for the remainder of his life. He composed two books of *laude* for Neri's Congregazione: *Il primo libro delle laudi* (4 vc.; 1565) and *Il secondo libro delle laudi* (2–8 vc.; 1570). The first volume holds simple, chordal settings of Latin and vernacular devotional texts; the second book is slightly more elaborate musically, with increased harmony and voicing, but without complex polyphony, so that the words might be clearly understood.

Giovanni Anerio

Giovanni Anerio (c. 1567–1630), composer, organist, and priest, was first associated with music professionally when he served as organist at the Oratorio del Ss Crocifisso at San Marcello. He was *maestro di cappella* at several churches in Rome and in Verona before going to Warsaw in 1624 to become court choirmaster to King Sigismund III of Poland. Anerio was a prolific composer. His *Teatro armonico* (Harmonic theatre; 1619), written for Neri's Oratory Congregation, contains 94 works with vernacular texts based on Biblical subjects or lives of the saints. Fourteen of the pieces are marked *dialogo,* and seven of those are of sufficient length to be considered oratorios. With them Anerio inaugurated the *oratorio volgare* (vernacular oratorio). The longest (about 20 minutes performance time) and most dramatic composition in the volume is *La conversione di S. Paolo* (The conversion of St. Paul). In it there are four soloists—Narrator (tenor), Saul (tenor), Voice from Heaven (bass), Ananias (tenor)—and double eight-part chorus. Organ bass is provided for accompanying the soloists; instruments double voices on the choruses. *La conversione di S. Paolo* and *Dialogo del figliuol prodigo* (Dialogue of the prodigal son) are the earliest known examples of obbligato (required) instrumental writing in vocal works, in Rome, in which instruments imitate vocal lines as well as play introductions, *ritornelli, sinfonie,* and double the vocal parts in the choruses.

The earliest printed works with the name *oratorio* in the title are two posthumously published libretti by poet Francesco Balducci (1579–1642): *La fede: oratorio* (Faith), over 450 lines concerning Abraham's sacrifice of Isaac, with solo and chorus roles; and *Il trionfo: oratorio* (Triumph), an allegorical poem of about 200 lines honoring the Virgin Mary.

By the middle of the seventeenth century, both *oratorio latino* (Latin oratorio) and *oratorio volgare* (vernacular oratorio) were written. Musical settings of the two types are similar; the only difference is in the language used for the texts. In the Oratorio del Ss Crocifisso, Rome, only Latin oratorios were performed; other churches permitted either type.

Among the most advanced oratorios c. 1650 are Giacomo Carissimi's *Daniele* (Daniel) and a half-dozen anonymous works, one being *Giuseppe: oratorio per la Settimana Santa* (Joseph: oratorio for Holy Week), the earliest known oratorio based on the Passion. All of these works have solo lines for a *Testo* (narrator), and each of the vernacular oratorios is divided into two *Partes,* each *Parte* concluding with a chorus. When these oratorios were performed in an Oratory, a sermon was delivered between the *Partes.* The music contains recitative, arioso, and aria types; all forms commonly used for opera arias are represented. Most of these oratorios use only the usual fundamental basso continuo instruments for accompaniment; some add two violins for interludes, *ritornelli,* and for doubling choral voices.

Giacomo Carissimi

Almost nothing is known concerning Giacomo Carissimi (1605–74) prior to 1623, when he is listed as a choir member at Tivoli Cathedral; in 1627 he was organist there. In 1629 he became *maestro di cappella* at Collegio Germanico, Rome, one of the most influential Jesuit educational institutions in the world. He retained that position until his death, though several other attractive positions were offered him. Frequently during 1650–60 he participated in performances at Oratorio del Ss Crocifisso. Carissimi is the first important composer of oratorios and was well known for his cantatas, of which at least 200 survive. He composed several Masses and numerous motets, also; in these he never ventured beyond the traditions of the forms.

Carissimi wrote both Latin and vernacular oratorios. All of his Latin oratorios are in one section only, which is normal for Latin oratorios of that time. For Latin oratorios he chose Biblical subjects from the Vulgate, usually from the Old Testament. Sometimes Scripture is used literally, sometimes paraphrased or supplemented. Since Carissimi credited no librettists, it is presumed that he prepared the texts himself. He termed the narrator *Historicus* (Storyteller), rather than *Testo,* and often used chorus for part of the narration. He did not shun experimentation. For example, two of his oratorios—*Damnatorum lamentatio* (Lament of the damned) and *Felicitas beatorum* (Happiness of the blessed)—seem to have been conceived as paired opposites, both in voicing and textual wording.

On the surface, Carissimi's music seems remarkably simple. However, when writing musical speech he took into consideration not only correct verbal accentuation but accurate and expressive articulation of phrases and sentences as well, so that each word or phrase fits into the whole with the appropriate expression of its emotional content. To achieve this, he used dissonance, ornaments, word painting, or whatever technical device seemed suitable; his compositional approach was similar to that of Monteverdi. *Judicium Salomonis* (The Judgment of Solomon) and *Jonas* exemplify this.

Much of Carissimi's music has been lost, but 14 of his oratorios survive. The best known of these is *Jephte* (Jephtha; composed before 1650), based on Judges xi: 19–40 (excerpt, DWMA115). The text is from the Vulgate, with some paraphrasing and some supplementation. Historicus sings the introduction to the story. In monodic recitative, Jephtha (tenor) vows: If the Lord will give the Israelites victory in the impending battle against the Ammonites, Jephtha will sacrifice to the Lord the first being that comes to greet him upon his return home. Then, in solo arias, duets, and choruses, the story of Jephtha's victory is told; imitation and *stile concitato* are used effectively. Historicus opens the next scene in *recitativo* narration, relating Jephtha's triumphant return to his home. His only daughter—whom, by his vow, he must sacrifice—comes to greet him, followed by several of her companions. In dialogue recitative, Jephtha explains the circumstances to his daughter (who is never named); she acknowledges that she must be sacrificed but requests permission to spend two months in the mountains with her companions bewailing her fate. Jephtha grants her request. A nine-measure chorus introduces the daughter's song, *Plorate, plorate colles* (Weep, weep hills), an affective recitative in which the cadences of her phrases are echoed by two of her companions (sopranos). The oratorio concludes with a six-voice choral lament, *Plorate filii Israel* (Weep, daughters of Israel), a madrigalesque piece with imitation and polychoric echo effects. This final chorus was much admired by later composers. Handel incorporated it in the chorus "Hear, Jacob's God!" in his oratorio *Samson* (1741).

The only composer after Carissimi to write Latin oratorios in quantity was his pupil Marc-Antoine Charpentier (c. 1645–1704), who composed about 50 of them and who transmitted the Latin oratorio to France. Carissimi's influence is apparent in the form and style of Charpentier's oratorios, e.g., *Le Reniement de St. Pierre* (St. Peter's denial). Among Carissimi's Italian contemporaries, the most important composer of Latin oratorios was Domenico Mazzochi (1592–65), who wrote seven, most of them called dialogues; they were published in *Sacrae concertationes* (Sacred concertos; 1664). Mazzochi composed some excellent vocal chamber music and wrote one opera, *La catena d' Adone* (The chain of Adonis; 1626).

During the reigns of Emperors Leopold I (r. 1658–1705), Joseph I (1705–11), and Charles VI (1711–40) the Viennese court was an important center of sacred dramatic music in the Italian language. All of these rulers were musicians, as well as patrons of music. Leopold I composed at least nine sacred dramatic compositions. His *Il sagrifizio d'Abramo* (Abram's sacrifice; perf. 1660) is the earliest oratorio known to have been performed in Vienna. Two of his oratorios (written in 1679 and 1682) have German texts, which is most unusual for Vienna at that time.

Women Composers of Dramatic Works

Between 1670 and 1725, several women were active in northern Italy and Austria as composers of opera and oratorio. Angiola Moratori Scannabecchi of Bologna (1662–1708) was both painter and composer. At least three of her paintings were hanging in churches in Bologna in 1988. Printed libretti for four of her oratorios survive; the music is lost. Three of those works were performed in the Oratory of St. Filippo Neri, Rome: *Il martirio di S. Colomba* (The martyrdom of St. Colomba; 1694), *Li Giochi di Sansone* (Samson's trick; 1694), and *L'Esterre* (The stranger; 1695). *Cristo morto* (The dead Christ) was performed for the Confraternity of Santa Maria della Morte on Good Friday evening, 1696.

Libretti survive for two operas and two oratorios by Maria Anna von Rachenau (c. 1651–c. 1710), nun and *Chormeisterin* at St. Jakob auf der Hülben. *Le sacre visione di S. Teresia* (The sacred vision of St. Teresia; 1703) is dedicated to Leopold I.

Manuscript scores and libretti are extant for four oratorios by Camilla de Rossi that were performed at the Viennese court during the reign of Joseph I: *S. Beatrice d'Este* (1705; libretto, Cardinal Pamphili); *Il Sagrifizio di Abramo* (Abram's sacrifice; 1708); *Il Figliuol Prodigo* (The prodigal son; 1709); and *S. Alessio* (St. Alexis; 1710).

Signora Caterina Grazianini's *S. Geminiano vescovo e protettore di Modena* (St. Geminiano, bishop and protector of Modena) was first performed in Modena, then given twice in Vienna, in 1705 and 1715. The music survives in manuscript.

Maria Margherita Grimani (fl. 1713–18) may have worked in Italy as well as in Vienna. The dedication of *Pallade e Marte* was dated 4 April 1713 at Bologna, and the work was performed 4 November 1713 in celebration of the name day of Emperor Charles VI. This was the first opera by a woman composer to be performed in the imperial court theater.

Grimani's two oratorios were also given there: *La visitazione di Elisabetha* (Elisabeth's visitation) was performed immediately after *Pallade e Marte* in 1713 and was given again in 1718; *Le decollazione di S. Giovanni Battista* (The beheading of St. John the Baptist) was presented in 1715. In Grimani's works, almost all recitatives are *secco,* and most of the arias are *da capo* form with basso continuo accompaniment; only a few arias have orchestral accompaniment.

Passion

A **Passion** is the story of the Crucifixion as recorded in the Gospels. The oldest Passion story included in the liturgy is that according to St. Matthew, which, by decree of Pope Leo I (r. 440–61), was to be chanted on Palm Sunday and on Wednesday of Holy Week. Two centuries later, the St. Luke Passion displaced the St. Matthew on Wednesday; from the tenth century, the St. Mark Passion was sung also, on Tuesday of Holy Week. The text was chanted by a single singer, but some ninth-century manuscripts suggest a dramatic approach to the presentation by indicating different manners of reciting or different pitch levels for the words of Christ, the *turba* (crowd), and the narrator. After c. 1250, the liturgical presentation approximated the early liturgical drama (p. 54), for it became customary to have the story chanted by three priests using contrasting ranges and tempos to represent Christ, the *turba,* and the narrator. Division of the Passion presentation among three singers became almost universal by the fifteenth century. (In some churches it is still chanted liturgically in that manner.) The first monophonic choral presentation of the *turba* occurred c. 1350.

Polyphonic settings of the Passion date from the fifteenth century. Passion plays were presented in which motet-style polyphony was used for only those portions of text representing *turba* participation in the Passion. This type of setting is known as **responsorial Passion.** A fifteenth-century treatise written in southern Germany relates how the three reciting tones of the three priests were combined to create the polyphony of the *turba.* However, the earliest surviving responsorial Passion is in an English manuscript dating from c. 1435. As the century advanced, two kinds of responsorial Passion settings were written: (1) the **choral** or **dramatic** Passion, in which portions of the text, including the *turba* and the words of Christ, are set polyphonically, and the remainder is monophonic; and (2) the **through-composed** or **motet** Passion, in which the complete text receives polyphonic setting.

In the sixteenth century, Passions composed for use in Italy and in Catholic churches in Germanic lands were the responsorial type, but the words of Christ were not set polyphonically. The four Passions Lassus composed for the Bavarian court chapel (1575–82) are responsorial; he wrote polyphonic motets for full chorus for the *turba* portions and set the words of individuals as *bicinia* and *tricinia,* sometimes using *falsobordone* (passages of root-position triads).

In Protestant Germany, Luther opposed "acting out the Passion in words and pretence," though he did not object to simple responsorial presentation of it. Nevertheless, both monophonic and polyphonic settings of Passion texts continued to be sung in Service on the four Sundays before Easter and during Holy Week through Good Friday. The two Passion settings (St. Matthew, St. John) made c. 1550 by Johann Walter, who was closely associated with Luther, became models for responsorial Passions in the Lutheran church. Walter's works were intended as examples of how the Passion should be sung. In addition to Walter's models, the setting by Antoine de Longueval (fl. 1507–22) was widely used in Germany. Longueval's four-voice motet Passion is the earliest known setting to incorporate portions of text from all four Gospels—termed a *summa Passion*—and thus include all seven words of Christ on the cross.

A model for motet Passions was *Die deutsche Passion . . . nach . . . Sancte Johanne in Figural-Gesang bracht* (The German Passion . . . according to . . . St. John, in polyphonic song; 1568) by Joachim à Burck (1546–1610). Johann Machold's (d. 1595) inclusion of the strophe, *O Jesu Christe, Gottes Sohn* (O Jesus Christ, God's Son) in his *St. Matthew Passion* (1593) inspired the practice of inserting strophic hymns or songs into the Passion.

With the rise of concerted music and the emergence of sacred opera came the **oratorio Passion,** which uses recitative, arioso, aria, ensembles, chorus, and a few purely instrumental pieces as well as instrumental accompaniment. The earliest oratorio Passions were those by Thomas Selle (1599–1663), whose *Johannespassion* (St. John Passion; 5 vc.; 1641) was the first to include instrumental interludes.

In the second half of the seventeenth century, it became customary to insert poetic meditations (solo arias, or recitative-aria combinations) as the Passion story progressed, and chorales associated with the Passion (for choir or congregational singing). The presentation usually commenced and concluded with a chorale. By adhering to a text taken from only one Gospel, a composer met the requirements of orthodox Lutheranism. Some writers prepared completely original Passion texts; this type is exemplified by C. F. Hunold's *Der blutige und sterbende Jesus* (The bleeding and dying Jesus; set by Keiser, 1704), a free paraphrase replete with graphic details. B. A. Brockes's libretto *Der für die Sünden der Welt gemarterte und sterbende Jesus* (Jesus, martyred and dying for the sins of the world), though an expressive free paraphrase, is less graphic. It attracted Keiser (1712), Telemann (1716), Handel (1717), Mattheson (1718), and others. Though J. S. Bach did not set it, he drew upon it for some portions of text in his *St. John Passion*. Settings of completely paraphrased libretti had little use in divine worship but were influential in the development of the cantata.

Heinrich Schütz

Heinrich Schütz (1585–1672; Insight, "Heinrich Schütz") is considered the greatest German composer of the seventeenth century; he is the first German composer to achieve international renown. Apparently, he did not compose any independent instrumental music, and all of his stage works are lost. Some secular and a considerable amount of sacred music—over 500 works in all—survives, presenting a panorama of Schütz's compositions from his first publication to his last works. Schütz began his compositional career by writing Italianate music with Italian texts; he composed only two volumes with Latin texts. His use of German texts and the fusion of German and Italian styles present in his music form the foundation of the German music composed during the remainder of the Baroque era. In one important

Heinrich Schütz. From a portrait by Christoph Spetner (1617–99). *(Original in Karl Marx Universität, Leipzig.)*

respect, Schütz's music differs from that of other major composers of sacred music of that time: few traces of chant or Lutheran chorale melodies are present.

Schütz's first publication, *Il primo libro de madrigali* (First book of madrigals; Venice, 1611), comprises 19 unaccompanied five-voice Italian madrigals, which he may have composed in connection with his lessons from Gabrieli. The pieces are stylistically similar to those in Monteverdi's Book V.

In 1619 *Psalmen Davids* (Psalms of David), Schütz's first collection of sacred music, was published. These motet and concerto settings of the Psalms reflect Schütz's training under Gabrieli at St. Mark's—the Venetian *concertato* style is apparent in Schütz's treatment of the soloists, multiple choruses, and instruments, but his settings are sensitive to the German texts. Schütz followed *Psalmen Davids* with a *summa* Passion setting, *Historia der . . . Aufferstehung . . . Jesu Christi* (Story of the . . . Resurrection . . . of Jesus Christ; 1623). He next published a volume of motets, *Cantiones sacrae* (Sacred songs; 1625). In these Latin motets, madrigalesque word painting colors basically conservative counterpoint

Example 15.10 Schütz's setting of (*a*) *Ego dormio, et cor meum vigilat* (I sleep, and my heart is vigilant), mm. 1–5, Motet XI; and (*b*) *toto corpore extensum* (whole body stretched out), mm. 16–18, Motet XXIII, are typical of the madrigalesque word painting he used in the Latin motets in *Cantiones sacrae* (1625). *(Source: Heinrich Schütz: Neue Ausgabe sämtlicher Werke, Band 8, p. 61; Band 9, p. 16.)*

(ex. 15.10). During 1626–27 Schütz devoted his compositional energies mainly to preparation of the so-called Becker Psalter (SWV 97a–256a; 1628. SWV = *Schütz-Werke-Verzeichnis,* the catalog of Schütz's works). The Psalter is a series of simple settings, in four-part harmony, of theologian Cornelius Becker's German paraphrases of Psalms.

In the spring of 1627, Elector Johann Georg I of Saxony took his Kapelle to Hartenfels Castle at Torgau for nuptial celebrations honoring his daugh-

ter Sophia and Landgrave Georg II of Hessen-Darmstadt. For those festivities Schütz composed several works, including the opera *Dafne*—the first opera created in Germany. That work is lost.

While on an extended visit to Italy in 1628–29, Schütz published *Symphoniae sacrae* (Sacred symphonies; SWV 257–76; 1629). This, his last book of Latin text settings, comprises motets. In all the *Symphoniae,* the accompanying instruments are those that became a more or less standard trio sonata ensemble: two violins, violone, and keyboard (organ); but

Heinrich Schütz

Heinrich Schütz's (1585–1672) early childhood was spent at Weissenfels, where he received music instruction from the local Kantor. Late in 1599 he became a choirboy at the court of Landgrave Moritz at Kassel. When Schütz's voice changed in 1608, he entered the University of Marburg to study law, but within a year the Landgrave sent him to Venice to study with Giovanni Gabrieli. Schütz remained in Venice until after Gabrieli died.

In 1613 Schütz returned to Moritz's court as organist, but the acquisition of his services soon became the subject of controversy between Moritz and Elector Johann Georg I of Saxony, who wanted Schütz at Dresden. Moritz was reluctant to release Schütz but agreed to lend him to the Elector for a time. For several years, Moritz tried unsuccessfully to regain Schütz from the Elector. In 1617 Schütz was named electoral Kapellmeister, a position he held to the end of his life, though he obtained leave of absence to spend several years at the royal court of Denmark.

Schütz married Magdalena Wildeck on 1 June 1619. The printed volume of his *Psalmen Davids* (Psalms of David) was ready for distribution shortly before the wedding and he included copies with the wedding invitations he sent to church and city councils throughout Saxony. Schütz's married life was of short duration; Magdalena died on 6 September 1625, after a brief illness. Schütz placed their two daughters, Anna (1621–38) and Euphrosina (1623–55), in Magdalena's mother's care. He never remarried.

During an extended visit to Italy in 1628–29, Schütz discussed various aspects of music with Monteverdi, secured some instruments and instrumentalists for the Dresden court, and published some sacred music. In autumn 1631 Saxony entered the Thirty Years' War, in alliance with King Gustavus II Adolphus (r. 1611–32) of Sweden. Economic pressures at the Dresden court were heavy; music resources at the chapel declined drastically. When Crown Prince Christian of Denmark invited Schütz to Copenhagen to direct the music at a forthcoming royal wedding celebration, he was eager to accept, but months elapsed before he could leave the Dresden court. In December, he was appointed Kapellmeister to King Christian IV (r. 1588–1648) but still retained his Dresden post. Schütz was in Copenhagen until mid-1635. Upon his return to Dresden, he sent copies of many of his works, both printed and manuscript, to Copenhagen; from time to time, over the years, he continued to do this—a fact that contributed to the survival of some of his works when fire and war damaged other libraries. Economic hardship compelled Schütz to leave many of his works unpublished. The war dragged on. There were no funds for training new personnel, and by 1639 the Dresden court chapel had dwindled to fewer than ten singers, most of whom lived in abject poverty because salaries had been delinquent for many months.

Schütz spent most of 1642–44 in Denmark as court Kapellmeister, then visited various German cities before returning to Dresden. He had been connected with the court at Brunswick-Lüneburg since 1638 and had encouraged the Duchess to compose. He was a frequent guest at Brunswick and Wolfenbüttel, and in 1655 was appointed senior Kapellmeister at Wolfenbüttel. During his lifetime he placed copies of many of his works in the Wolfenbüttel library.

In 1645, Schütz requested permission to retire from his position at the Dresden court. This was the first of many such petitions that either were ignored or brought him only a few months away from court. The Elector did permit him to spend winters in Weissenfels, but Schütz returned to court around Easter each year. Not until George II became Elector (1657) was Schütz given a pension and permitted to retire. He retained the title of Chief Kapellmeister, however, and continued to compose and to revise his works. Some of his finest works—the Passions and *Christmas Story*—date from his retirement years. After 1670 Schütz made his home in Dresden. He died there, peacefully, in November 1672.

Schütz's choice of solo and duet voicing varies considerably. In five instances, two *symphoniae* pair to form a long motet. *Symphoniae IX* and *X,* respectively, *Prima Pars* and *Secunda Pars* of the same motet, set selected verses from Song of Solomon, ch. iv. The instrumental *sinfonia* that commences *Symphonia X* provides contrast when the two *partes* are performed as a single large motet (DWMA116).

Vocal soloists in this motet are tenor and bass. Written without key signature, the *Prima Pars* commences in triple meter in D minor with bass singing Schütz's paraphrase of the opening words of Song of Solomon iv:1, *O, quam tu pulchra es* (O, how beautiful thou art). He states the long phrase completely, with little repetition of text or melody, though both harmonic and melodic sequences occur; the phrase cadences in hemiola rhythm (mm.12–13). The bass soloist then begins to restate the phrase, engages in imitative dialogue with the tenor, and the two voices cadence simultaneously. On their final cadence chord the violins begin their statement of the melodic material in imitation, and approach their cadence through hemiola (mm.46–47). Throughout the section, distinct polarity of treble and bass ranges is maintained. At times, instrumental and vocal groups are juxtaposed; at other times, they are combined and share in imitative presentation of the contrapuntal material. Schütz indulged moderately in word painting when describing the beloved's body; those short descriptive passages are in arioso style. *Symphonia IX* concludes with the entire ensemble cadencing (V–I) on an A-major chord spread over three octaves, while still maintaining instrumental polarity of treble and bass and polarity between vocalists and instrumentalists.

An instrumental *sinfonia* opens *Symphonia X,* the *Secunda Pars* of the motet, with imitative counterpoint in scalar passages in A-natural minor (Aeolian mode) over a walking bass line. As they cadence, the tenor enters, singing the instrumental melody two octaves lower. Except for its initial words, *Veni de Libano* (Come from Lebanon), his text uses most of the same adoring expressions found at the beginning of *Symphonia IX.* This half of the motet moves at a faster pace and contains longer melismas than the *Prima Pars.* The final cadence is approached through long tonic and subdominant pedals, harmonies that vacillate between major and minor, and the triple reiteration of an arpeggiated D-minor chord, before the final D-major chord is pronounced by the entire ensemble. The concluding phrase of text, *O quam tu pulchra es,* with voices and keyboard sounding the same d and a pitches that commence *Symphonia IX,* brings the motet full circle.

Many of the occasional works Schütz wrote have disappeared. For instance, a surviving libretto (without music) indicates that he composed a five-act opera-ballet on the Orpheus myth, performed at the wedding celebration of Prince Johann George and Princess Magdalena Sybilla of Brandenburg. Among Schütz's published occasional music is *Musicalische Exequien* (Funeral music; SWV 279–81), commissioned by the family of Prince Heinrich Posthumus of Reuss and performed at his funeral in December 1635. This work comprises a concerto in the form of a German Mass, and two motets, all written for soloists and choir with basso continuo accompaniment (violone and organ).

Two volumes of *Kleiner geistlichen Concerten* (Little sacred concertos) were printed (1636; 1639). These are motets for one to five solo voices, with basso continuo for organ.

Schütz published *Symphoniarum sacrarum secunda pars* (Sacred symphonies, part 2) in 1648; most of these works had been written previously. *Symphoniarum sacrarum tertia pars* (Sacred symphonies, part 3) appeared in 1650. In both volumes, German texts are set for solo voices with instrumental accompaniment by two violins, violone, and keyboard (organ); a few pieces in Part 3 have parts for chorus—some *ad libitum*—with those lines doubled by additional stringed instruments. Many of the works in Part 3 are cantatas, and their voicing varies considerably. For example, *O Herr, hilf* (O Lord, help) is for two sopranos; *Saul, was verfolgst du mich* (Saul, why persecutest thou me?) is for six soloists and double choir, with *ad libitum* doubling of choir parts by additional instruments. In the latter work, Schütz used *concertato* in a manner that anticipates *concerto grosso,* for the double choir parts (instrumentally doubled) merely double and reenforce portions of the soloists' lines and lend dramatic intensity to the text. Supposedly, Schütz composed Part 3 for the Dresden court chapel, which had increased in size after the Thirty Years' War ended with the Peace of Westphalia in 1648. However, as late as 1654, the status of that musical chapel was still precarious; salaries were very low, and payments were often delinquent.

Schütz was concerned about the quality of contrapuntal music being produced. To this end, he published a pedagogical work, dedicated to the Leipzig city fathers and intended for use in the training of choirboys at Thomaskirche. *Geistliche Chor-Musik . . . erster Theil* (Spiritual Choral Music . . . book 1; SWV 369–97; 1648) contains choral motets written according to the principles of traditional counterpoint, the *prima prattica.* Two years earlier, Schütz had been drawn into a dispute between Paul Siefert and Marco Scacchi concerning the quality of contemporary Italian composers' counterpoint. The *Geistliche Chor-Musik* collection was Schütz's practical response to the Seifert-Scacchi controversy, an encouragement for those who would train musicians to write strict counterpoint according to the rules of Palestrina's time.

In 1657 a book of small choral pieces appeared, *Zwölff geistliche Gesänge* (Twelve spiritual songs; SWV 420–31). Schütz authorized, but did not edit, this publication. His next major work was *Historia der . . . Geburth Gottes und Marien Sohnes, Jesu Christi* (Story of the birth of God's and Mary's Son, Jesus Christ; SWV 435; 1660), the so-called Christmas Oratorio. This is the earliest German setting of the Nativity story to have the evangelist's words sung in recitative instead of the traditional unaccompanied chants. Arias, choruses, and instrumental music, in *concertato* style, are included in the separate scenes of the story.

During 1665–66, Schütz composed three Passions: (1) *Historia des Leidens und Sterbens unsers Herrn und Heylandes Jesu Christi nach dem Evangelisten St. Johannem* (Story of the suffering and death of our Lord and Savior Jesus Christ according to the evangelist St. John; SWV 481a, 1665; rev. SWV 481, 1666); (2) *Historia . . . nach . . . St. Matheum* (Story . . . according to . . . St. Matthew; SWV 479, 1666); and (3) *Historia . . . nach . . . St. Lucam* (Story . . . according to . . . St. Luke; SWV 480, 1666). The three works are similar in style: narrative and dialogue are cast in unaccompanied recitative that is not chant but is reminiscent of it, and the chorus (the *turba*) is given *a cappella* contrapuntal settings resembling motets. All three Passions are modal. For the *St. Luke Passion* Schütz used Lydian mode on F, the traditional modality for this text; the *St. John Passion* is in Phrygian mode, and the *St. Matthew Passion* in transposed Dorian. Schütz's skill at portraying dramatic situations is apparent in these three works.

Nothing is known concerning the origin of Schütz's *Die sieben Wortte unsers lieben Erlösers und Seeligmachers Jesu Christi* (The seven words of our beloved Savior Jesus Christ; composed 1645, publ. 1873). There is no record of its performance during his lifetime, though parts in manuscript are extant. The work, which takes about half an hour to perform, is one of Schütz's finest compositions. *Die sieben Wortte . . .* is for five soloists (Christ and four evangelists) and chorus, with strings and basso continuo

(organ) accompaniment. The words of Jesus, in expressive monody, are always accompanied by two stringed instruments and basso continuo. In two instances, the evangelist quartet presents brief narration. The work is in Phrygian mode (on E, with no sharps or flats). It commences with a short five-part (SATTB) polyphonic setting of the first stanza of the hymn *Da Jesus an dem Kreuze stund* (Since Jesus on the cross was hung; DWMA117), followed by a *sinfonia*; the string ensemble includes two viola parts. After the seventh Word the *sinfonia* is repeated, and the composition concludes with polyphonic choral setting of the final stanza of the hymn. Throughout the work Schütz's mastery of syncopation is evident. The quiet, deeply devotional nature of the music is in accord with Schütz's religious views; this, coupled with the absence of performance data and the small dimensions of the composition, lead one to believe the work was composed for highly personal reasons.

Schütz's five *Historiae* (the three Passions, Nativity Story, Resurrection Story) and *Die sieben Wortte . . .* are the most significant Lutheran music in these semidramatic forms before J. S. Bach.

The *Teutsch Magnificat* (German Magnificat, SWV 494), Schütz's last completed composition, was published along with *Königs und Propheten Davids hundert und neunzehender Psalm . . .* (King and prophet David's 119th Psalm . . .) in 1671.

During his lifetime, Schütz was accorded unparalleled recognition as a composer. He was a master teacher, too, and his pupils were a credit to his teaching. Moreover, the extent of his concern, as Kapellmeister, for the welfare of his subordinates was unusual; he petitioned for payment of their delinquent salaries, and when money was not forthcoming, supplied their needs out of his personal funds. Unfortunately, with the exception of the Becker Psalter, Schütz's works fell into oblivion after his death and were not rediscovered until c. 1830. Arnold Mendelssohn (1855–1933), Philipp Spitta (1841–94), and Johannes Brahms (1833–97) were influential in promoting a renaissance of Schütz's music, but the Biblical cantatas of the *Symphoniarum sacrarum* volumes and the larger semidramatic works received the most attention. Not until after 1920 was there general recognition of his works and of his stature as composer.

Cantata

The precise meaning of the term **cantata** (literally, a piece to be sung) varied at different times during the seventeenth century. The term seems to have been used first by Alessandro Grandi (c. 1575–1630). His *Cantade ed arie* (Cantatas and arias; c. 1619) is a collection of 42 pieces for solo voice with *basso continuo* accompaniment. The pieces labeled "cantata" are strophic variations. However, for about a decade the term cantata was applied rather indiscriminately to *continuo*-accompanied vocal solos in various forms.

From c. 1625 through the remainder of the Baroque era, the cantata was one of the three principal forms of vocal composition, the other two being opera and oratorio. Most of the early cantatas were published in Venice, but the principal center of cantata composition in Italy was Rome, where the homes of the leading patrons of music provided fertile ground for the cultivation of vocal chamber music. Between 1630 and 1670 two main types of cantatas were composed: (1) short works containing a single aria and (2) longer compositions with a number of sections written as recitative, arioso, or aria, as the text dictated. The subject matter of cantatas varies considerably and includes amorous, didactic, or occasional material that is lyrical or quasi-dramatic in character.

The two most prolific cantata composers in Rome in the second quarter of the seventeenth century were Luigi Rossi (c. 1597–1653) and Marco Marazzoli (c. 1605–62). Marazzoli's extant cantatas number 379; about 300 of Rossi's survive. They wrote cantatas in a variety of forms, styles, and textures, and sometimes set the same texts. The most outstanding feature of Marazzoli's cantatas is the lyricism of the solo line. His harmonic language verges on being tonal, with a decided preference for major mode; he used more chromatic movement and dissonance than did Rossi. In the works of both composers, formal structures are clearly defined—strophic songs, strophic variations, binary, ternary, *da capo* arias, and songs with ostinato bass lines for the simpler cantatas and for sections in the longer ones; and recitative, arioso, and aria in the multisection ones. Rossi was especially skilled at moving smoothly from recitative to aria.

At mid-seventeenth century the two leading Italian composers of cantatas were Giacomo Carissimi and Antonio Cesti. Carissimi's vocal lines are mainly diatonic steps and broken triads; texts are set syllabically. Though he wrote some single aria strophic-variation cantatas, most of his cantatas are multisectional or multimovement, with clear distinction between recitative, arioso, and aria.

By 1670, the strophic-variation aria had been supplanted by the aria on an ostinato bass, and the cantata was almost totally patterned in clearly differentiated recitatives and arias, with the arias usually in *da capo* form. Alessandro Stradella (1644–82) and Agostino Steffani wrote cantatas of this kind. Stradella was one of the most versatile composers of his time. He composed a vast amount of music in his short lifetime and made a special contribution to the development of instrumental music by employing instrumental ensembles for accompaniment in many of his cantatas. He made clear distinction between recitative and aria but moved easily from one to the other. He preferred contrapuntal texture, and he favored the *concertato* aspect of *concerto grosso* ensemble (see p. 367) in accompaniment.

The greatest and most prolific composer of cantatas was Alessandro Scarlatti. Of his approximately 600 extant cantatas, more than 500 are for solo voice (usually soprano) and basso continuo. Many of these pieces were composed for Cardinals Ottoboni and Pamphili and other aristocratic patrons in Rome. Cantatas Scarlatti composed during his first stay in Rome (1672–84) reflect the influence of the older composers then working there. A majority of the cantatas he wrote in 1703–04 consist of two *da capo* arias each preceded by a recitative. This became a more or less standard pattern for secular cantatas composed during the eighteenth century, except in France.

Composers were actively writing cantatas in other Italian cities, also. In Bologna, Maurizio Cazzatti composed at least nine books of vocal music, most of them containing some solo cantatas and arias. Giovanni Maria Bononcini, of Modena, published two volumes of cantatas in 1677–78; he seems to have been the first to use the term *cantata per camera* (chamber cantata). His son Giovanni (1670–1747), whose works were known throughout Europe, wrote 12 duet cantatas and more than 300 solo cantatas, about a third of them with two violins and *continuo*. Many of his solo cantatas are still unpublished. Giovanni Legrenzi published two books of solo cantatas (Bologna, 1676; 1678) and one book of cantatas for two and three voices (Venice, 1678).

Barbara Strozzi (1619–64), adopted daughter of poet-librettist Giulio Strozzi (1583–1652) and pupil of Cavalli, composed at least six volumes of arias, madrigals, and cantatas in 1644–64. Several of her cantatas are very large works with a wide variety of writing, e.g., *Lagrime mie* from *Diporti di Euterpe,* Op. 7 (My tears, from Pastimes of Euterpe; 1659). One of Strozzi's works is a multisection wedding cantata. Some of her compositions have instrumental ensemble *ritornelli* and accompaniment. Many of the texts she set were by Giulio Strozzi.

Duchess Sophie Elisabeth (1613–76) of Brunswick-Lüneburg was encouraged by Schütz to compose. She had been trained at her father's court, Mecklenburg-Güstrow, where outstanding English instrumentalists were orchestra personnel. To escape war in 1629, she moved to the Kassel court, another active music center. In 1635, she married Duke August (the younger) of Brunswick-Lüneburg, founder of the Wolfenbüttel library, which became and has remained one of the most important repositories for music. Sophie was responsible for the establishment (in 1638) and continual upgrading of the Brunswick court orchestra; from 1638 Schütz was her musical adviser, and, after 1655, her composition teacher. Most of her surviving works are sacred songs. She was instrumental in establishing the tradition of performing ballets and theatrical works with music annually at birthday celebrations and composed for them. Representative of her festival cantatas is *Glückwünschende Freudensdarstellung* (Congratulatory presentation [Happy birthday gift]; 1652), for four soloists, four-part chorus, four strings and basso continuo.

In France, interest was concentrated on the *ballet de cour* and *tragédie lyrique* until c. 1700. When aristocratic society returned to the cosmopolitan atmosphere of Paris, rather than remaining centered in Versailles, the cantata began to flourish. Jean-Baptiste Morin (1657–1744), who served Philippe III, Duke of Orléans, was a pioneer in cantata composition in France. The Duke enjoyed Italian music and employed some Italian composers and musicians. Morin's first book of cantatas was published in 1706; a second followed in 1707. The works, which had circulated in manuscript earlier, combine French lyrical melody with its delicate ornamentation and elements of Italian arias, such as motto beginning, ostinato bass and accompaniment figures, *da capo* form, and trio sonata ensemble accompaniment. Soon other French composers were writing cantatas, and the genre flourished during the first quarter of the eighteenth century. Most prolific were Nicolas Bernier (1665–1734) with more than three dozen cantatas, and Louis-Nicolas Clérambault (1676–1749) with 25. The influence of Italian cantatas is apparent in the works of both men, but Clérambault, who wrote some of the finest French cantatas, was able to effect a real blend of Italian and French styles. In his masterpiece, *Orphée* (1710), for high voice with violin, flute, and basso continuo, French lyricism is imbued with Italian brilliance and warmth.

English composers wrote songs with basso continuo accompaniment but the term *cantata* was not used until 1710, when Walsh published Johann Pepusch's (1667–1752) *Six English Cantatas,* Book 1. *Six English Cantatas,* Book 2, and *12 Cantatas in English* appeared in 1720. Pepusch's cantatas are among the finest written in England. In structure, the works are Italianate—two *da capo* arias preceded and separated by recitatives, accompanied by basso continuo and one or two obbligato (required) instruments. Yet the harmony exhibits the English penchant for major tonality, and the melody displays typical English tunefulness.

The outstanding composer of English songs was Henry Purcell. *Orpheus Britannicus* (London, 1698) is a large collection of his vocal solos, duets, and trios. John Blow (1649–1708) published a similar collection, *Amphion Anglicus* (London, 1700). For ceremonial celebrations or state occasions, large works for soloists, chorus, and orchestra were commissioned. Purcell composed a number of these, including a setting of N. Brady's *Hail, bright Cecelia* for St. Cecelia's Day, 1692. That setting is scored for five soloists, chorus, and instrumental ensemble of recorders, oboes, trumpets, timpani, strings, and basso continuo.

Secular songs and cantatas were composed in Germany, but the cantata attained its highest development after 1700 as sacred music associated with the Lutheran church service. In the last half of the seventeenth century, music printing was at a low ebb in Germany, and repertoires were amassed in manuscript. Among the few collections of solo songs published were Adam Krieger's (1634–66) *Arien* (Arias; Leipzig, 1656) and *Neue Arien* (New Arias; Leipzig; 1667), each collection containing 50 songs; in the second edition (1676) of *Neue Arien* 10 songs were added. Texts of the songs vary from pastoral and mythological love poems to bawdy drinking songs. Most of the songs are for solo voice with basso continuo; 20 of them are for from two to five voices, and all are supplied with instrumental *ritornelli*. The *Neue Arien* are strophic songs, with each strophe in binary or bar (AAB) form, and five-part instrumental *ritornelli* between strophes. Seemingly, composers wrote few independent songs during the last decades of the seventeenth century; it is possible, however, that because of printing difficulties many songs did not sur-

vive. Also, the song was absorbed into the composite forms then current—opera, cantata, and oratorio. Among the few secular cantata collections printed were those by Telemann, who engraved and published many of his own works.

Summary

Monteverdi was a principal figure in the transition from Renaissance to Baroque in music. He realized that two styles of music could coexist and originated the idea and the terminology of two practices: *prima prattica* or *stile antico,* denoting Renaissance polyphony in which music took precedence over words; and *seconda prattica* or *stile moderno,* in which the text dominated the music. Baroque composers adopted the concept of two practices but with somewhat different connotations. For Baroque composers, *seconda prattica* denoted accompanied monody; Monteverdi believed either practice could be used in polyphonic music. He continued to write ensemble madrigals long after other composers abandoned them. Some of his church music is traditional Netherlands-based polyphony; in other sacred music outdated compositional techniques, e.g., cantus firmus, mingle with operatic elements.

Monteverdi's interpretation of Platonic precepts convinced him of music's power to move human affections. He used dissonance expressively, for affective purposes, and, in accordance with Plato's philosophy, associated certain rhythmic patterns with certain human emotions. Monteverdi was a master of the use of musical figuration to depict various human emotions. His affective use of rhythmic figures resulted in his creation of *stile concitato,* the excited style, featuring measured tremolo.

In Florence, the interests of the humanists and literati led to the creation of accompanied monody and led from there to an approximation of dramatic presentations in the manner of the ancient Greeks and

Romans. Opera resulted. Opera, and the similarly structured forms known as oratorio and cantata, were the main forms of vocal music composed during the Baroque era. But opera was not entirely new—it had many precursors: ancient Greek dramas, medieval liturgical dramas, religious mystery and morality plays, some trouvère plays, *intermedi,* dramatic madrigals and madrigal cycles, and the pastorale.

Peri's *Dafne,* the first opera, a Florentine court presentation in 1598, was soon followed by several operas on the Euridice-Orpheus myth, produced at Florence and Mantua. The Florentine composers relied heavily on recitative-type monody, but Monteverdi included strophic variations, arioso, and madrigals, and used ostinato figures and longer ground bass melodies. Monteverdi was interested in psychology, knew human nature, and was adept at characterization. His composition of a full-length comic opera (*opera buffa*) was unusual, as was his choice of subject matter for his last opera—historical events with human characters. *L'incoronazione de Poppea* is one of the finest operas composed in the seventeenth century.

Monteverdi moved from Mantua to St. Mark's, Venice, in 1612; operas by him were presented in private homes in the 1620s. By the early 1630s, the operatic center was Venice; there, the first public opera house opened in 1637. Venetian opera was spread throughout Italy by traveling opera companies and was extended to other lands by enthusiastic patrons who moved to other countries, by foreigners who experienced opera while visiting Italian courts, by Italian composers who secured appointments in other countries, and by foreign composers who studied and worked in Italy and carried the form back to their own lands. Italian-born Lully was primarily responsible for the creation of French opera, with its emphasis on *divertissements* and ballets. No national school of opera formed in England. Opera was slow getting started in Germany, where it was rooted in *Singspiel* and school drama. After the establishment of a German opera company in Hamburg (1678), German opera was enjoyed there for about 50 years. In Spain, Calderón invented the *zarzuela,* modeled after Italian opera but using spoken dialogue. Very early in the eighteenth century, operas were composed in Peru and Mexico.

Allegorical opera, bordering on being sacred, began in Rome in 1600, with the staging of *Rappresentatione di Anima, et di Corpo* in the Oratory del Chiesa Nuova; true sacred opera originated in Rome c. 1630, with the operas of Landi and the libretti of Rospigliosi.

Oratorio was an outgrowth of Neri's religious meetings in Rome, where it evolved from the musical dialogues of Anerio. Later oratorios resembled opera in musical design, but were not staged, and were usually on religious subjects. By mid-seventeenth century, both Latin and vernacular oratorios were written.

The Passion, a liturgical presentation for centuries, assumed the character of oratorio in the seventeenth century, using recitative, arioso, aria, ensembles, chorus, and a few purely instrumental pieces. The Passions of Schütz are the most significant Lutheran music in this semidramatic form prior to J. S. Bach.

In 1600, the term cantata denoted piece of vocal music. As the seventeenth century advanced, features of opera were absorbed by cantata, which, by 1650, was structured as a series of recitative-aria combinations. In the Lutheran church, the cantata was given an instructive function and placed in the liturgy, in proximity to the homily. The Lutheran cantata reached its height at the hands of J. S. Bach.

Baroque Vocal Music

Baroque Instrumental Music

During the seventeenth century the production of instrumental music increased steadily; by the end of the century instrumental music was on a par with vocal music in both quality and quantity. Four principal types of instrumental works were written: (1) dance music, either for dancing or stylized and intended for listening; (2) quasi-improvisatory works; (3) variations; and (4) pieces in imitative counterpoint, either (a) nonsectional works such as the *ricercar* or (b) sectional pieces of the *canzona* type, written for the most part in imitative counterpoint but sometimes including sections stylistically different. These categories are not mutually exclusive; for example, quasi-improvisatory style or variation technique might appear in any of the types. Moreover, the title given a piece does not always indicate its true character—a piece entitled *fantasia* might be a *ricercar* or might be in improvisatory style.

Instrumental Music Types

Pieces in Imitative Counterpoint

Most ricercars are nonsectional compositions of motetlike character with thematic material treated in continuous imitation. Generally, the pieces are of short to moderate length. Most ricercars are monothematic, but a number of polythematic ricercars exist. Terminology was not precise; this kind of composition might be labeled *ricercar, capriccio, fuga, verset, fantasia,* or with some other name. Eventually, the monophonic nonsectional ricercar merged into the fugue.

The term *fantasia* (imagination, whim) was frequently applied to a ricercar-type composition that was of considerable length and had a rather complex formal organization. An example is Jan Pieterszoon Sweelinck's (1562–1621) *Fantasia chromatica* (Chromatic fantasia), in Dorian mode (DWMA118). In this four-voice imitative piece for organ, the subject, a chromatically descending tetrachord from tonic to dominant, is introduced in the alto part and is restated immediately in the superius, accompanied by countersubject in the alto. Essentially, the subject remains unchanged throughout the 160-measure composition, though at times it appears in augmentation (note values doubled) and in diminution (note values halved). The counterpoint becomes more complex as the composition proceeds; many of the technical devices common to fugue are present. Sweelinck explored thoroughly all the possibilities inherent in the material. Compositions of this kind are difficult to classify, for they possess a dual nature—they are monothematic, imitative, and contrapuntal, as is a ricercar; they contain many elements of fugue, as does a ricercar; also, they are quasi-improvisatory in character.

In the seventeenth century, English composers wrote contrapuntal *fancies* or *fantasias* for chamber ensembles of strings without basso continuo. The short fugal sections characteristic of the English *fancy* are present in Matthew Locke's (c. 1622–77) *Fantazia* for a **consort** (ensemble) of four viols. The compositions John Jenkins (1592–1678) labeled *fancy* exhibit

Baroque Instrumental Music

1600	1625	1650	1675	1700	1725	1750

ricercar -

monothematic nonsectional ⎫
ricercar and canzona ⎬ merge into fugue

canzona -

sectional canzona becomes *sonata da chiesa*

contrapuntal fancy; fantasia -

dance music stylized - - - - - - - - -

  collections of dance music - - - - - - - - - - - - - - - - - -

                           1649 Froberger: suites of dances

1620s—grouping of   c. 1650 gigue included in suite
allemande-courante-sarabande

                                                      1693 order of movements in suite standardized

French lute *style brisé*
transferred to keyboard by Froberger and Chambonnières

keyboard toccata - - - - with fugato sections - - - - - with alternating free-fantasia

                                    and fugal sections - - - - toccata and fugue - - - - - - - - - -

                            various well-tempered tunings - - - - - - - - - - - - - - - c. 1735 equal
                                                               temperament

                                        fugue -

                       chorale-based organ compositions -

                                 keyboard sonata -
                                 1692 Kuhnau Sonatas

variation: theme and variation -

  continuous variation over ostinato bass -

characteristics of both ricercar and canzona; some of his *fancies* for two violins and bass resemble Italian trio sonatas in many respects.

During the seventeenth century, the canzona was not composed according to one definitive formal pattern but might be structured in any one of several ways: (1) in several contrasting sections, each having its own theme treated imitatively, in a manner resembling the points of imitation of a chanson, and with the final cadence prefaced by a cadenzalike passage, e.g., the anonymous *Canzona per l'epistola* (Canzona for the Epistle; DWMA119); (2) as a *variation canzona,* in which variations or transformations of a single theme serve as subject matter for the several sections, e.g., G. M. Trabaci's *Canzona francese* (French canzona); and (3) in several contrasting sections that are totally unrelated thematically and that vary considerably in length and musical style, e.g., Frescobaldi's *Canzona.* Many canzonas commence with the rhythmic figure ♩ ♪ ♪ or a variant thereof.

As the seventeenth century advanced, composers gradually altered the canzona by writing fewer sections but increasing their length; contrasting meters and tempos were designated, e.g., *Canzon detta la Vesconta* (Canzona called La Viscontessa) from Tarquinio Merula's (c. 1595–1665) second book of canzoni (1639). In some canzoni, homophonic sections alternated with contrapuntal ones. Eventually, each section became a self-sufficient movement, and the multisectional canzona became the multimovement *sonata da chiesa* (church sonata). In fact, the instrumental ensemble work Merula named *Canzon detta la Vesconta* could be considered a trio sonata.

Variation

Variation technique figured prominently in much of the instrumental music of the seventeenth century. The three principal types of variation in use are rooted in Renaissance compositional procedures. These types are: (1) cantus firmus variation, (2) melodic paraphrase variation, and (3) variation over an ostinato bass or chordal framework. Also, many composers wrote sets of variations on secular songs; **song variations** were favored by composers of harpsichord music late in the seventeenth century and became known later as **theme and variation.**

As the name implies, in **cantus firmus variation,** the melody was treated as a cantus firmus—it remained constant and virtually unchanged through all repetitions but usually was not retained in the same voice part in all variations. In each variation the melody was surrounded or supported by different counterpoint. Cantus firmus variation had considerable use in organ music, especially in chorale variations. Examples abound in Samuel Scheidt's (1587–1654) *Tabulatura nova* (New Tabulature; 3 vols.; 1624); *Warum betrübst du dich, mein Herz* (Why are you troubled, my heart) is one. *Tabulatura nova* was the first German publication of keyboard music notated in score. The first two volumes contain mainly sets of variations, including eight sets of cantus firmus variations based on Lutheran chorales. In the seven sets based on secular melodies paraphrase technique predominates. Volume 3 of *Tabulatura nova* was designed to meet the precise needs of a Lutheran church organist in Halle, Germany, and contains a repertory of liturgical music for the church year. The hymn settings are variation sets; in the first variation of each set, Scheidt treated each phrase of the chorale cantus firmus as a point of imitation.

In **paraphrase variation,** the contrapuntal harmonies remain constant, and in each variation the melody is altered by means of different embellishments. The melody is always apparent, however, and is usually retained in the uppermost part. Johann Adam Reinken's (1623–1722) *Partite diverse sopra l'Aria "Schweiget mir von Weiber nehmen"* (Diverse variations on the song "Say nothing to me about getting married") is an example.

In the late Renaissance and early Baroque eras, repeated chordal schemes with bass lines that were fixed successions of root-position triads served as the basis for some dance music—the *passamezzo, Romanesca, Ruggiero, La Folia,* and others. During the many repetitions of the bass line, or harmonic *ground,* as it became known, melodic and contrapuntal variation occurred within the chordal framework. Some of the bass lines were associated with treble melodies, e.g., the *Romanesca* and *La Folia,* but after their initial presentation in a piece those melodies were usually obscured by figuration. Each repetition of the harmonic pattern formed a *parte* or variation section; the entire composition was a *partita* or set of variations. Frescobaldi's *Partite sopra l'aria della Romanesca* (Variations on the Romanesca song) is one.

The polarized concentration on bass line and melody during the Baroque era resulted in emphasis being placed on the bass line itself as a ground for variations, and shorter *basso ostinato* patterns such as *passacaglia* and *chaconne* received increased attention as foundation for continuous-variation pieces. Originally, there may have been a distinction between *passacaglia* and *chaconne,* but through the years composers used the terms interchangeably to such an extent that attempts to definitively differentiate *passacaglia* and *chaconne* have been futile.

Dance Music

A wealth of dance music was produced during the seventeenth century—music for dancing; incidental music for dance scenes in operas, plays, and other spectacles; and stylized dance pieces for listening pleasure. Moreover, various elements of dance music infiltrated other music, both vocal and instrumental, e.g., the clear metric organization of the rhythm, specific rhythmic patterns, standardized chordal schemes, well-known ground bass and treble melodies. Structurally, most of the individual dance pieces were in binary form; some use was made of alternating form (such as *rondeau,* e.g., ABACADA) and continuous variation.

Dancing was cultivated by the nobility and by their middle-class admirers and emulators; there was an abundance of dancing-masters to assist in the pursuit of dancing skills, and some dance manuals were printed. Ballroom dancing was a daily pastime at court and an important part of state celebrations. The types of dances performed varied considerably and included stately processional dances, leaping dances, circle dances, and progressive long dances. Many dances popular during the Renaissance remained favorites in the seventeenth century, but as the century progressed gradual changes crept in, so that by the end of the century most of the dances had been transformed considerably, though they still retained their Renaissance names.

Dances

By 1600, the *basse danse* had disappeared; its position as an introductory dance was taken over by the *pavane*. Paired with the *pavane* was the *galliard,* a lively but not rapid dance. The galliard was one of the few dances men performed with their heads uncovered; when dancing the galliard, a man held his hat in his hand. In Italy in the early seventeenth century, the pavane was rare, but the galliard was a favorite dance. Early in the century, the *passamezzo* and *saltarello* were still used, but by c. 1640 the *passamezzo* was no longer danced.

The *allemande* and *courante* were still popular but were not always paired. By mid-seventeenth century the tempo of the courante had become much slower. In the second half of the century it was the preferred dance for inaugurating a court ball, but after 1700 the courante was rarely danced. Early in the seventeenth century, English composers wrote stylized versions of the *alman* for keyboard; *The Fitzwilliam Virginal Book* (1609–19) contains several.

The *zarabanda* (*sarabande*) appeared in Spain in the 1580s and by the early 1620s was known in Italy. Presumably, the *zarabanda* originated in Latin America. According to contemporary accounts, it was a dance so sexually suggestive that its performance was forbidden; persons caught dancing the *zarabanda* were whipped and exiled. The *chacona,* described as passionate, sensual, and wild, was sung and danced in Mexico in the 1590s; it reached Spain before 1605, and, despite its obscenity—or perhaps because the obscenity was considered humorous—the *chacona* became the leading Spanish dance during the first quarter of the seventeenth century. The *chacona*

became slower and more dignified as it spread through France and into Germany during the second quarter of the seventeenth century. The danced *passacaglia* was similar to the *chacona* but less unbridled. Seventeenth-century dance manuals do not include instructions for the *sarabande, chacona,* and other popular dances considered too crude or degrading for use at court.

The *jig* was sung and danced as part of court entertainment during the reign of Elizabeth I. In addition, jigs formed a substantial part of farces called *jiggs* and appeared as incidental music in plays; stylized jigs were written for performance by instrumental ensembles. A form of jig was introduced into France by Jacques Gaultier (died c. 1660), who worked as lutenist at the London court for about 30 years. The French called the piece *gigue;* soon *gigues* appeared in French collections of harpsichord and lute music. For both English and French, the word *jig* or *gigue* signified a style as well as a specific dance. The words *en gigue* were sometimes appended to other pieces, e.g., *allemande en gigue.* The gigue achieved popularity in Germany as a stylized dance form after 1650.

It should be noted that the dances changed considerably during the course of the century; by the end of the century, none of them was the same as it had been originally.

Suite

Many collections of dance music were published—more than a hundred such collections were printed in Germany in the first two decades of the seventeenth century—and dance music was included in collections of instrumental solo and ensemble music intended for use by talented, trained amateur musicians. Certain dances were printed as pairs, and in a few books sequences of dances were indicated. The earliest known use of the term *suytte* (literally, pieces following one another) for a group of dance pieces occurred in Estienne du Tertre's *Septième livre de danceries* (Seventh book of dance pieces; 1557). Tertre's *suyttes* were groups of *bransles* (fig. 16.1).

During the first quarter of the seventeenth century, there was a great deal of mobility and interchange among musicians of all nationalities. French

Figure 16.1 Table of contents of du Tertre's *Septieme livre de danceries* (1557) uses the term *suytte.*

musicians worked at the English court; Britain had royal connections with several northern European countries, and a considerable number of English musicians traveled and worked in northern Europe. Before the Thirty Years' War, many English composers had their works published in Germany. German collections of music included Polish dances (*Polischner Tanze*). Many persons went to Italy to study; musicians at the Spanish courts in southern Italy popularized the guitar and its music. This internationalism is reflected in the grouping of dance pieces into the *suite.*

English composers, especially those working in Germanic lands, seem to have been the first to group several dances that originated in different countries and to link the dances by thematic variation. German composers soon took up the practice. William Brade (1560–1630), an English viol player and composer working variously at Brandenburg, Bückeburg, and Hamburg, published a collection entitled *Newe ausserlesene Paduanen, Galliarden, Canzonen, Allmand und Coranten . . . auff allen musicalischen Instrumenten lieblich zu gebrauchen* (Selected new pavanes, galliards, canzonas, allemandes and courantes . . . for all appropriate musical instruments; 5 pts.; 1609). Two years later, German organist-composer Paul Peuerl (1570–c. 1626) published a volume of suitelike compositions, *Newe Padouan, Intrada, Däntz unnd Galliarda mit vier Stimmen* (New pavanes, intradas, German dances and galliards for four parts;

1611). These are variation suites: the basic theme is presented in the *Dantz,* and the other dances use variations of it. Grouping of pavane, galliard, courante, and allemande became common.

One of the most significant collections of grouped dances is J. H. Schein's (1586–1630) *Banchetto musicale* (Musical banquet; 1617). The volume contains 20 numbered groups of dances for five unspecified instruments ("but preferably viols") without basso continuo. As Schein stated in his Preface, the dances "correspond with one another in both mode and invention." Each group—Schein did not call the groups suites—is actually the combination of two paired dances, *pavane-galliard* and *allemande-tripla,* separated by a *courante.* The *allemande* and *tripla* are homophonic and not far removed from actual dance music; the *tripla* is a strict proportional reworking—a variation—of the *allemande* in triple time. Pavane and galliard are contrapuntal and stylized; the courante, in $\frac{6}{4}$ meter, is intermediate in style. There is thematic resemblance, and some sharing of melodic motives, among dances that are grouped.

The suite for keyboard or lute became a multimovement musical entity in three stages: (1) In the 1620s, three dances—*allemande, courante,* and *sarabande*—formed the core of the suite. (2) Around 1650, the *gigue* was often included with the other three dances, but the movements were presented in no established order. (3) By the last quarter of the seventeenth century, a standard pattern had been established for the order of presentation of the core movements of the suite. This may be illustrated by three collections of suites by Johann Jakob Froberger (1616–67). One autograph manuscript, dated 1649, holds five suites; four of them consist of *allemande-courante-sarabande,* and Suite No. 2 contains *allemande-courante-sarabande-gigue.* A second autograph manuscript, written before 1656, also contains five suites, each having four movements arranged as *allemande-gigue-courante-sarabande.* Note that all suites but one conclude with a *sarabande,* a slow dance. In a book of Froberger's suites published posthumously (1693), the *publisher* rearranged the order of the movements to conform with the pattern then standard: *allemande-courante-sarabande-gigue.* It is not known whether Froberger himself ever sanctioned the sequential order that ultimately became standard for the core movements of the Baroque suite: *allemande-courante-sarabande-gigue*. All of Froberger's suite movements are in binary form, with each half repeated; all movements of a suite are in the same key (DWMA120). The allemande is the most elaborate movement, and usually the allemande and courante have some limited thematic relationship.

Froberger wrote several pieces entitled *Tombeau, Lamentation,* or *Lamento;* each is in the style of an allemande and was used in lieu of the allemande in a suite. Perhaps the best known of these pieces is the *Lamento sopra la dolorosa perdita della Real Maestà di Ferdinando IV* (Lament on the deplorable loss [i.e., death] of His Majesty Ferdinand IV). This lament, which serves as allemande in Suite No. 12, is comparable to the French *tombeau* and is somewhat programmatic; it concludes with a three-octave ascending scale that symbolizes the emperor's ascent to heaven.

During his travels, Froberger observed and absorbed characteristic elements of French and Italian musical styles; he amalgamated these with German stylistic traits, and he produced keyboard works regarded as being distinctly German; this is particularly apparent in his toccatas. Through his keyboard suites he helped transfer to Germany the French stylistic concept of the various dances. His mastery of the so-called *style brisé* (broken style; see pp. 351–52) used by French lutenists and clavecinists is apparent in the *Lamento* previously mentioned.

The four dances German composers accepted as standard movements in the keyboard suite might be supplemented by an introductory movement (called *intrada, praeludium,* or some similar name) and/or one or more optional movements placed before or after the sarabande or after the gigue. Such optional movements might be *gavotte, bourrée, minuet, chaconne, loure, canarie,* or other stylized dances. Sometimes a dance—especially a courante or a sarabande—was followed by an ornamented version of that dance, called a *double*. The number of movements in a Baroque suite varies considerably—there may be as few as 3, especially in early suites, or as many as 30 (in some French suites); most of the Baroque suites contain 4 to 6 rather short movements. The addition of optional dance movements reflects French influence, for the French considered a suite more an anthology of dances than a strict sequence of movements in a multimovement work. The French are credited also with establishing the characteristic style and idiom of each of the dance movements.

The various movements of a suite contrast in meter and tempo, but all movements are in the same key, and most of the movements are in binary form. The *allemande* is in moderate tempo, duple meter, and usually is polyphonic in texture, with all parts sharing in a continuous flow of music written in small note values. Normally, the allemande commences with an **anacrusis** (upbeat); however, quite a few allemandes have no anacrusis.

The allemande is followed by a French *courante* (running) or an Italian *corrente*. Though the two words are literal synonyms, their musical connotation is not identical. Composers were not always particular about which of the two labels they chose for this movement and sometimes attached an Italian name to a movement in French style, or vice versa. At times, French and Italian styles were intermingled in a movement. The Italian *corrente,* in $\frac{3}{4}$ or $\frac{3}{8}$ meter, is filled with running notes and proceeds at a lively tempo. The French *courante* is in $\frac{3}{2}$ or $\frac{6}{4}$ meter but is more moderate in tempo; it is highly stylized, with subtle syncopations, and is somewhat more contrapuntal than the *corrente*. Typically, the courante uses dotted rhythms, such as ♩ ♪♪ | ♩ ♩ ♪ or ♩. ♪♪ | ♩. ♪♪ , which reflect the hopping character of the actual dance. Some use of hemiola is usually present, e.g., the combination of $\frac{3}{2}$ meter in one part with $\frac{6}{4}$ in another. Often, especially in early suites, the allemande and courante have some thematic relationship.

The *sarabande* is in a slow tempo and in triple meter, usually $\frac{3}{2}$. It commences on the beat, i.e., without anacrusis. The rhythmic pattern

♩ ♩. ♩ | ♩ 𝅝

is typical; note the slight cessation of motion and consequent agogic accent created by dotting the second note.

The *gigue* (Italian, *giga*) is in quick tempo, in compound duple or triple meter ($\frac{6}{8}$, $\frac{9}{8}$, $\frac{12}{8}$); occasionally, $\frac{4}{4}$ meter and dotted rhythms were used. Features of the melody are triplets and frequent wide leaps; imitative contrapuntal texture is common. Frequently, the gigue commences with an eighth note anacrusis; often the second section of the binary-form movement starts with a mirror inversion of the opening motive.

Quasi-improvisatory Compositions

Pieces in improvisatory style were written for solo keyboard or solo lute and were called *fantasia, toccata,* or *prelude.* The fantasia was aptly described by Mersenne, who wrote in *Harmonie universelle* (1636) that the musician might "employ whatever inspiration comes to him, without expressing the passion of any text." Fantasias vary considerably in length, form, and meter.

The composed *prelude* evolved from short improvisations made by instrumentalists checking the tuning (lutenists) or testing the touch (keyboard players) of their instruments. Church organists improvised short "preludes" to establish the mode and pitch of music to be sung during the liturgy. A composed prelude has no special form but usually is a self-contained piece. In the seventeenth century, French composers wrote a kind of prelude termed *prélude non mesuré* (unmeasured prelude)—a piece in free rhythm and without metric indications. Some of the earliest unmeasured preludes were written for lute by Denis Gaultier (in *La rhétorique des dieux*) and for harpsichord by Louis Couperin, Lebègue, and D'Anglebert.

Toccatas were composed in the late sixteenth century by Bertoldo, Diruta, Gabrieli, and others; many toccatas were written during the seventeenth and early eighteenth centuries. Toccatas vary considerably in content and design. In Merulo's toccatas, one hand is given brilliant runs and ornamental figuration to perform while the other hand plays predominantly chordal material. Both hands share in both types of material. Some of Frescobaldi's toccatas are reserved and mystical, without undue technical display, and well suited to the portions of the Mass for which they were intended, e.g., the toccatas in *Fiori musicali* that

are used at Elevation of the Host. His *Toccata di durezze e ligature* (Toccata with dissonances and suspensions), the eighth toccata in *Il secondo libro di toccata* (1627), was designed for use at Elevation. This piece is filled with chromaticisms but is devoid of virtuosic runs and figuration. Other toccatas by Frescobaldi are more brilliant and rhapsodic, with figuration in two or three lines simultaneously, e.g., *Toccata IX* (DWMA121).

Froberger transmitted Frescobaldi's toccata style to Austria. Some of Froberger's toccatas have many sections; continuity and systematic organization are apparent in the contrapuntal sections, in contrast with the rhapsodic figuration of sections in improvisatory style. Frescobaldi and Froberger notated their toccatas on two staves, a treble staff of six lines, and a bass staff of seven. Some of Froberger's toccatas were known in France and were transcribed for other instruments.

French Lute Music

The earliest known French suites with allemande-courante-sarabande nucleus are François Chancy's (d. 1656) six short suites for mandore (a small, lutelike instrument) published in *Tablature de mandure* (1629). Lute music flourished in France during the early seventeenth century and is highly significant historically, for the lutenists cultivated a musical style that not only was transferred to harpsichord but also influenced the entire French style of composition for more than a century.

Both lute and harpsichord are incapable of sustaining tones. Lutenists dealt with this problem by breaking the chords into arpeggiations and figurations, and by sounding the tones of melody, harmony, and bass individually, distributing them through the various registers of the instrument, in a more or less continuous flow of small note values. It was left to the listener to assimilate the component parts and complete the musical picture from the lutenist-composer's sketch. This presents no difficulty, for usually the melody is unclouded, phrases are clearly defined, and all basic elements of the music—melody, harmony, rhythm, and texture—are coordinated. If seventeenth-century lutenists had a special name for this style of writing, that name has not survived; in the twentieth century, the term *style brisé* (broken style) was coined to describe it. In conjunction with their special style of writing, lutenist-composers developed a system of *agréments* (graces, i.e., little ornaments) some of which they indicated in the notation by small symbols that served as stenographic signs; others were improvised, at the discretion of the performer. Composers of keyboard music adapted the lutenists' style to the harpsichord, along with the system of *agréments*. Some composers used the word *luthée* (literally, luted) in connection with keyboard music written in this style. Foreign musicians who visited in France—Froberger was one—became acquainted with these techniques and introduced them in their countries.

The most significant French contributions to seventeenth-century repertoire for lute were made by Denis and Ennemond Gaultier, who were cousins. Ennemond (1575–1651), called *le vieux Gaultier* (the old Gaultier), achieved fame at court as performer and lute teacher; though his lute solos were widely known, very few of them were printed during his lifetime. Denis Gaultier (1603–72), called *Gaultier de Paris* (the Paris Gaultier), played his lute in the salons of Paris; he had no court position. Compositions by Ennemond and Denis are similar in style, and some confusion exists with regard to authorship of some works. A number of pieces are signed only "Gaultier." There survive in manuscript approximately 75 dance pieces, mainly *courantes* and *allemandes,* and several harpsichord transcriptions of some lute compositions.

Livre de tablature (Tablature book; 1672) contains an equal number of pieces by Denis and Ennemond; these attributions are clear. Ennemond is represented by a lute suite in a collection entitled *Suittes facile* (Easy suites; 1703). Both *Pièces de luth sur trois differens modes nouveaux* (Lute pieces in three different new modes; c. 1672) and *La rhétorique des dieux* (The rhetoric of the gods; c. 1652), which the title pages indicate are by Denis, contain some pieces attributed to Ennemond in other sources. *La rhétorique des dieux* contains 56 stylized dances, grouped into 12 sets, one in each of the 12 modes. Each set comprises *allemande, courante, sarabande,* and a varied number of other dances in random order (fig. 16.2).

LA DEDICASSE.

Figure 16.2 *La Dedicasse,* in lute tablature, from Gaultier's *La rhétorique des dieux* (Paris, c. 1652). *(Source: Denis Gaultier,* La rhétorique des dieux, *Berlin, Kupferstichkabinett MS 142,* c. *1650, folios 25, 26.)*

La rhétorique des dieux concludes with a program suite—a *tombeau* (lament) for lutenist Henri L'Enclos (c. 1593–1649). In addition to being labeled *Allemande Grave, Courante,* and *Chaconne ou Sarabande,* each of the three movements was given a descriptive title. The Gaultiers were pioneers of the *tombeau* for lute and composed several of them. The instrumental *tombeau* follows the tradition of the *déplorátions* that Medieval and Renaissance poets and composers wrote in commemoration of an esteemed teacher or colleague at the time of his death.

Organ Music

At least two dozen composers made significant contributions to the development of organ music during the seventeenth and early eighteenth centuries; most of them worked in the northern and central parts of Germany, in Lutheran areas. In the southern territories, where Catholicism prevailed, the function of the organ was mainly to supply accompaniment for the Services; this included cantus-firmus-type compositions connected with the liturgy.

At the beginning of the seventeenth century, the chief composers of organ music were Jan Pieterszoon Sweelinck (1562–1621) of Amsterdam and Samuel Scheidt (1587–1654) of Halle. Sweelinck was one of the most famous and respected organists and teachers of his time. Among his pupils were the founders of the north German school of organists, which culminated in J. S. Bach. All of Sweelinck's instrumental music is for keyboard; none of it was published during his lifetime. He wrote in the established forms of the time, and he incorporated quasi-improvisational and variation techniques in many of his compositions. In most of his *toccatas,* homophonic or imitative sections are interspersed with sections of extended passage work. His monothematic *fantasias,* with imitation on tonic and dominant levels, are important forerunners of the monothematic *fugue.*

Scheidt's principal contribution to organ literature is his three-volume *Tabulatura nova* (see p. 347). His predilection for contrapuntal writing and variation technique, as well as his use of certain motivic figurations, reflect the influence of Sweelinck, with whom he studied for a time.

German organists and composers influential later in the century include Franz Tunder (1614–67) and his son-in-law and successor Dietrich Buxtehude (c. 1637–1707) at Lübeck; F. W. Zachow (1663–1712) of Halle, who was Handel's teacher; Johann Kuhnau (1660–1722), J. S. Bach's predecessor at Thomaskirche, Leipzig; Johann Christoph Bach (1642–1703) of Eisenach, the most important Bach musician prior to Johann Sebastian; and Johann Pachelbel (1653–1706) of Nuremberg and Erfurt. All of these organists composed vocal as well as instrumental music.

Three principal types of organ music were written: quasi-improvisatory compositions usually termed *toccata* but sometimes named *prelude* or *fantasia; fugue;* and *chorale*-based compositions. To a lesser extent, *passacaglias* and *chaconnes* were produced.

Toccata

The *toccata* retained its quasi-improvisational character and became a vehicle for virtuosic display, especially on the pedals. *Toccatas* by German composers were distinctive in their inclusion of passages featuring pedal work. The rhapsodic nature of the toccata was somewhat disciplined by the use of sequences,

either melodically or imitatively, and by the inclusion of sections of imitative counterpoint. Occasionally, a brief homophonic section was included. Pachelbel used sequences effectively in his short *Toccata in e minor.* The contrast between freedom and discipline may be seen in toccatas that commence quasi-improvisationally and include one lengthy fugal section; often, compositions of this type were entitled *Praeludium cum fuga* (Prelude *with* fugue). The *Praeludium cum fuga* by Buxtehude, DWMA122, is a toccata-type piece with several well-defined sections that contrast in tempo, meter, and style. The opening rhapsodic Largo is followed by a lengthy fugal Allegro in which the pedals participate actively. The third section, a Largo, features pedal passages that include long trills. Melodic and harmonic sequences figure prominently in several of the seven sections of the piece. The penultimate section, a four-measure Adagio, is sandwiched between a gigue-like Allegro and an imitative Allegro with driving rhythm.

The imitative contrapuntal (i.e., fugal) section of the toccata gradually was accorded increased importance and ultimately became an independent piece— a **fugue**—which often was coupled with and introduced by a quasi-improvisatory, virtuosic toccata, fantasia, or prelude, e.g., Johann Christoph Bach's *Praeludium und fuge* (Prelude *and* fugue).

Fugue

The term *fuga* (flight) was applied variously over the centuries to imitative works now known as **canons** and to pieces with imitative entries. The motetlike ricercar or fantasia, and those organ *canzoni* that are monothematic and nonsectional, were important forerunners of the independent **fugue.** Sweelinck might have named his *Chromatic fantasia* a *fuga* (DWMA118); in it he employed many technical devices that became standard in fugue: augmentation, diminution, the crowding of entries termed *stretto,* and variation of the subject. Frescobaldi's *Ricercare dopo il Credo* and some of G. Gabrieli's *canzoni* also represent early stages in the development of fugue.

Some of the early fugues were quite short. When Pachelbel became organist at St. Sebald in Nuremberg (1695), he composed 95 short fugues for use as preludes to establish the pitch for singing of the Magnificat at Vespers.

The fugue did not attain perfection until the major-minor system of key tonality had been fully developed. The viability of the fugue as a keyboard work was dependent upon the tempered tuning of keyboard instruments. The culmination of these developments resulted in J. S. Bach's production of *The Well-Tempered Clavier,* vol. I, in 1722—a series of 24 preludes and fugues, one in each of the major and minor keys, all suitable for performance on the same keyboard instrument, which had been tuned according to one of the well-tempered methods then current (see p. 414).

In its perfected form, the independent fugue is an imitative contrapuntal composition characterized by two types of sections that are not clearly marked off: (1) **expositions,** in which the subject is stated and is imitated on tonic and dominant tonal levels, and (2) **episodes,** which are usually modulatory and in which the subject does not appear in its entirety. Within the fugue there is a definite tonic-dominant tonal organization, and there is a sense that the musical material is being propelled energetically toward a climax that is ultimately resolved by the concluding measures of tonic key tonality. In contrast, the *ricercar* is modal (or more closely related to modality than to key tonality) and tends to move serenely and steadily toward its close without varietal disruption or effective climax.

Chorale-based Compositions

During the late seventeenth and early eighteenth centuries, composers used the chorale as basis for several kinds of compositions: (1) **chorale fugue;** (2) **chorale fantasia;** (3) **chorale partita,** also known as **chorale variations;** and (4) **chorale prelude.**

The chorale fugue is a short work in which the first line of a chorale is treated as the subject of a fugue. An organist might perform a chorale fugue in the Lutheran Service as preparation for congregational singing of the chorale; in other words, a chorale fugue served the same function as a chorale prelude. Pachelbel, Johann Christoph Bach, and other organists in central Germany were the principal composers of chorale fugues.

The chorale prelude (German, *Choralvorspiel*) is a rather short polyphonic setting of an entire chorale melody. The individual phrases of the chorale are not separated by interludes. Composers treated the chorale melody in various ways: (1) The entire melody might be presented in long note values and be retained in the uppermost part throughout the composition; (2) the entire melody might be written in long note values but the individual phrases be distributed successively among the several polyphonic lines; (3) the entire melody might be ornamented or paraphrased and retained in the superius; or (4) each phrase of the chorale melody might be treated as a point of imitation, as in a *chorale motet* or *chorale ricercar.* Buxtehude frequently paraphrased or embellished the chorale melody, as he did in his chorale prelude on *Nun komm, der Heiden Heiland* (Now come, Savior of the heathen). DWMA123 presents for comparison four chorale preludes written by different composers (Scheidt, Buxtehude, Pachelbel, and J. S. Bach) on the same melody, *Vater unser im Himmelreich* (Our Father in heaven). The chorale prelude attained culmination in the 45 pieces J. S. Bach wrote for his *Orgel-Büchlein* (see DWMA137).

The chorale partita, or chorale variations, is a set of variations based on a chorale melody. Scheidt made extensive use of chorale variation in his *Tabulatura nova* (1624), e.g., in *Warum betrübst du dich, mein Herz* (Why are you troubled, my heart; see p. 347). Pachelbel and J. S. Bach composed several chorale partitas in which the original proportions and often some other features of the preexisting melody were retained in each variation. An example is Bach's chorale partita on *O Gott, du frommer Gott* (O God, thou good God). The exact liturgical function of the chorale partita is not known; perhaps works of this kind were substituted for motets at times when a choir was not available.

The chorale fantasia is a large composition in which the chorale melody is freely and elaborately developed; usually each phrase appears several times with different treatment. Tunder and Buxtehude composed impressive chorale fantasias. Presumably, these works had no liturgical function but were expressly designed for performance in the Lübeck *Abendmusik* concerts, which attracted large audiences, especially in Buxtehude's time. Six of Tunder's extant organ chorale settings are chorale fantasias. A basic structural plan was to present each line of the chorale melody twice, once unadorned as a cantus firmus in long note values and once highly orna-mented. An example is Buxtehude's chorale fantasia on *Ich ruf zu dir* (I call to Thee). Chorale fantasias by Sweelinck and Scheidt are conservative in comparison with those produced later in the century. Two surviving chorale fantasias by Reinken are large-scale, virtuosic works, incorporating much ornamentation and passage work, echo effects, and frequent hand-crossing (one of his specialties).

Italian Composers

Girolamo Frescobaldi

Girolamo Frescobaldi (1583–1643), the leading Italian composer of keyboard music in the first half of the seventeenth century, wrote keyboard works in all of the forms then current. He was born in Ferrara, and it is presumed that he lived there until the court disbanded in 1597. He had organ lessons from Luzzaschi and was a prodigy on that instrument. Some of Frescobaldi's compositions reflect his awareness of musical developments at court—the embellishments Luzzaschi notated in the madrigals composed for the virtuosic *concerto delle donne,* the extreme chromaticism used by Gesualdo, and the polyphonic madrigal with harmonies and texture that were not far removed from the *seconda prattica* of which Monteverdi wrote.

By 1604, Frescobaldi was in Rome. Early in 1607, he became organist at the church of Santa Maria in Trastevere, and later that year he traveled to Brussels with the papal ambassador to Flanders. Frescobaldi returned to Italy early in 1608 and in July was named organist at St. Peter's, Rome. That position was not restrictive, and from time to time he played organ in other churches and religious institutions and played harpsichord at musical gatherings in apartments of several cardinals. He acquired several patrons, including Enzio Bentivoglio and, from c. 1612, Cardinal Pietro Aldobrandini. Occasionally, Frescobaldi negotiated (usually without success) for a court position, for instance, at Mantua shortly after Monteverdi departed for Venice. In 1628 Frescobaldi obtained leave of absence from St. Peter's to serve as court organist in Florence; he resumed duties as organist at St. Peter's in May 1634 and retained that post until his death.

Girolamo Frescobaldi. Engraving by J. Caldwell.

As early as 1609, Frescobaldi began to attract attention as a performer, and his reputation and professional standing increased steadily. By 1630 he was known throughout central Europe and was acclaimed as a teacher. Among his noted pupils was Froberger, who was granted leave from the Viennese court to study with him. Dietrich Buxtehude was acquainted with Frescobaldi's works, and J. S. Bach copied his *Fiori musicali.*

Although Frescobaldi composed both sacred and secular vocal music (Masses, motets, Magnificats, and madrigals), his reputation rests primarily on his instrumental works. Almost all of his compositions are notated in *partitura,* i.e., in open score, each voice of the music notated on a separate staff. His published instrumental works include a book of fantasias (1608); two books of toccatas (1615, 1627); four books of ricercars, canzonas, and capriccios (1615, 1624, 1626, posth. 1645); and *Fiori musicali di diverse composi-tioni, toccate, kyrie, canzoni, capricci, e ricercari, in partitura, a 4* (Musical flowers of diverse compositions, toccatas, kyries, canzonas, capriccios, and ricercars, in open score, 4 vc.; 1635). Both books of toccatas contain some dance pieces, and the second book of toccatas holds some liturgical works, also.

Frescobaldi's stated aim was to raise the quality of organ music and organ playing. To that end, he included in the prefaces of his published works didactic information concerning the proper execution of ornaments and tempos. He used tempo markings liberally—usually *Adagio* and *Allegro*—and advised the performer to commence a piece slowly so that succeeding phrases might seem livelier.

Frescobaldi's toccatas were designed for virtuosic display; they are structured in numerous sections that contrast sharply in character, thereby creating a kind of restlessness. Present in these works are complicated cross-rhythms, proportional changes, imitative counterpoint, considerable chromaticism, and much figuration, especially in the approach to the final cadence, which Frescobaldi sometimes marked *Non senza fatiga si giunge al fine* (Not without effort does one reach the end). All of these features are present in Toccata IX, from *Il secondo libro di toccate, canzone,* . . . (The Second book of toccatas, canzonas . . . ; 1627; DWMA121).

Frescobaldi's early canzonas have several themes treated in contrasting sections; some of the sections are quite short. His later canzonas are monothematic, with fewer and longer sections. Some are variation canzonas, in which variations of the single theme provide subject matter for the various sections.

Since mid-eighteenth century, *Fiori musicali . . .* has been Frescobaldi's most famous publication. Most of the music in the volume is arranged as three organ Masses: *Messa della Dominca, Messa delli Apostoli,* and *Messa della Madonna.* For the Ordinary of these Masses, Frescobaldi composed only the Kyrie; each Kyrie is a *cantus firmus* setting based on a chant that is identified by title: *Kyrie Orbis factor, Kyrie Cunctipotens Genitor, Kyrie Cum jubilo.* Toccatas, ricercars, and canzonas serve as substitutes for sections of the Proper of the Mass: Introit, Gradual, Offertory, and Communion. Each Mass contains toccatas to be played before the Kyrie, before some ricercars, and during Elevation of the Host; ricercars for use after the Credo and in some instances after the Communion; and canzonas for use after the reading of the Epistle and after the Communion. Introductory toccatas are quite short. Those short toccatas designed to precede ricercars create a kind of prelude-and-fugue structure; there are few examples of this kind of

pairing in Italian organ music. Toccatas to be used during Elevation of the Host are longer and more complex. Typical of the ricercars is *Ricercare dopo il Credo* (Ricercare after the Credo) from *Messa della Madonna* (DWMA124). It is monothematic, with a chromatic subject; commencing at m.24, the subject appears in augmentation, with a variant version of the countersubject inverted. For the last six measures, the alto line sustains a dominant pedal. The canzonas are considerably longer than the ricercars and are sectional, with contrasting tempo markings indicated; canzona subjects are less chromatic than those used for ricercars. Some are variation canzonas, e.g., *Canzona dopo l'Epistola. Fiori musicali* concludes with two capriccios that have no specified function in the Masses. Frescobaldi's capriccios exhibit no standard pattern; each displays individuality and is capricious, as its name implies.

Among Frescobaldi's works are some individual dance pieces—mainly *correnti* and *gagliarde*—and some *partitas*. Frescobaldi's *partitas* are sectional compositions, i.e., constructed in *partes*, and related to dance music and to variations. An example is *Partite sopra l'aria della Romanesca* (Sectional variations on the Romanesca song). In addition to the *Romanesca*, variations were written on *La Folia, La Monachina, Ruggiero,* and the various forms of descending-tetrachord pattern known as passacaglia bass.

Bernardo Pasquini

The most important Italian composer of keyboard music between Frescobaldi and Domenico Scarlatti (see p. 439) was Bernardo Pasquini (1637–1710). He was born near Lucca, spent his childhood in Ferrara, and by 1650 was living in Rome, where he worked for the remainder of his life. The names of those who taught him music are not known, but manuscripts in Pasquini's hand indicate that he made a thorough study of Frescobaldi's works by copying some of them, e.g., the entire *Il primo libro delle fantasie* (First book of fantasias). Pasquini became an outstanding virtuoso on both organ and harpsichord and was considered an excellent teacher. He served as organist at various churches in Rome and enjoyed the patronage of several aristocrats, including Queen Christina of Sweden, Prince Colonna, Cardinal Ottoboni, and Prince Giambattista Borghese.

Pasquini's talent was comparable with that exhibited by Frescobaldi earlier in the century and was equal to that of Corelli (see p. 375). Moreover, Pasquini and Corelli were friends, had some of the same patrons, and performed together in concerts, operas, and oratorios. In the musicians' guild, Pasquini became guardian (head) of the organists, and Corelli was guardian of the instrumentalists; they were admitted to the Arcadian academy at the same time, along with Alessandro Scarlatti.

As a composer, Pasquini made significant contributions to vocal as well as to keyboard music. Many of his operas, oratorios, cantatas, and motets have been lost. Surviving compositions indicate that in the development of Roman opera, Pasquini stands between Antonio Cesti and Alessandro Scarlatti.

Little of Pasquini's music was published. The primary source of his keyboard works is a four-volume autograph manuscript, which, it is believed, he compiled c. 1700 for the use of his nephew, who lived with him. Pasquini's surviving keyboard works include about 15 sets of variations, 4 *passacaglias,* 17 suites of dances and numerous individual dances, 34 toccatas, 11 imitative contrapuntal compositions (canzonas, ricercars, capriccios, a fantasia, and a *Fuga*), 4 sonatas for organ, and the figured bass part only for 28 three-movement (Allegro-Andante-Allegro) harpsichord sonatas.

The sets of variations are dance-related and include variations on the *Bergamasca* and two sets on *La Folia.* In the latter, some of the figuration is more idiomatic for violin than keyboard and may perhaps reflect Corelli's influence. The toccatas vary considerably in structure, length, and style. They contain brilliant passage work and figuration, sequences, and pedal points.

The suites constitute Pasquini's most significant contribution to the development of keyboard music in Italy; he was influential in establishing the keyboard suite there. His suites consist basically of *allemanda-corrente-giga* grouping, with the number and type of any additional dances varying. All of the dances are in binary form. (Several of Corelli's trio *sonate da camera,* Op. 2, published in 1685, have the same arrangement.)

German Composers

Dietrich Buxtehude

Little is known concerning the early life of Dietrich Buxtehude. At the time of his birth, the Duchy of Holstein, in which the town of Buxtehude was located, was under control of Denmark; Dietrich always considered Denmark his native country. After the death of Franz Tunder (1667), Buxtehude auditioned for the position of organist at the Marienkirche, Lübeck. He was appointed to the post on 11 April 1668, became a citizen of Lübeck on July 23, and on August 3 married Anna M. Tunder. Presumably, marriage to Tunder's daughter was one condition of Buxtehude's appointment. (Buxtehude imposed a similar requirement upon his successor—that condition deterred several excellent organists from applying.) For almost 40 years Buxtehude served as Marienkirche's organist. He died in May 1707 and was interred in the Marienkirche.

In addition to playing for Services and supplying requisite music therefor, Buxtehude reinstated the type of church concert known as *Abendmusik.* Tunder had held these concerts on weekdays, but Buxtehude moved them to 4 P.M. on Sunday—immediately after afternoon Service—and scheduled them on the last two Sundays of Trinity and the last three Sundays of Advent. Music at these concerts included oratorios or cantatas, vocal concertos, and arias, as well as organ works. A large part of Buxtehude's fame derived from the *Abendmusiken,* which were attended by musicians from all over Germany. Unfortunately, none of Buxtehude's music that is known to have been performed at these concerts is extant.

All but eight of Buxtehude's surviving vocal works have sacred texts. His extant secular works are wedding music; his 120 sacred compositions include cantatas, vocal concertos, chorale settings, and strophic arias.

Buxtehude's organ music was written for the typical north German organ with three manuals and an independent pedalboard, all capable of producing contrasting tonal colors. The organ he played at Lübeck had 52 stops, with 15 of them in the pedal; the pedalboard had a full complement of principals,

insight

Keyboard Instruments

Baroque Organ

The most important German organ builders were members of the Schnitger and Silbermann families. Arp Schnitger (1648–1719), the son of an expert woodcarver, learned the art of organ building from Berendt Hüss, his cousin. Hüss died in 1676, and Schnitger set up his own shop in Neuenfelde, south of Hamburg. While still in his 20s, Schnitger achieved fame as an organ builder and soon was accorded monopolies in certain areas of Germany. He·trained two of his sons, Johann Georg (1690–c.1734) and Franz Caspar (1693–1729) and took them into his shop when they had learned the art. After Arp's death, his sons worked in the Netherlands.

Arp Schnitger constructed more than 150 organs of all sizes. Many of his organs had three or four manuals and a pedalboard of 26 or 27 keys. The "natural" keys of the manuals were covered with ebony, beech, or strips of glazed pottery; the "sharps" had bone or ivory covering. Schnitger's organs had a four-octave compass, from **C** to **c'''**, with the lowest octave being a short one. Most Schnitger organs were in mean-tone temperament (i.e., octaves and ascending thirds tuned true, fifths narrowed) and were tuned about 3/4 of a tone higher in pitch than the standard **A = 440** now in use. Schnitger preferred to use metal pipes, probably because they were easier to make and to voice than wooden ones. J. S. Bach considered the Schnitger organ in Jakobikirche, Hamburg, one of the finest organs he ever played; that organ was still extant in 1987.

In Alsace, Saxony, and Dresden, the Silbermann brothers, Andreas (1678–1734) and Gottfried (1683–1753), were famous for building fine organs. Andreas settled in Strasbourg and trained two of his sons, Johann Andreas (1712–83) and Johann Daniel (1717–66), in the trade. From 1706 to 1710 Gottfried worked in partnership with Andreas in Strasbourg, then established his own shop in Freiberg. Later, Gottfried enjoyed the patronage of Frederick the Great. Several of Gottfried Silbermann's organs are still extant, including a three-manual, 44-stop organ built for Freiberg Cathedral in 1710–14, and a one-manual, 11-stop organ made in 1721–22 for St. Marien Church, Rotha.

Baroque organs were designed so that the performer could achieve a homogeneous blend of sound, yet could enhance and bring into prominence clearly and brilliantly any one of the polyphonic lines. Thus, the instrument was admirably suited for performance of both polyphonic and homophonic music. In the twentieth century, there has been great interest in accuracy of performance practices, and many organs have been built simulating Baroque specifications, especially along the lines of Silbermann instru-

mixtures, and reeds. It is not surprising, therefore, that in Buxtehude's organ works the pedals participate fully, even in the virtuosic display. His organ compositions are of three types: continuous variation over an ostinato, freely composed, and chorale-based. Buxtehude's three ostinato pieces—*Ciaconne in c minor, Ciaconne in e minor,* and *Passacaglia in d minor*—are among his best-known works. Both J. S. Bach and Johannes Brahms knew these compositions and were influenced by them.

All of Buxtehude's freely composed works contain fugal sections. Typically, he began this kind of piece with a prelude, then alternated fugal sections with quasi-improvisatory ones containing virtuosic passage work.

The chorale-based works are mainly short chorale preludes, with the chorale melody highly ornamented and placed in the top voice; the other three voices provide contrapuntal (usually nonimitative) accompaniment. These pieces use two manuals and pedals. Buxtehude's chorale fantasias are virtuosic pieces in which each phrase of the chorale melody is treated separately and is developed extensively, e.g., *Ich ruf zu dir* (I call to Thee). Buxtehude wrote a few chorale variations. His settings have only three or four verses and usually are for manuals only; some verses are *bicinia.*

Buxtehude did not publish any of his harpsichord music. There survive in manuscript 19 suites and 6 sets of secular variations. Almost all of the suites comprise *allemande-courante-sarabande-gigue;* occasionally, a *double* is inserted.

ments. Actually, Silbermann organs are heard at their best in performance of Bach's fantasias, toccatas, and fugues, but Schnitger organs render chorale preludes with finer subtleties.

During the Baroque era, the testing and proving of organs was considered very important. When a new instrument was completed, experts were invited (and were paid handsomely) to come from other cities to examine and test every detail of that organ's construction. J. S. Bach was in great demand as an organ prover; his opinions and suggestions were highly regarded. Bach praised the work of the Leipzig organ builder Johann Schiebe (c. 1680–1748), who in the 1720s enlarged the organs at Thomaskirche and Nicholaikirche (both three-manual instruments, with 36 stops) and in 1742–44 constructed a two-manual organ at Johanniskirche.

Clavier

The term *clavier* (French, keyboard; German, *Klavier*) is generally interpreted to mean harpsichord or clavichord. However, composers used the word *clavier* indiscriminately for keyboard music, and at times music designated for "clavier" may have been intended for performance on an organ. In the seventeenth and eighteenth centuries, the most famous builders of harpsichords were Flemish, especially, members of the Ruckers family in Antwerp. Builders in other countries include members of the Hass and Fleischer families in Germany; Tabel, Shudi, and Kirckman in England; Zenti and Cristofori in Italy; and the Blanchets, the Jacquets, and Taskin in France.

Members of the Jacquet family were master harpsichord builders. In the 1630s, Jehan Jacquet (d. after 1658), of Paris, was considered one of the best harpsichord makers of that time. His son Claude (c. 1605–1674) was equally talented; in 1987, one of Claude's harpsichords was in the Ringling Art Museum, Sarasota, Florida. Jehan's brother Marceau (dates unknown) and his descendants also built harpsichords.

Many harpsichord builders constructed clavichords also. A few clavichords built by J. C. Fleischer and H. A. Hass in the 1720s were still extant in 1988. Gottfried Silbermann was renowned for his clavichords; C. P. E. Bach used one of his instruments for almost half a century. In the early 1730s, Silbermann began to construct fortepianos with action similar to that used by Cristofori. J. S. Bach's adverse criticism of Silbermann's pianos resulted in several improvements, particularly, lighter action and stronger treble register. The piano was not widely used until the second half of the eighteenth century.

Buxtehude's only major publications during his lifetime were three collections of instrumental chamber music. The collection published in 1684 is lost. The other two, issued in 1694 and 1696, each contain seven sonatas for violins, viola da gamba, and harpsichord. Seven additional sonatas survive in manuscript.

Clavier Music

The types of music written for clavier (i.e., harpsichord and clavichord) during the late seventeenth and early eighteenth centuries include quasi-improvisational pieces, such as the toccata, fantasia, and prelude; fugues; variations, such as chaconne, passacaglia, and theme and variations; suites; and, after c. 1690, sonatas. Of these types, the two most important were the suite and the theme and variations.

Theme and Variations

During the last half of the seventeenth century, many composers wrote original themes for their sets of variations. Such a theme was a short songlike piece, called *aria, air,* or simply *thema* (theme). The theme was stated, then followed by a series of sections (often numbered), each a variation of the theme. For example, in 1677, Alessandro Poglietti (d. 1683) composed *Aria allemagna con alcuni variazioni* (German song with some variations) as a birthday gift for his patroness, the ruling Austrian empress. Empress Eleonore was 22; Poglietti wrote 22 variations. Composers did not completely abandon the use of borrowed thematic material, however. In the eighteenth century, theme and variations was used increasingly, not only as a separate composition, but as a movement—often the second—of a multimovement form.

(a)

(b)

Figure 16.3 (*a*) Excerpt from Kuhnau: *Sonata 4*, with the chorale melody (pitches marked x) placed uppermost; and (*b*) title page of the *Biblischer Historien* (Leipzig, 1700).

Suite

Many harpsichord suites were composed during the late seventeenth and early eighteenth centuries. In most of the suites published after 1690, the movements appear in allemande-courante-sarabande-gigue order, with optional dance(s) placed between sarabande and gigue. Several publications might be cited, among them Kuhnau's *Neue Clavier-Übung* (New Clavier-pieces; Part I, 1689; Part II, 1692), each volume containing seven suites.

Sonata

Before c. 1690, the term *sonata* was associated primarily with instrumental ensemble music. A few composers entitled isolated pieces for solo harpsichord *Sonata*, but these compositions had nothing in common with the ensemble sonatas of the time.

The solo harpsichord *Sonata in Bb* that Johann Kuhnau (1660–1722) included as the final piece in Part II of *Neue Clavier-Übung* (1692) contains five short sections, in slow-fast-slow-fast-slow order of tempo, the last slow section being repetition of the first. The internal structure and style of the sections closely resembles that of the Italian trio sonata. Two published collections of Kuhnau's harpsichord works consist entirely of solo sonatas: *Frische Klavier Früchte* (Fresh Keyboard Fruits; 1696), containing seven sonatas; and *Musicalische Vorstellung einiger Bib-*

lischer Historien (Musical representations of some Biblical stories; 1700), containing six. Each sonata in *Frische Klavier Früchte* consists of a succession of from three to six movements that contrast in tempo, key, thematic material, and style. The *Musical representations . . .*, better known as the "Biblical Sonatas," are multimovement programmatic compositions, each prefaced by a prose description of the particular Old Testament incident musically represented in the sonata. Each section is supplied with an Italian subtitle that designates the particular action or emotional state represented by that portion of the music. The six sonatas are: *The fight between David and Goliath; Saul cured by David through music; Jacob's wedding; Hezekiah, sick unto death and restored to health; Gideon, savior of Israel;* and *Jacob's death and burial.* In addition to being representations of Bible stories, the religious element is present in them in Kuhnau's symbolic use of chorale melodies. The chorale *Aus tiefer Not* (Out of great need) is the basic melody for the prayer of the Israelites before the battle in *The fight between David and Goliath.* In the first movement of the fourth sonata, Hezekiah's complaint is depicted through the chorale melody *Ach, Herr, mein arme Sünder* (Oh, Lord, my poor sins; fig. 16.3), the same melody J. S. Bach used for setting the chorale text *O Haupt voll Blut und wunden* (O Sacred Head sore wounded).

Kuhnau is credited with transferring the instrumental ensemble sonata to clavier and introducing that type of composition in Germany. He was also the author of a novel, *Der musicalische Quack-Salber* (The musical charlatan; 1700), which contains valuable information concerning the social status of musicians and musical practices of that day; by means of satire, Kuhnau criticized many performance practices that he considered incorrect or questionable.

French Composers

Jacques Champion de Chambonnières

Jacques Champion, Sieur de Chambonnières (1602–72), is considered the founder of the French school of harpsichord playing in the Baroque era. Almost nothing is known concerning the first 30 years of his life. His family name is Champion; his father was Sieur de La Chapelle, but Jacques acquired his maternal grandfather's noble title and was known as Baron or Marquis de Chambonnière. (He signed his name without the final s.)

By 1632, Chambonnières was working at the court of Louis XIII. Soon Chambonnières acquired a reputation for being a brilliant harpsichordist almost without peer and a talented dancer in court ballets. He remained at court after the death of Louis XIII (1643), even though the regent, Anne of Austria, had her own harpsichordist. Chambonnières was at the height of his career by 1650; he was praised throughout Europe as a distinguished performer and composer and was sought after as a teacher. Among his pupils were Louis Couperin (1626–61), Nicolas-Antoine Lebègue (c. 1631–1702), and Jean Henri d'Anglebert (1635–91), all of whom made substantial contributions to harpsichord technique and repertoire.

In 1657, Chambonnières's career took a turn for the worse, primarily because he experienced difficulty realizing basso continuo parts and could not supply suitable accompaniments. He was replaced as royal harpsichord teacher, and late in 1662 he resigned the remainder of his court duties in favor of D'Anglebert. No doubt Chambonnières still had a few pupils, and he continued to perform solos. To secure needed income, he published *Les pièces de clavessin* (Harpsichord pieces; 2 vols.; 1670). The books comprise an anthology of 60 individual pieces arranged into groups or suites; in each group, all pieces are in the same key. At least 142 of Chambonnières's harpsichord works survive in manuscript; all are dance pieces, mainly *allemandes, courantes, sarabandes,* and *gigues.*

Chambonnières's harpsichord playing was described as being delicate of touch, brilliant without undue display, and filled with the proper amount of imaginative embellishments. He is credited with being the earliest important French composer of harpsichord works written in the new *style brisé* idiom. His whereabouts during the years 1611–31 are not known; the manor of Chambonnière was just a few miles east of Paris, and Jacques may have been in Paris when Denis and Ennemond Gaultier were developing their distinctive lute style. Certainly, Chambonnières transmitted the *style brisé* to his pupils and to foreign musicians who heard him perform or who, like Froberger, had manuscript copies of some of his works.

Elisabeth Jacquet de la Guerre

Elisabeth-Claude Jacquet de la Guerre (c. 1666–1729) was harpsichordist, organist, and composer. A child prodigy, she first appeared in concert at the age of six. By the time she was ten, she had acquired a reputation for her remarkable talent in several areas of music: sight-singing difficult music, playing harpsichord, accompanying, improvising, transposing, and composing. She attracted the attention of Louis XIV, who encouraged her career. By 1684 she had married organist Marin de la Guerre, who died in 1704.

Elisabeth retired from public performance in 1717 but continued to compose. Her surviving works include the five-act opera *Cephale et Procris* (1694), a comic scene written for Théâtre de la Foire (1715), three volumes of cantatas (1708, 1711, and one undated), *Pièces de clavecin* (Harpsichord pieces; 1687), six sonatas for violin with basso continuo (1707), two violin sonatas with basso continuo for viola da gamba and organ (MS), four trio sonatas (MS), and some songs printed in various early eighteenth-century anthologies. A ballet and a *Te Deum* that she composed have not been located. The *Pièces de clavecin qui peuvent se jouer sur le viollon* ([14] Harpsichord pieces which may be played on the violin; 1707) comprise two suites (DWMA125). Included in the volume

Example 16.1 *Table des Agréments* from Jacquet's *Pièces de clavecin*, France. *(Copyright Editions de l'Oiseau-Lyre, S.A.M. Les Remparts, Monaco 1965. Reprinted by permission.)*

François Couperin le grand. Engraving (dated 1735) by Jean J. Flipart.

is a table of *agréments* (ex. 16.1) showing correct interpretation of the stenographic symbols Elisabeth-Claude used in her musical notation.

François Couperin *le grand*

François Couperin *le grand* (1668–1733), composer, harpsichordist, and organist, is considered the most important French musician between Lully and Rameau. Musical talent was present in large measure in several generations of the Couperin family; many Couperins were excellent organists. Louis Couperin (François's uncle) was organist at St. Gervais, Paris, from 1653 until his death in 1661; Charles (François's father) succeeded his brother and retained the position until his death (1679). By that time François's talent was recognized; officially, he was given the position when he became 18, but he served as deputy organist at St. Gervais long before then. After his father's death, François became the *protegé* and pupil of royal organist Jacques-Denis Thomelin (c. 1640–93) and in 1693 succeeded Thomelin. There were four royal organists; a different one attended the royal chapel each quarter of the year. By c. 1700, Couperin was recognized as the leading French composer; however, he did not receive another royal appointment until 1717, when he succeeded d'Anglebert as royal harpsichordist.

In 1689 François Couperin married Marie-Anne Ansault. Two of their four children were talented musicians: Marie-Madeleine (1690–1742) became a nun and was organist at Maubisson. Marguerite-Antoinette (1705–c. 1778) succeeded her father as court harpsichordist in 1730 when ill health forced him to relinquish the post. She was the first woman to hold that position, and she served also as harpsichord teacher to the king's daughters. She held both positions until 1741, when ill health forced her to resign. She was not a composer.

François Couperin published his first and only volume of organ works, *Pièces d'orgue* (Organ pieces) in 1690. Though he was only 21, the two organ Masses that comprise this volume are comparable in quality with those composed and published by the noted French organist Nicolas de Grigny (1672–1703) in his *Livre d'orgue* (1699). An **organ Mass** is a series of polyphonic compositions designed to replace movements of the Ordinary and Proper of the sung Mass; each organ movement is based on a Gregorian chant corresponding with that movement of the Mass. Couperin's organ pieces are not small works—the offertories, especially, are extensive and impressive. The *Pièces d'orgue* reveal Couperin's melodic gift, contrapuntal skill, and ability to handle current formal

Figure 16.4 Explanation of Ornaments Couperin published in *Premier livre de pièces de clavecin* (1713).

structures with ease. In the seventeenth century, the organ Mass was cultivated primarily in France and Italy (see Frescobaldi, p. 356).

Couperin composed some excellent instrumental chamber music (see p. 382), some secular songs and cantatas, and a considerable amount of sacred vocal music, but his more than 235 harpsichord pieces represent his greatest compositional achievement. Most of these pieces were published in four books entitled *Pièces de clavecin* (Harpsichord pieces; 1713, 1717, 1722, 1730). In each volume the pieces are grouped into what Couperin called *ordres;* the four volumes contain a total of 27 *ordres.* An *ordre* contains as few as 4 or as many as 24 small pieces; most *ordres* have from 8 to 15 of them. All pieces in an *ordre* are in the same or parallel tonality; e.g., the *Second ordre* contains d tonality pieces, both major and minor. A few pieces bear the names of standard suite movements (*allemande, courante, sarabande, gigue*). Most of the pieces have fanciful titles, such as: *Les papillons* (Butterflies); *Le Rossignol en amour* (The nightingale in love); *La reine des coeurs* (The queen of hearts); *La mysterieuse* (The mysterious lady); *Les matelotes provençales* (Provençal sailors). Several of the pieces are satirical. Included in the *Eleventh ordre*

is a five-movement (or five-act) satire entitled *Les fastes de la grande et anciénne Mxnxstrxndxsx* [sic] (The ostentatious displays of the great and ancient minstrels guild), a programmatic work portraying the activities of the company of *Ménétriers* (minstrels guild). It was not Couperin's intention that an *ordre* be considered a unified multimovement work to be performed as an entity. Rather, a performer was expected to exercise the option of selecting from an *ordre* the several pieces to be played (see DWMA126).

Couperin used three formal structures for his harpsichord pieces: binary, rondeau, and chaconne. In his *rondeaux,* the theme (labeled *rondeau*) is usually four or eight measures long; the episodes (termed *couplets*) vary in length and design. A few of the pieces labeled *chaconne* or *passacaille* are in rondeau form. This was not unusual; Elisabeth Jacquet de la Guerre, Louis Couperin, and Chambonnières also wrote *chaconnes* in *rondeau* form.

In some of his pieces, especially those of *allemande* type, Couperin used the so-called *style brisé* favored by lutenists. He was extremely careful to notate ornament symbols accurately, and he included in his publications a table explaining the meaning of the *agrément* symbols he used (fig. 16.4). In 1733,

Figure 16.5 Title page of Couperin's *L'Art de toucher le clavecin* (Paris, France, 1716).

François d'Agincourt (1684–1758) credited Couperin with standardizing the system of *agréments* (and, of course, the symbols representing the ornaments) then in use throughout France.

Couperin was an excellent harpsichord teacher. His two theoretical writings provide insight into his didactic methods and beliefs, and constitute valuable sources concerning performance practices in the early eighteenth century. *Regle pour l'accompagnement* (Rule[s] for accompaniment), which survives in manuscript at Bibliothèque nationale, Paris, states concisely the rules for accompanying from a basso continuo line. In *L'art de toucher le clavecin* (The art of playing the harpsichord; 1716, rev. 1717; fig. 16.5), Couperin reflected on various aspects of a pupil's early training in playing harpsichord; discussed fingering, *agrément* symbols and ornamentation (with specific examples), and other matters of performance practice; and suggested fingerings for difficult passages in the pieces published in Books 1 and 2 of *Pièces de clavecin*. Included in *L'art de toucher le clavecin* are eight *Preludes* designed to serve as teaching material and as introductory preludes to the *ordres* in the first and second books of *Pièces de clavecin*. (Two English translations of *L'art de toucher le clavecin* published in the twentieth century were available in 1988.)

Iberian Composers

The earliest surviving keyboard music printed in Portugal is *Flores de musica pero o instrumento de tecla & harpa* (Musical flowers for keyboard and harp; 1620), a collection of works by Manuel Rodrigues Coelho (c. 1555–1635), Portuguese organist and composer. Coelho served as organist at the Portuguese royal court from 1602 to 1633; *Flores de musica* is his only known work. The volume contains 24 *tientos* (imitative contrapuntal works similar to the Italian *ricercar*), approximately 100 versets for liturgical use, and 4 intabulations of Lassus's popular chanson *Susanne ung jour*. Several of the *tientos* are more than 200 measures long.

Francisco Correa de Araujo (c. 1577–1654) was born in Portugal but studied and worked in Spain. He served as organist in three churches: San Salvador, Seville (1599–1636); Jaén Cathedral, Easter (1636–40); and Segovia Cathedral (1640–53). At some time between 1626 and 1630, he attained priesthood, primarily on the strength of his organ playing. Correa's only surviving music is in his *Facultad organica* (Organ School; 1626), a theoretical treatise with a repertory of didactic organ music illustrating the points presented. *Facultad organica* contains 62 *tientos,* 3 sets of variations, 2 cantus firmus settings of sacred melodies, and 2 intabulations of chansons. The compositions are arranged progressively in order of increased difficulty, concluding with pieces that are very demanding technically. Correa is credited with being influential in establishing elements of the Baroque style of music in Spain, but most of his works are modal and contain elements of Renaissance style. He instructed that ornaments should be supplied tastefully, even if they are not specifically indicated. His compositions contain bold dissonances; he wrote chords in which a pitch and its chromatic alteration sound simultaneously, e.g., a c♮ sounding with a c♯. The more difficult works have an abundance of rhythmic complexities (ex. 16.2), including irregular groupings of equal notes.

The music of Juan Bautista José Cabanilles (1644–1712) brings to culmination the Iberian tradition of organ music that began with Cabezón and was continued by Coelho and Correa. When compared with contemporary seventeenth-century music

Example 16.2 Example of rhythmic complexities in Correa's music.

produced elsewhere in Europe, Cabanilles's music, like that of his predecessors, is in many respects more a development of Renaissance style than Baroque. Yet, Cabanilles's location in Valencia, a cosmopolitan city, enabled him to maintain contact with other musicians, especially those from southern Italy, and apprised him of international developments. His knowledge of *concertato* style is apparent in the eight sacred choral works that were discovered in the early 1970s; some of these pieces are for 12 voices, divided into two or three choirs.

The vast majority of Cabanilles's music is for organ: at least 200 *tientos,* approximately 170 versets for liturgical use, several sets of variations, some *toccatas,* and some dance pieces. His contrapuntal mastery is apparent in the *tientos,* most of which are polythematic. Three *tientos* are based on plainsong hymns; each phrase of the chant is treated imitatively, as in a chorale motet. Cabanilles's excellent short monothematic *tientos* are filled with sharp dissonances, surprising harmonic progressions, and unusual melodic intervals. He wrote many of the *tientos* for broken keyboard registration (*medio registro*), i.e., he assigned independent registrations to the upper and lower parts of the organ manual so that one hand might be soloistic.

Carlos de Seixas (1704–42), organist and harpsichordist, was the most important Portuguese composer during the first half of the eighteenth century. At the age of 14 he succeeded his father as organist at Coimbra Cathedral, and in 1720–42 served as organist at the royal chapel in Lisbon, where he was associated professionally with Domenico Scarlatti (see p. 439) for nine years. However, Seixas's surviving compositions do not reflect Scarlatti's influence.

Seixas wrote both choral and keyboard music, much of which has been lost. Eight sacred vocal works survive. Although eighteenth-century accounts indicate that he composed 700 keyboard works, only 88 have been located. Seixas used the terms *toccata* and *sonata* interchangeably. Some pieces are single-movement works that are typical Baroque toccatas. Others are sonatas containing from one to five movements, each in binary form. Viewed as a whole, Seixas's sonatas portray the transition between Baroque and Classical styles; among his surviving works are pieces exemplifying the various phases of that transition.

Spanish and Portuguese America

Spanish missionaries to America considered music an essential part of the religious teaching of native populations. By the end of the seventeenth century, every village and small town had from two to three dozen native musicians—instrumentalists as well as vocalists—capable of performing in choirs and small orchestras. Choirmasters and organists in the cathedrals were from Spain and Portugal, or had been trained in Europe, and were the most highly paid. Most, if not all, of the other instrumentalists listed in church account books were Indians—violinists, oboists, bassoonists, trumpeters, and harpists. Although purely instrumental music was cultivated in Spanish America, little notated music has been located. Three examples survive in Mexico: (1) an organ tablature, *Tiento de quarto tono, medio Registro, tiple del Maestro Fran.co correa . . .* (*Tiento* in fourth tone, split registration, treble by Maestro Francisco Correa . . . ; c. 1620); (2) *Método de Citara* (Cittern Method; mid-seventeenth century) containing dances, such as *pavana, gallarda, minuete, zarabanda,* and others; and (3) *Tablatura de Vihuela* (Vihuela tablature; c. 1740), containing approximately 50 types of dance music and transcriptions of 17 movements from sonatas by Corelli.

Very little is known about art music in Brazil prior to the middle of the eighteenth century. Both Franciscans and Jesuits sent missionaries to Brazil, and music was used in connection with their religious observances and in conversion of the natives. The earliest Brazilian art music that has been located was composed in 1759.

Summary

Throughout the seventeenth century, the composition of idiomatic instrumental music increased steadily; by the end of the century it equaled vocal music in both quality and quantity. Four principal types of instrumental music were written: dance music or stylized dance music intended for listening, quasi-improvisatory pieces, variations, and contrapuntal works of ricercar or canzona type. Stylized dance music evolved into the suite, in a basic format of allemande-courante-sarabande-gigue with additional movements optional. Fugue grew out of organ ricercar, and ensemble canzona eventually became *sonata da chiesa*.

The idiomatic style (later termed *style brisé*) developed by French lutenists was transferred to harpsichord, along with their systematized symbols for *agréments* (ornaments). French lutenists pioneered in composition of the *tombeau* (lament), related to the *déplorations* by which Medieval and Renaissance poets and composers honored deceased colleagues and teachers.

The finest Baroque organs were made by Arp Schnitger and Gottfried Silbermann. Members of the Ruckers family in Antwerp and the Jacquet family in France built excellent harpsichords; Fleischer, Hass, and Silbermann were noted clavichord builders. In the 1730s, Silbermann began to construct fortepianos according to Cristofori's principles, but the piano was not widely used until after 1750.

Three principal types of organ music were written: quasi-improvisatory pieces (usually named toccata), fugue, and chorale-based compositions. The latter category includes chorale fugue, chorale fantasia, chorale partita, and chorale prelude. Among important composers of organ works were Frescobaldi and Pasquini in Italy and Buxtehude in Lübeck, Germany.

Types of clavier music composed in the late seventeenth and early eighteenth centuries include quasi-improvisational pieces, fugues, variations, suites, and, after c. 1690, sonatas. Of these, the two most important types were suite and theme and variations. Composers making significant contributions to the development of clavier music include Kuhnau in Germany, and Chambonnières, Elisabeth Jacquet, and François Couperin *le grand* in France. Couperin's *L'art de toucher le clavecin* is an important source of information concerning performance practices. In Iberia, important organist-composers were Coelho, Correa, Cabanilles, and Seixas. Spanish missionaries considered music an important part of religious teaching, and choirmasters and organists in Spanish-American colonies were trained in Europe.

Ensemble Music

As early as the thirteenth century the Provençal word *sonada* was used in literature to denote a piece of instrumental music; in succeeding centuries, authors of literary works referred to instrumental pieces as *sonnade, sonada,* or *sennet*. The term was used by composers in the sixteenth century—Luis de Milán's *El maestro,* published in 1536, contains *villancicos y sonadas*.

Near the end of the sixteenth century, instrumental music developed rapidly, and several terms were used interchangeably and imprecisely in connection with ensemble music; those used most frequently are *sonata, sinfonia,* and *concerto*. Sometimes the terms *sonata* and *canzona* were used interchangeably, or together, as Vicentino used them in 1572: *canzon da sonar,* an instrumental song. Actually, the *sonata da chiesa* (church sonata) evolved from the canzona. As the sections of a canzona became longer and more individualistic in style, fewer sections were used per piece. Eventually the sections became independent and were "movements" of a multimovement composition that was no longer a true canzona but was a sonata of the type later known as *da chiesa*.

The Italian word *sonata,* the feminine past participle of the verb *sonare* (to sound, to play) meant merely a piece of instrumental music, in contrast with *cantata,* a vocal composition. In the early seventeenth century, *sonata* and *sinfonia* were used interchangeably to label instrumental interludes in vocal works, introductory sections preluding vocal compositions, or (rarely) a separate movement serving as prelude to a vocal composition. Later in the century, *sinfonia* was used to label a movement preceding a group of dances, as in G. M. Bononcini's *Sinfonie, allemande, correnti, e sarabande,* Op. 5.

In the second quarter of the seventeenth century, the word *sonata* was used more and more for an independent instrumental piece, but not until around the middle of that century was the designation *sonata* used with any degree of uniformity in meaning. Most of the instrumental works termed *sonata* were absolute (i.e., nonreferential, nonprogrammatic) music, were sectional or multimovement pieces of chamber music performed by one person per part, and had no connection with vocal music. Exceptions to these generalities did occur and do exist.

Around 1660, composers applied two technical designations to distinguish types of sonatas: Works designated *sonata* or **sonata da chiesa** (church sonata) were intended for performance in church, as part of the Proper of the Mass, as filler between Mass movements, or as Postlude (or very rarely as Prelude) to the Service. Pieces designated **sonata da camera** (chamber sonata) were intended for performance at court for diversion or in private concerts for a patron, at private concerts that were part of *Accademia* meetings, or at private or public concerts given in homes. A *sonata da camera* comprised a group of stylized dances, each movement properly identified (e.g., sarabande, corrente, etc.), but might commence with a nondance movement as introduction or prelude. In other words, a *sonata da camera* was really a kind of suite. In a *sonata da chiesa* the individual movements were labeled with tempo markings only, though some of the individual movements might actually be dances or dancelike in character.

Most of the sonatas composed in the last third of the seventeenth century were written for two treble instruments (usually violins) with basso continuo. The notation—three lines of music—gave rise to the term **trio sonata** for this kind of composition. Four performers were required for performance since the basso continuo line was played on an instrument capable of sustaining the notated pitches their full written value (usually a violoncello, viola da gamba, or violone) and was doubled on an instrument capable of supplying the implied supporting harmonies, which the performer improvised (usually harpsichord or organ). The accompanied solo sonata gained popularity after 1700; for its performance three instrumentalists were needed—the soloist (usually a violinist, flutist, or bass

violist) and two performers for the basso continuo accompaniment. Less frequent were unaccompanied solo sonatas, and ensemble sonatas, usually written for two to six stringed instruments, one per part. Many *sinfonie* and ensemble sonatas are stylistically indistinguishable from one another.

The word **concerto** was commonly used in Italy in the first half of the seventeenth century to denote vocal music accompanied by instrumentalists, especially church music. At times the term was used synonymously with *concertato* to mean vocalists and/or instrumentalists performing in opposition to, yet in agreement with, one another. The word was applied similarly to purely instrumental music during the Baroque era.

The first compositions that gave identity to the instrumental concerto were sonatas written for an orchestra divided into a small ensemble of soloists, called the *concertino* (little ensemble), and a larger instrumental ensemble, known as the *concerto grosso* (large ensemble). This kind of separation occurred in several instrumental works composed by Stradella c. 1675; he contrasted a *concertino* of trio sonata texture (two treble instruments playing in the same range plus basso continuo) with a *concerto grosso* of stringed instruments plus basso continuo. This kind of instrumentation was not standard specification but was the type most used by succeeding generations. It is not known exactly when or by whom the term **concerto grosso** was first applied to a composition for this kind of instrumental grouping, but the terminology was in use by around 1700. Corelli's *Concerti grossi,* Op. 6, became the most famous models of the form; these works were well known before their publication in 1714. Concertos written for a soloist with orchestral ensemble accompaniment were composed by Torelli, Albinoni, and Jacchini c. 1700.

Italy

In the seventeenth century, northern Italy was the leader in the production and performance of instrumental chamber music. This kind of music flourished especially at Venice, Modena, and Bologna, sites of the main development of the sonata.

Violin Making

The craft of violin making, begun in the sixteenth century, rose to unprecedented heights during the Baroque era—heights of excellence that have never been surpassed. Violins did not soon displace viols, however; viols were used throughout the seventeenth century and were preferred for performance of purely contrapuntal music. The most celebrated craftsmen making instruments of the violin family worked at Cremona, Italy. There Andrea Amati (c. 1510–c.1580) established his workshop at some time during the 1550s. Andrea, the first violin maker to become famous, built many instruments for Charles IX of France and painted the monarch's coat of arms on their backs. Violin making was a family business; patterns and procedures were transmitted from generation to generation. Andrea Amati trained two of his sons (Antonio and Girolamo) and his grandson Nicolo (1596–1684) to make violins, violas, and violoncellos. Nicolo constructed finer instruments than those of his grandfather, and taught the craft to many noted builders, including Andrea Guarneri (c. 1626–98) and Antonio Stradivari (1644–1737), both of whom trained some of their descendants and other talented pupils. Antonio Stradivari and Giuseppe Guarneri (1698–1744), grandson of Andrea, are considered the two greatest violin makers of all time. Stradivari made instruments for approximately 70 years; when he died, some of his carefully guarded trade secrets, such as his formulas for varnish, perished with him.

A violin made by Antonio Stradivari in Cremona c. 1697.

Venice

At St. Mark's, Giovanni Gabrieli adapted *cori spezzati* methods to the canzona and created an instrumental chamber music idiom. The talents of the cornettists, trombonists, and violinists working there inspired the composition of *concertante* music. After Gabrieli's death, the musical chapel at St. Mark's sank to a low ebb. It was reorganized and considerably improved during Monteverdi's tenure as *maestro di cappella* (1613–43); however, Monteverdi's only instrumental music was associated with his vocal works. The composition of canzonas and canzonalike sonatas was taken up by violin virtuosi such as Fontana and Marini, who were the two leading figures in the early development of the sonata, especially the solo sonata.

Almost nothing is known concerning the life and career of Giovanni Battista Fontana (died c. 1630) except that he was a native of Brescia and worked there and in Rome, Venice, and Padua. His only surviving compositions are sonatas, preserved in a posthumous memorial publication: *Sonate a 1. 2. 3. per il violino, o cornetto, fagotto, chitarone, violoncino o simile altro istromento* (Sonatas in 1, 2, 3 parts for violin, or cornett, bassoon, chitarone, 'cello, or other similar instruments; 1641). Of these pieces, 6 are for solo violin with basso continuo, and 12 are for two violins with basso continuo; some of the latter are supplied with a *concertante* part for violoncello or bassoon. All of the sonatas have numerous short sections contrasting in tempo, meter, and style. Some sections are homophonic, others contrapuntal with canzonalike imitation. In general, the writing is quite conservative. No strong tonal relationships are present; often the bass line is melodic and serves as another contrapuntal line rather than true accompaniment.

Violinist-composer Biagio Marini (c. 1587–1663) was born in Brescia and was working there c. 1608. From 1615 to 1620 he was employed as a violinist at St. Mark's, Venice, where Monteverdi was *maestro di cappella*. During 1623–49 Marini served at the court at Neuburg an die Donau, but he seems to have been away from court for long periods of time for travels in Belgium, Italy, and Germany. He moved back to Italy in 1649, and for the next seven years worked intermittently at Milan, Ferrara, and Vincenza. From 1656 until his death, he lived alternately in Brescia and Venice.

Marini's compositions were published in at least 22 volumes; 7 of those are lost and many of the surviving volumes are incomplete. His vocal works are mainly concerted pieces for a few voices with instruments. His most important compositions are the instrumental pieces for strings. An overview of several of the volumes gives a sampling of the kinds of instrumental music he wrote. *Affetti musicali*, Op. 1 (Musical affects; 1617), contains dance pieces, canzonas, sinfonias, and sonatas, for one to three violins or cornetts with basso continuo. In this volume Marini seems to have used the words "sinfonia" and "sonata" interchangeably. However, some of the *sinfonie* for one violin have basso continuo lines that are truly accompaniment; these seem to be the earliest datable examples of solo violin sonatas with basso continuo **accompaniment.** The solo line of the sonata *La Gardana* from Marini's Op. 1 is as idiomatic for cornett as for violin. *La Gardana* is *canzona*like in form, having short sections stylistically different and alternately slow and fast in tempo. The three solo *sinfonie* in Marini's *Madrigali e symfonie*, Op. 2 (Madrigals and sinfonias; 1618) are more violinistic and require double stopping. In these pieces the performance directive *"affetti"* (supply appropriate ornaments) appears for the first time in Marini's music (ex.16.3).

Arie, madrigali et correnti, Op. 3 (Arias, madrigals and *correnti*; 1620), contains a set of variations on the Romanesca melody and bass line, for solo violin

Example 16.3 Marini's designation *Affetti* directed the performer to embellish this passage in his *Sonata per il violino per sonar con due corde*, Op. 8 (1629).

with basso continuo. The sectional variations comprise four numbered *partes*, a *Galliarda*, and a *Corente;* most of the sections are in binary form, with both halves marked to be repeated. (Frescobaldi used the same aria melody and bass line, in the same tonality, for a set of variations for keyboard.)

In Marini's *Sonate, symphonie . . . e retornelli*, Op. 8 (1629, but dedication dated 1626), sonatas and sinfonias are clearly differentiated—sonatas are longer, with more varied structure, than sinfonias. Pieces in the volume are for one to six instruments. One solo sonata contains a section in *scordatura* (instrument mistuned); a *Capriccio* has triple-stops throughout; and there is an echo sonata for three violins. Works with these kinds of special effects reflect Marini's contact with German virtuoso violinists.

Marini's last surviving printed volume is *Per ogni sorte di strumento musicale diversi generi di sonate, da chiesa, e da camera*, Op. 22 (Sonatas, *da chiesa* and *da camera*, for all sorts of musical instruments of various kinds; 2–4 instrs. with basso continuo; 1655). The collection comprises six sonatas, four of them divided into separate sections. Though these are not movements *per se,* the pieces indicate clearly that composers were beginning to think of the sonata as a multimovement work.

Modena

When Ferrara reverted to the Papal States in 1598, Duke Cesare d'Este moved the family seat to Modena, and the center of musical activity there soon shifted from Modena Cathedral to d'Este court. Throughout the seventeenth century, d'Este patronage and the reputation of the court *cappella musicale* attracted outstanding artists, composers, singers, and instrumentalists from all over Italy.

Virtuoso violinist Marco Uccellini (c. 1630–80) attracted many to the court when he was head of instrumental music there (1641–47) and to the cathedral when he was *maestro di cappella* (1647–65). Uccellini initiated at Modena a tradition of violinist-composers that antedated the Bologna school by approximately 15 years. Seven of Uccellini's printed volumes of instrumental music are extant; Opp. 2–5 are mainly sonatas. He wrote triadic themes, and he modulated through the circle of fifths by means of sequences; his excursions into the keys of B major and E♭ minor were unusual in music for stringed instruments at that time. In Uccellini's music, the range used for violin extended to g‴ (sixth position). The solo violin sonatas in Op. 4 and Op. 5 contain *scordatura* passages, double-stops, wide leaps, and brilliant figuration. Uccellini's use of instrumental puzzle canons was a characteristic feature of the Modena school.

French influences invaded music at Modena after Alfonso IV d'Este married Laura Martinozzi, niece of Cardinal Mazarin, in 1665. Elements of French musical style appeared in the *sonata da camera,* in sets of dances, and in pieces labeled "in the French style." Those influences can be seen in some of the music composed by Giovanni Maria Bononcini (1642–78). A violin pupil of Uccellini, Bononcini was also a theorist. In 1671 he received a dual appointment as violinist at Modena Cathedral and chamber musician to Dowager Duchess Laura d'Este. From 1673 to 1678 Bononcini served as *maestro di cappella* at the cathedral and also as *capo degl' istrumentisti* (head of instrumentalists) at court.

Between 1666 and 1671 Bononcini published two volumes of trio sonatas, a volume of chamber sonatas, and two collections of dances. Three more volumes of sonatas (both *da camera* and *da chiesa*) and dance music (Opp. 6, 7, and 9) were printed in 1673–75. His Op. 8 is a practical treatise on theory and composition, *Musico prattico* (1673). Bononcini's predilection for counterpoint is discernible in even his earliest works. Instrumental canons, known as *artificii musicali,* are a feature of his work; he included puzzle canons in many of his works, especially in Opp. 2, 3,

and 5. Two books of *Cantate per camera* (Chamber cantatas; Opp. 10 and 12) for soprano or bass vocal solo, with *basso continuo,* and a volume of five-voice madrigals (Op. 11), appeared in 1677–78. Bononcini seems to have been the first to use the term *cantata per camera.*

Bononcini's *sonate da chiesa* in Opp. 1–6 are clearly related to the *canzona*; in the sonatas of Op. 9 slow homophonic movements alternate with fast contrapuntal ones. His mastery of counterpoint is apparent in the fugal movements of the *sonate da chiesa.* His writing for violin is refined, never exceeding third position in range. There are no *scordatura* sections. Though traces of modality are found in his works, his music reveals his knowledge of the principles of major-minor key tonality. Bononcini's sonatas for stringed instruments are considered the highest achievement of the late seventeenth-century Modena school of instrumental music.

The reign of Francesco II d'Este (1674–94) marked the most brilliant phase of music at the Modena court. In addition to commissioning compositions and stimulating musical performances at court, Francesco amassed an excellent library, helped establish the university, and encouraged the founding of the Accademia de' Dissonanti c. 1683. The music library at the Este court formed the bulk of the music collection of Biblioteca Estense, Modena. After Francesco's death, musical activities at the court declined; in 1734 the musical chapel had only nine members.

Bologna

The city of Bologna was an important commercial, cultural, and educational center (fig. 16.6) and was second in importance only to Rome within the Papal States. The University of Bologna, formally established in 1158, was noted for its offerings in literature and the humanities, jurisprudence, and medicine; in 1450 Pope Nicolò V sanctioned the establishment of a chair of music there. Several academies, most important of which was Accademia Filarmonica, stimulated, regulated, and consolidated all musical activities and strove to ensure a high level of performance. The Accademia Filarmonica was founded in 1666 by 50 Bolognese musicians. It held *esercizi* for composer members twice a week and *conferenze* for performer members once a week. The purpose of these

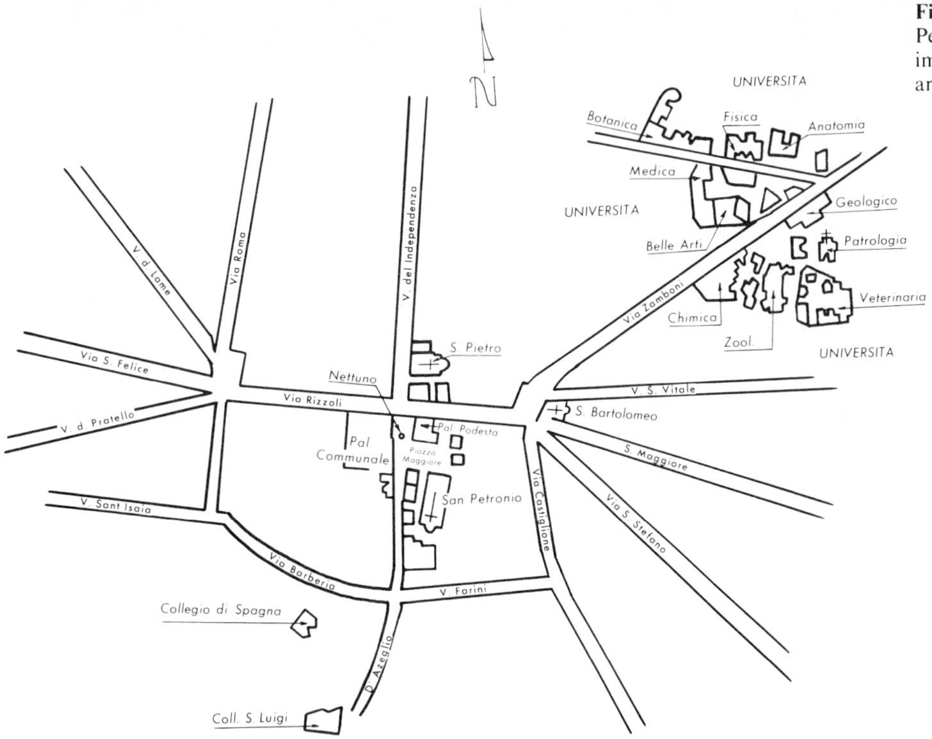

Figure 16.6 Location of San Petronio in relation to other important churches, the university, and colleges in Bologna.

meetings was to discuss theoretical works and to perform and analyze members' new compositions. Thus, the Academy could exercise control over its members, determine musical taste, and ensure an acceptable musical style.

Bologna's public musical life was centered in the chapels of its numerous churches. The basilica of San Petronio, planned to be one of the largest churches in Italy, became an important center of music in the seventeenth century. San Petronio's musical chapel was officially established by Pope Eugene IV in 1436; it was under the jurisdiction of a board of six laymen, members of the Bologna senate, who examined candidates and selected the ones to fill the positions. The number of excellent performers permanently employed in the musical chapel was fairly large; in 1661, 33 musicians were on the regular roster. On special occasions, such as the annual patronal celebration on October 4, additional vocalists and instrumentalists were hired, and the performing ensemble numbered more than a hundred. Although instrumentalists participated in performances at San Petronio as early as

the fifteenth century, they were first added to the chapel as regularly paid members in the late sixteenth century.

Acoustics in the church are superb. On either side of the high altar are choir stalls with musicians' galleries, each equipped with an organ—an ideal antiphonal arrangement. The older organ, made by Lorenzo di Giacomo da Prato c. 1470–75, is on the right-hand side (the Epistle side) as one faces the apse. The organ on the Gospel side was built by Baldassare Malamini and was installed in 1596; its tone is the lighter of the two instruments, and that organ was probably designed for continuo accompanying. The organs were rebuilt and revoiced in 1666 and were placed in new Baroque cases in 1675. Both original organs were still in use in 1988.

The famed Bologna school had its inception with the appointment of Maurizio Cazzati (1620–77) as *maestro di cappella* at San Petronio in 1657. Cazzati, who was born in Lucera, a town midway between Bologna and Mantua, was priest, violinist, composer, and

Baroque Instrumental Music

publisher. Between 1641 and 1657 he served at various times as *maestro di cappella* of churches at Mantua and Bergamo, of the Sabioneta court at Bozzolo, and of the Accademia della Morte at Ferrara. His appointment at San Petronio resulted from an impressive performance of some of his sacred works at the church of San Salvatore in Bologna in 1657. Cazzati remained at San Petronio until 1671, then moved to the Gonzaga court at Mantua where he served as *maestro di cappella* until his death.

During his tenure at San Petronio, Cazzati increased the number of instrumentalists employed and established the size of the musical chapel at 35 vocalists and instrumentalists who performed regularly for ecclesiastical functions. He encouraged the playing of string instruments to such an extent that excellent violinists from other parts of Italy were attracted to Bologna, and within a short time the city became the recognized center for violin playing. Cazzati contributed significantly to the repertoire of instrumental music, especially that for trumpet and strings. Ten of his 66 extant volumes of published music contain instrumental works; 5 of the collections contain a total of 54 sonatas of both melody-with-continuo and polychoral types. In addition, manuscripts in the Archivio di San Petronio contain many of his sonatas for one or two trumpets and strings; the presence of multiple string parts indicates that these pieces were performed orchestrally. All of the trumpet pieces in the San Petronio repertory are for trumpet in D. The trumpet sonatas by Cazzati are important precursors of Torelli's sonatas and concertos.

Cazzati's *Sonate a due, tre, quattro, e cinque, con alcune per Tromba,* Op. 35 (Sonatas for 2, 3, 4, and 5 [instruments], with some for trumpet; 1665), includes three sonatas for trumpet, violin, alto and tenor viols, and violone. These trumpet sonatas are homophonic; the other sonatas are polyphonic. The trumpet part is confined to the range between a' and a". In the preface to the volume Cazzati stated that a violin might be substituted if a trumpet player of sufficient capability was not available.

Cazzati's *12 Sonate a due istromenti cioè violino, e violone* (12 Sonatas for 2 instruments, namely, violin and violone; 1670) are considered the first published *solo* violin music of the Bologna school, because almost all of the violone line is identical with the basso

Example 16.4 Opening measures of each movement of Cazzati's *Sonata prima, "La Pellicana,"* from Op. 55.

continuo part for organ. For all 12 sonatas the cornetto is specified as an optional alternative for violin, and the solo part, which is neither virtuosic nor lyrical, is as idiomatic for cornetto as for violin. Range is limited to two octaves, c' to c'''. The sonatas are in four movements, with some thematic resemblance among movements of a sonata (ex. 16.4). Undoubtedly, the soloist was expected to ornament the slow second movements. Cazzati's restrained and serious approach to violin music is characteristic of the Bologna school; perhaps this reflects the religious atmosphere at San Petronio. In the Opus 35 trio sonatas for strings, e.g., "La Casala," broken chords and short sequential sixteenth-note figures appear; such passages were conceived violinistically and lie well within hand compass. Cazzati's writing for violin does not exhibit the lyricism found in music of subsequent Bolognese composers.

In his sonatas Cazzati used two general schemes: (1) monothematic, with short derivative motives used as bridges between restatement of the theme; and (2) polythematic, with movements divided into two sections, the second beginning in the dominant. In the slow movements of trio sonatas, often two motives are announced successively, in dialogue fashion.

Cazzati was not an outstanding composer. He is historically important because (1) under his leadership the musical chapel of San Petronio attracted excellent instrumentalists and composers to Bologna, e.g., G. B. Vitali and Arcangelo Corelli; (2) he composed and encouraged others to contribute to repertories for accompanied solo violin and for trumpet and strings; and (3) he included instrumental works of this kind liturgically in Services at San Petronio.

G. B. Vitali

Giovanni Battista Vitali (1632–92), a native of Cremona, studied counterpoint with Cazzati before joining the musical chapel at San Petronio in 1658 as singer and *violone da brazzo* player. When Cazzati left the chapel in 1671, Vitali was appointed *maestro di cappella*. In 1673, he moved to Modena to serve as one of two *vicemaestri di cappella* at Francesco d'Este's court. While working at Modena, Vitali retained his interest in events at San Petronio and often visited Bologna; it would not be incorrect to consider him a connecting link between the court and the church.

Although Vitali composed numerous vocal works, he is known mainly for his instrumental music; he contributed significantly to the development of the trio sonata. He specifically designated as *da chiesa* (for church) the trio sonatas of his *Sonate a 2 violini col suo basso continuo per l'organo,* Op. 2 (1667). Vitali's interest in counterpoint is reflected in the contrapuntal character of his sonatas. In fugal movements he seldom used episodes; rather, ideas seem to overlap in close imitation, making these movements compact. He excelled at writing compositions in which the same melodic material was presented in different rhythmic aspects.

Vitali's *Artificii musicali . . . ,* Op. 13 (1689) is a pedagogical work, systematically presenting 60 instrumental canons, 9 of them in the principal instrumental forms then in use. The pieces are presented in order of increasing difficulty. A *balletto* for two stringed instruments has one line written in the key of F♯ and the other in the key of G♭. One wonders whether the performers tempered their pitches or permitted clashing enharmonic polytonality to prevail. *Artificii musicali* seems to be the earliest collection of its kind in the Baroque era and is an important precursor of J. S. Bach's *Musikalisches Opfer* (Musical Offering).

Pietro degli Antonii

Pietro degli Antonii (1648–1720) spent his entire life in Bologna but worked as *maestro di cappella* at churches other than San Petronio. His compositions comprise operas and secular pieces as well as Masses, motets, and organ works. Of his five surviving collections of instrumental music, two consist of paired or separate dances (Op. 1, 1670; Op. 3, 1671); two comprise *sonate da chiesa* for solo violin with basso continuo (Op. 4, 1676; Op. 5, 1686); the other volume contains organ sonatas and versets (Op. 9, 1712). Degli Antonii was one of the first to write solo violin sonatas with a melodic line so lyrical and rhapsodic that the basso continuo is reduced to purely harmonic support. Only three of his trio sonatas survive. One of these, Sonata No. 5, is found in *Scielta della Suonate,* printed by Silvano in 1680. That publication is the earliest known anthology of sonatas and is one of five important sonata anthologies published in Bologna prior to 1706.

Degli Antonii was the only composer of the Bologna school to make the solo sonata his principal field of activity. His *Sonate a violino solo* are the only ones in the San Petronio archives printed in score instead of partbooks. In these sonatas, he employed the Neapolitan sixth (lowered supertonic), unprepared sevenths, deceptive cadences in which the leading tone is suspended but not resolved, and changed from minor to major tonality over the same root. Occasionally, the keyboard accompaniment enjoys modulatory excursions around the circle of fifths, while the solo violin is assigned sequential passages, e.g., in Op. 5, No. 6, *Grave.* Unlike the imitative fast movements written by Vitali, those of degli Antonii include episodes; he wrote nonimitative fast movements also in which the theme never appears in the bass. His predilection for lyrical and affective music is evidenced in a preponderance of slow movements labeled "Adagio affettuoso," "Aria grave," "Aria posata," and similarly.

Domenico Gabrielli

Not all of the virtuosi at San Petronio were trumpeters and violinists. Noted 'cellists include Petronio Franceschini (1650–81) and Domenico Gabrielli (1651–90). Gabrielli, a pupil of Franceschini, composed some of the earliest music for violoncello. His advanced performing technique is reflected in the florid passage work and the double-, triple-, and quadruple-stops included in his sonatas and ricercars for unaccompanied 'cello. His *Balletti, gighe, correnti, alemande, e sarabande,* Op. 1, comprises 12 paired dances, each pair in a different key, ranging from E♭ to A major and from C minor to B minor. There are extant six of Gabrielli's sonatas for one or two trumpets with orchestra, written specifically for performance at San Petronio. He included the 'cello as an obbligato (required) instrument in the trumpet sonatas and constructed a movement in one of the sonatas as a *concertante* duet for trumpet and 'cello with basso continuo—essentially, a trio sonata. The sonatas have from four to six movements, usually with slow and fast movements alternating. Gabrielli composed numerous vocal works in which he included 'cello as an obbligato instrument, and frequently he featured violin, 'cello, or trumpet in vocal arias of his operas.

Giuseppe Torelli

Giuseppe Torelli (1658–1709), virtuoso violinist and composer, contributed greatly to the development of concerto grosso and solo concerto and to the repertoire for trumpet and strings at Bologna. A native of Verona, Torelli moved to Bologna in 1682 and was admitted to the Accademia Filarmonica in 1684; during 1686–89 and again in 1701 he was regularly employed as an instrumentalist member of the musical chapel at San Petronio. From time to time, he performed as violinist at Parma, Modena, and other Italian cities and at Berlin, Ansbach, and Vienna.

More than 100 of Torelli's works exist only in manuscript. A majority of these compositions were written for trumpet(s) in D, violin(s), and/or oboe(s). Four volumes of his chamber music for strings were published in Bologna in 1686–88:

1. *Sonate à tre,* Op. 1, ten trio sonatas for violins and basso continuo. Seven of these *sonate da chiesa* each have four movements arranged in slow-fast-slow-fast order, with the second movement usually in a related key. Generally, first movements are chordal, second movements imitative, and fourth movements dancelike in character.
2. *Concerto da camera à due violini e basso,* Op. 2, 12 *sonate da camera* for two violins with basso continuo. Dances in the individual suites vary, but allemande, *corrente, balletto,* and gigue are represented, and each suite concludes with a gavotte, minuet, or sarabande.
3. *Sinfonie à 2. 3. e 4.,* Op. 3, twelve sonatas of which 6 are trio sonatas.
4. *Concertino per camera,* Op. 4, 12 sets of dance pieces for violin and violoncello, without basso continuo. These may be the earliest violin-'cello duos by a Bolognese composer.

In 1679, Torelli became interested in composing for trumpet. No doubt he was inspired by Giovanni Pellegrino Brandi, an excellent trumpet player, who, in 1679–99, participated in the annual celebrations whereby San Petronio honored its patron saint. For these celebrations, Torelli and other Bolognese composers wrote sonatas and sinfonias for solo trumpet and strings; a work of this kind was performed to begin the Mass and was followed by the Kyrie.

Torelli's Op. 5, *Sinfonie à tre e concerti à quattro* (1692), comprises six trio sonatas and six concertos. The concertos are orchestral works; Torelli instructed in the preface that multiple instruments are to be used per part. These seem to be the earliest printed instructions for orchestral performance. Similarly, Torelli indicated in the preface to *Concerti musicali,* Op. 6 (1692), that all passages marked "solo" are to be performed by a single violin; on all other parts three or four instruments are to be used. Two of the 12 concertos contain short solo episodes; these pieces foreshadow the approach of the solo violin concerto.

No traces of Torelli's published Op. 7 or its intended contents have been located. His Op. 8, entitled *Concerti grossi con una pastorale per il Santissimo Natale* (Concerti grossi with a pastorale for the most holy birthday [i.e., Christmas]), was published posthumously. Actually, only six of the pieces are concerti grossi; the other six are solo concertos. Because Torelli dated very few of his compositions, it cannot be determined whether any of his solo concertos antedated solo concertos written and published by Tomaso Albinoni in 1700 and Giuseppe Jacchini in 1701.

Some features of the fully developed Baroque solo concerto are apparent in Torelli's concertos. Most of them are structured in three movements, arranged in fast-slow-fast tempo pattern. Concerto No. 7 of Op. 8 is a representative example. In the Allegros, imitative *ritornelli* (sing., *ritornello*) alternate with soloist episodes using idiomatic figuration; in contrapuntal passages the top voice—the first violin—clearly dominates. (In a concerto movement, the term *ritornello* signifies the recurring passage performed by the orchestra or *tutti*.) The last *ritornello* is a recapitulation of the first. Torelli's Allegro themes are rhythmically vigorous and are colored by sequences and suspensions. The concerto's middle movement, in a related key, is for soloist accompanied by the basso continuo duo. That movement is ternary—two similar Adagios (the second shorter than the first) frame an Allegro characterized by broken chords and other figuration idiomatic to violin.

Arcangelo Corelli

Arcangelo Corelli (1653–1713; Insight, "Arcangelo Corelli") was highly regarded in Italy as violinist, composer, and teacher. He was adept at directing both instrumental and vocal music, and occasionally he assisted other composers by writing portions of their works. For example, he furnished the *Introduzione* (overture) and *Sinfonia* (overture to part two) for Lulier's oratorio *S. Beatrice d'Este* (1689) and led the orchestra in several performances of that work. The overture survives in manuscript. On two occasions in March 1689, Corelli led very large ensembles of singers and instrumentalists in performance of two Masses celebrating Queen Christina's recovery from an illness. Reportedly, Corelli composed a "*sinfonia with trumpets*" for one of those celebrations. This lends credence to the attribution to him of a Sonata in D for trumpet, two violins, and basso continuo; however, there is the possibility of a scribal error in the manuscript, and that trumpet piece may belong to Torelli.

Corelli prepared for publication six sets of compositions for stringed instruments, each set containing 12 works:

Sonate a trè, Op. 1 (Rome, 1681): 12 trio *sonate da chiesa* for two violins, violone or archlute, with bass for organ.

Sonate da camera a tre, Op. 2 (Rome, 1685): 11 *sonate da camera* and a chaconne, for two violins, and violone or harpsichord.

Sonate a tre, Op. 3 (Rome, 1689): 12 *sonate da chiesa* for two violins, violone or archlute, with bass for organ.

Sonate a tre, Op. 4 (Rome, 1694): 12 *sonate da camera* for two violins and violone.

Sonate a Violino e Violone o Cimbalo, Op. 5 (Rome, 1700): six *sonate da chiesa,* five *sonate da camera,* and theme and variations on *La folia,* for solo violin with violone or harpsichord.

Concerti grossi, Op. 6 (Amsterdam, 1714): 12 *concerti grossi* for obbligato soloist ensemble of two violins and violoncello, and optional large ensemble of two violins, viola, and bass. Eight of these *concerti* are *da chiesa.*

In addition, Estienne Roger of Amsterdam published (c. 1715) six *Sonate a tre* for two violins with basso continuo, as *Ouvrage posthume* of Corelli.

It is interesting to note that (1) the majority of Corelli's compositions are trio sonatas, the most fashionable ensemble music of the time; (2) the four volumes of trio sonatas were published first; and (3) in assembling his compositions, he observed the distinction between *da chiesa* and *da camera* sonata types and grouped pieces of similar character together. Moreover, he specified for the *da chiesa* trio sonatas the full sound of both violone and organ continuo; the *da camera* trio sonatas use *either* violone or harpsichord. According to the title page of *Concerti grossi,* Op. 6, these works may be performed as trio sonatas; both *concertino* 'cello part and *ripieno* bass are supplied with figures for keyboard realization. This can be interpreted in two ways: (1) that the figures supplied with the *concertino* 'cello part are to be realized by a keyboard player when the pieces are performed as trio sonatas; or (2) that two continuo keyboard instruments are to be used when the compositions are performed as *concerti grossi.* When each group has its own keyboard instrument, the small and large ensembles can be separated spatially, as they probably were when a *concerto grosso* was performed in Corelli's time.

Corelli's Style

In contrast to other Bolognese composers who have to their credit numerous Masses, cantatas, and operas, as well as instrumental music, Corelli wrote almost exclusively for bowed string instruments and wrote idiomatically for them. Very rarely does the violin part extend beyond third position. (The one exception in

insight

Arcangelo Corelli

Arcangelo Corelli (1653–1713), youngest of the five children of Arcangelo and Santa Raffini Corelli, was born a month after his father's death. The Corellis were prosperous landowners in Fusignano, a small town between Bologna and Ravenna, Italy, and Sra. Corelli was able to provide the children with education befitting the family's elevated social status. Arcangelo received music lessons from a priest in nearby Faenza, then studied at Lugo. At the age of 13, he went to Bologna to pursue classical studies, but upon hearing the musicians at San Petronio he determined to study the violin seriously. He studied in Bologna at least four years. In 1670, after due examination, he was admitted to the Accademia Filarmonica. Corelli's whereabouts for the next several years are not definitely known; from 1675 until his death, he worked primarily in Rome. However, he considered himself a member of the Bologna school; the title pages of his first three published works name him *Arcangelo Corelli da Fusignano, detto il Bolognese* (Arcangelo Corelli of Fusignano, called the Bolognese).

In Rome, Corelli was soon recognized as one of the leading violinists and an outstanding director of instrumental ensembles. The list of his performances is impressive. For a short time, he worked as chamber musician to Queen Christina of Sweden who, after her abdication, resided in Rome. Account books at the church of San Luigi list Corelli as leader of ten violins there in 1682; every year from 1682 through 1708, on August 25 (the day honoring the church's patron saint), Corelli performed at that church.

Arcangelo Corelli. *(The Bettmann Archive.)*

In 1684 Corelli began to take responsibility for and to perform in musical functions at the palace of Cardinal Benedetto Pamphili; in July 1687 Pamphili employed him as music master. Corelli and his pupil Matteo Fornari resided in an apartment at the palace. Frequently they performed

the six published volumes he prepared is the fifth-position f''' in m.97 of *Concerto Grosso,* Op. 6, no. 2.) The first three positions are the area of greatest comfort in playing the violin, especially on the Baroque violin, for the instrument's neck and fingerboard were considerably shorter and had a slightly different slant than that of modern stringed instruments. Also, the first three positions match in compass the range of the most gifted sopranos at a time when *bel canto* was considered the highest type of vocal art. Corelli seldom used the G string on the violin, for that string was made of uncovered gut and the sounds emitted by it were unlovely. (In fact, no pitches produced on the G string are used in the first, fifth, and seventh trio sonatas in Op. 1.)

Corelli's music is characterized by clear key tonality with no trace of modality; he seems to be the earliest composer to write exclusively in major-minor key tonalities. Except for an occasional chromatic alteration to create a diminished seventh chord or a Neapolitan sixth, Corelli's music is diatonic. He employed sequences systematically, using harmonic sequences to effect modulations and melodic sequences to extend a melodic line or as imitative dialogue. Composers of the Bologna school experimented with sequences that moved the tonality around the circle of fifths, and Corelli was no exception. Sometimes he modulated by means of harmonic sequences, then defined the tonality by a descending series of sixth chords (first-inversion triads), e.g., in the *Corrente* of solo

trio sonatas and *concertino* parts in *concerti grossi* with Spanish 'cellist G. L. Lulier (c. 1650–after 1708), who was also employed by Pamphili. Another who frequently performed with Corelli was Bernardo Pasquini, virtuoso harpsichordist and organist. Corelli led the orchestra for performances of several of Pasquini's works, including opera, and for at least one oratorio by Lulier. Pasquini and Corelli were members of the Congregazione ed Accademia di S Cecilia (the musicians' guild); each became head of his respective section of the guild—Pasquini, the organists; Corelli, all other instrumentalists.

When Pamphili moved to Bologna in 1690, Cardinal Pietro Ottoboni (nephew of Pope Alexander VIII) became Corelli's patron. Ottoboni held regular Monday evening academies at the palace. All visiting dignitaries and famous composers and musicians in Rome were invited to these concerts, and Corelli, whom Ottoboni treated as a friend, became acquainted with celebrities in all professions. Corelli directed the concerts and performances of operas at the palace and operas at Teatro Tor di Nona. He continued to compose music for his own and Fornari's performance. Account books indicate that Corelli contributed *concerti* and *sinfonie* for several special performances, but the specific compositions are not identified.

In April 1706, Corelli, Pasquini, and Alessandro Scarlatti were admitted to the Arcadian Academy; their patron, Ottoboni, was already a member. All members of the academy used pseudonyms—Corelli's activities there are recorded under the name Arcomelo Erimanteo.

After 1708 Corelli no longer performed in public. Late in 1712, his health deteriorated considerably, and he moved from the palace into his brother Giacinto's apartment, taking with him the vast treasure of paintings he had accumulated. Corelli died on 8 January 1713; he was interred in the church of Santa Maria della Rotonda—the Pantheon—in the chapel of St. Joseph. Though interment in the chapel of St. Joseph was restricted to architects, painters, and sculptors who were members of the Artistica Congregazione dei Virtuosi al Pantheon, Corelli was placed there by special indulgence of Pope Clement XI (r. 1700–21). For several years, some of Corelli's *concerti grossi* were performed in the Pantheon on the anniversary of his death. At Cardinal Ottoboni's suggestion, the Elector honored Corelli posthumously with the Marquisate of Landenburg.

Corelli had prepared his Will on 5 January 1713. He left one painting of his choice to Cardinal Ottoboni and a Breughel canvas to Cardinal Colonna; Corelli's brothers received the remaining 134 pieces in his art collection, which included landscapes by Poussin, a Madonna by Sassoferrato, several canvases by Trevisani, and other valuable items. Corelli bequeathed to Fornari his musical instruments, manuscripts, the plates of Op. 4, and the plates prepared for the unpublished Op. 6. Fornari arranged with Estienne Roger, Amsterdam, for publication of the *concerti grossi,* Op. 6 (1714).

sonata da camera Op.5, no.7. Both homophony and polyphony are included in each of Corelli's compositions; at least one of the fast movements—usually the second movement—is fugal or contains fugato passages. Corelli's linear counterpoint is harmonically based and is governed by key tonality. He wrote chains of suspensions frequently. Except in the trio sonatas of Op. 2, he seldom notated the so-called Corelli clash—the harmony created by the delayed introduction of a cadential leading tone so that it coincides with the anticipation of the tonic in an upper voice (ex. 16.5). However, there are some places where that dissonance could be created by improvised cadential ornamentation. Some of Corelli's cadences are of the type favored a century later by Mozart and other composers of the Classical era: a trill on the supertonic above a dominant seventh chord, resolving to the tonic (ex. 16.6). In the approach to the final cadence of a movement in triple meter, Corelli frequently used hemiola, e.g., by notating the penultimate measure of a $\frac{3}{4}$ movement in $\frac{3}{2}$ meter (ex. 16.7).

In some of the sonatas there is thematic relationship between movements; however, each movement is monothematic. Many of the slow movements of Corelli's compositions appear to be very sustained and bare; the performer was (and is) expected to ornament the written notes lavishly. When Corelli did not want such ornamentation he indicated that fact by the words *Arcate sostenuto e come stà* (sustained bowing

Example 16.5 Example of the so-called Corelli clash.

Example 16.6 This cadence from Corelli's Sonata Op. 5, No. 1, mvt. 2, with its cadenza and the cadential trill on supertonic over dominant seventh, is a direct precursor to the type of cadenza frequently used by Mozart. The + is the symbol used for a trill.

Example 16.7 Hemiola cadence concluding mvt. 3 of Corelli's Sonata Op. 5, No. 3.

Example 16.8 Excerpt from John Walsh's edition of Corelli's Op. 5 sonatas showing the type of ornamentation Corelli is said to have performed.

and as it stands) or simply *come stà* (as it stands = as written). That directive appears in the first Grave of *Concerto Grosso,* Op. 6, No. 8 (the "Christmas" concerto); in that short movement the parts, continually intertwining, move from beginning to end without arriving at a single intermediate cadence, and Corelli did not want his notation ornamented. In 1710, J. Walsh (London) published a pirated edition of Corelli's solo violin sonatas (Op. 5) in which the first six sonatas are lavishly embellished, supposedly with Corelli's own ornaments (ex. 16.8). (A twentieth-century edition of Walsh's publication is available.)

Trio Sonatas

In Corelli's trio sonatas, the two coequal upper parts move in the same range and are always in proximity but are separated from the bass by a wide interval. When the basso continuo includes a keyboard instrument, the harmonies of the realized bass line fill the space; however, a gap still remains between violins and 'cello. The two violin parts often cross, especially in imitative passages; in their moments of homophony they frequently move in parallel thirds. In many of the slow movements, chain suspensions create exciting harmonies. The tessitura within which the two

violins move is limited, usually being about two octaves. There is no evidence of virtuoso display. Several of the trios could be played entirely in first position; third position is never exceeded. The writing for 'cello is idiomatic, easily playable in the lower positions, and the tessitura is kept below violin range.

Many of Corelli's *da chiesa* trio sonatas comprise four movements, arranged in slow-fast-slow-fast order of tempo; in the majority of the trio sonatas (both *da chiesa* and *da camera*) all movements are in the same key. The *da chiesa* sonatas usually commence with a Grave or other dignified movement suitable for church. The second movement is fast and fugal, and the bass is an integral part of the imitation. Corelli's fugal and canonic themes are well conceived; J. S. Bach borrowed both the subject and countersubject of Corelli's *Vivace,* Op. 3, No. 4, and used them note-for-note in a Fugue in B minor for organ (BWV 579).

Corelli subjects his canonic themes to inversion, augmentation, diminution, and other contrapuntal devices and uses them in this manner in *da camera* as well as in *da chiesa* sonatas, e.g., the *Allemande,* Op. 2, No. 5. The *da camera* trio sonatas begin with a *Preludio,* followed by the more sedate dance-related movements, and conclude with a lively dance, such as a gigue or gavotte (see DWMA127).

Concerti grossi

The *concerto grosso* was still a relatively new form in Corelli's time, and the number and kind of instruments placed in the opposing ensembles varied. The instrumentation that Corelli chose to use became standard. The *concertino* is a string trio, possibly with its own continuo keyboard instrument; thus, the idiom of the trio sonata is projected against an orchestral background of strings with keyboard. The *ripieno* group never plays alone but is used to reenforce the *concertino;* the more difficult parts are reserved for the soloists. Orchestral parts are easy; the viola enjoys a real part and is not merely filler. In each of these concertos, one of the slow movements is in a contrasting key. The most famous of the *concerti grossi* is No. 8, called the "Christmas Concerto" because of Corelli's notation on the *Pastorale,* which he included as an optional final (6th) movement: *Fatto per la Notte di Nativitata* (Written for Christmas Eve).

Solo Sonatas

Each of the solo sonatas of Corelli's Op. 5 commences with a slow movement and concludes with a fast one. Each of the six *sonate da chiesa* compositions in that volume has five movements; the first three *sonate da camera* have four movements, the next two sonatas have five. Eight of the solo sonatas are in major keys and have one slow movement in the relative minor. Some of the solo violin sonatas appear deceptively simple on the printed page. They are technically demanding, however, and require command of both bowing and fingerboard techniques. *Moto perpetuo* movements, arpeggiations, rapid runs, double- and multiple-stops, and cadenzas appear in these pieces. Nothing is included merely for virtuoso display; every technical aspect is justified by the musical content of the movement as a whole. Many passages can be performed easily in second position; proper execution of

Example 16.9 A Phrygian cadence with hemiola and a Picardian final chord concludes mvt. 4 of Corelli's Sonata Op. 5, No. 1.

others requires sequential shifting through the three positions. There is no evidence that Corelli indicated any fingerings to be used; he did designate specific bowings, however.

Many characteristics of Corelli's style can be seen in *Sonata da chiesa,* Op. 5, No. 1 (DWMA128). The sonata comprises five movements unlabeled except for tempo indications. The first movement, in D major, is essentially in binary form. It opens with a two-measure Grave introduction, followed by a seven-measure interlude of arpeggiated chords that modulate to A major for another brief Adagio; these three sections are repeated exactly in transposition at the dominant level, with an extension of the final Adagio to close the movement in D. All of the Adagio sections are to be embellished by the violin soloist. The Allegro second movement, in D major, is polyphonic. The violin is given the first two statements of the fugue subject; double-stopping gives way to triple-stopping when the subject enters the fourth time. A vestige of the trio sonata texture remains in the solo violin sonata in the fugal fast movements, for the violin soloist is required to handle polyphonic presentation of the imitative thematic material through double- and multiple-stopping. In the penultimate measure of this movement Corelli notated a short cadenza that concludes with a trill on the supertonic over a dominant-seventh chord, then resolves to tonic (ex. 16.6). The third movement, also an Allegro in D major, is a *moto perpetuo* of 16th-note broken-chord figurations. The Adagio fourth movement is in b minor. As notated, the melody is lyrical and expressive, but it becomes even more beautiful when properly embellished. The movement concludes with a hemiola Phrygian cadence that moves through f♯ minor in a descending tetrachord to end on a Picardian F♯ major chord (ex. 16.9). The final Allegro is fugal, with the solo violin duplicating trio sonata texture by presenting imitative polyphony through double-stopping. The thematic material is related to that of the second movement, as is the formal plan.

One of the most difficult compositions in the Op. 5 set is Sonata No. 12, *La Folia* theme and 23 variations. In the late seventeenth century, the *folia* was a stately dance performed by a solo dancer; in France it was called *Folies d'Espagne* (Spanish lunacy), and in England it was known as *Farinelli's Ground*. Corelli used both the melody and the bass line of *La Folia* as theme for his set of variations. In this sonata he created variations with a triple role: variations of a melody, variations on a ground bass, and variations in bowing techniques.

Corelli's Influence

Corelli's published music was reprinted many times and was disseminated widely. By 1785, 35 editions of the trio sonatas, Op. 1, had been issued. His *concerti grossi* were especially favored in England. Numerous "Christmas concertos" were modeled after his Op. 6, No. 8; the *sinfonia* for strings in Handel's *Messiah* is stylistically similar to the last movement of Corelli's "Christmas concerto." Corelli's solo violin sonatas, Op. 5, were his most popular compositions; by 1800, 45 editions of the volume had been printed. Many composers imitated his compositional style; several composers patterned works after the last sonata (the *ciaconne*) of Op. 2, and especially the variations on *La Folia*. Tartini (see p. 454) used the *Gavotte* from solo sonata No. 10 as the theme of his *L'Arte dell' arco* (The Art of bowing), a set of 50 variations for the study of different bowing techniques.

As a conductor, Corelli had a reputation for being a stern disciplinarian, demanding that players of an orchestral section use uniform bowings. Corelli was the most influential violin teacher of his century. He attracted numerous pupils, many of whom became outstanding concert artists and teachers who transmitted Corelli's principles of violin playing to future generations. Among those pupils were Giovannni Battista Somis (1686–1763), Pietro Castrucci (1679–1752), Jean-Baptiste Anet (1676–1755), and Francesco Geminiani (1687–1762). Geminiani was one of

Henry Purcell.

the great violin virtuosi of his time; he worked principally in England, where he wrote numerous compositions and several treatises, including the very popular *The Art of Playing on the Violin* (1750), which was based on Corelli's teachings.

England

Henry Purcell

Henry Purcell (1659–95), organist and singer (bass and countertenor), was one of the greatest English composers of all time. As a boy, he was a chorister in the Chapel Royal. His compositional talents surfaced early; he is represented in Playford's *Catch that Catch Can* (1667) by the three-part song *Sweet tyrannes*. Purcell's voice broke in 1673 (earlier than normal), and he was assigned other tasks at court—assisting the keeper of instruments, tuning the organ at Westminster Abbey, and copying music. In 1677 he succeeded Matthew Locke as composer-in-ordinary for violins, and in 1679 he succeeded John Blow as organist at Westminster Abbey. From 1682 to 1695 Purcell was one of three organists attached to the

Example 16.10 Opening measures of *Sonata* from Act IV of *The Faerie Queen.* *(Source: Henry Purcell:* Complete Works, *Vol. 12, Copyright © 1912 Novella, Ewer & Company, London, England.)*

Chapel Royal; the others were John Blow and William Child. Purcell was active as composer and organist at Westminster Abbey and at court for the remainder of his life. He died in November 1695; his funeral was held in Westminster Abbey, and he was interred there, in the north aisle, adjoining the organ.

Most of Purcell's surviving music dates from after 1679. He made important contributions in several areas: the opera *Dido and Aeneas* (1689); "incidental" music for plays, e.g., Dryden's *The Indian Queen* (1695) and *King Arthur* (1691), to an extent that makes those plays semioperas; welcome songs and odes, the most significant being the *Ode for St. Cecelia's Day* (1692), an important forerunner of Handel's English oratorios; anthems, both verse and full, for Service and for special occasions such as coronations; more than 100 secular songs, some of which were included in the collection *Orpheus Brittanicus*; keyboard works, including eight harpsichord suites, some dances, and a few organ voluntaries; and a considerable body of instrumental ensemble music.

Purcell's compositional genius is especially apparent in his instrumental works. Available to him at court were recorders, oboes, trumpets, timpani, and strings. For *Dido and Aeneas* he used only strings; in *The Tempest* he added one oboe; for the other semioperas and plays he used all available resources. The ensemble "Sonata" played "while the Sun rises" in Act IV of *The Fairy Queen* is one of the earliest instrumental compositions to commence with a timpani solo (ex. 16.10). Purcell was a master in the use of canon and ground bass. He handled winds effectively,

writing obbligato lines for them in vocal solos and treating winds and strings antiphonally in ensemble music.

Purcell's independent ensemble music is divisible into two categories: works for viol consort, a medium virtually obsolete at that time; and sonatas for violins with basso continuo specified for bass viol and keyboard. His fantasias for viols and several of his *Ten Sonata's in Four Parts* (publ. posth., 1697) are found in the same manuscript, which is dated 1680. Modality is still present in the viol fantasias, but Purcell's knowledge of major-minor keys is evident. In the *Fantasia upon One Note* (1680), for five viols, the fourth part sounds no other pitch than middle C, but Purcell avoids monotony by using vivacious rhythms and all of the possible harmonic progressions. The two *In nomine* pieces (one for six viols, the other for seven) are traditionally English, with counterpoint enveloping the cantus firmus *Gloria tibi Trinitas* plainsong melody as notated by Taverner in the Benedictus of his *Mass Gloria tibi Trinitas* (see p. 274).

The *Sonnata's of III Parts* (composed c. 1680, publ. 1683) comprise 12 works for two violins, bass viol, and either harpsichord or organ. Purcell stated in the Preface that originally he did not intend to include keyboard. The *Ten Sonata's in Four Parts* are for two violins, bass viol, and basso continuo. Included in the volume is a long chaconne that is one of Purcell's finest instrumental compositions.

Supposedly, Corelli had a rather low regard for Purcell's sonatas. Perhaps that was because Purcell's sonatas are more English than Italian in style.

France

The French were slow to accept or write sonatas and concertos for string instruments. The first concertos written by a resident of France and published in that country were the four *concerti grossi* by Michele Mascitti that were included in his Op. 7, printed in Paris in 1727. Mascitti (c. 1663–1760), an Italian-born violinist, settled in Paris in 1704. His playing attracted the attention of the Duc d'Orléans, who arranged for him to perform before the King and his entire court. Mascitti became immensely popular with the French public, who (erroneously) considered him on a par with Corelli. In 1739 Mascitti became a French citizen by naturalization. All of Mascitti's printed works are for strings. They were issued in nine collections between 1704 and 1738, and comprise 100 solo sonatas (mainly *da camera*), 12 trio sonatas, and 4 *concerti grossi*. His works are patterned after Corelli's but he adapted that Italian master's style to suit French taste.

During the late seventeenth and early eighteenth centuries, when the violin and 'cello were becoming increasingly important, there flourished in Paris a school of bass viol (gamba) players and composers. At the center of that school was Marin Marais (1656–1728), noted viola da gamba player in the service of the French king. Marais wrote more than 550 compositions for one, two, or three bass viols (gambas), with basso continuo, which he published in five collections of *Pièces de violes* between 1686 and 1725. Additional bass viol pieces and four operas by Marais survive in manuscript. The vast majority of the *Pièces* are for one bass viol with figured bass. His *Pièces en trio pour les flûtes, violon, et dessus de viol* (Trios for flutes, violin, and treble viol), published in 1692, are considered the first trio sonatas to appear in France. By c. 1725, Marais was known throughout Europe as a virtuoso on the bass viol and an outstanding composer of music for that instrument. His works are historically important as marking the full flowering of bass viol (i.e., gamba) music in France.

François Couperin *le grand*

François Couperin *le grand* (see p. 362) also composed *Pièces de violes* (Paris, 1728) for bass viol and basso continuo. Couperin may have written trio sonatas as early as 1692; however, they did not appear

in print until decades later. In France there was controversy concerning the merits of French and Italian musical styles. Couperin admired the music of both Corelli and Lully, and attempted to maintain a neutral stand in the controversy by including in his music elements of both French and Italian styles. *Les nations: sonades et suites de simphonies en trio* (The nations: sonatas and sets of instrumental trios; 1726) contains four works, each comprising a sonata *da chiesa* and a suite of dances, for two violins with basso continuo. Titles of the works reflect nationalities: *La françoise* (The French lady), *L'espagnole* (The Spanish lady), *L'impériale* (The royal lady), and *La piemontoise* (The Piedmont lady). In each composition, Italy is represented by the sonata and France by the suite. Couperin stated in the Preface to *Les nations* that Corelli was his model and principal source of inspiration. Of these pieces, *L'impériale* most clearly shows Couperin's understanding of the Italian trio sonata concept of Corelli; in it there is lively and well-balanced interplay of musical ideas.

In other chamber music works, too, Couperin aimed to reconcile or to show the compatibility of French and Italian musical styles. In the Preface to *Les goûts-réünis* (The styles reconciled; 1724) he expressed his high regard for the Italian sonata, his belief that his composition of Italianate music was not disrespectful to his French heritage or to Lully, and his neutral position in the current controversy. *Les goûts-réünis* contains: (1) *Le Parnasse, ou L'apothéose de Corelli, grande sonade en trio* (Parnassus, or The apotheosis of Corelli, large trio sonata), for two violins and *basso continuo*; and (2) a series of eight *Nouveaux concerts* (New ensemble music) for unspecified instrumentation. The *concerts* are suites; *L'apothéose de Corelli* is a seven-movement *sonata da chiesa*.

Reconciliation of French and Italian styles is represented programmatically in *L'apothéose composé à la mémoire immortelle de l'incomparable Monsieur de Lully* (The apotheosis composed for eternal memory of the incomparable M. de Lully; 1725): Lully and Corelli meet on Parnassus; at first, their respective styles are juxtaposed. Then Apollo persuades the two composers that musical perfection will result from the union of French and Italian styles, and Corelli and Lully perform together, playing the two treble parts of a trio sonata.

Jean-Marie Leclair

Jean-Marie Leclair *l'aîné* (the elder; 1697–1764), violinist, composer, and dancer, is considered the founder and first great violinist of the French school. Among Leclair's outstanding pupils are J.-B. Saint-Sevin (known as L'abbé le fils), G. P. Dupont, Elisabeth de Haulteterre, and Pierre Gaviniès. Leclair was murdered with an engraving tool in the courtyard of his Paris home on 22 October 1764. Three suspects were apprehended: his second wife, who was a professional engraver; the gardener, who found the body; and Leclair's nephew, violinist G.-F. Vial. Evidence in the French Archives Nationales points toward Vial; however, he was never brought to trial, and the case is marked "Unsolved."

Leclair carried on the work of Couperin and achieved a modification of Corelli's style that suited French taste. To effect this synthesis, he combined elements of Lullian dance and French harpsichord and bass viol pieces with Italian sonata style. Leclair was well acquainted with Corelli's style, for he had studied with G. B. Somis, knew Geminiani, performed with and in duel against Locatelli, and may have studied with Locatelli. Leclair was well grounded in the French style also. His greatest rival as violinist was the brilliant Italian-born virtuoso Jean-Pierre Guignon (1702–74), also a pupil of Somis. When Guignon became a naturalized French citizen, the King bestowed on him the (long-vacant) title used by head of the medieval musicians' guild—*Roy et maître des ménétriers et jouers d'instruments* . . . (King and master of minstrels and instrumentalists . . .). Guignon may have equaled Leclair as a performer, but Guignon's trio and solo sonatas are inferior to Leclair's.

Leclair's earliest known works are 10 sonatas for violin and basso continuo in a manuscript anthology compiled c. 1721 that contains 69 violin sonatas by French and Italian composers. Leclair's 10 sonatas were included with others in his first two published volumes: *Premier livre de sonates* (First book of sonatas; 1723), and *Second livre de sonates* (Second book of sonatas; c. 1728). He composed several volumes of solo sonatas, at least one book of trio sonatas, and a dozen *concerti grossi*.

Leclair's music is technically difficult, with double- and multiple-stops, difficult figurations, excursions into high positions, and double trills. He wrote some entire movements in multiple-stops, occasionally writing a chord so extended in range that the thumb had to be used on the G-string to stop the lowest note of the chord. Leclair used a slightly longer violin bow than did Corelli, and the bowing techniques specified in his compositions reflect this advantage. Leclair's melodies are constructed in relatively short phrases, with ornaments in moderation but completely written out. The harmonies are tonal with some surprising chromatic progressions and occasional enharmonic modulations.

Germanic Lands

In Germanic territories the Thirty Years' War (1618–48) had a disastrous effect on all the arts. Courts and towns, impoverished by war, had little money for patronage of music and reduced the size of Hofkapelle, Kantorei, and Stadpfeiferei; more and more, composers wrote for small ensembles of vocalists and/or instrumentalists. Music printing almost completely halted; few volumes of music were printed during the last half of the seventeenth century and most of those were issued in Nuremberg. It was expensive and time consuming to produce music manuscripts in multiple copies; therefore, most of the music that was composed was designed for local use rather than for general circulation and public consumption.

Sonatas

The outstanding violinist-composers working in German and Austrian courts were Heinrich Ignaz Franz von Biber (1644–1704) and Johann Jakob Walther (c. 1650–1717). Biber, a native of Bohemia, served in 1660–70 as performer on several string instruments at the court of Prince-Bishop Karl at Olomouc, Moravia. The prince amassed a remarkable music library, which is catalogued and housed at Kroměříž Castle; most of the surviving manuscripts of Biber's compositions are there. In autumn 1670 Biber left Prince Karl's court without permission and at some time during the following winter became a member of the Salzburg court chapel. He was appointed Kapellmeister at Salzburg in 1684 and retained that position until his death. By 1670 Biber had achieved a reputation for being a formidable virtuoso on the violin, yet there is no record of his making professional concert tours. He was well known in

Munich and on two occasions was decorated by Emperor Leopold I (r. 1657–1705), who ennobled him in 1690. Biber's compositions include works for solo violin, instrumental ensemble, 3 operas (only 1 survives), at least 15 school dramas, and a good deal of sacred music.

The instrumental ensemble compositions consist of dance pieces and sonatas in four, five, six, or eight parts. Among the sonatas are works for solo trumpet with strings and basso continuo, for trumpets and timpani, for recorders with strings and basso continuo, and for strings with and without basso continuo. Biber's sonatas for solo violin reflect his own capabilities as a virtuoso performer. To play them, the violinist needed technical facility over the entire length of the violin fingerboard—seven positions, at that time. The eight sonatas for solo violin with basso continuo (*Sonatae violino solo*; 1681) contain polyphonic passages filled with multiple-stops and brilliant figuration above ostinato bass lines; some movements include passages requiring *scordatura* (tuning the strings other than in perfect fifths). *Scordatura* was used to achieve richer sonorities and special tone colors and to make obtainable multiple-stops not ordinarily possible on the violin (ex. 16.11).

All but two of Biber's so-called *Mystery* (or *Rosary*) *Sonatas* require *scordatura,* different for each sonata. The designation *Mystery* or *Rosary* derives from the fact that in one manuscript each of the first 15 of the sonatas is prefixed by a depiction of one of the 15 mysteries of the rosary; the 16th sonata, the *Passacaglia* for unaccompanied violin, has a picture of a guardian angel and child. It is believed Biber performed the *Passacaglia* at Salzburg Cathedral on 2 October 1676, the Feast of the Guardian Angel, and performed the other 15 sonatas in Services there later that October, the month the cathedral devoted to observance of Rosary Mysteries. The sonatas include several sets of variations, all using ostinato basses. Biber's polyphonic *Passacaglia* for unaccompanied violin is the most important precursor of J. S. Bach's D-minor *Chaconne*. The *Mystery Sonatas* were not printed until 1905.

Like Biber, Walther wrote compositions involving high positions, multiple-stops, and polyphony, but Walther adhered to conventional tuning of the violin.

Example 16.11 Some of the *scordatura* tunings specified by Biber for his *Mystery Sonatas.*

Only two collections of Walther's music are known: *Scherzi da violino solo . . .* (Scherzos for solo violin; 1676), with accompaniment specified for organ or harpsichord and one viol or lute; and *Hortulus chelicus uni violino . . .* (Musical garden for one violin; 1688), comprising two-, three-, and four-part polyphonic pieces to be played on one violin. Walther's solo violin music is replete with programmatic elements, e.g., imitations of birds, animals, other musical instruments, and an ensemble of violins.

Suites, Dance Music

Early in the seventeenth century, English violists working in Europe familiarized continental musicians with ensemble dance music for four or five viols; Netherlands, Danish, and German composers began to write similar pieces for groups of wind or stringed instruments. Pieces of this kind appear in Hans Leo Hassler's *Lustgarten neuer teutscher Gesäng, Balletti, Gaillarden und Intraden* (Pleasure garden of new songs in German, *balletti,* gaillards, and *intrade*; 1601) for four to eight voices and in Samuel Scheidt's (1587–1654) four-volume *Ludorum musicorum . . .* (Musical pastimes . . . ; 1621–22), also for four to eight parts. Pavane and galliard were paired, with related thematic material; allemande, courante, and other dance pieces were individual dances. Customarily, German musicians performed a dance that was written in duple meter, then by improvising transformed it to a second dance in triple meter; that second dance was called *Tripla* or *Proporz.* A set or **suite** of dances usually included allemande, courante, *intrada,* and paired pavane and galliard but had no specific order of arrangement. At the hands of German composers a suite of dances was expanded by progressive variation, all dances being thematically related; such a group is known as a **variation suite.** Frequently, the dances in a variation suite were unified by an initial motive, as medieval Masses were unified by a head motive. The variation suite reached a high point with Johann Hermann Schein's (1586–1630) *Banchetto musicale* (Musical banquet; 1617), a collection of 20 numbered groups of pavanes, galliards, courantes, and allemandes, arranged according to mode. Each allemande is supplied with a *tripla* in strict proportion, i.e., the *tripla* is a simple bar-for-bar reworking of the allemande in triple time. Schein did not call the groups "suites," though they are such; each group comprises pavane-galliard and allemande-tripla paired dances separated by a courante. Schein indicated that performance on viols was preferred but that any instruments might be used; there is no basso continuo part.

In the middle Baroque era, the paired pavane-galliard with which an ensemble suite usually began was gradually replaced by paired allemande-courante. Johann Christoph Pezel (1639–94) wrote hundreds of pieces of ensemble music for winds and for strings. This music was published in several collections, including *Hora decima musicorum* (Tenth hour of music; 1670), containing 40 sonatas for two cornetts and three trombones; and *Fünff-stimmigte blasende Music* (Five-voice wind music; 1685), containing 76 pieces of dance music for two cornetts and three trombones.

Johann Rosenmüller's (c. 1619–84) promising career at the Thomasschule in Leipzig was halted suddenly in 1655 when he was imprisoned on a morals charge. He escaped from jail and fled to Venice, where he worked as trombonist at St. Mark's and as composer at the Ospedale della Pietà. In 1682 he returned to Germany as court composer at Wolfenbüttel. Rosenmüller's surviving instrumental works include a collection of dances for three instruments with basso continuo (1645) and two volumes of ensemble *sonate da camera* (1667; 1682). The collection published in 1667 contains 11 sonatas, each comprising a sinfonia, allemande, courante, *ballo,* and sarabande, for five string instruments plus basso continuo. Each of the 12 sonatas in the collection published in 1682 has from three to five movements, one of which is usually repeated as the finale. None of the movements is designated as dance music; rather, the sonatas may be considered as an expansion of the sinfonia idea. Many movements are imitative or fugal; transitional sections are slow and chordal. The 1682 collection displays Rosenmüller's assimilation of the Italian style of sonata composition, which he helped transmit to the north.

Georg Muffat

The French musical style and the standards of ensemble playing imposed by Lully were transmitted to Germany by Georg Muffat and others. Muffat (1653–1704) considered himself German, though he was French by birth. He grew up in France and became thoroughly familiar with Lully's orchestral style. In 1680–82 Muffat visited Italy, where he studied with Pasquini and heard Corelli's *concerti grossi;* some of Muffat's ensemble sonatas were performed in Corelli's house. Muffat published those sonatas, which are based on the concerto principle of alternating groups, in *Armonico tributo* (Harmonic tribute; 1682). The multilingual prefaces to Muffat's published works are especially significant, for in them he presented detailed information concerning Corelli's and Lully's performance practices, including bowing technique and proper ornamentation. *Florilegium primum* (1695) contains seven orchestral suites for four and five parts with basso continuo; *Florilegium secundum* (1698) contains eight orchestral suites. Muffat's suites commence with a French overture—the first section in slow tempo, in duple meter, and filled with dotted rhythms; the second section fast and fugal, in triple meter. The five-part string texture reflects Lully's royal ensemble—*les 24 violons du roi* (the 24 violins of the king).

Other excellent orchestral suites appear in J. K. F. Fischer's *Journal du Printemps* (Spring Journal; 1695) and Johann Sigismund Kusser's (1660–1727) *Composition de musique suivant la méthode françoise* (Musical composition according to French style; 1682). Kusser seems to have been the first to add the French overture to the German orchestral suite. Both Telemann and J. S. Bach composed orchestral suites (see Ch. 17).

Summary

The principal types of compositions for instrumental ensembles were sonata (i.e., *sonata da chiesa*) and related forms, suite (*sonata da camera*) and related forms, and concerto. The *sonata da chiesa* evolved from the canzona. Though some sonatas were written for solo instrument with basso continuo, most of the sonatas composed during the last third of the seventeenth century were trio sonatas; a few sonatas were written for unaccompanied solo violin.

The word *concerto* was commonly used in Italy during the first half of the seventeenth century to denote vocal music accompanied by instrumental ensemble. Around 1675, composers began to write instrumental ensemble concertos—*concerto grosso* compositions.

The construction of instruments of the violin family rose to unprecedented heights in northern Italy during the Baroque era. The craftsmanship of Stradivari and Guarneri has never been surpassed. Northern Italy was the leader, too, in the production and performance of instrumental chamber music, with Venice, Modena, and Bologna being sites of the main development of the sonata. At Bologna, especially at the basilica of San Petronio, instrumental music flourished. Cazzati, G. B. Vitali, and degli Antonii are only a few of the many composers of violin and ensemble music who worked there. Domenico Gabrielli wrote for unaccompanied 'cello; Giuseppi Torelli contributed greatly to the development of *concerto grosso* and to the repertoire for trumpet and strings. Generally, Torelli used *ritornello* form for the first and last movements of his solo concerti, with the middle movement contrasting in tempo and design.

Arcangelo Corelli wrote almost exclusively for bowed string instruments. The majority of his published works are trio sonatas; one volume of solo sonatas and another of *concerti grossi* were issued. He seems to have been the first composer to write exclusively in major-minor key tonalities, with no trace of modality. He made systematic use of sequences, both melodic and harmonic, and was equally skilled in writing polyphony and homophony; his linear counterpoint is harmonically based. Corelli was the most influential violin teacher of the era; his many pupils carried his didactic principles to England and to all parts of continental Europe. They raised public regard for violin playing to the extent that, in the eighteenth century, violins supplanted viols.

Henry Purcell was one of the greatest English composers of all time. He made important contributions in several areas: opera, music for plays, occasional songs and odes, anthems, and instrumental pieces.

The French, who enjoyed viol music, were slow to accept other bowed string instruments or to write sonatas and concertos. François Couperin *le grand,* in addition to composing for keyboard, made important contributions to the repertoire of chamber music for strings, but J.-M. Leclair *l'ainé* is considered the founder and first outstanding violinist of the French violin school. The French musical style, and the standards imposed by court composer Lully, were transmitted to Germany by Georg Muffat and others. Orchestral suites by German composers were important forerunners of similar works by Telemann and Bach, e.g., the orchestral suites that Kusser commenced with French overture. The German virtuoso violinist Biber composed technically demanding sonatas for unaccompanied violin; his *Passacaglia* is an important precursor of J. S. Bach's *Chaconne* in D minor.

Great strides were made in the advancement of instrumental music during the seventeenth century. Even greater accomplishments were to come at the hands of master composers working in the first half of the eighteenth century.

Eminent Composers of the Early Eighteenth Century

Several different musical styles are apparent in the first half of the eighteenth century. The Baroque, with all grandeur, reached its height. In France the light-textured *style galant* (termed *rococo* by some historians) came into vogue and passed through two stages; in northern Germany *empfindsamer Stil* (expressive style) flourished. After 1730, Pre-Classical elements predicted the trend music would take in the last half of the century. (These styles are discussed in Chapter 18.) Some composers worked entirely within one style, while others incorporated two or more styles in their compositions. Composers were concerned with the music of their own time and wrote music that met the needs of their employment. Music was practical—didactic works were written for a composer's current pupils, not for future generations; theoretical treatises and performance manuals were written to explain current practices to interested contemporaries. Preservation of the historical past did not enter into consideration. All of these facts are visible in the lives and works of five eminent composers: Antonio Vivaldi, Georg Philipp Telemann, Jean-Philippe Rameau, Johann Sebastian Bach, and George Frideric Handel.

Antonio Vivaldi. *(The Bettmann Archive.)*

Antonio Vivaldi

Antonio Vivaldi (1678–1741) was born in Venice, where his father was a professional violinist at St. Mark's Church. Although Antonio had music lessons from his father and others at St. Mark's, he was educated for the priesthood and was ordained early in 1703. He did not follow that profession, however, because asthma, angina pectoris, or a combination of those diseases rendered him incapable of officiating at Services. Throughout his adult life he was nicknamed *il prete rosso* (the red priest) because of his red hair.

1675	1700	1725	1750	1775	1800

- - Baroque era -

- - *Style galant* -
     (first stage)   (second stage)

- - *empfindsamer Stil* - - - - - - - - - - - - - *Sturm und Drang*

- Pre-Classical - - - - - - - - - - - - -Classical era - - - - - - - - - - - - -

1678 - - - - - - - - - - - -Vivaldi - - - - - - - - - - - - - - - - -1741
              Baroque concerto

1681 - - - - - - - - - -Telemann -1767
              collegium musicum concerts
                1725 *Pimpinone*

1683 - - - - - - - - - Rameau -1764
                1722 *Traité de l'harmonie*
                   1737 *Castor et Pollux*

1685 - - - - - - - - - J. S. Bach -1750
                1722 *Das wohltemperirte Clavier*
                  1727 *Passion according to St. Matthew*
                    1731–42 *Clavier-Übung* Series
                      1740s *Die Kunst der Fuge*

1685 - - - - - - - - Handel -1759
           1711 *Rinaldo*   1741 *Messiah*
                         English oratorio
                         organ concerto

            1728 Gay and Pepusch
              The Beggar's Opera

c. 1700 Cristofori fortepiano

           1722 *Critica musica*

In September 1703, Vivaldi was appointed *maestro di violino* (violin teacher) at Pio Ospedale della Pietà, one of four *ospedali* (hospitals) in Venice. These hospitals were charitable institutions whose main purpose was to care for the sick or to supervise the education of indigent, illegitimate, or orphaned girls. The four *ospedali* provided for hundreds of girls, and musical training was an important part of the curriculum. By 1700, each *ospedale* employed a full-time *maestro di cappella* and two or more specialists to teach various instruments. Only the most talented girls—those of soloist or virtuoso caliber—were taught by the professional staff; proficient older girls trained the others, and some were permitted to accept as pupils children from outside the *ospedale*. Each *ospedale* had its own choir and orchestra and gave concerts regularly and frequently in the *ospedali* chapels.

An ensemble of approximately 40 girls—selected representatives from all four *ospedali*—performed on special occasions. The instrumentation and personnel varied considerably, depending on the talent available at the time. New music was programmed for each concert, much of it written by *ospedali* music teachers and other Venetian composers. The performances attracted large crowds and prompted donations and endowments to the institutions.

Gradually, Vivaldi's duties at the Pietà were expanded. In 1704 he was charged with teaching lessons on all string instruments, acquiring new string instruments for the orchestra, and supervising the maintenance of all string instruments owned by the Pietà. He was promoted to *maestro de' concerti* (master of concerts) in 1716. Vivaldi was associated with the Pietà until 1740, but he was away from the *ospedale* intermittently, sometimes for a year or longer, for various reasons: poor economic conditions affecting the institution's budget, or travels to perform or to arrange for opera productions in other cities. However, during Vivaldi's lifetime no other violin *maestro* was ever appointed at the Pietà.

By 1704 Vivaldi was composing. His pieces, like those of his contemporaries, were written for specific performers and occasions. When a dozen compositions of the same genre had accumulated, he had them published. His Op. 1, comprising 12 trio sonatas, was printed in Venice in 1705; a set of 12 sonatas for violin with basso continuo was issued as Op. 2 in 1709. Twelve concertos—four each for one, two, and four solo violins with string orchestra—form his *L'estro armonico,* Op. 3 (Harmonic whim, or Musical fancy), published in 1711 by Étienne Roger of Amsterdam, one of the finest music publishers of the time. *La stravaganza,* Op. 4 (Eccentricity), 12 concertos featuring solo violin, appeared in 1714. Concertos continued to pour from his pen—he composed hundreds of them, and they constitute the vast majority of his works.

Vivaldi wrote some vocal music, too. His father was involved with opera, and after 1710 Antonio pursued a career in that field, as both composer and impresario. His first opera, *Ottone in Villa* (Ottone at his country home), was performed in May 1713 at Vicenza, a resort town. Commencing in 1714, Vivaldi composed a number of operas for St. Angelo theater, Venice. Though he wrote at least 49 operas, only 21 are extant and some of those are incomplete.

The governors of the Pietà valued Vivaldi's contributions as composer and continued to commission works. For instance, in June 1715 he was paid for a Mass, a Vespers, the oratorio *Moyses Deus Pharaonis* (now lost), and more than 30 motets. In 1723 the Pietà commissioned him to compose two concertos per month and to rehearse and direct performances of them when he was in Venice.

Vivaldi considered himself primarily an opera composer, but his contemporaries thought he was more talented as a violinist than as a composer. After his death, he was virtually forgotten for several decades. When it was discovered that some of his works had been copied, studied, transcribed, or arranged by J. S. Bach, interest in Vivaldi was aroused. But not until c. 1905 were Vivaldi's significant contributions to the development of the concerto recognized. In the 1920s a great many of Vivaldi's autograph scores—presumably, his personal collection—were located and were placed in Biblioteca Nazionale, Turin. Since then, one of his Glorias and some of his concertos, especially *The Seasons,* have attracted considerable attention.

Vivaldi's Music

In addition to operas, Vivaldi's vocal music includes motets and psalm settings, Magnificats and Vespers, Masses and Mass movements, oratorios, sacred and secular cantatas, and serenatas. Most of the cantatas are for one soloist (soprano or alto) with basso continuo and consist of recitatives and arias in regular alternation.

A list of Vivaldi's surviving instrumental compositions includes approximately 90 sonatas (both trio and solo), 16 sinfonias, and more than 500 concertos with diverse solo instrumentation. About 350 of the concertos are for one solo instrument with string orchestra and basso continuo; approximately two-thirds of those 350 are for solo violin, and in the remainder, the solo is for bassoon, violoncello, oboe, flute, viola d'amore, recorder, or mandolin. (The instruments are listed in descending order of frequency.) More than 40 concertos are for two soloists, usually two identical instruments, and most often two violins. Unusual combinations, such as viola d'amore and lute, indicate the variety of talent possessed by the young women at the Pietà. About 30 concertos require more than two soloists; 60 are orchestral concertos (no individual soloists); and in 20 concertos the individual soloists combine to form the ensemble playing the *tutti* parts.

Vivaldi gave many of his concertos special titles alluding to the person for whom the piece was written, the soloist, the overall mood of the composition, an unusual technical feature of the work, or the program depicted. For example, 7 of the 12 concertos in *Il cimento dell'armonia e dell'inventione,* Op. 8 (The contest between harmony and invention; publ. c. 1725) are programmatic: Nos. 1–4, individually entitled *La primavera* (Spring), *L'estate* (Summer), *L'autunno* (Autumn), *L'inverno* (Winter)—collectively called *La stagione* (The seasons); No. 5, *La tempesta di mare* (Storm at sea); No. 6, *Il piacere* (Pleasure); and No. 10, *La caccia* (The hunt). Vivaldi wrote four sonnets, one describing each season, and included the appropriate poem with each of the first four concertos; the music portrays characteristics of the designated season.

Vivaldi's most important contributions to the development of music were made in connection with the concerto. He strengthened, perfected, and expanded the elements of Baroque concerto style and formal structure set forth by Torelli. But Vivaldi's themes are more concise and his rhythms more driving than those of Torelli. Moreover, Vivaldi transferred to his concertos the techniques he employed in writing opera arias: opposing soloist and ensemble, balancing tension with release, and concluding a movement with a synthesis of the musical ideas presented.

Most of Vivaldi's concertos contain three movements, in fast-slow-fast order of tempo, with the middle movement usually in a contrasting key closely related to that of the two Allegros. Though the three movements are not of the same length and character, they are of equal importance. The final Allegro is usually shorter and more animated than the first; the slow movement is lyrical, expressive, and sometimes passionate, and for this movement the orchestral instrumentation is reduced. In the two outer movements, orchestral *ritornelli* alternate with solo episodes. Vivaldi lengthened both *ritornello* and solo passages. Though the soloist clearly dominates the ensemble and the composition, it is apparent that the orchestral and soloist music were conceived as a unit, for the orchestra does not merely accompany. The *ritornelli* are highly organized and function as consolidating and stabilizing factors between the passages of idiomatic, brilliant figuration by which the soloist advances the musical plan. The concerto's opening measures precisely indicate the tonality of the work, e.g., by spelling out the tonic triad or arpeggiating the tonic chord, by iterating the key note vigorously several times, or by a scale (ex. 17.1).

Though Vivaldi frequently borrowed from himself, reworking themes and entire movements and reusing them, his musical style is not static or stereotyped; he was aware of contemporary trends and kept

Example 17.1 The opening measures of Vivaldi's concerti emphasize the tonic key: (*a*) Op. XI, No. 2, mm. 1–2; (*b*) Op. III, No. 6; (*c*) Op. III, No. 5.

pace with the changing times in which he lived. His instrumental music is primarily homophonic, with counterpoint used incidentally. His early solo and trio sonatas display Corellian traits; his sinfonias, *ripieno* (orchestral) concertos, and some solo concertos composed after c. 1726 exhibit characteristic features of Pre-Classical style, e.g., balanced phrases, homophonic texture, triplet sixteenths, melodic sighs, and carefully placed ornaments. Some of the concertos in *La cetra,* Op. 9 (The Lyre; 1727), are in Pre-Classical style. An example is Op. 9, No. 2, mvt. 2 (ex. 17.2; DWMA129).

Vivaldi's concertos and sinfonias served as models for some compositions by J. S. Bach and other composers. The overall plan of the Baroque concerto and the concept of solo-tutti contrast developed by Vivaldi were transmitted to later eighteenth-century composers and still survive in concertos and other forms of instrumental music.

Georg Philipp Telemann

In the early and middle eighteenth century, Georg Philipp Telemann (1681–1767) was considered the leading German composer. He was extremely prolific—more than 4000 of his compositions are extant—and wrote French, Italian, and German music in Baroque, Pre-Classical, and Rococo styles. Besides adding considerable music to most categories of the repertoire, he made significant contributions in the areas of music theory, music education, and concert organization.

Example 17.2 Measures 115–20 of the solo violin part of the Largo of Vivaldi's *La cetra*, Op. 9, No. 2, contain the triplet 16th notes and melodic sighs characteristic of Pre-Classical style. *(Source: Le opere di Antonio Vivaldi: La Cetra [Amsterdam, 1728], ed. G. F. Malipiero [Milan: Ricordi, 1952], Vol. 126, pp. 18–19.)*

Telemann was the youngest of two sons in an upper-middle-class Magdeburg family. There were no musicians among his ancestors, but all of the men had been educated at some university, and most of them, including Georg's father (d. 1685) and brother, had become clergymen. In 1685, Georg was enrolled at the Magdeburg Gymnasium and Domschule, where he studied Latin, rhetoric, and dialectic. He received no special training in instrumental music, but by the age of 10 had learned to play several instruments, including flute, violin, and keyboard. He studied the pieces written by the school's Kantor and tried to compose music, too. When Telemann was 12, he attempted to compose an opera. At that point, his mother deprived him of his instruments, forbade any further involvement with music, and sent him to school at Zellerfeld. There, in addition to academic studies, he learned of the association between music and mathematics. He taught himself more about composition and wrote some pieces that the local *Stadt-pfeiferei* performed. (*Stadtpfeiferei* were professional musicians employed by the city.) In 1697, Telemann went to Hildesheim to study. While there, he wrote

Georg Philipp Telemann. The name of the artist is unknown.

incidental music for several school dramas and, with other Protestant students, performed cantatas in the Catholic Church.

On visits to Hanover and Grunswich he first encountered French and Italian instrumental music and Italian opera. He studied the compositional styles of Corelli and Steffani and tried to write similarly.

In 1701 Telemann entered Leipzig University to study law. (The university law curriculum provided the best education available, and many persons not intending to practice law embarked upon that course of study.) Although he concealed his compositional endeavors, his roommate discovered one of the pieces and arranged for its performance at Thomaskirche. That performance was the turning point in Telemann's life. The mayor of Leipzig commissioned him to compose a cantata every two weeks for use in Thomaskirche. From then on, music was Telemann's lifework. During his student days at Leipzig, Telemann met Handel, who had already attracted attention in the musical world. They became good friends and frequently exchanged ideas.

In Leipzig, Telemann quickly became involved in many musical activities. In 1702 he founded a *collegium musicum,* a group of students who met to perform all kinds of music, much of it newly composed. He arranged for the *collegium* to give public concerts regularly and programmed sacred and secular music indiscriminately. In the same year, he became music director of the Leipzig Opera. He composed several operas for performance there and employed student singers and instrumentalists, as well as professionals. From time to time over the next 20 years, Telemann wrote operas for performance at Leipzig.

When a new organ was installed at Neukirche (the university church) in 1704, Telemann was appointed organist there. He agreed to serve as church music director also and to arrange for his *collegium* to present sacred music concerts at the church regularly. Johann Kuhnau (1660–1722), Leipzig city music director and Kantor at Thomaskirche, became indignant at Telemann's involvement in so many activities, primarily because Telemann achieved results that Kuhnau had believed impossible—cantatas sung at Thomaskirche every Sunday and fine music at Services and in concerts at the university church. More-

over, students whom Kuhnau thought should be singing at Thomaskirche were using their talents at Neukirche, in *collegium,* and at the Opera. The city fathers heeded Kuhnau's complaints—they forbade Telemann to work at the Opera.

In 1705 Count Erdmann II of Promnitz appointed Telemann court Kapellmeister at Sorau (now in Poland). There, Telemann and Erdmann Neumeister (1671–1756), the court chaplain, became friends. Between 1695 and 1742, Neumeister wrote nine cycles of cantata texts, each cycle containing texts for all Sundays of the church year, and some extra texts for special feasts. The cycles were of three types: (1) Biblical verses and poetic aria texts, and an occasional chorale—texts to be set to music for soloists and chorus; (2) madrigalesque poetry, suitable for musical setting as recitative and aria, in the manner of Italian secular solo cantata; and (3) a combination of the foregoing two types, which became the standard cantata in the eighteenth century. Telemann set two of the cycles that Neumeister prepared for the court at Eisenach, and J. S. Bach used portions of Neumeister's cycles in several of his works.

Telemann was appointed Kapellmeister at the Eisenach court in 1708, where he composed chamber music, overtures, and concertos for the orchestra. It was there that he met J. S. Bach, and another lasting friendship began. In 1709 Telemann married Louise Eberlin of Sorau. She died two years later, shortly after the birth of their daughter.

In 1712 Telemann moved to Frankfurt, where he was city music director and Kapellmeister at Barfüsskirche. For the church Telemann composed at least five cycles of cantatas for the liturgical year, and for the city he wrote whatever music was needed for civic affairs. Though he had no teaching assignment, he assumed the task of training the schoolboys for choir singing. He directed the Frauenstein Society *collegium musicum* and organized weekly public concerts. His new chamber and orchestral works and oratorios were among the pieces programmed. A special concert was arranged at Barfüsskirche in 1716 for performance of his setting of J. H. Brockes's Passion oratorio libretto, a text in which the Biblical account is infiltrated by dramatic and allegorical elements. Keiser, Handel, Mattheson, and others also set Brockes's text, and J. S. Bach used parts of it.

Telemann acquired citizenship in Frankfurt in 1714, through marriage to Maria Textor. From time to time, he received employment offers from other courts and used those offers to bolster his position at Frankfurt. Occasionally, he visited other cities to hear special performances and in that connection met noted composers and performers.

Without making formal application for the position, but upon Neumeister's recommendation, Telemann was invited by the city of Hamburg to be Kantor of the Johanneum and music director for five churches. He accepted. There the demand for new music was immense: two new cantatas for each Sunday, a new Passion annually, additional cantatas, odes, and oratorios for church and civic ceremonies and special events. Despite his busy schedule, he found time to participate in opera, direct the *collegium musicum,* and arrange for public concerts. The two most famous *collegia musica* in Germany were at Leipzig (founded by Telemann) and Hamburg (founded in 1660 by Matthias Weckman). Telemann was solely responsible for the establishment of public concerts in Hamburg; after 1722, both aristocracy and middle-class citizens attended them.

Some city council members objected to Telemann's unassigned activities with public concerts and opera, and the council forbade his participation in theatrical and operatic performances. He retaliated by applying for the position of Kantor at Leipzig's Thomaskirche, the vacancy having been occasioned by Kuhnau's death. Six men applied for that position; one was J. S. Bach. Telemann received the appointment, but the Hamburg council refused to release him. Instead, they raised his salary and ceased objecting to his involvement with public concerts and opera. Later in 1722 Telemann was named music director of the Hamburg Opera and held that position until the Opera closed in 1738. Operas by Handel and Keiser, as well as his own, were presented frequently. Telemann composed light opera of both comic and satirical types as well as *opera seria.* Perhaps his greatest operatic success was *Der geduldige Socrates* (The patient Socrates; 1721). Telemann's comic opera *Pimpinone, oder Die ungleiche Heirat* (Pimpinone, or The unequal marriage; 1725) was first performed as an intermezzo; it anticipated Pergolesi's *La serva padrona* by about eight years. Both *Socrates* and *Pimpinone* contain elements of *opera buffa* style, such as patter (rapid singing of many syllables on one note) and ensembles.

Telemann began publishing his works while he was in Frankfurt. Usually, he personally engraved the music on the copper plates, and he arranged for all details of publication and sale of the music. He wanted to get printed music into the hands of middle- and lower-class citizens and wanted that music suitable for performance at home, because many sizable families had their own instrumental and/or vocal ensembles. With this in mind, he made simplified arrangements of some of his works and indicated alternate or optional instrumentation for others. In this regard, parts and instrumentation designated *obbligato* are required; *ad libitum* parts and instrumentation are optional.

Between 1725 and 1740 Telemann published at least 44 items, 43 of them under his own imprint, including: (1) an untitled cycle of 72 cantatas for the church year; (2) *Harmonischer Gottes-Dienst, oder Geistliche Cantaten zum allgemeinen Gebrauche* (1725–26), a cycle of 72 sacred cantatas for general use; (3) *Musique de table partagée en Trio Production* (Dinner music, in three productions; 1733), three sets of chamber music compositions for a variety of instruments, each set comprising an overture, a quartet, a concerto, a trio, a solo, and a *Conclusion à 7*; (4) *Fantaisies pour le Clavecin: 3 Douzaines* (36 Harpsichord fantasies; 1733), the first and third dozens Italianate, the second dozen in French Pre-Classical style; and (5) *Singe-, Spiel-, und Generalbassübungen* (Vocal, instrumental, and thoroughbass studies; 1733), which includes, among other music, a collection of 48 strophic secular songs for home use.

Late in 1737 Telemann visited Paris and was shocked to find that many of his compositions had been published there without his consent. However, the publication of pirated music was common in Europe in the eighteenth century.

The earliest music periodicals appeared in the second decade of the eighteenth century in Germany. They were of two kinds: (1) critical journals such as Johann Mattheson's (1681–1764) *Critica musica,* the first music journal (1722); and (2) periodicals containing music, such as *Der getreue Musikmeister* (The faithful music master). The latter, which had only four pages, seems to have been the first music periodical to be issued regularly, once every two weeks. It contained both vocal and instrumental music; some of Telemann's sonatas appeared first in that periodical. (An interesting feature of this kind of periodical is the fact that the printed music broke off when space ran out; the composition was continued from that point in the next issue.)

After 1740 Telemann's creative activity decreased considerably. He continued to compose Passions and to set oratorio texts by young poets; perhaps his attraction to oratorio resulted from his continued correspondence with Handel. Some of the music in Telemann's oratorio *Die Tageszeiten* (The Times of day; 1734) anticipates Haydn's *Die Jahreszeiten* (The Seasons), e.g., *Chor der Seligen* (Chorus of the blessed), in which the soloist is supported by chorus.

Telemann's three autobiographies, written in 1718, 1729, and 1739, provide some valuable insights concerning his life and beliefs. Musical activities did not totally consume Telemann's waking hours. He had an absorbing interest in rare plants—an avocation that, he said, provided consolation in times of hardship. Occasionally, Handel contributed to that collection.

Telemann's Music

From Telemann's voluminous compositional output, works in the following categories survive: (1) sacred cantatas (5 published cycles, each containing 72 cantatas; at least 1100 individual cantatas); (2) festal church music for funerals, inaugurations, special thanksgiving, and other ceremonial events; (3) Masses, oratorios, Passions and Passion oratorios, psalm settings and motets; (4) occasional vocal music for weddings, academic, political, or civic military ceremonies; (5) operas (7 complete operas and portions of a dozen others); (6) secular cantatas (56 complete) and serenades; (7) Lieder; (8) a lute suite; (9) keyboard pieces (mostly harpsichord), including suites, fantasies, chorale preludes, fugues and fughettas; (10) instrumental solo and ensemble works, including concertos, sonatas, overtures, sinfonias, divertimentos, and various other chamber music. There is evidence that he wrote much more music that has been lost. In addition, Telemann edited and published selected works by approximately 20 other composers and treatises by Haltmeier, Kellner, and G. A. Sorge.

Telemann's oratorios are transitional between the Baroque and Classical eras. His operatic experience infiltrated his sacred music to the extent that he used musical imagery to express the text and its meaning. Much of his music displays Pre-Classical elements. The *style galant* is visible in the song collection in *Singe-, Spiel-, und Generalbassübungen*. These songs conform to Telemann's belief that a melody should be comfortable to sing, and that a strophic poem should be set to a single stanza of music that is suitable for every poetic strophe and yet adequately conveys the meaning of each individual verse. The songs contain no extremes of register and no virtuosic ornamentation.

Much of Telemann's instrumental music is not technically demanding. Some of his pieces are written in Baroque counterpoint; in others, such as the keyboard works he called *Galanterie-Fugen,* he combined Pre-Classical and Baroque characteristics. For many of his keyboard and chamber music pieces he rejected the learned (contrapuntal) style of the Baroque in favor of the *galant,* using uncomplicated melodies cast in clear, periodic phrases, with accompaniment subordinate to melody. Some of his quartets (none of which use classic string quartet instrumentation) are conversational in style, e.g., those in *Musique de table.* Some of the harpsichord fantasies of 1733 exhibit incipient sonata form.

Telemann's Influence

In the eighteenth century, a patron or employer controlled the amount and kind of music a composer produced, and an employee's sphere of activity was defined by the nature of his position. Telemann refused to be bound by such limitations. He disregarded and ultimately broke down barriers between sacred and secular. He violated the conventions of his time by writing operas and being involved with the theater when he held the post of Kantor, by including sacred and secular music on the same concert program, and by the fact that public concerts he promoted and directed were not associated with any institution. Telemann was influential in bringing all kinds of music to the people, by encouraging student musicians to perform in *collegia musica* and opera as well as in church, by establishing public concerts at which a variety of sacred and secular selections were performed, and by preparing and publishing editions of music suitable for performance by amateurs. He ensured reasonably correct performance of some of the music by including instructional material in the publication.

Where music education and music theory are concerned, Telemann's aims were not fully realized. He wanted to write and publish material that would enable amateurs to compose music reasonably well and perform the music of others properly. To this end, he included in *Fortsetzung des Harmonischen Gottes-dienstes* (Sequel to Harmonious Divine Service) the basic principles of recitative composition and in *Harmonischer Gottes-dienst* (Harmonious Divine Service) rules on the proper performance of recitative. Similarly, in *Singe-, Spiel-, und Generalbass-übungen,* he gave instructions for writing out the inner parts when only a polarity of treble and bass was given and for realizing a basso continuo line at the keyboard.

Telemann's music was forgotten for many decades, and other persons were credited with contributions that he made to the development of music in history. Only in the twentieth century has his true stature been realized.

Jean-Philippe Rameau

Jean-Philippe Rameau (1683–1764), organist and clavecinist, composer, and theorist, was the most important French musician in the eighteenth century. He received his early musical training from his father, who was organist at St. Étienne Church in Dijon; there is no record that Jean-Philippe had any other formal music instruction. He was the seventh of eleven children; his parents intended that his career be in law, but his interests lay in music. The authorities at the Jesuit school to which he was sent reported to his parents that he spent more time on music than on his required studies and asked that he be removed from their tutelage. Not until he was 18 did his parents agree that music should be his profession.

Rameau visited Italy for several months during 1701. In January 1702 he was employed as temporary organist at Avignon Cathedral, and in May he became organist at Clermont Cathedral in Auvergne. He resigned that post in 1706 and went to Paris, where he served for a time as organist to the Jesuits and Mercredians and published ten stylized dance movements as *Premier livre de pièces de clavecin* (First book of

Jean-Philippe Rameau. Portrait by J. A. Aved. Original painting in Musée des Beaux-Arts, Dijon. *(Photo © Art Resource.)*

harpsichord pieces; 1706). When his father became ill in 1709, Rameau returned to Dijon and assumed his father's duties as cathedral organist. From 1713 to 1715 he worked as organist to the Jacobins in Lyons, then returned to Clermont Cathedral, where he remained until c. 1722. Then he moved to Paris, but he seems to have had no regular employment during the next nine years.

While at Lyons and Clermont, Rameau composed some psalm settings and secular cantatas and wrote the first of his theoretical treatises, *Traité de l'harmonie reduite à ses principes naturels* (Treatise on harmony reduced to its natural principles), published in Paris in 1722. A second treatise, *Nouveau système de musique théorique* (New system of music theory), appeared in 1726. These two publications made Rameau famous as a theorist. However, that was not his goal. He was interested in continuing theoretical research and experiments, but he wanted to write music, especially opera. For several years, his endeavors to interest a librettist were unsuccessful. Meantime, some secular cantatas and two more books of his harpsichord pieces were published: *Pièces de clavecin avec une méthode sur le mécanique des doigts* (Harpsichord pieces, with a fingering method; 1724) and *Nouvelles suites de pièces de clavecin* (New sets of harpsichord pieces; c. 1728).

In 1726 Rameau married 19-year-old Marie-Louise Mangot, a talented singer, who, in later years, performed some of his music in public. Rameau earned a living by teaching some pupils to play harpsichord and by composing some incidental music (*divertissements*) for musical comedies performed in the popular Fair Theaters. Those sketches, written by the poet Piron, combined spoken dialogue with airs and dances. In 1732 Rameau became organist at Ste. Croix-de-la-Bretonnerie, and from 1736 to 1738 he occupied a similar position at the Jesuit Novitiate Church.

At some time before 1731, Piron introduced Rameau to Alexandre-Jean-Joseph Le Riche de la Pouplinière (1693–1762; see Insight, "Le Riche de la Pouplinière"), a wealthy financier and patron of the arts. For 22 years (1731–53) Rameau was employed by La Pouplinière as organist, clavecinist, orchestra conductor (conducting from the keyboard), composer-in-residence, and clavecin teacher to Mme de La Pouplinière, *née* Thérèse des Hayes. From 1744 to 1753 the Rameau family occupied an apartment in one of La Pouplinière's Paris residences. While employed by La Pouplinière, Rameau had ample opportunity to hear his own works performed, for he had to write music on demand for all sorts of occasions.

At La Pouplinière's, Rameau met the noted poet-playwright Abbé Simon-Joseph Pellegrin (1663–1745) and realized his ambition to write operas. Pellegrin provided him with a libretto entitled *Hippolyte et Aricie* (Hippolytus and Aricia), based on Euripides' *Hippolytus* dramas. Rameau's *tragédie lyrique* was performed in 1733, first at La Pouplinière's, then at L'Opéra. Pellegrin was 70; Rameau was 50.

Performance of *Hippolyte et Aricie* at L'Opéra touched off one of the pamphlet wars for which the French are noted. Supporters of Rameau (*Ramistes*) praised his accomplishment, while others (*Lullistes*) deemed his writing too Italianate and declared him a traitor to Lully and the French opera tradition. In the preface to his next work, the opera-ballet *Les Indes galantes* (The gallant Indies; 1735), Rameau expressed his admiration for Lully and his loyalty to

insight

Le Riche de la Pouplinière

Alexandre-Jean-Joseph Le Riche de la Pouplinière (1693–1762), a wealthy financier and patron of the arts, was *fermier général* (tax collector) of France under King Louis XV from 1721 to 1738. La Pouplinière especially enjoyed music and literature, spent a large part of his income on them, and furthered the careers of many authors and musicians, including Rameau, Johann Stamitz, and F.-J. Gossec. At his palatial estate at Passy, he maintained an orchestra, hiring additional musicians when necessary. That orchestra was probably the first to include clarinets and trombones as regular members; later, these instruments were introduced into the orchestra at L'Opéra. Music was a vital part of the established routine at La Pouplinière's château at Passy. Mass was conducted in the private chapel on Sunday; concerts were presented on Saturday, Sunday afternoon and evening, and several times during the week. Pre-première performances of many compositions were given for private audiences at La Pouplinière's château before the "première" public performances of those works in Paris.

---

traditional French opera, but the Lullistes were not placated. The partisans continued to dispute after each successful performance of an operatic work by Rameau.

Les Indes galantes comprises a prologue and four self-contained *entrées* (acts), each act entitled and set in a different remote, exotic locale: *Le Turc généreux* (The generous Turk) takes place on an island in the Indian ocean; *Les Incas du Pérou* (The Incas of Peru); *Les fleurs* (Flowers), a Persian festival; *Les sauvages* (The savages), set in an American forest. The music is quite dramatic and emotional at times. Perhaps the best of the four acts is *The Incas of Peru,* which includes a Feast of the Sun and a spectacular volcanic eruption provoked by the leading character, Huascar.

The opera *Castor et Pollux* (Castor and Pollux) appeared in 1737; many persons consider it Rameau's masterpiece. The plot concerns brotherly love and relates that portion of the mythological story wherein Castor is slain in battle and Pollux, inconsolable for the loss of his twin, begs Jupiter (their father) for permission to give his own life as ransom for that of Castor. The opening scene, set at Castor's tomb, combines intense grief with ritual; to commence a work in this manner was a rather shocking novelty in eighteenth-century French opera.

In 1739 the opera *Dardanus* and the opera-ballet *Les fêtes d'Hébé* (Festivals of Hebe) were composed and performed. *Les fêtes d'Hébé* comprises a prologue and three *entrées*: *La poésie* (Poetry), *La musique* (Music), and *La danse* (Dance). Lyric, tragic, and pastoral aspects of all three arts are presented.

Two of Rameau's *comédie-ballet*s, *La Princesse de Navarre* (The Princess of Navarre) and *Platée*, were composed for performance at Versailles in 1745 as part of the nuptial festivities for the Dauphin and Infanta Maria Teresa of Spain. After the performance of *La Princesse de Navarre*, the king expressed his appreciation by granting Rameau an annual pension and bestowing on him the honorary title *Compositeur du cabinet du roy* (Chamber music composer to the king). Also, he paid all expenses for publication of the work.

Rameau wrote almost two dozen more stage works, some having only one act, and many of them commissioned for special occasions. The most important of these compositions is the *tragédie en musique* (musical tragedy, i.e., serious opera) *Zoroastre* (Zoroaster; 1749).

In 1753 Rameau ceased working for La Pouplinière and moved back to the Paris residence he had occupied before 1744. He composed, conducted scientific investigations concerning music theory, and wrote about his findings. From time to time, he became involved in polemics. In addition to the Lulliste-Ramiste controversy, he was drawn into the dispute over the respective merits of French and Italian music, the *Querelle des bouffons* (Buffonist War), and he engaged in heated arguments with Jean-Jacques Rousseau and Jean d'Alembert over erroneous statements made in *Encyclopédie* articles about music. In May 1764 Rameau was ennobled. He died in Paris less than two weeks before his 81st birthday.

Rameau's Music

Rameau's extant music includes 4 books of clavecin solos, 1 clavecin solo published separately, 1 volume of chamber music, 4 nonliturgical motets or psalm settings, 6 secular cantatas, and about 30 stage works. The cantatas and motets are the least important.

Stage Works

Hippolyte et Aricie and other operas by Rameau correspond with the general plan followed by Lully and Quinault. A long *divertissement* of singing and dancing is included in each act. The drama is advanced mainly by recitative, usually accompanied and quite melodic; Rameau's recitatives are more melodic than those of Lully, who advocated rather strict adherence to natural declamation. Often, there is no distinct stylistic contrast between recitative and aria. Rameau used three basic forms for his arias: (1) binary (AB); (2) ternary (ABA, or da capo); and (3) rondeau (more than one repetition after contrast, as in ABACA or longer). Some orchestral accompaniments are quite descriptive, e.g., the measured tremolo in the plea to Mars in Act I of *Dardanus* and the birdsongs in *Ramage des oiseaux* (Warbling of birds) in *La Temple de la gloire* (The Temple of Glory). Choruses and action dances are important in Rameau's operas; usually, they are closely associated with the drama and sometimes contribute to the action, e.g., the chorus of demons guarding Hell in Act III of *Castor et Pollux*.

Rameau's music reveals his understanding of the characters in his operas and the situations in which they are involved. In Act II of *Hippolyte et Aricie* a modulatory chromatically descending sequence is used to convey terror; in the tomb scene of *Castor et Pollux* a descending chromatic scale symbolizes desolation. That scene is an excellent combination of intense grief and ritual. Pollux's plea that he substitute for his brother, *Ma voix, puissant maître du monde* (My voice, powerful master of the world), is sung in Act II. A contrasting mood—one of blissful tranquillity—is depicted when Castor, having been redeemed through the sacrificial act of his twin, views the Elysian fields and sings *Séjour de l'éternelle paix* (Abode of eternal peace; DWMA130).

The overtures to Rameau's early operas follow the basic formal structure of the French overture used by Lully, but the fast sections are less contrapuntal than those of Lully. Many of Rameau's overtures, e.g., that of *Hippolyte et Aricie,* contain thematic material that is heard later in the operas. Overtures to later operas are more varied; some are programmatic, such as that of *Zoroastre*; some are tripartite like an Italian overture.

Keyboard Music

If Rameau composed any organ music, it has not survived. His extant keyboard music comprises 53 clavecin solos and a volume of chamber music—*Pièces de clavecin en concerts,* published in 1741—that contains five suites for harpsichord, violin or flute, and viol or another violin. All of the solos except his transcriptions of five of the concerted pieces and *La Dauphine* were composed before he began writing opera. He extemporized *La Dauphine* at royal wedding festivities in 1747 and later notated it, but it was not published until 1895.

The imitative linear counterpoint or lutelike arpeggiated harmonies in a few of the keyboard pieces are reminiscent of the late Renaissance or very early Baroque. Some pieces are clearly Baroque; others exhibit stylistic features of Pre-Classical music, such as triplet 16ths and melodic sighs. *L'Enharmonique,* with its numerous chromatic alterations, 64th notes, some quintuplets, and frequent abrupt changes of expression, seems to anticipate Rococo or *Sturm und Drang* (storm and stress) pieces by C. P. E. Bach (DWMA131). At times, it seems that Rameau desired more than the harpsichord was capable of giving—he wrote arpeggiations covering the entire compass of the keyboard and long tied notes that the instrument could not sustain.

Prefatory material in Rameau's books provides notated examples designating precisely how the embellishment symbols he used are to be interpreted, and, in Book II, instructions and exercises for fingering that specify use of the thumbs—though standard practice today, this fingering was relatively new in Rameau's time. Hand crossing is designated; long roulades in 64th notes and rapid arpeggiations spanning more than three octaves require hand-over-hand technique, e.g., conclusion of *Les trois mains* (Three hands; ex. 17.3).

The ten compositions in Rameau's *First book of clavecin pieces* might be considered a suite, though he did not call them that. Two are in A major; the remainder, in A minor. The *Prelude* commences with a lutelike quasi-improvisatory section, written without barlines. The other nine pieces are in binary form, some with full harmony written out, others with only treble and unfigured bass notated.

Example 17.3 Rameau: *Les trois mains,* mm. 35–44, presents a 16th-note arpeggiation over four octaves, followed by 64th-note *roulade* and cadence. *(Source:* Pièces de clavecin, *revised edition, 1731.)*

The second book contains 21 genre pieces and stylized dances. Rameau orchestrated at least 13 of his clavecin solos and incorporated them in his stage works, e.g., the *Musette en rondeau* and *Tambourin* from Book II, used in *Les fêtes d'Hébé.* Book III contains two suites of intermingled dance and genre pieces. Rameau transcribed for harpsichord solo five pieces from his chamber music suites. Some of the pieces in these books are quite simple; others, like *La Forqueray,* are virtuosic.

Rameau's clavecin pieces reveal his mastery of the instrument; collectively, they form a repertoire that is a panorama of past styles, contemporary practices, and future developments in harpsichord music.

Treatises

It is significant that Rameau applied in his compositions those principles he set forth in his theoretical treatises. He regarded music as a science and sought to establish that its universal harmonic principles derive from natural causes. His most important and most influential treatise was his first, *Traité de l'harmonie* (fig. 17.1). As Rameau matured, so did his ideas about music theory. He knew the writings of Zarlino, Mersenne, Sauveur, and other acousticians and theorists and based his own ideas on their investigations as well as on his own. The principles Rameau formulated clarified the compositional practices of his own time, served as a springboard for investigations by succeeding generations of theorists, and have been basic to and influential in the understanding of harmony for two centuries.

Rameau believed that harmony is the foundation of all music; in fact, melody is derived from harmony. He began his study of harmony by investigating the physical nature of a fundamental sound, then proceeded to consider harmonic generation, harmonic inversion, and the fundamental bass. These are his conclusions:

1. A vibrating body generates a fundamental tone whose component parts (partials) form what is called the overtone series. The first, second, and fourth partials produce the primary consonances—octave, perfect fifth, and major third; when combined, they form the perfect chord. The octave is considered a replica of the fundamental sound; therefore, the major triad derives from the overtone series. (The third partial produces the perfect fourth, which was discounted because it is the inversion of the fifth and forms an octave with the octave.) Rameau experienced difficulty when he tried to explain the derivation of the minor triad through natural principles; he did establish the melodic minor scale, however.

2. The chord is the most important element in music. Chords are built of thirds, and a triad may be expanded by the addition of one or more thirds, provided two major thirds are not stacked successively; in this manner chords of the seventh and ninth are created.

3. The identity of a chord is determined by its root; inversion does not change the chord's identity but merely weakens the chord. In a series of harmonies, the important factor is the root-progression of the chords (the *fundamental bass*), not the notated bass notes.

4. The primary chords, in order of importance, are the tonic, dominant, and subdominant; other chords are related to and are secondary to these. This is the concept of functional harmony.

5. Modulation may be effected by a change in function of a chord—the principle of modulation by pivot-chord. (Essentially, Rameau was applying to harmony and key tonality the pivot-pitch principle used by Guido in mutation from one hexachord to another: To mutate, enter the pitch by its name in one hexachord and quit it by its name in another hexachord.)

Rameau sought to explain the derivation of the diatonic scale by proceeding upward through a series of fifths (c-g-d'-a', etc.) and reducing the pitches to close proximity; however, the fourth scale degree was missing. A satisfactory explanation for the derivation of that pitch eluded Rameau for some time. Ultimately, he explained it through the triple geometric progression 1:3:9, placing the tonic in the center and flanking it by fifths (f:c:g). This accounts for his naming the fourth the **sub**dominant—the fifth below the tonic.

Johann Sebastian Bach

The ancestry of J. S. Bach (1685–1750) can be traced, through genealogical data he recorded, to Veit Bach (d. 1577), baker and cittern player in Thuringia. Most of Veit's descendants possessed some degree of musical talent, which they used in positions under municipal government and/or church patronage. The Bachs were proud of their musical heritage. Children received musical training from parents or other relatives; when a son was born, it was presumed that his vocation would be music. Most of the Bachs were instrumentalists, usually keyboard players, and some made instruments; a few wrote music. J. S. Bach copied 20 of their compositions into the *Alt-Bachisches Archiv* (Bach Ancestral Record) that he maintained. An abundance of musical talent

Johann Sebastian Bach. Painted by Elias Gottlieb Haussmann in 1748. *(W. H. Scheide Library, Princeton.)*

taught him to play violin. His mother died in 1694, and his father soon remarried. After Ambrosius died (early in 1695), Sebastian's stepmother was financially unable to maintain the household, so Sebastian and his brother Jacob went to live with their older brother, Johann Christoph (1671–1721), organist at Ohrdruf. At the Ohrdruf Lyceum, Sebastian received a broad, enlightened education that included religion and singing; Christoph gave him keyboard lessons and probably trained him to assist with organ repairs.

Sebastian moved to Lüneburg in April 1700. There he studied at St. Michael's School and sang treble in the *Mettenchor* (Matins choir) until his voice changed. While at Lüneburg he became acquainted with Georg Böhm (1661–1733), organist at the Johanniskirche, and traveled to Hamburg to hear Johann Adam Reinken (1623–1722), organist at the Catharinenkirche and leading organist of the north German school. Though Bach successfully auditioned for the organist position at Lüneburg's Jakobikirche in 1702, an older man received the appointment, and Bach soon decided to leave Lüneburg.

On 4 March 1703 he obtained a minor position as orchestral violinist and court musician at the Weimar court of Duke Johann Ernst. Bach's stay there was short. In June, he was invited to examine and play the new organ at Neukirche, in Arnstadt, and, as a result of that performance, was appointed organist there in August. (Neukirche was renamed for Bach in 1935.) Bach's duties at Neukirche were light, so he had ample time for organ playing. At that time, his primary interest was performing. He requested four weeks' leave to visit Lübeck to hear the aging Buxtehude perform but stayed away almost four months and thereby jeopardized his job. While at Arnstadt, Bach began to compose organ music. Also, he accepted some organ pupils; among them were J. M. Schubart (1690–1721) and J. C. Vogler (1696–1763). For the remainder of his life Bach attracted pupils.

At Easter, 1707, Bach successfully auditioned for the post of organist at Mühlhausen; the first version of his Cantata No. 4, *Christ lag in Totesbanden* (Christ lay in bonds of death), was probably performed as part of that hearing. His duties for the city and St. Blasius Church began in July, and in October he married Maria Barbara Bach, a distant cousin.

was inherited by J. S. Bach, who was famous in his own day as virtuoso organist and consultant on organ building.

In the last quarter of the seventeenth century, several Bachs held important positions in Thuringia. Johann Ambrosius (1645–95) was court trumpeter and town music director at Eisenach; his twin brother, Johann Christoph (1645–93), was a court violinist and town musician at Erfurt. Their cousin Johann Christoph (1642–1703), musically the most important member of the family before Johann Sebastian, was organist and harpsichordist in the Eisenach court chapel; his brother Johann Michael (1648–94), town clerk and town organist at Gehren, was an instrument maker and composed excellent chorale motets.

Johann Sebastian Bach, born at Eisenach on 21 March 1685, was the youngest of the eight children of Johann Ambrosius Bach and Maria E. Lämmerhirt (1644–94). Sebastian attended the local Latin School where he received a general humanistic-theological education that included singing; his father

Bach resigned at Mühlhausen in July 1708 to become court organist for Duke Wilhelm at Weimar; there, Bach wrote many of his organ pieces. However, his violin playing was not neglected, and in March 1714 he was named Konzertmeister, also. Duke Wilhelm regarded his musicians as servants and required them to wear special livery on ceremonial occasions. This *hajdúk* garb, modeled after mountain bandit gear, was a type of national costume worn in Hungarian and some Polish courts at that time. Bach was required to wear *hajdúk* attire when he performed in the court orchestra. During those Weimar years Bach became acquainted with Telemann, who worked in Eisenach from 1708 to 1712. Six of Bach's children were born at Weimar, including Wilhelm Friedemann (1710) and Carl Philipp Emanuel (1714); Telemann was Emanuel's godfather.

When J. S. Bach was appointed Kapellmeister at the Cöthen court of Prince Leopold in August 1717, Duke Wilhelm refused to release him. Bach was so adamant in demanding his release that the Duke had him imprisoned on November 6. Finally, on December 2, Bach was dismissed in disgrace and was succeeded as court organist by his pupil Schubart.

Prince Leopold enjoyed music; he sang bass and could play violin, viola da gamba, and harpsichord well. Frequently, he sent Bach to other cities to examine and/or purchase keyboard instruments. On one such trip in 1719, Bach was near Halle and tried in vain to contact Handel, who was visiting there. Over the years, Bach made several attempts to contact Handel, but the two men never met.

It was customary for the prince to take several musicians with him when he traveled, and on several occasions Bach accompanied him to the Carlsbad spa. Upon returning from such a trip in July 1720, Bach learned that Maria Barbara had died and that her funeral had already been held. During Bach's temporary depression after his wife's death, he considered taking a church organist position, and he auditioned by playing for more than two hours on the organ at Catharinenkirche, Hamburg, before city officials and 97-year-old Reincken, who praised him highly for his ability to extemporize on a given theme. Yet, when offered the organist post at Jakobikirche, Hamburg, Bach declined. In 1721 he became acquainted with court-singer Anna Magdalena Wilcke (1701–60), and they married on 3 December 1721. She was a competent musician and made many of the fair copies of her husband's works. On several occasions in later years, when Bach returned to Cöthen to perform, Anna Magdalena went with him and sang at court.

At Cöthen Bach was expected to provide music for special holidays, ceremonies, and court entertainment, but he had no church responsibilities. Most of the pieces he composed there are for clavier or are instrumental chamber music. Among the latter are the *6 Suites a Violoncello Solo senza Basso* (6 Suites for unaccompanied violoncello; c. 1720); six violin and harpsichord sonatas (1717–23); and *Sei Solo à violino senza Basso accompagnato* (Six solos for unaccompanied violin; 1720), commonly referred to as Sonatas and Partitas for unaccompanied violin. Also, he completed the so-called Brandenburg Concertos (1711–21). Several didactic volumes were produced during this time: *Clavier-Büchlein vor Wilhelm Friedemann Bach* (Little book of keyboard pieces for Wilhelm Friedemann Bach; 1720), which contains, among other pieces, the *15 Inventions* (publ. 1723) and *15 Sinfonias* (publ. 1723); the first volume of *Das wohltemperirte Clavier* (The well-tempered clavier; 1722); and much of the first *Clavier-Büchlein für Anna Magdalena Bach,* which contains the first five French suites and other pieces.

In December 1721 Prince Leopold married, and since the princess did not care for music, Bach soon decided to look for other employment. There was a vacancy at Leipzig, occasioned by the death of Kuhnau, and Bach was among the six who applied. The position was prestigious, and employment by the city of Leipzig offered greater economic security for his family and educational advantages for his sons, though Bach considered it a social step down from his court post. Telemann was the committee's first choice, but he declined the offer; Graupner, too, rejected the invitation. The Leipzig officials then offered Bach the position, though they deemed his talents mediocre. He accepted the appointment but refused to assume all the duties that had been Kuhnau's.

In mid-1723 Bach moved to Leipzig and was employed there as Kantor at Thomasschule and Music Director of Leipzig—not as organist—for the rest of his life. He was responsible for the music at Leipzig's four principal churches (Thomaskirche, Nicolaikirche, Neukirche or Mattaeikirche, and Petrikirche), for the musical training (both vocal and instrumental) of Thomasschule pupils, and for supplying whatever music the town council required for civic ceremonies and special occasions. The number of Thomasschule pupils was sufficient to form the four church choirs; choirboys, university students, and professional town musicians performed together at civic ceremonies. Thomasschule was a boarding school for boys, and pupils there ranged in age from 12 to 23. Medical data indicates that in the seventeenth and eighteenth centuries puberty occurred later than it does in the twentieth century, and some of Bach's older pupils at Thomasschule had soprano and alto voices of solo quality and several years of practical experience. For any performance Bach had at his disposal at least 16 singers and an equal number of instrumentalists. On special occasions or for performance of a Passion 40 singers could be assembled. Kuhnau had introduced the performance of Passions in Leipzig in 1721, and Bach continued the practice but alternated the annual Passion presentation between Thomaskirche and Nicolaikirche.

At St. Peter's, only plainchant was sung, but the other churches required polyphony. Bach personally directed at St. Thomas's and St. Nicholas's (the civic church) on alternate Sundays, and he assigned to others the duties at St. Peter's and St. Matthew's (the university church). As Introits, sixteenth-century Latin motets were sung, accompanied only by harpsichord, and the congregation sang well-known hymns, but new organ music, e.g., chorale preludes, was needed. In the Lutheran Service, the cantata served a liturgical function. On Sundays and feast days, a cantata was performed between the Gospel reading and the homily; if the cantata was in two parts, the first part was sung after the Gospel reading and the remainder after the homily. Bach was required to provide a cantata for each Sunday and each church feast, Passion music for Good Friday, and Magnificats for Vespers for three feasts. For Leipzig he planned five complete cycles of cantatas for the church year (i.e., about 60 cantatas annually). Two cycles were completed, composition of the third cycle was interrupted, and portions of the others have not survived. The *Passion according to St. Matthew* was probably composed in conjunction with the fourth cycle of cantatas and was performed as early as 1727, then revised for use in 1729 and 1736. Sometimes, when Sebastian did not have a new cantata ready, his church choirs performed the excellent cantatas written by his cousin Johann Ludwig Bach (1677–1731); Sebastian's copies of Ludwig's cantatas are extant.

Bach composed music for weddings and funerals and received extra fees for this. He taught music lessons, gave concerts in other towns, and examined and tested new and rebuilt organs. In 1725 he started a second *Büchlein* (Little book) for Anna Magdalena, and in 1726 he began to publish some keyboard music. Six *Partitas* BWV 825–30 (BWV = *Bach Werke Verzeichnis,* Bach Works Catalog) were first printed singly (1726–31); later, they were assembled as *Clavier-Übung* (Keyboard-practice), Volume I. (The catalog of J. S. Bach's works was prepared by Wolfgang Schmieder c. 1950. Sometimes the abbreviation S., for Schmieder, is used instead of BWV.)

Bach became director of the Leipzig *collegium musicum* in April 1729. Perhaps he assumed the additional responsibility because he needed extra money to support his expanding family—beginning in 1723, a child was added to the family annually. Or, he may have wanted opportunities to compose and perform more secular music. Possibly, this extracurricular activity served as release from tensions caused by controversies with the headmaster at Thomasschule. Under Bach's direction, the *collegium* presented concerts regularly on Wednesdays. In summer, the concerts were given outdoors from 4 to 6 P.M.; in winter, they were presented in a coffee house from 8 to 10 P.M. There is no record of all the music that was performed or how much of it was Bach's. Frequently, performers and composers visiting Leipzig participated in the performances. After 1733, the *collegium* performed some secular cantatas by Bach that in style and dramatic character approximate opera. In fact, he called this kind of cantata *dramma per musica* (musical drama). Bach directed the *collegium musicum* during 1729–37 and 1739–41. The organization was no longer in existence in 1744; performances in 1743 by the *Grosses Concert,* a group of 16 performers directed by J. F. Doles, may have been a factor in the demise of the *collegium.*

In 1733 Bach composed the Kyrie and Gloria of the *Mass in B minor* and sent them to the Elector of Saxony at Dresden with an application for the title of court composer. The request seems to have been ignored, and Bach was not accorded that title until he applied a second time, in 1736. Then, in appreciation, he played a two-hour organ recital at Frauenkirche on 1 December 1736.

During the controversial 1730s at Thomasschule, when the headmaster was more interested in academics than music, many of Bach's church works included movements that were parodies of earlier compositions, principally cantata movements. Among these are four *Missae Breves*, the *Passion according to St. Mark*, the *Mass in B minor*, and the *Oratorio tempore Nativitatis Christi* (Oratorio for the season of Christ's birthday), the so-called Christmas Oratorio that was performed in six sections for six feasts between Christmas Day 1734 and Epiphany 1735.

Bach continued to publish his music and kept a stock of works by other composers for distribution. He collaborated on G. C. Schemelli's *Musicalisches Gesang-Buch* (Musical Songbook; 1736), composing three of the hymn melodies and editing all the bass lines. In 1735 *Clavier-Übung*, Volume II, was printed, and in 1737 he began work on Volume III, which was published in 1739. Also, between 1738 and c. 1742 he compiled the 24 preludes and fugues that constitute the book now known as *Das wohltemperirte Clavier*, Volume II. Bach became interested in Renaissance-style polyphony, studied the works of those who wrote in that contrapuntal style, and made transcriptions and arrangements of many of them. For example, from Pergolesi's *Stabat mater* came Bach's Psalm setting *Tilge, Höchster, meine Sünden* (Most High, blot out my sins). And, during these years, Bach taught private pupils and gave organ recitals. In 1741 he went to Berlin to visit his son Carl Philipp Emanuel, court harpsichordist to King Frederick the Great of Prussia (r. 1740–86), and traveled to Dresden to visit Count von Keyserlingk. The *Aria mit verschiedenen Veraenderungen* (Aria with diverse variations)—the so-called Goldberg Variations—may have been commissioned by the Count. They were published c. 1742 as the fourth and final volume of *Clavier-Übung*.

Example 17.4 King Frederick the Great's theme, used by Bach for the pieces in *Musikalisches Opfer*.

In August 1742 Bach composed his last secular cantata, a *cantata burlesque* known as the Peasant Cantata. It was performed on an estate near Leipzig to honor Carl Heinrich von Dieskau, new lord of the manor. The cantata is folklike in character; its style reveals that Bach was aware of Pre-Classical developments and could incorporate elements of that style in his own work.

Between 1742 and 1745 Bach composed the *Symbolum Niceum* (Nicene Creed, the Credo), and c. 1748 assembled the *Mass in B minor*. Around 1745 he began to revise some of the organ chorales written at Weimar, then prepared the six organ transcriptions of cantata movements that Schübler published c. 1749—the so-called Schübler Chorales.

In May 1747 Bach again visited the royal court, this time at the king's invitation. Frederick the Great, a flautist, was seriously interested in music and asked Bach's opinion of the new Silbermann fortepianos at court. Bach frankly pointed out their faults; later, he supplied Silbermann with suggestions for improving the instrument, and Silbermann followed his advice. King Frederick provided Bach with a theme and requested him to extemporize canons and fugues upon it (ex. 17.4). Bach obliged but thought he had not done his best. When he returned to Leipzig, he composed *Musikalisches Opfer* (Musical Offering)—two ricercars, a trio sonata, and ten canons, all based on the king's theme—and sent them to the king, with this Latin acrostic: ***Regis Iussu Cantio Et Reliqua Canonica Arte Resoluta*** (At the king's command, the melody and additions worked out in canonic style). In deference to the king, Bach included flute in the instrumentation.

At some time in the mid-1740s Bach wrote a compendium of fugal composition—*Die Kunst der Fuge* (The Art of Fugue). A complete autograph of an early version of this composition is extant. In his last years he began revising this, and as he revised, he prepared the work for publication. He had continued to supervise the printing of his works, and, from time to time, his sons had assisted him; Johann Christoph probably worked with his father on *The Art of Fugue*. Bach died before the revision had been completed, and one of his sons, presumably Emanuel, published the incomplete revision in 1751. The organ chorale *Vor deinen Thron* (Before Thy throne; BWV 668) was included to lend completeness to the publication.

In June 1747 Bach joined the Correspondirende Societät der Musikalischen Wissenschaften (Society of Musical Sciences). As a scientific work, he submitted to the Society a six-voice triplex canon—three simultaneous two-voice canons—on *Vom Himmel hoch* (From heaven on high; BWV 769). This is the music Bach is holding in the portraits painted by Elias G. Haussman in 1746 and 1748 (see p. 400). Bach was hesitant about joining the Society and was not an active member, but that may have been due to health problems rather than mere apathy. Shortly before 1745, Bach began experiencing eye problems. He had cataracts, and when he was almost totally blind he underwent two operations by English eye specialist John Taylor (March, April 1750). Complications ensued; Bach never regained his eyesight, and his physique was weakened. On 28 July 1750 he suffered a stroke and died a few hours later. His body was interred in St. John's cemetery.

Bach's modest estate, consisting principally of his manuscripts and numerous harpsichords and string instruments, was divided among his widow and nine surviving children. Wilhelm Friedemann received most of the manuscripts. When in financial need, he sold the various individual compositions to individual purchasers; thus, the music was scattered and almost all of it lost. Anna Magdalena received the parts to the cycle of chorale cantatas—the second liturgical cycle Bach composed for Leipzig—and gave them to the Thomasschule. Most of C. P. E. Bach's share was acquired first by Georg Poelchau, then by Berlin Königliche Bibliothek, which became Preussische Staatsbibliothek. These holdings, which constitute the most important collection of Bach's surviving works, were divided in time of war, so that a single disaster could not destroy all of them. In 1985 the collection was still divided, one part at Staatsbibliothek, West Berlin, another at Deutsche Staatsbibliothek, East Berlin, and some works believed lost had been recently located in Krakow, Poland. Very few of the items owned by Johann Christian have survived; the location of material received by the other five brothers and sisters is unknown. From time to time, one or two compositions have been located; in 1984, 38 organ chorales were found in manuscripts at Yale University. Five of these had been considered lost; the other 33 were previously unknown compositions. In addition to original manuscripts, there survive numerous copies made by Bach's pupils and copyists he employed.

Influences

Many factors influenced Bach's career: (1) a working knowledge of both Renaissance and Baroque contrapuntal techniques; (2) an awareness of the techniques, styles, and forms used by his contemporaries at home and abroad—composers older and younger, as well as those of his own generation—and assimilation of the best of their stylistic characteristics into his own work; (3) a thorough understanding of voices and instruments and of vocal and instrumental virtuosity; (4) craftsmanship, perseverance, and planning, coupled with family pride, talent, and personal genius; (5) the eighteenth-century patronage system, by means of which an employer dictated, controlled, and stimulated an individual's artistic production; and (6) a religious conviction that the primary purpose of his life and his work was to glorify God. Bach was well-educated in theology and interpreted the Biblical and liturgical texts he set to music from a theologian's viewpoint; this is evident from his marginal notes in his Bible and his copy of Abraham Calov's three-volume commentary on the Lutheran Bible. Bach's religious conviction is expressed overtly in dedications and by inscriptions such as the letters J. J. (*Jesu, juva,* Jesus, help) and S. D. G. (*soli Deo gloria,* To God alone be glory) that appear at the beginning and end of his cantatas or the letters I. N. J. (*in nomine Jesu,* in Jesus's name) above the first piece of music in Wilhelm Friedemann's *Clavier-Büchlein* (fig. 17.2).

Figure 17.2 Preliminary page from Bach's manuscript for *Clavier-Büchlein vor Wilhelm Friedemann Bach.* Note the religious inscription "I.N.J." at the top of the page and Bach's fingerings indicating use of the thumb.

Bach's Music

Bach wrote effectively in almost all genres used during the late Baroque era. Though he composed no operas *per se,* the secular cantatas designated *dramma per musica* and the *Passion according to St. Matthew* demonstrate his ability to write expressive dramatic music in operatic style. Bach wrote few single compositions; he planned cycles or sets, volumes, and series of volumes methodically. When he composed, he followed rhetorical principles, as did many of his German contemporaries. Invention—finding the musical idea, melody, or theme—was the first step; next came outlining, and planning the composition; finally, elaborating on the idea and notating the finished product. For example, to a chorale melody he added the bass, then the middle parts; when writing a fugue, he invented the subject, sketched out the entries, planned the harmonies, then wrote the piece. When Bach transcribed, adapted, or arranged works of others, he improved upon the original. Unlike Telemann, who wrote music for dissemination to the general public, Bach composed for the capabilities of performers he knew.

Symbolism pervades Bach's music. In addition to the Baroque *Figurenlehre* used to denote the affections, he included alphabetical and other types of numerology and chiasma—the symbological relationship between the Greek letter *chi* (χ), Christ, and the cross. In fact, Bach could write his name chiasmatically:

Vocal Music

Cantatas

Most of Bach's secular cantatas and more than one-third of his sacred ones have been lost. The sacred cantatas are of various types. Bach used texts from the Lutheran Bible, from chorales, combined Biblical and chorale texts, and wrote some himself. A chorale might be used (1) as final movement of a cantata; (2) to open and conclude a cantata; (3) at beginning, middle, and ending; or (4) alternately with another text. Bach's earliest extant cantatas date from Mühlhausen and are mainly settings of Biblical or chorale texts. (The cantata numbers are the BWV numbers of the works, i.e., Cantata No. 4 is BWV 4.)

Cantata No. 4, *Christ lag in Totesbanden,* was originally written at Weimar c. 1707; that early version was first performed at Mühlhausen, then was revised for performance at Leipzig in 1724. Bach based the cantata on seven stanzas of Luther's Easter hymn, published with the chorale tune in 1524. In accordance with Luther's terminology, Bach called the stanza-movements of his cantata Versus. The cantata opens with a 14-measure Sinfonia that Bach may have designed as his alphabetical numerological signature: BACH = 2 + 1 + 3 + 8 = 14. (Other symbolism present in Bach's setting is too detailed for analysis here.) The complete Lutheran chorale melody in its original tonality forms the cantus firmus, recognizable in each Versus; the seven Versus, treated as chorale variations, are arranged in Machaut-like

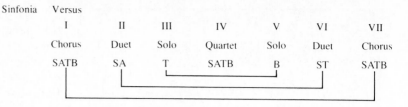

Figure 17.3 Diagram of the symmetrical structural plan of Cantata No. 4.

symmetry (fig. 17.3). The central movement, *Es war ein wunderlicher Krieg* (It was a wonderful battle), is a chorale motet.

Cantata No. 80, *Ein' feste Burg ist unser Gott* (A mighty fortress is our God), was composed in 1715 and revised c. 1724 for performance at Leipzig on the Feast of the Reformation. The cantata commences by presenting the first stanza of the chorale as a chorale fantasia in D major for all performing forces (DWMA132). The voices, each doubled by a string instrument, present each phrase of text fugally. In J. S. Bach's original scoring, two oboes (as *dux*) and violone with organ (as *comes*) present the chorale melody as cantus firmus in canon at the distance of one measure. In Bach's notation, these parts were the two outer parts, written on the top and bottom staves of the score. Was Bach thus symbolizing the all-encompassing nature of God as mighty fortress? After Sebastian's death, someone, presumably Wilhelm Friedemann Bach, slightly revised the cantata by adding timpani and three trumpets to the instrumentation. However, Bach's plan to enclose the entire performing ensemble within the chorale melody was not disturbed, for the first trumpet, in *clarino* register, doubles the oboe an octave higher (mm. 22–28).

The second stanza of Luther's chorale is presented as a soprano-bass duet in D major; while the soprano sings the chorale text, the bass sings a commentary on it. Their accompaniment is structured as a trio sonata—oboe, unison violin and viola, and basso continuo—with oboe doubling soprano. Bach used nonchorale poetic texts in movements 3 and 4. The third movement, for solo bass with continuo, is a pathos-filled recitative supported by unstable chromatic harmonies, followed by an arioso in F♯ minor; the fourth, an aria in B minor for solo soprano with continuo. In the fifth movement (D major) the chorale melody returns, sung in unison by the choir, with

a flowing yet energetic orchestral accompaniment in eighth and sixteenth notes. Nonchorale poetic texts are inserted for movements 6 and 7, which are, respectively, a recitative (B minor) and arioso (D major) for solo tenor with continuo and a duet for tenor and alto with accompaniment in trio-sonata texture provided by oboe da caccia, violin, and basso continuo. The cantata concludes with the fourth stanza of the chorale (D major) in simple four-part harmony suitable for performance by all present in the sanctuary; instruments double vocal lines in the appropriate registers.

Cantata No. 140, *Wachet auf, ruft uns die Stimme* (Awake, a voice is calling us; Matt. 25:1–13) relates the Biblical parable of the five wise and five foolish maidens. The cantata was first performed at Leipzig on 25 November 1731. Bach's planning may be seen in the symmetrical pattern of his seven-movement cantata, which is based on the *Wachet auf* chorale composed c. 1597 by Philipp Nicolai (1556–1608). Bach placed the three stanzas of Nicolai's hymn at the beginning, middle, and end of the cantata. The stanzas of the chorale present the theological interpretation of the parable, the union of God with His people and the union of Christ with the Church. The text used for the other four movements is based on portions of the Song of Solomon; perhaps Bach wrote the words for these movements himself.

Chorale variations form the opening movement, with the chorale melody, as cantus firmus in long note values, sung by the sopranos; the other voices have imitative counterpoint. The second and third movements, respectively, a tenor *secco* recitative and a soprano-bass dialogue, balance movements 5 and 6, an *accompagnato* recitative for bass and a soprano-bass duet. The words used for these movements parallel the chorale text by presenting another interpretation of the parable—the relationship between Jesus and an individual believing Soul. The bass represents Jesus; the soprano, the longing Soul. In the fourth movement, upper strings present a flowing melody as solo, then repeat it as countermelody to the chorale tune, which is sung in unison by tenors. The final movement is a simple four-part harmonization of the chorale tune, designed for performance by all present at the Service.

In Leipzig, secular cantatas were performed on various special occasions, such as weddings, anniversaries, birthdays, name days, visits of dignitaries, installation of city officials, school celebrations, and even some housewarmings. Performances were given at the Thomasschule, the university, *collegium musicum* concerts, or private homes of persons being honored. Plots of secular cantatas were usually rather simple, with mythological, allegorical, or pastoral characters. The best-known of Bach's secular cantatas are the *Kaffee Kantata* (Coffee Cantata; BWV 211; perf. c. 1734) and the so-called Peasant Cantata (BWV 212; perf. August 1742). Both are based on texts by Picander.

Motets

Since Bach wrote motets for special occasions only, there is no reason to believe he composed more than the six that survive. The occasion for his creation of *Lobet den Herrn alle Heiden* (Praise the Lord, all nations; Ps. 117) is not known; *Singet dem Herrn ein neues Lied* (Sing unto the Lord a new song) was written for the birthday of Friedrich August, King of Poland and Elector of Saxony; the other four motets were first sung at funeral or memorial services. Bach's motets were probably performed by the church motet-choir, with continuo accompaniment.

Jesu, meine Freude (Jesus, my joy; 1723), is the longest of the motets and comprises 11 movements symmetrically arranged (fig. 17.4). The music is based on Johann Crüger's chorale tune, *Jesu, meine Freude* (1653); for text, Bach used six chorale verses and Romans 8:1–10. Motet verses 1 and 11 are musically identical, setting hymn stanzas 1 and 6 to four-part (SATB) harmonizations of the chorale melody (E minor). The second movement, for five voices (SSATB), is a binary in which the text (Rom. 8:1) is set twice, the first presentation commencing in E

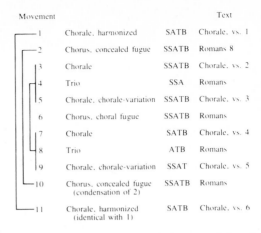

Figure 17.4 Diagram of the symmetrical structural plan of the motet *Jesu, meine Freude.*

minor and cadencing in B minor, the second progressing from B minor to tonic E minor (DWMA133). In each presentation, the last half of the Bible verse is treated fugally. Whereas Handel's vocal fugues are obvious, Bach frequently concealed fugues within the musical fabric, as he did in this motet. All five voices are singing when the tenor introduces the subject, which is gradually woven into the counterpoint at two-measure intervals as it is assumed by each of the other voices (ex. 17.5). Bach set the text expressively, with appropriate word painting. For example, "no condemnation" is emphasized by repeating and enisling the word *nichts* (no; mm. 2–4); sinning by "walking according to the flesh" (*nach dem Fleische wandeln*) is depicted by the melodic descent of a diminished fifth and a long melisma (mm. 37–44; ex. 17.5).

Movement 3 sets the second hymn stanza as a five-voice chorale. In the fourth movement, for SSA trio (or semichorus), the meaning of the Biblical text (Rom. 8:2) is musically depicted by the divergent counterpoint of the alto part. The movement ends on an open octave, b-b'. The fifth movement (E minor; 5 vc.) commences with a V₇–I progression in A minor and arrives at E minor with the fourth chord. This movement is a chorale-variation in which the music at times soars, rages, and is serenely sustained, as the text dictates. Movement 6 is a five-voice choral fugue in G major, concluded by an Adagio in B minor. The hymn text returns in the seventh movement (E minor;

Example 17.5 *Jesu, meine Freude,* mvt. 2, mm. 27–43, contains a fugue.

SATB), with the unadorned chorale melody in soprano and a moving accompaniment in the other voices. Movement 8 is an alto-tenor-bass trio (or semichorus) setting of Rom. 8:10, in C major, characterized by extensive melismas on the words *Geist* (Spirit), *Leben* (life), and *Gerechtigkeit* (righteousness). The movement concludes with a Phrygian cadence on an E-major chord as a dominant preparation for the A-minor tonality of the next section. In the ninth movement, a four-voice (SSAT) chorale-variation setting the fifth verse of the chorale, altos sing the chorale melody in four-measure phrases widely separated by rests. The other three contrapuntal lines form an independent musical entity that effectively sets the text. Musically, movement 10 is a condensed version of movement 2; movement 11 is identical with movement 1.

Oratorios and Passions

In 1734–35 Bach wrote three multimovement works that he referred to as oratorios. All are parodies of earlier cantatas supplemented by new material. In their use of Gospel texts, they form a link with the Lutheran *historia* and thus with the Passion. For his *Oratorium tempore Nativitatis Christi* (Christmas Oratorio; BWV 248) Bach borrowed from Cantatas Nos. 213, 214, 215, and 248a (now lost). From the reworked and new material he formed six cantatas, with differing instrumentation and voicing; they were performed individually on December 25, 26, 27, 1734, and January 1, 2, and 6, 1735. Biblical passages from Matthew 2:1–11 and Luke 2:1–21 are set as recitative; the narration differentiates these cantatas from others by Bach. Arias and chorales provide commentary. *Kommt, eilet und laufet,* the Easter Oratorio (BWV 249), was performed as a cantata on Easter, 1725, then revised as an oratorio. Cantata No. 11, *Lobet Gott in seinem Reichen* (Praise God in His kingdom) is known as the Ascension Oratorio. Many of the Biblical choral settings are new music.

Bach's *Necrology* indicates that he composed five Passions. Two of them have survived complete: the *Passion according to St. Matthew* (BWV 244), and the *Passion according to St. John* (BWV 245). The text and portions of an early version of the *Passion according to St. Mark* (BWV 247) are extant, but the only known complete copy of the revised version disappeared—probably was destroyed—during World War II. In 1987, two of the Passions could not be accounted for. A spurious *St. Luke Passion* to which Bach made some additions exists (BWV 246). Some portions of the *St. Matthew Passion* were written as early as 1725; an early version of the work was performed in 1727, then repeatedly revised for performances in 1729, 1736, and the 1740s. All of Bach's Passions contain several four-part harmonizations of chorale melodies. The melody of the so-called Passion Chorale, *O Haupt voll Blut und Wunden* (O, sacred Head, sore wounded), which appears with simple four-part harmonizations five times in the *St. Matthew Passion,* was originally composed as a secular Lied by Hassler (see p. 236).

The *Passion according to St. Matthew* is for double chorus, soloists, double (duplicate instrumentation) orchestra, and two organs. The Gospel text, taken from Matthew 26 and 27, is narrated by tenor (as Evangelist) in solo recitatives and by chorus (colorplate 17). Often the chorus has words of direct dialogue and thus participates in the action. Interspersed with the narration are chorales, arias, and some recitatives (actually, ariosos). The words of the added recitatives and arias were written by C. F. Henrici (1700–64), a Leipzig poet whose *nom de plume* was Picander; he supplied librettos for many of Bach's cantatas. This Passion is a massive work—its performance takes approximately four hours. Because of its length, Bach divided it into two Parts, so that in the Good Friday Service half of the Passion could be performed before the homily and the remainder after it. Part I opens and closes with great chorale-fantasias. The alto solo that commences Part II is taken up by chorus; the Passion concludes with a chorale-based movement whose words of mourning balance those of the opening chorale-fantasia.

The *St. Matthew Passion* music is expressive and dramatic and closely akin to opera in many instances, e.g., Nos. 69–70, the alto recitative (actually an arioso) *Ach, Golgotha!* (Oh, Golgotha!) and aria *Sehet, sehet, Jesus hat die Händ* (See, see, Jesus' hands [outstretched]). The last presentation of the Passion Chorale is followed by the Evangelist's recitative relating, with descriptive accompaniment by organ, the rending of the Temple veil. The ensuing passage, *Wahrlich, dieser ist Gottes Sohn* (Truly, this is the Son of God), is one of the most effective short choruses ever written (DWMA134). Many of the choruses contain concealed fugues. Two choruses of No. 59 provide examples of overt and concealed vocal fugues: *Lass ihn kreuzigen!* (Let him be crucified!) commences with the fugue subject; in *Sein Blut komm über uns* (Let His blood be upon us) the fugue subject is surrounded by other counterpoint.

Masses and Magnificats

In the Lutheran church, Magnificats were sung at Vespers, especially at Christmas and Easter. During his first year at Leipzig Bach composed a Magnificat in E♭ that included four Christmas pieces (BWV 243a). At some time between 1728 and 1731, the composition was revised in the key of D and the Christmas music deleted (BWV 243); in its revised form, the Magnificat is suitable for use at Vespers on any major feast day. The work is scored for SSATB choir, soloists, and instrumental ensemble with basso continuo.

Though Bach's *Mass in B minor* has a liturgical text, it is not suitable for performance in either a Roman Catholic or a Lutheran Service, primarily because of its vastness. In Bach's time, the Latin *Missa brevis*—a short Mass, Kyrie and Gloria—(with Lutheran additions) was still used in some Leipzig churches, including Thomaskirche. The *Mass in B minor* was not composed as a unit but is a compilation Bach made c. 1747–49 of Mass sections written at various times, some of the sections containing parodies of movements of other Bach works. For this reason, the performing resources vary considerably from movement to movement. Kyrie and Gloria were composed as a unit and were sent to the Elector of Saxony in 1733. The Sanctus was first performed on Christmas Day, 1724. The Credo, assembled and composed in the 1740s, is remarkable in many respects: its overall structural symmetry (fig. 17.5), the use of Gregorian chants as cantus firmi in the *Credo in unum Deo* and *Confiteor* sections, the symbolic central location of the *Crucifixus,* the latter's ostinato bass, and the representation within this movement (as well as throughout the Mass) of various styles of composition, e.g., both Renaissance and Baroque

polyphony, the combination of Palestrina-style counterpoint with basso continuo in *Confiteor,* and the Italian trio-sonata accompaniment to the bass solo in *Et in Spiritum sanctum Dominum.* It should be remembered that Bach usually used more instrumentalists than vocalists when performing an orchestrally accompanied work. However, throughout this Mass care was taken so that the singers were not overpowered.

Bach's interest in Renaissance polyphony led him to write arrangements of Mass movements by other composers; several of these survive. In addition, he composed four *Missae breves,* in F, A, G, and G minor; all are for three or four soloists, four-part choir, and orchestral (mainly strings) accompaniment.

Chorales and Songs

Approximately 375 of Bach's chorales survive. The chorale collections he made were probably used in his teaching; Emanuel wrote that his father used chorales to teach his students to realize figured bass and then required them to write bass lines to given melodies.

The only extant source of individual arias and songs by Bach is the *Notenbüchlein für Anna Magdalena Bach* (Little music-book for Anna Magdalena Bach), dated 1725. (This little book has no title but bears on its cover "AMB 1725." It contains both vocal and keyboard music and is called both *Clavier-Büchlein II* and *Notenbüchlein.*)

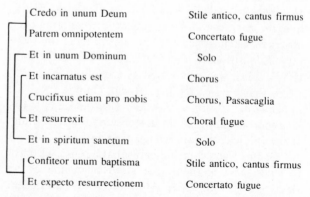

Credo in unum Deum	Stile antico, cantus firmus
Patrem omnipotentem	Concertato fugue
Et in unum Dominum	Solo
Et incarnatus est	Chorus
Crucifixus etiam pro nobis	Chorus, Passacaglia
Et resurrexit	Choral fugue
Et in spiritum sanctum	Solo
Confiteor unum baptisma	Stile antico, cantus firmus
Et expecto resurrectionem	Concertato fugue

Figure 17.5 Diagram of the structural plan of the Credo of Bach's *Mass in B minor.*

Keyboard Music

Bach composed keyboard works in an almost unbroken succession from early in his career until his death. The earliest of his works that can be dated is the *Capriccio in B♭* (Capriccio on the departure of his most beloved brother; BWV 992), composed c. 1703. This is program music in which each movement is headed descriptively.

Bach wrote specifically for organ *or* clavier (harpsichord or clavichord), and his keyboard music is not interchangeable, with the exception of the chorale partitas and the small organ chorales in *Clavier-Übung,* Volume III. In most of Bach's organ works pedalboard is obligatory. The clavichord has only one manual; though its tone is small, it is a very sensitive instrument capable of producing some delicate shadings. The two-manual harpsichord, with octave strings and stops, can double sounds in three octaves, change tone quality, and produce broad contrasts; its sound carries farther than that of the clavichord. Clavichord music can be played on harpsichord, but the reverse is not possible. Bach did not write for the fortepiano, though he probably knew of its existence by 1722 when Mattheson wrote about it. The fortepiano was invented by Bartolomeo Cristofori (1655–1731), around 1700 (see Insight, "The Fortepiano").

Clavier-Übung Series

Bach published four volumes of keyboard music under the title *Clavier-Übung* (Keyboard-practice), a title that had been used previously (1689, 1692) for two books of music by Johann Kuhnau, Bach's predecessor at Leipzig. The word "practice" in Bach's title does not denote that the volumes contain exercise or study material but should be interpreted in the sense

insight

The Fortepiano

The fortepiano (now called "pianoforte") was the invention of a single individual, Bartolomeo Cristofori (1655–1731), keyboard instrument maker and custodian of musical instruments at the court of Prince Ferdinand de' Medici, in Florence, from 1690 to 1731. Cristofori began making an *arpicembalo che fà il piano e il forte* (harpsichord that can play soft and loud) in 1698. By 1700 he had completed at least one of the new keyboard instruments whose strings were activated by hammerstrokes instead of by plectra. Cristofori's early pianos were intended to be placed in outer cases patterned after Italian harpsichords, i.e., wing-shaped. Three wing-shaped instruments had been built by 1709. Cristofori's basic principles of piano construction were sufficient for the demands made upon the instrument throughout the eighteenth century. Three instruments built by Cristofori in the 1720s survive; the one at Metropolitan Museum of Art, New York City, has a range of four and a half octaves (fig. 17.6). Gottfried Silbermann learned of Cristofori's piano through an article in Mattheson's *Critica musica,* and began his experimental piano construction in the 1730s. Early Silbermann pianos that survive have action identical with that Cristofori used.

Figure 17.6 Fortepiano made by Cristofori in 1709. *(Crosby Brown Collection of Musical Instruments, Metropolitan Museum of Art, New York City.)*

of performance practice—the works in the four volumes illustrate various styles, forms, and performance practices of Bach's day.

Clavier-Übung, Volume I (1731), was published as Bach's "Opus 1." In it he printed the six Partitas (BWV 825–30) that he had already published singly (1726–31); Nos. 3 and 6 of these are in the second *Clavier-Büchlein* for Anna Magdalena Bach. Each partita contains the four standard suite movements—allemande, courante, sarabande, gigue—and one or more extra pieces known as *galanteries*: prelude, aria, menuet, gavotte, rondeau, *burlesca,* scherzo, etc. Each suite commences with a large-scale movement as a prelude, but the titles and styles of the first movements vary considerably. The opening movements of the six Partitas are, respectively, *Praeludium,* Sinfonia (in three sections, like an Italian overture), Invention, French overture, *Preambulum,* and Toccata. The harpsichord suite was popular in the early eighteenth century. With these Partitas Bach attained the ultimate; they are the finest representations of the mature Baroque suite.

In *Clavier-Übung,* II (1735), Bach published two works in different styles: *Concerto nach italiänische Gusto* (Italian Concerto; BWV 971); and *Ouvertüre nach französicher Art* (Overture in French style; BWV 831), a large Partita in B minor for two-manual harpsichord. (Bach entitled some other suites *ouvertures.*) The Italian Concerto exemplifies the transcription to harpsichord of a concerto for solo instrument and orchestra; dynamic markings are used effectively to differentiate the solo, played on one manual, from the orchestral *tutti,* played on the other. The Partita shows Bach's knowledge of French musical style.

Clavier-Übung, III (1739), contains organ works. The first piece in the volume is a Prelude in E♭; the last piece is a Fugue in E♭, a triple fugue, commonly referred to as the "St. Anne Fugue" because one of the three fugue subjects is derived from the St. Anne hymn tune (ex. 17.6a) attributed to William Croft (1678–1727). The key of E♭, the three themes in the Prelude, and the three Fugue subjects (ex. 17.6b) symbolically represent the Trinity. Moreover, the Prelude and the Fugue each have three main sections. The Prelude and Fugue are usually performed together, as though they were composed and printed as

a single work. Placed between the Prelude and Fugue in this volume are 21 chorale arrangements (9 for Mass, 12 for Catechism) and 4 duets. Bach included three arrangements of the chorale *Allein Gott in der Höh' sei Ehr* (Only God in Heaven is Lord) and two arrangements of each of nine other chorale melodies, one arrangement designed for a two-manual organ with pedalboard, and a smaller-scale arrangement for manuals only (DWMA135). This is liturgical music; the central doctrines of the Church are represented by the chorale themes.

Clavier-Übung, IV (1742), *Aria mit verschiedenen Veraenderungen* (Aria with diverse variations), is one of the finest sets of variations ever written. Bach presented a copy of the music to Count Keyserlingk, who may have commissioned the work for his harpsichordist, J. T. Goldberg; from this comes the popular title "Goldberg Variations." Bach composed the music for a two-manual harpsichord and indicated at the head of each variation whether it was for one or two manuals. The Aria, which opens and closes the work, appears untitled as the 25th composition in Anna Magdalena Bach's *Clavier-Büchlein* of 1725. It is logical, therefore, to presume that J. S. Bach composed it. The Aria is a sarabande, a symmetrical binary in G major in $\frac{3}{4}$ meter; both halves are to be repeated. The 32-measure bass line of the Aria serves

Example 17.6 (*a*) First phrase of hymn with "St. Anne" melody in soprano; (*b*) the three subjects of Bach's triple fugue, BWV 552.

as the basis for 30 free and canonic variations, in various forms, meters, moods, and styles. Some are Baroque; some are Pre-Classical, with an abundance of triplet 16ths and melodic sighs; others approach Rococo in style. Logically, to mark the beginning of the second half of the variation set, Bach wrote Variation 16 as a French overture. He composed a series of nine canons, from unison through ninth, arranged them in ascending intervallic order, and spaced them evenly throughout the work, as Variations 3, 6, 9, 12, 15, 18, 21, 24, and 27. The 30th and last variation is labeled *quodlibet*. Bach included in it two German tunes that were popular in his day: *Ich bin so lang bei dir nicht g'west* (It's been so long since I've been at your house) and *Kraut und Rüben haben mich vertrieben* (Cabbage and turnips have driven me away; ex. 17.7). Bach's sense of humor is apparent here and at other places in these variations. After Variation 30 appears the directive: *Aria da capo e Fine* (Repeat the Aria). Thus, the variations are framed. The unified structure of the composition indicates that Bach intended it to be played in its entirety. Yet, he wrote sectional variations, so that if perchance the insomniac Count Keyserlingk fell asleep while his harpsichordist, Goldberg, was playing the piece, there was a convenient stopping-place at the end of each variation. At some time after 1742, Bach added to his personal copy of this work a series of 14 perpetual canons on the first eight measures of the Aria's bass line (BWV 1087). He arranged these canons progressively in order of increasing difficulty, the final one being a quadruple proportion canon.

Didactic Works

The *Clavier-Büchlein* Bach prepared for Wilhelm Friedemann in 1720 contains, along with some instructional theoretical data and some music by other composers, Bach's 15 two-part *Inventions* (BWV 772–86), the 15 three-part *Fantasias* later published as *Sinfonias* (BWV 787–801), several of the pieces known as *Twelve Little Preludes,* and some of the preludes used in *Das wohltemperirte Clavier* (fig. 17.7).

(a) Ich bin so lang bei dir nicht g'west

(b) Kraut und Rü-ben ha-ben mich ver-trie-ben,

Example 17.7 The first phrases of two popular tunes Bach incorporated in variation 30 of the "Goldberg" Variations.

Figure 17.7 These manuscript pages from Bach's *Clavier-Büchlein vor Wilhelm Friedemann* hold early versions of the preludes in C major and C minor that J. S. Bach published in *Das wohltemperirte Clavier* in 1722.

Eminent Composers of the Early Eighteenth Century

Volume I of *Das wohltemperirte Clavier,* published in 1722, contains 24 preludes and fugues, presented in ascending chromatic order of key tonality, commencing with C major. As the title indicates, all pieces could be played on a single clavier with well-tempered tuning, but whether Bach meant "equal temperament"—the division of the octave into 12 equal semitones—is debatable. Several kinds of well-tempered tunings were in use experimentally in the late seventeenth and early eighteenth centuries. The first person to openly advocate equal temperament seems to have been Rameau, in *Génération harmonique* in 1737.

Bach modeled *Das wohltemperirte Clavier* after *Ariadne musica* (Musical Ariadne) by Johann Kaspar Ferdinand Fischer (c. 1670–1746). Fischer's book, which may have been in existence as early as 1702, was published in 1715. Its title implies that Fischer was exploring key tonality and tempered tuning much as mythological Ariadne investigated the minotaur's maze. *Ariadne musica,* written for organ, contains 20 miniature preludes and fugues in 19 major and minor keys and in Phrygian mode on E; the pieces are arranged in ascending order of key tonality, commencing with C major. Comparison of *WTC* I and *Ariadne musica* reveals some thematic resemblance between some fugues in the same key. Bach's preludes in *WTC* I are actually *études,* for each is concerned with and concentrates on at least one technical problem in a musical context. The two- to five-voice fugues in Bach's volume summarize concisely the various aspects of monothematic fugal writing. Even the old-style ricercar is represented (*WTC* I, C♯ minor). Each subject is introduced clearly; the fugal counterpoint and its harmonic progressions are developed logically (DWMA136).

Between 1738 and c. 1742, Bach compiled a second volume of *24 Preludes and Fugues,* arranged in the same manner as *Das wohltemperirte Clavier.* The compilation is commonly referred to as *Das wohltemperirte Clavier,* Volume II, though Bach did not give it that title.

Bach planned the *Orgel-Büchlein* for instructional purposes. Its title page reads: "Little Organ Book, wherein a beginning organist is given instruction in diverse ways of developing a chorale, and for improving pedal technique also, since in these chorales the pedal is considered essential." A rhymed couplet follows: "To honor the Most High God alone, To instruct my fellow-men." It is apparent from the autograph that Bach had planned to write a series of 164 miniature chorale preludes for the entire liturgical year. However, only 46 were completed (BWV 599–644), and most of those were composed at Weimar. In all of them, the chorale melody is recognizable and is most often in the top voice (DWMA137). When treated canonically, the melody is usually given to the two outer voices (soprano and pedals), e.g., in *In dulci jubilo* (BWV 608). In *Christum wir sollen loben schon* (We shall indeed praise Christ; BWV 611), which is quite elaborate, the chorale is in the alto. Some of the chorale preludes contain word painting and symbolism, e.g., *Durch Adams fall ist ganz verderbt* (Through Adam's fall everything was spoiled; BWV 637). The chorale melody is highly ornamented in *Wenn wir in höchsten Nöthen sein* (When we are in direst need; BWV 641).

Harpsichord Suites

In addition to the six Partitas in *Clavier-Übung,* I, Bach composed two sets of six suites each. These are commonly known as the *French Suites* (BWV 812–17) and the *English Suites* (BWV 806–11), though Bach did not so designate them. Nor do the titles describe the styles of the music—some dances in the *English Suites* are more French than English, and in the *French Suites* there are some Italian *correntes.* Early versions of *French Suites* Nos. 1–5 are in the first *Clavier-Büchlein für Anna Magdalena Bach;* the *English Suites* were written at Weimar c. 1715. Each suite contains the standard four stylized dances (allemande, courante, sarabande, gigue) and additional short movements. Each *English Suite* commences with a prelude. In some of the suites, a movement is followed by a *double,* an embellished version of the movement it follows. In the first *English Suite* two *doubles* follow Courante II. In performance, if the harpsichordist does not wish to add embellishments to that Courante, either *double* may be substituted. There are two Gavottes in *English Suite No. 3* and two Menuettes in *English Suite No. 4;* in both instances, the second dance serves as Trio to the first,

Example 17.8 The subject of Bach's fugue BWV 543 uses bariolage-type figuration for three measures, commencing on the fourth beat of the second measure.

and a *da capo* is required to conclude the dance movement. (Gavotte I–Gavotte II–Gavotte I without repeats.)

Other Clavier Works

Among Bach's surviving clavier works there are numerous miscellaneous suite movements, preludes and fugues, fantasias, and toccatas. The most significant of these are the *Chromatic Fantasia and Fugue* in D minor (BWV 903), composed at Cöthen, and the Toccatas in F♯ minor (BWV 910) and C minor (BWV 911). Also, there survive 16 keyboard concertos that are transcriptions or arrangements of concertos by Vivaldi, Telemann, Marcello, and other composers as yet unidentified.

Other Organ Works

Early in Bach's career, when he was employed as organist, he seems to have concentrated on composing organ works—chorale preludes, chorale-partitas (chorale-variations), fantasias, toccatas, preludes, and fugues. In some of these compositions, pedal work figures prominently. Bach's early interest in pedal virtuosity is evidenced by his *Pedal Exercitium* (BWV 598), pedalboard improvisations that were notated later. The *Fantasia and Fugue in G minor* (BWV 542), composed at Cöthen c. 1720, combines quasi-improvisational sections with contrapuntal interludes. The *Passacaglia in C minor* (BWV 582) is prelude to a large double fugue; for one of the fugue subjects Bach used the first half of the passacaglia theme. Bach's fugue subjects vary considerably, from chorale types to Italianate figuration such as *bariolage* (in BWV 543, *Fugue in A minor*; ex. 17.8). In some instances, elements of the subject seem to engage in conversational dialogue on two levels, e.g., in BWV 542.

The chorale-partitas are in four groups. The first two sets and a portion of the third were written c. 1700–07; the fourth set, five canonic variations on the Christmas chorale *Vom Himmel hoch da komm' ich her* (From heaven high I come; BWV 769), was composed c. 1747.

The so-called Schübler Chorales (BWV 645–50) are organ transcriptions of cantata movements. Perhaps the best known of these is *Wachet auf* (BWV 645), from Cantata No. 140, mvt. 4.

Among Bach's last works are *Musikalisches Opfer* (BWV 1079; see p. 403) and *Die Kunst der Fuge* (The Art of Fugue, BWV 1080). Bach did not specify instrumentation for *The Art of Fugue*. Presumably, he intended the work for keyboard but notated the music in open score so that the individuality of each voice would not be obscured. *The Art of Fugue* comprises a series of *Contrapunctus* that illustrate all kinds of fugal devices and various types of monothematic fugues from the simplest to the most complex. All of the fugues are based on the same subject, though countersubjects vary. In the published version, the last *Contrapunctus* breaks off after Bach entered, as countersubject, the musical spelling of his name.

(a)

B A C H

(b)

B A C H

Bach incorporated (*a*) the musical spelling of his name in (*b*) this countersubject used in *Die Kunst der Fuge*.

The Art of Fugue may be considered the third compendium in Bach's series on the composition of monothematic fugues—a series begun in 1722 with *Das wohltemperirte Clavier*.

Orchestral Works

Much of the orchestral music Bach wrote at Cöthen and for the Leipzig *collegium musicum* has been lost. Among the surviving works are the six so-called

Brandenburg Concertos (BWV 1046–1051). The autograph manuscript bearing dedication of the pieces to Christian Ludwig, Margrave of Brandenburg, is dated 24 March 1721. However, it is believed that Bach selected these six pieces from a series of similar concertos he had composed during the previous decade and assembled a packet of music, which he sent to the Margrave. Bach did not refer to the concertos as component parts of a single work but called them *Concerts avec plusieurs instruments* (Concertos with several instruments). Moreover, the third and sixth are *ripieno* (orchestral) concertos, and the other four feature soloists. The first, third, and sixth concertos exhibit a relationship with some cantatas Bach composed at Weimar. Thematically and structurally, these six concertos are Italianate and reflect Vivaldi's influence.

The six "Brandenburg Concertos" are significant because they use a variety of instrumental combinations rather than the standard Italian *concerto grosso* instrumentation. Winds and brass are included in the *concertino* of Concertos Nos. 1 and 2. Concerto No. 3 is scored for three violins, three violas, three cellos, and basso continuo. In Concerto No. 5, the soloists are flute, violin, and harpsichord; this seems to be Bach's first use of transverse (German) flute. Concerto No. 6 calls for two violas, two viole da gamba, violoncello, and basso continuo; Bach used this combination of low strings in some cantatas written at Weimar. In Concerto No. 6, the two viola parts are written in close canon.

Bach composed several concertos for solo instruments with string orchestra, many of them featuring harpsichord. There survive seven concertos for solo harpsichord with orchestra, three for two harpsichords, two for three harpsichords, and one for four harpsichords. The latter is an arrangement of Vivaldi's Op. 3, No. 10, for four violin soloists; most of the other harpsichord concertos are arrangements of violin or oboe concertos by Bach or other composers. There are extant also two concertos for solo violin and string orchestra, in E major (BWV 1042) and A minor (BWV 1041); a concerto in D minor (BWV 1043) for two violins with string orchestra; and a concerto for flute, violin, and harpsichord, with strings (BWV 1044).

The four *Ouvertures* (BWV 1066–69) are orchestral suites. The slow movement of the third *Ouverture* has been arranged for violin and keyboard as *Air for the G String*. Suites 1 and 4 exhibit French characteristics; the inclusion of timpani and three trumpets in Suites 3 and 4 indicates that these were for outdoor performance.

Chamber Music

Ensemble chamber music by Bach includes six sonatas for violin and harpsichord (BWV 1014–19), three sonatas for viola da gamba and harpsichord (BWV 1027–29), and six sonatas for transverse flute and harpsichord (BWV 1030–35). Most of these appear to be *sonata da chiesa* works, but in several of them the harpsichord is given the dual role of melody instrument and continuo accompanist; thus, a trio sonata texture is projected.

Bach composed a *Partita* in A minor (BWV 1013; c. 1720) for unaccompanied flute, seven large works for lute, and two sets of works for solo violin and solo 'cello. The *Six Solos for unaccompanied violin* (BWV 1001–06; 1720) comprise three sonatas and three partitas, arranged so that every four-movement sonata is followed by a partita of five or more movements. The sonatas are constructed according to the formal pattern of the Italian *sonata da chiesa*; the partitas are sets of stylized dances. The C-major fugue of the Third Sonata is extremely polyphonic for a violin; its subject was derived from the Lutheran hymn for Whitsuntide, *Komm, Heiliger Geist* (Come, Holy Spirit). Undoubtedly, that sonata was intended for performance in church. The D-minor *Ciaconne* that concludes the Second Partita is technically difficult also; in many passages the melody is embedded in arpeggios and full chords and must be brought to the fore. This set of works, a landmark in violin literature, was probably composed for Torelli's pupil Johann Georg Pisendel, whom Bach met at Weimar. (See fig. 17.8.)

The *Six Suites for unaccompanied violoncello* (BWV 1007–12; c. 1720) mark a high point in literature for that instrument. The Fifth Suite calls for *scordatura* tuning of the 'cello—the highest string is lowered to g; the Sixth Suite was written for a five-string instrument.

Figure 17.8 Bach's manuscript for unaccompanied violin Sonata No. 1, mvt. 1. *(Source: J. S. Bach autograph manuscript, 1720, University of Tübingen Library.)*

Figure 17.9 Some of the alterations made in violin and bow construction during the last half of the eighteenth century are apparent when the instrument Leopold Mozart is playing in this portrait, printed in his treatise in 1756, is compared with the instrument pictured at the right, which was used by his **grandchildren in the 1790s.**

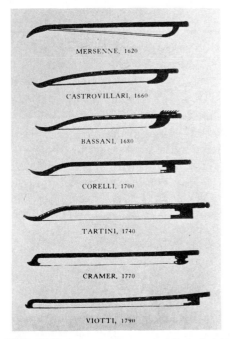

Figure 17.10 Violin bows used by seventeenth- and eighteenth-century virtuosi who were master teachers are representative of the changes that were being made in bow construction. *(From H. Abele,* The Violin and its Story, *1905.)*

The violins, violas, and violoncellos of Bach's day and those in use in the twentieth century differ structurally in several respects; surviving instruments of the violin family that were built before c. 1750—instruments by Amati, Guarneri, Stradivari, and other luthiers—have been adapted for modern use. A few of the differences are: (1) at mid-eighteenth century, the violin fingerboard was about two and one-half inches shorter than it now is; (2) the neck of the instrument was approximately one-half inch shorter and was not as flat as it now is; (3) the bridge was slightly shorter and was flatter (less arched), which may have facilitated the rendition of chords and polyphonic music. The violin and viola chinrest had not yet been invented. In performance, the instrument rested on the player's collarbone and was supported by the upper chest (fig. 17.9). The bow was shorter, with a higher arch; there was no uniform way of regulating tension of bow hair, and most violinists controlled that tension with the right thumb (fig. 17.10).

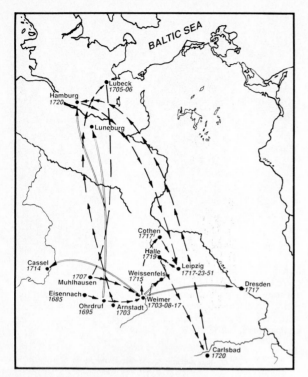

Figure 17.11 All of Bach's journeys were made to cities in Germanic lands.

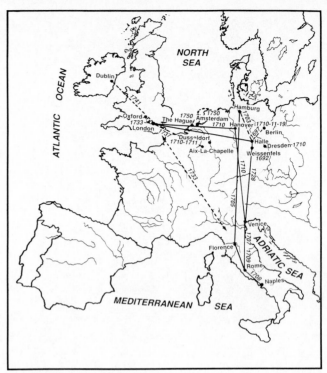

Figure 17.12 Handel's travels were much more extensive than Bach's.

Like other composers of his time, Bach borrowed considerably from himself and from others. He used the material indiscriminately, incorporating borrowed sacred music into secular instrumental pieces, and vice versa. Several movements from the *Solos for Unaccompanied Violin* were reused; e.g., the Sixth Partita (BWV 1006) was arranged for lute; its *Praeludium* became the orchestral sinfonia for Cantata No. 29, *Wir danken dir, Gott* (We thank Thee, God); and the second movement of the First Sonata became an organ fugue.

George Frideric Handel

George Frideric Handel was born in Halle, on 23 February 1685. At an early age, he showed an interest in music, but his father, Georg Händel (1622–97), a barber-surgeon, denied him an instrument, partly because he wanted the boy to have a career in law. Somehow, George gained access to a clavier and practiced diligently. On a family visit to the ducal court

of Saxe-Weissenfels, where George's half-brother was employed, George astonished everyone by playing the organ. At the Duke's urging, arrangements were made for George to study music with F. W. Zachow, organist at Liebfrauenkirche, Halle. Zachow taught him harmony, counterpoint, and composition as well as keyboard and violin lessons; he shared his personal music library with George and encouraged him to examine, copy, and imitate the styles of the composers represented there.

In February 1702 Handel entered the University of Halle, and in March he (though Lutheran) became organist at the Calvinist Domkirche. A year later, he moved to Hamburg, obtained a position as an orchestral violinist—later, as harpsichordist—at the Opera, and taught private music lessons. Reinhard Keiser was Hamburg Opera director at that time. At Hamburg, Handel and Johann Mattheson (1681–1764) became friends; together, they visited Dietrich Buxtehude (1637–1707) at Lübeck to investigate the possibility of one of them succeeding him as organist,

George Frideric Handel. Portrait in oils, made c. 1748, by Philippe Mercier. *(Archiv für Kunst und Geschichte, Berlin.)*

tatas for performance at weekly (Sunday) concerts. Of the approximately 150 cantatas he wrote while in Rome, more than 100 survive.

On April 7 and 8, 1708, Handel's *Oratorio per la Resurrezione di Nostro Signor Gesù Christo* (Oratorio for the resurrection of our Lord Jesus Christ) was presented at Ruspoli's palace. Stylistically, the oratorio is operatic, and those performances were spectacular. The 45-piece orchestra was led by first violinist Arcangelo Corelli, and his patron, Cardinal Ottoboni, attended the first performance, at which famed operatic soprano Margherita Durastanti sang the role of Maddalena. For the second performance Durastanti was replaced by a castrato because Pope Clement XI (r. 1700–21), who attended, objected to a woman singing in opera. Papal decree forbade opera in Rome, but composers dodged the prohibition by writing cantatas and oratorios in operatic style.

Handel wrote other music while in Italy, including three large-scale Latin motets that were performed in church at Vignanello in 1707: *Dixit Dominus* (Ps. 109/110), *Laudate pueri Dominum* (Ps. 112/113), and *Nisi Dominus* (Ps. 126/127). These are ambitious works for soloists, choir, and several instruments with basso continuo. In Naples, he composed *Aci, Galatea e Polifemo* (Acis, Galatea, and Polyphemus; 1708) for a ducal wedding. Late in 1709, in Venice, he met Cardinal Grimani, who prepared the libretto for *Agrippina*. That opera, first performed on December 26, was repeated 27 times during the carnival season.

Handel's visit to Italy was a shaping force in his career. His mobility permitted him to meet the leading composers, attend performances of their works, and observe their styles. He learned about the composition of opera, oratorio, chamber cantata, concerto, and solo and trio sonatas in the places those forms originated. Among the composers he met were Alessandro and Domenico Scarlatti, Corelli, Caldara, Vivaldi, Gasparini, Lotti, and Perti. From Alessandro Scarlatti, Handel learned to write long-breathed melodies in *bel canto* style. In performance, he demonstrated his superior organ-playing talent and proved his equality with Domenico Scarlatti at the harpsichord. At Ruspoli's, he made many advantageous professional contacts; several persons who performed his works in Rome joined him in London in later years.

but when they learned that marriage to Buxtehude's daughter was requisite for the position, they lost interest. (J. S. Bach also declined, for the same reason.)

While in Hamburg, Handel composed three operas. *Almira* and *Nero* were performed early in 1705; *Almira* was a success but *Nero* (now lost) a failure. In *Almira,* French and Italian styles are mingled. The third opera was divided and produced at Hamburg Opera in 1708 as *Der beglückte Florindo* (Happy Florindo) and *Die verwandelte Daphne* (Transformed Daphne). Probably, Handel wrote a number of his instrumental and keyboard pieces while in Hamburg and revised them later.

In autumn 1706, at the invitation of Prince Ferdinand de' Medici, Handel went to Italy and remained there until February 1710. He visited Florence, Venice, and Naples and spent several months of each of those years in Rome at the estate of a wealthy layman, Francesco Ruspoli, who employed him as a household musician. Handel received no regular salary but was expected to compose secular can-

While in Italy, Handel received and accepted invitations to visit Hanover and England. In June 1710 he was appointed Kapellmeister to George Louis, Elector of Hanover, but was granted a year's leave of absence before assuming responsibilities there, so he could visit London. Handel stayed in London eight months; he was received at Queen Anne's court, concertized, visited Queen's Theatre (the opera house), and composed *Rinaldo,* which was performed there 24 February 1711. *Rinaldo* drew satirical comments from Addison in Steele's *The Spectator* but was performed 15 times during the next three months. It was the most successful of Handel's London operas. In April, John Walsh published some songs from *Rinaldo*; this was the first printed music identified with Handel's name. *Rinaldo* required a sizable orchestra and a large cast, including three alto castrati— Nicolini sang the title role. All of the music was not new; Handel borrowed some from his earlier works, a practice he continued all his life.

After this success, Handel returned to Hanover and, for the next 15 months, wrote chamber and orchestral music for the 18 court instrumentalists. In 1712, he obtained permission from the Elector to visit London again. There, he composed during the daylight hours and performed in the evenings. From 1713 to 1716, he lived at Lord Burlington's home, where he became acquainted with Arbuthnot, the Arnes, Gay, Pepusch, and other English composers. Handel composed at least four new Italian operas, and *Rinaldo* was revived, but there were no outstanding successes. Queen Anne commissioned him to compose works commemorating the Peace of Utrecht; he composed an Ode for Queen Anne's birthday (February 6); and his *Te Deum* and *Jubilate* were performed in St. Paul's Cathedral in July 1713 (fig. 17.13).

Queen Anne died in 1714, and, via the genealogical route outlined in the Act of Succession (1701), the throne passed to the Elector of Hanover, who became George I, King of Great Britain (r. 1714–27). (In 1707 England and Scotland had joined in a parliamentary union as the kingdom of Great Britain.) George's accession was opposed by a pretender to the throne, whose followers rallied in his support in 1715; this Jacobite Uprising delayed the opening of the opera until February 1716. The story that Handel had

Figure 17.13 St. Paul's Cathedral, London, whose architect was Christopher Wren, is the first cathedral to be completed during the lifetime of its architect.

incurred the Elector's disfavor by overstaying his London leave, and that he placated George I through performance of the *Water Music,* is probably untrue. It is doubtful that Handel was ever in disfavor with George. In fact, Handel received large pensions from the King and Queen and was music instructor to the royal princesses. Handel did compose special music— presumably, the three *Water Music* suites—for performance by 50 instrumentalists on a barge during a royal procession on the Thames River 17 July 1717.

During the summer of 1716, Handel visited his relatives in Halle and may have gone also to Hamburg, where *Rinaldo* had been performed in 1715. During that visit, he acquired Brockes's Passion oratorio poetry; Handel's setting was performed in the refectory of Hamburg Cathedral in March 1719.

Late in 1716 Handel returned to London and revised some of his operas for performance that season. At the end of June 1718 the opera house closed permanently. That summer James Brydges, then Earl of Carnarvon, and soon thereafter Duke of Chandos, employed Handel as resident composer. Brydges maintained a group of singers and instrumentalists, a composer, and a music director at his palace and private chapel. At the time of Handel's appointment, Johann Pepusch (1667–1752) was music director. For Chandos, Handel composed 11 anthems, a *Te Deum* in B♭, and two masques in English: *Acis and Galatea,* on a libretto by John Gay; and the first version of *Esther.* In these works, violas and alto voice are seldom used, but there are three tenor parts; perhaps the highest was sung by a countertenor.

Though Handel invested in the speculative financial-commercial scheme known as the South Sea Bubble, its bursting in 1720 had relatively little effect on his finances. He was a salaried employee of the Royal Academy of Music, a promotional organization formed during the 1718–19 winter by a sizable group of nobles, with the king's support, for the purpose of firmly establishing Italian opera in London. As music director, Handel recruited from Europe several outstanding singers who had performed his works in Rome. Subscriptions were sold, and the Academy opened in April 1720; it remained active until 1728. For it Handel composed a number of operas; some of his finest *opere serie* were written and performed in 1723–25: *Giulio Cesare in Egitto* (Julius Caesar in Egypt), *Tamerlano,* and *Rodelinda. Admeto* (1727), in which Handel had to balance the roles played by rival singers Faustina Bordoni and Francesca Cuzzoni, was a success in spite of the fact that the singers' rivalry incited obnoxious comments from opposing factions in the audience.

A number of factors contributed to the collapse of the Royal Academy—temperamental singers, rivalry among composers, public factions supporting opposite sides of the internal squabbles, plus the fact that Londoners were becoming weary of an art form in a foreign language most of them did not understand. Pepusch and Gay were aware of the language problem and wrote in English *The Beggar's Opera,* a ballad opera in which sections of spoken dialogue alternate with songs set to the tunes of popular ballads.

Its plot concerns crime and prostitution in London and satirizes the political situation in England at that time. *The Beggar's Opera* was performed 29 January 1728 at Lincoln Fields and was repeated 61 times. The success of *The Beggar's Opera* cut into Handel's profits, but his popularity did not suffer. His music was printed (with and without his permission) and sold: complete operas in score, overtures in parts, individual numbers on single sheets.

In 1721, Handel was appointed composer to the Chapel Royal. Special royal events required new music, such as the four anthems performed in Westminster Abbey at the coronation of George II (r. 1727–60). Music at that ceremony was performed by 47 singers and an orchestra of approximately 160. One or more of those anthems has been performed at every subsequent British coronation.

Early in 1727 Handel became a naturalized British citizen; he moved into a house (still standing) on Brook Street. In November, some of his music was performed in Bristol, the first English performance of his works outside of London.

In 1729, Handel and Johann Heidegger (1666–1749), an impresario, leased King's Theatre for five years and planned a subscription series of operas to be produced there. The venture had little success at first, despite the presentation of new Handel operas and the revival of formerly successful ones. In the spring of 1732, the children of the Chapel Royal gave three private performances of Handel's oratorio *Esther* (a revision of the masque) at the Crown and Anchor Tavern; the choruses were sung by the Westminster choirs. That was the first performance of oratorio in London. Costumed singers (most of them boys) acted the drama; the choirs were placed between the stage and the orchestra, "after the manner of the Ancients." A problem arose when Princess Anne requested Handel to transfer the performances to King's Theatre, and the Bishop of London forbade stage presentation of a sacred subject in the opera house. But Handel revised and enlarged the score, and *Esther* was performed "in the manner of the Coronation Service," without action, and with books in the choirboys' hands.

Then began serious rivalry with the Opera of the Nobility, a company headed by the Arnes, who featured the most famous European singers and included in their production series pirated performances of Handel's works. The battle became difficult when Handel's own compositions—e.g., *Ottone,* with Farinelli in the title role—were used against him. Handel retaliated in various ways—with revisions, enlargements, pasticcios, macaronic English-Italian texts, dances, and ballet *à la* Lully—but drew small audiences. Even *Orlando,* one of his best operas, played to a small house in January 1733.

In July 1734 Handel moved his stage productions to Covent Garden. The following spring he produced several oratorios. Gradually, oratorio performances were moved closer to the Lenten season, and by 1745 it had become standard practice in England to perform oratorios during Lent. In 1735, when casting about for something new to attract large audiences to his productions, Handel remembered that he was an organ virtuoso and announced that he would perform organ concertos between acts of his oratorios. To meet his need, Handel created the concerto for organ and orchestra. He composed (and partially improvised) at least four organ concertos that spring; they became a regular feature of the oratorio season. For the performance of the oratorio *Deborah* he used a new organ, advertised as a new invention; no doubt this was the organ mechanically attached to the harpsichord so that both instruments could be operated from one. With such an instrument Handel could be soloist, conductor, and continuo player! At that time, organs equipped with pedals were rare in England; in only one of Handel's organ concertos (Op. 7, No. 1) are some passages marked *Pedale,* and that concerto may have been written for performance in Europe. Handel's virtuosity at the organ should not be compared with that of J. S. Bach, for the instruments they used and composed for differed considerably. Six of Handel's organ concertos (Op. 4) were published in 1738, and six more in 1740.

Handel continued to compose operas until January 1741, though his own company and that of his rivals closed in June 1737. Handel lost money on the venture but was never bankrupt. From 1738 to 1741 Heidegger produced Handel's operas. His last great operatic success was *Alcina* (1735); even the excellent operas *Serse* (Xerxes; 1738) and *Deidamia*

(1741) met with public indifference. Meantime, Handel wrote other stage works, such as his setting of Dryden's ode *Alexander's Feast* (1736).

On 13 April 1737 Handel suffered a stroke that caused slight mental impairment and temporarily paralyzed his right arm so that playing and conducting were impossible. Within six months he recovered sufficiently to continue his musical activities, but for the next four years his health was somewhat impaired. In July 1738 he began writing *Saul*; it was performed the next January, with a huge orchestra that included three trombones, a carillon, and organ. *Exodus* (later renamed *Israel in Egypt*) was written within a month and performed in April 1739; in September he set Dryden's *Ode for St. Cecelia's Day.* (St. Cecelia, patron saint of music, is honored on November 22.) By October 30 he had composed the 12 *Grand Concertos* (Op. 6) for strings.

Throughout his life, Handel assisted charitable organizations; he was generous with financial donations, loaned copies of his works to provincial organizations for festivals, and performed numerous benefit concerts. When the Fund for the Support of Decayed Musicians (later called the Royal Society of Musicians) was established in May 1738, Handel became a patron; he helped support the Foundling Hospital, established in 1740. His reputation for generosity brought him a joint invitation from the Duke of Devonshire and the governors of three charitable institutions in Ireland to aid their causes by giving a series of concerts in Dublin. Between August 22 and 14 September 1741, Handel prepared the English oratorio *Messiah*; some of the music was newly composed, but a good deal of it was borrowed from earlier works. The libretto, prepared by Charles Jennens, is based on the Bible and the Psalter of the Anglican Prayer Book.

Handel arrived in Dublin in mid-November. He played organ recitals, conducted some of his anthems in churches, arranged for a series of six subscription concerts, and followed those with another six. On 27 March 1742 the *Dublin Journal* announced that "Mr. Handel's new Grand Oratorio" would be performed "For the Relief of the Prisoners in the several Gaols, and for the Support of Mercer's Hospital in Queen's Street, and of the Charitable Infirmary on the Inns

Mrs. Cibber. Portrait by John Faber. *(Owned by Gerald Coke, Esq.)*

Figure 17.14 Handel penciled Mrs. Cibber's name at the top of this manuscript page of "O thou that tellest good tidings from Zion" from *Messiah*, thereby assigning her this solo for the Dublin première of the oratorio.

Quay." Public rehearsals for *Messiah* began on April 9, and the oratorio was performed in Neale's Music Hall on the 13th. Most of the soloists came from London; in Dublin Handel engaged Susanna Cibber (1714–66) as an alto soloist (fig. 17.14). Mrs. Cibber, sister of composer Thomas A. Arne, was an excellent actress; she had a small mezzo-soprano voice but she used it effectively. The audience was deeply moved by her singing of "He was despised." Handel's oratorio *Saul* was given on May 25, and *Messiah* was repeated on June 3. At all of the oratorio performances Handel played organ concertos. Crowds attended the concerts, the works were received with enthusiasm, and a considerable sum was raised for the charities. However, when *Messiah* was performed in London, on 23 March 1743, it was a failure, primarily because many persons considered presentation of Biblical words in a playhouse blasphemous. *Messiah* was not accepted by London audiences until Handel presented it in benefit performances at Foundling Hospital Chapel in 1750.

Handel had been under considerable pressure, and in April 1743 he suffered another slight stroke from which he soon recovered. When the Prince of Wales requested a new opera, Handel composed *The Story of Semele*. Next he wrote the Dettingen *Te Deum* and anthem (*The king shall rejoice*), performed 27 November 1743. In 1744–45 came the oratorios *Joseph and his Brethren* and *Belshazzar* and the musical drama *Hercules*. Again Handel experienced health problems but continued to compose and to perform organ recitals. His next major work was the oratorio *Judas Maccabeus*, inspired by the English victory at Culloden (16 April 1746). When the king commissioned martial music "with no fiddles" for the fireworks display at Green Park to celebrate the Treaty of Aix-la-Chapelle (1749), Handel wrote *Music for the Royal Fireworks*.

He began composing the oratorio *Jephtha* in 1751. Then glaucoma and cataract caused loss of sight in his left eye and weakened the other. Treatment by specialists and surgeries by William Bromfield and John Taylor were unsuccessful but blindness did not deter Handel. He performed from memory or improvised, and he dictated his compositions to J. C. Smith.

Eminent Composers of the Early Eighteenth Century

In September 1758 Handel became ill; he died at home on 14 April 1759. In accordance with his wishes, his body was interred in the south transept of Westminster Abbey; he had requested a private funeral but thousands attended. In his Will, Handel provided funds for a monument by Louis François Roubiliac; this was unveiled in Westminster Abbey in July 1762. Reportedly, the sculptor portrayed Handel accurately.

Handel was witty and possessed a good sense of humor, but he became quite angry at times. He had no close friends among composers except Telemann, who was miles away. Handel respected Rameau and admired Purcell's music but openly voiced dislike of the work of contemporary English composers. Handel never married; the bulk of his estate was inherited by a niece in Germany. He willed his harpsichord, scores, and music books to Smith, who eventually presented them to King George III; they are now in British Museum.

Handel composed music rapidly. Comments made by his contemporaries indicate that ideas came to him at the keyboard or as he read through a libretto, and he planned the music mentally, then notated his mental image. His talent for improvising is apparent in the ways he worked out an initial motive. Occasionally, he made sketches; often he revised works. He borrowed from himself and from others, sometimes reworking the borrowed material and at other times using it verbatim. His mature style is eclectic, with the various elements he selected smoothly woven into his musical fabric. Basically, Handel's style is Italianate, with added French, German, and English elements. He learned from Keiser how to orchestrate for woodwinds and from Corelli how to write for string instruments; the influence of Alessandro Scarlatti is apparent in his vocal works. Handel's odes indicate that he knew Purcell's. Handel was trained to write stage music; his orchestration is suited to the subject matter and to the talents of those he wanted to sing the roles. He wrote a good deal for high male voices; if good alto castrati were not available, he assigned male roles to female singers. In the assignment of roles, many composers thought of singers as voices rather than persons; if the vocal range and quality were suitable, it made no difference whether male or female was cast in a role.

Vocal Music

Handel is best known as a composer of oratorios, particularly, as the composer of *Messiah*. However, his career was principally in the field of opera—from 1705 to 1741 he composed and conducted operas; he wrote almost 40 of them. His 3 masterpieces of 1724–25—*Giulio Cesare, Rodelinda,* and *Tamerlano*—surpass operas written by his contemporaries. In *Tamerlano* he first used clarinets in the opera orchestra. During Handel's lifetime, his operas were performed in London, Hamburg, and Rome; there is no record of any Handel opera being performed anywhere between 1755 and 1920. A revival of Baroque opera began in Germany in the 1920s and gradually spread to other countries; some of Handel's best operas are being performed again.

Twentieth-century producers of Baroque operas must decide whether to give authentic performances or to adjust the operas to fit modern ideas of staging. When Handel's operas were performed in the eighteenth century, the curtain rose at the beginning of the opera, after the overture, and did not descend until the end of the last act. Pairs of panels (back flats) meeting in center stage were fit into grooves and could be pulled apart by the operation of a single machine to "open" a new scene (fig. 17.15). Intermediate curtains were not used until c. 1750. Scene changes were made quickly in view of the audience; the musical structure was designed with this in mind. In some operas Handel wrote special music to cover scene changes, e.g., the hunting chorus in *Deidamia* (Act II); more often, the music was designed to point up the changes. Usually, at scene changes Handel shifted the key. In most scenes there is a gradual tapering off of characters in view. Almost all acts conclude with one person remaining on stage; hence, most acts end with a soloist singing a large aria.

Stage lighting was by tallow candles and oil lamps. In England, the house lights—candles in chandeliers—remained on throughout the performance. Members of the audience were provided with programs containing the Italian words and their English translation.

In his operas Handel used three basic types of subject matter: (1) historical, as in *Giulio Cesare*; (2) mythological, as in *Admeto*; and (3) romantic, as in

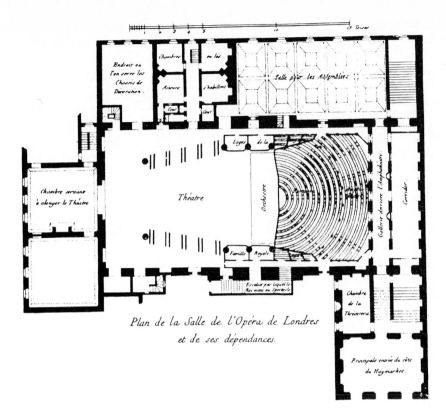

Figure 17.15 Plan of interior of King's Theater. *(Source: G. Dumont,* Parallèle de Plans des plus belles salles de Spectacle, *published 1764.)*

Plan de la Salle de L'Opéra de Londres et de ses dépendances.

Orlando. The supernatural element—sorcery, witchcraft, magic transformation—figures in five operas, e.g., in *Orlando* and *Alcina*; for Handel's special effects, the full complement of Baroque theatre machinery was required.

The operas Handel composed in Hamburg show his indebtedness to Keiser; those he wrote in Italy and during his first years in London reflect the influence of Alessandro Scarlatti and Caldara. Except for its final number, *Rinaldo* consists entirely of recitative-aria pairs. As his operatic style matured, Handel became more inventive and manipulated recitatives and arias to suit his musical purposes. At times, he built up to an aria by approaching it through recitative and arioso. Some accompanied recitatives are intensely emotional; arias exhibit numerous different designs. Recitative is not always followed by aria; two arias may occur in succession, or one aria might interrupt another. Sometimes two arias are combined to form an extended duet; occasionally, for humor or

irony, an aria is transposed and given to another character to sing back to its original interpreter. Occasionally, a **cavatina** (aria without *da capo*) is tucked in. Handel understood human nature, could characterize well, and was able to translate comic situations as well as serious emotions into effective music; he did so in *Agrippina* and in *Serse*. In some operas Handel associated certain keys with particular characters, e.g., in *Admeto*; later, this procedure would be favored by Richard Wagner.

The English oratorio was Handel's innovation. Its most significant feature—highly contributory to its success—is that its libretto is in English. Handel could never speak English without an accent, but he made accurate and masterful musical settings of that language as it was used in the eighteenth century.

Contributory to Handel's invention of the English oratorio was the fact that the middle-class English appreciated familiar Bible stories but the Bishop of London intervened against stage performance of them.

Handel realized that middle-class English people had turned against Italian opera, yet he was reluctant to abandon writing for the theater. He described many of his oratorios as "sacred dramas," and he included in their music many operatic structural devices. Handel recognized that oratorio had advantages: (1) without costumes and scenery, it was less expensive to produce; (2) since there were no scene changes, no entrances and exits, fewer changes of key were needed; (3) virtuoso singers were unnecessary; (4) a small professional chorus, such as the Westminster choir and the Chapel Royal choirboys, could be used more often. Note that Handel used an all-male chorus and that it was small. Handel's oratorios deal with human experiences and a moral is apparent, but they were intended to be historical and dramatic rather than religious presentations. They are for performance in the concert hall, not in church. Their plots have a double connotation—the personal plights of the characters and the fate of the nation or humanity. *Semele,* with its moral "Don't tempt the gods," is variously considered opera, oratorio, or opera-oratorio.

Handel was a master of choral writing. This is seen not only in his oratorios but in his anthems—e.g., those written for the Duke of Chandos and for the coronation of George II. In the oratorios, the chorus narrates, comments upon the action, and participates in it; often, the chorus becomes alive and personal, rather than aloof and impersonal. In his great choral fugues, Handel balances polyphonic sections with blocks of homophony. The voice leading is smooth, and the parts lie within the most effective part of their vocal ranges. Where maximum fullness is desired, the chord pitches are in close position (the four parts brought close together) with upper voices in middle register and tenors and basses rather high. Rests are used most effectively, with general pauses like open windows between massive blocks of sound, especially just before final cadences, e.g., *Hallelujah* chorus. Affective and pictorial symbolism is present in the oratorios, as in much Baroque music; examples in *Messiah* include "Every valley," where the mountain and hill are brought low, and the crooked made straight; and, the twisting figure depicting straying in "All we like sheep." (See DWMA138.)

Handel's church music includes Latin psalm settings for use in a Roman Catholic Church; the Brockes *Passion,* which is Lutheran; and Anglican music composed for performance in royal ceremonies (coronations, funerals, weddings, victory celebrations) or private chapels (Chandos and Foundling Hospital anthems). Though Handel was Lutheran, chorales seldom appear in his music.

It is estimated that Handel composed 150 cantatas during his stay in Rome. More than 100 survive. Approximately 75 are with basso continuo accompaniment; the remainder use various instruments. Handel reused portions of some of these cantatas in his operas. Some of the longer cantatas for more than one voice, such as *Aci, Galatea e Polifemo* and *Apollo e Dafne,* are in essence one-act operas.

More than 40 songs by Handel are extant. Approximately 2 dozen of these are English; 8 are Italian, 9 are French, 1 is Spanish. Some have survived on songsheets, others in eighteenth-century anthologies.

Instrumental Music

Most of Handel's orchestral writing was done in connection with his stage works; the *Water Music* and *Music for the Royal Fireworks* were commissioned. The *Water Music* comprises three suites for different instrumental groups. The *Music for the Royal Fireworks* is on a larger scale, written for 37 woodwinds, 18 brass instruments, and 3 timpani; Handel added string parts (doubling winds) for a later performance.

The 6 *Concerti Grossi,* Op. 3, were published in 1734 but probably written earlier. These are often erroneously called "oboe concertos," most likely because two oboes are included in the instrumentation. In two of the concertos (Nos. 1 and 3) recorders are used also. The 12 *Grand Concertos,* Op. 6 (1739), for strings, are on a par with Bach's *Brandenburg Concertos.* Handel expanded *sonata da chiesa* structure by adding one or two movements, usually in dance rhythms, to the standard slow-fast-slow-fast pattern. In each concerto, one of the Allegros is fugal. These concertos exhibit a variety of moods, and Handel's improvisational talent and inventiveness are reflected in the varied treatment given the thematic material. There exist also 3 *Concerti a due cori* (1747–48) for two groups of winds with string orchestra.

The organ concerto was invented by Handel to supplement and enhance his oratorio productions. Each concerto can be related to the oratorio for which it was created. The first set of six concertos, Op. 4, dates from 1735–36; No. 6 of this set was originally a harpsichord concerto written for the performance of *Alexander's Feast*. The second set of six concertos was published in 1740 without opus number; a third set, written in 1740–51, had posthumous publication as Op. 7 in 1761. Two more concertos were published in 1797. Handel's designation of the first set as being "for harpsichord or organ" is indicative of their character. In all of the organ concertos there are many *ad libitum* indications and many opportunities for improvisation. These pieces are most effective when played on a small organ with a small orchestra; a continuo harpsichord is required.

Chamber Music

During Handel's lifetime, four sets of his sonatas for one or two melody instruments with basso continuo were published: (1) Op. 1, 12 sonatas for transverse flute, recorder, violin or oboe, with basso continuo; (2) Op. 2, 6 trio sonatas for two flutes, oboes, or violins, with basso continuo; (3) 3 sonatas for flute and basso continuo; (4) Op. 5, 7 trio sonatas for violins or flutes, with basso continuo. Unfortunately, autographs of all of the sonatas of Op. 1 are not extant, and Handel's intended instrumentation for each of these sonatas is not known. The sonatas in this group are mainly *sonata da camera* type and show Corelli's influence. The Sonata in D major, No. 13, for violin and basso continuo, survives in autograph; it was not in the original Op. 1 and is the finest of the solo sonatas.

Keyboard Works

Two volumes entitled *Suites de pièces pour le clavecin* (Keyboard suites) were published in 1720 and 1733; each book contains eight suites. From the first book of suites comes the *Passacaille* in G minor and the set of variations in E major known as *The Harmonious Blacksmith*. The *Aria* in B♭ from the first suite in the second book was used by Johannes Brahms as the theme for his *Variations on a Theme by G. F. Handel*, Op. 24 (1861). In 1735 Walsh published six *Fugues or Voluntarys for the Organ or Harpsichord*.

There survive also a *Klavier-büch aus der Jugenzeit* (Clavier book from youth) and isolated keyboard works that cannot be dated. In general, Handel's harpsichord works are inferior to those of J. S. Bach and Domenico Scarlatti.

Summary

Bach, Handel, Rameau, Telemann, and Vivaldi were talented craftsmen who achieved success and eminence in their own time. During the early and middle eighteenth century Telemann was considered the leading German composer; in the twentieth century, Bach is regarded as one of the most important composers of all time. The works of these five men demonstrate their competence in traditional composition, their awareness of current trends, and their ability to reconcile the conflict between contrapuntal and homophonic styles. They achieved the ultimate with the established forms and styles of the late Baroque, and, when those forms would not suffice, created some new forms. Each was aware of what the others were doing, though they seldom (if ever) had personal contact with one another.

Bach studied the music of other noted composers, including Vivaldi, absorbed the best features into his own musical style, and infused that blend with his originality and genius. In many forms, his music attained a degree of excellence that has never been surpassed, e.g., fugue, theme and variations, organ chorale and chorale-prelude, harpsichord partita, sonatas and suites for unaccompanied violin and unaccompanied violoncello, and Passion. Though Bach wrote no operas, he understood operatic style and used it in some of his cantatas and Passions. The didactic keyboard works he created for his children and pupils have become staple educational repertoire. As organist, technician, and acoustician, he frequently counseled instrument builders, and he made suggestions that contributed to the improvement of the fortepiano.

Telemann brought music to the middle classes by editing and publishing music suitable for amateurs to use at home, by organizing *collegia musica,* and by establishing a regular series of public concerts. He broke down barriers between sacred and secular music by programming both types on the same public concert and by composing and directing operas while employed as Kantor in the Lutheran church.

Vivaldi, Handel, and Rameau excelled at writing opera. In addition, Vivaldi broadened and perfected the Italian Baroque solo concerto. When opera proved unprofitable financially, Handel created the English oratorio and, as an adjunct to it, the organ concerto. As a composer of choral music, Handel is peerless; his masterful choral fugues have never been equaled.

Rameau built on the operatic foundations laid by Lully and carried French opera to greater heights. He scientifically investigated and clearly explained in his treatises the principles of harmony and key tonality underlying the music of his time—principles that remained valid for music composed in the succeeding centuries.

It should not be forgotten that each of these men was composing music to meet immediate needs—to fulfill the requirements of his own employment, to benefit and enrich the lives of his own generation. That much of their music has become standard repertoire and continues to provide enrichment is in itself a tribute to their greatness.

Eighteenth-Century
Pre-Classical Music

During the eighteenth century, the political and cultural complexion of Europe changed considerably. Russia, "Westernized" under Tsar' Peter the Great (r. 1689–1725), became a European power. The central-European Germanic provinces remained disunited, each under its own ruler, and collectively governed (nominally) by a Holy Roman Emperor who almost always was chosen from the Austrian Habsburg dynasty. Within the empire, there were frequent boundary disputes caused by envious neighbors with territorial ambitions. Perhaps the most envious was King Frederick II ("the Great") of Prussia (r. 1740–86), who seized Silesia from Maria Theresa (r. Austria 1740–80) and coveted other territory. Though Maria Theresa directly inherited the Habsburg lands of her father, Emperor Charles VI, in 1740, a woman was ineligible for election to the imperial throne. Only gradually was Maria Theresa acknowledged as ruler, by Austria in 1740, Hungary in 1741, Bohemia in 1743. In 1745, Maria's husband, Francis I, was named Holy Roman Emperor; he was succeeded by their son, Joseph II, in 1765. Italy, too, was an aggregation of states, rather than a true nation, and lacked even nominal central leadership. Britain was a colonial and sea power, with strong Germanic ties acquired when the Elector of Hanover became King George I of England (r. 1714–27).

France was an absolute monarchy, and, under Louis XIV (r. 1643–1715), it became the most powerful nation in Europe. Louis XIV was an avid patron of the arts, especially music, and his Versailles court with its many cultural activities provided the model for other European courts. The reigns of Louis XV (1715–74) and Louis XVI (1774–89) became increasingly corrupt, inefficient, and seemingly directionless; ultimately, the Old Régime (i.e., the absolute monarchy) collapsed during the French Revolution.

The Enlightenment

The period in European history variously referred to as "The Enlightenment" or "The Age of Reason" began around 1685, gathered momentum during the next 50 years, and continued until the outbreak of the French Revolution (1789). The movement was humanitarian and secular, against superstition and the supernatural, and skeptical about religious authority and dogma. Its leaders believed in the "dignity of man," sought the betterment of humanity through proper education, and placed emphasis on reason and on knowledge gained through experience (empiricism) and scientific experiments. Knowledge, acquired through proper education, provided power to

The Pre-Classical Period

1700	1710	1720	1730	1740	1750	1760	1770	1780	1790	1800

- - - - Louis XIV (d. 1715) ◄- - - - - - - - - - - - - - - Louis XV (r. 1715–74) - - - - - - - - - - - - → Louis XVI - - -French
                                                                    (r. 1774–89) Revolution

Tsar' Peter the Great - - - - - - - - -
of Russia   (d. 1725)   Frederick II (the Great) - - (r. 1740–86) - - - - - - - - - - - - -
                                               of Prussia

Maria Theresa (r. 1740–80) - - - - - - - - - - - - - - - -
of Austria

Joseph II (r. 1765–90) - -

- George I - ► George II (r. 1727–60) - - - - - - - - - - - ►George III (r. 1760–1820) -
(r. 1714–27)

                                                     American
                                                   Revolution

The Enlightenment Era

- Baroque era -

- - *style galant* -

                              - *empfindsamer Stil* - - - - - - - - - - - - - - - - - *Sturm und Drang*

                                              - - - - Classical Era - - - - - - - - - - - - - - - - -

Rise of public concerts:
collegium musicum   *Concert spirituel*   Bach-Abel concerts
                                       (1725–90)   (1765–81)

Invention of Piano

                            Use of Well-tempered & Equal temperament

Baroque concerto -

                                     Pre-Classical concerto - - - - - - - - - - -Piano concerto -

Italian opera *sinfonia* - - - concert *sinfonia* - - - symphony -

                                  Keyboard sonata   - Clarinet used in symphony - - - - - - - - - - - - - - - - - -

                                    Accompanied keyboard sonata

               Rameau: *Traité de l'harmonie*   Treatises on Performance:
                           1722   Quantz, C. P. E. Bach, Tartini, L. Mozart

                           D. Scarlatti: Keyboard sonatas

                        D. Alberti: Sonatas

                        - - C. P. E. Bach fl. -

                                            J. C. Bach fl. - - - - - - - - - - -

                        - J. Stamitz fl.

                            Gossec fl. -

---

achieve liberation from the various evils that beset humanity. Humanitarian ideals were embodied in the American colonies' Declaration of Independence, drafted by Thomas Jefferson, and in the United States Constitution.

During the Enlightenment, science, rationalism, and freedom advanced considerably. One expression of the ideas of tolerance and brotherly love was the formation of fraternal organizations such as the Freemasons. Formally founded as a fraternal Lodge in England in 1717, Freemasonry spread throughout Europe and to the American colonies; among its

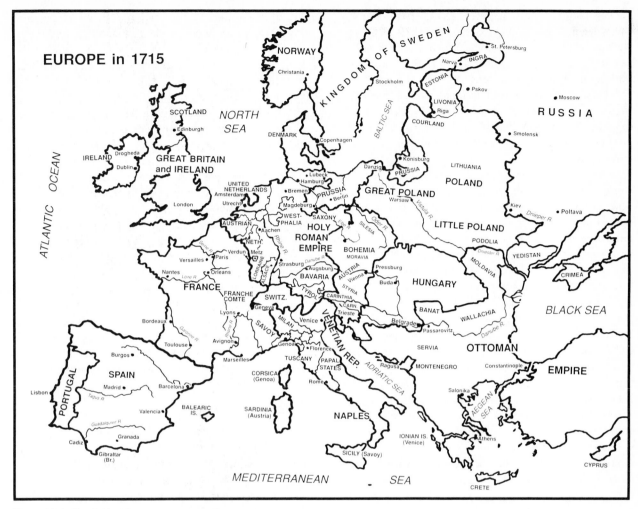

EUROPE in 1715

Figure 18.1 Europe in 1715.

members were rulers (Frederick the Great, Joseph II of Austria), statesmen (Benjamin Franklin, George Washington), philosophers (Lessing), authors (Swift), poets and dramatists (Klopstock, Schiller, Goethe, Beaumarchais), composers (Mozart, Haydn), and other talented persons from both upper and middle classes.

Some rulers were "enlightened" despots, e.g., Frederick the Great, Catherine II of Russia (r. 1725–27), Emperor Joseph II (r. 1765–90); others were merely despots. Louis XVI, in the early years of his reign, was enlightened but gradually became purely despotic.

The roots of The Enlightenment extend back to medieval times, to reaction against Church authorities who sought to dominate every phase of life, public and private, secular as well as religious. However, the obvious beginnings of the eighteenth-century movement were in England, in the writings and scientific experiments of such men as John Locke (1632–1704), Isaac Newton (1642–1727), his associate Edmond Halley (1656–1742), and David Hume (1711–76). On the Continent, impetus was provided by articulate Frenchmen who were acquainted with those Englishmen's ideas—Montesquieu (1689–1755), Voltaire

Eighteenth-Century Pre-Classical Music

(1694–1778), Denis Diderot (1713–84)—and by Swiss-born Jean-Jacques Rousseau (1712–78), who worked in France. These men referred to themselves as *philosophes* (philosophers), though all were not philosophers, in the true sense.

Diderot wrote several influential essays of musical criticism. More importantly, he planned and organized the production of the *Encyclopédie* (1751–76), 28 volumes whose articles stirred up enough controversy to make them a causal factor in the French Revolution. The *Encyclopédie* was not a reference work, as is a modern encyclopedia; rather, each volume was intended to be read from cover to cover. Rousseau wrote the articles on music for the *Encyclopédie*. Also, he expressed his ideas on education and politics in two books meant to be read in conjunction, *Émile* and *Social Contract* (1762). Voltaire's bold writings brought him imprisonment in the Bastille, and later, from time to time, self-imposed exile in countries where courts were more tolerant of his beliefs. He was welcome at the Prussian court of Frederick the Great. In that cosmopolitan atmosphere, Voltaire's influence was extensive. He reached, among others, the German critic Lessing (1729–81), and philosophers Moses Mendelssohn (1729–86) and Immanuel Kant (1724–1804). In *Was ist Aukfklärung?* (What is Enlightenment?; 1784), Kant revealed his own philosophy, a synthesis of empiricism and rationalism, and answered his essay's title question with the words *Sapere aude!* (Dare to know!). Voltaire's influence is seen also in the writings of Italians Francesco Algarotti (1712–64) and Cesare Beccaria (1738–94).

By the mid-1780s, most of the *philosophes* had died. Just as living conditions had prompted and influenced their thinking, so had their ideas affected living conditions. The issue of individual rights vs. state rights (and its resolution) shows this.

Aspects of Musical Life

The rise of a more or less independent spirit, leading from the accordance of divine right to kings to a belief in human rights and brotherhood, is exemplified in France and North America in revolution and is reflected in activities of the musical world. The general rise of the middle class to an influential position brought with it the popularization of art and learning, treatises written in the vernacular, novels and plays depicting ordinary people with everyday emotions, literature in prose, and public concerts. As music printing increased, instructional materials found their place on the market and developed from mere statements of principles to methods containing exercises and études for practice. Around mid-century, numerous "do-it-yourself" instruction books, especially for learning to play the violin, were on the market. The manufacture of keyboard instruments increased considerably. Books of songs and keyboard music designed for use by amateurs in their homes were readily available, and title pages with pictures of ladies playing instruments seem to indicate that some of the publications were intended for women. Music journals were issued more or less regularly, containing all sorts of music news—reviews, criticism, lists of newly published music, announcements of concerts, and even, so far as space would permit, some printed music. When space ran out, the piece was broken off (sometimes in mid-measure) and was continued from that point in the next issue of the magazine.

Public Concerts

The term **concert,** used for a public nontheatrical performance of music, came into existence in England in the late seventeenth century. During the Commonwealth era, when court activities were nonexistent, music patronage came into the hands of upper-middle-class citizens, and performances of music were presented in private homes and businesses. In 1672, violinist John Banister (1625–79) set aside a room of his house for the presentation of public subscription concerts; his series lasted six years. In 1678, Thomas Britton (1644–1714), an amateur musician, sponsored free concerts given every Thursday in a long, narrow room over his small-coal shop in London. However, it was decades before a systematically organized public concert series was established in England—the Bach-Abel concerts, organized and managed by C. F. Abel (1723–87) and J. C. Bach (1735–82), both capable impresarios. Their series, which presented 10 to 15 concerts annually, began 23 January 1765 and concluded on 9 May 1781.

Though public opera houses were operated in various continental European cities in the seventeenth century, there was no great interest in public concerts of nontheatrical music until the 1720s. Private performances at courts and in the homes and palaces of wealthy patrons entertained the aristocrats and nobility; middle- and lower-class citizens enjoyed music at church, and many of them participated in family amateur music making. Commencing in the 1720s and continuing through the century, the public concert developed significantly. Telemann, while employed at Frankfurt (1712–21), made concerts by the *collegium musicum* a feature of civic musical life by inaugurating regular public concerts by that group. In 1722–23, Telemann scheduled regular *collegium musicum* concerts in Hamburg, and musicians in other German cities followed his lead. J. A. Hiller (1728–1804) mounted a series of subscription concerts (*Liebhaberkonzerte,* concerts for amateurs or music-lovers) in Leipzig in 1762, which continued through 1768 and led to the establishment of the *Gewandhaus Konzerte* in 1781.

In France in 1725, oboist Anne Danican Philidor (1681–1728) negotiated a three-year contract with the government that permitted the presentation of a series of public performances, known as *Concert spirituel,* during those seasons when theaters were closed because of ecclesiastical regulations. At first, these concerts were given during Lent and consisted principally of vocal sacred music; gradually, the scope of the endeavor was extended to other religious days and seasons and to include secular and purely instrumental music. The *Concert spirituel* was in existence in Paris from 18 March 1725 until 1790. Works by prestigious composers from all over Europe were presented at these concerts. Several other concert organizations were founded and were active for a limited time. Besides the public concerts, many wealthy patrons in and around Paris entertained invited guests at weekly concerts in their homes. La Pouplinière maintained an orchestra and presented concerts regularly in his home at Passy from 1731 to 1762. Mme de Pompadour (1745–64) was a lavish patron of music and theater.

In North America, concerts "in an English manner" were presented by visiting companies in Boston in 1731 and in Philadelphia from 1734. The first concert of record in New York was organized by Charles Pachelbel (1690–1750) in 1736. Pachelbel became organist at St. Philip's Church, Charleston, South Carolina, in 1737 and sponsored concerts in his home in Charleston. It was not long before prominent citizens in other colonial cities did likewise.

Pre-Classical Styles

The term "Pre-Classical" is generally applied to those styles of eighteenth-century music that led to and were absorbed into the "Classical" style exhibited in the mature works of Mozart and Haydn. Though "Pre-Classical" is sometimes used loosely to refer to any eighteenth-century music before c. 1770, the term most appropriately encompasses the French and Italian *galant* style (French, *style galant*; Italian, *galante*), the north-German *empfindsamer Stil* (literally, sensitive style), and the latter's extension into *Sturm und Drang* (storm and stress). The Pre-Classical grew out of the Baroque, and coexisted with it, but was in some respects more or less a reaction to it. Many composers wrote in both Baroque and Pre-Classical styles.

Style Galant

As the center of cultural activity shifted from the church to the salon, *style galant* came into being in aristocratic and courtly circles. *Galant* music is light and graceful, elegant, sometimes witty, and, above all, pleasing to the ear upon first hearing. It is thin-textured homophony, characterized by simple melodies in short phrases, uncomplicated harmonies, and a slower harmonic rhythm than that used by Baroque composers. Major key tonalities were preferred. Notated music began to take on a different appearance, for instead of always notating only treble and bass lines and relying on the harpsichordist to supply the inner parts, as was customary in Baroque music, some composers of Pre-Classical music wrote down the complete harmony. Figured bass was not discarded but had some use throughout the eighteenth century. However, the bass line lost the independence and leadership it had enjoyed (especially in Baroque counterpoint) and functioned as support for and accompaniment to the melody. The inner voices merely

Example 18.1 (*a*) Murky bass. (*b*) Alberti bass. (*Example* b *source: Domenico Alberti:* Sonata 3 *in* Eb *major, mvt. 2. MS 35973, Biblioteca del Conservatorio di Musica, Naples, Italy.*)

supplied filler harmonies. Lest the slower harmonic rhythm with static harmonies become boring, broken chord figurations were used: **murky bass,** and, after c. 1735, **Alberti bass.** A murky bass is an accompaniment in broken octaves (ex. 18.1a). More popular was the Alberti bass, named for Domenico Alberti (c. 1710–40), who seems to have been the first composer to have made frequent use of it. The technique consists of a broken triad figuration, created by playing the notes in this order: lowest, highest, middle, highest (ex. 18.1b). Alberti, equally famous as opera singer and harpsichordist, composed (after 1736) more than 36 harpsichord sonatas, each structured with two movements; in them, the Alberti bass figuration appears often.

Style galant retained the decorativeness of Baroque music but dispensed with grandeur. In its maturity, *style galant* employed explicitly designated ornaments, appoggiatura sighs, Lombardic rhythm (; sometimes called the "Scottish snap"), feminine cadences (final cadence chord on weak beat of measure), melodic triplet sixteenth notes, and fussy dynamic contrasts. Representative examples of *style galant* instrumental music may be found in François Couperin's keyboard works, Jean-Marie Leclair's violin sonatas, Tartini's violin concerti, and in those optional eighteenth-century dance movements of suites known as *galanteries,* e.g., menuet, gavotte, *bourrée, loure.*

Empfindsamer Stil

After the death of J. S. Bach, German music was dominated by a form of *style galant.* Johann G. Harrer (1703–55), Bach's successor at Leipzig, was an outspoken advocate of it. In northern Germany, after c. 1750 the style was given new expressiveness and became *empfindsamer Stil,* the sensitive style. In *empfindsamer Stil,* the Baroque idea of an entire composition expressing only one basic affect was supplanted by the belief that, within a piece, there should be a continual change of expression or affection, together with appropriate changes in dynamics. J. J. Quantz (see also p. 445) advocated using all levels of dynamic shading, from *ppp* to *fff,* and stressed the necessity of avoiding the alternation of *piano* and *forte,* which would produce the terraced dynamics of Baroque music. Expressive nuances were of utmost importance. They were a feature of C. P. E. Bach's keyboard playing; the clavichord, his preferred instrument, could respond to his subtle shadings. In the works of C. P. E. Bach, *empfindsamer Stil* reached a high point. His music is finely nuanced, with periodic melody constructed in short phrases, and supported by light-textured accompaniment. He stated that the human singing voice provided the model for good instrumental melodic writing; melodies should be free of excessive ornamentation and should be simple enough so that beautiful tone quality and expressive nuances could be appreciated. At times, Bach's melodies are speechlike, bordering on operatic recitative. Never did he write melody merely to tickle the ear; his expressive, intimate music was designed to touch and move the listener. "Play from the soul," Bach wrote. He himself was moved when he played the clavichord.

Sturm und Drang

Sturm und Drang was a movement in German literature c. 1760–85 with the artistic aims of frightening, shocking, stunning, or overcoming with emotion. Adherents of the movement believed strongly in personal freedom, especially freedom from conventions that shackled artistic creativity. The most representative form of *Sturm und Drang* was drama, but parallel movements arose in all the arts. Authors penned "Gothic" novels such as Horace Walpole's *The Castle of Otranto* (1764). Artists sought to convey terror by painting storms, shipwrecks, macabre scenes, and nightmarish visions, e.g., Henry Fuseli's *The Nightmare* (colorplate 18).

In instrumental music by German composers, the emotional expressions and contrasts of *empfindsamer Stil* sharpened and intensified to become passionate outbursts characteristic of *Sturm und Drang*. Some of C. P. E. Bach's "Prussian" Sonatas and symphonies, and the dark, stormy moods portrayed in some of Joseph Haydn's minor-key symphonies written c. 1770, e.g., Nos. 44 and 49, are *Sturm und Drang* expressions.

In opera, an arena of combined arts, librettists created frightening situations that composers and set designers intensified with their music, costumes, and staging. Examples may be found in the works of Jommelli, Traetta, and Georg Benda, and Classical composers produced some magnificent, terrifying scenes: Gluck's scene with the Furies in *Orfeo ed Euridice* (Orpheus and Euridice; 1764); the tomb scene in Mozart's *Lucio Silla* (1772); and the conclusion of *Il Don Giovanni* (1787). In *Sturm und Drang* scenes like these, seeds of nineteenth-century German Romantic opera were sown.

Formal Structure

Some formal patterns preferred by Baroque composers remained in favor. Most *Lieder* and other art songs were strophic (same music for all stanzas). In opera, the *da capo* (ABA) aria reigned supreme. Occasionally, some German composers carved away the *da capo* section and wrote **cavatinas.** A cavatina is a small aria in which there is no reprise of the A section. An example is K. H. Graun's *Godi l'amabile,* in *Montezuma* (1755; DWMA139).

For most of their instrumental pieces, Pre-Classical composers used binary form but enriched, modified, and expanded that pattern. As a result of this modification and expansion, a new form emerged, albeit in an embryonic or incipient stage—a form that would be perfected by Haydn, Mozart, and other Classical composers and that nineteenth-century theorists would call **sonata form.** (There is no record that eighteenth-century composers ever gave this kind of formal structure that special name.) Sonata form was the most important structural design principle in instrumental music from the Classic period to the twentieth century.

The evolution of sonata form from simple binary may be summarized and diagrammed as in example 18.2. A simple binary form consists of two complementary main sections, A and B, each of which is usually marked to be repeated. (With repeats, the pattern is AABB.) The piece opens in the tonic key and modulates to a closely related key, where it cadences; the second section begins in that key and modulates to the tonic key in sufficient time to clearly establish the tonic before cadencing (ex. 18.2a). If the piece is in a major key, modulation is usually made to the dominant; if the piece is minor, modulation is to relative major. Often, the musical material commencing the B section is a transposition of the opening measures of the piece (ex. 18.2b); occasionally, eighteenth-century composers inverted the melodic motive when using it to begin the B section (ex. 18.2c). In the eighteenth century, **cadence rhyme** was common, i.e., the cadence at the end of the A section was transposed to the tonic for the final cadence (ex. 18.2d). Sometimes the rhyming termination was extended backwards, by including the approach to the cadence in the transposition (ex. 18.2e).

It was not unusual for Pre-Classical composers to go a step further and duplicate the opening measure(s) of the piece when returning to the tonic key near the conclusion of the B section (ex. 18.2f). Sometimes a composer restated all of the A section, in its original key, as conclusion to the B section—of course, making the necessary harmonic adjustment to ensure cadencing in the tonic key (ex. 18.2g). A binary form in which the first section is substantially returned, in its original key, in the final portion of the second section, is called a **rounded binary.** With repeats, the formal pattern of such a binary is AABABA. Rounding a binary could lengthen its second section considerably and make the form asymmetrical.

Example 18.2 The evolution of sonata
form from simple binary form.

(a) Simple binary form   ‖: A :‖: B :‖   (= A A B B)

‖: Tonic → Related .. Cadence :‖: Related ...→ Tonic .. Cadence :‖
              key   key

Major: I   →   V   Dominant   Dominant   →   Tonic   I

Minor: i   → Relative   Relative   →   Minor   i
               major   I   major   tonic

(b) Transposition of beginning of A section used to begin B section

(c) Inversion of beginning of A section used to begin B section

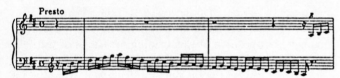   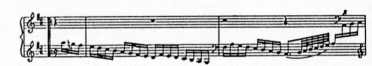

(d) Binary form with cadence rhyme

‖: Tonic → Dominant .. Cadence :‖: Dominant → Tonic .. Cadence :‖
                                                            Rhyme

(e) Binary form with cadence rhyme and approach to cadence also transposed

‖: Tonic → Dominant .. Cadence :‖: Dominant → Tonic .. Cadence :‖
                                                          Rhyme
                                              with approach to
                                              cadence transposed

(f) Binary form with cadence rhyme, approach to cadence transposed, and
opening measures of A section returned simultaneously with return
to tonic key

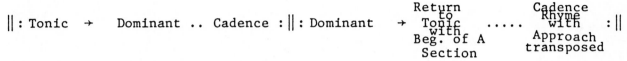

‖: Tonic → Dominant .. Cadence :‖: Dominant → Return to Tonic with Beg. of A Section ..... Cadence Rhyme with Approach transposed :‖

(g) Rounded binary

‖: A :‖: B A :‖ (= A A BA BA)

‖: Tonic → Dominant .. Cadence :‖: Dominant → → Double Return: of Tonic & of all or most of A section ... .Cadence :‖ (Tonic Key) Rhyme

Eighteenth-Century Pre-Classical Music

When composers began to manipulate the thematic material in the B section of a rounded binary form—to fragment and develop the thematic material and to venture into keys beyond the dominant—**sonata form** came into existence. German composer J. G. Harrer composed movements in sonata form, with respectable developments, in the 1730s. Movements in **incipient** sonata form—i.e., movements with B sections exhibiting some manipulation of thematic material but without true development sections—appear in the keyboard works of Domenico Scarlatti and C. P. E. Bach. Incipient sonata form occurs in Bach's *Sonata* in F major, mvt. 1 (1742).

Sonata Form

The term **sonata form** refers to the constructional principle of a movement, not the form of the multi-movement work called "sonata." (The terms "sonata-allegro" and "first-movement form" are limiting misnomers and should be avoided. Sonata form does not require any specific tempo, neither is its use limited to the first movement of a multimovement work.)

Sonata form was not described by theorists before the 1790s, though it had been in use for about 50 years. H. C. Koch (1749–1816) seems to have been the first to give an adequate description of it, in his *Versuch einer Anleitung zur Composition* (Treatise on Composition, 3 vols.; 1782–93). Koch's treatise is an extensive treatment of composition; his descriptions of forms, with "formal models" (music examples), make his essay a major contribution. Koch did not use the term sonata form, but described that kind of formal structure as binary, written in two distinct units, each unit usually marked to be repeated. He explained that this kind of binary contains a two-part tonal structure (i.e., tonic-to-dominant; dominant-to-tonic) expressed in three main sections (statement of material; manipulation of material; restatement of material).

From the viewpoint of the Pre-Classical composer and the eighteenth-century theorist, then, sonata form was a monothematic rounded binary form in which: (a) the first section established the tonic key, then modulated to dominant (or relative major) where it cadenced; (b) the second section commenced in dominant (or relative major), developed (i.e., manipulated) previously stated material and increased tension by modulating into keys more remote than dominant; then (c) made a strong, clear return to the tonic key and, simultaneously, began a restatement of the material of the first section in the tonic; and (d) upon completion of the restatement, cadenced in the tonic (fig. 18.2). However, composers did not always follow that pattern strictly. Rarely, in the first section of a composition in minor, a composer modulated to the dominant minor key. Moreover, the theme stated at the outset might generate subsidiary thematic material, but the most important factor in the formal pattern was **tonality**—statement of key, digression to a closely related key and then to more remote keys, and return to the original key.

Though eighteenth-century composers made frequent use of sonata form in single- and multiple-movement compositions, they never referred to it by that name. Perhaps the frequent use of the form in works entitled "Sonata" prompted a nineteenth-century theorist to term it "sonata form." By mid-nineteenth century the term was in use, and theorists analyzing this form called the first section "exposition," the first part of the second section "development," and the restatement "recapitulation."

The Baroque *sonata da chiesa* gradually disappeared, supplanted by a different kind of multimovement composition called "sonata." Though the vast majority of Pre-Classical sonatas were for solo keyboard, some were written for other instruments, e.g., Quantz's flute sonatas and Tartini's violin sonatas. In

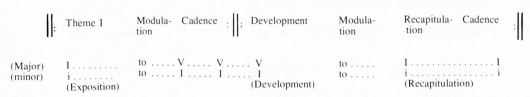

Figure 18.2 Diagram of monothematic sonata form.

the 1730s and 1740s, Mondonville and other Parisian composers wrote sonatas for keyboard with violin accompaniment. The Baroque trio *sonata da chiesa* existed into the Classical period—Gluck and Haydn wrote works of this type. Eventually, it was supplanted by true trios: the piano trio (violin, 'cello, piano) and the string trio (2 violins, 'cello). Also, the trio sonata was forerunner of the piano quartet and the string quartet.

The first real flowering of the Pre-Classical sonata for solo keyboard came after 1735, with the works of Domenico Scarlatti (though he called them *essercizi*, or studies), Domenico Alberti, C. P. E. Bach, and many lesser-known Italian and German composers. Alberti and Scarlatti wrote two-movement works; most of Bach's have three. After 1740, a three-movement fast-slow-fast structural plan resembling that of the Italian opera overture (*sinfonia*) was used increasingly. It comprised an Allegro, a lyrical Andante that was usually quite short, and a Finale with dancelike rhythm, often a *gigue* or *menuetto*. That the Pre-Classical sonata bears little resemblance to Baroque *sonata da chiesa* is due primarily to cultural interests of the time. Relatively few sonatas were written expressly for use in church. Rather, they were intended for performance at court, in public and private concerts, and by amateurs at home. Some sonatas were designed for teaching purposes, e.g., Scarlatti's *Essercizi* and Arne's *Lessons*.

Domenico Scarlatti

Domenico Scarlatti (1685–1757), composer, teacher, and performer, was born in Naples; he was the sixth of the ten children of Alessandro Scarlatti and Antonia Anzalone. Nothing is known about Domenico's early life. Presumably, he was educated in Naples and may have received his musical training from his father. Alessandro was aware of Domenico's talent and sought to further Domenico's career by directing its path.

In September 1701, Domenico was appointed organist and composer at the royal court at Naples, where his father was *maestro di cappella*. No compositions survive from those months of employment. From June to October 1702, father and son visited the Medici court at Florence. Possibly, during that visit

Domenico met Bartolomeo Cristofori, who was making keyboard instruments at that court. Domenico resumed work at Naples in October and composed two operas for performance there in 1703. The following spring Alessandro ordered Domenico to accompany Nicolini (Nicolò Grimaldi, alto castrato; 1673–1732) on a journey from Naples to Venice, with stops at Rome and Florence. Alessandro hoped his son would secure a position at the Florentine court. In his letter of recommendation to Ferdinand de' Medici, Alessandro stated that he did not want Domenico to work in Rome and that he had "forcibly removed" him from Naples because his talent was not the right kind for that court. Furthermore, Alessandro wrote, he did not want to hinder Domenico's career. Domenico did not remain in Florence, nor did he return to Naples. He went instead to Venice, and nothing is known concerning the next four years of his life.

Domenico Scarlatti. Painted c. 1740 by Domingo Antonio de Velasco. *(Institutiçao José Relvas, Alpiarça.)*

From 1709 to 1713 Domenico was employed as composer at the private court of exiled Polish queen Maria Casimira, in Rome. For performance there he composed a cantata, an oratorio, and six operas. While in Rome, he attended the weekly chamber music recitals given at the palace of Cardinal Pietro Ottoboni. There Scarlatti became acquainted with Corelli, met Handel, and formed a friendship with Thomas Roseingrave, who later arranged for publication of some of Scarlatti's music in England. Late in December 1713, Domenico became *maestro di cappella* of the Basilica Giulia, in Rome, and early in 1714, he secured an additional appointment, as *maestro di cappella* to Marquis de Fontes, Portuguese ambassador to the Vatican. Thus, Scarlatti was composing music for both sacred and secular use. Because Alessandro was still interfering in his affairs, Domenico took legal action against him in 1717, but this brought only temporary relief. In August 1719 Domenico resigned his positions in Rome and moved to Portugal, where he served as *mestre* of the patriarchal chapel in Lisbon until 1728. The records pertaining to his employment in Portugal were probably destroyed in the disastrous earthquake that almost obliterated Lisbon on 1 November 1755. Between 1719 and 1728, Scarlatti returned to Italy three times. In 1724, he visited Rome, where he met Quantz and may have met Farinelli (Carlo Broschi; 1705–82), famed Italian soprano castrato. Fourteen years later, Farinelli and Scarlatti were working together at the Madrid court. In 1725, Domenico spent some time with his ailing father in Naples, and in 1728, he went back to Rome to marry 16-year-old Maria Caterina Gentili. He never again left the Iberian peninsula.

In Lisbon, Scarlatti's responsibilities included the music education of King John V's daughter, Infanta (Princess) Maria Barbara, and Don Antonio, King John's younger brother. A lasting bond was formed between the princess and her teacher; for her he created many if not all of the approximately 555 keyboard "sonatas" that are his most significant work. In 1728, when Maria Barbara married Spanish Crown Prince Fernando, Scarlatti was among those who accompanied her to Madrid. The last 28 years of his life were spent there.

Little is known of Domenico Scarlatti as a person. The legend that he was too fat to cross his hands at the keyboard is belied by a portrait of him made c. 1740 by Domingo Antonio de Velasco. That painting, located in 1956, depicts Scarlatti as slender, with prominent cheekbones and chin.

Until 1719 Scarlatti had a career in opera, without much success. His departure from Italy in 1720 brought freedom from Neapolitan (and his father's) domination. His new position presented opportunities beyond composing and performing music for court use—to develop his capabilities as teacher, to provide new keyboard music that would interest his royal pupils yet challenge and develop their talents (especially those of Maria Barbara), and to incorporate in that music the characteristic sounds and customs of Iberia. He could experiment with a new compositional style and test the viability of new ideas. For the next 35 years he wrote keyboard pieces—the "sonatas" for which he is acclaimed.

Scarlatti was influential principally in the Iberian peninsula and in England. His influence can be seen in the work of Antonio Soler (1729–83) and Sebastián de Albero (1722–56), both of whom he knew. Some of Scarlatti's sonatas were published in England in 1738, probably through the influence of Farinelli.

Scarlatti's Music

Several persons have edited and/or catalogued Scarlatti's sonatas, each according to his own method. Sonatas bearing L. numbers were catalogued by Alessandro Longo; those with K. numbers by Ralph Kirkpatrick; those with P. numbers by Giorgio Pestolli; and those with G. numbers by Kenneth Gilbert. In the principal manuscript sources, many of the pieces seem to have been grouped by pairs; there is no proof that Scarlatti composed them in pairs, though he may have arranged some of them that way later.

Each piece (sonata, or sonata movement) is an *étude*; each presents in pedagogical and musical context at least one consistently recurring problem of physiological, technical, or musical difficulty that requires of the player both mechanical application and musical interpretation. Included are hand crossing, rapid reiteration of notes, arpeggio figurations extending the full length of the keyboard, and patterns requiring use of the thumb.

Scarlatti's sonatas differ considerably from the typical Baroque binary, though outwardly they follow that form. The piece commences in tonic and, if major, progresses to dominant; if minor, the progression is to relative major. A thin double bar or a repeat sign marks the conclusion of the first half of the piece. The second section reverses the progression, moving from dominant or relative major back to tonic. Usually there is indication that both halves are to be repeated (fig. 18.3). Frequently, there is cadence rhyme, that is, the final cadence is a transposition to tonic of the cadence that concludes the first section of the sonata (Sonata in B♭, L.56, mm. 21–22 and mm. 40–41). Cadence rhyme is sometimes quite extensive (Sonata XI, C minor). There is no recapitulation, but often the binary is rounded, i.e., the opening measures of the sonata are brought back prior to the transposed final cadence. One of the sonatas, K.159, closely approximates Classical sonata form; in several sonatas the first part of the second section is developmental, evidencing that Classical sonata form is incipient.

Characteristics of Scarlatti's sonatas include: (1) frequent use of the *acciaccatura* (literally, crushed grace note), a lower auxiliary note briefly sounded simultaneously with its resolution (ex. 18.3a and b; also, Sonata L.429, mm. 2–6); (2) blurred or obscured resolutions; (3) vamping; (4) phrase elision; (5) bold modulations achieved by means of chromatic alteration; and (6) a rather plain sequential pattern enhanced or surrounded by an auxiliary line of chromatic filigree. The term **vamp** describes a section of indeterminate length that conveys the impression of stalling or waiting for the entrance of important musical material. Scarlatti frequently used vamping to commence the second section of a sonata, the vamp containing a repeated figural pattern that somewhat resembles a solo passage from a Vivaldi violin concerto (ex. 18.3c; also, L.26, mm. 73–76; L.429, mm. 52–55). At times Scarlatti wrote a phrase several measures long and brought it to cadence, then repeated it but replaced the cadential measure(s) with the initial measures of a new phrase; thus, in repetition, the phrase was elided and the retained portion served as impetus or booster to the new material.

Among areas of special concern in performance practice are: the correct interpretation of Scarlatti's ornaments, and Scarlatti's manner of drawing long curved lines above or below the final measures of the first half of a sonata to indicate the omission of those measures when repeating the section; often, the measure beginning the second section is identical with one of those omitted, as it is in Sonata in D major, K.535 (ex. 18.4).

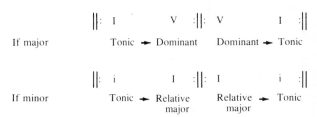

Figure 18.3 Diagram of typical binary structure of a Domenico Scarlatti sonata movement.

Example 18.3 (*a*) An *acciaccatura* as notated; (*b*) an *acciaccatura* as performed, all notes being sounded together initially but the crushed notes being released immediately; (*c*) vamping, as used in Scarlatti's Sonata in A minor, K.175 (L.429), mm. 27–32.

Example 18.4 Scarlatti's use of long curved lines above and/or below the final measures of the first half of a sonata indicates the omission of those measures when the section is repeated. *(From Sonata in D major, K.535.)*

Ornamentation symbols used in Iberia in the eighteenth century do not always correspond with those used elsewhere in Europe; no treatise has been located that definitively explains all the markings used by Spanish and Portuguese composers. The very small notes Scarlatti wrote as graces can be interpreted as appoggiaturas, and the trill symbols are clear. The directive *Tremulo nell' A la mi re*—note the use of Guido's nomenclature—in mm. 56–58 of Sonata in D Major (K.119; DWMA140) can be interpreted as an inner trill and is not difficult to perform (ex. 18.5). But the meaning of Scarlatti's *tremulo* directive is not always apparent. In some pieces, it seems improbable that he intended *tremulo* to mean "trill." Possibly, those sonatas were intended for performance on clavichord, and the word *tremulo* indicates an ornamental vibrato similar to the *Bebung* C. P. E. Bach enjoyed playing.

It is not likely that all of Scarlatti's keyboard sonatas were written for harpsichord. At least three of them—K.287, K.288, K.328—were for organ. Maria Barbara owned clavichords and single-escapement pianos whose hammers produced a delicate sound. Most of her harpsichords had one manual with two registers and a five-octave range; the tones they produced were clear but delicate—very different from sounds produced by Flemish and German harpsichord reproductions built in the late twentieth century.

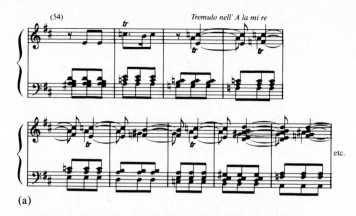

(a)

(b)

Example 18.5 Scarlatti's directive "Tremulo nell' A la mi re" in mm. 54–62 of Sonata in D major, K.119, (*a*) in a modern edition and (*b*) in an early printed edition of the work.

Pre-Classical Concerto

The formal structure of the concerto for solo instrument and orchestra that Vivaldi established was followed by Pre-Classical composers and was infused with *galant* characteristics. Vivaldi wrote solo concerti for violin, violoncello, flute, oboe, or bassoon, with an orchestra of strings and basso continuo. Solo concerti for these instruments were written by Pre-Classical composers, too, either for performance by themselves or by a specific pupil or patron. J. J. Quantz (1697–1773), flautist and teacher of King Frederick the Great of Prussia, wrote more than 300 flute concerti (as well as more than 200 flute sonatas) for performance by the king. J. S. Bach created the concerto for solo keyboard and string orchestra when he transcribed and adapted for harpsichord some of Vivaldi's concerti.

In the Pre-Classical era, Bach's sons contributed a great deal to the development of the solo keyboard concerto: Wilhelm Friedemann Bach (1710–84) composed 6 of them; Johann Christoph Friedrich Bach (1732–95) wrote at least 6; Johann Christian Bach (1735–82) wrote more than 30; and C. P. E. Bach (1714–88) wrote more than 50. Joseph Haydn was influenced by C. P. E. Bach's keyboard concerti; those by J. C. Bach influenced Amadeus Mozart, who perfected Classical concerto form.

Many of C. P. E. Bach's concerti are in minor keys. Most of his concerti have three movements; a few have four. The opening movements follow the ritornello form used by Vivaldi. Bach's writing, especially in the slow movements, is in *empfindsamer Stil*—the soloist's part is brilliant, as well as expressive.

J. C. Bach was the first to adopt the piano for public performance. He encouraged its use as solo instrument by stating in the titles of some of his works that they were suitable for piano, e.g., *Sei concerti per il cembalo o piano e forte,* Op. 7 (Six concertos for harpsichord or pianoforte; 1770). In that day, the tone of the piano was small, so Bach balanced it with trio-sonata orchestral instrumentation: Violin I, Violin II, and basso continuo. Some of Bach's concerti have three movements, most of them have only two. Stylistically, they are infused with *galant* elements. Themes are well defined, and melodies are Italianate. In the fast first movements of his concerti, Bach merged elements of ritornello and sonata form, opening the movement with an orchestral section, entirely in tonic key, that resembles the first section (the exposition) of a sonata-form movement. At the conclusion of the recapitulation, the soloist improvised a cadenza; a coda brought the movement to conclusion. Slow movements of Bach's concerti resemble arias. Bach wrote his concerti for his own performance; he was not only soloist, but keyboard continuo player as well. This meant that the harpsichordist (or pianist, as the case might be) performed throughout the composition. Also, at that time the composer-keyboard player usually was the conductor.

Carl Philipp Emanuel Bach

C. P. E. Bach was the chief representative of north German *empfindsamer Stil* and one of the four principal composers active during the last half of the eighteenth century. The others were Gluck, Haydn, and Mozart, who are considered Classical composers. Bach also produced some works that are in Classical style. Besides being a prolific composer, Bach was a theorist, keyboard teacher, and virtuoso performer.

Emanuel, second surviving son of Johann Sebastian and Maria Barbara Bach, was the most famous of Bach's sons. In fact, Emanuel's fame surpassed that of his father in the decades immediately following Sebastian's death. From the time of his birth Emanuel was surrounded by music. Sebastian Bach determined that his sons should have the best possible education. At Cöthen they attended the Lutheran seminary to receive basic theology in their own faith; at Leipzig they were enrolled at the Thomasschule, where they received a thorough education that included music study with their father. Sebastian was the only music teacher Emanuel ever had. His instrumental study was confined to keyboard—he seems never to have been interested in any other instrument—and he was exposed to a wealth of material from his father's didactic works. The Bach home was filled with music; rehearsals were held there, and distinguished musicians were frequent visitors. Emanuel's musical experience was broad, covering sacred and secular instrumental and vocal music of many styles and nationalities and in all genres except opera.

From 1731 to 1738 Emanuel was both full-time university student and professional musician. His university studies were in law, for that curriculum provided the most thorough liberal education a man could acquire. While attending Leipzig University (1731–34), he lived at home and served as musical assistant to his father. After transferring to the University of Frankfurt-an-der-Oder in September 1734, he earned his living by teaching keyboard lessons and by composing music for public concerts or special occasions.

Emanuel's earliest known composition is a small *Minuet in C* (1731) that he personally engraved while his father supervised the task. Before Emanuel moved

Carl Philip Emanuel Bach.

Figure 18.4 Adolf Menzel's painting *Frederick's Flute Concert at Sans Souci* depicts Frederick the Great playing the flute and C. P. E. Bach at the keyboard. Quantz is standing at the extreme right, almost out of the picture. *(Neue Nationalgalerie, West Berlin.)*

to Frankfurt, he had written five keyboard sonatas, six keyboard sonatinas, a keyboard suite, seven trios, a flute solo, an oboe solo, two harpsichord concertos, and some chamber music that he revised years later. During the next four years he enlarged that list by at least a dozen more instrumental works.

In 1738 Emanuel entered the service of Crown Prince Frederick of Prussia, who at that time employed 18 musicians to perform chamber music. Well-known composers among the group were Franz and Johann Benda, K. H. and J. G. Graun, and J. J. Quantz. The prince usually participated in performances (fig. 18.4). Though conditions were not always to Emanuel's liking, he served Frederick for about 30 years. Bach was not the only accompanist among the court musicians; his compositions were seldom performed at court, and his salary was very low. On the other hand, he had ample time to teach, compose, and write. He was already planning an essay on playing keyboard instruments. Some of his best friends in Berlin were authors, bankers, and other businessmen; he knew Sara Levy (Mendelssohn's great-aunt), who was assembling a library of works by Bach family

composers. In 1742 Emanuel witnessed the establishment of the Berlin Opera and learned about dramatic music from performances there. However, he never composed an opera.

In 1744 Emanuel married Johanna Danneman. Their three children were not musicians; their youngest child, Johann Sebastian (1748–78), became an accomplished painter. Often, well-known writers and musicians visited in Emanuel's home. He was generous in assisting young musicians who came to Berlin to establish their careers.

The most influential of the many compositions Emanuel wrote while at the Berlin court were solo keyboard pieces, including the six "Prussian" Sonatas (1743) and six "Württemburg" Sonatas (1744). Another excellent work is the *Magnificat* (1749).

Publication of the first part of *Versuch über die wahre Art das Clavier zu spielen* (Essay on the true art of playing keyboard instruments; 1753) established Emanuel Bach's reputation as the leading keyboard teacher of that time. He published a revised version of the treatise in 1757; it was reprinted several times, and translations circulated in other countries. In the late twentieth century, Bach's *Essay* is considered one of the most important practical treatises on music written in the eighteenth century—a standard guide to all aspects of keyboard performance practices in that century. Emanuel stated rules clearly and authoritatively and illustrated them with music examples.

Emanuel may have felt compelled to write his *Essay* because he knew Quantz was preparing a treatise on flute playing. Quantz's *Versuch einer Anweisung die Flöte traversiere zu spielen* (Instructional essay on playing the transverse flute) appeared in 1752. His book contains only five chapters on flute playing; the remainder of the essay concerns almost all phases of musical performance. Quantz's treatise is the most comprehensive and reliable source of information about the eighteenth-century flute and its playing technique. Both Quantz and Bach wrote for the one-keyed (Db key) conical transverse flute developed by Hotteterre, the standard model during the first half of the eighteenth century. It was built in three sections, and its seventh finger hole was controlled by a key.

When J. S. Bach died, Emanuel took into his home his young half-brother, Johann Christian. Also, after 1750 Emanuel maintained close contact with Telemann, who was his godfather; Telemann became almost a second father to him. Emanuel was not content with his court employment; several times during the 1750s, he applied for other posts, without success. One of those unsuccessful applications (1755) was for the position at the Thomasschule vacated by his father's successor. Conditions at court worsened after Prussia became involved in the Seven Years' War (1756–63). Busy defending his kingdom, Frederick lost interest in his musical establishment. Monetary values decreased, and court employees were paid in almost worthless paper money. Emanuel renewed his search for a new position, often consulting with Telemann when applying. When Telemann died (1767), Emanuel was named his successor at Hamburg. However, Frederick was reluctant to release Bach and did so only after Emanuel pretended to be in ill health. Actually, Emanuel's only ailments were trembling hands and occasional severe attacks of gout, problems he had had most of his life.

Bach's association with the Prussian court was not completely severed. When he left the king's employ, Frederick's youngest sister, Princess Anna Amalia

insight

Princess Anna Amalia

Princess Anna Amalia (1723–87), youngest daughter of Frederick Wilhelm I of Prussia, was an accomplished keyboard player, a capable violinist and flautist, and a composer. Her first music lessons were from her brother; then she studied with Berlin organist Gottlieb Hayne. During 1758–83 Johann P. Kirnberger (1721–83), pupil of J. S. Bach, was Anna Amalia's resident Kapellmeister; with him she studied counterpoint and composition. Anna Amalia's setting of Ramler's oratorio libretto *Der Tod Jesu* (The Death of Jesus) preceded that by K. H. Graun. Kirnberger used an excerpt from it as a model in his composition treatise *Die Kunst des reinen Satzes in der Musik*. Anna Amalia composed some arias, chorales, songs, marches, and sonatas. Several of her surviving works have been published, including a *Sonata for Flute* (F major) and a *Trio Sonata*. She amassed a library that contained several thousand books and more than 650 musical items, including autograph scores by J. S. and C. P. E. Bach, Handel, Hasse, Kirnberger, Telemann, and others. She bequeathed her entire library to the Berlin Joachimsthalschen Gymnasium. In 1914 the music portion was transferred to the Royal Library and is now divided between the German government libraries in East and West Berlin.

(1723–87; see Insight, "Princess Anna Amalia") to whom Emanuel had dedicated his six *Sonatas with Varied Repeats* (1760), named him her *Kapellmeister von Haus aus* (nonresident chapelmaster).

In March 1768 Bach became Kantor of the Johanneum (the Lateinschule) at Hamburg; he worked there for 20 years. In many respects, his position paralleled that his father had held at the Thomasschule. Emanuel's duties included providing music for approximately 200 performances annually for five churches, plus music for the school and for special civic, political, and religious ceremonies and occasions of all kinds. It was a tremendous workload—for instance, ten Passions were needed within 13 days—yet, he managed to remain healthy and to produce all that was required of him. He taught keyboard lessons, performed, and published music. In 1768 he arranged for a series of concerts to be given at Hamburg in which he performed harpsichord concertos and programmed music by J. S. Bach, Telemann, Handel, Haydn, Gluck, and others. Emanuel published a serial, *Musikalisches Vierley* (Musical Quarterly; 1770), a compilation of keyboard pieces, chamber music, and songs with keyboard accompaniment, by various composers, for general popular use.

Bach continued to entertain visiting dignitaries at his home; Burney, Klopstock, Lotti, Reichardt, and Gottfried van Swieten were some who visited him. Charles Burney (1726–1814) was gathering material for his book *The Present State of Music in Germany, the Netherlands, and the United Provinces* (publ. 1773). Bach's ability to improvise and the ardor with which he played amazed Burney. Emanuel's discussions with Klopstock and other poets concerning the esthetic association between music and words were influential in his setting of poetry expressively but with music subservient to text.

For van Swieten, Austrian ambassador to Prussia, Emanuel composed six symphonies (W182 = H657–62; 1773) and dedicated to him the third collection of six *Sonaten für Kenner und Liebhaber* (Sonatas for connoisseurs and amateurs; 1781). When van Swieten returned to Vienna at the conclusion of his diplomatic tour of duty, he actively championed the music of J. S. and C. P. E. Bach and Handel by arranging for performances of their works at weekly concerts. Through van Swieten, Mozart became acquainted with this "old" music. Awareness of Emanuel Bach spread to other countries. Haydn played some of his keyboard sonatas; Diderot requested harpsichord music for his daughter. C. G. Neefe (1748–98), who later taught Beethoven, knew Emanuel's keyboard music and Sebastian's *The Well-Tempered Clavier*.

During the last 20 years of his life, C. P. E. Bach was required to be primarily a composer of church music. Yet, his greatest contributions and his finest works were produced in other areas. A good many of his choral works have been lost. Among his extant sacred works are psalm settings, chorales, cantatas, numerous Passions, and the oratorios *Die Israeliten in der Wüste* (The Israelites in the wilderness; 1769) and *Auferstehung und Himmelfahrt Jesu* (Jesus' resurrection and ascension; c. 1777). Emanuel's oratorios are the best written in Germany during that era. It is unfortunate that he was employed in a position demanding a vast amount of choral music but

in an era in which Lutheran church music was declining. The place of choral music in the life of the congregation was changing; use of the traditional chorale in the Service had diminished. Sebastian Bach had been able to compose music setting integrated texts that reconciled Orthodox and Pietist leanings, but when Emanuel was working in Hamburg the rationalistic and Pietistic had come to the fore. He realized that, under the circumstances, he could not write the kind of integrated church music that his father had provided. Although it was Emanuel's job to supply requisite music for the churches, this choral music became of secondary importance to him, and many times he adapted works of others or prepared a *pasticcio* (patchwork) to meet his needs.

C. P. E. Bach's Music

Keyboard Works

Bach created music on two levels: to meet his own high standards and to please his patron and/or appeal to the public. His finest compositions are 6 collections of keyboard pieces for connoisseurs and amateurs (W55–59, W61); next in importance are 12 keyboard concertos (W41–47) and 10 symphonies (H657–66). ("W" numbers are those in Wotquenne's thematic catalogue; "H" numbers are from Helm's catalog.)

Emanuel's first composition was written for his own instrument, and he continued to compose keyboard works all his life. The harpsichord was the preferred keyboard instrument in Emanuel's time; he performed on it, and he composed for it. However, he preferred the clavichord, which was capable of producing subtle and expressive shadings. Moveover, on the clavichord he could produce the *Bebung* (literally, tremolo) or vibrato, because the metal tangent remained in contact with the string until the player's finger released the key. Emanuel's fantasias, rondos, and some of his sonatas sound best when played on clavichord. He aimed to express his thoughts and emotions effectively without using words, and these works indicate that he could do so. Present in them are abrupt changes of mood, remote modulations, and the characteristics of *empfindsamer Stil*—melodic sighs, triplet sixteenths, sudden dynamic changes, Lombardic rhythmic figures, chromaticism, and various kinds of ornaments indicated by symbols and miniature notes. (Examples are: Fantasia in G minor, Fantasia in C minor, and Sonata in A major, H186 = W55/4, Poco Adagio.) The fantasias reflect to some degree Emanuel's ability to improvise. His works of this kind are reminiscent of Sebastian's fantasias and were influential in Mozart's composition of piano fantasias. Emanuel composed his last five sets of keyboard sonatas (1780–87) for pianoforte.

Many of Bach's keyboard sonatas are rather conservative. Some were written for popular consumption, such as the sonatas *für Liebhaberin* (for lady amateurs; W54; c. 1765–66).

Bach's sonatas are usually in three movements, in fast-slow-fast order of tempo. The structure of the outer movements indicates that he knew sonata form: they are in binary form, with a kind of development and a recapitulation in the second half. Bach had a tendency to develop themes as soon as he stated them, rather than wait for the development section; consequently, the development section immediately after the double bar is rather short. Usually, the slow movements are through-composed. However, the *Cantabile* second movement of the third sonata from his first set of *Sonatas for connoisseurs and amateurs* (1779) is in sonata form. Its development displays the motivic variation that is a central characteristic of Bach's work. His choice of key for some of his sonatas was unusual; e.g., F minor was rarely used in the eighteenth century. Both Haydn and Beethoven were influenced by Bach's Sonata in F minor.

Orchestral and Chamber Music

Bach's concertos for harpsichord and orchestra are virtuosic keyboard works, designed for his own performance. He adapted ten of the concertos for other solo instruments, and in each instance the adaptation is idiomatic. Basically, the concertos follow Vivaldi's formal plan: three movements, in fast-slow-fast order of tempo. However, the outer movements are a blend of ritornello and sonata form.

Bach wrote 12 compositions for solo harpsichord and orchestra that he called "sonatinas." In these concertato-type works the solo harpsichord music is often quite virtuosic; for this reason the sonatinas are sometimes classified as miniature concertos. The sonatinas resemble suites, however, for they contain from two to ten short movements in binary or miniature sonata form, and all movements are in the same key.

C. P. E. Bach was one of the principal symphonists of the north German school. Some of his approximately 20 symphonies are in *empfindsamer Stil;* the four *Orchester-Sinfonien mit 12 obligaten Stimmen* (Orchestral symphonies with 12 required parts; W183 = H663–66; 1776) exhibit the fire and energy of *Sturm und Drang.* The 12 obbligato parts are for two flutes, two oboes, two horns, bassoon, and five-part string orchestra. A figured bass part is included, indicating that harpsichord was expected but not obligatory; 'cello and bassoon parts generally (but not completely) duplicate the figured bass line. There are no minuets. Symphony No. 3 (H665; F major) has three movements: Allegro di molto, Larghetto, and Presto (DWMA141). The first movement is in classical sonata form, with two themes, though the development is rudimentary. The general tone of the movement foreshadows Beethoven; in fact, Beethoven borrowed the first theme for inclusion in his second symphony. The Larghetto (D minor) commences as a duet for violas and 'cellos and retains a two-voice structure throughout; keyboard is *tacet.* The Presto finale is binary.

Emanuel's chamber music includes solo sonatas with basso continuo; trio sonatas; harpsichord/violin and harpsichord/flute duets; chamber sonatas that are trios (not trio sonatas) for two instruments and harpsichord; and three quartets for flute, viola, violoncello, and harpsichord, written in Classical style, with balance of parts, thus foreshadowing the piano quartet. There is also the *Clavier-Fantasie mit Begleitung einer Violine* (Keyboard-fantasia with accompaniment of one violin; 1787), subtitled on the manuscript *C. P. E. Bachs Empfindungen* (C. P. E. Bach's Perceptions), in F♯ minor. This composition may reflect the influence of Johann Schobert (c. 1735–67), Silesian harpsichordist and composer, who was known particularly for his sonatas for harpsichord with violin accompaniment. Emanuel Bach was among the first composers to elevate the keyboard from its accompanist/continuo status and make it an equal partner in chamber music or give it a leading role in ensemble music.

Vocal Music

C. P. E. Bach composed approximately 300 songs with keyboard accompaniment. These are strophic settings—usually there are many strophes—in which the poetry is more important than the music. For this reason, the harmony is intentionally thin. Three lines of music are notated for keyboard, with the top line doubling the vocal melody. Though the settings are simple, they are effective and the music is appropriate to the general tenor of the poetry. About 60 percent of the songs set sacred texts.

Emanuel seldom wrote fugues or used Baroque counterpoint. He did not disdain counterpoint; it simply did not fit the style of music he espoused. The *Magnificat* (1749) contains a rare instance of his use of fugue, in the *Sicut erat in principio* section. The subject of that fugue has been compared with that used by Mozart in the Kyrie of his *Requiem*. Bach combined ancient and modern styles in *Heilig* (Holy; 1778) by writing homophonic music for antiphonal SATB choirs, with three trumpets, two oboes, bassoon, timpani, strings, and basso continuo.

The Symphony

The symphony took its name from and was a direct outgrowth of the Italian opera overture (*sinfonia*) in use during the last two decades of the seventeenth century. However, the Pre-Classical symphony is indebted to several other forms—especially, trio sonata and Baroque concerto (solo, concerto grosso, and orchestral)—for certain internal details of structure, texture, style, and instrumentation.

Usually, the overture to an early eighteenth-century Italian opera served merely to advise the audience that the opera was about to commence, and it bore no thematic relationship to the opera it prefaced. Consequently, an opera overture could be performed as an independent piece on other occasions, for instance, in a concert or at a banquet. Dual usage of this kind was common around mid-century. Moreover, many opera overtures were published as *sinfonie* without reference to the operas for which they had been written.

Around 1730, composers began to write concert *sinfonie,* following the tempo plan Alessandro Scarlatti devised in 1681 for his opera overtures: three

movements, in fast-slow-fast order, with the finale being dancelike in character and usually in triple meter ($\frac{3}{8}$ or $\frac{3}{4}$). Scarlatti's instrumentation was copied, too—strings, pairs of brass and woodwind, with basso continuo for bass (usually 'cello) and keyboard. After 1730, the instrumentation used most frequently was strings, two oboes, two horns, and basso continuo; this combination became the standard Pre-Classical orchestra. Occasionally, a piece would call for flutes instead of oboes, but not for oboes *and* flutes, since it was common for the same persons to play both instruments. Of course, composers wrote for whatever combination of instruments was at their disposal; this might be only strings with basso continuo, and the number of strings might be as few as three or four.

The number of independent symphonies known to have been written between 1730–40 is quite small. Among the few composers making substantial contributions to the repertoire during that decade were G. B. Sammartini (1701–75) in Milan and J. G. Harrer, who was then working in Dresden. Harrer had studied in Italy; most of his works, vocal as well as instrumental, are Italianate and Pre-Classical in style. He wrote at least 27 symphonies. None of his music was published during his lifetime, and, as of 1988, no modern edition of Harrer's symphonies had been published.

Sammartini is credited with the earliest datable concert symphony using rudimentary but recognizable sonata form; however, this *sinfonia* was originally the overture to his opera *Memet* (1732). He wrote some two-movement symphonies (fast-minuet) but usually constructed his symphonies in three movements: the first movement in sonata form or an approximation thereof; the slow, lyrical second movement characterized by expressive chromaticism and *galant* ornamentation; and the third movement—truly a Finale—either in concise sonata form or a minuet in $\frac{3}{4}$ meter. Sammartini recognized the functional difference between an opera overture (which prefaces a larger work) and a concert *sinfonia* (complete in itself), and he designed the symphony Finale so that it would bring the multimovement work to an impressive conclusion (DWMA142). Sammartini's early symphonies are scored for strings and basso continuo and are thin-textured. Several of them might be called orchestral trio sonatas, or trio symphonies. In most of the 37 symphonies he wrote between c. 1740–58, he included either two trumpets or two horns. His 12 late symphonies (c. 1759–74) are Classical in style, with independent parts for the two oboes, and with 'cello and bass often separated (instead of doubling each other and the basso continuo). Sammartini's influence on W. A. Mozart's symphonies, particularly the slow movements, is apparent.

Though sonata form eventually became the accepted (and expected) structural pattern for the first movement of a symphony, many of the early *sinfonie* used other forms, such as binary, rounded binary, or exposition-recapitulation (no development). In fact, pure sonata form rarely occurs. Rather, within the basic outlines of that form, there were many variants.

Composition of concert symphonies in the Italian style spread into other areas of Europe by Italians who secured positions outside Italy and by northern European composers who returned to their native lands after studying or working in Italy for a time. Occasionally, composers wrote four-movement symphonies, with a minuet or gigue-like finale. After 1740, the symphony gradually supplanted the Baroque concerto as the leading form of concerted instrumental music and has retained that status in the succeeding centuries. In 1760, Parisian music publishers listed in their catalogs more symphonies than either concerti or string quartets.

Other composers whose works were important in the early history of the symphony include Italian opera composers Nicolò Jommelli, who worked at Stuttgart, and Baldassare Galuppi; Johann Stamitz at the Mannheim court; J. G. Graun and C. P. E. Bach at the Prussian court and later at Hamburg; Georg Monn and G. C. Wagenseil at Vienna; L. G. Guillemain and F.-J. Gossec in Paris (fig. 18.5).

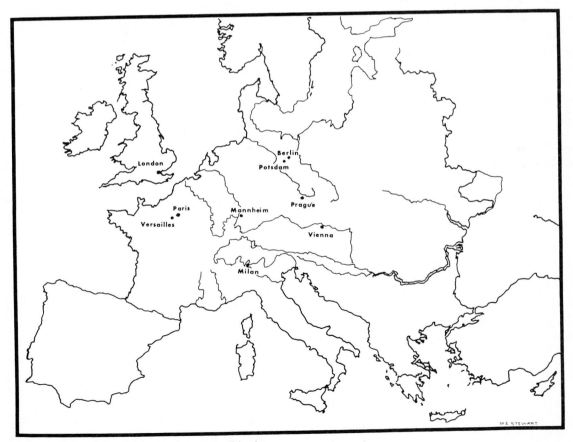

Figure 18.5 The principal centers of symphony composition in the eighteenth century.

Eighteenth-Century Pre-Classical Music

Mannheim

Mannheim was founded in 1606 as a fortress and supported virtually no musical life before 1720. The choice of Mannheim as Electoral center was unexpected—the result of political and physical circumstances. In 1718, when Karl Philip became Elector Palatine (r. 1718–42) and transferred his court from Innsbruck to Heidelberg, he found Heidelberg Castle in deplorable condition, having suffered considerable damage during the War of the Spanish Succession (1701–14). The Elector sought more favorable surroundings, and on 18 November 1720, moved his entire court to Mannheim. His retinue included 53 musicians, who had followed the Elector from his previous courts at Breslau, Innsbruck, and Düsseldorf. Music at Karl Philip's court consisted of concerts and church music; there was no opera until a suitable theater was constructed in the palace in 1742. (That opera house, described as one of the most beautiful of its time, was destroyed during the seige of 1795.) Karl Philip died on the last day of 1742 and was succeeded by his granddaughter's husband, Prince Karl Theodor (b. 1724; r. 1743–99).

Elector Karl Theodor maintained his court at Mannheim until 1778; then, when he became Elector of Bavaria also, merged the Mannheim court chapel with that at Munich, his new location. Several factors contributed to Mannheim's rise to prominence as a center of music. (1) The Palatinate was at peace while its court was at Mannheim. (2) Karl Theodor was a performing musician, as well as patron of science and the arts. He played several instruments well and enjoyed playing chamber music with members of his *Hofkapelle*. During his tenure, the size of the court chapel increased considerably. (3) Johann Stamitz (1717–57), a virtuoso violinist and an excellent teacher who had joined the *Hofkapelle* c. 1741, soon was promoted to *Konzertmeister*. Stamitz was a strict disciplinarian who insisted that every instrumentalist be properly trained and perform with the utmost accuracy and precision. To this end, he himself taught some of the string players. After Stamitz's death, his successor, Christian Cannabich (1731–98), was even more pedantic. (4) Most of the musicians at the Mannheim court were exceptional in that they were virtuoso soloists as well as superb ensemble players. Many were also excellent composers.

Example 18.6 (*a*) The "Mannheim roll." (*b*) The "Mannheim rocket."

The orchestra at Mannheim became the largest and finest in Europe. In 1756, Stamitz had at his disposal 56 instrumentalists: 20 violins, 4 violas, 4 'celli, 2 double basses, 4 horns, 4 flutes, and pairs of oboes, bassoons, and timpani, as well as 12 trumpets. Two clarinets were added in 1758. The ensemble was famous for precision of attack, uniform bowing in the string sections, and the ability to produce the slightest dynamic nuances. Among the effective special effects that brought acclaim to the orchestra were (a) extended crescendos and diminuendos, ranging from softest *pianissimo* to loudest *fortissimo*, (b) unexpected general pauses that created great windows of silence, (c) measured tremolo, (d) the "roll," scale passages in measured tremolo, coupled with crescendo (ex. 18.6a), and (e) the so-called Mannheim rocket (*Raketen*), the rapid upward arpeggiation of a chord over a wide range (ex. 18.6b). Discipline lay at the heart of the orchestra's fine performances. Stamitz, Konzertmeister as well as conductor, controlled the ensemble with slight movements of his bow, a nod of his head, or a glance.

Johann Václav Anton Stamitz

Stamitz (1717–57) received his early musical training from his father and attended the Jesuit Gymnasium in Jihlava, Bohemia. The Bohemian Jesuit schools produced some of the foremost musicians in Europe at that time. In 1734, Stamitz entered Prague University but studied there for only a year. His whereabouts between 1735 and 1741 are unknown; presumably, he was concertizing as virtuoso violinist. In 1741, he was employed as a string-instrument player at the Mannheim court. Soon, he was promoted to first violinist, then to Konzertmeister, and in

1750 was awarded the newly created post of Director of Instrumental Music. Under his direction, the Mannheim orchestra became the most renowned ensemble of the time.

In August 1754, Stamitz went to Paris for a performance of one of his symphonies at *Concert spirituel.* He lived and worked at La Pouplinière's palace, and performances of his works—symphonies, orchestral trios, a Mass—met with great success. Stamitz returned to Mannheim in autumn, 1755, and worked at the Electoral court until his death, at age 39.

Stamitz composed chamber music, concertos, symphonies, orchestral trios, cantatas, and liturgical music, including at least one Mass. He wrote no solo keyboard works or operas. His symphonies and ten orchestral trios are his most important works; approximately 60 of his symphonies are extant. His early symphonies are scored for strings with basso continuo; occasionally, he included two horns. In later works, he used two horns, two oboes *or* two flutes, and in 5 of the symphonies, two trumpets and timpani. There were clarinets in La Pouplinière's orchestra, and Stamitz included two clarinets in some of the symphonies he wrote in Paris.

For the most part, Stamitz reenforced what the Italians were doing in the transference of *sinfonia* as opera overture to *sinfonia* as concert symphony. His principal innovation in symphonic writing is his adoption of the four-movement structural plan: a fast first movement in sonata form, a slow second movement, minuet and trio third, and a Presto or Prestissimo finale. He seems to have been the first composer to use that formal design consistently; it occurs in more than half of his extant symphonies and in nine of his orchestral trios. Often, the first movements have two themes, with presentation of the second theme assigned to winds. Since there were excellent wind-instrument players at Mannheim, Stamitz treated winds independently much of the time, rather than having them double string parts. As might be expected, Stamitz's symphonies contain all of the Mannheim mannerisms—dynamic surprises and nuances, melodic sighs, the "roll," the "rocket."

Representative of Stamitz's symphonic writing is *Sinfonia a 8* in D major (*La Melodia Germanica*, No. 1; written c. 1755; DWMA143). It is scored for two horns, two oboes, strings, and basso continuo; 'cellos and double basses play the basso continuo line. (Since double basses are transposing instruments, this produces octaves.) In this four-movement work, the second movement is in A major; the others are in D major. Movements I, II, and IV are longer than most Pre-Classical symphony movements, and Stamitz's orchestral technique is more advanced than that found in most symphonies at this time. The first movement (Presto, Common meter) commences with three hammer strokes on the tonic sounded by full orchestra, followed by a flourish and the Mannheim "roll." In fact, most of the Mannheim mannerisms are present in this Presto. The movement is bithematic, violins announcing the first theme in tonic key, and oboes presenting the second theme in parallel thirds in the dominant while violins provide an A pedal in reiterated eighth notes. Melodic sighs are plentiful. The development section (24 measures long) commences with a "roll" (m. 58). In the recapitulation (m. 82), the second half of the first theme is restated, then the first half of it, and the second theme. The movement concludes with the "roll." The slow movement (Andante non Adagio, $\frac{2}{4}$, A major) is in simple binary form, with both halves repeated. The scoring, for strings and basso continuo, is reduced to three-voice writing much of the time. Tonality returns to D major for the third movement, a typical Menuet with Trio. Winds are prominent in the Trio, but in the Menuet they double string parts most of the time. The Prestissimo finale (D major, $\frac{2}{4}$) is in sonata form. In its first section, three themes are presented; new material is introduced in the short development section. A portion of the first theme is omitted from the recapitulation.

Vienna

In the eighteenth century, Vienna lay at the crossroads of European civilization. As the seat of the Holy Roman Empire, it exerted widespread cultural influence, though, much of the time, more brilliant musical performances were heard in Paris. Reputedly, Maria Theresa had a fine singing voice; however, troublesome affairs of state prohibited her from devoting much time to music, though the *Hofkapelle* was maintained and excellent composers and musicians were employed there. More important was the patronage of numerous aristocratic families, such as the Esterházy, Lobkowitz, and Lichnowsky, whose musical establishments provided a favorable climate for musical talent.

Viennese attention, during the Pre-Classical era, seems to have been directed primarily toward Italian opera and the cultivation of chamber music, though a few composers produced symphonies in profusion. One who did so was Georg C. Wagenseil (1715–77); 82 symphonies by him are extant. His symphonies were performed frequently and were disseminated internationally. Wagenseil was a native of Vienna; he was raised in the atmosphere of the imperial court, where his father and grandfather were employed. Trained by court musicians, principally J. J. Fux, Georg became an excellent keyboard player and teacher. He began to compose while in his teens, and until 1745 wrote liturgical music almost exclusively. For the next five years, he concentrated on opera; after 1756, instrumental music interested him most. His numerous keyboard sonatas and symphonies follow a three-movement scheme: fast-minuet-fast, or fast-slow-minuet. In general, the symphonies have small dimensions and three-voice texture. First movements are *galant* in style and, viewed chronologically, reflect Wagenseil's increasing command of the principles of sonata form. The slow movements of his early symphonies contain many Baroque elements, but gradually the writing becomes lighter, more delicate, more *galant*. Likewise, the finales gradually become more substantial; in the late symphonies, frequently the finale has rondo form or $\frac{2}{4}$ meter.

Georg Monn (1717–50) is ranked with Wagenseil as a leading Viennese composer of symphonies. However, Monn's works were not accorded international acclaim, as were Wagenseil's, since none of Monn's music was published during his short lifetime. He has been credited with composing, in 1740, the earliest known four-movement symphony with minuet-and-trio third movement. It is his only four-movement symphony. All of the movements—Allegro, Aria, Menuetto, Allegro—are short, and all are in D major. Monn's symphonic style is conservative. All of his symphonies have small proportions and usually exhibit trio sonata texture (no viola); he seldom included horns, and many of his themes are motivic.

František Xaver Dušek (1731–99), Bohemian composer, pianist, and teacher, received his early musical training at a Jesuit Gymnasium, then studied with Wagenseil in Vienna. Around 1770, he returned to Prague, where his home became an important center of musical life and a gathering place for foreign musicians visiting Prague. Dušek was one of the most important native Bohemian composers of secular music in the last half of the eighteenth century. Among his extant works are 20 string quartets and 40 symphonies that vary stylistically from *galant* to Classical. In his three-movement symphonies, the order of movements is fast-slow-fast; in the four-movement ones, and in most of the string quartets, a fast-slow-minuet-fast pattern is followed. First movements are bithematic, in sonata form, with brief development sections; a few finales are extensive rondos. Occasionally, Dušek's melodies contain Bohemian idioms.

Paris

In Paris, between c. 1723 and 1789, music was dominated by opera. At those times when religious regulations forbade theatrical presentations, public concerts were scheduled by the *Concert spirituel*. In addition, concerts were given almost every day somewhere in or near Paris at some patron's home. The *Opéra* orchestra, which averaged 48 members, performed at *Concert spirituel* and gave private concerts in homes of aristocrats who did not have their own ensembles. The *Concert spirituel* was one of the central institutions in Parisian nonoperatic life. Important local musicians and visiting artists often performed their own compositions there. The journey from Mannheim to Paris could be made with relative ease, and composers from the Mannheim court frequently appeared at *Concert spirituel*.

Louis-Gabriel Guillemain (1705–70) seems to have been the first Parisian to compose symphonies. Guillemain, a violinist, studied with G. B. Somis in Italy, then returned to Paris in 1737 to become one of the highest paid and most popular musicians at the court of Louis XV. Guillemain wrote only instrumental music, largely sonatas or trio sonatas for violin(s). His 12 symphonies are extant: *VI Symphonies dans le goût italien en trio,* Op. 6 (6 trio symphonies in Italian style; 1740) and *Second livre de*

François-Joseph Gossec. Lithograph made by J. Boilly in 1820.

symphonies . . . en trio, Op. 14 (Second book of trio symphonies . . . ; 1748). As the titles state, these are trio symphonies (for two violins and basso continuo), Italianate and *galant* in style. They follow the three-movement fast-slow-fast scheme, with each of the fast movements clearly in sonata form, though their developments are minimal.

The most important symphonist working in Paris after 1756 was François-Joseph Gossec (1734–1829). Gossec came to Paris from the Netherlands (from a Walloon area now in Belgium) in 1751, with a letter of introduction to Rameau, who was then directing La Pouplinière's orchestra. A vacancy in the orchestra had just occurred, and Gossec was hired immediately to play violin and bass. He worked for La Pouplinière until 1762. There, Gossec played under Stamitz's direction in 1754 and became acquainted with compositions of the Mannheim school.

Gossec was a prolific composer of all kinds of music. He wrote approximately 50 symphonies, of which 47 survive. Between 1756 and 1762, he composed 25 symphonies (4 sets of 6, plus 1 individual work). His *Symphonie in D* (1761) is one of the first orchestral works in France to use clarinets. Gossec favored the clarinet and did a great deal to promote its use.

Gossec began writing for theater in 1757, and he concentrated on composing opera after La Pouplinière's death (1762). In 1769 Gossec founded the *Concert des Amateurs* (Music-lovers' concerts), supported by public subscription; only instrumental music was performed at those concerts, and Gossec wrote some symphonies for them and conducted some. He was the first to conduct a Haydn symphony in France (1772). The symphonies Gossec composed after his Op. 3 (the first set of 6) are four-movement works, with Menuet. The sonata-form fast movements are bithematic, and his writing contains Mannheim mannerisms. It is surprising that Gossec did not include trombones in any of his symphonies, especially since he used trombones in his operas and liturgical music.

During 1773–77, Gossec was one of the three directors of *Concert spirituel*. He continued to compose for *L'Opéra* and served as one of its directors until 1784. That year, *L'École Royale de Chant* (Royal Singing School) was established, as part of *L'Opéra,* and Gossec became its director. Between the time of his appointment and the outbreak of the French Revolution, his only compositions were six symphonies.

Gossec was very supportive of the Revolution. He resigned his post at *L'Opéra* in order to direct the *Corps de Musique de la Garde Nationale* (National Guard Band). He and other composers sympathetic with the aims of the Revolution created an extensive repertoire of patriotic works for outdoor performance by huge massed ensembles. Gossec's *Hymne à l'Être Suprème* (Hymn to God; 1794) was performed, under his direction, by a chorus of 2400, accompanied by an orchestra of 1600. Gossec was made a Chevalier of the Legion of Honor soon after that order was created (1804).

When the Paris Conservatoire was established in 1795, Gossec was named one of its five Inspectors, as well as Professor of Composition. He and others on the composition and voice faculties formulated the courses of study in composition and singing used there. In 1816, Gossec resigned from his posts at the Conservatoire and lived in retirement until his death, at Passy, in 1829.

Gossec made major contributions to the development of music in France by promoting use of the clarinet, providing a vast repertoire of military wind ensemble music, helping establish the Paris Conservatoire and creating instructional materials for its curriculum, as well as by composing symphonies. Beethoven and Berlioz knew Gossec's works and were influenced by them.

Treatises

Around the middle of the eighteenth century, several important treatises concerning performance practices were written by men who were recognized as outstanding performers, teachers, and composers. J. J. Quantz's *Versuch einer Anweisung die Flöte traversiere zu spielen* (see p. 445) was translated into French and published simultaneously in Berlin and Paris in 1752. The following year, C. P. E. Bach's *Versuch über die wahre Art das Clavier zu spielen* was published in Berlin. Leopold Mozart's *Versuch einer gründlichen Violinschule* (Essay on the fundamental principles of violin playing) appeared in Augsburg in 1756; and in Paris in 1771 P. Denis published Giuseppe Tartini's *Traité des Agrémens de la Musique* (Treatise on ornaments in music). These writings provide valuable information not only about playing flute, keyboard, and violin, but about the proper performance of all kinds of eighteenth-century music. All of these treatises were available in English translation, as well as in their original languages, in 1987.

Giuseppe Tartini

Giuseppe Tartini (1692–1770), composer, theorist, performer, and teacher, was the most renowned Italian violinist in mid-eighteenth century. He was especially noted for the perfection of his bowing technique. Violinists from all over Europe were attracted to his "School of the Nations" at Padua, where he taught advanced violinists by the lecture method. Among his pupils were the prominent violinists and com-

Giuseppe Tartini. Oil portrait by unknown artist. (*Conservatorio Musicale G. B. Martini, Bologna.*)

posers Pietro Nardini (1722–93), Signora Maddalena Lombardini-Sirmen (1735–c. 1786), Pierre de la Houssaye (1735–1818), and Giovanni Francesco Nicolai (leading violinist in Rome in 1770). Signora Sirmen, who had a brilliant career in Paris, continued her studies by correspondence; a lesson-letter Tartini wrote to her in March 1760 has been published many times.

Several of Tartini's students copied his *Regole per arrivare a saper ben suonar il Violino* (Rules for learning to play the violin well); French and Italian manuscript copies are extant. Tartini himself never published this treatise, but after his death Pietro Denis published it in French (1771). A modern multilingual edition entitled *Traité des Agréments de la Musique* was published in 1961. The treatise, whose rules for ornamentation are applicable to both vocal and instrumental music, was in existence before 1756; Leopold Mozart pirated large portions from it for his essay on violin playing.

Figure 18.6 Title page of Maddalena Lombardini-Sirmen's *Six Sonates,* from an undated early edition published at The Hague.

Tartini wrote several other theoretical treatises, at least two of which were published. His accompanied violin sonatas and virtuosic violin concertos—approximately 135 of each—and numerous *sinfonie* considerably enriched the repertoire. Tartini's concertos follow the three-movement fast-slow-fast pattern used by Vivaldi, with the slow movement in a related key. After 1740 Tartini began to combine ritornello with binary form for the outer movements; Nardini expanded the form in the first allegro to an approximation of sonata form. In his music Tartini blended elements of *style galant* and *empfindsamer Stil* with northen Italian characteristics; his works are predominantly Pre-Classical in style.

Leopold Mozart

Leopold Mozart (1719–87) was born in Augsburg and received his education at the Gymnasium and Lyceum of the Jesuit school there. After earning a baccalaureate degree in philosophy at the Benedictine university in Salzburg, he rejected his parents' plan that he become a priest and chose to study music. As his capabilities increased, so did his reputation; ultimately he became deputy Kapellmeister to the Prince-Archbishop of Salzburg. In November 1747 Mozart married Anna Maria Pertl (1720–78). When it appeared that their children Maria Anna and Amadeus were prodigies, Leopold jeopardized his own career to promote theirs. His career was at its height in 1760, but the children's concert tours and Amadeus's career took him away from his court post often, and he had little time for musical composition.

In 1756 Mozart published his *Versuch einer gründlichen Violinschule,* an important source on eighteenth-century performance practices and musical taste. Mozart incorporated many of the ideas of "a well-known Italian violinist" (Tartini) in his essay. The book circulated widely in France and Germany, was reprinted many times, and was published in a modern English translation in 1948.

Music in America

In Spanish colonies in the New World, from the first days of colonization, missionaries had paid special attention to the importance of music in converting the natives to the Catholic faith. It is not surprising, therefore, that in the eighteenth century the Catholic Church was the most important cultural, economic, social, and political influence. In New Spain (Mexico) the principal centers of musical activity were the large cathedrals—Mexico City Cathedral, Puebla Cathedral, and the Cathedral of Valladolid (now Morelia) in the province of Michoacán. Almost all of the music that has survived from the eighteenth century is sacred, a good deal of it with instrumental accompaniment, which would indicate that, at least in composed music, sacred music predominated. A number of instrumentalists—more strings than winds—are listed on cathedral rosters.

Some secular and some purely instrumental music was written, however. One manuscript of purely instrumental music is extant from the eighteenth century. Entitled *Tablatura de vihuela* (Vihuela music), it contains vihuela transcriptions of some of Corelli's trio sonatas, a sonata by Samuel Trent (about whom nothing is known), and approximately 50 types of dance music, including *seguidilla, jota, folia española,* and many others.

Figure 18.7 Location of the principal centers of musical activity in New Spain.

cate, there must have been a local orchestra (at either the school or the church) capable of performing them.

Eighteenth-century music in South American colonies is meager, and, to date, all of the compositions that have been located are sacred music. In the North American colonies, music by European composers was enjoyed early in the century, but art music by native-born American composers did not appear until after 1750.

The second opera known to have been composed in the New World, *La Parténope,* by Manuel de Zumaya (c. 1678–1756), was performed at New Spain's viceroyal palace on 1 May 1711. Unfortunately, only the libretto survives. Zumaya, a native of Mexico, received his musical training as a choirboy at Mexico City Cathedral. He became a priest c. 1700, was appointed one of the three organists at the cathedral in 1708, and in 1715–39 served as *maestro di capilla* there. From 1739 until his death, he was *maestro di capilla* at the cathedral in Oaxaca, his native city.

At Valladolid, the *Colégio de Santa Rosa,* a convent for orphan girls, was founded in 1738. In connection with the *Colégio,* an *escoleta de música* (school of music) was founded c. 1740 and flourished. Daily music lessons were included in the curriculum at the convent. In the *Colégio* archives are several pieces of instrumental music in manuscript, among them two *sinfonias* in Pre-Classical style, each scored for violin I, violin II, viola, bass, two oboes, and two horns. The *Obertura* in D major by Antonio Sarrier (unknown) has three movements: an Allegro, bithematic, in sonata form; a lyrical Andante, in binary form; and a *Fuga* marked Presto. The other *obertura* is by Antonio Rodil (also unknown). If these *oberturas* were performed at the convent, as the presence of the music in the *Colégia* archives seems to indi-

Summary

During the eighteenth century, the political and cultural complexion of Europe changed considerably. The "Enlightenment," a humanitarian movement, placed emphasis on reason and on knowledge gained through proper empirical education. Science, rationalism, and freedom advanced considerably. Freemasonry spread throughout Europe and to America. The rise of a more or less independent spirit, leading from accordance of divine right to kings to a belief in human rights and brotherhood, culminated in revolution in France and in North America.

The general rise of the middle class to an influential position brought changes in musical activities, too. As music printing increased, music for amateur use flooded the market, especially tutors for learning to play an instrument, books of songs, and keyboard music. Music journals containing all kinds of music news (and some music) were issued more or less regularly. After 1720, public concerts of nontheatrical music were performed frequently in many of the larger European cities; in the 1730s some European musicians concertized in the American colonies.

The term "Pre-Classical" comprises those styles of eighteenth-century music that led to and were absorbed into the "Classical" style of Mozart and Haydn: *style galant, empfindsamer Stil,* and the latter's extension into *Sturm und Drang. Galant* music is light, graceful, elegant homophonic music, characterized by simple melodies, short phrases, uncomplicated harmonies, and a slower harmonic rhythm than that used in the Baroque era. Lest static harmonies become boring, murky and Alberti basses were used. At its peak, *style galant* employed ornaments in moderation, an abundance of appoggiatura sighs, Lombardic rhythms, melodic triplet sixteenth notes, and fussy dynamic contrasts. In northern Germany after c. 1750, the *galant* was given new expressiveness and became *empfindsamer Stil*, the sensitive style. Its principal exponent was C. P. E. Bach, whose music is finely nuanced, with periodic melodies constructed in short phrases and supported by light-textured harmonic accompaniment. *Sturm und Drang* resulted when the emotional expressions and contrasts of *Empfindsamkeit* were sharpened and intensified to become passionate outbursts and dark, stormy moods. *Sturm und Drang* was most effective in opera.

Some formal patterns preferred by Baroque composers remained in favor: strophic songs, *da capo* arias, ritornello concerto movements, binary form. New forms emerged: the cavatina and sonata form. Sonata form evolved as composers expanded and modified binary form. Gradually, the Baroque *sonata da chiesa* was supplanted by the multimovement sonata, which at first was written principally for solo keyboard. The first real flowering of the Pre-Classical sonata for keyboard came after c. 1735, with the works of Domenico Scarlatti, Alberti, C. P. E. Bach, and many lesser-known Italian and French composers. Some early sonatas had only two movements, but after 1740 most sonatas followed a three-movement scheme: Allegro, lyrical Andante, dancelike Finale. As used by Pre-Classical composers, sonata form, the constructional principle of a single movement, was an expanded and modified rounded binary form. Usually, the first movement of a multimovement sonata was in sonata form.

The formal structure of the concerto for solo instrument and orchestra that Vivaldi established was followed by Pre-Classical composers. J. S. Bach created the concerto for solo harpsichord and string orchestra when he transcribed and adapted for harpsichord some of Vivaldi's concerti. Bach's sons contributed much to the development of the solo keyboard concerto—Emanuel Bach's concerti influenced Joseph Haydn; J. C. Bach's influenced Amadeus Mozart. J. C. Bach was the first to adopt the piano for public performance and to publish piano concerti.

C. P. E. Bach was one of the four principal composers active during the last half of the eighteenth century. (The others were Gluck, Haydn, and Mozart.) Emanuel Bach, a prolific composer, contributed largely to vocal as well as instrumental music literature. He composed many keyboard sonatas and concerti and was one of the principal symphonists of the north German school.

The concert symphony was a direct outgrowth of the Italian opera overture (*sinfonia*). Significant contributions to the development of the independent symphony were made during 1730–40 by G. B. Sammartini, who is credited with the earliest datable concert symphony using rudimentary but recognizable sonata form. He usually constructed his symphonies in three movements: a fast first movement in sonata form; a slow, lyrical second movement characterized by expressive chromaticism and *galant* ornamentation; and a finale designed to bring the multimovement composition to an effective close.

The cosmopolitan atmosphere of the age fostered spread of the Italian concert *sinfonia* northward into Europe. Important centers of symphony composition existed at Mannheim, Vienna, Paris, and Potsdam; composers making notable contributions to the development of the concert symphony include J. Stamitz, C. P. E. Bach, Monn, Wagenseil, Guillemain, and Gossec. Most of the Pre-Classical symphonies were constructed in three movements; occasionally, four movements were written, with the last movement usually a minuet or a gigue. Under Stamitz's direction, the Mannheim court orchestra became the finest in Europe; some orchestral performance practices Stamitz instigated have become standard and are still observed.

Music was an important influence in Spanish colonies in the New World and was included in the curriculum in cathedral and convent schools. Though most of the composed music was sacred and vocal, orchestral instruments were used in concerted works as well as for accompaniment, and some purely instrumental music was written. Two surviving Pre-Classical concert *sinfonie* indicate that, at least in Mexico, composers were aware of symphonic developments in Europe.

Several important treatises by Pre-Classical composers provide valuable information concerning performance practices of the time: Quantz's essay on flute playing, Leopold Mozart's book on violin playing, C. P. E. Bach's essay on playing keyboard instruments, and Tartini's treatise on ornaments.

Vocal Music

Italian Opera

The Arcadian neoclassical reform that occurred in Italian literature in the late seventeenth century effected some changes in the structure of the Italian opera libretto. In the area of drama, literary neoclassicists were concerned primarily with the purity of dramatic types, the purposes of drama, the concepts of decorum and verisimilitude, and the observation of the three unities of time, place, and action. Neoclassicists recognized only two kinds of drama as legitimate forms—tragedy and comedy—and insisted that there be no mixing of tragic and comic elements in a drama; each form had its own rules with regard to type of plot, characters, and style. However, literary reformers were only partially successful in their attempts to subject opera libretti to such strict regulation, for the amorous intrigues common to opera plots often involved a mixture of character types.

When the libretto was purged of comic elements, *opera seria* (serious opera) resulted. Usually, *opera seria* plots were based on heroic stories dealing with affairs of state, the downfall of rulers, or similar events, and included a conflict of passions. Almost always, by the end of the opera the main characters had been extricated from their dilemmas. The poetic style was lofty. Apostolo Zeno (1668–1750) was a leader in the pan-Italian Arcadian movement. He and contemporary poets observed the three unities, decreased the number of arias in an opera, and considered carefully the function of those arias and their placement within the opera. In 1718 Zeno became court poet to Emperor Charles VI but accepted that appointment under the condition that he not be required to write comedy or occasional poetry. When Zeno retired in 1729, Pietro Metastasio (1698–1782) succeeded him at court.

Metastasio

Metastasio became the greatest Italian dramatist and poet of his era. Because he encountered no serious rivals, he was able to shape and dominate *opera seria*, though his most important libretti were written before 1740. During the eighteenth and early nineteenth centuries, his 27 three-act heroic opera libretti were set more than 800 times by different composers. In the late 1720s, Metastasio carried opera libretto reform to fruition by standardizing *opera seria* format. Actually, he was aided by circumstances. Economic conditions at Italian opera houses could not support large expenditures for spectacle, so extravagant *divertissements* were out of the question. Casts were smaller, and there were only three acts, with fewer scene changes. Generally, Metastasio's cast numbered six or seven characters, the trio of principals being *primo uomo* (leading man, a castrato), *prima donna* (leading lady, a soprano), and a tenor (as father, king, mentor, or in some similar role); and secondary characters including *secondo uomo* (also a castrato), *seconda donna,* and whoever else was requisite to the plot. Frequently, a "magnanimous tyrant"—a favorite character in the eighteenth century—was included.

Though Metastasio always considered music an accessory to his dramas, the fact that his poetry was set to music exercised considerable influence on the structure and style he used. The libretto settled into an alternation of unrhymed recitative (to propel the narrative) and strophic aria (for commentary, reaction, and reflection). Occasionally, a duet was inserted; larger ensembles were rare. After presenting the overture, the orchestra had little to do except accompany the singers. Most recitatives were *secco,* with minimal harmonic support supplied by the usual basso continuo duo; only at points of heightened dramatic action was *recitativo accompagnato* used. Musical interest was centered in the arias. Italian singers were the finest in Europe. Excellent training had given them absolute control over their voices, so they were able not only to sing simple melodies beautifully but also to embellish such melodies properly and with virtuosity. The talents of certain singers attracted the public to attend opera performances repeatedly. Thus, both librettist and composer were encouraged to concentrate on arias.

Judiciously, Metastasio distributed the arias within the opera in accordance with the importance of the characters (apportioning them with discretion so as not to provoke an unwritten scene between jealous singers) and positioned an aria at the end of a scene, usually culminating in the singer's exit. The poet skillfully varied the verse, at times leading the audience to expect an action other than that which ultimately resulted. It was the composer's task to ascertain that successive arias differed to some degree in musical style. Almost invariably, composers set arias in *da capo* form, but within that basic ABA outline, considerable variance was possible. The A and B sections might be of equal length, or the B section might be quite short. Tonally and melodically, an aria might resemble a rounded binary, with the A section cadencing on the dominant and the B section commencing in that tonality with an inversion of the melody. Or, the orchestral introduction might be treated as a ritornello, recurring between phrases or couplets of the text. By c. 1760, some composers were writing arias with a tonal plan that approximated sonata form: the first A section functioning as exposition and cadencing in the dominant, the B section serving either as contrast or as development and moving farther afield tonally, and the return of the A section being treated as recapitulation. In any case, the *da capo* pattern provided ample opportunity for a singer to improvise ornaments on the return of the A section and permitted the insertion of a long virtuosic cadenza just prior to the final cadence.

Concentration of musical interest in the aria gave rise to numerous abuses. Many singers, capitalizing on personal popularity, arbitrarily demanded that poets and composers include additional arias and alter others to provide greater opportunity for virtuosic

Figure 18.8 Title page of the composer Benedetto Marcello's satire *Il teatro alla moda.*

display. If their demands were not met, singers substituted arias for which they were famous, regardless of the musical and dramatic unsuitability and the ethical impropriety of such action. Sometimes the *da capo* section of an aria was embellished to extremes. Critics and some composers decried the rampant abuses but their words of condemnation had no immediate effect. Joseph Addison's (1672–1719) essays in *The Spectator* (London, c. 1711–12) and composer Benedetto Marcello's (1686–1739) satire *Il teatro alla moda* (The fashionable theater; Venice, c. 1720; fig. 18.8) point out specific instances of operatic abuses. Important reforms were not forthcoming until the mid-1740s, when *empfindsamer Stil* and middle-class ideas were becoming influential.

In the late 1720s and early 1730s, opera composers began to use the new *galante* (Italian; French, *galant*) style—music with periodic melodies, lightly accompanied, presented in a manner that aimed to be immediately pleasing. Leonardo Vinci (c. 1690–1730) seems to have been the first to do so; his melodies are simple and fresh, yet elegant. He made no attempt to portray musically (by means of affect) the emotional state of the character singing an aria. He was one of the first to write, in ritornelli, arpeggiated figures propelling upwards in a crescendo in the manner of the so-called Mannheim rocket figure. Other composers working in Italy at this time and beginning to use *galante* style in operas include Nicola Porpora (1686–1768), Johann Adolph Hasse (1699–1783), and Giovanni Battista Pergolesi (1710–36). Vinci, Pergolesi, and Hasse all set Metastasio's *Artaserse* in distinctively different ways (as did countless later composers).

Pergolesi

Both *galante* and the older style of opera are present in the work of Pergolesi. His setting of Metastasio's *Adriano in Siria* was commissioned by King Carlos of Naples (r. 1734–59) for performance on his mother's birthday, 25 October 1734. The *primo uomo* role of Farnaspe was composed for soprano castrato Caffarelli, who had recently become a member of the king's musical chapel. Caffarelli, ranked second only to the great soprano castrato, Farinelli, was as famed for his arrogance, obstinacy, and insolence, as for his virtuosic vocal talent. Pergolesi had to alter Metastasio's libretto considerably to cope with Caffarelli's demands. Not only were the three arias assigned to Farnaspe extended, but alterations to those arias affected the number, character, and placement of arias assigned to other members of the cast. Metastasio's libretto contains 27 aria texts; Pergolesi had to omit 8 of them, and he substituted different texts for 9 others.

One of Pergolesi's finest operas is his setting of Metastasio's *L'Olimpiade,* commissioned for performance in Rome during Carnival, 1735. It contains intensely expressive, lyrical melodies structured in periodic phrases. Some scenes have no arias but are written entirely in simple (*secco*) recitative. In *L'Olimpiade,* the aria is assigned a new function—to bring the action in a scene to climax rather than summarizing it. An aria of this type requires stanzas that increase the tension, and for setting such a text *da capo* form is inappropriate. Pergolesi's treatment of *Se cerca, se dice* (If searching, asking; fig. 18.9; DWMA144) was a model for others setting that text. *Ne giorni tuoi felici ricordati di me* (In your happy days remember me), the love duet that concludes Act I, is a masterpiece of lyrical intensity. Pergolesi's instrumental writing in *L'Olimpiade* is characterized by an abundance of measured tremolo in *stile concitato,* and Lombardic rhythmic figures.

The separation of tragedy and comedy advocated by neoclassicists was observed, yet the two kinds of drama were combined when the acts of an *opera seria* were interlaced with and separated by the acts of a comic *intermezzo.* Sometimes the *intermezzo* was accorded greater acclaim than the *opera seria.* Such was the case with *La serva padrona* (The maid as mistress; 1733), which Pergolesi composed as *intermezzo* for his opera *Il prigionier superbo* (The proud prisoner; 1733). *La serva padrona,* written for three characters—a soprano, a bass, and a mute—with accompaniment by strings and basso continuo, clearly displays Pergolesi's genius for setting comic scenes and character depiction. The story concerns a clever girl who, through intrigue, rises in social status from servant to mistress in the home of a wealthy old bachelor. The plot was not new; eight years earlier, Telemann had used a similar one for his *Pimpinone.* Telemann's *intermezzo,* too, had only two singing roles and was popular as an independent comic opera.

Because *La serva padrona* originated as an *intermezzo,* it has no overture. The work opens effectively with a short aria sung by the irascible Uberto as he waits for the maid to answer his summons. His mounting anger and his frustration at her slow response are depicted through sequences rising in pitch and sustained tones that drop an octave. Serpina's first aria portrays her wit and determination and her scorn for Uberto. Most of the music is in major, but that sung by Uberto is almost always in flat keys, while Serpina's is written in sharps. Not all of the arias are *da capo.* Much of the time, the melodic line is disjunct, and, though there is much repetition of short motives, the music is never monotonous. Unexpected accents on off-beats produce comic effects. Each act concludes with an excellent duet (DWMA145).

Figure 18.9 Manuscript page of *Se cerca, se dice* from Pergolesi's opera *L'Olimpiade.* *(Source: MS 2287, Bibliothèque royale de musique, Brussels.)*

Almost immediately after its première, *La serva padrona* was staged independently; soon it became a favorite with traveling opera troupes and was performed throughout Europe, reaching Paris in 1746. Performances of it there in 1752 touched off the *Querelle des Bouffons* (Bouffon War)—the controversy over relative merits of French and Italian elements in opera (see p. 467). In the twentieth century, *La serva padrona* is still popular; it takes less than an hour to perform.

Hasse

Hasse studied in Hamburg and joined the Hamburg Opera Company in 1718, as a tenor. Late in 1721 he visited Venice, Bologna, Florence, and Rome, then went to Naples, where he studied with Alessandro Scarlatti for a few years. Hasse completely assimilated the Italian operatic style and soon became one of the most successful opera and *intermezzo* composers in Naples. His *Artaserse* was produced in Venice in February 1730; *Dalisa* and *Arminio* soon followed, with mezzo-soprano Faustina Bordoni (1700–81) as *prima donna.*

Faustina and her celebrated rival, soprano Francesca Cuzzoni (c. 1698–1770), were the first *prime donne* to achieve international acclaim and were ranked among the finest singers of the era. Faustina was from an aristocratic Venetian family, and, under the guidance of Benedetto Marcello, studied singing

Faustina Bordoni. Painted by Rosalba Carriera in 1757. *(Ca' Rezzonico, Venice.)*

with M. Gasparini. In addition to her remarkable singing voice, she was endowed with acting ability, beauty, and a charming personality. During the 1720s, she sang the leading female roles in many of Handel's operas in London; in 1728–31, she sang in various cities in northern Italy. Faustina married Hasse in 1730, and for the remainder of her life her career was inseparably linked with his.

Early in 1730, Hasse was appointed Kapellmeister to the Elector of Saxony and was associated with that court for approximately 30 years. He was not restricted to Dresden by his position but could produce his operas wherever opportunities presented themselves. By 1750, Hasse was Europe's most successful opera composer. Approximately 75 of his operas are extant.

Though Hasse had set some of Metastasio's texts in the 1730s, his appreciation for Metastasio's neoclassical libretti deepened during the 1740s. Frederick the Great and Dresden court poet Francesco Algarotti (1712–64), who were enthusiastic about Metastasio's work, were largely responsible for this. As Hasse and Metastasio worked together in 1743–44, a close friendship developed between them. Hasse became Metastasio's favorite composer, justifiably, for he complied with the librettist's requests, heeded his suggestions, and composed music that complemented the poetry perfectly. Hasse set 24 of Metastasio's libretti, some more than once. The last Hasse-Metastasio collaboration was *Il Ruggiero* (1771; fig. 18.10). Its production evoked Dr. Burney's comment that Metastasio and Hasse were the two halves of a whole, each endowed with the genius, good taste, and judgment that made of one a superior lyric poet and of the other a comparable lyric composer.

In Hasse's *opere serie,* the orchestral accompaniment was (at Metastasio's suggestion) minimal and transparent. With no orchestral distractions, attention was focused on the lyricism and fluidity of the vocal line. He constructed beautiful melodies that are elegant and smoothly flowing and supported them with simple harmonies. Hasse was an excellent dramatist but disciplined his use of music for theatrical effects. He set supernatural scenes exceptionally well, and the accompanied recitatives in *Artaserse* are superb.

Figure 18.10 Scene from Hasse's opera *Il Ruggiero,* as performed in Milan in 1771. From Metastasio's *Oeuvres complète,* publ. Paris 1780/82.

Gradually, in Hasse's operas, *da capo* aria was displaced by abridged *da capo* or *dal segno* types, and by 1771 he was writing some through-composed arias, e.g., *Ho perduto il mio tesoro* (Ah, my treasure [is] lost), in *Il Ruggiero.* Also, the number of arias per opera decreased. Hasse placed an average of 30 *da capo* arias in each of the operas he composed during the 1730s; *Il Ruggiero,* his last opera, contains 16 arias, only 6 of them *da capo.*

As Hasse carried the Italian *galante*-style setting of neoclassical *opera seria* to Dresden in the 1730s, other Italian-trained opera composers transmitted that style to other courts. Nicolò Jommelli (1714–74) went to Vienna and later to Stuttgart; Tommaso Traetta (1727–79) went to Vienna and on to Mannheim.

Jommelli

Jommelli received his basic musical training as a choirboy at the cathedral in his hometown, Aversa, then studied in Naples for three years. Hasse, Leo, and other composers working in Naples during Jommelli's student years were influential in shaping his compositional style. Jommelli's career as a composer of stage works was launched with two comic operas performed in Naples in 1737; his first *opera seria,* staged in Rome in 1740, secured for him the patronage of Cardinal Henry Benedict. The following year, Jommelli moved to Bologna where his setting of Metastasio's *Ezio* was produced; more important to Jommelli's career was the lifelong friendship formed at Bologna with Padre Martini, with whom he studied for a time.

Soon Jommelli was enjoying a successful career in Italy as an opera and oratorio composer. In 1749, he was appointed *maestro coadiutore* (coadjutor master) to the papal choir in Rome and subsequently supplied that choir with a large repertoire of instrumentally accompanied liturgical choral works, principally in *concertato* style. He continued to compose operas, fulfilling commissions from a half-dozen Italian cities.

In his operas Jommelli used orchestral resources advantageously. He frequently treated first and second violins as separate textural lines, sometimes scored an independent part for viola, and used dynamic markings abundantly, especially crescendo. Orchestral innovations that often are credited (erroneously) to Stamitz and the Mannheim school—the use of a contrasting second theme in the dominant key, contrasting passages (or sections) for pairs of instruments, the "Mannheim rocket"—really originated with Jommelli in *sinfonie* composed in the 1740s. His *sinfonie* were heard in Germany before 1750 and in Paris soon thereafter.

In 1749 the Vienna court commissioned Jommelli to set Metastasio's *Achille in Sciro.* While in Vienna, he observed composers' use of ensembles and chorus scenes in their operas, and when he returned to Italy he began to incorporate ensembles in his operas and wrote more substantial final choruses. Also, in the operas he composed during the 1750s, Jommelli increased the number of accompanied recitatives and reduced the number of *secco* recitatives and arias.

Jommelli was at the height of his career in 1753. His liturgical music was sung at the Vatican, his *opere serie* were performed throughout Europe, and traveling troupes included his comic operas in their repertoires. In fact, the performances that provoked the notorious *Querelle des Bouffons* in Paris included Jommelli's *Il paratajo* (The tapestry) as well as Pergolesi's *La serva padrona.*

Several Kapellmeister positions were offered Jommelli in 1753, and he chose the one at Stuttgart. There he had almost unlimited resources and absolute control over every aspect of opera producton except choice of subject matter. Duke Karl Eugen's (r. 1737–93) interests were French-oriented; he enjoyed ballet and the elaborate staging of French operas, and he imported well-known French choreographers, including J. G. Noverre (1727–1810). At Stuttgart, Jommelli composed operas that were cosmopolitan in style, and he used orchestral resources to the fullest. Between 1755 and 1767 he increased the size of the orchestra from 24 to 47 and included pairs of winds (except clarinet) and brasses, and percussion. His treatment of instrumental music in opera changed the role of the orchestra from accompanist to equal partner with the singer.

While at Stuttgart, Jommelli composed at least two Masses, a *Miserere,* and a *Te Deum.* He had retained the right to visit Italy from time to time, and c. 1769 he returned to Naples. For the remainder of his life, he divided his time and energies between Neapolitan and Lisbon courts. Between 1769 and 1777 the royal Portuguese theaters presented at least four Jommelli operas each year.

Johann Christian Bach

Another composer of Italian *galante*-style opera who studied with Padre Martini in Bologna and worked in Naples for a time was Johann Christian Bach (1735–82), youngest son of J. S. Bach. Christian served for a short time as second organist at Milan Cathedral—he had converted to Catholicism in 1757—before turning to opera composition. After successful performances of several of his works, including settings of Metastasio's *Artaserse* (1760), *Catone in Utica* (Cato in Utica; 1761), and *Alessandro nell' Indie* (Alexander in India; 1762), Bach visited London to write operas for King's Theater. London became his home. Though he was a versatile and prolific composer, skilled at writing various forms of instrumental and vocal music in *galante* style, opera was one of his main interests. Twelve of his operas survive, all Italianate in style. Among his London productions are *Orione, ossia Diana vendicata* (Orion, or Diana avenged; 1763) and *La clemenza di Scipione* (Scipio's mercy; 1778).

In 1766 Bach met soprano Cecilia Grassi (c. 1740–82), who came to London to perform as *prima donna* in serious operas at King's Theater that season. Grassi's theatrical talent was modest; reportedly, her voice was sweet, and she sang with perfect intonation. Bach composed several cantatas for her, and during 1773–76 she performed regularly in Bach-Abel concerts. At some time after 1776, she married Bach.

Traetta

Tommaso Traetta studied in Naples in 1738–48 and began to write both comic and serious operas. During the early 1750s, he came in contact with Jommelli and contributed four arias to Jommelli's *Ifigenia in Aulide* (Iphigenia in Aulis; 1753). In 1758, Traetta was appointed to the court at Parma with the assignment of combining elements of French *tragédie lyrique* with Italian elements in opera. As his fame spread, he received commissions from Vienna, Turin, and Mannheim. Elector Palatine Carl Theodor of Mannheim desired greatly to surpass the neighboring Stuttgart court, and Traetta, with the Mannheim orchestra at his disposal, was inspired to compose excellent *sinfonie* and other instrumental music for operas.

As did Jommelli, Traetta instituted some opera reforms. He relied heavily upon orchestral color for expressive effect, wrote many accompanied recitatives, and structured arias in forms other than *da capo*, sometimes using *cavatina*. In Vienna, he was influenced considerably by Gluck's operas. For instance, Traetta's *Ifigenia in Tauride* (Iphigenia in Tauris; 1763) is noticeably indebted to Gluck's *Orfeo ed Euridice* (1762).

Enthusiasm for opera declined at Parma, and in 1765 Traetta accepted an appointment as director of the Conservatorio dell' Ospedaletto, Venice. While there, he composed conventional Italian *opere serie* for the public theaters. In 1768, he succeeded Galuppi as singing teacher and musical director of the opera at the court of Tsarina Catherine II of Russia (r. 1762–96), at St. Petersburg. For her he produced his operatic masterpiece, *Antigone* (1772), in which the influence of Gluck's *Orfeo ed Euridice* is again apparent. Caterina Gabrielli (1730–96), who had created the leading roles in several of Traetta's and Gluck's operas, was *prima donna* in this one, also. In *Antigone* Traetta repeatedly used a few easily identified motifs, e.g., a figure depicting sobbing. Such motivic repetition may have been commonplace at the time, but until that fact is proven, it must be assumed that Traetta anticipated techniques of later importance in opera.

Intermezzo

In the eighteenth century, the term **intermezzo** (pl., *intermezzi*) was used to denote a comic interlude sung between the acts of an *opera seria*. The *intermezzo* can be traced back to entertainments presented between the acts of plays during the early Renaissance. Once the curtain covering the stage set had been drawn, it could not be replaced, and the set remained exposed between acts. *Intermezzi*—then usually termed *intermedi*—covered those gaps in the dramatic performance when no one was on stage. The earliest *intermedi* consisted of music played behind the scenery and functioned merely to mark off the acts in the drama. Gradually, visible interludes were used; mimed, danced, and sung entertainments were presented between acts. At the Medici court in Florence during the early sixteenth century, costumed entertainers appeared between acts, and each interlude was designed to point up the passage of time between the action in the segments of the drama it separated. As *intermedi* became longer and more spectacular, the time element disappeared.

In the monodic operas of the early seventeenth century, *intermedi* figured prominently as divisions between acts. Moreover, some sixteenth-century *intermedi* provided subject matter for operas, e.g., Rinuccini's libretto for Peri's *Dafne*. By the end of the

Commedia dell'arte

The *commedia dell'arte* (comedy of artisans) was an actor-centered, improvised form of comic drama that appeared in Italy in the 1540s and flourished for about two centuries. The actors were professionals—skilled improvisators, endowed with imagination and ready wit and adaptable to almost any kind of audience and playing condition. Equipped with only skeletal scripts that sketched out the main turns of event in a few basic plots, they relied upon their ingenuity to flesh out comic drama suited to current conditions and the locale in which they found themselves. Use of local dialect(s) was an important feature of the presentation. Since no parts were written, the dialogue was always new and fresh.

There was a set of stock characters, most of them wearing standard costumes (now regarded as "traditional") and masks. Included were two elderly men (parent, guardian, or professionals), two *zanni* ("madcap" male servants), a maidservant, a pair of lovers, and one or two other persons, as needed. In Italy, the two lovers played unmasked and spoke in elegant Tuscan; most of the others used dialect(s). Standard guardian types were: Pantalone, a miserly old merchant, usually Venetian; *il Dottore* (the doctor), a boring and pedantic Bolognese lawyer whose lengthy speeches led one to question his learning; and Capitano—later Scaramuccio—a military adventurer or cowardly soldier who boasted of his conquests in war and love. Typical *zanni* were Pulcinella, hunchbacked and with a large nose; and Arlecchino, a nimble, witty servant but a capricious and heartless lover. Two *zanni* were characterized as witty fool and comic rustic. Columbine (dovelike, gentle), a maid, was Arlecchino's female counterpart. Once assigned a certain role, a performer always played that role and acted consistently and realistically. Female roles were played by women.

Itinerant troupes spread the *commedia dell'arte* throughout Europe. Everywhere it remained essentially the same, though some slight modifications were made. Between 1750 and 1800, the *commedia dell'arte* gradually died out. However, its use of regional dialect and its stock characters and style influenced and left their marks on ballet, *intermezzo* and comic opera, the dramas of Shakespeare and Molière, and some poetry and novels. From time to time, traces of *commedia dell'arte* have appeared in works by twentieth-century authors and composers.

---

seventeenth century, the scenic spectacles presented between acts often included the comic servants of the opera cast. Sometimes the *intermedi* were of greater interest than the drama itself.

Occasionally, in the eighteenth century, short ballets were still used as *intermezzi,* but more often, comic scenes were presented. At Naples, until c. 1720, *intermezzi* related to the subject and cast of the *opera seria* were incorporated into almost every new opera. Elsewhere in Italy, particularly in Venice, dramatically independent comic *intermezzi* were written and were set to music by the composers of the serious operas with which they were first performed. The *intermezzi* used with an opera followed a continuous plot; thus, in performance the acts of a serious opera and a short comic one were interlaced.

The *Commedia dell'arte* (Comedy of artisans), centuries old, was a model for librettists writing *intermezzi.* Borrowings from it include stock characters with their traditional names, comic antics, disguises, tricks, and regional dialects (see Insight, "*Commedia dell'arte*").

In the second quarter of the eighteenth century, the *intermezzo* entered its golden age, especially in Naples. Hasse, Pergolesi, and almost all composers working there composed some of them. Stock characters and more or less standard plots were used. One of the most common *intermezzo* plots concerns a cunning woman, cast as maidservant, widow, or shepherdess, who plays a trick on her male partner or traps him into matrimony—or both. Frequently, the lady's name is in accord with her character, for instance, Vespetta (little wasp) in Telemann's *Pimpinone* and Serpina (little snake) in Pergolesi's *La serva padrona.*

In its maturity, the *intermezzo* assumed a rather rigid musical format. The libretto, usually in two acts, was designed for two singing roles and often included one or two mute characters. Each act contained two or three *da capo* arias, separated by *secco* recitatives, and concluded with a duet. The music was homophonic, with melodies cast in short phrases and supported by simple harmonies. Not infrequently, local dialects were used for part or all of the texts. Only later, when an *intermezzo* was performed independently of the drama for which it was created, did it require an overture.

As early as 1716, itinerant troupes included *intermezzi* in their repertoire. Perhaps the most notorious performances were those given at Paris during the 1752–54 seasons by Bambini's troupe from Strasbourg, occasioning the *Querelle des Bouffons*.

Opera buffa

Opera buffa (comic opera) and *intermezzo* developed contemporaneously in the eighteenth century. *Opera buffa* is a full-length opera with a comparatively large cast of characters with singing roles. Usually, the cast included a pair of young lovers, whose plans for marriage were hindered by some misunderstanding or ban; generally, the lovers exploited their elders' foolishness to their own advantage. Other characters included professional persons whose foibles were deliberately exaggerated—a rich merchant, an unscrupulous lawyer, a bungling doctor, a clumsy servant—for, according to belief then current, comedy should instruct the audience through caricature. Often, these professional portrayals reflect the stock characters of *commedia dell'arte*. Other features of comic opera were exploitation of the bass voice, use of ensemble finale, and regional dialects. In those *opere buffe* containing both serious and comic characters, the serious characters spoke in Tuscan and the comic characters in dialect.

The earliest known full-length *opera buffa* produced in the eighteenth century was Antonio Orefice's (fl. 1708–34) three-act opera *Patrò Calienno de la Costa* (Father Calienno of Costa), written in Neapolitan dialect. It was presented at the Fiorentini Theater, Naples, on 1 October 1709. Soon Naples became a center for comic opera. At Rome, after c. 1736, comic operas were given during Carnival; in Venice they were presented regularly during opera seasons in the 1740s. Most of the early comic operas were written by composers trained in or born in Naples, such as Leonardo Vinci (c. 1690–1730), Leonardo Leo (1694–1744), and Nicola Logroscino (1698–c. 1765).

Baldassare Galuppi (1706–85), a native of Venice, was the first composer of *opera buffa* to receive international acclaim. He did so with *Il filosofo di campagna* (The country philosopher; 1754). The comic operas Galuppi composed after 1749, especially those setting the satiric fantasy libretti of Carlo Goldoni (1707–93), are especially fine. Both Leo and Logroscino used the ensemble finale, but Galuppi closed the acts of his comic operas with a kind of chain finale—a series of short sections linked together and culminating in the ensemble finale. This effect may be credited to Goldoni, who in his libretti enlarged the scope of the ensemble finale: in length, in number of participants, and in density of plot. Goldoni altered and refined comic opera in other ways, too. He increased the importance of the stage setting by creating libretti that demanded beautiful scenery. By accelerating the action and simplifying the plot, he reduced considerably the amount of recitative required and was able to increase the ensemble effects. Thus, the composer was stimulated to use a greater variety of musical forms. One of these was the **arietta,** a short, through-composed solo that was not followed by the singer's exit from stage.

It is significant that at this time, in Venice and in Vienna, it was the librettist who regulated and controlled the form of the drama and thus the form of the music. The poet distributed the musical numbers according to the requirements of the drama and the specifications of the opera director and company that was to produce the work. Rarely was a composer consulted when a libretto was being written. However, an opera director might make drastic changes in a work to suit his singers or because of the facilities available.

Commencing c. 1750, Goldoni and other poets began to create some comic opera plots that differ in character from the traditional ones—plots that are sentimental or pathetic and that sometimes contain an element of tragedy while still being basically humorous. This kind of comic opera was called *dramma giocoso* (jocular drama). Goldoni wrote three libretti of this type for the Bourbon court at Parma in 1756; one was *La buona figliuola* (The good girl), an adaptation of Samuel Richardson's novel *Pamela, or Virtue Rewarded* (publ. 1740). In its 1760 setting by Niccolò Piccini (1728–1800), *La buona figliuola* became the most popular comic opera of the decade.

Another important work of this type is Giovanni Paisiello's *Il barbiere di Siviglia ovvero La precauzione inutile* (The Barber of Seville, or The useless precaution; 1782), composed for the St. Petersburg court. Paisiello's *dramma giocoso* sets Petrosellini's adaptation of Beaumarchais's comedy (written in 1774), which dealt with current political issues semiseriously. *Dramma giocoso* attained perfection at the hands of W. A. Mozart, in *Il Don Giovanni* (1787).

Light Opera Outside Italy

In all light opera other than Italian, spoken dialogue was used instead of recitative, and in each country light opera was given its own distinctive name.

Opéra comique

The French form of light opera was called *opéra comique*. The earliest known play that interspersed spoken French dialogue with solos and duets is the pastourelle *Le jeu de Robin et de Marion* written by trouvère Adam de la Halle c. 1285. About 450 years later, entertainments of similar construction, known as *comédies mêlées d'ariettes* (plays mixed with little songs), were popular in Paris; however, in those *comédies* the dialogue was considerably expanded by bawdy jokes inserted extemporaneously by the entertainers.

From late medieval times, a type of entertainment called *sotie* (farce) was given at the two Paris *Théâtres de la Foire* (Fair Theaters) during the pre-Easter and summer seasons. Stock characters in these farces included a pretty maiden named Columbine, her lover Arlequin, the old father Cassandre, and the greedy servant Paillasse or the rascal Scaramouche. In mid-seventeenth century, these farces made extensive use of instrumental accompaniment, but after 1670 the use of music was severely restricted by Lully's royal patents.

In 1697, activities of the Comédie-Italienne were suppressed in France, and the Fair Theaters acquired their repertoire, some of which had been published. Included were comedies with considerable musical content—overtures, dances, parodies of Lully's operas, and **vaudevilles.** Originally, *vaudevilles* were strophic songs on all sorts of courtly subjects, but during the reign of Louis XIV, *vaudeville* texts became topical, satirizing court and political happenings. The popular melodies were often reused, with many different sets of words. Musically, the tunes resemble folk songs, being rather short and in a narrow range, with a persistent rhythmic pattern and with words set syllabically.

In 1707, when theatrical monopolies prevented the Fair Theaters from presenting spoken dialogues, they circumvented the restriction by miming the scenes and displaying the actors' lines on large placards. Words of the *vaudevilles* were similarly presented for group singing by the audience, and a claque was scattered through the crowd to lead the singing. Many of the songs were structured as couplets with a refrain. In 1715, publicity notices referred to these entertainments as *opéra-comique.* A year later, the Fair Theaters secured permission from the Opéra (in return for payment of 35,000 livres annually) to present "spectacles mixed with music, dances, and *symphonies* under the name Opéra-Comique."

As *opéra comique* developed, more original music was added. For several years, Rameau earned his living by writing music for the Fair Theaters. The entertainment gradually expanded, and each act concluded with a **vaudeville final**—all of the important characters were assembled on stage and each of them sang one or two verses of a *vaudeville.* Beaumarchais's drama *Le mariage de Figaro* concludes in this manner. Between 1735 and 1750, *opéra comique* was refined considerably; the rustic element was retained but much of the coarseness was removed. The ensemble finale remained an important feature of *opéra comique,* and its influence was felt in *opera seria,* e.g., Gluck's *Orfeo ed Euridice.*

Querelle des Bouffons

For decades there had been a debate on the relative merits of French and Italian music, though for a time attention had been diverted by comparison of Rameau's and Lully's operas. In August 1752, Eustache Bambini's Italian troupe performed Pergolesi's *La serva padrona* at the Académie Royale de Musique, Paris, between the acts of Lully's *Acis et Galatée.* This touched off another exchange of pamphlets, letters, and articles—the *Querelle des Bouffons.* Despite the controversy (on which Bambini and his nine colleagues did not comment), the troupe performed Pergolesi's *intermezzo* 20 more times and presented 11 other *intermezzi* before leaving Paris in March 1754. Their departure was hastened and the pamphleteering was suspended by the successful revival of two Rameau operas, *Castor et Pollux* and *Platée,* in January and February. The controversy stimulated production of *opéras comiques.* Even Jean-Jacques Rousseau (1712–78), whose involvement in the debate was pro-Italian, composed *Le devin du village* (The village soothsayer; October 1752), a one-act *intermède* with airs and couplets in French *galant* style and a *vaudeville final.* The work remained a popular favorite for about 60 years (DWMA146).

Grétry

A native of Belgium, André-Ernest-Modeste Grétry (1741–1813) dominated the field of *opéra comique* during the last half of the eighteenth century and made important contributions to the development of serious opera as well. Grétry was trained as a choirboy and violinist at the collegiate church of St. Denis in Liège, then attended the Collège de Liège in Rome (1761–65). In Italy he heard Pergolesi's *opere buffe* and began to write *intermezzi.* In 1767, Grétry moved to Paris where, after 1768, he achieved success with his *opéras comiques.* Of his more than 60 stage works two-thirds are *opéras comiques.* His works were performed throughout Europe, including Russia. One of the finest eighteenth-century *opéras comiques* and one of Grétry's greatest successes is *Les fausses apparences, ou L'amant jaloux* (False appearances, or The jealous lover; 1778).

Grétry was a master of ensemble writing and was adept at characterization. He used orchestral resources economically but effectively and wrote accompaniments that supported and emphasized the text without detracting from it. Dances are included in all of his stage works. All of these features appear in *Richard Coeur-de-lion* (Richard the Lion-hearted; 1784), which is noteworthy in several respects: (1) In it Grétry made rudimentary use of *Leitmotif* (a kind of musical label for a character, place, thing, or idea). (2) It is an early example of **rescue opera,** a forerunner of Cherubini's *Les deux journées* (The two days; 1800) and Beethoven's *Fidelio* (1805). In rescue

opera, the hero is in peril of death but is saved through the heroic endeavors of a devoted friend. Richard the Lion-hearted is rescued by his trouvère friend, Blondel. (3) Some of the airs and dialogues reflect the new romanticism entering music, e.g., the romance *Une fièvre brûlante* (A burning fever). Beethoven was acquainted with *Richard Coeur-de-lion*—he wrote a set of eight variations for piano on *Un fièvre brûlante* (1798).

During the Revolutionary period, many *opéras comiques* dealt with political and social issues of the time. *Opéra comique* flourished well into the nineteenth century and was a significant factor in the further development of opera.

Ballad Opera

Though Italian opera was performed in England over a long period of time, French opera seems to have had little influence in Britain. Grétry's *Richard Coeur-de-lion,* which was of interest primarily because of its subject matter, was presented in English translation in 1784. From time to time, some farces were given by traveling troupes from the Théâtres de la Foire. It is possible (but has not been proven) that John Gay (1685–1732) and Johann Pepusch (1667–1752) attended some performances of *comédies en vaudeville* presented in London by those Parisian companies, and from them they conceived the idea of creating a **ballad opera.** A ballad opera is a play, usually comic, in which spoken prose dialogue is interspersed with verses set to traditional tunes or currently popular melodies. In England in the eighteenth century these melodies were derived from a variety of sources, not the least of which were the "dancing-master" books then being published.

John Gay was the first English librettist to insert familiar melodies into spoken dialogue; he placed 69 such tunes within *The Beggar's Opera,* which was performed with great success in London on 29 January 1728. For this, the first English ballad opera, Johann Pepusch composed an overture and the bass lines for the tunes. The story concerns the depravity of many lower-class persons then living in London and parallels such evils as robbery and prostitution with political wiles and professional abuses. The music itself is not without political satire, e.g., the tune *Walpole* is included. Some of the roles are caricatures of politicians then active and criminals who had been executed for their crimes.

The success of *The Beggar's Opera* provided incentive for a multitude of similar works by Gay and other English authors, including Henry Fielding, Colley Cibber, Henry Carey, and Charles Coffey. Not all of the subjects were political and social; some were historical, patriotic, or mythological, usually with a satirical twist. Rarely were the composers identified; however, T. A. Arne (1710–78) wrote some. Ballad operas were performed throughout Britain and were enjoyed by all social classes, whereas Italianate opera was available only in London and only to the wealthy. The popularity of *The Beggar's Opera* was renewed in the twentieth century, when a modern version, *Die Dreigroschenoper* (The Threepenny Opera; 1928), was created by Bertolt Brecht (1898–1956), with music by Kurt Weill (1900–50). *Die Dreigroschenoper* has remained an outstanding popular success in America as well as in Europe.

One of the most significant ballad operas was Coffey's (d. 1745) *The Devil to Pay, or The Wives Metamorphosed* (1731), which influenced the north German *Singspiel*. When the Prussian ambassador to England heard a performance of *The Devil to Pay* in London in 1736, he arranged for C. W. von Brocke to translate it into German. That translation, with the English music, was performed in Berlin in 1743 under the title *Der Teufel ist los*. In 1752, a more suitable translation was made by C. F. Weisse, and new music was provided by J. C. Standfuss (died c. 1760). In 1766 the entire work was rewritten by Weisse as a *Singspiel*; some of Standfuss's music was retained and some new music supplied by J. A. Hiller.

English ballad operas were produced in the American colonies, commencing with John Hippisley's (1696–1748) *Flora, or The Hob in the Well* (1729), presented at the Courtroom, Charleston, South Carolina, on 8 February 1735, and Coffey's *The Devil to Pay*, given there early in 1736. *The Beggar's Opera* was among selections performed by a traveling troupe that visited Philadelphia and New York c. 1750. Some Americans attempted to write ballad operas c. 1770, but had little success.

Singspiel

The form of light opera that arose in north and central Germanic lands was known as **Singspiel.** In 1598 the designation *Singspiel* was applied to plays containing some music, and during the seventeenth century the term was commonly used to connote stage works containing vocal music. *Singspiel* had a variety of predecessors, including medieval mystery plays and all kinds of secular plays with music performed by traveling troupes. The latter presentations usually included a comic character whose name changed according to the area in which the performance occurred; in Germany he was called Pickelhäring or Hanswurst. Italian *commedia dell'arte* companies that traveled from place to place affected the development of *Singspiel* both directly and indirectly—directly, through their presentations in Austria and southern Germany, and indirectly, through the influence of the Comédie-Italienne on the repertoire of the Paris Théâtres de la Foire. The immediate sources of north German *Singspiel* were the French *comédies mêlée d'ariettes* and English ballad opera. Germans were aware of the popularity of ballad operas in London, and it was not long before translations and adaptations of them were on the boards in Germany.

After the Hamburg opera venture failed in 1738, the only permanently located troupe performing German-language *Singspiel* was the Hanswurst company at Vienna's Kärntnertor Theater. The comedians at that theater were the first to present true *Singspiel* and had done so from c. 1710. Their plays, given in the vernacular, contained scenes featuring peasants or servants (who used regional dialect) and included music. The members of that company were actors and actresses who could also sing; music was accessory to the comedy.

The persons most significant in the rise of *Singspiel* in northern Germany in the eighteenth century were dramatist-poet C. F. Weisse (1726–1804) and composer J. A. Hiller, who collaborated on a dozen of them. The plots usually concerned artisans or lower- to middle-class people who maintained a satirical attitude toward any who threatened their simple pastoral life; the comic element and, of course, some romantic interest were included. The dialogue was spoken in vernacular prose, with music occurring at emotional peaks. Hiller's vocal solos were fairly simple strophic songs; rarely, he inserted some recitative and an aria. Dances and marches were included, and frequently a *vaudeville final* was used.

Though Johann von Goethe (1749–1832) and other authors attempted to raise the standard of *Singspiel,* their efforts had only limited success; most composers seemed to find it difficult to combine a libretto of high quality with rather simple music that had popular appeal. The best eighteenth-century composer of *Singspiel* was W. A. Mozart. Among his contemporaries, excellent *Singspiel* music was written by Georg Benda (1722–95), Karl Ditters von Dittersdorf (1739–99), Christian Neefe, J. F. Reichardt (1752–1814), and Johann R. Zumsteeg (1760–1802). Dittersdorf and Benda were especially skilled at musical characterization, and Dittersdorf's musical humor is exceptional.

In northern Germany, the *Singspiel* gradually acquired Romantic characteristics and eventually merged with early nineteenth-century German Romantic opera. By the beginning of the nineteenth century, only slight differences remained between opera with spoken dialogue and true *Singspiel,* and the distinction is not always readily perceived. In southern Germany and Austria, farces and lighter music were preferred. In Vienna, in 1778, Emperor Joseph II instituted the German National-Singspiel, with the intention that native composers and poets would write vernacular works of high quality that would become popular. Unfortunately, despite the best efforts of director and emperor, the greatest successes were German translations of foreign works. The National-Singspiel closed in 1788.

Secular Song

Although composers throughout Europe seem to have been occupied primarily with writing operas, cantatas, oratorios, and church music, a good deal of secular song was composed. Undoubtedly, much more existed than has survived. Many of the songs written during the first half of the eighteenth century exhibit extreme simplicity. For the most part, this can be attributed to the *galant* ideals and the general high regard for sincerity, lack of affectation, and even sentimentality.

French Songs

In France, in the first half of the eighteenth century, the term **romance** was used to denote a strophic song usually recounting an ancient love story but occasionally concerning an historical event of gallantry. The melody was simple and lyrical, in a rather narrow range, the harmony thin, and the mood sentimental. Around mid-century, composers began to incorporate romances in *opéras comiques*; J.-J. Rousseau was one of the earliest to do so, in *Le devin du village* (1752). When romances were included in *opéra comique,* minimal orchestral accompaniment was provided; for solo romances only the melody and basso continuo were notated. Printed collections of romances were available before 1770. J. P. A. Martini (1741–1816), a German composer active in France, is credited with being the first in France to publish songs with complete piano accompaniment rather than basso continuo; the first of his six collections of chansons and romances appeared in 1775. In the 1780s, the romance was a popular favorite at court; reportedly, even Marie Antoinette (1755–93) composed one.

Near the end of the seventeenth century, some French poets began texting (or parodying) preexistent instrumental pieces, especially dance music, thereby creating solo songs. The practice spread to Germany, where it was taken up by university students. Albrecht Kammerer's manuscript book, dated 1715, contains dance music for keyboard, with texts added. Two decades later, such manuscript books served as direct models for Sperontes and other German poets who published collections of similar songs.

German Songs

In the last quarter of the seventeenth century, when the Italian cantata and opera became popular in Germany, selections from those kinds of works filled the published song collections. Melodies became increasingly more florid and operatic in style, and *da capo* form superseded strophic structure. Because such songs were too difficult for most amateur singers (and professionals were busy singing opera), these collections were not as popular as earlier anthologies of Lieder had been; this is reflected in the drastic decline in the number of anthologies of *Generalbass Lieder* (solo songs with basso continuo) issued during those years.

At the beginning of the eighteenth century, collections of sacred solo songs with basso continuo accompaniment became popular, but there was a dearth of secular Lieder publications. Because of this, the first three decades of the eighteenth century have been dubbed *Die Liederlose Zeit* (The Songless Era). In the 1730s conditions improved somewhat. In 1733, the first volume of J. V. Rathgeber's (1682–1750) *Tafel-Konfekt* (Table confections) appeared; it held a varied selection of crudely constructed dance songs and drinking songs. Collections of parody Lieder—piano music with incidental texts—soon followed. One of the most significant of these was assembled by Johann S. Scholze (1705–50), a German poet, who used the *nom de plume* Sperontes. The first volume in Sperontes's anthology, *Die singende Muse an der Pleisse* (The muse of song on the Pleisse [River]; 1736), contains 68 musical selections and 100 poems. It became so popular as household music that Sperontes published three additional volumes (1742, 1743, 1745), each containing 50 songs. The entire collection was revised and reissued in 1751 as a complete edition, containing 248 pieces of music with 250 poems. The keyboard pieces Sperontes selected for *Die singende Muse . . .* are minuets, polonaises, and marches written in *style galant*. In the first edition, only melody and basso continuo line were notated; Sperontes did not underlay the text but printed the poem separately, as though it were an afterthought, at the end of the keyboard music. The fact that some pieces in Sperontes's and similar parody collections were decidedly unvocal, and others caused unnatural declamation of the text, prompted the publication of critical essays establishing rules for proper composition of Lieder. In his book *Von der musikalischen Poesie* (Concerning musical poetry; 1752), Christian Krause (1719–70) stated that a *Lied*: (1) should be relatively short; (2) should have a melody resembling a folk song (*volkstümlich*), easily singable by an amateur; (3) should express the mood and meaning of the text; and (4) should have a simple accompaniment sufficiently independent that the melody could be sung without it.

Of equal significance is the fact that Sperontes's publication instigated the publication of collections of newly composed Lieder. In 1736, Johann Gräfe, a German poet for whom musical composition was an avocation, assembled a collection of 36 newly composed Lieder, entitled *Samlung . . .* (Collection . . .),

which he published the following year. The anthology was plainly intended to counterbalance and provide competition for *Die singende Muse . . .* and probably was meant also as a mild protest against texting piano music. Three additional volumes were issued (1739, 1741, 1743), each containing 36 Lieder. The songs were by various composers, including C. P. E. Bach.

After 1750, Berlin was the principal center of Lieder composition, with Franz Benda, C. P. E. Bach, and K. H. Graun the leading figures. Their songs are strophic, with text set syllabically to expressive melodies resembling folk song and with very simple keyboard accompaniment kept subordinate to the vocal line. Thus, they are in accord with Krause's recommendations and the philosophy of *empfindsamer Stil*. All of these Berlin composers are represented in *Oden und Melodien* (Odes and Melodies), a volume of Lieder published by Krause in 1753.

Johann Ernst Bach (1722–77), son of Johann Bernhard Bach (a cousin of Johann Sebastian), published one of the earliest collections of **ballads,** through-composed settings of long narrative poems, with changing moods. His *Sammlung auserlesener Fabeln* (Collection of selected stories) appeared in 1749.

A second Berlin school of Lieder composition arose c. 1770, with Johann A. P. Schultz (1747–1800), J. F. Reichardt, and C. F. Zelter (1748–1832) the chief composers. During the second half of the eighteenth century, there was a surge in Lieder composition—more than 750 collections of Lieder were published in Germany, whereas during the first half of the century only 40 collections were issued. Music journals such as *Musikalisches Wochenblatt* (Musical Weekly; Vienna) and *Der Freund* (The Friend; Berlin) included Lieder in their issues. The increase in production of Lieder continued steadily, well into the nineteenth century.

Masses and Motets

During the first half of the eighteenth century, most composers of opera wrote Masses also. Though some persons continued to write Masses in *stile antico,* the operatic style invaded much of the church music. Thus, a *stylus mixtus* (mixed style) was created, in which solos were quite florid and resembled operatic arias, and some choral sections were provided with independent orchestral accompaniment and instrumental interludes, while others were in *stile antico* with instrumental doubling of the vocal lines. Choruses with independent orchestral accompaniment were homophonic, with words set syllabically, and sometimes were structured in forms usually associated with instrumental music, e.g., French overture and incipient sonata form. It became customary for the *Amen* endings of the *Gloria* and *Credo* to be written as fugues, and often *empfindsamer Stil* was used for the *Crucifixus*. Even J. S. Bach's *Mass in B minor* is a mixture of styles, but the disparity is partly due to the fact that he originally planned only a Kyrie-Gloria Mass of the type used in Lutheran worship, then added to it. In Lutheran areas of Germany, composers continued to produce chorale-motets with vernacular texts from the Bible.

Local conditions and traditions played an important part in determining the style used for church music. In Italy, both Masses and motets were affected by the current operatic forms. In Venice, the church music that emanated from the conservatories was written mainly for female voices, with a few male voices added for choral sections. Antonio Lotti (1667–1740), organist at St. Mark's and also an opera composer, preferred *stile antico* for Masses.

The Roman Catholic areas of south Germany and Austria were strongly influenced by Italian opera. At Dresden, Hasse used a mixture of styles for choral sections and wrote solos as florid and operatic as arias, especially those for soprano (probably intended for Faustina). At the imperial court in Vienna, J. J. Fux (1660–1741), a conservative composer with strong loyalty to the traditional counterpoint of Palestrina, composed about 80 Masses. He recognized and used three distinct styles: (1) strict *stylus a cappella* (unaccompanied traditional counterpoint); (2) a *stile antico* that was not quite as strict, with vocal parts doubled by violins, trombones, and organ; and (3) *stylus mixtus*. He described all three in his treatise *Gradus ad Parnassum* (Steps to Parnassus; 1725),

which became a standard textbook on traditional counterpoint and is still influential. The treatise is written as dialogue between a student, Joseph (representing Fux), and a master teacher, Aloysius (representing Palestrina).

In France, Louis XIV and Louis XV preferred Low Mass and favored motets. Customarily, Mass in the royal chapel included three motets: a choral *grand motet* (large motet), a *petit motet* (small motet) sung at Elevation, and a motet setting of Psalm 19:10 (French Prot. 20:10), *Domine salvum fac regem* (Lord, save the king), which served as a salutation to the king and closed all Masses. A *grand motet* consisted of a psalm setting for solo voice(s), ensemble, and five-part chorus, with a five-part orchestra doubling the choral lines and providing interludes and independent accompaniment for ensembles and soloist(s). Court composer Michel-Richard de Lalande (1657–1726) wrote more than 70 *grands motets* and 7 settings of *Domine salvum fac regem* for the royal chapel. In style, a *grand motet* by Lalande closely resembles a German cantata—it contains solos (arias) and ensembles interspersed with polyphonic choruses. Lalande's *grands motets* were considered masterpieces and, after 1725, one of them was included in each program presented at the *Concert spirituel*. André Campra wrote at least 60 motets, and in 1723–41 he composed for the royal chapel 25 *grands motets* that contain both homophonic and polyphonic choruses, double fugues, virtuoso arias, and pieces with ostinato basses. French composers continued to write motets (both *grand* and *petit*) for the Versailles chapel until the time of the French Revolution.

After 1750, no continuous line of motet development can be traced. The motet never regained the prominent position it held during the Middle Ages and Renaissance.

Summary

The reform of Italian literature that effected separation of tragic and comic elements in drama caused dramatists to purge the opera libretto of comic elements, thus creating *opera seria*. Because Metastasio had no serious rivals, he was able to shape and dominate *opera seria.* The standard libretto required an alternation of recitative and *da capo* aria, with an occasional small ensemble and very little work for the orchestra. Concentration of musical interest in the arias gave virtuoso singers a measure of power that they were quick to grasp and abuse. Critics agitated for reforms that were slow in coming.

Tragedy and comedy were combined in a stage presentation when comic *intermedi* were performed between the acts of a serious opera. Sometimes an *intermezzo* achieved greater notoriety than the *opera seria,* as did Pergolesi's *La serva padrona.* Composers trained in Naples transmitted the Italian *galante*-style setting of *opera seria* to other lands—Hasse took it to Dresden, Jommelli to Vienna and Stuttgart, and Traetta to Vienna and Mannheim. Jommelli and Traetta made opera reforms that eliminated some abuses.

Opera buffa and *intermezzo* developed contemporaneously in the eighteenth century. Most of the early comic operas were written by composers trained in or born in Naples. Features of comic opera were the ensemble or chain finale, exploitation of the bass voice, and the inclusion of regional dialect(s). Gradually, poets began to write some comic opera libretti that contain elements of tragedy or that are pathetic or sentimental, while still being basically humorous—a kind of comic opera called *dramma giocoso.*

In France, light opera, known as *opéra comique,* evolved from farces and *vaudevilles* given at the Fair Theaters. Between 1735 and 1750, *opéra comique* was refined considerably, but the rustic element was retained, and the *vaudeville final* remained an important feature of the genre. Performances of Italian *intermezzi* in Paris in the 1752–54 seasons ignited and fueled the *Querelle des Bouffons* and stimulated the production of French light opera. Later, political and social issues became subject matter for *opéras comiques.* Grétry contributed to the development of both *opéra comique* and serious opera; his *Richard Coeur-de-lion* is an early example of rescue opera.

Italian opera was in vogue in London but was not a profitable business there. The success of Gay's *The Beggar's Opera* in 1728 stimulated production of ballad operas on a variety of subjects, usually mingled with satire. English ballad operas and French *comédies mêlée d'ariettes* were the immediate sources of north German *Singspiel,* though the *Singspiel* had a variety of more distant predecessors. Most significant in the rise of *Singspiel* were librettist C. F. Weisse and composer J. A. Hiller. Eventually, the north German *Singspiel* merged with early nineteenth-century German Romantic opera.

Though composers seem to have concentrated on stage works, a considerable amount of secular song was produced. In France, the romance appeared; at mid-century romances were incorporated in *opéras comiques.* Some French poets created solo songs by texting preexistent keyboard pieces; the practice spread to Germany, where, in the mid-1730s, several volumes of such songs were issued. Sperontes's *Der singende Muse . . .* and similar publications instigated the production of collections of newly composed Lieder written in *empfindsamer Stil* and put an end to the so-called Songless Era. After 1750, Berlin was the principal center of Lieder composition, with F. Benda, C. P. E. Bach, and K. H. Graun the principal composers of the first Berlin school. Hundreds of collections of Lieder were printed during the second half of the eighteenth century, and the increase in production of Lieder continued well into the nineteenth century.

Most composers of opera also wrote church music. Some continued to write in *stile antico,* but operatic style infiltrated much of the church music and created a mixed style. To a great extent, local conditions and traditions determined the style used for church music. In Italy, both *stile antico* and *stylus mixtus* were used. Catholic areas of south Germany and Austria were strongly influenced by Italian opera. In France, where the kings preferred Low Mass and motets, the *grand motet* flourished and, after 1725, became a feature of *Concert spirituel* programs. In Lutheran areas of Germany, some chorale-motets were composed; that form attained perfection with J. S. Bach. The motet never regained its former prominence in church music, and after 1750, no continuous line of motet development can be traced.

The Classic Era

During the last half of the eighteenth century, Austria, through the Hapsburg dynasty, governed much of Europe, for the Emperor and Empress of the Holy Roman Empire were also the elected heads of several other countries. As the ideas of tolerance, brotherly love, and consideration for the worth and dignity of the individual regardless of rank spread through the land, Emperor Joseph II (r. 1780–90) attempted to rectify injustices, to improve literacy by educating the people, and to promote religious tolerance. German became the official language of the empire. However, Leopold II (r. 1790–92) quickly revoked much that Joseph had decreed.

Within the Holy Roman Empire, there were numerous church states, such as Salzburg, closely allied with Rome. Archbishop Colloredo (r. 1771–1803) endeavored to institute reforms that were in accord with enlightened ideas, but he met with opposition because those reforms would have eliminated deeply rooted traditions. The Archbishop fled Salzburg a few hours before Napoleon's troops entered the city on 10 December 1800. Upon Colloredo's formal abdication in 1803, Salzburg ceased being an ecclesiastical state. Napoleon entered Vienna in 1805 but did not set up his establishment at Schönbrunn castle until 1809.

Gradually, middle-class citizens achieved greater importance politically, economically, and culturally. Interest in the arts increased. Musical amateurs sought and obtained instruction from professional musicians or published tutors; family and neighborhood music making was an essential part of life. Near the end of the century, there were many traveling virtuosi. Musically informed listeners paid admission to attend public concerts, and those who could afford to do so sometimes commissioned works. A great deal of music was composed, but much of it was lost because it was never published. "Publication" did not necessarily mean printing; publishing houses sold manuscript copies of music, too. Copyright protection was virtually nonexistent.

The church remained an important patron of music, and at monasteries music was copied and preserved in their libraries. Secular court and aristocratic patronage began to wane; musicians could no longer rely on that for total support. For most of his life, Joseph Haydn enjoyed the patronage of the Esterházy family and accepted the measure of servitude that went along with it. Mozart found such obeisance obnoxious and left the Salzburg court, but in Vienna, as an independent musician, he struggled to provide a decent living for his family. Beethoven was accepted as an independent artist-composer and was more successful financially.

Customarily, the chronological boundaries of the Classic era in music have been set at c. 1750 and c. 1825. Indeed, the roots of Classicism do extend back to 1750 (and even earlier) and tap the resources of both Pre-Classical and late Baroque styles. However,

The Classic Era

1750	1775	1800	1825

Holy Roman Emperor: 1765 ◄- - - - - - - - Joseph II - - - - - - - - ►1790–92 ◄- Francis II - ►1806
                                                            Leopold II

France: Louis XV - - - - - - - - - - - - ►1774 ◄- Louis XVI - - - - - - ►1789 French Revolution
                                                            1793–94 Reign of Terror
                                                                Napoleon ◄- - - - - - - - - ►1813
                                                                Congress of Vienna 1814–15

1775 - - - - - 1783 American Revolution

c. 1770 Classical style firmly established

by 1750 *concerto grosso* out-of-date

divertimento, serenade fl. c. 1750 - - - - - - - - - - - - - - - - - - c. 1785

c. 1765 *symphonie concertante* - - -

1768 J. C. Bach, fortepiano solos in concert

1770 piano concerto -

1780s Mozart perfects piano concerto

1757 F. X. Richter string quartets

1780s Haydn and Mozart mature string quartets

c. 1770 structural pattern of four-mvt. symphony standardized

1786 flute études -
1787 violin études -
c. 1800 piano études -

- - toward opera reforms - - - - - - - - - - - -   1790s song cycles written in England
Gluck fl. - 1787
            1767 *Alceste*   1779 *Iphigénie en Tauride*
C. P. E. Bach (b. 1714) - 1788
F. J. Haydn (b. 1732) - 1809
                                                            "London" symphonies
                                                            The Creation
        1756 - - - W. A. Mozart - 1791
                                                1787 *Il Don Giovanni*
                                                1791 *The Magic Flute*
America:
        1759 Hopkinson: *My Days have been so wondrous free*

                c. 1779 Antes: chamber music

        - - - Billings: fuging tunes

the Viennese idiom that exemplifies the music of the Classic era—the idiom that distinguishes the "Classical" era—emerged c. 1770 as a distillation of elements of the *galant* and *empfindsamer* styles synthesized with elements of the learned (contrapuntal) style. This synthesis was achieved by Joseph Haydn more fully than by his contemporaries, and the Viennese Classical style was firmly established in the instrumental works he created in the 1770s. Haydn's works were widely disseminated in Europe in the 1780s, and a more or less universal cosmopolitan musical language resulted. This musical language may be seen to best advantage in the middle and late works of Haydn, the late works of Mozart, and the early works of Beethoven and Schubert. By c. 1820 musical Romanticism was well under way. (Beethoven is considered in Ch. 20, Schubert in Ch. 21.)

The Classic style is characterized by clarity, balance, and restraint. In their works, composers attempted to pursue a middle ground between the too easy and the too difficult. They sought to create music that had universal appeal, with a degree of simplicity that prevented it from becoming mentally taxing to listeners, music that was refined without being stiff. Form was important; most of the music was constructed in regular phrases and periods. A basically homophonic texture prevailed, with counterpoint used for contrast or for developmental purposes. Instrumental melodies, especially those in slow movements of multimovement works, frequently resemble operatic arias, e.g., the slow movements of Mozart's *concerti* K.191, K.595. Folk or folklike elements—melodies resembling or based on folk song, folk dance rhythms, drones—were incorporated in multimovement works (exs. 19.12 and 19.19). Instrumental color became a significant factor in defining a theme (ex. 19.15). Harmony and rhythm were as important as melody. No really new harmonic materials were introduced, but harmonies were treated differently and were used functionally in a wider sense, with concern for chordal relationships between keys as well as within a key. Major tonalities predominate. Harmonic rhythm, which had slowed during the Pre-Classical era, was a significant factor in articulating large-scale forms, as well as in sustaining individual phrases. Harmonic clarity was important; when moving from one key to another, the tonality was established clearly at the beginning and end of the modulation. However, the functional tonic-to-dominant (and its reverse) was gradually expanded by employing secondary dominants, and within the modulation, pivot chords might function subtly. Methods of development changed from being the restatement of a portion of a phrase in several different keys to being fragmentation and working out of thematic material, and, as the era progressed, composers selected themes with more regard for developmental possibilities than for melody.

Principal Genres and Forms

The principal genres of music composed during the Classic era were symphony, sonata, solo concerto, chamber music, and opera. All are multimovement forms, and each has its roots in types of music written in the Baroque and Pre-Classical eras. To each genre the prominent Classic era composers gave new dimensions. Opera reforms begun by Jommelli, Traetta, Gluck, and others are in evidence in Mozart's mature works; with Mozart, opera rose to unprecedented heights. Haydn's experimentation, inventive imagination, and productivity contributed more to the development of the symphony than any other single composer. He and Mozart developed a characteristic style for the string quartet. In Mozart's works, the solo concerto—especially that for keyboard—attained perfection. Both Haydn and Mozart wrote some excellent piano sonatas, but it was Beethoven who brought that genre to a peak.

The structural principle most often used for a movement was sonata form (or a variant thereof). Next in frequency of use was theme and variations, a favorite form for improvisation; many compositions of this type were never written down.

The Sonata

In the 1770s, hundreds of composers wrote solo keyboard sonatas, frequently with titles conveying the option *cembalo o fortepiano* (harpsichord or piano). Not until c. 1785 did the word *cembalo* begin to disappear from titles. During the last decades of the eighteenth century, the accompanied keyboard sonata—usually with violin as the accompanying instrument—became popular. Most of the piano/violin sonatas by Mozart and Haydn fall into or are not far removed from this category. In Beethoven's piano/violin and piano/'cello sonatas, the two instrumentalists are equal participants in chamber music.

The Symphony

By the late 1780s, many symphonists had adopted a four-movement structural scheme that has come to be considered the standard pattern of the Classical symphony. Haydn's 12 "London" symphonies and

Movement	Tempo	Key	Form
First	Fast	Tonic	Sonata form
Second	Slow	Related key	Ternary, sonata form, abridged sonata form, theme and variations, or rondo
Third	Moderately fast	Tonic *	Compound ternary
Fourth	Fastest	Tonic	Sonata form, rondo, or sonata-rondo

*Trio is almost always in a related key.

Figure 19.1 Outline of structural scheme of four-movement Classical symphony.

Mozart's last 3 symphonies provide excellent examples of this scheme, which may be outlined as shown in figure 19.1.

From time to time, composers altered the internal structure of a movement. The most significant modification was the addition of a slow introduction to the sonata-form first movement. Leopold Hofmann (1738–93) of Vienna, a prolific composer of symphonies, seems to have been the first to do this consistently, commencing as early as 1761. Many slow introductions are characterized by dotted rhythms, thus indicating that the concept of a slow section as introduction to a fast sonata-form movement was

insight

The Piano (I)

On 2 June 1768, in London, for the first time the fortepiano was used in concert as a solo instrument; J. C. Bach, the soloist, used a "square" (actually rectangular) piano made in England by J. C. Zumpe (1735–83). (See fig. 19.2.)

During the last half of the eighteenth century, Johann Andreas Stein (1728–92) of Augsburg was one of the greatest German makers of keyboard instruments. Amadeus Mozart, according to his letters, preferred Stein fortepianos because the action (individual escapement) was better; on other pianos, the hammers blocked and stuttered.

The Stein piano of Mozart's time had a compass of five octaves, from F' to f'''. Normally, the naturals on the keyboard were covered with ebony, and the sharps were covered with bone or ivory. Inside the piano, the narrow hammers were covered with leather. In the upper register, Stein pianos produced clear and very bright tones; pitches in the bass register were round and full, and, because strings were very thin, bass tones sounded clearly. Many eighteenth-century pianos were equipped with right and left knee-levers that served the same function as the sustaining pedal on the modern piano (to lift the dampers); this allowed a richer tone. Dynamic gradations from *pp* to *ff* were possible. Though the fortepiano had limited tonal volume, it was able to hold its own against the small orchestra used at that time (fig. 19.3).

Figure 19.2 In Johann Zoffany's painting *The Cowper and Gore Families* (1775), the lady is playing a Zumpe-style square piano. *(Yale Center for British Art, New Haven, Conn.)*

Figure 19.3 A Viennese fortepiano, by J. A. Stein, dated 1780. In Museum of Fine Arts, Boston. Leslie Lindsey Mason Collection.

probably derived from the French overture. Commencing a symphony with a slow introduction became common practice in the late 1780s but was not done invariably. Mozart wrote slow introductions for only 3 of his symphonies (Nos. 36, 38, 39); 11 of Haydn's "London" symphonies have slow introductions. On the other hand, Mozart's decision not to repeat the development-recapitulation section of the sonata-form first movement of his "Paris" Symphony (No. 31, K.297) was exceptional at the time.

The Concerto

Johann Christian Bach played a major role in the development of the Classical concerto, particularly the concerto for piano and orchestra. Though Bach was one of the chief masters of *style galant,* several of his *Six Concertos,* Op. 1 (1763), *Sei concerti per il cembalo o piano e forte* (Six concerti for harpsichord or pianoforte, Op. 7; 1770) and *A Third Sett of Six Concertos,* Op. 13 (1777) are stylistically more Classical than *galant* and often are described as sounding "Mozartean." In reality, Mozart is indebted to Bach for some of his stylistic traits.

Bach commenced each of the concerti in his Op. 1, Op. 7, and Op. 13 sets with a fast movement, as did Vivaldi, but modified Vivaldi's first-movement structural pattern by combining elements of Baroque concerto-ritornello and sonata form. Such a movement can properly be termed **sonata-concerto form.** In fact, in 1793 H. C. Koch described it as such. He wrote: "The concerto's first *Allegro* contains three principal periods which the soloist performs, and which are enclosed by [i.e., are alternated with] four secondary periods played by the orchestra as ritornelli" (*Treatise on Composition,* III, p. 333). This ritornello-solo alternation is the Baroque concerto aspect. Koch then stated that the three principal solo

sections followed the same basic structural scheme and harmonic pattern as the first movement of a symphony. (At that time, the term "sonata form" was not in use.) Koch considered the first solo section the *Anlage* (exposition) of the movement, with the responsibility for laying out the main themes in the proper tonalities; the first ritornello opened and closed in the tonic and served as introduction.

As written by Bach, the concerto's first movement consists of four distinct sections: orchestral ritornello, *concertante* exposition, modulatory fantasia, and recapitulation (fig. 19.4).

Detailed internal construction of the first movement is as follows: (1) an orchestral ritornello that usually remains in the tonic key and contains the principal theme (and sometimes the second theme, also), a transition, and closing (cadential) material; (2) a *concertante* section resembling the exposition (i.e., the first section) of a sonata-form movement, in which the soloist presents the first theme in the tonic key and new thematic material in the dominant, interspersed with portions of the orchestral ritornello and concluding with the orchestral ritornello closing material in the dominant key; (3) a modulating section more like a free (but controlled) fantasia than a true development, moving into more distant keys before returning to dominant key and usually concluding with the soloist playing a long trill on the dominant and a short cadenza; (4) full recapitulation of all thematic and ritornello material, now presented in the tonic key, concluding with a long cadenza improvised by the soloist and followed by the orchestral ritornello closing material as coda (fig. 19.5; (DWMA147).

Some of Bach's keyboard concerti have only two movements. In his three-movement concerti, the second movement is arialike. Usually, the finale is a minuet or a rondo or may contain elements of both.

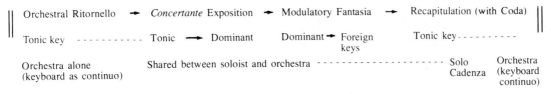

Figure 19.4 Outline of structure of first movement of concerto for keyboard and orchestra used by J. C. Bach.

The Classic Era

Orchestral Ritornello			Concertante Exposition				Modulatory Fantasia	Recapitulation with Cadenza and Coda		
Theme 1	Transition	*Closing	**Theme 1	Transition (portion of ritornello)	**Theme 2	Closing (portion of ritornello)	Some thematic material in modulatory sequences. Ends with long trill on dominant, by soloist, and short cadenza.	Themes and portions of ritornello, now in tonic key. Ends with sustained I $^6_4$ chord.	Improvised by soloist. Ends with long trill cadencing into tonic chord.	Closing portion of ritornello
Tonic key			Tonic key		to Dominant key		Dominant key to foreign keys to dominant preparation for the tonic.	Tonic key		Tonic key

*Orchestral ritornello may include Theme 2, in tonic key.

**Soloist may present new material also.

Figure 19.5 Detailed outline of internal structure of first movement of concerto for keyboard and orchestra used by J. C. Bach.

It is significant that, when the Mozarts were on tour and visited London in 1764–65, Amadeus met J. C. Bach. In 1767, when Mozart wanted to write concerti, he began by making arrangements of isolated movements from sonatas by other composers. Sometime between 1767 and 1772, he arranged three of J. C. Bach's piano sonatas (from Op. 5; publ. 1766) as three concerti for keyboard and orchestra (K.107), using the same orchestral instrumentation as Bach's Op. 1 and Op. 7 (two violins, basso continuo). Bach's concerti were Mozart's models when he composed his first original piano concerto (K.175; 1773).

For his concerti, Mozart adopted the three-movement fast-slow-fast overall scheme favored by Vivaldi. Mozart constructed a concerto's first movement according to the sonata-concerto form used by Bach but gradually modified and refined that pattern, retaining its basic ritornello and adding full-scale sonata-form features (fig. 19.6). Gradually, Mozart changed the modulatory free fantasia section into true development and ultimately gave the concerto, as a whole, symphonic dimensions. Strings remained the core of the orchestra, but instrumentation was augmented to include flute, two oboes, two bassoons, and sometimes two clarinets, two trumpets, and timpani. Mozart's last piano concerto, K.595, though somewhat reserved and lacking the soloistic virtuosity of some of his other concerti, exemplifies his symphonic treatment of the form (DWMA148). The second movement of a Mozart concerto is an instrumental aria; usually, the third movement is a kind of rondo.

Though no two of Mozart's sonata-concerto movements are exactly alike, he did follow a basic structural pattern. The opening orchestral ritornello normally includes both first and second themes, plus *tutti* closing (cadential) material, and remains in the tonic key. Most often, the *concertante* exposition commences with the soloist stating the first theme; after appropriate transitional material, the second theme is stated in the dominant, followed by a portion of the orchestral ritornello in the dominant. The third section resembles a sonata-form development, with tensions achieved through wide modulations, thematic fragmentation and manipulation, and, occasionally, the addition of some new material. This section concludes with a dominant preparation—and usually the soloist plays a long trill over a dominant chord—leading into the next section, full recapitulation of thematic and ritornello material, now in the tonic key. The recapitulation concludes with a sustained orchestral I$_6$ chord. Next, the soloist improvises a cadenza, concluding it with a trill on the supertonic over a V_7 chord; the trill terminates with a small figure termed *Nachschlag* ( ; ex. 19.1). This trilled

Example 19.1 The conclusion of a soloist's improvised cadenza: a long trill on the supertonic harmonized by a V_7 chord, the trill terminating with a *Nachschlag*, and the dominant-seventh chord resolving to the tonic.

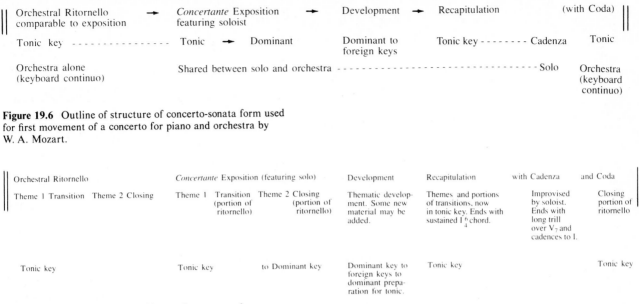

Figure 19.6 Outline of structure of concerto-sonata form used for first movement of a concerto for piano and orchestra by W. A. Mozart.

Figure 19.7 Detailed outline of internal structure of concerto-sonata form used by W. A. Mozart.

dominant-seventh chord is a signal to the orchestral players (whose conductor, in Mozart's time, was either the pianist or the first violinist) that the cadenza has concluded and that the next chord, resolving the dominant-seventh to the tonic, will commence the coda. The closing orchestral ritornello constitutes the coda (fig. 19.7; DWMA148).

String Quartet

The string quartet came into being c. 1745 when viola was added to the trio sonata ensemble and keyboard deleted. For a time, either 'cello or bass might be used as the lowest instrument; sometimes the part was marked simply "Bass." Isolated examples of true quartet writing appeared earlier, e.g., Alessandro Scarlatti's *Quattro sonate a quattro per due violini, violetta e violoncello senza cembalo* (Four quartet sonatas for two violins, viola, and violoncello without keyboard; 1720). Basically, Scarlatti's quartets are Baroque in style, except for the dance movements with which each quartet concludes; the compositions exhibit balance of musical interest among parts. Genuine string quartet literature seems to have evolved from *divertimenti* and from quartet-symphonies

(quartets that are transcriptions of symphony movements), such as those written in the 1740s by Johann Stamitz and other Pre-Classical symphonists at Mannheim and by Georg Monn at Vienna.

Franz X. Richter (1709–89), a Moravian, and one of the foremost of the Mannheim composers, wrote more than 40 pieces of chamber music. Of these, the 6 string quartets forming his Op. 5 (written c. 1757; publ. 1768) are the most significant. In some ways, these quartets are conservative: each has only three movements, most of them in binary form; there is considerable use of imitative counterpoint. The finale of No. 2 is labeled *Fugato presto*. In other respects, Richter was considerably in advance of his contemporaries: the use of minuet as finale (Nos. 3 and 4); a real development section in some movements; great responsibilities given to viola and 'cello, thus producing balance among parts, e.g., No. 3, mvt. 1 (ex. 19.2; DWMA149). In the Op. 5 quartets, Richter anticipated the genuine quartet style of later Classical composers, a style Johann von Goethe likened to serious conversation between four intellectual equals (fig. 19.8).

The Classic Era

Example 19.2 Richter: String Quartets, Op. 5, (*a*) No. 2, mvt. 1, mm. 26–32; (*b*) No. 3, mvt. 1, mm. 19–38. *(Source: Denkmäler der Tonkunst in Bayern, Vol. XXVII/Jg. 15 of orig. ed., p. 13, pp. 22–23.)*

(a)

(b)

Chamber Music with Piano

True chamber music that included piano—ensemble music in which the keyboard was on a par with the other members of the ensemble, rather than dominating or accompanying them—developed slowly during the Classic era. Before c. 1760, the keyboard (usually harpsichord) played an essential but supporting role in ensemble music: fleshing out the skeletal treble-bass notation by supplying the harmonies, augmenting the musical texture, and maintaining the rhythmic flow. As the Baroque trio sonata waned, and the basso continuo was gradually phased out, the 'cello found its place in chamber music in the string quartet. There was increased interest in the piano, but it was still a relatively new instrument and did not blend easily with strings or wind instruments. Composers writing for small instrumental ensembles that included piano either allowed the keyboard to dominate

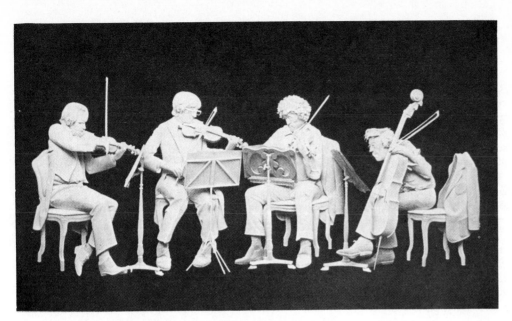

Figure 19.8 Paper sculpture, *The Rehearsal,* by Siegfried Reinhardt, 1976. *(Used with Mr. Reinhardt's permission.)*

the ensemble or relegated the piano to accompaniment status. Not until the 1780s were composers able to achieve tonal balance and genuine dialogue among the instruments of a chamber music ensemble that included piano. In piano trios, Mozart solved the problem by writing a good deal of the piano part between the musical lines of 'cello and violin.

Divertimento

By 1750, the Baroque *concerto grosso* was out-of-date. The *concertato* principle was not abandoned, however; it frequently found expression in light, entertaining types of ensemble music—compositions of similar construction but variously labeled *divertimento, serenade, cassation,* or *notturno*—and, after 1765, in the *symphonie concertante.*

Almost all court composers in south Germany, Austria, and Bohemia wrote *divertimento*-type music. Much of it was created for special occasions, for it was music suitable as background for social events, and the instrumentation varied according to the performing forces available at the time. Generally, the music was intended for a small ensemble—strings, or winds, or a mixture of the two—and was performed by one person per part; some pieces were written for small orchestra. A *divertimento* might consist of from two to nine movements, most of them in binary form, arranged so that tempi contrast. During the 1760s, a five-movement structural plan was common: Allegro-Minuet-Andante-Minuet-Allegro. The eventual omission of the first Minuet produced the multimovement plan that ultimately became standard for the Classical string quartet.

Joseph and Michael Haydn and Leopold and W. A. Mozart were among the many composers writing numerous compositions of *divertimento* type. W. A. Mozart's most important *divertimenti* are K.247, K.287, and K.334, all for two horns and solo strings, and all written for Salzburg families. His last serenade, *Eine kleine Nachtmusik,* K.525 (A little nightmusic; 1787), for string quintet, originally contained five movements; the second movement, presumably a Minuet, is lost. *Eine kleine Nachtmusik* has remained a popular favorite but in the twentieth century is usually performed by string orchestra.

The greatest significance of the *divertimento*-type composition is the exclusion of basso continuo from the ensemble. The absence of harpsichord accompaniment paved the way for Classical chamber music, such as string quartet, and for the disappearance of keyboard from the orchestra. Not until the end of the eighteenth century was the harpsichord completely eliminated as a requisite member of the orchestral ensemble. Though Haydn did not include basso continuo in the scores of his 12 London symphonies, there is evidence that, when the works were first performed, he was at the keyboard supporting the orchestral harmonies.

The Étude

The **étude** emerged during the Classic era and by 1800 had become an important teaching tool. An étude is a complete musical composition featuring at least one consistently recurring problem of physiological, technical, or musical difficulty that requires of the player not only mechanical application but proper study and correct interpretation as well. In contrast, an **exercise** is a chiefly mechanical note pattern of undetermined length, designed for the player's drill on a certain specific technical aspect of his instrument. In other words, an exercise is never, strictly speaking, a complete *musical* composition.

When, around 1700, persons began to write and publish method books and tutors for learning to play the violin, they included for practice small dance pieces; these pieces were usually in binary form. As the violin increased in popularity and esteem during the eighteenth century, an interested public desired instruction and more methods were published; these became more comprehensive in contents, both verbally and musically. Not only was more music included, but the compositions were longer and were designed to cope with technical difficulties. By mid-century, page-long études were included in some methods. Usually, such pieces were entitled "Caprice" or "Lesson for . . ." and the didactic purpose of each study was clearly indicated. These études were not confined to technical problems; equally important

was the matter of taste (style) or expression. The étude had no form that could be considered exclusively its own. However, many of the early études were in binary form.

Books composed solely of compositions that were designated as études began to appear in Paris after 1785. Detel's *Étude* for flute is listed in Sieber's catalog for 1786. Antonio Bartolomeo Bruni's (1757–1821) *Caprices & Airs variés en forme d'études pour un violon seul* (Caprices & varied airs in the form of études for one unaccompanied violin; 1787) seems to have been the first publication for the violin to use the word "étude" in the title and to indicate in print that caprices and varied airs could be études. Some of those airs with variations are melodies from Bruni's operas. His second volume of violin études, *Cinquante études* (Fifty études), appeared c. 1795. Similar volumes were published by other violinists working in Paris, e.g., Federigo Fiorillo (1788), Rodolphe Kreutzer (c. 1800), and Pierre Gaviniès (1800), and have become standard instructional repertoire.

Books of études for piano appeared early in the nineteenth century. The most important of these were prepared by pianists of the London school (see Ch. 20), e.g., Cramer's *Studio per il pianoforte* (Studies for piano; 1804–10) and Clementi's *Gradus ad Parnassum* (Steps to Parnassus; 1817–26).

Symphonie concertante

The **symphonie concertante,** an orchestral form featuring two or more virtuoso soloists, appeared in the late 1760s, became very popular during the 1770s, flourished until c. 1830, then almost disappeared. The rise of *symphonie concertante* was influenced primarily by social conditions: expansion of the public concert, an audience of middle-class citizens who enjoyed virtuosic display, the use of larger orchestras (though still small in comparison with twentieth-century ones), and improved social status of musicians. Usually, excellent local musicians—music teachers, orchestra section principals, and sometimes the composer—were the soloists in a *symphonie concertante*. A bond, as though of kinship, linked local

performers and the *bourgeois* audience. The performances attracted pupils to the teachers and increased sales of the composer's manuscript or printed music.

A majority of the extant *symphonies concertantes* are three-movement works that, in structure and style, closely resemble the Classical concerto for soloist and orchestra. The remainder have two movements, or, rarely, four.

The earliest composers of *symphonies concertantes* worked in Paris or at Mannheim. Paris publishers printed their works, and soon Paris became the principal center of *symphonie concertante* composition. Among the numerous composers contributing to the genre there were F.-J. Gossec, Ignace Pleyel (1757–1831), and G. M. Cambini (1746–1825), who wrote about 80. J. C. Bach composed 15 excellent *symphonies concertantes* for performance in London and Paris; at Mannheim, Christian Cannabich composed 12, and Karl Stamitz (1745–1801) wrote more than 30.

Both Haydn and W. A. Mozart contributed to the repertoire. Haydn wrote only one full-fledged work of this kind—the *Symphonie concertante* in B♭, Op. 84 (classified by Hoboken as Symphony No. 105), for violin, oboe, 'cello, and bassoon soloists with orchestra; the work was written for the Salomon concerts in London in 1792. Mozart composed at least six *symphonies concertantes*. His first, called *Concertone,* K.190 (1773), is in C major, with solos for two violins, oboe, and 'cello, and is *galant* in style. The masterful *Sinfonia concertante* in E♭, K.364 (1779), for violin and viola soloists and orchestra, is Classical in design but calls for *scordatura* viola. Mozart raised the viola tuning a half-step to achieve greater tonal brilliance, as well as to provide greater convenience in performing the virtuosic passages.

The *symphonie concertante* never completely disappeared. Isolated examples exist among the works of nineteenth- and twentieth-century composers.

Christoph Willibald Gluck

Although Gluck (1714–87) composed 8 trio sonatas, 18 symphonies, 5 ballets, and numerous sacred and secular vocal pieces, he is remembered primarily for his work in the field of opera. Little is known concerning Gluck's early life. He was born in Bohemia and, presumably, received some training in singing and in playing instruments at school. However, as a musician and composer, he seems to have been largely self-taught. From 1727 to c. 1735 he was in Prague, where he earned his living by making music as best he could—performing with church choirs or at neighborhood fairs, and, for a short time, serving as organist at Tyn Church.

After spending two years (1735–37) in Vienna, he secured an orchestral position at the Milan court of Prince Melzi. While there, Gluck became acquainted with the works of Italian symphonists and opera composers, including G. B. Sammartini, but there is no documentary evidence that he studied with

Christoph Willibald Gluck. Portrait by J. S. Duplessis, painted in Paris in 1776. *(Oesterreichische Nationalbibliothek, Portraitsammlung, Vienna.)*

Sammartini. Gluck's first opera, *Artaserse,* on Metastasio's libretto, was produced in Milan in December 1741. Its success brought commissions from Venice, Turin, Crema, and Milan for seven more operas. After the production of *Ippolito* in Milan early in 1745, Gluck went to London, where he wrote two operas for the Haymarket Theater. Neither was very well received. He had greater success with his *verrillon* concerts. (The *verrillon* is a set of musical glasses, tuned by being filled with different quantities of water and played by striking them with small sticks or rubbing dampened fingers around the rims.) While in London, he met Handel and attended performances of some of his works.

Between 1746 and 1752, Gluck visited Hamburg, Dresden, and Vienna. For the reopening of Vienna's Burgtheater in May 1748, he composed *Semiramide.* That opera was especially appropriate, in view of the recent European opposition to Maria Theresia as ruler of Austria, for it concerns the legendary Semiramis, who, disguised as a man, reigned in Babylon as King Ninus.

In summer 1748, Gluck again began to travel about, directing operas and performing concerts (including *verrillon*) in Dresden, Hamburg, and Copenhagen. While in Copenhagen in 1749, he consulted with Johann A. Scheibe (1708–76), an influential music critic. Scheibe's theories on opera may have influenced Gluck's composition somewhat—at least, the two men shared some of the same opinions. Scheibe's ideas, published in the preface to his *Singspiel, Thusnelde* (1749), included the following: (1) the orchestral overture or prelude should lead directly into the first scene of the opera; (2) even recitative can express the passions; and (3) various ascending levels of recitative (e.g., *secco* to *accompagnato* to *arioso*) can be used to lead into aria, which in turn rises to emotional heights. In *La contesa de' numi* (The strife of the gods; 1749), Gluck caused the orchestral introduction to Act I to lead directly into Jupiter's accompanied recitative, which links the prelude with the ensuing drama. This did not make Gluck a "reformer"—it was but a very small step in that direction.

For the next two years, Gluck divided his time between Prague, Munich, and Vienna. In Vienna, in 1750, he married Maria Bergin. From 1753 to 1761 he served first as Konzertmeister and then as Kapellmeister in the household of the imperial field marshal. Financial stringencies engendered by the Seven Years' War caused the orchestra to be disbanded in 1761.

Meantime, Gluck's interests had taken a different turn. In 1752, Count Giacomo Durazzo (1717–94) was appointed assistant director of theatrical affairs at Vienna, and in 1754 sole director, with responsibility for everything connected with the Burgtheater and the Kärntnertor. Each of those large theaters had its own actors, ballet troupe, and orchestra. Also, in 1752 a French drama company was brought to the Viennese court to perform drama, ballet, and *opéra comique*. Durazzo imported *opéras comiques* from Paris and engaged Gluck to adapt them to Viennese taste. Gradually, instead of merely adapting the music, Gluck began to replace the French music with pieces of his own; however, he did not alter or replace any of the ballet music. Eventually, he composed complete *opéras comiques*. His first was *La fausse esclave* (The false slave; 1758); he wrote seven more before the end of 1761. Gluck's experience with the French company provided him with a wealth of knowledge concerning stage productions, including ballet.

When given the opportunity, Gluck wrote *opera seria*. In 1754 he set Metastasio's revision of *La cinesi* (The Chinese ladies), and the following year he was commissioned to compose *L'innocenza giustificata* (Innocence justified) for the emperor's birthday. For the latter work, Durazzo prepared a libretto that, though it incorporated aria texts by Metastasio, differed from Metastasian opera conventions. But Metastasio was not completely cast aside. When Gluck was commissioned to compose an opera for Carnival season in Rome in February 1756, he chose Metastasio's *Antigono*. The cast was selected with strict adherence to traditional operatic conventions in Rome—all solo roles (even the principal female ones) were sung by men. Their brilliant performance of *Antigono* obtained for Gluck the patronage of Cardinal Albani (1692–1779) and the Cavalier of the Golden Spur award from Pope Benedict XIV (r. 1740–58).

Gluck worked in Vienna until the end of 1762. His activities during the late 1750s were primarily concerned with French stage works, but in the autumn of 1760 Italian opera was revived in Vienna. The following winter Raniero de Calzabigi (1714–95) arrived in Vienna, won the confidence of the court chancellor, and met Durazzo, who introduced him to choreographer Gasparo Angiolini (1731–1803) and Gluck. Calzabigi had lived in Paris for more than a decade; he had experienced the *Querelle des Bouffons* and was well-acquainted with ballet, opera, and Metastasio's operatic ideals. His early works reflect Metastasio's influence, but by 1755 Calzabigi had become aware of the problems plaguing opera production, had developed a critical attitude toward Metastasio, and had formed definite views concerning opera esthetics. Calzabigi, Angiolini, and Gluck shared ideas and opinions and collaborated in creating the *ballet d'action* (dramatic ballet) *Don Juan, ou Le festin de pierre* (Don Juan, or The stone banquet; perf. October 1761). Their combined talents produced a coalescence of dance, music, and pantomime. The ballet was performed 11 times in 1761, and Gluck borrowed seven items from it for later operas, including *Orfeo ed Euridice* (Orpheus and Euridice; 1762), *Iphigénie en Aulide* (Iphigenia in Aulis; 1774), and *Armide* (1777).

Gluck's "Reform" Operas

For Gluck, Angiolini, and Calzabigi, their most important collaboration in 1762 was *Orfeo ed Euridice* (perf. October 5). Calzabigi instigated that work, and the three men were frequently in consultation while the opera was in preparation. Gluck wrote the role of Orpheus specifically for the castrato Gaetano Guadagni (c. 1725–1792), whose excellent interpretation of the role contributed greatly to the opera's success. Traces of Baroque opera remain in *Orfeo ed Euridice*—the mythological tragic ending is averted by the god Amor, and the work concludes with a ballet and a jubilant chorus.

The drama is divided into three acts, each containing two scenes. When the curtain rises, Orpheus is standing at Euridice's grave; the music is a simple but rich choral *tombeau* (lament) in C minor, appropriately accompanied by solemn tones of trombones and trumpets and punctuated by Orpheus's grief-stricken cries. The *ballo* that follows is functional, providing exit music for the chorus, and, in uplifting E♭-major tones, bringing consolation to the bereaved husband. Thus, at the very beginning of the opera, drama, music, and ballet are unified. The usual *secco* recitative-exit aria combination found in Italian opera is not present here. Instead, there is a sense of dramatic continuity, to which Gluck's choice of tonalities contributed considerably. Orpheus's simple strophic lament, interrupted by a short *accompagnato* recitative, is at times echoed orchestrally by strings and *chalumeau* (a reed instrument, ancestor of the clarinet). The echo effect is in complete accord with his natural surroundings in the scene. Orpheus's *Chiamo il mio ben* (I call my beloved) is in typical Pre-Classical style, with melodic sighs, judiciously placed measured graces, a hint of Lombardic rhythm, and sudden shifts from *forte* to *piano,* yet the echo effect is reminiscent of Carissimi's *Jephte* (see p. 332).

In the two scenes of Act II, serene pastoral and threatening infernal scenes and moods are juxtaposed. Amor, god of Love, permits Orpheus to descend into Hades, where, through the power of his music, he seeks the release of Euridice. At first, his simple song is met with terrifying "NO!" responses chorused by the Furies (DWMA150). The Furies' ballet, with threatening postures, plus appropriate dissonance and orchestral instrumentation, heighten the dramatic tension. Finally, Orpheus wears down their resistance and obtains permission to lead his beloved out of the Underworld, provided he does not look back to ascertain that she is following him. Once they have recrossed the river Styx, her safety is assured. The entire act is a masterpiece.

In the catastrophic third act, Orpheus, being part-human, responds to Euridice's appeals and clasps her in his arms, then realizes that by so doing he has lost her forever. *Che farò senza Euridice?* (What shall I do without Euridice?) he sings. Amor, pitying him, comes to the rescue and, by touching Euridice, restores her to life. The opera concludes with an ensemble finale reminiscent of the *vaudeville final*—a trio, followed by a series of dances, the last of which is a *chaconne*.

Che farò senza Euridice? (DWMA151), Orpheus's lyric lament, became one of the most famous opera arias of the eighteenth century. Its lyric simplicity, balanced phrases, the melodic sighs in the vocal line, and broken chord figurations in the accompaniment, typify the Classical style then emerging (ex. 19.3).

Orfeo ed Euridice contains no *secco* recitative. From the outset, chorus and ballet participate functionally in the action. In this opera, French and Italian elements were blended; music, drama, and dance were no longer separate entities but merged and became fused, thus creating a unified theatrical production.

In 1774, Gluck prepared a new version of *Orfeo ed Euridice* for performance in Paris. Castrati were not used there, so the Orpheus role was altered to accommodate a tenor, necessitating some adjustments in keys; a new aria for Amor was inserted in Act I, and the dance of the Furies from *Don Juan* was added in Act II.

During the next five years, Gluck wrote several stage works, including *Il trionfo di Clelia* (Clelia's triumph; 1763) and *La rencontre imprévue* (The unexpected meeting; 1764), a three-act *comédie mêlée d'ariettes*. *La rencontre imprévue* was one of Gluck's most successful works. Mozart is indebted to it for portions of his *Die Entführung aus dem Serail* (The abduction from the harem).

Gluck's setting of Calzabigi's tragedy *Alceste* (Vienna, 1767) exhibits his mature style and his fusion of Italian, French, and German operatic elements.

Example 19.3 Measures 1–17 of Orfeo's aria *Che farò senza Euridice?* from Gluck's *Orfeo ed Euridice. (Source:* C. W. Gluck: *Sämtliche Werke, ed. R. Gerber, G. Croll et al., publ. by Bärenreiter, Kassel, Basel.)*

When *Alceste* was published (Paris, 1769), Gluck stated his reform aims in the dedication: (1) to compose music devoid of superfluous ornamentation, expressive of the text, and appropriate to the circumstances in the drama; (2) to construct each aria in a form suited to the situation, rather than relying on traditional *da capo,* in which the repeats serve only to foster vocal pyrotechnics; (3) to remove the sharp contrast between recitative and aria by using more *accompagnato* recitative and *arioso,* and avoiding *secco* recitative; and (4) to relate the overture to the ensuing drama.

Gluck was not the first to attempt to reform opera. His stated objectives are directly related to the principles advanced by Scheibe. Others, notably Francesco Algarotti (1712–64), in *Saggio sopra l'opera in musica* (Essay on opera; 1755), had agitated for similar reforms, as well as for control over the unruliness of Italian theater audiences. Reforms had been undertaken by Jommelli, Traetta, and K. H. Graun. Graun's *Montezuma* (1755), on a libretto written in French prose by Frederick the Great and translated into Italian by Tagliazucchi, was known to Gluck. In *Montezuma* Graun used *cavatina* as alternative to *da capo* aria.

Actually, Gluck did not accomplish all of his stated aims in *Alceste,* but the objectives that were realized did much to equalize the balance between music and drama. The overture, which leads without a break into the first scene, is truly a tragic introduction to the opera; the D-minor tonality and the dark tones of the three trombones help convey gloom. The arias are not all structured with *da capo,* but there is a lengthy aria (replete with superfluities) that delays the action considerably. Though much of the recitative is *accompagnato,* there is some *recitativo secco.* As in *Orfeo ed Euridice,* the chorus participates effectively in the action. The tragic mood persists almost to the end; then comes Apollo, *deus ex machina,* to dispel tragedy and effect a happy ending.

Gluck's next reform opera, *Paride ed Elena* (Paris and Helen; 1770), was not a success. Part of the problem was Calzabigi's drastic alteration of the mythological story; he blamed himself completely. Noteworthy in *Paride ed Elena* is Gluck's incorporation of themes from the opera in the overture, as Handel had done in *Deidamia.*

Influential in Gluck's career was his move to Paris in November 1773. His interest in Racine's *Iphigénie en Aulide* had produced a ballet on that subject in 1765, and in 1772 he planned an opera. With it, he hoped to revive and reform French *tragédie lyrique* and attract the patronage of Archduchess Marie Antoinette. In an open letter to the editor of the *Mercure de France* early in 1773, Gluck explained his artistic objectives. *Iphigénie en Aulide* had its première in Paris on 19 April 1774; because of the death of Louis XV in May, some of the scheduled repeat performances were canceled. Gluck revised *Iphigénie en Aulide* (perf. Paris, 1775), then returned to Vienna, where he had been appointed court chapelmaster.

In May 1777 he went back to Paris; there, in September, *Armide* was produced. When Gluck and Piccinni (1728–1800) both began setting Quinault's *Roland,* a heated controversy—another "paper" war, Piccinnists vs. Gluckists—developed. Gluck abandoned his project and returned to Vienna; Piccinni's opera was produced in January 1778. Both Piccinni and Gluck set *Iphigénie en Tauride* (Iphigenia in Tauris), and this time Gluck persisted; his opera, presented in Paris in May 1779, is a masterpiece. In it he successfully blended the traditional Lully-Rameau *tragédie lyrique* with Italian *opera seria* and eliminated several problems that had plagued Italian opera. The drama is developed by musical means; ballet and chorus are integrated with the action; and resolution of the dramatic situation is effected by human means rather than by Diana as *dea ex machina.* Gluck chose the instrumentation carefully and used instruments effectively—especially trombones—to support the action and characterization. One example is the horrifying chorus in Orestes's dream whose accompaniment includes three trombones (ex. 19.4). At times Gluck interrupted an aria by recitative, as he had done in *Orfeo ed Euridice* and *Iphigénie en Aulide.* *O malheureuse Iphigénie* (O unfortunate Iphigenia) is another example of Gluck's melodic gift.

Iphigénie en Tauride marks the summit of Gluck's operatic writing. It is a four-act opera of large proportions, employing soloists, chorus, orchestra, and ballet in a manner that balanced drama and music. With it, he evidenced his mastery of opera in Classical style. A German version of *Iphigénie en Tauride* was produced in Vienna in 1781, and Mozart learned much by attending all of the rehearsals. Other opera composers influenced by *Iphigénie en Tauride* include Hector Berlioz (1803–69) and Richard Wagner.

Gluck completed one more opera, *Echo et Narcisse* (Echo and Narcissus; 1779), which was a failure; he contemplated writing another but was prevented from doing so by a series of strokes that were temporarily paralytic. He did set six of Klopstock's poems for solo voice and keyboard (1786). Near the end of his life, Gluck composed a dark-toned *De profundis* (Out of the depths) for four-part chorus and orchestra. Shortly before his death, he gave a copy of it to Antonio Salieri (1750–1825), who directed its performance at Gluck's funeral.

Gluck's historical significance lies principally in his ability to establish an equilibrium between music and drama, to effect some reforms of *opera seria,* to revitalize *opéra comique,* and to blend elements of French *tragédie lyrique,* Italian *opera seria,* and German opera into a cosmopolitan Classical opera style. The balance he achieved between music and drama was a step toward the later music dramas of Richard Wagner. Gluck did not found a school, though his influence was felt by generations of opera composers. Simplicity is a prime factor in his style. He

Example 19.4 Mm. 1–10 of the Chorus of Furies in Act III, Scene 4 of *Iphigenie en Tauride*. Gluck's use of three trombones, *sforzando,* on the scale passages intensifies the horror of the scene. *(Source: Eulenberg score E.E.4700, pp. 136–37.)*

was a master of characterization and the portrayal of human emotions. Often he used the orchestra to express subconscious urges of which a character was unaware; to do so, he placed in the orchestra motifs that depicted emotions the exact opposite of those the character was expressing overtly. He was keenly aware of the importance of timing and adeptly positioned details in exact relationship to the total effect of the drama. He employed dramatic irony skillfully, frequently using the audience's foreknowledge of the mythological story for this purpose, e.g. Agamemnon's ruse to kill Iphigenia. (Later, Berlioz used audience foreknowledge similarly in *Les Troyens*.)

Franz Joseph Haydn

Although Franz Joseph Haydn (1732–1809) is recognized, along with W. A. Mozart (1756–91), as having composed music that most clearly exemplifies the perfected Classical style, Haydn lived through, experienced, and participated in many musical style changes, all of which are reflected to some extent in his music—the last stages of the Baroque, the Pre-Classical *galant,* rococo, and *empfindsamer* styles, the time of *Sturm und Drang,* the development and maturation of Classical style, and the encroachment of early Romanticism. Haydn and Mozart are jointly credited with developing and perfecting the Classical symphony and string quartet.

Franz Joseph Haydn. Painted by Rössler.

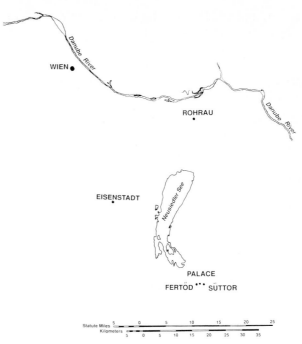

Figure 19.9 Most of Haydn's life was spent a short distance from his birthplace, Rohrau. Eszterhazá stands between the present towns of Fertöd and Süttor.

His Life

Joseph Haydn was born in Rohrau, Lower Austria, a geographical area of mixed population—Austrian, Hungarian, Croatian, Moravian, and Slovakian (fig. 19.9). To which of those ethnic groups the Haydn family belonged is not definitely known. Joseph was the second of the 12 children of Mathias and Anna Koller Haydn; 2 of the other children, Michael (1737–1806) and Johann Evangelist (1743–1805), also had careers in music. Mathias, like his father and four of his brothers, was a wheelwright, but he wanted Joseph to become a priest. Music was part of Haydn's home life; all of the children were expected to participate in family music making and neighborhood concerts. Joseph had a fine singing voice, an asset for a priest.

At the age of six, Joseph was sent to Hainburg to live with a distant relative, a schoolmaster. Upon recommendation of the parish priest, in 1740, Haydn auditioned and was accepted as a choirboy at St. Stephen's Cathedral, Vienna; he served there as a chorister and soloist until his voice changed, c. 1750. The cathedral choir school concentrated on preparing the choirboys for singing the church music; there was some training in playing musical instruments but no music theory or composition lessons. Before Haydn left St. Stephen's, he had begun to compose church music. A *Missa brevis* in F, conjecturally dated 1749, is extant.

Haydn was sufficiently skilled on harpsichord, organ, and violin to earn a meager living in Vienna in 1750–60 by giving keyboard lessons, playing in orchestras and for church Services, and, in general, accepting whatever musical jobs came his way. He lived in a small attic room in the Michaelerhaus, where the dowager Princess Maria Esterházy (mother of Paul Anton and Nikolaus) occupied the first floor and Metastasio lived on the third floor. Through Metastasio, Haydn met Nicola Porpora (1686–1768), composer and singing teacher, who employed him as accompanist. This association with Porpora profited Haydn greatly, for, in addition to learning a good deal about singing and composition, he came in contact with prominent musicians, such as Gluck. However, as a composer, Haydn seems to have been largely self-taught. That he diligently studied Fux's *Gradus ad Parnassum* is apparent from the marginal notations in his copy of it.

In 1758 or 1759, Haydn was appointed music director to Count Karl Morzin, who spent winters in Vienna and summers in Lukavec, Bohemia. For Morzin, he composed some *divertimenti* for wind instruments (mainly, for pairs of oboes, horns, and bassoons), and his first symphony, in D, for strings, two oboes, and two horns. Four other symphonies with this same instrumentation may have been written for Count Morzin.

In November 1760 Haydn married. He had hoped to wed Josepha Keller, but when she entered a convent, he agreed to marry her elder sister, Maria Anna Aloysia (1729–1800). The marriage was not a happy one.

On 1 May 1761 Haydn contracted to serve Prince Paul Anton Esterházy (b. 1711; r. 1734–62) as House Officer and *Vice-Kapellmeister* in Eisenstadt. By terms of the document, which survives, Haydn was subordinate to Gregor J. Werner (1693–1766), *Ober-Kapellmeister,* in the area of choral music only. The contract spelled out Haydn's responsibilities, as well as some regulations pertaining to his personal behavior and dress. He was responsible for the care of the music and musical instruments belonging to the estate and for the training and supervision of the instrumentalists. He was required to compose whatever music the prince required, was forbidden to give away or sell copies of that music, and was not to compose any music for any other persons without special permission. As Haydn's fame grew, he was permitted to accept commissions from others and to arrange for publication and distribution of his compositions. Though the terms of the contract seem quite restrictive, they were not unusual at that time. Frequently, patrons assigned musicians other household tasks and required them to wear special clothing. However, the beneficial aspects of patronage far outweighed the restrictions. In addition to providing regular income for composers plus lodging for themselves and their families, it assured performance of their works. More-

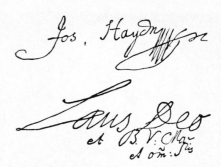

Figure 19.10 Haydn's signature and the religious inscription he customarily placed at the conclusion of a composition.

over, under the patronage system composers were constantly prodded to produce new works, for the emphasis was on new music, not repeat performances of works written previously. Haydn, in the comparative isolation of the Esterházy estate after 1766, was forced to rely upon his ingenuity and was free to experiment. By his own admission, composition was difficult for him; many times he prayed for ideas. He regarded his musical talent as a gift from God. At the beginning of a composition, Haydn inscribed the words *In nomine Domini* (In the name of the Lord), and at the conclusion of the work *Laus Deo* (Praise God), and sometimes added *et B. V. Ma. et om̄i S^{tis}* (and Blessed Virgin Mary and all the Saints) (fig. 19.10). Situations at court sometimes provided inspiration for a composition, e.g., Symphony No. 45, the so-called Farewell Symphony, was written as a hint to the prince that the musicians were anxious to return to the city.

The Esterházy orchestra was small, but excellent; in 1761, it had only 10 to 12 members. Haydn increased its size, but it never numbered more than 25. Among its members were violinist Luigi Tomasini, 'cellists Joseph Franz Weigl and Anton Kraft, and horn players Thaddeus Steinmüller and Karl Franz. The concertos and concertolike works Haydn composed during his first years at Eisenstadt reflect the measure of their talents and the high standard of music at the Esterházy court. A number of those compositions have become standard repertoire, e.g., two of the 'cello concertos, and Symphonies Nos. 6, 7, and 8, which are entitled *Le matin, Le midi,* and *Le Soir* (Morning, Noon, and Evening), and which verge on being *concerti grossi.*

Prince Paul Anton died in March 1762 and was succeeded by his brother Nikolaus (b. 1713; r. 1762–90), whose lavish expenditures for court entertainments earned for him the sobriquet "the Magnificent." Before his accession, Nikolaus had spent considerable time at his hunting lodge near Süttör, south of the Neusiedler See (fig. 19.9). He now had this dwelling rebuilt and enlarged to a palace, which he named "Eszterháza." At first, it was used only as a summer residence; commencing in 1766, Nikolaus moved his court there for most of the year. He kept the chapel choir at the Eisenstadt palace, however.

When Eszterháza was completed, there were two large music rooms and two theaters, one for opera and one for marionette plays. Haydn wrote at least five puppet operas; only one (*Philemon und Baucis*) is extant. Customarily, two operas were produced per week; these were mainly light operas, some of them written by Haydn but most of them imported. Haydn wrote a great deal of *Tafelmusik,* as well as music for the two concerts that were given each week, whether or not the prince was present. Additional concerts, with special music, were given when there were visiting dignitaries at court. Chamber music was performed almost daily in the prince's private chambers. Nikolaus played 'cello, viola da gamba, and baryton (fig. 19.11), a large string instrument similar to the bass viola da gamba but equipped with two sets of strings. The set passing over the fretted fingerboard was bowed; the other set of six alongside the fingerboard vibrated sympathetically with those bowed, or might be plucked. Two members of the Esterházy orchestra also played baryton, so the prince could enjoy listening to baryton music when he was unable to participate in performances. Among Haydn's extant works are 126 trios for baryton, viola, and violoncello; 12 *divertimenti* for 2 barytons and bass or 'cello; and a duet for 2 barytons. The popularity of the baryton was short-lived; the instrument became obsolete early in the nineteenth century.

In 1766 Werner died, and Haydn was appointed Ober-Kapellmeister, with full responsibility for all musical activities at the Esterházy court. This meant he could compose church music, which had always interested him. While in Esterházy employ, Haydn began a personal catalog of his works; he maintained this listing, in a somewhat unorganized manner,

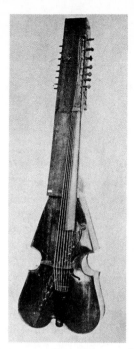

Figure 19.11 This baryton was made in Austria in 1779. *(The Crosby Brown Collection of Musical Instruments, The Metropolitan Museum of Art, New York City.)*

throughout his life. In 1776, he prepared an autobiographical sketch for publication. He considered himself primarily a composer of vocal music; perhaps, because he was a singer, it was natural for him to do so. Also, at that time, few of his instrumental works were known outside Eszterháza.

At some time during the early 1780s, Haydn and Mozart became acquainted. The association between the two composers over the next several years proved beneficial to both, especially in the areas of symphony and string quartet composition.

Haydn remained in the employ of the Esterházy family until shortly after the death of Prince Nikolaus. Nikolaus's son, Prince Anton (b. 1738; r. 1790–94) did not share his father's love for music and disbanded the orchestra. Since there was not much work for Haydn at court, he acquired a residence in Vienna and moved there in 1790. Shortly thereafter, he accepted a commission to compose some symphonies for the London orchestra, and, under management of impresario Johann Peter Salomon (1745–1815), worked in London from January 1791 to July 1792

Example 19.5 *Canon cancrizans a tre* submitted by Haydn for the honorary Doctor of Music degree he received from Oxford University.

Example 19.6 First phrase of the melody of Haydn's "Emperor" hymn. Translation: God! protect Franz the Emperor.

and from February 1794 to August 1795. In England, Haydn composed a number of works, including the 12 "London" symphonies, conducted numerous concerts, and performed at court. He became interested in British folk songs, began to collect them, and made arrangements of hundreds of them for solo voice with instrumental accompaniment.

On 8 July 1791 Oxford University conferred upon Haydn an honorary Doctor of Music degree. The "exercise" he submitted was a *canon cancrizans a tre* setting the text "Thy voice, O Harmony, is divine" (ex. 19.5). As part of the entertainment at this Oxford event, his Symphony No. 92 was performed; hence, its name, "Oxford" Symphony.

On his travels between London and Vienna in 1792, Haydn passed through Bonn, where he heard a talented young pianist-composer named Beethoven, examined some of his music, and encouraged him to come to Vienna. A pupil-teacher relationship between the two failed because of incompatibility.

Late in 1795 Haydn resumed limited service as Kapellmeister for the Esterházy family. Prince Nikolaus II (b. 1765; r. 1794–1835) was especially fond of church music and annually commissioned a new Mass to celebrate his wife's name day. Haydn wrote six Masses for those celebrations. There was more time now for Haydn to compose works of his own choice. He wrote a few string quartets and some sacred music, including a *Te Deum* in C, a vocal version of *Die Sieben letzten Worte* . . . (The Seven last words . . . 1795–96), and six English psalm settings.

While in England, Haydn had been particularly impressed by the British national anthem and wanted a hymnlike anthem for his country. In 1797 he composed *Gott! erhalte Franz den Kaiser* (God! protect Franz the Emperor) as a birthday gift for the emperor (ex. 19.6). The song was introduced to the public on 12 February 1797, the emperor's birthday. For many years the piece, known as the *Emperor's Hymn,* served as Austria's national anthem. In 1922, Haydn's music was supplied with new words, commencing *"Deutschland, Deutschland, über alles"*—the new text was A. H. H. von Fullersleben's (1798–1874) adaptation of a poem written by the Minnesinger Walther von der Vogelweide (c. 1170–c. 1230). During Hitler's régime, Haydn's music was used for the Nazi party song. In the 1980s, the same music, with still another set of words, served as national anthem for the German Federal Republic. The music appears also in several Protestant hymnals with the text "Glorious things of thee are spoken, Zion, city of our God."

At some time during the mid-1780s, Haydn met Baron Gottfried van Swieten, at whose home in Vienna a small group of musicians gathered on Sundays to study the music of Bach and Handel. A decade later, van Swieten prepared the libretti for Haydn's oratorios *Die Schöpfung* (The Creation; 1796–98) and *Die Jahreszeiten* (The Seasons; 1799–1801). Van Swieten was instrumental in promoting the first performances of those works.

Haydn spent his last years in Vienna. Occasionally, he attended concerts, the last one being a performance of *Die Schöpfung,* which Salieri conducted at the university on 27 March 1808. The choir consisted of boys and men, and the orchestra was very small.

Haydn, in weakened condition, was at his home in the suburb of Gumpendorf when Napoleon entered Vienna in mid-May 1809. After the city surrendered, the General ordered a guard of honor before Haydn's home. The aged composer died quietly at home on May 31. On June 1 (the feast of Corpus Christi) his remains were interred in Hundsturm Cemetery. The

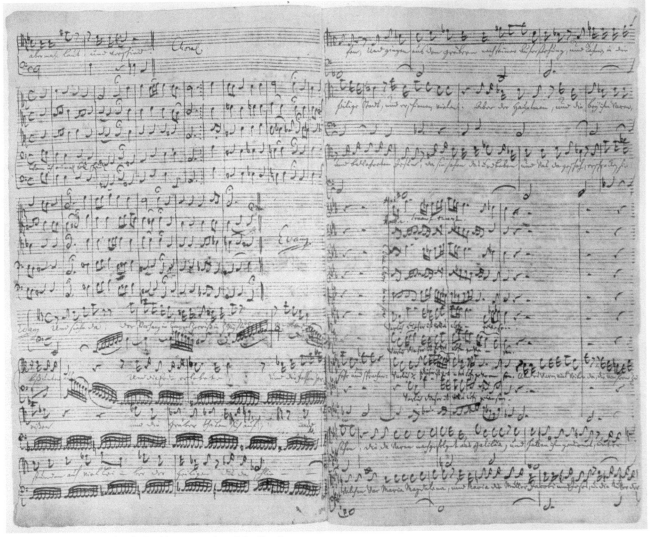

Plate 17 Two pages of J. S. Bach's manuscript of the *Passion according to St. Matthew*. Bach wrote Scripture passages in red ink. *(MS P 25, Deutsche Staatsbibliothek, Berlin.)*

Plate 18 Henri Fuseli. *The Nightmare*, c. 1781, oil on canvas,
30¼″ × 25″. *(Goethe Museum, Frankfurt-am-Main.)*

Plate 19 Anne Louis Girodet. *The Burial of Atala,* 1808, oil on canvas, approx. 6'11" × 8'9". Atala vowed lifelong virginity, but fell in love with a young savage. Rather than break her vows, she committed suicide; her lover and a priest bury her in the shadow of the cross. *(The Louvre, Paris.)*

Plate 20 Francesco Goya. *The Third of May, 1808*, painted in 1814, oil on canvas, approx. 8'8'' × 11'3''. *(Museo del Prado, Madrid.)*

Plate 21 Felix Mendelssohn. Aquatint landscape painted at
Thun 11 July 1847. Original in Mendelssohn-Archivs der
Staatsbibliothek, Preussischer Kulturbesitz, Berlin. *(Courtesy
Allen County Public Library, Fort Wayne, Indiana, owner of
Mendelssohn Aquarellenalbum No. 660.)*

Plate 22 Cloister scene, Act III, of Meyerbeer's *Robert le Diable*. Original in Bibliotheque de l'Opera, Paris. *(© Erich Lessing/Magnum Photos.)*

Baron Gottfried van Swieten. Pastel by V. Clavareau. *(Historisches Museum, Vienna.)*

following day a Requiem Mass was offered at Gumpendorf Church; two weeks later a memorial service was held in the Schottenkirche, Vienna, with Mozart's *Requiem Mass* being performed. Years later, Haydn's remains were moved to the Bergkirche in Eisenstadt.

Haydn's Music

The exact number of compositions Haydn wrote is not known. The only catalog made during his lifetime was compiled by Haydn himself, with some later entries by some of his students, and is incomplete and unreliable. In 1919, Anthony van Hoboken (1887–1983) began to collect first and early editions of famous composers' works and amassed over 5000 items, more than one-fifth of them by Haydn. Hoboken prepared the first thematic catalog of Haydn's works. Later, other musicologists prepared catalogs of specific genres of Haydn's compositions. In the following discussion of Haydn's works, the opus numbers of the string quartets and the numbers of the symphonies and keyboard sonatas correspond with those in Hoboken's catalog.

Vocal Works

It is natural that Haydn, trained as a choirboy, commenced his career as a composer by writing sacred vocal music. The compositions known to be products of his youthful years in Vienna, e.g., the *Missa brevis* in F and a *Salve regina* in E, are works of a talented, noninnovative composer. The *Missa brevis,* for two soprano soloists and four-voice choir, is mainly homophonic, with accompaniment scored for typical Baroque trio sonata instrumentation (two violins and basso continuo). The *Salve regina,* provided with similar instrumental accompaniment, is slightly more Italianate and *galante,* indicating Porpora's influence.

While employed by Count Morzin and during the years the Esterházy court was located at Eisenstadt, Haydn wrote no church music. Only after succeeding Werner as Kapellmeister (1766) did Haydn resume composition of Masses and liturgical settings. All of his Masses, from the simplest to the most complex, are sincere expressions of faith and devotion. The *Cäcilienmesse* (Cecilia Mass; 1766) is a cantata-type Mass, constructed as a succession of self-contained arias and choruses. The *Missa Sancti Josephi* (St. Joseph Mass; c. 1679) conveys a greater sense of continuity, for the solos, instead of being self-contained entities, lead into and blend with the choruses. This work is known also as the *Great Organ Mass* because of the *concertante* organ part in the Benedictus.

An Austrian official requested Haydn to compose the *Mariazeller Messe* (Mass for Mariazell; 1782) for the monastery of Mariazell in Styria. As in the great Masses of the late Baroque, fugues conclude the Gloria, Credo, and Agnus Dei. For the Benedictus, Haydn adapted an aria from his opera *Il mondo della luna* (The world of the moon).

Haydn composed no more church music for 14 years. This hiatus was probably caused by his compliance with an imperial decree restricting the use of orchestrally accompanied music in church during the years 1783–92 and his reluctance to write music that was *a cappella* or used only organ accompaniment. Haydn did not immediately resume composition of church music once the imperial ban was lifted. Probably, he was not requested to write any sacred music

The Classic Era

and his time was spent fulfilling commissions for purely instrumental works. Between 1796 and 1802, he composed six Masses for Prince Nikolaus II Esterházy. Each of these Masses exhibits individuality of character, but they have some common structural elements. All six Masses are scored for SATB soloists, four-voice choir, and orchestra, including timpani and two trumpets—the *Lord Nelson Mass* has three trumpets but no winds—plus basso continuo for organ. Haydn's masterful symphonic style is apparent not only in the orchestral music but in the manner in which symphonic formal principles are permitted to infiltrate the vocal music without negating the traditional structure of the Mass. For example, the Gloria and Credo are sectional, in conformity with the traditional treatment of their texts; both movements commence in fast tempo, then move into an Adagio in a contrasting key, before concluding with the customary Baroque choral fugue.

Two of the Masses are directly related to conditions in Europe: *Missa in tempore belli* (Mass in time of war; also known as *Paukenmesse,* or Kettledrum Mass; 1796) and *Missa in angustiis* (*Lord Nelson Mass*; sometimes called the *Imperial Mass*; 1798). Supposedly, in the latter work, the use of trumpets in the Benedictus represents the heralding of the news of Lord Nelson's victory at the Battle of the Nile.

Missa Sancti Bernardi von Offida (Mass for St. Bernard of Offida; 1796) is better known as *Heiligmesse* because Haydn used the hymn *Heilig, heilig* (Holy, holy) in the Sanctus. Similarly, the *Schöpfungs-Messe* (Creation Mass; 1801) derives its name from the fact that a theme from the oratorio *Die Schöpfung* (The Creation) is used in the *Qui tollis* and *Miserere* sections. In the *Harmoniemesse* (sometimes called the *Wind-band Mass*), Haydn used winds prominently. Presumably, the *Theresienmesse* (Theresia Mass; 1799) was named for the Empress.

Haydn composed only three true oratorios. *Il ritorno di Tobia* (The Return of Tobias; 1774–75) is an Italian oratorio, composed mainly of arias, with only a few choruses. Haydn's last two oratorios, written after he visited England, reflect his knowledge of Handel's *Messiah* and *Israel in Egypt.* Haydn's first acquaintance with Handel's oratorios may have come at van Swieten's weekly gatherings in Vienna, but it was not until Haydn heard the works performed in London that he was inspired to write another oratorio. Salomon had given him a copy of John Milton's *Paradise Lost* (written 1667–74), and Haydn requested van Swieten to consider it as material for an oratorio. Van Swieten not only prepared the libretto for *Die Schöpfung* (The Creation), basing it on material from *Genesis* as well as *Paradise Lost,* he supplied Haydn with detailed instructions for setting it.

Die Schöpfung (1796–98) is scored for SATB soloists, four-part chorus, and full orchestra, including three trombones and timpani, with basso continuo for harpsichord. There is only one alto solo, almost at the end of the work. The instrumental preludes, introductions, and interludes are effective program (i.e., descriptive) music. Symbolism is evident throughout the oratorio, in the choice of keys and instrumentation, and in word painting. Storms and the crashing sea are presented in D minor, a key Haydn had used for other "storm" works. Flashes of lightning are depicted by flute, and *divisi* lower strings portray great whales and other sea creatures being created and multiplying. (The string bass part calls for C', which was then its lowest open string, rather than the E' commonly in use c. 1810.) *Die Schöpfung* commences in C minor and, after touching on several transient tonalities, settles into C major as God makes order out of chaos. C major—the key associated with glory, power, majesty, and heaven—is used for God's creation of mankind, but the oratorio concludes in B♭, tonally depicting the fall of Adam and Eve. Especially impressive is the opening "Representation of Chaos," with its Romantic harmonic coloring, followed by recitative and chorus, and the choral proclamation, "And there was LIGHT!" climaxing on a great C-major chord. Other choruses, e.g., "The Heavens are telling," are almost as masterful. The well-known aria "With verdure clad" is an excellent depiction of nature, and, from time to time, Haydn inserted delightful bits of musical humor into this oratorio.

The libretto for *Die Jahreszeiten* (The Seasons) was also prepared by van Swieten (after Brockes's translation of James Thomson's poem). The oratorio contains some powerful choruses, excellent accompanied recitatives and arias, and pleasant rural depictions of the changing seasons, but, considered

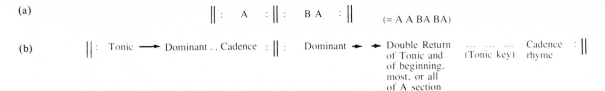

(a) ‖: A :‖: B A :‖ (= A A BA BA)

(b) ‖: Tonic ⟶ Dominant .. Cadence :‖: Dominant ➤ ➤ Double Return ... ... Cadence :‖
of Tonic and (Tonic key) rhyme
of beginning.
most, or all
of A section

Figure 19.12 Diagram of rounded binary form: (*a*) overall structural scheme; (*b*) detail of key tonality within the structural scheme.

overall, it is less consistent in quality than *Die Schöpfung*. Into the composition of *Die Schöpfung* Haydn poured the wealth of his knowledge of composition—blended the styles and forms associated with symphony, Mass, opera, and traditional oratorio—to create a masterpiece that is a worthy successor to Handel's *Messiah*. In fact, after *Die Schöpfung* was published (1800), its popularity equaled that of *Messiah*.

Many of the secular cantatas and stage works that Haydn composed for the Esterházy court have been lost or survive only in fragments. Records indicate that most of his 15 Italian operas were *opera buffa* or *dramma giocoso* types. Two of his three serious operas, *Armida* (1783), a three-act *dramma eroico* (heroic drama), and *Orlando paladino* (1782) were well received. *Orlando paladino,* which is noteworthy for effective characterization, was performed in at least two dozen European cities within a decade of its première. Haydn did not indulge in experimentation when composing operas, as he did when writing symphonies and chamber music. Frequently, he expressed a desire to visit Italy, so that he might observe operatic developments there, but he was never able to do so. He openly acknowledged Mozart's superiority in the field of opera.

Haydn wrote approximately 50 solo songs with keyboard accompaniment. At least 9 of the 14 songs with English texts, composed in 1794 and 1795, are settings of poems by Anne (Mrs. John) Hunter (1742–1821). Among Haydn's fine, small vocal works are 13 part songs (three- and four-voice) with keyboard accompaniment. Moreover, folk-song repertoire was considerably enriched by the more than 400 arrangements of British folk songs—Scottish, Irish, Welsh, Gaelic, and Celtic airs—that Haydn and some of his pupils prepared for English publishers.

Keyboard Works

Keyboard works occupy a relatively minor place among Haydn's compositions. There are approximately 50 sonatas, a handful of concertos, several sets of *Tema con variazioni* (Theme with variations), and a few miscellaneous pieces such as the *Capriccio* in G and the *Fantasia* in C (both publ. 1789).

All of the early sonatas, written in 1750–67, are in major keys and are closely related to the Viennese *divertimento*. In fact, Haydn labeled many of them as such. For Sonatas Nos. 1 and 2 he used the Baroque title *Partita*. Most of the extant early piano sonatas have three movements—Nos. 6 and 8 have four—with all movements of a work in the same key. The second or third movement is usually a minuet with trio. The first movement (and also the last movement when it is not minuet/trio) is a rounded binary in which the first section modulates to dominant (fig. 19.12). In the second section, the "b" music is not systematically developed, though there are excursions into other keys. The return to tonic key does not constitute a true recapitulation but only a reference to the principal theme through restatement of its opening measures and presentation of the first section's cadential passage in the tonic (cadence rhyme). Thus, the binary is "rounded." The slow movement, when not a minuet, has a *cantabile* melody in the *galant* style popular at the time, with accompaniment that incorporates figuration of the "Alberti bass" type.

The sonatas written c. 1770–80 (Nos. 20–39) reflect the influence of C. P. E. Bach, a debt Haydn openly acknowledged. For four of the sonatas Haydn chose minor keys: No. 20, C minor; No. 32, A minor; No. 34, E minor; No. 36, C♯ minor; in these sonatas, the music is more expressive and intense. In Sonata No. 25 (E♭), the minuet is canonic; in No. 26 (A), it is *al rovescio,* i.e., the second half is the retrograde of

The Classic Era

Example 19.7 Haydn's Sonata No. 52, mvt. 1, mm. 1–4.

Allegro

the first half (DWMA152). The last movement of Sonata No. 20, an Allegro in C minor in $\frac{3}{4}$ meter, is like a *moto perpetuo* in a single rhythmic pattern.

Haydn's mature Classical style is present in some of the sonatas of the last group. Sonatas Nos. 49 (E♭), 51 (D), and 52 (E♭) are excellent works. They were written after Haydn visited London where pianist J. L. Dussek loaned him one of the latest English pianos. Sonata No. 52 is a large three-movement work whose first movement, an Allegro, is in Classical sonata form. Its chordal first theme is shown in example 19.7. Extremes of range, rapid scale passages, and figuration are important features of the movement. (Remember that Haydn's keyboard had a range of only about six octaves.) The second movement is an Adagio in E major, an unusual key relationship and tempo for Haydn. The movement is *galant* in style, with a simple, expressive theme that is presented as a complete binary, each half marked to be repeated. The middle section of this movement, in E minor, may be regarded as a variation and slight expansion of the second half of the binary; this variation concludes with an arpeggiated dominant-ninth chord extending over several octaves. There is a brief rest; then, the E-major opening theme recurs, beginning simply as though in recapitulation but soon becoming another ornamental variation of the entire binary. The Presto final movement is virtuosic. The first theme is reminiscent of folk dance, with drone bass. At the conclusion of the development, there is a dominant-seventh chord followed by a brief cadenzalike Adagio; then comes recapitulation. In stature, Sonata No. 52 is comparable with Haydn's mature string quartets.

Chamber Music

In the last half of the eighteenth century, a prince's chambers were often the setting for concerts that included symphonies and other orchestral works, as well as compositions designed for smaller ensembles and soloists. The works programmed on such concerts, and the concerts themselves, were frequently referred to as **chamber music.** However, very early in the nineteenth century, the term chamber music took on a different connotation—ensemble music performed by one person per part. Haydn composed chamber music of both types.

The catalog of Haydn's chamber music includes duos, trios, quartets, quintets, and sextets for strings; sonatas for violin and keyboard; piano trios; and trios, quartets, sextets, octets, and nonets for various combinations of string and wind instruments. In developing the string quartet, Haydn made his greatest contribution to chamber music. But Haydn did not originate the string quartet.

Haydn's early quartets (1762) provide examples of both *divertimento* and transcription types: Op. 1, No. 5 (B♭) was derived from what was originally Haydn's first symphony; the other quartets of Op. 1 and those of Op. 2 are *divertimenti*. Each quartet has five movements, binary in form, and usually arranged Fast–Minuet–Slow–Minuet–Fast. First violin is prominent; viola doubles either second violin or 'cello.

Before Haydn turned again to string quartet composition, he wrote 40 symphonies. That experience is reflected in the six quartets of Op. 9 (1768–70). In these four-movement works the first-violin part is brilliant; undoubtedly, it was designed for Luigi Tomasini, *Konzertmeister* at the Esterházy court from 1767 to 1808. Occasionally, the other instruments share in the thematic material, and viola and 'cello are accorded some independence.

In the quartets of Op. 17 (1771) and Op. 20 (1772), the first violin part is quite virtuosic at times, with double-stops, arpeggiation, use of highest register, and flashy string-crossing, but there is more equality in distribution of thematic material among the four instruments. To some degree, this equality results from increased use of imitative and invertible counterpoint. Half of the Op. 20 quartets conclude

Fuga a 4ᵗʳᵒ soggetti
Allegro
sempre sotto voce

Example 19.8 Measures 1–6 of Haydn's String Quartet, Op. 20, No. 2, mvt. 4, a fugue with four subjects.

with a *Fuga* employing more than one subject. In these movements, fugue is treated as a compositional technique—counterpoint used to enrich homophonic texture—rather than as a polyphonic form. The opening measures of the finale of Op. 20, No. 2, *Fuga a IV Soggetti* (Fugue with 4 subjects), are given in example 19.8. Each quartet has four movements, but placement of the Minuet has not been firmly established—it vacillates from second to third movement. In fact, in Haydn's string quartets the position of the Minuet was never firmly established. Whether he placed it second or third seems to have depended on where he thought it would exert the most influence in stabilizing the overall tonic key tonality of the quartet.

Some of the *Sturm und Drang* expressive elements that color the symphonies written in the early 1770s appear also in the Op. 17 and Op. 20 quartets. All of the Op. 20 quartets have marked individual differences. In some of the sonata-form first movements, Haydn employed a device used frequently in his symphonies—the *fausse reprise* (false recapitulation). One instance of this occurs in Op. 20, No. 4, mvt. 1, m. 21 of the development. True recapitulation occurs at m. 217 of the movement and is preceded by statement of the opening measures in the subdominant (ex. 19.9).

Haydn wrote no more string quartets for almost a decade; then, in 1781, the six Op. 33 quartets appeared. With these works, Haydn began using the designation "string quartet"; previously, he called his pieces in this genre "divertimenti." The Op. 33 quartets are variously called "Russian" because Haydn wrote them for Grand Duke Paul of Russia, and "*Gli Scherzi,*" supposedly because in each quartet a movement labeled *Scherzo* replaced the Minuet. Haydn never again used the term *scherzo* in his string quartets. Basically, these *scherzi,* four of which are second

movements, are still minuets but are lighter in mood and have faster tempo indications than usual. The Italian *Gli scherzi* literally means "Jokes," and when these movements are played too fast, Haydn's humor is lost. That humor occurs in other movements, too, and is conveyed through melodic character, false starts, pizzicato, placement of half-cadences where full ones are expected, and, in the Finale of No. 2, through an abrupt, unexpected conclusion.

When the Op. 33 string quartets appeared, Haydn stated that they were written "in an entirely new, special way." In general, they are light, happy music, with some folklike themes, and the slow movements seem especially expressive and emotional. However, some of the melodies are more elaborate rhythmically and contain more distinctive intervals. Haydn broke down those melodies and developed some of the motivic fragments contrapuntally. Haydn's "new, special way" of writing is thematic development using contrapuntal devices in a homophonic relationship. The development section of Op. 33, No. 2, mvt. 1 is an example (DWMA153). The most popular quartet of the Op. 33 set was No. 3 (in C), filled with grace notes that have given it the nickname "The Bird."

A single quartet in D minor constitutes Op. 42, written c. 1783–85. Stylistically, it displays characteristics of Haydn's early and middle periods of quartet writing. During the remainder of the decade, Haydn wrote 18 string quartets. The 6 *Prussian* quartets, Op. 50 (1787), dedicated to King Friedrich Wilhelm II (r. 1786–97), reflect the fact that the Prussian king was an accomplished 'cellist. The other 12 quartets were written for and dedicated to Johann Tost, a wealthy merchant who played violin. Tost published them in three sets, as Op. 54 (3 quartets, 1788), Op. 55 (3 quartets, 1788), and Op. 64 (6 quartets, 1790). In general, these four sets of chamber

The Classic Era

(a)

(b)

(c)

Example 19.9 Haydn's String Quartet, Op. 20, No. 4, mvt. 1: (a) mm. 1–6; (b) mm. 132–40, a *fausse reprise* near beginning of development section; (c) mm. 206–24, return of the opening measures in the subdominant key, followed by actual recapitulation at m. 217.

works parallel in quality and stylistic traits the symphonies composed during the late 1780s. However, the first movements of Haydn's quartets do not have the slow introductions that characterize his symphonies. This is not a lack, but an advantage—such introductions would have impaired the intimacy of the quartets. The quartets composed prior to Op. 50 contain relatively few passages formed from fragments of chromatic scales; there is a noticeable increase in chromatic passages in the Op. 50 and Op. 64 quartets and in *The Seven Last Words*. Doubtless, the amount of chromaticism Haydn used in these works is directly related to his awareness of that characteristic of Mozart's music and the association between the two composers during the years Haydn composed these quartets.

Haydn's late quartets include Op. 71 (3 quartets, 1793); Op. 74 (3 quartets, 1793); Op. 76 (6 quartets, 1797); Op. 77 (2 quartets, 1799); and Op. 103 (1803), his last quartet, which he struggled with for several years and then abandoned after completing only the slow movement (B♭ major) and the Menuetto (D minor). The key Haydn intended for Op. 103 is a moot question; the work is usually referred to as being in B♭ major, yet the Menuetto—normally constructed in the tonic key of the composition—is in D minor!

In the Op. 71 and Op. 74 quartets, written after Haydn's first visit to London, the first movements are supplied with introductions varying in length from two or three chords to several Adagio measures. This addition was not merely transference of an orchestral technique; rather, it resulted from Haydn's observance that, in London, chamber music was often performed in concert rooms, as entertainment for listeners and not primarily for the performers' enjoyment. Haydn did not regard the introductions as solely prefatory material; usually, that music was woven into the fabric of the entire movement. Tendencies toward romanticism characterize these works, especially Op. 74—an expanded harmonic palette, sudden shifts of tonality to remote keys, far-ranging modulations, and formal liberties such as development within recapitulation or telescoping of development and recapitulation.

The Op. 76 quartets are intensely expressive and reveal the maturity of Haydn's style. They abound in passages illustrative of his continual experimentation, which at times was quite bold, his development and enrichment of forms through new uses of compositional techniques, the expansion of his harmonic vocabulary, and his exploration of remote key tonalities. Several of these passages are noteworthy: (1) in No. 1, mvt. 1, the audacious quasi-fugato presentation of the first theme, with statement of the first phrase by unaccompanied 'cello, answered by unaccompanied viola (ex. 19.10a); (2) in Nos. 1 and 3, commencement of the Finales in the parallel minor key; (3) in No. 2, the descending fifths in the opening theme of mvt. 1, which give rise to a preponderance of fifths in the movement, thereby generating the name *Quinten* (Fifths) for the quartet (ex. 19.10b); and the *Hexen Menuetto* (Witches' Menuet), a two-voice canon between violins in octaves and viola and 'cello in octaves (ex. 19.10c); (4) in No. 3, mvt. 2, a simple presentation of Haydn's hymn *Gott! erhalte Franz den Kaiser,* followed by four variations wherein the complete melody, unaltered, is presented in turn by second violin, 'cello, viola, and first violin; (5) in No. 5 (D major), the romantic Largo (F♯ major; excerpt, ex. 19.10d); and (6) in No. 6 (E♭ major), the *Fantasia, Adagio,* which commences in B major—though there is no key signature, and each chromatic alteration is notated—and proceeds through at least 10 keys before settling into B major. In each of the Op. 76 quartets, the slow movement is second, and the Menuetto third. All of the minuets have the character of *scherzi* and bear Italian tempo markings denoting that they are to be played quickly. This same kind of Menuetto appears in the "London" symphonies.

Haydn's last two completed string quartets, Op. 77, Nos. 1 (G major) and 2 (F major), are his last completed large-scale instrumental works. Composed in 1799 as sonatas for flute and piano, Haydn transcribed them for string quartet (publ. 1802) for Prince Lobkowitz, who played violin and 'cello. These works mark the summit of Haydn's string quartet writing. Found in them are the subtle wit and the other stylistic traits that characterize Haydn's other late quartets and symphonies.

(a)

(b)

(c)

(d)

Example 19.10 Excerpts from Haydn's String Quartets, Op. 76: (*a*) No. 1, mvt. 1, mm. 1–10, quasi-fugato presentation of first theme; (*b*) No. 2, mvt. 1, mm. 1–2, the descending fifths contributory to the quartet's nickname, "Quinten"; (*c*) No. 2, mvt. 3, mm. 1–5, beginning the canon; (*d*) No. 5, mvt. 2, mm. 1–4, lyrical first theme, romantic harmonies.

The Classic Era

Example 19.11 Haydn: Symphony No. 7, mvt. 2, mm. 16–20, one of several recitative-like violin solo passages in the movement.

Symphonies

When considering Haydn's 104 symphonies, it must be remembered that he wrote for a patron, that the instrumentation of a composition was determined by that of the orchestra at his disposal, and the degree of difficulty of the work was geared to the capabilities of the members of the patron's performing ensemble. A keyboard instrument is required for all of Haydn's first 50 symphonies; though he seldom specified it thereafter, he continued to use it, even for the "London" symphonies. He played the keyboard part in the London premières of those works.

Haydn's first five symphonies were written for Count Morzin; symphonies Nos. 6–81 were designed for the Esterházy orchestra. Most of the early symphonies are scored for two oboes, two horns, and strings, with basso continuo. Commencing with No. 20, other wind instruments were occasionally included, e.g., two trumpets in No. 20, two English horns in No. 22. Not until 1779, beginning with No. 70, was flute added consistently.

For his early symphonies, Haydn maintained no standard structural plan. Many of them have the three-movement fast-slow-fast formal structure derived from expansion of the Pre-Classical *sinfonia*: an Allegro in tonic key; an Andante in contrasting tonality, usually parallel minor or subdominant; and a Minuet or an Allegro with gigue characteristics (e.g., No. 19), in tonic. A few of the early symphonies are in four movements. Some of these, e.g., Nos. 21 and 22, follow a structural pattern resembling Baroque *sonata da chiesa*: Andante–Allegro–Minuet–Presto, with all movements in the same key, and the individual movements in binary form. Yet, No. 3 (1762) exhibits the overall scheme that became standard in the Classical symphony: Allegro (G major), Andante moderato (G minor), Minuet/Trio (G major), and Allegro (G major). The slow movement, for strings alone, is in rudimentary sonata form; the Minuet is canonic, and the final Allegro contains some fugal writing.

Symphonies Nos. 6, 7, and 8 also have the four-movement structure of the Classical symphony. All three feature violin and 'cello soloists and are to some degree programmatic. Symphony No. 7 resembles Baroque *concerto grosso* in the writing for a *concertante* trio of two violins and violoncello, an instrumentation identical with the Baroque trio sonata ensemble commonly used as *concertino* of the *concerto grosso*. There is a suggestion of opera, too, in the *recitativo* passages for solo violin in the Adagio of No. 7 (ex. 19.11).

Symphony No. 31 in D major, nicknamed the "Hornsignal" Symphony, has several distinctive features: (1) It is scored for four horns instead of the usual two, and the first movement commences with the solo horn-call that gave the symphony its nickname. (2) The Adagio, featuring solo violin, uses a melody whose opening phrase closely resembles an old Netherlands song of thanksgiving. (3) The fourth movement consists of theme with six variations and a concluding Presto unrelated to the theme. When first printed (Paris, 1785), this work was designated *symphonie concertante*.

Haydn wrote few symphonies in minor keys, but in 1768–73 he composed five of them: Nos. 26, 39, 49, 44, and 52 (in that order). Symphonies Nos. 44 and 52 exhibit a degree of expression closely akin to that of *Sturm und Drang*. The *Trauer* (Mourning) Symphony, No. 44, commences Allegro con brio with a monothematic sonata-form movement in which Haydn begins to develop the theme in the exposition; further development occurs in the middle section of the movement. The Minuet (in tonic E minor), a canon at the octave, is placed second; its Trio is in parallel major. The third movement, an Adagio (E major) (DWMA154), in which the violins are muted, is one of the loveliest slow movements Haydn ever composed. The Presto finale is monothematic, in sonata form with an abbreviated recapitulation.

In 1771–74, Haydn composed the symphonies catalogued as Nos. 42–48, 50–52, 54–56, 64, and 65. Though each of these works has individual characteristics, all of them exhibit some common features: They are on a larger scale than earlier symphonies, with greater harmonic richness, with modulatory excursions farther afield in the development sections, and with greater intensity of expression. Abrupt and unexpected dynamic changes occur, and in slow movements the strings are muted. In No. 47, both the Minuet and Trio are written *al rovescio*. (The Minuet of Sonata No. 26 in A, written in 1773, is constructed similarly.)

For several of these symphonies Haydn chose keys that were exceptional in the eighteenth century: No. 45 is in F♯ minor; No. 46, in B major; and No. 49, in F minor. The inner tonal scheme of No. 45, the "Farewell" Symphony, is also exceptional. The opening Allegro is in F♯ minor; the slow second movement, in A major; the third movement, in F♯ major; and the Presto finale, in F♯ minor, but before concluding, it moves into an Adagio that commences in A major and ends in F♯ major. Extramusical reasons occasioned the Adagio conclusion—in this section, Haydn gradually reduced the instrumentation, and when a musician finished playing his part, he packed up his instrument, blew out the candles on his music stand, and departed. Only two performers remained to conclude the work. (History records that Haydn's hint was effective—the prince permitted the musicians to say a temporary "Farewell" to Eszterháza and return to the city.) Another feature contributes to the individuality of Symphony No. 45— Haydn introduced a new theme in the development section of the first movement. This is the only symphony in which he did so.

In the sonata-form movements of symphonies written in the 1770s, Haydn was fond of using a *false reprise*—in the development section, after some development has occurred, the first theme returns as though commencing the recapitulation but is abandoned in favor of continued development before actual recapitulation occurs. The surprise element is important and is seen in harmonies, key relationships, and deviations from traditional structural patterns.

In the symphonies composed during the 1780s, Haydn sometimes used sonata-rondo form in the last movement. Basically, this construction resembles a seven-part rondo (ABACABA), with the first ABA treated as exposition, the C section being developmental, and the last ABA section being recapitulation (the B music presented in the tonic key; fig. 19.13). Haydn first used sonata-rondo for the finale of a symphony in 1782, in Symphony No. 77. He did not introduce the form, however; Mozart had used it previously. An interesting feature of the finale of Symphony No. 77 is Haydn's use of dominant pedal (sustained for nine and ten measures) during the third and the last presentations of the rondo theme.

In 1785, Haydn accepted a commission from the cathedral at Cadiz, Spain, to compose some instrumental music appropriate for Good Friday Service. *Die sieben Worte des Erlösers am Kreuze* (The seven words of the Savior on the cross) resulted: an introduction, seven orchestral sonatas, and *Il terremoto* (The earthquake). When performed at Cadiz Cathedral, each sonata was preceded by an accompanied recitative by a baritone singing the appropriate words of the Savior.

In 1785–86, Haydn composed the "Paris" Symphonies, Nos. 82–87, for performance at the Concerts de la Loge Olympique, Paris. Several of these symphonies have nicknames, derived from musical passages in the works, e.g., No. 82, *L'Ours* (The Bear),

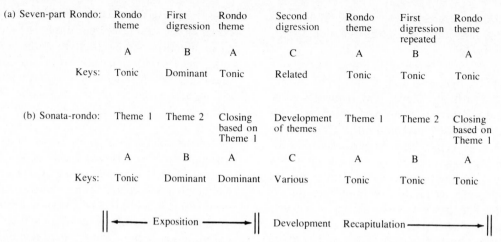

(a) Seven-part Rondo:	Rondo theme	First digression	Rondo theme	Second digression	Rondo theme	First digression repeated	Rondo theme
	A	B	A	C	A	B	A
Keys:	Tonic	Dominant	Tonic	Related	Tonic	Tonic	Tonic

(b) Sonata-rondo:	Theme 1	Theme 2	Closing based on Theme 1	Development of themes	Theme 1	Theme 2	Closing based on Theme 1
	A	B	A	C	A	B	A
Keys:	Tonic	Dominant	Dominant	Various	Tonic	Tonic	Tonic

‖ ◄——— Exposition ———► ‖ Development Recapitulation ———► ‖

Figure 19.13 Comparison of seven-part rondo form and sonata-rondo form.

so-called from the drone bass accompaniment in the dancelike finale. Symphony No. 85, *La Reine* (The Queen), contains variations on a French melody that was a particular favorite of Marie Antoinette. In the 1780s, Haydn began to effect a change in the kind of principal theme he used for the opening movement of a symphony. Instead of writing the triadic or scalar type of theme that emphasized the tonic, as Baroque and Pre-Classical composers had done, he constructed simple, pliant themes suitable for fragmentation and development. Moreover, he distributed the thematic material among all orchestral instruments instead of assigning it to only one or two sections of the orchestra.

Symphonies Nos. 88–92 (1787–88) were commissioned by private individuals (Johann Tost, Comte d'Ogny, and Prince Oettingen-Wallerstein). No. 92, the "Oxford" Symphony, is one of Haydn's most popular orchestral works.

Haydn's symphonic writing culminates in the two sets of "London" symphonies, Nos. 93–98 (1791–92) and Nos. 99–104 (1793–95). These are large works composed for a large orchestra and exhibit Haydn's mastery of symphonic writing. In most of these symphonies, the first movement is in traditional sonata form but commences with a long, slow introduction, featuring the dotted rhythms commonly associated with the first section of a French overture. Not

always does this introduction begin in the designated key of the symphony—e.g., Symphony No. 104 is in D major, but its first movement opens in D minor (DWMA155). Nor are developmental features reserved for the middle section of the form; they may infiltrate the entire movement. In only one of these symphonies (No. 101) does the development section commence in the dominant key; instead, Haydn used mediant, submediant, or a plagal key (subdominant or supertonic). The long introduction is balanced by increased length of the coda, which often is developmental. Haydn's fondness for folk songs is apparent in his choice of thematic material—first and fourth movements of No. 104 provide examples of folk-song-*like* themes (ex. 19.12). In Symphonies Nos. 99, 100, 103, and 104, the melody used as first theme is restated in the dominant as the second theme; this substantiates current belief that it is the change of key tonality rather than melodic content that defines the secondary theme in a sonata-form movement. As if to prove the point, in some works Haydn stated the thematic material twice in the tonic key in the recapitulation (e.g., No. 104, mvt. 1). The movement's closing theme is clearly defined.

In the "London" symphonies, most of the second movements are theme and variations. Though the third movements are structured as Minuet/Trio, the tempo is much faster than that of the courtly dance.

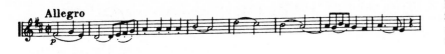

(a)

(b)

Example 19.12 Some themes in Haydn's Symphony No. 104 resemble folk song melodies: (a) mvt. 1, theme 1; (b) mvt. 4, theme 1.

In accordance with tradition, instrumentation is reduced for the Trio. (Incidentally, the Trio was so-named because originally that section was often performed by an instrumental trio.) Customarily, the Trio is in a related key. In No. 104, the Minuet is in D major (the key of the symphony) and the Trio in B♭ major, an unusual choice but a preview of the preference nineteenth-century composers would exhibit for the drop of a third in tonality. In some of the Minuets and the Trios, the second section of the music is developmental. Finales are very fast, in sonata form or sonata-rondo; all are in duple meter. Humorous touches color several of the Finales.

Two trumpets and timpani are included in all of the "London" symphonies; in No. 100, the "Military" symphony, triangle, cymbals, and bass drum are added in the second and fourth movements. Sometimes the trumpets are given independent parts instead of doubling horns; similarly, 'cellos frequently have music different from that of the string basses. In the last set of six symphonies, only No. 102 does not require two clarinets.

Several of these symphonies acquired nicknames from unusual features of their second movements—e.g., the steady ticking rhythm in the slow movement of No. 102, the "Clock," and the crashing *forte* chord concluding the subdued presentation of the theme in the second movement of No. 94, the "Surprise."

An overview of Haydn's symphonies reveals a variety of formal patterns and a diversification of inner structural schemes that prevented the symphonies from becoming stereotyped. In developing thematic material, he adeptly balanced counterpoint with homophony. All of the movements were increased in length and complexity, not just the outer ones. Haydn's imagination, inventiveness, and constant experimentation brought the symphony to Classic proportions and to a level of development that fostered the masterworks of Beethoven.

Concerti

Haydn did not consider himself a soloist and did not concertize; his concerti were written for others to perform. The several concerti written before 1765 are Pre-Classical in style.

The piano Concerto in G (c. 1770) was composed for Maria Theresia Paradis, for whom Mozart also wrote a concerto. The Concerto in D for harpsichord or piano and orchestra (publ. 1784) uses Classical three-movement format. Contrary to custom, orchestral forces (two oboes, two horns, strings) are not reduced for the slow movement. In the finale, *Allegro assai; Rondo all' Ungarese* (Hungarian Rondo), Haydn probably used authentic Hungarian gypsy or folk melodies.

Of the surviving violin concerti, that in G major is the finest. The 'cello concerti were written for Eisenstadt 'cellists, the C-major work (c. 1765) for Joseph Weigl, and that in D major (1783) for Anton Kraft. The D-major concerto contains brilliant and virtuosic technical effects designed to display Kraft's talent: harmonics, octaves, passages labeled *sul G* (on the G string) and *sul D.*

Not all of Haydn's concerti are for traditional instruments. In 1786, he accepted a commission from King Ferdinand IV of Naples (r. 1759–1825) for five concerti for two *lire organizzate.* The *lira organizzata,* very popular in the 1780s, was a kind of hurdy-gurdy with a set of organ pipes somewhat like Panpipes built into its body; its sound was penetrating, but not loud.

The Classic Era

Haydn created his *Concerto per il clarino* in E♭ (Trumpet Concerto; 1796) for Anton Weidlinger (1767–1852), the trumpet player who, c. 1793, invented the keyed E♭ trumpet. In Haydn's concerto, a large-scale symphonic work, the trumpet is treated not only as a military/martial instrument but as one capable of virtuosity, lyricism, and chromaticism. Weidlinger's trumpet had five keys that were played by the left hand while the performer held the instrument with his right hand. All chromatic tones between concert b♭ and c''' were available on the E♭ keyed trumpet, and Haydn's music displays the extremes of the range. In accordance with custom, space is provided for a cadenza in the first movement. The second movement is a lyrical solo in A♭ major, written for the middle register of the instrument. The finale, a brilliant sonata-rondo, makes great technical demands upon the soloist, e.g., in the original version, calling for e♭''' (concert c''') in mm. 216–17. Weidlinger performed Haydn's concerto in 1800. Shortly thereafter, the work fell into obscurity and was not brought to light until 1929. It has risen in popularity since 1950 and has been performed frequently in the late twentieth century.

The keyed trumpet became obsolete soon after the piston-valve trumpet was introduced by Berlin instrument maker Heinrich Stölzel (1772–1844) in 1814. However, the score of Bellini's opera *Norma* (1831) calls for two keyed trumpets. Around 1760, Anton J. Hampel (c. 1710–1771) began the practice of inserting his hand into the bell of his horn to lower pitch; thereafter, some trumpets were built with two double bends in the tubing to shorten the instrument sufficiently so that trumpeters might follow similar procedure. Such trumpets, called **stop trumpets,** were usually built in F, with alternate crooks to change to a lower key. **Slide trumpets** had been used by tower watchmen since the late fourteenth century. In London, in the late 1790s, J. Hyde invented a chromatic slide trumpet in F, which remained in use in England throughout the nineteenth century.

Wolfgang Amadeus Mozart

Johann Chrysostom Wolfgang Amadeus Mozart (1756–91), born in Salzburg, Bavaria (Austria), was the seventh and last child of Leopold and Anna Pertl Mozart. Only two of their children survived infancy: Amadeus and Maria Anna (1751–1829; Insight, "Maria Anna Mozart"). Amadeus demonstrated extraordinary musical talent by the time he was four; before he was six he was composing music. Because that music was notated by Leopold, it is impossible to determine exactly how much of it Amadeus actually composed.

Amadeus never received any formal schooling; most of his musical training came from his father. At the age of six, the boy was a harpsichord virtuoso; soon he became an excellent organist and violinist also. Maria Anna's musical talent almost equaled her brother's. When Leopold realized that his children were unusually gifted, he decided to promote and exhibit their talents. In January 1762, he took them to Munich, where they played harpsichord for the Elector of Bavaria. It was the first of many journeys that filled most of the next decade of Amadeus's life. Also in 1762, the Mozart family visited Vienna, where the children performed in the homes of nobles and for Empress Maria Theresa in Schönbrunn palace; in 1763 the Mozarts went to Paris and in 1764 to London. Usually, they stopped at every significant music center *en route* so Amadeus could perform. Eventually, his talents were displayed in all of the principal cities and courts of Germany and Austria, as well as in France, England, Holland, and Italy. Frequently, he was subjected to tests, such as sight reading and improvising upon a given theme, to prove he was truly a prodigy. His extraordinary musical memory was astounding—he could accurately reproduce a work after hearing it only once, a capability he retained throughout his life. In many respects, the tours during Amadeus's impressionable years were beneficial; he met important composers and performers and was exposed to different musical styles. Elements of those styles appeared in his own compositions; some were used for a time and then rejected, others were absorbed into his musical style.

Wolfgang Amadeus Mozart. Detail from Joseph Lange's unfinished oil painting of Mozart at the piano (c. 1783). Original is in the Mozart Museum, Salzburg, Austria. *(New York Public Library.)*

insight

Maria Anna Mozart

As a child, Maria Anna Mozart, called "Nannerl," evidenced talent as a keyboard performer that almost matched her younger brother's. She received her first lessons from her father in 1758 and experienced her first success in public performance when the Mozarts made a musical tour to Munich in January 1762. Nannerl participated in the family's musical tours until c. 1769; thereafter, she was permitted to perform only at home. She then turned to musical composition, which pleased Amadeus, who examined and commented favorably upon her work. None of her music survives. In 1784, she married J. B. von Berchtold zu Sonnenburg (1736–1801), a councillor at St. Gilgen. After her husband's death, Nannerl moved to Salzburg, where, until she became blind in 1829, she taught piano lessons. Her diaries and letters provide important information concerning the Mozart family.

In Paris, early in 1764, Amadeus's first published compositions appeared—two pairs of sonatas for keyboard and violin, his Op. 1 (K.6, 7) and Op. 2 (K.8, 9). Six sonatas of the same type (K.10–15) were issued in London in 1765; six more (K.26–31) were printed at The Hague in 1766. In all of these sonatas, the keyboard part is self-sufficient, and the violin provides accompaniment. Harpsichord sonatas with violin *ad libitum* were especially favored by Johann Schobert (c. 1735–67), a German composer active in Paris in the 1760s. The influence of Schobert's keyboard works, particularly his Op. 3 D-major sonata, is apparent in these early Mozart works. Schobert's music made a lasting impression on Mozart; borrowings from Schobert's sonatas appear in some of Mozart's piano concertos and later keyboard sonatas, e.g., Sonata in A minor K.310, whose Andante contains a quotation from Schobert's Sonata Op. 17, no. 1.

During the 15 months the Mozarts spent in England, Amadeus became acquainted with the sonatas and symphonies of J. C. Bach and C. F. Abel. In Chelsea, near London, Amadeus composed his first symphonies.

In autumn 1767, the Mozarts visited Vienna and several cities in Bohemia, then spent about a year in Vienna. By that time, Amadeus had composed arias and scenes for voice and orchestra; now, Leopold encouraged him to write an opera. *La finta semplice* (The feigned simpleton), a full-length *opera buffa*,

was completed but was not produced until May 1769, at Salzburg. However, other compositions by Amadeus were heard in Vienna in 1768: (1) a one-act *Singspiel, Bastien und Bastienne,* performed in October at the home of Dr. Franz Mesmer (1734–1815), inventor of "magnetism therapy" (mesmerism, hypnotism); (2) a festal Mass, K.139, performed at the dedication of Waisenhauskirche in December. Most of 1769 was spent in Salzburg, where Amadeus composed another Mass and several other sacred works, some minuets, and three instrumental serenades for university ceremonies. Late in October, he was appointed honorary Konzertmeister at the Salzburg court.

Between mid-December 1769 and March 1773, Leopold and Amadeus made three extensive journeys to various Italian cities. In addition to performing and sight-seeing, Amadeus had some counterpoint lessons from G. B. Martini (1706–84) at Bologna, met the celebrated castrato Farinelli, and, at Florence, formed a friendship with the precocious English violinist-composer Thomas Linley (1756–78; Insight, "Thomas Linley"), whose talents closely paralleled his own. That friendship was good for Amadeus, for it made him realize that he was not unique.

insight

Thomas Linley

Thomas Linley, a native of Bath, England, was writing music and was concertizing on the violin by the age of seven. In several respects, his early life paralleled that of Mozart. Linley had two musically talented and precocious sisters: Elizabeth (1754–92) and Mary (1758–87), both excellent sopranos. The Linley children received their early musical training from their father, Thomas (1733–95), a composer and singing teacher. Young Thomas studied composition with William Boyce in England, then studied violin with Pietro Nardini in Italy. Linley returned to England in 1771, concertized extensively, and was acclaimed as an outstanding violinist. During the last five years of his life, he composed a vast amount of music: at least 20 violin concertos, 2 sets of violin sonatas, several cantatas, operas, anthems, an oratorio, and other works. Only about two dozen of his works have been located; all are of consistently high quality. Some of his operas were among the first performed in Canada. Linley's untimely death, in a boating accident while on holiday with his family, was a tragic loss to English music.

Thomas Linley. Portrait by Thomas Gainsborough, c. 1773. *(Dulwich College Gallery, London.)*

In Italy, Amadeus became acquainted with works of leading Italian composers. The influence of G. B. Sammartini (c. 1700–75) of Milan is apparent in several of the symphonies Mozart wrote at this time. In general, Sammartini's symphonies are characterized by a texture similar to that of chamber music, with frequent passages of dialogue between instruments, intense rhythmic drive, varied treatment of sonata form, and structural continuity achieved by frequent elision of themes and/or sections. Slow movements are rich in lyricism and in imitative passages. Some portions of Sammartini's late symphonies have been described as "Mozartean," when, in reality, it was Mozart who assimilated characteristics from Sammartini. In Italy, Mozart composed his first seven string quartets: K.80 (1770) and K.155–60 (1772–73); they also reflect Sammartini's influence.

While in Rome, the Mozarts visited Sistine Chapel, where they heard Allegri's *Miserere* for double choir sung. Its notation was a carefully guarded secret, but Amadeus reproduced it after hearing the work once. A few months later (June 1770), the pope named Amadeus a Knight in the Order of the Golden Spur.

Most significant of the compositions Amadeus wrote during these years in Italy are two *opere serie* that were produced in Milan: *Mitridate rè di Ponto* (Mithridates, King of Pontus; December 1770) and *Lucca Silla* (December 1772). For Venanzio Rauzzini, *primo uomo* of *Lucca Silla,* Mozart wrote the motet *Exsultate, jubilate* (Rejoice greatly, jubilantly; K.165; soprano, orch.), a three-movement work that concludes with a brilliant *Alleluia*.

After several months' stay in Salzburg in spring 1773, Leopold took Amadeus to Vienna, where the youth heard Haydn's Opp. 17 and 20 string quartets and absorbed some features of Viennese musical style. Haydn's quartets inspired Amadeus to compose another set of six, K.168–73, in which some of those characteristics took root. For example, K.168 and K.170 have full-fledged fugues as finales—but fugues more like Fux's than Bach's. These finales are the first complete fugues in Mozart's secular works; undoubtedly, they were inspired by those in Haydn's Op. 20.

Back in Salzburg, in December 1773, Mozart wrote his first original piano concerto, K.175 (D major) and his first string quintet, K.174 (B♭ major), modeled after a quintet by Michael Haydn, court musician at Salzburg from 1763 to 1806. Mozart's choice of quintet instrumentation—a second viola added to string quartet—was probably determined by the fact that he enjoyed playing viola and may have participated in the work's initial performance.

Salzburg, 1773–1781

The Mozarts spent most of the time between October 1773 and November 1781 in Salzburg. In that provincial atmosphere Amadeus was discontent, but all of his applications for court positions elsewhere were fruitless. In late 1773 and in 1774, he composed the earliest of his works to find a place in concert repertoire—Symphonies K.183 (G minor) and K.201 (A major) and the Concerto for Bassoon and Orchestra (K.191)—works that attest his maturity. From this time forward, his compositions reveal an increase in his musical stature, and his individuality comes to the fore. Elements of styles experienced on his travels are visible in his writing and blend in varying degrees to produce a cosmopolitan, "Mozartean" flavor. Present are Italian lyricism (e.g., lyrical second themes, arialike slow movements), *style galant* (melodic sighs, triplet sixteenths, measured tremolo), Germanic seriousness with emphasis on counterpoint and greater formal complexity, and the expressive intensity of *Sturm und Drang*. Symphony No. 25 (K.183), often referred to as "the little G minor," is Mozart's second minor-key symphony and indicates his awareness of his contemporaries' use of minor keys—especially G minor—in works whose musical intensity is comparable with that depth of feeling expressed in *Sturm und Drang* literature.

Since Amadeus and his father both held appointments at the Archbishop's court—Leopold as court musician (from 1743) and deputy Kapellmeister (from 1763), and Amadeus as Konzertmeister (1769–77) and court organist (1779–81)—both Mozarts were expected to compose and perform church music regularly. Archbishop Hieronymus (Count Colloredo, r. 1772–1803) preferred short Masses with Epistle sonatas. In addition to Masses, among the sacred works Amadeus composed in 1772–80 are 17 short, single-movement Epistle sonatas written for performance in Salzburg Cathedral. Fourteen are trio sonatas for two

violins, organ, and "bass"; in another, two trumpets are added, and the other two require a small orchestra composed mainly of winds.

A commission Mozart received in 1774 for an *opera buffa* for the Carnival season in Munich resulted in *La finta giardiniera* (The feigned gardener); Leopold went to Munich with Amadeus for the January 1775 performance. Amadeus's earliest surviving piano sonatas date from the time of that Munich visit: Sonatas K.279–283 (in C, F, B♭, E♭, and G, respectively), which were written as a group, and K.284 (D major), the only one of the six published during Mozart's lifetime. His other significant works in 1775 are the concerti for violin and orchestra: K.207 (B♭ major), K.211 (D major), K.216 (G major), K.218 (D major), and K.219 (A major). For whom they were composed is not known; they may have been written simply because, as court Konzertmeister, Amadeus thought he should write something for the instrument associated with that position. He played them, and so did Antonio Brunetti, who joined the Salzburg court in 1776. For Brunetti, Mozart wrote two new movements: Adagio K.261 as substitute for that in K.219 and Rondo K.269 to replace that in K.207. These concerti show Mozart's steady development in the genre. From this time forward, he continued to write concerti, though he never composed another for solo violin. (The "Adelaide" Concerto, K.271a, in D, is spurious.)

When, in 1777, the Archbishop denied the Mozarts' several requests for permission to travel so that Amadeus could perform at other courts, Amadeus requested his release. In response, the Archbishop dismissed both father and son but soon reinstated Leopold. Amadeus was delighted to be released. He loathed being regarded as a servant and could not understand why musicians had to work under a feudal-type patronage system. He hoped his forthcoming tour would bring both fame and a lucrative position. Late in September, he and his mother set out, traveling to Munich, to Augsburg, and to Mannheim, where they remained several months before going to Paris. In each city, Mozart's endeavors to obtain a good position failed.

509

In other respects, the tour was not unproductive, though there were some grievous times. At Mannheim, Mozart observed orchestral practices and was fascinated by the clarinet. He renewed acquaintance with Cannabich, met Kapellmeister Holzbauer and flautist J. B. Wendling, and fell in love with soprano Aloysia Weber (c. 1761–1839). Through Wendling, Mozart obtained a commission from a Dutch flautist for three flute concerti and four flute quartets. Mozart wrote idiomatically for flute, but his antipathy for the instrument made composing these works difficult for him. He completed only two concerti (K.313 in G, K.314 in D) and two quartets (K.285 in D, K.285a in G). Two keyboard sonatas composed at Mannheim, K.309 in C major (for Cannabich's daughter) and K.311 (D major), together with K.310 (A minor) written in Paris, were published later as Op. 4. A sonata for piano and violin, K.296 (C major), written for the daughter of Amadeus's Mannheim landlord, engendered a further set of six, K.301–306, begun in Mannheim and completed in Paris. In most of these sonatas, the violin plays a subordinate role, just a step above being accompanist for the piano. Several theme-and-variations pieces were written in Paris, including that based on the French air *Ah, vous dirais-je maman* (Ah, I would like to tell you, Mother; K.265). Mozart was adept at improvising variations and undoubtedly created many sets that have not survived because they were never notated.

In Paris, the director of the *Concerts spirituel* commissioned Mozart to write a symphony for the program on Corpus Christi (June 1778). Mozart thus was confronted with composing for a large orchestra and in a style compatible with Parisian taste. He combined Mannheim and Paris styles in the symphony he prepared, No. 31, K.297. Also, Mozart became interested in *sinfonia concertante,* then popular in Paris, and composed in this genre several pieces featuring winds.

In July, Amadeus's mother contracted fever and died. When Amadeus broke the news to his father, Leopold urged his son to return to Salzburg. He did so, but by a circuitous route, through Strasbourg, Mannheim, and Munich. In Munich, he again saw Aloysia Weber but found her more interested in her career than in him. Mozart was enthusiastic about her singing, and in the ensuing years that enthusiasm never flagged. He created the role of Madame Herz in *Der Schauspieldirektor* (The Impresario; 1786) for Aloysia, and she was Donna Anna in the first Vienna performance of *Il Don Giovanni* (1788). For Aloysia's older sister, Josepha (c. 1759–1819), also a soprano, Mozart wrote the part of Queen of the Night in *Die Zauberflöte* (The magic flute; 1791).

In mid-January 1779, Amadeus finally returned to Salzburg. He was dejected, and with good reason: He had found no suitable position and knew he could not earn his living concertizing; his expenditures had hurt family finances; relations with his father were strained; his mother had died; he had fallen in love and had been rejected. Now, he willingly accepted an appointment as organist to the Archbishop. In addition to playing organ in the cathedral and at court, his duties included teaching the choirboys and composing whatever music was required. During the next two years, he wrote some Masses and Psalms settings, several symphonies, concerti, and serenades and began a *Singspiel* that he never completed. The most significant of these works are the "Coronation" Mass (K.317; C major), considered his finest Salzburg Mass, and the *Sinfonia concertante* (K.364; E♭) for solo violin and viola with orchestra.

In the summer of 1780, Mozart was commissioned to compose an opera for Munich and wrote *Idomeneo*. While the opera was in rehearsal in Munich, he made many revisions, trimming his original score considerably. The performance was postponed until 29 January 1781 and was quite successful. While in Munich, Amadeus composed several short vocal pieces, the Oboe Quartet (K.370, F major), and three piano sonatas (K.330–332) that are among his most popular keyboard works.

Meantime, the Archbishop and his retinue had gone to Vienna for festivities celebrating the imperial accession of Joseph II, and in mid-March Amadeus was summoned there. When several opportunities to perform before the emperor were denied him by the Archbishop, Mozart again rankled at the conditions of his servitude and requested release. At first, his request was denied, but, in June, after a stormy interview with the Archbishop, Mozart was dismissed and was literally kicked out of the Archbishop's presence.

The Vienna Years

Amadeus decided to remain in Vienna and took lodging with the Webers. Aloysia had married Joseph Lange in 1780, and now Amadeus's name began to be linked with that of her younger sister, Constanze (1762–1849). To squelch the rumors, Amadeus moved elsewhere but maintained contact with the family. During the winter of 1781–82, the friendship between Constanze and Amadeus deepened; on 4 August 1782 they were married in St. Stephen's Cathedral. In fulfillment of a vow made at that time, Amadeus began to write the Mass in C minor (K.427) but completed only Kyrie and Gloria. Most of the Sanctus and its Benedictus were notated and the Credo was begun, but, for an unknown reason, they were abandoned. On 25 October 1783, the Kyrie and Gloria, supplemented by other Mass movements previously composed by Mozart, were performed at St. Peter's in Salzburg. Constanze sang one of the soprano solo parts. Her voice was well trained and pleasing, but she was not gifted with outstanding musical talent.

Amadeus's first few years in Vienna were prosperous, though he had no permanent position or patron, no steady income. He had several pupils, and his talents as pianist and composer were in demand. His first Vienna publication was a set of six sonatas for piano and violin (K.296, K.376–80; 1781). Composition of *Die Entführung aus dem Serail* (The abduction from the harem) occupied much of his time during the spring of 1782. That *Singspiel* was favorably received when produced at Vienna's Burgtheater in July; it remained in the repertoire there for several years. Many of Mozart's finest compositions—most of the works responsible for his being considered a great composer—were written during the Vienna years. During this decade, his compositions were influenced principally by works of J. S. Bach and Joseph Haydn. In 1782, Amadeus became acquainted with Baron van Swieten, and for several years he attended the weekly gatherings at van Swieten's home that were devoted to studying the music of Handel and Bach. In those sessions, Mozart was introduced to *The Well-Tempered Clavier, The Art of Fugue,* and other Bach works. He reorchestrated some of Handel's oratorios, arranged five fugues from *The Well-Tempered Clavier,* Volume II, for string quartet (K.405), and composed a *Fugue in C minor* (K.426) for two pianos.

Constanze Weber Mozart. Portrait by Joseph Lange, c. 1782. *(Hunterian Art Gallery, Glasgow University, Scotland.)*

(That he made other arrangements of Bach's fugues is dubious.) After 1783, Mozart used counterpoint increasingly.

In 1781, poet Lorenzo da Ponte (1749–1838) came to Vienna; he achieved his first success as opera librettist working with Mozart. Their collaboration produced the operas *Le nozze di Figaro* (The marriage of Figaro; 1786), *Il Don Giovanni* (Don Giovanni; 1787), and *Così fan tutte* (Thus do they all; 1790), an *opera buffa.*

Between December 1782 and January 1785, Mozart composed his finest string quartets: K.387, K.421, K.428, K.458, K.464, K.465. Published as a set, in 1785, they were dedicated to Haydn. In 1782, Symphony No. 35 (K.385) was created for a Haffner family celebration; Symphony. No. 36 (K.425) was dashed off for a concert at Linz in 1783. For about three years, Mozart wrote no symphonies. Then, Symphony No. 38 (K.504; 1786) was written for performance at Prague. A year and a half later, in approximately six weeks in summer 1788, Mozart composed his finest symphonies, Nos. 39–41 (K.543, 550, 551). In 1785–86, he wrote six piano concerti, including K.466 (D minor) and K.467 (C minor); the former became his most popular piano concerto in the nineteenth century. Between 1787 and 1791, he wrote the string quintets K.515–16, K.593, K.614, and created the excellent Clarinet Quintet, K.581 (A major; 1789) for clarinetist Anton Stadler (1753–1812).

Gluck died in 1787, and Mozart hoped to be appointed to fill that vacancy at court. He was named Imperial Chamber Music Composer, at a small fraction of Gluck's former salary. Even such a minor appointment for Amadeus would have pleased Leopold, but he did not live long enough to learn of it; he died in May 1787. Amadeus turned over to his sister all of Leopold's estate except the music manuscripts.

Amadeus became a member of a Vienna Lodge of the Brotherhood of Freemasons in 1784. The ideals of Freemasonry and his affiliation with the Brotherhood meant a great deal to him. He translated some elements of Masonic ritual into musical symbols, which he incorporated into some of his works, e.g., *Die Zauberflöte* (The magic flute), and wrote a number of compositions for Masonic occasions. Among them are *Mauerische Trauermusik* (Masonic Funeral Music, K.477; 1785); the lovely Adagio in B♭, K.411 (1785), for two clarinets and three basset horns; and the Cantata, K.623 (November 1791), his last completed composition. During the last years of his life, when he had few pupils, commissions, or playing engagements, Mozart felt no compunction about entreating his fellow Masons to assist him financially. Neither Amadeus nor Constanze could manage money very well, but they never experienced abject poverty. They had six children, only two of whom survived to adulthood: Carl Thomas (1784–1858) and Franz Xaver (1791–1844). Both sons were talented musically; Franz, like his father, played piano and composed.

In addition to some purely Masonic works, during 1791 Amadeus completed *Die Zauberflöte,* a *Singspiel; La clemenza di Tito* (The clemency of Titus), an *opera seria;* Piano Concerto in B♭, K.595; Clarinet Concerto in A, K.622; the motet *Ave verum corpus* (Hail, true body; K.618; D major; SATB, strings, organ); and began the *Requiem* (K.626). Mozart had

not written church music since he abandoned composition of the C-minor Mass in 1783. He composed *Ave verum corpus* for use by choirmaster Anton Stoll at Baden, near Vienna.

The *Requiem* was commissioned anonymously by Count Franz Walsegg zu Stuppach, a dilettante who enjoyed commissioning works and having them performed in his own chapel as his own compositions. He intended to use the *Requiem* as a memorial Service for his deceased wife. Mozart worked on the Mass intermittently in 1791 but gave priority to other works. The Mass was still unfinished at the time of his death and was completed by his pupil and close friend, Franz Xaver Süssmayr (1766–1803). Undoubtedly, Mozart and Süssmayr had discussed the composition.

W. A. Mozart died on 5 December 1791. There was no public ceremony honoring him, and no crowds attended his funeral. He was buried in a mass grave at St. Marx churchyard, outside the city limits; the location of that grave is unknown.

Mozart's Works

Mozart seldom used opus numbers or dated his works. No extensive catalog of his music was available until 1862, when Ludwig von Köchel (1800–77) published his *Chronologisch-thematisches Verzeichnis* (Chronological-thematic catalog; 1862) of Mozart's known works, a chronological listing with **incipits** (the first few measures) of the theme of each movement and some documentary data pertinent to each work. Subsequent musicological discoveries have altered some of Köchel's findings, and his *Verzeichnis* has undergone some revisions; however, Mozart's works are still referred to by K. (Köchel) numbers.

Church Music

Mozart began writing church music in 1766 and wrote Masses, motets, and other sacred music fairly regularly until c. 1781. However, only a few of those compositions are considered major works. With the exception of *Missa in honorem sanctissimae Trinitatis* (Mass in honor of the most holy Trinity; K.167; 1773), the Masses and other sacred works Amadeus composed for Salzburg are concise and somewhat austere (though not lacking ingenuity), in conformity with the Archbishop's views concerning music in worship. For instance, Colloredo insisted that a complete

Mass Service, with an Epistle Sonata included, should last no longer than three-quarters of an hour, a demand that restricted the music to *Missa brevis* proportions. The "Coronation" Mass (K.317, C major; 1779), a *Missa brevis* written for the ceremonial crowning of a statue of the Virgin in a church near Salzburg, is less condensed. Like the other Masses, it is scored for SATB soloists, four-part choir, and orchestra; counterpoint appears in the customary places (e.g., the conclusions of Gloria and Credo), and the fashionable operatic idiom and symphonic orchestral writing are present. Though Mozart never completed the Mass in C minor (K.427), it is considered one of his finest Masses.

The *Requiem,* too, is a major work. Mozart finished the Introit and Kyrie and wrote out in draft score (i.e., voice parts, figured bass line, indications for instrumentation) the eight sections from *Dies irae* through *Hostias.* Süssmayr composed Sanctus and Benedictus, Agnus Dei, and *Lux aeterna* to complete the work. Both Baroque and Masonic elements infiltrated the *Requiem.* One subject in the double fugue in the Kyrie is often mentioned as a borrowing from Handel; however, this seems to be a stock figure used by many composers. Only in the *Rex tremendae majestatis,* the *Recordare,* the *Confutatis,* and the *Lacrimosa*—the last four connected movements of the *Dies irae*—does the *Requiem* match in quality Mozart's great C-minor Mass.

The motet *Ave verum corpus* (1791) is a small masterpiece, basically homophonic, with perfect voice leading and with polyphony introduced where it is most effective.

Operas

It is not odd that, at an early age, Mozart was attracted to opera; it would have been stranger had he not been. The eighteenth century was dominated by Italian opera; in addition to its obvious presence in performances, its influence was felt in other vocal forms, both sacred and secular, and in the structure of Classical instrumental forms such as the symphony, sonata, and string quartet. Yet, with all his talent for the dramatic, Mozart did not specialize in opera. It is evident that he regarded opera as primarily a multimovement *musical* composition rather than a dramatic production in which music was an auxiliary, and he incorporated within his operas a variety of musical forms that he adapted to dramatic means.

Bastien und Bastienne (1768), *La finta semplice* (1768), *Mitridate, rè di Ponto* (1770), and *Lucca Silla* (1772) are works by a talented young composer who did not yet fully understand characterization and musical depiction of drama. Nor is there anything exceptional about *Il rè pastore* (The shepherd king; 1775). *La finta giardiniera* (The feigned gardener; 1774) is a conventional Italian *opera buffa.* As its title implies, there is pretense in the form of disguises and mistaken identities; there are also dramatic inconsistencies, some of them created by the unsynthesized presence of both comedy and tragedy. The two ensemble finales provide a foretaste of Mozart's ultimate capabilities in writing that kind of closing scene. The autograph score for Act I of *La finta giardiniera* was lost, but the opera survived in a *Singspiel* version that Mozart made in 1780. Fortunately, a copy of the original Italian score was located in Brno, Czechoslovakia, in 1965, and the original version appears in the *Neue Mozart-Ausgabe* (New Edition [of] Mozart [Works]) published in 1978.

Idomeneo, rè di Creta (Idomeneus, King of Crete; Munich, 1781) marks the beginning of Mozart's maturity as an opera composer. Basically, *Idomeneo* is a conventional *opera seria* of the old Metastasian type—recitatives regularly alternating with arias, few ensembles, brilliant coloratura arias requiring improvised cadenzas, a principal role for a male soprano. However, in accordance with eighteenth-century reforms, most of the recitatives are accompanied, and there are some large choral scenes. Some of the latter are reminiscent of scenes in operas by Rameau or Gluck, especially the terrifying finale of Act II, wherein a storm arises, the monster appears, tonalties of the music change rapidly, and the frenzied chorus cries out repeatedly, "*Il reo qual è?*" ("Who is the guilty one?"). Mozart's acquaintance with French opera is apparent, too, in his inclusion of ballet; contrary to current custom, he composed the ballet music himself. Mozart consistently associated certain motives with individual characters and their emotions (e.g., Electra's jealousy) and used tonalities for special effect. Electra's disorientation is depicted not only through her actions and words, but also musically, by a C-minor recapitulation in a D-minor aria!

Die Entführung aus dem Serail (The abduction from the harem; Vienna, 1782) has a Turkish setting—use of Turkish background was very popular in the eighteenth century—and Mozart's orchestra includes characteristic instruments of the Janissary, the military bodyguard of Turkish sovereigns: cymbals, triangle, and bass drum, plus the exotic tones of clarinet and basset horn. Though the opera is a *Singspiel,* it is not the traditional type. The action is carried on almost exclusively by means of the spoken dialogue, but this opera contains more music than the usual *Singspiel.* Perhaps this is because Emperor Joseph II had insisted that the *National-Singspiel* (the imperial opera house) employ opera singers, preferably virtuosi, rather than actors relatively untrained in singing. Moreover, Mozart made some concessions to the singers, notably, the coloratura arias designed to display the virtuosity of soprano Catarina Cavalieri (1760–1801), who created the role of Constanze. (Catarina, considered one of the finest singers in Vienna in 1777–93, sang principal roles in several Mozart operas, e.g., Donna Elvira in *Il Don Giovanni* and the Countess in *Le nozze di Figaro.*) Mozart did not use coloratura merely for its own sake or to placate a singer but to delineate drama inherent in the text. Moreover, in this opera he notated every grace and cadenza, thereby eliminating the possibility of improvisation by the singers. He enlarged considerably the role of Osmin, the harem overseer, who, when enraged, becomes incoherent and illogical; Mozart's music superbly characterizes Osmin. The opera concludes traditionally, with a *vaudeville final*—a rondeau in which each participant is expected to sing a strophe, followed each time by a refrain sung by all on stage, but Osmin, enraged and confused, sings instead his vengeance music from Act I. With *Die Entführung aus dem Serail* Mozart elevated *Singspiel* from comparatively amateur status to an artistic level; therein lies the work's significance.

Lorenzo da Ponte supplied the libretti for Mozart's next three operatic successes. For *Le nozze di Figaro* (The marriage of Figaro; Vienna, 1786), he adapted P.-A. Beaumarchais's (1732–99) comedy *Le mariage de Figaro* (written 1781, perf. 1784), particularly diminishing the subversive aspects that were in accord with revolutionary thought prevalent in France at the time but retaining the basic clash between aristocracy and lower classes. Central to the opera are love and class conflict; present in abundance are irony and satire. The solution of the conflict was some ground gained by the underprivileged class. Often, the term "absolute musicality" is used to describe Mozart's music, meaning that his music does not reflect events in his personal life or the world about him. Such a blanket statement is inaccurate. Mozart, da Ponte, and Beaumarchais were well aware of social inequalities and oppression and had experienced them to some extent, for all three men had lower-class backgrounds. Because of their respective talents, they had gained a degree of acceptance in the highest social circles. In several operas, Mozart censured and ridiculed the aristocracy; his personal experiences sharpened his psychological insight so that he could aptly delineate character and use musical satire effectively.

Mozart did not label *Le nozze di Figaro* an *opera buffa,* but a *commedia per musica* (comedy through music); actually, it is a *dramma giocoso,* for both tragedy and comedy are present in it. The humor is not that of situation comedy but is dramatic and often is underlined with irony. There is, of course, some delightful text painting, e.g., the melodic intervals matching Figaro's measuring and Susanna's fainting with a declining scale. However, Mozart's music is not a succession of set pieces but a well-coordinated multimovement composition, and for some of those movements, he adeptly used symphonic formal structures. For example, in Act II, the strong wills of the Count and Countess conflict with regard to Susanna, who is present but hiding; tensions increase before the conflict is resolved. Ingeniously, to fit the dramatic situation, Mozart wrote the trio (No. 13; DWMA156) in miniature sonata form—first theme, modulation to dominant, second theme, closing theme, ten measures of development, full recapitulation in tonic, coda. The form and the three singers take the dramatic situation seriously; only for the audience is it comic. Through Mozart's excellent writing, the singers transform stock figures into real persons participating in and reacting to actual happenings. Mozart's ability to characterize is particularly effective in his ensemble writing, especially in the ensemble finales where, gradually, all of the characters are assembled on stage and all threads of plot and subplot are gathered together and cumulatively woven into the fabric, to effect either a climax or the final solution. In *Le nozze di Figaro* ensembles play a more important role than in Mozart's previous dramatic works; in fact, the number of ensembles and arias is almost equally balanced. The opera commences with a duet between Figaro and Susanna; subtly, this advises the audience that the emphasis is not on Figaro as hero but on the *marriage,* an ensemble (French *ensemble,* together). Mozart's point is lost when the opera is referred to as "Figaro."

Il dissoluto punito, ossia: Il Don Giovanni (The libertine punished, or Don Juan; Prague, 1787), a two-act *dramma giocoso,* concerns divine retribution rendered a libertine and blasphemer. The Don Juan legend originated in Seville and had been presented in drama since c. 1615 and in opera since 1713, but in Mozart's work the Don appears for the first time as a real person—a bold, romantic rebel, who is charming, selfish, ruthless, and unrepentant. Mozart's music portrays him superbly.

The opera is a synthesis of comedy and tragedy—the comedy of the Don's continual conquests and the situations in which he finds himself because of his amorous desires; the tragedy of murder, divine vengeance, and punishment by death. As in Shakespeare's plays, moments of comedy occur in many serious scenes. Donna Elvira constantly complains about the Don jilting her; her plight is pathetic, but she is subjected to frequent ridicule in "asides" that evoke audience laughter. When Leporello, the Don's valet, endeavors to console her by giving a detailed account of his master's amorous conquests, his rendition of the catalog aria is humorous. For a time, the listener takes him seriously, then realizes that he is exaggerating. Occasionally, the orchestra adds its musical laughter as it helps Leporello tally the numerous victims in various countries. *Madamina, Il catalogo è questo* (Young lady, this is the catalog . . . ; DWMA157b) is the most entertaining aria in the opera.

Mozart composed the overture last (DWMA 157a). A sonata-form movement in D major, it opens with a dignified introduction in D minor that, except for the absence of trombones, uses the same instrumentation, key, and musical material associated with the awesome appearance of the Commandant's statue at the climax of the opera. In the last half of the eighteenth century, trombones were still associated primarily with church music, and in *Il Don Giovanni* Mozart restricted their use to those times when the Statue and the demons associated with it appear on stage. Elements of nineteenth-century German Romantic opera are present in those scenes.

As in traditional, pre-reform Italian opera, much of the action in *Il Don Giovanni* is conveyed through *secco recitative.* However, Mozart rarely used *da capo* aria. The arias and duets are not always static or reflective; at times they represent dramatic developments. Such is the case in the little duet *La cì darem la mano* (There we will join hands) sung by Don Giovanni and Zerlina, the peasant girl he has asked to come to his villa. She hesitates, wavers (*vorrei e non vorrei,* I want to and yet I don't), then makes her decision—*Andiam!* (Let's go!). Immediately, the mood and tempo of the music change: the pleadingly tender Andante becomes a brisk and purposeful Allegro. Many examples could be cited to illustrate Mozart's careful attention to detail—often his treatment is subtle—in his comedies.

Così fan tutte, ossia La Scuola degli Amanti (Thus do they all, or The school for lovers; Vienna, 1790), on an original libretto by da Ponte, is a melodious, lighthearted work in the tradition of old Italian *opera buffa,* with the usual two pairs of lovers, mistaken identities and the resultant confusion, and ultimate resolution of the problem to the satisfaction of all participants. This is the only one of Mozart's operas published during his lifetime.

The music for *La clemenza di Tito* (The clemency of Titus; Prague, 1791), an *opera seria* commissioned for the festivities celebrating Leopold II's coronation as King of Bohemia (r. 1790–92), was written hastily at a time when Mozart was under financial and physical strain. In many respects, this is a conventional serious opera, and the restrained style Mozart used for the music is well suited to the topic and to the modified Metastasio libretto. At first a failure, the opera has attained a degree of acceptance.

On the other hand, *Die Zauberflöte* (The magic flute; Vienna, 1791) was successful immediately and has remained so. The idea of "magic" was much in vogue during the eighteenth century, and "magic" plays, stories, and operas were written in abundance.

The libretto for *Die Zauberflöte,* by Emanuel Schikaneder (1751–1812), is a collage of ideas borrowed from other authors' writings and runs the gamut from simple buffoonery to impressive solemnity, from childlike belief in magic to the sublime. Considerable machinery is required for the many magic effects. Some characters are enigmatic, appearing to be evil but ultimately revealed as being good. Papageno is a comic of the "Hanswurst" type (p. 469).

The opera's story extols the virtues of love, forgiveness, tolerance, the brotherhood of man—all important in Freemasonry, which was a moral and political force at this time in history. Both Mozart and Schikaneder were active in the local Masonic lodge, and the opera's connections with Freemasonry were neither accidental nor secret; Masonic symbols appeared on the printed libretto. Also, the mystical and perfect number three figures prominently in the opera: the overall key of the opera is E♭ major, and there are three temples, three doors, three genii, three attendants to the Queen of Night, three repeated chords, and three of other items. The great German dramatist Johann von Goethe, who also was a Freemason, commented that the higher meaning of the opera would not escape the initiate. What that higher meaning is, neither Mozart nor Goethe ever disclosed.

Die Zauberflöte is a *Singspiel* in the sense that it uses spoken dialogue and contains humorous scenes. However, Mozart's label for it—*grosse Oper* (great, or grand, opera)—is more appropriate; it is probably the first and is certainly one of the great modern German operas. (See fig. 19.14.) The music is Germanic in character, even to the use of a Lutheran chorale as basis for the duet of the Men in Armor (Act II), which is constructed as a kind of Baroque chorale prelude. The mood of much of the music is solemn. The rich, dark tones of basset horns and three trombones are prominent in several places. Mozart included some recitatives and wrote appropriate musical declamation for dialogue in German. His music fits perfectly the accents and rhythm of the German language and is sufficiently flexible to move from declamatory to arioso passages without disturbing the musical flow. An excellent example occurs in the first finale, in the scene between Tamino and the High Priest.

Figure 19.14 A contemporary drawing of a scene from the first production of Mozart's *The Magic Flute* at Theater auf der Wieden, Vienna, 1791. *(Mander & Mitchenson collection.)*

Mozart's use of keys is important, for it hints at procedures that would be followed to a greater extent in the nineteenth century, especially by Richard Wagner. Though the key of *Die Zauberflöte* as a whole is E♭ major, certain keys are consistently associated with specific kinds of persons or situations: G major for comic characters, G minor in painful situations, F major for the priests, and C minor for the otherworldly, regardless of whether evil, holy, or benign. Moreover, several themes are recurrent.

With *Il Don Giovanni* and *Die Zauberflöte* Mozart brought opera to heights never before scaled. In his hands the *Singspiel* became an art form, and the first steps were taken in the establishment of a national German opera. Through his psychological insight and skillful characterization, attention is focused on the individual person, and that person's relationship to and interaction with others. No longer is expression of an abstract emotion—an affect—central to the composition. Symphonic styles were adapted to operatic writing. In the three operas written with da Ponte, Mozart dealt with serious social issues of his time, using instrumentation, tonality, and sharp differentiation of musical styles to illustrate the chasm between social classes. It was not Mozart's intention to institute operatic reforms, nor did he make great changes in the theatrical forms of his day. His fusion of the comic and the serious, his ability to maintain

Example 19.13 Mozart: Symphony No. 1, K.16, mvt. 1, theme 1.

the action on both levels, and the depth of characterization he brought to the operatic stage were important factors in the development of opera.

Symphonies

Mozart wrote approximately 50 symphonies, some of them now lost. The development of his compositional skills and the changes in his musical style may be seen clearly in his symphonies, for their composition was spread over almost all of his professional career. The first 4 were written in a few weeks in 1764; the last 3, in about six weeks in 1788. His symphonic style evolved as his models changed: from J. C. Bach (1764); to the Viennese school of Georg Monn, Wagenseil, and Holzbauer (1767); to Sammartini and other Italian masters of the *sinfonia* (1770); to Stamitz, Cannabich, and others of the Mannheim school; and to F. J. Haydn (after 1772). In Mozart's last 3 symphonies, elements of these various influences coalesce with his individual characteristics and produce the symphonic style that is "Mozartean."

In Chelsea, England, in 1764, eight-year-old Amadeus copied two symphonies—one was K. F. Abel's Op. 7, No. 6—and composed four others. Two of those symphonies were preserved from the time of their composition. Two others, of which Köchel saw only fragments, K.16a in A minor, and K.19a in F major, were believed lost but were located in 1980 and 1983, respectively.

Symphony No. 1 in E♭, K.16, is scored for two oboes, two horns, strings, and basso continuo. A short three-movement work in Pre-Classical *sinfonia* style, it reflects Amadeus's acquaintance with works of J. C. Bach. The first movement (Allegro molto, $\frac{3}{4}$ meter) approximates sonata form, with three themes, the first of them outlining the tonic triad (ex. 19.13). The short development section consists of repetitions of the first theme in different keys; that theme does not appear in the recapitulation. The slow movement (Andante,

‖ : Exposition : ‖ : Development Recapitulation : ‖ Coda ‖

Figure 19.15 Diagram of Mozart's construction of the sonata-form movements of his Symphony No. 29, K.201, with exposition repeated, development-recapitulation repeated, followed by coda.

C minor, $\frac{2}{4}$) is in binary form; the finale (Presto, E♭, $\frac{3}{8}$) is a rondo. Mozart's orchestral treatment of all of the instruments is idiomatic, with sensitivity to tone colors and careful use of the winds to reenforce harmonies, to provide accents, and, about 50 percent of the time, to double the strings.

For the symphonies he wrote in Vienna in 1767 (K.43, K.45, K.48) Mozart used the four-movement plan favored by the Viennese symphonists, but he reverted to three-movement *sinfonia* pattern for some of the Italianate works he created in 1770 (K.74, K.81). In 1772–74, Mozart composed 17 symphonies, almost evenly divided between three- and four-movement structure. Haydn's influence is apparent in some of the four-movement works, notably Symphonies No. 20, K.133 (D major; 1772), and No. 25, K.183 (G minor; 1773). Mozart wrote only three minor-key symphonies, two of them in G minor, both filled with intense emotion.

Symphony No. 29, K.201 (A major; 1774), is scored for two oboes, two horns, and strings—the same instrumentation as Amadeus's first symphony. Three themes of contrasting character are presented in the exposition of the sonata-form first movement (Allegro maestoso, $\frac{4}{4}$); a new theme is introduced in the development. Measured tremolo is used extensively. The recapitulation almost exactly duplicates the exposition. Both halves of the movement are marked to be repeated. Then comes a coda based on the first theme, here treated imitatively (fig. 19.15). The Andante second movement (D major; $\frac{3}{4}$), in sonata form with an abbreviated development section, is also structured with a coda to be played after both sections of the movement have been repeated. There is some use of polyphony in conjunction with presentation of the first theme. The melodic writing in this movement is quite ornate; this, plus the fact that the strings are muted, creates an effect of delicacy. Menuetto with Trio constitutes the third movement. Dotted rhythms are a feature of the Menuetto; in

The Classic Era

contrast, the Trio melody is lyrical. The symphony concludes with a bithematic, sonata-form Allegro con spirto (A major; $\frac{6}{8}$), in which the melodic first theme is presented against an ostinato line. Mozart began the development section with sequential treatment of the first theme, modulating through several keys—a characteristic feature of his development procedure—then continued the modulations through sequences used imitatively. As in the first and second movements, the coda follows repetition of development-recapitulation section.

Four years elapsed before Mozart wrote another symphony. Then, for the *Concert spirituel* in June 1778, he composed Symphony No. 31, K.297, a three-movement work in D major. The Paris orchestra was larger and contained more winds than orchestras for which he had written previously; in addition to strings, K.297 requires pairs of flutes, oboes, clarinets, bassoons, horns, trumpets, and timpani. This is Mozart's first symphony with clarinets. Paris audiences were accustomed to hearing works by Mannheim composers, as well as those by Gossec and other Parisians; therefore, Mozart designed his "Paris Symphony" accordingly, incorporating features of both Mannheim and Parisian styles. Even without a minuet/trio movement, K.297 was longer than any of his previous symphonies; because of this, he did not repeat the development-recapitulation section of the first movement. Moreover, he had to rewrite the slow movement because his original Andante was too long.

Mozart's last six symphonies—K.385, K.425, K.504, K.543, K.550, and K.551—have become a part of standard orchestral repertoire and are frequently performed. Symphony No. 35, K.385 (D major; 1782), known as the "Haffner" Symphony, originated as a six-movement serenade (but *not* the "Haffner" Serenade, K.250) written for Sigmund Haffner for a family celebration. Mozart created the four-movement symphony by deleting the serenade's opening march and second minuet.

In 1783, Mozart hastily wrote Symphony No. 36, K.425 (C major) when he was in Linz, Austria, and discovered he had no symphony with him for the concert there. His next symphony, No. 38, K.504 (D major; 1786), a three-movement work without a minuet, was first performed in Prague. In both the "Linz" and the "Prague" symphonies, the first movement commences with a slow introduction, something Mozart used in only one other symphony, No. 39, K.543. (The symphony Köchel catalogued as No. 37, K.444, is by Michael Haydn.)

Mozart's last three symphonies are masterpieces of the genre. In comparison with his other symphonies, these compositions have more extended forms, more complex development sections, and exhibit greater use of counterpoint, chromaticism, and unifying motives among the movements of a work. The extensive counterpoint in these symphonies reflects Mozart's interest, at that time, in the polyphonic works of J. S. Bach and Handel.

Each of these symphonies has four movements, arranged in the same order, with the slow movement in a related key. The wind instrumentation of each of the symphonies differs slightly: Symphony No. 39, K.543 (E♭ major), has no oboes; Symphony No. 41, K.551 (C major; nicknamed "Jupiter"), has no clarinets; Symphony No. 40, K.550 (G minor), has neither trumpets nor timpani and in its first version had no clarinets. Moreover, in K.550 the two horns (in B♭ and G) are treated individually rather than as a pair. The three symphonies differ vastly in mood. The E♭-major symphony is the most cheerful of the three; the C-major sounds majestic and victorious; the G-minor is filled with intense emotion and passion, at various times conveying grief, pain, or joy (DWMA158).

Outstanding features of Symphony No. 40 are its concentration on the second, especially the minor second, its chromaticism, and Mozart's skillful use of counterpoint. The minor second appears at the outset, in the reiterated "melodic sigh" motif that forms much of the first theme—a theme whose melody hovers around the dominant pitch and mentions the tonic g only slightly (in m. 4; ex. 19.14a). In the slow movement, the imitative entry of second violins creates a hammering harmonic second and is accompanied by chromaticism (minor seconds) in the bass (ex. 19.14b). Minor seconds occur in the second measure of the Menuetto theme (ex. 19.14c). In the Finale's first theme, the "melodic sigh" atop the "Mannheim rocket" and the chromaticism in the winds' response provide more minor seconds (ex. 19.14d). The violin melody of the second theme, presented *piano* (mm. 70–85), is filled with minor seconds (ex. 19.14e). In every movement of this symphony, the first theme commences on an upbeat.

(a)

(b)

(c)

(d)

(e)

Example 19.14 Mozart: Symphony No. 40, K.550: (*a*) mvt. 1, mm. 1–5; (*b*) mvt. 2, mm. 1–6; (*c*) mvt. 3, mm. 1–3; (*d*) mvt. 4, mm. 1–4; (*e*) mvt. 4, theme 2.

The Classic Era

Example 19.15 Mozart: Symphony No. 40, K.550, mvt. 1, theme 2.

The opening movement, Molto Allegro (G minor), is in sonata form. A general pause (m. 43) calls attention to its chromatic, lyrical second theme, which is divided between strings and winds (ex. 19.15).

Counterpoint plays a large role in the sonata-form second movement (Andante, E♭), whose first theme, with its hammering rhythm, is presented imitatively by upper strings. In mm. 44–46, the *forte* E♭-minor seventh chord and the ensuing chromatic dissonances (ex. 19.16) probably were an aural shock in the 1780s.

Tonality returns to G minor for the last two movements. Themes of the Menuetto (Allegretto) and its Trio (in parallel major) suggest Austrian folk dance and folk song. In the Allegro assai finale, also in sonata form, constant alternation of *piano* and *forte* adds to the agitation. Tension is created almost immediately in the development section by unison utterance, *forte,* of an altered version of the "rocket," followed by stabbing downward leaps of a diminished seventh—the sevenths marked by wedges to indicate sharp staccato articulation, and punctuated by rests (mm. 126–132). Modulations around the circle of fifths and contrapuntal treatment of the "rocket," used in stretto three times (mm. 160–174), further increase tension. The development section concludes *forte* on an F♯ diminished-seventh chord; after a general pause (mm. 205–

Example 19.16 Mozart: Symphony No. 40, K.550, mvt. 2, mm. 43–46.

206), the double return (to tonic key and opening measures of the movement) for recapitulation commences *piano.*

Mozart's mastery of developmental techniques, and of symphonic structure, is apparent in his last three symphonies.

Example 19.17 Mozart: Piano Sonata K.331, mvt. 3, mm. 1–5. Turkish Janissary music was extremely popular when Mozart wrote this sonata. The graced figure would, of course, be performed as four equal 16th notes.

Solo Keyboard Works

A performing pianist, Mozart made a significant contribution to the repertoire for solo piano. His surviving solo keyboard works consist primarily of 17 sets of variations, 18 sonatas, and some fantasias. The independent theme-and-variations sets are charming but not distinctive. Theme-and-variations compositions were very popular in Paris, and, in general, Mozart's sets of variations follow the Parisian pattern: If the theme is in a major key, one variation is in minor; if the theme is in duple meter, one variation is in triple time; and one variation is an Adagio. The 12 variations on the old French nursery rhyme *Ah, vous dirais-je maman* provide a representative example. That melody is better known in America as "Twinkle, twinkle, little star."

The solo sonatas are three-movement works usually constructed according to the following scheme: First movement in sonata form with contrasting themes; second movement, either Adagio or Andante, exhibiting expressive lyricism; third movement, a lively rondo that in two instances (K.311, K.333) includes a cadenza.

In the six sonatas composed in 1775, the K.279–283 group and K.284, *style galant* is apparent, as is also the influence of Haydn and C. P. E. and J. C. Bach. The middle movement of K.284, labeled *Rondeau en Polonaise, Andante* (A major), is a simple rondeau whose theme has polonaise rhythm. The finale (D major) comprises theme and 12 variations, most of them as virtuosic as any in the independent sets.

Mozart ranked K.309 (C major) and K.311 (D major), written in 1777, among his most difficult sonatas. By then, he was using a Stein piano. The small, light hammers (some of them were hollow) of Stein pianos with individual escapement levers contributed to ease of performance of rapid passages, especially those containing repeated notes (see Insight, "The Piano (I)," p. 478).

Sonata K.310 (A minor; 1778), is Mozart's first minor-key sonata. Of sonatas K.330–332 (1781), K.331 (A major) has become a perennial favorite, though it is not typical of Mozart's sonata writing. Its structure is unusual: The Andante grazioso first movement, in A major, presents an 18-measure rounded binary theme, followed by six highly expressive, difficult variations. The middle movement is an A-major Menuetto with Trio in D major. The finale reflects the current interest in Turkish Janissary music. Labeled *Alla Turca* (in Turkish style; ex. 19.17), it is a rondo in A minor with an A-major refrain.

Sonata K.333 (1784), in B♭ major, is an excellent example of Mozart's mature style. The opening Allegro reflects the influence of J. C. Bach, especially his Sonata in G major, Op. 17, No. 4.

When published in Vienna in 1785, the Sonata in C minor, K.457, was prefaced by the *Fantasia,* K.475, also in C minor. Pairing of this kind seems to imply that continuous performance was intended, though the Sonata was composed seven months earlier than the *Fantasia.* Both compositions are indebted to similar works by C. P. E. Bach. The *Fantasia* is constructed in six distinct sections, the last being a return to *Tempo primo* and the initial material, as a kind of recapitulation. Its concluding measure is a dashing three-octave C-minor scale that ends on a C-minor chord spanning the same distance. The Sonata commences *forte* with a staccato arpeggiation of the tonic chord, played in octaves, and the sonata-form first movement gathers strength as it proceeds. This, Mozart's most forceful sonata, presages the development of the sonata in Beethoven's hands. In fact, Sonata K.457 exerted considerable influence upon Beethoven. The second movement, in E♭ major, is a lovely Adagio whose main theme, in its successive presentations, is furnished with increasingly elaborate embellishments. Then, the same driving force that

The Classic Era

Example 19.18 Mozart: Sonata K.457, Finale, theme 1.

Molto allegro. (n.d. Autograph)

propels the first movement of the sonata is present in the syncopated triadic theme that begins the finale (ex. 19.18). However, in the finale, silences—general pauses—diminish the power and permit the intrusion of an element of despair, the *pathétique* character of C-minor tonality. (DWMA159.)

Undoubtedly, Sonatas K.545 (C major) and K.570 (B♭ major) were written for instructional purposes. The Sonata in D major, K.576 (1789), Mozart's last piano sonata, is his most difficult one. In its three movements there is no trace of the Alberti bass that characterizes many of Mozart's piano works; instead, other kinds of broken-chord figurations are used. The movement contains much skillfully written counterpoint. The A-major Adagio middle movement is, as usual, filled with elaborate figuration; this movement also served as a model for Beethoven. The strength of the Allegretto rondo finale is not weakened by the fact that it contains much that is *galant*.

Concerti

Mozart's chief contributions to the historical development of instrumental music are his treatment of the concerto and his perfection of Classical concerto structure. The composition of concerti—especially those for piano and orchestra—occupied him throughout his compositional career. Moreover, his choice of piano (rather than harpsichord or clavichord) as his solo keyboard instrument did much to promote the use of that instrument.

Mozart's earliest concerti for keyboard and orchestra (K.37, 39, 41; Salzburg, 1767) are arrangements of sonata movements by other composers. Subsequently, he arranged three sonatas from J. C. Bach's Op. 5 as keyboard concerti (in D, G, and E♭, K.107; 1772). The influence of J. C. Bach on Mozart's career should not be minimized.

The 23 original concerti Mozart composed for piano and orchestra may be divided into four chronological groups: (1) those written in Salzburg in 1773–79 (K.175, 238, 246, 271, the three-piano concerto K.242, and the two-piano concerto K.365); (2) those written in Vienna, 1782–83 (K.413, 414, 415); (3) those written in 1784 (K.449, 450, 451, 453, 456, 459); and (4) those written in 1785–91 (K.466, 467, 482, 488, 491, 503, 537, 595). Fourteen of the 17 concerti composed during the Vienna years were created for Mozart's own performances. The sharp decline in his popularity as soloist after 1786 is reflected by the fact that he wrote no piano concerto in 1787, only 1 in 1788 (K.537), and no more until 1791 (K.595). All of Mozart's piano concerti are of high quality.

For his first original piano concerto, K.175 (1773), Mozart added two trumpets and tympani to the standard orchestral instrumentation. The work is longer and somewhat more complex than J. C. Bach's concerti. The finale of K.175 exhibits both *galant* and "learned" (contrapuntal) elements.

Mozart did not write another piano concerto until 1776. In the interim, he composed a bassoon concerto and five violin concerti. For these, he reverted to the orchestration then standard: two oboes, two horns, strings, basso continuo. In the bassoon concerto, K.191 (B♭; 1774), Mozart's writing is completely suited to the instrument. The slow movement is a lovely, lyrical aria.

The five concerti for violin and orchestra, all written in 1775, are: K.207 (B♭ major) and K.211 (D major), which display some Baroque characteristics; K.216 (G major), which begins with a theme from an aria ritornello in *Il rè pastore*; K.218 (D major), whose first movement is a blend of concerto-ritornello and sonata form; and K.219 (A major), which concludes with a Menuetto. Of the five, the last three are richer and of greater depth and are excellent examples of his mature style. They have been performed frequently in the twentieth century. The slow movement of K.216 is especially beautiful. Within the finale of K.218 Mozart wrote both a gavotte and a **musette.** (A musette is a dancelike piece characterized by a sustained drone such as that produced by the eighteenth-century musette, the French bagpipe.)

Mozart resumed composition of piano concerti in January 1776. Within the next 12 months, he produced K.238 for himself, the triple concerto K.242 for three lady amateurs, K.246 for Countess Lützow, and K.271 (Eb; January 1777) for Mlle Jeunehomme. Of these, K.271 is the most substantial. In its Andantino (C minor), the first minor movement in a Mozart concerto, strings are muted. In the Presto finale, Mozart interpolated a stately Menuet in Ab with four variations.

Two years elapsed before Mozart wrote another piano concerto. His next two concerti were for flute—K.313 in G, K.314 in D (1778). They are idiomatic, pleasing, nonvirtuosic works. While in Paris in April 1778, he composed two double concerti: K.299 for flute and harp and the *Sinfonia concertante* in Eb, K.364, for violin and viola, a masterful piece of *concertante*-symphonic writing.

Early in 1779, for his sister and himself, he wrote K.365 (E major; two pianos and orch.), which may be considered a companion piece to (but not quite equal to) K.364. Mozart aimed at moderation in the three piano concerti composed for his own use in Vienna during fall-winter 1782–83, K.413, 414, 415—"midway between the too easy and the too difficult," he wrote his father—and he achieved that aim.

For his friend Ignaz Leutgeb (c. 1745–1811), Mozart wrote three horn concerti in Eb: K.417 and K.447 in 1783; K.495 in 1786. Despite the fact that Mozart's autograph scores contain numerous jocular remarks at Leutgeb's expense, some of this music makes real demands of the soloist, especially K.447.

Two of the concerti (K.449 in Eb, K.453 in G) that Mozart composed in the spring of 1784 were intended for his pupil, Barbara Ployer; the other two, K.450 in Bb and K.451 in D, were for himself and were, he wrote his father, "*concerti* that are bound to make the performer sweat." The G-major concerto is lovely, at times passionate, at times expressively tender; some of its modulations go far afield. Commencing in 1784, Mozart added a flute and two bassoons to the concerto orchestra; for K.451 he added two trumpets and timpani, also. Later that year, he composed K.456 (Bb) for Viennese virtuosa Maria Theresia von Paradis (1759–1824) to perform on an extended concert tour in Paris and London. Paradis, daughter of imperial court secretary Josef von Paradis, was also a composer; most of her works are lost.

The reason Mozart composed K.459 (in F; December 1784) is not known; presumably, the concerto was for his own use. He performed it, with trumpets and timpani in the orchestra, along with K.537, at coronation festivities in October 1790. The trumpet and timpani parts are lost; certainly, those instruments added brilliance to the military effect of the first movement. Mozart included two trumpets and timpani in the orchestra for all of his remaining piano concerti except K.488 and K.595.

Mozart's D-minor concerto, K.466 (February 1785), his first concerto in a minor key, was the one of his concerti most frequently performed in the next two centuries. It is a dramatic work, filled with pathos and passion—a work that Beethoven knew and one for which he wrote cadenzas. The solo and orchestral parts are sharply contrasted. Some of the themes in the first movement are introduced by and belong exclusively to the soloist. Strong contrasts exist among the movements, too. Mozart's choice of key for the Andante is unusual—Bb, the subdominant of the relative major—a shift in tonality that might be expected from Beethoven 15 years later. Mozart's next concerto, K.467 in C major (March 1785), is symphonic in sound. Its Andante, in F, is an expressive aria (in ABA form) presented by the piano against a background of muted strings; the C-major finale is a sonata-rondo.

During winter 1785–86, Mozart wrote three piano concerti—K.482 in Eb, K.488 in A, K.491 in C minor. Again, he altered the orchestral instrumentation, substituting two clarinets for the oboes in K.482 and K.488 and not using trumpets and timpani in K.488. The first two of these concerti are lighter than those written earlier in the year, as though Mozart sensed that his popularity was slipping, and he wished to regain the favor of Viennese audiences. Certainly, he did so with K.482. When he performed it in a subscription concert in Vienna, the audience so appreciated the slow movement, an Andante in C minor, constructed as theme and variations, that he had to repeat it immediately. This seems to indicate that in the late eighteenth century applause was rendered after each movement of a multimovement work instead of being reserved until the end of the last movement. Or, possibly, Mozart did not play all three movements of the concerto as a unit; in that era, it

Example 19.19 (*a*) Mozart: Concerto No. 27 for Piano and Orchestra, K.595, Finale, theme 1. (*b*) Beginning of folk-song melody *Komm lieber Mai und mache die Wälder wieder Grün*.

(a)

(b)

was not unusual for the movements of a multimovement work to be performed individually and interspersed with other items on a concert program.

For K.491, Mozart used the richest orchestration he ever employed in a piano concerto: one flute, pairs of oboes, clarinets, bassoons, horns, and trumpets, plus timpani and strings. The sound produced was indeed symphonic. This C-minor concerto is another that Beethoven admired. Mozart's 25th piano concerto, K.503 (C major; December 1786), is a grandiose work, conveying a triumphant, victorious mood. Often considered the counterpart of K.491 (C minor), its immediate predecessor, it may be regarded also as an intensification of K.467 (C major).

The so-called Coronation Concerto, K.537 in D, was written for Lenten concerts in 1788, and Mozart played it at the Dresden court in 1789. He took this concerto and K.459 with him when he went to Frankfurt for the imperial coronation in 1790, and he performed both of them at the festivities. The "Coronation Concerto" is a festive work, but, as it now exists, the solo piano part is only an approximation of what Mozart intended it to be, because he merely sketched an outline of the solo and filled in most of the music from memory when performing it. The orchestral parts were notated completely.

Mozart completed his 27th and last piano concerto, K.595, in B♭, on 5 January 1791 and performed it on March 4 as part of a recital given by clarinetist Joseph Bähr in the concert hall of court caterer Jahn in Vienna. This B♭ concerto is a serene work, "Classical" in every respect. In it, Mozart's complete mastery of concerto composition is evident; the first movement is a textbook example of concerto-sonata form (DWMA148). The first theme of the last movement closely resembles and may have been inspired by the folk song *Komm lieber Mai und mache die Wälder wieder grün* (Come, dear May, and make the woods green again; ex. 19.19).

The Concerto in A for clarinet and orchestra, K.622 (October 1791), was written for Anton Stadler. In this concerto, Mozart exploited all registers of the clarinet without undue exhibition of virtuosity and provided no opportunity for the soloist to improvise cadenzas. The apparent simplicity of the concerto is at times deceptive; that apparent simplicity is what makes this concerto so effective.

Chamber Music: Quartets

Mozart's 26 string quartets may be divided into two basic groups: the 16 quartets written in 1770–73, works numbered K.80, K.136–138, K.155–160, and K.168–173; and the 10 quartets composed in 1782–90, consisting of the 6 dedicated to Haydn (K.387, K.421, K.428, K.458, K.464, K.465), one dedicated to F. A. Hoffmeister (K.499), and the so-called Prussian quartets (K.575, K.589, K.590).

Originally, Mozart's first quartet, K.80, written in Italy in 1770, had only three movements: Adagio, Allegro, Menuet/Trio, all in G major. The Rondo fourth movement was added in 1773. This quartet reflects the influence of the north Italian trio sonata: second violin has many passages in thirds, sixths, and tenths with first violin; viola and 'cello provide accompaniment.

Mozart gave his next nine quartets only three movements each. The three quartets written in Salzburg in 1772 (K.136–138) are structured alike, with principal interest in the violin parts, opening themes built on tonic chord figures, and, in sonata-form movements, sectional developments in which only one theme is used at a time. The six quartets K.155–160, composed in Italy in 1772–73, are in *concertante* style—upper against lower strings, or solo violin against second violin and viola, with 'cello *continuo*. Strong, sudden dynamic contrasts indicate Mannheim influence.

Example 19.20 Mozart: Oboe Quartet, K.370, Finale, mm. 90–103. Note the meter change for oboe at m. 95.

Quartets K.168–173 (1773) are Viennese in style and reflect Mozart's acquaintance with Haydn's Op. 17 and Op. 20 quartets. Each of these Mozart works has four movements, with Minuet included; there is considerable use of counterpoint, resulting in greater independence of parts and more importance accorded the three lower instruments. The Andante first movement of K.170 is theme and variations; K.168 and K.173 have fugal finales.

Between 1773 and 1782 Mozart wrote no string quartets. In 1777, he accepted a commission for a set of three flute quartets (fl., vln., vla., 'cello), but only one of them is considered completed, the three-movement K.285 (D major). Throughout that quartet, the flute has a prominent role but is treated soloistically only in the Adagio second movement, wherein the strings are relegated to pizzicato accompaniment. The three-movement quartet for oboe, violin, viola, and 'cello (K.370, F major; 1781), written for oboist Friedrich Ramm of Mannheim, is excellent. The oboe does not dominate, yet is given ample opportunity to exhibit its capabilities. An unusual feature in the Rondo finale, written in $\frac{6}{8}$ meter, is a passage in which the oboe presents a melody in $\frac{4}{4}$ meter while the strings continue in $\frac{6}{8}$ (ex. 19.20).

Mozart seldom composed without having either a commission or a professional need for a particular work. Yet, between December 1782 and January 1785, he wrote six string quartets for purely personal reasons. Inspired by Haydn's Op. 33 quartets, and stimulated by a desire to show his esteem for the older composer, Mozart determined to honor Haydn with a series of string quartets that would, at the same time, display his own compositional capabilities. In dedicating the quartets to Haydn, Mozart referred to them as "fruit of a long and laborious endeavor." The completed quartets do not reveal that Mozart experienced any difficulties whatsoever in their composition—indeed, they are Mozart's finest string quartets. However, the numerous alterations Mozart made in the autograph manuscript support his statement. Undoubtedly, this set of Mozart's quartets surpassed any that Haydn had composed up to this time, and, in their turn, influenced Haydn's later string quartets, especially with regard to chromaticism.

The Classic Era

Example 19.21 Mozart: String Quartet in C major, K.465 ("Dissonance" Quartet), mvt. 1, mm. 1–11.

These "Haydn" quartets are a heterogeneous set, each quartet being to some extent individualistic, yet all having some traits in common. Mozart's only use of a slow introduction in a string quartet occurs in the first movement of K.465 (C major), a contrapuntal introduction replete with cross-relations, seconds, and other dissonances that belie the movement's C major tonality and cause the composition to be known as "Dissonance Quartet" (ex. 19.21).

Dissonant imitative counterpoint occurs in the first movement of the sombre D-minor quartet (K.421), also. On the other hand, the mood of the Bb-major quartet (K.458; "The Hunt") is light. The hunting theme with which its first movement commences (and from which the name of the quartet is derived) does not recur until the coda, where it is treated imitatively. This is the only quartet with a development section that does not quote from the exposition; instead, the development presents new thematic material. The second movement, in Bb major, is a short Menuetto with Trio; the third, an Adagio in Eb major, has rich, romantic harmonies. A sonata-rondo finale with three themes concludes the quartet.

Though these six quartets elicited praise from Haydn, they brought Mozart more criticism (especially concerning the dissonant C-major K.465) than commissions. He wrote only four more quartets: K.490 (D major, 1786), in which the sonata-form movements are colored by unusual modulations and un-

expected occurrences of developmental passages; and the three "Prussian" quartets (K.575, 1789; K.589, K.590; 1790).

The quartets Mozart wrote during the last decade of his life exhibit the characteristics of his mature style: instrumental themes of a vocal nature; short chromatic lines; a good deal of harmonic freedom; pervading thematic development; considerable use of counterpoint, forming a closely knit texture.

Chamber Music: Quintets

Mozart composed nine quintets: six for strings, two for one wind instrument and the string quartet complement, and one for piano and winds. His first string quintet (K.174) was written in 1773, shortly after he became acquainted with G. B. Sammartini's string quintets in Italy; 14 years elapsed before he wrote another. By this time, he knew the quintets of Michael Haydn and Luigi Boccherini, but, instead of using two 'celli as they did, Mozart employed two violas to widen the tonal expanse without great gaps in texture. The two string quintets he composed in April and May 1787, K.515 in C major and K.516 in G minor, are masterpieces. They are direct antitheses in mood and character, the C-major quintet exhibiting classical serenity (though it is by no means bland) and the G-minor work depicting depths of emotion and a style more romantic in nature. In this respect, as well as in keys, they are comparable with his last two symphonies (K.550, G minor; K.551, C major), composed a few months later.

Most of Mozart's string quintets commence with an upward arpeggiation of the tonic chord. In K.516, the first theme of the opening Allegro incorporates also the descending chromaticism that colors many of Mozart's second themes. The opening theme dominates the first movement, and elements of that theme appear in other movements, e.g., the ostinato bass figure of the second Adagio. In texture, K.516 is very contrapuntal. In this quintet, the order of the movements, and the keys used for them, do not conform to the pattern generally considered standard for multi-movement Classical works. The opening movement, a sonata-form Allegro in G minor, is followed by a Menuetto in G minor (Allegretto) with Trio in G major. The Adagio ma non troppo third movement, played on muted instruments, is an 82-measure abridged sonata form (i.e., lacking development section) in E♭ major. Next comes a 32-measure Adagio in G minor, notated as a separate movement but actually serving as slow introduction to the Allegro finale, a lengthy (297 measures) rondo in G major.

Mozart's genius as a composer of chamber music is fully revealed in the Clarinet Quintet in A major, K.581 (1789). He wrote idiomatically for clarinet, with due regard for its timbre, registers, agility, and finer subtleties. In this quintet, he did not allow the clarinet to become the soloist; nor did he so imbed it within the ensemble that its distinctive characteristics were overshadowed. Rather, he created a texture in which there is perfect tonal balance. Leadership in introducing themes is divided between clarinet and first violin, but all of the instruments share in later presentation of the thematic material. In the Finale, a set of variations, Mozart's treatment of the various instruments is especially remarkable.

Chamber Music with Piano

The change in the role of the keyboard from soloistic domination to equal partnership in the ensemble may be seen in Mozart's works—in the piano trios, the piano quartets, and especially in the 33 sonatas for violin and keyboard. In the 16 early sonatas (K.6, 7; K.8, 9; K.10–15; K.26–31), the violin provides accessory accompaniment to the keyboard. The harpsichord (or piano) part is self-sufficient; if the violin part were deleted, a keyboard solo sonata would remain.

To some degree, duetting, dialogue, and sharing of thematic material occurs in Sonatas K.301–306, written in Mannheim and Paris in 1778. However, in many passages the musical sense would not be damaged if the violin line were omitted. Not until 1781, in Sonatas K.376–80, did Mozart achieve genuine violin-piano partnership. The Sonata in B♭, K.481 (1785), which Mozart wrote for and performed with the brilliant young Mantuan violinist Regina Strinasacchi (1764–1839), is a masterpiece, as is also the Sonata in A, K.526 (1787). Both sonatas contain slow movements of great beauty.

Among Mozart's chamber music with piano are other works that must be considered masterpieces: the Piano Quartets K.478 in G minor (1785) and K.493 in E♭ major (1786); and the Piano Trios K.502 in B♭ major (1786) and K.542 in E major (1788).

Other Composers

Dozens of excellent composers were active in Europe in the late eighteenth century. Vienna attracted many, at least transitorily; some remained there, but most moved on to other Austrian and German cities, to Italy, and to France. Leopold Gassmann (1729–1774) and Antonio Salieri (1750–1825) obtained posts at the imperial court and remained in Vienna.

Antonio Salieri

Salieri was born near Verona and received his early musical training in Italy. When in Venice in 1766, Gassmann noticed Salieri, brought him to Vienna, and guided his further education. At the imperial court Salieri met Metastasio and Gluck and learned a good deal about opera composition from them. The performance of Salieri's *Armida* at the Vienna Burgtheater in 1771 marked the beginning of his career as an opera composer. He composed more than three dozen operas, and during 1778–1804 he enjoyed operatic successes in Italy and Paris, as well as in Vienna.

In 1774 Salieri succeeded Gassmann as imperial court composer and Italian opera conductor, and in 1788 was appointed court Kapellmeister, also. Thus, while still in his twenties, Salieri held one of Europe's most important musical posts. He served at the imperial court for over half a century. Salieri was a prolific composer. In addition to operas, he composed

Antonio Salieri. Unsigned oil painting. *(Gesellschaft der Musikfreunde, Vienna.)*

cantatas and other secular pieces, oratorios, Masses and other sacred works, and orchestral and chamber music. Moreover, he exerted considerable influence as a teacher. Among his outstanding pupils were Beethoven, Czerny, Liszt, Schubert, and Weigl.

Salieri acquired a reputation for intrigue, justifiably. But the widespread rumor that he poisoned Mozart is not true. There is no record that Salieri ever did anything to harm Mozart.

Johann Rudolf Zumsteeg

J. R. Zumsteeg (1760–1802), 'cellist and composer, served as music master at Carlsschule military academy in Stuttgart from 1785 to 1794 and held several important posts at the Stuttgart court: solo 'cellist (1781–94); director of German music at the theater (1791–93); Kapellmeister (1794–1802). His numerous compositions include Masses, sacred and secular cantatas, operas, 'cello concerti and other instrumental works, and almost 300 Lieder and ballads.

Zumsteeg's long ballads—some almost 1000 measures long—were published singly; his shorter songs were issued in collections, e.g., the seven volumes entitled *Kleine Balladen und Lieder* (Little ballads and songs; 1800–1805).

As Kapellmeister, Zumsteeg did much to promote performance of the neglected operas of Mozart. The influence of Jomelli is apparent in Zumsteeg's early operas, but his last three *Singspiele—Die Geisterinsel* (The Ghost Island; 1799), *Das Pfauenfest* (The Peacock Festival; 1801), and *Elbondocani* (1803)—reflect his knowledge of Mozart's operas, especially in characterization, treatment of ensembles, and melodic style. The subject matter of those *Singspiele*—the world of magic, medieval chivalry, and Oriental fairy tale—indicates the trend toward nineteenth-century German Romantic opera.

The many Lieder and ballads Zumsteeg composed after 1791 are historically significant because they lie midway between the works of the second Berlin school and the songs of Franz Schubert. Zumsteeg set most of the well-known ballad texts of his time, and his settings served as models for works by later composers. Schubert patterned his early ballads (written in 1811–16) after Zumsteeg's and set some of the same texts, sometimes using the same key tonality and meter, e.g., *Die Erwartung* (Expectation) and *Ritter Toggenburg* (Knight Toggenburg). Zumsteeg was one of the earliest composers to use recitative effectively in lyric song. In his ballads, he made extensive use of descriptive figurations; his ability to depict mood was excellent. Some of his ballads are Romantic, e.g., his 950-measure, through-composed setting of Bürger's *Lenore* (1798), the story of a girl waiting for her lover to return from war. He has been killed and returns as a ghost to carry her away to their nuptial bed, the grave. Two of Zumsteeg's finest Lieder are his settings of Kosegarten's *Nachtgesang* (Nightsong; in *Kleine Balladen und Lieder,* Volume I; 1800), and von Salis's *Das Grab* (The Grave; in Volume IV; 1802; DWMA160). The brief strophic setting of *Das Grab* (F minor) is a masterpiece of solemn emotional depth—an F-minor chord sounded four times as introduction, followed by an eight-measure strophe that is to be repeated.

Music in North America

In the British colonies in North America, subscription and benefit concerts of instrumental and vocal music written by European composers (e.g., Handel, J. C. Bach, Abel, Stamitz) date from the 1730s. However, the first music by native-born North American composers did not appear until the second half of the century. Those composers include Francis Hopkinson (1737–91), James Lyon (1735–1794), William Billings (1746–1800), and John Antes (1740–1811).

Early in the eighteenth century, singing schools resulted from a desire among ministers to improve the quality of singing in their churches. These schools were not formal educational institutions but instructional sessions devoted to teaching singing and music note reading. The publication of tune books with instructional introductions commenced in the 1720s and continued throughout the century. Some tune books contained only melodies and were designed to be used with metrical versions of Psalms texts; in other tune books, texts were included.

James Lyon's tune book *Urania or A Choice Collection of Psalm-Tunes, Anthems, and Hymns* (1761) is a compilation of 96 pieces, most of them for four voices. It was the first publication to identify works by native American composers and contains the first printed compositions by Lyon, Hopkinson, and William Tuckey (1708–81). Lyon is represented by three psalm tunes and two anthems; his "Let the Shrill Trumpet's Warlike Voice" is one of the earliest anthems by an American composer. *Urania* was the first American tune book to include English **fuging-tunes,** a type of composition that soon became an American favorite. A typical fuging-tune has two sections, the second of them marked to be repeated. The piece begins as a simple four-part chordal harmonization of a psalm tune—the tune is in the tenor—which is brought to cadence, usually on the tonic. The second section commences with the **fuge**—successive contrapuntal entrances of the four voices, with a semblance of imitation; after all voices have entered, chordal harmonization is resumed and continues to the end of the section (ex. 19.22; DWMA161). In some fuging-tunes, the fuging section incorporates more than one imitative passage.

In 1770, William Billings, a Boston tanner and self-taught musician, published his first tune book, *The New-England Psalm-Singer.* This, the earliest tune book to contain only American music, was the first printed collection of sacred music by a single American composer. Among the approximately 125 compositions in the volume are psalm and hymn tunes, anthems, canons, and fuging-tunes. Perhaps the most famous of the pieces are the four-voice canon *When Jesus Wept* (fig. 19.16; DWMA162) and *Chester,* which was later equipped with several additional stanzas and became a popular Revolutionary War song. Billings published a total of six volumes of vocal music, the last of them appearing in 1794.

Francis Hopkinson, a Philadelphia native, was an attorney by profession and had many avocational interests. A staunch American patriot, he was a member of the Continental Congress, signed the Declaration of Independence, designed government seals and the nation's first flag, and served as a judge from 1779 until his death. He was a skilled draftsman, an excellent literary satirist, and a talented amateur musician who performed as harpsichordist and organist,

Example 19.22 Beginning of the *fuga* section of a *fuging-tune*.

The Classic Era

Figure 19.16 Billings's *A Canon of 4 in 1,* "When Jesus wept," is printed at the lower right on this page from his *The New-England Psalm-Singer* (1770).

Figure 19.17 Hopkinson's secular song "My days have been so wondrous free" in the manuscript book of songs he labeled "Francis Hopkinson, his Book." In the Library of Congress, Washington, D.C.

composed, designed an improved type of harpsichord plectrum, and invented a new instrument—the bellarmonic. The bellarmonic was similar to Franklin's glass harmonica but had metal instead of glass bowls. Hopkinson is the first known native American composer of vocal music. His secular song *My days have been so wondrous free* (1759), a setting of a poem by Thomas Parnell (1679–1718), is one of several original compositions Hopkinson copied into his personal music book in 1759–60 (fig. 19.17). Included in that oblong manuscript book is *An Anthem from the 114th Psalm* (dated 1760), which may antedate any anthem composed by James Lyon.

Late in 1788, Hopkinson's *Seven Songs* appeared, the first printed collection of secular songs by a single American composer. Actually, the collection contains eight songs—as Hopkinson explained, the eighth song was added after the title page was engraved. "My gen'rous heart disdains" is a delightful rondo (DWMA163). Stylistically, Hopkinson's melodies are Pre-Classical, but his music is notated in the Baroque manner, as melody fitted only with figured (or unfigured) bass.

Several American diplomats were knowledgeable about music. Benjamin Franklin (1706–90) played guitar, sticcado-pastorale (a kind of miniature xylophone with glass bars), and, after hearing music played on tuned glasses, invented the glass harmonica (fig. 19.18). The glass harmonica became popular in Europe during the last quarter of the eighteenth century; at least a dozen composers wrote music for it, including W. A. Mozart and Beethoven. Franklin did not compose the scordatura string quartet that sometimes is attributed to him.

Thomas Jefferson (1743–1826) was a fine violinist, and he frequently invited friends to Monticello, his home, to make music. He owned sufficient music to accommodate requests for either vocal or instrumental selections, solo or ensemble. After the federal library was burned during the War of 1812, Jefferson sold the books in his personal library to the federal government. Included were nine writings about music; these formed a nucleus for the Music Division of the Library of Congress.

Benjamin Carr (1768–1831) was born in London, where he studied music and learned the music pub-

Figure 19.18 Benjamin Franklin's glass harmonica. *(*National Geographic Magazine, *July 1975.)*

lishing trade. In 1793, he emigrated to Philadelphia; there he was influential as publisher, editor, concert promoter, teacher, conductor, organist, and singer. His works written between 1794 and 1800 include a ballet, two ballad operas, several piano sonatas, and the *Federal Overture* (1794). After 1800, Carr composed about 60 songs and much sacred music; of the latter, the most significant is the collection *Masses, Vespers, Litanies, Psalms, Anthems, & Motets* (1805). His songs are settings of substantial poetry, e.g., by Shakespeare and Sir Walter Scott. Carr's **song cycle,** *Six Ballads from the Poem of the Lady of the Lake,* Op. 7 (1810), appeared shortly after Scott's work was published (ex. 19.23). A song cycle consists of a group of songs, each complete in itself, that have something in common, e.g., all of the texts concern the same topic, or relate a series of events, or may be by the same poet. Several English composers wrote sets or cycles of songs in the 1790s, but the practice was not imported to continental Europe until after 1813. Carr's songs, intended for performance by professional singers, are sensitive, through-composed settings, with

Example 19.23 Measures 1–14 of Benjamin Carr's *Ave Maria*, from his song cycle *Six Ballads from the Poem of the Lady of the Lake*, Op. 7 (1810). *(In Benjamin Carr,* Selected Secular and Sacred Songs, *Eve R. Meyer, editor. Copyright A-R Editions, Madison, WI.)*

good balance maintained between voice and accompaniment. In this respect, they anticipate the style of Schubert's and Schumann's art songs.

John Antes is considered the first American-born composer to have written chamber music. Born in Frederick, Pennsylvania, he was educated by the Moravian Brethren at Bethlehem, where music occupied an important place in communal living. There, he learned to make harpsichords and string instruments and crafted the first violins, violas, 'cellos, and string basses built in America. Several of Antes's instruments are extant and were in playable condition in 1988. In 1764, Antes emigrated to England, then to Germany, where he was ordained into the ministry by the United Brethren (Moravians); late in 1769 he was assigned to their missionary post in Cairo. While in Egypt, Antes composed a set of six quartets, which, in 1779, he sent to Benjamin Franklin who was then at Passy, France. Unfortunately, those quartets are lost. Antes was recalled to Europe in 1781 and subsequently was assigned to work in England. His *Tre Trii, per due Violini e Violoncello,* Op. 3 (Three Trios, for two violins and violoncello) were published in London c. 1790 (DWMA164). Each trio has three movements whose tempi differ, with the middle movement in a related key. Antes was a talented composer, well versed in vocal and instrumental techniques; he was aware of the prevailing musical style of his time. Stylistically, the music is Classical and sounds quite Haydnesque. In addition to the Trios, Antes's extant music consists of 35 concerted anthems and solo songs and about 55 hymns. His finest concerted work—in fact, one of the finest in the entire Moravian repertory—is *Go, Congregation, Go— Surely He has borne our griefs,* for soprano solo, four-part chorus, and strings (DWMA165).

It should be noted that Antes, though American-born, composed music after he left America. However, his music—especially his hymns and sacred concerted compositions—was known and was used by Moravians living in America. During the last half of the eighteenth century, European-born Moravians living in America composed a large amount of music for use by Moravians in Moravian communities in eastern Pennsylvania (Bethlehem, Nazareth, Lititz) and at Salem (now Winston-Salem), North Carolina. The Moravian Church placed strong emphasis on music, both congregational (hymns) and concerted (anthems, sacred duets and solos, instrumental pieces), and a great deal of music was written by composers within the Moravian Church itself. However, this music was intended for use exclusively by Moravians and had little or no direct influence on the main stream of American music.

The vast majority of secular music performed in Canada from the time its first settlements were founded until the middle of the nineteenth century was folk music brought there by French and British immigrants. Roman Catholic and Jesuit missionaries from France established settlements in Canada early in the seventeenth century, and, using hymns and adaptations of folk songs, began to teach religion to the Indians. For this purpose Jean de Brébeuf (martyred by Iroquois, 1649) wrote the Huron carol *Jesous Ahatonhia* (Jesus is born; 1642); its monophonic music bears some resemblance to the French folk song *La jeune pucelle* (The young maiden). Fr. Charles-Amador Martin (1648–1711), of Quebec, is credited with composing the monophonic chants for the *Prosae* sections of the Office for the Holy Family. Some of the anonymous sacred music in the seventeenth-century manuscripts in the Ursuline archives in Quebec—music known to have been used during the tenure of Mother Marie de St. Joseph at the Ursuline convent (1639–52)—may have been written by clergy living in Quebec. Some instrumental music was used in church; there was a church organ in Quebec as early as 1661.

British settlers came to Canada in the eighteenth century and vied with the French for control of the land. Gradually, Britain gained territory—through the Treaty of Utrecht (1713), by a decisive battle on the Plains of Abraham (Quebec, 1759), and by the Treaty of Paris (1763)—until it had complete control of Canada. James Lyon, who served as a minister in Nova Scotia in 1765–71, may have used *Urania* there.

Concerts of music, as well as music lessons, were provided by military bands stationed at the forts, but the music performed was by well-known European composers. In Canada, musical composition was an avocation. Joseph Quesnel (1779–1809), who settled in Canada in the 1770s, composed two ballad operas, *Colas et Colinette* and *Lucas et Cécile,* for which the vocal parts survive. *Colas et Colinette* (1788; perf. Montreal, 1790), with a total cast of five, was a prose comedy interspersed with 14 musical numbers— ariettes, duos, and a final chorus sung by the complete cast.

Summary

The Viennese Classical idiom is a synthesis of elements of *galant, empfindsamer,* and learned styles. This synthesis was achieved by Haydn more fully than by his contemporaries, and the Viennese Classical style was firmly established in the instrumental works he created in the 1770s. Haydn's works, widely disseminated in the 1780s, influenced other composers to the extent that a more or less universal cosmopolitan musical language resulted. This musical language, which is characterized by clarity, balance, and restraint, may be seen to best advantage in the middle and late works of Haydn, the late works of Mozart, and the early works of Beethoven and Schubert.

The Classic Era

Though composers continued to write Masses and operas, most of the music written in the Classic era was instrumental. The principal genres of instrumental music composed between c. 1770–c. 1820 were symphony, sonata, solo concerto, chamber music, and opera. The structural principle most often used for a movement was sonata form, or a variant thereof (sonata-rondo, sonata-concerto, abridged sonata). Next in frequency of use was theme and variations.

Haydn contributed more to the development of the symphony than any other single composer. Among his symphonies are excellent examples of the various stages of that development. By the late 1780s, a four-movement structural scheme became standard, with sonata form used for first and last movements, and Minuet/Trio for third. Often, the sonata-form movements had slow introductions. Gradually, the orchestra was increased in size; by 1800, the instrumentation for symphonies included trumpets, clarinets, and timpani.

Haydn and Mozart developed a characteristic style for the string quartet and composed sets of quartets that are basic to the repertoire. J. C. Bach introduced the concerto for piano and orchestra, with first movement containing features of both ritornello and sonata form. In Mozart's hands, the solo piano concerto attained perfection. He retained the three-movement overall scheme favored by Vivaldi but modified Bach's first-movement pattern by adding full-scale sonata-form features. Usually, the second movement of a Mozart concerto is an instrumental aria; the third movement is a kind of rondo. Ultimately, Mozart gave the concerto, as a whole, symphonic dimensions. The *symphonie concertante,* featuring two or more virtuoso soloists with orchestra, flourished between c. 1780–c. 1830, then almost disappeared. *Divertimenti* and similar works (*cassation, notturno, serenade*) for small ensemble served as suitable background music for social events. Books of didactic pieces termed *études* appeared in Paris after 1785. The earliest of these publications were for flute and for violin; London pianist-composers published books of études for piano early in the nineteenth century.

Though Haydn considered himself primarily a composer of vocal music, and wrote numerous operas, Masses, and other sacred and secular vocal works, his most significant contributions were made in the instrumental realm. His two oratorios are worthy successors to Handel's *Messiah* and constitute his most important contribution to vocal repertoire.

Gluck was one of several composers who worked to reform opera and achieved considerable success. But Mozart brought *opera seria* and *Singspiel* to unprecedented heights. In several respects, *Die Zauberflöte,* a *Singspiel,* foreshadows nineteenth-century German Romantic opera; *Il Don Giovanni* is a *dramma giocoso* masterpiece. Zumsteeg was instrumental in promoting performances of Mozart's operas in Stuttgart. Zumsteeg's Lieder and ballads lie midway between the works of the second Berlin school and the songs of Schubert.

Haydn and Mozart composed some excellent piano sonatas, but it was Beethoven who brought that genre to a peak. In fact, several innovations barely perceptible in Haydn's instrumental works (e.g., commencing a symphony in a key other than its tonic, and modulation to a key a third removed) were brought to fruition by Beethoven.

In America, singing schools resulted from a desire to improve the quality of singing in church. This led to the publication of instructional tune books. The first music by native-born North American composers—Francis Hopkinson, James Lyon, William Billings, and John Antes—appeared in the second half of the eighteenth century. Hopkinson was the first native-born American to compose a secular song; Antes was the first American to write chamber music. Diplomats Benjamin Franklin and Thomas Jefferson were competent performers. Franklin invented the glass harmonica; when Jefferson shared his personal library with the federal government, he provided the nucleus of the Music Division of the Library of Congress. Benjamin Carr, an Englishman active in Philadelphia, composed one of the earliest song cycles.

The vast majority of the secular music performed in Canada from the time of its first settlements until the middle of the nineteenth century was folk music brought there by French and British immigrants. Fr. Martin, of Québec, wrote some monophonic chants for Offices. Canada was controlled by Britain after 1763, and concerts of European music, as well as music lessons, were provided by members of military bands stationed at forts. Late in the century, ballad operas were popular; vocal parts from two ballad operas by Quesnel survive.

From Classicism to Romanticism

In the last decades of the eighteenth century, the humanitarian ideals and theories of the philosophers of the Enlightenment became realities of life, engendering powerful emotions and actions. The search for liberty, equality, and fraternity led to revolution in America and France. The American colonies' Declaration of Independence, formulated in 1776, asserts that all men are created equal. The United States, the first new nation to free itself from imperial domination, established a constitutional federation based on a Bill of Rights and representative government that is still in existence and that has had a major impact on civic ideals throughout the world. The French, through their Revolution, experienced constitutional representative government, a revolutionary dictatorship based on mass terror, and Napoleon Buonaparte's military leadership, with his European conquests and his imperialistic seizure of power. The French presented a powerful example—perhaps the first complete one—of popular mass nationalism and a national army. The Holy Roman Empire came to its end in 1806. Throughout Europe political attitudes changed, new standards of social equality gradually appeared, and codes of law were altered. At the Congress of Vienna (1814–15), a brilliant gathering of most of the rulers and all of the leading statesmen of Europe, national boundaries were established as the map of Europe was redrafted for the purpose of stabilizing Europe and establishing a reasonable balance of power.

In France, on 25 April 1792, poet-composer C.-J. Rouget de Lisle (1760–1836) wrote the *Chant de guerre pour l'armée du Rhin* (War song for the Rhine Army). That song, frequently sung by the Marseilles Volunteer Batallion, became known as *La Marseillaise* when it was adopted in 1795 as the French national anthem.

Through appointed Commissions, France's postrevolutionary government sought out and appropriated for preservation in national archives all important music manuscripts and valuable musical instruments. In August 1795 the government legally established the Conservatoire National de Musique (Paris Conservatory); it was intended that the Conservatoire should provide free or almost free tuition in music for all talented pupils, without distinction as to rank or social position. This was the first step toward the gradual establishment, commencing in 1822, of 56 national music schools throughout France. Musical compositions commissioned to commemorate military victories and governmental successes were performed at celebrations held regularly during the several decades following the French Revolution. This created a vast repertoire of music for wind band, massed choruses, and orchestra. The effect of such celebrations was felt in other countries, in creative works centered around heroism, e.g., poems and dramas, operas, funeral marches, sonatas, and symphonies. In opera, the strong feelings, suspense, and dramatic tension of revolutionary and postrevolutionary times found expression in libretti based on actual revolutionary events, rescue plots, and included crowd scenes.

From Classicism to Romanticism

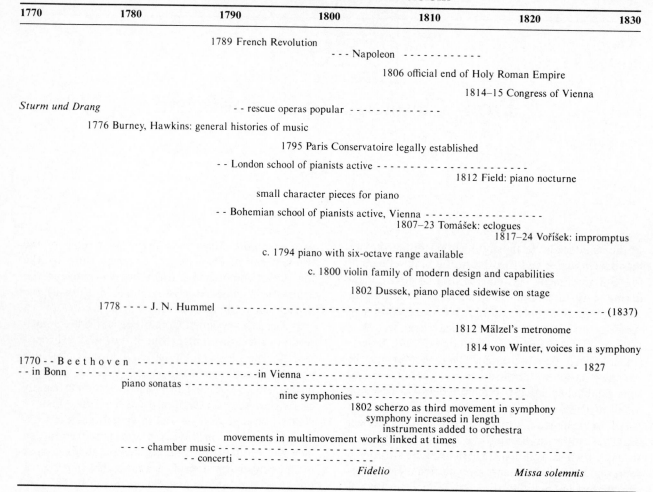

1770	1780	1790	1800	1810	1820	1830

1789 French Revolution

- - - Napoleon - - - - - - - - - - -

1806 official end of Holy Roman Empire

1814–15 Congress of Vienna

Sturm und Drang

- - rescue operas popular - - - - - - - - - - - - -

1776 Burney, Hawkins: general histories of music

1795 Paris Conservatoire legally established

- - London school of pianists active -

1812 Field: piano nocturne

small character pieces for piano

- - Bohemian school of pianists active, Vienna - - - - - - - - - - - - - - - - -

1807–23 Tomášek: eclogues

1817–24 Voříšek: impromptus

c. 1794 piano with six-octave range available

c. 1800 violin family of modern design and capabilities

1802 Dussek, piano placed sidewise on stage

1778 - - - - J. N. Hummel - (1837)

1812 Mälzel's metronome

1814 von Winter, voices in a symphony

1770 - - B e e t h o v e n - 1827

- - in Bonn - in Vienna -

piano sonatas -

nine symphonies -

1802 scherzo as third movement in symphony

symphony increased in length

instruments added to orchestra

movements in multimovement works linked at times

- - - - chamber music -

- - concerti -

Fidelio   *Missa solemnis*

Many composers became interested in folk music. Hundreds of settings of folk songs were published, and some folk-song melodies were used as themes in sonatas and symphonies. There was increased interest in early music, too, and in 1776 two general histories of music were published: Charles Burney's (1726–1814) *A General History of Music from the Earliest Ages to the Present Period* and Sir John Hawkins's (1719–89) *A General History of the Science and Practice of Music*. However, those histories are more valuable for contemporary views of music than for historical accuracy.

The London School of Pianists

London, because of its rich concert life, active publishing houses, and a prosperous piano industry that produced instruments of superior quality and efficiency, attracted foreign musicians, especially pianists. In the 1790s, the group of important pianists working in London included Muzio Clementi (1752–1832; Italian), J. B. Cramer (1771–1858; German), Jan L. Dussek (1760–1812; Bohemian), and John Field (1782–1837; Irish). By 1800, George Pinto (1785–1806; English) had joined them.

Clementi won acclaim first as performer and composer of harpsichord and piano music, then as teacher. After moving to London in 1785, he manufactured pianos and also published music. His firm issued the first editions of about a dozen of Beethoven's major works. Clementi's influence on succeeding generations of pianists and composers of piano music was tremendous. Among his noted pupils were Cramer, Field, Dussek, and Meyerbeer. Beethoven knew Clementi's piano sonatas and used them in his teaching; moreover, those sonatas directly influenced some of Beethoven's piano sonatas. Clementi's most important didactic works are *Introduction to the Art of Playing on the Piano Forte,* Op. 42 (1801), and *Gradus ad Parnassum* (Steps to Parnassus; 3 vols.: 1817, 1819, 1826), a collection of 100 keyboard pieces that is a compendium of Clementi's works covering approximately 45 years.

As a performer, Cramer was noted for his expressive legato touch; in the nineteenth century, that type of touch became a stylistic norm. Although Cramer wrote many compositions for piano, the only work of his that is widely known in the twentieth century is *Studio per il pianoforte* (Studies for piano; 2 vols.: 1804, 1810), a set of 84 studies. This comprehensive technical *opus* was used by Beethoven and other nineteenth-century pianists in their teaching.

Dussek enjoyed a brilliant career as a pianist in Europe. After moving to London c. 1788, he frequently performed at Salomon's concerts, and in that connection he became acquainted with Haydn. In 1799, Dussek returned to continental Europe to concertize and became Kapellmeister to his former pupil, Prince Louis Ferdinand of Prussia (1772–1806), an outstanding pianist and a fine composer. From 1807–12 Dussek worked for Talleyrand in Paris. Dussek's late works (c. 1793–1812) are characterized by frequent modulations to remote keys, altered chords, nonharmonic notes, and much chromaticism. Except for the chromaticism, Beethoven assimilated into his sonatas all that Dussek had to offer. The influence of Dussek's Op. 35 and Op. 39 sonatas on Beethoven's sonatas is particularly noticeable. One similarity is shown in example 20.1. Stylistic elements present in Dussek's Sonata XIII (Op. 35, No. 3; C minor; 1797; DWMA166) appear in sonatas Beethoven and Chopin

Example 20.1 (*a*) Dussek: Sonata, Op. 39, mvt. 1, mm. 1–4; (*b*) Beethoven: Sonata, Op. 10., No. 1, mm. 1–5.

composed later. Dussek's influence can be seen also in compositions by Schubert, Liszt, and other Romantic composers.

Dussek was one of the few composers of that era who wrote idiomatically for harp. His wife, *née* Sophia Corri (1775–1847), concertized as harpist and pianist and composed music for both instruments. After Dussek's death, she established a music school in Paddington.

Field was one of the first to write small character pieces for piano—nonprogrammatic pieces somewhat like songs without words. Previously, pianist-composers had been content with sonatinas, sonatas, sets of variations, fantasias, fugues, and rondos; Field composed some works in those forms, too. In England, the rapidly rising middle class participated actively in music making and favored short works over multimovement compositions and large works with long-range emotional effects. In 1812, Field invented the *nocturne* for piano and used it not only as an independent piece (DWMA167) but as a movement in a multimovement work and as a section within a movement. Field had an expressive, delicate touch and cultivated an artistic, sensitive style of piano playing characterized by singing melodies and a quasi-improvisatory air. His compositions were designed to exploit the piano's capabilities—percussive, harmonic, melodic, sustaining—without becoming mere technical display. Field greatly influenced the playing style of Chopin and the compositions of Chopin, Liszt, Mendelssohn, and others.

From Classicism to Romanticism

Pinto was the most daring composer of the London school. His *Grand Sonatas* (Op. 3; 1803) exhibit a degree of romanticism comparable with that of Chopin and Liszt. The Sonata in E♭ minor, Op. 3, No. 1 contains passages that are striking parallels with some in the first movement of Beethoven's Sonata No. 31, Op. 110 (A♭ major; 1821). Pinto was influential in the English revival of J. S. Bach's music c. 1800, when London musicians began to discuss *Das wohltemperirte Klavier.*

Bohemian Pianists

Active in Vienna during the late eighteenth and early nineteenth centuries were several Bohemian pianist-composers who made significant contributions to piano literature: Václav Jan Tomášek (1774–1850), Jan Václav Voříšek (1791–1825), and Johann Nepomuk Hummel (1778–1837).

Tomášek, who was largely self-taught, was an excellent teacher. Among his outstanding pupils were Voříšek and Eduard Hanslick. Though Tomášek venerated Mozart, he did not limit himself, in either performance or composition, to Mozart's style. Tomášek was a prolific composer, writing operas and other stage works, sacred and secular choral compositions, orchestral and chamber music, as well as piano pieces. In addition to 7 sonatas and 5 sets of variations, his works for piano solo include 15 rhapsodies, 3 dithyrambs, 6 caprices, and 42 pastoral pieces that he called **eclogues.** The eclogues (1807–23) are light, lyrical pieces with uncomplicated textures and are not technically demanding (ex. 20.2; DWMA168). Schubert knew Tomášek's eclogues; many of Schubert's works and the eclogues have common features, e.g., the sudden reappearance of a major-tonality theme in the minor, or a minor-key theme presented in the major, and doubling in thirds and sixths. Among Tomášek's hundreds of songs—part songs, Bohemian art songs, and Lieder—are settings of many poems by Schiller and Goethe, including *Erlkönig* (Erlking). Two of his best songs are *Nähe des Geliebten* (Near the beloved; Op. 53, No. 2)—a through-composed setting—and *Mignons Sehnsucht* (Mignon's longing; Op. 54, No. 1). Generally, his Lieder have lyrical melodies, lightly

Example 20.2 Tomášek: *Eclogue,* Op. 66, No. 6, mm. 1–4.

embellished, with simple accompaniments incorporating right-hand figuration and broken-octave or Alberti bass.

Voříšek received his early musical training from his father, who taught him many of Mozart's works. While still a child, Voříšek toured in Bohemia as a keyboard virtuoso. Though he completed university studies in law and practiced law for a time, he abandoned that profession for a musical career. He studied harmony, counterpoint, and composition with Tomášek, who stressed the importance of counterpoint and of Bach's *Das wohltemperirte Klavier.* Because of his enthusiasm for Beethoven, Voříšek moved to Vienna, for, musically, Prague favored the Classicism of Mozart, an attitude Voříšek considered reactionary.

Rhythmically and thematically, Voříšek's music reflects his admiration for and knowledge of Beethoven's piano works; both composers frequently used rhythmic displacement to effect a climax. However, Voříšek's use of diminished chords and chromatic progressions is more like that of Schubert and Chopin. In Vienna, Voříšek and Schubert became friends, and their compositions reflect this to some extent— Voříšek's vocal music shows Schubert's influence, and Schubert's piano music was influenced by Voříšek. Voříšek pioneered the piano character piece, Romantic in style, usually ternary in form, which he entitled rhapsody, eclogue, or impromptu. His *Impromptus,* Op. 7 (1822), *Impromptu* in B♭ (1817), and *Impromptu* in F (1824) preceded and strongly influenced Schubert's impromptus. (DWMA 169.)

Hummel, too, was a child prodigy. When he was eight, the family moved from Pressburg (now Bratislava) to Vienna, and his father, music director of Theater auf der Wieden, took him to Mozart for keyboard lessons. For two years (1786–88), the boy studied with Mozart and lived in the Mozart home;

then Mozart discontinued the lessons and recommended that Hummel concertize. Later, Hummel studied for a short time with Clementi. During the 1790s, Hummel had lessons in counterpoint from Albrechtsberger, in vocal composition from Salieri, and on organ from Haydn—the same persons with whom Beethoven studied. From 1804 to 1811, Hummel served as deputy Kapellmeister at the Esterházy court; thereafter, he held similar positions at Stuttgart and Weimar. In 1813, he married Elisabeth Röckel (1793–1883), a well-known opera singer.

Beethoven's quick success in Vienna was somewhat traumatic for Hummel. The playing styles of the two men distinctly differed, and their pupils and admirers took sides and continually quibbled in a kind of pseudo-warfare, thus creating two schools of piano playing in Vienna c. 1800. Hummel limited his performance repertoire almost exclusively to his own music and that of Mozart, and his style was Mozartean—a restrained Classicism, neat and delicate, with emphasis on fluent technique and textural clarity; he was able to create an illusion of speed without actually taking a rapid tempo. Beethoven produced a full tone and stressed technical power and dramatic execution; his music incorporated orchestral effects and a wide range of dynamics. Hummel formed the link between the style of Mozart and Clementi and that of Schubert, Mendelssohn, and Chopin, a chain of piano playing that bypassed Beethoven. Professionally, Hummel was Beethoven's greatest rival in Vienna; yet, despite some stormy interludes, the two pianists managed to remain friends.

Hummel was a prolific composer and wrote music for all performing media then current and in all genres except the symphony. In that genre, he felt intimidated by Beethoven's genius. Hummel's compositional style is basically Classical, though works written after 1814 are tinged with Romanticism and contain chromatic passing tones, secondary dominants, and modulations by thirds. In many of his manuscripts there are figured bass indications, an archaic procedure in direct contrast with his nineteenth-century harmonic vocabulary. In the early nineteenth century, Hummel stands as one of the foremost representatives of late Classicism, while Beethoven points toward Romanticism.

Ludwig van Beethoven

Ludwig van Beethoven (1770–1827) was born in Bonn, Electoral seat of Cologne, and grew up in court surroundings. At the time of Ludwig's birth his father, Johann van Beethoven (c. 1740–92), was a tenor at the Electoral court, and his grandfather, Ludwig (Louis) van Beethoven (1712–73), was Kapellmeister there. Ludwig was the second of Johann's seven children, only three of whom survived infancy; his younger brothers, Kaspar Anton Karl (1774–1815) and Nikolaus Johann (1776–1848), played important roles in Ludwig's life.

When Ludwig was very young, his father taught him to play piano and violin; after the age of eight, Ludwig received organ lessons from various local organists and a relative taught him viola and violin. Beethoven had no formal education beyond elementary school; in later life, though he attained a high level of literacy through self-education, he continually experienced difficulties with spelling, punctuation, and mathematics. In 1779 Christian G. Neefe (1748–98) was employed at court as musical director of a theatrical troup; soon, he became court organist. From him Beethoven received music lessons—organ, counterpoint, and composition—and learned Bach's *Das wohltemperirte Klavier*. At that time Beethoven's hands were still small and his fingers stubby, but he was determined and mastered the preludes and fugues. By 1782 he was sufficiently proficient to be Neefe's assistant and to serve as deputy organist when Neefe was away from court. In 1783, Neefe hired Ludwig as orchestral harpsichordist at court, a responsible position that exposed him to all musical genres and the variety of styles then current.

By 1782, Beethoven was composing music deemed worthy of publication, though his early works were issued without opus number (WoO): [9] *Variations on a March by Dressler* (1782), and three piano sonatas dedicated to Elector Maximilian Friedrich (1783). There survives only the solo part (with orchestral cues) of an unpublished piano concerto in E♭ written in 1784.

Ludwig van Beethoven. Oil painting by Willibord J. Mähler, 1815. *(Gesellschaft der Musikfreunde, Vienna.)*

When Maximilian Franz, brother of Emperor Joseph II, became Elector in 1784, Beethoven began to receive a small salary for his work as organist. His duties were light; there was time for composition and music lessons. He taught piano lessons, studied violin with Franz Ries (1755–1846), and in 1785 composed a set of three piano quartets (publ. 1828). In 1787 Beethoven visited Vienna and, while there, met Mozart. The Vienna visit was cut short by Beethoven's mother's illness and subsequent death (in July). Then, his father began drinking heavily and in 1789 was dismissed at court; Ludwig, at age 19, assumed responsibilities as head of the family. For the next four years he played viola in the court chapel and theater orchestras. At least twice he was commissioned to compose cantatas for special occasions, but the works were not performed. He composed (anonymously) the music for the *Ritterballett* performed by Bonn nobility in 1791. That summer his 24 variations (for piano) on Righini's *Venni amore* were published.

Throughout his life Beethoven was comfortable in the presence of aristocracy and nobility; among his friends in Bonn were Count Waldstein, the von Breunings, and the Kochs. When the court orchestra accompanied the Elector on official trips, Beethoven took advantage of opportunities to meet well-known musicians. At Aschaffenburg early in 1791, he astounded pianist-composer Johann Sterkel (1750–1817) by improvising variations in Sterkel's distinctive style. In 1790, only Mozart was ranked higher than Beethoven in ability to improvise variations on a theme.

When Haydn stopped at the Bonn court in 1792 on his way back to Vienna from London, Beethoven showed him the funeral cantata he had written to honor Emperor Joseph II, and Haydn invited Beethoven to Vienna. At the urging of friends, especially Count Waldstein and the von Breunings, Beethoven obtained leave from court, and in November went to Vienna; except for short stays not far from the city, he lived there the rest of his life. For approximately a year, he studied with Haydn; then Haydn returned to London. Meantime, Beethoven had become disillusioned with Haydn's teaching and had gone in secret to Johann Schenk (1753–1836) for counterpoint and composition lessons. In 1794–95 Beethoven studied counterpoint with J. G. Albrechtsberger (1736–1809), and in 1801–02 took lessons in setting Italian texts from Antonio Salieri.

In Vienna, as in Bonn, Beethoven acquired friends among the nobility. In the Austrian capital, the aristocracy devoted much time and money to music, and a performer of Beethoven's caliber was welcomed. Some Viennese maintained private orchestras (Prince Lobkowitz), opera companies (the Esterházy), and chamber ensembles (Count Razumovsky); others (Baron van Swieten) organized private concerts. Patronage was on the wane, however, and in Vienna Beethoven had no patron and no steady job. How, then, did he earn his living? His principal resources during his first few years in Vienna were playing piano at gatherings in the halls and salons of aristocrats, appearing as assisting artist in concerts given by other musicians, teaching piano lessons to wealthy pupils, and publishing some compositions by subscription, i.e., soliciting orders for printed copies of a work, paying for its publication, and selling the copies at his own price. From time to time, his lodging was provided by

insight

The Piano (II)

John Broadwood (1732–1812) began manufacturing "square" pianos in England c. 1767 and by c. 1785 had made many improvements in the mechanics and design of the instrument. He improved the escapement, attempted to equalize string tension, and continually sought to produce an instrument capable of greater volume of sound and increased dynamic flexibility. By 1800, piano keyboards had been changed from black naturals and light or white-topped chromatics to the white naturals and black chromatics of the modern keyboard. Broadwood preferred the wing-shaped ("grand") piano, with three unison strings per note provided throughout the compass of the instrument and with three pedals. Thus, a composer could specify and expect true *una corda, due corde,* and *tutte le corde* responses. Haydn, Clementi, Dussek, Field, and Beethoven were among the first composers to write pedaling instructions in their piano music. Haydn's designations are rudimentary and insignificant in comparison with Field's; for Field's and for Beethoven's music, pedaling is crucial. From c. 1791 until well into the nineteenth century, the leading pianists used Broadwood instruments. Beethoven's last piano sonatas would have been virtually impossible without the Broadwood piano he received from London in 1818.

Dussek was the first (in 1802) to have the piano placed sidewise on the stage so that the audience could view the performer's right profile. He encouraged Broadwood to extend the compass of the piano from five to five and one-half octaves (F'–c'''') in 1791, and upwards to six octaves (F'–f'''') in 1794. Not all keyboards had the extended range, however. During the first quarter of the nineteenth century, range continued to be expanded. Beethoven, in his sonatas, often carried the bass to the piano's lowest note, but not until Op. 106 (the *Hammerklavier Sonata;* 1817–18) was that pitch below F'. A bass passage written in octaves would, of necessity, become a single line when continued octave doubling would have required pitches lower than F'. The full 88-key keyboard considered standard on modern pianos was not available until c. 1830.

Figure 20.1 Beethoven's last piano, a gift of the Viennese piano manufacturer Konrad Graf, has quadruple rather than the usual triple strings. The instrument is in Beethoven-Haus, Bonn.

In 1796, Érard *frères,* of Paris, began to manufacture grand pianos in the English style. In 1808 they patented a repetition action and in 1821 patented a second one that greatly improved the player's ability to repeat notes rapidly. Érard's repetition action became the basis of virtually all double escapement actions in the twentieth century.

Though the Austrian firm headed by Konrad Graf (1782–1851) is considered a manufacturer of fine instruments rather than an innovator, they began early in the nineteenth century to use quadruple stringing on pianos in an endeavor to increase volume and gave Beethoven one of their pianos (fig. 20.1). Beethoven used Broadwood and Érard pianos much of the time and is said to have preferred Broadwood.

---

certain aristocrats, e.g., Prince Lichnowsky. After Beethoven had been in Vienna long enough to establish his reputation, he gave some concerts of his own, received commissions for some compositions, sold performance rights to some of his works (usually for

a six-month period), and was paid for some dedications. From time to time, he received monetary gifts from friends, and for a few years (c. 1809–c. 1813) he benefited from an annuity set up by three aristocratic friends. Once his reputation was established,

From Classicism to Romanticism

and when hearing problems began to plague him, he refused to perform at private parties to which he had been invited. Undoubtedly, there were times when money was scarce, but Beethoven seldom resorted to composing "hack work."

For the first half-dozen years in Vienna, all went well for Beethoven. By 1795 both of his brothers were also living in Vienna and were gainfully employed. Then, Beethoven began to experience some difficulty hearing. The affliction, which he regarded as a temporary illness, gradually worsened, and he sought medical aid. When he realized that neither medicine nor spas could heal or alleviate his malady and that ultimately he faced total deafness, he despaired. He was barely 30, yet the end of his career as virtuoso pianist was in sight. The struggle within himself was intense; more than once he contemplated suicide. Finally, at Heiligenstadt in autumn 1802, he came to terms with his dilemma. With great strength of character, he determined that, despite encroaching deafness, he would pursue a career as composer. He wrote a letter to his brothers—a letter intended to be read after his death and kept secreted until that time—in which he described his trauma and explained his decision to mingle with society only when necessity demanded such contact. In this document, known as "the Heiligenstadt Testament," Beethoven stated that he had already been "hopelessly afflicted" for six years. His words convey his anguish:

> Ah, how could I possibly admit an infirmity in the *one sense* which ought to be more perfect in me than in others, . . . I cannot do it, therefore forgive me when you see me draw back when I would have gladly mingled with you. . . . For me there can be no relaxation with my fellow-men, no refined conversations, no mutual exchange of ideas. . . . If I approach near to people a hot terror seizes upon me and I fear being exposed to the danger that my condition might be noticed. . . . What a humiliation for me when someone standing next to me heard a flute in the distance and *I heard nothing,* or someone heard a *shepherd singing* and again I heard nothing. Such incidents drove me almost to despair, a little more of that and I would have ended my life—it was only *my art* that held me back. Ah, it seemed to me impossible to leave the world until I had brought forth all that I felt was within me. . . . I hope my

Ludwig van Beethoven. Detail of an oil painting by W. J. Mähler c. 1804. *(Historisches Museum, Vienna.)*

determination will remain firm to endure until it pleases the inexorable Parcae to break the thread. Perhaps I shall get better, perhaps not, I am ready.— Forced to become a philosopher already in my 28th year, oh it is not easy, and for the artist much more difficult than for anyone else.— (Thayer's *Life of Beethoven,* rev., ed., E. Forbes, Princeton, 1967, I, 304–06.)

After making his decision in Heiligenstadt, Beethoven returned to Vienna and composed prolifically for several years. Between 1802 and 1812, he wrote the majority of his symphonies, six piano sonatas, three piano *concerti,* three piano trios, the opera *Fidelio,* five string quartets, incidental music for three plays, and several other works. After 1808 he no longer performed in public as piano soloist, though he participated in chamber music from time to time. His last performance as pianist was 11 April 1814 when his "Archduke" Piano Trio was first performed.

Occasionally, Beethoven attempted to meddle in his brother Johann's affairs but was rebuffed. Also, from time to time, Ludwig showed interest in some young lady and considered marriage but either was rejected or lost interest. The lady in whom he was most interested was never named in his correspondence; usually, because of Beethoven's words in a passionate letter to her dated 6 July 1812, she is referred to as "the immortal beloved" (*unsterbliche Geliebte,* immortal or eternally beloved one). Some convincing evidence supports the conjecture that she was Antoine Brentano, aristocratic, married, and unattainable. It is believed Beethoven composed the song cycle *An die ferne Geliebte* (To the distant beloved; Op. 98; 1816) with her in mind.

Between 1813 and 1818, Beethoven's compositional activity slackened, and there was a corresponding decrease in his income. His finances were further affected by the depreciation in Austrian currency that resulted from the Napoleonic War and by the fact that, in 1812, Prince Kinsky, one of the contributors to Beethoven's annuity, was killed in a fall from his horse. Financial need made Beethoven venture out into society in search of commissions, which resulted in his writing some rather mundane works for public events, such as the pieces performed at the Congress of Vienna.

The death of Beethoven's brother Kaspar on 15 November 1815 precipitated another crisis. In accordance with Kaspar's Will, his widow and Ludwig were appointed co-guardians of Kaspar's only child, Karl, then nine years old. To Ludwig, such an appointment was untenable, for he disapproved of the boy's mother and doubted her capabilities as guardian. Litigation over the issue lasted until July 1820, when, after appeal to the emperor, the final decision favored Beethoven. Meantime, Beethoven experienced some illnesses, and from this time on his health deteriorated. Moreover, by 1818 his deafness had deepened to the extent that any communication with him had to be written. Extant conversation books are one-sided, indicating that he replied orally.

After the matter of Karl's guardianship was settled, Beethoven's compositional activity increased. Between 1820 and 1826 he created a number of masterpieces, including Piano Sonatas Nos. 30–32; Symphony No. 9; the *Missa solemnis;* String Quartets Opp. 127, 130–32, 135; and the *Grosse fuge,* Op. 133. By this time, many persons considered him the world's greatest living composer.

Beethoven received another crushing blow in late July 1826, when Karl attempted suicide. After Karl recovered from his gunshot wounds, Beethoven, with the help of Stephan von Breuning, arranged for him to enter the army as a cadet in Baron Joseph von Stutterheim's regiment. As a token of gratitude to Stutterheim, Beethoven dedicated the C♯-minor string quartet (Op. 131) to him.

In late September 1826, Beethoven, who had not been feeling well, went with his brother Johann to the latter's country estate at Gneixendorf (near Krems). When Beethoven returned to Vienna in December, he was seriously ill. In the ensuing months, his condition (cirrhosis resultant from hepatitis) worsened and was complicated by pneumonia. When he realized that the end was near, he prepared his Will, leaving his entire estate to Karl. On 26 March 1827 Beethoven died. It is estimated that 10,000 persons attended his funeral.

Personal Characteristics

At age 30, Beethoven was an attractive man, dark complexioned, with dark brown deep-set eyes and black hair. Though he was not tall, he was stocky of build and of lofty bearing. There was about his countenance a look of determination. He had tremendous vitality, and his energy was seemingly boundless. His disposition was that of an autocrat. At times domineering, self-willed, and quick to anger, he was equally quick to remorse, to self-incrimination for hurts he caused others, and he could be wonderfully kind. Visible in his character are traces of self-sufficiency and arrogance. His pride is apparent in his personal life in his decision to avoid society rather than disclose his increasing deafness, and in his career in his desire to present to the world as his Op. 1 his three Piano Trios (1795), though he had composed and published some excellent music earlier. The sketchbooks in which he jotted down and revised his musical ideas—a practice acquired from Haydn—provide a record of his creativity and work methods, document his constant striving for perfection of his musical ideas, and indicate also his desire for continual self-improvement.

Beethoven was raised a Catholic but seems to have cared little for the highly formalized aspects of that religion. That he envisioned God as being very personal is evidenced by papers found among his estate. He was not a pantheist, though he perceived

God in nature and in everything in the world about him. Beethoven loved the out-of-doors; he enjoyed taking long walks in the countryside (and took a sketchbook with him). Usually, he spent the summer months in small villages rather than in Vienna. In many respects, Beethoven was a representative of the Enlightenment. His delight in nature, his interest in the brotherhood of man, his belief in a personal God, all found places in his music—and all concur with Enlightenment thinking.

In later life, deafness and serious illnesses wrought changes in Beethoven's character and disposition. His hair greyed, his complexion became florid, and often his appearance was unkempt. In direct contrast with his lack of concern for his personal appearance and the cluttered state of his lodgings is the high regard he maintained for himself as musician and composer and for his compositions. His esthetic doctrine was the same as that of poet Johann Schiller (1759–1805)—that it is the moral obligation of a work of art to uplift and ennoble an audience.

Beethoven's Music in General

Grouped according to genre, Beethoven's music includes the following completed works: 9 symphonies, plus the so-called Battle Symphony, *Wellington's Victory;* 2 independent orchestral concert overtures (e.g., *Coriolan Overture,* inspired by but never performed with Collin's tragedy *Coriolan*); incidental music for 6 dramatic presentations, including *Egmont* and *Die Ruinen von Athen* (The Ruins of Athens); 2 ballets, the most significant being *Die Geschöpfe des Prometheus* (The Creatures of Prometheus); the opera *Fidelio;* 2 Masses (in C and in D); the oratorio *Christus am Ölberge* (Christ on the Mount of Olives); the *Fantasia* ("Choral Fantasy"; piano, vcs., orch.); a violin concerto, 5 piano concerti, and a triple concerto (piano, violin, 'cello, and orch.); 9 piano trios; 32 large sonatas for piano; 10 sonatas for violin and piano and 5 for 'cello and piano; at least 20 sets of variations for solo piano; 2 *Romances* for violin and orchestra; and 16 string quartets plus the *Grosse Fuge* (Grand Fugue) in B♭. In addition, he wrote many Lieder and other songs, arias, *scenas,* several pieces for wind band, short piano pieces, almost 200 arrangements of folk songs with piano trio accompaniment, and numerous pieces of miscellaneous types.

Ludwig van Beethoven. Oil painting by Ferdinand Waldmüller, 1825.

Beethoven's personality and his beliefs are inherent in his music. His boundless energy is found in driving rhythms, in pressing fugues (Op. 59, No. 3, mvt. 4), in the quiet murmuring of a babbling brook (Symphony No. 6, mvt. 2), and in robust marches that serve also to provide relief from tension, to change the mood, or to engender humor (Symphonies Nos. 3 and 9). He expressed humor in a variety of other ways, of which the following are but a few: the delayed entrance of an instrument (timpani, in Symphony No. 9, mvt. 2); pitch limitations imposed on an instrument (bassoon's "do" and "sol" in Symphony No. 6, mvt. 3); general pauses that interrupt the rhythmic flow (Symphony No. 5, mvt. 1, recapitulation). The various moods that colored Beethoven's disposition—even his abrupt shifts between contrasting moods—are present in his music: tenderness, joy, exuberance, sadness, melancholy, and the serenity and peace that he found while walking down a country lane.

Many of Beethoven's themes are constructed from small motives. Motivic generation of thematic material and motivic development figure prominently in his style; he subjected motives to incredible degrees of modification. Frequently, he used one or more *fortissimo* or *sforzando* chords (as in the *Eroica*) or a chromatically rising or falling passage coupled with a *crescendo* to herald a theme's arrival (e.g., Op. 18, No. 3, mvt. 4, mm. 53–56). Often, in sonata-form movements of piano sonatas, he presented the first theme *piano* but recapitulated it *forte* (e.g., Op. 2, No. 1, mvt. 1, mm. 1–2, mm. 101–02). Habitually, he directed attention to a new theme by prefacing it with a rest (as did Mozart) or a diametrically opposed dynamic (e.g., *sf* or *ff* prior to *pp* entrance of theme). General pauses served also to effect unexpected modulations to remote keys.

When composing, Beethoven disregarded the comfort and convenience of the instrumentalist. He considered only the pitches, timbres, and effect he desired, and it mattered not at all to him whether the production of a passage was difficult or awkward. Probably, bass players and 'cellists suffered most because of this. See, for example, *Serenade,* Op. 8, mvt. 5, mm. 52–55, 'cello part; or, Symphony No. 5, mvt. 3, Trio, bass part. Beethoven's difficult orchestral string bass parts probably stem from his acquaintance with Domenico Dragonetti (1763–1846), virtuoso string bass player, and no doubt some of the horn parts were written with the talents of virtuoso Giovanni Punto (Jan Stich; 1746–1803) in mind.

Moreover, Beethoven was an innovator. In some of his youthful works, written in Bonn, he was already experimenting. After he mastered Classical forms and style, his harmonic language became more forceful and daring, his modulations bolder. He used augmented sixth chords (the so-called German, Italian, French, and mixed sixths) effectively. Sudden modulations, especially to keys a third above or below the tonic—a striking departure from the modulations expected in that era—became a lifelong feature of his style. Nor was he more cautious where form was concerned. To Beethoven, form was not a mold into which music was to be poured—his music could not be so confined. Rather, form was an elastic band, expandable at any point, capable of containing all that needed to be expressed without ever becoming so distorted that its identity was lost or so extended that it snapped. Beethoven never shattered form; he stretched it.

Through his experiments with form, modulations, developmental processes, and instrumentation, music's horizons broadened considerably. Frequently, his compositions puzzled his contemporaries and drew their critical comment. Yet, his music influenced other composers, not only those of his own time, but many in later generations as well.

Style Periods

Customarily, Beethoven's music is divided into three chronological periods, based on stylistic differences exhibited in the music: (1) early works composed at Bonn and Vienna, 1782–c. 1802; (2) works composed in or near Vienna, c. 1803–c. 1815; (3) late works, composed c. 1815–1827. However, the first style period must be subdivided and the youthful works Beethoven wrote at Bonn, 1782–1792, considered separately from the early works he composed in Vienna, 1793–c. 1802. It must be stressed that divisions such as these are not clear-cut; works produced near the end of one period may exhibit style characteristics of the next, and vice versa.

Bonn, 1782–1792

From the Bonn period, approximately 40 works survive. A dozen of them were written during 1782–85: four piano sonatas, three piano quartets, two rondos for piano, *Variations on a March by Dressler* (C minor), and two songs. That most of these works were published is significant.

The most substantial of these early works are the three piano quartets and the three so-called Elector's Sonatas (ded. to the Elector of Cologne; publ. 1783) in Eb, F minor, and D. These are three-movement sonatas, in a style combining early Classical and *empfindsamer Stil*. The passionate mood of the F-minor sonata links it with Beethoven's later piano sonatas in that key (Op. 2, No. 1; and the *"Appassionata,"* Op. 57; DWMA170). The use of F minor was not common then, though C. P. E. Bach, who frequently wrote in minor keys, composed three keyboard sonatas in F minor; Beethoven knew many of Bach's works. Beethoven began the sonata-form Allegro assai first movement of his F-minor sonata with a Larghetto maestoso introduction, a few measures of which return in the development section; he used this feature in several later sonatas. The Andante is highly embellished; the Presto finale, dramatic and passionate. The D-major sonata is larger in scope and more brilliant than the others. Each of the three piano quartets (in Eb, D, and C) was modeled after a specific piano/violin sonata by Mozart (K.380, 379, 296; publ. 1781). The significance of these early sonatas and quartets lies in Beethoven's awareness of and interest in Viennese Classical style and in his high regard for the multimovement sonata.

During the next few years—years marked by his brief visit to Vienna, his mother's illness and death, his father's irresponsibility, and Ludwig's concern for the family—Beethoven seems to have written very little music. The only complete work that survives from 1786 is a trio for piano, flute, and bassoon. After 1789, however, he completed several sets of variations for piano, based on themes by others; some Lieder, and concert arias with orchestral accompaniment; a funeral cantata for Emperor Joseph II (d. 1790) and a cantata for the accession of Emperor Leopold II; and an Octet in Eb for pairs of winds (1792; later revised; publ. as Op. 103, 1830). In addition, there survive some sketches and many fragments of movements intended for a symphony, a piano concerto, and sonatas. The best of the late works from the Bonn period are the sets of variations and the cantatas; moreover, they contain seeds of later works. The funeral cantata (SATB, 4-vc. chorus, orch.) opens and closes with an excellent, expressive chorus in C minor. Beethoven reused material from the soprano aria of that cantata in *Fidelio*. In the eighteenth century, C minor was regarded as the *pathétique* key; Beethoven would use it often in later works.

Vienna, 1793–c. 1802

During his first years in Vienna, Beethoven composed primarily for piano. It was as an improviser—a creator of variations on a theme—that he first impressed Vienna. Very few of those variations were written down. At first, Beethoven may have felt somewhat intimidated by the accomplishments of Haydn and Mozart and shied from writing symphonies and concerti. As his horizons expanded, he branched out into many genres. In addition to 20 piano sonatas, the compositions he created during his first decade in Vienna include concert arias, Lieder (e.g., the extended Lied *Adelaide,* Op. 46), two piano concerti, three violin/piano sonatas (Op. 12), two 'cello/piano sonatas (Op. 5), three string trios (Op. 9), six string quartets (Op. 18), the ballet *Die Geschöpfe des Prometheus* (Op. 43), two symphonies, many pieces for Viennese social life (e.g., ballroom dances, marches, sets of variations), and some pieces for mechanical clock.

He revised some of his Bonn works and used some of the sketches made at Bonn in new compositions. For example, in 1795 he thoroughly recomposed the wind Octet in Eb to create a version for string quintet (Op. 4, publ. 1796; see also Op. 103). He mastered Viennese Classical style and sonata form, which was central to it. Beethoven always considered publication of his works important and wanted to be certain his first Vienna publication was worthy; he was in Vienna more than two years before publishing a work. His 3 Piano Trios, Op. 1, (in Eb, G, and C minor) appeared in 1795. Haydn counseled against publication of the C-minor work, yet it was the most popular of the three. Beethoven frequently chose minor keys, especially C minor, as the main tonality of his large works or for movements within them. Three piano sonatas composed in 1793–95 were published as Op. 2 in 1796; the first of these, in F minor, was modeled after C. P. E. Bach's F-minor Sonata No. 3.

At the outset, Beethoven's impatience with authority and discipline became evident. In multimovement forms, he experimented with the balance of the movements and varied their character. Moreover, he did not always use the same number of movements. Of significance is his view of the multimovement sonata as an expansive form in which all movements work toward a climax in the finale.

As the 1790s drew to a close, Beethoven began to write string quartets, concerti, and symphonies. Also, he was more innovative. His harmonic language became more forceful and daring, his modulations bolder. Often, contrary to tradition, he commenced a composition on a chord other than the tonic or even in a tonality other than the main key of the piece (e.g., Symphony No. 1).

Vienna, c. 1803–c. 1815

In this period Beethoven's compositions reflect the greater maturity and depth of character he attained through his personal battle at Heiligenstadt—the strength emanating from the inner conflict, mental anguish, and physical pain caused by the cruel blow fate had dealt him, and his determination to rise above it. This is seen especially in the several "heroic" works: *Sinfonia Eroica, Fidelio,* and the incidental music for Goethe's drama *Egmont*—incidental music in which Beethoven included a *Siegessymphonie* (Victory symphony). It is important to realize that in these heroic works Beethoven was honoring a person as hero, not commemorating heroism in general and certainly not the circumstances or event that occasioned the heroism. In this respect, his music differed from the French revolutionary works—symphonies, marches, choruses by Gossec, Bruni, Méhul, and their contemporaries—though they influenced his music. However, it is possible to interpret Beethoven's portrayal of heroism in a broad sense, as depicting heroism in overcoming difficulties—struggle with victory triumphant. Strength and a sense of power and/or victory are conveyed through the music of Piano Concerto No. 5 (Eb; "Emperor") and the "Waldstein" and "Appassionata" piano sonatas, also.

This period was dominated by orchestral works: Symphonies Nos. 3–8, the last three piano concerti, the violin concerto, and the *Fantasia,* Op. 80. Instruments were added to the orchestra as Beethoven needed them, e.g., piccolo, contrabassoon, and three trombones in Symphony No. 5, and four horns in the *Léonore* overtures. In all of Beethoven's instrumental writing, the parts became more and more demanding technically, e.g., the string bass part in Symphony No. 5, mvt. 3, Trio. And, as instruments were improved, Beethoven's demands became greater.

Increasingly, Beethoven expanded the dimensions of form, and he blurred dividing lines by disguising or varying material in the recapitulation or by connecting movements of a multimovement work. Development sections grew long and complex, and codas were expanded to become virtually second development sections concluding with quasi-recapitulation reference to the first theme. Often, Beethoven used theme groups or a multitude of themes and motives, all conceived for their developmental possibilities. Frequently, an introductory motive or theme was designed with regard to later incorporation of all or part of it into the form as a whole, e.g., the introductory phrase of Sonata No. 17 (Op. 31, No. 2) or the cyclic motive of Symphony No. 5. This kind of thematic recurrence was not entirely new in Beethoven's works—he had put the introductory measures of Sonata No. 8 (Op. 13) to similar use—but the treatment was more expansive in Op. 31, No. 2. Frequently, the first theme of a fast movement was constructed so that it needed completion, e.g., in Symphony No. 3, mvt. 1, the first theme, based on the Eb-major triad, concludes on a C♯. It was not uncommon for a first theme to generate all others within a movement or a work.

Beethoven's innovations were bolder and his stylistic changes more radical in his string quartets and piano sonatas than in his symphonies, a fact that made his contemporaries reluctant to accept works like the Op. 59 quartets. A sense of the dramatic pervaded many of the works of this period, e.g., the somber, very intense F-minor *Quartet serioso,* Op. 95. Beethoven concluded several of his minor-key compositions with a movement or coda in the parallel major, almost as though paying homage to old rules governing the Picardian ending. (Examples are Symphony No. 5; Quartet, Op. 95; Sonata No. 27, Op. 90.) Adverse criticism did not deter Beethoven but elicited from him words to the effect that posterity would understand his music—the first indication that a composer thought of his works being performed by later generations.

Vienna, c. 1815–1827

Between 1815 and the time of his death, Beethoven produced his most abstract and most sublime music. His principal works from this period are the song cycle *An die ferne Geliebte,* the last five piano sonatas, the *Diabelli Variations,* the *Missa solemnis,* Symphony No. 9, and the last six string quartets.

Outstanding characteristics of Beethoven's last style period are: (1) the meditative quality of his works, (2) development of thematic material to the seeming exhaustion of all its potentialities, (3) increased use of counterpoint, and (4) the blurring of

From Classicism to Romanticism

demarcations between theme groups, between sections of a movement, and even between movements of works. In addition to expanding transitions and bridge passages, Beethoven wrote a kind of merging bridge passage in which he gradually shifted from one musical area to another without pinpointing the exact moment of transition. His predilection for the flatted submediant key, and for modulations by thirds (rather than by harmonic degree, i.e., the fifth), is apparent to a much greater degree than in the previous style period. Also, he included passages of instrumental recitative and arioso in many works and showed a deeper concern for the use of lyricism within sonata form.

Beethoven studied, as did many other nineteenth-century musicians, the works of Bach, Handel, Palestrina, and more ancient composers; he incorporated some of their techniques in his works. Handel's choral fugues were models for those Beethoven wrote in the *Missa Solemnis*. Beethoven carefully researched Zarlino's *Istitutione harmoniche* and used the correct modes—Dorian and Lydian, respectively—for the *Et incarnatus* of the *Missa Solemnis* and the third movement of String Quartet, Op. 132. Medieval hocket technique appears in the fourth and fifth movements of the C♯-minor String Quartet, Op. 131 (e.g., mvt. 5, mm. 85–95). Moreover, during these years Beethoven seems to have had a penchant for writing canons and created many occasional ones for his friends.

Beethoven was aware of the new musical genres being used in England and touched on areas that received greater attention from his European contemporaries and later nineteenth-century composers, e.g., the song cycle (*An die ferne Geliebte*) and small character pieces for piano, such as *Für Elise* (For Elise) and the *Bagatelles,* especially Op. 126 and the last four of Op. 119, which influenced Schumann and Brahms.

After 1815, Beethoven's use of the principles of variation and fugue increased. Each of these compositional techniques can be used, and were used by Beethoven, in several ways: (1) as an independent composition (*Variations in C minor,* WoO 80, variations upon a harmonic ground; *Diabelli Variations,* theme-and-variations; and the *Grosse Fuge*); (2) as a movement of a multimovement composition (Symphony No. 5, mvt. 2, variations on two themes; Sonata No. 31, Op. 110, *Fuga* finale; a fugue as Var. 32 of the *Diabelli Variations*); (3) as a technique within another formal plan for a single movement (the variations within the finale of Symphony No. 9; the fugue within the sonata-form finale of *String Quartet,* Op. 59, No. 3). Beethoven skillfully embedded fugue and variation techniques in sonata form and in the complete sonata structure.

Piano Sonatas

The piano sonata occupies a central position in Beethoven's work. Since he composed piano sonatas throughout his life, each of his stylistic periods is represented in them. In this genre he introduced and experimented with new ideas, new procedures, and new interpretations that he incorporated in other works.

The sonatas Beethoven wrote in Bonn have been considered previously. Approximately two-thirds of his piano sonatas were composed between 1793 and 1802; stylistically, the 3 written in 1802 fit into his second Vienna period. In formal structure, Sonatas Nos. 1–20 vary considerably. Ten of them (Nos. 1–4, 7, 11–13, 15, 18) are constructed in four movements; 2 have only two movements (Nos. 19, 20); the remainder have three. Sonata form was used for first movements in the first 13 sonatas composed (Nos. 1–11, 19, 20); finales are usually some type of rondo. The minuet, when included, is not the elegant Classical type; often, Beethoven replaced it with a livelier movement, such as scherzo, e.g., Op. 2, No. 2. Sometimes he omitted both minuet and scherzo, e.g., Op. 10, Nos. 1, 2; Op. 13. However, the four-movement Sonata No. 18 (Op. 31, No. 3) contains a Scherzo (Allegretto vivace) as second movement and a Menuetto/Trio (Moderato e grazioso) as third. Sonata No. 12 (Op. 26; A♭) contains no sonata-form movement; the work commences with an Andante con Variazioni (theme and variations), has a Scherzo/Trio second movement, a *March funebre sulla morte d'un Eroe* (Funeral march on the death of a hero; A♭ minor) as third movement, and concludes with an Allegro rondo.

Among those whose works influenced Beethoven's writing for piano during his first decade in Vienna and thereafter were Muzio Clementi, whose piano sonatas of the 1780s and 1790s were particularly influential, Haydn, C. P. E. Bach, and Dussek. All of them used minor keys, especially C minor and

F minor. The finale of Clementi's F-minor sonata, Op. 10, No. 6 (1784), in particular, exhibits characteristics found in Beethoven's works of the middle and late 1790s. Both Clementi and Dussek were fond of major-minor parallelism or dualism—moving from C major to C minor within a movement or using a passage in Eb minor to prepare for a section in Eb major. However, at this time, such parallelism was common procedure in compound ternary form, e.g., Menuetto in major, Trio in minor. Clementi's works were probably responsible, to a great extent, for the full texture, octave doublings, *moto perpetuo* (perpetual motion) sections, and active, middle-register accompaniments in Beethoven's sonatas, as well as some of the harmonies then considered abrasive. Dussek also wrote full-textured music, with full chords, passages in octaves and thirds, rapid scale passages, and much figuration. He frequently modulated to remote keys and often colored his music with altered chords and nonharmonic tones.

Beethoven absorbed a great deal that other pianist-composers had to offer. However, to imply that Beethoven's style of piano writing was derived principally from outside influences would be erroneous. Though outside influences are important and stylistic similarities (and even direct borrowings) can be pointed out, Beethoven's innate talent and his originality—his invention of musical material and his ingenuity in treatment of it—must not be minimized.

The three sonatas Beethoven published as Op. 2 (1796) were dedicated to Haydn and reflect his influence as well as that of C. P. E. Bach. Beethoven's F-minor sonata (Op. 2, No. 1) contains several *galant* characteristics: the "Mannheim rocket" that commences the work, triplet eighths and sixteenths, frequent use of broken octaves, and Alberti figuration in the bass. Beethoven used rondo form frequently. In Op. 2, No. 2 (A major), both second (Largo appassionato, D major) and fourth (Rondo, grazioso; A major) movements are rondos; the third movement is Scherzo with Trio (A major/A minor).

Of the Op. 2 sonatas, No. 3 (C major) is the most brilliant and the most difficult to perform. Its first movement, an Allegro con brio in sonata form, contains concise motives conducive to variation and other developmental procedures. Figuration abounds—broken octaves, arpeggiations, Alberti bass, and other

Example 20.3 Beethoven: Sonata No. 4, Op. 7, mvt. 1, mm. 1–4.

types. Beethoven borrowed the *cantabile* second theme (in G minor) from an unpublished piano quartet he wrote in Bonn c. 1785. At m. 218, recapitulation of the closing theme is interrupted by an Ab-major chord (the flat submediant); the next 13 measures contain sweeping passages more characteristic of the soloist's part in a concerto than of a sonata. A I_6^4 chord is sounded, and an unbarred cadenza—a cadenza typical of a concerto—is notated; a 25-measure coda brings the movement to a close. The Adagio second movement is an alternating form based on two well-defined sections, in E major and E minor, respectively; the key relationship to the overall tonic of the sonata is unusual. Scherzo with Trio (C major/A minor) forms the third movement. The long Allegro assai finale is a rondo; prolonged trills—sometimes simultaneous trills on three notes—are a feature of its coda.

Sonata No. 4 (Op. 7; Eb major; 1796–97) is Beethoven's first real masterpiece in this genre. The figure opening the sonata-form first movement recurs throughout the movement as a unifying device, much needed because of the diversity of themes (ex. 20.3). The coda is the longest Beethoven had written up to this time; in structure, it foreshadows future codas he would write. The second movement is a lovely Largo in A major (ternary form, with coda). Though not so labeled, the Allegro third movement is a scherzo in Eb major, with a Minore trio (Eb minor) that is a *moto perpetuo* in triplets. Realizing that a fast Finale would spoil the effectiveness of the previous movements, Beethoven concluded Op. 7 with a long seven-part Rondo to be played Poco Allegretto e grazioso.

On the whole, the three sonatas of Op. 10 (comp. 1796–98) are representative of Beethoven's first Vienna period; yet, when they were published (1798), many critics considered them too experimental. Sonata No. 8, Op. 13 (C minor; 1798) was named

Pathétique (touching, moving) by Beethoven, perhaps because of the affect formerly associated with its key. Beethoven gave programmatic titles to only two of his piano sonatas; the other is No. 26. The *Pathétique* Sonata is in three movements: (1) A sonata-form Allegro di molto e con brio introduced by a dramatic, solemn Grave whose first three measures recur, slightly altered, to commence the development and the coda. (2) A long, lyrical Adagio cantabile in A♭ major (submediant key) constructed as a five-part rondo; the 16-measure rondo theme is in binary form. (3) A seven-part Rondo (Allegro; C minor), with coda, as finale.

Beethoven labeled each of the two sonatas of Op. 27 (1800–01) *quasi una fantasia* (fantasialike). Both sonatas must be considered experimental works. Neither has a sonata-form first movement; rather, fantasia elements are present in the first movement of each work, and elements of sonata form appear in the finale of each sonata—the climax toward which the preceding movements work. In Op. 27, No. 1 (E♭ major), the movements succeed one another without breaks; the finale is a sonata-rondo containing a cadenza. In Op. 27, No. 2 (C♯ minor), the first two movements are played without a break. The C♯-minor sonata is popularly known as the "Moonlight" Sonata. The nickname derives from the sonata's first movement, which, when performed on a piano of the type Beethoven used in 1801, could very well make a listener think of moonlight.

The greater freedom of form, more audacious choice of keys, and more remote modulations that characterized the sonatas composed during the last years of Beethoven's first decade in Vienna continued to be features of works written during his second Viennese style period. Of the 7 sonatas (Nos. 21–27) that he wrote in 1803–15, Nos. 21 and 23 are the most significant.

Sonata No. 21, Op. 53 (C major; 1803–04), was composed during a relatively serene period in Beethoven's life, after he had come to terms with the reality of his increasing deafness. Because the work is dedicated to Count von Waldstein, it has become known as the "Waldstein" Sonata. Originally, the sonata contained three expansive movements: a C-major Allegro con brio, an F-major Andante, and a

C-major Rondo. When Beethoven played the work for friends, they judged it too long, and he agreed. Moreover, he deemed the Andante second movement harmonically inappropriate to the sonata as a whole. Some of its most effective modulations are approached in a manner that adds strangeness to their beauty—a characteristic of nineteenth-century Romantic works. After due consideration, Beethoven removed the Andante from the sonata and in 1805 published it as a separate work, without *opus* number and without dedication; it is often referred to as *Andante favori*. To replace the deleted slow movement, Beethoven wrote an F-major *Introduzione* (Adagio molto) that leads, without pause, into the Rondo finale (Allegretto moderato; C major).

The sonata-form first movement of the "Waldstein" Sonata commences *pianissimo* in bass clef with two measures of reiterated chords; in both exposition and recapitulation, the first theme is stated twice, slightly varied the second time. The *dolce* and very *legato* second theme, in the mediant key of E major, also enters softly. Throughout the sonata, there is an abundance of many types of figuration, much of it thematic. Often, fast rhythmic motion offsets the fact that the harmonic rhythm is slow. Prolonged trills, sometimes placed between left-hand figuration and upper-voice melodic line, and extensive scale passages in octaves alternating between hands (and played *pp*), are features of the Rondo finale. The "Waldstein" Sonata is a masterpiece that attests Beethoven's ability to tastefully control virtuosic elements rather than flaunt them flamboyantly.

Sonata No. 23, Op. 57 (F minor; 1804–5), named "Appassionata" by the publisher, is a dramatic three-movement work. The outer movements, especially, exude strength. A sense of tragedy and strength is apparent from the sonata's very beginning, conveyed in the dark tones of the F-minor first theme, with its dramatic dotted rhythms and its unharmonized first measures doubled two octaves lower (ex. 20.4). Basically, the theme is an extended tonic-to-dominant progression; however, its sequential repetition on the flatted supertonic (Neapolitan) moving to its dominant (VI) certainly must have shocked Beethoven's contemporaries. The second theme group commences in A♭, the relative major, then moves to A♭ minor.

Allegro assai.

Example 20.4 Beethoven: "Appassionata" Sonata, mvt. 1, mm. 1–8.

Example 20.5 Beethoven: "Appassionata" Sonata, mvt. 1, the four measures preceding the Coda.

Adagio.

Le-be-wohl!

p espressivo

Example 20.6 Beethoven: Sonata, Op. 81a, *Lebewohl!* motive.

Just prior to the Più Allegro coda to the movement, the music dwells on a figure not unlike the cyclic motive of the Fifth Symphony (ex. 20.5). The Andante con moto (Db major), a 16-measure theme with four variations, proceeds directly into the finale, an Allegro non troppo (F minor) in which a new theme is introduced in the development section. Only the development-recapitulation section of the finale is marked to be repeated; in the second ending, tempo is gradually but quickly increased to Presto for the coda. Except for eight measures of transition in the recapitulation and six measures in the coda, the entire finale is in minor tonalities.

Five years elapsed before Beethoven composed another piano sonata. Then, late in 1809, he wrote two small ones (No. 24, F♯; No. 25, G) and began a third. Sonata No. 24, Op. 78, has been neglected by performers but is a real gem and was a favorite of Beethoven. Its two short movements, both in F♯ major, are fast.

Of substantial proportions is the programmatic Sonata No. 26, Op. 81a (Eb; 1809–10), dedicated to Beethoven's pupil and friend, Archduke Rudolph, a talented pianist. To the sonata Beethoven affixed the title *Das Lebewohl, Abwesenheit, und Wedersehen* (Farewell, absence, and return), and, in the Adagio introduction to the first movement, labeled the *Lebewohl* motive (ex. 20.6), which recurs in the ensuing Allegro. The single theme generates all others in the sonata. Beethoven wrote no program for the sonata, and the music is not descriptive; rather, it is an expression of high regard and deep feelings. The brief

Andante, in the relative key of C minor, aptly depicts loneliness. The second movement moves into the third without a break; the mood of the finale is exultant.

In notating Sonatas Nos. 27 and 28, Beethoven again broke with tradition by heading the movements with German instructions instead of Italian tempo markings.

Between 1817 and 1822, Beethoven composed his last five piano sonatas, Nos. 28–32. All are characterized by exceptional developmental techniques, more frequent use of polyphony, especially fugal sections, still more daring harmonies and remote modulations, and thematic or motivic relationships between movements. Sometimes a passage of dramatic recitative interrupts the flow of a movement. Beethoven showed a decided preference for modulating to or writing movements in the flatted submediant key, and at times he did this subtly, enharmonically. Often, a remote modulation is prefaced by a general pause rather than by dominant preparation. Several of the last sonatas present the performer with some tremendous technical difficulties.

In the powerful *Hammerklavier Sonata,* No. 29, Op. 106 (Bb; 1817–18; ded. to Archduke Rudolph), the pianist is confronted with formidable technical problems. Counterpoint is present in abundance. Subtle thematic relationships exist among first themes

From Classicism to Romanticism

Example 20.7 Beethoven: "Hammerklavier" Sonata, Op. 106. (*a*) Conclusion of mvt. 2; (*b*) mvt. 3, mm. 1–2.

(a)

(b)

of the movements of this work. The opening sonata-form Allegro (B♭) is majestic and grandiose; its long exposition is to be repeated—there are first and second endings—and its contrapuntal development section is extensive. The Scherzo with Trio (B♭ major/B♭ minor) follows Classical form except for the insertion of a 32-measure Presto with a Prestissimo cadenza prior to return (written-out) of the Scherzo. The musical quibbling among A♯, B♭, and B♮ in the coda must be interpreted harmonically in terms of *enharmonic* relationships (with B♮ = C♭). For the extremely long Adagio sostenuto, performed *appassionato e con molto sentimento,* Beethoven used F♯ minor—enharmonically, G♭ minor, the flatted submediant minor key—a shocking shift in tonality (ex. 20.7). This type of enharmonic key relationship occurs also in his C-minor and E♭-major concerti. The Adagio is meditative, with moods ranging from somber melancholy through serenity to brightness. A quasi-improvisatory Largo serves as modulating introduction to the 390-measure Allegro risoluto finale (B♭ major), a three-voice fugue that ultimately has three subjects and two countersubjects. Beethoven skillfully used all kinds of

fugal techniques, but his counterpoint is neither purely Classical nor purely Baroque, and there are some interesting deviations: displacement of beat, reversal of accent, and the *sempre dolce cantabile* three-voice fugue in D major on a third subject (mm. 240–68)—a fugue within a fugue—followed by fugal treatment of first and third subjects in combination (mm. 269–84).

Beethoven's last three piano sonatas are his most introspective ones. In them he evidenced little concern for traditional formal patterns and the Classical overall structural scheme of the sonata—almost as if he deliberately tried to violate established conventions. Consistently, he displaced the slow movement; Scherzo/Trio were disguised; sonata form, when used, was treated with considerable freedom. In the terse but free sonata-form first movement of Sonata No. 30, Op. 109 (E major; 1820), a Vivace ma non troppo theme in Lombardic rhythm alternates with a rhapsodic Adagio espressivo (B major). Tempo of the E-minor second movement is Prestissimo; the finale, Andante molto cantabile ed espressivo (E major), comprises a 16-measure theme in binary form, with six rich variations.

In Sonata No. 31, Op. 110 (A♭; 1821–22), the first theme is genesis of all the others. The lyrical first movement (Moderato, A♭ major), in free sonata form, contains rhapsodic passages and has a very short development section. In the Allegro molto middle movement (F minor, the submediant minor), Beethoven used a Silesian folk melody. The movement's concluding Picardian chord (F major) is heard as dominant to the B♭-minor opening of the finale, which commences Adagio, ma non troppo with a tripartite modulatory introduction—lyrical Adagio, dramatic *Recitativo,* and *Arioso dolente* (A♭ minor)—then, without a break, moves into a three-voice *Fuga* (A♭ major), tragic in mood. Still with no break between sections, the *Arioso* returns, varied, in G minor. In the middle of its final measure, another *Fuga* (G major) begins—actually, developing material presented in the first fugue and using as subject the inversion of the first fugue's subject. The many contrapuntal devices Beethoven used become complex and include stretto, augmentation, diminution, and stretto with double diminution. The sonata concludes triumphantly, *ff,* with a four-measure, rippling arpeggiation of the A♭-major chord.

Beethoven's last sonata, Op. 111 (C minor; 1822), has only two movements, unrelated, yet complementary: (1) an *appassionato* C-minor first movement with Maestoso introduction and (2) a C-major Adagio consisting of *Arietta* theme with four variations (in $\frac{9}{16}$, $\frac{6}{16}$, and $\frac{12}{32}$ meters), a coda that recapitulates the theme, and an impressive epilogue that concludes with a great crescendo passage that suddenly drops from *f sf* to *p* and *pp* for the last measure. Gustav Mahler (1860–1911) borrowed the C-minor melody from the first movement for his *Resurrection Symphony.*

Variations

The 21 sets of variations Beethoven wrote for piano are basically of two types: (1) those based on songs and arias that were popular at the time—pieces prepared for public performances, or originating as improvisations created in public performances and later notated, and (2) those with original themes, or with thematic material unrelated to popular music—more serious works comparable with the piano sonatas in degree of difficulty and mood. Compositions in the first category include variations based on arias from operas by Dittersdorf, Paisiello, Salieri, Süssmayr, von Winter, and Grétry. In the second category are the *"Eroica" Variations,* in E♭, Op. 35, and *Thirty-two Variations* in C minor, WoO 80. The latter is a chaconne—variations on an eight-measure ground that is a series of harmonic progressions.

More significant is the work entitled *33 Veränderungen über einen Walzer* (33 Variations on a Waltz), Op. 120. In 1819, the Viennese composer-publisher Anton Diabelli (1781–1858) wrote a waltz theme that he submitted to 50 composers with the request that each of them write a variation on it, so that he might publish a composite set. All but Beethoven complied with the terms of the request. Beethoven considered Diabelli's theme inconsequential—he called it a "cobbler's patch"—yet made from it a masterly set of 33 variations that many critics consider comparable to J. S. Bach's "Goldberg Variations." None of Beethoven's variations is included in Diabelli's composite set; instead, in 1823 Diabelli issued Beethoven's set as a separate publication. In Beethoven's variations, written in contrasting moods, styles, and *tempi,* the theme is transformed rather than merely varied. At times, it is reduced to a harmonic skeleton, and, in the 22nd variation, it is so freely metamorphosed that Beethoven could convert it, without incongruity, into a variation of Leporello's *Notte e giorno faticar* (Working night and day), from Mozart's *Il Don Giovanni.* The 31st variation, an expressive, ornamented Largo, resembles a Bach Adagio; Var. 32 is a fugue; the final variation commences as a Classical Menuetto but becomes highly stylized and very elaborate. Beethoven's "Diabelli Variations" served as model for sets of variations by later nineteenth-century composers, e.g., Brahms's 25 *Variations on a Theme by Handel.*

Beethoven composed sets of variations for chamber ensembles, also. One of the loveliest of these sets is based on Mozart's *La cì darem la mano,* from *Il Don Giovanni,* and is for two oboes and English horn (1795). Beethoven incorporated variation technique in large multimovement compositions, too: in symphonies (Nos. 3 and 9, finale; No. 5, mvt. 2) and in his late sonatas and string quartets, as slow movements (Quartet, Op. 131, mvt. 4), and occasionally as finale (Sonatas Op. 109 and Op. 111).

Chamber Music

Throughout his life, Beethoven was interested in chamber music. As a youth in Bonn, he composed chamber music; his first published works in Vienna were the three Piano Trios, Op. 1; during the last years of his life, he wrote string quartets. Yet, in no single category of chamber music is there a complete panorama of his style changes. He wrote no piano trios after 1811; his piano quartets (for piano and three other instruments of various kinds) were produced before 1798. His first string quartets (Op. 18) were begun in 1798, and he composed no string quartets between 1810 and 1823. His violin/piano sonatas and 'cello/piano sonatas were written in 1796–1815.

Trios with Piano

In addition to the three piano trios and three piano quartets completed at Bonn, several other chamber music works begun at Bonn were completed or rewritten in Vienna. Among the latter are the three Piano Trios (E♭, G, and C minor) published as Op. 1 (1795). Present in these trios are two devices that became characteristic of his style: themes constructed from repetitions of a short motive, and sudden modulations to keys a third above or below the tonic. Each of the trios follows the Classical four-movement structural scheme of the complete sonata, with the third movement being either Menuetto/Trio or Scherzo/Trio. The third Piano Trio is the most significant of the three. Its first, third, and fourth movements are in C minor, the two outer movements in sonata form. In the third movement, a conventional Menuetto/Trio, the Trio opens with a motive used at the close of the first movement, a unifying device Beethoven used to greater extent in later works. The variations in the second movement (Andante con Variazione, E♭) are imaginative transformations of the theme rather than mere ornamented versions of it.

The Trio in B♭, Op. 11 (publ. 1798), for piano, clarinet, and 'cello, is not distinctive. In 1808 Beethoven composed the two Piano Trios, Op. 70, in D and E♭. The D-major Trio is a closely-knit, passionate, three-movement work constructed from a minimum of motivic materials. Its nickname, "Ghost Trio," derives from the mysterious and expressive

Example 20.8 Beethoven: Piano Trio, Op. 70, No. 1, mvt. 2, theme 1. In 1808 Beethoven used this same theme in sketches he made for the witches' scene in Act I of H. J. von Collin's unfinished opera libretto *Macbeth*.

Example 20.9 Beethoven: Piano Trio, Op. 97, mvt. 3, theme.

character of the D-minor second movement, Largo assai ed espressivo (theme 1, ex. 20.8). In contrast, the E♭ Trio is, for the most part, a quiet work.

The so-called *Archduke Trio* in B♭, Op. 97, written rapidly in March 1811 for Archduke Rudolph of Austria (1788–1831), is magnificent. It comprises four movements: (1) Allegro moderato, B♭, in sonata form but with the second theme in the submediant (G) rather than the conventional dominant; (2) an imaginative Scherzo in E♭, whose Trio commences with a chromatic theme in B♭ minor; (3) Andante cantabile, ma però con moto, D major, theme with five variations and coda, which moves without a break into (4) an energetic Rondo finale. The Andante cantabile is one of Beethoven's loveliest movements. The simplicity and nobility of the theme is remarkable (ex. 20.9). Its melody is recognizable and its harmonic framework is maintained throughout the variations, which are presented in successively smaller note values.

Example 20.10 Beethoven: String Quartet, Op. 18, No. 3, mvt. 1, theme 1. The quartet opens on the dominant and arrives at a tonic D-major chord at the beginning of measure 3, with the resolution of a 4–3 suspension on the second half of the beat.

String Trios

Before composing string quartets, Beethoven wrote several string trios in complete sonata structure, in which violin, viola, and 'cello are equal participants: Op. 3, in E♭ (before 1794); and the three trios of Op. 9, in G, D, and C minor (1797–98). Also for string trio is a multimovement *Serenade* in D (Op. 8; 1797) that opens and closes with a March. The *Serenade* is excellent, but it is not easy and is seldom performed.

Beethoven had available for rehearsals and first performances of his chamber music for strings an experienced quartet headed by first violinist Ignaz Schuppanzigh (1776–1830). Beethoven first became acquainted with Schuppanzigh when his quartet performed weekly Friday morning concerts at the home of Prince Lichnowsky, where Beethoven had lodgings. In 1808, Schuppanzigh formed a quartet that Count Razumovsky supported until 1814—a quartet considered the finest in Europe. The ensemble rehearsed several times a week, and Beethoven attended the rehearsals more or less regularly. It was Schuppanzigh's quartet who complained about the strange harmonies of the Op. 59 quartets and to whom Beethoven replied that later generations would understand them—an indication that Beethoven's thinking was revolutionary, too, and that he intended his music not only for his contemporaries but for future generations to enjoy. Beethoven was the first of the great composers to have at his disposal instruments of the violin family in their modern construction—with fingerboard and neck lengthened and their slope altered, bridge more highly arched, longer bows with newly developed frog to control hair tension—and his writing for strings shows that he took full advantage of the increased range and the more advanced bowing techniques made possible by those constructional changes.

String Quartets

Beethoven's quartets are considered the backbone of string quartet literature. The six quartets of Op. 18 (F, G, D, C minor, A, B♭; written 1798–1800) were not planned as a set but were grouped for publication, in accordance with eighteenth-century custom. Actually, Op. 18, No. 3 (D major) was composed first, but the least adventurous work was placed first when the pieces were published. In general, the D-major quartet follows the Classic models of Haydn and Mozart with regard to general outline of form and tempo. Key relationships within and among movements are not conventional, however. Audacious touches include: (1) the sustained melodic seventh that begins the quartet on the dominant of the key and is a basic idea (as interval or rhythmically) throughout the sonata-form first movement (ex. 20.10); (2) the development section of the first movement commencing in the parallel minor key rather than the customary dominant; (3) the unusual length of the slow movement (Andante con moto), which is in B♭, the flatted submediant key; (4) in the third movement—a scherzo, though not so labeled—the written-out repeat of the D-major first section after the Minore trio (D minor) to permit repetition of the first section (customarily, not repeated on *da capo*) at the upper octave.

The Op. 59 quartets (1805–06) are representative of Beethoven's mature style of quartet writing. They were commissioned by Count (later Prince) Andrei Razumovsky (1752–1836), Russian statesman, patron of music, and competent violinist, who especially enjoyed chamber music and often played second violin in quartets. The quartets, in F, E minor, and C, respectively, are related by Beethoven's use of Russian folk-song melodies in the finale of the F-major

From Classicism to Romanticism

Example 20.11 The Russian melody *Slava* (Glory), as presented by viola in the trio of Beethoven's String Quartet, Op. 59, No. 2, mvt. 3.

and the third movement of the E-minor works, and by an original melody resembling a Russian folk song in the slow movement of the C-major one. *Slava* (Russian, Glory; ex. 20.11), incorporated in the E-minor quartet, was used also by Musorgsky in the coronation scene of his opera *Boris Godunov* (see pp. 735–36).

The Op. 59 quartets differ radically from Beethoven's earlier quartets in many respects. The movements are of larger proportions than those of previous quartets, and Beethoven's ability to write long, complex developments is evident. Some of the codas resemble second developments. Beethoven was more daring with regard to tonal relationships and formal structure, blurring and disguising sectional divisions within movements and sometimes linking movements. All movements of Op. 59, No. 1, are in sonata form. Only one section of that quartet is repeated—that containing the Russian theme, the exposition of the Finale. In the F-major first movement, an Allegro, the exposition opens on the dominant, the development commences in the tonic, and the recapitulation does not remain in the tonic. The 474-measure second movement, an Allegretto vivace e sempre scherzando in B♭, is colored by excursions into unexpected keys and sudden dynamic contrasts. The Adagio molto e mesto third movement, in F minor, ends with a cadenzalike passage in 64th notes for first violin, whose last note, a sustained trill on c″, carries over into the Allegro F-major finale and provides background for the 'cello's presentation of the Russian theme.

In Op. 59, No. 2, Beethoven placed the four movements in Classical order of tempo and used for them the keys of: (1) E minor, (2) E major, (3) E minor with E major trio, and (4) E minor. Such shifting of tonality between parallel major and minor keys was unusual.

The C-major quartet (Op. 59, No. 3) is the finest of the set. The work opens with a diminished-seventh chord on f♯, proceeds with a slow introduction (29 meas.) in which no key is established, then barely touches upon a C-major chord, *piano*—the first chord of the Allegro vivace—before embarking on an extensive modulatory section that eventually cadences into C major and establishes it as tonic in measure 43. The movement is richly colored by dominant-seventh and augmented-sixth chords, and the melodic minor second figures prominently. Modified sonata form was used for the melancholy Andante con moto quasi Allegretto, in A minor. The third movement is a Menuetto with Trio (C major/F major). After the Menuetto *da capo,* a coda brings the movement to a close on the dominant seventh of C, and the directive *attacca subito* moves the music immediately into the fourth movement. Throughout the first three movements, Beethoven used counterpoint effectively, but his most brilliant contrapuntal writing occurs in the Allegro molto (C major) sonata-form finale, the climax of the quartet. The first theme is presented as the subject of an energetic fugue that commences on the dominant of C and is answered on the dominant of G. In the recapitulation, a countersubject in staccato half notes provides the harmony.

In 1809 Beethoven wrote one quartet, Op. 74, in E♭, the "Harp" Quartet, nicknamed for two passages of pizzicato arpeggios in its first movement. Beethoven labeled his F-minor quartet, Op. 95 (composed 1810), *Quartet serioso.* This, his shortest and most intense quartet, is filled with chromaticism and is somber in tone. The work has no slow movement. Though the third movement is a scherzo in form, it is not such in spirit. Only the brief, light Allegro that, as coda, concludes the F-minor finale in F major, furnishes a fleeting moment of brightness.

Fourteen years elapsed before Beethoven wrote another string quartet; then, during the next three years, he created six of them. Total deafness, serious illness, and family problems had caused him to become increasingly introspective; this is reflected in his last quartets. The incentive to compose more chamber music was supplied in 1822 by Prince Nikolai Galitzïn, a 'cellist, who wrote Beethoven from St. Petersburg and commissioned "one, two, or three" quartets. For him Beethoven composed Op. 127 (E♭; 1824), Op. 132 (A minor; 1824–25), Op. 130 (B♭; 1825–26), and, as part of Op. 130, the *Grosse Fuge* that later became Op. 133 (B♭; 1825–26).

Originally, Op. 132 was planned as a four-movement work. Composition of the quartet was interrupted by Beethoven's severe illness in April 1825, an experience that caused him to head the quartet's third movement *Heiliger Dankgesang eines Genesenen* . . . (A convalescent's sacred song of thanksgiving to God, [written] in the Lydian mode). The hymn is presented in chorale style in the Molto Adagio first section of the movement (ex. 20.12a) and is followed by an Andante labeled *Neue Kraft fühlend* (Feeling new strength). Molto Adagio and Andante sections alternate within the movement, forming a kind of rondo structure: ABA′B′A″. In the second and last Molto Adagio segments, the hymn is treated more or less as a chorale motet (ex. 20.12b). The brief fourth movement commences *Alla marcia, assai vivace* (A major)—another instance of Beethoven using a march to relieve intensely emotional feelings. The march, a binary, is followed by a recitative-like section rather than a trio. The recitative proceeds without pause into the A-minor Allegro appassionato fifth movement, which concludes with a long coda in A major.

The quartet in B♭, Op. 130, was the third of the set composed for Galitzïn but was published earlier than the A-minor work, Op. 132. In its original completed form, Op. 130 was a six-movement quartet concluding with the *Grosse Fuge*. However, the quartet was badly received when first performed, and the blame was placed on its Finale. At the suggestion of publisher Matthias Artaria (1793–1835), Beethoven removed the *Grosse Fuge* from Op. 130, and Artaria published it as an independent string quartet,

(a)

(b)

Example 20.12 From Beethoven's String Quartet, Op. 132, mvt. 3: (*a*) the opening measures; (*b*) a portion of the second Molto Adagio section.

Op. 133 (B♭). The single-movement work commences with an *Overtura* (Introduction; G major) that presents the first of the two principal themes upon which the quartet is based (ex. 20.13). In the ensuing Allegro (in B♭) that theme is stated in diminution. Then the word *Fuga* appears above a new theme, and a double fugue is begun. Both themes are used, separately and together, in the several fugal sections that make up the piece, and both themes are developed extensively. The fugue is sometimes strict and obvious, sometimes free, sometimes hidden. The movement concludes with a brief Allegro molto e con brio section that is a simple summary of the subjects.

Example 20.13 From Beethoven's *Grosse Fuge,* Op. 133: (*a*) *Overtura,* theme 1; (*b*) mm. 26–32, in which theme 1, stated in diminution, becomes part of a double fugue.

(a)

(b)

Beethoven delayed writing a new Finale for the Op. 130 quartet until late in 1826; it is the last movement he completed before his death. On the whole, Op. 130 is a bright quartet. Its first two movements, Adagio ma non troppo; Allegro (sonata form with slow introduction) and Presto (scherzo/trio), are in B♭ major. Placed third is the slow movement, a D♭-major Andante con moto designated to be played *poco scherzando*. The fourth movement, *Alla danza tedesca* (In the style of a German dance), is a minuet (G major) with a waltzlike trio, but rather than *da capo* Beethoven developed the thematic material. A slow, expressive *Cavatina* (E♭) forms the fifth movement; Beethoven claimed that never before had he

written a melody that affected him so much. The *Cavatina* closes with a diminuendo to *pianissimo,* at which dynamic level the viola states the murky pedal that begins the new Finale Allegro, a sonata-rondo in B♭. Beethoven did not completely delete the *Grosse Fuge* from this quartet; melodic and tonal elements of the original finale are embedded in the new one.

The C♯-minor quartet, Op. 131, has seven movements designed to be performed without a break. The traditional complete sonata structural scheme appears as movements 2, 4, 5, and 7. The unity of the work lies in the uninterrupted succession of its movements, which may be outlined as shown in figure 20.2. In the coda of the fifth movement all four instruments

Movement	1	2	3	4	5	6	7
Key	C# minor	D major	B minor to E major	A major	E major	G# minor	C# minor
Tonal Relationship	Tonic	Neapolitan, or as V/V (dominant of dominant)	Relative minor of D, to dominant of A	VI of C# minor, or subdominant of E	Relative major of C# minor	Dominant of C# minor	Tonic
Form	Free fugue	Modified sonata form	Recitative serving as introduction to mvt. 4	Theme and variation	Scherzo with Trio	Introduction to mvt. 7: in Rounded Bar form	Sonata form

Figure 20.2 Outline of Beethoven's String Quartet, Op. 131.

Example 20.14 (a) Keys of the first four movements of Op. 131; (b) motive stated in mm. 1–2 of Op. 132.

are required to play an 18-measure passage staccato, *pianissimo,* and *sul ponticello* (bowed near the bridge)—this is the earliest use of *sul ponticello* in string quartet music.

Quartets Opp. 132, 130, 133, and 131 form a cycle with melodic, motivic, and tonal relationships. The four-note motive that opens Op. 132, the first of the four quartets to be composed, appears within the initial theme presented in the *Overtura* of the *Grosse Fuge,* occurs again at the beginning of the fugal Allegro (ex. 20.13), and is embedded in the thematic material of all quartets in the cycle. Moreover, the keys of the first four movements of Op. 131 form the motive, as stated in the first two measures of Op. 132 (ex. 20.14). Many other relationships could be pointed out. The entire cycle displays Beethoven's contrapuntal skill and his technical mastery of string quartet composition.

The F-major quartet, Op. 135, a relatively short, four-movement work composed at Gneixendorf in summer/autumn 1826, is not part of the cycle.

Ensemble Sonatas

Beethoven wrote the two 'cello/piano sonatas of Op. 5 (F major, G minor; 1796) for Jean-Pierre Duport (1741–1818), Prussian court 'cellist, and himself to perform at court, but when published the sonatas were dedicated to Prussian King Frederick William II (r. 1786–97), also a 'cellist. The title page states that the works are "For harpsichord or piano with violoncello *obligato,*" the word *obligato* [sic] indicating that the 'cello part is vital to the ensemble. These are the earliest sonatas written for 'cello and keyboard in which the keyboard is not considered a *continuo* instrument.

Each sonata has only two movements: a fast sonata-form movement with Adagio introduction, and a fast rondo.

The Sonata in A major, Op. 69 (1807–08), is a masterpiece of ensemble literature for 'cello. The sonata has three movements, none of them slow. Throughout the work, the musical material is shared equally by 'cello and piano. The 'cello, alone, commences the first movement (Allegro, ma non tanto; sonata form) but does not state the entire first theme; it is completed by the piano. Then, the roles are reversed. Dialogue exchanges between the two instruments occur throughout the movement. Next comes a Scherzo with a syncopated theme and a smoother Trio. A short Adagio cantabile introduces the Allegro vivace finale, in which Beethoven took full advantage of the 'cello's range, color, and technical possibilities.

The two sonatas of Op. 105 (C major; D major; 1815) do not fully exhibit stylistic characteristics of either of Beethoven's last two periods. These sonatas

From Classicism to Romanticism

Example 20.15 Passages in Beethoven's Violin/Piano Sonatas, Op. 12, demanding precise coordination of performers in timing and articulation: (*a*) No. 1, mvt. 1, m. 1; (*b*) No. 1, mvt. 1, mm. 91–92; (*c*) No. 1, mvt. 1, mm. 188–96; (*d*) No. 3, mvt. 2, mm. 55–60.

are shorter than his others for 'cello/piano but display increased use of counterpoint, more textural variety, and greater freedom of form.

Beethoven's violin/piano sonatas had predecessors in works by Haydn and Mozart, but Beethoven carried the genre far beyond those works. Nine of his sonatas were written in 1797–1803; the tenth was composed in 1812. Four of the sonatas (Nos. 5, 7, 10) are structured with four movements, according to the complete sonata scheme; each of the others has three. No two sonatas—in fact, no two movements—are exactly alike.

When the three sonatas of Op. 12 (D, A, E♭; 1797–98; publ. 1799, ded. to Salieri) appeared, Beethoven's contemporaries were unappreciative of them and were highly critical of his harmonies and modulations. In addition to contemporary Classical traits, the works exhibit traces of *style galant* and elements of emerging Romanticism. The Op. 12 sonatas are youthful works but contain some difficult and highly sophisticated passages (ex. 20.15): (1) unison writing that includes chords that the violinist must play *non arpeggiando* to agree with either crisply articulated piano chords (No. 1, mvt. 1, m. 1) or piano figurations containing the top note of the violinist's chord (No. 1, mvt. 1, mm. 91–92); (2) opposing rhythms and figurations that must be integrated (No. 1, mvt. 1, mm. 188–196); (3) chain figurations (No. 3, mvt. 2, mm. 55–60). In Op. 12, No. 3, the material is almost ideally distributed between the two instruments; frequently, Beethoven placed the violin line in the middle of three-part writing.

The third and fourth sonatas, Op. 23 (A minor; 1800) and Op. 24 (F major; 1800–1801) seem to have been intended as a pair but were published separately (1801) and are almost never programmed together, though the so-called Spring Sonata is a perfect complement for the tense outer movements of the A-minor work. The "Spring" Sonata has become a favorite; part of its charm is its simplicity, which is at times deceptive. Neither of the sonatas is easy.

Beethoven's last five violin/piano sonatas are true duos. The three sonatas of Op. 30 (A, C minor, G; composed 1801–02)—especially the C-minor sonata—contain difficult cross-rhythms, trills and small cadenzas to be played as duets, chain passages, long scales, and often the violin line is integrated in the middle of the three-voice writing. The C-minor

Example 20.16 Beethoven: Violin/Piano Sonata, Op. 96, mvt. 4, mm. 272–86, long run followed by imitative flourish.

sonata is a long, grandiose work that makes enormous demands on the performers.

Beethoven prepared the "Kreutzer" Sonata, Op. 47 (A major; 1802–03) for a concert he performed with violinist George Bridgetower (c. 1779–1860) in May 1803. In order to have a new sonata ready in time, Beethoven quickly finished the first two movements of an A-major sonata on which he was working, stripped the fourth movement from Op. 30, No. 1 (which had not yet been published), and appended it as Finale: Presto to those two movements. At the concert, the audience demanded an encore of the middle movement, an Andante with four variations, some of them virtuosic. Before Op. 47 was published (1805), Beethoven and Bridgetower had a disagreement, and Beethoven dedicated the sonata to violinist Rodolphe Kreutzer (1766–1831). However, Kreutzer claimed he did not understand the work and refused to play it. Beethoven's subtitle for the sonata reveals a great deal about the character of the work: *Sonata per il Pianoforte ed uno Violino obligato in uno stile molto concertante come d'un Concerto* (Sonata for piano and one required violin in a very *concertante* style, like a concerto).

Beethoven designed his G-major sonata, Op. 96 (1812), for French violinist Pierre Rode (1774–1830). The work is dedicated to Archduke Rudolph, who, with Rode, first performed it in December 1812. The sonata contains numerous difficult passages for both instruments, such as the lengthy run that concludes with a flourish and an arpeggiation up to d'''' (ex. 20.16). Beethoven was always particular about indicating dynamics. One of the most trying passages—

certainly, a test of the dynamic sensitivity of the duo—is the 12-measure crescendo from *pp* and the ensuing 15-measure diminuendo back to *pp* in the Trio of the second movement of Op. 96.

Symphonies

Beethoven's nine symphonies form the core of modern symphonic repertoire. They have influenced, in one way or another, all symphonies written since they were composed. Beethoven's symphonies attest his mastery of Classical style and forms, show the development of his individualistic style as a composer of symphonic orchestral works—his innovative treatment of harmonies, keys, thematic material, and forms—and, in his last symphony, the introspective character of his last works. At the heart of this development is his view of the structure of a single movement as sonata *principle* rather than sonata *form*.

Beethoven's first two symphonies were composed near the end of his first decade in Vienna. Symphony No. 1, Op. 21, in C major, has Classical proportions and form and uses as third movement the traditional Minuet/Trio (though it sounds much like a scherzo). The orchestral instrumentation is standard for the time: pairs of flutes, oboes, clarinets, bassoons, horns, trumpets, timpani, and strings. However, Beethoven gave winds more than the usual degree of prominence. The influence of Haydn's "London" symphonies is reflected in Beethoven's use of slow introductions to the first and fourth movements, and that of Mozart's Symphony No. 40 is apparent in the *fugato* opening of the sonata-form second movement. In other respects, the C-major symphony is the work of a talented, self-assured composer writing a *Grand Symphony* designed to please no one other than himself. The Adagio introduction to the sonata-form first movement provides a sample of Beethoven's harmonic audacity. Instead of the expected solid statement of the symphony's C-major tonality, the first chord is a dominant seventh in the key of F, and the first measure presents a perfect authentic cadence in F major. This is followed by a deceptive cadence in C and a dominant seventh-to-tonic progression in G (ex. 20.17a). For the ensuing seven measures the ear debates the final outcome of tonality that seems to waver between G and C major. Then unison strings utter an

(a)

(b)

Example 20.17 Beethoven, Symphony No. 1: (*a*) mvt. 1, mm. 1–4; (*b*) mvt. 1, theme 1; (*c*) mvt. 4, mm. 1–14, introduction and beginning of theme 1.

ascending G-major scale harmonized with a dominant seventh of C; there is a rapid descent of a harmonic degree, and the exposition commences, Allegro con brio, with a *piano* C-major chord. The marchlike first theme firmly proclaims C-major tonality (ex. 20.17b). The 5½ measure Adagio introduction to the Finale is also unusual, and humorous. After the *ff* pronouncement of a sustained G pitch, a C-major scale that commences on its dominant is timidly released in segments gradually increasing in length. There is a

(c)

brief general pause. Then, Allegro molto e vivace and *piano,* the complete scale begins the vivacious first theme (ex. 20.17c). The entire Finale is light and animated.

Symphony No. 2, Op. 36, in D major (1802), lies on the border between Beethoven's first and second Vienna style periods. It, too, opens with an Adagio introduction, but this one is much longer and much slower, and it proclaims D as tonic before exploring other tonalities. A questioning motive in the introduction (ex. 20.18a) recurs with an extension in the

first measure of the Finale, where it is part of a larger interrogation (ex. 20.18b) that finds its answer in the coda of that movement (ex. 20.18c). The trilled motive is almost identical with the one that opens C. P. E. Bach's Symphony No. 3 (ex. 20.18d). The Second Symphony's outer movements have long, developmental codas, and a new theme is introduced in the coda to the Finale. In the sonata-form slow movement, a richly melodic Larghetto (A major), the first theme is in two eight-measure strains (a theme group),

Example 20.18 (*a*) Beethoven, Symphony No. 2, mvt. 1, mm. 28–30; (*b*) Beethoven, Symphony No. 2, *Finale,* mvt. 4, mm. 1–3; (*c*) Beethoven, Symphony No. 2, mvt. 4, mm. 423–42, string parts; (*d*) C. P. E. Bach, Symphony No. 3, mvt. 1, mm. 1–6.

each repeated with different instrumentation; there are three other themes. The third movement, labeled *Scherzo,* is characterized by frequent sharp contrasts in dynamics, timbre, instrumentation, and tonality.

Symphony No. 3, Eroica (Heroic), in E♭ (1803), is one of Beethoven's most important works. According to legend, General Bernadotte, French ambassador to Vienna, suggested to Beethoven in 1798 that he write a work to honor Napoleon Buonaparte. At that time, Beethoven and countless others regarded Napoleon as a great representative of the common people working to bring about the republican aims of liberty, equality, and fraternity. The idea of writing a symphony for such a hero appealed to Beethoven. By 1803 he had completed the work, which

he planned to entitle "Bonaparte." (He never intended to dedicate the work to Napoleon.) However, when he learned that Napoleon had had himself proclaimed emperor, Beethoven became so incensed that he destroyed the original manuscript's title page. On the copy, the name "Bonaparte" was scratched out so violently that a hole was torn in the page (fig. 20.3). (Note that Beethoven did not destroy and did not change any of the music.)

French revolutionary music—particularly, the marches and grand symphonies of Gossec and his contemporaries—influenced Beethoven when he composed his *Sinfonia Grande.* Beethoven's third symphony is a spacious work. None of its four movements has a slow introduction. In fact, the only introductory material consists of the two crisp, *forte,*

(c)

(d)

From Classicism to Romanticism

Example 20.19 Beethoven, *Sinfonia Eroica*: (*a*) mvt. 1, mm. 1–8, two introductory notes and first theme; (*b*) mvt. 1, mm. 284ff., theme transformed.

E♭-major chords with which full orchestra commences the symphony (DWMA171). The first theme—based on the notes of the E♭ triad—is bass, befitting a hero, and is announced by 'cellos, then taken over by horns. (In this symphony, Beethoven added a third horn to the orchestra.) The simplicity of the theme is counteracted by the unexpected C♯, which hints at heroic daring deeds (ex. 20.19a). Here, it resolves upward through D to E♭, but in the recapitulation it precipitates a modulation to the key of F (mm. 402–07). What seems to be a new theme in the development (m. 284ff.) is actually **thematic transformation**, the modification of a theme so that, in a new context, it appears to be different but actually constitutes the same elements (ex. 20.19b). Thematic transformation, an application of the principle of variation, was exploited by nineteenth-century composers (especially Liszt) for unification purposes. Near the end of the development section of the *Eroica*'s first movement, while violins play tremolo *ppp* in dominant-seventh harmony, the first horn enters with the first theme, in the tonic key (m. 394). The effect was shocking—as if the horn player had miscounted and had entered too soon! But dominant-seventh harmony persists until m. 398, then resolves to E♭ and recapitulation begins. The first theme figures prominently in the coda, and the transformed theme introduced in the development is also brought back in the coda (m. 581ff.)—this was novel.

A solemn *Marche funebre* (Funeral march; Adagio assai) in C minor constitutes the symphony's slow movement. The minor tonality of the *Marche*, its dotted rhythms and muffled drums (also simulated in the string bass parts) are conventional; the *Maggiore*

Trio (C) is a eulogy. The Scherzo (E♭) is exceedingly fast and is *sempre pianissimo* and staccato for its first 90 measures; in its Trio, the three horns, maintaining the heroic E♭ tonality, present the principal phrases alone, as a trio. Beethoven had used the theme of the Finale before—in the finale of *Prometheus*, as a *contredanse*, and for the set of piano variations, Op. 35 (1802). His use of the Prometheus theme here may be a symbolic reference to heroism—the courage of an individual striving for victory over hopeless odds. In the Allegro molto (E♭) Finale of the *Eroica*, it is again treated as theme with variations, but several other themes are introduced, one of them marchlike. Counterpoint figures prominently; several variations are developed fugally. The movement concludes Presto, its last two crisp E♭ chords matching those that began the symphony.

It was Beethoven's custom to work on several compositions at the same time. This was the case with his Fourth and Fifth—and possibly his Sixth—Symphonies, all composed between 1806 and 1808. Symphony No. 4, Op. 60, in B♭, was completed in 1806 and was first performed (1807) in the Vienna home of Prince Lobkowitz. Because the Fourth Symphony is lighter in weight and mood than the others, it usually receives little attention. However, it is an adventurous work, though conventional in overall form. It is the only Beethoven symphony that uses only one flute. The Adagio introduction to the first movement is the longest Beethoven had yet written. All of the sonata-form movements—the second movement is abridged sonata with development in the recapitulation—use theme groups rather than single themes; all four movements have codas. By this time, use of theme groups was fairly common.

Undoubtedly, Symphony No. 5, Op. 67, in C minor (1807–08), is Beethoven's best-known symphony. It is a cyclic work whose opening motive

—the first notes of the yellowhammer's song—colors the entire work and is found, rhythmically or melodically, in every movement. To some persons, this symphony seems to represent Beethoven's determination to achieve success in the field of music despite his deafness—the C-major Finale of the C-minor symphony signifying ultimate victory. During World War II, the symphony's dominating motive was likened to the letter V in Morse Code (· · · —) and became a symbol of Victory.

The Allegro con brio first movement conforms with the general outlines of Classical sonata form. The movement commences in C minor in which key the principal motive is stated first as introduction (mm. 1–5) and then as first theme; second and third themes are presented in the relative major, Eb, in which key the first section ends. After the section is repeated, development occurs, followed by recapitulation, with some digression from expected procedure: the insertion of a small cadenza for oboe, and return of the second theme in C major. The coda is long and developmental. Beethoven chose the submediant key, Ab, for the Andante con moto, a set of variations on two themes, the first graceful and flowing, the second somewhat martial (though in $\frac{3}{4}$ time). The third movement, marked Allegro, is actually an irregular Scherzo with Trio and concludes with a transitional passage that leads directly into the Finale. The Scherzo opens in C minor with a "Mannheim rocket" figure similar to that commencing the Finale of Mozart's Symphony No. 40 (ex. 20.20). Mozart's theme is bright, but Beethoven's, presented by lower strings, is mysterious and threatening. The Scherzo's close is neither major nor minor—it is a short, unharmonized, orchestral C. Imitative counterpoint is a feature of the C-major Trio. Only its first section is literally repeated; at the end of the second section, what seems to start a *da capo* of the Scherzo blends into a long bridge passage colored by the cyclic motive. Softly,

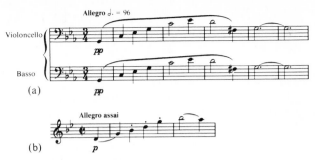

Example 20.20 (*a*) Beethoven, Symphony No. 5, mvt. 3, mm. 1–5, theme 1; (*b*) Mozart, Symphony No. 40, K.550, mvt. 4, mm. 1–2. Both themes use the "Mannheim rocket" followed by a melodic sigh.

timpani sound the motive, then, by subtly altering the rhythm until the beats blur into a roll, make the transition to the quadruple meter of the triumphant C-major Finale. For the Finale, Beethoven added to the orchestra a piccolo, a contrabassoon, and three trombones; this seems to have been the first use of these instruments in a symphony, though Gossec, Gluck, and Mozart had used trombones in opera orchestras.

Symphonies Nos. 5 and 6 were first performed on 22 December 1808, in Vienna, as part of a Beethoven *Akademie* (concert) that included several movements of the Mass in C; Concerto No. 4 (G major; piano, orch.); the aria *Ah, perfido!*, Op. 65 (voice, orch.; première); and the "Choral Fantasy," Op. 80 (C minor; première).

Beethoven's sketchbooks contain many verbal remarks about his Symphony No. 6, Op. 68, in F major (1808). In addition to *Sinfonia pastorella* (Pastoral Symphony), he referred to the work as being "recollections of country life." He did not attempt to depict actual scenes; as he stated at the beginning of the score, the music was "more the expression of feeling than of tone-painting." Instrumental music that was inspired by or that attempted to describe a nonmusical idea, scene, story, or event was not new in the nineteenth century, though it became very popular then. It was well established by 1700 (see Kuhnau, p. 360) and can be traced intermittently in earlier centuries (see Sakadas, p. 11). There are many eighteenth-century musical depictions of landscapes

From Classicism to Romanticism

and of feelings aroused by observation and/or contemplation of them, e.g., concerti by Vivaldi (p. 389). Franz Liszt (1811–86) is credited with being the first to apply the term **program music** to descriptive or referential music.

Beethoven's *Pastoral* Symphony has five movements, each with a programmatic title: (1) "Awakening of pleasant feelings on arriving in the country"; (2) "Scene by the brook"; (3) "Happy gathering of country folk"; (4) "Thunderstorm"; (5) "Shepherd's song: Happy and thankful feelings after the storm." Basically, Beethoven followed the structural scheme of the Classical symphony, but, when the peasants' merrymaking was interrupted by a sudden summer storm, what was more logical than to interrupt symphonic structure by inserting an additional movement to depict that storm? To maintain continuity in the musical description, movements 3, 4, and 5 are played without a break.

As usual, Beethoven was very conscious of tone color. For the last two movements, two trombones and two trumpets were added to the orchestra, and the shrill tones of piccolo color the storm. For the murmuring of the brook in the Andante, Beethoven wrote harmony for second violins, violas, and two muted solo 'cellos; the other 'cellos duplicate the string bass line. In the coda of the Andante, flute, oboe, and clarinet imitate the calls of nightingale, quail, and cuckoo; earlier in the symphony, the yellowhammer's alternate call and the trilling of other birds are heard. The first theme of the third movement resembles and may actually be an Austrian folk song; the shepherd's song, in the last movement, closely parallels a melody in Haydn's Symphony No. 6, *Le Matin,* a work Beethoven undoubtedly knew.

Piccolo, trombones, and contrabassoon are not in the orchestra for Beethoven's Seventh and Eighth Symphonies. Symphony No. 7, Op. 92, in A major (1811–12), is a Romantic symphony, exhibiting contrasts and dualities. The entire first movement is one of sudden contrasts—remote modulations, changes in dynamics (e.g., immediate shifts from *ff* to *pp*), changing melodies above *ostinato* pitches or figures. An overall duality exists in (a) the stability afforded by *ostinati* and (b) the instability created by sudden changes. Throughout the symphony, Beethoven used an abundance of *ostinato* figures, often two measures long, and scales.

The long Poco sostenuto introduction to Symphony No. 7 is sometimes listed as a separate movement, but its last several measures constitute dominant preparation for and transition to a sonata-form Vivace (ex. 20.21), the real first movement (though marked "II"). The rhythmic figure ♩♪♪♩ dominates the Vivace. The Allegretto (A minor) is characterized by a different rhythmic figure, strongly marked, and persistent: | ♩ ♪♪ | ♩ ♩ | ; two lovely, lyrical melodies appear in the movement, also. When the symphony was first performed, the audience demanded an encore of the Allegretto. In the Presto (F; trio in D), elements of scherzo/trio and rondo are combined to create a five-part ABABA form: Scherzo-Trio-Scherzo-Trio-Scherzo. There is a very short coda. The Finale (Allegro con brio, A major; sonata form with coda) is the climax of the work. The movement opens on the dominant, with an E-major explosion that the ear accepts as a tonic chord. After the air clears, an explosive E_7 jolts the ear with its D♮. Again, a general pause allows the air to clear. The first theme commences in E major, surrounded by E pedals and with *sfz* accents on the weak beat of the measure. In contrast with the control exhibited by the *ostinato* rhythm of the second movement, the Finale seems unconstrained, filled with revelry and fury, rough and sometimes wild humor.

Beethoven composed Symphony No. 8, Op. 93 (F major) in four months during late spring/summer 1812. In overall form and tonal scheme, the symphony is traditional. None of the movements has an introduction. The two outer movements are in A major, in sonata and sonata-rondo form, respectively, with long codas. The second movement, an abridged sonata form in B♭, is labeled Allegretto scherzando (in a playful mood). In the regularity of its rhythm Beethoven parodied the steady tapping of his friend Mälzel's chronometer (predecessor of the metronome; Insight, "Mälzel") as it marked the time. Moreover, the first theme is that of a canon Beethoven had jotted down for Mälzel the previous spring. The Tempo di Menuetto third movement (F major) reflects that combination of geniality and good humor the Viennese term *Gemütlichkeit*. The music's apparent simplicity belies its difficulty; melodies are so exposed that the slightest imperfection could destroy their beauty. In the Trio, the horns play one of the

Example 20.21 Beethoven, Symphony No. 7, mvt. 1, mm. 57–67, bridge from Introduction to Vivace. For ten measures the music consists almost entirely of reiterated e pitches that do not cadence into A major until the fifth measure of the exposition.

insight

Mälzel

Johann N. Mälzel (1772–1838) received musical training from his father but chose to become an inventor. Among his inventions was the Panharmonicon, a mechanical "instrument" (or automatophone) activated by bellows and pinned cylinders and capable of reproducing orchestral or wind ensemble music. Mozart, Haydn, and Beethoven were among those writing music for Panharmonicon use, e.g., Beethoven's *Wellington's Victory*.

Another of Mälzel's inventions was the chronometer, a pendulum device for determining the tempo for performance of a musical work. Using such a chronometer, Beethoven placed "metronome" marks on many of his compositions. While in Amsterdam in 1815, Mälzel learned of a better chronometer designed c. 1812 by Dietrich N. Winkel (1780–1826). Mälzel recognized the possibilities in Winkel's double-pendulum design—using an oscillating rod weighted at both ends—and appropriated it but added a scale of tempo divisions. Mälzel named the apparatus "Metronome" and patented it as his own invention. Though Winkel took Mälzel to court and won the lawsuit, the device is still known as Mälzel's Metronome (fig. 20.4).

Mälzel also made ear trumpets, several of which Beethoven owned and used.

Figure 20.4 One of Mälzel's metronomes. *(Gesellschaft der Musikfreunde, Vienna.)*

---

loveliest melodies ever written; in counterpoint the clarinet is required to sound the highest note (f‴) of which it was capable then. The Finale is vivacious and bright. In it, the timpani are tuned in octaves, perhaps for the first time in symphonic music. In the second part of the first theme group, Beethoven suddenly inserted a seemingly wrong note—a C♯—assigned to full orchestra *fortissimo*; not until the recapitulation, when the "wrong" note recurs, did Beethoven disclose its ultimate purpose—modulation to F♯ minor.

Symphony No. 9, Op. 125, in D minor (comp. 1817–23), the "Choral" Symphony, is Beethoven's longest symphony. He incorporated into this work musical ideas and sketches that covered a period of 30 years. As early as 1793, he had indicated his desire to compose a setting of Schiller's ode *An die Freude* (To Joy); at that time, his plans had no connection with a symphony. Ultimately, in his use of *An die Freude,* Beethoven set only those stanzas concerned with the universal brotherhood of man through joy and its basis in an eternal heavenly Father's love. Thematically, Symphony No. 9 is clearly related to the "Choral Fantasy." The first three movements of the symphony are expansions of traditional forms: The D-minor sonata-form first movement opens with a slow introduction commencing on the dominant—the open fifth A-E, sustained and *pianissimo*—and concludes with a long, developmental coda of the type that, by this time, was expected of Beethoven. Structurally, the second movement is a compound ternary incorporating elements of fugue, scherzo, and sonata form. Beethoven's humor is apparent in the tardy entrances of the timpani (tuned in octaves). This movement is another example of Beethoven's ability to organize a movement around a single rhythmic motive. The slow movement, placed third, is an alternating form comprised of two contrasting themes with variations—a chorale-like Adagio theme in $\frac{4}{4}$ meter and an Andante moderato melody in triple meter.

The fourth movement is unique, not in its inclusion of voices—that had been done previously, e.g., in 1814 by Peter von Winter (1754–1825)—but in its formal structure. It is really a cantata, though Beethoven always referred to it as *Variationen*; it does comprise choral and instrumental variations upon two themes. The movement opens with a *fortissimo* discord (which is truly striking when there is no long pause after the third movement) and a clamorous fanfare in which all but strings participate. Representative portions of the three previous movements pass in review, each in appropriate key and tempo, as if auditioning; each is rejected, via instrumental recitative. Then, on the dominant of D major, winds suggest a new theme, which is accepted and is extended into the melody that has become the *Hymn to Joy*. The song is repeated four times, with different instrumentation; there is transition to D minor and recapitulation of the movement's stormy introductory measures. Then, baritone soloist remonstrates, "Oh, friends, not these strains! Instead let us sing more pleasant and more joyful ones!" Different combinations of solo and choral voices, with orchestra, present three stanzas of *To Joy,* with some variations in the music. A brief transition culminates with heightened joy in the words "with God!" At this point, to relieve the high dramatic tension, Beethoven inserted a brisk *alla marcia* variation in $\frac{6}{8}$ meter (in B♭) for winds with piccolo and "Turkish" military percussion added to the instrumentation. Solo tenor and male chorus sing a portion of the fourth strophe of Schiller's ode; after an orchestral interlude—a double fugue, with both subjects derived from the hymn melody—chorus and orchestra repeat the ode's first stanza. For the next section of the cantata three trombones are added to the orchestra. The music becomes majestic, the mood devotional. Chorus and orchestra introduce a new theme, and the tempo slows to Adagio when the chorus implores the world's millions to seek and adore their Maker. As the last words are sung softly against tremulous orchestral background, the movement reaches a high point of mysticism. Tonality returns to D major for the next variation, an energetic Allegro in $\frac{6}{4}$ meter; now the rhythmically altered hymn melody

and the lyrics of the first stanza are combined with the theme and text the chorus has just presented. For many years this section of the cantata was considered unsingable because of the high tessitura of the vocal parts. The movement's Prestissimo coda is a brilliant development of both themes, presented by chorus and full orchestra. The symphony concludes orchestrally; the final progression from A in the winds down to a quick unison D by the orchestra recalls the open fifths of the symphony's first sounds.

While working on the second movement of Symphony No. 9 in July 1822, Beethoven wrote to Ferdinand Ries, in London, and through him made arrangements to write a symphony for the London Philharmonic Society. Certainly, throughout 1823, as Beethoven worked intermittently on the Ninth Symphony, he must have had in mind the instrumentation and capabilities of the London orchestra. When the symphony was completed, arrangements were made for the London Philharmonic Society to have performance rights to the work (in England only) for 18 months. However, Beethoven never abandoned plans for a première performance of the Ninth Symphony in Vienna.

Works for Solo Instrument(s) and Orchestra

There survive only portions of the three concerti (for piano, violin, oboe) that Beethoven worked on as a youth at Bonn. During his first decade in Vienna, he composed three piano concerti for his own use and two *Romances* for violin and orchestra (Op. 50, F major; Op. 40, G major). The first two concerti (No. 1 in C; No. 2 in B♭) are uncomplicated; No. 3, in C minor, is more difficult.

Between 1803 and 1809, Beethoven composed three more solo concerti, two for piano and one for violin; a triple concerto (for piano, violin, 'cello); and the *Fantasia,* Op. 80. The Violin Concerto, Op. 61, in D major (1806), is one of the finest ever written; solo and orchestral parts are ideally balanced.

The piano part of the triple concerto, it is believed, was written for Archduke Rudolph; the other piano works were for Beethoven's own use as concert pianist, and he did give Concerto No. 4, Op. 58, in G major, and the *Fantasia* their first performances. For

From Classicism to Romanticism

all of his concerti Beethoven used the overall fast-slow-fast structural scheme, with the middle movement in a related key, and the finale a rondo. The G-major concerto is unusual in that it commences with solo piano presenting the first theme; then the orchestra enters and continues the exposition.

In Concerto No. 5, Op. 73, in Eb major, the so-called Emperor Concerto, Beethoven again deviated from Classical sonata-concerto structure. In the first movement, he prefaced the orchestral exposition with quasi-improvisational dialogue between orchestra and soloist; when this material is reintroduced as transition from development to recapitulation, it is apparent that the "improvisation" was a calculated part of the design. Customarily, the soloist was given *carte blanche* to extemporize a lengthy cadenza at the conclusion of the recapitulation, but at this point Beethoven wrote in the music, "Do not create a cadenza but immediately attack the following" and notated his own cadenza—the latter portion of it accompanied by the orchestra. The slow second movement, in the remote key of B major, expresses enharmonically Beethoven's penchant for the flatted submediant key. According to Beethoven's pupil, Karl Czerny (1791–1857), the hymnlike melody used in the second movement was derived from an Austrian pilgrim song. Near the end of that movement, a modulation to the dominant key of Eb is achieved by a single semitone progression downward from B to Bb, and there, as the soloist hints at the impetuous Rondo that is to come, second and third movements are linked and blended together without pause.

At some time between composition of Concertos Nos. 4 and 5 Beethoven acquired a new piano—a larger, more resonant instrument with a full six-octave keyboard (F'–f''''); he used the entire range in the "Emperor" Concerto. In that work the piano is equal partner with the orchestra; there are a few places where the orchestra plays a lesser role.

The Eb-major concerto was completed in Vienna in 1809 when the city was experiencing the ordeals of Napoleonic War and military occupation. By this time, Beethoven's hearing was so impaired that he no longer appeared in public as soloist. Czerny, who performed the Eb concerto in public in 1812, may have been the first to do so. In his lessons from Beethoven, Czerny was given material from C. P. E. Bach's *Versuch,* studies for perfecting legato technique, and some of Beethoven's works. As a performer, Czerny was particularly known for his authentic interpretation of Beethoven's works; for several years, commencing in 1816, Czerny gave all-Beethoven programs weekly in his own home. Czerny was well known in Vienna as an excellent piano teacher; among his numerous pupils were child prodigies and *virtuosi,* including Anna Caroline von Belleville Oury (1808–80), Sigismond Thalberg (1812–71), and Franz Liszt. As a teacher, Czerny's most important contribution, historically, was transmitting Beethoven's ideas, techniques, and interpretations to young Franz Liszt. Czerny was a prolific composer of works in all genres but is best known for his pedagogical works—the thousands of exercises and études he wrote reflect the changes in the mechanics of the piano and in the techniques of piano playing that were occurring during his lifetime. Most significant among Czerny's published pedagogical works are his *Complete Theoretical and Practical Pianoforte School,* Op. 500 (1839), and the little-known treatise entitled *School of Extemporaneous Performance* (Volume I, Op. 200; Volume II, Op. 300), important because of its information on nineteenth-century performance practices and improvisation techniques.

Large Vocal Works with Orchestra

As previously mentioned, on two occasions in 1790, the Elector of Cologne commissioned Beethoven to write cantatas: on the death of Emperor Joseph II, the Elector's brother; and on the accession of Emperor Leopold II, another brother. For unknown reasons, neither cantata was performed. Yet, those works are a landmark in Beethoven's career, for Haydn saw in them sufficient evidence of outstanding talent to invite Beethoven to Vienna to study with him.

In 1803, Emanuel Schikaneder asked Beethoven to write an opera for Theater an der Wein. Beethoven agreed to do so, moved to lodgings in the theater, and began to set Schikaneder's libretto *Vestas Feuer* (The Vestal Fire). However, by the end of the year that project had been abandoned. Meantime, Beethoven seized upon the opportunity to give a concert at the theater on 3 April 1803. For that program he hastily composed the short oratorio *Christus am Ölberge*. The other works performed were his First and Second Symphonies, and Piano Concerto No. 3 with Beethoven as soloist. For all but Symphony No. 1, that was the first performance.

At that time, French operas were in vogue in Vienna, especially those by Luigi Cherubini (1760–1842) and Étienne-Nicolas Méhul (1763–1817). Cherubini's rescue opera *Les deux journées* (The two days; 1800) was so popular in Vienna that it was staged at rival theaters on successive nights. Beethoven knew the opera, and it was, to some extent, the model for his next operatic venture, a setting of Bouilly's *Léonore ou L'Amour conjugal* (Léonore, or Married love). J. F. Sonnleithner prepared the German libretto. The plot, based on an actual happening during the French Revolution, concerns the unjust imprisonment of Florestan and his rescue by his heroic wife, Léonore, disguised as "Fidelio" (the faithful one). There is the usual subplot involving two lovers, the jailer's daughter (Marzelline) and the porter (Jaquino), characters akin to the servant-lover pair in eighteenth-century comic opera.

Beethoven's *Léonore,* in three Acts, was first performed on 20 November 1805, a few days after Napoleon's armies had entered Vienna. The opera was not enthusiastically received, for various reasons: (1) It was too long and was poorly organized. (2) Those who usually were supportive of Beethoven's work were not in the audience—because of the political situation, many of the nobility, aristocrats, and Beethoven's friends had fled the city.

Over the next nine years, the opera (both music and libretto) underwent considerable revision and was condensed into two Acts. Beethoven composed another new overture—he had already written two—for the 1806 version. This time the work was presented as *Fidelio,* though Beethoven still considered it *Léonore*. After only a few performances, Beethoven withdrew the production. For the version produced eight years later, he wrote still another overture, one of programmatic character containing thematic material from the opera. All four overtures survive, but only the last is known as the "Overture to *Fidelio*"; the others are, respectively, "*Léonore* Overture" No. 1, No. 2, and No. 3.

Fidelio is a typical rescue opera, containing a blend of suspense, personal loyalty, and the triumph of good over evil. That blend is apparent in the dungeon scene in which Fidelio saves Florestan's life. Also present in *Fidelio* are elements that foreshadow German romantic opera. Though the work is a *Singspiel,* with spoken dialogue, Beethoven effectively used **melodrama** to open the horror-filled scene in which Rocco and Fidelio dig the grave of Pizarro's intended murder victim, Florestan. (A melodrama is a stage piece without singing but with action and speaking that is accompanied by or alternates with orchestral music.) Throughout the opera, tensions are relieved by elements of comic opera, e.g., in the subplot, and in the bass aria sung by Rocco, "*Hat man nicht auch Geld beineben*" (If only one had money at hand). The music in *Fidelio* is not always easy to sing, for Beethoven set not only the text but also its implications. There are places where he seems to have forgotten that he was writing for voices.

Beethoven did not find writing opera easy, but the genre interested him. At various times, he began operas but had to abandon them. For instance, his work on *Macbeth* was halted abruptly when Collin, who was preparing the libretto, died. Beethoven's continued interest in dramatic works found expression in incidental music for plays: ten pieces for Goethe's *Egmont* (1809–10); nine for Kotzebue's *Die Ruinen von Athen* (1811); ten for Kotzebue's *König Stephan* (1811); and four for Duncker's *Leonore Prohaska* (1815). Also, he composed another cantata, *Meerestille und glückliche Fahrt* (Calm sea and prosperous voyage; Goethe text; 1814).

The Mass in C, Op. 86 (SATB soloists, 4-vc. choir, orch.), commissioned by Prince Nikolaus Esterházy II for commemoration of his wife's name day, was performed at Eszterháza on 8 September 1807. Undoubtedly, Beethoven regarded the commission as both an honor and a challenge, for he realized he was following in Haydn's footsteps.

On 24 April 1819 Archduke Rudolph was created a cardinal and on June 4 was appointed Archbishop of Olmütz, in Moravia. Beethoven determined to honor his friend and pupil by composing a *Missa Solemnis* for his installation. The Mass in D, Op. 123 (SATB soloists, 4-vc. choir, organ, orch.) resulted.

Beethoven began the Mass in 1819, but several illnesses and litigation concerning his nephew interfered, and the work was not completed until 1823. Meantime, he had composed his Ninth Symphony. Beethoven thought that he was out of touch with Viennese taste and began negotiations for performance of the Mass in Berlin. When his friends learned of this, they petitioned him in writing to have the concert in Vienna. The first performance of the complete Mass occurred in St. Petersburg, Russia, on 6 April 1824, but the Kyrie, Gloria, and Credo were performed in a concert at Kärntnertor Theater, Vienna, on 7 May 1824. Other works on that program were Symphony No. 9 and the Overture in C, Op. 124.

Beethoven approached composition of the Mass seriously, for he intended the work to be a statement of his personal faith. Certainly, it is a universal statement as well. At the head of the Kyrie he wrote: *Von Herzen—Möge es wieder zu Herzen gehen!* (From the heart—may it go again to the heart!). Over both Kyrie and Sanctus are the words *Mit Andacht* (With devotion). It is evident from Beethoven's letters that he did a considerable amount of research, both liturgical and musical, as he wrote the Mass. In addition to early treatises, he had at his disposal the sacred music in the Archduke's library. The completed composition reveals Beethoven's acquaintance with and knowledge of liturgical and theological traditions as well as musical ones. For example, his setting of the Agnus Dei is unusual in that he made three (instead of two) complete presentations of *Agnus Dei, qui tollis peccata mundi, miserere nobis* (Lamb of God, who takes away the sins of the world, have mercy upon us)—the triple literal acclamation used in the ninth and tenth centuries (see Ch. 4)—before the *dona nobis pacem* (give us peace). The orchestral episodes in this movement are treated much as tropes to a chant.

In addition to writing music appropriate to the text, Beethoven filled that music with historical and liturgical symbolism. In the *Et incarnatus est,* he composed a quasi-chant melody in Dorian mode. (Beethoven owned a copy of Zarlino's *Istitutione harmoniche,* in which it is stated that Dorian is the appropriate mode for modesty and chastity.) *Mortuos* (death) was depicted in two ways: by a rest or

Example 20.22 (*a*) A typical Kyrie *topos* (traditional formula); (*b*) Beethoven, *Missa solemnis,* beginning of Kyrie.

by "dead" chords, i.e., those lacking the third. Not only is there text painting but also musical depiction of the celebrant's actions, e.g., a rising vocal line used for a line of text during which the celebrant raised his arms. The Kyrie commences with the traditional Kyrie text formula (i.e., a *topos*) used for a *Missa Solemnis* (ex. 20.22).

Omnipotence is expressed powerfully, with trombones, e.g., Gloria, m. 185ff.; Credo, m. 221ff. Beethoven interpreted the text according to the German *Bible,* wherein the Latin word *tuba* was translated *Posaune* (trombone; cf. Exodus 19:16). To express the extremes of the Last Judgment, Beethoven caused trombones to play in Ab minor (seven flats, and minor)! In keeping with tradition, he concluded the Gloria and Credo with fugues. For *Et vitam venturi saeculi* (and life everlasting) in the Credo he used the triad to symbolize perfection and fulfillment of life after death, and a very subdued dynamic level to express the peace of everlasting life. Many additional examples can be cited.

Though trumpets and drums were normally used in a *Missa Solemnis* for especially festive occasions, Beethoven's inclusion of a military fanfare not unlike that used in battle (Agnus Dei, m. 170ff.) was unusual but appropriate. Archduke Rudolph was a member of the imperial family, and the archangel Gabriel, protector of the imperial residence, was also patron of the trumpeters' guild. Moreover, it was Emperor Joseph II, Rudolph's grandfather, who had introduced trumpets and drums to the imperial dragoons in 1774. In this same Mass movement, after the military fanfare, Beethoven wrote a fugato (m. 216ff.) on a subject he consciously borrowed from Handel's "Hallelujah" chorus.

Beethoven considered the *Missa Solemnis* his greatest composition. In scope, excellence, and sincere expression of faith, it is comparable to J. S. Bach's *Mass in B minor*. Beethoven's *Missa Solemnis* is too long and too elaborate for liturgical use. Moreover, he took some liberties with the liturgical text, in repetition of some phrases (e.g., in the Gloria and Agnus Dei). Nevertheless, the *Missa Solemnis* is a symphonic depiction, pictorial and symbolic, of everything that the Mass was and is intended to represent.

Summary

The French Revolution and its aftermath had cultural as well as political consequences. Creative works centered around heroism; dramas and operas used rescue plots, and dramatic tension was heightened by crowd scenes. Music was affected also through government appropriation of manuscripts and valuable instruments for preservation in national archives, the establishment of the Paris Conservatoire, and the creation of a vast number of commemorative works for massed ensembles.

At the time of the Revolution, several important European musicians, particularly pianists, deserted Paris for London where they found a rich concert life, a rising middle class eager to participate in music making, active publishing houses, and piano manufacturers continually working to produce instruments capable of greater volume of sound, increased dynamic flexibility and technical facility, and with wider compass. The London school of pianist-composers included Cramer, Clementi, Dussek, Field, and Pinto. Cramer and Clementi wrote didactic works still used by many piano teachers. Field, who invented and made extensive use of the *nocturne* for piano, greatly influenced the playing style of Chopin and the compositions of Chopin, Liszt, and others. Beethoven knew Dussek's works and absorbed all that he had to offer; some striking parallels are present in the sonatas of these two men.

The leading Bohemian composers active in Vienna were Tomášek, Voříšek, and Hummel. Tomášek and Voříšek pioneered in the composition of Romantic character pieces for piano. Schubert knew and was greatly influenced by Tomášek's *eclogues* and Voříšek's *impromptus*; Voříšek's vocal music reflects Schubert's influence. Pianistically, Hummel was Beethoven's chief rival in Vienna. Hummel's style was Mozartean—a restrained Classicism, neat and delicate, with emphasis on fluent technique and textural clarity. Beethoven produced a full tone and stressed technical power and dramatic execution; his music exhibited orchestral effects and a wide range of dynamics. Hummel linked the style of Mozart and Clementi with that of Schubert, Mendelssohn, and Chopin; Beethoven's playing style was transmitted by Czerny to Liszt.

As a young man, Beethoven became thoroughly familiar with the Viennese Classical style of music and mastered, then extended, that style. At the height of his career as pianist, hearing problems hampered him; as deafness encroached, he gradually withdrew from social contacts until he became almost a recluse. In seeking release from personal problems, he grew more and more introspective and explored the depths of music's possibilities. In Beethoven's works, one finds a synthesis of Viennese, Parisian, and English musical styles. In its turn, Beethoven's music became the source of many features of nineteenth-century Romantic music. Beethoven's music cannot be considered either Classical or Romantic in style; rather, it bridges those two styles, and is, at the same time, individualistic.

Customarily, Beethoven's music is divided into three main chronological style periods: (1) youthful works written at Bonn, 1782–1792, and early works composed in Vienna, 1792–c. 1802, when he mastered Classical style and began to experiment within the general outlines of traditional sonata structure; (2) works composed in Vienna, c. 1803–c. 1815, a period dominated by orchestral and "heroic" compositions; and (3) late works, composed c. 1815–1827, in which boundaries are blurred, counterpoint is prominent, themes and motives are developed to their utmost, often through fugal and variation techniques.

Beethoven composed in all the genres of music current during his lifetime. The *Mass in D,* which he considered his masterwork, is comparable to Bach's *Mass in B minor,* and the "Diabelli Variations" are on a par with Bach's "Goldberg Variations." Beethoven's piano sonatas, string quartets, and symphonies form the backbone of standard repertoire in their respective categories.

The piano sonata occupies a central position in Beethoven's work. In his sonatas he introduced and experimented with new ideas, procedures, and interpretations that he incorporated in other works. Sonata No. 4, Op. 7, is Beethoven's first real masterpiece in this genre; the three sonatas of Op. 10 are stylistically representative of Beethoven's first Vienna period. The "Waldstein" and "Appassionata" sonatas exhibit the greater freedom of form, more audacious choice of keys, and more remote modulations typical of his second Viennese style period. His last three sonatas, Nos. 30–32, are his most introspective ones and display characteristics of his last style period.

In the early string quartets, especially Op. 18, No. 3, experimentation is mingled with Classical tradition. The "Razumovsky" quartets (Op. 59) are representative of Beethoven's mature style of quartet writing; in them, he was more daring with regard to tonal relationships and formal structure, blurring and disguising sectional divisions within movements, and sometimes linking movements. The late quartets Opp. 132, 130, 133, and 131 form a cycle with melodic, motivic, and tonal relationships. The C♯-minor quartet, Op. 131, Beethoven's last large-scale composition, fully exhibits characteristics of his late style.

The Op. 5 sonatas are the earliest sonatas written for 'cello and keyboard in which the keyboard is not considered a *continuo* instrument. The last five of Beethoven's ten violin/piano sonatas are true duos; the C-minor sonata (Op. 30, No. 2) makes enormous demands on the performers. Beethoven's Violin Concerto is one of the finest ever written; Piano Concertos Nos. 4 and 5 and the "Ghost" and "Archduke" Trios are frequently performed.

Beethoven's symphonies attest his mastery of Classical style and forms, show the development of his individualistic style as composer of symphonic orchestral works—his innovative treatment of harmonies, tonalities, thematic material, and forms—and, in his last symphony, the introspective character of his last works. At the heart of the development of Beethoven's style is his view of the structure of a single movement as sonata *principle* rather than sonata *form.* His orchestral writing reveals his knowledge of improvements made to individual instruments and advancements in performing techniques. The opera *Fidelio* and *Sinfonia Eroica* are typical of the "heroic" works Beethoven composed in the years following his Heiligenstadt decision. The *Eroica* is one of Beethoven's most important works. Its length, formal structure, general programmatic character, Beethoven's choice of thematic material, and his developmental procedures (which include thematic transformation, fugue, and variation) make it a landmark in symphonic literature. Symphony No. 5, Beethoven's best-known symphony, marks the first use of trombones in a symphony. It is a cyclic work of large proportions, with long developments and developmental codas. The *Pastoral* Symphony was the springboard for composition of numerous programmatic symphonies. Symphony No. 9, though not the first symphony to include voices, was unique in having a cantata within its Finale.

In one way or another, Beethoven's compositions have affected all music since his time. Much nineteenth-century Romantic music is rooted in his work. Throughout that century, his sonatas, symphonies, string quartets, violin concerto, and last piano concerto were viewed as standards for achievement and provided models to be emulated.

21

Beethoven's Contemporaries

Revolution did not bring either peace or freedom to the French people. By a *coup d'état* in 1799 Napoleon Buonaparte seized the reins of the government, and proclaimed, "The Revolution is ended." In his hands, the Republic became first the Consulate (1799–1804), then an empire. Through military conquests and the establishment of puppet rulerships, Napoleon expanded his empire considerably, extending his control over the Low Countries, western Germanic lands, a large part of Italy, and into Iberia. Thus, he upset— almost destroyed—the European "balance of power." Not only did his armies ravage the land, but in his desire for personal and national aggrandizement, Napoleon looted the conquered territories, transported their art treasures to France, and established museums in various cities to house them. From Italy alone he took more than 500 original artworks. Napoleon's downfall came at the hands of Britain and three countries that had formerly been France's allies—Austria, Prussia, and Russia. After suffering military defeat, he abdicated in April 1814 and was exiled to Elba. Yet, so great was his following that, *in absentia,* he assembled an army of 1500, and on 1 March 1815 he returned to France, regained control of the government, and held power for a hundred days before being decisively defeated at the Battle of Waterloo and being banished to St. Helena in the south Atlantic.

The Congress of Vienna (1814–15), by its deliberations, redesigned the map of Europe (fig. 21.1) and restored the European balance of power. With the consent of the Congress, control of the French government was restored to the former royal dynasty and entrusted to Louis XVIII (r. 1814–24). The French government was required to pay a large indemnity, and the art treasures that Napoleon had looted were returned to their rightful owners.

Austria was ruled by Francis I (r. 1792–1835), with the aid of his powerful adviser, Prince Metternich (1773–1859). Metternich was a distinguished statesman; his tenure as Austria's chancellor of state (1809–48) is known as "The Age of Metternich." In Eastern Europe, and in parts of central Europe, the aristocratic political and social order still functioned.

In the New World, the idea of colonies acquiring independence, as the United States had done, spread to Latin and South America, and one by one Spanish and Portuguese colonies became small autonomous countries. The boundaries of the United States were extended westward through Jefferson's purchase of the vast Louisiana Territory from France in 1803, and, by the time the French and Indian War ended (1815), Britain had secured control of Canada.

Beethoven's Contemporaries

1790	1800	1810	1820	1830

- - 1792 → Francis I, of Austria - →(1835)

1809 - Metternich - →(1848)

1799 → Napoleon in power - - - - - - - - - - - - - →1814→ - - - Louis XVIII - - →1824

Charles X 1824 - - - - - - - - - 1830

1814–15 Congress of Vienna

1803 Jefferson makes Louisiana Purchase

c. 1810 term "Romantic" applied to music - - - - - - - - - - - - - - - - - - -

- - Paris becomes opera capital of the world -

rescue operas popular - - - - - - - - - - - - - - - - - - -

1800 Cherubini: *Les deux journées*

1805–14 Beethoven: *Fidelio*

opéra comique - - - political -Romantic and comic - - - - - - - - - - - -

- - spectacular *tragedie lyrique* - grand opera - -

1807 Spontini: *La Vestale*

1809 Spontini: *Fernand Cortez*

Auber: *La Muette de Portici* 1828

1808 Goethe: *Faust,* Part I

1813 Spohr: *Faust* (perf. 1816)

1816 Hoffmann: *Undine*

1821 Weber: *Der Freischütz*

German Romantic opera - - - - - - - - - - - - - - -

reminiscence motif - - - - - - - - - - - Leitmotif - - - - - - - - - - - - -

1813 Mayr: *Medea in Corinto*

1816 Rossini: *Il barbiere de Siviglia*

Rossini: *Guillaume Tell* 1828

1810 Scott: *The Lady of the Lake*

1812 Grimm's Fairy Tales

Carl Loewe (1796–1869) ballads, Lieder -

Franz Schubert (1797–1828) Lieder, symphonies, Masses, piano music -

1815 *Erlkönig*

Momens musicals 1823–27

Impromptus 1827

During the first quarter of the nineteenth century, the arts prospered in France. Napoleon commissioned many works, established competitions, and awarded prizes for various forms of art. Painting, sculpture, architecture, the manufacture of porcelain and glassware, figurines, tapestries, and needlepoint flourished. Several Arcs de Triomphe were erected, and the Temple of Glory that Napoleon commissioned, which was completed after his downfall, became La Madeleine, a church. One of Napoleon's favorite artists was Jacques Louis David (1743–1825),

painter of "Buonaparte Crossing the Alps." Napoleon and Josephine both enjoyed music—concerts were given at the palace, in the Tuileries Gardens, and in Josephine's apartments—but Napoleon preferred the theater and opera and exercised considerable control over their subject matter and production. In fact, his code of regulations for the theater, drawn up in October 1812, is still in effect.

The age was colored by romanticism, with its subjectivity, its emphasis on the expression of personal feelings and emotions, its interest in nature and

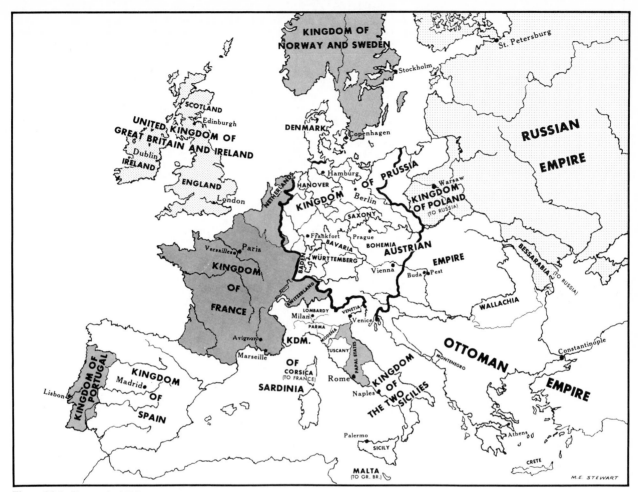

Figure 21.1 Europe in 1815.

in the spiritual and supernatural (both religious and demonic). These traits found expression in the novels of Sir Walter Scott, the lyric poetry of William Wordsworth, John Keats, Percy Bysshe Shelley, and Lord Byron, in Goethe's drama *Faust,* and in many pieces of art. Women, too, gained recognition as authors, though some published under male names— Mme de Staël, Aurore Dudevant (George Sand), and later Mary Ann Evans (George Eliot). Anne Louis Girodet's (1767–1824) painting *The Burial of Atala* (colorplate 19), based on Chateaubriand's novel *Atala,* simultaneously presents passionate love, death and burial, and pure religion. *Los Caprichos* (Ca-

prices), a series of etchings and aquatints created by Spanish artist Francesco Goya (1746–1828), is a commentary on various topics, including witchcraft, demons, fantasy, and social conditions. Goya's war paintings, particularly *The Third of May, 1808* (colorplate 20), depict the horror and brutality of Napoleon's invasion of Spain. Landscapes painted by England's John Constable (1776–1837) won gold medals when exhibited in France, and Joseph M. W. Turner's (1775–1851) treatment of light in his watercolors foreshadowed the work of French impressionists late in the century.

Table 21.1 Romantic Dualities

Contradiction: Relationship between	Solution or Treatment	Representative examples

Words and Music	Equal partnership of text and musical setting:
	  a. in Lied
		Schubert: *Erlkönig*
		         Gretchen am Spinnrade
		Schumann: *Der Nussbaum*

	b. in Opera and Music Drama	Wagner: *Tristan und Isolde* *Der Ring des Nibelungen*

	Composers as Authors:
	  a. of essays about music
		Schumann: *Davidsbündlerblätter*
		       An Opus Two; New Paths
		Weber: *Notices* (re: operas produced)
		Wagner: *Bayreuther Blätter*
		      (re: his stage works)

	b. of poetry, libretti for setting	Wagner: stage works: *Tristan und Isolde Die Meistersinger; Der Ring des Nibelungen;* others
	c. of stories, novels	Hoffmann: *Fantasiestücke* Weber: *Tonkunstlers Leben*
	Inclusion of vocal music in instrumental forms	Beethoven: *Symphony No. 9* ("*Choral*") Loewe: *Piano Sonata in E major* Liszt: *Eine Faust-Symphonie*

	Instrumental works based on vocal music	Schubert: Quintet, *Die Forellen*
		     Quartet, *Der Tod und das Mädchen*
		     Wandererfantasie for piano

	Program music (referential music)	Beethoven: *Symphony No. 6* ("*Pastoral*") Berlioz: *Symphonie fantastique* Liszt: *Les Préludes;* symphonic poems Loewe: *Mazeppa,* tone poem for piano
Composer and Audience	Composer writing for: a. specific performer(s) both commissioned and noncommissioned	Schubert: for Vogl; duets for Esterházy pupils; for Slavík and von Bocklet
	b. performance before circle of friends	Schubert: for *Schubertiaden* (Vienna) Rossini: for *Samedi soirées* (Paris)
	c. unknown performers, unknown future audiences	Beethoven: Quartets, Op. 59; other works
	d. personal expression without regard for audience	Beethoven: Quartets, Op. 59; other works

Romantic Music

The words "romance" and "romantic" stem from *lingua roman* (literally, Roman tongue), the "Low" Latin tongue and the vernacular European languages derived from it, and are related also to the French noun *le roman* (romance, novel, story), a long narrative poem written in the vernacular, e.g., the fourteenth-century *Le roman de la rose* and *Le roman de Fauvel* (see p. 127). The term "Romanticism" (German, *Romantik*) began to appear in essays on music around 1810 and seems to have been used first in connection with Beethoven's music. However, nineteenth-century Romanticism in music had its roots deep in eighteenth-century Classicism—it was not a break with Classicism but an extension, alteration, and expansion of it. Romantic traits are visible in some of C. P. E. Bach's *Sturm und Drang* pieces, in some of Haydn's symphonies written c. 1768–1774, and in several of Mozart's late works. In fact, some musicologists debate the classification of some of those Haydn symphonies as *Sturm und Drang* and consider them early manifestations of Romanticism.

One of the basic characteristics of Romantic music is its boundlessness, its seeming disregard for or freedom from limitations. In an article published in *Allgemeine musikalische Zeitung* in 1813,

Table 21.1 Romantic Dualities—Continued

Contradiction: Relationship between	Solution or Treatment	Representative examples
Individual and Crowd (Masses)	Virtuoso composer-performer(s) with or without orchestra, accompaniment	Paganini, Liszt, Chopin, Weber, others
	Single performer in solo recital	Clara Schumann
	Conductor directing with baton, and standing between audience and performers	Spohr, Weber
	Composer(s) not recognized performer(s)	Wagner, Auber
Professional and Amateur	Composer showing concern for amateur music making in home, community, in addition to writing works for own use.	Schubert: works for family quartet, neighborhood orchestra, and brother's school groups Liszt: transcriptions of symphonies, stage works, etc. for piano
Religious (godly) and Irreligious (demonic) aspects of the Supernatural Sacred and Secular	Combining both aspects in the same work, juxtaposed or used separately	Berlioz: *Symphonie fantastique*
	Inclusion of liturgical texts in secular works	Liszt: *Dante Symphony* Mahler: *Symphony No. 8*
	Settings of liturgical texts not suitable for church Service:	
	a. too large, or with repetitive phrases	Beethoven: *Missa solemnis*
	b. intended for memorial to war dead or personal friends	Berlioz: *Grande Messe pour les morts* *Te Deum laudamus* Verdi: *Requiem Mass* (for Manzoni)
	c. text set is not standard one	Brahms: *Ein deutsches Requiem*
Urban and Rural	Composers living and working in urban centers, writing for urban audiences, preoccupied with Nature, especially in its "wild" state, and composing program music of landscapes, seascapes, etc.	Beethoven: *Symphony No. 6* (*"Pastoral"*) Mendelssohn: *Hebrides Overture* (*"Fingal's Cave"*) Schumann: *Symphony No. 1* (*"Spring"*)
	The wildness of Nature depicted in opera scenes, settings	Weber: *Der Freischütz*
National and Cosmopolitan or International	Inclusion of folk song and folk dance elements, of own and of other countries	Chopin: mazurkas, polonaises Beethoven: Quartets, Op. 59 (Russian)
	Expression of patriotism, national sentiment	France: Commemorative works *Opéras comiques*
	Interest in Eastern exoticism	*à la Turk* and *Janissary* movements; new orchestral colors; new harmonies
	Collecting, preserving folk music	Brahms

E. T. A. Hoffmann stated that music "is the most romantic of all the arts . . . for its sole subject is the infinite." Indeed, music does border on the infinite, for it is intangible, invisible, and fleeting, existing only in time. Often, composers relied on tone colors, harmonies, and rhythms to express the feelings and deeper meanings that, for them, words could not relate sufficiently. In the nineteenth century, there was a great outpouring of **program music**—referential music, instrumental music (and, occasionally, vocalized tones without words) that described, characterized, presented, interpreted, or was inspired by a nonmusical subject or idea that the composer indicated by title, explanatory remarks, or prefatory material. An early nineteenth-century Romantic example is Beethoven's *Pastoral Symphony,* which he stated was an expression of his *feelings* rather than a musical description of pastoral scenes and events.

Another feature of Romantic music is the presence of a blend of opposites—contradictory factors woven into the musical fabric so skillfully that they appear as intriguing dualities rather than harsh contrasts or clashes of principle. These are detailed, with representative examples, in table 21.1.

Many of the same traits that characterize Romantic art are manifest in Romantic music—subjectivity, the expression of personal feelings, sentimentality, a preoccupation with nature (especially in its wild state), an interest in the world of magic and fairy tale, an intrigue with all aspects of the supernatural (sacred, eerie, demonic), a desire for freedom from the limitations of conventional formal patterns and harmonic rules. The emphasis placed on individual characteristics varied from region to region, but the basic traits remained fairly constant. Underlying Romantic music was the desire to be original and forge into the future unrestrained by limitations of the past, a yearning for expansion, and experimentation in the production of new harmonies and tone colors that resulted in the improvement of standard instruments and the invention of new ones.

The humanitarian emphasis on individual worth and the Enlightenment ideals of the "brotherhood of man" brought a new awareness of the individual, and in the search for individual identity there came not only a desire for originality and personal expression but a search for one's roots. The value placed on one's personal and national ancestry was balanced by musicians' and artists' high regard for their artistic heritage. This led to increased interest in folk song and a search for, study of, and performance of works of great composers of the past, especially J. S. Bach, Handel, and Palestrina. At times, however, those works were seen through Romantic eyes, e.g., the piano accompaniments that Schumann and Mendelssohn provided for Bach's *Six Solos for Unaccompanied Violin,* works that are complete in themselves as Bach wrote them. Performances of masterpieces by Bach and Palestrina led to publication of the first editions of their "Complete Works" later in the century, and the search for and location of those works brought into existence the science of historical musicology.

Music in France

In France during the first half of the nineteenth century musical interest centered on opera, and Paris became the opera capital of the world. Early in the century the focus was on *opéra comique*. It spread throughout Austro-Germanic lands, became popular, and dominated opera repertoire there. Italian opera composers were attracted to Paris and stayed to write French (rather than Italian) operas.

Opéra comique

During the Revolutionary period, the light, sentimental, mildly satirical kind of *opéra comique* was considerably overshadowed by a type that dealt seriously with political and social issues and aimed to edify rather than to entertain. Spoken dialogue and melodrama were retained, comic elements were minimized, and plots included common folk (e.g., fishermen, peasants, tradesmen) in key roles. Rescue operas were plentiful, many of them incorporating horror, violence, and highly spectacular scenes of natural catastrophes—fires, storms, earthquakes, volcanic eruptions. A number of early *opéras comiques* with themes of martyrdom were merely Revolutionary propaganda and have little artistic value, but later works, by composers such as Cherubini and Méhul, have real artistic merit.

For about a decade, serious all-sung opera, which the French produced at L'Opéra (sometimes known as Académie Royale de Musique, and by other names), was pushed far into the background by the successes of *opéra comique*. There were two main reasons for this: (1) The various governments encouraged the composition of works with themes that could stir up patriotism, and they viewed *opéra comique* as an appropriate vehicle for this. (2) For several years, two rival theaters flourished, each with its own group of composers who frequently competed by writing *opéras comiques* on the same subject. In 1801 this rivalry ceased because both theaters failed. The surviving participants formed a single company, which opened a theater in 1802. Gradually, the French public grew weary of weighty subjects in *opéra comique,* and lighter types of *opéra comique* again came into vogue. Some are comic; others have Romantic plots. The music consists of simple, melodious *ariettes* (vocal solos, or airs) with light-textured orchestral accompaniments, ensembles, and usually some dance pieces. Among the most important *opéras comiques* of this type in the 1820s and early 1830s were François-Adrien Boieldieu's *La Dame blanche* (The white lady; 1825), Daniel-François-Esprit Auber's *Fra Diavolo*

(1830), and Ferdinand Hérold's *Zampa, ou La fiancée de marbre* (Zampa, or The statue bride; 1831) and *Le Pré aux clercs* (The field of honor; 1833). Both *Fra Diavolo* and *Zampa* have remained in opera repertoire, and the overture to *Zampa* is frequently performed as a concert piece.

French interest was attracted by Italian comic opera when Giaochino Rossini's *L'italiana in Algieri* (The Italian woman in Algiers; Venice, 1813) was performed in Paris early in 1817. Rossini (1792–1868) came to Paris late in 1824 as director of Théâtre-Italien and remained there five years, at first directing his own Italian operas and introducing works by other Italians; then, when he had command of the French language, he composed French operas for L'Opéra. His influence on French opera was all-pervasive.

Luigi Cherubini

Luigi Cherubini (1760–1842), a native of Florence, Italy, received his musical education there and began his career as a composer of church music. In 1778–84, he studied with Giuseppe Sarti (1729–1802), noted Neapolitan opera composer, and wrote eight operas that were performed in various Italian cities. Cherubini spent the next three years in London, where he wrote three operas for King's Theatre. Then he moved to Paris and worked there for the rest of his life. For half a century, Cherubini was a dominating figure in French musical life. He made major contributions in the areas of opera, church music, and music education.

From 1793 to 1842 Cherubini served the French government as an educator. In 1793, he was appointed Inspector of Instruction, with teaching responsibilities, at the newly formed Institut National de Musique. Two years later, when by government decree the Institut became the Paris Conservatoire, Cherubini was named one of its five inspectors, the others being Gossec, Grétry, Le Sueur, and Méhul. Cherubini worked with other faculty members to draw up acceptable curricula in harmony, *solfège,* and counterpoint, and he published several pedagogical writings, including a textbook on counterpoint and fugue (1835). He was a master of counterpoint in an era when polyphonic compositions were *passé.*

Luigi Cherubini.

Soon after settling in Paris, Cherubini began to achieve success with his operas. Interspersed among some mediocre operas were several excellent ones: *Lodoïska* (1791), *Médée* (1797), and *Les deux journées, ou Le porteur d'eau* (The two days, or The water carrier; 1800). *Les deux journées,* performed throughout Europe, was translated into German and was known in Germanic lands as *Der Wasserträger.* Never again did Cherubini achieve the measure of success with opera that *Les deux journées* brought him, though he composed operas until 1833. After 1803 his popularity as opera composer declined, for various reasons: poor libretti; a change in Parisian taste to favor the lighter, tuneful type of *opéra comique* written by Boieldieu; Napoleon's expressed dislike of Cherubini's works; and the emergence of the new type of spectacular grand opera composed by Spontini and favored by Napoleon. Cherubini's importance in the history of opera lies in his expansion of *opéra comique* movements, his use of the genre to deal seriously with dramatic situations and contemporary issues, and his enriched orchestration. He was especially concerned with convincing dramatic portrayal, expressive recitative, and effective writing for ensembles. Most of his opera overtures are sonata-form movements with slow introductions.

Lodoïska, a *comédie heroique* (heroic comedy), is a rescue opera: Lodoïska, imprisoned in the castle of the evil Baron Dourlinsky, is rescued by her beloved, Floreski, with the aid of a horde of benevolent Tatars. Spoken dialogue is used; there are some comic scenes, and some revolutionary music with triadic melodies and simple harmonies. For local color, Cherubini used the polonaise. Cherubini's music (both operas and Masses) was greatly admired by Beethoven, who had at hand copies of *Lodoïska* and *Les deux journées* when he composed *Fidelio.* Floreski and Lodoïska may have served as Beethoven's models for the characters Florestan and Leonore in *Fidelio.*

Médée is concerned with psychological conflict—the inner conflict of Medea, who, unsuccessful in her attempts to win back Jason, rejects her two children by him, and, in revenge, murders them. Through vocal tessitura, fluctuations of tempo, sudden extreme dynamic contrasts, unexpected pauses and interruptions of the melodic line, new orchestral colors, and other devices, Cherubini portrayed Medea's mental anguish and inner conflict.

Les deux journées deals with social injustice and its rectification: a Savoyard family of water carriers rescues unjustly persecuted aristocrats; the prisoner escapes hidden in a water cart. The story was based on actual recent events, but for the opera the setting was transposed back to mid-seventeenth-century France. Spoken dialogue is used; melodrama in the last two acts is superb. Ensemble singing predominates, e.g., a chorus of soldiers (Act II) and a bridal chorus (Act III). There are only two solos in the opera; they occur at the beginning of the opera and contain motives that recur throughout the work, e.g., the refrain of Anton's romance.

In 1816 Cherubini was appointed one of the joint superintendents of the *Chapelle Royale*; thereafter, most of his compositions were church music: seven Masses (two are coronation Masses), two Requiem Masses, numerous motets and short sacred pieces. In writing church music Cherubini was deliberately conservative because he believed that musical effect should be subordinate to liturgical function; only where the text admitted it was he expressively dramatic or emotional.

Cherubini's best Masses are the two Requiems; their *Dies irae* sections are among the finest ever composed. The C-minor Requiem (1816) was commissioned by the French government to commemorate the anniversary of the execution of Louis XVI. Cherubini created a setting sufficiently universal to honor all who died in the Revolution, or even any great person. The Mass is for SATB chorus and orchestra; there are no soloists. Though the work won immediate acclaim and has continued to be regarded highly, it was not universally accepted in the nineteenth century. In 1834 the Archbishop of Paris objected to its performance at Boieldieu's funeral because women's voices were included. Cherubini determined to write a Requiem Mass that could not be barred from his own funeral for the same reason. He scored his D-minor Requiem Mass (1836) for TTB chorus and orchestra but wrote the first tenor part quite high, almost in countertenor range. In some chordal passages, he subdivided the voice parts. High tenor voices were fairly common in France in the early nineteenth century, and Cherubini's use of them had several advantages, including greater freedom in chord-spacing, and the tone color of the high tessitura in the male voice. Most tenors were trained to carry their voices into falsetto register with ease when a lyrical passage required them to do so.

Étienne-Nicolas Méhul

Méhul (1763–1817) was educated at a Franciscan convent and probably was intended for priesthood. Reportedly, his chronic ill health prevented that; ultimately, he contracted tuberculosis. At the age of ten, Méhul was sufficiently accomplished as organist to serve at the convent. He was taken to Paris c. 1779, and, failing to gain admission to Lavaldieu Abbey, began to teach lessons on keyboard instruments. After publishing two volumes of keyboard sonatas (1783, 1788), he decided on a career in composition. However, he resumed teaching in 1793, as a faculty member of the Institut National de Musique, and, in 1795, of Paris Conservatoire. As did other French composers, Méhul wrote numerous Revolutionary and commemorative patriotic pieces, mainly, vocal solos, and choral works accompanied by orchestra or wind band.

Around 1789, Méhul became interested in *opéra comique* and made significant contributions to the repertoire. His 40 stage works include operas, *opéras comiques,* and 4 full-length ballets that were produced at L'Opéra. In his operas, he made considerable use of recurrent motives, e.g., the "motto theme" of guiding Love that recurs throughout *Mélidore et Phrosine* (1794), a tragic tale of love thwarted by jealousy. Features of *Ariodant* (1799) are comparable with those found later in German Romantic opera: a medieval courtly setting, opposed "good" and "evil" couples, jealous love, recurrent motives. Méhul's most important *opéra comique* is *Joseph* (1807); he treated the Biblical story simply and used various types of music, including old hymns, dramatic ensembles, and some simple tunes with uncomplicated harmonies. Méhul was concerned that the music for each stage work create an atmosphere appropriate to the setting of the plot. Some of his works require large performing resources; crowd scenes became a prominent feature of French operas. His overtures are especially noteworthy for their incorporation of musical materials that occur in the opera and for tone painting.

Méhul's symphonies, five of which survive, also reveal his awareness of orchestral color and his experiments with timbres. Frequently, he wrote 'cello parts in the tenor register, subdivided the string sections, and required horns to play stopped notes, even at rapid tempos. Méhul was the most important French symphonist between Gossec and Berlioz.

Many of Méhul's works were performed throughout Europe. Printed copies of his music circulated widely. German Romantic opera composers became acquainted with his *opéras comiques* and were influenced by them, especially in orchestral scoring and the use of recurrent or **"reminiscence"** motives. Certainly, Weber's operas reflect his knowledge of Méhul's works, and similarities between some of the musical figures cannot be mere happenstance (ex. 21.1).

All-sung Opera

Between the Revolution and the 1820s there were very few great successes at L'Opéra. Under the Empire, Napoleon wanted productions at L'Opéra to portray the grandeur of France and do so with Classical de-

Example 21.1 (*a*) Méhul: *Mélidore et Phrosine*, beginning of overture; (*b*) Weber: *Der Freischütz*, beginning of overture.

corum but with spectacle that glorified himself, e.g., triumphal processions that reflected his own. Napoleon could control productions because he reinstituted the system of Privilège, which the Revolutionary government had abolished in 1790. Under that system, which was begun in 1507, publishers and theaters were required to obtain a Royal Privilège (License) in order to print or perform a work. In 1797, the Revolutionary government imposed a tax on published music and required music publishers to have their publications stamped, upon payment of certain fees. That law remained in effect until c. 1841.

Two of the earliest nineteenth-century spectacular operas were *La Vestale* (The Vestal virgin; 1807) and *Fernand Cortez* (1809), both by Gaspare Spontini (1774–1851). These works were significant forerunners of the monumental operas produced at L'Opéra in the second quarter of the century. Then, the term **grand opera** was used to refer specifically to the most monumental, spectacular operas produced at L'Opéra. The earliest successful grand opera was *La muette de Portici* (The mute girl of Portici; 1828) by Auber and Scribe. Another was Rossini's *Guillaume Tell* (William Tell; 1829).

Gaspare Spontini

Details of the first 25 years in the life of Italian composer Gaspare Spontini are sketchy. Apparently, he did not begin to study music seriously until he was 19. From 1796 to 1802 comic operas by him were produced in Italy, but most of those works are lost. Early in 1803, Spontini went to Paris, where he taught singing and composed some *opéras comiques*. The production of a revised version of his *La finta filosofa* (The pseudo philosopher; 2 Acts, 1799; 3 Acts, 1804) brought him the patronage of Empress Josephine and his appointment as composer of the Empress's private music.

Spontini's first great success in Paris came in 1807 with *La Vestale* (The Vestal virgin). The plot concerns a Roman Vestal virgin, Julia, who is condemned to death because she violated her vows and allowed the sacred flame on Vesta's altar to go out; at the last moment, she is saved by a supernatural bolt of flame that relights the fire. The opera requires enormous performing resources for the pageantry of processions and ceremonies—there are massed choruses and long instrumental pieces. Dialogue is in recitative; arias are filled with Italianate lyricism, but the harmonies are conservative, basically moving between tonic and dominant. Doubtless, Spontini's ability to combine elements of French *tragédie lyrique* with Italian lyricism accounted for *La Vestale*'s success.

Napoleon may have suggested the subject for Spontini's next opera, *Fernand Cortez* (1809), because of its political implications—the emperor saw in Cortez's conquest of Mexico a parallel with his own invasion of Spain. After 24 performances of the opera, the government suppressed it, perhaps because audiences did not perceive the parallel. Spontini revised the opera in 1817; the new version became part of standard repertoire at L'Opéra and was performed more than 200 times. *Fernand Cortez* provides an excellent example of Spontini's ability to present opposing ideas by using contrasting musical forces simultaneously and through distance effects: Three soloists on stage sing of their apprehension at the Aztecs' refusal to release their prisoners; simultaneously, as from a distance, an off-stage chorus sings joyfully in the belief that the prisoners have been released. As the trio becomes increasingly anxious, the chorus gradually draws nearer and finally appears on stage for a confrontation of the opposites as climax to the scene.

Spontini composed only three more works for L'Opéra. The last of these, *Olimpie* (Olympia; 1819) a *tragédie lyrique* laden with spectacle, contains some of his finest music.

Though Spontini became a naturalized French citizen in 1817, he worked in Berlin from 1819 to 1841, as *Generalmusikdirektor* to King Friedrich Wilhelm III (r. 1797–1840), with duties principally as opera conductor. The three operas that Spontini composed for Berlin audiences indicate that he was attempting to write German Romantic opera; however, threads of French *tragédie lyrique* and grand opera are woven into all of them. In 1842 Spontini returned to Paris. His few works after 1840 are pieces of church music and some songs.

In the history of French opera, Spontini occupies a transitional position. His *tragédies lyriques* are a continuation of the traditional form of French opera with large choruses and huge spectacles; thus, he adds a vital link to the chain formed by Lully, Rameau, and Gluck—a link between Gluck and Hector Berlioz (see p. 667), who stated he was influenced by *La Vestale* and *Fernand Cortez*. At the same time, *La Vestale* and *Fernand Cortez* are important forerunners of the new genre of grand opera, the spectacular works performed at L'Opéra during the period of its greatest magnificence (see p. 657).

Daniel-François-Esprit Auber

Auber (1782–1871), a pianist, did not decide on a career in music until 1803. In 1805 one of his short comedies attracted the attention of Cherubini, who accepted him as a pupil. Although Auber composed numerous instrumental and sacred vocal works, his most significant compositions are his operas, most of which set libretti by Eugène Scribe (1791–1861). Auber's first operas were failures, and, disheartened, he wrote no music for almost five years. Financial need and Cherubini's encouragement caused him to resume composition in 1820. For a time, in 1823, Auber imitated Rossini's vocal style; in 1824, he sought a purely French style. Then, wisely, he began to combine the two, eventually achieving a synthesis and mingling humorous—sometimes mordant wit—and Romantic elements, as he did in *Fra Diavolo*. (The actions of Fra Diavolo, leader of an outlaw band of robbers, fully justified his name, Brother Devil.)

In 1828 Auber and Scribe were commissioned to write a "*grand opéra*" for L'Opéra. *La muette de Portici* (The mute girl of Portici) resulted. Based on history (the Neapolitan insurrection led by Masaniello against the Spanish in 1647), the opera contained spectacular crowd scenes and colorful ballets. (Even the eruption of Vesuvius was included, though that occurred in 1631!) When performed in Brussels in 1830, *La muette de Portici* was instrumental in inciting the Belgians to revolt against the Dutch. Though Auber and Scribe collaborated in creating grand operas until 1851 and *opéras comiques* until 1861, in quality they never surpassed *La muette de Portici*. After 1840, Auber's style changed somewhat, and he wrote a more lyrical, more serious type of *opéra comique,* of which *Manon Lescaut* (1856) is the best example. The music Auber wrote before 1840 is conservative, characterized by diatonic harmonies and melodies with occasional chromaticism, dotted or dancelike rhythms, and homophonic texture. In later works he used richer harmonies, more chromaticism, and wider modulations.

Grand Opera

The new style of opera—grand opera—was firmly established as a result of the joint endeavors of librettist Eugène Scribe, composer Giacomo Meyerbeer, and Louis Véron (see also Ch. 22). Standards for grand opera were set by several masterpieces—*Robert le diable* (Robert the devil; 1831) and *Les Huguenots* (The Huguenots; 1836) by Meyerbeer (1791–1864), *Gustave III* (1833) by Auber, and *La Juive* (The Jewess; 1835) by Jacques Halévy (1799–1862)—all on libretti by Scribe.

Scribe was primarily responsible for developing the grand opera libretto. Usually, his plots have historical (or quasi-historical) settings that provide ample opportunity for crowd scenes and spectacle, including ballet. Central to the drama are passionate human relationships and the effect on them of conflicting forces—human, natural, or supernatural—over which the characters have no control. Often, that conflict had some contemporary relevance. In preparing a libretto, Scribe paid careful attention to the dramatic framework, delineated characters whose personalities and fortunes permitted effective musical contrasts, and adeptly created sequences of scenes that work up to a grand finale.

Meantime, some important changes had occurred at L'Opéra. Coal gas lighting, first used in London's Drury Lane Theater in 1817, was safe and controllable. In 1822 it was used for the first time at L'Opéra to light the stage for *Aladin, ou La lampe merveilleuse* (Aladdin, or The wonderful lamp), a work begun by Nicolas Isouard (1775–1818) and completed by Angelo Benincori (1779–1821). For that production, scene designer Pierre Cicéri (1782–1868) and painter Louis Daguerre (1787–1851; the inventor of the diorama and the photographic daguerrotype process) created realistic sets in which they applied the new scenic techniques already being used in popular Parisian theaters. In 1822, as a private enterprise, Cicéri founded a workshop that manufactured and sold reproductions of sets used at L'Opéra. Through shops of this kind, some of which sold costumes and properties also, a fairly uniform international style of opera-staging was gradually established.

Music in Austro-Germanic Lands

In Austro-Germanic lands, the most significant contributions made by Beethoven's contemporaries during the first three decades of the nineteenth century were in the areas of solo song (*Lied*) and opera. The general tenor of musical and literary works created in France at the time of the Revolution struck a responsive note among authors and composers in Germanic lands, where the various political states had no overall unity as a nation. Authors, in their search for a national consciousness, used as subject matter folklore and legends, as well as political themes and actual incidents; composers converted those poems into ballads and Lieder, those stories, dramas, and fairy tales into *Singspiele* and operas. In the nineteenth century, literary nationalism extended to historical novels and dramas with common folk as major characters.

The philosopher Johann G. Herder (1744–1803) considered music basic to all culture and education. He was interested in folk song and folk poetry and, in 1778–79, published two collections of *Volkslieder* (folk songs)—in fact, he coined the term *Volkslied*. Germany had no native opera tradition; Italian opera had flourished at German and Austrian courts, and in the late eighteenth century French opera was gaining a strong foothold. Joseph II's endeavor to establish a German opera company at the imperial court theater in 1777 was unsuccessful. Herder advocated a German national opera based on traditional materials. Moreover, in one of his several essays on music, he expressed his idea of opera becoming a unified theatrical work in which all of the arts merged—the kind of *Gesamtkunstwerk* (complete, collective artwork) that Richard Wagner created decades later.

Among the leading Romantic poets was Clemens Brentano (1778–1842), whose importance to music is primarily as coeditor, with Joachim von Arnim (1781–1831), of the collection of folk poetry entitled *Das Knaben Wunderhorn* (The boy's magic horn; 1805–08). Poems from that collection inspired settings by many nineteenth- and twentieth-century composers, including Gustav Mahler and Charles Ives (see Ch. 25). The most significant collection of fairy tales was *Kinder- und Hausmärchen* (Children's and family fairy tales, 2 vols.; 1812–15; better known as "Grimm's Fairy Tales"), written by Jakob (1785–1863) and Wilhelm (1786–1859) Grimm.

German nationalism found a place in opera gradually, as elements of magic and the supernatural were transferred to *Singspiel* and it became infused with Romantic components. One of the earliest of the "magic" *Singspiele* was Mozart's *Die Zauberflöte* (1791). Operas by Cherubini, Méhul, and other Parisian composers were popular in Austro-Germanic lands during the first decade of the nineteenth century, and, in reaction, German composers incorporated some features of French rescue operas and *opéras comiques* in their own stage works. Two German operas—E. T. A. Hoffmann's *Undine* (perf. Berlin, August 1816) and Ludwig Spohr's *Faust* (comp. 1813; perf. Prague, September 1816)—prepared the way for Carl Maria von Weber, who firmly established German Romantic opera in *Singspiel* with *Der Freischütz* (The free marksman; Berlin, 1821) and in *opera seria* with *Euryanthe* (Vienna, 1823). Gradually, recitative supplanted spoken dialogue, but melodrama was retained for special effects.

German Romantic opera, though popular, was relatively short-lived; the last important one was Wagner's *Lohengrin* (perf. 1850). The significance of the genre lies not merely in its expression of German nationalism, but in the striving of German composers, especially Weber, to effect a synthesis of the various related arts collaborating in the production of an opera and thereby create a self-contained work of art, a *Gesamtkunstwerk*. These composers prepared the way for Wagner, whose music dramas of *Der Ring des Nibelungen* (The Ring of the Nibelungs) are the ultimate *Gesamtkunstwerk* and contain elements of German Romantic opera.

In its definitive form, German Romantic opera is characterized by: (1) plots based on German legend, fairy tale, myth, or medieval history; (2) scenes of country life and nature in its wild state; (3) a cast of characters that includes supernatural beings, nobility, and common folk—the naive and pure, the evil, and the supernaturally possessed; (4) elements of magic and the supernatural treated as powerful forces capable of threatening, influencing, directing, or dominating the lives of humans; (5) the ultimate triumph of good over evil, as salvation or redemption, or even "rescue"; (6) use of simple, folklike, Germanic melodies, with harmonies and orchestral timbres appropriate to the dramatic situation.

Ludwig Spohr

Ludwig Spohr (1784–1859) was the leading German minor composer in the first half of the nineteenth century. He achieved fame first as a virtuoso violinist, concertizing throughout Europe, at first singly, and from 1806 to 1822 with his wife, noted harpist Dorette Scheidler (1787–1834). Spohr attracted violin pupils from all over Europe. In addition to contributing a vast amount of literature to violin and harp repertoire, he made a major contribution to violin playing when, c. 1820, he invented the "violin-holder," i.e., the chin rest, which has become a standard addition to the instrument. Spohr's placement of the device directly over the tailpiece, in the middle of the base of the instrument (fig. 21.2), indicates the manner in which the violin was held at that time. Spohr was a competent conductor, and he was one of the earliest to conduct with a baton instead of using a roll of paper or a violin bow.

As a composer, Spohr was prolific and versatile. Besides writing for violin and for harp, he composed 13 operas, 10 symphonies, some concert overtures and

Ludwig Spohr. Self-portrait, in pastels, 1807. *(Landesmuseum, Brunswick.)*

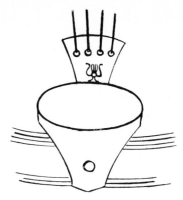

Figure 21.2 Spohr's "violin-holder," now called chin rest, was attached to the violin by the instrument's tailpin and extended over the tailpiece.

other orchestral pieces, 4 clarinet concertos of mediocre quality, 34 string quartets, 4 double string quartets, about 2 dozen other pieces of chamber music of various kinds, more than 90 solo songs, some part songs, a Mass, at least 5 oratorios, and numerous other sacred and secular choral works. His finest oratorio is *Der Fall Babylons* (The fall of Babylon; 1840). The double quartets are interesting—they are not string octets but are for two opposed string quartets.

Spohr was a thorough craftsman. He admired the Viennese Classical composers, and much of his music is Classical in form, but his compositions reflect also his knowledge of works by Méhul, Spontini, and Cherubini. In use of chromaticism, Spohr was strongly influenced by Cherubini. The stylistic developments Spohr effected in his operas were of far-reaching significance and foreshadow Wagner's work in several respects: the associative use of recurrent themes, later called *Leitmotifs*; the writing of through-composed (German, *Durchkomponiert*) rather than number opera; and his choices of harmonies and orchestral timbres to create atmosphere.

As a youth, Spohr became acquainted with Mozart's *Die Zauberflöte* and *Il Don Giovanni,* but not until 1806 did he attempt to write an opera. His first success in that genre came with *Faust,* composed in 1813 but not produced until September 1816, in Prague, where Carl Maria von Weber conducted its première. That two-act opera was not pure *Singspiel*; some recitatives were included. An important feature of *Faust* is Spohr's systematic use of "reminiscence motives" and "harmonies of the then and now"—an associative system of melodies and harmonies woven into the fabric of the entire opera. In *Faust,* these motives and harmonies function as psychic symbols. Reminiscence motives are used to a greater extent in *Zemire und Azor* (1819), a two-act fairy-tale opera whose plot centers on the Romantic idea of redemption. Spohr achieved his greatest operatic success with *Jessonda* (1823). Its exotic setting (India) permitted him to use chromaticism effectively. *Jessonda* is sung throughout and illustrates Spohr's endeavor to avoid number opera. By using recitative instead of spoken dialogue, and by progressively enhancing recitative until it attained the level of arioso, he was able to create a through-composed opera.

Though Spohr continued to compose operas, his later works had only limited success. Perhaps one reason for this was the fact that, after he accepted a lifetime appointment as Kapellmeister at the Kassel electoral court (1822), he no longer concertized. Once he became attached to a court, he became allied with the nobility; he ceased being a cosmopolitan virtuoso—an independent artist—with popular appeal to those who sought social independence from the nobility.

E. T. A. Hoffmann

Ernst Theodor Amadeus Hoffmann (1776–1822) was trained for and embarked on a career as lawyer and judge. As a child, he had received some training in music and painting and had continued those studies at Königsberg University. He had always been more interested in music than in law and, in 1799, began to compose. After he was transferred to Warsaw in 1804, he abandoned the legal profession for a career in music.

From 1809 to 1815, Hoffmann wrote essays on music and reviews of compositions and performances for *Allgemeine musikalische Zeitung,* but until 1813 the articles were published without by-line. After 1815, he reviewed only performances. As critic, he carefully distinguished between the analysis of compositional technique and the interpretation of musical content. His writings on music were highly respected throughout the nineteenth century. In addition to criticism, Hoffmann authored *Fantasiestücke* (Fantastic tales) inspired by music. Wandering through many of those stories is the eccentric Kapellmeister Johannes Kreisler, a Romantic musician figment of Hoffmann's imagination. Many of Hoffmann's tales inspired music, e.g., Tchaikovsky's ballet *The Nutcracker,* Schumann's *Kreisleriana,* Offenbach's *Les Contes d'Hoffmann* (The Tales of Hoffmann), and others. Hoffmann's most important contribution was probably literary—providing plots and referential material for other composers' works.

As a composer, Hoffmann was fairly prolific; many of his works have been lost. His most significant composition is the Romantic opera *Undine* (1816), a number opera based on a German fairy tale by Friedrich de la Motte-Fouqué. Its plot concerns the infusion of a soul into the water spirit Undine, a faithless knight, and the spirits' revenge on human faithlessness. Included in the cast are simple fishing folk and a pious priest. Scenes of medieval splendor contrast with scenes of wild and unspoiled nature; there are choruses of earth and water spirits. In much of the

music, Hoffmann conveys the sound of water rushing. *Undine* was performed in Berlin 14 times, and Carl Maria von Weber attended some of those performances.

Carl Maria von Weber

Weber (1786–1826), one of the leading German composers of the early nineteenth century, also worked to effect much-needed reforms in the theater. From early childhood, he was at home in the theatrical world. His mother was an actress-singer; his father, once Kapellmeister to the Bishop of Lübeck, was musical director of a theatrical company. Carl was a frail child, with a damaged hipbone that caused him to limp. Not until he was nine did he have competent instruction in music. His best instruction came a year or so later from Michael Haydn under whose watchful eye Weber composed six fughettas for piano (publ. 1798). He next studied piano and composition in Munich, where he wrote a Mass (rev. 1802; publ. 1926) and his first opera, *Die Macht der Liebe und des Weins* (The power of love and of wine; 1800; lost). In Freiberg, he wrote another opera, *Das Waldmädchen* (The forest maiden; perf. 1800; fragments extant), and in Salzburg, where he again studied with M. Haydn, Weber revised the Mass and composed his third opera, *Peter Schmoll und seine Nachbarn* (Peter Schmoll and his neighbors; 1801–02; perf. 1803; dialogue lost). Meantime, he had written a few songs, some choral canons, and several short piano pieces.

Hoping to study with Joseph Haydn, Weber went to Vienna; instead, he studied for about nine months with Georg J. Vogler (Abt Vogler; 1749–1814), whose teaching helped shape the careers of many composers, including Giacomo Meyerbeer and Peter von Winter. On Vogler's recommendation, 17-year-old Weber was appointed Kapellmeister at Breslau; there, Weber's attempts to reform conditions in the theater were unpopular. At that time, Weber was fascinated by lithography and dabbled in engraving. One night he accidentally drank some nitric acid stored in a wine bottle and suffered intensely for weeks; his vocal cords were permanently damaged.

From autumn 1806 to July 1807 Weber worked at the Carlsruhe court; there, he composed two C-major symphonies, some variations, and the Horn

Carl Maria von Weber. *(Shaffer Archive.)*

Concertino (rev. 1815). He next found employment at Stuttgart as secretary to the Duke of Württemberg and taught some piano lessons there. He wrote six piano duets for teaching purposes, a dozen songs, a cantata, incidental music for a play, and the Romantic opera *Silvana* (1808–10). By then Weber had become a virtuoso pianist. For his own use he composed a set of variations on an original theme, *Momento capriccioso, Grande polonaise,* and the Piano Quartet in B♭. Weber's friends at Stuttgart were the city's poets and intellectuals. He began to write critical articles on music and started a novel, *Tonkunstlers Leben* (A composer's life), which he never finished. Weber's status at Stuttgart was jeopardized by his father, whose meddling created financial difficulties that resulted in the Webers' banishment from the area.

To earn the money to settle his Stuttgart debts, Weber concertized. He resumed studies with Vogler at Darmstadt and composed Piano Concerto No. 1 (C major), six violin/piano sonatas, the Clarinet Concertino (E♭ major), and *Abu Hassan,* a *Singspiel.* At this time, he read the fairy tale *Der Freischütz* and determined to use it for an opera, but his chosen librettist had other priorities.

On his concert tours, Weber made valuable friends but composed few significant works—two clarinet concerti commissioned by the king (No. 1, F minor; No. 2, E♭ major; 1811), a bassoon concerto (F major; 1811), and Piano Sonata No. 1 (C major; 1812). The waltz was becoming popular, and he wrote six sets of waltzes for piano and one set for wind ensemble.

Early in 1813, Weber became theater director and conductor at Prague. He completely reorganized the theater system, then produced Spontini's *Fernando Cortez.* Works by Cherubini, Méhul, Boieldieu, and other French composers followed. Weber's familiarity with those operas directly influenced his own opera composition—some of his characters have prototypes in them. Gradually, Weber changed the theater repertoire. In January 1814 he presented Mozart's *Il Don Giovanni;* later that year he staged Beethoven's *Fidelio.* At Prague, Weber had little time for composition for several reasons: (1) The Prague public had not been receptive to some of the repertoire changes, and Weber decided to introduce unfamiliar works by writing articles on them for newspaper publication. (2) Health problems plagued him—chest pains, sore throat, aching hip. (3) When he returned from treatment at a spa, or from vacation, he found standards at the theater deteriorating. (4) Soprano Caroline Brandt joined the company in December 1813; Weber fell in love with her but could not persuade her to marry him then. Weber's most important works from the Prague years are *Leyer und Schwert* (Lyre and Sword; Volumes 1 and 3, solo vc. with pno.; Volume 2, unaccompanied male chorus), a clarinet quintet (B♭; 1815), the cantata *Kampf und Sieg* (Combat and Victory; 1816), and the *Grand duo concertant* (cl., pno.; 1816), a brilliant multimovement concert piece for two virtuosi. *Leyer und Schwert* (Volumes 1, 2, 1814; Volume 3, 1816) comprises settings of Körner's patriotic poems of the same name; Weber's TTBB part songs of Volume 2 are among the earliest of many such patriotic outpourings in Germanic lands in the nineteenth century.

Weber moved to Berlin in autumn 1816 and concentrated on composing. Among the works he wrote at this time are piano sonatas No. 2 (A♭ major) and No. 3 (D minor) and *Die Temperamente beim Verluste der Geliebten* (Emotions on the loss of the beloved; 4 songs; 1816), one of the earliest song cycles, composed only a few months later than Beethoven's *An die ferne Geliebte.*

In mid-January 1817, Weber became *Musikdirektor* at Dresden and was faced with the task of developing German opera in a court and city atmosphere dominated by Italian operas, Italian composers, and Italian singers. He began by completely reforming every aspect of the theater, then introduced some French operas. Again, he considered writing an opera on *Der Freischütz* but had time to compose only officially commissioned works, such as incidental music for the play *Der Weinberg an der Elbe* (Weinberg on the Elbe), in which Richard Wagner (1813–83) appeared as an angel.

Caroline and Carl married in Prague in November 1817. Upon returning to Dresden, Weber resumed his theater work, began *Der Freischütz,* and composed two offertories (1818) and two Masses (E♭, 1817–18; G, 1818–19). In the spring of 1819 he was ill with tuberculosis but by summer was well enough to write some piano pieces: *Aufforderung zum Tanze* (Invitation to the dance), *Rondo brillante, Polacca brillante,* and part of Piano Sonata No. 4 (C minor; completed in 1823). In 1820 he wrote some incidental music and began but abandoned the comic opera *Der drei Pintos* (The three Pintos; completed by Gustav Mahler, 1888).

In 1821 Weber sketched an F-minor piano concerto that ultimately became *Konzertstück* (Concert piece), and he completed *Der Freischütz.* The opera's première in Berlin's new Shauspielhaus was an outstanding success, a triumph that was repeated in theaters in most of the principal German cities and in Vienna. Everywhere but in Dresden, where for six months intrigues prevented its performance, *Der Freischütz* was popular, for Germans considered it truly representative of their folk heritage. Vienna impresario Barbaia (see also p. 615) requested Weber to compose a German Romantic opera for the 1822–23 season at Kärntnertor Theater, but Weber chose to set *Euryanthe* by Dresden poet Wilhelmine von Chézy (1783–1856). *Euryanthe* was well received in Vienna but was not really successful until sung by dramatic soprano Wilhelmine Schröder-Devrient (1804–60) in Dresden in 1824.

Though tuberculosis was making inroads and Weber knew he had only a few years to live, he accepted a commission from London for an opera, studied English, composed *Oberon* (1825–26), and went to London to rehearse and conduct it. While there, he concertized in order to earn as much money as possible for his wife and two small sons. Weber died in London on 5 June 1826 and was interred in Moorfields Chapel. In 1844 Richard Wagner arranged for transfer of the remains to Dresden and composed two works for the interment services: *An Webers Grabe* (At Weber's grave; *a cappella* male chorus), and *Trauermusik* (Funeral music; band) on themes from *Euryanthe.*

Weber's Music

Weber contributed to the development of music in several areas but most significantly in opera: his theatrical reforms, his desire for unification of the arts involved in opera production, and his definitive establishment of German Romantic opera with *Der Freischütz* (1821). Elements of German Romantic opera are present in the earliest of Weber's surviving operas, *Peter Schmoll . . .*—bourgeois characters in important roles, nature, fate, resolution of the situation through intervention of a holy man, melody resembling folk song. They are exhibited to a greater extent in *Silvana,* the story of a knight wooing and winning a mute girl living in the woods. There is, of course, a villain (a bass), and a huntsmen's chorus. Since *Silvana* uses a revision of the libretto and some of the music from *Das Waldmädchen,* elements of German Romanticism in Weber's music probably extend back to 1800.

Der Freischütz tells a story that mingles human and supernatural, good and evil: The hunter Max must win a shooting match to obtain the post of head ranger and the hand of Agathe, his beloved. Kaspar, in league with the devil through Samiel, persuades Max to use "free" bullets (hence, he is the "free" marksman) that can be directed magically to their mark. At midnight, in Wolf's Glen, seven bullets are cast according to forbidden rites. In the competition, six bullets hit the target; the seventh strikes Agathe, who is protected from death by a bridal wreath an old hermit has blessed (benevolent supernatural power). Kaspar has failed to secure Agathe for the devil and dies. Max confesses his duplicity, is to be banished for a year, then may marry Agathe.

Much of *Der Freischütz* takes place at night, and effective lighting is important. Weber replaced candle lighting with Swiss Argand burners that used a cylindrical wick and glass tubing; the light from Argand's oil lamps was more flexible and could be made brighter than candlelight. *Der Freischütz* is a *Singspiel,* a number opera with spoken dialogue. However, Weber skillfully used dialogue to lead into the singing, sometimes bridging dialogue and song with melodrama, thus creating longer scenes and avoiding pure number opera. An example of this is the scene in Wolf's Glen (DWMA172).

In his use of recurrent motives and associative key tonalities and tone colors, Weber anticipated some of Wagner's techniques. In *Der Freischütz* the key of C major is associated with benevolent powers; D major, with the natural, normal, healthy world. Samiel, being evil, never sings. He is represented musically by piccolo trills. The diminished-seventh chord f♯-a-c-e♭ is associated with him and with evil, and the four notes of that chord provide the key scheme for the Wolf's Glen scene. In that scene, Weber freely used motives and phrases previously heard in the opera. In *Euryanthe,* he used the motive associated with Eglantine's deceit and a diminished-seventh chord similarly but more expansively, modifying the motive to adjust it to represent the various aspects of Eglantine's guile. Weber's systematic use of recurrent themes extended beyond the technique of *Reminiszenzmotiv* then in use. Recognizing this, F. W. Jähns (1809–88), Weber's biographer and cataloger of his works, invented the term ***Leitmotif*** (leading motive) to describe Weber's practice. A *Leitmotif* is a kind of musical tag or label, a recurrent clearly defined theme or coherent musical idea that is intended to represent or symbolize a person, thing, place, idea, state of mind, or even a supernatural force. Obviously, a *Leitmotif* is a unifying device. In *Euryanthe,* Weber further weakened the set aria and took an important step toward the development of music drama. At the beginning of Act III of *Euryanthe* Weber used a series of highly chromatic chord progressions in which the so-called Tristan chord (the first chord in Wagner's *Tristan und Isolde,* f-b-d♯'-g♯') figures prominently.

Though Weber was knowledgeable concerning instrumental music and his orchestrations are superb, his purely orchestral works are unimportant. The overtures to *Der Freischütz* and *Oberon* are in sonata form, constructed on themes from the respective operas; frequently, these overtures are played in concerts.

All but one of Weber's chamber music works (the Clarinet Quintet) include his own instrument, piano. His solo piano music reflects his knowledge of the styles of Dussek and Cramer. Weber was one of the best pianists of his day, and the works he wrote for his own concertizing are considered difficult by modern pianists. Weber had large hands with long fingers and exceptionally long thumbs; playing a four-note chord encompassing a tenth posed no problem for he could span a twelfth easily. He preferred the Brodmann piano, a Viennese instrument with lighter action and slightly narrower keys than twentieth-century pianos. The most popular of Weber's piano pieces is *Aufforderung zum Tanze* (Invitation to the Dance; D♭). A programmatic work in rondo form with introduction and epilogue, it was the first of many large concert works based on the waltz. In 1841 Berlioz orchestrated the piece (*L'invitation à la valse*).

Weber was one of the earliest conductors to stand at a podium and direct the orchestra with a thick baton that he grasped in the middle (fig. 21.3). He stood near the prompter's box at the opera, with winds and brass to his left, upper strings to his right, lower strings behind him.

Weber's writings include his partially completed novel *Tonkunstlers Leben,* critical essays, and some poetry and occasional pieces. His most important writings are the articles he published to inform the public about the opera theater and its repertoire. In these "notices," as he called them, each published a few days before a performance, he made critical comments concerning the opera and its composer and frequently discussed technical and esthetic details of the

Figure 21.3 Detail from John Hayter's lithograph (1826) depicting Weber conducting *Der Freischütz* at Covent Garden. (© *Art Resource.*)

composition and its production. In these critical articles, Weber anticipated the editorial writings of Robert Schumann (p. 647). Also visible in Weber's writings is a nationalistic vein—his constant concern for the advancement of German music and German musicians.

Lesser Composers of Opera

After Weber's death, the composition of German Romantic opera was carried on by a number of lesser composers, chief of whom was Heinrich Marschner (1795–1861). Marschner first attracted attention as an opera composer in 1820, when his *Heinrich IV und d'Aubigné* (Henry IV and d'Aubigné; 1818) was produced by Weber at Dresden. However, it was another eight years before Marschner tasted real success, first with *Der Vampyr* (The Vampire, based on Byron's *Lord Ruthwen*; comp. 1827; perf. 1828), then with *Der Templer und die Jüdin* (The Templer and the Jewess, based on Scott's *Ivanhoe*; 1829).

The finest of Marschner's 13 operas is *Hans Heiling* (1833). Briefly, this is its plot: Hans, half earth-spirit and half mortal, wants to renounce rule of his spiritual realm and become completely mortal so that he can wed a mortal. But he asks too much of his beloved, and she breaks with him; heartbroken, he returns to his spirit kingdom. In setting the libretto, which was originally intended for Mendelssohn, Marschner wrote a sung, through-composed prologue but used spoken dialogue for the body of the work, with some melodrama at the beginning of Act II. Stylistically, *Hans Heiling* stands midway between the work of Weber and that of Wagner. Marschner was adept at characterization, and at portraying psychological aspects of a drama, but tended to neglect aspects of local color. This is a defect in *Hans Heiling,* where, in endeavoring to provide a unified setting for the entire opera, Marschner made the spirit world too human.

With the success of *Hans Heiling,* Marschner's position as one of the leading German opera composers was assured. He was also a capable conductor and frequently served in that capacity at music festivals. Besides operas and other stage works, he wrote numerous piano pieces, more than 120 part songs and choruses for male voices, and approximately 425 works for solo voice—Lieder, ballads, *Gesänge* (songs).

In the area of German comic opera, Albert Lortzing (1801–51) made significant contributions. His aim was to provide entertainment, and he did so admirably. *Czaar und Zimmermann* (Czar and carpenter; 1837) and *Der Wildschütz* (The poacher; 1842) are excellent examples. From early childhood, Lortzing had participated as actor or singer in theatrical productions; this practical experience gave him a decided advantage when preparing libretti and composing operas. He always wrote his own texts and set them as number opera. A characteristic of his style is the effective introduction of dialogue, as interjections, in musical numbers. His humor is delightful, e.g., the rehearsal scene in *Czaar und Zimmermann,* where the choir misunderstands the choirmaster's instructions and repeatedly bungles entrances. Lortzing was skilled at characterization and especially excelled in writing comic bass roles, e.g., Van Bett in *Czaar und Zimmermann* and Baculus in *Der Wildschütz.*

Another composer of comic opera was Otto Nicolai, whose *Die lustige Weiber von Windsor* (The merry wives of Windsor; based on Shakespeare; 1849) is a mixture of Italian and German musical styles.

Lieder

Many singers and composers working in Austro-Germanic lands were as interested in Lieder and secular choral music as they were in opera. Some composers tried writing opera and had little success, e.g., Franz Schubert. Others, like Anna Fröhlich and Luise Reichardt, were teachers and/or chorus directors. Carl Loewe, internationally known baritone, was able to concertize in addition to holding municipal and church positions; thus, he could promote the circulation of his own Lieder and ballads.

Carl Loewe

Loewe (1796–1869) was born near Halle, in the Thuringian area. He received his first training in music from his schoolmaster father and was a choirboy in the church at Cöthen. By the age of 12, Loewe had some published songs and instrumental pieces. (Later, the *opus* numbers of these early works were suppressed.) For a few years, an annuity from Jerome Buonaparte, King of Westphalia under the French domination, enabled Loewe to continue piano and composition lessons. A devout Catholic, Loewe studied theology at Halle University. From 1820 to 1865 he worked in Stettin, as professor and Kantor at the Gymnasium and seminary, and from 1821 as municipal Musikdirektor and organist at St. Jacobus Cathedral. He continued to compose—piano sonatas, piano concerti, symphonies, string quartets, oratorios, operas, songs, and other sacred and secular vocal works. By 1835 he was famous throughout Germanic lands as composer, conductor, and singer. Then he undertook international concert tours to Austria, London, Scandinavia, and France; in Vienna, he was acclaimed as "the north German Schubert." Rarely did Loewe sing songs by other composers; many of his ballads need vivid interpretation, and at this he excelled.

Loewe was a prolific composer. His 6 operas and 17 oratorios are stylistically similar. Many of his piano sonatas are programmatic, and some are unusual, e.g.,

Op. 16, in E major, whose slow movement is a song for tenor. *Mazeppa,* Op. 27 (1830), called a *Tondichtung* (tone poem), is his best work for piano.

Loewe is remembered for his approximately 375 solo songs with piano accompaniment. Some of his finest songs are early works: the 31 *Hebräische Gesänge* (Hebrew Songs, Opp. 4, 5, 13, 14; comp. 1819–26, publ. 1825–27), and the 3 ballads of Op. 1 (publ. 1824). The latter comprise *Edward* (1818), *Der Wirthin Töchterlein* (The [female] innkeeper's little daughter; 1823), and *Erlkönig* (Erlking; 1818). Frequently, Loewe chose texts by Herder, Uhland, and Goethe, the poets represented in Op. 1. Loewe had a predilection for ballads. In setting them, he often used modified strophic structure, and he contrasted (but did not necessarily alternate) arioso with dramatic accompanied recitative, as he did in *Der Wirthin Töchterlein* and *Archibald Douglas* (Op. 128, 1857). In this type of opposition, Loewe followed and improved upon the practice of Zumsteeg, who had used a great deal of *secco* recitative in his ballads. The same kind of contrast is apparent in the through-composed setting of *Erlkönig.* Though melodically different, Loewe's and Schubert's (comp. 1815, publ. 1821) settings of Goethe's *Erlkönig* are similar in several respects—key (G minor), agitated piano accompaniment, a rise in pitch as the child becomes more frightened, the lilting words of the coaxing Erlking, use of recitative in conclusion (ex. 21.2)—but whether Loewe saw Schubert's work in manuscript is debatable. Loewe's setting of the old Scottish ballad *Edward* (Eb minor; DWMA173) is his best-known song. It is filled with dark, brooding sonorities, and the piano supplies supportive, illustrative, and/or dramatic music at appropriate places during the dialogue as Edward gradually works up to telling his mother that he has killed his father and finally reveals that she instigated the murder.

Many of Loewe's ballads are Romantic, with elements of horror, the supernatural, folklore, and fairy tale. Humor, rare in Romantic music, is present also. In Loewe's songs, as in Schubert's, the piano does not merely accompany the singer but enters into partnership with the voice in interpreting the poetry. For Loewe, the poem was of prime import; he composed a vocal line suited to the poem, with due secondary

(a)

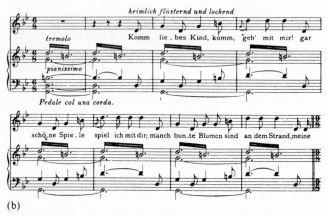

(b)

Example 21.2 Loewe's *Erlkönig*, Op. 1, Nr. 3: (*a*) mm. 1–4; (*b*) mm. 25–32; (*c*) mm. 80 to end of piece. *(Source:* Carl Loewes Werke: Gesamtausgabe der Balladen, Legenden, Lieder und Gesänge, *ed. Max Runze. Band XI. Leipzig: Breitkopf & Härtel, 1899–1904.)*

(c)

consideration for the style of narration and the descriptive effects. Never did he permit piano figuration to encroach upon the vocal line. He rarely wrote introductions or postludes, and when he did, they were brief.

Franz Peter Schubert

Franz Peter Schubert (1797–1828), the only great native Viennese composer, was the 11th child of Moravian-born schoolmaster Franz Theodor and Maria Schubert. Only 4 of their 12 children survived infancy: Ignaz, Ferdinand, Karl, and Franz Peter. Franz Theodor personally gave the children some

Franz P. Schubert. *(Courtesy of the Free Library of Philadelphia.)*

musical training, and family music making was important; both Ferdinand and Franz Peter wrote music specifically for performance by family members. Eventually, Ferdinand (1794–1859) became a highly respected educator in Vienna, held an organist-choirmaster position also, and was a minor composer of vocal music.

Franz Peter's violin and piano playing soon surpassed that of his father and brothers. When he was nine, he was sent to Michael Holzer, the Liechtental parish church organist, for further training—piano, organ, violin, singing, and harmony lessons. In 1808 he was accepted as a choirboy in the imperial court chapel and admitted to the Kaiserlich-königliches Stadtkonvikt (Imperial-royal City Seminary), the principal Viennese boarding school. There he was an excellent student, academically as well as musically. Soon he was promoted to leader of first violins in the school orchestra and conducted when the regular conductor was absent. Eventually, court Kapellmeister Antonio Salieri took over supervision of Schubert's musical training. At the school, Schubert formed a lifelong friendship with Josef von Spaun, who provided the manuscript paper Schubert could not afford to buy and took him to Kärntnertor Theater to see his first opera.

Schubert's earliest surviving compositions date from his Stadtkonvikt years and include *Fantasie* in G major for piano duet (D.1; 1810), six Minuets for winds (D.2d; 1811, lost and relocated in 1969), and the songs *Hagars Klage* (Hagar's lament, D.5; 1811), *Des Mädchens Klage* (The maiden's lament, D.6; 1811), and *Eine Leichenfantasie* (A funeral fantasy, D.7; 1811). During school vacations, Schubert enjoyed playing in the family string quartet—father played 'cello, Ignaz and Ferdinand played violins, Franz played viola. For this group, Franz composed many pieces, but only a few of his quartets written in 1811–14 have survived, and some of those are incomplete. The best of the early quartets is that in E♭ major, D.87 (1813). Schubert's works are generally known by their "D" numbers, according to the catalog of his works prepared by Otto Erich Deutsch (1883–1967).

Of the many works Schubert composed in 1813, the finest is Symphony No. 1 (D major, D.82). Near the end of 1813, he left the Stadtkonvikt, took a training course for elementary teachers, and in autumn 1814 began teaching in his father's school. He continued lessons with Salieri until the end of 1816. Schubert was rejected by military conscription authorities because his eyesight was defective, and he was too short (about five feet tall). In 1814, Schubert wrote the first work that brought him public attention: Mass No. 1 (F major, D.105), performed twice in October, as part of the centennial celebration at Liechtental Church and at the court church of St. Augustine. More importantly, on 19 October 1814 Schubert created his first masterpiece—*Gretchen am Spinnrade* (Gretchen at the spinning wheel, D.118), a setting of ten stanzas from Part I of Goethe's *Faust*. Later that year, Spaun encouraged Schubert to set Johann Mayrhofer's (1787–1836) *Am See* (At the sea, D.124) and arranged for the two men to meet. They became lifelong friends; in 1815 Schubert set Mayrhofer's two-act play *Die Freunde von Salamanka* (The friends of Salamanka, D.326) as a *Singspiel.*

Schubert taught in 1815 but disliked the work. Music filled his mind, and that year he composed more music than in any other single year of his life. Among those works are 2 symphonies (No. 2, B♭ major, D.125; No. 3, D major, D.200), 2 Masses (No. 2, G major, D.167; No. 3, B♭ major, D.324), 4 *Singspiele,* a piano sonata (C major, D.279), numerous dances for piano solo, a string quartet (G minor, D.173), a set of 10 Variations in F for piano solo (D.156), much choral music (most of it for male voices), and about 145 songs—settings of poetry by Klopstock, Körner, Goethe, Mayrhofer, Schiller, and others. In length the songs vary from very short, e.g., *Wandrers Nachtlied* (Traveler's night song, D.224; 1 strophe, 13 measures) to very long ballads, e.g., *Adelwold und Emma* (D.211; 610 measures, not counting repeats). Twenty measures of music (repeated for the 4 strophes) suffice for *Die Mainacht* (May night, D.194). Among the 30 settings of Goethe's poems are some of Schubert's finest and most famous songs, including *Heidenröslein* (Little heath rose, D.257) and *Erlkönig* (D.328). *Erlkönig* is probably Schubert's best-known song; many critics consider it his greatest.

In 1816 Schubert decided to devote all his time to composition, but not until late October did he abandon teaching, and then the break was only temporary. Instrumental in that move was his friend Franz von Schober, who provided him with temporary lodging. Another factor may have been the receipt of his first commission, which resulted in the cantata *Prometheus* (D.451; lost), performed at a private celebration held in the garden of Josef Witteczek's house in July. A few years later, that house, where Spaun had lodgings, was the setting for many *Schubertiaden,* evening concerts devoted to Schubert's music and attended by a circle of Schubert's friends and sometimes their families. It was for private social gatherings of this kind that Schubert wrote many of his songs; they were not intended for performance in public concerts. He was not a concert artist and was most comfortable performing chamber music or accompanying his talented friends.

Again, in 1816, Schubert was prolific. He wrote 2 more symphonies: No. 4, which he entitled *Tragic,* in C minor (D.427) and No. 5, in B♭ major (D.485). The B♭ symphony was first performed by a small private orchestra that had developed from the Schubert family quartet. Among Schubert's other works from 1816 are Mass No. 4 (C major, D.452; publ. 1825), 3 violin/piano sonatas (D.384, 385, 408; publ. 1836 by Diabelli as sonatinas), String Quartet in E major (D.353), and more than 100 songs. One of those songs, *Der Wanderer* (The traveler, D.489), became very popular.

Through Schober, in 1817, Schubert met baritone Johann M. Vogl (1768–1840), and another close friendship developed. Vogl, a member of the Vienna court opera, had sung the role of Pizarro in Beethoven's 1814 revision of *Fidelio* and was himself a composer of vocal music, but he is remembered as friend of Schubert and ideal interpreter of his songs. That was the way Schubert thought of him, too.

During most of 1817, Schubert was without gainful employment. That year he wrote approximately 55 songs, several piano sonatas and sonata movements, the violin/piano Sonata in A major (D.574), String Trio in B♭ (D.581), 2 overtures "in Italian style," and began Symphony No. 6 (C major, D.589; 1817–18). Of the songs, the most important are *Gruppe aus dem Tartarus* (Group from Tartarus, D.583), *Der Tod und das Mädchen* (Death and the maiden, D.531), and *Die Forelle* (The trout, D.550). Several years later, Schubert used material from *Die Forelle* and *Der Tod und das Mädchen* as the basis for variations movements in chamber music.

In autumn 1817 Schubert resumed teaching in his father's school but resigned in July 1818 to accept a position as music teacher to Count Johann Esterházy's two daughters. Early in 1818 two significant events brought Schubert's music before the public: In January his setting of Mayrhofer's *Am Erlafsee* (At Erlaf lake, D.586; September 1817) was printed in a periodical; it was the first of his works to be published. In March and again in May his C-major Italian overture was performed in concert and the performances were mentioned by the press. During the summer Schubert worked at the Esterházy residence at Zseliz, Hungary; in winter, the Esterházy family and Schubert returned to Vienna, where he continued teaching the daughters but resided with Mayrhofer. That those two piano pupils were of comparable talent is reflected in his compositions for them—about a dozen piano duets, including the Sonata in B♭ (D.617). In 1818 Schubert wrote only 14 songs, but that summer he composed a *Deutsches Requiem* (German Requiem, D.621), which his brother Ferdinand appropriated. Not until 1880 was Franz's authorship revealed.

During the next two years Schubert enjoyed being with his widening circle of friends; he composed, though he wrote few songs—22 in 1819 and 23 in 1820. Some of his music was performed in public concerts and at private gatherings other than *Schubertiaden* and his name was becoming more widely known. However, between February 1818 and November 1822 he made sketches for works that he never composed, began compositions that he never finished, and commenced others that he completed years later, e.g., Mass No. 5 (Ab major, D.678; 1819–22). Among the incomplete works is a string quartet in C minor (D.703), of which he finished only the first movement. Some sketches for an Andante in Ab major evidence that he considered writing additional movements. Known simply as *Quartettsatz* (Quartet movement), the composition marks a new seriousness, at times dark and occasionally restless, that appears in Schubert's later chamber music.

Vogl took Schubert home with him to Steyr for the summer of 1819. There, Sylvester Paumgartner commissioned Schubert to compose a piece of chamber music; the Quintet in A major (D.667) resulted. Written for piano, violin, viola, 'cello, and string bass, the work has five movements. Schubert, aware of Paumgartner's love for the song *Die Forelle,* constructed the quintet's fourth movement as variations on that Lied; from that movement comes the work's nickname, "The Trout Quintet."

Early in 1819 Schubert wrote *Die Zwillingsbrüder* (The twin brothers), a one-act *Singspiel* that was staged at Kärntnertor Theater in June 1820 with Vogl as both twins. The work had only a few performances but brought Schubert a commission to write the music for the three-act melodrama *Die Zauberharfe* (The magic harp; D.644)—music that he dashed off in about two weeks. The overture, an especially fine piece of music, has become known erroneously as the Overture to *Rosamunde*. Schubert wrote incidental music to Wihelmine von Chézy's *Rosamunde* in 1823 but composed no overture for that play.

Despite the fact that Schubert was becoming more widely known as a composer, publishers were neither anxious nor willing to issue his works. Perhaps the main reason for this was that Schubert did not concertize, and publishers believed that music by a nonconcertizing composer would not sell. In 1821 several of Schubert's friends had 20 of his songs published (as Opp. 1–8) by private subscription. In addition to benefiting from the circulation of his music, Schubert earned some money by selling dedications of the works. A few months later, the 36 waltzes for piano solo (D.365; 1816–21) and a set of 8 variations for piano duet (D.624; 1818) were published, and he was invited to contribute a variation on Diabelli's waltz theme for inclusion in that publisher's forthcoming printed collection.

Since c. 1812, Schubert had been writing choral pieces, many of them for male ensembles. One of the best of these is his setting of Goethe's *Gesang der Geister über den Wassern* (Song of the spirits over the waters, D.714; 2d version, 1821) for male double quartet (or chorus) accompanied by two violas, two 'cellos, and string bass. He continued to write solo Lieder, about a dozen in 1821 and 30 in 1822.

In Vienna, in August 1821, Schubert sketched out and partly scored his Symphony No. 7 (E major, D.729) but never finished it. (Since Schubert's death, two persons have edited or realized the sketches—in 1883 and in 1934—with less than satisfactory results.) Schubert abandoned work on the symphony when he went on vacation with Schober in September and they became absorbed in collaborating on the three-act opera *Alfonso und Estrella* (D.732; 1821–22).

Schubert's most important compositions in 1822 are *Wandererfantasie* for piano (C major, D.760; publ. 1823) and the "Unfinished" Symphony No. 8 (B minor, D.759). It is conjectured that work on the symphony was first interrupted by composition of the *Wandererfantasie,* and then several months of serious illness prevented him from resuming work on it. For the remaining few years of his life, Schubert would suffer increasingly from ever-deepening ravages of syphilis on his central nervous system. At some time in 1823, Schubert gave the autograph manuscript of the incomplete B-minor symphony to his friend Josef Hüttenbrenner for transmission to his brother Anselm, apparently as a gift. (Schubert had become acquainted with Anselm in 1815, when he, too, was studying with Salieri.) That manuscript contained the completed score of the first two movements and the first nine measures of the third. The remaining leaves in the gathering were blank; one sheet had been cut out. That missing page, found by Christa Landon (1921–77) c. 1968, contains the score for measures 10–20 of the third movement. Schubert's piano sketches for that movement have come to light, also, making it possible to construct the entire Scherzo/Trio. But there is no indication that Schubert ever planned a fourth movement. The "Unfinished" Symphony lay submerged, along with other Schubert works, in Anselm Hüttenbrenner's collection, until the 1860s; the symphony was first performed, as a two-movement work, on 17 December 1865. (In a twentieth-century edition the symphony has been completed, with Schubert's projected third movement, and, for finale, the first entr'acte of *Rosamunde* which is in B minor.)

The only significant piano solo Schubert wrote in 1823 was a piece in F minor that eventually became No. 3 in a set of six works published collectively in 1828 as *Momens musicals* [sic] (Musical moments; see p. 606). He wrote another of these (No. 6) in 1824 and the other four in 1825–27. In 1823 Schubert wrote only eight individual Lieder, four of them settings of Rückert's poems, including *Du bist die Ruh'* (You are rest, D.776). That year Schubert composed the first of his two song cycles on poems by Wilhelm Müller (1794–1827), *Die schöne Müllerin* (The fair maid of the mill, D.795). The 20 songs tell a story of the unrequited love of a young miller for Rose, the maid of the mill; when she rejects him, he commits suicide in the millstream. By 1824 publishers were more willing to print Schubert's songs—*Die schöne Müllerin* was available in Vienna in February.

Schubert was still very interested in stage works, though his operas had little success. In 1823 he composed the three-act opera *Fierabras* (D.796; first perf. 1897), which Kärntnertor Theater director Barbaia firmly rejected, albeit on theatrical rather than musical grounds. Schubert next accepted a commission to write incidental music for Chézy's Romantic play *Rosamunde*; the play had only two performances.

Schubert's entr'actes and ballet music for *Rosamunde* (D.797) are performed as concert pieces in the twentieth century.

In 1824 Schubert created three of his most important pieces of chamber music: the Octet (F major, D.803) and the string quartets in A minor (D.804) and D minor (D.810). During the summer, he again taught Esterházy's daughters at Zselig and wrote some more piano duets, including the Sonata in C major known as the "Grand Duo" (D.812). In each of the next four years Schubert wrote some four-hand piano pieces. In 1825 he composed for piano solo the sonatas in A minor (D.845) and D major (D.850) and may have begun writing Symphony No. 9 (C Major, D.944; c. 1825–28), commonly called the "Great C-Major" to distinguish it from Symphony No. 6, in the same key.

Schubert's vocal works in 1824 comprise only 3 choral pieces and 8 Lieder, but in 1825 his output of Lieder increased by 23 songs. Among them are settings of 5 songs from Sir Walter Scott's *The Lady of the Lake,* including *Ellens Gesang III* (Ellen's song III, D.839), Schubert's well-known *Ave Maria* (cf. Carr, p. 532). In 1826, Schubert wrote two dozen Lieder, including 3 Shakespeare songs and 4 *Gesänge aus Wilhelm Meister* by Goethe (Songs from *Wilhelm Meister,* D.877). One of the Goethe poems, *Nur wer die Sehnsucht kennt* (Only he who has known loneliness; also known as "None but the lonely heart") was set by many nineteenth-century composers, including Beethoven, Schumann, Tchaikovsky, Wolf, and Richard Strauss. Two of the Shakespeare songs are better known by their first lines than Schubert's titles: *Ständchen* (Serenade, D.889), generally referred to as "Hark, hark, the lark," and *Gesang. An Sylvia* (Song. To Sylvia, D.891), usually called "Who is Sylvia?"

The instrumental pieces Schubert wrote in 1826 include the String Quartet in G major (D.887), the Piano Sonata in G major (D.894), and *Rondo brilliant* (B minor, D.895; vln., pno.). The *Rondo* and the *Phantasie* (C major, D.934; 1827) were written for two Bohemian concert artists, violinist Josef Slavík (1806–33) and pianist Karl Maria von Bocklet (1801–81). The *Phantasie* indicates Schubert's recognition of the performers' talents and his knowledge of the

Figure 21.4 Moritz von Schwind's *Schubert Abend bei Josef von Spaun* (1826), a sepia drawing depicting a *Schubertiade* at Spaun's home. Schubert is at the piano; Vogl, at his right, is singing; Spaun is seated at Schubert's left, in the position of page turner. *(Historisches Museum, Vienna.)*

structural and technical capabilities of the most advanced instruments of the time. The violin part is not easy; to play it the violinist needed an instrument of modern dimensions and the Tourte-improved bow, whose resiliency would produce cleanly and easily the rapid spiccato passages. The pitch range covered in the violin part extends from g to e''''. The pianist needed a six-octave keyboard (F'–f'''') and used all of it but the top note. Slavík, the first modern Bohemian violinist to achieve international acclaim, was also a composer. He wrote at least two violin concerti, several sets of variations, and numerous other pieces for violin, but only a few of his works are extant. His sudden death at age 27 dashed hopes that he would become a second Paganini (see p. 670).

Schubert's major instrumental works in 1827 are the eight *Impromptus* for piano solo (D.899, D.935). No doubt his choice of title was influenced by Voříšek's *Impromptus,* which had been available in Vienna for several years. During November and December Schubert wrote the Piano Trio in E♭ major (D.929) that Bocklet, violinist Böhm, and 'cellist Linke performed on 26 March 1828. Sometime in 1827 or 1828 Schubert wrote the Piano Trio in B♭ major (D.898). Schubert composed a lot of vocal music in 1827: a *Deutsche Messe* (German Mass; D.872), several choral works including a setting of Grillparzer's *Ständchen* (Serenade, D.920) in two versions (alto solo with male voices, and with female voices), approximately 21 Lieder, and his second song

cycle, *Die Winterreise* (Winter journey, D.911). It comprises 24 songs, settings of Müller's poems. One of the Lieder is *Edward,* in Herder's translation (see Loewe, p. 595).

During 1826–27 numerous *Schubertiaden* were held in various Vienna homes. Schubert's circle continually widened, and a majority of those who gathered were not musicians. Some were artists who, like Moritz von Schwind, made drawings of Schubert with particular friends or sketched the groups at the gatherings (fig. 21.4).

Schubert was not well in 1828, yet he composed and participated in the gatherings or simply socialized with friends. Though he enjoyed playing music with friends and sometimes mentioned arranging a public recital, not until spring 1828 did he actually do so. He never wrote a piano concerto, nor did he ever make any sketches for one. He had no need for a concerto, for he was not a concert pianist. An all-Schubert program was presented on 26 March 1828, but the composer performed in it only as accompanist for five songs sung by Vogl.

The principal instrumental works Schubert composed in 1828 are 3 piano sonatas (C minor, D.958; A major, D.959; B♭ major, D.960) and the String Quintet in C major (D.956; 2 vln., vla., 2 vc.). His vocal compositions that year include Mass No. 6 (E♭ major, D.950), a few choral works, and 21 Lieder. Thirteen of the songs, settings of poems by Rellstab

Beethoven's Contemporaries

and Heine, were written in August and were published as a collection entitled *Schwanengesang* (Swan song, D.957; publ. 1829). *Schwanengesang* is not a song cycle. The publisher added to the collection a 14th song, a setting of Seidl's *Der Taubenpost* (The carrier pigeon, D.965a) that Schubert wrote in October 1828.

Every summer Schubert had gone on vacation with one of his friends, but in 1828 he was too exhausted to go. In September he went to live with his brother Ferdinand. There he finished the last three piano sonatas and the C-major string quintet; he played the sonatas at a friend's home the day after he completed them. In October he decided to write the song Anna Milder-Hauptmann (1785–1838), famed Berlin soprano, had requested of him—a work that would display her talents and extended vocal compass. Milder-Hauptmann, whose voice was described as being rich and flawless, had created the role of Leonore in Beethoven's *Fidelio* and sang in Vienna frequently. For her Schubert wrote *Der Hirt auf dem Felsen* (The shepherd on the rock, D.965; October 1828; voice, piano, clarinet obbligato). For text, he chose stanzas by Müller and combined them with some verses by Chézy. *Der Hirt auf dem Felsen* was Schubert's last completed song and is one of his loveliest. However, because of its wide compass (b to b″) and pseudo-yodeling effects (ex. 21.3), the vocal line is not typical of his writing. The piano accompaniment is supportive but neither descriptive nor interpretive.

By mid-November Schubert was very ill. He died on November 19 and was interred in Währing cemetery, in the fourth grave from Beethoven, whom he had greatly admired. Though Schubert and Beethoven lived near one another in Vienna, they had met only once—when Beethoven lay dying, in March 1827, Schubert went with some friends to see him. Many persons wrote poems eulogizing Schubert, and friends collected contributions for a monument-sculpture to honor him. Part of those funds were proceeds from a memorial concert given by Anna Fröhlich (1793–1880), Viennese soprano and pianist; Schubert had composed several works for her, for her sister Josefine (1803–78), who was an internationally known opera singer, and for their pupils. (Two other Fröhlich sisters were talented musically, and the Fröhlich home in Vienna was a center of musical activity.) Grillparzer, who had provided texts for several of Schubert's works, wrote his epitaph, which, in translation, reads: "Here the art of music entombed a rich possession, but even far fairer hopes."

Schubert's Music in General

Schubert was, in many respects, a Classical composer. Though he had no permanent position and no steady patron demanding specific works, many of his compositions were written to suit the talents of specific performers or ensembles—the Stadtkonvikt orchestra, the family string quartet, the neighborhood orchestra, his piano pupils, his brother Ferdinand's students or those of the Fröhlich sisters, the parish church choir, his circle of friends, Schuppanzigh's quartet, and so on. Schubert wrote no program music; only one of his instrumental pieces bears a special title of his choosing (Symphony No. 4, *Tragic*), and he left no clue to the reason for it. He used Classical formal structures, sometimes modifying them slightly, but making no radical changes. Not once, when using the four-movement complete sonata scheme, did he write a Scherzo/Trio second movement and place the slow movement third. He did, however, write a Scherzo in full sonata form for the third movement of the "Great C-Major" Symphony, follow that Scherzo with a Trio in rounded binary form, then call for *Scherzo da capo*. Schubert always used sonata form for the first movement. In some of his early works, he began the recapitulation of a sonata-form movement in the subdominant, and in the finale of the "Great C-Major" Symphony the recapitulation commences in E♭ major.

Schubert used some counterpoint in his Masses, e.g., imitative entrances of voices and fugal ending for the Gloria, but in his instrumental music he rarely used counterpoint for long stretches. Exceptions are the fugato sections in the finales of the *Wandererfantasie* (D.760) and the *Phantasie* (D.934). Though Schubert did not write extensive fugato passages in development sections, he used counterpoint skillfully, as he did when presenting portions of three themes simultaneously in the "Great C-Major" Symphony.

Example 21.3 This excerpt from Schubert's *Der Hirt auf dem Felsen* shows the wide range and pseudo-yodeling required of the vocalist. *(Source:* Franz Schuberts Werke: Kritisch durchgesehene Gesammtausgabe, *ed. J. Brahms, E. Mandyczewski, et al. Leipzig: Breitkopf & Härtel, 1864–97.)*

Schubert's violin/piano duos are filled with interesting, unobtrusive contrapuntal techniques, including rondellus (*Stimmtausch*) and canon.

Many of Schubert's compositional traits are already present in his youthful works. His characteristic techniques may be summarized as: (1) presenting the initial material in unison or in octaves; (2) using the opening material prominently in the development, but omitting it from the recapitulation; (3) concluding a movement with a citation of the material used at its commencement, either by using it to begin the coda or by making it the final statement; (4) stating the first theme of an instrumental work or the first melodic phrase of a song twice, perhaps with slight alteration the second time; (5) foreshadowing a section or a movement in the cadential motive that immediately precedes it; (6) preparing the ear to receive modulation to a certain key but abruptly shifting to a different one; (7) achieving modulation by a move of a third or via a Neapolitan progression; (8) abruptly shifting to the key of the second theme, but modulating carefully in preparation for the recapitulation; (9) fostering tonal ambiguity by wavering between major and minor or by simultaneously voicing pedals that are dominants in different keys; and

(10) writing out trill terminations rather than using symbols. Many of these traits can be found in the "Unfinished" Symphony.

Schubert's skill at modulating cannot be over-emphasized. At times, his modulations are extensive and complex; sometimes, they are concise and traditional; at other times, they are abrupt, effected by the intrusion of a single foreign note into a chord or by the insertion of a general pause and a leap into the new key. For example, a surprising modulation is made after an unexpected measure of general pause (m. 62) in the first movement of the "Unfinished" Symphony (DWMA174), and an effective sudden remote modulation from G major to B major occurs crossing from m. 200 to m. 201 in the fourth movement of the "Great C-Major" Symphony. Where key sequence was concerned, Schubert was often adventurous, and he used harmonies imaginatively—in this he was Romantic. One of his favorite technical devices was wavering, seemingly in tonal indecisiveness, between major and minor forms of a chord or a key, e.g., in the familiar *Ständchen* (Serenade) or *Das Heimweh* (Homesickness).

Vocal Music

There was not a lot of great church music produced during the first half of the nineteenth century. Schubert made six settings of the Roman Catholic Mass, and the last two of them—in A♭, D.678, and in E♭, D.950—are among the finest of that time. Much of the writing is homophonic, but Schubert supplied the traditional fugal endings where expected. The Mass in E♭, written just six months before his death, is a deeply religious and at times emotional outpouring. In Schubert's Masses, the apparent omission of portions of the standard liturgical text should not be regarded as an indication of the composer's personal beliefs. There was at that time a certain degree of laxity with regard to the Mass text, and undoubtedly Schubert set the text with which he was familiar. It should be remembered that in the late eighteenth century Joseph II had instituted some reforms that were revoked after his death, and that Enlightenment theories and beliefs had been strong in Vienna; it was not at all unusual to find slightly different versions of the liturgical text in use in the various parishes in Vienna in the early nineteenth century. Competent editors have carefully inserted the controversial "omitted" phrases of text without damaging the music. Therefore, musicological purists may perform the Mass as Schubert wrote it, and theological purists may perform it with the complete standard liturgical text. Two other excellent choral works by Schubert are *Der 92. Psalm* (The 92d Psalm, D.953; 5 soloists, mixed chorus, unaccomp.; 1828), a setting of the Hebrew text; and *Gesang der Geister über den Wassern,* for two four-part choirs of tenors and basses and a choir formed of the three lower string instruments. The three "choirs" were used in various combinations.

Schubert composed more than 600 Lieder. Formally, he used four basic types of text settings: (1) strophic, or strophic with a refrain, with each strophe (stanza) of text sung to the same music, e.g., *Heidenröslein, An Sylvia,* or *Edward*; (2) modified strophic, in which some of the strophes use identical music but changes are made in the music for parts or all of other strophes, e.g., *Die Forelle, Du bist die Ruh',* or *An den Mond*; (3) through-composed (German, *durchkomponiert*), in which the music provided for each strophe is different, e.g., *Erlkönig*; and (4) *scena,* which is sectional, with different episodes in varying *tempi* and moods, e.g., *Der Wanderer* (The Traveler, D.489) or *Die Erwartung* (Expectation, D.159).

Schubert's accompaniments vary considerably but are always suited to the text and melody of the song. In degree of difficulty for the pianist, the accompaniments range from very easy to very difficult. The folk-song-like *Heidenröslein* has a very simple accompaniment (DWMA175). For Goethe's *Meeresstille* (Calm sea, D.216) Schubert wrote rolled chords in whole notes, to be played *pianissimo*. The piano part for *Der Doppelgänger* (The shadow, or, The spectral self, D.957, No. 13) is an ominous knell that forms a ground bass with an ever-present f♯ pedal. In *Gretchen am Spinnrade* (D.118) the accompaniment represents Gretchen's restlessness and her thoughts as well as the whirring of the spinning wheel. (See ex. 21.4.)

(a)

Example 21.4 Excerpts from Schubert's Lieder illustrating various types of accompaniment he used: (*a*) *Heidenroslein*, mm. 1–4; (*b*) *Meeresstille*, mm. 1–4; (*c*) *Der Doppelganger*, mm. 1–8; (*d*) *Gretchen am Spinnrade*, mm. 1–4; (*e*) *Der Abend*, mm. 1–4. *(Source:* Franz Schuberts Werke: Kritisch durchgesehene Gesammtausgabe, *ed. J. Brahms, E. Mandyczewski, et al. Leipzig: Breitkopf & Härtel, 1864–97.)*

(b)

(c)

(d)

(e)

Schubert's setting of Goethe's *Erlkönig* resembles a miniature opera as the story dramatically unfolds (DWMA176). Besides the narrator, the characters in the dramatic poem are a father, a sick child, a horse, and the Erlking (specter of death). Schubert portrayed the different roles as he would have treated operatic actor-singers with different personalities and different vocal ranges. Before the narrator begins the story, the piano establishes the tonality and the mood by fourfold statement of the G-minor motive shown in example 21.5. The piano depicts the rhythm of the horse's hoofs and the father's anxiety as, with his ailing son in his arms, he rides homeward late at night. The boy becomes more and more frightened; with each utterance his voice rises in pitch as he tells his father about the Erlking, who, in dulcet tones, attempts to lure the child away. The father tries, unsuccessfully, to calm his son. When the text speaks of the groaning child, the piano rapidly reiterates a dissonant V_7 of C for a full measure, then moves through C minor, *fortissimo,* forcefully and chromatically into A♭ major. The riders reach their destination—the horse's hoofs are silent. Then, in *secco* recitative, *pianissimo,* the narrator states, "In his arms, the child was dead." The vocal line ends in the dominant (D) but the piano punctuates the sentence *forte,* with a V_7–I cadence in G minor—the typical conclusion for an eighteenth-century operatic recitative.

Schubert's earliest Lieder reveal the influence of Zumsteeg, especially in ballad settings. In fact, the two composers set some of the same poems in the same manner and even in the same keys. As Schubert grew older, he became more and more sensitive to the inner meaning, as well as the literal meaning and external pictorial details, of the poetry he set. He became adept at translating poetry into music, thus effecting the synthesis of music and words that created Lieder masterpieces such as the *Winterreise* song cycle. In Schubert's songs, piano and voice share the music in partnership. In this kind of Lieder writing, Schubert was a pioneer. It is understandable that publishers, seeing his music in manuscript but not hearing it performed, would regard it as unusual and hesitate to publish it. Unlike Loewe, Schubert did not promote his Lieder by concertizing.

Example 21.5 In Schubert's *Erlkönig,* mm. 1–3, this motive presented by piano establishes the mood and the key. *(Source: Franz Schuberts Werke: Kritisch durchgesehene Gesammtausgabe, ed. J. Brahms, E. Mandyczewski, et al. Leipzig: Breitkopf & Härtel, 1864–97.)*

If Schubert was not completely satisfied with a setting, or if he saw in a poem the possibilities for more than one musical interpretation, he wrote more than one setting. For example, he made five settings of *Nur wer die Sehnsucht kennt.* Schubert did not shy away from poems packed with emotion. He had available the lyric poetry of excellent authors, especially Goethe (1749–1832), Heine (1797–1856), and Müller (1794–1827), but he set texts by unknown and little-known writers and by his friends, as well as works by great authors. Schubert wrote some meaningful poetry but did not set it to music.

Piano Works

Among Schubert's keyboard works are several sets of character pieces: six *Momens musicals* [sic] (D.780, publ. 1828), eight *Impromptus* (D.899, Nos. 1–2 publ. 1827, Nos. 3–4 publ. 1857; D.935, publ. 1838), and three *Klavierstücke* (Piano pieces, D.946; comp. 1828) that were not published until 1868 when Johannes Brahms edited them anonymously. Schubert may have intended the *Klavierstücke*, composed in 1828, as part of another set of *Impromptus.* All of these pieces owe something to the *Eclogues* of Tomášek and the *Impromptus* of Voříšek but are not imitations of those composers' works.

Two of the *Momens musicals* had been published individually: No. 3, as *Air russe* (Russian air), in 1823, and No. 6, as *Plaintes d'un troubadour* (Laments of a troubadour), in 1824. Formally, No. 5 is binary; the others have alternating forms (ternary, or a kind of rondo). The *Impromptus* are larger works than the *Momens musicals.* Schubert wrote all of the *Impromptus* in flat keys, but the publisher transposed

(a)

(b)

Example 21.6 (a) The portion of Schubert's Lied *Der Wanderer* that generated the thematic material for his *Wandererfantasie* for piano; (b) beginning of *Wandererfantasie*, mvt. 2 (Adagio). *(Source: Franz Schuberts Werke: Kritisch durchgesehene Gesammtausgabe, ed. J. Brahms, E. Mandyczewski, et al. Leipzig: Breitkopf & Härtel, 1864–97.)*

No. 3 from Gb to G for the collection. The first *Impromptu* is the most elaborate one. *Impromptu* No. 3 is typical of Schubert's writing—a *cantabile* melody is accompanied by an arpeggiated sextuplet figure over chordal Romantic harmonies (DWMA177). Schumann regarded Nos. 5–8 as movements of an F-minor sonata; though the sequence of keys would be suitable, *Impromptu* No. 5 is not in sonata form, and, more importantly, Schubert gave no indication that he intended those four pieces as a sonata.

Schubert wrote 21 piano sonatas, but some are incomplete. Apparently, he planned to use the four-movement complete sonata scheme for most or all of them. His finest sonatas are the last three, composed in 1828: D.958, C minor; D.959, A major; and D.960, Bb major. Structurally, each has its first movement in sonata form; the second movement is a songlike Andante either in ternary or five-part alternating form; the third, either scherzo/trio or minuet/trio; the fourth, a kind of rondo. Thus, Schubert favored the Classical structure used by Beethoven in his early sonatas. However, Schubert's sonata-form movements

are devoid of the extensive, exhaustive type of motivic development found in Beethoven's piano sonatas. In the C-minor and A-major sonatas, Schubert introduced new themes in the development section instead of developing to the fullest the themes presented in the exposition. Stylistically, his songlike slow movements are akin to his Lieder; the third movements are light and dancelike. The tonal relationships in the Bb-major sonata are unusual: in the first movement, the second theme is introduced in the remote key of F♯ minor, then brought into the expected key of F; the second movement is in C♯ minor, the lowered mediant key in its enharmonic minor (i.e., Db minor = C♯ minor).

The *Wandererfantasie* (C major; D.760) is a cyclic work based on the line *Die Sonne dünkt mich hier so kalt* from Schubert's Lied, *Der Wanderer* (ex. 21.6). The fantasy comprises four movements designed to be played without a break. The work commences with an Allegro con fuoco, in C major, that is episodic, then moves into an Adagio theme-and-variations second movement that presents the song theme in C♯ minor and concludes the last variation with a passage in E major. The Presto that ensues is a Scherzo (A♭) with two Trios (D♭); the finale, an Allegro in C major, opens with a fugato. Intense rhythmic drive is a feature of the first Allegro.

Schubert's comments concerning piano playing, stated in a letter dated 25 July 1825, give some insight into the proper performance of his works. He was then vacationing with Spaun at Steyr and had participated in a performance of his four-hand piano sonata (D.812). He wrote, "Several people assured me that the keys become singing voices under my hands, which, if true, pleases me greatly, since I cannot endure the accursed thumping in which even distinguished pianoforte players indulge and which delights neither the ear nor the mind."

Chamber Music

From 1811 until his death Schubert was interested in performing and composing chamber music. His early chamber music, intended for school or family use, shows the influence of the orchestral works of Haydn and Mozart. Some movements in those early works follow traditional formal and harmonic patterns so strictly that they could serve as composition textbook examples. Not until 1816 did Schubert's own style begin to emerge in his chamber music.

Most of Schubert's chamber music was composed before the end of 1820—before he wrote the C-minor *Quartettsatz* (D.703; December 1820), the movement that marks the beginning of his maturity in the composition of chamber music. It is an excellent example of Schubert's mature writing for string quartet and is one of the few instances in which he used counterpoint to any extent. The main theme, only two measures long, is presented quasi-fugato but without regard for accepted rules of tonality for fugal answer. There is a countersubject—almost an exact inversion of the subject. The first subject appears also in counterpoint with the second theme, which is slightly lyrical. Schubert completed only three more string quartets: D.804 in A minor (comp. and publ. 1824); D.810 in D minor (comp. 1824; publ. 1831), known as *Der Tod und das Mädchen* because its second movement is theme and variations on a portion of that Schubert Lied; and D.887 in G major (comp.

1826; publ. 1851). In the *Quartettsatz* and in some of the sonata-form first movements of these quartets, Schubert used three key centers in both exposition and recapitulation, sometimes adjusting the order in which he recapitulated the material so that the movement would conclude in its basic key and with the thematic material that began it. For example, in the *Quartettsatz* exposition, the themes are presented in C minor, A♭ major, and G major; in the recapitulation, the second theme is returned first and the first theme last, and the keys used are B♭ major, E♭ major, and C major that eventually becomes C minor.

The A-minor quartet, intended for Schuppanzigh's quartet, has a somewhat similarly constructed first movement. This quartet contains melodic material used in several other Schubert works: the theme of the Andante was used later for an entr'acte in *Rosamunde* and also for the B♭-major *Impromptu* (D.935, No. 3); the beginning of the Menuet contains a melodic quotation from the line *Schöne Welt, wo bist du?* (Lovely world, where are you?) that commences Schubert's Lied D.677 (1819).

The D-minor quartet seems to many persons to be a musical essay on death. If this was Schubert's intention, he left no words to that effect. The second movement (Andante) of the quartet is based on his Lied, *Der Tod und das Mädchen,* and the chorale-like presentation of the theme records Death's steady approach toward the Maiden, as stated in Claudius's poem and Schubert's Lied. In the variations, the theme is in a low register much of the time. The Scherzo is very short; the Presto is a tarantelle, energetic to the point of frenzied wildness.

Schubert's last quartet, in G major, was the first work performed in his concert given 26 March 1828, the anniversary of Beethoven's death. The quartet is very long. In both first and last movements, tonality alternates between G major and G minor (or vice versa), and at times the rhythm becomes syncopated and forceful (ex. 21.7a). Some of the harmonies in the Andante are daring (ex. 21.7b)—at one point, Schubert causes a violin and viola to stubbornly remain in one key while the other two instruments begin a modulation.

Schubert's most important quintets are the Piano Quintet in A major, D.667 (comp. 1819; publ. 1829; see p. 599), and the String Quintet in C major, D.956

(a)

(b)

Example 21.7 Schubert, String Quartet, G major: (a) Mvt. 1, mm. 64–72, theme 2 uses syncopated rhythm. (b) In mvt. 2 (Andante, e minor), mm. 53–54, the harmonies were daring for that time. *(Source:* Franz Schuberts Werke: Kritisch durchgesehene Gesammtausgabe, *ed. J. Brahms, E. Mandyczewski, et al. Leipzig: Breitkopf & Härtel, 1864–97.)*

(a)

(b)

Example 21.8 Comparison of (a) Schubert's String Quartet in G major, mvt. 1, mm. 1–10, and (b) Schubert's String Quintet in C major, mvt. 1, mm. 1–13.

(comp. 1827; publ. 1850). The C-major Quintet (2 vln., vla., 2 vc.) is Schubert's chamber music masterpiece. The inclusion of a second 'cello allowed him to widen the range and group the instruments in various combinations of twos and threes. Present in the music are expressive, lyrical melodies, contrasting moods, complex rhythms. The opening of the quintet resembles that of the G-major quartet but is more effective (ex. 21.8). The five players sustain a C-major chord for two measures while increasing volume from *piano*

Beethoven's Contemporaries

to *forte*; then the chord changes to a diminished seventh, volume diminishes to *piano,* and the melody commences. The expectation of exquisite music that the opening measures arouse in the listener is amply fulfilled; this is one of the loveliest pieces of Romantic chamber music created in the first half of the nineteenth century.

Other significant chamber music by Schubert includes the Octet, the violin/piano works previously mentioned, and two Piano Trios, in B♭ major (D.898; publ. 1836) and E♭ major (D.929; publ. 1828), written in 1827–28 for performance by three of his acquaintances. The Octet was commissioned by Count von Troyer, a clarinetist working for Archduke Rudolph. Troyer knew Beethoven's Septet and asked Schubert to write a similar work. Schubert complied but added second violin to the instrumentation Beethoven had used. There are some structural and motivic similarities between the Septet and the Octet, e.g., each work has six movements, one being an Andante theme and variations, but there are definite stylistic differences. The fourth movement of the Octet uses a vocal duet (No. 12) from the *Singspiel, Der Freunde von Salamanka*. The duet and octet movement are even in the same key, C major.

Orchestral Music

Schubert wrote only three works for solo instrument and orchestra, all featuring violin: *Concertstück* (Concert piece, D major, D.345; 1816), *Rondo* (A major, D.438, with strings; 1816), *Polonaise* (B♭ major, D.580; 1817). In form, the *Concertstück* is a rondo with introduction; stylistically, it resembles a Mozart violin concerto. Whether Schubert intended the *Rondo* to be accompanied by string quartet or string orchestra has never been definitely determined.

Schubert's orchestral works consist of several overtures and nine symphonies. All of the overtures were composed before 1820; the two of his concert overtures that are best known are those "in Italian style" written in 1817, D.590 in D major and D.591 in C major.

Though Beethoven and Schubert both lived in Vienna and, undoubtedly, Schubert was familiar with Beethoven's symphonies, Schubert modeled his first six symphonies after those of Mozart and Haydn. The two Schubert symphonies most frequently performed in the twentieth century are the "Unfinished" No. 8 in B minor (D.759; publ. 1867) and the "Great C-Major" No. 9 (D.944; publ. 1840). The "Unfinished" Symphony is a Romantic work that displays well Schubert's feeling for orchestral color, his lyrical melodies, his skillful modulations.

The "Great C-Major" Symphony is very long. Portions of it contain repetitious figuration that some performers consider boring, but the work has tremendous rhythmic drive and is filled with intense emotional expression and beautiful melodies. The interval of a third figures prominently in melodies, rhythmic motifs, and tonalities throughout the composition. The second movement is a rondo in A minor. This symphony attests Schubert's ability to use counterpoint skillfully and unobtrusively and also reveals his flair for orchestral color. Some of his characteristic techniques are handled in an unusual manner, e.g., the opening theme is presented by two horns in unison *piano*, with a *pianissimo* echo, followed by a second statement of the theme by winds accompanied by strings. The first movement has three contrasting themes, in addition to the thematic material presented in the introduction; all of the themes, including the introduction, are fragmented and recombined in the development. In this work, Schubert used three trombones and frequently asked them to play *piano*. Then he went a degree further, and, at the end of the exposition in the first movement, wrote a *pianissimo* codetta for full orchestra, with the three trombones playing in unison! Had this symphony been performed when written, instead of decades later, the effect would have been novel.

Schubert's Contributions

Schubert made a vast and priceless contribution to music repertoire. He pioneered in writing Lieder in which words and music are so synthesized that the music is a translation of the poetry, and, in the last year of his life, used some harmonies and tonal effects that were striking, but his work had little effect on the development of music in history during the first half of the nineteenth century. At the time of his death, Schubert was not a major composer; he was prolific

Einfach und innig, die 2te Strophe mit dem Ausdruck der Verklärung

Wenn die Ro - sen blü - hen, hof - fe, lie - bes Herz,

pp

Example 21.9 Beginning of L. Reichardt's *Hoffnung. (Source:* The Artistic Soprano: A Collection of Standard Ballads and Arias. *Copyright © 1913 M. Witmark & Sons, New York, NY.)*

and was highly respected in his native city but little known outside of Austria. His stage works had little success. Before 1825, publishers were reluctant to issue his work, and relatively few of his compositions had been published by 1828. After his death, his compositions lay submerged for several decades, either in stacks of manuscripts on dusty shelves in publishing houses or in his friends' and acquaintances' libraries and collections. By the time his works surfaced—some of his greatest compositions did not come to light until the 1860s—any harmonies, modulations, or tonal innovations in which he actually pioneered had become ordinary musical language.

Luise Reichardt

Luise Reichardt (1779–1826), daughter of Johann F. Reichardt (1752–1814) and his first wife, Juliane Benda (1752–83), inherited musical talent from both parents. Her mother, a singer, composed some keyboard sonatas and Lieder; approximately 20 of her works survive. Luise's father, a violinist and pianist, was a prolific composer and authored many articles on music and musicians. When Luise was growing up, the Reichardt home was a meeting place for musicians, artists, writers, and other intellectuals. From time to time that circle was entertained by Luise's singing and piano playing.

By 1813 Luise had moved to Hamburg, where she taught singing and directed a women's chorus. She and her chorus were influential in the formation of the Hamburg Singverein (Singing Society) in 1819. In accord with views prevalent in the early nineteenth century, Reichardt regarded the composition of music decidedly secondary to her pedagogical career. Yet, she composed more than 100 songs and choral pieces, both sacred and secular, and most of them were published. Her first Lieder were included in a collection

with some by her father, issued in 1800. Two published collections of her songs were of sufficient importance to be reviewed in *Allgemeine musikalische Zeitung* (1806, 1827). Many of her songs remained popular throughout the nineteenth century; a few have been included in many anthologies in the twentieth century. One such song is *Hoffnung* (Hope) sometimes referred to by its opening line *"Wenn die Rosen blühen"* (When the roses bloom; or, In the time of roses; DWMA178). *Hoffnung* is comparable in style and quality with Schubert's *Heidenröslein.* The simple piano accompaniment is well suited to the folk-song-like melody (ex. 21.9). Reichardt's vocal lines are usually lyrical and the accompaniments quite simple, devoid of any special motivic interpretation of text.

Music in Italy

By the end of the eighteenth century, Austrian and German composers had assumed leadership in instrumental music. During the first half of the nineteenth century, the only area of instrumental music in which Italians produced works of any consequence was opera overture. Many of these were written in sonata form or a variant thereof and have become a part of standard concert repertoire as independent pieces. Church music continued to be a concern of Italian composers, but no outstanding works were created during the first half of the nineteenth century. Italy had a rich opera tradition, however, and early nineteenth-century Italian composers concentrated on musical theater. In Italy all opera was sung throughout; spoken dialogue made no inroads. Revolutionary opera and that dealing with contemporary social problems had little following in Italy, which was still a land of separate states (fig. 21.5).

Figure 21.5 Italian territories in the first half of the nineteenth century.

Italy was overshadowed by events in Paris, but Italian composers working in the French capital made significant contributions to the development of opera there. In fact, after beginning careers in Italy, the two greatest Italian-born composers of the time, Cherubini and Spontini, went to Paris and wrote French-language operas in the French manner.

The opera reforms advocated by Gluck and Jommelli had not been generally accepted in Italy; performances of the operas of Johannes Simon Mayr throughout the land did much to promote that acceptance. Also, the popularity of Rossini's comic operas throughout the Italian states was instrumental in effecting a unification of styles.

Johannes Simon Mayr

Mayr (1763–1845), a native of Bavaria, received his early musical training from his father, then studied composition in Italy. In Venice, Mayr first composed church music, oratorios, and cantatas. Peter von Winter and Piccinni urged him to write opera, and during 1795–1800 he wrote almost two dozen operas (both *seria* and comic) and one-act farces for Venetian theaters. Commencing with *La Lodoïska* (2d version, 1799), he provided *opere serie* more or less regularly for Milan's La Scala. With the production of *Ginevra di Scozia* (Guinevere of Scotland; Trieste, 1801), he gained renown throughout Italy.

From 1802 until his death, Mayr was *maestro di cappella* at the cathedral of Santa Maria Maggiore, Bergamo. He reorganized the cathedral choir school as Lezioni Caritatevoli de Musica and, under his supervision, that school provided its pupils, tuition free, a more complete course of study in music than was available in most Italian music schools at that time. From 1806 to 1815, Donizetti (1797–1848; see Ch. 22) was one of Mayr's pupils there.

Mayr composed 60 operas in 1794–1814 and wrote 8 more in the next decade. His masterpieces are *La rosa bianca e la rosa rossa* (The white rose and the red rose; 1813), and *Medea in Corinto* (Medea in Corinth; 1813), modeled after Cherubini's *Médée*. In his writing, Mayr put into practice many of the reforms advocated by Gluck. Consistently, instead of writing exit arias, Mayr had the *prima donna* or *primo uomo* sing a cavatina at the beginning of a scene and remain on stage for continuation of the action. He included a considerable number of ensembles in his operas. Through use of accompanied recitative, he skillfully constructed long dramatic segments in which several scenes were bridged; *Medea in Corinto* and *La rosa bianca . . .* provide excellent examples of this, a feature that later nineteenth-century composers incorporated in their operas. Mayr also used a device that Rossini adopted—the so-called Rossini crescendo: short motivic figures are repeated, over alternating tonic and dominant pedals, with gradually thickening orchestration to create a crescendo effect. In his operas, Mayr combined Italianate melody with German harmonies and an orchestration characterized by independent writing for winds. Frequently, he included obbligato passages.

After 1815, Mayr devoted most of his time to church music. There exist in manuscript more than 600 works that Mayr would not allow to be published; in addition to 4 published writings on music, at least 16 more survive in manuscript.

Gioachino Rossini

Gioachino Rossini (1792–1868) was the principal Italian composer working in Italy in the first quarter of the nineteenth century. His work, equally important in *opera seria* and *opera buffa,* marks the transition from eighteenth-century to nineteenth-century styles in Italian opera. After a successful career in Italy, he moved to Paris where he contributed significantly to the development of grand opera.

Rossini was born in Pesaro, a small city on the Adriatic coast of the Papal States. He became aware of opera at an early age, for his parents were musicians employed by a traveling opera company. Rossini's father taught him to play horn, and he had some music lessons from a local priest. In 1804 Rossini entered the Liceo Musicale in Bologna, where he studied composition and counterpoint with Padre Stanislao Mattei (1750–1825), singing, 'cello, and piano—courses that prepared him well for opera composition. Mattei, pupil of G. B. Martini, was particularly celebrated as a teacher. While a student, Rossini wrote a Mass and some other sacred music, some instrumental pieces, and a cantata (rather poor, though it won a prize and was performed at the Liceo). In 1805,

Gioachino Rossini. (Photograph.)

he sang the role of the boy Adolfo in Ferdinando Paer's (1771–1839) *Camilla* at Teatro del Corso, Bologna, and in 1806 was honored with membership in the Bologna Accademia Filarmonica.

Rossini's first opera, *Demetrio e Polibio* (Demetrius and Polibius), a two-act *dramma serio,* was commissioned c. 1808 by the tenor of an opera troupe, who may have tampered with the composition. It was not performed until 1812; by that time, Rossini had written several more operas. His career as opera composer really began in 1810, when Teatro San Moïse, Venice, commissioned *La cambiale di matrimonio* (The marriage contract). There were early indications that Rossini would be a prolific composer of operas—five of his works were produced in 1812, among them the sacred opera *Ciro in Babilonia* (Cyrus in Babylon, sometimes called an oratorio) performed at Ferrara during Lent; *La scala di seta* (The silken ladder) performed in Venice in May; and *La pietra del paragone* (The touchstone) performed at Milan's La Scala in November. Because Rossini composed operas in quick succession, he did a considerable amount of self-borrowing. Musical materials—

even entire pieces—from early works found their way into later compositions. *Demetrio e Polibio* was particularly serviceable in this respect.

Two of the four operas Rossini wrote in 1813 brought him international acclaim: *Tancredi* (Tancred, an *opera seria*) and *L'italiana in Algieri* (The Italian woman in Algiers, an *opera buffa*). In *Tancredi,* formal numbers are separated by *secco* recitative, in traditional eighteenth-century manner, but within the numbers there are important dramatic events. As did Mayr, Rossini opened a scene with a cavatina. This might comprise two successive lyrical sections (*cantabile* solo and *cabaletta*), or it might consist of a short lyrical solo, a nonlyrical choral interruption in a contrasting key, and *cabaletta* in the same key as the opening solo. An example of the latter type of cavatina is Amenaide's prayer scene *Giusto Dio che umile adoro* (Just God whom I humbly worship), Act II, *Tancredi.* By writing this kind of scene, a composer prevents an aria from freezing the action. A **cabaletta** is a short aria that has a persistent rhythm and a repeat that permits the soloist to improvise embellishments. When used in the finale of an act, the *cabaletta* (there called the **stretta**) is usually in a fairly rapid tempo, and there is mounting excitement.

Though castrato singing was declining in fashion, Rossini wrote a few castrato roles. The great soprano Giambattista Velluti (1781–1861) sang the role of Arsace in *Aureliano in Palmira* (December 1813). Usually, Rossini wrote leading roles for the natural male voice. However, in several operas he wrote **breeches** roles (male roles sung by women). In *Tancredi,* the role of the hero is for contralto and was first sung by Adelaide Malanotte (1785–1832).

Copyright laws were nonexistent in Italy then, and opera composers did not receive royalties from extra performances of their works but were paid for performances only when they participated in them. Therefore, it was to Rossini's advantage to compose many operas and, whenever possible, to be at the keyboard when those operas were performed. From 1813 through 1819, he had commissions from several theaters in Venice, Rome, and Naples and composed from two to four operas per year.

Neapolitan opera was becoming stagnant. In an effort to revitalize it, impresario Domenico Barbaia contracted with Rossini to serve as musical and artistic director for his theaters and to compose operas for them; Rossini retained the right to travel and to compose for other theaters. From 1815 to 1822, Rossini worked under that contract and gradually overcame Neapolitan resistance to his foreign invasion. For Naples Rossini composed principally *opera seria*. The initial opera under his new contract, *Elisabetta, regina d'Inghilterra* (Elizabeth, queen of England; October 1815), marks his first use of *recitativo accompagnato* (accompanied by strings). Accompanied recitative was not new to Naples, however, for Mayr had used it in *Medea in Corinto* (1813). Isabella Colbran (1785–1845), who had been Medea in Mayr's opera, created the role of Queen Elizabeth; that of Norfolk was sung by tenor Manuel García.

Colbran, the leading dramatic coloratura soprano of the early nineteenth century, sang opera in Barbaia's Teatro San Carlo from 1811 to 1823. Rossini designed leading roles in several of his operas to display her talents. Colbran and Rossini married in 1822. She retired from the stage in 1824, after a disastrous performance in Rossini's opera *Zelmira* in London. Colbran was also a composer; she wrote four volumes of songs.

Rossini followed *Elisabetta* with two works for Rome: the rescue opera *Torvaldo e Dorliska* (1815), and the comedy *Almaviva, ossia L'inutile precauzione* (Almaviva, or The useless precaution; 1816), based on Beaumarchais's play, *Le barbier de Séville* (The barber of Seville). *Almaviva* was chosen as title for Rossini's opera to distinguish it from Paisiello's (1740–1816) *Il barbiere di Siviglia* (1782). The only similarities between Paisiello's and Rossini's operas are the dramatic situations. Cesare Sterbini wrote new verse for Rossini's libretto, added chorus, and created the old servant Berta, who sings a substantial aria in Act II. Berta is not essential to the plot; in fact, her aria stalls its progress. Rossini wrote the role of Almaviva for Manuel García. Briefly, the story is this: Young Count Almaviva, the student, uses two disguises (soldier and music teacher) to win Rosina, ward of Dr. Bartolo, who intends to marry her for her fortune. Figaro, barber and factotum, becomes involved in all aspects of the plot. Ultimately, the Count wins Rosina, and Bartolo gets the fortune.

Il barbiere di Siviglia is Rossini's masterpiece, his best-known work, one of the great Italian comic operas of all time. Yet, *Almaviva* was a failure on opening night. Why? Perhaps the Roman audience interpreted Rossini's changes and his new style as lack of respect for Paisiello, who was still living, and whose *Il barbiere di Siviglia* was highly regarded in Rome. Perhaps any new opera on that plot would have been considered impertinent and would have been given similar reception. Rossini's contract called for three performances, and at least that many were given. When the opera was produced in Bologna during the summer of 1816, only the title was new, *Il barbiere di Siviglia*. The *Almaviva* performed in Rome on 20 February 1816 was essentially the same *Il barbiere di Siviglia* known in the twentieth century. It was the first opera sung in Italian in New York, brought there in 1825 by Manuel García and his opera troupe (Insight, "The Garcías").

In *Il barbiere di Siviglia* Rossini used *secco* recitative for much of the dialogue but wrote sectionalized arias and ensemble finales. The opera provides excellent examples of Rossini's style and musical wit. One such is Bartolo's very rapid patter song, *A un dottor della mia sorte* (To a doctor of my sort), for which Rossini used sonata form in subtle satire of the tutor's pedantry. Basilio's *La calunnia* (Slander; DWMA179) displays the "Rossini crescendo" at its finest. The orchestral phrase basic to the crescendo is first presented by strings, playing *sul ponticello, pianissimo* (ex. 21.10). With each repetition of the passage its register ascends and, gradually, orchestral forces are increased; strings return to normal bowing position, and articulation becomes staccato—an excellent musical depiction of spreading rumor!

Rossini wrote two more operas for Neapolitan theatres, then composed *La Cenerentola* (Cinderella; January 1817) for Rome and *La gazza ladra* (The thieving magpie; May 1817) for Milan. The operas Rossini wrote under his Neapolitan contract show (1) a gradual decrease in the number and prominence of solo arias, (2) an increase in the number and length

Example 21.10 Rossini, *Il barbiere di Siviglia*, "La Calunnia," mm. 18–24 of the Allegro. In m. 20 the strings present the basic figure that is repeated several times to produce the so-called Rossini crescendo.

of ensembles, (3) more use of accompanied recitative and use of a more dramatic type of accompanied recitative, (4) treatment of the chorus as an active participant in the drama, and (5) a growing tendency to notate embellishments rather than allow soloists to improvise them at will.

Rossini's 34th opera, the last he wrote for an Italian theater, was *Semiramide* (Venice, 1823), a tragedy: The Babylonian queen Semiramide, aided by Assur, has poisoned King Ninus, but instead of appointing Assur to rule with her, she chooses Arsace, who eventually turns out to be the long-lost son she had with Ninus. To avenge his father's murder, Arsace attempts to slay Assur, but Semiramide rushes between them and receives the fatal thrust. The opera is filled with Romantic elements: the festival, Ninus's ghost summoning Arsace to the king's tomb, the Magi's shocking revelation of Arsace's identity, the gloomy scene at the tomb when Semiramide is slain. In *Semiramide* Rossini used reminiscence motives effectively. At the première, the role of Semiramide was sung by Isabella Colbran, for whom it had been designed; that of Arsace, written for contralto, was sung by Rosa Mariani.

While in Italy, Rossini did not write opera exclusively. He composed a dozen cantatas, some incidental music, miscellaneous vocal pieces, and several sacred works, including a *Messa di gloria* (1820) in which he combined operatic and traditional nonoperatic compositional techniques.

The Rossinis left Italy in autumn 1823, traveling first to Paris to negotiate future work, then going to London. A Rossini season at King's Theater in 1824 was, for the most part, unsuccessful. Colbran was in poor voice; Rossini wrote no new works. In August 1824 Rossini contracted to become director of Théâtre-Italien in Paris and to write operas for that theater and L'Opéra. Under his direction, Théâtre-Italien attained its greatest glory. He produced not only his own works but Italian operas by other composers, including Meyerbeer's *Il crociato in Egitto* (The crusader in Egypt). That production launched Meyerbeer's career in Paris and marked the beginning of an enduring friendship between Rossini and Meyerbeer.

The only new opera Rossini composed for Théâtre-Italien was an occasional work, *Il viaggio a Reims, ossia L'albergo del giglio d'oro* (The journey to Rheims, or The Golden Lily Inn; 19 June 1825), a one-act *dramma giocoso* performed in conjunction with festivities at the coronation of Charles X. The plot of *Il viaggio . . .* is directly related to the coronation, and events in the opera take place in the course of a single day: Plans to attend the coronation of Charles X are foiled when no horses are available for the journey to Rheims, but guests at the Inn are resourceful—they organize a feast and, in the finale, toast the king and sing anthems from their native lands. The score of *Il viaggio a Reims* disappeared for a time, resurfaced c. 1850, then was lost again. Somehow, the autograph copy of the music found its way to the library of Santa Cecilia, Rome, and remained there uncataloged for over a century. The music came to light in the early 1980s, and the work

insight

The Garcías

Manuel García (1775–1832), Spanish tenor, was educated at Seville Cathedral's choir school. By the age of 18, he was well known in Spain as singer, composer, and conductor of opera. His *El seductor arrepentido* (The repentant seducer; 1802) was one of the earliest Spanish operettas. García worked in Paris from 1808 to 1811, then went to Italy to sing opera. There he met Rossini, and for him created the roles of Norfolk in *Elisabetta* (1815) and Almaviva in *Il barbiere di Siviglia* (1816). García was acclaimed internationally as singer. He sang Almaviva in the première of *Il barbiere di Siviglia* in Italian in London, Paris, New York, and elsewhere in the Americas.

García formed an opera company that included his family and three other singers and in 1825 brought Italian opera, sung in Italian, to America. The troupe performed 6 Rossini operas, Mozart's *Il Don Giovanni,* and some of García's more than 40 operas and operettas. Lorenzo da Ponte, librettist for *Il Don Giovanni,* was living in America and assisted with that production in New York. The García company remained in the New World until 1829, then returned to Paris. García was an excellent singing teacher. All four of his children, whom he taught, had careers in music: Josefa Ruiz-García, Manuel Patricio García, Pauline Viardot (1821–1910), and Maria Malibran (1808–1836).

Pauline Viardot excelled at singing highly dramatic roles. Her performances benefited the careers of several opera composers, including Gounod, Massenet, and Fauré; she was one of the first to perform Brahms's *Alt-Rhapsodie.* Viardot composed some operettas, some of which have remained in the repertoire, e.g., *Cendrillon* (1904), performed at Newport, Rhode Island, in 1971. Many of her songs have been published, some of them settings of Russian texts.

Manuel P. García (b. 17 March 1805, d. 1 July 1906, age 101), a baritone, sang opera professionally until 1829. After the García opera company returned to Paris, he taught singing and began to study the physiology of the voice. In 1840 he presented to the Académie des Sciences, Paris, his *Mémoire sur la voix humaine* (Report on the human voice), a treatise that formed the basis for all subsequent investigations into physiology of the voice. Also in 1840, his *Traité complet de l'art du chant* (Treatise on the art of singing) was published in Paris. García taught at Paris Conservatoire (1847–50) and at the Royal Academy of Music, London (1848–95). In 1855 he invented the laryngoscope, and for this Königsberg University awarded him a Ph.D.

---

was performed to open the Rossini Opera Festival at Pesaro in 1984. *Il viaggio a Reims* was given its American première on 12 June 1986 by the Opera Theater of St. Louis, Missouri.

Late in 1826 Rossini relinquished some of his responsibilities at Théâtre-Italien. He had been appointed *Premier compositeur du roi* (First royal composer) and *Inspecteur général du chant en France* (Inspector general of singing in France); now, he wanted to concentrate on writing music in the French style for L'Opéra. His first works along that line were revisions of two of his Neapolitan operas: *Maometto II* (Mohammed II; 1820) became *Le siège de Corinthe* (The siege of Corinth; 1826), a *tragédie lyrique*; and *Mosé in Egitto* (Moses in Egypt; 1818) became *Moïse et Pharaon, ou Le passage de la Mer Rouge* (Moses and Pharaoh, or The passage through the Red Sea; 1827), an *opéra.* The revisions were extensive, amounting to more than using the French language and adding ballet. New librettists altered the plots; the music was rewritten. Each opera was lengthened by one act. The setting of *Maometto II* was changed from Venice to Greece, in order to incorporate current events—the Greeks had risen against the Turks in a fight for independence that was to last until 1833. The role of Mohammed II was rewritten for tenor; arias were divested of much floridity and were less important; solo voices were combined with chorus dramatically.

Then, Rossini was ready to write new operas. Working with librettists Scribe and Delestre-Poirson, he composed *Le Comte Ory* (Count Ory; perf. August 1828), an *opéra comique* in which he incorporated some of the music of *Il viaggio a Reims.* In structure,

Beethoven's Contemporaries

Le Comte Ory is episodic (a structure that would be favored by Berlioz; see p. 667); it contains only one virtuosic aria.

For his next opera, Rossini used a historical, patriotic theme—the heroic ventures of William Tell during the Swiss struggle for freedom from oppression. *Guillaume Tell* (William Tell; August 1829) was Rossini's last opera. Produced when the Revolution of 1830 was brewing, the opera stirred the sympathies of the French for their own cause. *Guillaume Tell* is one of the first important grand operas. Rossini integrated spectacular crowd scenes, processions, and ballets into the story, and the chorus is central to the drama. The Swiss freedom fighters' ceremonial vow in the finale of Act II is magnificent. *Guillaume Tell* is the first opera in which Rossini used local color to any extent; for the *ranz des vaches* he used actual quotations from a Swiss cowherd's horn call. Characterizations are excellent; reminiscence motives are used effectively. In *Guillaume Tell* Rossini skillfully united Italian lyricism with French declamation and spectacle.

For the remainder of his life Rossini lived in semiretirement, in Italy (1836–55) and in Paris (1855–68). Various reasons for his failure to write another opera have been advanced: weariness, illness, marital problems, differences of opinion with the new administration of Théâtre-Italien and L'Opéra. All have a few grains of truth in them; none have been proven. There is some evidence that he intended *Guillaume Tell* to be his last opera. However, in 1829 he negotiated with the French government and Charles X a contract that provided Rossini a lifetime annuity and stipulated that he would write four new operas, one every other year. While the Rossinis were visiting Bologna, the Revolution of 1830 occurred, Charles X was dethroned, and Rossini's contract and annuity were canceled. He took legal action to get the annuity reinstated.

Rossini did not give up composition entirely. From time to time, he wrote cantatas and choral works for special religious and state occasions, other sacred and secular vocal music, and a few instrumental pieces. Most significant of these works are the *Stabat mater* (in its 2d version, 1841); the *Petite messe solenelle* (Little solemn Mass; Paris, 1864), commissioned by Countess Louise Pillet-Will for consecration of her private chapel; and *Péchés de vieillesse* (Sins of old age; 1857–68), 150 pieces of vocal and instrumental music that Rossini called albumleaves. These pieces of musical wit, which he did not want published, were created for performance at his *samedi soirées,* Saturday evening gatherings held at the Rossini home in Paris. Programs presented at those *soirées* were of sufficient consequence to receive reviews in Paris music journals. Rossini's albumleaves show that his musical ingenuity never diminished. He kept abreast of contemporary developments in music and sometimes was ahead of them. Some of the piano pieces are quite difficult, e.g., *Prélude prétentieux* (Pretentious prelude), whose fugal subject and parodies of contrapuntal devices reveal Rossini's serious study of and admiration for the works of J. S. Bach. Many of Rossini's other piano albumleaves and the *Petite messe* show this, too. From 1857 until his death, Rossini subscribed to the critical edition of Bach's works.

Isabella and Rossini legally separated in 1837; after her death in 1845, he married Olympe Pellisier. Since 1840 Rossini had suffered from a chronic disease that slowly worsened; he became seriously ill in autumn 1868 and died in November. He was buried in Père Lachaise cemetery, Paris, until Olympe died in 1887; then his remains were moved to Santa Croce, Florence. In his Will, Rossini provided for the establishment of a Liceo Musicale in Pesaro and two annual prizes in composition (for lyrics, and for music) to be awarded in Paris. His autograph music was left to the commune of Pesaro, and in the 1970s the Fondazione Rossini began work on a critical edition of his complete works.

Music in Iberia

Portuguese pianist-composer João D. Bomtempo (1775–1842) is considered one of the principal reformers of music in Portugal, which, at the beginning of the nineteenth century, was dominated by Italian opera. Among Bomtempo's works are two symphonies, six piano concerti, numerous piano pieces, some chamber music, and some sacred music. His finest work is the *Requiem Mass* (1819) in memory of the great sixteenth-century poet Camões. Bomtempo was the first Portuguese composer of symphonies. He created the Philharmonic Society and, through it, the first Portuguese symphony orchestra. In 1822, he began a regular series of concerts at which symphonies and chamber music of Haydn, Mozart, and Beethoven were performed. As Principal of the Conservatório Nacional de Musica, which he founded in 1835, Bomtempo was influential in transforming music teaching in Portugal.

After the French invasion of Portugal in 1807, the Portuguese royal court moved to Rio de Janeiro and did not return to Lisbon until 1821, shortly before Brazil achieved its independence.

In Spain, as in Portugal, music was dominated by Italian opera at the beginning of the nineteenth century. The most important Spanish composers left their native land to work in Paris, London, or Russia. In the case of guitar virtuoso Fernando Sor (1778–1839), the move was obligatory. He fought against the French at the time of their invasion but c. 1810 accepted an administrative post in the French government; after the French retreated (1813), Sor had to leave Spain. Sor's earliest surviving work is the opera *Il Telemaco nell' isola de Calipso* (Telemachus on Calypso's isle; 1797). While in Spain, Sor composed two symphonies, three string quartets, a cantata, a motet, and a Mass, none of which have been located. In Paris and London, he was acclaimed as much for his 33 Italian ariettas (vc., pno.) and ballets as for his guitar playing. His ballet *Cendrillon* (1822) brought fame to dancer Maria Mercandotti; it was performed more than 100 times in Paris and was chosen for the grand opening of Moscow's Bol'shoy Theater (1825). Stylistically, Sor's music owes a great deal to Mozart and Haydn. In the late twentieth century, Sor is best known for his contribution to classical guitar repertoire: approximately 70 compositions and *Méthode pour la guitare* (Guitar method; Paris, 1830).

Music in America

Latin and South America

Between 1810 and 1830 Latin American colonies began to gain independence; Mexico did so in 1821. The principal Mexican composer in the early nineteenth century was José M. Elizaga (1786–1842), who was instrumental in founding the Sociedad Filarmónica in Mexico City. In 1825, that society sponsored Mexico's first conservatory. Elizaga composed mainly church music in Classical style. He was well acquainted with the music of Mozart and Beethoven and pioneered in promoting performances of their music in Mexico.

Most of the performances at Coliseo Nuevo in Mexico City were by European artists, though a few comedies with music by native composers were presented. Until the 1820s, European troupes performed operas in Spanish translation. Manuel García and his company were the first to sing Italian opera in Italian in Mexico City when, on 29 June 1827, they performed Rossini's *Il barbiere di Siviglia*. Commencing in 1831, an Italian opera season was an annual event at Teatro Principal, and until 1871 even native-born composers had to write their operas in Italian to get them performed in Mexico City.

Before Brazil acquired independence (1822), most of the music making there was associated directly with church services. Around 1800, in Minas Gerais province, hundreds of native musicians and composers were active. Though the vast majority were members of local music guilds independent of the clergy, most of the compositions that have been located are Masses, motets, and other liturgical music. The only known work in the vernacular—portions of a Christmas oratorio (1789)—was found in 1967.

As a result of French invasion of Portugal in 1807, Queen Maria I (r. 1777–1816) and her son Dom João (regent for Maria 1799–1816; King John VI, r. 1816–26) moved the Portuguese royal court to Rio de Janeiro, where the establishment of a royal chapel stimulated musical activities considerably. However, Marcos Portugal (1762–1830), court *mestre de capela,* was enjoying great success producing his Italian operas in Europe and remained in Lisbon until 1811. Then he and his brother Simão (1774–c. 1842) went to Rio, Marcos resumed his previous court position, and Simão became royal organist. For almost a decade Marcos exercised what amounted to musical dictatorship at court and in the city. He produced several of his old Italian operas there as well as some new ones and composed a comic opera, *A saloia namorada* (A peasant girl in love; 1812), on a libretto by Brazilian poet Domingos C. Barbosa. Marcos's own catalog of his works lists 35 Italian operas, 21 Portuguese comic operas, and more than 100 pieces of church music. His sacred music is Italianate, and his operas are Neapolitan in style. When the Portuguese court returned to Lisbon in 1821, Marcos remained in Rio. He composed the Brazilian *Hino da independência* (Hymn of independence) first performed 12 October 1822.

From 1808 to 1811, José Mauricio Nunes García (1767–1830), a native of Rio de Janeiro and *mestre de capela* at Rio de Janeiro Cathedral, served as *mestre de capela* and music director at the Portuguese court. José Mauricio is considered one of Brazil's finest composers. Of his extant compositions, 225 are liturgical, 5 are instrumental, 5 are secular vocal works and include one opera. The influence of Viennese Classical style and traces of Baroque compositional practices (e.g., some figured bass) are apparent in his works. His masterpiece is the grandiose and deeply religious *Requiem Mass* (1816) commissioned for the funeral services of Queen Maria I. The Mass is scored for SATB chorus and soloists, with orchestra of strings, pairs of clarinets and horns, and "flutes, trumpets, and kettledrums *ad libitum.*"

In the La Plata River Viceroyalty, Buenos Aires was the most important city musically, with activity centered in the church and the theater. Plays with music (*tonadillas* and *zarzuelas*) were presented in Buenos Aires theaters in the late eighteenth century, and Italian operas were performed regularly after 1824. In the early nineteenth century, the city's musical life was strongly influenced by José Picassari (1769–1843), *maestro de capilla* of Buenos Aires Cathedral. In 1822 he established the Escuela de Música y Canto (School of Music and Singing) and helped found the Sociedad Filarmónica.

North America

During the first quarter of the nineteenth century, European professional musicians came to the United States to concertize and to give theatrical performances, chiefly ballad operas and plays with incidental music. Some of those professionals settled in America, e.g., oboist Gottlieb Graupner (1767–1836), organist George K. Jackson (1745–1823), and librettist Lorenzo da Ponte. The leading musical centers were Philadelphia, New York, and Boston. Polemical writings appeared debasing fuging tunes and other pieces by singing-school music masters and praising the works of Handel and Haydn. Late in 1815 a handful of American musicians and European professionals in Boston, including Graupner and Jackson, founded the Handel and Haydn Society for the performance of choral and instrumental music. The Society's first concert was presented on Christmas night by a chorus of 90 men and 10 women. Similar societies were established in other major cities. In 1825 Rossini's *Il barbiere di Siviglia* and Mozart's *Il Don Giovanni* and other Italian operas were performed in Italian in New York by Manuel García's opera company. Tune books were compiled and some popular songs written, but there were no outstanding American-born composers or performers during the first quarter of the nineteenth century.

In Canada, during the first two-thirds of the nineteenth century there was continuous westward territorial expansion; cultural activities were local and depended to a great extent on talents of local residents. The centers of musical activity were the local church, the coffee house, and, in larger communities, the military band. Gradually, local musicians organized community bands. Touring companies performed ballad operas in Quebec, Montreal, and Halifax. In 1820 Thomas Linley's comic opera *The Duenna* was presented in St. John's, Newfoundland; the first opera produced in Newfoundland, it played for almost two weeks, with proceeds benefiting local fire victims.

Summary

In the first half of the nineteenth century, musical interest in France was centered on opera. At first, the focus was on *opéra comique*—it became popular in Austro-Germanic lands, too, and, for a time, dominated the repertoire there. Paris became the opera capital of the world and attracted Italian opera composers who remained there and eventually wrote operas in the French style. For a time, *opéra comique* served as a vehicle for patriotism; then lighter types of *opéra comique* became the vogue. All-sung opera, though still performed, was pushed into the shadows until the 1820s.

Cherubini's rescue operas, particularly *Les deux journées,* served as models for similar operas by composers throughout Europe. Use of recurrent themes, or reminiscence motives, a feature of the operas of Cherubini, Méhul, and other composers working in Paris, led to the *Leitmotif* used by Weber. Auber, in his *opéras comiques,* achieved a blend of comic and Romantic elements, then turned to a more serious and more lyrical type. Parisian composers did not limit their writing to opera. Cherubini wrote some of the finest Catholic Masses produced during the first half of the nineteenth century, and Méhul composed symphonies. Many composers were concerned educators who helped formulate governmental educational policies, taught at the Paris Conservatoire, and determined its curricula.

Before 1820 very few all-sung operas were successful in Paris. Napoleon favored the spectacular, especially if it honored himself and France; through Royal Privilèges, he controlled what was staged. Two of the earliest nineteenth-century spectacular operas were Spontini's *La Vestale* (1807) and *Fernand Cortez* (1809), significant forerunners of the monumental grand operas produced at L'Opéra in the late 1820s. Spontini's *tragédies lyriques* were a continuation of the traditional French form of opera; thus, he forged another link in the chain—Lully, Rameau, Gluck, Spontini—that led to Berlioz. The earliest successful grand opera was Auber's *La muette de Portici* (1828), on a libretto by Scribe; another was Rossini's *Guillaume Tell* (1829). Through the joint efforts of Scribe, Meyerbeer, and Véron in the early 1830s, grand opera masterpieces were produced and standards established. Changes in theatrical practices in the 1820s—new methods of lighting and scenic design—greatly affected opera production.

In Austro-Germanic lands, the most significant contributions made by Beethoven's contemporaries were in the areas of solo song (Lied) and opera. Collections of folk (or pseudo-folk) poetry inspired many song settings; opera libretti were based on German fairy tales. German nationalism entered opera gradually through legend and fairy tale; elements of magic and the supernatural appeared in *Singspiele*. In 1816, Hoffmann's *Undine* and Spohr's *Faust* prepared the way for Weber, who firmly established German Romantic opera in *Singspiel* with *Der Freischütz* (1821)

and in *opera seria* with *Euryanthe* (1823). Gradually, recitative supplanted spoken dialogue in German operas, but melodrama was retained for special effects. Weber and other German composers strove towards *Gesamtkunstwerk,* a unification of all of the arts through opera. Weber's constant struggles to effect theatrical reforms did a great deal to improve standards of opera production. Minor German composers who made significant contributions to opera include Marschner and Lortzing. German composers did not limit themselves to opera. Spohr and Weber were competent conductors; Hoffmann was author, music critic, and painter. Weber, a virtuoso pianist, contributed to the repertoire for clarinet as well; his works for unaccompanied male chorus in *Leyer und Schwert* were among the earliest of many such patriotic German songs in the nineteenth century. Weber's published critical essays anticipated the editorial writings of Schumann.

Most important among the many composers of Lieder and ballads were Loewe and Schubert. Both were prolific composers writing in many musical media, but they are remembered chiefly for their solo songs with piano accompaniment. In his Lieder Schubert so synthesized words and music that his music was a translation of the poetry. Though overshadowed by Beethoven's accomplishments in the areas of symphony and chamber music, Schubert's late string quartets and last two symphonies are important contributions to the repertoire. Also, he composed some of the finest settings of the Catholic Mass written in the first half of the nineteenth century. Because many of Schubert's works were not widely disseminated during his lifetime and were disregarded, forgotten, or lost for some time after his death, they exercised little influence upon most of his immediate successors. Later in the century, as Schubert's works gradually came to light, they had significant influence upon the works of major composers.

Italy, which had held leadership in the musical world for so long, took a lesser role in the early nineteenth century. Many Italian composers were attracted to Paris; Cherubini and Spontini made significant contributions to the development of opera in France. Italy's rich opera tradition was not lost, however, for in Italy composers concentrated on opera.

Spoken dialogue made no inroads—all opera was sung throughout. Mayr, a Bavarian working in Italy, put into practice many of the operatic reforms advocated by Gluck and Jommelli and did much to promote acceptance of those reforms throughout nonunified Italy. Besides writing 60 operas, Mayr composed a vast amount of church music, taught, and greatly improved the quality of music education in his locale.

Rossini was the principal Italian composer working in Italy in the first quarter of the nineteenth century. His work, equally important in *opera seria* and *opera buffa,* marks the transition from eighteenth- to nineteenth-century styles in Italian opera. After a successful career in Italy, he moved to Paris, where he contributed significantly to the development of grand opera. Though Rossini preferred to write for the natural male voice, he occasionally wrote for castrati, and in several operas designed the hero's role to be sung by a woman. After the Revolution of 1830, Rossini ceased writing opera and turned to other types of composition. His most important nonoperatic work is the *Stabat mater.*

Manuel García, for whom Rossini designed the role of Almaviva in *Il barbiere di Siviglia,* performed Rossini's works throughout Europe and America. It was García's troupe who first performed opera in Italian in the United States and Mexico. Pauline García Viardot composed operettas and songs; her operatic performances promoted the careers of several French composers later in the nineteenth century. After a short career as singer, Manuel P. García became both scientist and singing teacher; he invented the laryngoscope and wrote the treatise that formed the basis for all subsequent investigations into physiology of the voice.

At the beginning of the nineteenth century, music in Iberia was dominated by Italian opera, but with Napoleon's invasions conditions changed. The Portuguese royal court moved to Brazil, and several Spanish and Portuguese composers pursued their careers elsewhere in Europe, e.g., guitarist Sor and pianist Bomtempo. Later, some composers returned to Portugal, as did Bomtempo; he was the first Portuguese composer to write symphonies.

Between 1810 and 1830 Latin American colonies began to acquire independence. The principal nineteenth-century Mexican composer was Elizaga, who wrote mainly church music. He was influential in founding Mexico's first music conservatory and promoted performances of Mozart's and Beethoven's music in Mexico.

In Brazil, hundreds of native musicians and composers were active; most of their known compositions are liturgical music. Marcos Portugal, court *mestre de capela,* composed Italian and Portuguese operas and church music that is Italianate in style. José Mauricio, one of Brazil's finest native composers, wrote mainly liturgical music in Viennese Classical style; his masterpiece is his Requiem Mass (1816). In the La Plata River Viceroyalty, Buenos Aires was the most important city musically, with activity centered in the church and in opera.

In the United States, European professional musicians concertized and gave theatrical performances. The leading centers of music were Boston, New York, and Philadelphia. Tune books were compiled and some popular songs were written, but there were no outstanding American-born composers or performers during those years.

In Canada the centers of musical activity were local—the church and the coffee house. In the larger communities, the military band was an important influence, inspiring local musicians to organize community bands. Touring companies from England performed ballad operas; Linley's comic opera, *The Duenna,* was the first opera produced in Newfoundland.

Musical Expansion in Mid-Nineteenth Century

Between 1825 and 1870, the two developments with the most significant social and political consequences were industrialization and the rise of nationalism. Of course, industrialization brought with it increased urbanization. Great factories with powered machinery appeared throughout Europe, and wealthy industrialists and merchants sought to dominate politics. Among the interesting industrial procedures was the Jacquard loom, invention of J. M. Jacquard of Lyons, in which a series of rectangular punched cards controlled the complex patterns of the silk threads weaving the fabric. Inspired by the principle of the Jacquard loom, London inventor Charles Babbage (1792–1871) designed (but never got around to building) an "Analytical Engine" operated by a kind of mechanized intelligence, i.e., a stored memory and programs encoded on spinning cylinders. Lady Ada Augusta Lovelace (1815–52), daughter of Lord Byron, in a published commentary (Geneva, 1842) on Babbage's engine, wrote that a machine of this type with pitches and harmonies encoded in its spinning cylinders "might compose elaborate and scientific pieces of music of any degree of complexity or extent." Lovelace stated that the machine could not *originate* anything but could carry out whatever it was programmed to perform. Thus, before the middle of the nineteenth century Lovelace advanced the idea of computer-generated music.

Britain was the leading industrial power between 1825 and 1870 and was the most stable politically. France was, in many respects, the culturally dominant nation but was unsettled politically. In the July 1830 Revolution, the Bourbon monarchy of Charles X (r. 1824–30) was overthrown. Louis Philippe (r. 1830–48) was crowned King of the French (not King of France) but was deposed in 1848 as a result of working-class uprisings. Then Louis Napoleon was named President. He soon approximated dictatorship and assumed the title Emperor Napoleon III. That régime collapsed during the Franco-Prussian War (1870).

There were numerous uprisings in other European countries. The doctrine of nationalism—the establishment of states according to nationality of peoples instead of on the basis of dynastic inheritance or intermarriage—gained strength. The Italian people, who for centuries had lived in separate kingdoms, duchies, and republics, were finally united, in several steps (fig. 22.1), as a kingdom under King Victor Emanuele I of the House of Savoy. Unification of the German people as an empire under Kaiser Wilhelm I (and his minister Otto von Bismarck) occurred after Prussia successfully waged war with France in 1870. There was unrest in America, too, and the Civil War was fought (1861–65) to preserve the republic and national unity. The patriotism and nationalism

Nineteenth-Century Musical Expansion

1800	1825	1850	1875

Revolution of 1830   Revolution of 1848   1861–65 Civil War in United States

1809 - Abraham Lincoln -1865

Suez Canal opened 1869

1848 Marx-Engels: *Communist Manifesto*

Unification of Italy } 1871
Unification of Germany }

- - - - Cecilian movement -

c. 1825–70 Britain the leading industrial power; France culturally dominant

increase in amount of program music -
character pieces for piano -

1840 - - first complete solo recital

- - voices increasingly included in symphonies - - -

concert overture -

revival of J. S. Bach's works - - Bach Gesellschaft founded

piano becomes the most important solo instrument -

opéra comique -

Bizet: *Carmen* 1875

lyric opera -1859 Gounod: *Faust*

c. 1855 *opéra bouffe* fl.

grand opera - begins to diminish
1831 Meyerbeer: *Robert le diable*

1856–58 Berlioz: *Les Troyens*

opera semiseria -
1831 Bellini: *Norma*

Mendelssohn - - - - - - -1836 *St. Paul;* 1846 *Elias*

Robert Schumann: 1840 Lieder

1830 Berlioz: *Symphonie fantastique*

1843 { Leipzig Conservatory founded;
{ Clara and Robert Schumann on faculty

1842 New York Philharmonic Society founded

---

rampant throughout the Western world found expression in the arts. In music, nationalism became increasingly apparent during the last half of the century.

The first stirrings of socialism and socialistic labor movements appeared. Among those producing thought-provoking publications on economic and social conditions were Friedrich Engels and Karl Marx, authors of *Communist Manifesto* (1848). Their ideas were welcomed not only by factory workers but by people experiencing crop failures at that very time. Those crop failures caused many persons to emigrate to America.

The arts—architecture, painting, sculpture, literature, and music—were important, and philosophers discussed them and wrote about them. Georg F. W. Hegel (1770–1831) taught a course on esthetics, which Mendelssohn attended; Hegel's *Lectures on Aesthetics* were published posthumously

Figure 22.1 The unification of Italy may be viewed as the expansion of Sardinia. The extent of Sardinia (*a*) in January 1859; (*b*) in August 1859; (*c*) in April 1860; (*d*) after October 1860. Notice how The Patrimony of St. Peter (The Papal States) has diminished.

(1835–38). Some patronage of the arts still existed, but, for the most part, success for the musician meant concertizing and gaining public acclaim. The concert-going populace had changed; no longer was it an elite group of the wealthy and aristocracy but consisted of persons from all walks of life. And, more and more, women were breaking out of the domestic mold and were manifesting their talents in the arts—writing and publishing novels and poetry, composing and publishing music, directing choral ensembles, and concertizing.

Vocal Music

Nineteenth-century composers wrote several kinds of vocal music: (1) accompanied solos (Lieder, ballads, romances, and other solo songs, including arrangements of folk songs); (2) part songs and choruses, chiefly on secular texts, for male, female, or mixed ensembles, unaccompanied or accompanied; (3) sacred music intended for use in church Services; (4) large works for chorus and orchestra, with or without vocal soloist(s), intended for concert performance (oratorios, cantatas, and single- or multi-movement independent pieces); and (5) operas. A number of symphonic works incorporated chorus and/or soloist(s) in one or more movements.

Without a doubt, some of the loveliest choral-orchestral works written in the nineteenth century are those of Johannes Brahms, especially *Alt-Rhapsodie* (Alto rhapsody, Op. 53; 1869) and *Gesang der Parzen* (Song of the Fates, Op. 89; 1882). Both works are settings of poems by Goethe.

In the nineteenth century, the terms "oratorio" and "cantata" were not clearly differentiated. Though a cantata might be either sacred or secular, most of them are secular; usually, cantatas are shorter and less dramatic in character than an oratorio. Among the excellent cantatas composed in mid-nineteenth century are Mendelssohn's *Die erste Walpurgisnacht* (The first Walpurgis night, 1832, rev. 1843) and R. Schumann's *Das Paradies und die Peri* (Paradise and the Peri; 1843).

Customarily, a composer labeled a work "oratorio" if it dealt with a sacred subject (not necessarily Biblical) and there was a part for narrator (*historicus,* evangelist); however, the narration might be given to chorus. Some Romantic oratorios were based on religious legends, e.g., Liszt's *Die Legende von der heiligen Elisabeth* (The Legend of St. Elisabeth; 1862); others concern the life and work of martyrs, e.g., Loewe's *Johann Hus* (Jan Hus, 1842). The subject matter of an oratorio might be either contemplative or dramatic in character; however, an oratorio is not intended to be staged, nor are the singers specially costumed for its performance. Among the numerous oratorios on contemplative subjects are Spohr's *Die letzten Dinge* (The last Judgment; 1826), and César Franck's *Les béatitudes* (The beatitudes; 1879). The finest nineteenth-century oratorios are Mendelssohn's *Paulus* (St. Paul; 1836) and *Elias* (Elijah; 1846). Excellent choral writing is vital to an oratorio, and Mendelssohn's expertise in this regard placed his works second only to Handel's in the eyes of the English.

Hundreds of part songs were written during the nineteenth century. Many of them were patriotic and were engendered by the frequent political uprisings in European countries between 1825 and 1875. Other part songs were written for performance at music festivals in Germany and in Britain or for use by the choral societies that existed in almost every German city and town. Only a few of the part songs, those by major composers such as Brahms, have had frequent performances in the twentieth century.

Most nineteenth-century composers wrote some church music. In the area of liturgical Service music, the finest Catholic Masses were composed by Cherubini, Schubert, and Liszt. Rossini's *Stabat mater* is excellent, though operatic in style. Liszt and Mendelssohn were among those writing Psalms settings; Samuel S. Wesley wrote 27 anthems for the Anglican church.

Quite a few large works on sacred subjects were written for performance in church but were not intended for and were not appropriate for liturgical Services. Representative of such works are Berlioz's *Grande Messe des Morts* (a Requiem Mass; 1837) and *Te Deum laudamus* (1849), conceived for military-political commemorations; Verdi's *Requiem* (1874) and Brahms's *Ein deutsches Requiem* (A German Requiem; 1868) were written as memorials to specific individuals. In the twentieth century, these works have been performed in concerts.

Cecilian Movement

Commencing around 1825 and continuing through the remainder of the nineteenth century, there was increasing interest in the music of Palestrina and other composers who wrote liturgical *a cappella* polyphony. That interest generated a movement that fostered a return to use of *a cappella* choral music in the church, particularly music in the style of Palestrina. (Whether Palestrina's music actually was performed *a cappella* is debatable, but in the nineteenth century that was believed to have been the case.) As an offshoot of this, there arose c. 1848 a movement that advocated use of Gregorian chant in its purest form. In some regions, this meant strict adherence to the *Editio Mediacaea* published in 1614, the edition prepared by Palestrina and Annibale Zoilo after the meetings of the Council of Trent. In other areas, particularly those in accord with the beliefs of the Solesmes school, there was a desire to go back even further, to the St. Gall Codex and the choral style of the late Middle Ages.

The movement was in direct opposition to the views of the Enlightenment, which sought complete integration of instrumental and vocal music in liturgical Services.

The reform movements had very little effect on actual practice during the first half of the nineteenth century. In France the movement was strong; it not only approved but established use of *a cappella* choral music and Gregorian chant in Services. In Germany in 1869 the Allgemeine Cäcilien-Verein (General Cecilian Society) was formed for the purpose of eliminating integrated music from Services; in 1870 Pope Pius IX officially sanctioned that Union and its stated purposes. The Cecilian movement—named for St. Cecilia, patron saint of music—spread rapidly, and in many regions there was strict demarcation between styles of church and secular music. Contemporary nineteenth-century musical developments were considered untenable where church music was concerned; composers who wrote sacred music that integrated instrumental/vocal and secular/sacred styles found their works unacceptable for performance within the church.

One result of the Cecilian movement was the improvement of singing in the church—by choirs, congregation, and clergy. A provision of the 1903 *Moto Proprio* (edict) of Pope Pius X stressed the importance of this and made musical education of the clergy compulsory.

Another result was the preparation and publication of new editions of liturgical chantbooks. The *Regensburg Edition,* based on the *Editio Medicaea,* and advocated by the Society of St. Cecilia, appeared in 1875. Both it and the *Editio Medicaea* were supplanted by the *Editio Vaticana,* prepared in compliance with the 1903 *Moto Proprio* of Pope Pius X. After Vatican Council II, under papal directive, the Benedictine monks of Solesmes prepared and published new editions of all of the chantbooks, in accord with the recommendations made at meetings of that Council. One of the publications is a *Graduale Triplex* containing three comparative versions of the chants: the neumes of the Laon manuscript printed above the modern square notes in black, the neumes of the St. Gall manuscript printed in red below the modern square notation (fig. 3.7).

Instrumental Music

Instrumental music composed during the nineteenth century includes orchestral works, chamber music, compositions for solo instrument with orchestral or keyboard accompaniment, and solo piano pieces. Any of these instrumental types might be **program** (descriptive or referential) music or **absolute** (nonreferential or "pure") music. The orchestral works were principally symphonies, concert overtures, and stylized dance music. All of the types of symphonies can be related to those of Beethoven. Programmatic works are related to his *Pastoral Symphony*; cyclic works, those with movements that are linked, and those that commence in one key and conclude in another, are related to his Fifth Symphony. Symphonies that include vocal soloists and chorus stem from his "Choral" Symphony, the Ninth. Unconventionality of formal structure may derive from his Sixth Symphony, which has five movements, or from his Ninth, which places the slow movement third and the Scherzo second. That four-movement structural scheme became rather common in chamber music, too, especially string quartets. "Heroic" symphonies, and those with thematic transformation, have their roots in Beethoven's *Sinfonia Eroica.* Aside from an unconventional introduction, Beethoven's First Symphony is conventional absolute music, as are also his Second, Fourth, Seventh, and Eighth Symphonies.

Almost all of the chamber music written in the nineteenth century is absolute music and is of traditional types: sonata, trio, quartet, quintet, and other ensemble music with one person per part.

A majority of the solos with orchestral accompaniment are concerti. The principal solo instruments were piano and violin; a few solos were written for 'cello and for clarinet. In fact, throughout the nineteenth century, the piano was the most important solo instrument and was considered the musical instrument indispensable in every middle- and upper-class home. Any person aspiring to some degree of gentility learned to play the piano. For it composers wrote dance pieces (waltz, mazurka, polonaise, and others); character pieces (ballade, barcarolle, berceuse, impromptu, *moment musical,* prelude, romance, and others); concert études; solo sonatas; variations; and fantasias.

Piano Playing

During the nineteenth century, after the deaths of Beethoven and Schubert, several styles of piano playing were evident. As piano construction improved, pianist-composers wrote music that was increasingly more demanding technically, and in the 1830s Liszt composed some pieces that required the full keyboard (88 keys). John Field, pupil of Clementi, and Johann N. Hummel, who as a child studied with Mozart, bridge the Classical style of their teachers and the Romantic style of Chopin and Liszt. Both Field and Hummel played with clarity, brightness, and elegance, as did Chopin and Liszt, with never a suggestion of pounding or "thumping." Chopin and Schubert stated firmly their dislike of such forceful playing. Field was first to use the pedal as an integral part of the piano; in his music, as in Chopin's, proper pedaling is vital for the wide-spaced harmonies in the left-hand part.

Successful pianists who aimed to impress with showmanship and audacity include Louis Moreau Gottschalk (1829–69), Sigismund Thalberg (1812–71), and Friedrich Kalkbrenner (1785–1849). Their compositions are of lesser quality than those of Chopin and Liszt and seldom are performed in the twentieth century.

The impressive, colorful pianists whose technical display did not detract from their effective interpretation of the music were Franz Liszt (1811–86), Anton Rubinstein (1829–94), and Hans von Bülow (1830–94). All three were composers. Von Bülow, pupil of Friedrich Wieck and later of Liszt, was well known as a conductor. Rubinstein, a Russian pianist-composer whose successful concert career began when he toured Europe in 1854, was influential in improving music education in Russia. With the assistance of Duchess Elena Pavlovna, he founded the Russia Musical Society, whose concerts he conducted, and established St. Petersburg Conservatory (1862). He was director of the Conservatory until 1867, when he again concertized in Europe.

Liszt was considered the finest pianist of his time (see Ch. 23). He greatly admired virtuoso violinist Niccolò Paganini, and, like him, wore a black suit and adopted a rather haughty posture and impressive mannerisms. Liszt determined to do for the piano what Paganini had done for the violin, and in his compositions and performance style he exploited the piano's capabilities in a manner previously unknown. His *Transcendental Études* contain some of the most difficult piano music ever written. Liszt was the first to play a complete solo recital (London, 1840), unassisted by and not shared with other musicians. His repertoire was vast, and his recital programs included works by his predecessors and contemporaries as well as his own original compositions and his piano transcriptions of orchestral overtures and symphonies.

The outstanding pianists with solid musicianship, concern for correct interpretation, and technical perfection without pretentious display or pointless bravura were Felix Mendelssohn-Bartholdy (1809–47), Clara Wieck Schumann (1819–96), and Johannes Brahms (1833–97). All three were composers, and Mendelssohn and Brahms were excellent organists.

Liszt preferred to teach master classes rather than private lessons. Czerny, his teacher, gave up a career as performer in order to devote his time to teaching. In the second half of the nineteenth century, teaching became a career for many who considered performing of secondary importance. One of the finest teachers was Theodor Leschetizky (1830–1915), a pupil of Czerny. Leschetizky stressed thorough knowledge of every detail of the music and complete concentration on the music while performing it. Among his most famous pupils were Ignace Paderewski, Artur Schnabel, and Ossip Gabrilowich.

Music in Austro-Germanic Lands

Though there was no Austro-German empire after 1806, close ties existed between Austria and the German states throughout the nineteenth century. After the Congress of Vienna, Germany was even more divided than it had been previously. The search for a national identity found expression in the music of German composers, as well as in literature.

The most important music publishing houses were in Leipzig, but others existed in large German cities, and music printed in Vienna was readily available throughout Germany. As the nineteenth century advanced, there was increased interest in the music of great composers of past generations, particularly Bach, Handel, Palestrina, and Gabrieli. Published volumes of music by Palestrina and Gabrieli began to appear in the 1830s, and by mid-century some plans were made for preparation and publication of complete editions of their works. Composers and scholars became interested in searching out old music, and many persons amassed private collections of manuscripts. By 1850, music of the past had found a place in concert repertoire. Such music was not merely of historical interest—composers studied the compositional techniques and incorporated them into their own compositions.

Beethoven's achievements in symphony and string quartet were so highly regarded that, for a time, many composers hesitated to work in those genres. However, throughout the century all kinds of music were composed, especially solo pieces of small size, such as Lieder and character pieces. Romanticism flourished in Germanic lands and was evident in subjects of operas, in program music, and in choral part songs, particularly those for male voices. Choral societies existed in almost all cities and towns. In Vienna, dancing was a popular pastime, and the waltz was the favorite dance. Weber's *Aufforderung zum Tanze* had brought the waltz into the concert hall, and later composers wrote numerous sets of waltzes for concert performance.

The founding of Leipzig Conservatory (1843) and the Berlin Hochschule für Musik (1868) was followed by the establishment of conservatories in other major German cities. Outstanding musicians at these schools provided excellent instruction in all areas of music. Considerable importance was attached to teaching, to serving as director of a conservatory, or being conductor-director of an opera house or of a society that presented a regular season of concerts.

Warsaw: Frédéric Chopin

Pure Romanticism is seen in most of the piano music of Frédéric Chopin (1810–49), a native of Warsaw. Chopin's mother, who was Polish, had had sufficient musical training to be able to sing well and to teach piano; his father, who was French, taught French language and literature in a boarding school the couple operated. At the time of Frédéric's birth, the Grand Duchy of Warsaw was part of the Kingdom of Saxony; technically, Chopin was a citizen of a Germanic land.

Frédéric Chopin. Portrait by Eugène Delacroix (1838). *(The Louvre, Paris.)*

The three Chopin children received excellent general education, and both Frédéric and his older sister, Ludvika, had piano lessons from a local musician in Warsaw. (Though Ludvika did not have a career in music, and there is no indication that she had sufficient talent to pursue such a career, she composed some mazurkas.) Frédéric had both literary and musical talent: at age seven, he was writing poetry, could improvise, and composed several pieces, including a polonaise (published) and a march (lost). By 1818, when he made his first public appearance as a piano soloist in a concerto, Chopin knew that he wanted a career in music. During his high school years (1823–26), he also studied music at Warsaw Conservatory and in 1825 composed a *Rondo* in C minor, his Op. 1 (publ. 1825). In 1826 he performed two benefit concerts, enrolled at Warsaw Conservatory, and began composing piano music for his own use. His *La cì darem la mano varié pour le piano, avec accompagnement d'orchestre* (Variations on [Mozart's] *La cì darem la mano* for piano with orchestral accompaniment, Op. 2; publ. 1830) was followed by a Sonata in C minor (Op. 4; 1827), *Rondo à la Mazurka* (Op. 5), and nine *Mazurkas* (Opp. 6, 7). His composition teacher decided, after comparing the sonata with Chopin's other works, that Chopin composed better music when he was not forced to follow established rules.

Hearing performances by Hummel (1828) and Paganini (1829) fired Chopin's zeal for music. In 1828, he had accompanied a professor on a trip to Berlin; there he had heard music by Handel and Mozart—music that he could not hear in Warsaw, where the basic musical diet offered the public was Italian opera. Chopin decided in 1829 that he needed to see more of Europe and hear more of its music. At that time, he was not especially interested in composing music except for his own use. Primarily, he wanted to play the piano, and he wanted to broaden his horizons. However, he went to Vienna, arranged to have some works published, and in August performed a successful concert of his own music—his Op. 2, the concert rondo *Krakowiak* (F major, Op. 14; 1828), and some improvisations—at Kärntnertor Theater. After a second successful concert, he returned to Warsaw and composed more music, including his two piano concerti and some études. He planned a concert tour in Germanic lands and into Italy, but political uprisings preceding the Revolutions of 1830 delayed his departure. In the spring of 1830, he played a concert at Warsaw's National Theater. His virtuosic performance, coupled with the Polish character of his compositions, caused an enthusiastic public to view him as a national composer, but in a short time his glory diminished in Warsaw. Moreover, as a professional he did not experience concert successes comparable with those he had enjoyed as an amateur. In 1830, Schumann heard Chopin play his *La cì darem la mano* variations and wrote the highly complimentary article *Ein Opus II,* in which he pointed out Chopin's genius as composer of piano music.

Political conditions precluded Chopin's planned trip to Italy late in 1831, so he set out for Paris. En route, he learned that the Russians had captured Warsaw. The concert he performed in Paris in February 1832 received excellent reviews in the journals, and his acceptance there was assured. He moved in the highest social circles and counted among his friends well-known authors, painters, and composers. But he decided that a career as a virtuoso performer was not for him—he did not enjoy performing concerts before large audiences. He limited his concert

appearances to once or twice a year, and sometimes those were as second pianist to another artist. During his entire career, Chopin performed only about 30 public concerts. That number is low not because he was not invited to give concerts, but because he chose not to do so. No other performer achieved so great a reputation with so few concerts. In some respects, Chopin's temperament as a performing musician must have been similar to that of Schubert, for he preferred to perform in salons before small audiences or at gatherings of his friends. Actually, Chopin's style of playing, with its subtle nuances and his use of sustaining pedal to blur harmonies and blend tones, was more suited to a small audience. He, like Schubert, disliked forceful playing—"pounding" or "banging" on the keys.

To earn his living, Chopin taught. Because he could and did command high fees, most of his pupils were of high social standing. Though he enjoyed teaching, his real interest lay in composing, and it was not long before he was recognized in Paris as a composer and could earn his living by composing.

In 1836 Chopin experienced bouts of serious illness, and his health declined; by 1838, his ailment had been definitely diagnosed as tuberculosis. As the illness progressed, his compositional output diminished; in 1844 he wrote only the B-minor Sonata.

Over the years, he had several love affairs. That of longest duration (1837–47) was with French novelist Aurore Dudevant (1803–76), who used the *nom de plume* George Sand. After Chopin broke with Sand, his health deteriorated rapidly, and composition no longer interested him. In February 1848, almost on the eve of the Revolution, he performed in a concert in Paris, then went to visit a former pupil in Britain and gave several performances there. When he returned to Paris in 1849 he was quite ill. He died on October 17. In compliance with his request, Mozart's *Requiem Mass* was performed at his funeral; the service was held at La Madeleine, and special permission had to be obtained for women to sing there. Three of Chopin's pieces were performed also: the *Marche funèbre* from the Sonata in B♭ minor, orchestrated; and organ transcriptions of the A-minor and B-minor *Préludes,* Op. 28.

Example 22.1 Frequently Chopin's use of dissonance was daring: (a) *Mazurka*, Op. 7, No. 2, mm. 22–26; (b) *Scherzo*, Op. 20, mm. 591–601. *(From F. F. Chopin: Dziela wszytkie [Complete Works] 1949–1961, edited by I. J. Paderewski. Copyright © 1953 Instytut Fryderyka Chopina, Warsaw, Poland. (a) from Vol. X [Mazurkas]; (b) from Vol. V [Scherzos].)*

Influences and Style

The composer-performers most influential on Chopin's playing and composing were Field and Hummel. Polish national dances and melodies were shaping forces on Chopin's music, and, possibly, he knew the mazurkas, polonaises, and nocturnes of Polish pianist Maria Szymanowska (1789–1831). Another important influence was the kind of piano available to him, and its technical capabilities. Without the double escapement action Érard invented and patented in 1821, it would not have been possible for Chopin to articulate clearly the rapidly repeated notes that appear so often in his music. Also, the leather-covered hammers contributed to the soft tone quality. (Pape of Paris began to use felt on hammers c. 1826, but this was not generally accepted until after 1850.)

Chopin did not write program music. His music is graceful, sensitive, expressive, and Romantic, and proper performance of it demands of the player impeccable technique and touch. Chopin's melodies are lyrical, of a vocal rather than an instrumental type. Usually, the melodies are periodic, eight measures long, and basically diatonic. Chopin was skilled at improvisation and preferred thematic variation rather than fragmentation as a developmental tool. Chromaticism was used to vary and develop themes. In Chopin's music there are grace notes, passing tones, and ornaments (both written out and indicated by symbols) in abundance. Repetition with variation and return after contrast were his basic formal procedures. Frequently, he used a kind of rondo; for instance, his *Nocturne* in E♭ major, Op. 9 No. 2 is constructed as A-A'-B-A''-B'-A'''-Coda-Cadenza-Cadence. Chopin's music is devoid of strict counterpoint and polyphony; he wrote only one fugue and one canon. In his harmonies, he used dissonance freely, daringly, shockingly (ex. 22.1). Often, he accomplished modulation enharmonically; sometimes he simply assumed a new key. At times, his melodies seem to be generated out of the harmonies he used, for he was adept at weaving melody into accompaniment figurations or weaving accompaniment figurations around melody. In much of his music, the rhythms are those associated with dances. Chopin used the *sostenuto* pedal not only to sustain a melodic line or a harmony, but, more importantly, to expand the compass of a chord and thus extend the harmony well

Example 22.2 Chopin used pedal to expand the compass of a chord and extend harmony beyond a normal handspan: (*a*) *Etude,* Op. 10, No. 11, mm. 1–6; (*b*) *Nocturne,* Op. 27, No. 1, mm. 1–8.

(a)

(b)

beyond the normal octave span of a hand (ex. 22.2). Proper pedaling is vital when performing Chopin's music.

Tempo rubato is an important characteristic of Chopin's music. His own explanation of his use of the term is: The hand playing the accompaniment adheres to strict tempo; the hand playing the melody relaxes the tempo, then unobtrusively accelerates it in order to resume synchronization with the accompaniment.

Chopin's Works

Chopin was a prolific composer. His piano solos include 26 preludes, 27 études, 21 nocturnes, 4 impromptus, 16 polonaises, 61 mazurkas, 20 waltzes, 3 sonatas, 4 ballades, 4 scherzi, fantasias, 4 variations, 4 rondos, marches, and numerous other pieces bearing such titles as *Barcarolle* (Op. 57, Op. 60), *Bolero* (Op. 19), *Bourrée* (2 WoO, publ. 1968), and *Tarantelle*

(Op. 43). He wrote 1 Fugue (A minor; 1841, publ. 1898) and 1 Canon (F minor; c. 1839, unpubl.). For piano and orchestra there are 2 concerti (F minor, E minor), *Variations on La cì darem la mano* (Op. 2), *Fantasia on Polish airs, Grand Polonaise in Eb,* and the concert rondo *Krakowiak*. Also, there are a piano trio, 3 chamber music works for 'cello and piano that he wrote for a 'cellist friend with whom he enjoyed playing, a set of variations for flute and piano, and 19 songs on Polish texts.

There are two single *Preludes,* in Ab major (WoO; 1834, publ. 1918) and C♯ minor (Op. 45; 1841), and the set of *24 Preludes* (Op. 28; 1836–39; publ. 1839). The Op. 28 *Preludes* are short independent pieces, one in each major and minor key. They are arranged in the volume in major-minor pairs, commencing with C major and A minor, and proceed first in ascending numbers of sharps, then in descending numbers of flats. *Prelude* in E minor, Op.

Example 22.3 Chopin: *Étude,* Op. 25, No. 11, mm. 1–6. The dirge-like tolling figure that begins the *Étude* serves as basis for the piece. *(From F. F. Chopin: Dziela wszystkie [Complete Works] Vol. II, edited by I. J. Paderewski. Copyright © 1949 Instytut Fryderyka Chopina, Warsaw, Poland.)*

28 No. 4 (DWMA180), is a one-part form 25 measures in length. In tonality, it moves from tonic to dominant, with a half-cadence in m. 12; restatement of the melody commences in tonic in m. 13 and concludes on a dominant-seventh chord in m. 23. After a half-measure rest, a strong cadence covers the last two measures. An expressive but simple lyrical melody is accompanied by chords in a persistent eighth-note rhythm. When restated in the second half of the *Prelude,* the melody is embellished.

Each of the two volumes of *Études,* Op. 10 and Op. 25, contains 12 studies; in addition, Chopin wrote 3 études for Moscheles's *Méthode* (1839). There are études in most of the 24 major and minor keys; apparently, Chopin planned to write a cycle of études, then altered his plan. Each étude deals with a particular pianistic problem of either technique or musicianship. In concern for musicianship, style, and proper interpretation, Chopin's études go beyond those of Clementi. Chopin seems to have been the first pianist to write études with sufficient musicality to be performed in public without revealing their underlying pedagogical purpose. The E-major *Étude,* Op. 10 No. 3, was Chopin's favorite; its apparent simplicity is deceptive. Most of the Op. 25 études are very demanding. The A-minor *Étude,* Op. 25 No. 11, the "Winter Wind" étude, commences Lento with two statements of the dirgelike tolling figure on which the entire composition is based (ex. 22.3; DWMA181). That dismal theme appears in the *Marche funèbre* and the A-minor *Prelude,* also. Chopin wrote the four-measure introduction to the A-minor *Étude* as an afterthought; the body of the study is an Allegro con fuoco in which one hand steadily reiterates harmonizations of the somber theme, while the other hand is a whirlwind of activity in 16th notes.

Chopin's mazurkas and polonaises were some of the earliest nineteenth-century music based on national idioms. His *Rondo à la Mazur,* Op. 5, and a *Mazurka* in G major were published in 1826; that year, Maria Szymanowska's *24 Mazurkas* were published in Leipzig. Though Chopin made no direct quotations from Polish dances, he used their characteristic rhythms, melodies, and harmonies in his works. The mazurka originated near Warsaw; the name of the dance derives from the folk who lived in that area, the Mazurs. Actually, there are three types or regional variations of mazurka: the *mazur,* the *obertas,* and the *kujawiak.* All use triple meter, with the second or third beat of the measure stressed. The raised fourth degree of the scale, a feature of the Lydian mode, is characteristic of Polish music and of Chopin's mazurkas. Many of Chopin's mazurkas are in some kind of rondo form, as is also his concert showpiece *Krakowiak.*

The stately processional-type Polish dance that, sometime in the seventeenth century, the French named "polonaise" had existed for centuries. Stylized instrumental versions of it were composed as early as the seventeenth century, and in the eighteenth century some were written by Bach, Handel, Couperin, and others. However, in Chopin's hands, the polonaise became a symbol of Polish nationalism. The most popular and the finest of his polonaises is that in A♭ major, Op. 53 (1842).

Chopin's nocturnes are subjective, introspective, expressive pieces. Clearly, they were influenced by those of Field, though Chopin's harmonies are more complex. Chopin's skill at improvisation is apparent in his nocturnes; this, along with Romantic harmonies, enriched them considerably. Usually, each time the melody recurred Chopin embellished it increasingly, and occasionally he inserted small cadenzas. This may be seen in his *Nocturne* in E♭ major, Op. 9 No. 2. In several respects that work resembles Field's *Nocturne* in A major, No. 9. A greater similarity exists between Chopin's *Nocturne* in A♭ major, Op. 32, and Field's *Nocturne* No. 5, in B♭ major. Both nocturnes convey a nostalgic atmosphere (DWMA167 and 182).

Chopin's C-minor Piano Sonata, a student work, was unsatisfactory to both his teacher and himself, and he waited more than a decade before attempting another. In 1837 he composed a *Marche funèbre* as an isolated composition; three years later, he wrote three movements to surround it and thus created his second Piano Sonata (B♭ minor; Op. 35). It is a Romantic work, structured according to the mid-nineteenth-century view of the complete sonata—in four movements, with Scherzo/Trio placed second and the slow movement third, but with a most unusual Finale. The first movement commences with a four-measure Grave introduction. Two contrasting themes, the first motivic, the second elegiac, are presented in the exposition and are developed. Only the second theme returns in the recapitulation; the first theme is basis for the coda. The second movement is a brilliant Scherzo with Trio. Next comes the ponderous *Marche funèbre*. The sonata climaxes with a 25-measure Presto filled with chromatic passages played by both hands an octave apart. Chopin's third and last Piano Sonata (B minor, Op. 58; 1844) is more conventional: a sonata-form Allegro maestoso, a brief Scherzo with Trio, Largo, and rondo Finale. Typically, Chopin was unorthodox in writing recapitulations of sonata-form movements. Usually, he returned the second theme first; sometimes he omitted the first theme or returned it in a key other than the tonic.

As they now exist, Chopin's two concerti, No. 1 in E minor (Op. 11; 1830; publ. 1833) and No. 2 in F minor (Op. 21; 1829–30; publ. 1836) are piano solos with meager orchestral accompaniment and orchestral interludes. The original orchestrations for both works have been lost; that used with the E-minor Concerto is the result of some editing, and the same may be true of the F-minor orchestral parts.

In the composition of instrumental ballades, Chopin seems to have had no predecessors. Reportedly, his first two ballades (G minor, Op. 23; F major, Op. 38) were inspired by ballads of Polish poet Adam Mickiewicz (1798–1855). Chopin's ballades are large one-movement works constructed according to the principle of repetition after contrast. A characteristic of the ballades is Chopin's consistent use of one of the themes varied or transformed each time it reappears.

Chopin's significance in the development of music lies in his ability to write music particularly suited to the piano, taking full advantage of its unique capabilities rather than attempting to draw from it orchestral sonorities. He thoroughly understood the piano of his day, viewed it as a solo instrument, and made the most of its distinctive, expressive qualities. His hands were small, and his fingerings were often unorthodox, yet his playing was virtuosic. His best compositions are those in which he was unhampered by traditional forms: ballades, nocturnes, preludes, and études.

Felix Mendelssohn (Bartholdy)

Felix Mendelssohn (1809–47) grew up in a cultured environment provided by his parental home and by the city of Berlin, where, as a result of the Enlightenment, there was some social equality for citizens who followed the Jewish faith. The Mendelssohns themselves provided their children's early education, including music lessons. (All four children had musical talent; Rebekka sang and Paul played 'cello.) When the two older children, Fanny and Felix, showed exceptional pianistic talent, they had lessons from Ludwig Berger (1777–1839). Felix had violin lessons and painting/drawing lessons also and evidenced talent in both areas. Later, he created some beautiful landscape watercolors (colorplate 21) and wrote some poetry.

Felix Mendelssohn. Portrait by Edward Magnus (1845). Original in Mendelssohn-Archiv, Berlin. *(Courtesy of the Free Library of Philadelphia.)*

insight

Marie Kiéné Bigot

Pianist Marie Kiéné (1786–1820) received her early musical training from her mother. In 1804 Marie married Paul Bigot, librarian to Count Razumovsky. She had access to all music (even new manuscripts) in the Count's library. While living in Vienna, she performed in concert, often as partner of violinist Ignaz Schuppanzigh. She knew Salieri, Haydn, and Beethoven and played some of their music in their presence. All of those composers highly praised her playing. The Bigots moved to Paris in 1809; there Mme Bigot moved in musical circles that included noted composers such as Cherubini. Bigot lost his life in the 1812 Russian campaign, and Mme Bigot earned her living by teaching. From time to time, she composed; some of her piano pieces were published in Vienna and Paris.

In 1816, when Abraham Mendelssohn (1776–1835) was assigned government business in Paris, he took his family along; there, Fanny and Felix received piano lessons from Marie Bigot (see Insight, "Marie Kiéné Bigot"). That year Abraham Mendelssohn had his children baptized as Christians; a few years later he converted to Christianity and adjusted the family name to Mendelssohn-Bartholdy. Felix signed his name "Felix Mendelssohn Bartholdy." Both Christian and Enlightenment beliefs were important factors in Felix's career.

When the Mendelssohns returned to Berlin, Fanny and Felix had theory and composition lessons from C. F. Zelter (1758–1832), noted composer of

Lieder, who was director of the Berlin Singakademie. Mendelssohn's great-aunt, Sara Levy (1763–1854), had recommended Zelter as teacher. Levy had been a harpsichord pupil and patroness of W. F. Bach and had known C. P. E. Bach; she had appeared as harpsichord soloist at the Singakademie on several occasions in 1806–08, while Zelter was director. Levy had acquired a large library of music (much of it in manuscript) composed by members of the Bach family. She made her library available to Zelter, members of the family, and the Singakademie. Zelter taught J. S. Bach's works to his pupils and promoted the performance of Bach's works in Germany. Zelter and Bach's music were shaping forces in the careers of Fanny and Felix Mendelssohn.

Felix's earliest surviving compositions bear date 1820; probably, the earliest of these is the small piano piece labeled *Recitativo,* in Largo tempo. In 1820–21 he worked to master counterpoint and sonata form; compositions written then include seven *sinfonie,* four piano sonatas, a cantata, some *Singspiele,* about two dozen small piano pieces, and a few songs. Those early works were performed, even the *Singspiele,* at musical gatherings in the Mendelssohn home. After 1825, that home was a most important cultural center in Berlin. Several times a week persons gathered there to hear and discuss literature, to view and discuss art, or for a musicale.

In 1821 Zelter took Felix to meet Goethe, and their friendship began. Goethe influenced Mendelssohn's life and work significantly. In 1822 Mendelssohn began to write concerti and other works in large forms. Representative of this stage in his development are the Piano Concerto in A minor and the Violin Concerto in D minor (both WoO; 1822), the latter Mozartean in style. It soon became evident that Mendelssohn would be a prolific composer—in 1822 he wrote the first of his several psalm settings, the Magnificat in D (chorus, orch.), some solo songs, some part songs for male chorus, a piano quartet, and three fugues for piano. By 1825, his mature style was manifest; it is apparent in the Octet in E♭ for strings, Op. 20, whose scherzo was inspired by Goethe's poetry about Walpurgisnacht.

Regularly, on Friday mornings, Zelter held practices at his home for the purpose of singing little known music by Bach, Handel, and other old masters. There, Mendelssohn first heard Bach's Passion music, and he was overjoyed when, at Christmas 1823, his grandmother gave him a copy of Bach's *St. Matthew Passion*. Commencing in 1827, a small choir met weekly at the Mendelssohn home to sing some of that Passion music. Early in 1829, Mendelssohn, actor Eduard Devrient (1801–77), and Zelter made plans for the Berlin Singakademie to perform Bach's *St. Matthew Passion* that spring. Performance of the work—the first in almost a century—took place on March 11, with Mendelssohn conducting, and was repeated ten days later, and again on Good Friday. "To think," Mendelssohn commented to Devrient, "that it should be an actor and a Jew who give back to the people the greatest of Christian works."

Abraham Mendelssohn traveled a good deal and took either his whole family or his sons with him, giving them opportunities to meet composers, artists, literati, and other important persons all over Europe. The Mendelssohns were financially secure and insisted that Felix spend several years traveling in foreign countries. In 1829 he visited friends in London and had a few lessons from pianist Ignaz Moscheles (1794–1870), who introduced him to musical circles. As composer or performer—sometimes both—Mendelssohn participated in four large concerts in London. His Symphony No. 1 (C minor; 1824) was performed, and also his Concerto in A♭ for two pianos, with Mendelssohn and Moscheles as soloists. At another concert, Mendelssohn performed Beethoven's "Emperor" Concerto. Britain became an important part of Mendelssohn's life; he returned year after year to participate in music festivals, especially those at Birmingham. On his 1829 journey, he visited Scotland, where he thought of composing a Scottish Symphony—it became reality in 1842. A trip to the island of Staffa inspired an overture, *Die einsame Insel* (The solitary isle).

In 1830 Mendelssohn declined the offer to fill the chair of music at University of Berlin. That year he visited Italy, and during the next few years he traveled widely in Europe and England. He also composed, performed, and conducted concerts. In fact, he was already recognized as an excellent conductor. Mendelssohn was always a sensitive person, and the deaths of Goethe and Zelter in 1832 deeply distressed him. He applied for the position of director of the Singakademie, as successor to Zelter, but Zelter's deputy was chosen.

Mendelssohn began an in-depth study of Handel's oratorios, made arrangements of many of them, and conducted performances of them in Düsseldorf. For a time he worked at a theater where he produced and directed operas by Weber and Mozart.

Early in 1835, Mendelssohn was named conductor of the Leipzig Gewandhaus orchestra. During the decade of his tenure there, he did much to improve standards of orchestral performance, the quality of programs presented, and economic and social conditions for orchestral players. He programmed music by historically significant composers as well as works by his contemporaries. When Robert Schumann located Schubert's "Great C-major" Symphony and brought the music to Leipzig, Mendelssohn gave the work its world première (21 March 1839) at Gewandhaus. Often, he invited outstanding soloists to perform with the orchestra; Clara Wieck Schumann performed there 21 times with him as conductor. He encouraged many, singers as well as instrumentalists, by inviting them to perform at Gewandhaus. He organized chamber music concerts, arranged for performances of cantatas and oratorios, and from time to time he appeared as solo pianist or organist and programmed some of his own compositions. In 1840 he conducted a performance of the *St. Matthew Passion* at Thomaskirche, where Bach had first presented it. It is not surprising that the University of Leipzig conveyed upon Mendelssohn an honorary doctorate.

In March 1837 Mendelssohn and Cécile Jeanrenaud (1817–53) were married. The happy couple had five children.

Friedrich Wilhelm IV became King of Prussia in 1840 (r. 1840–58) and involved Mendelssohn in some of his reforms. For instance, the king's desire for a revival of Greek tragedy with some music caused Mendelssohn to write incidental music for Sophocles's *Antigone* and *Oedipus at Colonos*. For the next two years, Mendelssohn divided his time between Berlin and Leipzig. In 1843 he was named director of the Berlin Cathedral choir (all male voices) and director of the opera orchestra. Meantime, in 1840 he convinced King Friedrich August II of Saxony of the need for a music conservatory in Leipzig, and when the Leipzig Conservatory opened in 1843, Mendelssohn was its first director. He designed the curricula and assembled an outstanding faculty. Despite all of these demands on his time, he continued composing and performing. A highlight of each year was his trip to Britain for the Birmingham Festival.

Though Mendelssohn did not feel well during 1846, he fulfilled his teaching and conducting responsibilities, performed, and composed. The news of his sister Fanny's sudden death on 14 May 1847 was a blow from which he never fully recovered. His last completed work was the String Quartet in F minor (Op. 80); he considered it a Requiem for Fanny. In October he suffered a series of slight strokes; he became seriously ill on November 3 and died the next day. His remains were interred in Trinity Cemetery, Berlin, near Fanny's grave.

Mendelssohn's Style

Viewed overall, Mendelssohn's compositions reveal him to be essentially a Classical composer, albeit with some Romantic tendencies, particularly the ability to convey ideas or paint scenes musically. He wrote in traditional forms; when he altered those forms, his modifications did not obscure the traditional patterns. He had a high regard for his musical heritage, studied and performed the works of Bach, Handel, and Mozart, and applied in his own works many of the principles that governed theirs. Mendelssohn could write counterpoint without pedantry, included fugato passages in his large instrumental works, and in his oratorios wrote choruses that incorporated both homophonic and fugal sections. Others who influenced his works include Zelter, Goethe, Beethoven, and Shakespeare. As a composer, Mendelssohn was not a pioneer. He wrote lovely lyrical melodies and frequently used the diminished-seventh chord, but his musical language was more Classical than Romantic. Chromaticism played a relatively small role in his music. His orchestrations are superb and show his thorough understanding of orchestral instruments and his ability to use their tone colors effectively.

Orchestral Works

Mendelssohn's orchestral works comprise 13 *sinfonie,* 5 symphonies, and 6 overtures. There is also an early overture for winds (C major, Op. 24; 1824). The introductory fanfares of the C-major Overture, Op. 101 (1826) have given it the nickname "Trumpet Overture." The other overtures are programmatic; most of them are in sonata form. *Ein Sommernachtstraum* (A Midsummer Night's Dream; 1826), based on Shakespeare, was first performed as an independent overture at one of Carl Loewe's concerts in Stettin. (On the same program Mendelssohn and Loewe performed a double concerto and a work by Weber for two pianos. It was Mendelssohn's first appearance in a public concert.) In 1842, when Mendelssohn wrote incidental music for a production of Shakespeare's *A Midsummer Night's Dream,* he used this overture. *Ein Sommernachtstraum* takes the listener on a delightful excursion into a fairy-tale world; the music is often described as "elfin." (Mendelssohn's other incidental music for *A Midsummer Night's Dream* consists of *Scherzo, Intermezzo, Nocturne,* and *Wedding March.*) *Ruy Blas* (1839) was based on and served as overture to Victor Hugo's play; Mendelssohn also supplied a *Romance* for that play.

The other overtures were intended as concert pieces. *Meeresstille und Glückliche Fahrt* (Calm sea and Prosperous voyage; 1828), based on two poems by Goethe (*Meeresstille* and *Glückliche Fahrt*), is constructed in two contrasting sections, each suited to the mood of the respective poem. *Die Hebriden* (The

Figure 22.2 Fingal's cave on the small island of Staffa.

Hebrides, Op. 26; 1830) is a revised, more expansive version of *Die einsame Insel,* the musical seascape/landscape inspired in 1829 when Mendelssohn visited the small island of Staffa and saw Fingal's Cave with its basalt pillars that, in some respects, resemble organ pipes (fig. 22.2). Portions of the overture sound quite organistic. *Die schöne Melusine* (The lovely Melusine; 1833) portrays moods and events in the legend of the mermaid Melusine.

The 13 *sinfonie* came to light in 1960. Mendelssohn wrote 10 of them as composition exercises for Zelter; the others are youthful works, 1 (unnumbered) being a single contrapuntal movement in C minor. All of the *sinfonie* are for string orchestra; however, No. 8 exists in two versions, one with winds. These works show the influence of Bach and Handel, as well as Viennese Classical style.

For his five symphonies, Mendelssohn used a four-movement structural scheme but occasionally altered Classical formal patterns. Symphonies Nos. 3 and 4 ("Scottish" and "Italian") are the best known of Mendelssohn's symphonies. The "Italian" and "Reformation" Symphonies were not published until the complete edition of Mendelssohn's works appeared in the 1870s.

Symphony No. 1 (C minor, Op. 11; 1824) is stylistically like the *sinfonie;* in fact, Mendelssohn numbered it 13. Symphony No. 5 (D major, Op. 107; 1832) is known as the "Reformation" Symphony because it was planned for celebrations commemorating the Lutheran Reformation and the Augsburg Confession; however, those celebrations did not take place. The sonata-form first movement opens with a fugato (ex. 22.4a) on a motive that begins with the psalmodic formula that commences both the *Magnificat in the Third Tone* (LU,215) and the *Nunc dimittis* (LU,271). The slow introduction includes statements of the "Dresden Amen" (ex. 22.4b, c), and strings state that Amen again in a four-measure Andante just before the recapitulation. In the Allegro vivace second

(a)

(b)

(c)

Example 22.4 Mendelssohn's "Reformation" Symphony, mvt. 1: (*a*) score reduction of the fugato beginning, mm. 1–5; (*b*) "Dresden Amen" as presented by strings in mm. 33–36, in mm. 38–41, and in the Andante preceding the recapitulation; (*c*) the liturgical "Dresden Amen," J. G. Naumann's (1741–1801) harmonization of a traditional melody for use at the Royal Chapel, Dresden.

movement—a scherzo/trio, though not so labeled—winds and strings are treated antiphonally several times. In contrast, the short third movement, an Andante, makes little use of winds; its recitative-like melody is entrusted to first violins, accompanied by the other strings, and only occasionally do winds make a brief comment. A G pitch sustained by 'celli and string basses links the Andante with the Finale, which constitutes variations on Luther's chorale *Ein' feste Burg ist unser Gott*. For the Finale, the instrumentation is increased by contrabassoon, serpent, and three trombones. Mendelssohn used trombones sparingly in his music, only including them in movements associated in depth with church music.

Symphony No. 4, "Italian," (A major, Op. 90; 1832–33) was inspired and begun when Mendelssohn visited Italy but was completed in Germany. The symphony follows standard Classical four-movement form, with the finale being a Neapolitan *saltarello* in A minor. Symphony No. 2, *Lobgesang* (Hymn of Praise, B♭ major, Op. 52; 1840) was written for Leipzig's commemoration of the 400th anniversary of the invention of printing. In some respects, this symphony resembles Beethoven's Ninth. The first three movements of the *Lobgesang* are instrumental; the last is a long cantata (twice as long as the three instrumental movements) for vocal soloists, chorus, and orchestra and concludes with a great choral fugue. The introduction to the symphony's sonata-form first movement uses the dotted rhythms characteristic of the beginning of a French overture. The second movement has a folk-song-like melody such as Haydn might have used; the third movement is theme and variations.

Mendelssohn made sketches for a "Scottish" symphony in 1829, but that was the last symphony he completed. The four movements of Symphony No. 3, "Scottish," (A minor, Op. 56; 1842), are to be played without a break. Though passages from the introduction to the first movement serve as introductions to the other three movements, this symphony is not a cyclic work. The second movement (F major) is the scherzo; the Adagio (A major) comes third.

Concerti

Mendelssohn wrote seven concerti for soloist(s) and orchestra: three for one piano (A minor, 1822; No. 1 in G minor; 1831; No. 2 in D minor; 1837); two for two pianos (E major, 1823; Ab major, 1824); and two for violin (D minor, 1823; E minor, 1844). The E-minor Violin Concerto is one of the finest of all time, comparable with those of Beethoven, Brahms, and Sibelius. Mendelssohn was an excellent violinist, and in this work his writing for the instrument is demanding but idiomatic. He structured his E-minor concerto according to the traditional three-movement overall scheme but linked the movements to ensure that the work would be performed as a unit. The first movement (DWMA183), in modified sonata form, begins with one and one-half measures of orchestral introduction rather than the customary orchestral exposition (ex. 22.5a). Both first and second themes are lyrical. The cadenza is written out and serves as transition between development and recapitulation; arpeggiations in the cadenza overlap the return of the first theme in the orchestra. At the end of the first movement, a sustained B pitch voiced by bassoon as dominant of the E-major chord pivots to become leading tone of C major and link first and second movements. In the C-major Andante, the soloist is required to supply a portion of the accompaniment to the melody line of the second theme (ex. 22.5b). A modulatory 14-measure Allegretto non troppo commencing in A minor links the second movement with the finale, an Allegro molto vivace in E major. Mendelssohn's humor comes to the fore in the opening of the finale, as the orchestra firmly pronounces the tonic chord *fortissimo* and the soloist replies *pianissimo* with a *scherzando* arpeggiation of the dominant-seventh chord. After an 8-measure debate as to whether the melody should commence on tonic or

dominant (ex. 22.5c), the orchestra is victorious, and the soloist plays the first theme *pianissimo e leggiero* in the tonic. Soloist and orchestra share the coda. Structurally, this concerto goes a step beyond Beethoven's "Emperor" Concerto. Mendelssohn, in using a brief introduction instead of an orchestral exposition, making the cadenza functional, and linking all movements, provided a model for other composers.

Chamber Music

Mendelssohn's chamber music includes three piano trios, four piano quartets, seven string quartets, two string quintets, a sextet (D major, Op. 110; 1824; vln., 2 vlas., vc., bass, pno.), the Octet (Eb major, Op. 20; strings; 1825), six sonatas, and some lesser works. There are two sonatas for violin/piano, two for 'cello/piano, one for viola/piano, and one for clarinet/piano.

The most important of these chamber music works are the Octet, the Piano Trios in D minor (Op. 49; 1839) and C minor (Op. 66; 1845), and the three String Quartets of Op. 44 (D major, E minor, Eb Major). The two Piano Trios are frequently performed—many persons consider them the most excellent examples of Mendelssohn's chamber music. Of the quartets, the Eb-major work is the finest. In it Mendelssohn again reversed the order of the two middle movements, placing the lively scherzo second and following the slow movement with a brilliant finale. Mendelssohn's last completed quartet, in F minor (Op. 80; 1847), is somber. The Octet, considered the earliest of Mendelssohn's mature works, is not a double string quartet (though it has that instrumentation) but an eight-voice composition. Its four-movement structure follows the Classical pattern, except for tonality: the outer movements are in Eb, the Andante in C minor, the Scherzo in G minor. The Scherzo is excellent. In it there are bits of humor and some of the same "elfin" lightness that characterizes *Ein Sommernachtstraum*.

Keyboard Solos

Mendelssohn was a superb pianist and an excellent organist. For organ he composed *Three Preludes and Fugues* (Op. 37; 1837), *Six Sonatas* (Op. 65; 1845), several single Fugues and single Preludes, some chorale settings, and some lesser works. As might be expected, the Preludes and Fugues and the Sonatas show

Example 22.5 Mendelssohn, Concerto in E minor for violin and orchestra: (*a*) mvt. 1, mm. 1–6; (*b*) mvt. 2, mm. 55–57, where solo violin plays the melody and measured *tremulando* accompaniment to it; (*c*) ambivalence between tonic and dominant at the beginning of the Finale (reduction of score). (*Source:* Standard Violin Concertos. *Copyright © 1924 D. Appleton and Co.)*

Bach's influence. The Sonatas are uneven in quality—Third and Sixth are best and are frequently performed by church organists as prelude or postlude to a Service.

Mendelssohn wrote numerous solo piano works, ranging in type from sonatas and large fantasias through preludes and fugues to *Lieder ohne Worte* (Songs without words) and other small character pieces. There are 48 *Lieder ohne Worte,* published in sets of six, and a few individual ones. The characteristic titles of most of these pieces were supplied by publishers; Mendelssohn, who disapproved of such appellations, titled only three of them (*Barcarolle, Duo,* and *Chanson populaire*). The name "Song without Words" is appropriate; most of the *Lieder ohne Worte* resemble untexted accompanied solo songs and are in ternary form, with the second A section an expansion of the first rather than an exact repetition of it. Mendelssohn wrote several piano works that he called *Capriccio, Caprice,* or qualified as being *a capriccio*. The term *capriccio* was not new. It was used during the seventeenth and eighteenth centuries as a noncommittal title for keyboard, violin, or viol pieces cast in a variety of forms. In the nineteenth century, the term was used in various ways but usually for small character pieces. Mendelssohn used it to denote a work of fanciful or humorous character.

Mendelssohn's six piano sonatas were written before 1828; he wrote only one other piano work that he referred to, in a subtitle, as a sonata (Op. 28). Apparently he found that idiom unsuitable for what he had to say pianistically.

The most noteworthy of his piano works are *Rondo capriccioso* (Op. 14; 1824), *Six Preludes and Fugues* (Op. 35; 1835–36), the *Fantasia* subtitled *Sonate écossaise* (Scottish sonata, F♯ minor, Op. 28; 1833), and *Variations sérieuses* (Serious variations, D minor, Op. 54; 1841). The Op. 35 preludes are actually études, for each prelude is concerned with a specific technical problem or device. Bach's influence is apparent in the fugues. Of the preludes and fugues, the first, in E minor, is the finest. *Variations sérieuses* is brilliant, idiomatic, difficult but not virtuosic. The 16-measure theme is itself serious and is irregular in form; each of the 17 variations that ensue explores a different technique; the work concludes with a brilliant coda. The *Fantasia* in F♯ minor is in three move-

ments, to be played without a break. Structurally, it is similar to Beethoven's Op. 27, No. 2 sonata (*quasi una fantasia,* C♯ minor). Mendelssohn's work commences with an Andante in F♯ minor in ternary form, moves via a brief *agitato* transitional passage into an Allegro con moto in A major (a scherzo in mood, and equipped with a trio, but in duple meter), and concludes brilliantly with a sonata-form Presto in $\frac{6}{8}$ meter, in F♯ minor.

Stage Works

Early in his career, Mendelssohn was interested in composing stage works. Between 1820 and 1823 he wrote a *Lustspiel* (comedy), a *Singspiel,* and three comic operas. The dialogues for two of the comic operas and for his opera *Der Hochzeit des Camacho* (Camacho's Wedding; 1825) are lost. The works were probably performed at musicales in the Mendelssohn home. The one-act comic opera *Die Soldatenliebschaft* (The soldier's love affair; 1820) and *Die beiden Pädagogen* (The two pedagogues; 1821), a one-act *Singspiel,* were produced in Wittenberg and Berlin, respectively, in 1962. In 1829 Mendelssohn wrote a one-act *Liederspiel*. During the next 17 years he wrote no operas but composed incidental music for a half-dozen plays, including *A Midsummer Night's Dream* and *Ruy Blas*. A three-act opera, *Loreley,* begun in 1847, was unfinished when Mendelssohn died.

Vocal Music

Mendelssohn's most significant large works for vocal soloists, chorus, and orchestra are his two oratorios *Paulus* (St. Paul; 1836) and *Elias* (Elijah; 1846). A third oratorio, *Christus* (Christ), was never completed. Mendelssohn wrote these works after he had participated in the revival of Bach's *St. Matthew Passion* and after he had studied Handel's oratorios intensively and had arranged performances of many of them. *Paulus* and *Elias* reveal Mendelssohn's mastery of choral writing and establish him as a worthy successor to Handel and Haydn in the composition of oratorios. Not only did Mendelssohn include in these works all of the types of music Handel used—recitatives (both *secco* and *accompagnato*), arias, homophonic and fugal choruses—but, as Bach had done in his *St. Matthew Passion,* Mendelssohn inserted harmonized chorales. Undoubtedly, Mendelssohn saw a direct relationship between the story of St. Paul and himself—his Jewish heritage, persecution, conversion to Christianity, and his own personal faith. In *Paulus,* the narration is done by several soloists and sometimes by the chorus, instead of by a single *historicus* or narrator. The overture is based on the chorale *Wachet auf,* and that chorale, either harmonized or as basis for a choral movement, recurs within the oratorio. One of the lovely arias in *Paulus* is *Doch der Herr vergisst der Seinen nicht* (But the Lord is mindful of His own), for contralto.

Elias, written for and performed in English at the Birmingham Festival in August 1846, was more popular in Britain than in continental Europe. (The work was published in German in 1847.) The oratorio, based on I Kings 17–19, opens with a short Prologue in which Elijah (bass soloist) voices the prophecy of no rain. Then comes the Overture, which proceeds directly into the first chorus, the plea of the people for help. The chorus, representing the people, is vital to *Elias,* and Mendelssohn's choral writing is superb. The climax of Part I of the oratorio is the resolution of the confrontation between Elijah, prophet of Jehovah, and the people, worshipers of Baal—the bass recitatives of Elijah interspersed with the crowd's choral pleas to Baal, and, after Elijah's prayerful aria "Lord God of Abraham . . . ," and the quartet's advice to "Cast thy burden upon the Lord," the crowd's dramatic choral response to Jehovah's answer, "The fire descends from heav'n!" (DWMA184). The story of Elijah really ends with the choral report of his being taken up into heaven in the fiery chariot ("scene" No. 38). That is where Mendelssohn wanted to end his oratorio. However, the librettist persuaded him to add another aria, recitative, and two choruses of commentary. Using the words of Psalm 8:1, the final chorus triumphantly praises God and concludes the oratorio with a sevenfold Amen. For the large choral numbers, Mendelssohn used full orchestra, including three trombones, ophicleide, and organ. The distinctive tone quality of the ophicleide, a brass instrument now obsolete, cannot really be replaced by modern instruments (see Insight, "Ophicleide").

Mendelssohn composed six secular cantatas, the finest being *Die erste Walpurgisnacht* (Op. 60; chorus, orch.; 1832). Inspired by Goethe's poem, the highly dramatic cantata concerns the legendary custom of

insight

Ophicleide

The ophicleide, an instrument now obsolete, was introduced c. 1817 by Halary, a French instrument maker, and patented by him in 1821. It is a keyed brass instrument with a strictly conical bore, a wide bell, and a cup-shaped mouthpiece. Actually, the instrument might be described as a very large, upright keyed bugle, and the quality of the tone it produces is comparable with that of a tenor cornet (also obsolete). The ophicleide has a compass of three octaves. The first ophicleides were bass instruments built in C and B♭, but a "family" of ophicleides of various sizes and keys—alto, contralto, bass, contrabass—was soon developed. The B♭ bass ophicleide was the size most widely used, and when played well its tone is full and resonant. Among the composers who wrote important orchestral parts for ophicleide were Spontini, Mendelssohn, Schumann, Verdi, and Wagner. In the twentieth century, ophicleide parts are usually assigned to the orchestral tuba, but it cannot really replace the characteristic ophicleide tone quality.

The ophicleide was the immediate ancestor of the saxophone. Around 1840, Adolphe Sax was repairing an ophicleide and wanted to hear what its sound would be if he substituted a clarinet (reed) mouthpiece for the normal cup-shaped brass one. Thus, he conceived a new instrument—the saxophone.

Bass ophicleide, as pictured on the title page of V. Caussinus's *Solfege-Méthode pour l'Ophicleide Basse,* Paris, c. 1840.

greeting springtime in revelry resembling a witches' sabbath on the night of St. Walpurgis's feast day, April 30.

Mendelssohn's church music is varied in scope and includes works for Catholic, Lutheran, Anglican, and Jewish Services. For the Anglican church, he composed a *Te Deum* . . . (1832), *Nunc dimittis* (1847), *Jubilate* (1847), and *Magnificat* (1847), all with English texts. His Psalms settings are in a variety of forms. Some are similar to cantatas, others are motets; some are *a cappella,* others have instrumental accompaniment, sometimes including instruments that raised theological objection. Some of the Psalms settings (e.g., Op. 78, Op. 91) were written, at the king's request, for the Berlin Cathedral choir. Others were composed for use in Leipzig. The original setting (lost) of Psalm 100 was commissioned by the Neue Tempelverein for dedication of the new Jewish Temple at Hamburg and was for four-voice choir and small orchestra; the existing version is for *a cappella* chorus.

Some of the music on liturgical texts, e.g., *Te Deum* . . . (1826), was written for the Berlin Singakademie, as were also many short community songs. Mendelssohn wrote many part songs—the vast majority of them for male chorus—for German and English music festivals, such as the Lower Rhine Music Festival and those held at Birmingham and in Wales.

While studying with Zelter, both Felix and Fanny Mendelssohn began writing Lieder. More than 110 solo songs and 13 duets by Felix survive. Although they are singable and melodious, the art songs are his weakest compositions.

Influence and Contributions

Mendelssohn was the leading German composer during the second quarter of the nineteenth century and was highly regarded throughout Europe as conductor, performer, and composer. In all three capacities, he participated in music festivals in Germany and Britain. He was in great demand as conductor and conducted at concerts in all the major cities of Germany and Britain. As a pianist, he did much to promote interest in the concerti of Beethoven and Mozart.

Mendelssohn composed well over 250 pieces in nearly all genres and made especially valuable contributions to the repertoire in his oratorios *Paulus* and *Elias* and the E-minor Violin Concerto. He was instrumental in the nineteenth-century revival of Bach's music, through performance of the *St. Matthew Passion* and other works. He programmed Handel's oratorios, also, though often they were presented in altered and somewhat Romanticized versions—sometimes with living tableaux. Mendelssohn was equally cognizant of the work of his contemporaries and promoted the careers of many symphonists (Schumann, Gade, Berlioz) by programming their works in Leipzig. He assisted performers such as Joseph Joachim (1831–1907) and Jenny Lind (1820–87) by presenting them as soloists at Gewandhaus. As director/conductor of the Leipzig Gewandhaus orchestra, Mendelssohn strove for higher standards of orchestral playing and for better economic and social status of the instrumentalists; he planned programs that would acquaint audiences with works from various historical periods. He was instrumental in founding Leipzig Conservatory (1843) and, as its director, assembled an outstanding faculty that included Clara and Robert Schumann, Ferdinand David, Carl F. Becker.

Shortly after Mendelssohn's death, his friends in Leipzig and in Britain founded scholarships in his honor. The Mendelssohn scholarship is one of the most highly valued prizes in Britain; its first recipient was Arthur Sullivan (1856). In 1878 the Mendelssohn Stiftung (Foundation) was established in Germany, and Mendelssohn scholarships were awarded annually from 1878 to 1934. Then the Nazi régime discredited Mendelssohn's accomplishments because of his Jewish background, and the Foundation was forced to cease operations. The awarding of Mendelssohn scholarships was resumed in Germany in 1963.

Fanny Hensel

Fanny Mendelssohn Hensel (1804–47), older sister of Felix Mendelssohn, was a fine pianist and composer. Her earliest known composition is a Lied written for her father's birthday in December 1819. Over the years, she continued to compose Lieder, and they comprise the bulk of her known works.

Fanny Mendelssohn Hensel. Drawing by her husband, Wilhelm Hensel. *(Historical Pictures Service, Inc.)*

Abraham Mendelssohn was strongly opposed to Fanny having a career in music; he believed that the only career for a woman was that of housewife, and with this Fanny's brother Felix agreed. Felix was well aware of Fanny's talent as composer, for brother and sister customarily examined and criticized each other's compositions. Felix included some of Fanny's Lieder in two of his collections of solo songs with piano accompaniment. Three of the songs in his Op. 8 (1828) are Fanny's: *Das Heimweh* (Homesickness), *Italien,* and *Suleika und Hatem,* the latter for two voices and piano. Felix's Op. 9 (1830) includes Fanny's *Sehnsucht* (Longing), *Verlust* (Bereavement), and *Die Nonne* (The Nun).

In October 1829 Fanny married court artist Wilhelm Hensel (d. 1861), who urged her to publish some of her music. However, she made no arrangements for publication of her work under her own name while her father lived. Then, though Felix's opinion had not changed, two of her Lieder—*Die Schiffende* (The one sailing; 1837) and *Schloss Liebeneck* (Liebeneck castle; 1839)—were included in published song collections. Fanny's first public appearance as piano soloist occurred in 1838 when she performed Felix's Piano Concerto No. 1.

Fanny, her husband, and their son (Sebastian) spent the winter of 1839–40 in Italy. That winter she composed a good deal and, with others, performed for the circle of their friends, which included composer Charles Gounod, then in Italy as winner of a Prix de Rome. When the Hensels returned to Berlin, Fanny occupied herself with housewifely duties but continued composing and participating in the Sunday musicales at the Mendelssohn home. After her mother's death (1842), Fanny planned the concerts and sometimes performed in them as pianist and as director of a choral group that rehearsed regularly once a week. Three volumes of her music were published in 1846, *6 Lieder für 1 Singstimme mit Pianoforte* (6 songs for 1 voice with piano, Op. 1), *4 Lieder ohne Worte für Pianoforte* (4 Songs without words for pianoforte, Op. 2), and *6 Gartenlieder* (6 a cappella part songs, SATB, Op. 3). In 1847 three books of her piano pieces and another volume of six Lieder were issued (Opp. 4, 5, 6). Her Piano Trio, Op. 11, was first performed at a musicale in the family home in April 1847.

On 14 May 1847, Fanny became ill while rehearsing a group for a performance of Felix's *Walpurgisnacht* at a Sunday concert; she died that night. Several volumes of her works were published posthumously: *2 Bagatellen* (2 Bagatelles, piano; 1848), *4 Lieder ohne Worte* (4 Songs without words, Op. 8; 1850), two books of Lieder (Opp. 9, 10; 1850), the Piano Trio (Op. 11; 1850), and *Pastorella* (for piano; 1852). Her character pieces for piano indicate that she was aware of current trends.

Hensel composed more than 250 Lieder, and, in addition to the instrumental works mentioned, she is known to have composed one overture and five vocal works with orchestra. About a hundred of her Lieder, and perhaps other works, are in private collections. Many of her early Lieder resemble folk songs and are strophic; those written after 1829 are more sophisticated, in a variety of formal structures—strophic, modified strophic, through-composed, ternary—and in the songs written during the 1840s there are bolder harmonies, enharmonic modulations. Viewed generally, Hensel's known songs exhibit stylistic variety. Occasionally, the piano doubles the vocal line, but usually there is independence of voice and keyboard. Sometimes the vocal melody is projected against reiterated pedal notes; sometimes chords are broken into figurations. Phrases are in irregular lengths (two, three, or four measures); often piano and voice share in melodic interplay. Some of her Lieder are comparable with works by Robert Schumann. Schubert may have been an influence in songs Hensel wrote after 1840, for she played some of Schubert's songs from manuscript while in Italy that year. Of course, Felix was an influence, since they customarily shared opinions about each other's compositions.

Among Hensel's works are German, French, Italian, and English songs. Her choice of poets is comparable with that of Schubert, and includes Goethe, Heine, Müller, Eichendorff, and little-known poets who were members of the Mendelssohn circle. It was not unusual for Fanny and Felix to set the same texts, e.g., Goethe's *Erster Verlust*. Fanny and Schubert set some of the same poems, e.g., Mignon's song, *Kennst du das Land* (Do you know the land) from Goethe's *Wilhelm Meister*. Hensel's setting, written in 1822, differs from most of her early works in being through-composed.

In the 1980s, as a result of increased awareness of the role of women in music history, many of Hensel's compositions were published and recorded. Certainly, she should be considered a significant composer of Lieder in the second quarter of the nineteenth century.

Robert Schumann

Robert Schumann (1810–56) was the youngest (fifth) child of August Schumann, an author, publisher, and bookseller in Zwickau, Saxony. Robert was educated in a local private school and received music lessons from local musicians. In 1820 Schumann began studies at Zwickau Lyceum, where, from time to time, he played piano in musical programs. In 1822 he wrote his first musical composition, a setting of Psalm 150 for SA soloists, piano, and orchestra; later that year he composed an overture and a short chorus. Those works were performed by his friends. Around that time, his literary talent surfaced in some poems and short prose articles. His father printed some of the writing in one of his own publications. Throughout Robert's life, he maintained a dual interest in literary writing and musical composition and succeeded in both fields.

August Schumann died in 1826. During the next year Robert formed three habits that stuck with him for years: drinking champagne excessively, keeping a detailed and explicit diary, and becoming infatuated with pretty girls. The first habit he eventually overcame; the second supplies interesting biographical details; the third was the most costly to him, for through it he contracted syphilis.

Schumann completed his studies at Zwickau Lyceum in March 1828 and entered Leipzig University as a law student. That year he heard Clara Wieck perform and arranged to study music with her father. Over the next few months, Schumann composed a group of songs, eight polonaises for piano, a set of

Robert Schumann. Lithograph by J. Kriehuber, 1839. Original in Robert-Schumann-Haus, DDR. *(Courtesy of the Free Library of Philadelphia.)*

variations for piano duet, and a piano quartet in C minor. He gave these early works opus numbers (ignored by cataloguers), an indication that he was thinking about a career in music. Only the polonaises were published, but not until 1933.

Schumann studied at Heidelberg University in 1829 but maintained contact with Wieck and requested from him Schubert's waltzes and music by Hummel, Czerny, and Moscheles. In 1830 Schumann resumed law studies at Leipzig University but soon abandoned them. He continued music lessons with Wieck and, as was customary, had living quarters in his teacher's house. Before long, he became dissatisfied with Wieck's teaching—Wieck devoted most of his time to Clara, and frequently they were away for concerts—and approached Hummel for piano lessons, without success. For a while, Schumann studied thorough-bass and counterpoint with Heinrich Dorn (1804–92), but much of the time Schumann's attitude and work were lackadaisical, and Dorn discontinued the lessons.

In 1830 Schumann composed the music that became his published Op. 1—*Thème sur le nom "Abegg" varié pour le pianoforte* (Theme on the name "Abegg" with variations, for piano)—influenced by Meta Abegg and by Moscheles's *Alexandre* variations. Throughout his life, Schumann translated names into musical motives for his works, including ASCH, EHE, and, of course, BACH.

Meantime, Schumann turned to literary writing. He invented fictitious names for his friends, his associates, and himself—Master Raro, Florestan, Eusebius, Julius, Zilia, and others—names that appear in his writings for years. In 1830 Schumann heard Chopin play his *Variations on La cì darem la mano.* Schumann procured the music, found he could not master it, and wrote the essay *Ein Opus II* (An Opus Two) in which he made salient remarks about the music and proclaimed through one of his fictitious characters, "Hats off, gentlemen, a genius!" That article, published in *Allgemeine musikalische Zeitung* in December, was the first of Schumann's critical essays on music.

Schumann heard Paganini play in 1830 and was more impressed with his compositions than his virtuosity. A few years later, Schumann based two sets of concert études (Opp. 3, 10) on Paganini's *Caprices.*

Piano playing was becoming difficult for Schumann. The fingers of his right hand, especially middle and index fingers, were weakening. This was formerly attributed to his possible overuse of some kind of mechanical device to improve his technique. (Such devices were available, and their use was advocated by some teachers but not by Wieck.) It is now believed that the weakness was a side effect of treatment Schumann received for syphilis. When he realized that a career as performer was out of the question, he concentrated on composing and on literary activity. Wieck, Schumann, and some friends established the *Neue Leipziger Zeitschrift für Musik* (Leipzig New Journal for Music) and began publication in April 1834. In 1835 the journal was renamed *Neue Zeitschrift für Musik* (*NZfM*); Schumann was its editor for about a decade. At Wieck's home, in 1835, Schumann met Chopin, Moscheles, and, more importantly, Mendelssohn, who, as director of Leipzig Gewandhaus, would be influential in his career. Schumann's most significant article for *NZfM* that year was a long essay on Berlioz's *Symphonie fantastique.*

From time to time, Schumann had been involved with various young women and had extricated himself from at least one engagement. In 1835 he became attracted to Clara Wieck. The two young people fell in love, and in 1837 they decided to marry. For months Wieck evaded a direct answer to Schumann's request for Clara's hand, then refused. Certainly, Wieck viewed Schumann's personality and financial prospects in the proper perspective; also, Wieck was motivated by his personal and financial interest in Clara's career as a performing artist. Undoubtedly, Wieck's objections fueled the romantic fires. Parental permission was required by law; Clara and Robert had to go through long, unpleasant legal proceedings before securing permission to marry in 1840.

During those years, Schumann had composed piano music that was published, and the *NZfM* had prospered. He had always been interested in Schubert's music, and, in 1839, when he learned that Ferdinand Schubert had some of Franz's manuscripts, Schumann visited him. He located in Ferdinand's possession a number of Franz's unpublished works, including the "Great C-major" Symphony, and shared his discovery with Mendelssohn, who gave that symphony its first performance.

Schumann decided in 1840 that he needed a doctorate and inquired as to the proper procedure for obtaining one. On the basis of his achievements as composer, author, and editor, the University of Jena granted him an honorary doctorate. The degree was conferred in March.

In February 1840, Schumann embarked on a year of song composition; he wrote more than a hundred Lieder that year. Many of them—some of his finest Lieder—are love songs. The majority are solos with piano accompaniment; six are part songs for male voices. Most of the songs were published in groups, the volumes containing from 3 to 26 songs. Sometimes a volume was devoted to settings of poetry by a single author, e.g., Eichendorff (Op. 39), Lenau (Op. 90), Rückert (Op. 101), Goethe (Op. 96), and the two masterly song cycles, *Frauenliebe und -leben* (Woman's love and life, Op. 42; von Chamisso's poems) and *Dichterliebe* (Poet's love, Op. 48; Heine's poems).

Clara encouraged Robert to write a symphony. In 1832, he had made sketches for a G-minor symphony but had completed only its first movement (publ. 1972). Late in January 1841, he made sketches for a symphony in B♭, and this time followed through, completing in February his Symphony No. 1, originally entitled *Spring Symphony* (Op. 38). Mendelssohn conducted its first performance at Gewandhaus in March, on a concert presented by Clara. This spurred Robert to more orchestral writing: *Overture,*

Scherzo, and Finale (E minor/E major; Op. 52); *Fantasie* (A minor; pno, orch.); Symphony No. 2 (D minor), revised in 1851 and renumbered as Symphony No. 4 (Op. 120). At the publisher's insistence in 1845, two movements were added to the *Fantasie,* and it became the Piano Concerto in A minor (Op. 54).

Another genre of music soon captured Robert's attention—opera. He adapted Thomas Moore's (1779–1852) narrative poem *Lalla Rookh* for text. Ultimately, Schumann's work became the Romantic cantata, *Das Paradies und die Peri* (Op. 50; 1843), for solo voices, chorus, and orchestra. It was first performed at Gewandhaus in December 1843, with Schumann conducting; the first rehearsal was his first experience as conductor.

In 1842 Schumann turned to chamber music and in swift succession produced three string quartets (A minor, F major, A major). Later that year he wrote a piano quintet (A major) and a piano quartet (E♭ major). More chamber music followed, but he was dissatisfied with the works and used the material in pieces for other media in later years.

Berlioz visited Leipzig in 1843 to conduct some of his work at Gewandhaus, and Schumann talked with him at length. That April the Leipzig Conservatory opened, and Mendelssohn appointed both Schumanns to the piano faculty. Clara, in the last stages of pregnancy with their second child, assumed her teaching duties a bit later.

Schumann was offered editorship of *Allgemeine musikalische Zeitschrift* but declined. For five months in 1844, the Schumanns were on concert tour in Russia. Clara's performances and success weighed heavily upon Robert, and he became melancholy. He composed little and in August experienced a nervous breakdown. At the end of 1844, the Schumanns moved to Dresden. They had acquired a pedalboard for their piano, and Robert wrote 16 pieces for pedal-piano (Opp. 56, 58, 60); he designated the *Six Fugues on B-A-C-H* (Op. 60) as suitable for either pedal-piano or organ. In December Schumann speedily drafted a C-major symphony; completed in 1846, it became his Symphony No. 2. Sporadically, during 1844–53 he worked on *Szenen aus Goethes "Faust"* (Scenes from Goethe's *Faust*; vocal soloists, chor., orch.). However, in 1846 a continual singing sensation in his ears inhibited his creativity for months.

It was as though Schumann felt a compulsion to compose in all genres. In April 1847 he again determined to write an opera. After seeing Friedrich Hebbel's (1813–63) drama *Genoveva* (1843), he decided to use the medieval legend of Geneviève as basis for his opera. He chose to combine material from Hebbel's play with Ludwig Tieck's (1773–1853) drama on the subject but demanded that the librettist delete several interesting and important details of the story. When the librettist refused, Schumann cobbled together the libretto that he set. Yet, it is not the libretto but the music that is weak. Schumann's libretto contains forest scenes, black magic, a ghost, and flames engulfing a witch, but the music lacks the dramatic power, the strength, and the excitement that could have produced an opera comparable with Weber's *Der Freischütz*. Nevertheless, *Genoveva* (Op. 81; 1847–49) *is* German Romantic opera. It contains folk-song-like strophic duets and effective choruses; it is sung throughout but uses arioso rather than recitative, and instead of systematic use of *Leitmotif* as in Weber's opera, Schumann used some reminiscence themes.

Schumann experienced spurts of activity during which he composed rapidly and produced several works; then something would distress him, and he would be unproductive for months. The death of his youngest child in June 1847 did not upset him greatly, but he was shocked by Mendelssohn's death in 1847 and was spurred into activity by being named director of the Dresden Liedertafel, a male singing society. During the next year and a half, Schumann composed choral works, chamber music, instrumental solos with orchestra, songs, and piano pieces. Among the piano works were *Album für die Jugend* (Album for the young, Op. 68) and *Waldscenen* (Forest scenes, Op. 82), the latter inspired by Heinrich Laube's (1806–84) accounts of hunting expeditions in *Jagdbrevier* (Hunting anthology; 1841). In 1849 Schumann set the nine Goethe poems that form *Lieder und Gesänge aus Wilhelm Meister* (Lieder and songs from *Wilhelm Meister,* Op. 98a) and the *Requiem für Mignon* (Requiem for Mignon, Op. 98b). Though political revolutionary activities in Dresden in May 1849 caused the Schumanns to take refuge in a nearby town, Robert's composing was interrupted only briefly.

In 1850 Schumann became municipal music director of Düsseldorf. However, things soon began to go amiss there, and increasingly there was dissatisfaction with his work as conductor. His general health and mental stability steadily deteriorated, and medical treatment had no appreciable effect on his condition. By 1854 the situation had worsened to the extent that the choir refused to perform under his direction. Clara seemed not to realize the extent of his illness and his incompetency as music director—she blamed Robert's colleagues for his difficulties with the choir. He still composed, though there were periods of apathy, and wrote several large works for chorus and orchestra, including a Mass (Op. 147) and a Requiem Mass (Op. 149).

In 1853 Schumann wrote piano accompaniments for Bach's *6 Solos for Unaccompanied Violin* and 6 'cello *Suites*; he did not understand that for those works piano accompaniments are superfluous. Also, he wrote accompaniments to Paganini's *24 Caprices for Unaccompanied Violin*. The many compositions Schumann created in 1853 include a Violin Concerto (D minor; publ. 1937) and *Fantasie* for violin and orchestra (C major, Op. 131) both for Joseph Joachim (1831–1907), whose playing excited Schumann. Joachim brought his friend Johannes Brahms to call on the Schumanns; that visit inspired Schumann's essay *Neue Bahnen* (New Paths), praising Brahms's piano playing and compositional talent.

In February 1854 Schumann asked to be taken to an insane asylum; instead, his doctor advised bed rest. Only after Schumann attempted suicide by plunging into the Rhine River was he placed in a private mental institution near Bonn. There he remained for the rest of his life. Brahms and Joachim visited him from time to time, but because Clara's visits upset him considerably, she stayed away until just a few days before his death (29 July 1856).

Contributions and Style

Schumann was a Romantic composer. His main contributions were in the areas of vocal music, especially Lieder, and piano music. He usually composed at the keyboard, and he included piano in almost all of his works. In fact, he thought pianistically. In many of his Lieder the piano does not merely accompany the voice; rather, voice and piano are partners, with the vocal line adding another tone color to the piano music. *Der Nussbaum* (The walnut-tree; DWMA185) is an example. In no way does this lessen the quality of the Lieder—it enhances the quality. Many of Schumann's piano pieces and Lieder were composed in groups, sets, or cycles.

Though he admired Bach's music, Schumann could not comprehend the self-contained character—the completeness—of Bach's solos for unaccompanied violin and unaccompanied 'cello. Bach was an important influence in Schumann's music, particularly in the mature works. So was the music of Beethoven, Schubert, Chopin, Paganini, Weber, Hummel, and Clara Wieck. Often, Schumann quoted from the works of others; one of the undisguised instances of a lengthy quotation is his use of *La Marseillaise* in *Die beiden Grenadiere* (The two grenadiers). From Clara he borrowed themes and motives, and works of hers inspired him to create similar ones. Clara's encouragement and her urging that he write in large forms was an important factor in his composition of symphonies.

Much of Schumann's music is programmatic, but in many instances the program was not disclosed. He explained in a letter the association between *Papillons* (Butterflies, Op. 2; 1829–31) and Jean Paul's (Jean Paul Richter, 1763–1825) *Flegeljahre* (Years of Indiscretion). Some of Schumann's piano pieces have programmatic titles that were assigned as afterthoughts and had no bearing upon the composition of the music. Schumann concealed from the world a great deal of the intensely personal part of his music. Much of his music is introverted, associated with the private world of his thoughts and feelings and with events in his life. His fantasy world contributed, too; from it came the "larvae" and "butterflies," and the descriptive names he assigned to his associates and himself: Master Raro, Zilia, Florestan, Eusebius, and the others in the illusory League of David of which Schumann was the self-appointed leader. These characters appear in his critical writings and in his music, e.g., *Davidsbündlertänze* (Dances of the League of David, Op. 6, 1837), *Carnaval* (Op. 9, 1834–35), and his article *Ein Opus II*. No doubt Schumann's liking for Heine's poetry stemmed from the hidden or double meanings found in many of those lines. Literature of all kinds served as inspiration for Schumann, though the literary associations in his music are not always obvious. Schumann's fondness for translating names or words into musical motives has been mentioned.

In the performance of Schumann's piano pieces, correct pedaling is extremely important. Also, careful attention must be paid to rhythm, for often Schumann used cross-rhythms and syncopation.

Piano Music

Schumann's music for piano is idiomatic and varies from moderately easy pieces for children to difficult concert works. Character pieces make up the majority of his piano works and are his most important contribution to piano literature. Some, like *Arabeske* (Arabesque) and *Blumenstück* (Flowerbed), are individual pieces, but most of the character pieces are grouped in sets or cycles. Thus, each group forms a large work that is usually performed from beginning to end. In some of the groups each individual piece is complete in itself. However, throughout *Davidsbündlertänze,* Schumann presents the two sides of his personality, Florestan (passionate and extrovert) and Eusebius (dreamy and introvert), and some of the pieces are complementary. Some sets are composed of very short pieces: *Kinderscenen* (Scenes from Childhood), *Waldscenen, Papillons, Davidsbündlertänze. Album für die Jugend* contains delightful little pieces for children. Large character pieces form the cycles entitled *Phantasiestücke* (Fantasy pieces), *Kreisleriana* (Pieces about Kreisler), *Nachtstücke* (Night pieces), and *Noveletten* (Novelettes). E. T. A. Hoffmann's writings about the fictitious Kapellmeister Kreisler inspired both *Phantasiestücke* and *Kreisleriana.*

Carnaval: scènes mignonnes sur quatre notes (Carnaval: miniature scenes on four notes) is a programmatic cycle of 21 short character pieces, most of them dancelike, with thematic variation. The four notes were derived from the letters ASCH, the name of the town in which Schumann's friend Ernestine von Fricken lived. The German notation of the letters can be interpreted as either A-E♭-C-B♮ (ASCH) or A♭-C-B♮ (AsCH), and Schumann used both in *Carnaval*. One of the small pieces is entitled *ASCH-SCHA: Lettres dansantes* (ASCH-SCHA: dancing letters), the rearrangement of the letters representing their order of appearance in Schumann's name. Instead of being announced at the outset, the theme is stated in long note values in a section entitled *Sphinxes,* placed between the eighth and ninth pieces; this short insert is omitted when *Carnaval* is performed. Among the miniatures in the set are *Florestan* and *Eusebius* (representing Schumann), *Chiarina* (Clara), *Estrella* (Ernestine), *Chopin* (a nocturne), and *Paganini* (a virtuosic piece) (DWMA186).

Schumann's most important large works for piano are the Piano Concerto (A minor, Op. 54), *Phantasie in C* (Op. 17), and *Symphonische Etüden* (Symphonic études, Op. 13, C♯ minor). The Concerto's first movement, originally called *Fantasie,* reflects Schumann's knowledge of Beethoven's "Emperor" Concerto. The second movement, an *Intermezzo* in F, concludes, after a long general pause, with a rapid A-major scale that extends into the first measure of the Finale (Allegro vivace, A major). All movements bear some thematic relationship.

The *Phantasie in C* is in three large movements. The first, in C minor, is in sonata form, freely treated; the movement features thematic variation rather than thematic development, and the recapitulation is abbreviated. In the coda, reference is made to the melody of the sixth song in Beethoven's *An die ferne Geliebte* cycle. The second movement is an expansive scherzo in E♭ major, with two trios; the Finale, in C major, is slow.

For the *Symphonische Etüden* Schumann borrowed a theme from Ernestine von Fricken's father and constructed massive and diverse variations on it. In 9 of the 12 études the theme is clearly visible as melody or supporting bass line; in the others the material is treated freely. Schumann wrote three other sets of études. Two sets, each containing 6 études, are based on Paganini's *Caprices for Unaccompanied Violin*; another set comprises free variations on a theme from the Allegretto of Beethoven's Symphony No. 7.

Schumann's three piano sonatas (F♯ minor, G minor, F minor) each contain four movements and follow the traditional structural scheme. The sonata-form first movements are less than satisfactory because of Schumann's inability to develop the thematic

material in the development section. The slow movement of the F-minor Sonata consists of four variations on a theme by Clara.

Chamber Music

In 1842 Schumann composed six chamber music works: three string quartets (A minor, F major, A major, Op. 41), a piano quintet (E♭ major, Op. 44), a piano quartet (E♭ major, Op. 47), and *Phantasie-stücke* for piano trio (Op. 88). Both sides of Schumann's personality, the dreamy and the passionate, are present in the quartets. The piano quintet is excellent and is frequently performed. Its second movement, in C minor, is a march, slow and funereal, with an *agitato* F-minor Trio. Next comes a Scherzo with two Trios that give rondo shape to the movement. The work concludes with a joyous finale in C minor.

Schumann composed three Piano Trios: Op. 63 in D minor (1847), Op. 80 in F major (1847), and Op. 110 in G minor (1851). The finest is Op. 63. In its first movement, a new theme introduced by the piano in the development section resembles Schubert's Lied, *Der Kreuzzug* (The Crusader); its accompaniment in the strings is *sul ponticello.*

In 1851 Schumann wrote two sonatas: one in A minor (Op. 105) for piano and violin; one in D minor (Op. 121) for violin and piano. There *is* a difference in the musical emphasis.

Symphonies

Schumann's symphonies are Romantic works, filled with lyricism, and often the internal structure of their movements is unorthodox. His first complete symphony reveals that, though he could and did write idiomatically for the various instruments, he had difficulty thinking orchestrally and did not take full advantage of the tone colors an orchestra offered. The first rehearsal of Symphony No. 1, the *Spring Symphony* (B♭ major; 1841), brought the shocking realization that the opening horn call had been notated too low for the stopped pitches to sound out well, especially when played *forte.* At Mendelssohn's suggestion, the passage was transposed up a third. Originally, Schumann intended to label each movement with a descriptive title related to Spring; that would have been appropriate to the character of the

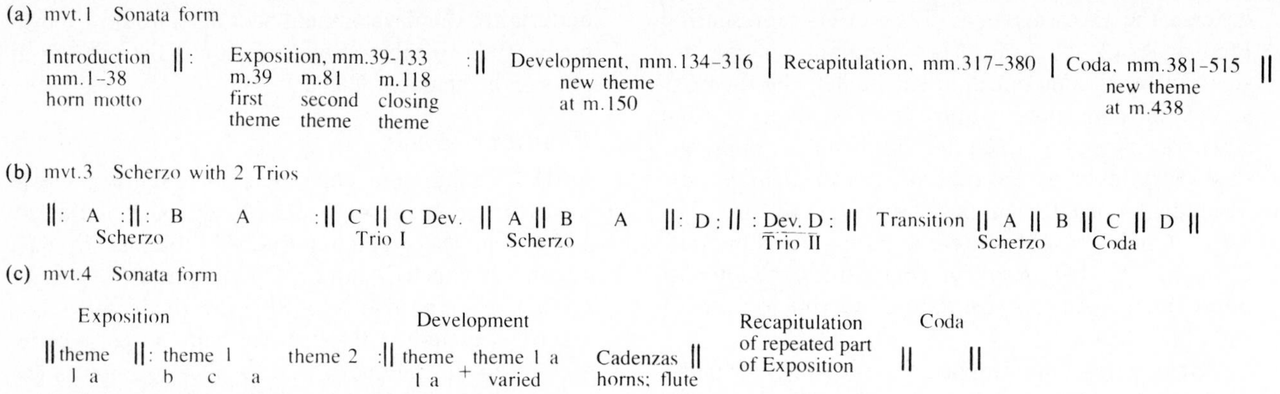

(a) mvt.1   Sonata form

| Introduction
mm.1–38
horn motto | ‖: | Exposition, mm.39-133
m.39   m.81   m.118
first   second   closing
theme   theme   theme | :‖ | Development, mm.134–316
new theme
at m.150 | Recapitulation, mm.317–380 | Coda, mm.381–515
new theme
at m.438 | ‖ |

(b) mvt.3   Scherzo with 2 Trios

‖: A :‖: B   A   :‖ C ‖ C Dev. ‖ A ‖ B   A   ‖: D :‖ :Dev. D: ‖ Transition ‖ A ‖ B ‖ C ‖ D ‖
  Scherzo   Trio I   Scherzo   Trio II   Scherzo   Coda

(c) mvt.4   Sonata form

| Exposition | | Development | | Recapitulation | Coda |

‖theme ‖: theme 1   theme 2 :‖ theme   theme 1 a   Cadenzas ‖   of repeated part   ‖   ‖
  1 a   b   c   a   1 a + varied   horns; flute

Figure 22.3 Diagrams of formal structure of some movements of Schumann's Symphony No. 1, Op. 38, the "Spring" Symphony: (*a*) mvt. 1, Sonata form; (*b*) mvt. 3, Scherzo with two Trios; (*c*) mvt. 4, Sonata form.

music. The first movement, portraying Spring's awakening, is in sonata form with introduction and coda, but the development section is minimal, and a new lyrical theme is introduced in the coda (m. 438; see fig. 22.3a). The songlike Larghetto (E♭ major) that follows is a five-part rondo in which Schumann used dissonance expressively. Near the end of the coda, trombones intone a figure anticipating the theme of the Scherzo; the Larghetto concludes with a transitional passage that leads directly into the D-minor Scherzo. That Scherzo movement is written out. It has two Trios, one in triple and one in duple meter, thus forming a five-part rondo (fig. 22.3b); a coda follows the last return of the Scherzo. The development section of the Finale uses thematic variation rather than thematic development (fig. 22.3c) and is unusual in that all strings except basses play constant tremolo.

The numbering of Schumann's four symphonies does not reflect the order of their composition. He composed a second symphony (D minor) in 1841 but revised it before it was published in 1851 as Symphony No. 4. Its four movements are to be played without a break; in them there is thematic interrelationship—the slow introduction to the first movement provides germinal motives for thematic material of all four movements. In both the first and last movements of the D-minor symphony, as in the first movement of the *Spring Symphony,* Schumann introduced a new lyrical theme near the end of the movement.

The significance of the D-minor symphony lies in the novelty of its structure, and the fact that it is so closely woven.

As he did in the *Spring Symphony,* Schumann began his Symphony No. 2 (C major; comp. 1845–46; publ. 1847) with a slow introduction having a motto theme presented by brass and containing thematic material used in succeeding movements. In the Finale, he again introduced a new lyrical theme near the end of the movement. At Düsseldorf, in the space of five weeks, Schumann composed Symphony No. 3 (E♭ major; Op. 97; November–December 1850), the "Rhenish" Symphony. The work has five movements, two of them slow. Schumann had visited Cologne shortly before writing this symphony; that visit and the installation of Archbishop von Geissel as Cardinal, which took place at Cologne Cathedral, inspired the symphony's impressive fourth movement.

Vocal Music

Schumann is the true successor to Schubert in composition of Lieder. Schumann's Lieder are not as spontaneous as those of Schubert, but they are filled with lyricism and Romantic harmonies. The settings vary from accompanied melody to works in which piano and voice enjoy true partnership, e.g., *Der Nussbaum,* in which the voice begins a phrase and the piano completes it (ex. 22.6a). In other songs, after the piano has taken over the melodic line, the vocalist

Example 22.6 (*a*) *Der Nussbaum*, mm. 37–42, and (*b*) *Lieb'*
Liebchen, mm. 15–24, are representative of voice and piano
sharing melody in Schumann's Lieder. *(From* R. Schumann:
Werke, Vol. 13, edited by Clara Schumann. Breitkopf & Härtel,
Leipzig, 1881–93.)

enters with the same material, e.g., at the end of each
strophe of *Lieb' Liebchen* (Dear little darling) from
Liederkreis (ex. 22.6b).

Schumann and Schubert set some of the same
poems, but their settings differ considerably, e.g., the
songs from Goethe's *Wilhelm Meister*. As did
Schubert, Schumann used various formal types—
strophic, modified strophic, through-composed—depending on his sensitivity to the meaning of the poetry.
In the same way, he selected the type of accompaniment for his melodies, and his Lieder exhibit a great
variety of accompaniment types. Sometimes the accompaniment contains or hints at the presence of a
countermelody. Schumann almost always wrote a
piano prelude and postlude to his songs; sometimes
the postlude spoils the overall effect. In *Die beiden
Grenadiere,* the quiet concluding chords detract from
the stirring majesty of the vocal line and *La Marseillaise.* Schumann gave *Die beiden Grenadiere*
modified strophic setting (DWMA187), as he did

Mondnacht (Moonlight night; DWMA188). The
latter song exhibits extreme musical economy, eight
measures of the music recurring several times in its
three short strophes. Schumann set translations of
foreign-language poems as well as German ones, and
works of his little-known contemporaries as well as
those of noted authors. The song cycles *Dichterliebe*
and *Frauenliebe und -leben* are excellent.

In addition to solo songs, Schumann wrote many
duets, trios, quartets, and part songs for female, male,
and mixed choral groups. Most of the part songs were
written with the Dresden singing societies in mind.
The best of Schumann's choral works are the large
works for vocal soloists, chorus, and orchestra, such
as *Das Paradies und die Peri, Szenen aus Goethes
Faust,* and *Requiem für Mignon.*

Schumann completed only one opera, *Genoveva.*
He planned another but barely began it in 1844. His
only other dramatic work was incidental music for
Byron's *Manfred* (comp. 1848–49).

Critical Writings

Schumann's critical essays take the reader into the fantasy world in which he lived much of the time; the articles are interesting and informative. In some instances, they aided composers' careers, particularly Chopin and Brahms. Schumann made some excellent observations, but his judgments were subjective. This is apparent in the conversations of the fictional *League of David,* which he headed, and whose members advocated the kind of music he composed.

Clara Wieck Schumann

Clara Schumann (1819–96), one of the leading pianists in the nineteenth century, was the daughter of Marianne Tromlitz (1797–1872) and Friedrich Wieck (1785–1873), both of whom were musical. Marianne, a talented singer and pianist, sang the soprano solos in public performances of Mozart's Requiem (1816) and Beethoven's C-Major Mass (1817) and appeared as piano soloist at Gewandhaus on several occasions during 1821–24. Wieck was a self-taught musician who developed a philosophy of education and a system of teaching that was most effective, as evidenced by several of his pupils, e.g., Hans von Bülow, and Wieck's daughters, Clara and Marie. Besides teaching, Wieck owned a business where he sold pianos and had a music lending library in Leipzig. Marianne and Wieck were legally separated in 1824, and he obtained custody of all but the youngest child. Marianne soon remarried; four years later, Wieck did, too.

Though Wieck gave all of his children adequate care, he lavished his attention on Clara and dominated every area of her life. The education in music that he gave her was thorough and practical, but her general education was neglected. Clara did not speak at all until she was almost five, and when she did begin to talk, haltingly, it was rumored that her hearing was impaired. She had learned a little piano before her parents separated; after the separation Wieck established a strict regimen of music study for her: piano, violin, singing, theory, harmony, counterpoint, and composition lessons. In addition, there were long daily walks, for physical exercise was essential. Social contacts were important, and Clara was always present at the gatherings of musicians and literati that took place in the Wieck home. In 1828, Wieck took Clara

Clara Wieck Schumann. *(Da Capo Press.)*

to Dresden where she gave a few private performances. On 20 October 1828, at Leipzig's Gewandhaus, nine-year-old Clara played in her first solo concert. Two years later she performed her first complete public recital in the same hall.

In 1828 Robert Schumann heard Clara perform, was impressed by her playing, and arranged for lessons with her father. Over the next nine years, Robert and Clara became friends, and the friendship deepened into love, but Wieck denied them his permission to marry. Clara was internationally acclaimed as a concert pianist, and her father was reluctant to relinquish his hold upon her life and career. Only after lengthy legal battle was the couple permitted to marry in 1840.

At that time, it was customary for concert artists to include at least one of their own compositions on their programs. Clara had learned to improvise, could make variations, and could include music of that kind. By 1830 she was composing, and by the time she and Robert were married, her piano works Opp. 1–11 had been published. Her Op. 7 is a Piano Concerto in A minor, with string orchestra (or quintet) accompaniment.

Clara continued to concertize after she married, despite the fact that, over the next fourteen years, she had eight children. Undoubtedly, it was necessary for her to work to help meet household expenses. Sometimes she and Robert went on tour together, leaving a maid in charge of the children; sometimes Clara went alone or with another woman. From time to time, Clara wrote some music, but she deferred to Robert's greater talent in that field and usually submitted her compositions to him for criticism. Some of her works contributed to or inspired his compositions. She preferred to include his works on her recital programs rather than her own, but sometimes she included both. On 13 January 1833 her program included, among other works, her own *Caprices en forme de Valse* (Caprices in the form of waltzes, Op. 3; 1832), two of Schumann's "Paganini" études, several *Mazurkas,* and a Chopin *Nocturne.*

Clara was one of the first concert artists to present recitals alone, without assisting artists. She enjoyed playing chamber music and playing sonata recitals, such as those she did with Joachim. When appearing as a soloist, she always played from memory.

After Leipzig Conservatory was established, both Robert and Clara served on the faculty. Reportedly, Mendelssohn invited Wieck to teach there, too, but he declined. During Robert's long illness and after his death it was necessary for Clara to concertize in order to support the family. After 1855 she rarely composed. By that time she had 23 published works with opus numbers, and some without; an additional 15 or 16 works remained unpublished. She continued to include Robert's compositions on her programs but also performed works by Chopin, Liszt, Brahms, and other contemporary composers.

Clara Schumann was the first woman to have a successful international career as a concert pianist. She maintained a rigorous concert schedule until 1873; then she reduced her schedule somewhat, though she believed she should perform in about 50 concerts per year. She concertized until she was past 70; her last public appearance was with E. Welcker, another Conservatory teacher, in a performance of Brahms's *Variations for Two Pianos on a Theme by Haydn,* on 12 March 1891.

In 1878, Clara joined the faculty of Hoch Conservatory, Frankfort-am-Main, as principal piano teacher. She was an excellent teacher, and, though she considered students' individual differences, she insisted that her students master technique, play with seeming relaxation, pay attention to minute details, and interpret the music in conformity with the composer's era and style. She instructed, "Play what is written; play it *as* it is written."

In 1877, after being assured of Brahms's assistance, Clara contracted with Breitkopf & Härtel to prepare a critical edition of Robert's complete works. She relied heavily upon Brahms for advice and for the actual editing of the orchestral, choral, and ensemble works. He prepared the supplementary volume, too.

Clara died in her home in Frankfurt-am-Main on 20 May 1896, while listening to her grandson Ferdinand play, at her request, some of Robert Schumann's music.

Her Music

In addition to the Piano Concerto, a remarkable composition for a 15-year-old, Clara Schumann's works comprise a Piano Trio (G minor, Op. 17; 1846, publ. 1847), a Piano Concertino (F minor, 1847), *Drei Romanzen* (3 Romances, Op. 22; vln./pno.), about 40 piano pieces, 26 Lieder, a few part songs, and cadenzas for concerti by Beethoven and Mozart. Many of her Lieder are excellent, e.g., *Liebst du um Schönheit* (Lov'st thou for beauty; Op. 12, No. 2; DWMA189). The three settings of Rückert's poems that constitute Clara's Op. 12 were combined with nine of Robert's and published as *Zwölfe Gedichte aus "Liebesfrühling"* (12 Poems from *Springtime of Love,* his Op. 37).

The piano pieces are chiefly character pieces, variations, and stylized dances (polonaises, waltzes). The 6 pieces in *Soirées musicales* (Musical evenings, Op. 6; 1835–36)—Toccatina, Ballade, Nocturne, Polonaise, and 2 Mazurkas—indicate that Clara knew Chopin's compositions, and perhaps those of Maria Szymanowska as well. Szymanowska, who concertized internationally from 1815 to 1828, performed in Leipzig in 1823, and most of her approximately 60 piano pieces were published there in 1820–25.

Clara's finest composition is her Piano Trio. Shortly after the Trio was published, Robert composed his first Piano Trio (Op. 63). Clara compared her work with his and belittled her own talent. Yet, Mendelssohn praised her work, and the Trio was the work of hers that was most frequently performed in the nineteenth century. Clara composed only two works according to the four-movement complete sonata scheme: an unpublished *Sonatine* (Allegro, Scherzo, Adagio, Rondo; 1841–42) and the Piano Trio (Allegro moderato, Scherzo, Andante, Allegretto). Note that in both works she placed the scherzo before the slow movement. In the development section of the Trio's Finale, Clara skillfully wrote a fugato.

Music in Denmark

Until the middle of the nineteenth century, very little music by Danish composers was known internationally. Music had flourished in Denmark, and several important European composers, e.g., Schütz, had worked at the Danish court. In the nineteenth century, plays (with and without music), operas, and *Singspiele* were performed at the Royal Theater, and the Royal Orchestra presented numerous concerts. There were two Danish composers of significance in the nineteenth century: Johann Peter E. Hartmann (1805–1900) and Niels Gade (1817–1890).

Johann Peter E. Hartmann

Hartmann's father was a violinist in the Royal Orchestra and organist-choirmaster at Garnisonkirke; his mother was a tutor at court. Johann received an excellent education, both general and musical. Though he completed university studies in law and held a government position, he pursued what might be called a full career in music. He was organist at Vor Frue Kirke, composed music, conducted concerts, and taught at Siboni conservatory. In 1829 he married Emma Zinn (1807–51), who composed songs and published them under the pseudonym Frederik Palmer.

Hartmann traveled outside Denmark and was acquainted with some of the leading European musicians and knew their works, but his music was not influenced by their musical styles. Schumann knew and reviewed some of Hartmann's works, particularly the Piano Sonata in D minor, Op. 34. His masterpiece, the opera *Liden Kirsten* (Little Christine; 1846) was performed at Weimar in 1856. For the most part, however, Hartmann's music was known only in Denmark. Much of his music is quietly nationalistic, containing elements of folk music, traditional hymns, national songs, and, in his operas, the atmosphere of medieval ballads. His surviving works include three operas, incidental music for several plays, two ballets, four concert overtures, two symphonies (G minor; E major), three violin/piano sonatas, other chamber music, numerous piano and organ pieces, much vocal music, including sacred and secular songs, cantatas, and choruses.

Niels Gade

Though Niels Gade had musical parents and Niels evidenced musical talent at an early age, lack of funds prevented him from receiving any systematic musical training until he was 15. In 1833, he was accepted in the Royal Orchestra as a junior violinist. By that time he was composing, but after he heard his early orchestral overtures performed he destroyed most of them.

Gade's first important compositions were the ballet *Faedrelandets muser* (The Fatherland's muses; 1839) and the concert overture *Efterklange af Ossian* (Echoes from Ossian, Op. 1, 1840). With that overture, which was awarded the Copenhagen Music Society prize, Gade came to the attention of Spohr and Mendelssohn. Gade's next important work, Symphony No. 1 (C minor, Op. 5; 1842) was not accepted for performance by the Royal Orchestra, but Mendelssohn programmed it at Gewandhaus in 1843 and brought Gade to Leipzig, as assistant conductor of Gewandhaus Orchestra. In 1847 he succeeded Mendelssohn as conductor of that orchestra.

Soon after war broke out between Denmark and Prussia in 1848, Gade returned to Copenhagen. He reorganized the Copenhagen Musical Society and established a permanent orchestra and choir. Gade held an organist post from 1851 to 1890, served as director and professor at Copenhagen Academy of Music in 1866–90, and composed much music. A few of his works reflect Mendelssohn's influence, e.g., the string

Octet, the *Koncertstykke,* and some scherzo movements. Mainly, however, Gade's works have a distinctly Danish character. For a time in the late 1850s, he included material from Norse mythology in his vocal works, and he was caught up in the contemporary Ossian (or pseudo-Ossian) vogue. Though some of his compositions have programmatic titles, he seems not to have been affected to a great extent by musical Romanticism. In fact, after 1860, he tended more and more to withdraw from it. Gade's extant compositions include nine symphonies, seven overtures, keyboard works for organ and for piano, chamber music (mostly for strings), several pieces for violin and orchestra, ballets, operas, incidental music to plays, sacred and secular cantatas, choral works, and songs.

Gade is historically significant because he introduced some elements of Romanticism into Danish music and helped initiate the national Romantic movement that influenced the next generation of Danish composers. Much of his own music is individualistic, personal. In some of it, he combined Scandinavian traits with some characteristics of German music. After 1860, Gade was gradually overshadowed by the new generation of Scandinavian composers, particularly Edvard Grieg (1843–1907).

Music in France

In France during the second quarter of the nineteenth century, music was dominated by opera. To be sure, there were concerts, both public and private, at which symphonies and chamber music were performed, songs were sung, and famed virtuosi played—Paganini, Chopin, Liszt, young Joachim—but it was opera that reigned, especially grand opera. The success of grand opera in the 1830s was due to the combined efforts of a half-dozen very talented persons: Véron, the director of L'Opéra; Scribe, the librettist; Meyerbeer, the composer; Cicéri and Duponchel, the scene designers; and Auguste Levasseur, the claque leader.

Grand Opera

Opera and theater had succeeded in France because they were enjoyed by royalty and were government supported. Government control was broken temporarily during the French Revolution but was resumed under Napoleon. From 1811 until the 1830 July Revolution, the operation of theaters and opera houses in Paris was under the general supervision of the national Superintendent of Theater and was subsidized by the government. Immediately after the Revolution of 1830, government long-term contracts with dramatists, librettists, and composers, e.g., that between Charles X and Rossini, were canceled. In February 1831 the royal theater was placed under the control of the Minister of the Interior. Government subsidy was gradually withdrawn from L'Opéra, and its operation was leased for six-year periods to a director-entrepreneur who was personally responsible for its financial success or failure. The first person to hold that lease was Dr. Louis Véron (1798–1867), a physician and journalist who had founded the *Revue de Paris* in 1829. Véron knew his own money was at stake—he viewed L'Opéra as a business venture and operated it as such. He had managerial ability and wanted financial success. Therefore, he studied carefully all aspects of opera production and determined to employ the best talents available for everything connected with it. When Véron resigned in 1836, L'Opéra was secure musically and financially. Moreover, he had made a profit—only Lully had done so before him.

Véron began by having the auditorium redecorated and revamped; he reduced the number of boxes containing six seats and increased the number containing four. To gain the support of the bourgeoisie, he held opera balls (masked balls) that were financially profitable, and he removed the "No Admittance" sign from the stage door. He reviewed the personnel roster carefully, culling out the deadwood and reducing salaries where he could, especially in orchestra, chorus, and ballet. Then he considered carefully the choice of librettist, composer, set and costume designers, and even the leader of the claque. Véron was aware of the most successful productions in the late 1820s—Auber's *La muette de Portici* and Rossini's *Guillaume Tell*—and determined to produce works of that kind. After all, those works followed along the traditional lines of Lully's *tragédie lyrique* and Gluck's *tragedia per musica.*

Véron chose Eugène Scribe (1791–1861) as librettist. Scribe had worked in vaudeville, had written libretti for *opéra comique,* and his first venture at L'Opéra, *La muette de Portici,* had proven successful. Scribe knew how to capture audience attention and retain it; he could supply the right amount of diversion (*divertissements*) and could keep a complicated plot under control. His libretti were not adaptations of plays or books but were original scripts based on or related to historical events. His boldest and most successful libretti dealt with issues of political and religious freedom, e.g., *La muette de Portici, La Juive* (The Jewess), *Les Huguenots.* Because Scribe was of the bourgeoisie, he could understand and express their attitudes. In his libretti, Scribe blended Romanticism with the conventional elements of opera. Throughout Véron's tenure at L'Opéra, Scribe was his preferred librettist. Just as Lully had relied on Quinault, and eighteenth-century composers of opera had turned to Metastasio, so Véron depended on Scribe to create effective libretti. Scribe never failed him.

Véron selected Scribe's *Robert le diable* (Robert the devil) as the first grand opera to be produced in newly remodeled L'Opéra. Scribe had originally intended *Robert le diable* as *opéra comique* and in 1827 had discussed it with composer Giacomo Meyerbeer (1791–1864). At that time, Meyerbeer rejected the idea.

Giacomo Meyerbeer (original name, Jakob Beer), a native of Berlin, had studied composition with Zelter, B. A. Weber, and Abt Vogler. Meyerbeer was a virtuoso pianist of the caliber of Hummel and Moscheles but chose not to concertize. Early in 1816 he went to Italy to collect national folk songs, met the leading performers and librettists, and began to compose Italian operas. The musical climate seemed favorable, so he remained in Italy. During the next nine years he wrote six Italian operas, including the semiserious melodrama *Margherita d'Anjou* (Marguerite of Anjou; 1820), and all were successful. His greatest success in Italy came with *Il crociato in Egitto* (The crusader in Egypt; Venice, 1824), which was equally successful when performed in London (1825) and in Paris (1826). Though he never acquired a permanent home in Paris, after 1825 he spent several months a year working there.

In 1831 when Véron and Scribe cast about for an experienced opera composer, they had comparatively few choices. Rossini had decided not to write any more operas, Auber was setting another of Scribe's libretti, Spontini was working in Germany, and Cherubini was considered too old, though in 1833 he did set Scribe's *Ali-Baba ou Les quarante voleurs* (Ali-Baba or The forty thieves) for production at L'Opéra. So Meyerbeer was approached again about composing the music for *Robert le diable,* as a through-composed opera. This time he was receptive, for he had witnessed the success of *La muette de Portici* and *Guillaume Tell.* When performed, on 21 November 1831, *Robert le diable* brought Meyerbeer the greatest success he had ever known. In 1836 he and Scribe experienced similar success with *Les Huguenots. Robert le diable* and *Les Huguenots* are considered the definitive works that established the style of French grand opera.

The plot of *Robert le diable* concerns the contest between Good and Evil for a man's soul, a contest in which the devil uses all possible means but still loses. In composing the music for *Robert le diable,* Meyerbeer drew upon several models: the orchestration of Mayr, the choral writing of Spontini, and the vocal solos of Rossini. There were flaws in Meyerbeer's writing, but the overall composition was excellent. He was especially effective in realizing in his music the full dramatic and emotional potentials of a situation. The soloists, some of whom had been trained by Manuel García, used a blend of French and Italian singing styles. Though grand opera is sung throughout, there are few arias. The arias that are included occur at the beginning of a scene and usually are interrupted from time to time by ensemble or choral interjections. Thus, the solo is incorporated within the dramatic scene, and the singer remains on stage after singing the aria. The chorus participates in the action. There are excellent examples of this in *Les Huguenots,* e.g., Act II, Scenes 7 and 8; Act IV, the scene including the duet and continuing through the Benediction of Daggers, which is the final stretto; Act V, the *scena* with trio. (See DWMA190.) In 1831 L'Opéra had a superb chorus master in Jacques Halévy (1798–1862), who was also a talented composer. In 1835 he achieved outstanding success with his setting of Scribe's *La Juive,* a masterpiece, and one of the finest grand operas of the 1830s.

The success or failure of an opera is determined by more than just the quality of its music and its libretto. Many contributing factors must be taken into account. Among these are stage setting, costumes, and properties. Véron and his two scene designers, Edmond Duponchel (1795–1868) and Pierre Cicéri (1782–1868), were very much aware of this. In their production of grand opera, the scenery was not merely background but environment and was closely allied with the action. The designers made the stage setting as authentic and realistic as possible—Duponchel was architect as well as artist. They insisted on accuracy in costuming, used real objects (instead of wooden or other imitation ones) as properties, and replaced flat backdrops with dimensional-effect scenery that extended the space considerably. Cicéri and Duponchel were well acquainted with the panoramic treatment of scenes in the tableaux of the popular *spectacles d'optiques,* and the revolving floors used in connection with diorama, and they used as many of these devices and effects as they could in the production of grand opera. For example, in the cloister scene in Act III of *Robert le diable,* Duponchel based his realistic setting on an actual cloister, Montfort-l'Amaury. In that *divertissement* scene, nuns long-dead arise from their graves, cast off their musty habits, and dance in the pale moonlight (colorplate 22). Achieving the proper sepulchral effect of pale moonlight over a cemetery was no problem with the new, controllable gas lighting. House lights were lowered during the production; stage lights were dimmed during scene changes. So effective were the sets for *Robert le diable* that sets for later works were measured by them. In view of the importance attached to stage settings, and the popularity of tableaux entertainments in Paris, it is understandable that Hector Berlioz (see p. 667) wrote operas constructed in **episodes,** without dramatic continuity, placed in tableaulike settings.

Another important factor in the success of *Robert le diable* was the claque, which, firmly persuasive, guided audience taste. Auguste Levasseur, claque leader, studied the libretto, attended rehearsals regularly, and knew the singers and dancers. His claque, well-trained and responsive to his signals, was scattered strategically among the audience. (The theatrical term for this is "papering the house.")

The characteristics of the musical construction of French **grand opera,** as defined by the most successful productions in the early 1830s, particularly Meyerbeer's *Robert le diable* and *Les Huguenots,* are these: Grand opera is sung throughout, but there are relatively few arias and almost no pure recitative. Those arias that are included occur at the beginning rather than at the end of a scene, and the soloist remains on stage at the conclusion of the aria. In style, the solo songs are less elaborate and may be narrative; the lyricism of solo song is secondary to movement of the drama. Usually a solo is interrupted by choral or ensemble interjections that may occasion dialogue sections. Instead of dialogue via recitative, arioso is used. The language of the libretto does not interfere with the music. Much of the action takes place in festive settings such as processions, mass meetings, and social gatherings. Ensembles of all sizes, from trios to full chorus, are an important part of the drama. The spectacular choral and ballet *divertissements,* in accord with historical events, are woven into the drama and the music so that they contribute to the continuity of the plot; they serve to relax audience attention briefly but do not permit it to stray from the story. For example, *La Juive* takes place in the fifteenth century, at the time of the Great Schism when there were three rival popes, and when anti-Pope John XXIII and Emperor Sigismund arranged a meeting at Constance in an attempt to end the Schism. The pomp connected with the circumstances provided ample material for crowd scenes and ceremonial spectacles.

All of the most important grand operas produced at L'Opéra in the 1830s—those that established the course of French opera—were on libretti by Scribe: Meyerbeer's *Robert le diable* (1831), Auber's *Gustave III* (1833), Halévy's *La Juive* (1835), and Meyerbeer's *Les Huguenots* (1836). None were adaptations of plays; all were new scripts with stories akin to the Gothic romances that were popular literary fare in Europe. Both common folk and aristocracy were included in the plots, and each plot involved a major decision related to historical and sometimes contemporary issues—a decision with which the audience could empathize. For example, in *La Juive* Rachel can escape her terrible fate if she renounces her religion; Valentine, in *Les Huguenots,* must choose between life with Catholicism and death with her Huguenot lover.

Duponchel succeeded Véron as director of L'Opéra in 1835 and managed it until 1849. French grand opera was produced throughout the nineteenth century, though to a lesser extent after 1850. Patriotic themes were popular during the Revolution of 1848. When Louis Napoleon came into power (r. Pres. 1848–52, Emperor 1852–71), he placed L'Opéra, then experiencing financial deficit, back under government control.

Grand opera, as a type, was not confined to Paris. The influence of French grand opera is apparent in works by Italian and German composers: Bellini's *I Puritani* (The Puritans; Paris, 1835), Verdi's *Les vêpres siciliennes* (Sicilian vespers; comp. 1839, Scribe libretto; Paris, 1855) and *Aïda* (Cairo, 1871), and Wagner's *Rienzi* (1842). Touches of grand opera appear in other works by Wagner and in some twentieth-century operas.

Opéra comique

Almost all of the composers of serious opera wrote *opéras comiques* also and Scribe wrote libretti for both kinds of settings. Operas were produced in two different theaters in Paris, L'Opéra admitting only large-scale works sung throughout, and L'Opéra-Comique producing only works with spoken dialogue. When government subsidies were withdrawn after the Revolution of 1830, L'Opéra-Comique experienced financial difficulties, and, a few months after the successful première of Hérold's *Zampa* (May 1831), was forced to close for a short time. The Paris riots in June 1832 caused another closing that lasted until the end of September. When L'Opéra-Comique reopened, *Zampa* became part of the repertoire. Shortly after Hérold's *Le pré aux clercs* (The field of honor; December 1832) was produced, he died and never realized its tremendous success. Before 1900, it had more than 1500 successful performances at L'Opéra-Comique. Both *Zampa* and *Le pré aux clercs* are the romantic type of *opéra comique*.

Scribe wrote the libretti for 6 of the 14 new operas produced at L'Opéra-Comique in 1833–40. In fact, Scribe and Auber dominated *opéra comique* for approximately half a century. Between 1813 and 1869 Auber composed 34 *opéras comiques,* and all but 6 (the first 4 and the last 2) were on libretti by Scribe.

Among them were *Leicester, ou le château de Kenilworth* (Leicester, or Kenilworth Castle; 1823), based on Scott's novel; *Fra Diavolo* (Brother devil; 1830); *Le domino noir* (The black domino; 1837); *Les diamants de la couronne* (The crown diamonds; 1841); and *Manon Lescaut* (1856). Auber's last *opéra comique, Rêve d'amour* (Love's dream; 1869) was in essentially the same style as his early works—dealing with amusing situations, witty and worldly without emotional depth, with uncomplicated music, usually in a major key. Casts were comparatively small. The plots were either romantic or semiserious drama or comedy and sometimes a mixture of both. In *Fra Diavolo,* romantic and comic elements are mingled. These facts indicate that, so far as style and content were concerned, music at L'Opéra-Comique was relatively stagnant betwen c. 1825 and 1870.

Bizet

Georges Bizet (1838–75) worked as rehearsal accompanist at L'Opéra-Comique while he was studying composition at Paris Conservatoire. Bizet was an excellent pianist and could have pursued a concert career had he chosen to do so. Instead, he became a composer. After winning the Prix de Rome (1857) and spending the required years composing music in Italy, he returned to Paris and began to compose operas. In 1866 he signed a contract with Carvalho to compose some works for Théâtre-Lyrique. After Carvalho became director of L'Opéra-Comique (1868), Bizet wrote some *opéras comiques* for production there. His greatest work is *Carmen* (comp. 1873–74), produced at L'Opéra-Comique in March 1875.

Carmen did not follow traditional lines. In fact, it was so different from the usual *opéras comiques* that it was a failure. The audience was shocked and puzzled by it; they considered some of the situations coarse and obscene. The plot was neither Romantic nor comic, but serious—a tragedy. For the first time, a murder was enacted on stage. The spoken dialogue was neither affected nor obscene, but that typically used by cigarette-factory workers and the other types of characters depicted, at that time. The same can be said of the situations in the story. Bizet presented characters realistically, in true-to-life situations, with normal reactions. The dramatic mezzo soprano Célestine Galli-Marié (1840–1905), a petite young lady

Figure 22.4 A contemporary drawing of the Habanera scene in Act I of Bizet's *Carmen* in the first production of the work, Paris, 1875. Don José, at the left, is busy with his equipment, while Carmen sings and teases him with her flower.

with a vibrant personality, created the role of Carmen. Bizet included in the music a folk song from Ciudad Réal, used for Carmen's song *Coupe-moi, brûle-moi* (Cut me, burn me; Act I). The entr'acte to Act IV is based on a song by Manuel García. Bizet thought he was using an authentic folk song for the *Habanera*, but he learned later that it was *El arreglito, Chanson Havanèse* (A little arrangement, Havanese song) by Spanish composer Sebastién de Yradier (1809–65) and put a note in the vocal score acknowledging that fact.

Viewed historically, *Carmen* is a landmark in the history of *opéra comique*. It is excellent, and with it Bizet brought *opéra comique* to a peak. More importantly, through use of a serious subject, and presentation of a tragedy with spoken dialogue, Bizet

destroyed the artificial line of demarcation between *opéra comique* and *opéra*. *Carmen* could not have been performed at L'Opéra because of its spoken dialogue, and Théâtre-Lyrique was no longer in existence. Technically, the subject was too serious for L'Opéra-Comique, but Carvalho decided to produce the opera. Bizet's realistic portrayal of characters and situations in *Carmen* had considerable influence on the composition of *verismo* (realism) operas at the end of the nineteenth century.

Before his death (June 1875), Bizet prepared the vocal score, without the spoken dialogue, for publication, and it was issued later that year. After Bizet's death, his friend, American composer Ernest Guiraud (1837–92), substituted recitatives for the spoken dialogue, so that the work might be performed at L'Opéra, and toned down some of the scenes. The recitatives spoil the opera. For one thing, they remove from it the portions of melodrama that were so effective. Attempts have been made to restore the opera to its original state, but, as of 1988, all of the original spoken dialogue had not been located.

Lyric Opera

In France, c. 1845, there were three principal theaters producing operas: L'Opéra, for large-scale serious works in French, such as grand opera, that were sung throughout; L'Opéra-Comique, for lighter, non-tragic works in French with spoken dialogue; and Théâtre Italien, for Italian operas. Composers writing French operas that were sung throughout but were on a smaller scale than grand opera experienced difficulty getting their works produced. In 1847 the Opéra National was founded with the express purpose of producing French operas that were rejected by L'Opéra-Comique because they were sung throughout and that could not be performed at L'Opéra because they were considered too small or too light. Moreover, the new theatre, whose name was changed in 1852 to Théâtre-Lyrique, did not deny production to mid-scale works with spoken dialogue. Many composers writing operas for production at Théâtre-Lyrique gave their works the designations *opéra lyrique* or simply *opéra*; if the opera had spoken dialogue, the composer might label it *opéra dialogué,* as did Charles Gounod (1818–

93). The subject matter of many of the operas produced there was romantic drama or fantasy. Théâtre-Lyrique was at its height during 1856–68, while baritone Léon Carvalho (1825–97) was director. The theater closed in 1870 because of financial difficulties during the Franco-Prussian War.

Several operas by Bizet were produced at Théâtre-Lyrique, including *Les pêcheurs de perles* (The pearl-fishers; 1863) and *La jolie fille de Perth* (The pretty girl from Perth; 1867). In 1863 Part II of Berlioz's *Les Troyens* was staged at Théâtre-Lyrique. Among the most successful productions there were Gounod's *Le médecin malgré lui* (*opéra comique*; 1858), *Faust* (*opéra dialogué*; 1859), and *Roméo et Juliette* (*opéra*; 1867); and Ambroise Thomas's (1811–96) *Mignon* (1866), a melodious, expressive work based on Goethe's *Wilhelm Meister.* Thomas had a strong cast for *Mignon,* with Célestine Galli-Marié as Mignon and Marie Cabel as Philine. The roles of Marguerite (in *Faust*) and Juliet were created by soprano Marie Miolan-Carvalho (1827–95).

Gounod's *Faust* concerns only that portion of the legend dealing with the love story of Faust and Marguerite and the destruction of both lovers through Mephistopheles's treachery. In *Faust,* the spectacular element is present but is reduced in importance; characters are more humanized than in many grand operas of the time. Marguerite's ballad *Il était un roi de Thulé* (There was a king of Thulé) has a tinge of modality and delightful conversational interruptions; the "Jewel Song" is excellent. Both songs are in a style appropriate to Marguerite's character. Gounod's ability to write meaningful, expressive, lyric melody is apparent. *Faust* is almost never performed as originally written, for in 1860 Gounod converted it to grand opera and substituted recitatives for the spoken dialogue; later, he added a full-length ballet, so that *Faust* was suitable for performance at L'Opéra. Gounod is seen at his best in *opéra comique.*

Opéra bouffe; Operetta

Pure comic opera was almost nonexistent in Paris during the first half of the nineteenth century. In 1850 Jacques Offenbach (1819–80), a 'cello virtuoso, was appointed conductor at Théâtre Français, a theater producing spoken drama in Paris. He attempted to get some of his stage music produced, to little avail,

so he decided to produce some of his works himself. He rented a small wooden theatre on the Champs-Elysées, the Théâtre Marigny, renamed it Les Bouffes Parisiens (Parisian comedies), and on 5 July 1855 presented the first in a series of programs of short comic pieces. The endeavor proved successful. In 1856 he moved to a larger theater, and by 1858 Parisians were interested in *opéra bouffe* (comic opera). Though he concentrated on one-act works, he produced some with two. His first triumph came with *Orphée aux enfers* (Orpheus in the underworld; 1855) satirizing the Orpheus myth. *La chasse,* the music played while Orpheus and Euridice are attempting to flee from Hades, is that of the Cancan. *Orphée aux enfers* was followed by a series of successes, chief of which were *La belle Hélène* (Beautiful Helen; 1864), satirizing the story of Helen of Troy; *Barbe-bleu* (Bluebeard; 1866); and *La vie parisienne* (Parisian life; 1867). Frequently, Offenbach achieved humor by quoting music that was familiar to the audience and substituting satirical words or using the borrowed themes in incongruous situations. In his works, the music is always more or less subdued, and the words are never obscured by it. Offenbach composed approximately 90 comic operas and operettas. **Operettas** are musical theatrical works, light and sentimental in character, with spoken dialogue, and with some dancing. Offenbach wrote some ballets, also, and *Les contes d'Hoffmann,* depicting three stories by E. T. A. Hoffmann as episodes in Hoffmann's love life. Ernest Guiraud orchestrated *Les contes . . .* for Offenbach.

Operettas became popular in Vienna after 1860, in England during the last quarter of the century, and in the United States after 1900. The principal Viennese composers were Franz von Suppé (1819–95) and Johann Strauss II (1825–99). Many of Strauss's 16 operettas have become part of standard repertoire, especially *Die Fledermaus* (The Bat; 1874).

Louis-Hector Berlioz

Louis-Hector Berlioz (1803–69) was the oldest of the six children of Dr. L.-J. Berlioz, a well-to-do and highly respected citizen of La Côte-St. André, France. Hector's mother was a devout and strict Catholic; his father's intellectual pursuits were wide, his views liberal. As a child, Hector was much interested in literature. He had flute and guitar lessons and, without

Hector Berlioz. A photograph made c. 1865.

Berlioz wrote an operatic setting of de Florian's ode *Estelle et Némorin*; later, he burned it and some other early works. Though Berlioz disliked the idea of a career in medicine, he continued medical studies until he obtained his baccalaureate in physical sciences (1824). Then music occupied his time. When funds from home were cut off, he worked as a chorus singer and taught lessons. He was not an outstanding performer but played flute and guitar well. In 1826 he enrolled at the Conservatoire as a composition student and wrote the opera *Lénor, ou les derniers francs juges* (Lénor, or the last French judges), which was never performed.

Between September 1827 and March 1828 Berlioz had three experiences that greatly affected his life and work: He attended performances of Shakespeare's plays, including *Hamlet* in which Harriet Smithson acted; he heard Beethoven's symphonies (Nos. 3 and 5) for the first time; and he read Gerard de Nerval's (1808–55) translation of Goethe's *Faust*. Beethoven's symphonies turned Berlioz's attention from vocal to instrumental music, particularly the symphony; his infatuation for Smithson was translated into *Symphonie fantastique*; Shakespeare's plays and Goethe's *Faust* became the basis for several compositions. A few years later, Berlioz introduced Liszt to Goethe's *Faust* through the French translation. Berlioz's interest in literature never flagged. He maintained a lifelong interest in Vergil's *Aeneid,* Shakespeare's plays, Goethe's *Faust,* and works by contemporary French authors—this is reflected in his compositions.

Berlioz competed four times for the coveted Prix de Rome before he finally composed a cantata worthy of the honor. Only a fragment of that work, *La mort de Sardanapale* (The death of Sardanapale, 1830), survives. The cantata he submitted for the 1828 competition, *Herminie* (Erminia, based on Tasso), contains the melody he used for the *idée fixe* (obsession), the recurrent theme in *Symphonie fantastique*.

Winning the Prix de Rome was important to Berlioz; he hoped it would give his career the boost that it needed so badly, but he did not really want to leave Paris. He was enjoying an eventful life—one that would be increasingly colored by passionate romances, triumphs and disappointments, and even scandal. In 1830, he was romantically involved with

a tutor, acquired a basic knowledge of harmony by studying Rameau's *Traité de l'harmonie* and other theoretical treatises. Apparently, he did not have access to a keyboard instrument; in fact, he never became a pianist. While in his early teens, he began to write music and in 1819 submitted some of it to publishers. *Le dépit de la bergère* (The shepherdess's spite), a **romance,** was accepted and published. A romance is a lyrical, strophic song on an epic or amorous subject.

Berlioz received a bachelor's degree in Grenoble in 1821, and, to please his father, entered medical school in Paris. He was attracted to opera, and one of the first performances he attended was Gluck's *Iphigénie en Tauride*. Gluck's music had a lasting influence on Berlioz's style. In 1822 Berlioz arranged for composition lessons with Le Sueur. The following year

pianist Camille Moke, and he was in Rome only a short time when he became concerned because he had not heard from her. He went back to Paris to check on her, learned that she had married Camille Pleyel, and planned to shoot them both. Fortunately, he was deterred. Berlioz returned to Rome but did not remain in Italy for the full two years expected of Prix de Rome recipients. While in Italy, he composed the musico-literary *Le retour à la vie* (Return to life), later named *Lélio,* and in Nice he wrote overtures based on Shakespeare's *King Lear* and Scott's *Rob Roy.*

Berlioz had been obsessed with Harriet Smithson (1800–1854) since he first saw her on stage. He pursued her relentlessly, despite the fact that he had not even met her and she spurned his proffered attentions. When Berlioz returned from Italy, he finally met Smithson and, after a whirlwind courtship during the course of which he attempted suicide, they were married in 1833. The marriage was not the happy one Berlioz envisioned.

During the 1830s, Berlioz earned very little from composition. To earn a living, he resorted to writing and penned numerous critical articles for *Gazette musicale, Journal des débats,* and other influential French papers. He was better known in Parisian music circles as critic than as composer. In 1832–42 he participated as conductor in from two to five concerts per year in Paris—concerts shared by several artists and an orchestra. Because he strongly advocated strict adherence to composers' notated music, and he realized that many performers and conductors altered music freely, Berlioz did not want others to conduct his compositions. For the next two decades, he went on a number of concert tours in Germany, conducting performances of *Roméo et Juliette, Symphonie fantastique,* and his concert overtures. For 12 years, commencing in 1842, he toured frequently with mezzo soprano Marie Recio (1814–62). For her he composed *Les nuits d'été* (Summer nights; 1840–41) and other songs.

From time to time, Berlioz served as chief conductor at national commemorative celebrations and composed works for such affairs. His most significant commemorative works are *Grande messe des morts* (Large Requiem Mass; 1837) and *Te deum laudamus* (1849). In the early 1840s, he worked on his *Grand traité d'instrumentation et d'orchestration modernes* (Large treatise on modern instrumentation and orchestration, Op. 10; publ. 1843).

Harriet Berlioz had been paralyzed for several years and died in 1854. A few months later, Marie Recio and Berlioz were married (1855). Marie's mother lived with them, and, after Marie's death (1862), cared for Berlioz who was in ill health. During the last six years of his life, Berlioz composed almost nothing and spent his time working on his *Mémoires.* He died on 11 March 1869.

Style Characteristics

Characteristics of Berlioz's style are: (1) effective and free use of counterpoint, including the combination of melodies or themes first presented separately, and fugato sections in which successive entries do not adhere to traditional tonic-dominant practice; (2) treatment of the bass line as a melody placed contrapuntally against another melody in an upper voice; (3) construction of melodies in irregular phrase lengths; (4) use of chromatic inflections (especially the flatted submediant pitch) in basically diatonic melodies, for purposes of characterization or expression of mood; (5) use of basically Classical harmonic vocabulary in nontraditional manner, with progressions chosen for expressive reasons rather than the expected functional ones; (6) frequent use of recurrent themes, theme transformation, and thematic variation, e.g., *Harold in Italy, Symphonie fantastique*; (7) orchestration centered on instrumental color, sometimes combining dissimilar instruments to achieve the desired coloristic blend, and considering as standard orchestral instrumentation some instruments formerly included only for special effects, e.g., English horn and harp; (8) spatial distribution of voices and/or instruments (e.g., performers offstage) for special effects.

Berlioz was concerned not only about the sound of his music *per se* but about the suitability of the music to the size and acoustics of the hall in which it was to be performed. In other words, with Berlioz as with Gabrieli (see p. 280), the spatial distribution of sound was important. This was equally crucial in choral and in instrumental music. Berlioz's achievements in orchestration were remarkable. His orchestration treatise was the first textbook written on that subject. It is still used in some schools.

Berlioz's significance for the development of music in history lies in his symphonies (particularly the first three), his orchestration treatise, and his epic opera *Les Troyens* with which he brought the French style of opera to a peak. The nineteenth century knew only truncated versions of that work so could not appreciate it as the masterpiece that it is. In the main, Berlioz was an individualist, a Romanticist, relatively unaffected by the work of his contemporaries but aware of and influenced by the music of Beethoven and Weber, and to a lesser extent by Gluck, Spontini, and (in his early operas) Méhul. The many grandiose works written to commemorate French military victories, the Revolution, and other political events also had some effect on Berlioz's works.

Berlioz had a penchant for program music. Just as Schubert was able to translate poetry into sound and create a miniature drama from a Lied (e.g., *Erlkönig*), so Berlioz could synthesize programmatic ideas with orchestral music to create drama without words (e.g., *Symphonie fantastique*).

Instrumental Music

Berlioz's orchestral works comprise four symphonies, five overtures, and *Reverie et caprice* for violin and orchestra (1841). Of the overtures, *Le carnaval romain* (Roman carnival; 1844), a brilliant orchestral piece based on material from his opera *Benvenuto Cellini,* is the one most frequently performed. It is constructed, as are most of Berlioz's overtures, with an introduction consisting of a brief Allegro followed by a slow section, then the main Allegro. The other overtures are: *Waverly* (c. 1828) and *Intrada di Rob Roy Macgregor* (Overture on Rob Roy Macgregor; 1831), both based on novels by Scott; *Le roi Lear* (King Lear; 1831); and *Le corsaire* (The Corsican; 1844).

Symphonie fantastique: Episode de la vie d'un artiste (Fantastic symphony: Episode in an artist's life; 1830) was Berlioz's first symphony. In it he aimed to create a large-scale orchestral composition that was a unified whole rather than a set of movements that could be performed individually, and a work that possessed dramatic and lyric significance. He did so. The work is unified in two ways: through a recurrent theme (ex. 22.7) and through the musical unfolding of the drama. The printed program the composer provided the audience outlines the events experienced by a young man in delirium after seeking release from the anguish of unrequited love by taking opium. In the translation of those experiences into music, the Beloved became an *idée fixe,* a recurrent theme (sometimes transformed or varied rather than literal), a glittering thread woven into the fabric of the symphony. Berlioz was that lovesick lad; Harriet Smithson was the Beloved, whom, at that time, he had not even met!

Notwithstanding the authenticity of the stated program Berlioz provided, the symphony is autobiographical to a greater degree in that it reflects numerous shaping forces in Berlioz's life between the ages of 12 and 27: (1) his infatuation as a 12-year-old for Estelle Duboeuf; (2) his liking for Vergil's *Aeneid* and concern for the plights of mythological Dido and Phaedra; (3) his mother's devout religious beliefs and his own professed atheism; (4) his proximity to French revolutionary ideas, the guillotine, and the execution of André Chénier; (5) his medical studies and the psychiatric term in vogue, *idée fixe*; (6) his reading of De Quincey's *Confessions of an English Opium Eater* and Chateaubriand's *Genius of Christianity*; (7) his intellectual experiences in Paris— Shakespeare, Hoffmann, Goethe's *Faust,* Hugo's *Ronde du Sabbat*; (8) his study of Beethoven's music and Weber's *Der Freischütz*; and (9) musical themes designed for some of his own early compositions. Not even the *idée fixe* was new—Berlioz had used it in a cantata (1828) to represent the female warrior Erminia, ill-fated beloved of the Christian knight Tancred (in Tasso's *Gerusalemma liberata*).

Structurally, *Symphonie fantastique* reveals Berlioz's knowledge of Beethoven's symphonies in at least three ways: (1) it is cyclic (Fifth Symphony); (2) there are five movements (Sixth Symphony); (3) the slow movement is placed third instead of second (Ninth Symphony). Berlioz's awareness of Beethoven's Fourth and Sixth Symphonies is apparent in the musical depiction of the "Scene in the Fields," which constitutes the third movement of *Symphonie fantastique*.

The first movement of *Symphonie fantastique*, labeled "Reveries, Passions," is in sonata form with introduction and coda. Winds and muted strings create a mood of reverie, playing a C-minor melody originally used by teen-aged Berlioz in his setting of de Florian's pastorale, *Estelle et Némorin*. The principal theme, the *idée fixe,* is presented in C major by flute and violins in unison. The second movement, "A ball," is a graceful waltz in A major, featuring strings and harps; the middle portion of the movement is devoted to the *idée fixe,* voiced first by flute and oboe with string tremolo accompaniment, then reiterated by clarinet and flute. The third movement is a pastorale, a "Scene in the Fields" in which English horn and oboe simulate the echoing and dialogue of Alpenhorns, using the Swiss *ranz des vaches* (cowherds' horn call) that Berlioz enjoyed when visiting his grandparents at Meylan. The Beloved's presence is felt when flute and oboe play the *idée fixe*. The pastoral mood is interrupted by timpani rumblings—thunder at first distant, then moving closer; the serene melody piped by shepherds continues to the end of the movement. In the fourth movement, "March to the Scaffold," the man dreams that because he has killed his Beloved, he is condemned, led to the guillotine, and executed. Timpani prelude the approach of the solemn procession, whose march is based on a G-minor scale and its inversion. Tension mounts; a brilliant climax is achieved in the coda. Clarinet ponders the *idée fixe*; a great G-minor chord crashes (descent of the guillotine blade), and ominous G-major chords

conclude. The finale is "A Witches' Sabbath" in which he envisions his funeral, his Requiem a burlesque (DWMA191). It is an eerie scene, with C clarinet caricaturing the *idée fixe* to depict the witchly transformation of the Beloved, and polyrhythmic orchestral parts signifying confusion. E-flat clarinet more extensively mocks the Beloved. Solemn tolling of bells is heard in the distance. Violas and oboe timidly propose a dance tune but are effectively silenced. (Berlioz knew the Finale of Beethoven's Ninth Symphony, too.) The *Dies irae,* liturgical Sequence of the Requiem Mass, is sounded in augmentation, then in the usual temporal values, and then in diminution and syncopated, each time an octave higher. Low strings commence the witches' round dance, presented fugally; ultimately, it is combined with the *Dies irae* (combination of melodies is another resemblance to the Finale of Beethoven's Ninth). Strings playing *col legno* (with the wood of the bow instead of the hair) add to the diabolic glee. This movement has been called "the first symphonic presentation of the macabre in the literature."

Verbally and financially, Niccolò Paganini encouraged Berlioz to write *Harold en Italie* (Harold in Italy; 1834), his second symphony. In this four-movement work, the solo viola represents Harold, who observes Italian scenes. Though Berlioz gave each movement a descriptive title, he supplied nothing more to aid the listener in interpreting the music. The programmatic work is cyclic; the recurrent theme appears unchanged in the four movements. In the finale, as in Beethoven's Ninth Symphony, themes of the preceding movements are recalled, and, of course, new themes are presented. Throughout the symphony Berlioz used counterpoint effectively, e.g., combining the viola melody contrapuntally with the other themes in each movement. The solo viola is treated idiomatically and is not limited to its special theme but is given other melodies and accompanying figures as well. The variety of blends of instrumental colors that Berlioz used in this work produces exquisite sonorities. *Harold en Italie* is an important contribution to symphonic repertoire, especially because it features solo viola.

Berlioz called *Roméo et Juliette* a dramatic symphony. The work has a choral introduction, three instrumental movements corresponding to the first three movements of a traditional symphony, and a choral finale. The purely instrumental movements are *Fête chez Capulet* (Festival at the Capulet home); *Scène d'amour* (Love scene), the slow movement; and *La reine Mab* (Queen Mab), a scherzo/trio. The introduction, which describes the feuding Capulets and Montagues and gives a basic outline of the story, contains choral recitative and solos for tenor and contralto. In his preface to the work, Berlioz stated that he chose to depict the central portions of the drama orchestrally because instrumental music could be more powerful and more deeply expressive than music limited by words. The climax of the finale is the choral presentation of the reconciliation of Montague and Capulet families and the Oath; the latter is as effective as that of the Swiss in Rossini's *Guillaume Tell.*

La reine Mab, the third movement, is sometimes played as a concert piece and usually is listed on the program simply as "Queen Mab Scherzo." The scherzo is a whirlwind *moto perpetuo;* the Trio moves at half the speed of the scherzo. Instead of *da capo* repeat of the scherzo, Berlioz wrote a new orchestration of that section when he returned it. Berlioz depicted the fairy world with delicacy and lightness. Strings are muted, violins and 'celli are scored *divisi,* and players are called upon to use techniques associated at that time with solo playing: spiccato and ricochet bowings and natural and artificial harmonics sustained for many measures. Berlioz was specific in his directives to performers and indicated precisely in the music how he wanted a passage played. This is a directive in *La reine Mab*:

> *Coup frappé avec une baguette sur une Cymbale ordinaire. Il faut tenir la Cymbale suspendue avec la main gauche et frapper avec la main droite.* (Blow struck with a sponge mallet on an ordinary cymbal. The suspended cymbal must be held with the left hand and struck with the right hand.)

The *Grande symphonie funèbre et triomphale* (Large funeral and triumphal symphony; 1840) was commissioned by the French government for a commemoration honoring participants in the July 1830 Revolution. Berlioz scored his three-movement memorial work for large military band, a suitable instrumentation for the out-of-doors performance. Later, for an indoor performance of the work, he added strings; still later, he added six-part chorus (SSTTBB)

with a patriotic text. Portions of the music were borrowed from earlier compositions. The three movements are in different keys: the opening movement, an impressive *Marche funèbre* (Funeral march) is in F minor; the *Oraison funèbre* (Funeral oration), in G major; the finale, *Apothéose* (Apotheosis), a triumphal march in B♭ major.

All of Berlioz's orchestral works are programmatic; his treatment of melodies and harmonies and his orchestrations are Romantic. Though he viewed form as flexible, he never completely discarded sonata form and the complete sonata structure. He seemed not to regard the various musical media as separate and distinct entities, but merged vocal and instrumental, soloist(s) and large ensemble, and always did so effectively. He wrote no piano music, and the few pieces of chamber music he wrote as a youth are lost.

Operas

Berlioz composed six operas; four survive complete, and each of them is different. His first opera, *Estelle et Némorin,* written in 1823, is not extant. Only five numbers survive from his second opera, *Lénor ou Les derniers francs juges* (1826). Its plot is semipolitical, with a medieval setting in the Black Forest, and involves the common people—the real heroes—liberating the region from the domination of a tyrannical ruler and his ruthless judicial court. The influence of German Romantic opera is apparent, particularly, Weber's *Der Freischütz,* with which Berlioz was familiar.

Benvenuto Cellini (1834–37), an *opera semiseria* (sung throughout), was not a success when performed at L'Opéra in 1838. At that time, Paris audiences preferred lighter, more entertaining subjects, works with more than a touch of comedy or with great spectacles. *Benvenuto Cellini* has some crowd scenes, and both comic and serious elements are present in the opera, which concerns the Renaissance artist Benvenuto Cellini (1500–1571), a superb goldsmith and sculptor. The opera presents a chain of episodes rather than unfolding a plot, and audiences were not ready for that at L'Opéra. However, staged episodes were not new to Paris—entertainments of that kind were presented in the popular theaters, in the tableaux of *spectacle d'optique* and diorama.

Since his childhood, Berlioz had been fascinated with Vergil's *Aeneid*. Around 1850 he began to plan an opera based on the second and fourth books of that epic poem and in 1856 commenced a libretto. By 1858 he had completed the music but made some revisions during the next five years. *Les Troyens* (The Trojans) is a monumental five-act grand opera. Because of its epic proportions, Berlioz could not secure patronage for it to be performed at L'Opéra. In order to obtain a performance of part of the work, he divided the opera: Acts I–II became Part I, *La Prise de Troie* (The Capture of Troy), the fall of Troy as a result of the ruse of the wooden horse; Acts III–V, Part II, *Les Troyens à Carthage* (The Trojans at Carthage), the story of Queen Dido of Carthage, Aeneas's sojourn at Carthage, and the fate of the Trojan people. Part II was performed at Carvalho's Théâtre-Lyrique in November 1863 and was well-received, but Carvalho made drastic cuts after the first performance. *La prise de Troie* had its première at Karlsruhe in December 1890. The first act is massive and presents the armistice, the celebration outside the walls of Troy, and the fateful entry of the wooden horse into the city. The second act is the shortest of the five, with two balanced scenes.

Les Troyens is a scene opera containing many large choral and ballet presentations, always appropriately placed and never included merely for spectacle or theatrical effect. This work lacks the glitter of many of the grand operas of the 1830s. Though it deals with an epic story, *Les Troyens* is not a boring narration, and the large scene-complexes present only the essential stages of the action. Berlioz's characterization is superb—even the appearances of specters are convincing. The music seems to contain less chromaticism than his earlier works because he restrained the use of chromaticism to instances where it would be most effective, e.g., in laments. The vocal lines are expressive, clean, and devoid of superficial opulence; there are few appoggiaturas and suspensions. Berlioz shaped his harmonies to convey effectively the emotions appropriate to each scene. The music of the final scene, Dido's death and funeral pyre, is magnificent.

Les Troyens is the most important French opera written in the nineteenth century, yet the nineteenth century barely knew it. The opera was not performed in its entirety during Berlioz's lifetime. In fact, Berlioz never heard Part II performed completely. This opera, Berlioz's masterpiece, places him at the peak of a long tradition of opera in France, a tradition that begins with Lully and proceeds through Rameau, Gluck, Spontini, and Meyerbeer—to Berlioz.

Berlioz's last opera, *Béatrice et Benedict* (1860–62), is an *opéra comique* written to fill a commission from Baden-Baden. Again, he prepared his own libretto, based on Shakespeare's *Much Ado about Nothing*. The comic Somarone does not appear in Shakespeare's play; Berlioz invented the character to satirize pompous, pedantic Kapellmeisters. The opera contains 15 numbers interspersed with spoken dialogue. Each of the two acts contains three choruses and scenes for one, two, or three voices; there is an additional air and duet in the first act. The music is much lighter in texture than that of *Les Troyens*. The drinking song, with its guitars, is delightful, and the nocturne (a duo) that concludes the first act is excellent.

Choral Works

In 1828–29 Berlioz composed *Huit scènes de Faust* (Eight scenes from *Faust*) based on Nerval's French translation of Goethe's *Faust*. Later, the eight scenes were expanded and combined with an arrangement of the *Rákóczy March* and other music to form *La damnation de Faust* (The damnation of Faust; 1845–46), which Berlioz called a dramatic legend. A blend of the symphonic and dramatic, it is intended for concert performance, not staging, though the score contains stage directions to explain the course of events. The musical presentation does not relate a continuous story but comprises 20 scenes, organized in four main sections. The work is for three soloists (Faust, Marguerite, and Mephistopheles), seven-part chorus (alto is not divided), and orchestra. Chorus is important, participating as penitents, students, soldiers, sylphs, carousers, occupants of Heaven and Hell. Some of the music is strongly chromatic (Faust's "Invocation to Nature"); some music is simple and resembles folk song (Marguerite's "King of Thulé"). There are a few recurring themes. The *Rákóczy March* is merely an inserted number; it has nothing whatsoever to do with the Faust legend. *Le damnation de Faust* is dedicated to Liszt, who also wrote a large symphonic work based on *Faust*.

L'Enfance du Christ (The infancy of Christ; 1850–54) is a mixture of opera, oratorio, and symphony. It is frequently referred to as an oratorio, though Berlioz never regarded it as such. He called it a *trilogie sacrée* (sacred trilogy). The work is in three parts, which were composed separately and later combined: *Le songe d'Hérode* (Herod's dream), the last to be written; *La fuite en Egypte* (The flight into Egypt), the first section composed; and *L'arrivée à Saïs* (The arrival at Saïs), presenting the apochryphal account of the Ishmaelites welcoming the Holy Family. The role of narrator is most important in the second part. As in *La damnation de Faust,* the score is supplied with stage directions, but the work was never intended for staging.

La damnation de Faust and *L'enfance du Christ* represent a compromise between the stage works with which Berlioz so desperately wanted to achieve success and the symphonic works for which he could more easily secure performance and which he believed would be accepted more readily.

Frequently, Berlioz was called upon to compose works for national commemorative celebrations. The most important of those works are the *Grande messe des morts* (Requiem Mass; 1837) and *Te deum laudamus* (1849)—monumental and deeply religious works that require enormous performing resources, both vocal and instrumental. The huge proportions and ceremonial character of these works is directly related to the French tradition of massed ensembles performing out-of-doors in commemoration of Revolutionary events. The Requiem Mass, structured according to traditional liturgical format, was designed for performance in the church of Les Invalides, which could accommodate the huge orchestra and massive choir. Spatial separation of performers is a feature of both the *Te Deum . . .* and the Requiem Mass. This is a link with the distant as well as the immediate past, stretching back three centuries to Giovanni Gabrieli's use of *cori spezzati* at St. Mark's in Venice and also relating to the use of many ensembles that participated individually, in combination, and *en masse* in the post-Revolutionary commemorative celebrations held in Paris. The *Tuba mirum* of the Requiem Mass provides an example. For it, extra brass and timpani are required. At each of the four corners of the large orchestra, there is placed a supplemental group of brass instruments and a pair of timpani.

The *Te deum laudamus* was intended for use in a military celebration for the return of the French army from Italy in 1832, but Berlioz did not finish it in time. The 1849 score of the work calls for full orchestra, organ, tenor soloist, and two choirs of 100 singers each. Late in 1851, Berlioz added a third choir, composed of 600 children, to sing in unison and "to represent the people who, from time to time, add their voices to the ceremony of praise." Berlioz's knowledge of Bach's *St. Matthew Passion* is apparent, not only because of the children's choirs but in the use of counterpoint. Berlioz conducted the first performance of his *Te Deum . . .* at the Church of Saint-Eustace, Paris, on 30 April 1855. According to his account of the performance, the organ was at one end of the church, the orchestra and two choirs at the other. The organ is seldom heard simultaneously with the rest of the performers, and its spatial separation from them is necessary. Where the children's choirs were situated is not known. At the Saint-Eustace performance (and also when he served as principal conductor for various ensembles in different locations out-of-doors) Berlioz controlled tempo by means of a special metronome whose electrical pulsations were transmitted simultaneously to subconductors in the various locations.

The *Te Deum . . .* comprises eight movements, of which two are purely instrumental: a *Prelude* as third movement and at the end a *March* designed as processional for visible pageantry, including presentation of the Colors. Berlioz instructed that these movements should be omitted when the *Te Deum . . .* is performed on occasions that are neither for thanksgiving after a victory nor for a service of military character. Therefore, in an ordinary concert, these two movements should be omitted.

At various times in the *Te Deum . . .* the music appropriately conveys majesty, brilliance, and soft supplication. The final choral movement, *Judex crederis esse venturus* (We believe that Thou wilt come to be our judge), is some of the most powerful music ever written. Berlioz considered that movement "the most imposing thing" he had ever composed.

Among Berlioz's works are several choral compositions small in scope but monumental in style, designed for national commemorations. There are also serene, contemplative works (*Méditation religieuse*;

1831) and pieces of exquisite delicacy (the ballade *Sara la baigneuse,* Sara the bather, for three separate choruses and small orchestra). Berlioz wrote numerous songs for solo voice(s) and orchestra. Among the finest of these are *Les nuits d'été,* settings of six poems by T. Gautier (1811–72).

Berlioz as Author

As did many nineteenth-century composers, Berlioz prepared some of his own libretti, wrote critical articles that appeared in Paris journals, and authored fiction and fantasy. His essays on music contain valuable information concerning compositions, performances, performers, and new instruments; he prepared short biographies of outstanding composers and his own *Mémoires.* He was one of the first to advocate firmly that music should be performed as written, in the style of the composer's era, not modernized in performance or published in editions that adapted the original notation to contemporary practices. His important treatise on instrumentation and orchestration was mentioned previously.

Minor Composers

Among the minor composers in France in mid-nineteenth century were Louise Dumont Farrenc (1804–75) and Camille Moke Pleyel (1811–75). Both were outstanding performers and excellent teachers—they were among the few women to become faculty members at significant music conservatories before 1850.

At the age of fourteen, Camille Moke was performing concerti in public concerts; by 1830 she was on the music faculty of a girls' school in Paris. She was engaged briefly to Berlioz, but in 1831 married Camille Pleyel (1788–1855). When they separated in 1835, she resumed concertizing in northern Europe and England. Sometimes she appeared on the same program with Liszt, and performed four-hand compositions with him. From 1848 to 1872 Mme Pleyel taught piano at Brussels Conservatory. She composed several piano pieces, including *Rondo parisien* (Parisian rondo, Op. 1), and some fantasias.

Mme Farrenc, a talented pianist of professional stature, was Professor of Piano at Paris Conservatoire from 1842 to 1873. In the nineteenth century, she was the only woman musician at the Conservatoire to hold a permanent position of that rank. Her first published compositions, works for piano, appeared in 1825. Among her compositions are two overtures, three symphonies, a nonet for winds and strings, a sextet for piano and winds, two piano quintets, a string quartet, two piano trios, two violin/piano sonatas, a 'cello/piano sonata, and numerous piano pieces. The *Nonet* (E♭, Op. 38; 1849) was especially acclaimed; Joachim participated in its première (Paris, 1850). Mme Farrenc's pedagogical works include *30 Études* in all the major and minor keys, and more than 50 other études. With her husband, Aristide Farrenc (1794–1865), she compiled, edited, and published a collection of keyboard compositions by earlier composers, *Le trésor des pianistes* (Pianists' treasure, 23 vols.; Paris, 1861–74).

Music in Italy

In Italy during the nineteenth century musical interest was centered on opera. To many Italian composers, success in music was synonymous with success in opera. Most Italian composers wrote a good deal of church music, secular songs, and some instrumental works, but they either turned to composition in other genres after having a career in opera or considered other genres of lesser importance. A noteworthy exception was Niccolò Paganini.

Niccolò Paganini

Virtuoso violinist Niccolò Paganini (1782–1840) not only dazzled the world with his exceptional technical skills and his effective musical interpretation, he attracted the attention of other nineteenth-century composers and performers to the extent that several emulated his virtuosity in their own performances and in their compositions. Paganini also played mandolin and guitar exceptionally well; he composed solos for all three instruments, wrote some chamber music that included them, and created some music for orchestra and voice.

Paganini began concertizing at the age of 12 to earn money for violin and composition lessons. From 1801 to 1807 Niccolò and his oldest brother, Carlo (1778–1830), also a violinist, played in the national orchestra at Lucca. In 1805, Niccolò became solo violinist at the court of Napoleon's sister, Princess Elise

Niccolò Paganini. Lithograph by Maurir.

Baciocchi, ruler of Lucca. On 1 January 1808 the Princess replaced the orchestra with a string quartet, with the Paganini brothers as violinists. Niccolò, disappointed because he was never offered the *maestro di cappella* post, decided in December 1809 to become a concert artist. He could play the concerti of Kreutzer, Rode, and Viotti and the 24 caprices in Pietro Locatelli's (1695–1764) *L'arte del violino*—his own 24 unaccompanied *Caprices* (c. 1805) were more difficult. He had mastered the techniques of the noted violinists of his time. Moreover, he had developed a few techniques with which other violinists were as yet unfamiliar, such as ricochet bowings, left-hand pizzicato, and double-stops in harmonics. His hands were large, his fingers long and slender, and by extension he could play in three positions without shifting. He had a predilection for playing an entire composition on one string, particularly the G string; when gauged

strings were available, he used thin gut strings so that the upper strings would break more easily and he would be forced to complete a piece on only one string.

From 1810 to 1828 Paganini concertized throughout Italy, creating a furor wherever he played. The *Allgemeine musikalische Zeitung* carried reviews of his performances, though he did not perform outside Italy until 1828. By then he had composed five concerti and numerous technically difficult solos. He was adept at making variations; many of his pieces feature them.

During part of 1822–23, Paganini was so ill that he could not concertize; it was the first of his many bouts with catarrhal phthisis, a wasting away of the tissues of the throat, a tubercular disease that in turn claimed his vocal cords, his violin playing, and his life. In 1824 he met singer Antonia Bianchi; their son Achille was born in July 1825. While Paganini's liaison with Bianchi lasted, she assisted in some of his concerts and performed his vocal compositions; when they separated in 1829 (they never married) Paganini obtained custody of Achille and by court action in 1837 legitimized him.

In 1828–34 Paganini concertized internationally. He began with 14 concerts in Vienna, concerts on which he programmed orchestral works by Beethoven, Mozart, and Haydn, as well as his own works. Those concert programs reveal an interesting performance practice, e.g., the performance of symphonies and concerti by movements rather than as complete entities. Though the movements were performed in their proper order, solos or movements of other works were performed between them. Paganini was not only a virtuoso soloist, he was an excellent quartet player and performed the quartets of Haydn, Mozart, and Beethoven.

In the early 1830s Paganini became very interested in the viola, and in 1833 he encouraged Berlioz to write an orchestral work featuring viola. Berlioz anonymously inserted a notice in the January 20 *Gazette musicale* to the effect that he was to compose a "dramatic fantasy" for orchestra, chorus, and solo viola and that Paganini would play the viola part. By the time Berlioz completed *Harold in Italy,* Paganini's health had deteriorated, and he could play few concerts.

Paganini returned to Italy in 1834. During 1835–37 he served on the administrative commission of the ducal theater at Parma; in 1837–38 he invested heavily in the Casino Paganini in Paris, which featured musical entertainment and illegal gambling. In October 1838 he was critically ill and completely lost his voice; thereafter, he communicated by writing. Before leaving Paris in December, he attended a Berlioz concert at which *Harold in Italy* was performed. Paganini indicated his appreciation of Berlioz's work by giving him 20,000 francs, sufficient to support him while he composed *Romeo et Juliette.*

During the last years of his life, Paganini's health deteriorated steadily. For a brief time, he worked as a dealer in bows and string instruments in Marseilles. He visited Genoa in autumn 1839, then went to Nice to spend the winter. Nothing is known of the last two weeks of his life; he died on 27 May 1840 without absolution or extreme unction, and the Bishop of Nice, regarding him as a nominally excommunicated sinner, prohibited interment of the remains in consecrated ground. For five years, the embalmed body was stored in various places; in 1845 Achille was granted permission to have a Requiem Mass recited for his father, and the Grand Duchess of Parma authorized interment at a private villa. Finally, in 1876, the Bishop's orders were revoked, and Paganini's remains were moved to a cemetery in Parma.

Many violinists and composers were influenced by Paganini's compositions as well as by his technical wizardry and his beautiful tone quality when playing Adagio melodies. Only the German school of violinists (Spohr, Joachim) was adamantly opposed to his style. Paganini's virtuosity was a shaping force in the style of Liszt, who, after hearing Paganini in 1832, determined to do with the piano what Paganini had done with the violin. Several composers used one or more of Paganini's compositions as the basis of or models for their own works, among them, Chopin, Liszt, Schumann, Brahms, and Rachmaninov. Paganini's 24 *Caprices for Unaccompanied Violin* have become standard study and performance repertoire. Tone quality was very important to Paganini. He owned two complete quartets of Stradivari instruments, for matched tone quality in playing string quartets. One quartet of Stradivari instruments is the property of the Corcoran Gallery, which loans them to reputable performing quartets in the United States.

Italian Opera

In accordance with tradition, the clear separation between *opera seria* and *opera buffa* was preserved until almost the middle of the century. (Remember that in Italy all opera was sung throughout, even *opera buffa.*) Only gradually did Romantic elements infiltrate Italian opera, and never did they permeate to the same extent as in Germany or France. There were two main reasons for this: the many independent states each with its own traditions and restraint on the part of the librettists. Felice Romani (1788–1865) and Salvatore Cammarano (1801–52), who prepared libretti for Mayr, Donizetti, Bellini, and a few for Verdi, used only moderate amounts of Romanticism. They derived plots from European literature and fairly recent history rather than from ancient history and mythology—British literature and English history were especially favored—but they modified the Romantic elements. Verdi worked closely with Piave and other librettists and firmly controlled every aspect of his operas. He was Romantic only in his concern for realistic portrayal and characterization. In other respects, he followed tradition. Though tradition was strong for composers, some changes were made. As Rossini had gradually supplanted the castrato hero with a contralto, so later composers supplanted the contralto hero with a tenor. Bellini was the first Italian composer to write typically Romantic roles for tenor. Verdi included roles for baritone and for *basso cantante,* a firm singing bass.

Paris attracted and kept many Italian composers and fine performers. The principal Italian composers of opera during the second quarter of the nineteenth century were Gaetano Donizetti and Vincenzo Bellini. Donizetti, trained by Mayr, was the direct precursor of Giuseppe Verdi, who dominated the Italian opera scene from 1842–1893. (Verdi is discussed in Ch. 23.)

Gaetano Donizetti

Gaetano Donizetti (1797–1848) was the fifth of six children in an extremely impoverished family in Bergamo, Italy. Fortunately, in 1806 the Cathedral of Santa Maria Maggiore in Bergamo opened its free music school, with J. S. Mayr as director. Donizetti was accepted in the first class of students and received excellent, thorough training in music. Mayr was a

Gaetano Donizetti.

shaping force in Donizetti's career: In 1814 he arranged for Donizetti's further study with Padre Martini in Bologna; in 1818, Mayr helped him secure a contract to compose operas for a company performing in Venice; and in 1822, when Mayr was unable to fulfill a commission for an opera for Rome, he turned over his contract to Donizetti. The success of that opera brought a contract from Barbaia, and Donizetti went to Naples as successor to Rossini. Between 1822 and 1830, Donizetti composed 24 mediocre operas for production there. That these operas bear some resemblance to Rossini's style may indicate a deliberate attempt on the part of Donizetti to follow in Rossini's footsteps in pleasing Barbaia and the Neapolitan public.

With his 31st opera, *Anna Bolena* (Anne Boleyn; Milan, 1830), an *opera seria,* Donizetti experienced his first major success. The role of Anne Boleyn was created by soprano Giuditta Pasta. *Anna Bolena* was the first of Donizetti's works to be performed internationally. Donizetti composed rapidly; he wrote several operas a year in addition to other works. After

writing five more mediocre operas, he again achieved success with the comedy *L'elisir d'amore* (The elixir of love; 1832), an adaptation of a Scribe libretto, and *Lucrezia Borgia* (1833), based on Victor Hugo's play.

In 1835 Rossini invited Donizetti to write an opera for Théâtre-Italien, Paris. Though that opera, *Marino Faliero,* was overshadowed by other Paris productions, Donizetti's visit to Paris was educational. It revealed the caliber of musical and dramatic talent in Parisian *opéra comique,* and it provided his first exposure to French grand opera (Halévy's *La Juive*). Donizetti returned to Naples for production of his serious opera *Lucia di Lammermoor* (September 1835) and attempted to write opera in French style, with ballet and with more ensembles than he had been including. Then he began to develop a distinctive style of his own. He returned to Paris in 1838 and in 1840 had two successful productions: *Les martyrs,* a grand opera, at L'Opéra and *La fille du régiment* (The daughter of the regiment) at L'Opéra-Comique. His *opera buffa, Don Pasquale,* was produced at Théâtre-Italien in January 1843.

Donizetti wrote more than 600 compositions, including 70 operas, over 100 songs, some vocal chamber music, numerous pieces of church music, 2 oratorios, more than 2 dozen cantatas, 19 string quartets, 3 string quintets, miscellaneous pieces of other instrumental chamber music, some piano solos and duets, about 15 *sinfonie,* and a few other orchestral works. Among the sacred music is a Requiem Mass written in memory of Bellini. Of Donizetti's operas, the most important are: the *opere serie, Anna Bolena, Lucrezia Borgia,* and *Lucia di Lammermoor;* the *opéra comique, La fille du régiment;* the *comica, L'elisir d'amore;* and the *opera buffa, Don Pasquale.*

Don Pasquale is considered Donizetti's comic masterpiece, yet some of the most striking segments of it, and of the comedy *L'elisir d'amore,* are not at all comic. This signals the beginning of a breaking down of the traditional distinction between *opera seria* and *opera buffa.* Donizetti favored the libretti of Romani and Cammarano, both of whom had excellent sense of the dramatic in opera. Mingled with elements of nineteenth-century Romanticism (used in moderation) in Donizetti's operas are passages of *secco* recitative, totally unaccompanied, and sections in which the accompaniment is minimal. On the other hand, some arias are quite florid. Donizetti's music is not as brilliant as Rossini's nor does it have the sincerity and earnestness conveyed by Verdi's music. Yet, those works Donizetti composed after 1835 point directly to the early works of Verdi.

Donizetti was influenced in the composition of opera by the resources at hand—the types of voices in the particular opera company, the demands of the leading singers. His sense of humor came to the fore on at least one occasion when he notated a brief cadenza virtually impossible to sing (and that would have been inappropriate if it had been sung), as if to say that no matter what he wrote the singer would alter it. A distinctive characteristic of Donizetti's melodies is the fact that many of them are based on a descending or an ascending scale. Though his music is expressive, and he could bring out the dramatic or the humorous in a given situation, he did not use daring or chromatic harmonies, and he seems to have always considered the vocal line(s) as being of greater significance than the orchestral accompaniment.

Donizetti is seen at his best in his comic operas. *Don Pasquale* and *L'elisir d'amore* have been part of opera repertoire since they were first produced; *La fille du régiment* has been performed frequently in the twentieth century.

Vincenzo Bellini

Vincenzo Bellini (1801–35), a native of Sicily, received his musical training first from his father and then from his grandfather, both of whom were composers and music teachers. In 1819 Vincenzo entered Naples Conservatory where, among other things, he studied the instrumental music of Haydn and Mozart. Bellini's first published composition, a *romanza,* appeared c. 1825, but by that time he had written a number of sacred works. Customarily, at the time a student completed the course of study at Naples Conservatory, one of that student's dramatic works was given public performance. Therefore, Bellini's *opera semiseria, Adelson e Salviri,* was performed by a cast of male students at the Conservatory. As a result of that performance, Bellini received a commission for an opera for Teatro San Carlo and composed *Bianca e Fernando* (1826). The librettist was Romani, with

Vincenzo Bellini. *(© Art Resource.)*

whom Bellini formed a sincere friendship and a lasting collaboration; Romani supplied libretti for all of the rest of Bellini's operas except the last one.

In 1827 Barbaia commissioned an opera from Bellini for La Scala. The success of that work, *Il pirata* (The pirate), brought Bellini other commissions. During 1827–33 he and Romani collaborated on eight operas, six of them successful. Bellini's earnings from commissioned operas were more than sufficient to supply all of his living, and he moved in the highest social circles.

Bellini learned from his failures. *La straniera* (The foreign woman; Milan, 1829) was criticized for its lack of coloratura; critics considered it too declamatory. In succeeding operas Bellini included more coloratura but carefully regulated its use. After a failure with *Zaira* (1829), Bellini found success again with the *opere serie I Capuleti e i Montecchi* (The Capulets and the Montagues; 1830) and *La sonnambula* (The sleepwalker; 1831). But when *Norma* was performed at La Scala in December 1831, Bellini proclaimed it a fiasco. His judgment was faulty—he had created a masterpiece. *Norma* is the story of a Druid high priestess and her unfaithful lover, Pollione, a Roman proconsul. Giuditta Pasta (1797–1865), talented Italian soprano, created the title role. By that time Bellini had established a lasting friendship with Pasta, who, for at least a decade, was acclaimed as the greatest soprano in Europe. Her voice was not perfect, but she had an extended range and could sing lyric and dramatic roles equally well. She created the title role in Donizetti's *Anna Bolena* and the leading role (Amina) in Bellini's *La sonnambula.* In 1833, in a performance of *I Capuleti e i Montecchi,* she sang the part of Romeo. After Bellini met Pasta, he designed the leading soprano roles in most of his operas to suit her talents, and when his operas were performed under his direction in London and Paris in 1833, she sang those roles in most of them.

When Bellini returned to Milan after the Paris performances, he spent several months resting. In 1834, to fill a commission for Théâtre-Italien, he composed *I Puritani* (The Puritans; Paris, January 1835); that libretto was by Carlo Pepoli, a fact that disturbed Romani considerably and caused a temporary rift in his friendship with Bellini. After the successful performance of *I Puritani,* Bellini stayed in Paris. Suddenly, in mid-August, he became seriously ill, and on September 23 he died. A few days later, Théâtre-Italien opened the season with *I Puritani.* For Bellini's funeral service, a four-voice *Lachrymosa* was arranged on the theme of the tenor melody in Act 3 of *I Puritani.*

Bellini was a man with strong emotions; he was proud and a bit egotistical. In the short span of seven years he had earned a very large measure of success, and, at the time of his death, he stood on the brink of even greater achievements.

Bellini's music was influenced by Rossini, Zingarelli (his teacher at Naples Conservatory), his working-friendships with Romani and Pasta, and the folk music of Sicily much of which had been absorbed into art music. The lyrical style of Bellini's early music was derived from Rossini; gradually, Bellini controlled and narrowed that lyricism and infiltrated it with emotion. He set text carefully, with due regard for correct declamation and also for the proper mood of the phrases. He demanded of Romani an emotional libretto, filled with exciting situations. In composing music to fit those situations, Bellini sought a balance between *bel canto* lyricism and dramatic tension. He constructed melodies in broad curves built from small segments; this may be seen in *Casta diva,* the cavatina and prayer scene from Act II of *Norma* (DWMA192). That scene provides an example of the manner in which an aria was incorporated into a scene containing sections in different tempi and involving ensemble participation. This was not new with Bellini; Mayr and others used it effectively. In *Casta diva,* the melodic climax comes at the end; Bellini used motives sequentially to build phrases and to build to that climax. When repeating phrases, he embellished them (*Casta diva,* mm. 109–26). Many of his melodies feature scale passages in semitones (*Casta diva,* m. 118ff, or mm. 151–54); he often wrote passages with ever-widening pitch intervals (mm. 155–61). He tended to select a rhythm and have it permeate an entire piece or a great section of it.

Bellini did not limit his composition to opera. He wrote numerous sacred and secular vocal works and pieces for keyboard and for orchestra. Many of those compositions are still in manuscript. As of 1988, no complete edition of his works had been issued.

Music in England

Since the time of Handel, England had especially favored the oratorio. Oratorios and part songs were an important part of the many music festivals in England. The provincial festivals helped promote the formation of choral societies and the singing of part songs and glees. Festivals were held throughout the land—at Leeds, York, Norwich, Bristol, Sheffield, and elsewhere—but that at Birmingham was the most significant. Birmingham regularly commissioned choral works, particularly oratorios, by continental composers. After Mendelssohn first visited Britain and was charmed by it, he returned there annually for over a dozen years, and the English took him to their hearts. The affection of the English for oratorios influenced Mendelssohn to write them—*Paulus* was performed there twice in 1836, and *Elias* was composed in August 1846 for the Birmingham festival that month.

Other oratorios that had premières at English festivals were Spohr's *The Fall of Babylon* (1842), Gounod's *La rédemption* (The Redemption; 1882), and Dvořák's *St. Ludmilla* (1886).

Since the time of Purcell, the only English composer whose work was known internationally was young Thomas Linley, whose music seems to have been soon forgotten after his untimely accidental death in 1778. In the nineteenth century Britain was again represented among those internationally acclaimed. Irish singer-composer Michael Balfe (1808–70) first had a career as opera singer (baritone) in Paris and Italy. He rose to sudden fame as an opera composer with the successful première of *The Siege of Rochelle* at Drury Lane in October 1835. His greatest success came with *The Bohemian Girl* (1843), which became popular in Europe and was translated into French, Italian, and German. Balfe composed 29 operas, a ballet, a few songs, a piano trio, and a piano/'cello sonata.

During the last quarter of the nineteenth century Arthur S. Sullivan (1842–1900) attained fame with his operettas and comic operas, especially those setting libretti by W. S. Gilbert. *Trial by Jury, The Gondoliers, H.M.S. Pinafore, Yeomen of the Guard,* and *The Mikado* are still popular favorites. Behind the comedy in many Gilbert-and-Sullivan operettas is satire of specific conditions (political and cultural) in England at that time. Sullivan composed many works of more serious nature, including the oratorio *The Prodigal Son* (1869), Anglican anthems and other Service music, a *Te Deum* . . . performed in St. Paul Cathedral (1902), choral works with orchestra, orchestral and chamber music, and much vocal music, some of which is excellent and most of which is never performed.

In the area of English church music, the work of Samuel S. Wesley (1810–86) was outstanding. His career as cathedral organist began in 1826 and continued until his death; his longest terms of service were at Winchester Cathedral (1849–65) and Gloucester Cathedral (1865–76). Wesley's several Services and 27 excellent anthems were an important contribution to Anglican church music. His music is specifically English, and though some of his anthems show the possible influence of Mozart's *Ave verum corpus* or the counterpoint of Bach, whose music he knew well,

Wesley's style is distinctive. In some of his long anthems, he incorporated recitative, arialike solos, and fugal sections. He also composed some organ music for use in Services, secular and sacred songs, choruses, and part songs, and some piano solos. Wesley was influential in promoting the performance of Bach's music in England.

Music in North America

United States

Between 1825 and 1875 many immigrants came to the United States from European countries, especially from Britain and Germany. Some came to join friends and relatives already living here; others came because of unfavorable or revolutionary political conditions in their native lands or the European crop failures in 1848. Musicians came to concertize for a while and then returned to Europe. Among the virtuoso performers concertizing in America in 1843–57 were Norwegian violinist Ole Bull (1810–80), soprano Jenny Lind (1820–87), whom P. T. Barnum brought to the United States, German soprano Henriette Sontag (1806–54), and pianist Sigismond Thalberg (1812–71).

Music in the United States in the nineteenth century was of two basic kinds: so-called popular music, which was naive and untrained, and cultivated or art music based on European models. There were reasons for this duality. The United States was undergoing vast and rapid territorial expansion, and the settlements within the country's boundaries were of three types: (1) pioneer settlements with little or no contact with cultural events outside one's own community; (2) new towns with limited outside contact; and (3) established urban centers, such as New York, Philadelphia, and Boston. In general, the nineteenth-century view of music was that it belonged in the province of women, foreigners who came specifically to concertize or to teach music, and the effeminate.

Art music was of five general kinds (stated in the order of importance): church music, songs, piano music, orchestral or ensemble music, and opera. In all categories except the first, individuality and subjectivity were highly esteemed. Church music was given priority because it was functional music; there was great concern for good singing in church Services and

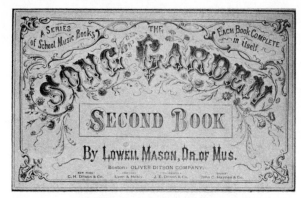

Figure 22.5 Lowell Mason: *The Song Garden,* Second Book, published by Oliver Ditson, Boston, in 1864.

meetings. Among those who taught in singing-schools, composed hymns, and worked for the cause of music education were Lowell Mason and William B. Bradbury.

Lowell Mason (1792–1872) composed over 1200 hymns with simple four-part harmony and adapted as hymns hundreds of melodies by other composers. He placed the melody in either the tenor or the soprano. Among Mason's best-known hymns are *Olivet* ("My faith looks up to Thee") and *Missionary Hymn* ("From Greenland's icy mountains"); these are found, with melody in soprano, in many Protestant hymnals in the twentieth century. For a dozen years (1813–24) Mason taught in singing-schools and compiled a collection of songs suitable for singing in Sunday school. He pioneered in music education by getting singing introduced in four public schools in Boston on an experimental basis in 1837, by setting standards for that teaching through doing it personally and without salary at first, and by composing and publishing collections of songs suitable for use in that teaching (fig. 22.5).

William Bradbury (1816–68), a native of Maine, received both singing and instrumental music lessons at home. In the 1830s he attended some of Mason's classes in Boston, then served for more than a year as singing-school teacher in Maine. After 1841, he worked in churches in New York, began teaching singing-school classes there, and organized annual festivals in which hundreds of children sang. As a result of those festivals, singing was introduced into New York public schools. In addition to 28 anthems and more than 800 hymns, Bradbury wrote 78 secular songs, some patriotic male choruses, and other vocal music.

In the area of song, there were many persons setting sentimental, nostalgic verses to music for voice with piano accompaniment. Many of these were used at home or in community concert programs. Some are of the "tear-jerker" variety, e.g., Bradbury's *The Lament of the Blind Orphan Girl,* simple tunes and harmonies in strophic settings of sad sentimental lyrics. Some texts were set as melodrama, and, during the Civil War Years, many were patriotic. Part songs for three or four unaccompanied male voices also served as entertainment music at home or in concerts. *Männerchor* (male singing societies) were organized at Philadelphia in 1835 and in several other cities. Also, **glees** (part songs for entertainment) were brought over from England and generated composition of similar songs by Americans.

America's principal song writer in mid-nineteenth century was Stephen Collins Foster (1826–64). Foster was born in Pennsylvania and never visited many of the southern communities about which he wrote. He was raised in a typical middle-class home where music making was a part of family life. Basically, he was self-taught in music, much of his knowledge of musical composition coming from his interest in and study of the works of Mozart, Beethoven, Weber, and a few other masters. Foster had a gift for melody and could harmonize those melodies fairly well. His first published song was *Open Thy Lattice, Love* (1844). Foster was the first American-born composer to earn his living entirely from song writing; he did so for the last fourteen years of his life. Instead of selling his songs outright to publishers, he arranged for royalties.

Foster wrote approximately 150 songs of all kinds, many of them love songs addressed to or about a lady who was unattainable. *Jeanie with the Light Brown Hair* is an example. Some songs use pentatonic scales and resemble Irish folk songs—Foster's ancestry was Irish. Other songs indicate that Foster knew Rossini's music. When minstrel shows became popular in the 1840s, Foster contributed some songs to the repertoire of the "Original Christy Minstrels." His songs

Stephen Foster.

Louis Moreau Gottschalk. *(The Bettmann Archive.)*

differed from the usual minstrel song in that he portrayed black persons experiencing the same kinds of emotions as white persons and feeling them just as deeply. After 1850, Foster wrote some songs that he called "plantation songs," nostalgic songs that reminisce on bygone days, e.g., *My Old Kentucky Home* and *Old Folks at Home*. His last songs were patriotic, related to the Civil War.

Piano Music

There were several prosperous piano manufacturing firms in the United States in mid-nineteenth century. Chickering, in Boston, made both "square" (rectangular) and grand varieties. Heinrich Steinweg (Henry Steinway) established his firm in New York in 1850; Mason & Hamlin began business in 1854. Hundreds of composers were writing and publishing piano solos in sheet music—musical trifles usually constructed as theme and variations or fantasias, related to the ability to improvise.

Louis Moreau Gottschalk (1829–69) was the first American musician to be acclaimed internationally as a virtuoso performer. When Gottschalk showed musical aptitude at the age of four, his parents saw to it that he had private music lessons. In 1842, at the teacher's suggestion, Gottschalk was sent to Paris for further study. Then 13, he was refused admission to Paris Conservatoire because he was not a French citizen, but at the age of 20 he was invited to judge examinations there! When Gottschalk returned to the United States in 1853, he was a seasoned concert artist of virtuoso caliber. He had concertized in Europe and had played for Chopin and Berlioz. For the remainder of his life, Gottschalk was almost continually on concert tour in Europe and America.

Gottschalk was a prolific composer not only of hundreds of piano solos and works for piano and orchestra but of symphonies, marches, operas, and accompanied vocal solos, as well. Some of his finest piano works stem from the years he spent in the Antilles, e.g., *Souvenir de Porto Rico* (1857), and while on tour in South America, he wrote *Grand tarantelle* (1868). Many of his piano pieces and some of his symphonies bear programmatic titles, e.g., Symphony No. 1, *La nuit des tropiques* (Night in the tropics, 1858); Symphony No. 2, *A Montevideo* (Montevideo; 1868). When on tour in Latin and South America, Gottschalk organized festivals at which huge ensembles—300 to 600 instrumentalists—performed his programmatic symphonies and other orchestral works. In his use of large performing ensembles, he was like Berlioz.

One characteristic of Gottschalk's style is the frequent quotation of snatches of anonymous works or works by other composers; in his use of quotations as musical and psychological devices, Gottschalk presages Charles Ives. The piano solo *Le banjo* (1855) is an example of this. Wherever Gottschalk lived and worked, he absorbed all of the Creole, Latin American, Spanish, and Negro rhythms that surrounded him, and these appear in his music. His treatment of some of these rhythms is closely akin to the ragtime and jazz that emerged at the end of the century.

Orchestral Music; Opera

The mid-nineteenth century witnessed the founding of the first permanent orchestra in the United States—the Philharmonic Symphony Society of New York, established in 1842. The Boston Symphony was the next, founded in 1881.

Comparatively little orchestral music was written by American composers at this time. The Moravians were musically active in Pennsylvania but wrote their music primarily for their own communal use. An orchestral overture and two symphonies by Charles Hommann (c. 1800–c. 1840) are known, and William H. Fry (1813–64) wrote at least four programmatic symphonies (most of them lost).

Two of George F. Bristow's (1825–98) symphonies, composed for and performed by the New York Philharmonic in 1856 and 1859, sound similar to those of Mendelssohn. Bristow's *Niagara Symphony* (1893), modeled after Beethoven's Ninth, is for soloists, chorus, and orchestra. Bristow wrote approximately 120 compositions, including overtures,

string quartets, piano pieces, an oratorio, cantatas, a Mass in C (1885), and the opera *Rip van Winkle* (1855).

The least significant genre of music in America in mid-nineteenth century was opera. Fry wrote three: *Aurelia the Vestal* (1841), which was never performed; *Leonora* (1845), the first opera by an American composer to be publicly performed; and *Notre Dame of Paris* (1864). The operas are in English and are not distinctive musically.

In the mid-nineteenth century, two American journalists concerned themselves with music. Fry, writing for the *New York Tribune,* championed the cause of American music, and, with Bristow, instigated the inclusion of American works on programs of the New York Philharmonic. John Sullivan Dwight (1813–93) wrote and published a weekly *Journal* devoted to music criticism and promotion of works by master European composers, especially Beethoven, Bach, and Mozart. Between 1852 and 1881, 41 volumes of Dwight's *Journal* were published. In them are critiques of concerts, discussions of new works, and significant writings by European authors concerning European composers, e.g., an English translation of Forkel's biography of Bach.

Canada

Marie Lajeunesse (1847–1930) was born near Montreal. She received her first training in music—piano, harp, and voice lessons—from her father. After a few public appearances in Quebec and Albany, New York, she went to Paris and Milan for further study. While abroad, she adopted the stage name Emma Albani. In 1870 she made her operatic début as Amina in *La sonnambula* and soon became one of Europe's leading dramatic sopranos. She performed also at the Metropolitan Opera in New York. Emma Albani was the first Canadian-born musician to be accorded international acclaim as a performer.

Pianist-composer Calixa Lavallée (1842–91), a native of Verchères, Quebec, received his first music instruction from his father, a music teacher, violin maker, and bandmaster. Later, Calixa studied at Paris Conservatoire. When he returned to America, he found it easier to make a living as a professional musician in the United States and settled in Boston. In 1880 he was asked to compose a Canadian national song for a festival in Quebec; *O Canada* resulted. In 1980 *O Canada* was officially declared Canada's national anthem. Many of Lavallée's numerous compositions have been lost. Among the surviving works are some cantatas, the operetta *The Widow* (1882), and some piano music. One of his best-known piano pieces is *Le papillon* (Butterfly).

Summary

The middle quarters of the nineteenth century were filled with increased industrialization, urbanization, and political unrest. The doctrine of nationalism gained strength and led to the unification of Italy and Germany. The first stirrings of socialism and socialistic labor movements appeared. The arts were important, but patronage was waning, and most musicians earned their living by teaching and by concertizing before audiences from all walks of life. Women were publishing their compositions, teaching, and concertizing.

Composers wrote several kinds of vocal music: accompanied solos, part songs and choruses, liturgical church music, large choral works with orchestral accompaniment, and operas. A number of symphonic works incorporated chorus and/or soloists in one or more movements. Church music was affected to some extent by the Cecilian movement, which advocated the use of Gregorian chant in its purest form and sought to eliminate integrated music from church Services in favor of Palestrina-style *a cappella* choral music. Two results of that movement were the improvement of singing in the church and new editions of liturgical chantbooks.

Instrumental music includes orchestral works, chamber music, compositions for solo instrument with orchestral or keyboard accompaniment, and solo piano pieces. Any of these genres might be program music (referential music conveying nonmusical ideas) or absolute (nonreferential) music. Most of the instrumental solos with orchestra are concerti. The piano was the most important solo instrument and was considered essential in the homes of all who aspired to some degree of gentility. For it composers wrote dance pieces, character pieces, études, sonatas, variations, and fantasias. Several styles of piano playing were evident, and, as piano construction improved, pianist-composers wrote music that was increasingly demanding technically and that took full advantage of the instrument's capabilities.

Music printed in Vienna and Leipzig was readily available throughout Germany. Published volumes of music by Palestrina and Bach appeared in the 1830s, and plans were made for editions of their complete works. By 1850, music of the past had found a place in concert repertoire. A number of music conservatories were established, e.g., at Leipzig and Berlin, with outstanding musicians on their faculties.

In lands under Austro-Germanic rule, music seems to have been dominated by composers who were superb pianists. Chopin composed music particularly suited to the piano, taking complete advantage of its unique capabilities rather than attempting to draw from it orchestral sonorities. Characteristic of his music are the interweaving of melody and accompaniment figures, *tempo rubato,* and use of the sustaining pedal to expand the compass of a chord beyond a normal hand span. His best works are those in which he was unhampered by traditional forms: ballades, nocturnes, preludes, and études.

Mendelssohn contributed a great deal to the development of music in many ways: by promoting the revival of Bach's music; by establishing and serving capably as director of Leipzig Conservatory; by conducting the Gewandhaus Orchestra; and by programming works by historically significant composers and fine works by contemporary composers whose careers needed assistance. He composed much music in nearly all genres and made especially valuable contributions to the repertoire with his E-minor Violin Concerto and the oratorios *Paulus* and *Elias*. Mendelssohn's sister Fanny was an accomplished pianist who composed, among other things, a fine Piano Trio and some excellent Lieder.

A Romantic composer, Robert Schumann's main musical contributions were Lieder and piano music.

In many of his Lieder the voice and piano are partners, sharing in the musical presentation of the poetry. Much of his instrumental music is programmatic, often covertly so. Through critical reviews of compositions and performances, Schumann exerted a favorable influence on the careers of several musicians, especially Chopin and Brahms.

Clara Wieck Schumann, one of the nineteenth-century's leading pianists, was the first woman to have a successful international career as a concert pianist. She served on the faculty of Leipzig Conservatory and was the principal piano teacher on the faculty of Hoch Conservatory. Her finest composition is her Piano Trio.

In France during the second quarter of the nineteenth century, music was dominated by opera, especially grand opera. The success of grand opera in the 1830s was due to the combined efforts of Véron, the director of L'Opéra; Scribe, the librettist; Meyerbeer, the composer; Cicéri and Duponchel, scene designers; and Auguste, leader of the claque. Grand opera is sung throughout, has few arias and almost no pure recitative, promotes much of the action through spectacular scenes strategically woven into the drama, and makes much use of ensembles of all sizes, particularly chorus. The most important grand operas produced at L'Opéra in the 1830s—those that established the course of opera in France—were on libretti by Scribe: Meyerbeer's *Robert le diable,* Auber's *Gustave III,* Halévy's *La Juive,* and Meyerbeer's *Les Huguenots.* Almost all composers of serious opera wrote *opéra comique* also. In the history of *opéra comique,* Bizet's *Carmen* was a landmark. Not only did it bring the genre to a peak, but, through use of a serious subject and presentation of a tragedy with spoken dialogue, it destroyed the artificial line of demarcation between *opéra comique* and *opéra.* Bizet's realistic portrayal of characters and situations presaged *verismo* opera. Some operas could not be performed at L'Opéra because they were too small or their subject matter and music were too light; such an opera was termed *opéra lyrique.* Other types were *opéra bouffe* (comic opera) and *operetta. Opéra bouffe* was instigated and popularized by Offenbach, whose *Orphée aux enfers* satirizes the Orpheus-Euridice myth.

Opera in France attained new heights with Berlioz's *Les Troyens.* Berlioz contributed significantly to symphonic literature with *Symphonie fantastique,* a cyclic work exhibiting many of the characteristics and dualities of Romanticism. His most important contribution to composition and to music education was his *Grand traité d'instrumentation . . . ,* the first textbook on orchestration. His critical writings contain valuable information concerning compositions, performances, performers, and new instruments. He was one of the first to advocate firmly that music should be performed as written, in the style of the composer's era, not modernized in performance or published in editions that adapted the original notation to contemporary practices.

Paganini, through his virtuosic performances and exploitation of all bowing and fingering techniques then available, did much to advance violin playing. Outstanding pianists emulated his virtuosity, and his works inspired compositions by pianists of his own and future generations.

Music in Italy was centered on opera. In accordance with tradition, a clear separation between *opera seria* and *opera buffa* (both sung throughout) was preserved until almost mid-century. Only gradually did Romantic elements infiltrate Italian opera, and never did they permeate to the same extent as in Germany or France. The principal Italian composers of opera during the second quarter of the nineteenth century were Donizetti and Bellini. Donizetti, trained by Mayr, was the direct precursor of Verdi, who dominated the Italian opera scene during the last half of the century.

Since the time of Handel, England had favored the oratorio, and oratorios by Mendelssohn, Spohr, Gounod, Dvořák, and other well-known composers were first performed at English festivals. The most significant English composers were Arthur Sullivan, in the field of operetta, and Samuel S. Wesley, who is considered successor to Purcell in the area of Anglican cathedral music.

Music in the United States was of two basic kinds: "popular" music and art music. Art music was of five general kinds: church music, songs, piano music, orchestral or ensemble music, and opera. Mason and

Bradbury both wrote numerous hymns, some of them still in use. Both men taught in singing-schools, and Mason pioneered in music education by getting singing introduced into Boston's public schools in 1837 and by setting standards for that kind of teaching. America's principal song writer in mid-century was Stephen Foster, the first American-born composer to earn his living entirely from song writing. Gottschalk, whose talent paralleled that of Chopin, successfully concertized in Europe and throughout the Americas. In some of his works, his treatment of rhythm is closely akin to later nineteenth-century ragtime and jazz, and in his use of musical quotations, he presaged the work of twentieth-century composer Charles Ives. In 1842 the first permanent symphony orchestra was established in the United States—the New York Philharmonic—but American composers wrote little music for its use. The few operas composed by Americans at this time were inconsequential. However, Dwight's weekly *Journal,* with its critical and informative articles on music, was a significant contribution.

Canadians active as professional musicians include singer Emma Albani, the first Canadian-born musician to win international acclaim as a performer, and pianist Lavallée, composer of Canada's national anthem.

Master Composers of the Late Nineteenth Century

In many European countries, much of the nineteenth century was filled with uprisings and revolutions of various kinds. In France, the Revolutions of 1830 and 1848 were followed by the Franco-Prussian War. And for Germanic peoples and Italians, uprisings and warfare ultimately brought national unification—the formation of the nations of Germany and Italy, both formally established by treaties signed in 1871 in the Hall of Mirrors at Versailles. Many authors, artists, and musicians became actively involved in the struggles of their compatriots to achieve national identity. Two such active participants were Richard Wagner in Germany and Giuseppe Verdi in Italy. Though Wagner wrote controversial articles, joined a revolutionary organization and took part in the uprisings it instigated, only covertly were his sentiments expressed in his music. Verdi lent his name to the Italian unification movement, served in parliament, and voiced his patriotic feelings through the mouths of characters in his operas. The revolution seems to have affected Franz Liszt only indirectly—through its effect on the lives of his associates who had to flee from their homes and who sought his protection. In fact, in the works of the five master composers of the late nineteenth century—Wagner, Verdi, Liszt, Brahms, and Bruckner—there is no great outpouring of music that is nationalistic *per se*.

Wagner and Verdi concentrated on opera and their masterworks brought that genre to unprecedented heights. Liszt coupled virtuosity with solid musicianship and promoted piano playing, as well as creating compositions that enriched piano and orchestral literature. Both Brahms and Bruckner were outstanding performers on keyboard instruments. Neither of them wrote program music, and both of them produced excellent symphonies and superb choral works.

Richard Wagner

Richard Wagner (1813–83), ninth child of Johanna and Karl F. Wagner, was born in Leipzig. Karl Wagner died shortly after Richard was born, and Johanna married Ludwig Geyer (1779–1821), an actor and poet employed at the Dresden court theater. In Dresden, Wagner received not only a general education but some music lessons and acquired some knowledge of theater as well. As a child, he sometimes had bit parts in operas and plays. In 1827 Frau Geyer moved her family back to Leipzig and sent Wagner to school at *Nicolai-gymnasium.* By then, the theater had captured his attention, and he wrote a play. In Leipzig there was ample opportunity to hear fine music, and after hearing some of Beethoven's symphonies, Wagner determined to learn more about music. He tried to teach himself composition, then arranged for harmony lessons. In 1830 he studied at Thomasschule; a year later he entered Leipzig University to study music but soon gave that up in favor of private lessons from the Thomaskirche Kantor. Those lessons resulted in a number of compositions,

Master Composers of the Late Nineteenth Century

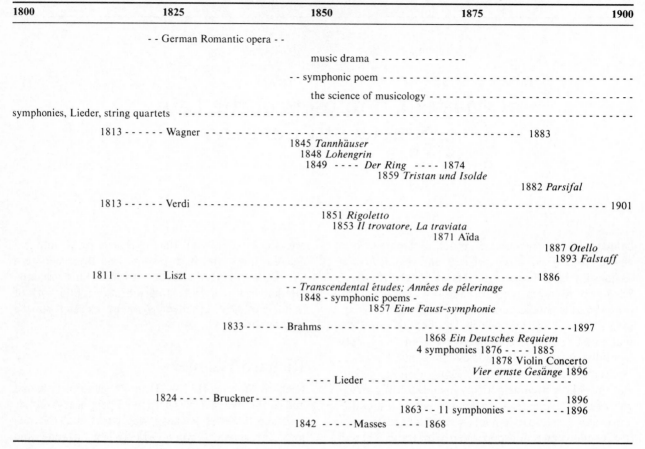

1800	1825	1850	1875	1900

- - German Romantic opera - -

music drama - - - - - - - - - - - -

- - symphonic poem -

the science of musicology -

symphonies, Lieder, string quartets -

1813 - - - - - - Wagner - 1883
                                    1845 *Tannhäuser*
                                    1848 *Lohengrin*
                                    1849 - - - - *Der Ring* - - - - 1874
                                          1859 *Tristan und Isolde*
                                              1882 *Parsifal*

1813 - - - - - - Verdi - 1901
                                    1851 *Rigoletto*
                                  1853 *Il trovatore, La traviata*
                                          1871 Aïda
                                                  1887 *Otello*
                                                  1893 *Falstaff*

1811 - - - - - - - Liszt - 1886
                             - - *Transcendental études; Années de pèlerinage*
                             1848 - symphonic poems -
                                  1857 *Eine Faust-symphonie*

1833 - - - - - - Brahms -1897
                                        1868 *Ein Deutsches Requiem*
                                    4 symphonies 1876 - - - - 1885
                                            1878 Violin Concerto
                                          Vier ernste Gesänge 1896
                          - - - - *Lieder* - - - - - - - - - - - - - - - - - -

1824 - - - - - Bruckner - 1896
                                     1863 - - 11 symphonies - - - - - - - - 1896
                              1842 - - - - - Masses - - - - 1868

---

including two piano sonatas (B♭ major, A major), a *Fantasia* (F♯ minor), some overtures, and a symphony (C major).

Primarily, Wagner was interested in stage music. In 1832 he wrote a libretto and composed his first opera, *Die Hochzeit* (The Wedding). Later, at his sister Rosalie's suggestion, he destroyed part of it. He looked for a suitable libretto for another opera but, after reading some that were offered him, decided that only he could write his libretti. On that, he never changed his mind.

During 1833 Wagner worked at Würzburg as chorus master and was involved in the production of French rescue operas and German Romantic operas.

There, he wrote the libretto and began to compose the music for *Die Feen* (The Fairies; 1833–34), based on Gozzi's play *La donna serpente* (The lady serpent). The work is a Romantic fairy tale opera, in the tradition of Marschner and Weber, and reflects Wagner's knowledge of their works. Next, he wrote *Das Liebesverbot* (Forbidden love; 1834–36), based on Shakespeare's *Measure for Measure*.

In 1834 Wagner began to write and publish articles on various aspects of drama, art, and music, some of them about specific compositions. Throughout his life he wrote essays of this kind for publication in such journals as *Neue Zietschrift für Musik* and *Gazette musicale*.

Richard Wagner. Photograph taken in 1880. *(Courtesy of the Free Library of Philadelphia.)*

Wagner became music director of Bethmann's theatrical company in 1834 and moved to Magdeburg with the company because he wanted to be near actress Minna Planer (1809–66). They married in 1836. From 1834 to 1836 Wagner produced major French, German, and Italian operas and learned a great deal about them. He hoped to produce several of his own works, but the company went into bankruptcy immediately after the première of *Das Liebesverbot* (1836).

For a few months in 1837 Wagner was music director at Königsberg Theater, then held a similar position at Riga. There, he produced operas by Mozart, Bellini, and Méhul and had opportunities to conduct some Beethoven symphonies and overtures by Weber and Mendelssohn. By the time Wagner began his fourth opera, he had a wealth of experience on which to draw. In Riga he began a grand opera, *Rienzi, der Letzte der Tribunen* (Rienzi, the last of the tribunes; 1837–40), a tragedy based on Bulwer-Lytton's book. In the spring of 1839 Wagner's work at Riga ended. Because he was heavily in debt and preferred to escape his creditors rather than find himself in debtor's prison, he left the country secretly. He and Minna embarked on a schooner for London, and en route, when the ship encountered stormy weather, Wagner thought of "The Flying Dutchman" legend—that became the subject of his next opera.

From London Wagner went to Paris where he completed *Rienzi* and wrote *Der fliegende Hollander* (The flying Dutchman; 1840–41). In 1842 he returned to Dresden. *Rienzi* was performed there in October and was his first operatic triumph. *Der fliegende Hollander* (perf. February 1843) was less successful. Nevertheless, Wagner was offered and accepted the position of conductor at Dresden. In 1844 he composed the *Trauermusik* (Funeral music; band) for Weber's interment services in Dresden.

At Dresden, Wagner wrote both *Tannhäuser* (1842–45) and *Lohengrin* (1845–48), but only *Tannhäuser* was performed there (1845). Wagner had strong feelings about political conditions in Germany and became a member of the revolutionary *Vaterlandsverein*. After participating actively in the uprising in May 1849, he had to flee from Dresden to avoid being imprisoned. He went first to Weimar, where Liszt aided him, then, with the assistance of other friends, fled to Zurich. While Wagner was in Switzerland, Liszt conducted the première of *Lohengrin* at Weimar (1850).

In Zurich, Wagner wrote some of his most significant essays on music, art, and drama, including *Die Kunst und die Revolution* (Art and Revolution, 1849), *Das Kunstwerk der Zukunft* (The Artwork of the Future, 1849), and *Oper und Drama* (Opera and Drama, 1851). Also, he began preparing the libretti (first drafted in prose, then written as poetry) for a cycle of music dramas based on material from the Icelandic *Edda* and the German *Nibelungenlied* (Song of the Nibelung), an anonymous thirteenth-century epic poem. Then he began writing some of the music. He did not compose the operas in the order in which they appear in the finished cycle, nor did he originally give them the titles they now bear: *Das Rheingold* (The Rheingold), *Die Walküre* (The Walkyrie), *Siegfried,* and *Götterdämmerung* (Twilight of the Gods). Together these four works constitute *Der Ring des Nibelungen* (The Ring of the Nibelung), which Wagner labeled *Bühnenfestspiel* (Festival presentation for theater) for a Prelude-evening and three days. Composition of the entire series took Wagner more than a quarter of a century (1848–74), yet the four music dramas are remarkably unified. He had completed the first two and part of the third by 1856, then other projects attracted him: five songs on poems by Mathilde Wesendonk (1857), *Tristan und Isolde* (1854–59), and *Die Meistersinger von Nürnberg* (sketched 1845; comp. 1861–67). When those works were finished, he resumed work on *Siegfried* and *Götterdämmerung* (completed 1874).

After Wagner had begun *Das Rheingold,* he designed a special kind of tuba, with tone quality midway between that of horn and trombone. In *Der Ring . . .* he used a quartet of those horns, which became known as **Wagner tubas.** Bruckner, Mahler, Stravinsky, and R. Strauss included Wagner tubas in some of their large orchestral works, and in the twentieth century Wagner tubas have been used in some film and television music.

Meanwhile, in 1864 King Ludwig II of Bavaria came to Wagner's rescue, paid his debts, directed him to come to Munich, and granted him a yearly allowance. But again in 1865 Wagner had to seek refuge in Switzerland for political reasons. In 1866 Minna Wagner died, and Wagner was free to marry Cosima Liszt von Bülow, with whom he had been having an affair for several years. Cosima left her husband in 1868 and, with the two of her daughters who were Wagner's, joined Wagner in Switzerland. Their son Siegfried was born in 1869. In 1870 Cosima obtained a divorce from von Bülow and married Wagner in August.

For some time Wagner had wanted a theater whose design would meet the needs of his stage works. In 1871 he acquired land in Bayreuth for a home (Wahnfried) and a theater. The cornerstone of the theater was laid in May 1872, and the building was completed by 1876. That year the first Bayreuth Festival was held in the new theater, and *Der Ring des Nibelungen* was performed in its entirety.

In 1845, when Wagner began work on *Lohengrin,* he had the idea for an opera on the subject of Parzival but did not begin sketching the music for that work until 1857. *Parsifal,* which he termed a *Bühnenweihfestspiel* (Festival of consecration in a theater), was completed and performed at Bayreuth in 1882. It was Wagner's last stage work and is the only one of his operas designed specifically for the Bayreuth theater.

Wagner had suffered from angina pectoris for several years, and, because of that, he frequently spent the winter months in Italy. While in Venice during winter 1882–83, he conducted a performance of his C-major Symphony and said that he wanted to write some one-movement monothematic symphonies. He never did so; on 13 February 1883 he suffered a fatal heart attack.

His Contributions

Wagner carried to completion the work in German Romantic opera begun by Weber and went beyond it to create music drama and approach the kind of *Gesamtkunstwerk* in stage music that Weber had striven toward. Wagner was extremely critical of the term "music drama" and would not have condoned its application to his stage works, yet he did not offer a more acceptable term. Wagner did not confine his compositional endeavors to opera, though he concentrated them there. He wrote orchestral pieces, chamber music works, choral music, and songs. Of the orchestral pieces, the C-major Symphony (1832) was performed several times during Wagner's lifetime and was the last work he conducted in public (1882); *Siegfried Idyll* (December 1870) was written as a gift to his wife; *Grosser Festmarsch* (Grand Festival March; 1876) was commissioned for the Centennial Celebration of the United States' independence and was performed in Philadelphia. In addition, Wagner wrote and published numerous essays on literary, musical, moral, and political issues; frequently his articles were controversial. He devised a new instrument and planned a new theater at Bayreuth.

His Music

Wagner was involved in every step of the creation of many of his stage works, from the time the idea for a new work came to him until the curtain fell at the conclusion of its première. He knew exactly what was meant by each word of the libretto and could accurately express in his music the dramatic truth of the text.

His early operas follow traditional lines. Only fragments survive from *Die Hochzeit,* his first operatic venture. *Die Feen,* his second stage work, is a Romantic opera in the tradition of Marschner, Weber, and E. T. A. Hoffmann. *Das Liebesverbot* reflects the influence of the Donizetti and Auber works that Wagner had conducted.

Rienzi is a five-act tragic grand opera in the style of Spontini's *Fernand Cortez* and Halévy's *La Juive.* Wagner had hoped that *Rienzi* would première in Paris but was disappointed. However, grand opera was still popular in Germany, and the Dresden performance was a decided success.

Der fliegende Hollander, a German Romantic opera of the martyr (or redemption) type, is based on a legend by Heine: A Dutch ship captain's sacrilegious oath dooms him to sail the seas until he is redeemed by a woman's fidelity; Senta, who loves him, provides that redemption. *Der fliegende Hollander* is a three-act through-composed scene opera, i.e., a work comprised of separate scenes that succeed one another. There were many such operas in the nineteenth century. The heart of this opera is Senta's ballad, sung in Act II, wherein she narrates the tale of the flying Dutchman whose portrait she has seen. Wagner sketched out the text and music of this ballad first, and from it the opera grew. In *Der fliegende Hollander* Wagner used only a few recurrent motives and used them as reminiscence motives rather than as full-fledged associative *Leitmotifs.* Themes used in the ballad appear as reminiscence motives elsewhere in the opera, including the overture.

For *Tannhäuser und der Sängerkrieg auf Wartburg* (Tannhäuser and the Singers' contest at Wartburg) Wagner combined two stories: the tale of Tannhäuser in *Das knaben Wunderhorn* and E. T. A. Hoffmann's tale of the guild singers' contest at Wartburg. *Tannhäuser* is another German Romantic opera of the redemption type, but Wagner merged with it elements of grand opera. The plot relates how Tannhäuser, after spending a year enjoying sensual pleasures at Venusberg, asks the pope for absolution from those sins; Tannhäuser receives that absolution only after the sacrificial death of Elisabeth, whose hand he wins as a result of his controversial participation in a singers' contest at Wartburg. All of the spectacular scenes in *Tannhäuser* are direct outgrowths of the story: the Venusberg ballet, the choruses sung by persons on pilgrimages to Rome, the song contest. There are numbers (set pieces) in *Tannhäuser;* this is typical of a song contest. Wagner wrote Tannhäuser's narrative of his pilgrimage to Rome (Act III) in a kind of flexible, semideclamatory style of arioso that, though new in Wagner's music, had been used by

Weber in *Euryanthe.* Wagner used this expressive semideclamatory style of writing extensively in his later operas; he called it *Sprechgesang* (speech song).

Lohengrin, considered the last important German Romantic opera, is based on Wolfram von Eschenbach's epic poem *Parzival* (see p. 118) and Grimm's fairy tale of the Swan Knight, with historical elements added by Wagner to justify the opera's tragic ending. In the nineteenth century, a tragic ending was acceptable only in historical works. The plot contains elements of both white and black magic. Taken literally, the plot deals with the trials of a wife's love—Elsa's love for Lohengrin, whose name she is not permitted to know. However, the character Lohengrin has been viewed as symbolically representing divine love descending in human form to give its blessing to humanity whose faith is too weak to accept it unquestioningly. The music of the Prelude, in A major, is interpreted as portraying the descent of the Holy Grail and its ascent back into heaven. *Lohengrin* contains some elements of grand opera—pageantry, processions, tableaux. Choruses are well written and effective; they are an important part of the opera, the chorus members serving either as participants in the action or as spectators who sometimes comment. Wagner's music is generally diatonic, with specific keys assigned to the major characters—A major (the key of the Prelude) for Lohengrin, E♭ major or A♭ major for Elsa, F♯ minor for Ortrud and for evil. In addition to similarities in plot, *Lohengrin* has other features in common with Weber's *Euryanthe:* the use of a few recurrent themes or associative *Leitmotifs,* the semideclamatory style of arioso. In *Lohengrin* the music is more continuous and greater use is made of scenes than in *Tannhäuser.*

Wagner was in Switzerland working on the series of Siegfried stage works that ultimately became *Der Ring des Nibelungen,* when he digressed to compose *Tristan und Isolde,* a work he referred to as an "Action." He began the poem in 1857 and completed the score in 1859. *Tristan und Isolde* is music drama, concerned with human character and emotions, and is devoid of spectacle. Wagner based his libretto on a medieval Celtic epic poem that relates the love story of Tristan and Isolde: By mistake, Tristan and the king's fiancée, Isolde, drink a love potion, fall in love, and meet secretly while the king is away. The king surprises them together, and mortally wounds Tristan; he is taken to Brittany, and Isolde goes there to try to heal him, but he dies in her arms. Grief stricken, she, too, dies.

In *Tristan and Isolde* Wagner uses *Leitmotifs* that are allegorical and associative and that are related to and derived from one another. Frequently, one *Leitmotif* is the inversion of another, e.g., Yearning and Suffering. Motives may be melodic, or harmonic, or a combination of both. The Yearning motive is not self-sufficient but is dependent on its underlying harmony. The same is true of the Love-potion motive, which is presented with the so-called Tristan chord (ex. 23.1).

The term "Tristan chord" derives from the first chord in *Tristan und Isolde,* f-b-d♯'-g♯', or an enharmonic spelling of that chord. In functional harmony, the chord can be explained as an altered diminished-seventh chord, with resolution effected by chromatic movement from g♯' to a', thus forming another seventh. That "Tristan chord" did not originate with Wagner; however, he sounded it without preparation, whereas other composers wove it into the musical fabric more subtly. For example, Gottschalk achieved a similar sound in his religious meditation *The Last Hope* (Op. 16, piano; comp. and publ. 1854) by writing a French sixth and resolving it to a dominant seventh by chromatic movement of the top pitch upward. Moreover, Gottschalk used the passage sequentially, just as Wagner did later in the *Prelude to Tristan und Isolde* (DWMA193). Gottschalk did not sustain the altered chord, however (ex. 23.2).

The "Tristan chord" is of special harmonic and dramatic significance in *Parsifal* as well as in *Tristan und Isolde.* Not only the "Tristan chord" but the entire harmonic vocabulary Wagner used in *Tristan und Isolde,* a harmonic vocabulary filled with daring chromatic progressions and bold accented appoggiaturas, is of historical significance in the breakdown of functional harmony and the advent of pantonality, atonality, and dodecaphony (see Ch. 25). A characteristic of Wagner's harmony in *Tristan und Isolde* is the ambiguous character of the chromatically altered chords. Wagner's chromaticism is founded in harmony, and there is the possibility that resolution of a

Example 23.1 The Prelude to *Tristan und Isolde* opens (mm. 1–6) with the Love-potion Leitmotif culminating in the so-called Tristan chord.

chromatically altered chord could be effected in any one of several ways. In other words, Wagner's harmony is tonal, but his use of altered chords and his unorthodox resolution of chromaticism pushed key tonality to the brink of dissolution. In chordal ambiguity lies the power of Wagnerian harmony in *Tristan and Isolde.*

In *Tristan und Isolde,* Wagner does not yet realize the full potential of *Leitmotifs* as essential building blocks; that remains for *Der Ring des Nibelungen.* The music of *Tristan und Isolde* is continuous throughout each act, though scenes are distinguishable. The orchestration of *Tristan und Isolde* becomes very dense. In Isolde's Love Death aria (DWMA194), Isolde's text is swallowed up in the symphonic sound and her voice becomes another tone color in the orchestral fabric even when the musical dynamic is *piano.*

Wagner began the libretto for *Die Meistersinger von Nürnberg* at Dresden in 1845; he composed the music in 1861–62. The story, set in the sixteenth century, concerns a Meistersinger guild's public singing contest in which Walther and Beckmesser are the chief competitors for the prize, the hand of the goldsmith's daughter in marriage. Wagner's music for *Die Meistersinger* is appropriate to the plot and its historical era. There are numbers and scenes in *Die Meistersinger,* and each act concludes with a massed finale, as in grand opera. The music is diatonic with conventional harmonies. Much use is made of aab structure, the traditional Bar form (two *Stollen* and an *Abgesang*) commonly used by the medieval Meistersinger.

Example 23.2 This excerpt from Gottschalk's piano solo *The Last Hope* contains passages that include a chord similar to the "Tristan chord" with a similar resolution.

Wagner modeled the character Hans Sachs after the real Meistersinger Hans Sachs (1494–1576), a master shoemaker who was a vital force in the activities of the Meistersinger guild of Nuremberg. Wisely, Wagner used some authentic Meistersinger music (e.g., the guild march) and set Hans Sachs's song *Wach' auf, es nahet gen dem Tag* (Awaken, the day approaches) in an approximation of typical Meistersinger style. In recognition of the historical Hans Sachs's activity during the Lutheran Reformation, Wagner opened the opera with a chorale. Moreover, he has the character Hans Sachs comment on the fact that Walther's song "sounded so old and yet was so new." Thus, Wagner linked historical past with controversial present; Sachs's comment could be applied to the music of *Die Meistersinger*—it "sounded so old and yet was so new." Part of that old sound is due to the fact that Wagner suppressed chromaticism in *Die Meistersinger*; when chromaticism is present, it is not often obvious. Some of the music is sentimental—a lot of the historical Meistersinger songs were. There is motivic linking between themes, and there are some recurring motives, e.g., the motive used at the very end of the opera, blending with the last chord, is the one with which the crowd mocked Beckmesser earlier. The opera conveys the idea of conflict between

the old and the new in the art of music, a conflict that was present in Wagner's life at the time. The rules of the guild are presented as antiquated, designed to preserve the old music; the expressive new music is regarded as unacceptable. The character Hans Sachs is a proponent of the new art, as is the Knight Walther von Stolzing. Sixtus Beckmesser, severe critic and town clerk who keeps the score, is against innovation; supposedly, he represents the critic Eduard Hanslick, who was outspoken in criticism of Wagner. In the music of *Die Meistersinger* Wagner not only presented the conflict between the old and the new, the historical past and the then present, he combined the musical techniques of the past with those of his own time.

Der Ring des Nibelungen is Wagner's masterpiece. Originally, he planned three music dramas concerned with the Siegfried legend, but after he had completed the trilogy of libretti, he realized the audience needed prefatory information concerning the ring and the gods' dilemma. Therefore, he wrote as informative material the poem *Das Rheingold* (The Rhinegold), which became the first music drama in the series—the "Prelude-evening" that explains the origin of the deadly magic ring and the need for a hero. The music dramas forming the trilogy about

Siegfried were intended to be performed in succession on the next three days (or evenings). As finalized, they are *Die Walküre* (The Valkyrie, female warriors who bear the bodies of dead heroes to Valhalla); *Siegfried*; and *Götterdämmerung* (Twilight of the gods, originally titled "Siegfried's death"; fig. 23.1a).

Der Ring des Nibelungen is the story of mythological events in the lives of Germanic gods and goddesses, humans, dwarfs, giants, and other beings, most of whom are greedy for gold and for the power wielded by a gold ring crafted from the stolen Rhinegold. Alberich, the dwarf who had the ring made, imbues it with a curse of death when he has to relinquish it. Thereafter, everyone who owns and wears the ring perishes—Siegfried, the hero, is slain; even the gods and their castle Valhalla are engulfed in flames. Ultimately, the ring is restored to the rightful guardians of the gold, the Rhinemaidens.

Behind the obvious story lies a symbolic one representing the creation and the end of the world, and, in a much smaller way, symbolizing the beginning, the living, and the end of a single human life. In a letter written to Liszt on 11 February 1853 Wagner said: "My new poem . . . holds the world's beginning and its destruction." The greed for the powerful ring fashioned from the Rhinegold and the struggles to attain it are symbolic of man's desire for money, worldly success, and power, and may be related to the Biblical statement that "the love of money is the root of all evil." Siegfried's destiny is death, and redemption is secured through Brunnhilde's loving sacrifice of herself in Siegfried's funeral flames.

From beginning to end, *Der Ring des Nibelungen* is a unified symphonic network of sound created from *Leitmotifs* that Wagner used in every imaginable way musically—at various times, they succeed one another, overlap or interlock, are rhythmically altered, transformed, transposed, and/or combined. In manipulating *Leitmotifs* Wagner used the contrapuntal techniques of Bach and the motivic development devices of Beethoven. There are *Leitmotifs* of association, presentiment, reminiscence, and presence. They represent characters, places, things, thoughts, premonitions, and have other associations. In *Der Ring* . . . the *Leitmotifs* become essential structural factors, the building stones of the musical edifice. The

(a)

(b)

Figure 23.1 (*a*) Joseph Huffmann's design for the final scene of *Götterdämmerung*—the final scene in *Der Ring des Nibelungen* series of music dramas. (*b*) The original setting for the Grail scene in *Parsifal*; Parsifal stands at lower right, observing the mystery. This setting was in use at Bayreuth until 1933. (*Sources: (a) Richard Wagner Archiv, Bayreuth; (b) "Mander and Mitchenson Collection."*)

vocal lines add their special timbres to the symphonic network to form the total musical picture. For Wagner, there was never a question of priority between text and music, voice and orchestra; they were of equal importance, and he treated them as such. Very often, the vocal line doubles an instrumental line (or vice versa). *Leitmotifs* may appear in the orchestra and not in the vocal line. Wagner used a very large orchestra in order to have available the instrumentation capable of producing the special timbres and effects that he needed in the music dramas.

The path of the gold can be traced musically through its *Leitmotif,* from the Rhinemaidens to the dwarf Alberich and Mime's forge, to Wotan, to the giant Fasolt and his brother who becomes the dragon Fafner, to Siegfried, and back to the Rhinemaidens (colorplate 23).

Ingenious as Wagner's use of *Leitmotifs* is, the *Leitmotifs* do not of themselves unify the music dramas or make Wagner's music great. Formal structure and keys are unifying factors also. The formal structure is not obvious but becomes apparent through analysis of the score. Frequently, sections of acts are organized in AAB or ABA form. In *Siegfried* there are ABA, AABA, and rondo forms. Each of the characters and important objects has an assigned key, and the relationships between characters, and between characters and objects, are reflected in the keys Wagner assigned to them. For example, Wotan is assigned Db major; when prophesied, Siegfried is in C minor, as hero he has Bb major, and at death returns to C minor; Wotan's female warrior Brunnhilde has Eb major; the Rhinegold first appears in G major (colorplate 24). Very few of the female characters are assigned major keys. The overall key of *Der Ring* . . . is Db major, the key of the chief god, Wotan, grandfather of Siegfried.

Another important item in Wagner's music is "infinite melody." Gluck and others had advocated the use of continuous music from the time the first note of the overture sounded until the curtain was pulled on the last scene. Some composers had accomplished that. Wagner advocated not merely continuous or endless melody but what he termed **infinite melody**—continuous expressive melody—and he achieved it in *Der Ring.* . . . In other words, to Wagner it was not the endless melody itself that was important but the expressive quality of that music at all times.

Parsifal (1882), Wagner's last theatrical work, presents a legend of the Holy Grail, with a basic theme of redemption through self-denial and sacrifice. A great deal of the presentation is via tableaux with sung narration (by the characters, not by a narrator). Parsifal's reactions are as important as his actions—

sometimes more so (fig. 23.1b). Changes of scenery such as those occurring as the result of magic were done by panorama, i.e., by sliding sets. (Revolving and sliding sets had been used in Paris for decades.) Viewed overall, *Parsifal* is constructed symmetrically, in *Bogen* (arch) form, with Acts I and III considered A and Act II, B. There is much that is traditional about the music of *Parsifal.* Choruses are important, and Wagner's choral writing is excellent. His use of separated choirs creates an effect resembling that of the *cori spezzati* of Gabrieli and other late Renaissance composers working at St. Mark's, Venice. For the Grail *Leitmotif* Wagner borrowed an old *Amen* formula that was sung at Dresden Hofkapelle when he conducted there, and the Prelude's first theme, the *Leitmotif* for the Last Supper, strongly resembles Gregorian chant.

There are great contrasts in the music of *Parsifal.* The music of Amfortas, befitting the agony he endures physically and mentally, is sometimes very dissonant and chromatic to the brink of atonality. The sorcery and intrigues of Klingsor and Kundry vary from extreme chromaticism to lush Romanticism. The music of the Grail is diatonic and at times churchlike. Within those different areas, Wagner makes even finer distinctions, e.g., that made in the diatonic music to differentiate the guilelessness of Parsifal, the purity of the Grail, the elevation of Parsifal to a position of leadership and guardianship of the Grail.

German dictator Adolf Hitler (1889–1945; chancellor 1933–45) especially favored *Parsifal* and when he was in power wanted it performed annually on Good Friday. Hitler owned several of Wagner's manuscripts; for a time, it was believed they were destroyed during World War II. Fortunately, before Hitler committed suicide, he sent those manuscripts to Scandinavia for safekeeping; they were located in the late 1970s.

Wagner's genius as a composer of theatrical music is unparalleled. In his music, he did not reject all that was traditional. Rather, he summed up all that had gone before. He was eclectic—he used every historical and traditional musical technique that would serve his purposes—from the composers of Gregorian chant, through the Meistersinger, Gabrieli, Bach, Mozart, Beethoven, Weber, and others—and shaped them and merged them expressively to create music that was so

Giuseppe Verdi.
(a) Photograph, 1853;
(b) photograph, 1888.

new it was considered radical. Wagner's music had a marked effect on late nineteenth-century and early twentieth-century musical developments. His use of orchestral color, his treatment of motives, his minimizing of divisions and subdivisions to the point where they were inaudible, and the symphonic character of his music dramas affected the work of symphonists as well as composers of operas. His treatment of key tonality and chromaticism, producing at times a measure of polytonality and verging on atonality, provided incentive for later composers to move into dodecaphony and pantonality/atonality.

Giuseppe Verdi

Giuseppe Verdi (1813–1901) was born in the village of Le Roncole, near Busseto, in Parma. At that time Parma was governed by the French; a year later, the area was under Austrian control. Verdi was barely a toddler when he showed an interest in music. Though his father was impoverished, he arranged for Giuseppe to have lessons from the organist and master of choirboys at the local church. When Verdi was about 9, the organist died, and Verdi was assigned some of

his duties. Not long thereafter, his father sent him to school in Busseto. There he received an excellent general education and had counterpoint and composition lessons from the municipal music director. At the age of 19, Verdi expected to enter Milan Conservatory but was denied admission because he failed to meet keyboard performance requirements. Disappointed but not discouraged, he arranged for private lessons with a local composer who had written some operas for La Scala.

In 1836 Verdi returned to Busseto as municipal music master, with secular duties only. He was required to teach vocal and instrumental music in the school and to conduct concerts. Programs of those concerts reveal that he wrote some orchestral pieces and some sacred and secular vocal works, but most of that music has disappeared. His first published compositions, songs, appeared in 1838. That year he worked on his opera *Oberto*. It had only moderate success when performed at La Scala in 1839 but brought Verdi a commission for three more operas. The first of them, the comedy *Un giorno di regno* (One day of reign; 1840), on a Romani libretto, was a failure. That experience may have turned Verdi against comedy; all of his other operas except the last one are serious. However, after 1850 he occasionally included comic roles in his serious operas.

Verdi's third opera, *Nabucodonosor* (Nebuchadnezzar; 1842)—the title was later shortened to *Nabucco*—was an outstanding success. The role of Abigaille was created by soprano Giuseppina Strepponi (1815–97), who, before she met Verdi, had been influential in getting his first opera produced. *Nabucco* was received favorably throughout Europe. *I lombardi alla prima crociata* (The Lombards on the first crusade; 1843), Verdi's fourth opera for La Scala, was another success.

Between 1842 and 1849 Verdi wrote 11 operas, all dealing in some way with heroism. Those works constitute the first of four distinctive groupings of Verdi's operas: (1) works concerned with heroism; (2) works relating to personal life (predicaments of ordinary people in everyday life, divorce, unmarried persons living together); (3) works showing French influence; and (4) the masterpieces based on Shakespeare's works.

Verdi's association with Francesco Piave (1810–76), librettist for 10 of his 27 operas, began with *Ernani* (1844) and continued intermittently until 1862. Piave and Verdi both felt intense patriotism for Italy and wanted a unified nation. A visible thread of patriotism is woven into all of the operas Verdi wrote before 1871. The Italians who attended performances of his operas were keenly aware of this. As Verdi's operas became more and more popular, Italians used his name as a slogan for unification of Italy under rule of the king of Sardinia. The cry, "Viva VERDI!" not only paid homage to a favorite native son, it expressed political hope: "Viva *V*ittorio *E*manuele, *R*e *D'I*talia!" Verdi's participation in plans for unification of Italy was not only through his music. He was a friend of Camillo Benso di Cavour (1810–61), prime minister to Vittorio Emanuele, and served as a member of the Italian Parliament from 1861 to 1865.

In the summer of 1847 Verdi went to London for the première of *I masnadieri* (The robbers). Soprano Jenny Lind, nicknamed "the Swedish nightingale," created the role of Amalie, and was a sensation. From London Verdi went to Paris to supervise some rehearsals for the production of *Jérusalem,* and while

Giuseppina Strepponi Verdi. Anonymous portrait in the Verdi home, Villa Sant'Agata, Busseto, Italy.

there he contacted Giuseppina Strepponi, whose singing had contributed to the success of *Nabucco*. Strepponi had studied at Milan Conservatory and had achieved her first successes in 1835, in Rossini's *Matilda di Shabran* and Bellini's *Norma* and *La sonnambula*. She first sang at La Scala in 1839 and had recommended that Verdi's *Oberto* be produced there. Strepponi had retired from singing opera in 1846 and was teaching singing in Paris in July 1847 when she and Verdi renewed their acquaintance. Their friendship deepened into a liaison, and they lived together openly for years before marrying in 1859. Giuseppina constantly encouraged Verdi and wrote many letters on his behalf; when he spoke of retiring, it was she who coaxed him into composing another opera.

The second major period in Verdi's opera composition covers the five operas *Luisa Miller* (1849), *Stiffelio* (1850), *Rigoletto* (1851), *Il trovatore* (The troubadour; 1853), and *La traviata* (The fallen woman, 1853). Each of these opera plots contains something very close to a situation in or an aspect of personal life, and most of them touched a condition in Verdi's own life.

Though Verdi was a successful composer and could have lived comfortably on the large fees he received from commissions and performances of his works, he maintained and managed his estate near Busseto, ascertained that the crops were properly tended, and that all was in order there. He was in tune with the land of Italy in a very real sense, as well as being in tune with its culture and involved in its politics.

After *La traviata* was produced, Verdi thought he needed a rest from composition and left Italy for a time. He was never completely free from composition, however, for he was always thinking about revising an old work or was casting about for a subject for a new one. A period of French influence in Verdi's opera composition began in 1853. That year he composed his first grand opera, *Les vêpres siciliennes* (Sicilian vespers, 1853). Its libretto was a revision of one Scribe intended for Donizetti and that was unfinished at the time of Donizetti's death. Verdi did not know until he was working on the opera that it came to him secondhand, so to speak. If he had known earlier, he probably would have rejected the libretto. Verdi's other important operas from this period of French influence include *Simon Boccanegra* (1857); *Un ballo in maschera* (A masked ball, 1859) based on Scribe's libretto for Auber's *Gustave III,* but with several major alterations made to avoid political problems in Italy; *La forza del destino* (The force of destiny, 1862); *Don Carlos* (1867); and *Aïda* (1871), a spectacular grand opera based on a scenario by Egyptologist A. E. Mariette.

Verdi's operas were performed internationally, and he received invitations to write new works for performance in major opera houses all over Europe. *Rigoletto* was performed at the Cairo Opera House in November 1869, and Verdi was asked several times to compose a new opera for Cairo. He rejected those requests until he saw a synopsis of Mariette's scenario for *Aïda.* After investigating the quantity and quality of performing resources at Cairo, Verdi decided to compose *Aïda.* Antonio Ghislanzoni prepared the libretto. Within two years of its première (Cairo, 1871), *Aïda* became an established part of international opera repertoire.

Meanwhile, Rossini had died (November 1868), and Verdi proposed that the leading Italian composers collaborate in writing a Requiem Mass as a Rossini memorial. The proposal was accepted, and Verdi composed the *Libera me* section, but the Mass was never performed.

In 1873, purely for his own pleasure and diversion, Verdi wrote a string quartet in E minor. It is quite good. That year Italian novelist Alessandro Manzoni died, and Verdi deeply mourned the loss of his good friend. It is strange that Manzoni's great Italian novel, *I promessi sposi* (The betrothed), was never used as an opera in the nineteenth century. Verdi proposed that Milan honor Manzoni with a memorial on the first anniversary of his death, and for that occasion Verdi composed his *Messa da Requiem.* The *Libera me* section of that Mass is the one Verdi had written for Rossini. In May 1874 Verdi's Requiem Mass was performed in the church of San Marco and was sung again in concert at La Scala. Manzoni was a devout Catholic; Verdi was a professed atheist, yet his Requiem Mass seems to be a sincere expression of Catholic religious faith. Verdi stated that his lack of religious faith was caused by mistreatment he had received from a priest while he was a choirboy. From time to time, Verdi included in his operas remarks about ecclesiastical cruelty and voiced through characters his criticism of the clergy.

After writing the Requiem, Verdi lived in semi-retirement. In 1874 he was elected to the Italian Senate, but he considered it an honorary post and never actively participated in Senate deliberations. In 1880 he composed an *Ave Maria* and a *Pater noster.* For almost six years he wrote no operas; then he was attracted to Shakespeare's *Othello.* Even before Verdi composed *Macbeth* (1847), he had been interested in Shakespeare's works, and from time to time he had thought about operas based on other Shakespeare plays. In 1879, Italian poet-composer Arrigo Boito (1842–1918), a close friend of the Verdis, prepared an *Otello* libretto and suggested that Verdi set it. Verdi

Figure 23.2 (*a*) Scene from first production of *Otello* at La Scala, Milan, 1887: Act II, Otello has just flung Iago to the ground. (*b*) A contemporary sketch of scene from Act II of the original production of Verdi's *Falstaff* at La Scala, 1893. Two women are hiding Falstaff in a large basket, and other persons are searching the house for him. Mrs. Quickly curtsies. Behind the screen, Nanetta and Fenton embrace. *(Figure a from Enthoven Collection; figure b from Collection of "Radio Times—Hulton Picture Gallery.")*

(a)   (b)

was interested, but it took Giuseppina's persuasion to convince him to write the opera. *Otello* was one of the two great masterpieces that crowned Verdi's career. With *Otello*, Verdi brought Italian tragic opera to its peak (fig. 23.2).

Verdi was not permitted to rest on those laurels. Boito gave him another Shakespearean libretto, *Falstaff*, based on *The Merry Wives of Windsor* and *Henry IV*. Verdi could not resist. When completed in 1893, Verdi's *Falstaff* took its place beside *Otello* as one of the great masterpieces of all time; with *Falstaff* Italian operatic comedy was brought to its peak.

Boito tried to interest Verdi in composing more Shakespearean operas—*Antony and Cleopatra* or *King Lear*—but Verdi was tired and considered himself too old. His last contribution to opera was a short ballet written for the Paris première of *Otello* in 1894. In 1889 Verdi wrote another *Ave Maria* for four-part unaccompanied chorus; he deemed it (rightly) inconsequential and did not want it performed. Between

composition of *Otello* and *Falstaff*, he wrote *Laudi alla Vergine Maria* (Praises to the Virgin Mary), and in 1895–97 composed a *Stabat Mater* and a *Te Deum laudamus*. These three pieces are excellent. All four sacred compositions were published together as *Quattro pezzi sacri* (Four sacred pieces; 1898).

Verdi's last contribution was not a musical composition. He financed the construction of Casa di Riposo per Musicisti, a home for aged retired musicians, in Milan. Verdi died on 27 January 1901, after having suffered a stroke a few days earlier.

His Music

A list of Verdi's works includes 28 operas, 3 major choral works, 3 instrumental compositions, and several vocal pieces. The 3 major choral works are *Messa da Requiem, Pater noster,* and *Quattro pezzi sacri*. Since 1950, Verdi's operas have experienced a real revival in the United States. Until the 1920s, only *Otello* and *Falstaff* received serious consideration.

Verdi consistently chose libretti based on literary works by major authors; though he used works by Romantic writers, he did not limit himself to that era. He chose authors from various countries—Britain, France, Germany, Spain, and Italy—and poetry, prose, and drama all supplied material. Represented are Shakespeare, with *Macbeth, Otello,* and *Falstaff;* Byron, with *I due Foscari* (The two Foscari) and *Il Corsairo* (The Corsaire); Schiller, with *Giovanna d'Arco* (Joan of Arc), *I masnadieri* (The robbers), *Luisa Miller* (based on *Kabale und Liebe,* Cabal and love), and *Don Carlos;* Scribe, with *Les Vêpres siciliennes* (Sicilian Vespers) and *Un ballo in maschera* (A masked ball); Dumas the Younger, with *La dame aux camélias* (Camille); Hugo, with *Ernani* and *Rigoletto;* Voltaire, with *Alzir;* Garcia Gutiérrez, with *Il trovatore* (The troubadours) and *Simon Boccanegra;* and Spanish dramatist de Saavedra, with *La forza del destino* (The force of destiny), based on *Don Alvaro, o La fuerza del sino,* though this last-mentioned opera contains some scenes from Schiller.

When choosing a libretto, Verdi looked for a subject that was bold and that contained emotional situations that could move at a fast pace. He worked closely with his librettists and maintained good working relationships with them, but he was demanding and made his requirements clear to them. He worked more than once with each of the librettists, except F. Romani. Cammarano, Solera, and Piave supplied most of his libretti, but Verdi insisted on a Scribe libretto for his first attempt at French grand opera. In the composition and production of his operas, Verdi reserved for himself the final determination of affairs—he checked every word of the script carefully, often changing words, paring phrases, or carving away entire sections that did not suit him, and he demanded that certain things be said in a certain way. Word choice was extremely important to Verdi, as was the proper musical setting of those words. He insisted that opera must not be acting or mere presentation of drama-in-song but the representation of persons involved in and reacting to realistic situations and events; this lies at the core of his success.

Verdi took a vital interest in all aspects of the production of his operas—the stage settings, costuming, the movement of the characters on the stage, their positions as they sang, and so forth. He made

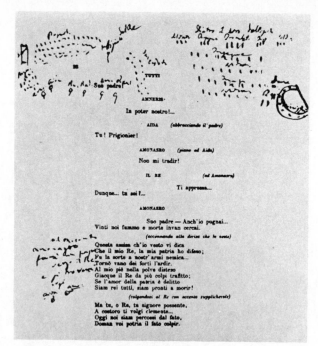

Figure 23.3 Page from a copy of the printed libretto of Verdi's *Aida* with his autograph notations made in 1872 concerning the position of singers on stage, and matters of interpretation. *(Pierpont Morgan Library, New York.)*

sketches in the libretto margins (fig. 23.3) and then personally prepared production manuals wherein he indicated precisely scene by scene such things as the placement of properties and the position of singers at key points in a scene. Those production manuals were published and some are extant. Verdi's great concern for proper staging and correct interpretation of his music dramatically and vocally manifested itself in his demand for countless rehearsals. One singer reported more than 150 of them!

Just as life in nineteenth-century Italy was colored by intense feelings of patriotism, so, as mentioned, there is present in Verdi's operas a strong but unobtrusive strand of Italian patriotism. Not only is patriotism present in his choice of subjects, in each opera it is in some of the lines his characters sing—lines filled with double meaning, suited to the character roles in the operas but also conveying his own intense patriotism. For Italians, the double meaning of those patriotic lines was obvious.

Verdi chose the subject matter and carefully edited the libretto first, with due regard for possible censorship and concern for local conditions at the site of the première. There were times when, because of political or religious censorship, he had to relinquish a subject he had selected, alter a plot, or effect a change of venue for a performance. Next he blocked out the general scheme of the opera, sketched out ideas, drafted vocal lines, wrote down the bass of the harmony and jotted down ideas for instrumentation as they occurred to him. Then he prepared the singers' parts, tested the keys of the pieces for suitability to the singers' voices, and made necessary adjustments. His harmonic plan was flexible, because he adjusted the material to fit the capabilities of the singers he had selected for the roles. Finally, he prepared the orchestration, writing the overture last of all.

A basic skeletal structural scheme is common to almost all of Verdi's operas. Most of them are constructed in four acts, in three acts with a prologue, or in three acts so organized that fourfold division of structure is visible. In the first main division (prologue or first act), one of the principal characters other than the heroine sings a solo with chorus; in the second or third scene, the heroine is introduced in a solo (usually of narrative character) with chorus. In either the second or third act, there is a large three-movement duet; both of the middle acts conclude with large ensemble finales, one of which might center on a stirring duet. At or near the beginning of the last act, there is a prayer scene (*preghiera*) for the heroine, often accompanied by chorus; and there is a death scene for the hero or a rondo finale for the heroine. It should be stressed that (a) this scheme is basic, and was varied in many ways, and (b) the scheme was not peculiar to Verdi; many other composers followed it.

The principal male singing voices basic to Verdi's cast were a strong baritone, a lyric tenor, and a firm bass (*basso cantante*); the type of soprano varied according to the specific characteristics of the heroine, and the nature of the supporting female role determined that voice type. He was adept at musical characterization.

Verdi drafted a large-scale harmonic plan for his operas but frequently modified that plan after he observed carefully the singer's optimum points. He used traditional tonal musical language, colored by the enriched harmonies of Romanticism. Frequently he used repeated figurations to arrive at the desired tonality, and then he would reiterate a pitch until the key was firm. He might use a diminished-seventh chord to pivot into a new key or move by a series of melodic thirds over a $^6_4$ chord.

Characteristically, as Verdi planned his operas, he made notations as to possible instrumental combinations for accompanying the singers. Frequently, he wrote at least one number that was orchestrated delicately, i.e., with only a few instruments of light tone quality. Often he used bits of instrumental solo prominently—harp, violin, flute, or 'cello. His vocal duets are distinctive in that he gave the participants dissimilar rather than similar material. Often he wrote baritone-soprano, father-daughter duets. The aria types he used vary considerably; usually his music moves fluidly from dramatic or free declamation through arioso to aria. Some scenes are broad, others are extremely condensed.

In the works Verdi wrote between 1839 and c. 1850, the influences of Rossini, Donizetti, and Saverio Mercadante (1795–1870) are the most significant. Mercadante, whose 60 operas never found a permanent place in standard repertoire because he was so completely overshadowed by Verdi, provides a link in the development of Italian opera during those few years in the 1830s when Rossini was no longer composing operas and Bellini was deceased, when Donizetti was beginning to achieve fame, and when Verdi's star had not yet risen. Mercadante's writing was uneven, but in some operas his orchestration was imaginative, his ensemble writing remarkable. In Verdi's early works, the influence of Donizetti is seen especially in the unison writing for chorus and in the regular and smoothly flowing melodies. Rossini and Mercadante possibly influenced the rapid-paced ensembles. From the time of Mayr, Italian composers had placed the aria within a scene and had linked recitative and aria with arioso or choral interjections.

Verdi's use of recurrent themes is particularly apparent in *Rigoletto, Un ballo in maschera,* and *La forza del destino.* Not only do themes recur within an opera, sometimes there is thematic similarity or recurrence between operas.

Master Composers of the Late Nineteenth Century

Verdi regarded *Rigoletto* as a landmark in his writing. Based on Victor Hugo's *Le roi s'amuse* (The king is amused), the opera libretto had to be changed in several ways before it was suitable for performance in Italy. The jester Rigoletto is directly related to the troupe of dwarfs Isabella d'Este maintained for entertainment purposes. In this opera Verdi included some satire, some comic touches. Two of the solos have remained popular favorites: Gilda's *Cara nome* (Dear name), a *romanza,* and the philandering Duke's *La donna e mobile* (Woman is fickle), sung twice in Act III. Its melody is cast in neat two-measure phrases and is provided with a strumming accompaniment. Duets are an important feature of *Rigoletto.* Here, Verdi again had opportunity to write a father-daughter, baritone-soprano duet. The semideclamatory recitative used in *Rigoletto* appears in Verdi's later operas, especially *Otello.*

Aïda is a number opera, but one with remarkable continuity. It contains much dramatic declamatory recitative, and the spectacular *divertissements* make it a monumental grand opera. Radames's *romanza, Celeste Aïda* (Heavenly Aïda), is impressive.

In *Otello,* to achieve unity of time and place Boito omitted Act I of Shakespeare's play; thus, all of the action could take place in Cyprus. The audience is apprised of the contents of Shakespeare's first act through the lyrics of the love duet at the end of Act I of the opera. Verdi's opera opens with a fierce storm, and Otello enters in the midst of it. The three main characters are introduced in the first Act, but none of them has a solo aria. Even the *brindisi* (drinking scene) is shared by Iago, two others, and the chorus. It is apparent at the outset that the leading characters are important because of their roles in the drama and not because they are singers. The action is not slowed to give a singer opportunity for virtuosic vocal display. Every part of a scene contributes to propelling the drama, e.g., the *brindisi* is a dramatic ensemble. Verdi accorded supremacy to voice, but he supported the vocal lines instrumentally and used instruments and orchestral techniques to enhance the text and the characterization. Iago's sinister personality is portrayed not only through his words and his actions, but

through well-placed chromaticism and ornaments: acciaccaturas, appoggiaturas, and a long trill followed by the drop of a fifth (DWMA195). Actually, in *Otello* Verdi produced a kind of "music drama" with continuous music and some associative figures (*not* Leitmotifs) used to characterize persons, but his music drama was still within the bounds of traditional Italian opera and was quite different from those of Wagner.

Falstaff seems shorter than it actually is because it moves along so rapidly. It is a witty comedy filled with puns and musical subtleties that play upon those puns—humor that can be appreciated most by persons who really know the Italian language. The humor is not only in the words and action, it is in the orchestration as well, e.g., the 'celli and piccolo playing four octaves apart in *Se Falstaff s'assottiglia.* In *Falstaff* Verdi skillfully combined recitative with aria, letting the music flow from one to the other, so there is no sense of recitative or aria *per se.* The opera abounds in melodic phrases and exhibits a kind of writing that Giuseppina described, in a letter to her sister, as "a new combination of poetry and music." In the last Act there is a song within a song, and much of the Windsor Forest scene in which the cunning wives outwit Falstaff is reminiscent of *A Midsummer Night's Dream.* The opera ends exuberantly with an ensemble finale—a fugue begun by Falstaff, *Tutto nel mondo è burla* (All the world is a joke).

Verdi must be considered a Classical-Romanticist. Romantic traits infiltrated his writing, but they were used to further the drama—the human actions and reactions—and not exploited. His treatment of nature, e.g., the storm scene in *Otello,* is an example. He followed the traditional lines of Italian opera established by Monteverdi in mid-seventeenth century and developed through the work of Steffani, Alessandro Scarlatti, Hasse, Mozart, Rossini, and Donizetti. Their work culminated in Verdi's Shakespearean masterpieces, *Otello* in tragedy, and *Falstaff* in comedy. In his insistence upon the realistic in details and staging, and in his regard for the presentation of events as human experiences with human reactions, Verdi paved the way for the *verismo* (realism) operas of Puccini.

Franz Liszt

The life of Franz Liszt (1811–86) was colorful and filled with opposites, as was the Romantic era in which he lived. He had the kind of personality that accepted and carried out responsibilities yet wanted freedom, that sought a priestly life within the church yet wanted all the world had to offer. He was restless and versatile, with a multifaceted career as virtuoso pianist, composer, author, and teacher.

Liszt's first piano teacher was his father, an official at the Esterházy court who also played 'cello in the court orchestra. In 1821 the Liszt family moved to Vienna; there Franz studied piano with Czerny and had composition lessons from Salieri, who was then quite old. At the age of 11, Liszt played in his first concert, in Vienna.

The Liszts moved to Paris in 1823, and Franz began to tour as concert artist throughout Europe. It was customary for several performers to share a concert program, assisting one another, or being accompanied and assisted by an orchestra. By 1827 Liszt had wearied of that kind of career and voiced his desire to become a priest. However, the death of his father (1827) and his own precarious health deterred him from embarking on religious studies. For a while, Liszt taught piano in Paris. At the same time, he read widely in an endeavor to compensate for his lack of a good general education. Between 1827 and 1830 he composed little music—for a young virtuoso pianist this is not surprising.

In 1831 Liszt heard Paganini for the first time. The great violinist's technical prowess so astounded Liszt that he determined to try to achieve comparable technical facility on the piano. Using as theme *La campanella* (The little bell), the melody from the Rondo movement of Paganini's B-minor Violin Concerto, Liszt composed a *Grand fantasia de bravoure* (publ. as Op. 2; 1834).

Liszt met Berlioz and Chopin in 1833. He formed a friendship with Chopin, and his observations of Chopin's playing brought more Romanticism into his own playing. Liszt became interested in Berlioz's works and made transcriptions of some of them, including *Symphonie fantastique*. Throughout his life, Liszt made transcriptions and arrangements of other composers' works—more than 400 of them survive.

Franz Liszt. *(Courtesy of the Free Library of Philadelphia.)*

He captured the orchestration fairly accurately—for some large orchestral works, such as those of Berlioz, that was not easy.

In 1834 Liszt was introduced to Aurore Dudevant (George Sand) and Countess Marie d'Agoult. Soon he and the countess began an affair. Around that time Liszt began to write articles on music for publication in various European journals; he discussed his material with the countess and she gave him valuable assistance with some of his writing. In 1835 she left her husband and lived with Liszt for the next eight or nine years. They had three children: Blandine (1835–62), Cosima (1837–1930); and Daniel (1839–59). The countess and Liszt traveled a good deal; he concertized, wrote, and composed much music. When they separated in 1844, he took their children to Paris to be educated.

Liszt was at the height of his career as a concert pianist in 1838. He is credited with being the first to perform a complete *solo* recital; he did so in London in 1840. That year, Liszt had his first experience conducting; he would do a great deal of that in the future. In 1842 he was appointed Grand Ducal Director of Music Extraordinary at Weimar.

There were other mistresses in Liszt's life after the countess, but he did not form another lasting liaison until he met Princess Carolyne Sayn-Wittgenstein in Kiev in 1847. From time to time, she requested a divorce so that she and Liszt might marry but could not obtain the pope's consent. In fact, the pope revoked his sanction on the eve of their antici-pated wedding day in 1861. The princess's husband died in 1864, but by that time Carolyne and Liszt had put aside thoughts of marriage. Carolyne was influ-ential in persuading Liszt to give up his career as per-former and devote his time to composition. Once that decision was made, he accepted the conducting post at Weimar as a permanent position. Between 1847 and 1858 he wrote most of the compositions that estab-lished his reputation as a major composer, the works for which he is known in the twentieth century.

At Weimar Liszt conducted major works by con-temporary composers as well as those of past gener-ations. Because of his willingness to perform works of promising composers, he attracted many of the avant-garde. At times, the fact that he programmed and conducted works by radical moderns created some dif-ficult situations in connection with his court position. For instance, he supported Wagner and championed his music when Wagner was a political refugee in Switzerland.

In addition to composing and conducting, Liszt taught piano lessons, and many talented pianists came to Weimar to work with him. One of his pupils was Hans von Bülow, a fine pianist who also became an excellent conductor. Liszt's daughter Cosima mar-ried von Bülow but later left him for Wagner, whom she eventually married in 1870, after having three children by him. That affair caused a serious rupture in Liszt's friendship with Wagner, a rupture that lasted until 1872. Though Liszt was party to affairs in his own life, he did not condone his daughter's.

In December 1858 Liszt resigned his position at Weimar. In 1859 his son died, and Liszt expressed his grief in the orchestral funeral ode *Les morts* (The dead).

Late in 1861, Liszt moved to Rome to begin re-ligious studies. He still composed but concentrated on religious music. In 1855 he had written a setting of Psalm 13 (How long wilt Thou forget me, O Lord?; tenor soloist, chor., orch.), and a *Missa solemnis* for the consecration of the basilica at Gran in 1856. In 1859 he had made settings of Psalms 23 and 137; in Rome, he revised those works and wrote settings of Psalms 116 (1869) and 129 (1881). He composed a *Missa choralis* (1865) based on Gregorian chant melodies, completed the oratorio *Die Legende von der*

heiligen Elisabeth (1857–62) and composed another, *Christus* (1862–67), and wrote *Via Crucis* (Stations of the Cross; 1879). When his daughter Blandine died in 1862, he composed, as memorial to her, variations on the passacaglia theme from Bach's Cantata No. 12.

In 1863 Liszt entered Oratorio della Madonna del Rosario and in 1865 took four minor orders in the Catholic Church, but he never became a priest. He continued to compose sacred music, including a Mass for the coronation of Emperor Franz Josef of Austria (r. 1848–1916) as King of Hungary (1867).

Teaching still interested Liszt. From 1869 until his death he made annual trips between Weimar, Rome, and Budapest to conduct master classes in piano playing. From time to time, noted composers visited him in Rome and sought his advice. Occasion-ally, he performed in charity concerts but no longer gave complete piano recitals. His last public perfor-mance was in Luxembourg in 1885, when he played three of his compositions in a concert sponsored by a music society. Liszt enjoyed hearing Wagner's music, and in July 1886 attended performances of several operas at Bayreuth, where his daughter Cosima maintained some control in the management of Wag-ner's interests. While in Bayreuth, Liszt became ill, pneumonia developed, and he died on 31 July 1886.

Style

In addition to Czerny, who, as teacher, transmitted to Liszt Beethoven's playing style, the most significant influences on Liszt's piano playing and compositional styles were Hungarian gypsy music, Field, Chopin, and Paganini. In his piano playing, Liszt, like Chopin, strove to make the piano transcend its actual limita-tions. He could caress the keys and draw forth inti-mate, delicate tones, or elicit from the instrument full, almost orchestral, sonorities. Emulating Paganini's violin virtuosity and showmanship, Liszt became the "Paganini of the piano." Liszt knew and performed Bach's preludes and fugues, Domenico Scarlatti's so-natas, pieces by Handel, and others. He played with brilliance and clarity, and his technique, shaped by Czerny, was flawless. Liszt's slender fingers were un-usually long, and he could play passages in tenths with no difficulty. He was as skilled a performer on organ as he was on piano.

Much of Liszt's music is monothematic, with the material for a work being derived from thematic transformation of either an initial theme or a germinal motive. He treated traditional formal patterns freely, particularly large forms. His harmonies are Romantic, and that Romanticism gradually increased, as he used more tritones, diminished and augmented chords, and chromaticism. After c. 1860, whole-tone scales appear more frequently in his works. Sometimes his harmonies clash to the extent that it seems he completely dispensed with the traditional rules governing harmony in key tonality—and perhaps in some instances he did.

Liszt's Keyboard Music

As was the case with most performer-composers, the type of piano music Liszt composed was directly related to his principal interests during a particular period in his life. His most virtuosic works were composed when he was concertizing actively, but his concert repertoire included works of other composers as well as his own compositions. In the virtuoso pieces Liszt composed for his own use, he exploited all of the piano's resources, sometimes notating the piano music on three staves, as he did in *Mazeppa* (ex. 23.3), the 4th of his 12 *Études d'exécution transcendante* (Transcendental études). *Mazeppa* exists as a symphonic poem, also; the piano étude is the more excellent version. Liszt composed and published simple versions of those études in 1827, then revised and expanded them, increasing the degree of difficulty considerably to make them "transcendental," and published them again in 1839; in 1851 he again revised them (republ. 1852). Ten of the études have programmatic titles; untitled are No. 2 in A minor and No. 10 in F minor. Though Liszt's *Transcendental Études* are excellent, they are inferior to Chopin's études musically.

Liszt composed 11 collections of character pieces. Of these the most significant are the three volumes entitled *Années de Pélerinage* (Years of pilgrimage); they contain some of his finest piano solos. The first volume, *Première année: Suisse* (First year: Switzerland; 1848–54, publ. 1855), holds nine short character pieces inspired by visits to Switzerland; one of the finest pieces in this set is *Au Bord d'une Source* (At the edge of a spring), a musical description of rip-

Example 23.3 Liszt: *Mazeppa,* mm. 7–12.

pling waters. Each piece in the second volume, *Seconde année: Italie* (Second year: Italy; 1837–49, publ. 1858), was inspired by an Italian poem or other work of art. Included in that volume are piano arrangements of three songs Liszt had written earlier, settings of Petrarch sonnets Nos. 47, 104, and 123. The largest piece in the volume is *Après une lecture de Dante, Fantasia quasi sonata* (After reading Dante, fantasia like a sonata). That piece, frequently called the "Dante Sonata," is a large, multisection, cyclic work that contains some very difficult passages. The third volume, *Troisième année* (Third year; 1867–77, publ. 1883), was also inspired in Italy. The pieces related to Villa d'Este, where Liszt spent part of each year, are the finest in this compilation. *Les jeux d'eaux à la Villa d'Este* (The fountains at *Villa d'Este;* DWMA196) is an important precursor of Ravel's (1875–1937) *Jeux d'eau* (Fountains; 1901) and of Impressionism (see pp. 777–78; see p. 772).

Among Liszt's excellent individual character pieces for piano are three comparatively little-known works: *Nuages gris* (Grey clouds; 1881; publ. 1927;

DWMA197), *La lugubre gondola* (The ominous gondola; 1882, publ. 1916), and *Schlaflos! Frage und Antwort* (Sleepless! Question and answer; 1883), a nocturne. These pieces are significant because of their experimental harmonies and unexpected chromatic modulations; the works are not technically difficult.

Few piano sonatas were written during the middle and late nineteenth century. Liszt wrote only one, Sonata in B minor (1852–53). Though the sonata is divided into three sections—Lento assai-Allegro energico, Andante sostenuto, and Allegro energico—it is actually one long, continuous movement. Three motives, or themes, are stated in the first section and undergo thematic transformation throughout the sonata. Structurally, the sonata resembles a symphonic poem. (See Liszt, Orchestral Music.)

Liszt wrote a number of piano pieces in dance forms—waltzes, *Ländler,* Hungarian dances, polonaises, mazurkas, and others. He composed a great deal of Hungarian music, resembling gypsy rather than authentic folk or nationalistic music. There are 20 *Hungarian Rhapsodies,* of which the 2nd, 11th, and 12th are pianists' favorites. Liszt's favorite was the 13th; it is one of the finest, but is seldom performed. The 15th is a version of his *Rákóczy March.*

Of Liszt's 11 works for organ, the most significant are the *Fantasie und Fuge über den Choral "Ad nos, ad salutarem undam"* (Fantasia and Fugue on the Chorale *Ad nos, ad salutarem undam;* 1850) and the *Präludium und Fuge über den Namen BACH* (Prelude and Fugue on the name Bach; 1855, rev. 1870). The *Fantasia and Fugue* is in three sections: (1) a fantasia using a theme borrowed from Meyerbeer's *La prophète;* (2) an Adagio on the chorale melody; and (3) a fugue with elements of fantasia. The *Prelude and Fugue on the name BACH* is a Romantic work. In the Prelude, the BACH motive is treated in various ways. The fugue commences with a chromatic passage, then the Bb-A-C-Bb motive appears in the pedals as ostinato bass for massive chords.

The hundreds of piano arrangements and transcriptions that Liszt made of symphonies, operatic selections, and other large works are an important contribution to the literature. By performing and publishing such works, Liszt made those compositions available to many persons who were unable to attend live performances of the original works.

Music for Piano and Orchestra

Liszt's music for piano and orchestra consists of two concerti (No. 1, Eb major, 1849; No. 2, A major, 1839); three Fantasias, one of them an expansion of the 14th *Hungarian Rhapsody* for solo piano; and *Totendanz* (Dance of death; 1849). Both concerti were revised several times before being published. The Eb-major concerto has four movements, thematically linked, and designed to be played without a break. Thematic transformation is present. Liszt knew Schubert's *Wandererfantasie* and obviously was influenced by it. The A-major concerto actually is a single-movement multisectional work, bearing more resemblance to a rhapsody than to the traditional concerto. The *Totentanz,* a *danse macabre,* was inspired by the frescoes *Il trionfo della morte* (The triumph of death) in Campo Santo Cemetery in Pisa, Italy. The composition is a set of variations on the *Dies irae* Sequence.

Orchestral and Chamber Music

Liszt did not write purely orchestral works until he was appointed court conductor to the Grand Duke of Saxe-Weimar. During the time he held that post (1848–61), he composed 2 symphonies and 12 single-movement programmatic works that he called **symphonic poems** (*sinfonische Dichtung*). His other orchestral works include *Two episodes from Lenau's Faust* (c. 1861), one episode being the *First Mephisto Waltz; Trois odes funèbres* (Three funeral odes; 1860–66); *Second Mephisto Waltz* (1880–81); the short occasional piece *Von der Wiege bis zum Grabe* (From the cradle to the grave; 1881–82); and five marches, one of them the *Rákóczy March* (1865). At first, Liszt had difficulty writing orchestrations, and he had assistance orchestrating several of his symphonic poems.

For each of his symphonic poems Liszt provided a synopsis, so the listener would know what the music was supposed to express. Liszt's symphonic poems were not meant to be pictorial or to tell a story, though they might at times depict scenes realistically. Rather, he sought to express his views relative to the extramusical material, and he always considered musical content of greater importance than referential depiction. This was the same as Beethoven's view of his Sixth Symphony. Though the symphonic poem was a product of nineteenth-century Romanticism, it had roots in such works as Beethoven's *Overture to Egmont.* Several of Liszt's poems were created as introductions or overtures to other works or are expanded versions of earlier compositions. *Mazeppa* is an expanded version of the fourth *Transcendental Étude; Orpheus* and *Tasso* were originally overtures. All of the symphonic poems exist also as arrangements for piano duet or for two pianos.

Each of the two symphonic poems, *Ce qu'on entend sur la montagne,* also called *Bergsymphonie* (What one expects on the mountain, or Mountain symphony; 1848–49) and *Die Ideale* (1857), could be considered a three-movement symphony compressed into a single movement. The best known of Liszt's symphonic poems is *Les préludes* (1848); it is the only one that has found a place in standard orchestral repertoire. The piece was originally written (1848) as introduction to *Les quatres élémens* (The four elements; unpubl.), a collaborative choral setting of four poems by Joseph Autran. When Liszt decided to use the introduction as a separate piece, he looked for a new literary program for it and selected the following commentary from the 15th of Alphonse Lamartine's (1790–1869) *Nouvelles méditations poétiques* (New poetic meditations): "What is life? Only a series of preludes to that unknown song whose first solemn note is sounded by death." Liszt mentioned also Lamartine's poem *Les préludes,* whose four large sections have a semblance of conformity with the sections of Liszt's music. The principle of thematic transformation is an important feature of *Les Préludes.* From one germinal motive Liszt derived many others (ex. 23.4).

Hamlet (1858), planned as an overture to Shakespeare's play, is the shortest of Liszt's symphonic poems and one of his finest. Here, Liszt painted a psychological portrait of Prince Hamlet. The work commences with a brief introduction, moves into a stormy Allegro, and concludes with a slow section that refers to the introduction and ends with a funeral march.

In *Eine Faust-Symphonie in drei Charakterbildern* (A Faust symphony in three character pictures; 1854–57) Liszt expressed his idea of the three main characters in Goethe's *Faust.* The symphony was conceived in three movements: *Faust, Gretchen,* and *Mephistopheles,* but three years after those movements were completed Liszt added a choral *Epilogue.*

Example 23.4 (*a*) Germinal motive and (*b*) three of the themes it generated in Liszt's *Les Préludes.*

For this symphony, Liszt included in the orchestra piccolo, third trumpet, and harp; on revision, brass and percussion were increased, and, for the *Epilogue,* organ, tenor soloist, and male chorus were needed. The slow introduction presents two of the symphony's main themes; thematic transformation is a feature of the Allegro impetuoso Faust movement that follows. The characterization of Gretchen is delicate, tender, youthful in sound. The Mephistopheles movement has no new themes; instead, in keeping with Mephistopheles's character, Faust's themes are parodied, and a short phrase is borrowed from *Malédiction,* an early work for piano and strings. The text of the choral epilogue is the *Chorus mysticus* from Goethe's *Faust,* Part II. The *Faust Symphony* is dedicated to Berlioz, who introduced Liszt to Goethe's *Faust.*

Liszt planned *Eine Symphonie zu Dantes Divina commedia* (A symphony on Dante's *Divine Comedy;* 1855–56) in three movements to correspond with the divisions of Dante's poem: *Inferno, Purgatorio,* and *Paradiso.* However, Wagner convinced him that it was impossible to portray Paradise musically, so he concluded the symphony with a Magnificat for women's voices.

Liszt composed only a few pieces of chamber music. Most of them are for violin and piano, including a four-movement sonata based on Chopin's *Mazurka in C♯ minor* (Op. 6 No. 2).

Vocal Music

Liszt wrote approximately 70 songs setting German, French, Italian, and Hungarian poems; one song has an English text. Among the Italian songs are the three Petrarch sonnets, which exist in two versions. Liszt composed several secular cantatas and began but never finished an opera.

Among Liszt's sacred choral works are numerous Psalms settings and liturgical works. There are two oratorios, *Christus* and *Die Legende von der heiligen Elisabeth*. The oratorios are too long—*Christus* contains some magnificent music but takes over four hours to perform. There are two Masses for SATB soloists, choir, and orchestra: the *Missa solemnis* performed at the basilica at Gran, Hungary, in 1856, and the *Hungarian Coronation Mass* commissioned for the coronation of Franz Joseph as King of Hungary in 1867. There exist also a *Missa choralis* (1865) for choir and organ and a *Requiem Mass* (1868) for male voices, brass, and organ; both were performed in Lwow. The Requiem Mass is filled with whole-tone themes and harmonies. An excellent composition from Liszt's late years is the *Via Crucis,* a large work for soloists, choir (or chorus), with either organ or piano accompaniment. It was not performed during Liszt's lifetime.

Contributions

Liszt made significant contributions to the development of music in history through his piano playing, his piano arrangements and transcriptions of major works by other composers, and his original compositions. He was influential also through the encouragement and assistance he gave others by programming and conducting their works. Liszt is credited with originating the symphonic poem, and his symphonic poems influenced other composers to create single-movement programmatic orchestral works. Among them were Bedřich Smetana (1824–84), whose symphonic poems include *Richard III* (1857) and the six in the cycle *Má Vlast* (My fatherland, 1874–79); César Franck (1822–90), who included a chorus in his *Psyché* (1888); and Camille Saint-Saëns (1835–1921) with *Le rouet d'Omphale* (Omphale's spinning-wheel, 1872) and *Danse Macabre* (1874).

Johannes Brahms

Johannes Brahms (1833–97) was the second of the three children in the family of J. J. Brahms, a string bass player in the Hamburg city orchestra. Both Johannes and his brother Fritz became musicians; probably, they received their first musical training from their father. At an early age, Johannes was sent to a local teacher for piano lessons, and by 1843 the boy was proficient enough to perform in a public recital. When it was suggested that he go on tour as a prodigy, his teacher intervened to prevent it. In 1846 Brahms began composition lessons with Eduard Marxsen (1806–87) and soon found a job arranging music for a small local orchestra. He gave his first solo piano concert in 1848.

During the revolutions of 1848, many Hungarian refugees came to Hamburg, and Brahms became interested in Hungarian gypsy music. He learned more about it when he accompanied violinist Eduard Reményi (1828–98) on a concert tour in 1853; Reményi taught Brahms how to play in Hungarian gypsy style and how to play *rubato* properly. Throughout his life, Brahms maintained an interest in Hungarian gypsy music and wrote many works flavored by it.

Another lifelong interest of Brahms was early music. In his childhood he began to visit libraries to copy and study music manuscripts, and as a youth he began to collect folk songs. Later, among his friends were some of the leading musicologists of his time, and he could intelligently discuss with them problems of performance practice and methods of editing early music (Insight, "Musicology").

In the 1850s Brahms formed a lifelong friendship with violinist Joseph Joachim (1831–1907). Joachim and Brahms devised counterpoint lessons for each other, exchanging assignments weekly. Joachim included in his work the pitches F-A-E, which he said represented his motto, *frei aber einsam* (free but lonely). Brahms responded by incorporating in his music the pitch sequence or chord F-A-F, *frei aber froh* (free but happy). That series of pitches appears in many of Brahms's works, and often he used chords constructed without the fifth of a triad.

Joachim introduced Brahms to Liszt and to Robert and Clara Schumann. When the Schumanns heard Brahms play some of his own compositions, they

Johannes Brahms. *(Courtesy of the Free Library of Philadelphia.)*

Until the second half of the nineteenth century, the scholarly study of music was considered a part of general music education. In 1863 Friedrich Chrysander (1826–1901) stated that such scholarship constituted a science comparable with other scientific disciplines. He called this discipline *Musikwissenschaft* (the science of music), a term that had existed since 1827 when the German music educator Johann B. Logier (1777–1846) used it in a narrower sense. This branch of music has since been termed **musicology,** meaning the scientific study of music, and defined by the American Musicological Society in 1955 as "a field of knowledge having as its object the investigation of the art of music as a physical, psychological, aesthetic, and cultural phenomenon." The historical branch of musicology received the most attention during the nineteenth century, when researchers and editors were concerned with locating and publishing works of great composers of the previous two and one-half centuries and with performing that music accurately. Late in the century, collecting folk music, editing it, and publishing it led to that branch of the science known as **ethnomusicology,** which brings sociological factors into the study.

recognized his genius, and Robert wrote the article *Neue Bahnen* (New Paths) in praise of Brahms's talents. Brahms became a staunch friend of all members of the Schumann family and was a mainstay to them during Robert's illness. Brahms's lovely *Alt-Rhapsodie* (Op. 53; 1869) was composed as a wedding song for the Schumanns' daughter, Julie.

From 1859 to 1862 Brahms lived in Hamburg. There, he founded and conducted a women's chorus and wrote a good deal of music for that group. In addition, he wrote some vocal solos with piano accompaniment. He was a superb organist, and in 1856 he composed several fine organ works: a Fugue in A♭ major (publ. 1864), two Preludes and Fugues (A minor, G minor; publ. 1927), and the chorale prelude and fugue *O Traurigkeit, O Herzeleid* (O sorrow, O heartache; publ. 1882). In 1857 he began *Ein deutsches Requiem* (A German Requiem), and in 1858 completed the Piano Concerto, Op. 15 (D minor), written for his own use. His Serenade No. 1 (D major, Op. 11; 1857–58) and Serenade No. 2 (A major; Op. 16; 1858–59) appeared in print in 1860.

Brahms moved to Vienna in 1862 and lived there for the rest of his life. He made friends there quickly, taught some piano lessons, and began concertizing. Brahms was an excellent concert pianist and was frequently away on tours in Germany, Austria, Hungary, Switzerland, Netherlands, and Denmark. On those tours he played only his own compositions. In 1863 he was named conductor of the Vienna Singakademie but

resigned after only one season; not until 1872 did he accept an appointment to another official position, when he became conductor of the Vienna Gesellschaft Konzerte, a post he held until 1875.

With the successful performance of *Ein deutsches Requiem* in 1869, Brahms was established as a composer. In 1873 his *Variations on a Theme by Haydn* (Op. 56) appeared. Other works followed, and soon he had more than 60 published works and was financially secure. Wisely, he had obtained royalty contracts for his music instead of selling the compositions outright to publishers. In 1876 Brahms and Joachim were offered honorary doctorates by Cambridge University; Brahms declined—he dreaded crossing the English Channel. The offer was repeated three times; still Brahms did not accept, but he sent along with Joachim the Symphony No. 1 (C minor, Op. 68) and it was performed on the occasion.

Brahms never married. He was pleased when Joachim married Amalie Weis (1839–98), famous mezzo-soprano, in 1863. Amalie was an excellent musician; Clara Schumann enjoyed giving song recitals with her and sharing some concert tours with her. Brahms was concerned when the Joachims experienced marital difficulties. When Joachim filed for divorce in 1881, Brahms sided with Amalie, and the Brahms-Joachim friendship chilled considerably. Fortunately, that rift between Brahms and Joachim was healed in 1887.

Brahms developed the habit of concertizing during the winter months and devoting summers to composition, though he did not adhere strictly to such a schedule. For several years he made regular trips to Italy to concertize, but he never wrote any Italianate compositions. During 1877–79 he concertized a great deal and wrote much music. His Symphony No. 2 (D major, Op. 73; 1877) and his only Violin Concerto (D major, Op. 77; 1878), the latter written for Joachim, were performed at the concerts commemorating the 50th anniversary of the Hamburg Philharmonic Society, in 1878. In 1879 Brahms accepted an honorary doctorate from the University of Breslau and submitted to them the *Academic Festival Overture*, Op. 80 (C minor). Later that year he composed the *Tragic Overture*, Op. 81 (D minor).

Brahms formed a number of friendships that were beneficial to his career. For instance, in 1881 Hans von Bülow offered him the services of the Meiningen court orchestra as a kind of rehearsal group. Other associations, such as that with 'cellist Robert Hausmann (1852–1909), brought inspiration or commissions for new works. In 1885 Hausmann played Brahms's E-minor Sonata for 'Cello and Piano (Op. 38) and his performance inspired Brahms to compose the F-major Sonata for 'Cello/Piano (Op. 99). Brahms then composed the two Violin/Piano Sonatas, Op. 100 (A Major) and Op. 108 (D minor), and the Piano Trio in C Minor (Op. 101), with the capabilities of Joachim, Hausmann, and himself in mind. The Concerto for Violin and Violoncello (A minor; 1887) was designed for the talents of Hausmann and Joachim, who gave that work its première in Cologne.

In 1891 Brahms met clarinetist Richard Mühlfeld (1856–1907) and, after hearing him perform Weber's clarinet compositions, decided to write something for clarinet. Quickly, he wrote the Trio in A minor (Op. 114) for clarinet, 'cello, and piano, and the Clarinet Quintet in B minor (Op. 115). The Quintet was first performed by Mühlfeld and the Joachim String Quartet; the Trio was performed by Brahms, Mühlfeld, and Hausmann, who was a member of Joachim's quartet. In 1894 Brahms composed two Clarinet/Piano Sonatas (F minor, and E♭ major, Op. 126) for Mühlfeld. It is interesting that for those sonatas, the "Horn" Trio, and the "Clarinet" Trio, Brahms supplied alternate parts for viola as substitute for clarinet and horn.

In 1896 Brahms composed a series of 11 chorale preludes for organ (publ. 1902); some of them are the finest written since the time of J. S. Bach. After Clara Schumann's death in 1896, Brahms composed *Vier ernste Gesänge* (Four serious songs, Op. 121) on texts that he selected from the German Bible. Though Brahms was not aware of it at the time, he was afflicted with cancer of the liver; he died on 3 April 1897.

Style

Though Brahms's music contains some elements of Romanticism, e.g., rich harmonies, lyric melodies, basically he composed in Classical style. Probably, he should be considered a Romantic Classicist. He was aware of what his contemporaries were doing, and at times stated that, where music was concerned, he had been born 30 years too late. He was a craftsman, with solid musicianship, and disliked flamboyance, brilliance, and bravura as showmanship. Everything in his music contributes to the innate musical coherence of the entire composition. Brahms had high regard for Classical forms and materials and was deeply interested in music of the past. His understanding of the value of counterpoint as a compositional technique is seen first in his desire to master it and then in his ability to use it effectively. Several of his compositions reflect his appreciation of Bach's works, e.g., his chorale preludes, the preludes and fugues, and those variations written as passacaglia/chaconne. Brahms was a master of rhythmic intricacies and rhythmic innovation. Frequently, he wrote cross rhythms, placed triplets against duplets, devised syncopations, or shifted metric accents.

Brahms wrote no program music. He did write some character pieces for piano, e.g., ballades, intermezzi. His music is filled with rich, velvety sonorities, and he especially favored the lower registers, at times omitting violins from his orchestration.

The vast majority of Brahms's music is for voice, but throughout his life he composed purely instrumental music. He was one of the finest pianists of his day and was an excellent organist. His personality is reflected in his works. Basically reserved, he was a deep thinker; though he sought the advice of friends, he relied on his own judgment when making decisions. There exist several manuscript versions of his works showing suggestions made by friends, particularly Joachim, for changes in specific passages of certain compositions; most often, Brahms ignored those suggestions. He needed sincere, warm friendships and made long-lasting ones, but he also required times of solitude—his music reflects both aspects.

Solo Keyboard Music

Brahms's keyboard works were designed primarily for his own use. Many of them are rhythmically complex, abounding in polyrhythms, syncopations, and rhythmic transformations. Counterpoint is present in abundance. Often, he used two melodic lines simultaneously, stating one simply and weaving the other into figuration; his Op. 116 *Intermezzi* provide examples. He began by writing piano sonatas, then moved to variations and character pieces. Each of his two piano concerti took him several years to compose, and a space of 20 years separates the two. Since he preferred to play only his own compositions in concert, it seems that, when concertizing, he was more comfortable playing variations, character pieces, and stylized dances—or that his audiences responded more favorably to those kinds of pieces. Brahms was a master of variation technique, a practice closely associated with improvisation. In large works he often incorporated thematic variation.

Most of Brahms's early works are for piano, and include three piano sonatas (No. 1, C major, Op. 1; No. 2, F♯ minor, Op. 2; No. 3, F minor, Op. 5); a Scherzo in E♭ minor; four Ballades (Op. 10, D minor, D major, B minor, B major); the Piano Concerto No. 1 (D minor, Op. 15; 1854–58), some gavottes, and several sets of variations, including *Variations and Fugue on a Theme by G. F. Handel* (B♭ major, Op. 24; 1861). The three piano sonatas—Brahms's only piano sonatas—are filled with rhythmic vitality and exhibit passages in thirds, parallel sixths, imitation, canon—all traits present in his mature style. The slow movement (Andante; C minor) of the C-major Sonata is theme and variations on an old *Minnelied* that commences *Verstohlen geht der Mond auf* (The moon rises stealthily); the melody is stated simply in the left hand, and it is varied four times. Brahms copied the lyrics in his manuscript. The third movement is a bright Scherzo in E minor, with Trio in C major. The Finale, a rondo with coda, recalls the principal theme of the first movement, with rhythmic transformation of the material. In the Op. 2 Sonata, Brahms again used theme and variations in the slow movement; the Finale is Romantic in character. The Op. 5 Sonata has five movements, in fast-slow-fast-slow-fast order of tempo, in the manner of a Classical *divertimento,* with second and fourth movements related. The second movement, in F minor, is elegiac, yet somewhat like a nocturne; the fourth movement, a sober Intermezzo in B♭ minor, is marked *Rückblick* (Reminiscence) and uses, in modified form, the principal theme of the second movement. The Finale is a rondo, freely treated. The *Ballades,* Op. 10, resemble rhapsodies; all are in some kind of ternary form (ABA, ABC).

The *Variations and Fugue on a Theme by G. F. Handel* is a masterpiece of variation technique. Handel's theme, used in the last section of his *Suite in B♭ major* for harpsichord, was equipped with five variations. Brahms wrote 25 and in them used all kinds of contrapuntal and harmonic devices. Variation 6 is a strict canon at the octave; canon occurs again in Variation 16; Variation 13 is a Hungarian rhapsody. The composition climaxes with a masterly fugue, which again reveals Brahms's study of Bach's works.

During Brahms's first 12 to 15 years in Vienna, he wrote very little piano music. When he resumed composing piano solos, he wrote chiefly variations and character pieces—rhapsodies, intermezzi, capricci, ballades, fantasias. The *Variations on a Theme by Paganini* (Op. 35; 1862–63) are based on the 24th of Paganini's *Caprices for Unaccompanied Violin.* Brahms wrote 28 variations, divided them into two sets, and provided each set with a finale. When all of the variations are performed, the finale at the end of the first set and the statement of the theme at the beginning of the second set should be omitted. Brahms subtitled the variations *Studien;* indeed, they are concert études. This composition, written for Brahms's personal use in concert, is extremely difficult technically.

An element of Hungarian gypsy music infiltrates many of Brahms's works. He composed some piano solos and duets that he entitled *Hungarian Dances,* and he made orchestral arrangements of three of those duets. None of the *Hungarian Dances* were given *opus* numbers. Because Brahms had collected and studied folk songs, he was able to write Hungarian dances that preserve the melodies, harmonies, and rhythms characteristic of gypsy music but that present the gypsy music with a higher degree of artistry than it has in its original folk-music status.

In 1892–93 Brahms published four collections (Opp. 116, 117, 118, and 119) containing a total of 20 character pieces, each in ternary form. The pieces are very concentrated, with less complicated harmonies than those found in the larger works. In the *intermezzi* there are no virtuoso elements; instead, there is simplicity of form, some rhythmic and harmonic elaboration, counterpoint, and thematic variation. Though the two E-major outer sections of *Intermezzo,* Op. 119, No. 2, contrast sharply with the Viennese-style middle section in E minor, all three sections are constructed on the same theme. Occasionally, Brahms placed the melody in an inner voice, e.g., in Op. 119, No. 3; Op. 118, No. 5; Op. 117, No. 1. The last of the 4 pieces in Op. 119 is a magnificent *Rhapsody* that commences in E♭ major and concludes in E♭ minor.

For organ, Brahms wrote a Fugue in A♭ minor (1856; publ. 1864), the chorale prelude and fugue *O Traurigkeit, O Herzeleid* (1856; publ. 1882), 2 Preludes and Fugues (A minor, G minor; 1856–57, publ. 1927); and 11 *Chorale Preludes* (Op. 122; 1896, publ. 1902). The early organ works were composed while Brahms was working at Düsseldorf and participating in counterpoint studies with Joachim. It is believed that Brahms wrote others, but they have not been located. In these works, Brahms's study of Baroque masters is apparent. The set of chorale preludes contains two versions of *Herzlich tut mich verlangen,* whose melody is better known as *O Sacred Head, now wounded,* the Passion chorale. The chorale prelude *O Welt ich muss dich lassen* (O world, I now must leave thee), which concludes the set, was Brahms's last composition. In general, the chorales are somber and convey an impression of preparation for impending death.

Chamber Music

After composing the early piano sonatas, Brahms reserved sonata form and complete sonata structure for his orchestral and chamber music works. Many of those chamber music pieces were composed for friends and are suited to their special talents. When writing for violin, Brahms frequently consulted Joachim. An isolated Scherzo in C minor (1853) was Brahms's contribution to a collaborative "F-A-E" violin/piano sonata dedicated to Joachim; R. Schumann and A. Dietrich composed the two outer movements. Joachim had the Scherzo published in 1906. Besides this Scherzo, Brahms composed 24 chamber music works. Those without piano include 2 string sextets (B♭ major, G major; for 2 vlns., 2 vlas., 2 vcl.), 3 string quartets, 2 string quintets (F major, G major; 2 vlns., 2 vlas., vlc.), and the clarinet quintet, Op. 115 (B minor). The latter is a masterpiece comparable with Schubert's clarinet quintet. Brahms's four-movement quintet amply displays the complete range and the artistic capabilities of the clarinet without treating it virtuosically; throughout the composition the clarinet remains on a par with the other participants in the ensemble. The quintet's finale is theme with five variations and coda; in the coda Brahms employs one of his favorite unifying techniques, recall of the composition's opening bars.

It is believed that Brahms wrote at least 24 string quartets. He was a perfectionist, however, and felt no compunction about destroying, revising, or changing instrumentation of works that did not meet his standards in their original format. Only 3 string quartets have survived: the C-minor and A-minor quartets of Op. 51 (c. 1873) and the B♭-major quartet, Op. 67 (1876). The Op. 51 quartets are in contrasting moods: the A-minor work is delicate and tender until one arrives at the energetic finale, which contains a bit of *czardas,* but the C-minor composition is more dramatic, rich, with a hint of melancholy. The A-minor quartet contains Joachim's F-A-E motto. Still another mood is conveyed by the B♭-major quartet—it is the most light-hearted of all Brahms's chamber music works. The finale, a set of variations, incorporates within its texture phrases from the first movement.

Brahms was dissatisfied with an early string quintet in F minor, written for two violins, viola, and two 'celli, and rewrote it as a sonata for two pianos, which he performed with Karl Tausig; still not pleased, Brahms remolded the composition as the Piano Quintet, Op. 34. In his other string quintets he used two violas. The String Quintet in F major, Op. 88, has only three movements. The second movement is an ABABA form in which a *sarabande* (Adagio) alternates with a *siciliano* (scherzo). Another unusual feature of this work (for Brahms) is the fugal exposition of the finale; this suggests the influence of Beethoven's Op. 59 No. 3 finale.

In 1853–54 Brahms wrote a Piano Trio in B major, Op. 8; more than 25 years later, he composed two more Piano Trios, Op. 87 in C major (1880–82) and Op. 101 in C minor (1886); then in 1889 he revised the Op. 8 trio. The Clarinet Trio in A minor, Op. 114, is not outstanding. Brahms composed the Horn Trio, Op. 40 (E♭ major; 1865) for natural (valveless) horn and demanded that it be used in the December 1865 performance of the work. Much of the charm of this Trio is due to its peculiar blend of timbres; the mellow tone quality of the horn colors the entire composition with a feeling for Nature. Although Brahms supplied alternate parts so that viola or 'cello might be used in lieu of horn, either substitution spoils the effect.

Seven of Brahms's chamber music works are duos for piano and another instrument: three violin/piano sonatas (Op. 78, G major, 1878–79; Op. 100, A major, 1886; Op. 108, D minor, 1886–88); two 'cello/piano sonatas (Op. 38, E minor, 1862–65; Op. 99, F major, 1886); and two clarinet/piano sonatas (Op. 120, F minor, E♭ major; 1894). Of the violin/piano sonatas, the D-minor is finest. All of the sonatas were written for specific persons and reasons, and each sonata is individualistic in some respect. In formal structure, the sonatas differ considerably from Brahms's other chamber music works. Only three of the sonatas are cast in four movements: Opp. 99, 108, and 120, No. 1. Each of the others has three, not always in the expected fast-slow-fast sequence; that occurs only in Opp. 78 and 100. The clarinet/piano sonatas are masterpieces.

Orchestral Works

The list of Brahms's orchestral works is not lengthy. There are two serenades, two concert overtures, four symphonies, a set of variations, two piano concerti, one violin concerto, and one double concerto (violin, 'cello). In addition, there are three *Hungarian Dances* (arr. from piano duets): No. 1 in G minor, No. 3 in F major, and No. 10 in F major. Most of these works were composed within the space of 14 years.

After much deliberation, Brahms decided in 1854 to compose a symphony and sketched out the work for two pianos, then attempted to orchestrate it. He found this very difficult, so altered his plans, and the projected symphony became Piano Concerto No. 1 (D minor, Op. 15; 1854–58). The piano part is not easy, but it is not a virtuosic solo with orchestral accompaniment. Rather, orchestra and soloist are treated as equal partners. Because soloist and orchestra have different thematic material, albeit remotely related, the first movement bears some resemblance to the *ritornello* concerto movements written by Vivaldi. The slow movement is solemn; the finale is a lively rondo.

In Piano Concerto No. 2 (Op. 83, B♭ major; 1878–81), soloist and orchestra are again treated as equal partners; however, in several places (especially in the development) the soloist must be aggressive to avoid being relegated to the position of accompanist to the orchestra. The concerto is unusual in having four movements instead of the usual three; Brahms inserted a Scherzo as second movement. Instead of writing that Scherzo in traditional compound ternary form, with *da capo* of the Scherzo after the Trio, Brahms wrote a free recapitulation of the Scherzo. The concerto does not open with an orchestral exposition but with an introduction (or prelude) in which soloist and orchestra engage in dialogue. The slow movement and the finale also have structural innovations.

The Violin Concerto (D major, Op. 77; 1878) is one of the great concerti in standard concert repertoire. Here, as always, Brahms was concerned with writing expressive, substantial music, not brilliance and bravura display. He demands of the violinist exceptional technique, but not virtuosity. Frequently, the violinist is required to play difficult double-stops and chords, to span large intervals, to move from high notes to low and from single pitches to double-stops in different positions with absolute accuracy. The orchestration is symphonic. The concerto follows the traditional three-movement scheme, commencing with an Allegro non troppo in sonata-concerto form. The orchestral exposition presents the basic material of the movement concisely and symphonically; the lyrical first theme, broad and sweeping, is stated immediately. The soloist's lengthy (46 mm.) opening passage, prefatory to statement of the first theme, is filled with rhythmic intricacies and a variety of bowing articulations that disclose at the outset the degree of difficulty of this masterwork. Brahms supplied the minor cadenzas for the concerto but left the major one for Joachim to improvise, and the one Joachim created (and notated) is Brahmsian in style. Soloist and orchestra conclude the movement together. The Adagio second movement (F major) is brief; the violin part consists almost entirely of beautiful arabesques. The movement ends on a sustained F-major chord. With an abrupt change of mood, soloist and orchestra plunge into the D-major rondo Finale, an Allegro *giocoso*

with melodies suggestive of Hungarian origin. After the movement is brought to triumphant climax in the recapitulation, orchestra and soloist indulge in a few measures of quiet meditation on the movement's opening motive, then conclude the work in partnership, with three *forte* D-major chords.

The double concerto (Op. 102, A minor; 1887), for violin and 'cello, is less gratifying for the soloists. When the work was being composed, Joachim and Hausmann urged Brahms to make their parts more difficult; in some passages, he complied. The concerto contains at least one reminiscence of Viotti's Violin Concerto in A minor, and here and there a hint of *concerto grosso,* though the music is nineteenth-century in style. This concerto was Brahms's last orchestral composition.

Serenade No. 1 (D minor, Op. 11; 1851–58) was originally intended for eight solo instruments; later, Brahms arranged the six-movement work for full orchestra. Serenade No. 2 (A major, Op. 16; 1857–60) is a *divertimento,* with five short movements. Its orchestration contains no violins, trumpets, or drums and includes only two horns. Much of the music is in the instruments' low registers.

Variations on a Theme of Haydn (B♭ major, Op. 56a; 1873) was inspired when K. F. Pohl, Haydn's biographer, showed Brahms the manuscript of an unpublished *divertimento* that it was believed Haydn had composed for Prince Esterházy's troops. (Haydn's authorship of the work has been questioned but not disproven.) Brahms was so taken by the second movement of the *divertimento* that he copied it into his notebook. Later, he used that movement, Haydn's harmonization of the *Chorale St. Antonii,* as theme for the Variations. Brahms made only one change in instrumentation—because the serpent had become obsolete, he had to substitute contrabassoon (see Insight, "Serpent"). In Brahms's orchestral work, eight winds state the theme, a rounded binary in B♭, with both halves repeated. In the eight variations that ensue, the chorale theme is present but is not always apparent—Brahms's variations are not transparent. The Finale is based on a five-measure ostinato that Brahms constructed from skeletal pitches of the first five bars of the theme. Though presented continuously in the bass, the ostinato sometimes appears imitatively in other voices. In conclusion, the chorale

insight

Serpent

The serpent, named for its serpentine shape, is a large bass-register woodwind instrument equipped with a cup-shaped mouthpiece made of ivory, bone, or horn. Constructed from approximately seven feet of conical, wide-bore wooden tubing, the instrument was serpentine-shaped from necessity—to keep its six fingerholes in a position easily accessible for playing. There are six open side holes, arranged in two groups of three, with the groups spaced about 12 inches apart. The mouthpiece is connected with the small end of the wooden tubing by a 12-inch metal crook that is curved almost at right angles. Like other instruments with cup-shaped mouthpieces, the serpent is capable of sounding partials of the harmonic series. A player could modify the pitches considerably. By lip adjustment, a player could lower a pitch by a fourth. Because of the considerable latitude in pitch available by lip adjustment, compass of the instrument varied between two and one-half and three octaves. It is surmised that the fundamental pitch of the earliest serpents was E, but most French instruments were built with D as fundamental, and in England the fundamental was C. The instrument is held vertically when played.

Invention of the serpent is attributed to Canon Edmé Guillaume of Auxerre, France, in 1590. At first, it was used solely for ecclesiastical purposes, primarily to double (at the unison) and support male voices singing liturgical chant. But by the middle of the eighteenth century, the serpent was being used in military bands. At some time in the seventeenth century, instrument makers gradually equipped the serpent with keys, and by 1800 three-keyed serpents were more or less standard. There were serpents in the wind band at the Esterházy estate when Haydn worked there, and he included the serpent in some of his *divertimenti*, e.g., the one containing his harmonization of the *Chorale St. Antonii*.

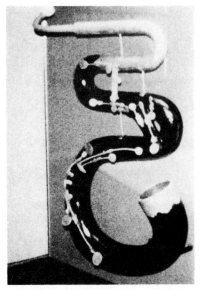

Figure 23.4 A serpent.

Originally, a serpent was made in two halves—carved from two large blocks of wood, usually walnut, shaped and hollowed out—and then fitted and glued together to make a tube that was covered with leather. Later, serpents were constructed by fitting together small segments whose halves were glued together; these, too, were covered with leather, and both ends of the wooden conical tube were strengthened with brass mountings. The serpent fell into disuse during the nineteenth century, and most of the serpents still in existence in the late twentieth century are in historical instrument collections.

---

theme is stated in augmentation, against rapid scales. In 1873 Brahms made a two-piano version of this composition; it is Op. 56b.

The *Academic Festival Overture* (C minor, Op. 80; 1880), submitted to the University of Breslau, contains a potpourri of student songs, including the familiar *Gaudeamus igitur*. Brahms wrote the *Tragic Overture* (D minor; Op. 81; 1880) as a companion piece to his first overture. (The reason for the title *Tragic* is not known.)

Unquestionably, Brahms was the greatest nineteenth-century symphonist after Beethoven. Brahms's four symphonies are absolute music, Classical in form, Romantic in expression and lyricism, masterworks that deservedly have found a place in standard symphonic repertoire. The symphonies abound in characteristics of Brahms's mature musical style: rhythmic intricacies, shifting metric accents, triplets against duplets, a melody in duple meter accompanied by

Example 23.5 The four basic motives of Brahms's Symphony No. 1, mvt. 1, all presented in the movement's introduction.

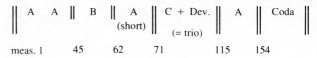

A	A	B	A (short)	C + Dev. (= trio)	A	Coda

meas. 1   45   62   71   115   154

Figure 23.5 Diagram of formal structure of Brahms's Symphony No. 1, mvt. 3.

triplet figurations, melodies combined in contrary motion, harmonies that omit the fifth of the chord but with octave-doubling of the root, avoidance of obvious cadences by devices such as elision or over-lapping phrases, "learned" counterpoint used non-pedantically. Like Beethoven, Brahms was adept at motivic development, often modulated to mediant or submediant keys, and frequently related movements and sections of a work by thirds, e.g., the keys of the movements of his Symphony No. 1 are, in order, C minor, E major, A♭ major (or, enharmonically, G♯), and C minor/major. Each of Brahms's symphonies contains four movements: the first in sonata form, the second in slow tempo, the third a modified scherzo or having some characteristics thereof, and the finale (in all but the Fourth Symphony) sonata form or a modification of it. The finale of the Fourth Symphony is a chaconne.

One of Brahms's contributions to the development of the symphony in the nineteenth century is his modification of the formal structure of the third movement. Another and more important contribution is his rejection of referential or programmatic concepts and his confirmation and reestablishment of the validity of abstract musical materials as basic building blocks of the symphony. Stylistically, Brahms's use of motives as basic concepts from which to build a symphony is comparable with Wagner's use of *Leitmotifs* as building blocks in the creation of the symphonic web of his music dramas. Both composers transformed their motives. Both men were using similar contemporary procedures but the manner in which they used them differed: Brahms believed and proved that the music itself was sufficient for the task; Wagner imbued the motives with associative features, used a greater number of motives, and created a more complex symphonic web.

Brahms composed his Symphony No. 1 (C minor, Op. 68; 1855–76) only after he had spent much time studying Beethoven's symphonies. The first movement of Brahms's C-minor symphony is intense and serious; it commences with a massive, slow introduction that presents the four basic motives from which the movement's themes are created (ex. 23.5). The development section is comparatively short. The coda commences with some development of the closing theme and concludes with a presentation of the movement's introductory material in miniature. The subsections of the movement's Classical formal structure are not obviously delineated; Brahms's treatment of cadences concluding the major subsections of the movement tend to obscure those divisions. The movement is unified through motivic integration of the subsections. The lyrical Andante sostenuto second movement (E major) is a ternary (ABA) with coda. In the second A section, Brahms returned one of the themes as a violin solo with full orchestral accompaniment, a technique reminiscent of Haydn, but Brahms's treatment of the material is decidedly Romantic. In the third movement, woodwinds predominate. That movement, an Allegretto (A♭ major) with Trio (B major), is treated as a kind of alternating form (fig. 23.5), although material is returned incomplete or is altered. The abridged sonata-form finale commences with an Adagio introduction that presents the main themes. The first theme is broad and lyrical, and resembles a chorale (ex. 23.6). In the exposition,

Example 23.6 Brahms: Symphony No. 1, mvt. 4, theme 1.

a horn solo leads into the second theme, whose first ten measures are supported by repetitions of a one-measure ground bass. The closing section contains two themes combined contrapuntally on two different tonal levels a third apart (C major and E minor). There is no development *per se*; the recapitulation returns the thematic material considerably varied. The coda uses material from the introduction, and the approach to the final cadence, which is plagal, incorporates a motive derived from the first theme.

Brahms's Symphony No. 2 (D major, Op. 73; 1877) is lighter, and more idyllic in character, and uses fewer themes than his First. Movements 1, 2, and 4 are in sonata form; all four movements use simple, lyrical melodies and also motivic relationships. A three-note semitone motive (D-C♯-D, and transpositions thereof) figures prominently in the themes of the first movement. Woodwinds are prominent. The Adagio is serenely beautiful, its first theme presented in simple homophony (an accompanied melody), but the movement is not devoid of rhythmic complexities. In the third movement, a short Allegretto in triple meter alternates with two Trios in *presto* tempo, one in $\frac{2}{4}$ meter, the other in $\frac{3}{8}$; thus, it forms a five-part rondo pattern (ABACA) with temporal, metric, and thematic contrasts. In commencing this movement, Brahms again combined material in two contrasting tonalities—an E-minor melody with Aeolian modal tendencies is fitted with G-major harmonies. The Finale is thematically complex, making considerable use of a motive related to the symphony's opening theme (D-C♯-D-F♯) for purposes of unification.

In Symphony No. 3 (F major, Op. 90; 1883) Brahms's personal motto F-A-F serves as germinal motif for thematic material in all four movements. A full F-major chord commences the majestic pronouncement of Brahms's motto, which is altered by a flatted A (F-A♭-F; ex. 23.7). The motto moves into the bass, then gradually pervades the first movement

(DWMA198). The second theme, in the mediant key of A major, consists of several variations of a single $\frac{9}{4}$ measure. The coda is based on the first theme and transitional material. The Andante second movement (ABA form) features winds; when returned, the A material is treated freely and supplied with new figuration. The third movement is a lyrical song with Trio; the rich romanticism of the first theme, introduced by 'celli, is balanced by the expressive melody violins present in the Trio. The Finale is dramatic, characterized by violent changes of mood. In the development, themes undergo augmentation and transformation of all kinds; the rhythm of the transition theme sounded by brasses is strongly reminiscent of the motive of Beethoven's Fifth Symphony. In the coda, the emotion that has colored the symphony subsides; with restatement of the motto and the material that began the symphony, the music draws to a serene close.

Symphony No. 4 (E minor, Op. 98; 1884–85) is the most economical of Brahms's symphonies. Here he used fewer and more condensed themes and motives. The Andante moderato second movement, in abridged sonata form, opens with unison presentation of a Phrygian melody (on E) that changes to E major in the fifth measure, where harmonization of the tune commences. The coda presents a version of the first theme harmonized by a diminished chord on G♯; after a restatement of the first theme as a Phrygian melody, the movement ends on an E-major chord. The third movement is a developmental form (ABA-dev.-ABA) in the mood and spirit of a scherzo with development instead of trio. Throughout the movement there is considerable thematic transformation. The Finale is a chaconne—a theme with 30 variations. The basic chaconne material is not preserved in its pristine state but is subjected to many transformations.

Example 23.7 The opening measures of Brahms's Symphony No. 3, mvt. 1, contain his musical motto, here written as both F-A-F and F-A♭-F.

Music for Solo Voice(s)

Brahms wrote approximately 300 songs for solo voice and piano, 20 duets, and numerous quartets. Throughout his life Brahms composed Lieder. He had great interest in German folk songs, collected them, and made arrangements of them for solo voice and piano. For the most part, his arrangements consisted of composing suitable accompaniments for the folk melodies, which, as much as possible, he retained in their original state. His arrangements were published in three large collections: (1) *Volks-Kinderlieder* (Children's Folk songs; 1858), 14 songs dedicated to the Schumann children; (2) 28 *Deutsche Volkslieder* (German Folk songs; arr. 1858, publ. 1926); and (3) 49 *Deutsche Volkslieder* (German Folk songs; 1894), printed in seven books each containing 7 songs. Brahms also published 18 *Liebeslieder* waltzes (Love songs; Op. 52) and 15 *Neue Liebeslieder* waltzes (New love songs; Op. 65) for vocal quartet, all supplied with optional four-hand piano accompaniment. For 9 of the Op. 52 *Liebeslieder* he furnished optional orchestral accompaniment. Also, he wrote a set of 11 *Ziegeunerlieder* (Gypsy songs, Op. 103; 1887) for vocal quartet and included 4 others in the Six Quartets, Op. 112 (publ. 1891).

Brahms knew the Lieder of Schubert and Schumann, and they were his models, especially those of Schubert. After Brahms had chosen a text that he wanted to set, he first wrote the melody and its bass line; these two factors determined the form and tonal plan of the Lied. In his sketches, he jotted down the harmonies by figuring the bass pitches. His formal options were the same as those open to Schubert: ballad, with elements of narrative recitative and arioso; strophic; modified strophic; and through-composed. He used all of them. Usually, for folk-song texts and melodies with folk-song flavor, he chose strophic settings; for other Lieder he seemed to favor modified strophic over through-composed structure. The names Goethe, Heine, Eichendorff, Uhland, and Rückert appear infrequently as authors of texts Brahms set; he preferred poems by lesser-known writers and his contemporaries. A number of Brahms's songs are settings of folk-song texts or of editions of such texts in published collections; he obtained several texts from *Das knaben Wunderhorn.*

Brahms's earliest surviving Lied, *Heimkehr* (Returning home, Op. 7 No. 6; 1851), contains elements of accompanied recitative and arioso and thus resembles some of the early ballad settings. Other works representative of his early Lieder, songs composed 1851–53, are in the Opp. 3, 6, and 7 compilations. Remarkable for its tone color is *An' eine Äolsharfe* (An Aeolian harp, Op. 19 No. 5; 1858) in A♭ minor/major.

One of Brahms's humorous Lieder is *Vergebliches Ständchen* (Unsuccessful serenade, Op. 84 No. 4; 1881), a slightly modified strophic setting of a traditional folk poem. Brahms labeled alternate stanzas *Er* (He) and *Sie* (She) and included the Lied in a group of songs to be sung by one or two voices, but whether he intended it to be sung by two persons is debatable; it is challenging to a soloist to be asked to characterize two roles when the vocal line has few differences. A song with similar subject matter, meant to be shared by two singers, is *Vor die Tür* (Before the door, Op. 28 No. 2). Brahms's interest in folk song is apparent in many of his Lieder, e.g., in *Wiegenlied* (Cradle Song, or Lullaby, Op. 49 No. 4; 1868), popularly known as "Brahms's Lullaby," an actual folk poem that he set characterisically with pedal tones

and open fifths. Woven into the accompaniment of *Wiegenlied* is the melody of an Upper-Austrian waltz song, whose text commences (in dialect) "*Du moanst wohl, du glabst wohl. . . .*" Brahms enjoyed combining melodies and could do it unobtrusively in his vocal music by tucking tunes into accompaniments, especially if the accompaniments involved figurations. Many times his use of that kind of polyphony—polyphony hidden in homophony—goes unnoticed. Another example of Brahms's use of folk-song texts is *Sonntag* (Sunday, Op. 47 No. 3; 1860), whose lines he obtained from the collection of *Alte hoch- und niederdeutsche Volkslieder* (Old high- and low-German [dialect] folk songs) edited by Uhland. Through his use of folk song, and his composition of melodies in the likeness and spirit of folk song, Brahms made an important contribution to nineteenth-century music.

Die Mainacht (May Night, Op. 43 No. 2) is one of Brahms's most beautiful and most serene songs. Another in the same Classic vein is *Sapphische Ode* (Sapphic Ode, Op. 94 No. 4). Equally lovely, but unusual, are the two songs of Op. 91, for alto, accompanied by viola and piano. In the accompaniment for the first song, *Gestillte Sehnsucht* (When I yearn no more; Rückert poem), the sighing wind is depicted by the violist's arpeggiated chords. In the second of the two songs, *Geistliches Wiegenlied* (Sacred cradle song, or, The Virgin's lullaby; text by Geibel from Lope de Vega), Brahms placed in the viola part the old German lullaby *Joseph lieber, Joseph mein* (Blessed Joseph, my Joseph). *Geistliches Wiegenlied* is remarkable for its use of cantus firmus technique, its emotional profundity, and its unusual timbres.

Brahms's love of nature is shown in *Feldeinsamkeit* (In a lonely meadow, Op. 86 No. 2). The majority of Brahms's songs are serious, and his late works are filled with contemplations on death. Outstanding examples are *Der Tod, das ist die kühle Nacht* (Death is like cool night, Op. 96 No. 1); *Auf dem Kirchhofe* (In the churchyard, Op. 105 No. 4), in which Brahms incorporated the Lutheran chorale *O Haupt voll Blut und Wunden*; and *Immer leiser wird mein Schlummer* (literally, Ever lighter becomes my slumber; sometimes given the English title, Fretful is my slumber; Op. 105 No. 2), which is deeply emotional.

Brahms wrote two excellent song cycles: *Romanzen aus L. Tiecks Magdelone* (Romances from L. Tieck's *Magdelone,* Op. 33) and *Vier ernste Gesänge* (Four serious songs, Op. 121). There are 15 *Romanzen,* arranged in five groups of three songs each. They are directly associated with Tieck's *Magdelone,* and for the music to be fully appreciated, program notes (or a narrator) should outline the story. Brahms's *Magdelone* songs have some musical relationship to one another, and at the end of the fifteenth song Brahms makes reference to the first one. Brahms made of each *Romance* a scene, with piano prologue, interlude(s), and epilogue.

Brahms's masterpiece of solo song is *Vier ernste Gesänge,* on texts he prepared from verses selected from both Old and New Testaments of the German Bible, including the apochryphal Ecclesiasticus. The dark mood of the first two songs is pessimistic; the third song tells of the blessedness of death for the world-weary person; the concluding song (DWMA199), through the love text from I Corinthians 13, extols the great power of love and asserts that love conquers even death. The vocal line is declamatory and varies between recitative and arioso in character; the piano part often sounds orchestral. The *Vier ernste Gesänge* were intensely personal to Brahms; he did not want them performed while he lived.

Choral Works

Brahms composed many choral works, sacred and secular, accompanied and unaccompanied, for various kinds of ensembles, but he wrote no operas or stage works. He composed one large secular cantata, *Rinaldo* (Op. 50; 1863–68) on a text by Goethe, set for tenor solo, four-part male chorus, and orchestra.

His important accompanied choral works are: (1) *Ein deutsches Requiem* (Op. 45; 1857–68); (2) *Alt-Rhapsodie* (Op. 53; 1869); (3) *Schicksalslied* (Song of Destiny, Op. 54; 1868–71), for four-part mixed chorus and orchestra; (4) *Triumphlied* (Song of triumph, Op. 55; 1871), based on Revelation 19, for baritone solo, eight-part chorus, orchestra; (5) *Nänie* (Op. 82; 1881), a lamentation, poems by Schiller, four-part chorus, orchestra; and (6) *Gesang der Parzen* (Song of the Fates, Op. 89; 1882), six-part chorus, orchestra.

The *Alt-Rhapsodie,* for contralto, male chorus, and orchestra, is one of the most beautiful choral works ever written. Three stanzas from Goethe's *Harzreise im Winter* (Winter journey to the Harz mountains) form the text. The first stanza is a recitative-like solo with orchestral accompaniment; the second is an aria in three sections. The male chorus does not enter until after the soloist has begun the third stanza, which contains a moving invocation to the "Loving Father." The *Alt-Rhapsodie* is not performed often, for the solo part is difficult to sing, and, to maintain the dark rich sonorities of the work, the soloist must have a wide range that does not become thin in the upper register. Mezzo soprano Amalie Joachim, whose voice was acclaimed for its rich tone quality, sang the solo when the work was first performed.

Brahms's greatest achievement in choral music is *Ein deutsches Requiem,* for soprano and baritone soloists, four-part mixed chorus, and orchestra (with organ optional). This was the work that brought Brahms to the attention of the musical world and firmly established him as a composer, especially as a composer of superb choral music. Brahms prepared the text for his Requiem from passages chosen from the German Bible, both Old and New Testaments. His work differs from the Latin Requiem Mass basically in that the Requiem Mass is a prayer for eternal peace for the souls of the dead, but *A German Requiem* seeks to console the living and to help them reconcile death and life. The Requiem Mass, when the *Dies irae* is included (and it was standard until after 1965), conveys the idea of Judgment after death; *A German Requiem* conveys hope, confidence, and promise. A Latin Requiem Mass is a religious Service intended to be sung in church; *A German Requiem* was intended for concert performance. German Requiems had been composed before the nineteenth century—Schütz's *Musikalisches Exequien* is one—but they were Requiem Masses, closely related in text and mood to the Latin Requiem Mass. Brahms's *A German Requiem* bears some resemblance to J. S. Bach's funeral Cantata No. 106, *Gottes Zeit ist der allerbeste Zeit* (God's time is the very best time); Bach sought to reconcile mankind with the thought of death and the promise of a better world beyond the grave. There are similarities of scoring, instrumentation, and format between Bach's work and Brahms's. *Ein deutsches*

Requiem is in seven interrelated sections. The words of first and seventh sections correspond, and the music near the end of the last movement is the same as that concluding the first movement. Movements 1, 2, 4, and 7 are choral; movements 3 and 6 contain the baritone solos; movement 5, added last, has the soprano solo. The third and fifth movements are compatible and stand in relationship to one another as lamentation (third) and deliverance (fifth). In the first movement, Brahms omitted violins, clarinets, and trumpets from the orchestra and subdivided violas and 'celli. When violins are used in the second movement, they are muted, and much of the time Brahms keeps them in middle to low register. (Bach did not use violins for Cantata No. 106.) *Ein deutsches Requiem* is filled with counterpoint; there is a fugue at the end of the third movement, and a great double fugue concludes the sixth movement.

Brahms was probably the most versatile and most accomplished composer in the nineteenth century after the death of Beethoven. He produced masterpieces in the areas of solo song, accompanied choral music, symphonies, and chamber music. He was the successor to Schubert and Schumann in the composition of Lieder and song cycle and to Beethoven in the areas of chamber music and symphony. In the composition of absolute music, he followed in the tradition of the great symphonists and string quartet composers Haydn, Mozart, and Beethoven.

Anton Bruckner

Schoolteaching, the monastery of St. Florian, and music were the main interests of Austrian composer Anton Bruckner (1824–96). He became interested in music when his mother, who sang in the church choir, took him to Mass with her. He received his first music lessons at the age of 4, when his schoolmaster-organist father began teaching him to play violin. Then he learned to play spinet and organ, and by the time he was 10 could substitute for his father as church organist. At the age of 11, Bruckner received his first theory lessons from an organist-schoolmaster cousin in a neighboring village—mainly, learning to realize figured bass at the organ. At that time, Bruckner first heard a Mozart Mass and Haydn's oratorios. After Bruckner's father died (1837), Mrs. Bruckner arranged with Michael Arneth, prior of St.

Anton Bruckner. *(Kulturamt der Stadt Steyr.)*

Florian, for Anton to enter that monastery as a chorister. There, in addition to general education, he studied music and had organ and violin lessons. In 1839 his voice broke, but he served as violinist at St. Florian for another year, then decided to become a schoolmaster-organist and took the one-year teacher-training course at Linz. Music lessons were part of that curriculum, but, in addition, he studied organ with cathedral organist August Dürrnberger (1800–1880), author of a standard text on harmony and figured bass. At Linz, Bruckner heard Masses by Mozart and Haydn, Beethoven's Fourth Symphony, and Weber's concert overtures.

From 1841 to 1845 Bruckner worked as schoolmaster in small Austrian villages, continued studying organ and theory, and composed some music. Extant from those years are a few organ preludes, some small sacred choral pieces, and two Masses.

Bruckner was appointed to the faculty at St. Florian in 1845 and worked there ten years, first as teacher, then as organist. All the while, he took theory and organ lessons, concentrating on Bach's works. In

1848 he inherited his friend Franz Sailer's Bösen-dorfer piano, and, for the rest of his life, he used it for composing. Bruckner's first notable works were written as memorials to friends: a Requiem Mass in D minor (1848) for Sailer and *Vor Arneths Grab* (At Arneth's grave; male chorus, 3 trombones; 1854) and *Libera me* (Deliver me; mixed choir, 3 trombones, organ; 1854) for Michael Arneth. For the installation of Arneth's successor at St. Florian in 1854, Bruckner composed a large *Missa solemnis* in B♭ minor for so-loists, choir, orchestra, and organ. Bruckner's skill as composer was now apparent, though he considered himself a schoolmaster and obtained, by examina-tion, two further teacher's training diplomas, one in high-school teaching, the other in organ playing and improvisation.

In 1855, at the insistence of concerned friends, he auditioned for and obtained the position of or-ganist at Linz Cathedral. He served there for a dozen years. In addition to cathedral duties, he played at the parish church, taught piano lessons, sang in the *Lied-ertafel* choral society *Frohsinn,* and eventually became conductor of that group. Immediately after moving to Linz, he arranged for private lessons in composition from Simon Sechter (1788–1867) of Vienna Conservatory. Sechter demanded that Bruckner compose no music other than that for his lessons. In 1861, when Sechter declared Bruckner's training completed, he applied to Vienna Conserva-tory for a diploma qualifying him to teach in music academies and passed the examinations with distinc-tion.

Bruckner was not yet satisfied with himself as composer—he never was—and studied with Otto Kitzler (1834–1915), who sometimes conducted the productions at Linz Municipal Theater. Kitzler in-troduced Bruckner to the styles of Beethoven, Men-delssohn, and other nineteenth-century composers, taught him orchestration and the principles of sonata form, and encouraged him to write orchestral music. Beethoven's music influenced Bruckner's symphonic writing considerably. Study with Kitzler was a turning point in Bruckner's life. Until he worked with Kitzler, Bruckner was a conservative craftsman, well versed in Classical, Baroque, and late Renaissance tech-niques. He could improvise a Baroque organ fugue and write a polyphonic motet or a Classical Mass, but Kitzler put him in touch with the musical styles of his own century.

Not until he encountered Wagner's music did Bruckner's compositional style change appreciably. After studying the score of *Tannhäuser* and hearing some of Wagner's music, Bruckner was convinced that Wagner was a master whose style was to be emulated. However, Bruckner was not, nor did he consider him-self to be, a revolutionary. He wrote a Symphony in F minor (unnumbered; 1863) and an overture that showed changes taking place in his style—more un-conventional harmonies, greater vitality in the music. In 1863–64 he composed a Symphony in D minor that he later rejected and labeled *Die Nullte* (0). Bruck-ner's individual, mature style is first seen in the Mass in D minor, which he called Mass No. 1 (1864; SATB soloists, SATB choir, orch., organ). (Actually, he had previously composed eight Masses, two of them Re-quiems.) From this point in his career, Bruckner sub-jected his works to constant revision. He seemed never to be satisfied with his work; he revised while working on a composition, after it was completed, and after it had been performed. Sometimes he revised the revi-sions. Not only was he extremely critical of his work, his self-esteem was low, an attitude fostered by the rejection of his symphonies by the Vienna Philhar-monic and his friends' comments that the symphonies were too long.

Bruckner attended all performances of Wagner's operas given in Linz, went to Munich for the first per-formance of *Tristan und Isolde,* met Wagner, and became his friend. With Wagner's permission, in 1868 Bruckner conducted a performance of the closing portion of *Die Meistersinger* given by the *Liedertafel Frohsinn* several weeks before the première of that opera. More and more, as the years passed, Bruckner allied himself with Wagner, met with him frequently, and attended the premières of *Der Ring . . .* and *Par-sifal.* Eventually critics such as Hanslick placed Bruckner in the "Wagner camp" and criticized his symphonies severely.

Around 1864 Bruckner began to study with Ignaz Dorn, who introduced him to the music of Liszt and Berlioz. Their styles had very little influence on the compositions Bruckner wrote at that time: Symphony No. 1 (C minor; 1865–66); Mass No. 2 (E minor; 1866); Mass No. 3 (F minor; 1867–68).

For more than a decade, Bruckner had spent long hours at his work and had been his own stern taskmaster in music study and composition. Eventually, he pushed himself to the limit of his endurance, and in 1867 experienced a nervous breakdown that caused him to spend several months in a sanatorium. When he had regained his health, he was offered a professorship at Vienna Conservatory, as successor to Sechter, but not until 1868 could his friends persuade him to accept that appointment. Some years later, he was named imperial court organist. He lived in Vienna for the remainder of his life.

Bruckner was a quiet person, deeply religious, intelligent, sincere, trusting, sometimes naive. He never married, though at times he considered marriage. Political affairs seemed not to bother him in the least, nor did a change of environment alter his life-style. He remained essentially rural in manners and customs; even when living in the heart of Vienna, he continued to use Upper-Austrian dialect and usually wore comfortable casual clothing. He was often filled with self-doubt and insecurity, though he was an excellent musician and a craftsman composer.

Bruckner's reputation as a superb organist spread rapidly; he was acclaimed internationally and traveled to major European cities to participate in international organ competitions and to perform recitals. On his recital programs he played his own compositions and improvised a great deal. It is most unfortunate that he never took time to write down those organ works; according to published reviews, they were magnificent. He notated only a few insignificant preludes and a single fugue for organ.

In 1870 Bruckner was appointed teacher of theory, organ, and piano at the teacher-training college of St. Anna, in Vienna. He continued to compose liturgical music. Especially notable are the Graduals *Os justi* (1879) and *Locus iste* ([How awesome is] this place; 1869), the Tract *Virga Jesse floruit* (The rod of Jesse blossomed; 1885), and the Antiphon *Tota pulchra es* (How beautiful thou art; 1878). Liturgical works on a larger scale include the *Te Deum laudamus* (C major; 1881–84) and *Psalm cl* (1892).

Bruckner spent most of his creative time and endeavor composing symphonies. He wrote Nos. 2 through 5 in 1871–76, Nos. 6 through 8 in 1879–87, and he worked on No. 9 from 1889 until the day of his death in 1896 and had not yet written the last movement. Bruckner's revisions of his earlier works hampered progress on the Ninth Symphony. As a whole, the symphonies were not successful during Bruckner's lifetime. The Vienna Philharmonic rejected them as "too daring" or "unperformable," and most conductors were unwilling to program them with their orchestras. When Bruckner did succeed in getting a symphony performed, the audience's and critics' reactions were equally unfavorable. This, together with urging by friends and pupils, caused Bruckner to make some drastic, and not always wise, reorchestrations, changes of instrumentation, long cuts, and other revisions. Hanslick did not help matters by accusing Bruckner of violating the symphonic tradition established by Beethoven. However, Bruckner's Symphony No. 7 was received favorably by audience and reviewers when performed by Leipzig's Gewandhaus Orchestra in 1884, and gradually other orchestras performed his symphonies, albeit in newly revised rather than original versions.

Bruckner died on 11 October 1896. Services for him were held in Karlskirche, Vienna, and in compliance with his request, his body was interred in the crypt beneath the great organ at St. Florian Monastery.

His Music

The music Bruckner composed before he was 39 is, for the most part, conservative and Classical in style, modeled after Mozart and Haydn. He could write liturgical music in Palestrina-style Renaissance polyphony and improvise or notate counterpoint in the Baroque style of J. S. Bach. In fact, throughout his life, when composing, Bruckner jotted down figured bass lines. Bruckner's style changed considerably after he heard Wagner's music, and his mature, individual style gradually became manifest. After he began to compose symphonies, he allowed himself to be persuaded by well-meaning but meddling friends and pupils that his works were too long, his harmonies too radical, his instrumentation incorrect—interference

Master Composers of the Late Nineteenth Century

that caused him to make drastic changes, often with unsatisfactory results. Both vocal and instrumental works were affected by those kinds of revisions. For this reason, the early published editions of Bruckner's works (some of the early publications issued as late as 1904, and some editions made in the 1930s) are considered unreliable and are seldom performed. Fortunately, Bruckner saved the original versions of many of his works and willed the sealed packet to the Vienna Court Library with instructions to forward the manuscripts to specified reliable firms for publication. In 1927 the International Bruckner Society was founded and began to prepare Bruckner's preferred versions of his symphonies for publication. The publications the Society issued after 1945 are considered the most authentic and definitive, for they are based on the manuscripts and sketches Bruckner preserved and on materials with corrections made in Bruckner's own handwriting.

Vocal Works

Bruckner wrote 19 accompanied secular choral pieces and 29 unaccompanied ones. Most of them are for male voices—the vast majority of choral ensembles in Germany and Austria were exclusively male. Only 2 of the surviving accompanied secular choral works are cantatas. Many of Bruckner's accompanied choral works, both sacred and secular, use trombones and/or keyboard (organ or piano, as appropriate). Bruckner's last completed composition was the symphonic chorus *Helgoland* (G minor; 1893) for male chorus and orchestra. It was the only work for male chorus in the packet bequeathed to the Court Library. *Abendzauber* (Evening magic; G♭ major; 1878), which is a representative example of Bruckner's Romantic writing for male chorus, calls for an interesting combination of performers: baritone soloist, TTBB chorus, three yodelers, and four horns. Austrian folk elements abound in works of this kind and also are tucked into scherzo movements in some of Bruckner's symphonies. Six solo songs by Bruckner are extant, three for alto, three for tenor, all with piano accompaniment.

There survive approximately 40 small sacred works on liturgical texts. One of the earliest of Bruckner's mature works in this category is a seven-voice *Ave Maria* written in Palestrina-style counterpoint; it is a serious, devotional work. Quite a few of Bruckner's motets are written in the ecclesiastical modes rather than in key tonalities. Five of his motets are superb: (1) the Gradual *Locus iste* (C major; for *a cappella* mixed choir; 1869) composed for the dedication of the votive chapel of the new Linz Cathedral; (2) the deeply moving Gradual *Os justi* (Lydian mode; 8–vc. *a cappella* mixed choir; 1879) used as Offertory in the 1880 performance of the Mass in D minor; (3) the Antiphon *Tota pulchra es* (Aeolian; tenor solo, SATB choir, organ; 1878) written for the silver jubilee of Bishop Rudigier of Linz; (4) the Tract *Virga Jesse floruit* (Lydian; *a cappella* mixed choir; 1885); and (5) the hymn *Vexilla regis* (Phrygian; *a cappella* mixed choir; 1892), first performed at St. Florian on Good Friday 1892. In the Alleluia that concludes the motet *Virga Jesse floruit* (ex. 23.8; DWMA200), Bruckner requires the tenors to leap an octave and sing a passage in falsetto range, while basses reiterate sustained E pitches.

Of Bruckner's five psalms settings, *Psalm cl* is the finest. In his *Te Deum* . . . (1883–84) the various sections are thematically interrelated. There survives also a Magnificat (B♭ major; 1852) for SATB soloists, mixed choir, orchestra, and organ.

Six complete Masses and a Requiem Mass (D minor; 1848–49) by Bruckner are extant; fragments and sketches of others survive. His first Mass (unnumbered; C major; 1842) is for alto soloist, two horns, and organ. The Mass in E minor (Mass No. 2; 1866) is a unique work. It was written for the dedication of the new Linz Cathedral and was first performed in the open air; therefore, Bruckner's choice of wind band as accompanying ensemble for the eight-part choir was excellent. However, he used accompaniment sparingly. In the polyphonic Sanctus, Bruckner used an adaptation of a theme from Palestrina's *Missa brevis*. Supporters of the Cecilian movement highly praised the contrapuntal style of several movements of this Mass. The Masses in D minor (Mass No. 1; 1864) and F minor (Mass No. 3; 1867–68) are often called symphonic Masses. Each is for SATB soloists, mixed choir, with full orchestra and organ accompaniment. Unquestionably, in these works

Example 23.8 Conclusion of Bruckner's motet *Virga Jesse floruit*.

Bruckner considered the words more important than the music, for he designed his music to enhance the liturgical text of the Mass.

Instrumental Works

Bruckner's surviving instrumental works comprise 10 piano solos, 2 piano duets, a few preludes and a fugue for organ, 5 pieces of chamber music, several marches for band, an orchestral overture (G minor; 1862–63) that is a student work, 11 symphonies and a few fragments of others.

Among his chamber music is a string quartet (C minor; 1862) that was located after World War II and was first performed in 1951; it is a student work of little consequence. The String Quintet (F major; 1879; 2 vlns., 2 vlas., vcl.) is excellent. It is in four movements, with Scherzo second and a lovely, rich Adagio third. Some of Bruckner's most beautiful instrumental music occurs in his Adagio movements.

Bruckner's symphonies are an important contribution to orchestral literature. As a student, he completed a symphony in F minor (1863), then wrote the D-minor symphony (1863–64) that he considered of so little value that he numbered it *Die Nullte* (0). Though his later symphonies are much finer, *Die Nullte* contains some excellent music. It has been performed several times by major American orchestras since 1975. The keys and composition dates of Bruckner's other nine symphonies are: No. 1, C minor (1865–66); No. 2, C minor (1871–72); No. 3, D minor (1873–77); No. 4, the so-called Romantic Symphony, Eb major (1874); No. 5, Bb major (1875–76); No. 6, A major (1879–81); No. 7, E major (1881–83); No. 8, C minor (1884–87); and the unfinished No. 9, D minor (1891–96). It is interesting that Nos. 0, 3, and 9 are all in D minor. With Symphony No. 3, Bruckner's genius for symphonic writing became apparent. Most of his symphonies were written for the standard-sized orchestra of his time. He never used English horn, bass clarinet, or piccolo and rarely used contrabassoon. In Symphony No. 7 he first used a quartet of Wagner tubas; he included them in the Eighth and Ninth Symphonies, also. Bruckner's orchestra sounds larger than it really is because he orchestrated in blocks of sound, with changes of instrumental color effected by using contrasting sections of the orchestra, and sudden changes of dynamics.

The general characteristics of Bruckner's symphonic writing are as follows: (1) use of traditional four-movement complete sonata structure with sonata form (or an altered version thereof) as first and fourth movements; (2) with the exception of Symphony No. 5, no introduction *per se* to begin the symphony; instead, the first movement begins with string tremolo, a *nebula*, that seems to be drawn from the air and gradually increases in volume; (3) thematic material presented according to standard procedure in the exposition of sonata-form movements, i.e., first, second, and third (closing) themes, but theme groups used rather than single themes; (4) frequently, themes in the second group are presented simultaneously rather than successively; (5) predilection for contrapuntal treatment of thematic material, through augmentation, diminution, and inversion (but never retrograde); (6) combination of thematic material, such as, simultaneous use of a theme and its inversion or a variant of the theme, or combining motives, phrases, and melodies, something Brahms also enjoyed doing (e.g., Symphony No. 3, mvt. 1, m. 101ff.; mvt. 4, m. 65ff.); (7) usually, recapitulation does not return material in its original state but presents a transformation of that material, a metamorphosis of it, so to speak; (8) very long codas that sum up all that has gone before, and, in first movements, usually conclude with a statement of the main theme (No. 8 is an exception) and, in finales, use the first theme of the first movement with the first theme of the finale; (9) lest the great length of the coda overbalance the other sections of the sonata-form movement, section lines are minimized by causing the climax of the development to coincide with the commencement of recapitulation, i.e., telescoping the end of the development with the beginning of recapitulation (e.g., Symphony No. 9); (10) frequent use of rhythmic figure combining a duplet with a triplet, e.g.,

(11) in Adagio movements, use of two groups of themes, the second, which Bruckner called *Gesangethema* (song theme), being more lyrical than the first; (12) strong thematic relationships between material in all movements, sometimes exact quotations of material previously used, sometimes variant or related material; and (13) a penchant for concluding a section with a rest that is a great window of sound (e.g., No. 7, Finale, m. 212), as Handel did in his choral writing, but Bruckner could and did write smooth transitions, also.

Despite the fact that these characteristics are common to Bruckner's symphonies, no two of the symphonies are structured exactly alike in every respect. Bruckner used quotations from his liturgical works and from other symphonies in a symphony movement, e.g., the Adagio of Symphony No. 9 contains references to the D-minor Mass and to Symphonies Nos. 7 and 8. The Finale of Symphony No. 5 is unique—a fusion of sonata form with double fugue. Bruckner presented a thematic motive first; that grew into the first theme and was used fugally; the third theme was presented and combined with the first and a double fugue created.

Bruckner dedicated his Symphony No. 9 "To my dear Lord" and prayed daily that he would live long enough to complete it. He referred to this symphony as his "farewell to life." The work exhibits most of the characteristics of his symphonic writing. The first movement (*Feierlich, Misterioso;* DWMA201) begins with a blur of sound created by strings producing a D tremolo that is soon strengthened by winds. From this "nebula" there emerges first a horn call, then a horn melody, to which strings reply *marcato*. Their response is extended by sequential repetition, a technique Bruckner employed frequently. The combination of gradual crescendo and string tremolo gives an impression of increased tempo as well as increased intensity. The first theme is stated majestically by full orchestra in unison. Immediately after the cadence Bruckner placed the first of many strategic General Pauses. Customarily, Bruckner telescoped development and recapitulation, and he did so in this movement. The last theme in the first group is not returned at the beginning of the recapitulation but is reserved for the coda. Portions of the movement resemble pastoral scenes painted by Smetana or Dvořák.

For second movement Bruckner wrote a Scherzo/Trio, which he commenced with one and two-thirds measures of rest. The D-minor tonality of the Scherzo is colored by a dissonant chord (e-g♯-b♭-c♯) stated and sustained at the outset by three clarinets and oboe and reiterated by violins and 'celli in pizzicato arpeggiation. The Trio (F♯ major) proceeds at a much faster tempo than the Scherzo—a reversal of Bruckner's usual practice. The third movement, an Adagio, begins with music that is both rich and desolate, with a profundity concealing gloom, Wagnerian in its breadth of sound. The movement's opening chromaticism obscures the key until tonic E major emerges at m. 7. Often the shadow of *Tristan . . .* seems to hover over the music. (Bruckner's score of *Tristan und Isolde* was without words—he cared only for the music.) In this movement, too, there are the usual sudden silences. A quietly beautiful coda, which refers to the symphony's first theme, to the Adagio of the Eighth Symphony, and to the opening of the Seventh Symphony, brings the Adagio of Symphony No. 9 to a serene conclusion.

Bruckner was the first composer to really extend the scope of the symphony beyond what Beethoven expressed in his Ninth Symphony. By so doing, he stood in direct opposition to many of his contemporaries, who believed that Beethoven had attained the ultimate in symphonic writing in his Symphony No. 9.

Summary

Throughout his life, Richard Wagner was interested in the theater and its music, and his most important contributions were made in those areas. Through his experiences as chorus master, conductor, and music director of theatrical and opera companies, he became well versed in every aspect of opera. From the first, he wrote the libretti for his own operas, and eventually he designed and built at Bayreuth a theater complex ideally suited to the production of his works. Wagner carried to completion the work in German Romantic opera begun by Weber and went beyond that to create music drama. With the four music dramas of *Der Ring des Nibelungen,* Wagner approached the kind of *Gesamtkunstwerk* Weber had been striving toward. Wagner was an eclectic composer, using every historical and traditional musical technique that would serve his purpose, but he shaped, merged, and manipulated those techniques in new ways, to create music that some critics considered radical. From beginning to end, *Der Ring* . . . is a unified symphonic network of sound created from *Leitmotifs* used in every imaginable way musically. Wagner's use of orchestral color, treatment of motives and *Leitmotifs,* obscuring of dividing lines, and the symphonic character of his music dramas affected symphonists as well as opera composers. His treatment of key tonality and chromaticism, frequently producing polytonality and sometimes verging on atonality, was a step toward the dodecaphony and pantonality of later composers. Certainly, *Der Ring* . . . is a landmark in the development of music.

Giuseppe Verdi, too, concentrated on opera. Unlike Wagner, Verdi did not write his own libretti, but he took a vital interest in the way those libretti were written and was involved in all aspects of the production of his operas. He followed the traditional lines of Italian opera but permitted Romantic traits to infiltrate when they furthered the drama. For Verdi, the prime purpose of the music was to support and reenforce expressively the human actions and reactions that constituted the drama. In insisting upon being realistic in details and staging, and in his regard for the presentation of events as human experiences with human reactions, Verdi paved the way for the *verismo* operas of Puccini. Verdi carried Italian opera to unprecedented heights with his two Shakespearean masterpieces: *Otello* in tragedy and *Falstaff* in comedy. In *Otello,* Verdi produced a kind of music drama with continuous music and some associative musical figures (not *Leitmotifs*) used to characterize persons, but his music drama was still within the bounds of traditional Italian opera and was quite different from the music dramas of Wagner.

Franz Liszt's closest approach to music drama was in his secular cantatas and oratorios. He first became famous as a virtuoso pianist and contributed a great deal to the development of piano playing and piano repertoire. Admiration for Paganini's virtuosity inspired Liszt to exhibit a comparable degree of technical proficiency and virtuosic display in his own playing. Like Chopin, Liszt strove to make the piano transcend its limitations. Liszt's piano arrangements and transcriptions of symphonies and operas by other composers form another significant contribution. To orchestral literature, Liszt added a new genre, the symphonic poem, a single-movement programmatic composition of symphonic proportions. Throughout his life, Liszt was deeply religious, and he composed some fine sacred music, including some Psalms settings, Masses, the Requiem Mass for Manzoni, and the *Via crucis.*

Johannes Brahms was a superb concert pianist, though he did not play with the virtuosic display that characterized Liszt's performances. Brahms was probably the most versatile and unquestionably one of the most accomplished nineteenth-century composers after the death of Beethoven. The vast majority of Brahms's music is for voice, but he never wrote an opera. He created masterpieces in the areas of solo song, accompanied choral music, symphonies, and chamber music. He was the successor to Schubert and

Schumann in the composition of Lieder and song cycle and to Beethoven in chamber music and symphony. In an era when many composers concentrated on program music, Brahms reenforced the position of absolute music in the concert hall. His four symphonies are absolute music, Classical in form, Romantic in expression and lyricism, masterworks that deservedly have found a place in standard symphonic repertoire. His Violin Concerto is one of the great concerti of all time. The *Alt-Rhapsodie* is one of the most beautiful choral works ever written, but Brahms's greatest achievement in choral music is *Ein deutsches Requiem,* the composition that first brought him to the attention of the musical world and firmly established him as a composer.

Anton Bruckner was renowned throughout Europe as a superb concert organist. Unfortunately, he improvised most of his organ compositions and never bothered to notate them. Bruckner composed some of the finest sacred choral music written in the late nineteenth century. His symphonies, like Brahms's, are absolute music and are an important contribution to orchestral literature. His Ninth Symphony is exceptionally fine. Bruckner was the first composer to really extend the scope of the symphony beyond what Beethoven expressed in his Ninth Symphony.

Late Nineteenth-Century—Early Twentieth-Century Music

The last quarter of the nineteenth century was colored by the growth of nationalism, both politically and culturally. There was a trend toward expansion—in business, in population, in aggressive territorial expansion (particularly into Africa and Asia), and in greatly increased performing resources called for by some composers. In several countries there was a move toward democracy, with control firmly in the hands of parliamentary governments based on equal male suffrage. (However, in Germany and Austria-Hungary the parliaments did not control the government.) Elementary education was compulsory in most western European countries, a fact that advanced literacy and increased the reading public. Realism is apparent in the novels of Émile Zola and Thomas Hardy, the short stories of Guy de Maupassant, the plays of Henrik Ibsen. But the Symbolist school of French poets—Stéphane Mallarmé (1842–98) was one—favored allusion rather than literal depiction. Personal independence was prized, and individual initiative led to innovations, especially in the arts.

Paris was the cultural capital of Europe. The international expositions held there in 1889 and 1900 presented much that was spectacular, including the Eiffel Tower, engineering triumph of bridge builder A. G. Eiffel (1832–1923). Other innovations are visible in the Impressionistic art of Monet (colorplate 25), Cézanne, Renoir, Degas (colorplate 26), and Pissaro and in the restless energy expressed by many of Auguste Rodin's (1840–1917) sculptures.

In music, composers had several paths from which to choose. Some post-Romanticists followed Wagner for a time; others, observing the extent of Wagner's expanded tonalities, were extremely innovative. Of course, some composers were conservative. Increased awareness of the accomplishments of great masters of the historical past (especially, Palestrina, Bach, Handel, and Beethoven) provided techniques to emulate and incorporate in contemporary compositions, and, in some cases, intimidated composers. This was particularly true of Beethoven's symphonies. The preeminence of Germanic composers began to fade, challenged mainly by nationalism and a new school of composition that arose in France.

Nationalism

Three kinds of nationalism are apparent in nineteenth-century music: (1) a nation's revival of its own folk song and the absorption of that folk song into the art music being composed, such as occurred in Germany early in the century; (2) a composer's use of a national element as an accessory to a basically cosmopolitan style or form of music, e.g., Chopin's stylized mazurkas and Liszt's rhapsodies on Hungarian gypsy tunes; and (3) a composer's use of national elements as subjects for and as basic features of a composition, e.g., Glinka's opera *A Life for the Tsar* and Smetana's *Má Vlast* (My fatherland). In nations such as Russia that had relied heavily on or had been dominated by music and musicians of other countries,

Late Nineteenth-Century – Early Twentieth-Century Developments

Growth of nonmilitaristic nationalism in art, literature, music
seen in opera, symphony, symphonic (tone) poem

c. 1888 symphonic suite

c. 1908 symphonic song cycle

Revival of *Märschenoper* in Germany

Realism in literature -

Verismo in Italian literature and opera - - - - - - - - - - - - - -

Paris the cultural capital of Europe -

Impressionism in art;

Symbolism in French poetry;

Impressionism/Symbolism in music

Increased interest in collecting folk songs; ethnomusicology -

1875 Harvard University establishes chair of music

Minstrel shows - Cakewalk; Ragtime; Blues; Jazz - - - - - - - - - - - - - - - - - - -

RUSSIA:
Dargomïzhsky (d. 1869)

Rise in importance of The Five:

(1837) Balakirev, the leader and mentor - 1910

(1835) Cui -1918

1880 *Musique en Russie*

(1839) Musorgsky - - - - - - - - - - - - 1881

1869 *Boris Godunov*

1874 *Pictures at an Exhibition*

(1844) Rimsky-Korsakov - 1908

1888 *Scheherezade*, symphonic suite

(1833) Borodin - - - - - - - - - - - - - - - - - - - 1887

1869–87 *Prince Igor*

(1840) Tchaikovsky - 1893

symphonies and ballets

1892 - - Scriabin - - - - - - - - - - - - - -1915
color-music relationship

c. 1910 *Prométhée*

---

native-born composers consciously endeavored to write music colored by or incorporating national and folk elements. Composers deliberately chose their nation's history, legends, and folklore as subjects for opera and program music, quoted snatches of folk song in vocal and instrumental compositions, used folk melodies as themes in orchestral works, and collected and published folk songs of their own lands. Distinctive features of this nationalistic music—the particular modal scales, harmonies, motives, melodies, rhythms, forms peculiar to or characteristic of the national idioms—gradually infiltrated the cosmopolitan music of Western Europe, and new styles of music arose.

1860	1870	1880	1890	1900	1910	1920	1930

CZECHOSLOVAKIA:
(1824) Smetana - - - - - - - - - - - - - - - - - 1884
nationalistic operas; symphonic poem cycle
Má Vlast (1872–80)

(1841) Dvořák - 1904
symphonies; operas; chamber music

(1854) Janáček - 1928
collecting folk songs; composing operas, choral and instr. music

SCANDINAVIA:
(1843) Grieg - 1907

1865 - - - Nielsen - (1931)

1865 - - - Sibelius - (1957)
nationalistic tone poems; symphonies (no works after 1930)

GERMANY, AUSTRIA:
1860 - - Hugo Wolf - 1903
Lieder

1860 - - Mahler - 1911
Lieder; symphonies; symphonic song cycle
integration of Lied and symphony

1864 - - Richard Strauss - (1949)
1889–98 tone poems; 1900–41 operas

FRANCE:
Cosmopolitan, traditional music (Franck, d'Indy)
French traditional music (Saint-Saëns, Fauré)
Impressionism in art; Symbolism in poetry
Impressionism/Symbolism in music (Debussy)

1862 - - - Debussy -1918
c. 1894 *Prélude à l'après-midi d'un faune*

1875 - - - Ravel - (1937)
Les Six: 1917 - - - 1922

BRITAIN: Interest in oratorio, music festivals continued

UNITED STATES:
Paine, MacDowell, Parker active

1874 - - - Charles Ives - (1954)
individualistic style; experimental

Ragtime (Joplin)   Rise of Jazz -

Russia

Until well into the nineteenth century, music in Russia was dominated by foreigners. Tsar Peter the Great (r. 1689–1725), in his desire to modernize his country, imported science, industry, art, and music from the West. During the reigns of Tsarinas Anne (r. 1730–40) and Elizabeth (r. 1741–62), Italian opera, translated into Russian, gained a real foothold. Though Araja set the Russian text for *Tzéfale i Procris* (Cephalo and Procris; 1755), and it was sung by an all-Russian cast, the work was still Italianate. Catherine II ("the Great"; r. 1762–96) maintained a magnificent theater at her St. Petersburg court and imported

Italian singers and composers, including (in order) Galuppi, Traetta, Paisiello, Sarti, and Cimarosa. Russians with promising musical talent were sent to Italy to study and returned to Russia to write inconsequential Italianate operas. Alexander I (r. 1801–25) preferred French opera and brought Boieldieu, as well as Germans and Italians, to work at court. In 1821, Irish pianist-composer John Field went to Russia to concertize and remained there to teach. Italian composer-conductor Catterino Cavos (1776–1840), who worked in St. Petersburg from 1797–1840, was the first to really explore Russian history and legends as source material for operas, e.g., in *Ivan Susanin* (1815), a story of heroism during the wars for independence at the beginning of the sixteenth century. However, no Russian musical compositions of real worth were created before Glinka (1804–57).

Mikhail Glinka was raised by his grandmother, who restricted his exposure to music to Russian folk songs. After her death (1810), Glinka lived with his parents and, for the first time, heard other kinds of music—Haydn and Mozart symphonies, and operas. Around 1817, Glinka was sent to school in St. Petersburg. He learned to sing and play piano, and in the 1820s he composed a lot of music. Among the works he completed are *Andante cantabile and Rondo* for orchestra (c. 1823, publ. 1955), two overtures (c. 1822–26, publ. 1955), several sets of variations and a few character pieces for piano, and many songs. The best of these early works are vocal solos with piano accompaniment, especially *A voice from the other world,* which is filled with chromaticism, unusual harmonies, and has a short passage in consecutive $\frac{6}{3}$ chords. Six of Glinka's early songs could easily be mistaken for genuine folk songs.

In 1830–33 Glinka visited Italy, then went to Berlin where he had some composition lessons and wrote some songs and piano pieces. In 1834 his father died, and Glinka returned to Russia. He decided to compose an opera and chose as plot the story of Russian peasant-hero Ivan Susanin. When Glinka requested permission to dedicate the opera to the Tsar, Nicholas I (r. 1825–55) exercised imperial censorship and named the work *A Life for the Tsar'* (1836). Basically, the music is Western, with elements of both Italian and French opera (ballet), but new to Russian

opera was Glinka's use of recitative; all previous Russian operas had used spoken dialogue. There are some recurring themes. The opera sounds as though it contains more authentic folk music than it really does— there are only two borrowed melodies. Glinka's orchestration is excellent. *A Life for the Tsar'* is a cornerstone in the history of Russian art music. Its success brought Glinka an appointment as *maître de chappelle* of the Imperial Chapel. He found the court singers in a deplorable state. By training them in basic rudiments of music, and by recruiting additional singers, he ultimately produced a magnificent choral ensemble of male voices, capable of performing eight-part harmony from very deep bass (down to $A\flat'$ or G'—below 'cello's lowest note) to fairly high soprano.

Glinka based his second opera, *Ruslan i Ludmila* (Ruslan and Ludmila; 1842), on a Pushkin fairy tale that is not specifically Russian and that is not really suitable for opera. The music evidences Glinka's liking for (1) thematic variation, (2) mediant relationships, (3) the flatted sixth degree, (4) descending chromaticism used for color or for sharp dissonance, and (5) changing-background technique, i.e., keeping a folk melody constant while changing the accompaniment background each time the melody is repeated. There is only one *Leitmotif,* the whole-tone scale associated with Chernomor.

Next, Glinka spent four years (1844–48) in Spain; there he composed two orchestral works on Spanish melodies. In 1848 he visited Warsaw, where he wrote some songs and his only other major work, *Kamarinskaya* (1848; orch.). In it he incorporated and juxtaposed the dance tune *Kamarinskaya* and the wedding song "From behind the mountains." Two techniques are used in the work: the changing-background principle and variation.

Glinka's music sounds Russian, and *A Life for the Tsar'* had some influence on Balakirev and Musorgsky.

The next important Russian composer was Alexander Dargomïzhsky (1813–69), who was employed in government service but had an adjunct career in music. He was a talented pianist and had violin lessons also, but he taught himself composition by borrowing Glinka's composition notebooks and studying them. Dargomïzhsky wrote many songs, but opera interested him most. In 1843 he resigned his post in the

Department of Justice and went to Paris, where he met the leading composers and became disillusioned with French opera. He returned to Russia, seriously studied Russian folk song, and began to write songs in which he combined the characteristic intonations of Russian speech and the melodic patterns of Russian folk songs. The value of his study is apparent in his third opera, *Rusalka* (1855). In many respects, it is Italianate in style, with recitatives, arias, set numbers, and choruses; however, the recitatives are basically declamatory with simple harmonic accompaniment. In mid-nineteenth century, Russia was experiencing social upheaval, and *Rusalka* is sometimes viewed as a vehicle designed to express the contemporary reaction against social inequality. Perhaps it was, but more probably Dargomïzhsky chose the Russian legend because of its dramatic possibilities.

Next, Dargomïzhsky wrote three orchestral pieces, *Kazachok, Baba Yaga,* and *Fantasia on Finnish Themes.* Of themselves, these works are not particularly outstanding; they are significant historically because they indicate a continuance of orchestral composition, begun by Glinka, an area in which later nineteenth-century Russian composers would make important contributions.

Sometime in the mid-1860s, Dargomïzhsky began his opera *Kamenniy gost* (The stone guest), Pushkin's version of the Don Juan story. In his quest for dramatic truth, Dargomïzhsky determined to set Pushkin's words virtually unchanged, as dramatic declamation, and hoped to avoid everything Italianate in structure. Some young Russian composers, especially César Cui and Modest Musorgsky, were very interested in what Dargomïzhsky was doing. When Dargomïzhsky's health failed, and he realized that death would prevent him from completing the opera, he requested Cui to finish the piano score and Musorgsky to orchestrate the work. All that remained for Cui to do was write the Prelude and finish the first scene. When performed (1872), *The Stone Guest* was a failure, but it was one of the most influential failures in the development of music, for it affected not only Russian music but that of the Western European composers who knew it. Dargomïzhsky sought to escape the bonds of key tonality and wrote the entire score without key signatures; he used some whole-tone scales and whole-tone harmonizations and some unusual modulations and radical harmonies. The opera is not devoid of Italian recitative or French phrases, but they are minimal.

Dargomïzhsky wrote about 90 songs with piano accompaniment. Some are excellent; many are romances in which elements of Russian folk song and Western European music are blended.

Moguchaya Kuchka, "Mighty Handful"

During the 40 years after the death of Nicholas I (d. 1855), Russia expanded in many ways: population, industry, agriculture, education of the people. In the 1860s there were strong feelings of nonmilitaristic nationalism, expressed in art, literature, and music. The main sources of materials for this new kind of nationalism were: (1) history (data on medieval Russia, Byzantium, the Eastern Orthodox Church, the Tatar Orient), and (2) the common man (his surroundings, his work, folk tales, folk songs, folk dances). Russian artists, authors, and composers relied on all of these.

Many musicians, both native and foreign, were active in Russia during those decades. By that time the Italian influence had faded, and a majority of the foreigners were Germans. The most significant of the Russians were the five whom critic Vladimir Stasov (1824–1906) called the *moguchaya kuchka* (mighty handful, powerful fist): Mily Balakirev (1837–1910), the acknowledged leader and mentor of the group, César Cui (1835–1918), Modest Musorgsky (1839–81), Nikolai Rimsky-Korsakov (1844–1908), and Alexander Borodin (1833–87). Those five men never referred to themselves by Stasov's term, nor was the term used in Russia by anyone other than Stasov. Actually, Stasov himself was as mighty a force as the others, not only through his many writings on art, literature, and music, but through assistance he provided the composers—suggesting subjects for compositions and ferreting out source materials for them. From 1854 until his death, Stasov held responsible positions at St. Petersburg Public Library. His writings on Russian music provide valuable information on the activities of musicians and composers who were his contemporaries.

The Russian Five, "The Mighty Handful," with Stasov. *Top row*: Balakirev, Stasov, Musorgsky; *bottom row*: Rimsky-Korsakov, Borodin, Cui.

From childhood, Mily Balakirev had been trained in music. His mother was his first piano teacher, and when he was 10 she took him to Moscow for a series of piano lessons with A. Dubuque, a pupil of John Field. Later, Balakirev studied theory with Karl Eisrich. In 1849 Eisrich introduced Balakirev to Alexander Ulïbïshev, a wealthy landowner who had a small orchestra and a large library of music. Ulïbïshev authored books on Mozart and Beethoven and had much of their music in his library. Balakirev lived in Ulïbïshev's home, played Beethoven's piano music for Ulïbïshev, and at the age of 15 was permitted to conduct rehearsals of the private orchestra that performed works by Mozart, Beethoven, Mendelssohn, and other European composers. While enrolled in the mathematics curriculum at University of Kazan (1853–55), Balakirev performed as pianist at social functions and taught piano lessons. Among his earliest compositions are *Grand Fantaisie on Russian Folksongs* (1852; pno., orch.), some songs (publ. 1908), and the first movement of a Piano Concerto in F♯ minor (1855–56). In 1855 Ulïbïshev introduced him to Glinka, who realized that Balakirev needed further instruction in theory/composition, but there

were no Russian textbooks on the subject and he could not read German. Glinka supplied Balakirev with some themes for new compositions, checked over the works when they were completed, and introduced Balakirev to Stasov.

Several times during 1857–58 Balakirev played some of his piano works in concerts. In 1857, at a private concert, he met César Cui, an officer in the Engineering Corps of the Russian Army. At that time, Cui knew very little about music. Balakirev introduced him to Dargomïzhsky. At Dargomïzhsky's home, Cui met Modest Musorgsky, a young military officer in the Preobrazhensky Regiment of the Guards. Musorgsky was a talented pianist and was interested in musical composition but had had no training along that line. They became friends, and Cui introduced Musorgsky to Balakirev. In 1861, Théodore Canille, who was teaching Nikolai Rimsky-Korsakov, a young naval cadet, introduced him to Balakirev, who encouraged Rimsky-Korsakov to compose. In 1862 Borodin, a chemistry student at the Medico-Surgical Academy, and a friend of Musorgsky, met Balakirev, who guided his compositional endeavors. Thus, the circle of musician-composers that Stasov termed the *moguchaya kuchka* was formed.

In general, the Five upheld these principles: (1) the music of the Russian people, religious and folk, should be used as a basis for art music—this was the new Russian nationalism; (2) strict German counterpoint and other techniques of Western European music might be ignored in order to allow the composer more freedom in creating art music; (3) realism was advocated; and (4) the spirit and style of nineteenth-century Romanticism was favored, as expressed in the music of Berlioz, Chopin, Liszt, and Schumann, and traditional Classicism was rejected.

In 1860 Balakirev began collecting Russian folk songs; he harmonized a number of them and published two collections (1866; 1898). In 1862 he was instrumental in founding the Free School of Music in St. Petersburg, in competition with the Conservatory. His work at the School, plus the hours he spent helping other composers in his circle, left little time for his own composing. Short works he completed; larger works bogged down, and some he never finished. He worked on his Symphony No. 1 (C major) for 33 years. His insistence on national themes, his general advocacy of musical nationalism, and his teaching that composers had the right to ignore all the traditional rules of Western European music if they so desired, caused antagonism among musicians and made for Balakirev many enemies. Moreover, between 1870 and 1881 he became involved in mysticism, and his compositional activity slackened while that of his colleagues increased. Not until after 1894 did he actively resume composing; in the next decade he wrote the majority (about 3 dozen) of his piano pieces and at least 20 songs. During this second period of compositional activity, he seemed to prefer traditional forms, though he altered them somewhat. For instance, his Piano Sonata in B♭ minor (1905) is a four-movement

work with sonata-form Andantino first movement, followed by stylized Mazurka, nocturne-like Intermezzo, and fast Finale.

Thus, Balakirev's compositional activity occurred during two short periods of creativity, separated by 25 years of silence. His surviving music includes 11 choral works, the majority of them for women's voices; 6 anthems for mixed chorus, 1 being *Cherubim Song;* 2 incomplete piano concertos; 2 symphonies (C major; D minor); 4 nationalistic concert overtures; 3 orchestral suites; *Romance* for violin/piano; approximately 50 piano works; and 45 vocal solos with piano accompaniment. One of his most significant compositions is the *Second Overture on Russian Themes* (1864), which he renamed *1000 let'* (1000 years) to commemorate Russia's chiliad (the 1000th anniversary of Russia's founding, see p. 59). The overture, slightly revised, was published in 1882 as the symphonic poem *Russia.* Another important work is the virtuosic Oriental fantasy *Islamey* for piano (1869), a very difficult work technically. It is based on three themes (Caucasian, Armenian) and has tremendous rhythmic drive (ex. 24.1). *Islamey* shows the influence of Liszt and in its turn influenced Debussy and Ravel.

Balakirev's significance for the development of music in history lies as much in his leadership as in his compositions. He did a great deal for Russian music simply by instilling in his colleagues and students the belief that Russian composers could rival Western European composers, particularly Germans. In his own works he did not completely reject traditional Western European methods but merged the Russian and Near Eastern with them. From Glinka he received training in the proper instrumental treatment of folk-music materials, then expanded and built on that training and transmitted what he learned to other Russian composers, e.g., Borodin, Musorgsky, and Rimsky-Korsakov. Balakirev was a dictatorial mentor; he did not merely suggest subjects to his colleagues, he supplied themes, insisted on certain keys (usually five flats or two sharps), and sometimes reworked portions of their compositions. He believed that composers, especially great composers, should be teachers and should pass their techniques on to their students. So firmly did he impress this upon his colleagues and students, that, from Balakirev's time to the present, great Russian composers have taught. In no other country is there such a continuous chain of music pedagogy.

César Cui, an expert on fortifications, was the weakest member of the Balakirev circle, yet through his critical articles was influential in Russian music for more than 50 years. He had little training in music before he met Balakirev but had tried to compose. The earliest of his extant works are two Scherzi for piano (1857), one based on the notes B-A-B-E-G, derived from his wife's maiden name, Bamberg, and the other labeled *à la Schumann;* he orchestrated both with Balakirev's help. Cui composed a large amount of music: 15 operas, 4 of them children's operas, e.g., *The Snow Giant;* more than 200 songs; some cantatas and other choral works, 3 string quartets and some other chamber music, at least a dozen orchestral pieces, and numerous piano pieces. His best works are miniatures, particularly the delicate ones, such as *Orientale,* one of the 24 violin/piano pieces in *Kaleydoskop* (Kaleidoscope, Op. 50; 1893). Cui was an ardent proponent of nationalism, but not all of his works are nationalistic. Most of his operas reflect the influences of Meyerbeer and Auber. Cui's operatic writing was highly respected by Dargomïzhsky, who requested him to complete *The Stone Guest.* Cui wrote the first comprehensive book on Russian music, *Musique en Russie* (publ. Paris, 1880). His second book on Russian music, *The Russian Song: A Study of its Development,* was issued in St. Petersburg in 1896.

Alexander Borodin, son of a Georgian prince, received an excellent general education, learned several foreign languages, and had lessons on flute and piano. Later, he learned to play 'cello. At age 14, he composed a piece for flute and piano and a string trio based on themes from Meyerbeer's *Robert le diable.* Boro-

din graduated from the Academy of Medicine in St. Petersburg, became an assistant professor there, and earned a doctorate in chemistry (1858). In 1859 he was sent to Western Europe for advanced study and to investigate scientific procedures in German universities. While in Germany in 1861, he met Katerina Protopopova, an excellent pianist, whom he married a few years later. In 1864 he became professor of organic chemistry at the Academy of Medicine in St. Petersburg. Borodin was internationally known in his field and wrote and published several important scientific papers. He was among the first to advocate the admission of women to the medical profession in Russia and instigated the establishment of medical courses at the Academy in 1872.

For Borodin, music was necessarily an avocation, but he composed music whenever he could find the time. Because he worked long hours in the laboratory and at the Academy, it took him several years to complete any large composition. He had met Musorgsky before he went to Germany and renewed that acquaintance upon his return to Russia; then he met Balakirev and the others of his circle. The first large work Borodin composed after meeting Balakirev was Symphony No. 1 (E♭ major; 1862–67). In general, the symphony follows traditional lines, but, in accord with nineteenth-century practices, scherzo/trio form the second movement and the slow movement (D major) is placed third. Borodin next wrote some songs. An opera-farce and an opera, *The Tsar's bride* (1867–69), have not survived. The opera *Prince Igor* and a second symphony were begun in 1869. Borodin chose unusual key relationships for the four movements of Symphony No. 2 (1869–76): sonata-form first movement in B minor, scherzo/trio in F major, slow third movement in D♭ major, Finale in B major. The motive shown in example 24.2 figures prominently in the first movement. The scherzo is remarkable for the rich colors of its orchestration; the slow movement is rather melancholy and somewhat oriental in sound. In contrast, the brilliant orchestration of the Finale is vividly colorful.

Stasov had sent Borodin the scenario for *Prince Igor,* and Borodin wrote the libretto from that. He worked on the music intermittently and composed other works—songs, chamber music, orchestral pieces, piano solos, and Act IV of the opera-ballet *Mlada*

Example 24.2 Borodin: Symphony No. 2, mvt. 1, theme 1. The opening motive of this theme is prominent throughout the work.

(1872), on which he collaborated with Musorgsky, Cui, and Rimsky-Korsakov. *Prince Igor* (1869–87) was not finished at the time of Borodin's sudden death from heart failure, and its completion was undertaken largely by Alexander Glazunov (1865–1936), with considerable assistance from his teacher, Rimsky-Korsakov. Fortunately, Glazunov had discussed *Prince Igor* with Borodin on more than one occasion and knew something of his plans for the opera. Glazunov wrote the overture, by piecing together sketches Borodin had made, relying on his memory of the overture as Borodin had improvised it for him one day when they had visited, and adding a few measures of his own here and there. It was a remarkable achievement for Glazunov. Throughout the overture the brilliance of the orchestration and the excellent choice of instrumentation for solo and duet passages are indicative of the superb training he received from Rimsky-Korsakov. In view of the facts that composition of *Prince Igor* extended over 18 years and that it was assembled and completed by two composers who were not involved in planning the work, it is not surprising that the opera seems to be a series of tableaux rather than a unified drama. Some of the arias are excellent, e.g., the two sung by Yaroslavna. The exotic *Polovtsian Dances* from Act II are frequently performed in orchestral concerts; one of those dances supplied the melody for the twentieth-century popular song *Stranger in Paradise.*

Two other excellent works by Borodin should be mentioned: the beautiful song he wrote at the time of Musorgsky's death, *For the shores of thy far land* (1881; Pushkin text), and the short orchestral piece *V sredney Azii* (In central Asia; 1882), one of a dozen works commissioned for use as background music for a series of living tableaux illustrating events during the reign of Alexander II (r. 1855–81).

Modest Musorgsky was the most talented and the most nationalistic of Balakirev's disciples. When he met Balakirev, Musorgsky knew a great deal about Russian folklore but very little about musical composition. When he was a very young child, his grandmother had taught him Russian folk tales and legends, and his mother had given him some piano lessons. Piano playing was easy for him; he learned quickly and played well. At the age of ten, he was taken to St. Petersburg for piano lessons but was taught nothing about form or harmony. His general education was acquired at preparatory school, then from a tutor; in 1852 he entered Cadet School of the Guards at St. Petersburg. He sang in the school choir, began to compose some music, and, on the advice of one of his religion instructors, studied the works of Bortniansky and other early nineteenth-century Russian composers. In 1857 Musorgsky, then a military officer, met Dargomïzhsky and Cui; they introduced him to Stasov and Balakirev. Soon Musorgsky persuaded Balakirev to help him with composition. With that guidance, Musorgsky wrote some songs and piano pieces; in 1858 he composed two piano sonatas (E♭ major; F♯ minor; lost), two Scherzi for piano (C♯ minor; B♭ major), and began an opera that he soon abandoned.

In 1858 Musorgsky began to experience nervous difficulties and resigned his military commission. From time to time, nervous disorders disrupted his career; those attacks may have been the early stages of epilepsy, but that disease was not diagnosed at the time. Russian serfs were emancipated in 1861, and for the next two years Musorgsky helped his brother manage the family estate. Then funds ran low, and he needed to find gainful employment; in 1863 he entered civil service, where he held responsible positions until his dismissal in 1867. He wrote a few songs and began another opera that he never completed. Shortly after his mother's death in 1865, Musorgsky had his first serious bout with alcoholism. Both diseases worsened over the years, and the combination of alcoholism and epilepsy eventually claimed his life. At the time of his death, many of his works remained unfinished; a number of them were completed by Rimsky-Korsakov and other composers.

Of the compositions that Musorgsky completed, there are extant: the opera *Boris Godunov* (1st version, 1868–69; rev. 1871–72); 4 choral works; 5 orchestral pieces, 1 being *St. John's Night on the Bare Mountain* (1867); approximately a dozen piano pieces;

(a)

(b)

Figure 24.1 Two of Victor Hartmann's art works that Musorgsky depicted musically in *Pictures at an Exhibition*: (*a*) *A Polish Jew, Sandomir*; (*b*) design for the chick costume for *Trilbi* ballet. (Pictures at an Exhibition, *published by International Music Company, New York, 1952.*)

at least 50 songs; and 3 song cycles, *Detskaya* (The Nursery; 1870–1872), *Bez solntsa* (Sunless; 1874), and *Pesni i plyaski smerti* (Songs and dances of death; 1874). He wrote no chamber music, no concerto, and barely began a symphony.

Musorgsky's songs rank among the finest written in the nineteenth century. Reportedly, he sang them most effectively at private gatherings. His songs portray various moods, among them, devotional (*Prayer;* 1865), satirical (*Oh, you, drunken sot!;* 1866), tender (*Lullaby;* 1865), comical (*Mephistopheles's song of the flea;* 1879). Some convey sobering and thought-provoking messages, e.g., *The Field-marshal* from *Songs and Dances of Death,* which communicates that in war the real Field-marshal and only victor is Death. For many of the songs Musorgsky wrote his own texts, e.g., *The Nursery* cycle; for others he used poems by noted Russian authors and translations of works by Goethe, Heine, and Rückert. All of Musorgsky's songs are in Russian. His music fits the natural declamation of normal Russian speech perfectly, and the songs lose much in translation. Phrases are usually asymmetrical, of uneven lengths. Melodic lines may be lyrical, or declamatory, or nonlyrical and individualistic, typical of the speech of the characters in the song, e.g., the satirical *Seminarist* (The Seminarian; 1866), wherein the seminary student's amorous thoughts invade his Latin declensions and even his intoning of a psalm (in mode VI) during Service. Incidentally, *Seminarist* was considered too shocking to be published in Russia; it was printed in Leipzig in 1870. Only in the twentieth century has it been viewed as Musorgsky intended it—as comic satire. Many of Musorgsky's melodies are modal or hint at modality; he carried modality over into his harmonizations, too. Frequently he used pedal points and sometimes short ostinato patterns. Musorgsky used chord streams 30 years before Debussy did so. Debussy spent a year in Russia where he heard some of Musorgsky's music and was influenced by it.

The best known of Musorgsky's piano pieces is *Pictures at an Exhibition* (1874; publ. 1886), a suite he composed after viewing an exhibit of architect-artist Victor Hartmann's works (fig. 24.1). From the more than 400 pieces on exhibit, Musorgsky chose 10 to depict musically and linked them by a *Promenade* that describes himself, as viewer, walking about the

Allegro moderato

Example 24.3 The Russian melody *Slava* (Glory).

exhibit. Musorgsky owned two of the drawings he translated into music; both have disappeared. *Pictures at an Exhibition* has been orchestrated by several persons; the best orchestration is that made by Maurice Ravel in 1921.

Musorgsky developed his libretto for *Boris Godunov* from two sources: Pushkin's play *Boris Godunov* (1825) and Karamzin's *History of the Russian State* (1818). The story is based on the long-held belief (since proven false) that Tsar Boris (regent for Fyodor, 1584–98; r. 1598–1605) murdered his nephew Dmitry, heir to the throne. The opera commences with Boris's coronation, then relates how a young monk pretends to be Dmitry and, in an attempt to usurp the throne, incites a revolt. Boris has brooded about his crime, and after he hears of a miracle that occurred at the real Dmitry's grave, collapses and dies.

Musorgsky's construction of the opera in scenes, rather than continuous drama, conforms with the structure of many literary works of the late nineteenth century. The original version of the opera consisted of seven scenes, but when the Imperial Opera rejected the work, Musorgsky expanded it to four acts with prologue. Segments of the opera were performed in various concerts in 1872 and 1873; the complete second version was performed in 1874. Basically, *Boris*

Godunov is a historical grand opera, with spectacular crowd scenes that are an essential part of the story. The work differs from nineteenth-century French grand operas in that Musorgsky created in *Boris Godunov* characters that are portrayed as humans—they are perceived by the audience as real people rather than as characters enacting a drama. Musorgsky paid great attention to characterization. For example, he used the same recurrent theme (*Leitmotif*) to represent the real Dmitry and Dmitry the Pretender. *Boris Godunov* presents not only a personal tragedy but the suffering of the Russian people, the masses. The people are the losers—the real heroes of *Boris Godunov*. The subject matter is extremely nationalistic, and it is so presented, with use of actual folk song and Russian Orthodox church music and many realistic details. The fierceness of medieval Russia, still existing in the sixteenth century, lives again in Musorgsky's music. This is musical realism.

The Coronation Scene in *Boris Godunov* is magnificent (fig. 24.2; DWMA202). The crowd sings its praise of Boris with the melody of the folk song *Slava* (Glory) as theme; the whole-tone scale is prominent (ex. 24.3). The pealing of many bells, representing Moscow's numerous cathedrals and churches, is most effective and realistic. The music is vigorous and vibrant. Boris's solo provides an excellent example of Musorgsky's ability to write in a style that is both expressive and flexible. Here, he united text with music so well that Boris's prayer has the effect of religious chant. The role of Boris requires a deep bass singer who can interpret expressively and convey the impression of great strength and power.

Acting in good faith, with the aim of making *Boris Godunov* acceptable to the public and less difficult to perform and to produce, Rimsky-Korsakov made and published two revisions of the work, with drastic alterations in Musorgsky's scores. Those changes destroyed much of the originality of Musorgsky's harmonies, modulations, and melodic lines. Rimsky-Korsakov removed many of Musorgsky's harmonic innovations—the harsh dissonances, chords structured in fourths and fifths, unorthodox and uninhibited modulations—that sounded strange then but actually added dramatic power and color to the music. Rimsky-Korsakov revised *St. John's Night on the Bare Mountain,* also. His versions present Musorgsky's music in a much more conventional light than it really was; Musorgsky was a daring, innovative, avant-garde composer. However, Rimsky-Korsakov did put *Boris Godunov* back into the repertoire in Russia. In 1908 musicologists expressed much dissatisfaction with Rimsky-Korsakov's revisions, and as a result of agitation for publication of the works with Musorgsky's original texts (unaltered), the Russian State Music Corporation began in 1928 to prepare an edition of Musorgsky's complete works that presents not only the original versions Musorgsky left but also all of the variant versions published by editors. Only when all of Musorgsky's music is available in its original form will his genius be fully recognized.

Nikolai Rimsky-Korsakov's autobiography, *Chronicle of My Musical Life,* edited and published by his son Andrey (1878–1940) in 1909, relates not only details of Nikolai's life but reveals much about musical activities in Russia during the years "The Five" were active. Since several of Rimsky-Korsakov's relatives had distinguished careers in governmental, military, or naval posts, it was natural that Nikolai would choose to enter the navy. One of his grandmothers, a priest's daughter, instilled in him religious devotion and great appreciation for Russian Orthodox liturgical music and ceremonies; the other grandmother, of peasant origin, imparted to him a love of folk song and legend. Both found places in his music.

His musical talent was apparent when he was quite young, and he had piano lessons from local teachers. His real interest in music was aroused when he heard Bortniansky's sacred music at a nearby monastery. At home he found the music for selections from Glinka's *A Life for the Tsar'* and dabbled half-heartedly at composition. While at the College of Naval Cadets (1856–62), he attended performances of operas by Glinka, Meyerbeer, Weber, and Rossini and heard for the first time some Beethoven symphonies and Mendelssohn overtures. But Glinka remained his favorite composer. During his cadet years, Rimsky-Korsakov took piano lessons from Théodore Canille, and through him, late in 1861, was drawn into Balakirev's circle.

At that time, Rimsky-Korsakov was trying to compose a symphony in E♭ minor, and Balakirev insisted that he continue to work on it. The first movement, scherzo, and finale were completed by 1862, but the slow movement was not finished until after Rimsky-Korsakov returned from two and one-half years of naval duty abroad. In 1866 Rimsky-Korsakov had time to discuss music with Dargomïzhsky and Balakirev's circle and to compose the *Overture on Russian Themes* and some songs and dance music. After beginning and abandoning another symphony, he wrote the symphonic poem *Sadko,* based on the legend of the minstrel Sadko (1867; rev. 1869, 1892). The composition reflects the influence of and contains borrowings from works by Glinka, Balakirev, Dargomïzhsky, and Liszt. (In 1894–96, Rimsky-Korsakov wrote the opera *Sadko.*)

In 1868 the Balakirev group regularly attended *soirées* at Dargomïzhsky's home and performed portions of *The Stone Guest* as Dargomïzhsky completed them. Among the other musically talented persons attending those *soirées* were the Purgold sisters, one of whom, Nadezhda, became Rimsky-Korsakov's wife. Discussions of opera at the *soirées* increased Rimsky-Korsakov's interest in that genre to the extent that he composed one, *The Maid of Pskov* (1868–72). Though it was well received when performed, he was not pleased with it and revised it twice (1876, 1898).

Rimsky-Korsakov was remorselessly self-critical. He constantly revised his compositions, and when he completed works left unfinished because of the deaths of his colleagues, he subjected those compositions to several revisions also.

In 1871 Rimsky-Korsakov was appointed professor of composition and instrumentation at St. Petersburg Conservatory. He knew very little about harmony, counterpoint, and form, but set about learning the basics in those areas and studied hard to keep ahead of his students. For a time, he became so involved with his studies that the others in the Balakirev circle thought he had turned traditional-classicist. Actually, he tried to write abstract music along traditional lines—a symphony (C minor), a string quartet (F major), a string sextet (A major), a quintet for piano and winds (B♭ major)—but found that it did not satisfy him nor did he think he did it well. Most of his 16 chamber music works are nonprogrammatic, contain a fair amount of counterpoint, and are more or less along traditional lines. But Rimsky-Korsakov's love of fantasy, folklore, and Russian history made program music and opera better areas in which to work.

From 1873 to 1884 Rimsky-Korsakov was Inspector of Bands for the Navy Department, also. In an endeavor to learn as much as possible about the various instruments, he purchased instruments and learned to play them. This, plus his thorough study of Berlioz's treatise on instrumentation, made Rimsky-Korsakov a brilliant orchestrator. He could orchestrate well because he knew from experience the various instrumental techniques, ranges, tone colors, and capabilities. He began to orchestrate some of his colleagues' works, first helping Cui and Dargomïzhsky, then finishing and editing Musorgsky's compositions and, after 1887, working with Glazunov in completing Borodin's *Prince Igor.* However, in working with the music of these composers, Rimsky-Korsakov tended to soften the dissonances, to reshape some of the chords and melodies, to delete portions, or to substitute a phrase here and there.

In 1874, Rimsky-Korsakov succeeded Balakirev as director of the Free School of Music, and in 1883 he became assistant superintendent of music at the Imperial Chapel (Balakirev was superintendent). In 1884 Rimsky-Korsakov's *Textbook of Harmony* was published (St. Petersburg). He wrote a treatise on orchestration, illustrated with more than 300 excerpts from his works. His son Andrey published that book, *Principles of Orchestration,* in 1913. It has been translated into French, German, and English and is still used at some universities as an orchestration text.

Besides teaching, orchestrating, and writing, Rimsky-Korsakov published two substantial collections of Russian folk songs, one of them (Op. 24; 1876) containing 100 songs, and composed a great deal of music: operas, orchestral works, some chamber music, piano pieces, and many songs. Over a 40-year period, he composed 14 operas and 1 opera-ballet, most of them unknown outside Russia. None of his operas is as fine as *Boris Godunov,* for he was not as adept at musical characterization as Musorgsky, probably because he regarded the music of prime importance, the drama second. However, Rimsky-Korsakov's finest vocal writing is found in his operas. Only *The Snow Maiden* (1880–81, rev. 1895), *Sadko* (1895–96), and *The Golden Cockerel* (1906–7) have been accepted internationally.

Rimsky-Korsakov wrote *The Golden Cockerel* during the summer of 1906, when he and his family were in Italy. The previous year, there had been much political and social upheaval in Russia, with strikes and riots, even at the Conservatory. In casting about for a subject for a new opera, he came upon a fairy tale that Pushkin had based on Washington Irving's *The Alhambra.* Pushkin had experienced unpleasant and unfair treatment at the hands of the rulers, and through his poetic satire *The Golden Cockerel* found a way of getting back at them. Rimsky-Korsakov's opera, in which the King kills the Astrologer, and in retaliation the Astrologer's cockerel attacks and kills the King, had political overtones in Russia. The satirical depiction of the aristocracy fit conditions in Russia at the time. Government censors recognized this and demanded removal of some of the lines. Rimsky-Korsakov's music reveals his knowledge of Wagnerian principles; *Leitmotifs* associated with the main characters are deftly woven into the symphonic fabric of the opera. In this work Rimsky-Korsakov's characters are delightful, though they are caricatures, and his scenic depictions are excellent.

Rimsky-Korsakov's reputation in the Western world rests on three orchestral works: *Spanish Capriccio* (also called *Capriccio espagnole;* 1887), *Scheherazade* (1888), and the overture *Russian Easter Festival* (1888). *Spanish Capriccio* resulted from Rimsky-Korsakov's desire to use Spanish themes for a virtuosic violin solo with orchestral accompaniment. The work has five short movements: (1) *Alborada,* a morning serenade or *aubade;* (2) Theme with variations; (3) *Alborada* for orchestra, a variation of the first movement; (4) *Scene and Gypsy Song,* containing cadenzas for flute, clarinet, harp, and violin; (5) *Fandango and Asturias,* stylized dance music based on an old Asturian dance tune. The work is exciting, buoyant, and vividly brilliant, filled with figuration patterns suited to each solo instrument and to each section of the orchestra. Rimsky-Korsakov himself evaluated it as a brilliant composition for orchestra, not a magnificently orchestrated piece.

Rimsky-Korsakov originated the **symphonic suite.** Romantic composers had written numerous short pieces based on fairy tales and legends but nothing that was symphonic in scope. He wanted to write a multimovement orchestral programmatic work that was not a symphony but that had the characteristic features of symphony, symphonic poem, and the nineteenth-century suite, a set of related pieces. He called this kind of work a symphonic suite.

Scheherazade is a four-movement symphonic suite based on episodes from *A Thousand and One Nights.* Rimsky-Korsakov gave the movements these titles: (1) *The Sea and Sinbad's Ship;* (2) *The Tale of Prince Kalender;* (3) *The Young Prince and the Young Princess;* (4) *Festival at Bagdad—The Sea— The Ship is Wrecked on a Rock Surmounted by a Bronze Warrior—Conclusion.* The suite is unified by cadenza-like introductions to movements 1, 2, and 4 and a cadenza-intermezzo in movement 3, all played by solo violin with harp accompaniment, representing Scheherazade telling her fascinating (and lifesaving) tales to the Sultan. The work is Romantic in its exotic Eastern colors and fairy-tale basis. Throughout the composition, the melodies are never overshadowed or impeded by other orchestral activity. The part-writing is well defined, as it always is in Rimsky-Korsakov's music. He handled the instrumentation expertly, (a)

combining different, unlike instruments to produce new tonal colors and effects; (b) contrasting the basic tone color of the same instruments in different registers; (c) contrasting individual instruments or groups of different instruments. To some extent, *Festival at Bagdad* foreshadows twentieth-century treatment of rhythm—in some sections rhythmic changes occur every few measures.

In writing the overture *Russian Easter Festival* Rimsky-Korsakov had two aims: (1) to depict the spectacle of a typical Easter morning Service at a cathedral of Russian Orthodox faith and (2) to convey the deeper meaning of that Service, a combination of Isaiah's prophesy of resurrection, the Gospel story of Jesus's resurrection, and the pagan symbolism and merry making that invaded Easter ritual. He did all of that. The very idea of composing an orchestral work based on Russian Orthodox liturgical materials was daring—for 1000 years church edicts had banned musical instruments from the sanctuary. Most of the themes used in *Russian Easter Festival* were derived from the *obikhod,* a collection of the most important canticles in the Russian Orthodox liturgy. Among those Rimsky-Korsakov used are "Let God arise!," "An angel wailed," "Let them also that hate Him flee before Him," and, in the coda, "Christ is risen!" There is a good deal of modality in *Russian Easter Festival.* The work is Romantic in its presentation of ritualistic pageantry, yet is a deeply devotional presentation of all that the Easter ritual represents in the way of sorrow, despair, joy, and hope.

Rimsky-Korsakov's importance as a teacher must not be minimized. He passed on to his students the legacy he received from Dargomïzhsky and Balakirev and that they had inherited from Glinka. Among Rimsky-Korsakov's composition students at St. Petersburg Conservatory were two generations of Russian composers: Alexander Glazunov (1865–1936), Anatoli Liadov (1855–1914), Mikhail Ippolitov-Ivanov (1859–1935), Igor Stravinsky (1882–1971), Sergey Prokofiev (1891–1953), Nikolai Miaskovsky (1881–1950), and Yulia Weissberg (1879–1942), who married Rimsky-Korsakov's son Andrey. Also, Nikolai Rimsky-Korsakov's influence is apparent in some of the compositions of Debussy, Maurice Ravel, Paul Dukas, and Ottorino Respighi.

Rimsky-Korsakov wrote both traditional and Romantic, abstract and program, nationalistic and non-nationalistic music. He was most successful with the Romantic, programmatic, and nationalistic types. His musical language was dual, also, sometimes diatonic and lyrical, sometimes filled with chromaticism or based on artificial whole-tone scales. His orchestrations are superb. The main influences in his style were Glinka, Balakirev, Liszt, and Berlioz. That he was an excellent composition and orchestration teacher is evident from the success of his pupils.

Nonnationalistic Russian Composers

Some Russian composers worked along traditional Western lines, composing programmatic and/or absolute Romantic music with few traces of nationalism. Three such composers were Anton Rubinstein (1829–94), Pyotr Tchaikovsky (1840–93), and Alexander Scriabin (1872–1915).

Anton Rubinstein was one of the nineteenth century's finest pianists, comparable with Liszt, and enjoyed international acclaim as a concert pianist. He and Henryk Wieniawski (1835–80), Polish violinist-composer, toured North America in 1872, presenting 215 concerts. In 1859 Rubinstein and Grand Duchess Elena founded the Russian Musical Society, an institution with a planned music curriculum that was decidedly pro-Western; the Society became St. Petersburg Conservatory in 1862. As director of the Conservatory (1862–67; 1887–93), Rubinstein did much to improve the status of musicians in Russia and to raise standards of performance, particularly in piano playing. However, in the 1860s he occupied a controversial position because of his espousal of Western European teaching methods and his outspoken attitude against nationalism in opera. Nevertheless, his advocacy of government-supported conservatories and opera theaters in every important Russian city and his ideas concerning the teaching of music in Russian schools are the basis for twentieth-century educational practices in Russia.

Only a few of Rubinstein's many works have achieved lasting popularity, among them the piano pieces *Melody in F* (Op. 3 No. 1) and *Kamennïy-ostrov* (Rocky island), Piano Concerto No. 4, and, in Russia, the opera *Demon* (The demon; 1871), which

Pyotr I. Tchaikovsky. *(Courtesy of the Free Library of Philadelphia.)*

has some nationalistic tendencies. Most of his music is Western European in style, reflecting particularly the influence of Mendelssohn and Meyerbeer. Rubinstein was the first Russian to achieve success as interpreter (pianist, conductor) of other composers' works and as composer.

Pyotr Tchaikovsky was exposed to Western European music from the time he was an infant—the family home was equipped with an orchestrion, a kind of automatophon controlled by pinned cylinders or punched cards that played orchestral music and excerpts from operas. When the family moved to St. Petersburg in 1848, Pyotr began to take piano lessons, and in 1850 he saw Glinka's *A Life for the Tsar'*. Tchaikovsky was educated at the School of Jurisprudence and, at the age of 19, became a government clerk in the Ministry of Justice. That work provided his living, but he was interested in music and arranged to take classes at the Russian Musical Society. Later, he studied composition with Rubinstein, and in 1863 resigned from the Ministry of Justice to become a full-time student at St. Petersburg Conservatory. To help meet expenses, he taught piano and theory lessons privately. In 1865 his graduation exercise, a cantata on Schiller's *An die Freude* (To Joy), won a silver medal. The following year, Tchaikovsky became professor of theory at Moscow Conservatory. There he met his future publisher and made friends who became powerful allies in later years. From that time on, he composed in earnest, often finding it very hard work.

Figure 24.3 A scene from Tchaikovsky's ballet *The Nutcracker.* (© *Martha Swope.*)

Frequently, he consulted other composers about his works and usually heeded their advice. Balakirev caused him to revise the *Overture-fantasy Romeo and Juliet* three times, and that work became Tchaikovsky's first real success. Much as he valued Balakirev's criticisms, Tchaikovsky never joined his circle.

In 1868–74 Tchaikovsky regularly contributed articles on music criticism to Moscow journals, and in 1871 his *Guide to the Practical Study of Harmony* was published. He made numerous trips to major European music centers and in 1891 visited the United States. For about 14 years (c. 1876–c. 1890) he enjoyed the patronage of Mme Nadezhda von Meck, a wealthy widow, who provided him an annual subsidy of 6000 rubles as well as commissioning works. Tchaikovsky and Meck never met; their association was maintained entirely by correspondence.

Tchaikovsky's surviving works include ten operas, three ballets; six numbered symphonies and the programmatic symphony *Manfred;* several concert overtures, orchestral fantasias, suites, and marches; three piano concerti; a violin concerto; *Variations on a Rococo Theme* for 'cello and orchestra; three string

quartets and a piano trio; numerous vocal works and piano solos. Many of his works have become part of standard repertoire: Symphonies Nos. 4 (F minor; 1877), 5 (E minor; 1888), and 6 (B minor; 1893); the ballets *Swan Lake* (1875–76), *The Sleeping Beauty* (1880–89), and *The Nutcracker* (1891–92); Piano Concerto No. 1 (Bb major; 1874–75); the Violin Concerto (D major; 1878); the *Overture-fantasy Romeo and Juliet* (B minor; 1869); *Serenade* (C major; 1880; strings); *Variations on a Rococo Theme* (A major; 1876). Tchaikovsky's Violin Concerto is one of the finest and one of the most difficult in the repertoire.

Every Christmas season *The Nutcracker* ballet is performed hundreds of times in the United States alone (fig. 24.3). In the *Danse de la fée dragée* (Dance of the sugarplum fairy) Tchaikovsky featured the *célesta,* a keyboard metallophone patented by Auguste Mustel in 1886. Tchaikovsky had seen the instrument in Paris and wanted to be the first to write an orchestral part for it. He was.

Much of Tchaikovsky's music is orchestral or involves an orchestra. Several of his symphonies are programmatic, though some are not overtly so.

Clarinetti in A

Violoncelli

Example 24.4 Tchaikovsky: Symphony No. 5, mvt. 1, mm. 1–6 of clarinet part, the first presentation of the motto theme.

Example 24.5 Tchaikovsky: Symphony No. 6, mvt. 2, mm. 1–8 of part for violoncelli—a waltzlike theme in $\frac{5}{4}$ meter.

Manfred, based on Byron's drama, was modeled after Berlioz's *Harold en Italie* and *Symphonie fantastique.* The opening theme of *Manfred* appears in each of the work's four movements much in the manner of the *idée fixe* of *Symphonie fantastique* and the theme in *Harold en Italy. Manfred* contains some of Tchaikovsky's finest orchestral writing and deserves to be heard more often. Symphonies Nos. 4, 5, and 6 are frequently performed. Symphony No. 4 is absolute music; subjective programmatic sketches exist for Nos. 5 and 6, the Fifth concerning Tchaikovsky's homosexuality and the Sixth expressing his depressing, fatalistic view of life. Symphony No. 5 is a cyclic work—its motto theme, borrowed from Glinka's *A Life for the Tsar',* is presented at the outset by clarinets in their chalumeau register and appears in all four movements (ex. 24.4). Tchaikovsky's liking for the waltz is apparent in his treatment of some of the thematic material of the first movement, and the third movement is a waltz. The lush Romantic melody of the second movement was used for a popular song in America in the twentieth century. Symphony No. 6, which Tchaikovsky labeled *Pathétique,* was his last work. In general, the coloring of its first and last movements is dark and the mood is gloomy; in the first movement trombones sound a portion of the Russian Orthodox Requiem.

Nationalism is present to some extent in Tchaikovsky's early works and in the operas *Evgeny Onegin* (Eugene Onegin; 1877–78) and *Charodeyka* (The sorceress; 1885–87). Folk songs and other Russian materials appear in some of his other works but not as conscious nationalism. Dance tunes and rhythms,

especially waltzes, characterize all of his music except the sacred works. Tchaikovsky had a gift for writing broad, lyrical melodies of great beauty, which he harmonized and orchestrated effectively. However, such melodies usually are not suitable for thematic development, and this explains, at least in part, the long-standing criticism that one of Tchaikovsky's weaknesses is his inability to manipulate material in thematic development. His music is rhythmically strong, and he enjoyed using unusual meters, e.g., the $\frac{5}{4}$ of the waltzlike second movement of Symphony No. 6 (ex. 24.5).

The textures and harmonies Tchaikovsky used are basically Western European; in his later works he increasingly included seventh chords. His chromaticism is decorative rather than fundamental, but, frequently, in a major key, he built a triad on the flatted submediant. Glinka did this, too. Tchaikovsky was a master of instrumental color and was adept at combining instrumental timbres to achieve the exact tone color he wanted, e.g., the blend of English horn and viola on the second theme in *Romeo and Juliet* and the combinations used to achieve exoticism in *The Nutcracker.*

Tchaikovsky's music has remained popular in Russia and has always had approval and support of the Soviet government.

The music of Alexander Scriabin is in no way related to the new nationalism. Scriabin studied piano diligently from early childhood and became a concert pianist, though he was not a virtuoso. In concerts, he performed works by Bach, Chopin, Liszt, Mendelssohn, and Schumann, as well as his own compositions.

Example 24.6 Beginning of Scriabin's *Poème fantasque*, Op. 45, No. 2. The "Scriabin sixth" chord is indicated by an x.

The music of Chopin and Liszt exercised considerable influence over Scriabin's style, especially in the works written before 1903, e.g., the *Twenty-four Preludes,* Op. 11 (1888–96). As a result of temporary injury to his right hand, Scriabin became interested in developing left-hand technique and composed two pieces for the left hand (Op. 9; 1894). In 1898 he joined the faculty of Moscow Conservatory and wrote a *Rêverie* (orch.) and two symphonies that show some influence of Tchaikovsky.

Around 1900, many persons in Russia were preoccupied with philosophical and mystical ideas. Scriabin became interested in the writings of Nietzsche, then was drawn to the theosophical teachings of Mme Blavatsky and Annie Besant. As Scriabin became increasingly preoccupied with theosophical ideas, his way of life and his compositional style changed. In 1903 he resigned from the Conservatory, left his wife and family, and concertized in Europe and America for the next six years. Many of the piano pieces that he wrote then bear such titles as *Enigme* (Enigma), *Poème languide* (Languid poem), *Caresse dansé* (Danced caress).

For his early music, Scriabin chose keys far removed from C major. Habitually, he began a piece with harmonies remote from the work's tonal center, then moved into it. For a time (c. 1903–07), he gravitated toward C major, perhaps because its key signature lacks sharps and flats. Eventually, in his late works, he dispensed with key signatures entirely and based a work on a few selected pitches that form a set (or series) that he transposed or otherwise manipulated for linear and chordal use. A few of the pieces Scriabin wrote in 1903–7 are decidedly Impressionistic, e.g., *Poème languide* (DWMA203). (Impressionism is discussed on p. 772.) Scriabin's music abounds in fourths and tritones (used both linearly and harmonically) and all kinds of sixth chords—French,

German, and the so-called Scriabin sixth consisting of an augmented triad with an added whole tone (ex. 24.6). He frequently used the ♭II chord. Whole-tone scales with an added nonharmonic pitch also figure prominently in his writing.

Scriabin was a superb miniaturist. This is apparent from his Preludes, the finest of which are Op. 11 and Op. 74, written at the beginning and end of his career (DWMA204, Op. 74 No. 3). For longer works he favored single-movement structure, often with a semblance of sonata form; in multimovement works, his music usually moves from one movement to another without pause. An example is *The Divine Poem* (Symphony No. 3, Op. 43; 1904), in three continuous movements that share thematic material, recurrent or related figurations and harmonies. This work requires a very large orchestra, with four of each woodwind instrument, the horn section doubled, and subdivided strings. *Le poème de l'extase* (Poem of ecstasy; 1905–8) comprises a symphonic poem and a verse poem. It is a transitional work exhibiting a blend of his early tonal and mature styles.

Rimsky-Korsakov and Scriabin had discussed the color possibilities of music, for both composers related musical pitches to colors, but in different ways. Scriabin expressed his views of color-music relationship in *Prométhée, le poème de feu* (Prometheus, poem of fire, Op. 60; 1908–10), for piano, orchestra, textless voices, and a *clavier à luce* (light-keyboard) though such a keyboard of colored lights did not exist. Scriabin's tonality-color scheme is shown in figure 24.4. The music for the light-keyboard is in two-part notation: The lower part (or color), is like pedal point, designed to fill the concert hall with a basic atmosphere of light, whose color changes are intended to portray a "spiritual evolution" taking place in the listeners as the music is perfomed. The upper part reflects actual harmonic changes in the music (ex. 24.7).

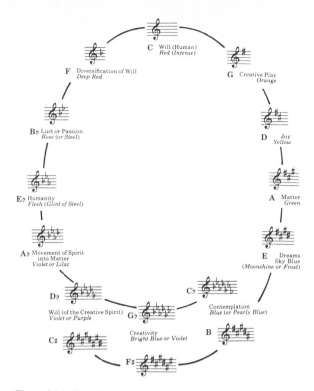

Figure 24.4 Scriabin's color-key scheme for *Prométhée*.
*(Copyright © 1980 Ernst Eulenburg Ltd., London. All Rights
Reserved. Used by permission of European American Music
Distributors Corporation, sole U.S. and Canadian agent for
Ernst Eulenburg, Ltd.)*

Example 24.7 Page 1 of the published score of Scriabin's
Prométhée, depicting Chaos. Notation for the light keyboard
(Luce) is on the top line. *(Copyright © 1980 Ernst Eulenburg
Ltd., London. All Rights Reserved. Used by permission of
European American Music Distributors Corporation, sole U.S.
and Canadian agent for Ernst Eulenburg, Ltd.)*

Scriabin's program for *Prométhée* does not adhere
to the myth about the Titan who, at Zeus's command,
made men from mud and water and so pitied them
that he stole fire (the flame of wisdom) from the gods
and gave it to mankind. Rather, Scriabin filled his
music with theosophical symbolism. The work opens
with a widespread chord (the "mystic chord") sounded
pianissimo for several measures—a representation of
the Mists (or Original Chaos) from which the universe was shaped. Scriabin formed this so-called
mystic chord by selecting six pitches from the natural
harmonic series of C and rearranging them to form a
chord structured in fourths (ex. 24.8). At m. 5 of the
introduction muted horns present the Creative Principle; at m. 21 muted trumpets depict the instant of
fire-giving. In several respects, this introduction resembles the opening of Bruckner's Ninth Symphony.
The exposition of *Prométhée* symbolizes the Dawn of

Human Consciousness, with the piano (mm. 30–31)
portraying Man as microcosm against the macrocosm
of the orchestral music (the Cosmos). *Prométhée* received its first satisfactory performance in September
1975 by the University of Iowa orchestra, with colors
and pitches coordinated according to Scriabin's
scheme and projected by laser apparatus devised by
Lowell Cross.

Example 24.8 Scriabin's mystic chord and its derivation from the harmonic series.

Example 24.9 Scriabin's Sonata No. 5, mm. 263–64, using the mystic chord.

The "mystic chord" appears either literally or transposed in several of Scriabin's mature works, e.g., Sonata No. 5 (ex. 24.9). After 1908, Scriabin seems to have based each of his works on a set of selected pitches and a chord structured from them, or vice versa, certainly an avant-garde procedure at that time. In his mature works he used no key signature—his last five piano sonatas have none—and at times his music approached pantonality/atonality. Harmonies were no longer functional, and in some of the pieces rhythm also dissolved. Forms became more condensed; he worked almost exclusively in single movements. The musical language Scriabin used during his last eight years was unique. His omission of key signatures may have stemmed originally from his knowledge of Dargomïzhky's *The Stone Guest,* and possibly his use of fourths may be related to Musorgsky's daring harmonies. Scriabin had no successors—unless one considers as very remotely related the mysticism of Olivier Messiaen's music.

Czechoslovakia

The country now known as Czechoslovakia was created in 1918 from the Habsburg territories of Bohemia, Moravia, and Slovakia. Slovakia had been conquered by the Magyars in 906 and had become part of Hungary. The kingdom of Bohemia, under strong Přemyslid rulers, dominated Moravia and formally incorporated it as a margraviate in 1029. Bohemia suffered from imperial invasions and Hussite wars during the fifteenth century but remained autonomous, even after the Habsburg Holy Roman Emperor, Ferdinand I, was crowned King of Bohemia (1527). During the sixteenth century, emperors and nobility maintained excellent musical chapels at their castles in Prague. However, in 1620, after the Habsburgs defeated the Bohemian nobility at the Battle of

Blaník, the Bohemians and Moravians lost their autonomy and were taken into the Habsburg Empire as virtual provinces. Moreover, they were forced to adopt the imperial language (German) and religion (Catholicism). The seat of the government, the Imperial Court at Vienna, attracted the leading Bohemian musicians. Through the years there was an undercurrent of resentment in the Bohemian people that did not really surface until the nationalistic movement in the nineteenth century. The Bohemian language (which eventually became the Czech language) was not used by musicians until the beginning of the nineteenth century. However, its use in the arts was openly encouraged in 1862 when a Provisional Theater for Czech drama and music opened in Prague and Count Harrach sponsored a competition for operas and libretti. In May 1919 it was formally decreed that "Czech" (Bohemian) should be the official language of "Czecho-Slovakia." In Moravia there was growing interest in folk song before the middle of the nineteenth century. In 1835 František Sušil published the first of his collections of Moravian folk songs. His work was continued by František Bartoš and Leoš Janáček. Czechoslovakia's first great nationalist composer was the Bohemian Bedřich Smetana.

Bedřich Smetana

Bedřich Smetana (1824–84) was raised in a German-language household, attended schools that gave instruction in German, and did not learn to read and write the Bohemian language until the 1860s. His training in music began early; his father taught him to play violin and he had piano lessons from local musicians. He was sent to the Academic Gymnasium in Prague, but instead of studying, he attended concerts and composed chamber music (lost) that he played

Bedřich Smetana. *(Historical Pictures Service.)*

with friends. In Prague he met Liszt. When Smetana's father learned what was happening, he sent Bedřich to the gymnasium in Plzeň. There, in 1840–43, Smetana studied diligently, but he also played piano for dancing at homes of the wealthy. At that time he met Kateřina Kolářová, with whom he played piano duets and for whom he composed many piano solos and duets (lost); in 1849 he and Kateřina married.

Smetana decided to become a professional musician and moved to Prague. From 1844 to 1847 he was resident piano teacher to the family of Count Thun; in their home he met several noted composers, including Clara and Robert Schumann. During those years, Smetana studied harmony, theory, and composition. He was a virtuoso pianist, and could play the most difficult works of Liszt and Weber, yet his concerts in Bohemia were not well attended. Nor did he have success when he opened a music institute. He had been composing piano music and dedicated *Six characteristic pieces* (Op. 1; 1847–48) to Liszt, who arranged for their publication.

The June 1848 Revolution in Prague failed—the Bohemians were not even able to secure official use of their own language. Smetana was unhappy with the political situation. Moreover, his *Triumph-*

Symphonie (1853–54), written to honor Franz Joseph, and containing Haydn's "Emperor" hymn, had gone unnoticed by the emperor. In 1856 Smetana went to Sweden, where he concertized as soloist and in chamber music groups, accepted directorship of a choral society, opened a singing school for ladies, and composed some character pieces and dance music, especially polkas.

By this time, Smetana and Liszt had become friends; Smetana had visited Liszt in Weimar and had heard some of his symphonic poems. Those works inspired Smetana to write three symphonic poems based on dramas: *Richard III* (1852; Shakespeare); *Wallensteins Lager* (1859; Schiller); and *Hakon Jarl* (1859–60; Oehlenschläger). Each symphonic poem is directly related to the drama and presents musically a series of episodes from it, with descriptive themes representing the important characters. The single-movement *Hakon Jarl* proceeds through four sections that follow the structural pattern of a four-movement symphony (allegro, slow section, scherzo, finale).

Kateřina died in 1859; the following year Smetana married Bettina Ferdinandova. He considered living permanently in Sweden, but his patriotism for Bohemia was too strong. In 1861, when he learned of plans for a Provisional Theater for Czech plays and operas and of a competition for a national opera, Smetana returned to Prague. There had not been many Czech operas—František Škroup's (1801–62) *Drátnik* (The Tinker; 1826) was the first; its style is Mozartean. Jiři Macourek's *Žižka's Oak* (1847), concerning the warrior Jan Žižka, is more nationalistic.

Smetana's opera *Braniboři v Čechách* (The Brandenburgers in Bohemia; 1863) has a historical plot (with some inaccuracies for the sake of greater drama). It concerns a time when Bohemia was overrun with German troops and when there was a young prince with a ruthless guardian. In some respects, the plot resembles *Boris Godunov. The Brandenburgers in Bohemia* is sung throughout; the orchestral music is continuous, and the music does not sound like folk song. Smetana's opera was awarded the prize, but the critics, expecting folklike entertainment and receiving drama, accused Smetana of being Wagnerian.

Smetana believed that composers of nationalistic music should not adhere strictly to folk songs but should employ contemporary compositional techniques and forms. He did a great deal to promote late nineteenth-century music as well as nationalism in Bohemia.

Smetana designed his second opera for entertainment. Originally written in two acts, with spoken dialogue, the comedy *Prodana nevěsta* (The bartered bride; 1863–66) was a success from the outset. It is the only one of Smetana's operas to become popular outside Czechoslovakia. In 1870 Smetana expanded it to three acts, with recitatives replacing the spoken dialogue. Part of the opera's charm is its apparent simplicity, with melodies reminiscent of Bohemian folk song and realistic characters with individual personalities. There is a drinking chorus, and there are national dances—polka, *furiant, skočná*. Smetana's achievement is all the more remarkable when one realizes that at that time he did not know the Bohemian language well.

From 1866 to 1874 Smetana was principal conductor of the Provisional Theater. He increased the repertoire considerably, adding 16 Czech operas (only 2 were his own) and 42 major works by European composers. After the diversion of *The Bartered Bride,* Smetana returned to his original aim: to compose a series of operas based on national history and legend that would feed nationalistic sentiments and glorify his native land. For his next opera he chose a subject from legend, *Dalibor* (1865–67). Set in the fifteenth century, the opera tells the story of the knight Dalibor who was imprisoned in the Tower because he killed the Burgrave to avenge the death of the minstrel Zdeněk. Daliborka Tower still stands and is pointed out to visitors to Czechoslovakia. In *Dalibor* Smetana achieved unity through recurring themes and used thematic transformation effectively. Dalibor's theme undergoes many transformations and appears throughout the opera. Smetana had used thematic transformation previously, in the symphonic poem *Wallensteins Lager.*

Smetana's fourth opera, *Libuše* (1869–72), was designed to commemorate the founding of the first Bohemian dynasty. Smetana specified that *Libuše* not be placed in opera repertoire but be reserved for special national festivals and commemorations. The opera relates the circumstances of the marriage of Queen Libuše, founder of the Přemyslid dynasty, who prophesied future greatness for Bohemia and envisioned a series of heroes. *Libuše* was first performed at the opening of the National Theater in 1881. So effective is Smetana's nationalism in this opera that its performance was banned while Nazis occupied the country and again when USSR took over Czechoslovakia. The music of *Libuše* reflects Wagner's influence, for musical themes are associated with characters in the manner of the *Leitmotif. Libuše* is a magnificent work. Despite Smetana's directive, its performance should not be reserved for special national commemorations.

While working on *Libuše,* Smetana was inspired to write *Má vlast* (My fatherland; 1872–80), a cycle of six symphonic poems depicting various aspects of Czech legend, history, and scenery: (1) *Vyšehrad,* the old royal castle; (2) *Vltava,* the Moldau River; (3) *Šarka,* the legendary Amazon heroine; (4) *Z českých luhuv a háju* (From Bohemian fields and groves); (5) *Tábor,* the city of Tabor and Hussite events there; and (6) *Blaník,* White Mountain. Smetana's programs for the symphonic poems differ somewhat from the ones usually printed with the music and the recordings. Two principal themes used in *Vyšehrad* recur in the cycle; in fact, these themes open and close the cycle. In the first symphonic poem whole-tone progressions are used. *Vltava* (DWMA205) is a picture of nature with fleeting glimpses of Czech customs and history revealed as one follows the course of the river from its sources in two tiny streams in the Šumava forest until it joins the Elbe beyond Prague. Both *Tábor* and *Blaník* are based on the fifteenth-century chorale, *All ye warriors of God,* one of the oldest Hussite hymns. Smetana dedicated *Má vlast* to Prague. It has become traditional for a leading Czech orchestra under the baton of a distinguished Czech conductor to perform *Má vlast* in its entirety annually on May 12, the anniversary of Smetana's death, to open the Prague Spring Festival. While working on *Vyšehrad,* Smetana's hearing began to fail, and before he had completed *Má vlast* he was totally deaf.

He did not confine himself to work on *Má vlast* but wrote other things at the same time. His next three operas are not particularly nationalistic, though they contain some actual folk songs. *Dvě vdovy* (The Two Widows; 1873–74) is a comedy, originally French, but with alterations that transplant it to Bohemia; *Hubička* (The Kiss; 1876) is romantic, with humor and pathos; and *Tajemství* (The Secret; 1877–78) is a comedy about a secret that was broadcast. *The Secret* is richer in songs than *Hubička;* some of the drinking songs are clever. Pilgrims, in a night procession to the chapel, sing a chorus written in folk style.

Smetana's last completed opera, *Čertova stěna* (The Devil's Wall; 1879–82), is a satire directed against those in the church who scheme to get power and wealth. There is comedy and also Romanticism of the type Weber used in *Der Freischütz.* Themes and motives are associated with the characters in the manner of *Leitmotif.* Beneš the hermit and Rarach, his devil counterpart, are identical—the two characters have the same theme—and are portrayed as being present at the same time, but only one is visible to the other characters and to the audience. The dual role is challenging for a singer-actor. The Devil's Wall is a Czech landmark, a great barrier of rocks that looks like piers of a ruined bridge stretching across the Moldau at Vyší Brod; according to legend, it was thrown across the river by the devil. In all of Smetana's operas except the original version of *The Bartered Bride,* he used continuous orchestral music, *accompagnato* recitative, declamatory arioso, and aria.

The long list of Smetana's compositions includes other orchestral music (absolute as well as program), sacred and secular choral works, a few solo songs with piano accompaniment, and some chamber music. His two string quartets, in E minor and D minor respectively, are excellent. The first quartet is autobiographical, *Z mého života* (From my life).

Smetana was concerned primarily with establishing a repertoire of nationalistic music for his native land, and he did so. He cared little whether it was performed outside Czech boundaries. Antonin Dvořák (1841–1904) was also a sincere patriot and nationalist composer, but achieved his greatest success outside Bohemia.

Antonin Dvořák. *(Shaffer Archives.)*

Antonin Dvořák

Dvořák's ancestors were butchers and innkeepers and he was expected to follow one of those trades. Nevertheless, he learned the German language and had lessons on viola and organ and in music theory. He assisted in his father's butcher shop for only a short time, then decided, at whatever cost, he would be a musician. In 1857 he entered Prague Organ School to train as church musician. When he graduated in 1859, he had his certificate and second prize but no church position, no piano, and no money for purchasing study scores. He was an excellent violist and found work in a small orchestra playing in restaurants and for dances. In 1862 he was hired as violist in the opera orchestra at the Provisional Theater. There he worked under Smetana's direction and learned a great deal about nineteenth-century music by performing it.

By 1865 Dvořák had composed two operas, two symphonies, a Mass (B♭ major; lost), a song cycle, a 'cello concerto with piano accompaniment, some chamber music, and some piano pieces. Smetana encouraged him by performing a few of those works, but much of Dvořák's music was rejected, a fact that caused him to become extremely self-critical of his writing. In 1874 he submitted 15 compositions in the Austrian competition for poor young artists and was awarded the prize. Brahms, who was one of the judges, influenced Simrock to publish some of Dvořák's works, and Simrock commissioned others. In 1878 he published more than a dozen of Dvořák's compositions. Soon other publishers began to request his music. Brahms also promoted Dvořák's career by interesting Europeans in performing his works. Dvořák's chamber music, especially, was frequently performed by reputable European ensembles such as the Joachim Quartet. By 1880 Dvořák had written four more symphonies, a piano concerto, a violin concerto, the first set of orchestral *Slavonic Dances,* the *Slavonic Rhapsodies,* ten string quartets and numerous other chamber music works, many keyboard pieces, a *Stabat mater,* other sacred and secular choral works, some songs, and four more operas. His one-act comic operas with plots about peasants were especially popular. From time to time, Dvořák was asked to write a German opera for performance in Vienna, but he always refused, usually on the ground that he was a Czech.

Dvořák spent much time during 1884–92 traveling throughout Europe, participating in concerts as conductor and violist. In 1884–85 he composed for the London Philharmonic what he considered his finest symphony, No. 7, in D minor. That London commission was, to him, a definite challenge. Symphony No. 7 follows traditional four-movement structure: sonata-form first movement, a melancholy Poco Adagio second, a Scherzo resembling a *furiant* third, and a powerful Finale that concludes on a major chord. From beginning to end, the symphony is filled with intense emotional expression. Technically, it shows Dvořák to be a master of thematic manipulation; in the first movement, the development is concise. Dvořák was correct—the Seventh *is* his finest symphony, but his Symphony No. 9 is far more popular.

In 1891 Dvořák received an honorary Ph.D. from the University of Prague and an honorary Mus.D. from Cambridge University. He composed, on com-

Example 24.10 Dvořák: Symphony No. 9, "From the New World," mvt. 1, theme 1, the motto theme.

mission, a Requiem Mass for performance at Birmingham (October 1891) and a *Te Deum laudamus* for performance in New York at celebrations commemorating the fourth centenary of the discovery of America (October 1892). Dvořák came to New York in 1892 to serve as director of the National Conservatory of Music and spent most of the next three years in the United States. During his holidays, he visited Bohemian communities throughout the country, especially that at Spillville, Iowa. He became interested in the music of black Americans, too. How much Dvořák's music was influenced by that of black Americans cannot be determined, for previously he had used "Scottish snap" rhythm, minor keys with flatted seventh degree, and some pentatonic scales. While in the United States, Dvořák was inspired to compose several works that are considered "American," including Symphony No. 9, *Z nového světa* (From the New World; E minor; 1893); the "American" String Quartet (No. 12, F major; 1893); and "American" String Quintet (E♭ major; 2 vln., 2 vla., vcl.; 1893). Symphony No. 9 is a cyclic work; its motto theme appears in every movement (ex. 24.10). A melody closely resembling the spiritual *Swing low, sweet chariot* is heard in the first movement (DWMA206). The broad, lyrical melody of the Largo has been adapted as a song and is popularly known as "Goin' home." In the Finale, themes from the previous movements are recalled, in the manner of Beethoven's Ninth Symphony's Finale. Despite the evidence of American-inspired themes, such factors as modal melodies, use of the flatted seventh scale degree, and dronelike accompaniment lend a Bohemian flavor to Dvořák's Ninth Symphony. Dvořák wrote for the standard symphony orchestra of his time, sometimes including English horn, but seldom using harp, bass clarinet, or contrabassoon. He thoroughly understood the timbres and techniques of orchestral instruments and used them effectively.

Between 1895 and 1904 Dvořák composed his 13th and 14th string quartets, a 'cello concerto, his first symphonic poems, some songs, and five operas. The two quartets, in G major and A♭ major, are some of Dvořák's finest chamber music. In his last three operas, *Čert a Káča* (The Devil and Kate; 1899), *Rusalka* (Nymph; 1900), and *Armida* (1902–3), he applied some Wagnerian principles.

From time to time, the influence of other composers—Mendelssohn, Schubert, Wagner, for example—can be detected in Dvořák's music, but Brahms exerted the greatest influence on his career. All of Dvořák's music, whether program or absolute, contains elements that mark it Bohemian. National characteristics appear in his dance pieces, in the rhythms of dance movements or sections of his string quartets and other chamber music, in his programmatic overtures, in the subjects of some of his operas, and in many of his songs. Certainly, one of Dvořák's important contributions was making the music of Bohemian composers known outside the boundaries of his own country.

Leoš Janáček

Like his grandfather and father, Leoš Janáček (1854–1928) became a teacher and musician. He attended the choir school at the Augustinian monastery in Old Brno, Moravia, at a time when the school was under the influence of the Cecelian movement; no instrumental music was taught, and vocal music was *a cappella*. He spent three years at the German College, completed the teaching curriculum at Czech Teachers' Institute, and taught without pay for the required two years at the Institute School. Then he studied for two years at Prague Organ School. In 1875 he returned to Brno to conduct the monastery choir and the middle-class all-male choral society. Soon he admitted women to the choral society, and by supplementing that group with the monastery choir and Institute pupils he had sufficient forces to perform large choral works.

Janáček's earliest works were liturgical pieces and a Mass (lost) written c. 1870; in 1877 he composed an *a cappella* offertory *Exaudi Deus* and a *Suite* for string orchestra. He decided he needed further study in composition, obtained leave from the Teachers' Institute, and spent 1879–80 in Leipzig,

Leoš Janáček.

studying at the university and privately; in 1880–81 he studied at Vienna Conservatory. Then he returned to Brno, founded and became director of an Organ School at which other music courses were taught also. Not until 1885 did he resume composing. He dedicated to Dvořák a set of four choruses for male voices, works whose bold modulations shocked Dvořák. Next Janáček composed the opera *Šarka* (1887–88), which was not performed until 1925.

In 1888 Janáček helped František Bartoš (1837–1906) collect folk songs in northern Moravia and assisted in preparing that collection for publication. Janáček made arrangements of some of the folk song melodies, e.g., *V Lašské tance* (Dances from Lašsko), and used some folk songs in several compositions: *Suite* for orchestra (Op. 3, 1891), a folk ballet, and the one-act opera *Počátek románu* (The beginning of a romance; 1891). The opera music was chiefly folk dances with vocal lines added.

Janáček's next opera, *Jenůfa* (also called *Její pastorkyňa,* Her foster-daughter; 1894–1903), is quite different from his first two, which are number operas. In *Jenůfa* Janáček relied heavily on musical monologue; there are some choruses but few duets and ensembles. Moreover, the folk melodies he incorporated are well integrated and do not dominate the music.

In 1904 Janáček resigned from the Teachers' Institute. During the next 12 years he wrote three more operas, a Mass and several other liturgical settings, some secular choruses, a few cantatas, a symphonic poem, and a little chamber music. Real recognition did not come to Janáček until 1915–16 when the Prague National Opera accepted *Jenůfa* into its repertoire.

Among the excellent works Janáček created during the last decade of his life are the operas *Kat'a Kabanová* (1919–21), *Přihody Lišky Bystroušky* (The adventures of the vixen Bystrouška; 1921–23), *Věc Makropulos* (The Makropulos affair; 1923–25), and *Z mrtvého domu* (From the house of the dead; 1927–28). In *The adventures of the vixen Bystrouška,* he specified use of children's voices, because of the animals, but in the other operas he did not want children's voices used. In his vocal music, especially in his late works, he showed decided preference for soprano and high tenor parts and tended to use alto solo voices sparingly. While he was writing *Jenůfa* he studied carefully the patterns of speaking voices to determine what he called their "speech-melody"—the rhythms and pitch inflections of voices in normal speech—and he studied the changes various moods and emotions caused in those speech patterns. He incorporated what he learned into the writing of the musical monologues in his operas. He wanted to set prose, rather than poetic, libretti. Much of the time, the orchestra and the vocal lines have different themes—they are seemingly detached from one another—yet, at the important points, they merge and are united lyrically and rhythmically.

After 1905, Janáček preferred to notate his music without key signatures; his string quartets, violin sonata, and other works do not have specified keys. Because of his interest in Moravian folk songs, he was predisposed toward modality and pentatonic scales. Also borrowed from Moravian folk song are the use of mirror rhythms and the technique of immediately repeating a phrase or melody but displacing the rhythm in the repetition.

One of Janáček's outstanding choral works is *Glagolská mše* (Glagolitic Mass; 1928), setting an Old Slavic text. The *Mass* is extremely difficult to sing, for the tenor parts are very high. Janáček's finest instrumental works are the two string quartets (No. 1, 1923; No. 2, 1928); the Violin Sonata (1921); *Mlada* (Youth; 1924; wind sextet); and *Sinfonietta* (1926), his last completed orchestral work. *Sinfonietta* exemplifies his technique of creating sections through expansion and variation of a motive and forming movements from several short sections each of which is repeated. At first glance, the score indicates a large orchestra heavy with brass: 9 trumpets in G, 3 trumpets in F, 2 bass trumpets in B♭, 4 tenor tubas, 1 tuba. However, each of the five movements is scored for a different combination of instruments, and no single movement employs all of them. The symphony *Dunaj* (Danube, 1923–28), unfinished when Janáček died, was completed in 1948 by his pupil Osvald Chlubna (1893–1971) and was given its North American première by the St. Louis Symphony in May 1988.

As a composer, Janáček was nationalistic and avant-garde. The editions of Moravian folk songs he collaborated on are the most authentic of Bartoš's set. Janáček's work with Moravian folk materials stimulated further research in Czechoslovakia and elsewhere. The Organ School he founded was the basis for Brno Conservatory. In addition, he contributed some excellent music to the repertoire in several genres.

Scandinavia

Sweden

In Sweden, during the first half of the nineteenth century, most of the musical activity was in the hands of the middle class. Music societies were established in major cities, and in mid-century three music publishing firms were active. By 1866 Stockholm Conservatory was providing a good music curriculum. Around mid-century, quite a few Swedish musicians studied at Leipzig Conservatory and introduced Romantic elements into a Swedish style that had been primarily Classic. In the late nineteenth century, the outstanding Swedish composer was Johan A. Söderman (1832–76). He wrote much incidental music for approximately 80 plays. Most of his other extant works are vocal; a few orchestral pieces, a piano quartet, and a piano fantasia survive. Söderman's works are historically significant because of his incorporation of stylistic elements from folk music—rhythms of folk dance, melodic and harmonic details that give the music authentic Swedish flavor.

The first symphony orchestras were established in Sweden c. 1900. Almost all of the music of Hugo Alfvén (1872–1960) is programmatic, much of it descriptive of Sweden and colored by folk music elements. *Midsommarvaka* (Midsummer vigil; orch.; 1903) is an example. He wrote five symphonies; in the finale of Symphony No. 2 and in the scherzo of Symphony No. 5 he used the melody of the Swedish chorale *Jag går mot döden var jag går* (I go toward death wherever I go). Pianist-composer Wilhelm Stenhammar (1871–1927) wrote in a style influenced by Beethoven and Brahms, tinged with Swedish color but without quotations from folk material. His orchestral *Serenade* (F major; 1911–13, rev. 1919) contains some Impressionistic passages.

Norway

Norway achieved independence from Denmark in 1814 but was united with Sweden from 1814 to 1905. During the nineteenth century, Norwegian nationalism increased, with periodic agitation for independence. Virtuoso violinist Ole Bull (1810–80), in addition to concertizing throughout the world, published a collection of folk song melodies arranged for piano (1852) and helped found the Norwegian Society for the Advancement of the National Element in Art and Literature (1859). During the last decade of his life, Bull spent winters in the United States and summers in Norway. Many authors—Thackeray, Ibsen, George Sand, Mark Twain, and others—were intrigued by his playing and his personality and mentioned him in their writings. Few of Bull's compositions were published, and many of his works are lost. Most of those that survive are technically difficult—some are in four-part polyphony playable only with a special violin bridge or bow. In some of his ensemble pieces, e.g., *Norges fjelde* (Norway's mountains; 1832) he included the Norwegian Hardanger fiddle, a kind of violin with sympathetic strings, and incorporated some Norwegian folk songs and the *slåtter,* a Norwegian dance. Other works contain folk tunes or melodies with folklike character.

Otto Winter-Hjelm (1837–1931) was instrumental in founding the first Norwegian music academy (1864). He composed much music, both vocal and instrumental, and is credited with being the first Norwegian to write symphonies (No. 1, 1861; No. 2, 1862, first perf. 1916).

Richard Nordraak (1842–66) was, with Grieg, one of the founders of Euterpe, a music society formed in 1864 to promote the works of young Scandinavian composers. Nordraak's music is strongly nationalistic. He composed the Norwegian national anthem, *Ja, vi elsker dette landet* (Yes, we love this land; 1864), originally written for unaccompanied male chorus. His extant works constitute six songs, five *a cappella* choruses, some piano solos, and a fragment of a symphony movement.

Norway's most important nationalist-Romantic composer was Edvard Hagerup Grieg (1843–1907). He had his first music lessons from his mother, Gesine Hagerup Grieg, an excellent amateur pianist who performed a great deal in and around Bergen. Edvard's father was British consul at Bergen, and musical gatherings were held regularly at the Grieg home. Edvard began to write music c. 1857; his piano playing attracted the attention of Ole Bull, who influenced the Griegs to send Edvard to Leipzig Conservatory. Edvard detested the pedantic methods at that school but enjoyed the concert life of Leipzig.

Until 1864 Grieg's musical associations were principally German and Danish; he knew almost nothing about Norwegian nationalism and Norwegian folk music until he spent the summer of 1864 with Ole Bull at Osterøy. After meeting Nordraak in 1865, Grieg determined to write nationalistic-Romantic Norwegian music. His first compositions influenced by Norwegian folk idioms are *Humoresker* (4 Humoresques, Op. 6, piano; 1865). The Piano Sonata, Op. 7 (E minor; 1865) and piano/violin Sonata No. 1 (F major; 1865) are not nationalistic, but national traits reappear in the first set of *Lyric Pieces* (Op. 12, piano; 1867). Grieg's most important and one of his finest works for piano is his *Ballade in Form von Variationen über eine norwegische Melodie* (Ballade in the form of variations on a Norwegian melodie, G minor, Op. 24; 1875–76), theme and variations on the folk song *Den nordlandske bondestand* (The northern peasantry). Some of his best work is the incidental music he wrote for plays, especially the 23 pieces for Ibsen's *Peer Gynt* (1874–75)—music for solo voices, chorus, and orchestra. When heard consecutively, in the order in which they occur in the play, those 23 pieces have tremendous dramatic impact. This is not apparent in the arrangement of the 8 pieces selected to form the two orchestral *Peer Gynt Suites.*

Other significant works by Grieg include the Piano Concerto (A minor, 1868); ten sets of *Lyric Pieces, Folkelivsbilleder* (Pictures from country life, Op. 19; 1870–71); three piano/violin sonatas (F major, 1865; G major, 1867; C minor, 1886–87); and the string quartet in G minor (1877–78). The third piano/violin sonata contains some Impressionistic passages and some irregular phrasing. That sonata is remarkable for its overall unity and for the thematic concentration in its first movement. The string quartet was the model for Debussy's string quartet, also in G minor (1893). Grieg, in his quartet, used chromatically altered chords within functional tonal harmony, occasionally wrote parallel chords and chord streams, and sustained chords as pedals for moving parts. Much of the time the participants play double-stops and chords. The entire quartet is based on a bit of melody from the song *Spillemaend* (Minstrel), one of the six settings of Ibsen's poems comprising Grieg's Op. 25 (1876).

National characteristics appearing in Grieg's works from time to time are the Hardanger fiddle, drone basses, modal tendencies in melodies and sometimes in harmonies, particularly Lydian and Aeolian, and national dance rhythms, especially the *slåtter* in which $\frac{3}{4}$ and $\frac{6}{8}$ meter rhythms are combined.

The principal Danish composer at the end of the nineteenth century was Carl Nielsen (1865–1931), son of painter Niels Jørgensen. In accordance with Danish custom, Carl's surname was derived from his father's given name (son of Niels = Nielsen) and was so recorded at his baptism. Nielsen's parents were amateur musicians, so he heard a great deal of music at home. He learned to play violin, cornet, and piano and as a child enjoyed imitating on his violin the songs his mother sang to him. He became interested in Bach's *Das wohltemperirte Klavier* and played the string quartets of Haydn and Mozart with his friends. In 1884–86, Nielsen studied at Copenhagen Conservatory and concentrated on violin. Though Mozart was the composer Nielsen most admired, the few compositions that he wrote before 1886 reflect Haydn's style.

In 1889 Nielsen was employed as a second violinist in the royal chapel; there he became acquainted with Wagner's music by playing it. In 1890–91 he traveled in Europe; in Paris he met Anne Marie Brodersen, sculptress, and they married. When they returned to Denmark, he completed his Symphony No. 1 (G minor, Op. 7; 1890–92); in it Brahms's influence is apparent.

Around 1900 Nielsen's personal compositional style began to emerge, and within the next decade it was well established. That style is rooted in Classicism and was strongly influenced by the village music he heard as a child. Its basic structural elements are melody and rhythm, frequently, a driving rhythm. His early works show his preference for tonal functional harmony with rather fast harmonic rhythm. In the 1890s, in an endeavor to create music that had more intense expression, he began to use what he termed "extended tonality"—to consider all 12 semitones within a key as being autonomous, each pitch directly related to the tonic. This allowed free use of chromaticism within a key. Thus, Nielsen regarded his music as being in a certain key but he could modulate freely from one key to another because he was not dealing with functional harmony. Intervals, too, were considered equal—there was no functional difference between major and minor thirds or between major and minor sevenths. Because of this, his music sometimes sounds quite modal. Polytonal and atonal passages appear in his late works. He created unaccompanied themes first and preferred concise motives to melodies; the themes then dictated the harmonies. He was adept at motivic development, thematic variation and transformation, and was skilled at counterpoint. Nielsen's treatment of phrasing underwent change also. In his early works, he used symmetrical phrases, usually four measures long; gradually, he worked toward the metrically free phrasing that appears in his late works. Polyphony became more and more important to Nielsen, and in his Symphonies No. 4 ("The Inextinguishable"; 1916) and No. 5 (1922) he wrote "group polyphony," treating groups of orchestral instruments polyphonically.

Nielsen composed operas, incidental music for plays, cantatas, songs, choral works (both *a cappella* and orchestrally accompanied), chamber music, concertos, and orchestral works. His finest orchestral work and the one that best exemplifies his mature style is *Symphony No. 3: Sinfonia espansiva* (Expansive symphony, Op. 27; 1910–11). His string quartets, Op. 14 (E♭ major; 1898) and Op. 44 (F major; 1919), are excellent; his best-known work is probably Symphony No. 5 (Op. 50, 1922).

Finland

Finland had no significant composers of art music until after 1750; then, the composers studied in Germany and wrote music that was German in style. At the time of the Reformation, Finland had become Lutheran, and the chorale occupies a central place in Finnish church Services. In 1809, Finland became a grand duchy in the Russian empire, and in Finland, as elsewhere, there were strong feelings of nationalism. One of the political issues in the 1890s was use of Finnish as the national language. Not until 1917 did Finland achieve independence.

The two leading composers in Finland in the 1880s were Robert Kajanus (1856–1933) and Martin Wegelius (1846–1906), natives of Helsinki. Wegelius was influential in the area of music education, founded Helsinki Music College (1882), and taught Jean Sibelius. Kajanus founded the first permanent orchestra in Helsinki (1882). He, too, influenced Sibelius's career, for it was his symphonic poem *Aino* (1885), based on Finland's epic poem *Kalevala,* that inspired Sibelius to compose music based on the *Kalevala.* Kajanus's orchestra first performed Sibelius's *Kullervo,* and Kajanus commissioned other works from Sibelius, and, with the Helsinki orchestra, recorded several of Sibelius's symphonies.

Jean Sibelius (1865–1957) was born in a small village in south central Finland. His father, a doctor, died when Jean was very young, and the three Sibelius children, all of whom had some musical talent, were raised by their mother and grandmother. Sibelius received his general education in Finnish schools and did not begin serious study of the violin until he was 14. He played in the family trio and hoped to become a virtuoso performer but never attained that goal. His first compositions were chamber music: a violin/'cello piece written when he was 10; a Piano Trio (A minor), a Piano Quartet (E minor), and a violin/piano Sonata (D minor), all written in 1881–82.

Jean Sibelius.

In 1885 Sibelius enrolled at Helsinki University to study law but soon abandoned that to study harmony, counterpoint, and fugue with Wegelius. Sibelius had his heart set on a performing career and auditioned for orchestral posts as far away as Vienna. He was attracted to the music of contemporary Russian composers, especially Tchaikovsky (whose music Wegelius did not like), and planned to study with Rimsky-Korsakov in 1889. When that did not materialize, Sibelius went to Berlin for a counterpoint course. There he heard a great deal of orchestral and chamber music and attended many opera performances. His hopes to study with Brahms were dashed when Brahms refused to receive him. Sibelius then went to Vienna, where he studied composition, drank a great deal, and, though he had little money, hobnobbed with high society. Up to that time, with the exception of three songs and a couple of piano pieces, all of his compositions were chamber music.

From the time he was a child in school, Sibelius had been interested in Swedish nature poetry, Norse legend, and the saga of Finland, the *Kalevala.* After hearing Kajanus conduct a performance of his *Aino* in Berlin, Sibelius decided to write some orchestral music, turned to the *Kalevala* for inspiration, and wrote *Kullervo,* a very large five-movement symphony whose central movement, "Kullervo and his Sister," incorporates soprano and baritone solos and male chorus. From the quality of the vocal writing and the dramatic propulsion of that movement, it is apparent that Sibelius could have written opera, had he chosen to do so. He did write many songs and fine choral works. Sibelius's feelings of nationalism were strong and deep-seated; he expressed them musically by describing his country and by depicting its legends, rather than by consciously incorporating folk materials into his music. He was interested in folk music, and its rhythms and modality sometimes colored his compositions, but he did not collect folk music and he did not deliberately use it in his works. Thus he differs from other nationalists of his time.

After the première of *Kullervo* (1892) Sibelius was recognized as Finland's leading composer. His next orchestral works were *En saga* (1892); two tone poems *Skogrsået* (The wood nymph; 1894) and *Vårsång* (Spring song; 1895), both unpublished; and *Lemminkäis-sarja* (Lemminkäinen suite; 1895). That suite is a powerful symphonic work, consisting of four large movements: *Lemminkäinen and the island maidens, Lemminkäinen in Tuonela, The swan of Tuonela,* and *Lemminkäinen's return.* Sibelius subjected the suite to numerous revisions and withheld some of the movements from publication for years. Usually, *The Swan of Tuonela* is performed as an independent piece.

Late in 1897 the Finnish government awarded Sibelius a small state pension, in acknowledgement of his musical achievements, then extended it to a life pension. In 1899, for a pageant presented at the Press Pension Celebrations, Sibelius wrote *Scènes historiques* (Historical scenes) and *Finlandia.* At that time, Finnish patriotism was running high, and some of the celebrations amounted to rallies. *Finlandia* fueled the patriotic fires considerably. A portion of that symphonic poem has become a hymn and is included in many Protestant hymnals (ex. 24.11).

Sibelius continued to write music based on the *Kalevala* but did not confine his instrumental writing to programmatic works. He composed seven symphonies, some overtures and other orchestral pieces, an excellent and difficult violin concerto (D minor; 1903), two violin/piano sonatas (D minor, F major), almost two dozen other works for violin and piano, some string quartets and other chamber music, incidental music for plays, numerous songs, and many choral works. His last string quartet, *Voces intimae* (Intimate voices, D minor; 1909), is excellent. Important programmatic orchestral works, besides those already mentioned, are the fantasia *Pohjolan tytär* (Pohjola's daughter; 1906) and *Tapiola* (1926). The

Example 24.11 (*a*) Sibelius: *Finlandia,* theme 3. (*b*) First phrase of a hymn based on theme 3 of *Finlandia.*

finest of his symphonies is No. 6, but it is seldom performed, perhaps because it is neither heroic nor majestic and on first hearing seems totally different from the others.

Sibelius's symphonic achievements are summed up in his Symphony No. 7 (C major, Op. 105; 1924), which he called *Fantastica sinfonica* (Fantastic symphony). It is a highly unified work whose single movement cannot be squeezed into any stereotyped formal pattern. The music undergoes changes in character and tempo, suggesting now a scherzo, then a slow movement or an intermezzo, merged so skillfully that one can only approximate the point at which the changes actually occur. Sibelius's mastery of thematic metamorphosis is evident; often he selected minor figurations for elevation to positions of greater importance, for instance, choosing a transitional figure for extensive development. One theme in the symphony seems to have special significance—a majestic trombone passage in C major that is presented three times, each time becoming stronger and nobler.

In general, Sibelius's music is sombre, serious, grand, majestic, and sweeping at times. In some works he wrote phrases seemingly conversational between two solo instruments and long solo passages. Some of the compositions he wrote c. 1908–9, when he underwent several operations for suspected throat cancer and had to give up alcohol and cigar smoking, are austere, with passages as bleak as frozen tundra. In 1914 he visited the United States, taught at New England Conservatory, Boston, for a short time, and composed *Aallottaret* (The oceansides). During World

War I, the October 1918 Revolution in Finland, and the ensuing civil war instigated by Finnish communists, Sibelius composed very little. In the 1920s he wrote much music but only four major works: his last two symphonies, incidental music for Shakespeare's *The Tempest,* and *Tapiola.* After 1929 he composed nothing. He was not sympathetic with the kinds of music composers were writing, except for that of Bartók. Sibelius especially disliked the music of contemporary French composers. Though he promised an eighth symphony, it was not forthcoming; if he worked on one, he destroyed it. In the 1930s, his orchestral writing was influential in northern Europe, England, and America, e.g., it is evident in Samuel Barber's First Symphony (1935–36), a one-movement work.

German and Austrian Composers

During the last decades of Romanticism in Germany and Austria, significant contributions were made by three major composers: Hugo Wolf (1860–1903), Gustav Mahler (1860–1911), and Richard Strauss (1864–1949).

Hugo Wolf

The composition of Lieder, developed by Schubert and Schumann, and to which Brahms made valuable contributions, was brought to another peak by Hugo Wolf. Wolf aspired to write opera—he greatly admired Wagner—and did not want to be just a songwriter, for he considered songs an inferior form of art music. Yet, history remembers Wolf as a great composer of songs.

Wolf was born in Styria, a German-speaking area of Yugoslavia, but worked mainly in Vienna. From childhood until within a few years of his death he was always poverty stricken. His family was musical, and his father gave him violin and piano lessons; he learned some theory from his teacher at the village primary school. There was a Wolf household orchestra in which Hugo and his teacher played. When Wolf was eight, he attended an opera performance for the first time, and it made a lasting impression on him. At the Benedictine Abbey boarding school, he was proficient in music studies, but incompetent in other areas, and was transferred to another school. He attended several secondary schools for short periods of time; he

Hugo Wolf.

was not a good student, was inattentive, was regarded as being too independent, and sometimes was a discipline problem. During those years, he composed some absolute music along Classical lines; reportedly, it was not very good, and most of it has not survived. However, two pieces dedicated to his father convinced him that Hugo should study at Vienna Conservatory. Among his fellow students at the Conservatory was Gustav Mahler. The two became friends, and later, when Wolf was in dire circumstances, he shared Mahler's lodgings.

While in Vienna, Wolf attended opera performances regularly. When Wagner was there in 1875, Wolf visited him, showed him some music he had written, and asked his opinion of it. Wagner advised him to write in larger forms. Wolf took that advice and attempted to write a symphony that he never completed. The same fate befell an early string quartet and several other large works that he commenced.

In 1875 Wolf began to write songs. The first of his songs that he considered worthy of publication was *Morgentau* (Morning dew; June, 1877); it is the first of the *Sechs Lieder für eine Frauenstimme* (Six songs for a female voice) published in 1888. Many of the texts he set in 1877 are by early nineteenth-century poets and concern romantic love or world-weariness (more aptly described by the German word *Weltschmerz*).

Wolf stated in letters to friends that in composing Lieder he was following in the tradition of Schubert and Schumann, and indeed Wolf's early Lieder reveal those influences, especially that of Schumann. The vocal line in some of Wolf's early songs bears resemblance to plainchant and psalm intonations that he sang in the choir at the monastery. In many of the early songs, Wolf really wrote piano music, with the text set to its top line. Wolf considered worthy of publication only 15 of the many songs he wrote before 1888.

Around the middle of 1878, Wolf chose more serious texts, sometimes even gloomy poetry, filled with renunciation and remorse; sometimes he wrote at the head of a manuscript the German word for renounce. At that time he knew he had contracted syphilis, and he was undergoing treatment for it. Throughout his life, Wolf's choice of texts and subjects for his music was directly related to circumstances in his personal life and his attitudes toward those circumstances. When he was romantically involved, he wrote Lieder about love and sexual passion; when he experienced recurrence of syphilis, he became depressed and derogatory toward women and chose material that blamed women for evils brought upon men. His personality had always been moody, and he found it difficult to get along with people; however, his periods of severe depression, his antagonism toward former friends, and his extended periods of solitude were all related to the encroachment of disease upon his central nervous system. Also, he deeply resented his short stature; his height was five feet, one and one-half inches, comparable with that of Schubert.

In 1879 Wolf visited Brahms, whom he considered conservative, showed him some of his songs, and asked his advice. Brahms told him to study counterpoint, an idea Wolf rejected immediately. That year Wolf associated with a group of young Wagnerites in Vienna, and his admiration for Wagner became more deeply entrenched. In 1883 Wolf considered composing an opera, along Wagnerian lines, but could find no libretto that suited him. At that time he rejected Rosa Mayreder's libretto *Der Corregidor,* which he did set in 1895. That text, based on Alarcon's play *El sombrero de tres picos* (The Three-cornered hat), blames women for men's injuries. Instead, Wolf composed a symphonic poem, *Penthesilea,* depicting the story of the Amazon queen who led her warriors to Troy where she fell in love with Achilles, was defeated by him, and in retaliation, incited her war hounds to shred him to bits. Wolf's symphonic poem shows Liszt's influence in its thematic transformation and treatment of harmonies.

In 1884, Melanie Köchert and her husband secured Wolf's appointment as music critic of the *Wiener Salonblatt.* For three years, Wolf published in that Sunday journal his outspoken articles on compositions and composers. Those articles are colored by his personal opinions—for instance, he was highly critical of Brahms, very supportive of Wagner. Wolf's knowledge of Wagner's operas was thorough, and his articles on them are important.

Wolf and Melanie became lovers, and in 1888 he experienced a year of song like that of Schumann in 1840–41. By early 1889, he had set 13 Eichendorff texts and 51 Goethe poems; in 1890 he composed settings for German translations of 44 Spanish songs. The Lieder are excellent. He had learned to write piano accompaniments independent of the declamatory vocal line, and he could effectively manipulate motives in the accompaniment; thus, his Lieder became more expressive and more dramatic. In 1888 he began to publish his Lieder, and his songs were first sung in public recitals. His music received favorable recognition, and from that time his fame spread.

In 1892–94 Wolf was ill and wrote nothing original. During two months in early summer 1895, he composed *Der Corregidor;* it was highly successful when performed in 1896. Wolf's last songs, settings of German translations of Michelangelo poems, were written in March 1897. Then he became insane. Initial treatment proved ineffective; he attempted to drown himself and had to be institutionalized for the remainder of his life. He died on 22 February 1903. His remains were interred in Vienna Central Cemetery near the graves of Beethoven and Schubert.

Wolf's mature compositional style first appeared in his settings of poems by Mörike (1887–88). Wolf considered the poetry more important than the music, published most of his Lieder under such titles as *Gedichte von Mörike* and *Gedichte von Goethe* (Poems of Morike, Poems of Goethe), and usually printed at the head of a Lied the poem that formed its text. He regarded his music as translations of the poetry rather than settings of it; each volume was a musical translation of poetry, not a volume of songs. For each volume of Lieder he had an overall plan; therefore, the volume became his large-scale work, with the individual Lieder as its movements or sections. Motivic relationships link some of the Lieder. Actually, the degree of Wolf's talent had to be as great as that of the poets or he could not have created such masterful settings.

Wolf set only those poems he believed had not been set adequately by other composers, or that had not been set previously, and his settings differ from those made by other composers in formal structure, treatment of the vocal line, types of harmonies and rhythms used, and general interpretation or expression of the meaning of the text. For example, his settings of Mignon's songs from Goethe's *Wilhelm Meister* differ from the several written by others, and his *Nun wandre Maria* (Ocaña poem) and *Die ihr schwebet* (Lope de Vega poem) in the *Spanisches Liederbuch* (Spanish Songbook; 1891) differ greatly from Brahms's settings. Wolf preferred to write modified strophic or through-composed settings; when he did write a strophic setting, he made slight alterations when the music was repeated. Wolf intended his music to expressively dramatize the poem; thus, each Lied was a miniature drama. The vocal line has no greater importance than the accompaniment; in fact, the accompaniment maintains the continuity of the Lied through the interludes that link the vocal phrases. This Wolf had learned from his study of Wagner's operas. Wolf, like Wagner, considered the voice another tonal color in the total fabric of the music.

Wolf's music is tonal; he let the structure of the poetry dictate the harmonies, and within a key he used chromaticism and dissonance to create expressive intensity as dictated by the poem. His music abounds in nonfunctional augmented sixth chords. Sometimes he effected harmonic changes subtly, through enharmonic modulations (e.g., G♭ major becoming F♯ minor in one of the Mignon songs). In some songs Wolf used progressive tonality, e.g., commencing in C and moving through E♭ to conclude in G, or beginning in E♭ and progressing through G♭ to end in C♭. Such

modulations were prompted by his search for greater expression. Rarely, a song has two tonal centers in keys a third apart, e.g., *In dem Schatten meiner Locken* (In the shadow of my tresses; DWMA207). Wolf associated a key with a specific mood and had the expression of a poetic text in mind when he chose a certain key for a Lied. Therefore, when one of his songs is transposed, it loses part of the specific expression with which Wolf imbued it. Also, most of Wolf's mature songs contain psychological details whose expressive intricacies in the musical interpretation are not immediately apparent. Many of his Lieder have a basic four-part (not four-voice) texture. This can be seen in *Anakreons Grab* (Anakreon's grave; Goethe poem; 1888; DWMA208). *Anakreons Grab* is one of a few songs that Wolf orchestrated.

Among Wolf's published books of Lieder are volumes of poetry by Mörike (53 songs), Eichendorff (20 songs), Goethe (51 songs), Michelangelo (3 songs), 2 *Spanisches Liederbucher* (Spanish Songbooks; one containing 10 sacred songs, the other containing 34 secular songs), 2 *Italienisches Liederbucher* (Italian Songbooks, one holding 22 songs, the other holding 24). Many of the songs in the *Spanisches Liederbucher* are exquisite; the *Italienisches Liederbucher* hold masterpieces. Besides writing Lieder, the opera *Der Corregidor,* and the symphonic poem *Penthesilea,* Wolf composed a String Quartet (D minor; 1878–84), *Intermezzo* (E♭ major, str. qrt.; 1886), *Italienische Serenade* (Italian Serenade; str. qrt.; 1887), a few piano solos, and 5 unaccompanied and 14 accompanied choral works. The programmatic *Italienische Serenade* is related to Eichendorff's novella *Aus dem Leben eines Taugenichts* (From the life of a good-for-nothing), which tells of a young violinist who leaves home to get away from his father and either attracts or antagonizes people by his playing. The work was written when Wolf found himself in a similar situation.

Gustav Mahler

Gustav Mahler's compositional talent was concentrated in two spheres: the Lied and the symphony. His work enriched both areas—the Lied was supplied with orchestral accompaniment; the symphony was infiltrated by the Lied. Mahler was an excellent conductor of opera as well as orchestral music, and in his

Gustav Mahler.

interpretations insisted upon accuracy down to the most minute detail. His own compositions are filled with numerous and intricate directives relative to dynamics, *tempi,* and other matters pertaining to performance.

Mahler was born in Bohemia and grew up in a village culturally rich in music and art. As a child, he learned many folk songs and received lessons in piano and music theory from local musicians. He played piano well and at the age of ten performed in his first public concert. In 1875 he passed the entrance auditions in piano at Vienna Conservatory but decided to pursue the composition course. For graduation in 1878 he submitted a Scherzo for piano quintet. That work, along with many of his early compositions, has been lost. At the Conservatory, Mahler attended Bruckner's lectures but stated emphatically that he was not a pupil of Bruckner. In Vienna Mahler became acquainted with Wagner's music, and, as did Wolf, joined a Wagnerite circle of musicians and social politicians. Mahler also took classes in philosophy and other subjects at the University of Vienna.

During 1878–81 Mahler composed his first important work, the dramatic cantata *Das klagende Lied* (The song of sorrow), for which he prepared the fairytale text. At the same time, he worked on an opera,

Rübezahl (the name of a sprite), which he never completed. Wolf was also interested in that subject and became angry when he learned that Mahler was using it. Of Mahler's endeavors, only the libretto survives. In 1880 Mahler composed three Lieder for tenor and piano on his own poems (first perf. 1934). Two of those Lieder have the kind of progressive tonality that characterizes many of Mahler's works: *Im Lenz* (In spring) begins in F major and ends in A♭ major; *Winterlied* (Winter song) commences in A major and concludes in F major. The third song, *Maitanz im Grünen* (May dance on the green), is in D major. In 1880–83, Mahler composed a group of five more Lieder for voice and piano; these form the first volume of *Lieder und Gesänge* (Lieder and songs, 3 Volumes, publ. 1892).

From 1883 to 1897 Mahler worked as conductor or director of theaters in various Austrian, Hungarian, German, and Bohemian cities. In most of the theaters, he found conditions deplorable and set about improving them. He was autocratic in his demands for higher performance standards. In Leipzig, he conducted Weber's operas for the first time and met Weber's grandson, who showed him Weber's sketches for the comic opera *Die drei Pintos;* Mahler completed that opera. In 1888 he met Tchaikovsky and Richard Strauss, and a lifelong friendship with Strauss developed. From 1897 to 1907 Mahler was director of the Vienna Opera. There he did a great deal to change the tastes of audiences who, at that time, favored French grand opera. In 1901 he met and fell in love with Alma Schindler (1879–1964; see Insight, "Alma Schindler Mahler"), who was studying composition in Vienna. Before they married in 1902, Mahler exacted from her the promise that she would give up her composing. In 1907 Mahler was appointed principal conductor of the Metropolitan Opera, New York, and in 1909 he became conductor of the New York Philharmonic. He spent the winter concert seasons in the United States and the summers in Europe. From 1907 he had suffered from a heart ailment; this was complicated by a bacterial infection in 1911, causing his death on May 18.

Mahler's works include nine completed symphonies, the symphonic song cycle (sometimes called a song-symphony) *Das Lied von der Erde* (The song of the earth; 1908–9), three song cycles for voice and

Alma Schindler Mahler

Alma Schindler studied counterpoint and composition with Austrian composers Josef Labor (1842–1924) and Alexander von Zemlinsky (1871–1942), both of whom also taught Schoenberg. Schindler met Mahler in 1901 when he was conductor of the Vienna Opera. Mahler knew Alma was writing Lieder but had never seen any of her work. Apparently, he surmised that it was of some worth, for, when a serious relationship developed between them, he advised her in a letter dated 20 December 1901 that she would have to give up composing, because a compositional rivalry between husband and wife would be bizarre. He asked, "Isn't it possible for you to consider *my* music as *yours*?" Alma loved him enough to comply with his request but always resented it. She did not destroy all of her compositions but kept some in a portfolio. As with most couples, there were times of marital crisis. At such a time in summer 1910, Alma came upon her husband playing some of her Lieder. Subsequently, he encouraged her to compose and arranged for publication of five songs she had written c. 1901 (*Fünf Lieder*). Four years after Gustav's death, Alma's *Vier Leider* (Four Lieder) was published, and in 1924 *Fünf Gesänge* (Five Songs) appeared. Since she did not date her work, it is difficult to determine when the songs were composed. However, *Der Erkennende* is a setting of a poem Franz Werfel (1890–1945) wrote in 1915. Alma Mahler's music is tonal but at times is greatly expanded by a generous supply of chromatic alterations. Her ability to write effective counterpoint is evident. Usually, the vocal line is independent of the accompaniment, and often it is completely surrounded by the accompaniment harmonies.

---

orchestra, the dramatic cantata *Das klagende Lied,* and several volumes of Lieder. A tenth symphony, unfinished at the time of his death, was constructed from his sketches by Deryck Cooke in 1951 (perf. 1976). The song cycles are *Lieder eines fahrenden Gesellen* (Songs of a wayfarer; 4 songs; 1883–85), *Des Knaben Wunderhorn* (The boy's magic horn; 12 songs; 1892–98), and *Kindertotenlieder* (Songs about the deaths of children; 5 settings of Rückert poems; 1901–4). Volumes 2 and 3 of *Lieder und Gesänge,* for voice and piano, are also settings of *Des knaben Wunderhorn* poems.

In its medieval setting, depiction of nature, and use of magic, *Das klangende Lied* reflects the influence of German Romanticism and Weber's operas; Wagner's influence is apparent also. Mahler used different keys to represent certain events, such as the murder, the flower, and the bone that becomes a flute and sounds the sorrowful song revealing the murderer. For this cantata Mahler used a large orchestra, and in the last scene he combined an offstage band playing festive music with the catastrophe being presented by those visible on stage. Many of the vocal melodies in *Das klagende Lied* are directly related to Bohemian folk song.

In *Lieder eines fahrenden Gesellen,* setting four of Mahler's own texts, the key changes as the hero travels; this gave rise to the term "narrative key tonality." The first song opens in D minor and closes in G minor; the second moves from D major to F♯ major; the third from D minor to E♭ minor; the fourth from E minor to F minor. "Progressive" and "narrative" tonality are different names for the same practice—changing keys as the music unfolds and concluding in a key other than that which begins the work. The practice is further evidence of composers' search for greater expression than that afforded them through adherence to the rules of traditional harmony.

The song cycle *Kindertotenlieder* contains no maudlin sentiment, no wallowing in grief, no mere acceptance of or resignation to a whim of fate that brought death to children. Instead, there is a richness expressive of the depth of love of father for child, deep emotion over tragic loss, and calm serenity in the assurance of God's protection and the promise of eternal life. The music says this as well as the poetry. Orchestral interludes between phrases of text seem to indicate soul-searching reflection; though they occur frequently, they do not disrupt the train of thought of the lyrics and are vital to the continuity of the compositions. In these five songs Mahler proved that a selective instrumentation need not imply a thin orchestration (No. 5, DWMA209); the balance is exactly as it should be. Mahler felt an affinity with Rückert and considered him one of Germany's greatest poets. In 1901 Mahler made settings of five other poems by Rückert. In those settings, Mahler treated the vocal solo as one of the contrapuntal lines.

Essentially, Mahler's consideration of the vocal line was similar to Wolf's, except that Mahler was writing orchestral accompaniments.

Probably, Mahler knew from his youth the Arnim and Brentano collection *Das knaben Wunderhorn.* Those poems provided him material for several sets of songs, and, in turn, his songs provided source material (in music and subject matter) for other compositions. The Second, Third, and Fourth Symphonies are closely linked with his *Des knaben Wunderhorn* songs.

Mahler's Lieder and his symphonies are interrelated. He based symphonies and symphony movements on some of his Lieder, used Lieder in his symphonies, and borrowed from Lieder for symphony themes. The kind of progressive tonality that occurs in many of his Lieder appears in his symphonies also. Symphonies Nos. 1, 6, and 8 are the only Mahler symphonies that begin and end in the same key; No. 6 is conventional in that movements 1, 3, and 4 are all in A minor. Most of Mahler's symphonies are programmatic, though he removed traces of his original programs from some of them. A few of his symphonies require enormous performing resources. In other symphonies, though his scores call for a very large orchestra, he does not use all of the instruments at the same time; the instrumental forces are available for the special instrumental combinations he needs. To depict the sound of medieval fiddle in the *danse macabre* in Symphony No. 4, Mahler used *scordatura* solo violin, with all four strings tuned a whole tone higher than normal tuning. (Saint-Säens used *scordatura* solo violin in his *Danse macabre.*) In Symphonies Nos. 4 and 5, Mahler relied more heavily on winds than on strings as the basis for his orchestra. In Symphonies Nos. 1, 2, and 8, he placed some instruments offstage. Only four of his symphonies have the traditional four movements, Nos. 1, 4, 6, and 9. When Mahler used sonata form for a symphony movement, he might return to the proper key for the recapitulation but usually he did not return the thematic material in the order in which it was originally presented. He followed Beethoven, Berlioz, and Liszt in using soloists and choral ensembles in some of his symphonies: Nos. 2, 3, and 8 have parts for soloists and chorus; No. 8 uses two choruses; No. 4 requires a soprano soloist.

Mahler originally planned his first symphony as a kind of tone poem in two parts, with five movements in all. With that in mind, he gave each part and each movement a programmatic title. Later he deleted the titles, and at one time named the symphony *Titan.* At another time, he stated that the symphony represented victory achieved by every gifted man in overcoming his Roquairol, his self-reflecting, scoffing, imperiling spirit. After the first three performances of the symphony, Mahler revised the work and removed the original second movement, *Blumine* (Flowers). That movement is identical with a piece of incidental music he wrote for the play *Der Trompeter von Säkkingen* (The Trumpeter from Säkkingen) in 1884. Since 1966, several orchestras in United States and England have performed the symphony as a five-movement work, with *Blumine* as second movement. Songs figure prominently in Mahler's Symphony No. 1, but it is a purely instrumental work. For the first movement, he borrowed liberally and literally from *Ging' heute Morgens über Feld* (O'er the fields I went this morning), the second of his *Songs of a Wayfarer.* In the Scherzo/Trio, he used short motives from his song *Hans und Grethe* (Hansel and Gretel), and in movement three he quoted literally the final section of *Die zwei blauen Augen* (Two blue eyes), the fourth of the *Songs of a Wayfarer.* In that Rondo third movement, the satirical *A Funeral March in Callot's Manner,* he used a D-minor adaptation of the well-known round *Bruder Martin* (in French, *Frère Jacques*) and for one alternate theme-section combined the folk song *Auf der Strasse stand ein Lindenbaum* (On the street is a linden tree) and the *Hatscho,* a dance typical of the Jihlava area in which Mahler grew up. In the Finale of the symphony, themes from the other movements are recalled.

Symphonies Nos. 5, 6, and 7 are closely related to the *Kindertotenlieder* cycle as well as to *Das knaben Wunderhorn.* The symphonic song cycle *Das Lied von der Erde* was originally conceived as the eighth symphony. The work is based on seven poems from Hans Bethge's translation of *The Chinese Flute,* which Mahler set for tenor and alto soloists and orchestra.

Mahler's actual Symphony No. 8 is sometimes called "Symphony of a Thousand" because of its enormous performing resources, both instrumental and vocal. It is the first completely choral symphony.

In this work Mahler made two statements: in Part I, an affirmation of Christian faith and belief in the power of the creative Holy Spirit, through use of the ninth-century hymn *Veni, Creator Spiritus,* and in Part II, a belief in the redemption of mankind through love, as Goethe presented it in Part II of *Faust,* in the *Chorus mysticus.* (Liszt had used this in his *Faust Symphony.*) Mahler's polyphonic treatment of the *Veni, Creator Spiritus* stemmed from his great interest at that time in the works of J. S. Bach; Bach's influence is seen, too, in the inclusion of boys' choir and in Mahler's choice of E♭ as the overall key of the symphony, the key Bach closely associated with the Trinity. Much of the Baroque, as Mahler viewed it, is present in the symphony's first movement.

Throughout much of his life, Mahler was preoccupied with thoughts of death. Several of his symphonies, particularly the last three (8, 9, 10), and *Das Lied von der Erde* are often viewed in this light. The "Farewell" motive used by Beethoven appears in several of Mahler's works, and in the fourth movement of the unfinished Tenth Symphony Mahler wrote the words *Leb' wohl* (Farewell) several times. His Ninth Symphony is sometimes regarded as expressing his premonition of his own death. Perhaps it does, but it is possible that he considered it a requiem for his daughter. The first movement of that symphony lacks the multitude of performance directives usually found in Mahler's works; instead, as pointed out by Alban Berg, it centers on cumulative use of the *crescendo.*

Mahler's music is tonal, with many of the melodies in his orchestral works borrowed from songs. The increased use of counterpoint after 1900 resulted from his study of Bach's works and his great admiration for Bach's music. Mahler was exceptionally skilled at orchestration. He could write delicate music for a chamber ensemble just as effectively as he wrote powerful music for a massive orchestra. One example is the introduction to the Adagio of Symphony No. 8, where an ensemble of 11 selected wind, keyboard, and string instruments playing very softly introduce the *Chorus mysticus.* In his symphonic writing, Mahler built on the work of his nineteenth-century predecessors, especially Beethoven, Berlioz, Liszt, and Bruckner, in the inclusion of voices, thematic transformation, and expanded form and tonality. Mahler extended the symphony beyond the massive proportions and programmatic content of post-

Richard Strauss. *(Courtesy Free Library of Philadelphia.)*

Romanticism, and through the incorporation of the Lied, use of expanded harmonies and progressive tonality, he elevated the symphony to an unprecedented height.

Richard Strauss

Richard Strauss (1864–1949) grew up in a musical atmosphere. His father was horn player in the Munich Court Orchestra, and, from an early age, Richard was permitted to attend rehearsals and performances of Classical and early Romantic music. His father kept from him the music of contemporaries such as Wagner. As a child, Richard had piano and violin lessons, and at the age of 11 received instruction in theory, harmony, and instrumentation. But he wrote his first composition when he was 6, and for the rest of his life he composed music, though he was almost middle-aged before he thought of himself as a composer. His primary career was conducting.

Example 24.12 Upward-sweeping theme presented in mm. 1–6 of Strauss's *Don Juan*.

Strauss never attended a music conservatory. After elementary and gymnasium schooling, he entered Munich University, where he studied philosophy, art history, and esthetics. In Munich he heard Wagner's music for the first time and was fascinated by it. His admiration for Wagner's music was lifelong, yet he did not attempt to compose music in that style.

By 1885, Strauss had written a great deal of music, including two symphonies (D minor, F minor), some overtures and orchestral serenades, a violin concerto, a horn concerto, a 'cello/piano sonata, a string quartet, some piano trios and other chamber music, some choral music, and some Lieder. One of those songs, *Allerseelen* (All Soul's day), ranks among his finest. Strauss was well known among musicians at the Munich court, and it was natural that his music would be performed there; however, some of his works were known in other Austrian cities—his Violin Concerto was played in Vienna in 1882.

In 1885 Strauss was appointed assistant conductor to Hans von Bülow at Meiningen and within weeks succeeded von Bülow, who resigned. Though inexperienced at conducting, Strauss learned quickly. While at Meiningen, he became interested in Wagner's writings and delved into Schopenhauer's philosophy. He was impressed with the idea of couching new music in new forms, was attracted to Liszt's symphonic poems, and decided to try composing works of that kind. In 1886 he wrote *Aus Italien* (From Italy), descriptive of his visit to Italy that summer. He called the work a symphonic fantasy; in type, it is a four-movement programmatic orchestral work that cannot be classified as either symphony or symphonic poem but lies midway between the two. Its third movement, instead of having development, contains an episode.

One of Strauss's harmonic devices is to prepare a modulation for a distant key but shift into tonic instead. This technique made its first appearance near the end of the third movement of *Aus Italien*.

Strauss's Tone Poems

In *Macbeth* (1886–88) Strauss's handling of symphonic poem is still immature, but with *Don Juan* (1888–89) he proved his mastery of the structure. He preferred to call his works **tone poems.** *Macbeth* and *Don Juan* are single-movement works in sonata form, with self-contained episodes in the development section. *Macbeth* is a psychological study of Macbeth, not a musical retelling of Shakespeare's play.

Don Juan is based on three excerpts from Nikolaus Lenau's unfinished *Don Juan* poem—fragments that are philosophical rather than descriptive. Lenau's hero (and Strauss's) is a man in ceaseless pursuit of the unattainable—the ideal woman, the perfect love—a man who prefers death rather than a life filled with ashes remaining from meaningless conquests. Musically, Don Juan seems to bound on the stage with the virtuosic upward-sweeping opening theme (ex. 24.12). Strauss's brilliant orchestration attests his mastery of orchestral effect and tone color and his understanding of the scope of orchestral instruments. The work contains several items that became trademarks of Strauss's style: a broad, upward-sweeping opening passage; use of solo instruments or of a section playing in unison to introduce thematic material; presentation of an important melody relatively late in the work. It is significant that when Strauss employs a solo violin in dialogue with the orchestra, the soloist remains an integral part of the ensemble rather than being set apart from the group.

Violoncello.
Contrabass.

Example 24.13 Theme representing *Wissenschaft*, used for fugue in *Also sprach Zarathustra*. The theme contains all 12 notes of the chromatic scale, and 3 different rhythms.

Strauss stated that *Tod und Verklärung* (Death and transfiguration; 1889) portrays an artist on his deathbed, who recalls his youth and unfulfilled idealism; at death, his soul is transfigured. Reportedly, when Strauss was dying, he remarked to his daughter-in-law that it was just as he had described it in *Tod und Verklärung.*

Strauss's next four orchestral works—*Till Eulenspiegels lustige Streiche, . . .* (Till Eulenspiegel's merry pranks, . . . ; 1894–95), *Also sprach Zarathustra* (Thus spake Zarathustra; 1895–96), *Don Quixote* (1896–97), and *Ein Heldenleben* (A Hero's life; 1897–98)—consolidated his position and brought him recognition as the leading German composer of his day. He was considered a "modern" composer because of the large orchestra, the realistic effects that he used, and the changes in formal structure in his works. *Till Eulenspiegels lustige Streiche, . . .* describes in detail that scamp's mischievous pranks. Above the introduction Strauss penned "Once upon a time . . ." and above the coda he wrote "Epilogue." His choice of rondo structure is appropriate for the work, for, though Till resolves to reform, he remains a prankster; the rondo theme, representing Till, unifies the episodes depicting his pranks. The work is delightfully humorous. Extra instruments, e.g., clarinets in different keys, are required for the orchestra.

Also sprach Zarathustra is based on Nietzsche's poem expressing the doctrine of a superman. Formally, Strauss's composition is a one-movement free fantasia unified by the motive C-G-C. There is artificiality in the fugue theme, obviously contrived to contain all 12 pitches of the chromatic scale and thus represent the omniscience of *Wissenschaft* (science; ex. 24.13). Some polytonality is present in the work.

Don Quixote, fantastische Variationen über ein Thema ritterlichen Charakters (Don Quixote, fantastic variations on a knightly character's theme), based on Cervantes's novel, describes the adventures of Don Quixote and his faithful companion, Sancho Panza. A solo 'cello represents the knight; Panza's theme is stated by bass clarinet and bass tuba. The

music is conversational at times, and resembles *sinfonia concertante* as well as symphonic poem. In contrast with Till, the personalities of Don Quixote and Sancho Panza are altered by their experiences; therefore, Strauss's choice of theme and variation with thematic transformation is appropriate for his presentation of them. Again, his philosophy—new ideas require new forms—is apparent. Strauss's ten "fantastic variations" incorporate transformations of the themes he assigned to Don Quixote (in D minor) and Sancho Panza (in F major). In depicting Don Quixote's encounter with the sheep, Strauss used a technique of maintaining a constant pitch but changing its color kaleidoscopically by having various instruments enter and drop out. Arnold Schoenberg used the technique more than a decade later and termed it *Klangfarbenmelodie* (tone-color-melody; see p. 821).

In *Ein Heldenleben,* Strauss is the hero, the Kapellmeister whose professional life is depicted in the tone poem's six sections. His wife is represented by solo violin. *Sinfonia domestica* (Domestic symphony; 1902–3), a one-movement work in four sections, portrays the Strauss family's home life. *Eine Alpensinfonie* (An Alpen symphony; 1911–15), describes in 22 sections a full day spent in the mountains. All of Strauss's orchestral works from *Don Quixote* through *Eine Alpensinfonie* require a very large orchestra. *Sinfonia domestica* calls for four saxophones, and *Eine Alpensinfonie* uses an orchestra of 150 players. However, seldom if ever are all of the instruments used at the same time.

Opera Conductor and Composer

From 1886 to 1889 Strauss served as third conductor at the Munich Court Opera, then went to Bayreuth and Weimar to conduct. At Weimar his conducting skills developed until, during the 1890s and 1900s, he was recognized as one of the three great Austro-Germanic conductors, the other two being Mahler and Felix Weingartner (1863–1942). Strauss met Mahler in 1887, and they became friends. Mahler encouraged Strauss to continue composing *Macbeth* at a time when Strauss was ready to cast that work aside. At Weimar Strauss met Pauline de Ahna (1862–1950); they married in 1894. A talented soprano, de Ahna sang leading operatic roles at Bayreuth, e.g., Isolde in *Tristan und Isolde,* and concertized. For her, Strauss wrote many excellent Lieder, commencing with the four songs, Op. 27, that were his wedding gift to her. One of the finest of his more than 200 Lieder is *Traum durch die Dämmerung* (Dream in the twilight, one of three songs in Op. 29; 1895). Strauss's Lieder deserve wider recognition than they have been accorded.

Strauss's work as opera conductor and his association with Pauline caused him to try writing opera. For his first, *Guntram,* which centers on redemption through a woman, he prepared his own libretto and designed the heroine (Freihild) role for Pauline. The opera was not successful, and in retaliation for the criticism he received, Strauss wrote another, the one-act *Feuersnot* (literally, distress caused by fire; 1900–1901), a satire on Munich's philistinism. For his next opera, *Salome* (1 Act; 1903–5), Strauss used a libretto by Wilde, a fantasy on the Biblical account of Herod's execution of John the Baptist. The music in *Salome* is beautiful, but the plot is gruesome, with gory details, such as Salome's singing a soliloquy to John's bloody disembodied head, which she caresses and kisses. Strauss's themes are short, and *Leitmotifs* woven into the musical fabric create dissonant polyphony. The orchestra is unusually large; Strauss used instrumental timbres most effectively and colored the music with harsh dissonances also. Though Strauss worked within established tonality and assigned keys to his music, in many places dissonance completely obliterates any sense of the designated key. Salome's *Dance of the Seven Veils* is especially beautiful and is often performed as a separate orchestral piece. The performance of *Salome* drew mixed reactions. Critics and audience were both shocked, but whereas critics were repelled by the violence and lust and considered the opera blasphemous, audiences were attracted by it.

Salome was followed by another one-act opera with dramatic female roles and bloody violence, *Elektra.* The libretto was by Hugo von Hofmannsthal (1874–1929), with whom Strauss established a

Example 24.14 (*a*) Motive representing *Elektra.* (*b*) Germinal chord for musical material in *Elektra. (Source: Strauss* Elektra, *copyright © 1908 A. Furstner, renewed 1936.)*

working relationship that lasted until Hofmannsthal died. *Elektra* presents the mythological story of Electra, whose mother has slain Agamemnon; Electra and Orestes avenge their father's death by murdering their mother. In *Elektra* Strauss's dissonances are even sharper than those in *Salome,* and repetition, dynamics, and accentuation reenforce the dissonant sounds. Actually, *Elektra* is a one-act music drama. As did Wagner, Strauss wrote continuous music and used *Leitmotifs* systematically—ex. 24.14a shows the one for Elektra. Note that the two chords progress by a tritone. Strauss assigned special keys to characters: Bb major for Agamemnon, Eb major for Chrysothemis, and bitonality with Elektra, sometimes A major/Eb minor, and C major/E major with her triumph. Moreover, as Liszt and Scriabin had done, Strauss generated the harmonies from a single germinal chord (ex. 24.14b).

Performance of *Elektra* evoked critic and audience reactions similar to those for *Salome.* At this point, Strauss's reputation as an opera composer was established in the minds of critics—he was a talented, daring, modern composer who wrote music that shattered conventions and was filled with ugly, cacophonous sounds. But it was not this that caused Strauss to effect a change of style in his next opera. Rather, it was the realization that he could not top what he had done in *Elektra.* He and Hofmannsthal next collaborated on the three-act comedy *Der Rosenkavalier* (The Knight of the rose; 1909–10), a witty, romantic, farcical opera. In style, it reverts to eighteenth-century Classicism, with Mozartian melody and lightness. Strauss's inclusion of waltz in the opera is, of course, anachronous. There are three important soprano roles in the opera; Oktavian is a breeches role. The trio sung by the three sopranos near the end of the opera is exceptionally well written. Strauss's change of style was totally unexpected, and his continued composition of operas along the same lines earned for him a new reputation—conservative composer. *Der Rosenkavalier* was well received, his later operas were not.

Strauss's next opera was a hybrid, innovative and experimental—and a failure. He arranged a two-part program, presenting as Part I Molière's *Le bourgeois gentilhomme,* and as Part II the one-act opera *Ariadne auf Naxos* (Ariadne on Naxos; 1912). Soprano Maria Jeritza (1887–1982) created the role of Ariadne. Strauss revised the work (1916) by deleting the Molière play and substituting for it a Prologue, a presentation of The Composer. Still the opera did not succeed, though in addition to Jeritza as Ariadne, the cast included soprano Lotte Lehmann (1888–1976). Audiences, who enjoyed being shocked, did not appreciate Strauss's changed techniques.

Strauss's next stage work was a ballet for Diaghilev, impresario of Ballet Russe. Then Strauss resumed opera composition, and wrote nine more. *Intermezzo* (1917–23) is remarkable for several reasons: (1) For the first time since *Guntram,* Strauss prepared his own libretto. (2) The two-act opera is autobiographical, with scenes of home life orchestrally linked. (3) In an endeavor to promote naturalness, Strauss wrote almost all of the dialogue in a kind of speech-recitative, with chamber orchestra accompaniment. He insisted that the dialogue be sung *mezza voce.*

Each of Strauss's last seven operas differs in some way. This was in accord with his belief (and Schopenhauer's) that new ideas require new forms. His last opera, *Capriccio* (1941), which he called a "conversation piece," is almost as delightful as *Der Rosenkavalier. Capriccio* concerns a widowed Countess who is in love with a poet and a musician. A one-act opera, *Capriccio* is economical, elegant, and refined. It concludes with the main character singing a soliloquy.

Strauss had worked in and around court all of his life but had paid relatively little attention to political activities. In 1933, for the first time, he experienced real political difficulties with the Nazis under Hitler's chancellorship. As a caring musician, Strauss agreed to substitute as conductor of *Parsifal* at the 1933

Bayreuth Festival, when, in protest against the Nazi's treatment of Jews, the conductor originally hired refused to conduct. Later that year, Joseph Goebbels, the Nazi minister of propaganda, established a state music bureau and, without consulting Strauss, named him president of it. When Hitler and Goebbels learned that Strauss was then working with a Jewish librettist, Stefan Zweig (1881–1942), Strauss's position was terminated. For a time, Strauss and his household—his daughter-in-law was Jewish—had to leave the area. Then, as casualties of World War II, came the destruction of the Munich National Theater in 1943 and the loss of opera houses in several major cities. After the War, Strauss composed *Metamorphosen* (1945) as an elegy for the previous German musical life he had known. The work is a study for 23 solo string instruments and is Neo-Classic in style. Neo-Classicism is visible in several of Strauss's late works. His last compositions are *Vier letzte Lieder* (Four last songs; 1948), for soprano or tenor with orchestra. Strauss died quietly, of heart failure, on 8 September 1949.

Engelbert Humperdinck

Engelbert Humperdinck (1854–1921), pianist, organist, and composer, studied at Cologne Conservatory. Most of the compositions he wrote before 1874 were destroyed by fire. Several of his works were awarded prizes, e.g., the Mozart Prize of Frankfurt am Main (1876) and the Mendelssohn Prize of Berlin (1879). While in Italy in 1880, he met Wagner, who was impressed with his talent and requested his assistance with preparations for the première of *Parsifal.* Humperdinck worked closely with Wagner in 1881–82, then spent some time in Paris and in Spain. In 1887, Humperdinck accepted a teaching position at Cologne Conservatory, and for the next several years he served as advisor to publisher B. Schotts Söhne and as opera critic for *Mainzer Tageblatt* (Mainz Daily News). He was responsible for publication of some of Hugo Wolf's Lieder and for convincing Siegfried Wagner to follow a career in music. In 1890–96 Humperdinck taught at Hoch Conservatory, Frankfurt am Main, then moved to Berlin to teach master classes in composition.

Humperdinck was primarily a composer of vocal music. During the last two decades of the nineteenth century, there was a revival of interest in Germany in *Märschenoper* (fairy-tale opera). Humperdinck wrote several of them, including *Hänsel und Gretel* (Hansel and Gretel; 1893), *Die sieben Geislein* (The Seven little goats; 1895), *Dornröschen* (Sleeping Beauty; 1902), and *Königskinder* (King's children; 1910). His finest works are *Hänsel und Gretel* and the incidental music to four Shakespeare plays (*The Merchant of Venice,* 1905; *The Winter's Tale,* 1906; *The Tempest,* 1906; *As You Like It,* 1907).

Hänsel und Gretel is based on the Grimm brothers' fairy tale. The work originated as songs Humperdinck wrote for his sister in 1890. He expanded them into a *Singspiel,* then into a three-act *Märschenspiel* (fairy-tale opera with spoken dialogue; 1893). *Königskinder* went through similar stages of composition but became a melodrama before becoming a full opera. Humperdinck's melodies sound like folk songs though he seldom actually quoted folk music—he did use two folk-song melodies in *Hänsel und Gretel.* Mingled with the folklike simplicity of his melodies is a Wagnerian influence, seen in the choice of harmonies, some contrapuntal textures, and some recurrent motives.

Max Reger

The music of Max Reger (1873–1916) has remained little known and little appreciated outside of Germany and Russia. Reger's music is difficult to classify, for it contains a mixture of Baroque, Classical, and Romantic elements. He was an excellent organist and a prolific composer of organ music; in fact, he composed more organ music than any other German composer since Bach. Reger understood Renaissance and Baroque polyphonic styles, and from his knowledge of and liking for those styles developed a predilection for counterpoint; he was adept at the techniques of fugue and variation.

Reger greatly admired Bach. Though Reger was a devout Catholic, he based many works on Lutheran chorales, including several large chorale fantasias, *13 Chorale Preludes* (Op. 79b; 1901–03), *30 Little Chorale Preludes* (Op. 135a; 1914), and *52 Easy Chorale Preludes* (Op. 67; 1902). Some of the chorale preludes are very easy, others are quite difficult. Among

his organ works are two sets of Preludes and Fugues, an *Introduction, Passacaglia and Fugue* (E minor, 1913), and several pieces titled *Fantasia und Fugue,* one on B-A-C-H (Op. 46; 1900).

Though Reger knew the music of Wagner, and Wagnerian chromaticism invaded Reger's harmonies, he did not follow Wagner's style. Reger used chromaticism as an adjunct to functional harmony, thus expanding key tonality without destroying it. His combination of chromaticism with counterpoint makes his large organ works tremendously difficult technically, e.g., *Chorale Fantasia "Ein' feste Burg ist unser Gott"* (Op. 27; 1898) and *Chorale Fantasia "Wie schon leucht't uns der Morgenstern"* (How brightly shines the morning star, Op. 52; 1900). At places in these fantasias the chromaticism pushes key tonality to its very limits but still does not destroy it.

Reger wrote in all genres except opera. He was outspoken in his dislike of program music. Much of his chamber music, especially the violin/piano sonatas and string quartets, reflect his admiration for and knowledge of the music of Beethoven and Brahms. Two excellent works for two pianos are *Variations and Fugue on a Theme of Beethoven* (Op. 86; 1904) and *Variations and Fugue on a Theme of Mozart* (Op. 132a; 1914), the latter based on the theme from Mozart's Piano Sonata, K.331, mvt. 1. Another fine work is the orchestral *Variationen und Fuge über ein lustigs Thema von J. A. Hiller* (Variations and Fugue on a merry theme of J. A. Hiller, Op. 100, E major; 1907).

Verismo

In the late nineteenth century there was a trend toward naturalism, or realism, in European literature. This is seen in the writings of Émile Zola (1840–1902) in France, Giovanni Verga (1840–1922) in Italy, Henrik Ibsen (1828–1906) in Norway, Leo Tolstoy (1828–1910) and Anton Chekhov (1860–1904) in Russia, and in other European authors' works. Composers, in their operas, sought to duplicate the realism of spoken drama and the realism of life itself. Realism is apparent in works of the Russians—in Dargomïzhshky's *The Stone Guest* and Musorgsky's *Boris Godunov.* Italians used the term *verismo* for their works of this kind. Frequently, they chose characters from the lower classes, or from a "bohemian" kind of life, involved in situations generating violent and brutal passions, especially hatred, lust, and murder. Strong local color is present in all operas of this kind.

In a competition held in 1888 for a one-act opera, Pietro Mascagni (1863–1954) won first prize with *Cavalleria rusticana* (Rustic chivalry), based on Verga's novella of the same name. The opera, first performed in Rome in 1890, was an outstanding success, and within a year Mascagni was internationally famous. *Cavalleria rusticana* has been translated into a half-dozen different languages and has remained in the repertoire. None of Mascagni's later operas equaled it in popularity, though *Iris* (1898) came close. *Iris* is a three-act opera filled with exotic and shocking effects. In using a Japanese setting, Mascagni preceded Puccini by more than five years. Because of the tremendous popularity of *Cavalleria rusticana,* Mascagni's name has been associated almost exclusively with *verismo;* actually, only 2 of his 15 operas are that type. He composed secular and sacred choral music, including a Mass, Requiem Mass, and other liturgical works; about a dozen songs; a symphony, symphonic poem, and other orchestral pieces; some chamber music and several piano pieces. Most of his compositions have never been published.

Another *verismo* opera that has remained in the repertoire is *I Pagliacci* (The Clowns; 1892) by Ruggero Leoncavallo (1857–1919). The opera presents a play within a play, and a situation in which dramatic art becomes reality. The plot concerns a troupe of *Commedia dell'arte* players whose leader plays the clown role. He is a sensitive, suffering person who must always present a happy-go-lucky attitude toward the world. The play within the play closely parallels a situation in his private life; he acts realistically and murders his wife. Then he sings, "I am not a clown, but a man," and, in a stupor, announces, "The comedy is ended."

In his music, Leoncavallo used many seventh chords, and there is much movement by thirds. The melody *Ridi, Pagliaccio!* (Laugh, clown!) appears three times in the opera. Originally, Leoncavallo intended *I Pagliacci* as a one-act opera, but the enthusiastic applause after *Vesti la giubba* (Put on the smock) caused him to divide the work into two acts.

Giacomo Puccini. *(Artex Prints, Westport, CT.)*

Puccini

The chief exponent of *verismo* was Giacomo Puccini (1858–1924). In his early childhood, he knew he was expected to follow in his forebears' footsteps and become organist-choirmaster at San Martino, in Lucca. When he was 10 he joined the choir, and four years later became organist there. At the age of 17 he began composing, writing and improvising for Service use organ pieces in which he included bits of Tuscan folk songs and melodies from operas. He wanted to write an opera, and in 1884 entered a competition for a one-act opera. His entry, *Le villi,* received no mention, but when he played and sang excerpts from it at a private party, Arrigo Boïto decided to stage it, and Ricordi published it. After its performance, Puccini began to receive commissions for operas. The tremendous success of *Manon Lescaut* (1893), based on Abbé Prévost's novel, brought Puccini to the attention of audiences outside Italy.

Puccini wrote a total of 12 operatic works, if one counts as 3 works the triptych comprising the one-act operas *Il tabarro* (The tabard), *Suor Angelica* (Sister Angelica), and *Gianni Schicchi* (Johnny Schicchi), first performed at Metropolitan Opera, New York, 1918. Among Puccini's works that have remained in standard repertoire are *Manon Lescaut* (1893), *La bohème* (The bohemian girl; 1896), *Tosca* (1900), and *Madama Butterfly* (1904). Others frequently performed in the late twentieth century are *La fanciulla del West* (The Girl from the [golden] West; first perf., New York, 1910), and *Gianni Schicchi,* based on a few lines from Dante's *Inferno, xxx. Madama Butterfly* is based on the play *Madam Butterfly* written by David Belasco after he read a magazine article recounting a true story of an American naval lieutenant and a Japanese geisha.

Puccini was always aware of what his contemporaries were doing and kept abreast of new developments. There are some parallel fifths and Tristan-like chords in *Manon Lescaut;* in *La bohème* he used some chord streams and augmented triads; *Tosca* and *Madama Butterfly* contain some whole-tone scales. In *Tosca* Puccini used recurrent motives in the manner of reminiscence motives; not until *Turandot,* unfinished at the time of his death, did he begin to use *Leitmotifs* in the Wagnerian sense. Verdi's influence is seen in *Tosca,* in the use of ostinato passages to create suspense. A characteristic of Puccini's orchestral writing is double or multiple reenforcement of the vocal melody, a technique known as *violinata,* used also by Rossini, Bellini, and Donizetti. Puccini's orchestra supplies continuous music, but it is not symphonic. The orchestration and instrumentation are always appropriate to the details of the opera's plot, sometimes delicate, sometimes brilliant—whatever the dramatic situation dictates. It is important, when considering Puccini's stage works, to realize that he viewed opera not as music drama, but as **musical drama**—the drama more important than the music—yet he insisted that every element of the production be meticulously coordinated to produce a unified work of art (a *Gesamtkunstwerk*). To this end, he supplied even more precise stage directions than those of Verdi.

Besides operas, Puccini composed other vocal music, both solo and choral, a few orchestral pieces, and some chamber music.

France

At the close of the Franco-Prussian War, there was a kind of musical renaissance in France that at first was nationalistic. In February 1871 a group of French composers founded the Société Nationale de Musique for the purpose of encouraging French composers. The organization was motivated not only by patriotism,

but by a sincere desire to improve the quality of French music, to divest it of superficiality, and to promote it as a serious art with solid craftsmanship. Franck, d'Indy, Duparc, Leheu, and Bordes were among those involved, with Franck the first acknowledged leader of the group. The Society sponsored its first concert the following November. Other concert series were established, designed to promote the performance of contemporary orchestral and chamber music. The most influential conductor-directors of these were Jules Pasdeloup, Édouard Colonne, and Charles Lamoureux.

During the 1890s, there was also a revival of interest in music of the past. Editions of the works of F. Couperin, Rameau, Palestrina, and other noted early composers were prepared, and their music was performed. In 1894 the Schola Cantorum was founded in Paris by Vincent d'Indy, Charles Bordes, and Alexandre Guilmant. Originally, the school was intended to provide instruction in plainchant and Palestrina-style religious music, but gradually the curriculum offerings were enlarged to include instruction in all areas of music. The doors of the Schola Cantorum were open to all who could qualify, not just French citizens, and soon its reputation for excellence attracted students from all over Europe and from America. By 1900, it had become a decided challenge to the Paris Conservatoire.

All this activity in composition, performance, education, and scholarship elevated France to a position of world leadership in music in the first half of the twentieth century.

There were several overlapping and interdependent lines of development in French music after 1871. Two were basic: one followed cosmopolitan traditions and is seen in the work of César Franck and his pupils, especially d'Indy; the other, adhering to specifically French traditions, is apparent in the work of Camille Saint-Saëns and his pupils, particularly Gabriel Fauré. Later, another line of development appeared, based on French tradition, and influenced by the ideas of French Symbolist writers and Impressionist artists. Its principal exponent was Claude Debussy, whose music has been highly influential and has affected the work of many twentieth-century composers.

César Franck

Belgian-born César Franck (1822–90) became one of the leading figures in the development of music in France during the last quarter of the nineteenth century. As a youngster, he was denied admission to Paris Conservatoire until his father became a naturalized French citizen. In 1872, Franck himself had to be naturalized in order to become professor of organ at the Conservatoire. There, despite his colleagues' disapproval, he taught composition to the students in his organ classes. Among those pupils were Vincent d'Indy, Ernest Chausson, Gabriel Pierné, Henri Duparc, and Louis Vierne.

In 1858 Franck was appointed organist at Ste. Clothilde, where he had at his disposal one of the finest organs in Paris. Much of the music he wrote prior to that date is of little significance. However, his use of cyclic construction and thematic transformation in his First Piano Trio (F♯ minor; 1840) gave some indication of the trend his music would take. The same kind of thematic treatment appears in his *Grand pièce symphonique* (F♯ minor; organ; 1860). From 1858 to 1872, Franck was mainly occupied with church music. Among other things, he wrote *Prélude, fugue, et variation* (B minor; organ; 1862) and the *Messe à trois voix* (Three-voice Mass; STB, org., harp., 'cello, str. bass; 1860), into which he later interpolated the well-known *Panis angelicus* (Bread of angels; 1872).

Franck worked in traditional instrumental forms, and his music is characterized by theme transformation or cyclic treatment of themes, full harmonies enriched by melodic chromaticisms, logical part-writing, and clear counterpoint. At times, he juxtaposed chords that had some common pitches but that were otherwise tonally unrelated, a device practiced by Beethoven.

Franck's finest compositions are the symphonic, chamber music, and keyboard works written during the last dozen years of his life. The important keyboard pieces include *Prélude, choral et fugue* (1884; pno.) and *Prélude, aria et final* (1887; pno.), and *Trois chorals* (Three chorales; E major, B minor, A minor; 1890, organ). The chorales are not hymns but highly developed fantasias on original themes, the kind of piece Franck improvised at the conclusion of Service when he was organist at Ste. Clothilde. *Prélude, chorale et fugue* was originally planned as a prelude and fugue in the style of Bach; then Franck inserted the chorale. The composition is a masterpiece in piano literature. In the *Prélude, aria et final,* themes from the first two pieces return in the finale.

With his last three chamber music works—the Piano Quintet (F minor; 1879), the violin/piano Sonata (A major; 1886), and the String Quartet (D major; 1889)—Franck laid the foundation for modern French chamber music. These works, as well as his *Symphonie* (D minor; 1888), are cyclical. Frequently, Franck generated themes from two germinal motives, for contrast. This is the case in both the *Symphonie* and *Variations symphoniques* (1885; pno., orch.). In *Variations . . .* he treated the solo piano as a participant in the ensemble, rather than allowing it to dominate. Only a few of Franck's works are programmatic, the most significant being the symphonic poems *Le chasseur maudit* (The accursed hunter; 1882) and *Psyché* (orch., chor.; 1888).

d'Indy

In 1869 Vincent d'Indy (1851–1931), who had been a child prodigy as a pianist, decided to become a professional musician. Then the Franco-Prussian War intervened, and he served France in the National Guard. He studied composition with Franck in 1872–80 and later transmitted Franck's methods and cosmopolitan ideals to his own students. D'Indy actively supported the Société Nationale de Musique from the time of its inception, and in 1890 succeeded Franck as its president.

D'Indy was greatly interested in music education. In 1893 he was asked to assist with reorganization of teaching methods at Paris Conservatoire, and, as a result of that experience, he became one of the founders of the Schola Cantorum in 1894. Actually, the school opened its doors in 1896. Under d'Indy's direction after 1900, it rivaled the Paris Conservatoire in excellence of instruction. D'Indy saw to it that students learned Gregorian chant and the Palestrina style of composition and received thorough grounding in the music of Bach, Beethoven, Rameau, and other master composers. D'Indy published his instructional methods in a multivolume *Cours de composition musicale* (Course in music composition; 1903–33).

D'Indy did much to further the cause of symphonic composition in France. His most important compositions are *Symphonie sur un chant montagnard français* (Symphony on a French mountain air; 1886, actually his second symphony though not so numbered) for piano and orchestra; *Istar,* symphonic variations (1896); Symphony No. 2 (B♭; 1903); the Violin/Piano Sonata (C major; 1904), and the opera *Fervaal* (1897). The opera libretto, by d'Indy, is based on an ancient legend concerning Christian ethics and the ultimate triumph of Christian purity and love over pagan beliefs. Appropriately, the final choral scene includes the plainsong hymn *Pange lingua* (Sing, my tongue [the glorious battle]). That d'Indy used *Leitmotifs* in *Fervaal* reflects his appreciation of Wagner's techniques.

The influence of Franck is visible in d'Indy's giving the solo piano a subordinate but prominent role in *Symphonie sur un chant montagnard français,* as well as in his use of thematic transformation. The symphony's principal theme is a folk song from the Cévenole region where d'Indy lived for a time. For Symphony No. 2 d'Indy used an ambiguous germinal motive and for this reason declined to designate the work as being either major or minor. The symphony is cyclic, and throughout the work d'Indy combined germinal and nongerminal themes in an ingenious interrelationship.

Istar is a set of symphonic variations depicting the legend of the Assyrian goddess Istar as told in Idzubar's epic poem. In order to free her lover from Hades, Istar must walk through seven gates and gradually disrobe as she passes through them. After walking through the last gate, she is nude. Consequently, d'Indy began his composition with the most complex of the seven variations and concluded the work with a simple orchestral unison statement of the theme. Besides the main theme, d'Indy used two others: one representing Istar knocking at a gate, the other representing her passage through the gate. The first variation and the final presentation of the theme are in the key of F; each of the other variations is in a different key, portraying Istar's mood at that point

in her walk. In addition to displaying d'Indy's resourcefulness and his logical presentation of the material, from a purely musical standpoint *Istar* is a remarkable orchestral work.

Saint-Saëns

Camille Saint-Saëns (1835–1921) was a child prodigy who received piano lessons at the age of two and a half, evidenced talent for musical composition at the age of three, and before he was seven was playing organ and piano in public programs. At the age of seven, he was studying composition with Pierre Maleden (1806–c. 1848), who taught Gottfried Weber's (1779–1839) principles of harmonic theory. Those principles, which were more lax than Rameau's with regard to treatment of altered chords and resolution of dissonance, made a lasting imprint on Saint-Saëns's compositional style. In 1848 Saint-Saëns entered Paris Conservatoire to study organ and composition. By 1853 he had written a number of large works, including cantatas and symphonies. From 1857 to 1876 he served as organist at the Madeleine, and in 1861–65 taught at École Niedermeyer—his only professional teaching appointment—where Gabriel Fauré was one of his students. A close friendship developed between Saint-Saëns and Fauré that lasted for many years, with Saint-Saëns eventually being considered a kind of older relative in the Fauré family.

Saint-Saëns was one of the founders of the Société Nationale de Musique, but he withdrew from the organization in 1908 when the society began to perform works by contemporary foreign composers. His own music was basically that of the French tradition, conservative, with order and restraint, and couched in Classical forms. His orchestral writing attests his mastery of counterpoint and his ability to write full sonorities. Saint-Saëns was a craftsman. He was eclectic, and from time to time his music was colored by Romantic elements.

His finest and most representative compositions were written in the 1870s and 1880s. They include Piano Concerto No. 4 (C minor; 1875); Violin Concerto No. 3 (B minor; 1880); Symphony No. 3, the "Organ Symphony" (C minor; 1886); Sonata No. 1 for violin and piano (D minor; 1885); Sonata No. 2 for 'cello and piano (F major; 1905); and *Le carnaval des animaux* (The carnival of animals; chamber orch.,

2 pnos.; 1886). Both the piano concerto and the symphony commence in C minor and conclude in C major, use thematic transformation, and contain chorale melodies. In both works, the first two movements and the last two are played without a break. (In many of Saint-Saëns's multimovement works, movements are connected.) The symphony is scored for a large orchestra, with two pianos and an organ. Violin Concerto No. 3 is more lyrical, more musical, and less technically demanding than his previous two violin concerti. *Le carnaval des animaux,* a series of delightful parodies of well-known compositions, reveals Saint-Saëns's wit and his knowledge of instrumental techniques. It has become one of his most popular pieces.

Also significant are the opera *Samson et Dalila* (Samson and Delilah; 1877) and the symphonic poems *Le rouet d'Omphale* (Omphale's spinning wheel; A major; 1872) and *Danse macabre* (G minor; 1874). The latter work marks an early use of xylophone as an orchestral instrument.

Fauré

Gabriel Fauré (1845–1924) entered École Niedermeyer as a boarding student in 1854 and remained there for 11 years. The curriculum was oriented toward training students to be church organists and choirmasters and consisted mainly of organ and piano lessons, plainchant, counterpoint, and Renaissance polyphony. After the death of Niedermeyer (1861), Saint-Saëns taught the piano classes and expanded the course to include contemporary music and composition. Fauré studied with him there for 5 years and maintained contact with him after leaving the school. The training Fauré received at École Niedermeyer, with its emphasis on chant and church modes, and its special way of teaching harmony, according to Gottfried Weber's theoretical principles, strongly influenced his compositional style. The *Traité d'harmonie* (1889) of Gustave Lefèvre, son-in-law of Niedermeyer, explains those principles, which, among other things, favor the use of altered chords in a manner that alludes to remote keys without actual modulation to them.

Fauré began his professional career as church organist at Rennes (1866–70). During the Franco-Prussian War he served in the infantry, and thereafter he held various organist and choirmaster posts in Paris churches, finally working at the Madeleine. In 1896 he was appointed professor of composition at Paris Conservatoire, and in 1905–20 was director of that school. Among his many pupils were Charles Koechlin, J.-J. Roger-Ducasse, Florent Schmitt, Louis Aubert, Maurice Ravel, and Nadia Boulanger. Through Boulanger's teaching, Fauré's influence was extended to many twentieth-century composers.

Though highly regarded in France, in other countries Fauré is relatively unknown; outside of France only his Requiem Mass (1887), some of his chamber music, and a few of his songs are performed. He wrote only a few orchestral works and was dissatisfied with most of them. He was never completely comfortable with orchestration and did not hesitate to seek assistance from friends and pupils. He had help orchestrating the Requiem, the incidental music for *Pelléas et Mélisande,* and the opera *Prométhée.* In the area of chamber music Fauré made some real contributions, and several of his works have been accepted into standard repertoire: Sonata No. 1 for violin and piano (A major; 1875–76), Piano Trio (D minor; 1923), Piano Quintet No. 2 (C minor; 1921), and String Quartet (E minor; 1924).

Fauré is seen at his best in the intimate forms of music—chamber music, piano pieces, and songs. His earliest compositions (1861–62) are single songs of the French romance type, and his first piano pieces are three *romances sans paroles* (romances without words; c. 1863). His piano pieces consist of character pieces, principally nocturnes, barcarolles, preludes, impromptus, and valse-caprices. Until the 1890s Fauré wrote single, independent song settings; then he began to compose song cycles also, the first being *Cinq mélodies 'de Venise'* (Five melodies from Venice; Verlaine poems; 1891). Throughout his career, Fauré wrote songs and piano music, and the changes in his style over the years are apparent in those genres. His early music is Romantic, showing the influence of Schumann, Mendelssohn, and Saint-Saëns, with formal clarity and basic Romantic harmonies. Then Fauré's appreciation for the music of Liszt becomes apparent in his style. Next, in the late 1880s, there appear reflections of the ideas of Impressionist painters and the Symbolist poets whose stanzas he set, e.g.,

Verlaine's *Clair de lune* (Moonlight; 1887). Gradually, in the 1890s, Fauré's harmonies became bolder and more expressive, as seen in his setting of Verlaine's *La bonne chanson* (The good song; 1892–94) and the powerful music of the opera *Prométhée* (1900). That *tragédie lyrique* was designed for performance out-of-doors; in its original version the instrumental music was for three large wind bands, strings, and harps. Fauré's style, in his final period, became more economical and at times austere, with increasing harmonic boldness and more use of polyphony.

Despite the periodic stylistic changes, certain characteristics of Fauré's writing remained constant. His music was tonal, but he blended modality into it, and he treated harmonies rather freely. Many of Fauré's melodies are modal, but he seldom used the whole-tone scale. The flatted seventh scale degree and the plagal cadence figure prominently in his music. Major and minor seventh chords appear frequently. He did not consider seventh and ninth chords dissonant; hence, they required no resolution. Nor did an altered chord indicate an impending modulation—he often used altered chords and foreign notes without making a change in key. Because of his facility with altered chords, Fauré could and did modulate to remote keys swiftly and was able to return to the tonic key just as suddenly. However, he did not modulate as frequently as is generally believed. Typical of his harmony is alteration of the mediant (e.g., mobility between B♮ and B♭ in a piece that has a key signature of one sharp) with no thought of vacillating between major and minor and no intention of changing the tonality. At times he substituted the fourth for the third in a triad and blended the dissonance into a common pitch in the next chord. Fauré's treatment of rhythm is equally interesting. In many of his songs he established a rhythmic ostinato figure and used it so skillfully that it did not impart monotony to the piece. He used syncopation subtly, and frequently he combined duple and triple rhythmic patterns in cross rhythms, as did Brahms.

Fauré was a master of French song, the *mélodie,* and wrote more than a hundred of them. (The term *mélodie* was used after c. 1840 to denote a French solo song with accompaniment, most often a setting of serious lyric poetry.) Three principal collections were published (1879, 1897, 1908), each containing 20 songs. His best-known *mélodies* are *Lydia* (1865) and *Après un rêve* (After a dream; 1865), both in Volume 1, *Clair de lune* (Moonlight; 1887) in Volume 2, and *Au cimitière* (At the cemetery; 1888) in Volume 3. Little known, *Le don silencieux* (The silent gift; publ. 1906), is excellent. However, Fauré is seen at his finest in the song cycles *Cinq mélodies, La bonne chanson, La chanson d'Eve* (Eve's song; 1906–10), and *L'horizon chimérique* (The chimerical horizon; 1921). In most of these cycles, unity is achieved by two means: The poems are arranged so that they tell a story, and the songs share some common musical motives. For *La bonne chanson* Fauré selected nine poems from Verlaine's series, rearranged their order, and deleted from the long poems (the eighth and ninth songs) some stanzas that he considered inappropriate to the thoughts he wanted to convey. Though the music is quite varied, the *mélodies* are linked thematically by several common motives, and the last song, *L'Hiver a cessé* (Winter is over; DWMA210), recapitulates material from some of the other songs. *L'Hiver a cessé* concludes the cycle with an expression of great joy. When *La bonne chanson* first appeared, it created quite a furor. Many persons, including Saint-Saëns and Debussy, were shocked at the harmonic innovations, the degree of expression, the unusual treatment of the vocal lines, and the importance given the piano accompaniment. The overall form of the cycle and the manner of its unification were also innovations.

Because so little of Fauré's music has been performed outside of France, the full extent of his influence on other composers is not yet apparent. Certainly, his impact was far greater than is generally realized.

Impressionism

The first use of the term "Impressionism" as a label for a distinctive artistic style was by critic Louis Leroy, who, after viewing an art exhibit in Paris in 1874, published a derogatory article in which he referred to the artists as "Impressionists." The title of one of the paintings exhibited contributed to that term—Claude Monet's *Impression: soleil levant* (Impression: sunrise, 1872; see colorplate 25). Within a few years those exhibitors, who included Monet (1840–1926), Édouard Manet (1832–83), Edgar Degas (1834–1917), Auguste Renoir (1841–1919), and

Camille Pissarro (1830–1903), were commonly referred to as Impressionists, and the style of their work, Impressionism. Characteristics of that style are avoidance of sharp outlines and formal precision, reliance on the effect of light and color, and a certain fluidity of design. The paintings manifest both blurring and brilliance. They are representational but not graphic and usually not realistic. With brush strokes of pure color the artist suggested, and the viewer's eyes mixed the colors and firmed up the shapes. Impressionist painting existed in France prior to 1872 but was at its height in 1874–86.

There was a comparable movement in French poetry known as *Le Symbolisme*. Precursor of the movement was Pierre Baudelaire (1821–67), who, in works like the sonnet *Correspondances,* expressed his theories about the music of poetry and the symbolic relationships between sound and color. The movement did not gain ground until the 1880s, when Paul Verlaine's *Romances sans paroles* (Romances without words; 1874), Stéphane Mallarmé's *L'Après-midi d'un faune* (The afternoon of a faun; 1876), and similar poems became known. The extreme Symbolist movement of which Mallarmé was leader was at its height c. 1890 in the *décadent* circles. Symbolist poets sought to convey impressions and suggestions; the function of their poetry was not to describe but to evoke. Words were chosen for color, harmony, and evocative power; fluidity of line and strophe was important. Fauré, Debussy, and Ravel were among the many composers who made settings of Symbolist poetry.

When first applied to music, the term "Impressionism" was used in a disparaging sense, also. The Académie des Beaux Arts, after examining Claude Debussy's symphonic suite *Printemps* (Spring; orch., female chor.; 1887), the second composition he submitted as evidence of his work in Rome, recorded that the composition exhibited "vague impressionism" and lacked formal clarity. Debussy was cautioned against excessive use of color but did not heed that admonition. Generally, he has been considered the chief exponent of Impressionist music, though that is only one aspect of his style. He strongly opposed the label "Impressionism" and preferred to have his work associated with that of contemporary French writers and identified as "Symbolism." Impressionistic music

Claude Debussy. *(Free Public Library of Philadelphia.)*

is characterized by irregular phrases and blurring of formal outlines, avoidance of traditional harmonic progressions, use of streams of chords in parallel motion and altered chords with unresolved dissonances, and choice of instruments for their coloristic possibilities. Though the music is tonal, modality frequently appears within it, and often the leading tone is suppressed. Composers wanted to create an atmosphere, to suggest rather than define, to hint rather than to state. Therefore, Impressionistic music *is* vague and may seem as elusive and fragile as gossamer.

Debussy

Achille-Claude Debussy (1862–1918) did not come from a musical family. As a child, he received piano lessons and in 1872 was accepted in piano at Paris Conservatoire. In the summer of 1880, Debussy met

Example 24.15 (*a*) Musorgsky: *Okonchen prazdnij, shumnij den'* (1874), mm. 16–19; (*b*) Debussy: *Nuages* (1893), mm. 1–4, clarinet and bassoon parts.

(a)

(b)

Nadezhda von Meck, Tchaikovsky's patroness. She engaged Debussy as household pianist, and he spent several summers in her employ, the first in Italy and Vienna, the others in Moscow. Also in 1880, he enrolled in composition courses at Paris Conservatoire, and in 1884 he was awarded the Prix de Rome for his cantata *L'enfant prodigue* (The prodigal son). He stayed the minimal time—two years—at Villa de Medici in Rome and submitted the required compositions to the Académie. As has been noted, not all of his work pleased them.

He became interested in the music of Wagner and visited Bayreuth in 1888 and 1889. At the Paris World Exhibition in 1889, Debussy again heard Russian orchestral music and was introduced to the sound of Javanese gamelan. That year he became reacquainted with Musorgsky's songs and *Boris Godunov*. All influenced his work to some extent. An example is

Nuages (Clouds; from *Nocturnes;* 1897–99), whose opening measures resemble portions of Musorgsky's "The idle, noisy day is ended" (No. 3 in *Sunless;* 1874; ex. 24.15), and whose middle section simulates the distinctive sound of the gamelan. *Nocturnes* comprises three orchestral pieces: *Nuages, Fêtes* (Festivals), and *Sirènes* (Sirens), the latter piece including textless vocalization by female chorus.

By 1889, Debussy had become acquainted with several Symbolist writers and had set some of their poetry. He had written a number of works but was relatively unknown until his *La damoiselle élue* (French translation of part of Rossetti's *The Blessed Damosel;* soprano, female chor., orch.; 1888) was performed by the Société Nationale in 1893. At that time he was already working on *Prélude à l'après-midi d'un faune* (orch.; 1892–94; DWMA211), based on Mallarmé's poem. Debussy's composition is not

(a)

(b)

Solo flute.

Très modéré

p *doux et expressif*

Figure 24.5 (*a*) Sketch of a faun playing panpipes. (*b*) One solo flute, representing the faun, plays this melody in *L'après-midi d'un faune*, mm. 1–4.

descriptive program music in the usual sense, but suggests the faun's thoughts and emotions, and, through the flute solo, the faun's expression of those feelings as he played his Panpipes (fig. 24.5). The music is chromatic, vague, and fluid and becomes intensely emotional. It is more attuned to Symbolism than Impressionism, with the flute symbolizing the faun's own instrument and the music his emotional release. Debussy, like Handel, recognized the effectiveness of rests, the importance of silence in music; after the initial flute solo in *Prélude à l'après-midi d'un faune,* there is a complete measure (m. 6) of silence. Then the music recommences, *pianissimo.* The symphonic poem is a free treatment of sonata form, a kind of statement-departure-return with an element of rhapsody. The orchestration includes two harps, uses no bright brasses, and the only percussion instruments are antique cymbals (small discs that are struck together very softly and allowed to vibrate) sounded near the end of the piece. Much of the time the strings play very softly, are muted, or bow over the fingerboard.

One way in which Debussy influenced twentieth-century music was his treatment of the orchestra. He had learned a great deal about instrumentation and orchestration from Rimsky-Korsakov's works. Debussy used an orchestra of average size and included only those instruments whose colors would effectively paint the picture he wanted portrayed. Most often, he favored winds over strings, and he seldom doubled melodic lines. For effect, he relied on understatement.

In 1893, Debussy saw Maurice Maeterlinck's (1862–1949) symbolist drama *Pelléas et Mélisande* and decided to make an opera of it. Writing the vocal score took Debussy two years (1893–95), but he did not prepare the orchestration until 1901–2. *Pelléas et Mélisande* was first performed in April 1902; by 1912 it had been performed a hundred times. It is a landmark in French opera. The story, set in the imaginary kingdom of Allemonde, concerns the idea that all of life is determined and controlled by unseen forces. This, like other Maeterlinck dramas, expresses the thought that the only certain reality is death. Debussy gave text primacy over the music, for he believed music was usually too predominant in opera. Therefore, he wrote no arias and included no dances. The singing is a kind of recitative, set with due regard for proper declamation of the French language. Some recurrent themes are used, representing states of mind, but there are no *Leitmotifs* as Wagner used them. The music is soft, atmospheric; orchestral instruments were chosen for color, and no trombones were included. Tonality and modality are mingled in the harmonies. The opera is an expression of Debussy's philosophy that music should be a free art, truly representative of the fact that it cannot be contained, but exists in time and is borne on air. That freedom meant a relaxation of restrictions such as those that normally governed form, harmonic progressions, and rhythm. He expressed those ideas in the articles he wrote, as well as in his music. *Pelléas et Mélisande* may be considered, both musically and psychologically, a forerunner of Alban Berg's *Wozzeck.*

Pelléas et Mélisande is the only opera Debussy completed. He planned operas on some of Edgar Allan Poe's (1809–49) stories, particularly, *The Devil in the Belfry* and *The Fall of the House of Usher,* but did not complete them. For the latter opera Debussy planned three scenes; the two that he completed (*La chute de la maison Usher;* 1908–17) were performed at Yale University in 1977. In addition, Debussy composed incidental music for d'Annunzio's mystery play *Le Martyre de Saint-Sébastien* (1911) and the ballet *Jeux* (Games; 1913), which is not Impressionistic.

While Debussy was working on *Pelléas et Mélisande,* he composed *La Mer* (The Sea; 1903–5), comprising the three symphonic sketches *De l'aube à midi sur la mer* (From dawn to noon on the sea); *Jeux de vagues* (Play of waves), a study of light; and *Dialogue du vent et de la mer* (Dialogue of the wind and sea), a study of color and space. His other important orchestral work, *Images* (1905–12), also consists of three pieces: *Gigues, Ibéria,* and *Rondes du printemps* (Spring round-dances), all of which contain French folk songs. Both *Gigues* and *Rondes du printemps* foreshadow Stravinsky's *Le sacre du printemps* (The Rite of Spring; 1913). In fact, Stravinsky was present at the first performance of *Rondes de printemps* (1910). The fusion of timbres, unexpected dissonances, combinations of tonality and modality, and the unusual scales Debussy used in the work were shocking to many in the Paris audience, but those were some of the factors that influenced later twentieth-century music.

Many of Debussy's songs were written before 1885. However, his most important songs are two sets (three songs each) entitled *Fêtes galantes* (Galant festivals; 1891, 1904; Verlaine poems); *Chansons de Bilitis* (3 Louÿs poems; 1898); and *Trois ballades de Villon* (Three ballades of Villon; 1910).

Debussy and his compatriot Ravel were two of the most important composers of piano music in the early twentieth century. Most of Debussy's piano music was written after 1900. His only significant early piano pieces are the *Suite Bergamasque* (4 pieces; 1893, rev. 1905), which contains the well-known *Clair de lune* (Moonlight); and the *Suite: Pour le piano* (Suite: For piano; 1894–1901), which consists of prelude, sarabande, and toccata. His mature style is apparent in the collection *Estampes* (Prints;

1903), comprising *Pagodes* (Pagodas), *Soirée dans Granade* (Evening in Granada), and *Jardins sous la Pluie* (Gardens in the rain). In the oriental-sounding *Pagodes,* inspired by Balinese gamelan music, Debussy used a pentatonic scale. *Soirée en Granade* uses the *habanera* rhythm and imitations of guitar playing. In addition to figuration depicting water falling, Debussy incorporated in *Jardins sous la Pluie* two French songs for children, *Do, do, l'Enfant, do* and *Nous n'irons plus au Bois.* This is Impressionistic music, as are also the two sets of *Images* for piano (1905–7). The two books of *Préludes* (1910, 1912) each contain 12 titled pieces, individualistic and programmatic, e.g., *Voiles* (Sails, or Veils) and *La fille aux cheveux de lin* (The girl with the flaxen hair). *La cathédral engloutie* (The engulfed cathedral), from Book I, is frequently performed. Based on legend, the music depicts the watery depths, then the cathedral of Ys rising briefly out of the sea and sinking back again; the music is blurry, with rising parallel fourth chords, a bit of melody resembling chant, and deep bell-like chords. The *Préludes* provide an excellent cross-section of Debussy's piano writing. Each of the two books of *Études* (1915) holds six serious technical studies that are highly musical. Debussy's humor is seen in *Children's Corner* (1906–8; 6 pcs.), which satirizes Czerny in *Doctor Gradus ad Parnassum* and Wagner in *Golliwog's Cake-walk* (by quoting from *Tristan und Isolde*). The suite *En blanc et noir* (In white and black; 1915) has three pieces for two pianos.

Nor did Debussy neglect chamber music and solo instrumental music. Important contributions are the unaccompanied flute solo *Syrinx* (1913) originally written as incidental music for Mourey's *Psyché,* the *String Quartet* (1893), and three sonatas ('cello/piano, 1915; fl., vla., harp, 1915; violin/piano, 1917).

Debussy's influence has been far-reaching, touching almost every significant composer working during the first half of the twentieth century, and a good many after that time.

Ravel

Contemporary with Debussy, but slightly younger, was Maurice Ravel (1875–1937). After Debussy's death, Ravel was considered the leading French composer. Generally, Debussy and Ravel are regarded as the chief exponents of French Impressionism in music,

Maurice Ravel. *(Three Lions, Inc.)*

but, viewed overall, Ravel's music is less Impressionistic than Debussy's, and the musical styles of the two men differ considerably. Actually, Ravel mingled Impressionism and Classicism. He was more objective than Debussy and was more traditional than Debussy in choice and treatment of form. Ravel preferred to use modal (Phrygian and Dorian, especially) rather than whole-tone scales, and he did not write dominant ninth chords and augmented triads to the extent that Debussy did. Ravel's music is colored by chromaticisms, and his harmonies are complex, but they are, for the most part, diatonic and functional. He was generous with major sevenths and supertonic ninths and did not always resolve dissonances. Frequently, he wrote streams of parallel triads or other chords. Organum-like passages of consecutive fourths or fifths appear in several of his works, e.g., the song *Ronsard à son âme* (Ronsard to his soul; 1923–24) and the opera *L'enfant et les sortilèges* (The child and witchcraft; 1920–25). Other features found in many of Ravel's pieces are the interval of a falling fourth and the reiteration of an accompaniment figure or of a single pitch.

Many things influenced Ravel's music. During his childhood and youth, private lessons from distinguished pianists in Paris provided him with technical facility on the piano, though he never became a virtuoso. Then, he attended Paris Conservatoire (1889–85; 1897–1900), where, in Fauré's classes, he acquired the technical mastery of composition that enabled him to become a superb craftsman, attentive to minute details, and writing with clarity of form. Also, Ravel's style was affected by music he heard at the Paris World Exhibition in 1889: Russian music conducted by Rimsky-Korsakov and Javanese gamelan. Ravel was a brilliant orchestrator, knowledgeable concerning the coloristic possibilities of all instruments, and he used instrumental timbres effectively. However, he was primarily a pianist, and many of his orchestral works were conceived first for piano, then orchestrated.

At least partially, Ravel's interest in Iberian music was inherited from his mother, who was Basque; yet, his works reflect the pure Spanish music of Andalusia and of flamenco, rather than the Basque of his mother's region. Ravel's friendship with his Conservatoire classmate, Spanish pianist Ricardo Viñes (1875–1943), was another influential factor. Viñes performed most of Ravel's piano works.

Some features that became characteristics of Ravel's compositional style were present in his earliest works: use of traditional form for *Menuet antique* (1895; pno.), the Spanish idiom of *Habanera* (1895; 2 pnos.), the consecutive parallel intervals in *Entre cloches* (Amid bells; 1897; 2 pnos.). Later, he used *Habanera,* orchestrated, as the third of the four movements in *Rapsodie espagnole* (Spanish rhapsody; 1907–8). Dance forms, both old and modern, figure prominently among Ravel's compositions. Other works with Spanish flavor are the one-act comic opera *L'heure espagnole* (Spanish hour; 1907–8), *Alborada del gracioso* (Morning song of the buffoon) from *Miroirs* (Mirrors; 1904–5; pno.), and the well-known *Boléro* (orch.; 1928) written for dancer Ida Rubenstein. *Boléro* was, to Ravel, an essay in orchestration, with continual repetition of two 16-bar phrases (harmonized) over an ostinato rhythmic figure; the only variety is the orchestral *crescendo* effected by the cumulative entrances of instruments as well as by increased volume.

Ravel's most Impressionistic compositions are *Jeux d'eau* (Fountains; 1901), the five pieces constituting *Miroirs* (Mirrors; 1904–5), the three pieces in *Gaspard de la nuit* (1908), all for piano; and *Daphnis et Chloé* (1909–12), a three-movement choreographic symphony. *Daphnis et Chloé* requires a very large orchestra, a wind machine, and a chorus singing textless melody. In all but one instance, the choral vocalization is doubled instrumentally.

Ravel wrote some of the finest piano music in the literature. *Jeux d'eau,* written earlier than Debussy's *Jardins sous la pluie* and *Reflets dans l'eau,* was known to Debussy and may have influenced his works.

Jeux d'eau (DWMA212) was a natural outgrowth of Ravel's interest in the piano music of Liszt and the latter's musical depiction of the fountains at Villa d'Este in Rome. *Gaspard de la nuit* was based on excerpts from the poetry of Aloysius Bertrand (1807–41). The pieces in the suite are programmatic, with supernatural subjects: *Ondine,* the water-sprite who lures young men to their deaths by drowning; *Le gibet,* a macabre gallows scene; and *Scarbo,* a grotesque, evil dwarf. *Gaspard de la nuit* presents the performer with some tremendous technical difficulties. Programmatic piano music of a totally different kind is *Ma mère l'oye* (My mother goose; piano duet; 1908–10), a set of five miniatures written for the Godebski children.

Ravel's other major piano works are Neo-Classical: *Pavane pour une Infante défunte* (Pavane for a deceased Infanta; 1899), the three-movement *Sonatine* (1905), the seven *Valses nobles et sentimentales* (Noble and sentimental waltzes; 1911), and *Le tombeau de Couperin* (Lament for Couperin; 1917). The *Pavane . . . ,* a stately dance, is the best known of these works, especially in its orchestral version (1910), but *Le tombeau de Couperin* is Ravel's finest achievement for solo piano. The composition resembles a French harpsichord suite of Couperin's time, with six small movements: Prelude, Fugue, Forlane, Rigaudon, Minuet with musette for trio, and Toccata, each a replica of its eighteenth-century counterpart. In two respects the suite is nationalistic—it honors Couperin, and each movement is dedicated to the memory of a World War I victim. For piano and orchestra, Ravel composed two concerti, one in D major (1929–30) for left hand only, commissioned by Paul Wittgenstein (see Insight, "Paul Wittgenstein"); the other, in G major (1929–31), for Mme Marguerite Long. The D-major concerto has only one movement, an Allegro with Lento introduction, and contains a quasi-improvisatory episode with elements of jazz. There is a good deal of rapid figuration in the concerto, sweeping arpeggios, and a magnificent cadenza that reviews all of the themes. *Concerto for Left Hand* is an extraordinary work; it does not sound as though the performer is using only one hand.

insight

Paul Wittgenstein

Austrian pianist Paul Wittgenstein (1887–1961) made his début in 1913 in Vienna. In 1914, he was wounded in World War I and lost his right arm, but he determined to pursue a concert career by performing pieces for the left hand. This meant he had to commission or compose the works, since no repertoire for left hand alone existed. Outstanding composers rose to the challenge and accepted commissions to write works for him. Among the most significant compositions for piano (left hand) and orchestra are: Richard Strauss's *Parergon zur Symphonia domestica* (1924) and *Panathenäenzug* (1927), symphonic études in the form of a passacaglia; Maurice Ravel's *Concerto for Left Hand* (1929–30); Sergey Prokofiev's Piano Concerto No. 4 (B♭ major; 1931); and Benjamin Britten's *Diversions on a Theme* (Op. 21; 1940). Lesser composers also were commissioned to write works, and many concerti, sonatas, piano solos, and pieces of chamber music were created for Wittgenstein.

In 1939 Wittgenstein moved to New York, where he taught privately and at Manhattanville College of the Sacred Heart. He wrote and published a method for handicapped pianists, *School for the Left Hand* (1957). Because of Wittgenstein's determination and commissions, there is now available a repertoire of piano literature for pianists who are able to use only the left hand.

Classicism is apparent in Ravel's chamber music: a cyclic String Quartet in F major (1903), a Piano Trio (1914), a violin/piano Sonata (1922), and a 'cello/piano Sonata (1927). The Piano Trio, which contains some elements of Impressionism, is an especially important contribution to the repertoire.

Ravel wrote a considerable amount of vocal music, much of it for solo voice with piano. However, the two groups of solos for which he supplied chamber ensemble accompaniment—*Trois poèmes de Stéphane Mallarmé* (Three poems by Stéphane Mallarmé; 1913) and *Chansons madécasses* (Songs of Madagascar; 1926)—are his most significant contribution to vocal solo literature. The Mallarmé settings were inspired by Schoenberg's *Pierrot Lunaire,* which Ravel had heard in Berlin, but Ravel did not use *sprechstimme* (speech-song). *Chansons madécasses* resulted when Elizabeth S. Coolidge commissioned him to write a song cycle for voice accompanied by piano, flute, and 'cello. Ravel chose three works by the eighteenth-century Creole poet Evariste Parny and set them with simplicity, giving the performers independent lines in the manner of a quartet with emphasis on the soprano. Each song is different—a passionate love song, a savage incitement for revolt, and a pastoral piece. The music is economical, and the stark realism of *Aoua!*, the middle song, is unique among Ravel's works. From time to time, Ravel harmonized folk songs of various lands and made orchestral arrangements of other composers' works. The most notable of the latter is his orchestration of Musorgsky's *Pictures at an Exhibition* (1922).

Other Impressionist Composers

Impressionism is found in the work of other composers, both French and foreign. Among them are Albert Roussel (1869–1937), Florent Schmitt (1870–1958), and Déodat de Séverac (1873–1921) in France, Ottorino Respighi (1879–1936) in Italy, Charles Griffes (1884–1920) in United States, and the English composer Frederick Delius (1862–1934), who worked in France after 1888. One of Griffes's best-known Impressionistic works is *The White Peacock,* from *Roman Sketches,* Op. 7 (1915–16).

Roussel, a student of d'Indy, first composed in cyclical forms, then was influenced by Impressionism, and wrote, among other things, *Evocations* (1910–11) for soloists, chorus, and orchestra. His work, like Ravel's, exhibits clarity of form and phrasing. Next, Roussel was attracted by Indian music and incorporated Hindu scale forms, irregular meters, and ostinato figures in his opera-ballet *Padmâvatî* (1914) and the symphonic poem *Pour une fête de printemps* (For a spring festival; 1920). Finally, he turned to Neo-Classicism and produced several orchestral works in that vein, including the Suite in F (1926), the Concerto for small orchestra (1926–27), his Third and Fourth Symphonies (1930; 1934), and a Piano Concerto (1927).

Respighi's greatest success came with his symphonic poems *Le fontane di Roma* (The fountains of Rome; 1917) and *I pini di Roma* (The pines of Rome; 1924), each in four movements. The insertion of a phonograph recording of a nightingale's song in *I pini di Roma* was, at that time, an innovation.

Lili Boulanger

Lili Boulanger (1893–1918) grew up in musical surroundings. Her father's parents had both been awarded prizes at Paris Conservatoire; her father, who taught there, had won the Prix de Rome, and her mother was a talented singer, though not a professional musician. Her sister Nadia (see p. 844) was quite talented. Lili evidenced musical talent when she was very young. She had private lessons on piano, harp, violin, and 'cello and studied composition with Georges Caussade and Paul Vidal at the Conservatoire. In 1913, she was awarded the Prix de Rome for her cantata *Faust et Hélène* (Faust and Helen); she was the first woman to receive that award. Her stay in Rome was cut short by ill health. She knew her time was limited and worked hard to complete some major works before her death.

Lili Boulanger composed more than 50 pieces of music during her short life. Some of her finest works are *Du fond de l'abîme* (Out of the depths . . . , setting Ps. 130; 1914–17; alto, tenor, chor., orch., organ), a work that shows her capable of handling solo voices and large ensembles admirably; *Vieille prière bouddhique* (Old Buddhist prayer; 1917; tenor, chor., orch.); and *Piè Jesu* (Holy Jesus; 1918; mezzo, str. qrt., harp, organ). Her instrumental works include some chamber music, two symphonic poems, a few pieces for small orchestra, some songs, piano solos, *Ave Maria* for organ, and some instrumental solos for violin/piano and flute/piano. The *Nocturne* (vln., pno., 1911; DWMA213) is delicate, with impressionistic tendencies, and shows Debussy's influence. An opera, *La princess Maleine* (Princess Maleine, based on Maeterlinck), was unfinished at the time of her death.

Erik Satie

The eccentric composer Erik Satie (1866–1925) was highly influential in Paris during the first quarter of the twentieth century. He wrote in a style that was neither Impressionistic nor anti-Impressionistic but was extremely individualistic. Some elements of his late style were as avant-garde as some of the music produced in the 1960s.

As a youth, Satie had organ and piano lessons. In the early 1880s he enrolled in a harmony class at Paris Conservatoire but was lackadaisical about his studies and accomplished little. After completing a year's required military service (1886–87), he composed a few piano pieces, including three *Sarabandes* (1887) and the suite *Trois Gymnopédies* (3 Gymnopédies; 1888). In 1890, the oriental-sounding *Gnossiennes* (Gnostics) appeared. By then Satie had become interested in mystical religions and joined the *Rose + Croix* (Rosacrucian) movement headed by Joséphin Péladan. Satie became the official composer of the organization. Music he composed while active in the group (1891–95) has an aura of mysticism and contains unresolved ninth chords, successions of first-inversion triads, and melodies in ancient Greek modes. One such piece is *Salut drapeau!* (Salute the flag!; 1891), a Rosacrucian hymn on a text by Péladin. Some of Satie's pieces have foolish directives, e.g., *avec beaucoup de mal* (with much difficulty). *Vexations* (1893) contains instructions to repeat a passage 840 times in succession. Not until 9 September 1963, in New York, was *Vexations* actually performed as directed. On the other hand, some of Satie's music is serious. Between 1893 and 1895 he composed a *Messe des pauvres* (Mass for the poor), a Latin Mass with psalms settings, for chorus and organ. In 1891 Satie met Debussy, who became interested in the monodic style and modal-sounding harmonies of *Gymnopédies* and orchestrated two of them.

From 1905 to 1908 Satie studied counterpoint, fugue, and orchestration at the Schola Cantorum, with d'Indy and Roussel. Around this time, either in retaliation for critical comment about the form and content of his compositions or simply to caricature the music being composed by others, Satie began writing satirical pieces with humorous titles and bizarre directives for the performers. Among these are the piano duets *Trois morceaux en forme de poire* (Three pieces in form of a pear; c. 1903) and the piano solos *Embryons desséchés* (Dessicated embryos; 1913) and *Descriptions automatiques* (Automatic descriptions; 1913). The music is spare of texture, frequently written in only two parts; the sound is dry, capricious, witty. The notation of such pieces is avant-garde, sometimes with black notes on red staves, without barlines, without key signatures. Some of Satie's calligraphy is beautiful. The pages in the facsimile edition of *Sports et divertissements* (Sports and entertainments; 20 miniatures; 1914) are artwork worthy of framing. In the songs *Trois poèmes d'amour* (Three poems about love; 1914) Satie satirized the *e* that is silent when French words are spoken but is vocalized when they are sung.

Some of Satie's best work occurs in his ballets, *Parade* (1917), *Relâche* (Theater closed; 1924), and in the symphonic drama *Socrate* (Socrates; 1918), for four sopranos and chamber orchestra. *Parade* satirizes the activities of a small troupe of performers on tour. The orchestration of *Parade* calls for siren and typewriter. In *Relâche* jazz is included, perhaps for the first time in Paris. Satie's *Musique d'ameublement* (Properties music), created as background for intervals between selections at a concert, calls for instrumentalists stationed at various places in the concert hall to simultaneously play different music at different *tempi*.

Satie's music was misunderstood by many persons because he was so avant-garde. To some degree, his miniatures and sparse textures forecast the very compressed pieces of Webern, and the spatial separation of performers predicts similar requests by composers active after 1945. Satie's influence extended beyond the young composers who gathered around him and affected the work of Ravel, Edgard Varèse, John Cage, and others later in the century.

Les Six Français

In 1917 six students at the Paris Conservatoire began meeting together to share ideas about music. In June they began giving joint concerts, performing their own music and new music by others. In the group were Georges Auric (1899–1983), Louis Durey (1888–1979), Arthur Honegger (1892–1955), Darius Milhaud (1892–1974), Francis Poulenc (1899–1963), and Germaine Tailleferre (1892–1983). They called themselves *Les nouveaux jeunes* (The new youth). They were joined by author Jean Cocteau (1889–1963), who promoted their work in his articles in *Le coq et l'arlequin* (The cock and the harlequin). Also, they were attracted to Erik Satie whose work embodied some of their precepts.

Les Six, with Cocteau. Left to right: Milhaud, Auric, Honegger, Tailleferre, Poulenc, Durey, and Cocteau at the piano. Photograph, 1952.

In 1920 journalist Henri Collet referred to this student group as *Les six français* (The French Six). He wrote of them in the same sentence with the Russian Five, and he was not incorrect, for the two groups had in common a desire to compose music devoid of German characteristics. In addition, The Six advocated: (1) choosing subjects from everyday life for use in program music, operas, and ballets; (2) using machines as instruments or source material; (3) writing for nonconventional as well as conventional instruments; and (4) learning about styles other than those suited to the concert hall, e.g., circus band, jazz band, or café-cabaret entertainment, and writing in those styles if they so desired. They thought compositions should be brief, dry, and straightforward. Some of the individual works of The Six evidence that they acted on their beliefs. They collaborated in producing *Album des Six,* which contains piano pieces by each of them, and *Les mariés de la tour Eiffel* (The wedding party at the Eiffel Tower; 1921), a ballet-farce on a text by Cocteau. In *Les mariés . . .* there are two speaking voices, representing phonographs, that describe the mime of the ballet. The Six did not remain active as a group; even before Satie's death, they had

begun to lose cohesion. Their ideas about music changed somewhat, but all continued to compose to some degree. Their individual activities are discussed in Chapter 25.

Britain

England

In England, throughout the nineteenth century, there was continued interest in oratorio, opera, music festivals, madrigal singing, and old music. Various special societies were formed to undertake publication of particular works: the Purcell Society (Purcell's complete works), the Plainsong and Mediaeval Music Society (Sarum chantbooks), Musical Antiquarian Society (works of Byrd, Gibbons, Weelkes, and Wilbye). John Stainer published a number of chansons by Du Fay and his contemporaries, from MS Canonici misc. 213. The various music festivals and the London Philharmonic commissioned works by many European composers. English composers active between 1870–1920 include Edward Elgar (1857–1934), Ethel Smyth (1858–1944), Frederick Delius (1862–1934), Ralph Vaughan Williams (1872–1958), and Gustavus (von) Holst (1874–1934). Of those composers, only Holst and Vaughan Williams (see Ch. 25) were interested in English folk music.

Gustavus T. (von) Holst

From early childhood Holst practiced piano under the supervision of his father, a pianist and organist, but Gustav had no instruction in harmony, and little attention was paid to his youthful attempts at composition. He studied Berlioz's treatise on instrumentation and was largely self-taught where composition was concerned. Gustav had poor eyesight, suffered from asthma, and during his teens developed neuritis in his right arm. Finally, his father realized that Gustav could never be a concert pianist, and he was permitted to study composition at Oxford. He was a diligent student but was not brilliant; his student works were highly chromatic and were strongly influenced by Wagner's music, which he greatly admired. At Oxford Holst met and became a close friend of Vaughan Williams; throughout their lives, they shared with one another sketches of their works in progress.

While at Oxford, Holst conducted a choir that met at poet William Morris's (1834–96) home in Hammersmith. There he made two important contacts: he met Isobel Harrison, whom he married in 1901, and he was introduced to Hindu literature and philosophy. Holst became proficient in Sanskrit, read stories from the *Ramayana* and *Mahābharata,* and translated hymns from the *Rig Veda* (see Ch. 1). Hindu mysticism influenced several of Holst's works: *Hymns from the Rig Veda* (9 hymns; vc., pno.; 1907–8), *Choral Hymns from the Rig Veda* (4 sets; chor., instrs.; 1908–12), the one-act chamber opera *Sāvitri* (from *Mahābharata;* 1908), the three-act opera *Sita* (from *Ramayana;* 1900–1906), and some individual songs, e.g., *Invocation to the Dawn* (bar., pno.; 1902).

In 1903, Holst accepted a teaching position at a girls' school in Dulwich; in 1905, he became music director at St. Paul's Girls' School, Hammersmith, and taught there, with a few leaves of absence, until his death. He came to America to conduct and lecture at University of Michigan in 1923 and was visiting lecturer in composition at Harvard University in 1932. Holst had limited time for composition because, in addition to teaching, he conducted amateur choral ensembles, orchestras, and festivals. He was responsible for the first performance in England of some of J. S. Bach's cantatas.

Holst became interested in English folk songs in 1903 when Vaughan Williams shared with him some that he had collected. Acquaintance with modal folk songs changed Holst's syle and removed from it much of the chromaticism that colored his early works. This is apparent in *A Somerset Rhapsody* (orch.; 1906–7), which is based on folk song. He made choral settings of 12 Welsh folk songs (1930–31), at least two dozen English ones, and some traditional English Christmas carols.

Holst's best-known work is *The Planets* (1914–16), a suite of seven orchestral pieces, one for each of the planets then known to be in our galaxy. An eight-voice female chorus is included in *Neptune,* the last movement. Holst considered *Egdon Heath* (1927) his best work. Written in homage to Thomas Hardy (1840–1928), it is based on Hardy's description of the heath in *The Return of the Native.* One of Holst's finest songs is the short, deeply devotional *The Heart Worships* (1907). *The Hymn of Jesus* (1917), for two choruses, female semichorus, and orchestra, is a masterpiece. Holst incorporated in the work's Prelude the chants *Pange lingua* and *Vexilla regis,* both woven into the orchestral fabric and chanted vocally, and used as fundamental text this passage from the apocryphal *Acts of St. John:* "Ye who dance not know not what we are knowing." The music contains some sharp dissonances but conveys an overall sense of great exultation (DWMA214).

Holst was skilled at counterpoint and used a good deal of it in his later works; far from being pedantic, his counterpoint is filled with vitality. He was very economical and direct in his writing. For instance, he believed it unnecessary to use bridge passages to get from one theme or idea to another, and he was apt to stop a work abruptly rather than prepare for a final cadence. Bitonality occurs in some of his works; several vocal canons and the instrumental *Terzetto* are in three keys.

Imogen Holst (1907–84) prepared the thematic catalog of her father's works, wrote a biography of him, and a book about his music. She formed the Purcell Singers in 1953 and conducted them until 1967.

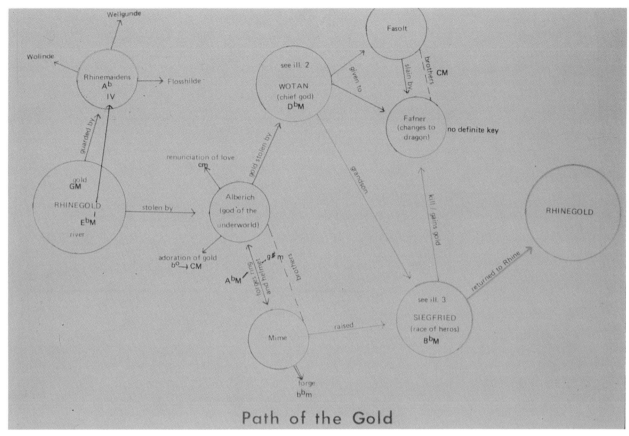

Wellgunde

Wolinde

Rhinemaidens
A♭
IV

→ Flosshilde

Fasolt

see ill. 2

WOTAN
(chief god)
D♭M

given to

brothers

slain by

CM

gold stolen by

Fafner
(changes to
dragon)

no definite key

guarded by

renunciation of love
cm

gold
GM

RHINEGOLD

E♭M

river

stolen by →

Alberich
(god of the
underworld)

grandson

RHINEGOLD

adoration of gold
b°→ CM

g♯m

brothers

A♭M — forges ring
and helmet

kill / gains gold

Mime

raised

see ill. 3

SIEGFRIED
(race of heros)
B♭M

returned to Rhine

forge
b♭m

Path of the Gold

Plate 23 Chart showing the Path of the Gold in Wagner's *Der
Ring des Nibelungen. (Courtesy Ellen Augustine, Goshen,
Indiana.)*

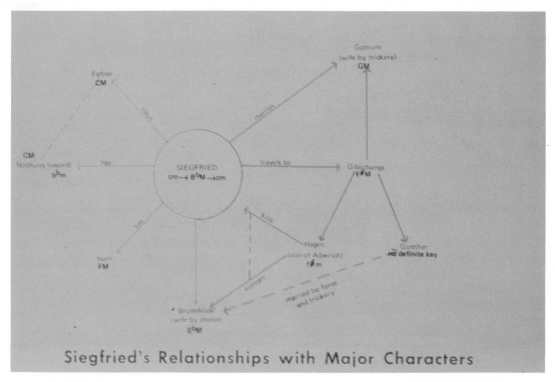

(a)

Plate 24 Siegfried's Relationships with Major Characters (*a*), and Wotan's Relationships with Major Characters (*b, facing page*), in Wagner's *Der Ring des Nibelungen. (Courtesy Ellen Augustine, Goshen, Indiana.)*

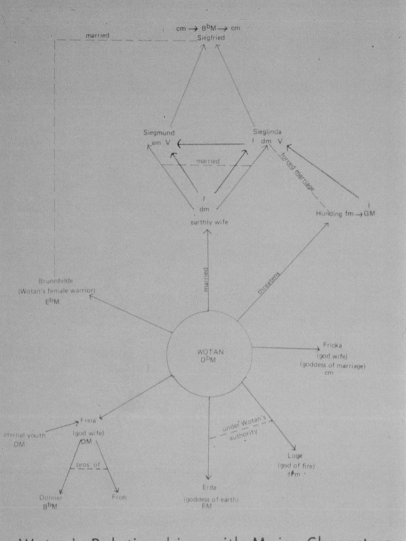

Wotan's Relationships with Major Characters

(b)

Plate 25 Claude Monet. *Impression: Soleil levant* (Sunrise), 1872, oil on canvas, 19⅝″ × 25½″. Present whereabouts of this painting is unknown; the work was stolen. *(Courtesy Cliche des Musées nationaux, Paris.)*

Plate 26 Edgar Degas. *Rehearsal on the Stage,* c. 1873, pastel,
21″ × 28½″. *(The H. O. Havemeyer Collection, The
Metropolitan Museum of Art, New York City.)*

Plate 27 Marc Chagall. *Green Violinist*, c. 1923, oil on canvas,
78″ × 42¾″. *(Solomon R. Guggenheim Museum, New York
City.)*

Plate 28 Fallingwater, the Kaufmann weekend house constructed in 1935–37 near Mill Run, Pennsylvania. Frank Lloyd Wright, architect.

Plate 29 Paul Cézanne. *Mountains in Provence,* c. 1886, oil on canvas, 25½″ × 31¾″. *(National Gallery, London.)*

(a)

(c)

(b)

Plate 30 Three panels from *The Isenheim Altarpiece*, painted by Matthias Grunewald c. 1510–15: (*a*) Engelkonzert (Angelic Concert); (*b*) Grablegung (Entombment); and (*c*) Versuchung des heiligen Antonius (The Temptation of St. Anthony). *(Sources: (a) © Scala/Art Resource, New York; (b) © Giraudon/ Art Resource, New York; (c) © Scala/Art Resource, New York.)*

Plate 31 Pablo Picasso. *Les demoiselles d'Avignon,* 1907, oil on canvas, 8′ × 7′8″. *(Museum of Modern Art, New York City.)*

Plate 32 William Hogarth. *A Rake's Progress,* c. 1733, oil on
canvas, 24½″ × 29½″. *(Sir John Soane's Museum, London.)*

Example 24.16 Elgar: *Enigma Variations*, original theme. (Copyright © 1899 Novello & Company, Ltd., Novello, Borough Green, Sevenoaks, Kent, England.)

She was one of the first women in Britain to conduct brass and military bands. Though she attended the Royal College of Music on a composition scholarship, she composed no significant works.

Edward Elgar

Elgar's only formal training in music consisted of a few violin lessons, but he learned a great deal from observation, at church, at his father's music store, and at meetings of choral societies. He played violin and bassoon well enough to participate in ensembles, substituted for his father as organist at St. George's Roman Catholic Church in Worcester, and conducted instrumental and choral ensembles in public programs. Elgar began writing music at the age of ten—incidental music for a family play. He used some of that music later in his two orchestral suites *The Wand of Youth* (No. 1, 1907; No. 2, 1908) and in incidental music for Pearn's play *The Starlight Express* (1915).

The composition that first brought Elgar national recognition is *Variations on an Original Theme,* better known as *Enigma Variations* (1898–99). Elgar explained carefully that, in addition to his original theme (ex. 24.16), which has 14 variations, another larger theme goes through the entire work, but he never revealed that theme or its meaning. Various conjectures have been made as to what that larger theme is; none has been proven. The first and last variations represent, respectively, Elgar's wife and himself; the other 12 characterize friends and a friend's bulldog. Most of the movements are headed by the three initials of the person portrayed.

The list of Elgar's compositions is long and comprises works in all genres. The piece that is heard most often is the first of his five marches entitled *Pomp and Circumstance* (D major; 1901). Of his five oratorios, the finest is *The Dream of Gerontius* (1900; Mez., T, Bar. soloists, chor., orch.), setting most of Cardinal John Newman's poem of the same title. The text concerns an ordinary man facing imminent death, judg-

ment, and eternity. Part I of the oratorio is filled with despair; Part II expresses hope in the vision of eternity. Elgar used representative motives, and the influence of Wagner's *Parsifal* is apparent. Elgar's music is expressive, with choral and orchestral music subtly integrated. Gerontius's solos vary from natural speech-rhythms to lyricism. When first performed, the oratorio was not well received and was criticized for being too theological. In fact, chorus members as well as audience disliked the most intense portions of it, especially that concerning Purgatory.

Another excellent work is *Falstaff* (1913), a "symphonic study" that portrays the gentlemanly side of Falstaff's character, visible through all events in his life.

Elgar did not quote folk songs in his works but did depict programmatically some English scenes and events, and some of his works evidence strong patriotism, as does *The Spirit of England* (1915–17; S or T solo, chor., orch.), his last choral work. Contributing to the "English" sound of Elgar's music are characteristic traits of late medieval English music, such as passages in parallel thirds and cross-relations. The oratorios *The Apostles* (1903) and *The Kingdom* (1906) provide examples.

Ethel Smyth

Ethel Smyth was born into a prosperous middle-class military family in Britain and received the general education typically given girls in England in the late nineteenth century. She knew as a child that she wanted to be a musician and was determined to study music in continental Europe. In 1877 she entered Leipzig Conservatory but, like many others, was not pleased with the kind of training she was receiving there, so she arranged for private instruction. Through her teacher, Heinrich von Herzogenberg, Smyth met many of the leading musicians of the time. She was a proficient pianist and a competent singer but was not of concert caliber in either area. Her first compositions were a String Quintet (1884), a violin/piano Sonata (1887), a 'cello/piano Sonata (1887), and two sets of Lieder (c. 1886). In 1891 she composed a Mass in D major (SATB soloists, chor., orch.), which was performed by the Royal Choral Society at Royal Albert Hall, London. After seeing the Mass, the German conductor Hermann Levi (1839–1900) urged Smyth to write an opera. She took his advice. Her first opera, *Fantasio* (1892–94), was performed in Weimar in 1898. Her second, *Der Wald* (The Forest; 1899–1901), with the forest setting of a German Romantic opera, has a Wagnerian-type theme of salvation through death. The heroes of the opera are the chorus of forest spirits (as was the chorus of people in Musorgsky's *Boris Godunov*).

Smyth's third opera, *Les Naufrageurs* (The Wreckers; 1903–4), is her finest and best-known work. It has never been performed in the original French, but it was translated into German and, under the title *Standrecht,* was performed in Leipzig and Prague in 1906. Smyth translated it into English and Thomas Beecham (1879–1961) directed it in London in 1909. *The Wreckers* shows Wagner's influence in use of *Leitmotifs,* the style of the contrapuntal writing, and the large orchestral resources. Smyth made effective use of chorus; in places, choral hymn-singing offstage accompanies singers on stage. The Prelude to Act II, "On the Cliffs of Cornwall," is descriptive sea music.

In 1910 Smyth was awarded an honorary Mus.D. by Durham University and in 1922 was made a Dame of the British Empire. She wrote three more operas: *Fête galante* (Galant festival; 1923) and the comedies *The Boatswain's Mate* (1913–14) and *Entente cordiale* (1925). Her other compositions include choral works with orchestral accompaniment, a double concerto for horn and violin with orchestra, about a dozen solo songs, and some chamber music. Her last composition, *The Prison* (1930), is a symphonic work for two soloists, chorus, and orchestra. Smyth's style is eclectic, not distinctively personal. Her operas clearly show the influence of Wagner and Arthur Sullivan. Smyth had literary talent, also. She prepared the libretti for all six of her operas, and, after deafness forced her to abandon her career as composer, she wrote ten books.

Frederick Delius

Frederick Delius was a member of a mercantile family that enjoyed amateur music making but regarded music unfavorably as a profession. Accordingly, he had music lessons but entered the family business. After proving unreliable there, he learned the basics of harmony and composition from a friend and entered Leipzig Conservatory. In Leipzig, Delius met Grieg, who persuaded Delius's father to allow Frederick to continue composing. Not until 1903 did Delius write any worthwhile music; none of his major works were performed in England until 1907.

Delius was not a nationalistic composer, and none of his works sounds particularly English, though he wrote program music on English subjects, e.g., *Brigg Fair: An English Rhapsody* (orch.; 1907). He composed several operas, incidental music for plays, concerti, orchestral works, chamber music, and choral and vocal pieces. Delius is seen at his best in works for soloists, chorus, and orchestra, such as *Sea Drift* (Bar., chor., orch.; 1903–4), a setting of poetry by Walt Whitman; and *A Mass of Life* (SATBar solos, chor., orch.; 1904–5), setting texts from Nietzsche's *Also sprach Zarathustra. A Mass of Life* reflects Delius's personal philosophy that everyone should live life to the fullest, realizing all potentialities of one's capabilities and talents, no matter what the cost, and fearlessly pursue life's course, in the knowledge that death is inevitable. Thomas Beecham conducted the first performance of *A Mass of Life* in 1909 in London and became a staunch supporter of Delius's music.

Delius's best-known work is the tone poem *On Hearing the First Cuckoo in Spring* (1912), the second of two works published as *Pieces for Small Orchestra*. The other piece, *Summer Night on the River* (1911), is Impressionistic. So is *In a Summer Garden* (1908), an orchestral rhapsody, free in form, with some sensuous harmonies, and at times rather pointillistic in the depiction of light and shade. In several of Delius's works for orchestra and chorus, the choral singing is textless, e.g., *A Song of the High Hills* (1911) and *Songs to be sung of a Summer Night on the Water* (2 songs for SATTBB chorus; 1917). On the whole, Delius's melodies are simple and are sometimes quite lyrical; his harmonies are Romantic, basically triadic, with secondary sevenths and dominant discords. In many of his works, harmony seems to be more important than melody.

Wales, Ireland, Scotland

In Britain, nationalism was more prominent in the music of Ireland and Scotland than in England itself. England had acquired those lands aggressively and had dominated them for several centuries, but the Irish and Scottish hope for their own kingdoms never died, and their pride in their national background was preserved in their literature and folk music. Music in England was cosmopolitan and had been dominated by foreigners since the time of Handel. Moreover, British composers had been subjected to all kinds of uncomplimentary comparisons with German musicians, even though most British composers received their training in Germany. There had been little opportunity anywhere for British composers. Near the end of the nineteenth century the tide began to turn.

The folk element was always present in the music of Wales. The Welsh treasure their Celtic heritage and have maintained links with their historical past through their unique language and their music. Thus, Welsh music was conscious nationalism with a different purpose than that of most countries in the nineteenth century. The *eisteddfod* (session), a competitive festival mainly for music and literature, originated in medieval times but became popular in the eighteenth century. The National Eisteddfod was established in 1880 and has been held annually since that time. The most important prizes are Chief Choral and Chief Male Voice. During the twentieth century, Welsh communities in the United States (Pennsylvania, Ohio, and elsewhere) have held *eisteddfods*.

Welsh composer Joseph Parry (1841–1903) composed songs and glees with Welsh texts and wrote the first Welsh opera, *Blodwen* (1878). Parry composed five operas, most of them on Welsh and English subjects, several oratorios and cantatas, some orchestral music, and edited and harmonized a six-volume collection of Welsh songs (*Cambrian Minstrelsie;* 1893). The most famous of his approximately 400 hymn tunes is *Aberystwyth* (1879); it is in many Protestant hymnals in the twentieth century.

Other Welsh composers who made significant contributions to choral music repertoire are David Evans (1834–1913) and David Jenkins (1849–1915). David V. Thomas (1873–1934) set medieval Welsh poetry to music, and the works of David de Lloyd (1883–1948) were greatly influenced by Welsh folk music.

Both Irish and English elements are present in the works of Dublin-born Charles V. Stanford (1851–1924), pianist-organist. Stanford was professor of composition at Royal College of Music (1883–1924) and professor of music at Cambridge University (1887–1924). Among his orchestral works are five Irish Rhapsodies (1901–14), two sets of Irish dances, *Symphony No. 3, "Irish,"* and *Irish Concertino* (vln., vcl., orch.). He published three volumes of Irish folk song arrangements (130 songs). Stanford's compositions include a Mass, several choral works, seven symphonies, and six operas, one being *The Canterbury Pilgrims.*

Alexander Mackenzie (1847–1935), the most important Scottish composer since the Reformation, came from a long line of musicians. A violinist, Mackenzie served as principal of Royal Academy of Music, London, from 1888 to 1924. His reputation as a composer was established by performances of his cantatas and oratorios at English festivals during the 1880s. Mackenzie prepared and published arrangements of Scottish folk songs, and many of his compositions contain folk-music elements. Among such works are the *Pibroch Suite* (vln., orch.; 1889); the *Highland Ballad* (vln., orch., 1893); *Scottish Concerto* (pno., orch.; 1897); three orchestral rhapsodies: *Scottish Rhapsody No. 1* (1880), *Burns, Scottish Rhapsody No. 2* (1881), *Tam o'Shanter, Scottish Rhapsody No. 3* (1911); the piano suite *In the Scottish Highlands* (1881). In addition, he composed a *Canadian Rhapsody* (1905) and the suite *London Day by Day.* Spanish violin virtuoso Pablo de Sarasate (1844–1908) first performed the works featuring violin; the *Scottish Concerto* was first performed by Polish pianist Ignace Paderewski (1860–1941).

United States

During the 1860s, the United States experienced Civil War and the assassination of President Lincoln, and after 1865 many areas of the country were badly in need of reconstruction. These circumstances influenced popular rather than serious art music, however, for most of America's composers were still European-trained and wrote music that reflected European styles. Very few American composers were inspired by or tapped for resources the wealth of indigenous

Example 24.17 Paine's use of thematic variation in the Prelude to *Oedipus Tyrannus,* Op. 35: (*a*) the theme, mm. 26–29, and its transformations in (*b*) mm. 55–57 and (*c*) mm. 78–80. *(Source: Paine's Prelude to Oedipus Tyrannus, Op. 35, copyright © 1881 Arthur P. Schmidt, Boston, M.A.)*

material that surrounded them—Indian tribal melodies, black spirituals, New England hymns, gospel songs. James Bland (1854–1911), one of the few who did, composed more than 700 popular songs, such as *Carry Me Back to Old Virginny* and *Oh, Dem Golden Slippers*. Between 1860 and 1920 American conservatories of music were founded—Peabody Institute in Baltimore and Oberlin Conservatory were the first—and private citizens financed the building of concert halls in major cities. European virtuosi and opera troupes concertized in the United States, noted composers came to teach for a while, and American concert programs were filled with music by European composers. The most important American composers during the last decades of the nineteenth century were James Knowles Paine (1839–1906) and Edward MacDowell (1860–1908).

Paine

Paine received his early musical training from Herman Kotzschmar, a German musician living in Maine, then, in 1858–61, studied in Berlin. On returning to America, Paine became organist at Appleton Chapel in Cambridge, Massachusetts, and presented a series of organ recitals and public lectures on various aspects of music. He joined the faculty of Harvard University in 1862, and, in 1875, when Harvard

became the first American university to establish a professorship of music, Paine was appointed to that post. Besides many organ works (most of them still unpublished), Paine's compositions include incidental music for plays, two operas, numerous choral works, a few songs, two symphonies, a symphonic poem, and some chamber music. Bach was the model for Paine's early organ works, but many of Paine's compositions reflect the influence of Mendelssohn, Schumann, and other German early Romanticists. The works written after c. 1880 show increased chromaticism and Chopinesque figurations, not always used to advantage, e.g., in Symphony No. 2. One of Paine's finest late works is the incidental music to Sophocles's *Oedipus tyrannus* (King Oedipus; 1880–81), particularly the Prelude, in which he effectively used thematic transformation (ex. 24.17).

MacDowell

As a child, Edward MacDowell studied piano with Juan Buitrago and Teresa Carreño (1853–1917). Carreño recognized the measure of his talent and encouraged study abroad. In 1876–78 MacDowell studied at Paris Conservatoire, then went to Germany for piano, counterpoint, advanced theory, and composition lessons. For several years he enjoyed a successful career in Europe as teacher, composer, and concert pianist. He returned to the United States in the autumn of 1888 and began his American concert career in Boston in November. When Columbia University established a chair of music in 1896, MacDowell was appointed to that professorship and retained it until 1904.

MacDowell's earliest works date from 1876; he composed nothing after 1902, when his health began to deteriorate. Many of his early works were published under the pseudonym Edgar Thorn. Mac-Dowell's compositions for piano include 2 piano concerti (A minor, D minor), 16 sets of character pieces, 4 sonatas, and some études. He wrote 2 orchestral suites, 4 symphonic poems, at least 42 solo songs, and more than 20 choral works. His music is tonal and shows especially the influence of Liszt, whom he knew, and Grieg. The styles of Schumann, Rubinstein, and Wagner were influential also. MacDowell's *Sonata eroica* (G minor; 1894–95) was modeled after Liszt's B-minor Sonata and shows some relationship to Liszt's *Eroica*. Most of MacDowell's instrumental compositions are Romantic program music. Some of the piano pieces are quite simple; others require virtuosic technique. Perhaps his best-known work is *To a Wild Rose,* from ten *Woodland Sketches* (1896). Other well-known sets of character pieces for piano are the eight *Sea Pieces* (1898) and ten *New England Idyls* (1901–2). In 1887 Mac-Dowell wrote several collections of piano pieces that are interpretations of poems: *6 Idyls after Goethe, Sechs Gedichte nach Heinrich Heine* (Six poems of Heinrich Heine), and *Vier kleine Poesien* (Four little poems). The poem interpreted is printed at the head of the piano piece.

Though MacDowell musically portrayed some New England scenes, he rarely used indigenous American materials in his compositions. Theodore Baker's *Über die Musik der Nordamerikanischer Wilden* (About the music of the North American savages) provided thematic material for MacDowell's orchestral *Suite No. 2, "Indian,"* but the chromatic harmonies and thick texture of the suite often obscure the Indian melodies. The suite is in five movements: "Legend," "Love Song," "In War-time," "Dirge," and "Village Festival." MacDowell was supportive of American composers and American music, but he believed strongly that the music should stand on its own

Princess Tsianina Redfeather.

merits and not be performed simply because its composer was American. He would not permit performance of his music on programs devoted solely to American music.

After MacDowell's death, his widow, pianist Marian Nevins MacDowell (1857–1956), converted their summer home into a working retreat (The MacDowell Colony) for artists, composers, and writers, and she helped support that cultural community by performing concerts of her husband's music. Since 1960 a MacDowell Medal has been awarded annually to a distinguished artist, composer, or writer.

Cadman, Farwell

The music of American Indians influenced the work of other composers, principally, Arthur Farwell (1877–1952) and Charles W. Cadman (1881–1946). Cadman was interested in Indian music, spent several months on Omaha and Winnebago reservations, made recordings of Indian songs, and arranged and published some of them. "At Dawning" and "From the Land of the Sky-blue Water" from *Four American Indian Songs* were very popular. He organized and presented a series of lecture-recitals with Omaha Indian Princess Tsianina Redfeather, mezzo soprano, a descendant of Tecumseh. Cadman used Indian melodies in many of his compositions. His most successful work was the opera *Shanewis or The Robin Woman* (1918), based on the life of Redfeather. *Shanewis* was performed by The Metropolitan Opera in 1918 and 1919.

Farwell, trained as an electrical engineer, was encouraged by MacDowell to make music his career. Farwell's primary interest was American Indian music, but he worked with Anglo-American folk song and the music of Spanish-Americans, blacks, and cowboys as well. Failing to find a publisher for his *American Indian Melodies* (1900), Farwell founded Wa-Wan Press, which published in beautiful volumes the music of contemporary American composers. Farwell's compositions cover a wide range, from *Navajo War Dance No. 1* to settings of Emily Dickinson poems, from preludes and fugues to *Polytonal Studies*.

Mrs. H. H. A. Beach

Amy M. Cheney (1867–1944) made her concert début as pianist in 1883 in Boston, and in October 1885 she performed Chopin's Concerto No. 2 with the Boston Symphony. In December 1885 she married Dr. H. H. A. Beach and thereafter used her married name in her career. She was the first American woman to achieve recognition as a composer of large forms. Her works include Mass in E♭ (1890), *Gaelic Symphony* (E minor; 1896), Piano Concerto (C♯ minor, 1899), the opera *Cabildo* (1932), a violin/piano Sonata (A minor; 1896), Piano Quintet (F♯ minor; 1898), Piano Trio (A minor; 1938), and numerous other piano pieces, choral works, and songs. Beach's Mass in E♭, premiered by the Boston Handel and Haydn Society in 1892, was that society's first performance of a composition by a woman. Her *Gaelic Symphony,* based on Irish folk melodies, is the first symphony composed by an American woman. The first performances of both the *Gaelic Symphony* (1896) and the Piano Concerto (1899) were by the Boston Symphony, with Beach as soloist in the concerto. After her husband's death (1910), Beach concertized in Europe for four years; in the 1920s she spent several summers composing at The MacDowell Colony. She

had a gift for melody and set the texts of her vocal works effectively and with correct declamation. Her most popular song was *The Year's at the Spring* (1899). The Sonata is Brahmsian, and the influence of Brahms and Liszt is seen in her piano works. In the Piano Quintet, her writing for piano is expressive and often rhapsodic, but the strings share in working out thematic material. A characteristic feature of the quintet is frequent use of Phrygian cadence.

Where music written and/or performed by women is concerned, Boston, in the 1890s, seems to have occupied a position comparable with that of the Medici court at Ferrara in the late sixteenth century. Mrs. Beach was not the only woman whose works were performed by the Boston Symphony. In 1893–96 that orchestra played several of Margaret R. Lang's (1867–1972, age 104) works: *Dramatic Overture,* the overtures *Totila* and *Wichitis,* and three arias for solo voice and orchestra. Helen Hood, Helen Hopekirk, and Mabel Daniels were active in Boston early in the twentieth century.

Foote, Chadwick, Parker

Among the New England composers active during the late nineteenth and early twentieth centuries and adhering to Classic-Romantic traditions were Arthur Foote (1853–1937), George Chadwick (1854–1931), and Horatio Parker (1863–1919). Foote, who had piano lessons as a child, had no intention of becoming a professional musician but changed his mind after studying with Paine at Harvard and earned the first master's degree in music granted by that university (1875). Some of Foote's finest works are *Ballad* (vln., pno.), Piano Trio No. 2 (B♭ major), and the Piano Quartet (1890). Most of his orchestral pieces were first performed by the Boston Symphony, and some have never been published, e.g., the overture *In the Mountains* (1886), which was performed also at the Paris Exposition in 1889. Foote wrote more than 100 solo songs, the best known being *The Night Has a Thousand Eyes, In Picardie,* and *I Know a Little Garden Path.* Other works by Foote include some cantatas, numerous keyboard pieces (piano, organ), three string quartets and other chamber music, a 'cello concerto, the symphonic poem *Francesca da Rimini,* and several suites. The Suite in E minor for strings (Op. 63; 1909) is excellent.

Chadwick began his professional career in music by serving for a year (1876) as head of the music department of Olivet College, Michigan, then spent several years studying organ and composition in Europe. On returning to America in 1880, he accepted an organist position in Boston. In 1882 he joined the faculty of New England Conservatory as teacher of harmony and composition and in 1897–1930 was director of that school. Many of Chadwick's works follow traditional Germanic lines, but he did not limit himself to that style. In several works he incorporated popular melodies and Afro-Caribbean syncopated dance rhythms, and in the scherzo of Symphony No. 2 (Bb major; 1883–85) he used a Negro melody. His opera *The Padrone* is the first American *verismo* opera; it concerns Boston landlords' and guarantors' exploitation of Italian immigrants. Chadwick advocated using the natural rhythms of American speech (i.e., prosody), and those rhythms appear in several of his works, e.g., the operas *Tabasco* and *The Padrone*. Representative examples of Chadwick's non-Germanic style are the symphonic ballad *Tam O'Shanter* (1917) and the orchestral suite *Symphonic Sketches* (A major; 1895–1904).

Parker received organ and piano lessons from his mother, then studied with Chadwick at New England Conservatory and went to Munich for further training in organ and composition. In 1894 he was appointed professor of theory at Yale University and was dean of the School of Music there in 1904–19. Most of Parker's compositions are choral works on religious or medieval subjects and include Latin motets, cantatas, oratorios, anthems, and occasional pieces. In addition, he wrote songs, hymns, chamber music, operas and incidental music, orchestral works, a few piano pieces, and numerous organ works. His masterpiece is the 11-movement oratorio *Hora novissima* (The last hour; 1893), a setting of portions of a twelfth-century Latin poem describing the glories of heaven. The Latin verses are metrically rigid, but Parker skillfully avoided that rigidity in various ways. Though he was awarded prizes for his operas *Mona* (1912) and *Fairyland* (1915), neither is in standard repertoire. On the whole, Parker's music is conservative, tonal, with well-defined melodies, diatonic harmonies, and traditional key relationships and formal structures. Only a few works written in 1901–11 show tendencies

Charles Ives. *(Bettmann Newsphotos.)*

toward tonally evasive harmonies and chromaticism, e.g., the lyric rhapsody *A Star Song* (for solo voices, chorus, orch.), the concert aria *Crépuscle* (mezzo, orch.), and *Mona*.

Ives

Charles Ives (1874–1954) was an individualistic composer who did not teach and who founded no school. His works were strongly influenced by transcendentalist philosophies and by the ideas about music instilled in him by his father, who was his first teacher. George E. Ives (1845–94), who had been an army bandmaster during the Civil War, was active in Connecticut as music teacher and conductor. He was not a composer but thoroughly understood traditional harmony, counterpoint, and the music of Bach. Moreover, George Ives was interested in quarter tones, polytonality, acoustics, and the effect of space in relation to performance. He gave Charles thorough grounding in all of these things, as well as lessons on organ, piano, drums, and cornet. In addition, Charles absorbed all of the features of the various kinds of music that were part of the small town in which he lived. Frequently, George required Charles to sing or play a melody in one key while playing the accompaniment in another key. Charles retained an interest in polytonality and later wrote some four-voice fugues with each voice in a different key, e.g., *The Shining Shore* (1897).

By the time Ives was 12, he was composing. When he was 14, he held a salaried position as church organist at Danbury Baptist Church, and for the next 16 years, he served as a church organist in whatever city he lived. Quotations from hymns and canticles are a feature of his compositions. Ives was adept at improvising and at making variations. One of his early compositions for organ is a set of *Variations on "America,"* first improvised, then notated c. 1891.

During 1894–98 Ives pursued a business degree at Yale and also enrolled in Horatio Parker's music courses there. Ives and Parker did not always agree on compositional procedures, for Ives considered music confined to traditional harmonies "stupid music," but he respected Parker's regulations and did not show him many of the nonconformist pieces he wrote. Parker's assignments to rewrite well-known Lieder texts set by outstanding composers posed no difficulty for Ives, since he had done that kind of resetting many times for his father. While at Yale, Ives composed more than 75 pieces, including *First String Quartet: "From the Salvation Army"* and *First Symphony.* From his teens, Ives's works were characterized by musical quotations, strong dissonance, and bitonality or polytonality. He could and did write music that followed the rules of traditional harmony but not by preference. His first symphony, written at Yale, follows tradition, but his second has five movements and is filled with musical quotations and dissonance. Ives believed, as did his father, that not every dissonance required resolution. In Ives's terminology, to write music without strong dissonance was to be "lily-livered," or to be a "Rollo." However, Ives was primarily a melodist and did not sacrifice melody for dissonance.

After graduating from Yale, Ives obtained work in a New York insurance firm, secured a position as church organist, and spent his free time on weekends and evenings writing music. In 1902, he resigned his organist post in order to have more time for composing. Unfortunately, he left many of his anthems

and organ works at the church, and they have been lost. After 1902, Ives's music gradually became more experimental and more aurally challenging. He tended to write orchestral works in sets, one of the most famous bearing the lengthy title *I. A Contemplation of a Serious Matter or The Unanswered Question. II. A Contemplation of Nothing Serious or Central Park in the Dark "In the Good Old Summertime"* (1905). The set requires two orchestras and two conductors, unsynchronized, and juxtaposes tonal and atonal music. Atonal music is prominent in the first piece, with tonal music in the background; in the second piece, the conditions are reversed.

A heart problem forced Ives to take a vacation from business obligations in 1906; then, he and his friend Julian Myrick started their own insurance firm. There was never any thought that music would be Ives's vocation. Composition was an important avocational outlet for him, and at that time he did not care whether his works were ever performed. In fact, in his opinion, it is impossible to perform some of his music. In the "Postface" to *114 Songs* he indicated that if the rights of some of the songs were observed, those songs would not be sung. Ives once said, "What has sound to do with music?" He was even more independent than Beethoven and composed for self-satisfaction. It sufficed for Ives to hear his music mentally and to express it by sketching out the notation.

He continued to compose during much of his free time and to stack up the compositions at home. Because of his seeming disregard for the value of his music, many of his works have been lost or survive only in fragments. Not until after he suffered a serious heart attack in 1918 did he consider sharing his music and begin to sort through his sketches and make fair copies of some of his works. By that time, he had written several orchestral sets, four symphonies, four violin/piano sonatas, some string quartets and other chamber music, two piano sonatas and other keyboard works, numerous choral works and partsongs, and well over 100 solo songs. He made a fair copy of the *Second Piano Sonata: "Concord, Mass. 1840–60,"* wrote *Essays before a Sonata* to accompany the music, had both printed privately in 1920, and gave copies to persons he thought might be interested in them. Next, he assembled a collection of his vocal solos, had the *114 Songs* printed privately in 1922,

and distributed those copies in a similar manner. The texts of several of those songs were by his wife, Harmony Twitchell Ives (1876–1969).

In 1927 Charles Ives met Henry Cowell (1897–1965), and the two composers found they had several things in common: (1) their musical innovations had not been influenced by avant-garde European composers; (2) their use of tone clusters as a viable compositional device had occurred independently of each other; and (3) their music was affected to some extent by vernacular and popular music in their surroundings and background. By 1927 Ives had almost stopped composing; his creativity had waned considerably, and any new works he commenced were soon abandoned. Cowell printed some of Ives's works in *New Music Quarterly* and introduced Ives to Nicolas Slonimsky (b. 1894), who conducted the first performances of Ives's *Three Places in New England* (c. 1912) in Boston and abroad.

Around 1927, pianist John Kirkpatrick (b. 1905) became interested in the *Concord Sonata* and determined to learn it, a task that took years to accomplish. When he performed the sonata in New York's Town Hall in January 1939, the work received a favorable review, and a recital devoted entirely to Ives's music was presented in New York a month later. From then on, Ives began to be recognized as a great American avant-garde composer.

The *Concord Sonata* consists of four programmatic movements: "Emerson," "Hawthorne," "The Alcotts," and "Thoreau." In this work, Ives aimed to present musically the spirit of the philosophical and literary views of the transcendentalists of Concord.

Each movement was designed to depict his impression of the person(s) for whom it was named. The sonata is a cyclic work based on two principal motives that appear in various permutations in all four movements: the four-note motive that dominates Beethoven's Fifth Symphony and a descending five-note figure that is first stated in octaves. Cowell called the first motive "epic," the second "lyric." (See ex. 24.18.)

In the first three movements of the sonata, meter signatures and barlines appear infrequently; when a barline is used, it points up a significant musical event, e.g., the first appearance of the Beethoven motive in the "Emerson" movement (ex. 24.18b). In the last movement there are no key signatures, no meter signatures, and no barlines. The "Hawthorne" movement, designated Scherzo, is a little lighter in character than the first movement. Tone clusters occur frequently, sometimes in rapid succession (ex. 24.19a). In one section of the movement, a board 14¾ inches long is used to depress silently the piano keys covering an expanse of two octaves and a second, so that an echo chamber is created within the piano, and those strings can vibrate freely and produce harmonics when other chords are played normally (ex. 24.19b). Quotations from familiar tunes are included in the "Hawthorne" movement, too—snatches of a circus march and *Columbia, the Gem of the Ocean.*

The sonata's third movement, "The Alcotts" (DWMA215), is simpler in texture, in keeping with activities in the Alcott home, and includes portions of familiar hymns, *Loch Lomond,* and the "Wedding March" from *Lohengrin.* The key signatures Ives used

Example 24.19 *"Concord" Sonata*, mvt. 2: (*a*) passage of tone clusters played faster and faster; (*b*) clusters requiring use of a board. *(From Charles Ives,* Piano Sonata No. 2. *Copyright © 1947 (Renewed) Associated Music Publishers.)*

(a)

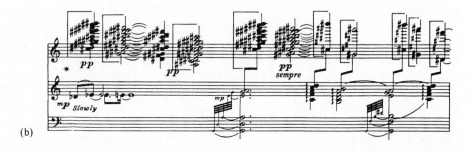

(b)

near the beginning of the movement openly indicate bitonality. Several chords in the "Thoreau" movement are designated "echo" and represent echoes over Walden Pond. In the last two-thirds of the movement, an ostinato figure recurs periodically. One instance of its use is in conjunction with an *ad libitum* flute melody that is intended to convey the sound of music floating over Walden Pond (ex. 24.20). Ives's associative use of quotations parallels literary authors' "stream of consciousness" technique—as writers used words, phrases, and quotations from other literary

works to invoke associations in the reader's mind, so Ives used musical quotations. He intended those quotations to be recognized.

In some works Ives does not quote at all, e.g., the songs *The Cage* (1906) and *Soliloquy, or a Study in 7ths and Other Things* (1907; DWMA216). *Soliloquy* commences with an unmeasured Adagio recitative-like section in which the singer chants or uses speech-song, over a three-chord ostinato accompaniment. In the ensuing Allegro, the metric unit is the 16th note, and the vocal melody is filled with major and minor sevenths and seconds. Ives systematically

Example 24.20 *"Concord" Sonata,* passage with flute near the end of mvt. 4. *(From Charles Ives,* Piano Sonata No. 2. *Copyright © 1947 (Renewed) Associated Music Publishers, Inc.)*

* Small notes in piano to be played only if flute is not used.

organized the accompaniment to consist of (1) four chords built note by note from the bottom up, each chord covering two measures; (2) a measure in which the successive chords are constructed of minor sevenths, perfect fifths, perfect fourths, alternate major and minor thirds, major seconds, and minor seconds; (3) a measure that reverses the foregoing constructional procedure and is almost the retrograde of the preceding chord series; and (4) four chords constructed note by note from top to bottom. For most of the Allegro, two measures of accompaniment correspond to one measure of melody.

The Cage resulted from Ives's observation of a boy watching a leopard pace back and forth in its cage. The song, written without barlines or meter signature, opens with piano introduction characterized by chords whose temporal value successively decreases. Almost all of the accompaniment chords are constructed of superimposed fourths or fifths. The vocal melody, mainly in eighth notes, moves stepwise in a persistent rising and falling pattern that depicts the monotony of the animal's pacing in its confined quarters. The last eight notes of the melody are a repetition of the first eight. To most listeners *The Cage* sounds atonal.

In Ives's musical style, no consistent line of development can be traced. He simply wrote to express his thoughts the way he wanted to, without regard for traditional rules of composition. He based at least one piece on a tone row, wrote some ragtime, and considered himself free to experiment in any way. His music is truly American, for he used indigenous musical material from various sources, and American literature, philosophy, and traditions were imbedded in his esthetic.

Cowell

Henry Cowell, pianist-composer and writer on music, maintained a lifelong interest in Irish folk melodies and legends. He was an innovative composer who wrote music spontaneously, even before he had formal training in music theory and composition. Before 1914 he had written more than 100 pieces of music. Among his innovative procedures was the use of large clusters of tones, which he called **tone clusters** and which he produced in *The Tides of Manaunaun* (c. 1912) by striking groups of piano keys with his hand or entire forearm. In *The Tides of Manaunaun,* which depicts huge waves aroused by the Irish god, the tone clusters are in the bass register, supporting a modal melody. The total effect is atonal. Though Ives and Cowell both used tone clusters, and arrived at their use independently of each other, it was Cowell who named them, and his use of them affected other composers' work, especially that of Bartók.

In several works written during 1915–19, Cowell initiated **indeterminancy** or the element of chance factors in performance. In *Quartet Romantic* (2 fl., vln., vla.; 1915–17) and *Quartet Euphometric* (str. qrt.; 1916–19), Cowell provided some harmonic guidance through the basic structure of a simple four-part theme, but most of the pitches are to be chosen freely. Another work using indeterminacy is *Ensemble* (chamber orch.; 1925). Indeterminacy was developed to a greater degree in some of Cowell's later works, and the principle was transmitted directly to his student John Cage.

It was Cowell who first had the idea of playing on the strings of the piano and then of placing foreign objects among the piano strings to create unusual sounds and new timbres. In the hands of John Cage, the latter technique developed into **prepared piano.** Cowell included music incorporating his experiments in his formal début recital played in Carnegie Hall in February 1924. Among his early works requiring the performer to play on the piano strings are *The Aeolian Harp* (1923) and *The Banshee* (1925). In *The Aeolian Harp,* piano keys are depressed silently with one hand while the other hand strums or plucks the piano strings. *The Banshee* requires an assistant to hold down the damper pedal while the performer plays on the piano strings (DWMA217).

Between c. 1935 and 1950 Cowell's music became increasingly conservative and tonal, with emphasis on folk music and early American hymnody. In general, conditions in America were economical, for the country was struggling to recover from the Great Depression. Works he created after 1950 show an endeavor to synthesize ethnic influences and his early innovative styles. Cowell was a prolific composer. Approximately 700 of his compositions survive, a majority of them still unpublished.

Jazz

Jazz, an American contribution to the development of music, emerged early in the twentieth century in southern United States, but some of its roots extend far back over the centuries, into the complex polyrhythms of African tribal music and the call-response (or leader-audience) nature of musical performance in African societies. Other factors in the development of jazz are the creation and manner of singing spirituals, gospel songs, and secular songs dealing with all kinds of personal situations and feelings—difficult working conditions, infidelity, loneliness, and others. The songs were improvised, then learned and (in variant forms) transmitted orally from one locality to another, from one generation to the next. Such songs were forerunners of the 12-measure **blues** that is fundamental in the development of jazz.

Blues are songs dealing with human problems—love, sex, poverty, and death. Somewhat more complex than ordinary work songs, a blues is constructed in 12 measures, divided into three equal phrases. Usually, the formal pattern is AAB, the second phrase being exact textual and melodic repetition of the first. Harmonically, the first line was totally in the tonic, the second line moved from tonic to subdominant, and the last line used a I-V-IV-I progression. Certain notes in the melody—the third and seventh degrees of the scale, and sometimes the fifth degree—are inflected or "bent" downward from their standard pitch; these are "blue notes" (ex. 24.21). The accompaniment is a vital part of a blues song and is constructed from the I, IV, and V chords of the normal major scale. Probably the earliest blues songs were accompanied by guitar. Guitarists can adjust tuning and bend tones, but when the accompaniment is supplied by piano, a harmonic clash is created between melody and accompaniment.

A blues is sung simply, often with considerable freedom because of the singer's individual vocal inflections of the melody. It conveys an impression of improvisation, and that the performer is personally identified with its message. Among well-known blues singers was Bessie Smith (1894–1937), whose finest performances were with Louis Armstrong in 1925.

Example 24.21 A blues scale.

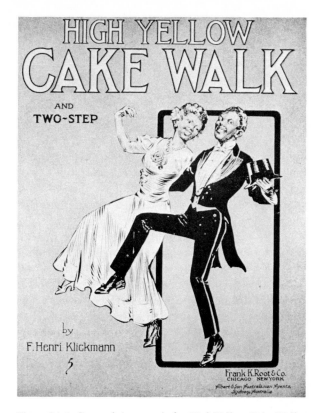

Figure 24.6 Cover of sheet music for *High Yellow Cake Walk*.

One of the last of the great blues singers was Alberta Hunter (1895–1984), who was still acclaimed for her public performances of blues in her 89th year.

Also important in the development of jazz were the blackface minstrel shows popular around the middle of the nineteenth century, the cakewalk, and ragtime. The **cakewalk** was a kind of processional dance done by couples parading or strutting around a square and improvising high stepping and other lively movements as they turned the corners. These "walkarounds," danced to fiddle and banjo tunes that were quite syncopated, became a feature of the parody-dances regularly held as part of black slaves' Sunday entertainments. Customarily, a prize—usually a cake—was given the couple whose movements in the walkaround were judged the most innovative. Hence, that dance became known as "cakewalk." The cakewalk became a fad in the 1890s, and cakewalk music was composed and published as sheet music (fig. 24.6). The cakewalk was known in Europe early in the twentieth century; Debussy incorporated it in a movement of his *Children's Corner* suite in 1905.

Ragtime was developed by black pianists and is akin to march music. The name derives from the fact that the rhythm is ragged, i.e., the pianist's right hand plays syncopated rhythms against a steady rhythm maintained by the left hand. Ragtime was not improvised. It is formally structured music intended to be performed exactly as notated. A ragtime piece usually consists of four **strains** (melodies), each 16 measures long, and each strain repeated (e.g., AA BB CC DD). The left hand maintains a steady rhythm in duple meter throughout the piece, while the right hand syncopates. Obviously, a rag contains no blue notes, since the piano is a structured instrument and cannot

"bend" notes. The most famous of all rags is Scott Joplin's (1868–1917) *Maple Leaf Rag* (1899).

Jazz is generally believed to have emerged in New Orleans early in the twentieth century, when small ensembles (bands) playing ragtime incorporated elements of blues. There was little recorded or notated jazz during the first quarter of the twentieth century. Early jazz relied heavily on improvisation, and improvisation is still considered a vital element of jazz. Supposedly, cornetist Charles ("Buddy") Bolden (1868–1938) was the first instrumentalist to play in jazz style. If this is true, jazz was in evidence before 1907, for Bolden's performing career ended in that year. After Bolden, came "King" Oliver (1885–1938), Louis Armstrong (1900–71), and others. Around

Louis Armstrong. *(The Bettmann Archive.)*

1910, the characteristic jazz ensemble consisted of cornet, clarinet/saxophone, trombone, and rhythm section. By 1920 jazz elements were being included in works of European composers. The New Orleans style of jazz reached a peak with Louis Armstrong and his "Hot Five" c. 1925. Armstrong was probably the greatest solo player in jazz. His cornet playing—his technique, expression, vibratos and "shakes"—served as a model for other jazz soloists.

Summary

During the last quarter of the nineteenth century, composers could choose conservatism, post-Romanticism, nationalism, Impressionism, or be innovative in a variety of ways. Three kinds of nationalism were apparent: a nation's revival of its folk music and absorption of it into art music, use of a national element as accessory to a basically cosmopolitan style, and use of national elements as basic features of a composition.

Russians and Czechoslovakians were foremost among nationalist composers. Until well into the nineteenth century, music in Russia was dominated by foreigners. No Russian musical compositions of real worth were created before Glinka's *A Life for the Tsar'* (1836). More influential was Dargomïzhsky, who sought to avoid everything Italianate, and used the Russian language, whole-tone scales and harmonizations, and notation without key signatures. Also significant were the five composers whom Stasov called the *moguchaya kuchka*: Balakirev, Cui, Musorgsky, Rimsky-Korsakov, and Borodin. The *moguchaya kuchka* is often viewed as a highly organized group that worked aggressively for Russian nationalism and totally rejected all aspects of Western European and traditional music. Such was not the case. The talents of the members of the group were not equal, and their interests were diverse. They did not totally reject the forms and techniques of traditional European music and break out new paths. Balakirev recognized and helped develop the latent talents of each of those he drew into his circle, but each of "The Five" promoted Russian nationalism in his own way. Balakirev instilled in his colleagues and students the belief that (a) Russian composers could rival Western European composers and (b) great composers should teach and pass on their techniques to their students. Musorgsky was the most talented and the most nationalistic of Balakirev's disciples. His opera *Boris Godunov* is a landmark in Russian music. Rimsky-Korsakov, in addition to writing a number of fine compositions, wrote a textbook on orchestration and was influential as the teacher of Glazounov and Stravinsky. Nonnationalistic Russian composers include A. Rubinstein, Tchaikovsky, and Scriabin.

Czechoslovakia's first great nationalist composer was Smetana, who encouraged the composition of Czech operas and is especially honored for his cycle of nationalistic symphonic poems, *Má Vlast*. Smetana was concerned primarily with establishing a repertoire of nationalistic music for his country; Dvořák made the music of Bohemian composers known outside of Czechoslovakia's boundaries. Janáček worked with Bartoš in collecting, editing, and publishing Moravian folk songs, founded an Organ School that was the basis for Brno Conservatory, and wrote some excellent music.

In Scandinavia, the most important composers were Södermann and Alfvén in Sweden, Grieg in Norway, and Nielsen in Denmark. Kajanus and Sibelius were the two leading composers in Finland.

In Austria and Germany, significant contributions were made by Wolf, Mahler, and Richard Strauss. Wolf brought the composition of Lieder to another peak. Mahler's talents were concentrated on the Lied and the symphony, and his work enriched both areas—the Lied was supplied with orchestral accompaniment, and the symphony was infiltrated by the Lied. He extended the symphony beyond the massive proportions and programmatic content of post-Romanticism, and through the incorporation of the Lied, the use of expanded harmonies and progressive tonality, elevated the symphony to an unprecedented height. Strauss is remembered primarily for his tone poems and a few of his operas. *Salome* and *Elektra* established his reputation as a daring composer whose music shattered conventions. With *Der Rosenkavalier,* he effected a complete change of style—to Neo-Classicism—that caught the musical world by surprise and altered his reputation to that of conservative composer. Most of Strauss's tone poems have either purely descriptive or philosophical programs.

During the last two decades of the nineteenth century, Germany experienced a revival of interest in fairy-tale opera. Humperdinck wrote several. Another development in opera in several European countries was *verismo* (realism). Its leading Italian exponent was Puccini.

There were several overlapping and interdependent lines of musical development in France after 1871. Two were basic: one followed cosmopolitan traditions and is seen in the work of Cesar Franck and his pupils, especially d'Indy; the other, adhering specifically to French traditions, appears in the work of Saint-Saëns and his pupils, particularly Fauré. Later, another line of development appeared, based on French tradition and influenced by the ideas of French Symbolist writers and Impressionist artists; its principal exponent was Debussy, and after him, Ravel. The term Impressionism was first applied to music in a disparaging sense, usually implying that a composition was vague and lacked formal and harmonic clarity. Impressionistic music is characterized by irregular phrases, blurring of formal outlines, avoidance of traditional harmonic progressions, use of streams of chords in parallel motion and altered chords with unresolved dissonances, and choice of instruments for their coloristic possibilities. The music is tonal, but modality frequently appears within it, and often the leading tone is suppressed. Composers aimed to create an atmosphere, to suggest rather than to define.

Satie was an eccentric composer with an extremely individualistic style that was neither Impressionistic nor anti-Impressionistic. Some of his music was very avant-garde. To some degree, his miniatures and sparse textures presage the extremely compressed pieces of Webern. A group of young composers associated with Satie in Paris in 1917 became known as *Les Six*: Auric, Durey, Honegger, Milhaud, Poulenc, and Tailleferre. Like the Russian "Five," they advocated writing music devoid of German characteristics. The Six did not remain active as a group, and their ideas about music changed somewhat, but all remained active to some degree.

In England, there was continued interest in oratorio, opera, music festivals, madrigal singing, and old music. Composers active between 1870 and 1920 include Elgar, Smyth, Delius, Vaughan Williams, and Holst. In Britain, nationalism was more prominent in the music of Ireland and Scotland than in England itself. The folk element was always present in the music of Wales. The Welsh treasure their Celtic heritage and have maintained links with their historical past through their unique language and their music.

In the United States, few composers were inspired by or tapped for resources the wealth of indigenous material that surrounded them—Indian tribal melodies, black spirituals, New England hymns, gospel songs. Between 1860 and 1920 the first American conservatories of music were founded, and concert halls were built in major cities, but concert programs were filled with music written by Europeans. The most important Amercan composers during the last decades of the nineteenth century were Paine and MacDowell. Their compositions were tonal, and, in general, show the influence of nineteenth-century European composers of Romantic music. On the other hand, the music of Farwell and Cadman reflects their interest in the music of American Indians.

Where music written and/or performed by women is concerned, Boston, in the 1890s, seems to have occupied a position comparable with that of the Medici court at Ferrara in the late sixteenth century. Mrs. H. H. A. Beach appeared as piano soloist with the Boston Symphony and was the first American woman recognized as a composer of large forms—Mass, symphony, piano concerto, and some chamber music. Other New England composers adhering to Classic-Romantic traditions were Foote, Chadwick, and Parker. One of America's most important and most individualistic composers was Ives. Ives and Cowell were innovative, had not been influenced by avant-garde European composers, used tone clusters, and to some extent were influenced by vernacular and popular music in their surroundings and background. In Ives's musical style, no consistent line of development can be traced. He wrote for self-satisfaction, expressed his thoughts as he wanted to, without regard for traditional rules of composition. Cowell, who was acquainted with Ives, named tone clusters, and his use of them affected the work of other composers, especially Bartók. In some works written in 1915–19, Cowell incorporated chance factors. He was first to play on the strings of the piano and to place foreign objects among the strings to create unusual sounds and new timbres.

Jazz emerged early in the twentieth century in southern United States, but some of its roots extend back into the complex polyrhythms of African tribal music and the call-response nature of musical performance in African societies. Other factors in the development of jazz include spirituals, gospel songs, secular songs dealing with personal situations and feelings, blues, cakewalk, and ragtime. Jazz is generally believed to have originated in New Orleans early in the twentieth century, when small ensembles playing ragtime incorporated elements of blues. Early jazz relied heavily on improvisation, and improvisation is still considered a vital element of jazz. The New Orleans style of jazz reached a peak with Armstrong and his "Hot Five" c. 1925.

25

Developments between the World Wars

World War I did not bring lasting peace. There were a few years of prosperity after the war, but most of western Europe experienced some degree of trouble during the 1920s—a general strike in Britain (1926), inflation in France, civil unrest and turmoil in Spain, a country that had remained neutral during World War I. Then, in 1929, the Great Depression began.

The quarter-century following the Treaty of Versailles (1919) was marked by increased nationalism in several countries and by an intense rivalry among the major powers for political world power, which created international tension. Naturally, each country considered its own ideology the best. In Russia, the Bolshevik Revolution of 1917 had toppled the Tsar. Under Lenin's leadership, Russia became the Union of Soviet Socialist Republics on 30 December 1922. After Lenin's death (1924), an internal power struggle ensued; eventually, Joseph Stalin (1879–1953) became the recognized leader. The Stalinist government aimed to suppress so-called capitalist imperialism and professed the fraternity and equality of man, but without spiritual or political freedom. In Italy, in 1919, Fascism was established by dictator Benito Mussolini (1883–1945). Fascism was characterized by the utmost nationalism, its aims being national unity, militaristic national expansion, class unity, and primacy of government and state. Violence, considered morally desirable, was fostered. In Germany, World War I had destroyed the old political hierarchy. A number of working-class movements arose, and the anti-Semitic National Socialist party (Nazi) emerged. Adolph Hitler (1889–1945) rose to party

leadership and, by the Enabling Act of 1933, became dictator of Germany. His goals were narrow and determined, colored by Nietzsche's theory of a super race, and the Hitler régime was filled with brutality and horror. Naziism in Germany and, to some degree, Fascism in Italy were suppressed at the expense of World War II (1939–45), more violent and horrible than the first because of the powerful weapons that had been invented.

Northern France had suffered much desolation during the World War I, but Paris still exuded a magnetism that attracted artists from all over the world. As political conditions and varying degrees of artistic censorship in Nazi and Fascist countries became intolerable, composers and artists fled first to Paris and then on to the United States.

The cultural arts were not immune from these earth-shattering events. Political and economic happenings always affect the arts to some extent and find expression in them. As the European political, social, and economic systems changed, so did literature and the other arts. Liberalism, rationalism, and irrationalism are all represented. Various styles are present in the artwork of Pablo Picasso (1881–1973). New movements in art included Dadaism (literally, "hobby-horse"), which was grotesque and often nonsensical; Surrealism ("super-reality"), an attempt to express subconscious feelings in weird, fantastic shapes, seen in the work of Salvador Dali (b. 1904); Expressionism, of which Marc Chagall (1887–1986; color-plate 27) was an exponent; and Abstraction, such as

Developments between the World Wars

1910	1920	1930	1940	1950

World War I (1914–18)   Depression - - - - - - - - - - - - -World War II (1939–45)

1917 Bolshevik Revolution

1917 - - - - Lenin - - - - 1924 - - - - - - Stalin - (1953)

1919 Fascism in Italy; Mussolini -1945

Rise of NAZI Party in Germany; - - - - - - 1933 Hitler, dictator - - - - - - - - - - - -1945

ART: - - Dadaism fl. - - - - - -Surrealism - - - - - -Expressionism - - - - - -Abstraction

Continuation of nationalism in music; folk music research: Janáček, Bartók, Kodály

Bartók: Synthesis of folk idioms in art music -1945
    percussive piano music;   string quartets;   *Mikrokosmos*

Orff: complete or "total" theater -

Vaughan Williams: operas (1924–29); symphonies (1912–57) -

Britten: operas, chamber operas - - - - - - -
(1941–71)

1932 Union of Soviet Composers, isolation from West

1917 Prokofiev: *Classical Symphony;* - Symphony No. 5, 1944

Shostakovich: 1925 - - - - - - 15 symphonies - (1971)

Second Viennese School: Schoenberg, Berg, Webern
Schoenberg: pantonal Expressionism; twelve-tone, serialism - (1951)
  Sprechstimme:
    1913 *Pierrot Lunaire*

Berg: Expressionist opera *Wozzeck* 1922;   *Lulu* (1928–35);   Violin concerto 1935

Webern: Pointillism; Expressionism -1945

    Les Six, as a group 1917–22; then separately -
            Durey: politically Communistic music
            Auric: stage and theater music
            Tailleferre: traditional music
            Honegger: stage and dramatic works; vocal effects, *Sprechstimme*
            Poulenc: *mélodie;* religious choral music
            Milhaud: lyrical, contrapuntal, polytonal works

    Neo-Classicism -
    Hindemith: *Mathis der Maler* 1932–35
           symphony and opera

Stravinsky: ballets;
    1913 *Le sacre du printemps* (polytonal, primitivism)
        1920 *Pulcinella* (Neo-Classicism) - *The Rake's Progress* 1951

Nadia Boulanger, master teacher -

         Copland: ballets - - - - - - - - - - - - *Appalachian Spring* 1944
         symphonies; *Fanfare for the Common Man* 1942

Gershwin: *Rhapsody in Blue* 1924   *Porgy and Bess* 1935

R. Crawford Seeger: String Quartet 1931

Thomson: *Four Saints in Three Acts* 1928

        W. G. Still -   Harris,   Piston,   Sessions

     Villa-Lobos -

            Ginastera -

       Chávez: Development of music in Mexico -

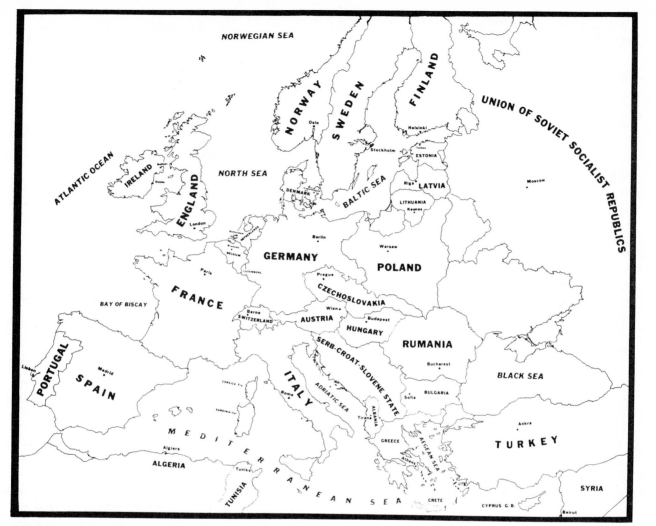

Figure 25.1 Europe in 1920.

the nonrepresentational geometric works of Piet Mondrian (1872–1944). In modern architecture, the principal creators were Frank Lloyd Wright (1869–1959; colorplate 28), Walter Gropius (1883–1969), and Le Corbusier (1887–1965).

In music, the economy that wartime conditions bring to a country and that occurred during World War I was reflected in the limited performing resources called for by some of the major composers. The rejection of traditional principles governing composition and the radical experimentation that characterized art also invaded the realm of music. There was also Neo-Classicism, a style in which the tradi-

tional and the new were synthesized. Nationalism, both overt patriotism and the conscious use of folk music, continued to be a major factor in the work of some composers. Others used folk music only incidentally, and still others did not use it at all. One distinctive school of composition arose—the Second Viennese School, which explored principles of dodecaphonic (twelve-tone) music advanced by Arnold Schoenberg. There were a few composers, e.g., Igor Stravinsky, whose work followed a path through many styles but espoused no single one of them permanently.

Developments between the World Wars

Integration of Folk and Art Music Styles

Folk music was an important aspect of the musical expression of nationalism. Composers quoted folk songs and dance tunes in their works and sought to absorb other elements of folk music into traditional styles. Popular music resembling folk song and dance also found its way into compositions. However, the availability of acoustic recording devices made collecting folk music easier and more accurate, so the material gathered could be studied objectively via ethnomusicological methods and techniques. Interest in and serious study of folk material became more widespread—many persons made regional collections, which they organized, edited, and published. One of the earliest scientific studies of folk music was that done by Janáček among the Moravians. The most extensive scholarly research in central European folk music was accomplished by Hungarian composers Zoltán Kodály (1881–1967) and Béla Bartók (1882–1945), who studied Magyar folk music first, then that of neighboring regions. Gradually, as scientific investigation of folk materials revealed the nature of those melodies, rhythms, harmonies, and forms, and the idiosyncrasies of the various regional musics became apparent, composers began to apply that knowledge in the creation of art music. Thus, the study of folk idioms generated new musical styles, and the scope of tonality was enlarged through the incorporation of the modal, pentatonic, or other scale patterns found in folk music. The most complete synthesis of folk idioms and art music was achieved by Bartók.

Hungary

Under the Compromise of 1867, Austria and Hungary had become a dual monarchy with Emperor Franz Joseph I of Austria (r. 1848–1916) as King of Hungary and with Vienna as one capital and Budapešt as the other. Magyars were the largest ethnic group in Hungary but constituted slightly less than 50 percent of the population. Among the other ethnic groups were the Croats, Serbs, and Slovenes. Many Magyars were discontent with the dual arrangement, wanted independence for Hungary, and, in the hope of eventually obtaining it, actively worked to "Magyarize" Hungary. By 1900 more than 90 percent of

Béla Bartók. *(The New York Public Library.)*

the officials and judiciary were Magyar; the Ugrian dialect of the Magyars became the official language and was used in the schools, though German was still spoken in many homes. Feelings of Hungarian nationalism and the desire for independence increased during the first decade of the twentieth century. In 1907 teachers might be dismissed if their students had not mastered the Ugrian language.

Bartók

Nationalism is closely interwoven with the career and compositions of Béla Bartók. Bartók was a virtuoso pianist who concertized, taught, composed, and made significant contributions as ethnomusicologist. Folk music, particularly that of his native Hungary, became one of his lifelong interests. Another was the piano and its music. Bartók's mother, a piano teacher, provided his first instruction on that instrument. Later, at Budapešt Academy of Music (1899–1903), he trained for a career as a concert pianist; he was an excellent accompanist, also, and played chamber music well. Composition was considered as an adjunct to a performance career.

While a student at Budapešt Academy, Bartók was disturbed by the fact that Hungarian composers of nationalist music were using pseudo (i.e., folklike popular songs) rather than authentic Hungarian folk materials as models for their works. In the early 1900s he wrote down a few songs that he heard Hungarian peasants singing, and c. 1905 he began to collaborate with Zoltán Kodály in gathering and cataloging ethnic musics of Hungary, Rumania, and other nearby Slavic countries. The cataloging system Bartók developed is still in use. Gradually, he expanded his research into other central European countries and into Turkey and

North Africa. He published several volumes of his editions of folk music, made arrangements of many folk songs, and assimilated folk materials into his own compositions.

In 1907 Bartók was appointed professor of piano at Budapešt Academy of Music, a position that provided a measure of financial security yet allowed him time to perform, compose, and continue folk-music research. For 27 years, he taught at the Academy and concertized, establishing his reputation internationally as a concert pianist. Usually, in concerts he performed only his own compositions. He wrote some purely pedagogical pieces, too. His *Mikrokosmos* (1926–37), originally intended for the instruction of his son Peter, is a six-volume progressive course in piano technique. The 153 pieces in the series range from simple one- and two-part pieces (in the first books) to extremely difficult works with complicated asymmetrical rhythms and bitonality (in the last book). Actually, the *Mikrokosmos* is a compendium of Bartók's style and of many of the compositional devices in use during the first half of the twentieth century.

Before 1902, Bartók wrote mainly piano pieces and songs; most of them are short pieces, Romantic in style, and relatively unimportant. Between 1902 and 1907, his attitude and his works became increasingly nationalistic. Strongly influenced by conditions at the Academy, he wore the Hungarian national style of clothing and insisted that his family not use German at home. Among the original nationalistic works he composed at this time are a violin/piano Sonata in E minor (1903), a Piano Quintet (1903–4), and the symphonic poem *Kossuth* (1903) honoring Lajos Kossuth (1802–94), the Hungarian nationalist leader during the Revolution of 1848. Bartók's first compositions to be given *opus* numbers appeared in 1904: *Rhapsody,* Op. 1, for piano, and *Scherzo,* Op. 2, for piano and orchestra. Then, in 1907, Kodály introduced Bartók to Debussy's music. Bartók was fascinated by the elements of folk music he detected in it and by Debussy's coloristic, nonfunctional treatment of chords.

Elements of Bartók's individual style began to manifest themselves soon after he became involved in collecting folk music and became increasingly apparent in the compositions he wrote in 1908–11.

Throughout his life he relied heavily on folk music, and often his innovations were stimulated by his research. Around 1908 he began to write melodies and harmonies based on modal and pentatonic scales; to combine modes or, as he described it, to color one with another; to construct chords by stacking fourths instead of thirds, or to use simultaneously the major and minor third (though he always placed the minor third uppermost); to use palindromic formal patterns; and to apply in his works the Fibonacci series of numbers and the "golden section." Many of these features appear in the 14 *Bagatelles* (Op. 6; 1908) for piano. Other significant works written by Bartók during these years are String Quartet No. 1 (Op. 7), *Two Pictures* (Op. 10; orch.; 1910); *Duke Bluebeard's Castle* (1911), his first one-act opera; and *Allegro barbaro* (1911) for piano. In addition to containing folk elements, the String Quartet reveals Bartók's knowledge of the quartets of Beethoven. *Allegro barbaro* exemplifies primitivism in music. It is percussive piano music, with driving rhythms, harsh chords in persistent ostinato patterns, melody of narrow range, and many repeated notes (ex. 25.1).

The libretto for *Duke Bluebeard's Castle* is by the Symbolist poet Béla Balázs, who adapted the Bluebeard legend to present symbolically humans' thirst for knowledge, and a moral—Curiosity can kill. (Balázs was also implying that in a marital relationship, some past events should remain behind closed doors.) Bluebeard gives his new wife, Judith, the keys to seven locked doors but warns her not to use them. Seeking information, she unlocks the doors in Bluebeard's presence and learns the fate of his previous wives. Each episode provides opportunity for dialogue. At the end of the opera, Judith silently walks through the seventh door to join her predecessors. The opera has only two singing roles, Judith and Bluebeard; a Prologue is spoken by the Bard. Bartók wrote chromatic Romantic music for Judith and pentatonic, folklike music for Bluebeard. Treatment of the vocal lines shows Bartók's knowledge of Debussy's *Pelléas et Mélisande.* Tonally, Bartók's opera moves from pentatonic F♯ (representing night) through D♯/E♭ to C major (the fifth door) and through A back to F♯ (darkness). Symbolic motives recur, and there is a quotation from Bach's *St. Matthew Passion.*

Developments between the World Wars

Example 25.1 Percussive, driving rhythms, harsh chords, persistent ostinato patterns used by Bartók in *Allegro barbaro*: (*a*) mm. 1–11; (*b*) mm. 28–32. *(ALLEGRO BARBARO © Copyright 1918 by Universal Edition; Copyright Renewed. Copyright and Renewal assigned to Boosey & Hawkes, Inc. Reprinted by permission.)*

(a)

(b)

During 1912–19, Bartók concentrated on teaching and folk music. He wrote few new works, the most important being String Quartet No. 2 (Op. 17; 1915–17), which contains a good deal of folk material. In 1919 he resumed concertizing, and wrote the piano score for the pantomime *The Miraculous Mandarin* but did not orchestrate it until 1923. The pantomime is a tragedy concerning the relationship between a primitive man and a civilized woman. The music is tonal but includes slow string *glissandi* designed to produce quarter tones. Political conditions in Hungary in 1920 hampered Bartók's career, and, though he wanted to concertize abroad, he was prevented from leaving the country until 1922. Moreover, performances of *Duke Bluebeard's Castle* and the ballet *The Wooden Prince* (1914–16) were prohibited in Hungary because Balász (the librettist and scenarist) was a political exile. In 1923 Bartók, Kodály, and other leading Hungarian composers were commissioned to write music for a Festival Concert commemorating the 50th anniversary of the merging of Pešt, Buda, and Óbuda into the city of Budapešt. For that concert Bartók composed *Dance Suite* for orchestra. Its five stylized dances exhibit his wide folkloric interests at that time: first and fourth are of Arabic derivation; second, third, and the *ritornello* are Magyar in spirit; fifth is primitive Rumanian.

During the next two and a half years Bartók composed very little. When he resumed composition in 1926, he began to use traditional forms and a great deal of counterpoint. *Out of Doors* (1927), a five-movement piano suite, is significant for the style of its fourth movement, "Night music," which Bartók simulated in several later works—the piano concertos, the Sonata for piano and percussion, and *Music for Strings, Percussion, and Celesta*. The Piano Sonata (1926), Piano Concerto No. 1 (1926), and Piano Concerto No. 2 (1930–31) were for his own performances. Both concerti are virtuosic. Bartók attributed his use of tone clusters in Piano Concerto No. 1 to Henry Cowell (see p. 793). Bartók did not limit his concert appearances to solo roles; sometimes he participated in chamber music or served as accompanist. *Rhapsody No. 1* and *No. 2* for violin and piano (1928) were written for concerts he played with Hungarian violinists Joseph Szigeti (1892–1973) and Zoltán Székely (b. 1903); later Bartók wrote orchestral accompaniments for both rhapsodies.

Between 1927 and 1939 Bartók composed String Quartets Nos. 3–6. As the *Mikrokosmos* provides a summary of Bartók's style through his writing for piano, so the six string quartets provide a summary of his style through chamber music. Bartók's six string

Example 25.2 In *Cantata profana*, mvt. 1, mm. 35–37, Bartók used invertible counterpoint and canon in the chorus parts. *(CANTATA PROFANA © Copyright 1934 by Universal Edition; Copyright Renewed. Copyright and Renewal assigned to Boosey & Hawkes, Inc. Reprinted by permission.)*

quartets are among the finest written since Beethoven's. String Quartet No. 4 is in five movements arranged in palindromic arch form, the two outer movements fast in tempo, the second and fourth being scherzi, and the third a slow movement, ternary in form. Its B section is the center of the entire work. The quartet is cyclic—a germinal motive presented at the outset provides material for other movements and also concludes the last movement. The first and fifth and the second and fourth movements share other related materials. The performers are required to play some difficult multiple stops and execute a variety of unusual techniques, including snap pizzicato, pizzicato glissando, pizzicato *sul ponticello,* and *col legno* chords. There is a good deal of counterpoint, and there is some bitonality. String Quartet No. 5 contains five movements also, but its central movement is a Scherzo surrounded by slow movements. That Scherzo is written in $\frac{4+2+3}{8}$ meter; its Trio, in very fast tempo, uses $\frac{3+2+2+3}{8}$ meter. The return of the Scherzo is a variation rather than a literal repeat of the original. In addition to the entire quartet being in arch form, some movements are themselves arches. The first movement uses a modified sonata form, with the recapitulation bringing back the themes in reverse order and inverted. The first theme is in B♭ major; the second

theme is in E, a tritone relationship—something Bartók would use again, often. The structure of the fifth movement is comparable with that of the first, using an inversion of the first movement's first theme and with the B♭-E tritonal relationship prominent throughout the movement.

Cantata profana (1930), subtitled *The nine enchanted stags,* for tenor and baritone soloists, double chorus, and orchestra, is Bartók's most important nonoperatic vocal work. Its text was derived from two versions of a Rumanian *colinda* (song). The music sounds as though it is filled with folk materials but actually contains none. Ostensibly in D, and beginning and ending in that key, it contains passages that are Mixolydian or that use the "acoustic" scale D-E-F♯-G♯-A-B-C-D or its inversion D-C-B♭-A♭-G-F-E-D. Structurally, the composition is symmetrical—a palindrome—or what Bartók called *Brückenform* (bridge form). The tonalities of the tripartite first movement spell out a D-minor triad; this is balanced by the last movement's three sections being in G, B, and D respectively, a G-major triad. Symmetry is found also in invertible counterpoint (ex. 25.2).

Many of the works Bartók wrote in the 1930s were commissioned, including String Quartet No. 5, by Elizabeth Sprague Coolidge; *Music for Strings, Celesta, and Percussion* (1937) and *Divertimento*

Developments between the World Wars

(1939), by Paul Sacher; Sonata for two pianos and percussion (1937), for Basle; Violin Concerto (1937) for Székely; and *Contrasts* (1938; cl., vln.; pno.), for Szigeti and Benny Goodman and first performed by them with Bartók at the piano. Clarinetist and violinist must each have two instruments, for *Contrasts* uses *scordatura* as well as *accordatura* tuning of the violin, and B♭ and A clarinets.

In the 1930s Bartók's open opposition to Fascism created problems for him. He wanted to emigrate but did not do so until after his mother died. He came to the United States in 1940 for performances with Szigeti and Goodman and returned later that year to take up residence. Besides concertizing, he cataloged Yugoslav folk music at Harvard University. For two years he composed nothing. Then he became ill with polycythaemia, a type of blood cancer. In 1943, he wrote *Concerto for Orchestra* (rev. 1945) to fulfill a commission from Koussevitsky for an orchestral work, and in 1944 wrote the Sonata for solo violin, but his quarter-tone version of the sonata's last movement remains unpublished. Bartók's last two works were Piano Concerto No. 3 (1945), written for his second wife, Ditta Pásztory (1902–82), with whom he had often concertized, and Viola Concerto (1945) commissioned by William Primrose. Bartók had not quite finished them when he died (26 September 1945). His friend, violist Tibor Serly (1901–78), had discussed those two works with him and completed them.

The compositions of Bartók's last style period, works written after 1937, are tonal, with much counterpoint. His use of thematic development and thematic transformation stems from Beethoven and Liszt, and from Liszt he learned to use germinal motives. As did Beethoven, Bartók often modulated to a mediant or submediant tonality, instead of moving to the dominant. Frequently he used foreign chords in a nonfunctional, nonmodulatory manner. The tritone figures prominently in many of his works. Most of the compositions written between 1908 and 1945 were influenced in some way by folk materials. Bitonality and polytonality appear in a good many of his compositions, but Bartók wrote neither atonal music nor twelve-tone serial music. Several of his late works contain most of the techniques that characterize his style, e.g., *Concerto for Orchestra* and *Music for Strings, Percussion, and Celesta.*

The celesta is by no means the featured solo instrument in *Music for Strings, Percussion, and Celesta.* The work is for two five-part string ensembles, side drums, cymbals, tam-tam, bass drum, tympani, celesta, harp, and piano. An ensemble seating plan was provided:

	Double Bass I	Double Bass II	
Violoncello I	Timpani	Bass Drum	Violoncello II
Viola I	Side Drums	Cymbals	Viola II
Violin II	Celesta	Xylophone	Violin IV
Violin I	Piano	Harp	Violin III

The entire composition is colored by tritone relationships, contrapuntal intricacies, and mirror and contrary motion techniques. The Andante tranquillo first movement (DWMA218), in A, is a fugue whose subject (ex. 25.3a) is presented in successive entries that move alternately in contrary motion around the circle of fifths from A to E♭ (i.e., A-E-D-B-G and so on); then the subject is inverted, and the tonality progresses from E♭ back to A. The tritone relationship between A and E♭, which is the secondary tonal center (rather than the traditional dominant), is reenforced in the movement's last three measures, played by first and second violins (ex. 25.3b). The dynamic level of the first movement gradually increases in intensity from the *pp* of muted strings at m. 1 to *fff* when E♭ is attained, then diminishes to conclude *ppp.* The second movement, a sonata-form Allegro in C, makes reference to the fugal subject of the first movement, albeit in altered form, and introduces some material that recurs in the fourth movement. There is some fugato in the development, and in the recapitulation the two string ensembles are treated antiphonally. The third movement, an Adagio in F♯ (a tritone away from the C of mvt. 2), is bridge form—Introduction-ABCBA-coda. The opening and closing measures have similar figuration, played by xylophone. The movement ends on the C-F♯ tritone. An interesting palindromic passage occurs at the center of this movement when two measures of music are repeated in retrograde (mm. 47–50). Some of Bartók's "night music" is in this movement, too. The fourth movement, an Allegro molto, exhibits many characteristics of Bartók's style: elements of Magyar folk music, driving rhythms, ostinato, and tone clusters.

(a)

(b)

Example 25.3 Bartók: *Music for Strings, Percussion, and Celesta,* mvt. 1: (*a*) mm. 1–4, the subject; (*b*) the last 3 measures (mm. 86–88.) *(MUSIC FOR STRINGS, PERCUSSION AND CELESTA © Copyright 1937 by Universal Edition; Copyright Renewed. Copyright and Renewal assigned to Boosey & Hawkes, Inc. Reprinted by permission.)*

Kodály

After Bartók emigrated to America, Zoltán Kodály worked alone collecting, scientifically studying, and codifying the folk music of central European peoples, especially in Magyar and Slavic regions. In addition to that work, he made significant contributions in the field of music education. Kodály did a great deal to advance the degree of musical literacy of young persons. He was concerned primarily with vocal music education, and many of the materials he used were derived essentially from folk music. In teaching sight-singing, he used mainly polyphony, and for that didactic purpose composed hundreds of two- and three-part exercises. The "Kodály method" is currently in use in many places in the Western world.

Naturally, folk elements infiltrated Kodály's compositions. However, he made no direct quotations from folk music. Rather, his mature works are an amalgamation of many influences—Bach-style counterpoint, the choral writing of Palestrina, Gregorian chant, and Hungarian folk music, including *verbunkos*. (The *verbunkos* originated as a Hungarian soldiers' dance consisting of two or more sections, alternating slow quasi-introductory material with very fast, wild music. Later, *verbunkos* became a ceremonial dance.) Kodály's music is basically tonal and diatonic, colored by modality, and, considered carefully, is more narrowly nationalistic than that of Bartók. Kodály attracted international attention with *Psalmus hungaricus* (1923), commissioned for the Budapešt 50th Anniversary Festival Concert. Written for tenor soloist, chorus, and orchestra, *Psalmus hungaricus* is a setting of Psalm 55, as translated by the sixteenth-century Hungarian poet-preacher M. K. Vég. The most popular of Kodály's compositions are the Singspiel *Háry János* (1926), based on the national legend of braggadoccio Háry János, teller of tall tales, and the six-movement orchestral suite (1927) derived from that comedy. Other important works by Kodály include *Marosszéki táncok* (Dances of Marosszék; piano, 1927; orch., 1930); *Galánti táncok* (Dances of Galánta; 1933), based on music from the Hungarian (now Czechoslovakian) countryside where Kodály grew up; and *Concerto for Orchestra* (1940), commissioned by the Chicago Symphony Orchestra.

Germany

Orff

German composer Carl Orff (1895–1962) was also greatly interested in the music education of elementary school children. Whereas Kodály was interested primarily in vocal music and the ability to sight-read fluently, Orff was concerned with rhythmic proficiency and fluidity of movement. After becoming acquainted with Jaques-Dalcroze eurhythmics, a method that correlated music and movement, Orff determined to use similar didactic methods in Germany and decided to train young adults as teachers of eurhythmics. To that end, he and Dorothee Günther (b. 1896) founded the Güntherschule in Munich in 1924 and prepared a curriculum in which music, dance, and gymnastics were highly coordinated. In teaching that curriculum, Orff used a wide variety of percussion instruments and commissioned instrument maker Karl Maendler to build special percussion instruments that would be easy to play. Some were modeled after Javanese gamelan bar-type instruments. Improvisation is a vital part of Orff's curriculum. He simplified the Jaques-Dalcroze methods so they were suitable for use with elementary school children, and he prepared a collection of carefully graded music exercises that have been published under the titles *Orff-Schulwerk* (Schoolwork; 1930–35) and *Musik für Kinder* (Music for Children; 1950–54). His didactic procedures were adopted in Germany first, then spread throughout the world.

Music education was not Orff's principal interest, however—that was complete or "total" theater, in which all aspects of words, music, and movement (action and dance) formed a cohesive whole. His models were ancient Greek drama and early Baroque Italian *rappresentazione* and opera. He began by making adaptations of several Monteverdi works, one being *Klage der Ariadne* (Lament of Ariadne; 1925; rev. 1940). Later works include Christmas and Easter plays, Bavarian peasant plays, and works based on Greek tragedies. Undoubtedly, Orff's most famous work is *Carmina burana* (Secular songs from Benediktbeuren; 1937), setting 25 thirteenth-century Latin and German poems found in Benediktbeuren Monastery in Bavaria. Also well known are the operas *Der Mond* (The moon; 1939) and *Die Kluge* (The wise woman; 1943), both based on Grimm brothers' fairy tales; and *Antigonae* (1949) and *Oedipus der Tyrann* (King Oedipus; 1959), both drawn from Sophocles. Orff's vocal lines are declamatory and rhythmically accented; orchestral accompaniments use simple harmonies in block chords. The

simplicity of his settings owes something to folk song, but the prominence given to chorus and the orchestral percussion suggest the possible influence of Stravinsky's *Les noces,* with which Orff was familiar.

England

Vaughan Williams

The career of Ralph Vaughan Williams (1872–1958), one of England's leading composers, covered a wide range of musical activities—he was composer, editor, arranger, author, teacher, conductor, and collector of folk song.

As a child, Vaughan Williams had piano lessons and received basic grounding in thorough-bass and harmony from an aunt and learned to play violin and organ. In preparatory school, he played viola in the school orchestra. Apparently, at one time he considered becoming an orchestral musician, but at Royal College of Music and Cambridge he concentrated on music history and composition. He studied composition with Max Bruch in 1897 and orchestration with Maurice Ravel in 1908.

The most important influence in Vaughan Williams's music was his English heritage, especially British folk song, music of the Elizabethan and Jacobean eras, and hymnody. His high regard for popular traditions is comparable with that of Bartók in Hungary. In addition, literature and the music of Handel, Bach, Ravel, and Debussy were influential. Vaughan Williams's friendship with Holst, whom he met in 1895, was an important factor, too. They criticized each other's work in progress and occasionally composed pieces for the same musical medium around the same time.

Throughout his life, Vaughan Williams maintained an interest in choral music. Some of his earliest compositions were unaccompanied part songs, and his first symphony, *A Sea Symphony* (1903–9), is for soprano and baritone soloists, SATB chorus, and orchestra. From 1905 to 1953 Vaughan Williams was principal conductor of the Leith Hill Music Festival, held annually (except during the wars) at Dorking. He wrote several choral works specifically for those festivals. Most of the performers at the festivals were amateurs, and to many of them Vaughan Williams provided their first acquaintance with the choral music

Ralph Vaughan Williams. *(The Bettmann Archive.)*

of Bach, Handel, Mendelssohn, and other outstanding composers. Several of Vaughan Williams's instrumental works were designed for performance by amateurs. His *Household Music* (1941), three preludes on Welsh hymn tunes, is for string quartet or other available instruments, and a section of his *Concerto Grosso* (1950) uses only open strings.

By 1903, Vaughan Williams was deeply interested in folk song, and in 1904 he became a member of the Folk Song Society. Over the years, he collected hundreds of folk songs. Some he incorporated in his compositions; some he arranged as choral works or accompanied vocal solos; others he edited and published in collections. The modality and the simplicity of folk song influenced his compositions considerably—some of his original melodies have been mistaken for folk songs or adaptations thereof. He arranged and published several collections of traditional English carols, and was coeditor of *The Oxford Book of Carols* (1928) to which he contributed several original carols.

Vaughan Williams was music editor of *The English Hymnal* in 1904–6. He included in the book some adaptations of folk songs and some of his own hymns, one being *Sine nomine* (literally, Nameless), better known by its opening words, "For all the saints . . ." (1905). The opening notes of that hymn follow a downward curve that became characteristic of many of Vaughan Williams's melodies. In fact, it may be considered a trademark of his style. Often, he combined it with harmonies that have a similar curve in contrary motion (ex. 25.4).

The years 1909–14 cover the first period of Vaughan Williams's mature writing. The benefit of his study with Ravel is seen in the chord streams, the rippling arpeggiated figurations, expressive chromaticisms, colorful musical imagery, and skillful orchestration. Vaughan Williams's style was unified, and elements of folk song had been assimilated into it. One of the most representative works of this period is the song cycle *On Wenlock Edge* (1908–9), a setting of six poems from A. E. Housman's (1859–1936) *A Shropshire Lad,* for tenor, piano, and string quartet. The music is filled with streams of parallel chords—first inversion triads, root-position triads, seventh chords, octaves with open fifths (ex. 25.5). The sound is more English than Impressionistic, recalling the English penchant for the full sonority achieved by complete triads, and the parallel $^6_3$ chords of fifteenth-century English discant. A sense of the dramatic is present, fostered by judicious use of chromaticism and dissonance as well as by the vocal line, which is simple but demanding.

Four other works from this period are significant: *Fantasia on a Theme by Thomas Tallis* (1910) for two string orchestras; *A London Symphony* (1912–13); the opera *Hugh the Drover, or Love in the Stocks* (1910–14); and *The Lark Ascending* (1914), a romance for violin and orchestra. All of these works were revised, some of them several times. Vaughan Williams was a perfectionist and revised many of his works, usually more than once.

The basis for the *Fantasia . . .* is a hymn tune by Tallis that appears as No. 92 in *The English Hymnal.* Vaughan Williams's composition commences with polyphonic treatment of phrases of Tallis's hymn, then presents the complete theme, as though it had grown out of the preceding music. Thereafter, the hymn tune undergoes development, with interplay between soloists from the sections and their respective string groups, as well as between

Example 25.4 Melodic curves typical of Vaughan Williams's writing: (*a*) Melody of the hymn *Sine nomine*; (*b*) *Toward the Unknown Region*, mm. 1–3; (*c*) *Pastoral Symphony*, mvt. 1, mm. 12–15 (score reduction.) *(Source: Example* a *copyright © 1906 Oxford University Press, New York, NY; example* b *copyright © 1918 Breitkopf and Härtel, Leipzig; example* c *copyright © 1924 (Renewed) J. Curwen & Sons, Ltd., New York, NY.)*

(a)

(b)

(c)

Example 25.5 Streams of chords used by Vaughan Williams in *On Wenlock Edge*: (*a*) I, mm. 1–2; (*b*) II, mm. 12–14; (*c*) III, mm. 1–4. *(ON WENLOCK EDGE © Copyright 1911, 1946 by Boosey & Hawkes, Ltd. Copyright Renewed. Reprinted by permission.)*

(a)

(b)

(c)

Example 25.6 Conclusion of Vaughan Williams's *Pastoral Symphony*: Melisma vocalized by soprano soloist while violins sustain high A pitches in octaves. All other performers are *tacet.* (Copyright © 1924, renewed 1952 J. Curwen & Sons, Ltd., New York, NY.)

the two string orchestras. The recapitulation is a variation of the opening material. The *Fantasia* mingles key tonality and modality, polyphony and homophony, and reflects somewhat the music of the Elizabethan era in which Tallis lived.

A London Symphony, Vaughan Williams's second symphony, is purely orchestral. It is traditional in form, with four movements, the third being a scherzo labeled *Nocturne,* and the fourth called *Epilogue.* The first movement opens with a Lento introduction, whose theme serves also as basis for the *Epilogue.* Vaughan Williams structured five of his nine symphonies with epilogues reflecting first-movement introductions; in the *Pastoral Symphony,* the epilogue is the concluding portion of the finale and reflects that movement's introduction. (Symphonies Nos. 8 and 9 are without epilogue.) *A London Symphony* is nationalistic, depicting various sounds of London, including Westminster chimes.

England had no tradition of native opera. In fact, it seemed almost as though there was a barrier against English opera. Vaughan Williams penetrated that barrier with *Hugh the Drover,* which he called a ballad opera. The songs are not limited to ballads, though the opera contains at least ten well-known tunes. The plot concerns life in a nineteenth-century Cotswold village. Because of wartime interruptions—Vaughan Williams served in the Royal Army Medical Corps during World War I—*Hugh the Drover* was not performed until 1924. During the next five years, Vaughan Williams composed three more operas: *Sir John in Love* (1924–28), *Riders to the Sea* (1927–29), and *The Poisoned Kiss* (1927–29). *Sir John in Love,* a four-act work for which Vaughan Williams wrote the libretto, is based on Shakespeare's *The Merry Wives of Windsor* and requires 20 soloists. Included in the opera is a Fantasia on *Greensleeves* that

is frequently performed as a separate piece. *Riders to the Sea* is a setting of Synge's one-act play. *The Poisoned Kiss,* a fun-filled three-act romantic extravaganza, differs from Vaughan Williams's other operas in using spoken dialogue.

During the years immediately following World War I, Vaughan Williams worked on the *Pastoral Symphony* (Symphony No. 3, completed 1921), in which he included voice. At the beginning of the finale, and again near the end of that movement, he placed a pentatonic, textless melisma for solo soprano, a feature that bears some resemblance to the long melismas of pure vocal sound found near the end of many English motets written during the Elizabethan era (ex. 25.6).

Several compositions Vaughan Williams wrote in the years between the two World Wars have a religious association, though only a few are liturgical. The neo-modal *a cappella* Mass in G minor (1920–21; SATB soloists, 8-part choir) was written at a time when there was renewed interest in Byrd's music and the polyphony produced by other English composers of that era who worked at Westminster Cathedral. The oratorio *Sancta civitas* (The Holy City; 1923–25), for tenor and baritone soloists, SATB chorus, semichorus, and distant chorus, opens with a quotation from Plato concerning the immortality of the soul, but the principal text is from Revelation. *Job* (1927–30), though on a Biblical subject, is a masque for dancing and is certainly not churchly. On the other hand, *Flos campi* (Flower of the field; 1925), for solo viola, chamber orchestra, and small SATB chorus singing textless music, is an interpretation of verses from *Song of Solomon.* The music flows continuously through six sections, each headed by a Latin quotation from that Biblical book. The opening of the piece is bitonal, and, though much of the music is rhapsodic and sounds

Developments between the World Wars

improvised, it has been carefully organized thematically. Without a doubt, *Flos campi* is the finest of the several works featuring solo instrument that Vaughan Williams created during this period.

Although Vaughan Williams stated that his fourth, fifth, and sixth symphonies are absolute music, many persons have considered them related to World War II: Symphony No. 4, in F minor (1931–34), as prophecy of it; Symphony No. 5, D major (1938–43), the hope for peace, especially seen in the serenity of its Finale; Symphony No. 6, E minor (1944–47), descriptive of war. In response to critics' search for extramusical implications in the Sixth Symphony, Vaughan Williams stated that its Epilogue could be verbalized as "We are such stuff as dreams are made on, and our little life is rounded by a sleep"—Prospero's words of farewell in Shakespeare's *The Tempest.* Symphony No. 6 is in four movements, played without a break. Two opposing moods are apparent in the composition—one violent, seen in its turbulent first movement; one serene, present in the fugal Epilogue, played softly throughout. In closing, strings vacillate between E-flat major and E minor, ultimately coming to rest on an E-minor chord that is not in root position.

Between 1905 and 1913, Vaughan Williams composed incidental music for nine stage works; in the 1940s, he wrote music for three radio dramas; and, in 1940 he began composing music for films. The most significant of his film scores was that for *Scott of the Antarctic,* with its portrayal of personal dedication, loyalty, and heroism, as well as a depiction of the polar wastes. That film music inspired a seventh symphony, *Sinfonia antartica* (1949–52), a five-movement work for soprano, small SSA chorus, and orchestra. Among the orchestral instruments is a wind machine, and quotations from Sir Robert Scott's journal occur in the symphony's epilogue.

A change that may be related to the *Sinfonia antartica*'s sharply contrasting musical ideas is apparent in the character of Vaughan Williams's last two symphonies, No. 8 in D minor (1953–55) and No. 9 in E minor (1956–57). Both are purely instrumental, neither has an epilogue, and sonata form was not used for the first movement of either of them. Both symphonies have parts for some unusual instruments—vibraphone in the Eighth Symphony, and three saxophones and a flugelhorn in the Ninth. Other unusual works from Vaughan Williams's last period are the Concerto in F minor for bass tuba and orchestra (1954) and the *Romance* in D♭ major (1951) for harmonica, strings, and piano, which was written for Larry Adler (b. 1914).

Certainly, Vaughan Williams's style is English, nationalistic in character without being tied to folk song, and at the same time highly personal. In his works archaic procedures from the Tudor era blend with those of his own times. Counterpoint and homophony, modes and keys are handled with equal skill, often incorporating shifts between major and minor harmonies, and including some polytonality (use or seeming use of three or more keys simultaneously). Vaughan Williams laid the groundwork for a tradition of English opera and did a great deal to establish the symphony as an important form in English music.

Britten

Benjamin Britten (1913–76) wrote a good deal of chamber and orchestral music, but his principal contributions lie in the area of vocal music, specifically, solo songs, choral works, and operas. Also, he wrote a large amount of challenging music for amateurs and children.

In the mid-1930s Britten composed the music for a series of documentary films, and in that connection met poet W. H. Auden (1907–73). A firm friendship developed. Over the years, Britten set a number of Auden's poems, and Auden supplied the libretto for *Paul Bunyan* (1941), Britten's first venture into opera. After its première (in New York), Britten withdrew the opera and did not permit its revival until June 1976 (BBC). A homosexual relationship and long-lasting musical partnership developed between Britten and tenor Peter Pears (1910–86) as a result of a series of recitals of English music the two men presented in 1937. Pears, whose talent inspired a number of Britten's vocal works, sang the leading tenor roles in most of Britten's operas. In 1939, when war was impending, Britten and Pears came to the United States; Auden had already emigrated to America. Britten returned to England in 1942 where, as a conscientious objector, he was exempted from military service. While in the United States, he composed at least a dozen works, including the Violin Concerto (1939),

Benjamin Britten.

the song cycles *Les illuminations* (Illuminations; tenor, strings; 1939) and *Seven Sonnets of Michelangelo* (tenor, piano; 1940), *Sinfonia da Requiem* (Requiem Symphony; 1940), and String Quartet No. 1 (D major; 1941). The *Sinfonia da Requiem* is programmatic, with movements entitled *Lachrymosa* (Tearful), *Dies irae* (Day of wrath), and *Requiem aeternam* (Eternal rest). Quite a number of Britten's works deal with the subject of death. Before 1942, Britten's output was predominately instrumental; thereafter, the majority of his compositions were vocal music.

Until the advent of Vaughan Williams and Britten, England had no native-born composer of the stature of Henry Purcell. In the twentieth century, there was a revival of interest in Purcell's music, and several of Britten's compositions reflect his knowledge of and appreciation for Purcell's works: String Quartet No. 2 (C major; 1945), written in tribute to Purcell; the song cycle *The Holy Sonnets of John Donne* (tenor, piano; 1945); *Rejoice in the Lamb* (SATB soloists, chorus, org.; 1943); and *The Young Person's Guide to the Orchestra* (1945), variations on a theme of Purcell followed by a fugue on an original

theme by Britten. After 1945, the only purely instrumental compositions Britten wrote were for specific individuals, e.g., the Sonata (C major; 'cello/piano; 1961), three Suites for unaccompanied 'cello (1964, 1967, 1971), and *Symphony in D for 'Cello and Orchestra* (1963) written for Mstislav Rostropovitch (b. 1927).

Shortly before Britten returned to England in 1942, the Koussevitsky Foundation commissioned an opera from him. *Peter Grimes* (1944–45) resulted. Constructed with a Prologue and three Acts, *Peter Grimes* is based on George Crabbe's poem *The Borough*. It concerns moral issues—innocence being the prey of violence, and the adverse effect of a community's unfounded suspicions—and graphically depicts living conditions in a small English seaside community. Peter Grimes, a rough fisherman, is suspected of having killed his apprentice. Peter is innocent, but most of the villagers consider him guilty and their unkind actions toward him reflect their beliefs. In the beautiful aria "Let her among you without fault cast the first stone . . . ," Ellen Orford remonstrates with the villagers for that cruelty. Eventually, Peter gets a new apprentice, whom he mistreats. One day, while dragging nets to the boat, the boy slips on the cliff and falls to his death. Peter, half-mad with despair, follows a villager's advice—he sails out to sea and sinks his boat. The opera's final scene is similar to the beginning of Act I—the same orchestral interlude is heard as a new day dawns on the borough and the people go about their daily work as usual. Peter has not yet been missed.

Britten set the narrative portions of the opera as *secco* recitative and used arioso and aria for solos. Besides accompanying the singers, the orchestra plays descriptive, mood-setting interludes between scenes and acts. There are some recurrent motives and figures, e.g., the leap of a ninth that is associated with Peter. The harmonies are basically triadic and traditional, but Lydian and Phrygian modes color the melodies. *Peter Grimes* is Britten's best-known opera.

Since, in 1945, only two opera houses existed in England, Britten decided to write chamber operas—works that require only a few singers and an orchestra of solo instruments and that can be performed on small stages. After composing *The Rape of Lucretia* (1946) and *Albert Herring* (1947), Britten saw the need for a chamber opera company, and in 1947 the English Opera Group was formed. In 1948 Eric Crozier (b. 1914), Pears, and Britten founded the Aldeburgh Festival, with facilities for producing chamber opera. By 1950 Britten's success as a chamber opera composer was well established. The large-scale opera *Billy Budd* was commissioned for the Festival of Britain in 1951, and *Gloriana,* the story of Queen Elizabeth I and Essex, was written for the coronation of Queen Elizabeth II in 1953. *Billy Budd,* as revised in 1960, has become part of English opera repertoire. Other operas, both full-length and chamber, followed. Significant among them are *The Turn of the Screw* (1954), *A Midsummer Night's Dream* (1960), *Death in Venice* (1973), and the one-act children's opera *Noye's Fludde* (1960), based on a Chester miracle play. For television production in 1971 Britten composed *Owen Wingrave,* a study in pacificism. Fundamentally, most of Britten's operas deal with social issues; *Albert Herring* is his only comic opera. Britten's works laid a firm foundation for the future of English opera.

Britten interspersed composition of operas and other works, most of them vocal. The most notable of the latter are the *War Requiem* (1961) and the cantata *Phaedra* (Mezzo, small orch.; 1975), written for Janet Baker. The *War Requiem,* performed at the consecration of the new Coventry Cathedral, is both a denunciation of war and a tribute to the British who died in World War II. The traditional liturgical Requiem text alternates with poems by Wilfred Owen, a war victim. Owen's lines are sung by tenor and baritone soloists; the Latin liturgical text is distributed among soprano soloist, boys' voices accompanied by organ, and chorus accompanied by orchestra.

Russia

In Russia after the Bolshevik Revolution in November 1917, cultural conditions differed vastly from those in western Europe. Education of the masses was a prime concern of the new government under Lenin and Trotsky. This meant that composers were expected to write music that supported and reenforced government ideals rather than create works for purely esthetic reasons. All of the arts were placed under state supervision in 1921, but composers were permitted some liberties, some individuality of expression. The Union of Soviet Composers was formed in 1932; its Resolution of 1932 decreed that all music should be socialistic and should be easily understood by the masses. Use of folk material was advocated, along with expression of "national feelings." Western modern music was banned, and performance of individualistic works, especially those with any semblance of modern techniques, by Russian composers was prohibited. Thus, Russia sought to isolate itself from the West.

News of the suppression of works, or composers' withdrawal of them because of severe criticism, reached the West. In 1936 two works by Dmitry Shostakovich (1906–75)—the opera *Lady Macbeth of the Mtsensk District* and the ballet *The Limpid Stream*—drew Party condemnation and critical attacks by *Pravda* (Truth, the Russian newspaper). In 1948 a number of works by Shostakovich, Sergei Prokofiev (1891–1953), Aram Khachaturian (1903–78), Dmitry Kabalevsky (b. 1904), and others were declared to be antidemocratic and in violation of regulations, particularly with regard to form. (Khachaturian may have been included merely because he associated with the other composers.) At that time, all art was supposed to be "socially significant communication."

Conditions gradually improved after the death of Stalin and were appreciably better when Nikita Krushchev (1894–1971) came into power. For instance, Shostakovich's Symphony No. 10 was accorded immediate acceptance and even hailed as a masterpiece. In 1958 the Communist Party's reversal of Stalin's 1948 decree lifted the ban on music by those composers who had been censured. Cultural agreements with other countries made possible the performance of new Western music in USSR, e.g., serial music, and works by Bartók and Hindemith. Russian composers who had emigrated were permitted to visit their native land.

Much of the music written by composers living in Soviet Russia is related to specific revolutionary events, heroes, or anniversaries. Other works implicitly convey Soviet ideology. Such music may touch the hearts of the Russian people and be easily understood by them, but comparatively few of those works have been accepted into Western repertoire, and the pieces most frequently performed are instrumental. A large body of music by Russian composers was created for films, and subsequently suites were derived from those film scores. Most of that music is unknown outside Russia. Conditions have continued to improve in USSR. The arts are not without censorship, but some modern music, with atonal, serial, or aleatoric features, has been written by some avant-garde composers and is performed in USSR, as well as abroad.

The most significant of the composers living in Russia between 1917 and 1945 are Prokofiev, Shostakovich, Khachaturian, and Kabalevsky. Works by all of them have entered Western repertoire. Khachaturian received international acclaim for his Piano Concerto (1936), Violin Concerto (1940), and the ballet *Gayane* (1942), which contains the popular "Sabre Dance." Khachaturian was particularly successful in Russia because his music incorporates regional materials, promotes Russian tradition, adheres to standard forms, and is not innovative. Many of his works reenforce Soviet ideology. In 1954 Khachaturian was named People's Artist of the USSR. His wife was composer Nina Makarova (1908–76), whose numerous compositions include a symphony and an opera. Her music is Romantic, with some Impressionistic touches.

Dmitry Kabalevsky, poet and painter as well as musician, began his career in music as an accompanist and a piano teacher. He wrote his first compositions for his piano pupils. He entered Moscow Conservatory in 1925 primarily because he wanted to be able to compose more effective teaching pieces; later, he became professor of composition there. Kabalevsky was a respected writer on music as well as a successful composer. His works exemplify the ideals of the Soviet Russian school of musical composition: diatonic melodies, harmonies basically tonal but not without dissonance, energetic rhythms, in traditional forms. In Russia Kabalevsky is best known for his vocal works (operas, cantatas, songs), but in Western countries his reputation rests on his instrumental music (symphonies, symphonic poems, concerti, piano sonatas and preludes).

Prokofiev

Sergei Prokofiev began composing at the age of five, and before he was ten had written several piano pieces, a symphony, and two operas. From 1904 to 1914 he

Sergei Prokofiev. *(The Bettmann Archive.)*

was a student at St. Petersburg Conservatory, where he formed a lasting friendship with Nikolay Myaskovsky (1881–1950) and received from him the advice and encouragement that he needed concerning his compositions. By the time Prokofiev graduated, he had written a number of works, the most important being Piano Concerto No. 1 (D♭ major; 1911). Though controversial at the time, it has remained in the repertoire, as has also Piano Concerto No. 3 (C major; 1917–21). In 1914 Prokofiev visited Paris, became intrigued with ballet, met Diaghilev, and received from him a commission for a ballet. The work that resulted, *Ali i Lolli,* was a failure but from it evolved the *Scythian Suite* (1915; orch.), relating to ancient Russian sun worship and strongly primitive.

Prokofiev's next significant work was the *Classical Symphony* (Op. 25; D major; 1916–17), notable for its anticipation of the Neo-Classical trend in early twentieth-century music that emerged a few years later. However, Prokofiev's anticipation was unconscious; he was merely attempting to write a symphony as Haydn might have, had he been living in 1917. The name "Classical" conveyed Prokofiev's hope that his work would become a "classic." Structured in four movements (sonata, ternary, gavotte with trio, rondo), and transparent in texture as were many Classical symphonies, this work has several features that became characteristic of Prokofiev's style, e.g., angular melody and ostinato. Prokofiev did not continue writing Neo-Classical music. His Symphony No. 2 (D minor; 1924–25) has only two movements, the second being theme and variations, and the first movement is quite dissonant.

From 1918 to 1936, Prokofiev lived outside Russia. He composed and concertized in western Europe and America, and after 1927 made several concert tours to Russia. His opera *The Love for Three Oranges* (1919) was first performed by Chicago Opera Company in 1921, with the composer conducting. Prokofiev prepared an orchestral suite from some of the music from that opera. Other frequently performed works written during these years are the symphonic suite *Lieutenant Kijé* (1934), Violin Concerto No. 2 (G minor; 1935), and *Peter and the Wolf* (1936; spoken narration, orch.), described as a "symphonic fairy tale" for children.

After the Union of Soviet Composers was established, Prokofiev received some Soviet commissions for works. He considered carefully the general guidelines that the Soviets had set up for composers, believed that he could comply with them, and in 1936 he returned to Russia to live. Yet, some of his works were severely criticized and rejected, and he had to rewrite several compositions to please Soviet and Union officials.

While on concert tour in United States in 1938, Prokofiev studied film music techniques in California. When he returned to Russia, Mosfilm commissioned him to write the film score for *Alexander Nevsky* (1938). Later, Prokofiev edited the music as a cantata, in seven sections, for mezzo-soprano, mixed chorus, and full orchestra. The film and cantata concern the heroism of Grand Duke Alexander (1220–63) and his Russian troops when they fought and defeated invading Teutonic Crusaders in a catastrophic battle fought on the ice of Lake Chud. In addition to stirring nationalistic Russian music, the cantata contains a Crusaders' chorale.

Prokofiev wrote numerous works in all genres. Of his seven symphonies, the *Classical* and the Fifth (B♭ major; 1944) are outstanding. Symphony No. 5 is an excellent example of Prokofiev's style, which may be described thusly: Nationalism is present but is min-

gled with Classical and modern features. Prokofiev adhered to traditional forms and was adept at motivic development. His music is tonal, with lyrical but angular melodies, strong motor rhythm, and sudden modulations to unexpected keys. *Basso ostinato* occurs frequently. The instrumental writing is idiomatic. Often, in places where the basic texture is thin, fuller sonority is achieved by having dissimilar instruments double the passages. Most of the symphonies include piano and harp.

Shostakovich

Dmitry Shostakovich received his first musical training from his mother, a professional pianist. In 1919 he entered Petrograd Conservatory, where he concentrated on piano and composition. He graduated in piano in 1923 and in composition two years later. As graduation composition, he submitted his Symphony No. 1 (F minor), a four-movement work modern in style. Both first and second movements—a sonata-form Allegretto with slow introduction and a scherzo marked Allegro—hint at serialism, with themes containing 11, 9, and 12 pitches, but serialism is not followed. The symphony is tonal throughout. In the Lento third movement, a lyrical melody characterized by wide leaps is typical of Shostakovich's melodic writing.

The symphony continued to interest Shostakovich—he composed 15 of them. In his symphonies, his stylistic traits are clearly revealed. *Symphony No. 2: "To October"* (C major; 1927), commissioned for celebration of the tenth anniversary of the Bolshevik Revolution, consists of a single movement in five sections, the last including chorus. *Symphony No. 3: "May First"* (E♭ major; 1930) is also a politically oriented one-movement work with chorus. All of his other symphonies are multimovement compositions, and only two others (Nos. 13 and 14) include voices. Though Shostakovich stated he felt the need of words in Symphony No. 7, he managed without them. Of his 15 symphonies, Nos. 2, 3, 7, 8, 11, and 12 are decidedly Russian in tone; the others are more contemporary and somewhat individualistic in style. Thus, there is visible in Shostakovich's work a dualism that reflects his vacillation between writing the kind of music he wanted to and fulfilling his moral and political obligations as a loyal Soviet citizen. In his

Dmitry Shostakovich. *(Historical Pictures Service.)*

last three symphonies, he seems to have returned to his youthful daring and to the experimentation that brought forth his First Symphony. In fact, of the last three "symphonies," only No. 15 is a truly orchestral symphony. Like his First Symphony, it is Neo-Classical, concisely written, in traditional four-movement form, with Scherzo third. In Symphony No. 15 Shostakovich quoted from a variety of sources, including the Fate motif in Wagner's *Der Ring . . .* and the *Vivace* of Rossini's *William Tell Overture.*

Seven of Shostakovich's symphonies are in minor keys, and most of them end in tonic major. The Third Symphony is especially dissonant. The Thirteenth is a setting of five poems by Yevgeny Yevtusenko (written in l961), the first of them decrying the harsh treatment and massacre of Jewish Russians at Babi Yar, near Kiev, in the Ukraine. The Fourteenth, in 11 short movements setting poems on death, also is closer to a song cycle than a symphony. It is scored for chamber ensemble of strings and percussion, with all string sections *divisi.* The seventh movement contains a four-voice fugue played *col legno.*

After writing the first three symphonies, Shostakovich became interested in writing for stage, and, among other things, composed the satirical opera *The Nose* (1927) and the ballet *The Golden Age* (1930), equally satirical, with brilliant orchestration. His next opera, *Lady Macbeth of the Mtsensk District* (1930–32), and the ballet *The Limpid Stream* (1934–35) drew harsh criticism and public condemnation from Russian political and cultural authorities and in *Pravda,* as did also Symphony No. 4 (C major; 1936). All three works were withdrawn. *Lady Macbeth . . .* reappeared, completely revised, as *Katerina Izmay-*

lova in 1956 and was favorably received. The opera realistically portrays the lascivious Katerina, whose homicidal activity is punished by imprisonment in a Siberian camp; there she murders a rival for her lover's affections and then commits suicide. In addition to sex and violence, there is some comedy and sentimentality.

Supposedly, Shostakovich wrote Symphony No. 5 (D minor; 1937) as acknowledgment of and in response to the "justified" criticism of his previous works. Actually, he made no concessions, though he did return to four-movement form. The work contains no folk materials and is not nationalistic. However, it was favorably received and has remained one of his most frequently performed works. Many of Shostakovich's symphonies commence with a slow movement; Symphony No. 5 opens with a Moderato in sonata form. Again characteristically, the first theme is given to bass instruments; here, it is presented in canon (ex. 25.7a). The second theme, introduced by first violins, abounds in wide leaps (ex. 25.7b). As is the case in most of Shostakovich's four-movement symphonies, the Scherzo is the second movement. It is a large ternary form, whose middle section serves as Trio and has reduced instrumentation. In the Largo third movement, melodies are lyrical but contain some wide leaps. Some of the contrapuntal writing resembles that of Vaughan Williams—melody and bass line, with a stream of parallel major triads in the inner voices. The Finale is festive, a sonata-form Allegro non troppo.

Symphony No. 7 (C major; 1941), popularly known as the "Leningrad Symphony," was Shostakovich's reaction to Hitler's invasion of Russia in 1941. The symphony quickly gained acceptance among the Allied countries, as well as in Russia, and became a symbol of Allied resistance against Naziism. Symphony No. 10 (E minor; 1953) is another that is performed frequently. Some persons consider it Shostakovich's finest symphony. Shostakovich personalized a number of his works, including the Tenth and Fifteenth symphonies, by placing within them his musical monogram, a transliteration of his Cyrillic first and last initials into German: D-SCH (D-Es-C-H), or D-E♭-C-B♮ in musical notation (ex. 25.8).

Example 25.7 Shostakovich: Symphony No. 5, mvt. 1: (*a*) mm. 1–3, strings present theme 1 in canon; (*b*) mm. 51–63, first violins present theme 2, a lyrical melody with wide leaps. *(From Dmitri Shostakovich, Symphony No. 5, Kalmus Miniature Score No. 165, Columbia Pictures/Belwin-Mills Publishing Corporation, Miami, FL.)*

(a)

(b)

(a)

(b)

Example 25.8 Shostakovich's musical monogram as used in Symphony No. 10, mvt. 3: (*a*) mm. 1–3, theme 1, based on the monogram; (*b*) closing measures, monogram stated by flutes and piccolos. *(From Dmitri Shostakovich, Symphony No. 10, Kalmus Miniature Score No. 158, Columbia Pictures/Belwin-Mills Publishing Corporation, Miami, FL.)*

Many persons consider Shostakovich the greatest symphonist of the mid-twentieth century. His Fourteenth and Fifteenth Symphonies are masterpieces but are still relatively unknown. He composed fine works in other genres, too. His 15 string quartets are a valuable addition to the repertoire; of them, Nos. 7 and 8 are the finest. The Piano Quintet (G minor; 1940) is also excellent.

The Second Viennese School

The name "Second Viennese School" has been applied to Arnold Schoenberg and his few private pupils at Vienna, especially Alban Berg and Anton Webern. From this small "school" there emerged a new style of music called **dodecaphony** or **twelve-tone music** (from Greek: *dodeca,* 12; *phonos,* sound), an atonal or pantonal style in which all 12 of the chromatic pitches in the octave were regarded as equals and none had any special function. (Schoenberg considered dodecaphonic music pantonal, i.e., a blend of all key tonalities, but most persons refer to it as being atonal.) Two of the principal factors generating the new style were: (1) the increasingly abundant use of dissonances in post-Romantic music, particularly, dissonances that remained unresolved and that were unrelated and unjustifiable in traditional harmony; and (2) a greater interest in and an ever-increasing use of linear counterpoint, whose motives and melodies dictated harmonies that, less and less frequently, followed the rules governing functional harmonies of key tonality.

During the first two decades of the twentieth century several composers, including Scriabin, Schoenberg, and Berg, wrote atonal music and music in which they considered the octave's 12 tones as being on a par. Dodecaphony and atonal music could not survive long without some system of order, however. Largely due to Schoenberg's efforts, an organizational system was developed that was put into operation in the 1920s, a system that became known as **serialism.** The name derives from the fact that a composer prearranged the order in which the 12 chromatic pitches were to be used, thus establishing a **Series** or **Tone Row**—the Original Row (O), which Schoenberg called *Grundgestalt* (basic pattern). Though the pitches were to be used in the specific order in which they appeared in the Row, the position of any one of them on the staff might be displaced by the distance of one or more octaves (octave displacement). Any two or more successive pitches might be combined to form a harmonic interval or chord. The Row need not always be used in its Original form but might be used in Retrograde (R), in Inversion (I), or in Retrograde Inversion (RI). Moreover, any or all of these four versions of the Row might be transposed to any step of the chromatic scale. Thus, 48 (12 × 4) possible versions of the Row were available to a composer. A **matrix** (also called a **grid**) showing those possibilities is figure 25.2. It should be readily apparent that what might seem, at the outset, to be extremely limiting, actually allows a composer considerable freedom.

Schoenberg was not the only composer in Vienna in 1913–23 who was seeking to develop a workable system for atonal music, though his principles were

O→ (ORIGINAL)	1	2	3	4	5	6	7	8	9	10	11	12	(EDARGORTER) ←R
1	E	F	G	Db	Gb	Eb	Ab	D	B	C	A	Bb	12
2	Eb	E	Gb	C	F	D	G	Db	Bb	B	Ab	A	11
3	Db	D	E	Bb	Eb	C	F	B	Ab	A	Gb	G	10
4	G	Ab	Bb	E	A	Gb	B	F	D	Eb	C	Db	9
5	D	Eb	F	B	E	Db	Gb	C	A	Bb	G	Ab	8
6	F	Gb	Ab	D	G	E	A	Eb	C	Db	Bb	B	7
7	C	Db	Eb	A	D	B	E	Bb	G	Ab	F	Gb	6
8	Gb	G	A	Eb	Ab	F	Bb	E	Db	D	B	C	5
9	A	Bb	C	Gb	B	Ab	Db	G	E	F	D	Eb	4
10	Ab	A	B	F	Bb	G	C	Gb	Eb	E	Db	D	3
11	B	C	D	Ab	Db	Bb	Eb	A	Gb	G	E	F	2
12	Bb	B	Db	G	C	A	D	Ab	F	Gb	Eb	E	1
RI	12	11	10	9	8	7	6	5	4	3	2	1	

(Left margin: I ↓ INVERSION / NOISREVNI ← EDARGORTER)

Figure 25.2 Matrix (or grid) for the Row Schoenberg used in *Suite für Klavier,* Op. 25.

those generally accepted. Another system, less efficient, was developed by Josef Hauer (1883–1959), who, for each composition, arbitrarily divided the 12 chromatic pitches into two hexachords but did not regulate the order of the pitches within each hexachord. In other words, he specified content but not order. Hauer and Schoenberg were in contact with each other in 1917–23, and Schoenberg arranged for performances of some of Hauer's atonal works. No doubt each composer profited to some degree from the work of the other. Disagreement arose between them when Hauer claimed to have originated the twelve-tone method. During the political turmoil in Austria in the 1930s Hauer receded into the background, though he composed stereotyped *Zwölftonspiele* (twelve-tone music) for the remainder of his life.

Berg and Webern, the most outstanding of Schoenberg's pupils, adopted his principles but used them in modification. Berg did not adhere to a single row for an entire composition or movement and often combined tonal and nontonal elements in a work.

Webern strictly adhered to serial principles, used one row per movement, and wrote highly ordered counterpoint, concentrated in extremely compressed forms. He used serial principles scientifically, creating rows whose variant forms, in transposition, reverted to the Original, and rows in which the intervals of the second hexachord, in retrograde, exactly duplicated those of the first hexachord. And what of Schoenberg himself? In his last style period, he tried to reconcile the principles of tonality and atonality. From time to time, he sought to return to the traditional tonal system but found himself returning to atonality and serialism.

At this point some clarification of terminology must be made. The terms **atonal** and **pantonal** are both used to describe music in which key centers of tonality are not clearly audible. Technically, those two terms are not synonymous. Atonal indicates the total absence of any center of key tonality, whereas pantonal indicates the presence of all tonal centers with none distinctive enough to be recognized or strong enough to exercise a tonal gravitation to itself. It has been mentioned that Schoenberg described his works as pantonal. **Dodecaphony,** meaning **twelve-tone music,** is the term applied to music based on series, sets, or rows containing all 12 chromatic pitches in the octave. A dodecaphonic composition is not necessarily atonal/pantonal; it may written in a key tonality. An ingenious composer can construct a series or row that reenforces rather than negates key tonality. Conversely, an atonal/pantonal composition is not necessarily dodecaphonic. A composition that is not based on twelve-tone techniques may be written in such a manner that no tonal center can be detected. These several terms must be clearly differentiated if one is to understand the music of many composers active after c. 1924.

Schoenberg

Arnold Schoenberg (1874–1951) was largely a self-taught musician. He became proficient enough on violin and 'cello to play in ensembles with friends and in an amateur orchestra conducted by Austrian composer Alexander Zemlinsky (1871–1942) and learned a great deal about musical composition by studying the scores of great composers. His first efforts at composition were some piano pieces and songs. Then, in 1894, he began to take counterpoint lessons from Zemlinsky and probably received other advice about

Arnold **Schoenberg**. *(Historical Pictures Service.)*

composition from him. By 1897 Schoenberg was composing works of sufficient quality to merit public performance. One of those pieces was a String Quartet (D major; 1897). By 1904 Schoenberg felt knowledgeable enough about composition to advertise for pupils. His advertisements attracted the attention of Alban Berg and Anton Webern, who became his first pupils.

Schoenberg's career as composer may be divided into five periods: (1) 1895–1908, characterized by tonal works that are post-Romantic in style, containing much chromaticism and reflecting the influence of Wagner, Mahler, and Richard Strauss; (2) 1909–14, when he dared to be different and composed dissonant pantonal Expressionistic works that defied or ignored the principles of traditional harmony; (3) 1914–23, a period of experimentation during which he formulated the twelve-tone method and serial principles but composed nothing for publication; (4) 1923–33, a period of dodecaphonic composition; and (5) 1934–51, a time when he sought to reconcile dodecaphony and key tonality, and, by his own statement, wanted to return to composing according to traditional principles of tonality but from time to time found himself slipping back into pantonality.

The first work to indicate that Schoenberg's musical personality would be distinctive was *Verklärte Nacht* (Transfigured Night, Op. 4; 1899) for two violins, two violas, and two 'celli. In 1917 he arranged it for string orchestra. *Verklärte Nacht,* based on a poem by Richard Dehmel, is one of Schoenberg's most frequently performed works. Its five sections, corresponding to the sections of Dehmel's poem, are played without a break. Containing sudden modulations, and filled with chromaticism clearly related to that of Wagner's *Tristan und Isolde, Verklärte Nacht* is an emotionally intense programmatic work. To write that kind of program music for string sextet was unusual.

Other post-Romantic tonal works from Schoenberg's first compositional period include the symphonic poem *Pelleas und Melisande* (1902–3), *Acht Lieder für Klavier und Singstimme* (Eight songs for piano and voice, Op. 6; 1904–5), *Sechs Orchesterlieder* (Six Songs with orchestra, Op. 8; 1903–5), and *Gurre-Lieder* (Songs of Gurre; 1900–11). *Pelleas und Melisande,* which is reflective of Strauss, is an extremely polyphonic work for a large orchestra but exhibits due regard for conventional tonality. Schoenberg had written all of the cantata *Gurre-Lieder* by 1901; he did not complete its orchestration until 1911. It is a massive work scored for five soloists, three four-part male choruses, an eight-part mixed chorus, and a huge orchestra. Readily apparent in the music is the influence of Wagner, particularly the wildness of *Die Walküre.* The last soloistic piece in *Gurre-Lieder,* presented just before the final chorus, is melodrama. The contrast between the last two numbers is most effective.

As Schoenberg's compositions grew increasingly more chromatic, he included in them an abundance of highly dissonant chords that he did not resolve. More and more, he was concerned with motivic units and their manipulation. Then he moved into the pantonality, or atonality, that characterizes the works of his second period. His first truly atonal works were *Drei Klavierstücke* (Three Piano Pieces, Op. 11; 1909) and *Das Buch der hängenden Gärten* (The book of the Hanging Gardens; 1908–9; vc., pno.), a setting of 15 poems by Stefan George. In the latter work, Schoenberg did not treat the piano as accompaniment to the vocal part but as an independent instrument, with different but compatible music. In these works, consonance is no longer primal, with dissonance being required to resolve to it. Rather, dissonance has become independent, on a par with consonance. Next Schoenberg applied his atonal style to orchestral music. Each of the *Five Orchestral Pieces* (Op. 16; 1909) has a programmatic title. The third of those

pieces, "Summer Morning by the Lake," was at various times entitled "Chord Colors" and "The Changing Chord" (DWMA219). Throughout the piece, which is ternary in form, a three-note motive (A-B♭-A♭ and transpositions of it) figures prominently. The opening and concluding sections of the piece contain sustained chords whose instrumentation is continually changing, unobtrusively, thus producing a flow of different tone colors. This is a form of **Klangfarbenmelodie** (tone-color melody), the technique of creating a melody from changing tone colors rather than from a succession of different pitches. It was used frequently by Schoenberg, often to point up motives.

Schoenberg wrote two important one-act dramatic works during this period. *Erwartung* (Expectation, Op. 17; 1909) is a surrealist **monodrama** for female voice and large orchestra. (In a monodrama, one person is responsible for unfolding the entire drama.) The plot concerns a woman wandering through a forest at night in search of her lover; finally, she stumbles over his dead body. Much of the time, the woman sings in dialogue with orchestral instruments, as though with persons. Tone colors are extremely important in this composition. The other work, *Die glückliche Hand* (The lucky hand, Op. 18; 1910–13), was, in a sense, a dramatic experiment, and for it Schoenberg wrote his own libretto. Performance of the work takes only 23 minutes. It requires a man and a woman who mime the action, a high baritone singer, six men and six women for the chorus, and a very large orchestra. Only the faces of the chorus are visible, painted green (or illuminated to appear green) and protruding through holes in purple velvet backdrop drapery. The chorus, whose function is similar to that of the citizens' chorus in ancient Greek tragedy, delivers its texts in a mixture of *Sprechstimme* (speechsong) and song. Expressionist works were not intended to be beautiful, pleasing, or even realistic. Rather, every detail involved in the performance of such a work is exploited in order to convey, as penetratingly as possible, inner thoughts, emotions, and experiences.

Schoenberg's unusual treatment of the voice that began in a small way with the melodrama in *Gurre-Lieder,* and continued through the various shadings of the voice in the monodrama *Erwartung* and the

Developments between the World Wars

choral mingling of *Sprechstimme* and singing in *Die glückliche Händ,* culminated in *Pierrot Lunaire* (Moonstruck Pierrot, Op. 21; 1912), the major work of this pantonal period. *Pierrot Lunaire* is probably Schoenberg's best-known work. Generally considered a cycle of 21 songs, the composition is actually a set of melodramas presented in *Sprechstimme* by a vocalist-reciter against instrumental accompaniment that varies from piece to piece. Each of the songs has different instrumentation. Five instrumentalists are needed, three of them doubling: piano, 'cello, flute switching to piccolo, clarinet to bass clarinet, violin to viola. Schoenberg selected 21 poems from the 50 in Albert Giraud's *Pierrot Lunaire* and arranged them in three groups of seven. Each of the poems has 13 lines arranged in Renaissance *rondeau* form, but the musical settings do not follow *rondeau* form. Schoenberg wrote the vocal line of all 21 pieces in *Sprechstimme,* using normal notation that indicates precise pitch and duration of each note but with an x through each note's stem to indicate that a special kind of delivery was required: ♪ . He supplied written instructions for singing *Sprechstimme,* in which he indicated that the rhythm must be absolutely strict, but that the notated pitch is merely touched upon at the outset of the note's value, then immediately rises or falls. He cautioned the reciter-singer never to really sing the pitches and never to "singsong" them. "It must not be reminiscent of song," he stated. For the instrumentalists, accuracy of dynamics and maintenance of strict rhythm is extremely important. In each of the pieces, a short initial motive generates the music for that entire piece. In No. 8, *Nacht* (Night; DWMA220a), which is a passacaglia, the generative motive contains ten notes. Though a three-note ostinato figure is ever-present, its note values are modified much of the time. The song is dark in color, well suited to the gloomy text, which depicts nightfall as giant black moths blotting out the sun's radiance and sinking earthward into people's hearts. Song No. 18, *Der Mondfleck* (The Moonspot; DWMA220b), for soloist and quintet—piccolo, clarinet, violin, 'cello, and piano—is brighter. It is the most contrapuntally complex piece of the entire cycle. There is a double canon *cancrizans*—one between the strings, the other between the winds—with the music becoming retrograde at the middle of the tenth measure. Simulta-

Example 25.9 Forms of the Row Schoenberg used in *Variations,* Op. 31.

neously with the double canon, the pianist plays a three-voice fugue whose subject is an augmented version (note values doubled) of the canonic melody between the winds. The piano music and the vocal line do not turn retrograde.

Between 1908 and 1913 Schoenberg's works gradually had become more and more dissonant, and most of them had not been well received by the public. Therefore, for almost a full decade, he worked behind the scenes, so to speak, and shared his compositions with the public only after he had devised a new style of composition to offer them. His first works in that new style were completed in 1923. In *Fünf Klavierstücke* (Five piano pieces, Op. 23) and *Serenade* (Op. 24) for chamber ensemble, the twelve-tone method was still experimental; a complete row appears in only one piece in each of those works. The first composition in which Schoenberg used a single twelve-note row throughout was the six-movement *Suite für Klavier* (Piano Suite, Op. 25; 1923). Other twelve-tone works followed, but not until he composed the orchestral *Variations,* Op. 31 (1927–28) were the possibilities of his twelve-tone system fully realized (ex. 25.9). A detailed analysis of that work, which consists of Introduction, nine variations, and Finale, could serve as a textbook on serial techniques. Schoenberg included the motive B-A-C-H (B♭-A-C-B♮) in the row for the *Piano Suite,* and in the *Variations.* The motive has greater prominence in the *Variations,* where it is played by trombones in the Introduction and at the end of Variation 2, and is used in counterpoint with the main theme in the Finale (DWMA221). According to Schoenberg, the Finale, which is itself a set of continuous variations, was modeled after Brahms's *Variations on a Theme by Haydn.*

After Adolf Hitler was elected Chancellor of Germany, Schoenberg, who was Jewish, decided to emigrate. He came to United States via Paris, settled in Los Angeles, and taught at California universities. In many of the compositions he wrote in America he combined serial techniques with tonality. In other works he adhered to the principles of traditional tonality. On the other hand, the Violin Concerto (Op. 36; 1936) and String Quartet No. 4 (Op. 37; 1936) are strictly serial atonal compositions.

Among the musical expressions of Schoenberg's Jewish faith are settings of several Psalms in Hebrew and *Kol Nidre* (Op. 39; 1938). The latter is a tonal work, a liturgical setting that Schoenberg hoped would find use in the synagogue. However, it was not accepted because he had written an introduction and had altered the text somewhat. *A Survivor from Warsaw* (Op. 46; 1947), for narrator, male voices, and very large orchestra, was written in response to a report of courageous Jews singing the *Shema Yisroel* during the Warsaw uprising. Schoenberg wrote the text himself and included in it the *Shema Yisroel,* the creed, acknowledging that God is One Lord, and the commandment to love Him.

Unfinished at the time of Schoenberg's death was the opera *Moses und Aron* (Moses and Aaron). The odd spelling of the name Aaron in the title resulted from Schoenberg's dread of the number 13; when he realized there were 13 letters in the title, he deleted one *a* from Aaron. Schoenberg had written the libretto for the opera and had composed Acts I and II in 1930–32 but had not written Act III. He based the entire opera on a single tone row. The work requires six soloists, chorus, and a large orchestra. Acts I and II have been performed, in a concert version (1954) and staged (1957). They are magnificent music.

Certain stylistic characteristics are visible in Schoenberg's compositions in all periods of his career: (1) melodies containing wide leaps; (2) the absence of vigorous, propelling rhythms; (3) emphasis on counterpoint, especially in the twelve-tone works; and (4) a penchant for constantly changing tone colors, particularly in orchestral works. In many of his pieces, the rhythmic beat is deliberately obscured through such techniques as dense texture, placement of rests on primary beats, frequent tempo changes, and sustained tones.

Alban Berg. *(Historical Pictures Service.)*

Berg

As a youngster, Alban Berg (1885–1935) played piano and enjoyed writing songs, though he had no formal training in composition. After completing his general education, he obtained clerical work in a government office. By chance, in October 1904 he noticed Schoenberg's advertisement for pupils and contacted him for lessons. Schoenberg became a close friend and his mentor, as well as his teacher; Berg studied with him for six years.

The compositions Berg wrote during his first years of study with Schoenberg—the *Sieben frühe Lieder* (Seven early songs; 1905–8) and the one-movement Piano Sonata (Op. 1; 1907–8)—are Romantic, stylistically reflecting Wolf, Mahler, and Schoenberg's tonal compositions. Atonality and originality emerged in the last of Berg's *Vier Lieder* (Four Songs, Op. 2; 1909–10) and the String Quartet (Op. 3; 1910). Several features of the quartet became characteristics of Berg's works: (1) use of scales that are largely (but not completely) whole-tone; (2) prolongation of a passage by melodic expansion of an interval, e.g., widening an interval from a second to a third to a fourth, etc.; (3) combining atonality with traditional forms, and suggestions of tonality with what is actually atonality.

Berg's *Fünf Orchesterlieder nach Ansichtskartentexten von Peter Altenberg* (Five orchestral songs after picture postcard texts by Peter Altenberg, Op. 4; orch. with voice; 1911), the "Altenberg Songs," are miniatures for a large orchestra. The work's last movement, *Hier ist Friede* (Here is peace), is a passacaglia on three subjects, one of them dodecaphonic. The very brief *Vier Stücke* (Four pieces, Op. 5; 1913; cl., pno.), when viewed overall, form a miniature sonata, with movements 12, 9, 18, and 20 measures long. A feature of Berg's mature works, and a factor that creates a kind of tension (between old and new), is the use of traditional form with powerful new music.

During World War I, Berg was employed by the War Ministry but found the time to compose *Drei Stücke* (Three Pieces, Op. 6; 1913–15; orch.) and to work on the opera *Wozzeck* (1917–22). He was inspired to write the opera in 1914 when he attended a performance of Büchner's play *Woyzeck* (written, 1837; first perf., 1913). The opera plot concerns a soldier (Wozzeck) who is badgered by his superiors and beset by poverty and whose frustrations ultimately drive him to murder his unfaithful mistress (Marie) and then commit suicide. Berg based his libretto on the second edition of Büchner's drama and reduced the number of scenes to 15. He constructed a three-act opera, with five scenes per act, each act being a cyclic self-contained form, and each scene being a self-contained movement or compositional form. Act I is a suite of five character pieces, in which Scene 1 is (according to Berg) a stylized version of a Bach *French Suite;* Scene 3 is a passacaglia. Act II, Scene 1 is in sonata form, and the entire Act—the longest in the opera—could be viewed as a five-movement symphony. Act III consists of five inventions (DWMA 222, Act III, Scene 2). Analysis reveals other formal patterns and traditional techniques: fugue, rondo, rhapsody, isorhythm, variations, and several more. Though *Wozzeck* is considered the first full-length atonal opera, there are semblances of tonality within it, e.g., in Act II, Scene 1. Berg's interest in numbers, his penchant for planning in number sequences, is apparent in this work, as in several of his other compositions. The music is continuous in *Wozzeck,* and *Leitmotifs* are important as a unifying device, but they are not as extensive as in Wagner's music dramas. As Debussy did in *Pelléas et Mélisande,* Berg used orchestral interludes to connect the scenes within an act. Another unifying device is the use of the same music at the opera's end and at the closing of the curtain on Act I. Berg designed his music to fit the opera so precisely that he hoped no one in the audience would be aware of the music *per se,* but attention would be concentrated on the social problems presented through the operatic drama.

Between 1923 and 1925 Berg composed the *Kammerkonzert* (Chamber concerto) for piano, violin, and 13 wind instruments. Thematic material for the three-movement serial work is derived from the letters of musical pitches found in the names Arnold Schönberg, Anton Webern, and Alban Berg, a technique resembling the *soggetto cavato* used by Josquin (see pp. 197–98). The *Lyrische Suite* (Lyric Suite; 1925–26) was commissioned and first performed by the Kolisch Quartet. In 1928 Berg arranged the suite's second, third, and fourth movements for string orchestra; that version is frequently performed. At some time he wrote a vocal finale for the work, for mezzo soprano solo with string quartet; this movement was discovered and first performed in 1979.

In 1928 Berg began a second Expressionist opera, *Lulu,* based on Frank Wiedekind's plays *Erdgeist* (Earth spirit) and *Die Büchse der Pandora* (Pandora's Box). In Berg's libretto, the two plays' seven acts became seven scenes in three acts. Berg had composed the entire opera but had not finished orchestrating the third act before his untimely death (1935) from systemic poisoning caused by an abscessed insect bite. Unfortunately, Berg's widow refused to release his manuscript for Act III; only after her death (1976) was the orchestration completed, and the entire opera performed (1979). Berg's music for *Lulu* is a combination of atonal, serial, and nondodecaphonic elements. As in *Wozzeck,* each act was designed as a musical form: Act I, sonata form; Act II, rondo; Act III, theme and variations. Within the acts and scenes are autonomous pieces, as in a number opera. Lulu represents female sexuality. In Act I she is seductive, powerful, and a murderess; in Act III she is murdered by Jack the Ripper. Some persons in the cast play dual roles—each of Lulu's victims in the first half of the opera becomes an avenger-character in the final scene—and, to reenforce that fact, Berg brought back, as highly telescoped recapitulation, the music of the first half of the opera.

Berg's last completed composition is the Violin Concerto, commissioned by violinist Louis Krasner (b. 1903). In April 1935, when Alma Mahler Gropius's 18-year-old daughter Manon died, Berg interrupted his work orchestrating *Lulu* to compose the concerto

Example 25.10: (*a*) Berg, Violin Concerto, mm. 134–37, introduction of chorale melody in imitation; (*b*) beginning of J. S. Bach's harmonization of the chorale *Es ist genug!*; (*c*) piano reduction of orchestral presentation of the chorale as used by Berg in mm. 142–45 of the Violin Concerto. In the Concerto Berg used Bach's harmonization transposed up a semitone.

as a memorial to her. The work is in two large movements, each containing two sections—Andante-Allegretto, and Allegro-Adagio—and each section having its own distinct formal pattern. The Allegretto is a Scherzo with two Trios, arranged as a palindrome: Scherzo–Trio I–Trio II–Trio I–Scherzo. Notated without a key signature, and with almost every note in the score preceded by a ♮, ♭, or ♯, the music is serial atonality so carefully structured that it permits Berg to allude to tonality. Some portions of the concerto are clearly tonal, e.g., that including Bach's chorale harmonization (ex. 25.10). The Andante commences with a ten-measure introduction consisting of arpeggiations closely akin to the pitches of the four open strings of the violin (ex. 25.11a). In the first four measures of that introduction, a series of six rising perfect fifths is presented. After a four-measure orchestral interlude, the soloist presents the row, which consists principally of four arpeggiated triads (alternately minor and major) constructed on

Developments between the World Wars

Example 25.11 Berg, Violin Concerto: (*a*) beginning of Concerto, arpeggiations of fifths; (*b*) the Row, as introduced by solo violin; (*c*) first phrase of the chorale, parallel in tonal structure to last four notes of the Row; (*d*) conclusion of concerto.

the pitches of the violin's open strings, plus a whole-tone tetrachord, all joined conjunctly (ex. 25.11b). The whole-tone tetrachord, in various guises, figures prominently throughout the concerto. The work is cyclic; the row appears in all four sections and in the finale is combined with the chorale *Es ist genug* (It is enough) as harmonized by Bach in his Cantata No. 60. That chorale melody commences with a whole-tone tetrachord; the row concludes with a whole-tone tetrachord (ex. 25.11c). The concerto concludes with five string soloists successively stating the row, their statements commencing with contrabass open-string E and extending upwards to violin g'''. While the violin

soloist sustains that high pitch, there is heard in the orchestra, very softly, as from a distance, the downward arpeggiation of the six perfect fifths that began the concerto (ex. 25.11d).

Berg's principal works are the operas *Wozzeck* and *Lulu*, the *Lyrische Suite* for string quartet, and the Violin Concerto. All provide excellent examples of his style. Though an exponent of atonality, Berg never completely relinquished Romanticism and tonality. In his treatment of twelve-tone music he differed from Schoenberg and Webern in several respects, principally in that Berg: (1) used dodecaphonic and nondodecaphonic episodes in the same work, and

Anton Webern. *(The Bettmann Archive.)*

sometimes in the same movement; (2) frequently supported a tone row with harmony in or suggesting a key; (3) sometimes used different rows (or sets) in the same work, and even in the same movement; (4) used retrograde and retrograde inversions of a row only in palindromes; and (5) usually wrote lyrical music.

Webern

Anton Webern (1883–1945) was Schoenberg's first pupil, coming to him shortly before Berg did in 1904 and remaining under his tutelage until 1908. Another of Schoenberg's pupils at that time was Egon Wellesz (1885–1974), then a student at University of Vienna. It is a credit to Schoenberg that his pupils absorbed his basic principles but developed individual compositional styles, rather than slavishly aping their teacher.

Like Berg, Webern was a native of Vienna. He played piano and 'cello and continued study of those instruments, along with harmony and counterpoint, at the University of Vienna. However, he concentrated on musicology and earned his Ph.D. in that field in 1906. His dissertation on Heinrich Isaac's *Choralis Constantinus II* (see p. 203) led to his edition of that liturgical music (publ. in *DTÖ*, Volume xxxii; 1909) and influenced the motivic treatment in some of his works.

After graduating, Webern worked as a conductor, though he had had no special training for that work. Experience provided proficiency, and soon he was receiving invitations to serve as guest conductor. Most of his energy was devoted to teaching privately, lecturing, and composing. Few of his works were pub-

lished, and he remained relatively obscure as a composer throughout his lifetime. Some of his lectures on dodecaphony, given during the early 1930s, were published in 1960 under the title *Der Weg zur neuen Musik* (The way to the new music). With the advent of Naziism and the consequent loss of some of his sources of income, Webern secured routine work from Universal Edition that he could do at home. He and his wife spent most of the World War II years at Mödling, but near the end of the war they moved to Mittersill, near Salzburg, to be near their daughters. There, on the evening of 15 September 1945, Webern was accidentally shot and killed by an American soldier investigating black market activities in the neighborhood.

Though Webern began writing music c. 1899, his output is not large, comprising 31 works with *opus* numbers and approximately an equal number of other pieces of various kinds. Most of the works are quite brief. The compositions with *opus* numbers may be separated into two groups, representing the two major periods of his compositional career after his study with Schoenberg: (1) Opp. 1–16, including 2 tonal works (Opp. 1 and 2) and 14 atonal ones, composed between 1908 and 1923; and (2) Opp. 17–31, the 15 dodecaphonic serial works composed between 1924 and 1945. Once Webern renounced key tonality, he did not recant; after he began to use serial techniques, he continued along that path. He made no attempt to write program music or to depict his impressions of things around him; rather, he sought to express inner thoughts through abstract music, and he did so succinctly. Some of his pieces and movements are very short, e.g., Op. 10 No. 4 has six and one-third measures; Op. 11 No. 3 has ten. His compositions bear generic titles—Four Songs, String Quartet, Symphony.

Webern reserved the designation "Op. 1" for the orchestral *Passacaglia* he composed in 1908. Actually, he had some justification for doing so; the music he wrote before studying with Schoenberg is of little consequence. The *Passacaglia* shows some influence of Brahms and Schoenberg with respect to variation techniques and of Mahler in the orchestration. Among the atonal works in the first group of pieces with *opus* numbers are eight sets of songs for one vocalist with

Example 25.12 Webern: *Fünf Stücke für Orchester,* I, last 6 measures. To conclude the piece, the same note is sounded successively by different instruments, producing *Klangfarbenmelodie.*

accompaniment; two sets of pieces for string quartet, including *Six Bagatelles* (Op. 9; 1911–13); two orchestral sets, one being *Five Pieces* (Op. 10; 1911–13); *Four Pieces* for violin and piano (Op. 7; 1910); and *Three Little Pieces* (Op. 11; 1913) for 'cello and piano. The compositions are concise, pointillistic, and emphasize dissonant intervals such as the minor second and major ninth. The word **pointillism** is used to describe athematic music seemingly constructed of isolated notes. The term was borrowed from art, where it connotes paintings consisting of dots or points of color that are blended into shapes by the viewer's eyes. Tone color was important to Webern, and the variation of timbres became a feature of his atonal pieces for instrumental ensembles. One instance of this occurs at the end of *Five Pieces* for orchestra, Op. 10, No. 1 (ex. 25.12). Often, Webern varied tone color to differentiate motives or to point up polyphonic entrances. Also, he varied tone colors by calling for different articulations, mutes, and other devices. Despite the changing timbres and registers, continuity of line is present in Webern's music, and he stressed the fact that the performer(s) *must* maintain that continuity. Variation of timbres considerably enriched the economy of means that characterizes Webern's works. Though he sometimes scored works for a large orchestra, e.g., *Six Pieces,* Op. 6, he included instruments for their timbral sonorities in particular passages rather than using them in orchestral ensemble. Webern recognized the significance of silence, too; rests play an important role in his works.

Between 1914 and 1924, Webern concentrated on vocal music; during that decade, he did not complete any purely instrumental compositions. By 1924, serial techniques had been developed, and he began to use these as extensions of variation technique. In Webern's second group of *opus* numbers, the works are highly contrapuntal and often contain canons, palindromes, and variations. He combined serial techniques with traditional ones and incorporated them in traditional forms; in this sense, his work is Neo-Classical. Gradually, in his orchestral works, he eliminated nonpitched percussion instruments and stopped writing harmonics and *col legno* in string parts. In his serial writing, Webern, like Schoenberg, sometimes reiterated a pitch. Frequently, he constructed a row from a series of small motives, or sets; then, in writing the composition, he might work with only a portion of the row, or with one of the motives, before going on to the next.

Webern imposed strict structural limitations upon himself, yet provided ample freedom to be creative. His Symphony (Op. 21; 1928; DWMA223) is an excellent example of this. The work is in two movements, the first in sonata form, the second, theme and variations with coda. Webern made sketches for a third movement but never completed it. Scored for chamber orchestra of nine solo instruments (violin 1 and 2, viola, 'cello, harp, clarinet, bass clarinet, and two horns), the music is highly concentrated, with a texture that never goes beyond four-part writing. For this work, Webern established a twelve-tone row whose Retrograde is identical with the Original transposed up an augmented fourth. He used only the Original and its Inversion in the first movement, and only the Original and its Retrograde in the second movement. The first movement, in addition to being in sonata

form, is a four-voice double canon with the Original row and its Inversion as subjects (ex. 25.13a). The row established for the second movement, and that forms the theme that is varied, is so constructed that its second half is the retrograde of the first half transposed up an augmented fourth (ex. 25.13b). The fact that the entire 11-measure theme is presented by clarinet, accompanied by horns and harp—that is, in a single timbral combination—is unusual in Webern's music. Seven variations are presented, the first and last being double canons; the movement concludes with an 11-measure symmetrical coda in which the Original and Inversion of the row are presented simultaneously, once.

Webern's last completed composition was Cantata No. 2 (Op. 31; 1941–43), for soprano and bass soloists, SATB chorus, and orchestra. It is one of his longest works, requiring slightly more than ten minutes for performance. The text is by Hildegard Jone, who wrote much mystical poetry. In some respects the cantata resembles some by J. S. Bach. It is in six sections: bass recitative and aria, female chorus with soprano solo, soprano recitative, soprano aria with chorus and violin obbligato, and final chorale for mixed chorus. The chorale directly reflects Webern's doctoral study of Isaac's music. Concerning the principal theme, Webern wrote: "The melody which the soprano solo sings in the introduction is supposed to be the law for everything that follows!" The music is written in long note values, resembling the "white notation" used during the Renaissance. The chorale is strophic, and the music is in strict canon; changes in meter occurring within the melodic line resemble mensural rhythmic alterations in the Masses and motets of Renaissance composers. In a letter to Jone (28 January 1944), Webern stated that the cantata was "basically a Missa brevis." The central message of the work is *Freundselig ist das Wort* (Blessed is the Word).

Not until after Webern's death was the significance of his work realized. Then, as the value of his contributions to serial technique became more apparent, he was recognized as a leader and his work was emulated by avant-garde composers internationally.

Example 25.13 Webern, Symphony, Op. 21: (*a*) mvt. 1, mm. 1–12, canonic use of various forms of the Row; (*b*) mvt. 2, theme. *(Copyright 1929 by Universal Edition. Copyright Renewed. All Rights Reserved. Used by permission of European American Music Distributors Corporation, sole U.S. and Canadian agent for Universal Edition.)*

Neo-Classicism

Near the end of World War I a reaction began to set in against late Romanticism. This movement, usually referred to as Neo-Classicism, began to gather momentum in the early 1920s and remained strong until after 1945. It is characterized by a preference for the objectivity of absolute music, greater emphasis on counterpoint (particularly, Bach-style counterpoint), economy of performing resources, and a revival of eighteenth-century traditional forms, with thematic material subject to techniques and compositional processes then favored. The prefix "Neo" indicates that the early music was not reproduced in its pure state but was modified by twentieth-century features, such as expanded tonality, modality, or atonality/pantonality. At times there was direct quotation of portions of an early work rather than mere allusion to it or parody of it.

Neo-Classicism was anticipated by Prokofiev in his *Classical Symphony*, which parodied Haydn's style, but Prokofiev did not continue in that vein. As a movement, Neo-Classicism began in 1920 with the performance of Igor Stravinsky's (1882–1971) *Pulcinella* (ballet with song, 1919–20), written in eighteenth-century Pre-Classical style and borrowing from Pergolesi and other composers of that era. In general, Stravinsky's style between 1920 and 1951 (*The Rake's Progress*) is Neo-Classical. Many composers turned to Neo-Classicism after having explored other styles. One such composer was Paul Hindemith (1895–1963), who began writing Neo-Classical music in the 1930s and continued in that style for the remainder of his life. Hindemith and Stravinsky are considered the chief exponents of Neo-Classicism. Among others who wrote in that style are the French composers known as *Les Six*.

The significance of Neo-Classicism lies in the historical awareness of early music by twentieth-century composers, and the fact that their appreciation and parodying of eighteenth-century music led to the revival of forms and characteristic styles of previous eras. Moreover, an unwillingness to accept twentieth-century musical sounds as suitable for church music caused composers to use as models sixteenth- and seventeenth-century styles and techniques such as Renaissance and Baroque counterpoint. In addition to the general back-to-Bach-and-Handel movement, composers in each country were motivated by nationalism to turn to the musical styles of the historical past in their own countries—the English, to the music of Byrd and Tallis; the Italians to Monteverdi, Gabrieli, and Palestrina.

Les Six—Later

Of the six young French composers who called themselves *Les nouveaux jeunes* and whom critic Collet dubbed *Les Six* (see Ch. 24), the most enduring music was written by Darius Milhaud, Arthur Honegger, and Francis Poulenc. The Six worked together only a few years; then each took a separate path.

In volume, Louis Durey (1888–1979) was least prolific of the group. Many of his pieces are miniatures. He wrote some fine chamber music, particularly, his first and third string quartets (1917, 1928), and some excellent songs, e.g., his setting of Jean Cocteau's *Le printemps au fond de la mer* (Spring at the bottom of the sea; 1920), for solo voice accompanied by ten wind instruments. After Durey joined the French Communist Party in 1936, his views toward music and his own compositions became more and more politically oriented. As Secretary-General of the Fédération Musicale Populaire (1937–56) and the Association Française des Musiciens Progressistes (1948–79), and as music critic of the Paris Communist newspaper, he urged composers to write nationalistic music based on folk songs, to be "democratic" in their choice of forms, and to avoid individuality. Among his communist-oriented works is *La longue marche* (The long march; tenor, chor., orch.; 1949), with text by Mao Tse-tung.

Although Georges Auric composed numerous songs and piano pieces in his youth, his most important contribution was to stage and theater music. He was one of the four pianists performing the première of Stravinsky's ballet *Les noces* (The Wedding) in 1923. Auric became acquainted with Russian impresario Sergei Diaghilev (1872–1929) and was commissioned by him to compose several works for the Ballet Russe. Particularly successful were *Les fâcheux* (The bores; 1923), based on Molière's play, and *Les matelots* (The sailors; 1924). Both ballets are Neo-Classical in style, with touches of humor. In the 1920s Auric wrote incidental music for at least eight plays, and in 1930–55 composed scores for a dozen films. He continued to write ballets until 1960. Works created in the 1950s reveal his awareness of avant-garde techniques. Both tonality and atonality are found in the ballet *Chemin de lumière* (Path of light; 1951), and, in some sections, serialism.

That Auric was highly regarded by his contemporaries is evidenced by his election to and years of tenure in influential administrative positions. From 1954 to 1977 he served as president of the Société d'Auteurs, Compositeurs et Editeurs de Musique (SACEM = Society of Authors, Composers and Editors of Music). As director of the Paris Opéra and Opéra-Comique in 1962–68, Auric did a great deal to revitalize opera in France. During those years his only compositions were two song settings. Though his retirement from the directorship was prompted by the desire to resume composing, he wrote just a few more works, all instrumental: *Imaginées I-IV* (I, fl., pno., 1968; II, 'cello, pno., 1969; III, cl., pno., 1971; IV, viola, pno., 1973) and *Double-jeux I-III* (2 pianos; 1970–71). Both sets of pieces are atonal but thematic, for cells derived from the tone row are the principal motives. The works attest that Auric remained in tune with current developments without relinquishing individuality or originality.

Many of Germaine Tailleferre's compositions follow along traditional lines established by Fauré and continued by Ravel, with whom she studied orchestration. She worked mainly in large forms—ballet, opera, *opéra comique,* concerto, sonata, string quartet—but wrote a few songs and single-movement instrumental pieces. Some of her keyboard pieces show Couperin's influence. She married an American author and visited the United States briefly in 1927. Her *Concertino for Harp and Orchestra* (1926) was written for and first performed by Boston Symphony Orchestra. Most representative of her style are her first violin/piano Sonata (1921), the ballet *Le marchand d'oiseaux* (The bird merchant; 1923), and *Ouverture* (orch.; 1932).

Arthur Honegger composed music in all genres. Between 1917 and 1930 he wrote a number of compositions with programmatic titles, the best known being the *Symphonic Movements* subtitled *Pacific 231* (1923) and *Rugby* (1928). Both works are strongly rhythmic and seem quite descriptive. However, Honegger considered them absolute music, and, lest

Mouvement symphonique No. 3 (1932–33) be similarly misunderstood, he refrained from subtitling it. Honegger's finest orchestral writing appears in his five symphonies, all absolute music, though the last three bear titles: *Symphony No. 3, Liturgique* (Liturgical; 1945–46), related to ecclesiastical ritual; *Symphony No. 4, Deliciae Basilienses* (Beloved Basel; 1946), written to honor Basel, Switzerland; *Symphony No. 5, Di tre re* (With three Ds; 1951), so-named because each movement ends on the note D sounded three times.

Stage and dramatic works make up the bulk of Honegger's music: operas and operettas, dramatic oratorios, incidental music for plays, ballets and pantomimes, radio and film scores. To the latter category Honegger contributed more than 40 film scores (in 1923–51) and 8 radio scores (in 1933–51).

In 1923 a concert performance of the dramatic psalm *Le roi David* (King David; 1921; staged 1921; rev. 1923) brought Honegger international recognition. The work is Neo-Classical, a number oratorio on the ancient Biblical subject, in which the scenes are linked by narration with orchestral background. Chorale-like melodies and polyphony reflect Honegger's admiration for Bach. The choruses, originally intended for amateurs, are not difficult to sing. In several subsequent stage works Honegger wrote more demanding speaking and singing parts, including *Sprechstimme,* humming, whispering, and screaming. One such work is the dramatic oratorio *Jeanne d'Arc au bûcher* (Joan of Arc at the stake; 1934–35), on a libretto by Paul Claudel (1868–1955). In it singing and speaking are well integrated. There are five speaking and five vocal solo roles, mixed chorus that speaks and sings, children's chorus, and a large orchestra. Designed to be staged, the work consists of a prologue and eleven scenes, some of them highly dramatic with tremendous emotional impact. Some of the music is quite dissonant, but into that dissonance Honegger blended dance tunes, folk songs, and Gregorian chant, all appropriate to the subject.

Francis Poulenc was a master of the *mélodie,* the French solo song with keyboard accompaniment, and wrote approximately 150 of them. Among his finest are the nine love songs constituting the cycle *Tel jour, telle nuit* (Such a day, such a night; 1936–37). The accompaniments for Poulenc's songs require "*beaucoup de pedale*" (much use of pedal) to produce the results he intended. The same is true of many of his piano pieces. The prime factor in his music is melody; it is supported by simple diatonic harmonies with passing dissonances, in a basically homophonic texture.

Another area in which Poulenc excelled is religious choral music. All of his work in this field was done after the untimely death of a close friend in 1935 caused Poulenc to draw closer to the Catholic faith. After visiting Notre Dame de Rocamadour, he composed *Litanies à la vierge noire* (Litanies to the black Virgin; 1936; fig. 25.3) for female chorus and organ. The following year he wrote the Mass in G for SATB chorus *a cappella*. Also notable is the *Gloria* (1961) for soprano soloist, chorus, and orchestra.

Poulenc did not shun stage music. He wrote several ballets and incidental music for about a dozen plays. In 1944 he composed his first opera, an *opera bouffe* based on Guillaume Apollinaire's play *La mamelles de Tirésias* (The breasts of Tirésias). The opera, which preserves Apollinaire's message against equality for women, reveals Poulenc's talent for musical satire. He imitated the style of the witty Parisian popular songs then current as well as mimicking the music of Debussy, Massenet, and Puccini. Poulenc waited almost a decade before beginning another opera, then wrote two that are quite different from his first: the three-act religious opera *Dialogues des carmélites* (Dialogues of the Carmelites; 1953–56) and the one-act monodrama *La voix humaine* (The human voice; 1958), a *tragédie lyrique*.

Darius Milhaud's voluminous output and the rapidity and facility with which he composed rival that of Telemann and Mozart. Moreover, he was very versatile. His works include operas, ballets, incidental music for plays, film and radio scores, orchestral compositions, chamber music, music for brass band, choral works, songs, keyboard works (piano, organ), and music for children. Of interest are several works of small dimensions: six chamber symphonies (1917–23), and three *opéras minutes* (miniature or chamber operas; 1927–28) parodying classical myths, operas about ten minutes in duration and requiring a minimum number of singers and instrumentalists.

Figure 25.3 The black Virgin statue at Rocamadour.

A native of Aix-en-Provence, Milhaud's deep appreciation of his Provençal heritage, the pastoral scenes of the region, and its folk music is apparent in a number of his compositions, especially, the orchestral *Suite provençale* (1936). As Paul Cézanne (1839–1906) painted Provençal landscapes (colorplate 29), so Milhaud translated the Provençal atmosphere into music.

While a student at Paris Conservatoire (1909–16), Milhaud's many friends in the city included artists and writers as well as musicians, and his association with Francis Jammes (1868–1938) and Paul Claudel were highly influential in his career. Both authors supplied him with libretti for operas and poems for songs, and he wrote incidental music for many of Claudel's plays. Claudel was diplomat as well as poet, and, while he served as French minister to Brazil (1916–18), he employed Milhaud as secretary. Brazil and its music impressed Milhaud deeply. After returning to France, he expressed his memories of Brazil musically in *Saudades do Brasil* (Souvenirs of Brazil; 1920–21), two suites of six dances each, written in two versions—orchestral, and piano. Also, he incorporated Brazilian music in the ballet *Le boeuf sur le toit* (The ox on the roof; 1919), which is set in the United States, and the two-piano work *Scaramouche* (1927). Although Milhaud suffered severely from rheumatoid arthritis, he traveled a great deal, and various musics of the countries he visited found their way into his compositions. On a visit to London in 1920 he heard jazz for the first time. This stimulated his interest in American popular music, but he did not experience authentic jazz played by black musicians until he visited Harlem, New York, in 1922. That inspired him to write the ballet *Le création de la monde* (The creation of the world; 1923) in which he included saxophones and elements of ragtime, blues, and jazz. This seems to be the earliest use of jazz and blues in an orchestral score.

Another influence in Milhaud's music was his Jewish ancestry. His pride in and reverence for this heritage was expressed in a number of works, the finest being *Poèmes juïfs* (8 Jewish poems; 1916), *Service sacré* (Sacred Service; 1947), portions of the ballet *Moïse* (Moses; 1940), the five-act Biblical opera *David* (1952), and his last work, the cantata *Ani maamin, un chant perdu et retrouvé* (Ani maamin, a song lost and found again; soprano, 4 reciters, chor., orch.), written for the 1973 Festival of Israel. *David,* commissioned for the celebration commemorating the 3000th anniversary of the establishment of Jerusalem as capital of Judea, was first performed in Jerusalem on 1 June 1954.

Milhaud's music is objective, characterized by lyrical melodies, formal clarity, skillful use of counterpoint, and bitonality or polytonality. Milhaud stated that he did not write polytonal chords solely for their dissonant effect but used them primarily to enhance diatonic melody. In other words, he used them as an artist uses color to point up specific things. Generally, in instrumental ensembles, Milhaud minimized polytonal dissonance by maintaining the tonal planes in different instrumental timbres. Once he discovered bi- and polytonality, that became a permanent feature of his music. Often cited as an example of Milhaud's contrapuntal skill, his String Quartets Nos. 14 and 15 may be combined to form an octet. A panorama of Milhaud's style is visible in his operas, which deal with a variety of subjects. A masterpiece,

the opera-oratorio *Christophe Columbe* (Christopher Columbus; 1928) on a libretto by Claudel, requires massive performing resources: 45 soloists, actors who do not sing, a very large chorus, and some film inserts. The music incorporates elements of Symbolism and Expressionism, some *Leitmotifs,* and in places uses chorus in the manner of the ancient Greeks. The work was first performed in Berlin in 1930, then lay untouched for almost 40 years, until Milhaud revised it drastically for a 1969 staging in Graz.

Hindemith

Paul Hindemith (1895–1963) experienced a multifaceted career as performer, composer, theorist, teacher, and author and made significant contributions in each of those areas. In 1904 he began studying violin and from 1908 to 1917 was a tuition-free student at the Hoch Conservatory in Frankfurt. He was virtuosic on violin and viola, an exceptionally accomplished performer on several other instruments, and particularly enjoyed playing string quartets. In 1915 he was employed as first violinist in the Frankfurt Opera orchestra and as second violinist in the Rebner quartet. His performance career was interrupted in 1917 when he was called into military service, but for much of the time he was assigned to a regimental band, and when World War I ended he was able to return to both of his previous positions.

Around 1912 Hindemith became seriously interested in composition. From time to time his works were performed by students at the Conservatory, and in 1919 he presented a public concert entirely of his own music that included two sonatas, a piano quartet, and the String Quartet, Op. 10. His compositions written between 1918 and 1923 adhere to no single style; rather, he seems to have been exploring stylistic possibilities, as well as seeking innovations. There are vast differences in the compositions written during these years, and some works show the influence of different eighteenth- and nineteenth-century German masters. A majority of Hindemith's early works are chamber music, the most important being *Kleine Kammermusik* (Little chamber music pieces; 1922) for wind quintet. In 1921 the performances of Hindemith's one-act operas *Mörder, Hoffnung der Frauen* (Murderer, hope of women; 1919) and *Sancta Susanna* (St. Susanna; 1921) attracted attention as much for their attitude toward sexuality as their innovative music.

Paul Hindemith. *(Historical Pictures Service.)*

However, Hindemith did not adopt the Expressionist style of those operas. By 1923, his works show a tendency to favor the forms, counterpoint, and rhythmic vitality that characterized Baroque music. This is apparent in the song cycle *Das Marienleben* (The life of Mary; 1922–23), a setting for soprano and piano of 15 poems by Rilke. Between 1936 and 1948 Hindemith revised the cycle and orchestrated six of the songs.

Hindemith's style changed in several respects between 1924 and 1933. For about two years, he continued writing Neo-Baroque works, with considerable use of linear counterpoint (often quite harsh harmonically) that deprived the bass line of much of its usual harmonic function. This is apparent in *Kammermusiken Nrs. 2–7,* six concerti for solo instrument and chamber orchestra. At times Hindemith altered orchestral balance by scoring works for an ensemble in which the number of winds and brasses equals that of strings. This is the case in *Concerto for Orchestra* (1925) and the three-act tragic opera *Cardillac* (1926; rev. 1952). Two other operas written in the 1920s are significant: the chamber opera *Hin und zurück* (There and back; 1927), constructed so that both action and music proceed to midpoint of the opera, then become retrograde; and the full-length comic opera *Neues vom Tage* (News of the day; 1929; rev. 1954), with timely subject matter and elements of popular music.

In 1927 Hindemith became professor of composition at the Berlin Hochschule für Musik. Teaching became one of his lifelong interests. His work at the Hochschule had several important results: (1) It aroused in him a desire to write music for instruments with minimal or deficient repertoire. He planned at least 25 sonatas but actually wrote 16. (2) It generated the text *Unterweisung im Tonsatz* (Instruction

in Composition, 3 Volumes, 1937, 1939, 1970). The first volume presents the theoretical principles; the second and third volumes contain, respectively, exercises for composition of two- and three-part compositions. The text was published in English under the title *The Craft of Musical Composition.* (3) It effected a change in his compositional style, bringing more lyrical melody, less dissonant counterpoint, greater use of functional tonal harmonies, and, in general, led toward the Neo-Classicism that remained typical of his music from 1933 to the end of his life. The change to more lyrical melody is visible in *Konzertmusik* (Opp. 48–50; 1930). (4) It shaped and strengthened his philosophy of music, which he expressed in the Charles Eliot Norton Lectures at Harvard University (1949–50) and in the book resultant from those lectures, *A Composer's World* (1952). Some knowledge of that philosophy is vital to understanding the music he composed after 1927.

Firstly, he believed that music must be understood as a means of communication between composer and the consumer of the music, i.e., between composer and performer and between composer and audience with performer as intermediary. Abstract music understood by and gratifying only its composer is not viable. It is the composer's responsibility to ascertain the needs and desires of the consumers of his product and to gratify them to the best of his ability. With the intent of narrowing the gap between composer and amateur performer, Hindemith wrote some music specifically for amateurs, e.g., *Spielmusik* (1927) and *Sing- und Spielmusiken für Liebhaber und Musikfreunde* (Vocal and instrumental music for amateurs and music-lovers; 1928–29). This is music to be performed for enjoyment, for fun, for play. He created several works specifically for children, e.g., the musical play *Wir bauen eine Stadt* (Let's build a city; 1930) and *Plöner Musiktag* (A day at summer music camp; 1932). Somehow, the word *Gebrauchsmusik* (music for use)—a term Hindemith thoroughly disliked—became associated with works of this kind. Closely related to "music for use" is didactic music, and Hindemith contributed to that category also. Especially notable is *Ludus tonalis* (Game of tonalities; piano; 1942). The work comprises a Prelude, a cycle of 12 fugues, 1 in each key, linked by modulatory interludes, and a Postlude. In

Example 25.14 Hindemuth, *Ludus tonalis*: (a) Prelude, mm. 1–2; (b) Postlude, last 3 measures. Note that (b) when turned upside down looks the same as (a). (© Schott & Co. Ltd., 1943. © Renewed. All Rights Reserved. Used by permission of European American Music Distributors Corporation, sole U.S. and Canadian agent for Schott & Co., Ltd.)

(a)

(b)

tonality the Prelude proceeds from C to F♯; the Postlude presents the music of the Prelude inverted and retrograde, thus moves from F♯ to C (ex. 25.14).

Secondly, Hindemith was convinced that a composer must be a performing musician and must have acquired familiarity with instruments through participation in ensembles. Only through practical experience can a composer understand how to write idiomatically and effectively for instruments. Theory without practice is fruitless.

Thirdly, Hindemith considered key tonality unavoidable. The manner in which the various pitches are naturally generated, as partials or overtones of a fundamental tonality, establishes their functional relationship to that central pitch and to each other. He explained this thoroughly in *Unterweisung im Tonsatz*.

Fourthly, he wholeheartedly endorsed the theory expressed in the writings of Plato, Ptolemy, St. Augustine, Boethius, and other ancient and medieval philosophers that the principles of order governing the acoustical ratios of musical intervals and the order within a musical composition symbolize and reflect, as microcosm to macrocosm, the principles that govern the orderly behavior of the universe. Hindemith expressed this part of his philosophy musically in his five-act opera *Die Harmonie der Welt* (The harmony of the world; 1956–57). The story concerns the endeavors of astronomer-mathematician Johannes Kepler (1571–1630) to discover the harmony of the world, and the name of the opera derives from the title of Kepler's treatise *Harmonices mundi* (The harmony of the world; 1619). The opera is a series of

dramatic tableaux, the music for the last being a passacaglia. Hindemith prepared a companion symphony to the opera and entitled its three movements according to Boethius's threefold classification of music: *Musica mundana, Musica humana,* and *Musica instrumentalis.*

Unquestionably, Hindemith's masterpiece is the opera *Mathis der Maler* (Mathias the painter; 1932–35). The plot concerns Mainz court painter Matthias Grünewald's (c. 1480–1528) decision to renounce art and devote his energies to political action during the Peasant's Revolt in 1525, and his realization, after the Revolt collapsed, that his action had accomplished nothing worthwhile, for he had to flee to northern Germany. At Halle, he returned to art. The opera, for which Hindemith himself wrote the libretto, is in seven scenes, each clearly in one overall key. Though essentially a number opera, continuity is maintained by links of recitative or arioso. At appropriate places, Hindemith incorporated plainchant and folk song in the music.

Hindemith's first symphony, also entitled *Mathis der Maler* (1934), is a companion piece to the opera and was completed two years before the opera was finished. The symphony is programmatic and tonal. Each of its three movements ("Angelic Concert," "Entombment," and "The Temptation of St. Anthony") represents one of the several panels of the altarpiece Grünewald painted (1510–15) for the monastic hospital order of St. Anthony at Isenheim (colorplate 30) and is at the same time a quotation from the opera. The first symphonic movement became the opera's prelude and furnished some music for the first scene of the sixth tableau; the second movement was used as an intermezzo in the opera's last tableau; the third was adapted for choral presentation in tableau six. Formally, melodically, and harmonically, the symphony is an amalgamation of traditional and twentieth-century musical resources. The three movements are arranged in fast-slow-fast order: the first movement in sonata form; the second, ABA' with coda (DWMA224); the third, a complex ternary with elements of rondo. Tonally, the symphony commences in G; the second movement modulates from D to C♯, and the third is in C♯ but starts with a recitative theme that contains all 12 tones.

The symphony *Mathis der Maler* provides an excellent preview of Hindemith's mature style, which is a synthesis of traditional and modern and reflects influences of major German composers from the sixteenth through the nineteenth centuries. Hindemith was very prolific and wrote works in every genre. Many of his compositions were written for specific performers. Among Hindemith's works frequently performed in America are *Mathis der Maler* symphony, *Symphonic Metamorphoses on Themes of Carl Maria von Weber* (1943), and the dance legend *Nobilissima visione* (Noblest vision; 1938) relating to the life of St. Francis of Assisi.

In a sense, the *Mathis der Maler* compositions reflect Hindemith's own situation in Germany at the time he was composing them. During the Hitler régime, Hindemith's concerts and his music were boycotted in Germany because he performed in ensembles with Jewish musicians. Moreover, his wife was Jewish. Hindemith was never expelled from Germany but thought it best to leave that country. He came to America and in 1946 became a United States citizen. From 1941 to 1953 he taught at Yale University, and for the next several years divided his time between Yale and University of Zurich. He died in Frankfurt on 28 December 1963.

Stravinsky

Without a doubt, Igor Stravinsky (1882–1971) was one of the twentieth century's most outstanding composers. He grew up in musical surroundings in Russia, where his father, Fyodor Stravinsky (1843–1902), was one of the principal bass singers at the imperial opera

Igor Stravinsky. *(Historical Pictures Service.)*

theater. In the hope that his children would become professional musicians, Fyodor provided them with music lessons and encouraged them to attend opera and ballet performances. Igor studied piano with a pupil of Anton Rubinstein, then had lessons in counterpoint and harmony. Nevertheless, he enrolled at St. Petersburg University to study law. One of his student friends there was Vladimir Rimsky-Korsakov, who invited Stravinsky for a visit in his home. Thus, Stravinsky met Nicolai Rimsky-Korsakov, who became his mentor and strongly influenced many of his compositions. In fact, Rimsky-Korsakov was a kind of second father to Stravinsky after his own father died. Stravinsky dedicated his Symphony No. 1 (Op. 1; E♭ major; 1905–7) to Rimsky-Korsakov, and when Rimsky-Korsakov died Stravinsky composed a dirge for wind instruments in his memory. That music has been lost. Years later, Stravinsky spoke of that dirge as his finest work prior to *L'oiseau de feu* (The firebird; 1909–10). His orchestral fantasy *Le feu d'artifice* (Fireworks; 1908) was written to celebrate the wedding of Rimsky-Korsakov's daughter Nadezhda. In Stravinsky's early works the influence of older Russian composers—Rimsky-Korsakov, Tchaikovsky, Borodin, and Glazounov—is apparent. There

Developments between the World Wars

is also some reliance on folk material. *Le feu d'artifice* reveals Stravinsky's knowledge of Dukas's *The Sorcerer's Apprentice* and Debussy's *Nocturnes*. From Rimsky-Korsakov Stravinsky learned to write harmonies and melodies based on the augmented fourth to portray supernatural characters and to use diatonicism with modal overtones for the principal human characters. Soon, he became adept at expressing psychological states and physical movements through music.

In 1909 Stravinsky visited Paris, where he attended some ballets and became acquainted with Diaghilev, who asked him to orchestrate some pieces for the Ballet Russe. Diaghilev, pleased with the orchestrations, then commissioned *L'oiseau de feu* (The Firebird) for the 1910 season. Stravinsky moved to Paris, the hub of international art at that time. Though he was almost 30, his career as a professional composer was just beginning. The success of *L'oiseau de feu* brought him commissions for other ballets: in 1911, *Petrushka,* and in 1913 *Le sacre du printemps* (The rite of spring), subtitled *Tableaux of Pagan Russia.*

Petrushka and *Le sacre du printemps* differ vastly, each in its own way, from Stravinsky's earlier works. The Oriental exoticism that colored *L'oiseau de feu* is no longer present, partly due to the nature of the new works, but also because Stravinsky's mature style was gradually emerging. The character Petrushka, Slavic counterpart of the French Pierrot, is a regular feature of the annual Shrovetide Fair at St. Petersburg. Stravinsky's ballet depicts a puppet who, suddenly endowed with life, is scorned and rebuffed by the Ballerina he loves and is destroyed in a brief struggle with his rival, the Moor. In portraying interaction between characters with such different personalities, Stravinsky superimposed scales, harmonies, melodies, and rhythms and used contrasting instrumentation. An example of this is found in the third tableau, where the Moor is courting the Ballerina—contrasting instrumental combinations present, in superimposition, the $\frac{3}{4}$ waltz rhythm of the graceful Ballerina and the $\frac{2}{4}$ rhythm of the rather clumsy Moor. That third tableau is bitonal, simultaneously presenting material in C major and F♯ major (though, in the scoring for B♭ clarinets the latter is written as G♭ major). The simultaneous arpeggiations of the

Example 25.15 (*a*) The "Petrushka" chord; (*b*) *Petrushka,* Part II, mm. 9–10, clarinets arpeggiate a C-major chord and the first inversion of an F♯-major chord (enharmonically, G♭ major) simultaneously. *(Example b: PETROUCHKA © Copyright by Edition Russe de Musique. Copyright assigned to Boosey & Hawkes, Inc. Revised edition © 1947, 1948 by Boosey & Hawkes, Inc.; Copyright Renewed. Reprinted by permission.)*

tonic chords of these keys gave rise to the epithet "Petrushka chord" (ex. 25.15). Stravinsky habitually composed his works at a muted piano, and his choice of these particular tonalities for contrasting voices may have been prompted by the fact that one passage uses only white and the other only black keys on the keyboard. Not all of *Petrushka* is bitonal, however. For some of the music Stravinsky used conventional diatonic harmonies. Also, he included Russian folk song modal melodies, a popular French air, and a waltz borrowed from Joseph Lanner (1801–43). Ostinato patterns appear often—they became a characteristic feature of Stravinsky's style.

In *Le sacre du printemps* Stravinsky used polytonality, polyrhythm, *ostinati,* and contrasting instrumental timbres much more extensively than he had in *Petrushka.* Strongly dissonant, with savage, pulsating rhythms, *Le sacre du printemps* was a musical counterpart to the primitivism being expressed in artworks at that time. So were Debussy's orchestral *Gigues,* with its pounding rhythm, and *Rondes de printemps,* with its distinctive timbres, unexpected dissonances, combined tonalities, and unusual scales—works that, undoubtedly, Stravinsky knew. Though these works foreshadowed *Le sacre du printemps,* they are mild in comparison with it.

Stravinsky's music and the dancers present the scenes of pagan Russia in two parts: "The Adoration of the Earth" (Introduction and 7 Scenes) and "The Sacrifice of the Chosen One" (6 Scenes). Within each of the main parts, the scenes follow one another without a pause. In preparing the sequence of scenes, Stravinsky worked with artist Nicholai Roerich, who was knowledgeable concerning ancient pagan rites in Russia. Basically, the ballet symbolizes primitive pagan tribes' adoration of the Earth as the Mother of all, the association of fertility with Spring, and the belief that death ensures the renewal of life, as evidenced by the earth's biological cycles. It is not surprising, therefore, that the ballet concludes with a sacrificial dance in which the chosen virgin dances until she dies from sheer exhaustion. The première of *Le sacre du printemps* on 29 May 1913 was the occasion of one of the largest theatrical riots Paris had known. The choreography of Vaclav Nijinsky (1890–1950), the costumes and stage settings of Roerich, and, to a lesser degree, the music, were considered ugly and were offensive to many in the audience. Probably, they had come expecting to view beautiful costumes and scenery, to hear Impressionistic or post-Romantic music typifying Spring, but received primitivism instead. Actually, the scenery, costumes, and musical style were dictated by the subject matter and were appropriate to it. There were those present who applauded the innovations, and undoubtedly there were as many shouts of approval as there were cries of derision. The critical outcry in artistic circles after the première of *Le sacre du printemps* was comparable with that occasioned by Pablo Picasso's painting *Les demoiselles d'Avignon* in 1907 (colorplate 31). Scathing reviews of the ballet and its music appeared in Paris journals. But the following April, when a concert version of the *Le sacre du printemps* was performed, critics praised it.

To achieve the timbral effect he desired, Stravinsky had to score *Le sacre du printemps* for a very large orchestra, with a greatly expanded woodwind section, extra brass and percussion instruments, but without celesta, piano, and harp. For the most part, the various instrumental choirs are treated as distinct entities, each having at times its own ostinato and its own key. Most of the different instruments are given solo passages, often in extreme ranges. The Introduction to Part I (DWMA225) is begun by bassoon voicing in its high register a Lithuanian folk melody in Aeolian mode. Gradually, the distinctive timbres of other woodwinds are added, sometimes challenging the tonality—the c♯ of the horns in measure 2, and the "black-key" melody of English horn at measure 10 challenging the "white-key" folk tune of the solo bassoon and generating the three bassoons' chromaticism at the *più mosso* (ex. 25.16). Many of the melodic fragments that appear later in the music have some relationship to the opening Lithuanian folk melody.

In Stravinsky's polytonality, one key seems to be fundamental, with the other(s) superimposed on it temporarily. For example, in the Introduction to Part II, the fundamental key is D minor. Frequently, Stravinsky used the bitonality of chords with roots a semitone apart, e.g., at the beginning of "Augurs of Spring," the simultaneous sounding of an F♭-major chord (enharmonically, E major) and a seventh chord on E♭ (ex. 25.17). This bitonality bears the same significance for *Le sacre du printemps* as the bitonal clarinet arpeggiations had for *Petrushka*.

Counterpoint is an interesting feature of *Le sacre du printemps*. Not only is there the counterpoint of melodic fragments and *ostinati,* but counterpoint of timbres, tonalities, and rhythms. Rhythm is probably the most outstanding feature of the work. As the music proceeds, the rhythm becomes increasingly significant, until, in the sacrificial dance, the frenetic rhythms dominate the music. A number of persons have stated that in *Le sacre du printemps* Stravinsky emancipated music from the tyranny of the barline. He did not dispense with barlines but, by continually shifting accents and/or changing meter signatures, made the barline the servant rather than the master of his music. Underlying those shifting accents and changing meter signatures is a basic pulse—the unit of beat remains the same, though the number of beats per measure and the placement of accents changes. Actually, Stravinsky used rhythm according to the additive manner of the ancient Greeks, in multiples of a *minimum* or basic unit (see Ch. 2). This kind of treatment produced a different result from that in traditional music written since c. 1600, when composers began to think of rhythm as subdivisions of a *maximum* value that filled a measure in which, predictably, the first beat was strong and the second weak. (For example, instead of thinking of a whole note as being divided into eighth notes, Stravinsky considered an eighth note as basic unit and used multiples

Developments between the World Wars

Example 25.16 Stravinsky, *Le sacre du printemps,* Introduction: (*a*) mm. 1–2; (*b*) mm. 9–10; (*c*) mm. 13–15. (*LA SACRE DU PRINTEMPS* © Copyright 1921 by Edition Russe de Musique. Copyright assigned to Boosey & Hawkes, Inc. Copyright Renewed. Reprinted by permission.)

of them, placing barlines where he needed them.) Some sections of *Le sacre du printemps* are much easier to play if the performer disregards meter signatures and barlines and simply thinks in terms of the basic underlying beat—the eighth note, or the sixteenth note, whichever it happens to be.

During World War I Stravinsky lived in Switzerland; he returned to Paris in 1920. His most important work from those years is *Les noces* (The wedding; 1914–17), a stylized portrayal of a Russian peasant wedding. He prepared the libretto from portions of the texts of Russian folk songs in Keriensky's collection. *Les noces* is in four choreographic scenes,

Example 25.17 Stravinsky, *Le sacre du printemps*, "Augurs of Spring," mm. 1–2, ostinato of F♭-major chord and first inversion of E♭ seventh-chord sounded simultaneously. *(LA SACRE DU PRINTEMPS © Copyright 1921 by Edition Russe de Musique. Copyright assigned to Boosey & Hawkes, Inc. Copyright Renewed. Reprinted by permission.)*

for four vocal soloists, four-part chorus, four pianos, and large percussion ensemble. Rhythm is the most significant feature of the composition. Throughout the work, each rhythmic change is proportionally related to that which it follows, as well as to a basic pulse (or beat) that underlies the entire work.

An economy of resources is apparent in most of the compositions Stravinsky wrote in 1913–23. Undoubtedly, this reflects wartime general economy to some extent, but it stemmed primarily from Stravinsky's desire to make contemporary art music available to people living in small communities. With that in mind, he decided in 1918 to write a stage work that could be performed by a few persons in small concert halls. *L'histoire du soldat* (The soldier's tale), which is to be "read, played, and danced," requires three actors, a female dancer, and seven instrumentalists who are representative of the various orchestral families—violin, string bass, clarinet, bassoon, cornet, trombone, and many percussion instruments played by one person. The instrumentalists are to be seen as well as heard, for they and their music participate in the action. The story, taken from a collection of Russian fables, is Faustian. It relates the adventures of a soldier who sells his violin (his soul) to the devil in exchange for a book that contains the answer to every

question. Though the soldier regains possession of the violin for a time, and by playing it effects a miraculous healing, ultimately the devil wins.

After *L'histoire du soldat,* Stravinsky wrote only one more work strongly colored by Russian nationalism—*Mavra,* a one-act *opera buffa* based on Pushkin's *The Little House at Kolomna,* and dedicated to the memory of Pushkin, Glinka, and Tchaikovsky. *Mavra* is a blend of Russian tradition and Italian opera and was the first of several works in which Stravinsky used a preponderance of wind instruments—of the 34 players, there are 2 violins, 1 viola, 3 'celli, and 3 string basses. His interest in writing for winds continued, as evidenced by the *Symphonies of Wind Instruments* (23 winds; 1920) and the *Octet* (winds; 1922–23). In *Chronicle of My Life,* Stravinsky discussed *Mavra* and nationalism in the arts. Among other things, he stated that Pushkin, Glinka, and Tchaikovsky were essentially cosmopolitan in their outlook but produced nationalistic works naturally and instinctively because they were Russian. On the other hand, the kind of nationalism expressed by "The Five" and others was deliberate and cultivated, "a doctrinaire catechism which they wished to impose." Stravinsky did not condone the remaking of an art that originally was an instinctive creation of the people. Therefore, he turned his talents in other directions.

Though he had no firsthand experience with ragtime, he dabbled in it and wrote *Rag-time* for 11 orchestral instruments (1918) and *Piano-rag-music* (1919). Then Diaghilev commissioned him to arrange for ballet some music attributed to Pergolesi. That ballet, *Pulcinella,* with chamber orchestra accompaniment, is a forerunner of the Neo-Classical period in Stravinsky's writing, a period that actually began with the *Octet* for winds and continued through the opera *The Rake's Progress* (1948–51).

In the early 1920s, Stravinsky decided that he needed to earn more money, and that he must perform more often as pianist and conductor, even if that meant he would have less time for composing. That decision turned his compositional endeavors in a new direction temporarily, for he wrote a number of piano pieces for himself: Sonata (1924); *Serenade* (A major; 1925); Concerto for piano with orchestra of winds, string bass, and timpani (1923–24); and *Capriccio* (pno., orch.; 1928–29). A few years later, for performance with his son Soulima (b. 1910), a professional pianist, Stravinsky wrote the Concerto for two pianos (no orch.; 1931–35). American violinist Samuel Dushkin (1891–1976) commissioned the Violin Concerto (D major; 1931), and Stravinsky wrote the *Duo concertante* (vln., pno.; 1931–32) to perform with Dushkin.

Stage works attracted Stravinsky's attention again in the late 1920s, and he composed the opera-oratorio *Oedipus rex* (Oedipus the king; 1927), and two ballets, *Apollon musagète* (Apollo, leader of the Muses; 1927–28; rev. 1947) and *Le baiser de fée* (The fairy's kiss; 1928). The scenario of the latter is rooted in a Hans Christian Andersen (1805–75) fairy tale, and Stravinsky constructed his music on piano pieces and songs by Tchaikovsky. *Oedipus rex,* based on Sophocles but with a Latin text, is an excellent work. However, it was not well received when first performed.

As a youth, Stravinsky left the Russian Orthodox Church. In 1926, he decided to rejoin the Church, and expressed the renewal of his faith in three sacred choruses on Slavonic liturgical texts. Later, when commissioned to write a symphonic work for the 50th anniversary celebration of the Boston Symphony Orchestra, he composed *Symphony of Psalms* (1930), an outstanding contribution to choral literature. In this work, the connotation of "symphony" is closely akin to Schütz's and Gabrieli's understanding of the word—a harmonious blend of voices and instruments—for Stravinsky intended that these "two elements should be on an equal footing." He achieved his aim. *Symphony of Psalms* is a setting of selected Latin verses from Psalms 38, 39, and 150 in the Vulgate (39, 40, 150 in KJV). The orchestral complement to the SATB chorus contains no violins or violas, includes a harp, two pianos, and brass instruments, and relies heavily on woodwinds (5 flutes, 4 oboes, English horn, 3 bassoons, contrabassoon). The composition is in three movements, one for each of the Psalms texts, presenting, respectively, lamentation and supplication, faith, and praise. The second movement (DWMA226) is a large bitonal double fugue—one in C minor for orchestra, one in E♭ major for chorus. Stravinsky frequently used relative keys in bitonal combination.

Most of Stravinsky's compositions written during 1927–45 were commissioned, including *Jeu de cartes* (The card party; 1936) for the American Ballet Company; *"Dumbarton Oaks" Concerto* (chamber orch.; 1937–38) for Mr. and Mrs. R. W. Bliss and named for their Washington, D.C., home; *Symphony in C* (1939–40) for Chicago Symphony Orchestra; and *Symphony in Three Movements* (1942–45) for the New York Philharmonic. Stravinsky was invited to teach at Harvard University for the 1939–40 academic year. In those lectures, which became his book *Poétique musicale* (Musical poetic; 1942), he set forth his philosophy and musical esthetics. Among his statements was the assertion that, in the composition of music, the more constraints a composer imposes on himself, the greater is his freedom. In his own work, he established certain limitations at the outset—sometimes very narrow—then moved within them as freely as possible. Obviously, Stravinsky's self-imposed limitations did not shackle his creative spirit.

In 1939 Stravinsky decided to make his home in the United States. He settled in California, and in 1945 became a naturalized United States citizen. While living on the West coast, he accepted some commissions for music for films. For some time he had wanted to write a liturgical Roman Catholic Mass, and in 1944 he began one; it was completed in 1948. Liturgical though the Mass is, rarely has it been performed in a church Service; its first performance was at La Scala, Milan.

Next, he decided to write an opera in English. *The Rake's Progress,* based on Hogarth's artwork (colorplate 32), is Stravinsky's longest stage work, lasting about two and a half hours. Librettists W. H. Auden and Chester Kallman supplemented Hogarth's morality-play drawings with three items: Mephistopheles, the three wishes fable, and a card game in which the Devil is defeated. *The Rake's Progress* is a Neo-Classical morality opera, dealing with the conflict of good and evil, and is replete with satire on many social customs of the time. Some of the ideas (but not the music) presented in *The Rake's Progress* resemble some thoughts expressed in *L'histoire du soldat, Le sacre du printemps,* and Stravinsky's melodrama *Perséphone* (1933–34). *The Rake's Progress* music consists of separate recitatives, arias, and ensembles in the traditional eighteenth-century manner; harpsichord is specified for the *continuo* accompaniment of the *secco* recitatives. There is also some melodrama. Undoubtedly, *The Rake's Progress* is one of the finest compositions written during the Neo-Classical era.

Stravinsky and Schoenberg resided comparatively near one another in California but were not particularly friendly. Stravinsky was wary of serialism and approached it cautiously when, after Schoenberg's death, he began to experiment with the techniques. That Stravinsky did so at all was largely due to the urging of Robert Craft, who served as Stravinsky's assistant in 1948–71. Stravinsky did not radically change his compositional style; he merely blended serial techniques into it. At first, he used rows of only 4, 5, or 6 notes. Only after he had used a full twelve-note series in some short movements of a work did he finally employ serial techniques throughout a composition.

When, in 1953, Boston University commissioned an opera from Stravinsky, he arranged for Dylan Thomas to prepare the libretto. However, Thomas died in 1954 and Stravinsky abandoned the project. Instead, he wrote *In memoriam Dylan Thomas,* an elegy in which prelude and postlude dirges for four trombones frame a setting, for tenor and string quartet, of Thomas's poem "Do not go gentle into that good night." In that work Stravinsky used a five-note row.

Stravinsky's next commission came from Venice for a work to be performed on the Biennial program in 1956. He responded with *Canticum sacrum ad honorem Sancti Marci nominis* (Sacred song to honor the name of St. Mark; 1955), for tenor and bass soloists, choir, and an orchestra without violins and 'celli. The work, specifically designed for performance in St. Mark's, is dedicated to the city of Venice. As prelude to the work, the two soloists sing the Latin dedication, accompanied by two trombones. *Canticum sacrum* . . . has a Biblical text and is in five short movements. In overall form, the composition is symmetrical, as were many of the works of J. S. Bach—first and fifth movements are choral, second and fourth are vocal solos. Moreover, the first and last movements are palindromic, i.e., the fifth movement is the retrograde of the first. In the three middle movements Stravinsky used two full 12-note rows that are inter-related, and in the middle movement there is some *cancrizans* writing. As did Schoenberg, Stravinsky reiterated notes in the series. However, Stravinsky's rows and his treatment of them reflect more of Webern than of Schoenberg. *Canticum sacrum* . . . is filled with symbolism of all kinds, including structural relationship with the edifice of St. Mark's and some numerological symbolism.

An important event in Stravinsky's life was a visit to his native Russia in 1962, after an absence of almost 50 years. When he returned to America, he wrote his first completely serial composition—*Threni: id est Lamentationes Jeremiae prophetae* (Lamentations of Jeremiah the prophet; 1962–63).

Most of the compositions Stravinsky wrote after 1953 are choral works. A number of them are elegies, including *Elegy for J. F. K.* (Elegy for John F. Kennedy; 1964; Bar. solo, 3 clarinets). With his own death in mind, Stravinsky composed the *Requiem Canticles* (1965–66), using text from the Gradual, Sequence, and final Responsory of the Requiem Mass.

Stravinsky was a versatile composer with mastery of all compositional techniques available to him. A survey of his compositions, with particular regard for his style, reveals its diversity. Yet, underlying that diversity there is unity. Though he moved from one genre to another, from one style to another, keeping in touch with contemporary trends, some things remained constant. He never completely abandoned key tonality though he wrote some atonal pieces. Many times, he worked with opposing tonal poles, and he used modality, bitonality, polytonality, and dodecaphonic techniques. Rhythm is perhaps the most important feature of all of his works. Rather than being governed by meter, he based his rhythms on the constancy of a minimum value and used multiples of that, making whatever adjustments were necessary in meter signatures and barline placement. The barline was not tyrannical but was subservient to his purposes. Silence was important to Stravinsky; he used rests effectively. Ostinato patterns figure prominently in his music; so does syncopation. Stravinsky understood instrumental and vocal tone colors and was a master of orchestration. Throughout his life, he built upon the excellent foundation he had received from Rimsky-Korsakov.

Nadia Boulanger

Nadia Boulanger (1887–1979) was a master teacher who influenced the careers of composers from many countries. Boulanger's paternal grandparents and her father were highly talented musicians; when he was 20, her father had received the Grand Prix de Rome for his cantata *Achille*. Ernest Boulanger (1815–1900) was 62 when he married the 18-year-old Russian Princess Raissa Mychetskaya; Nadia, born a decade later, was their second child. Nadia studied solfège, harmony, organ, and composition at Paris Conservatoire and was awarded several prize medals for outstanding work there, including, in 1908, the second Grand Prix in composition, for her cantata *La Sirène* (The siren). After the death of pianist-composer Raoul Pugno (1852–1914), she completed his unfinished opera *La Ville morte* (The dead city). For a number of years she was organist at La Madeleine, Paris.

Boulanger's teaching career began in 1909, when she was assistant in the organ class at Paris Conservatoire and also began to take private pupils. Her teaching was the principal source of income for the Boulanger family. From 1920 to 1939 she taught music history and other subjects at École Normale de Musique, Paris, and when the American Conservatory was founded at Fontainebleau in 1921, Walter Damrosch asked her to join the faculty as teacher of harmony. In addition, she taught a large number of private pupils at her home. Lessons there covered all aspects of music, especially analysis, composition, and conducting. Boulanger was an excellent conductor. She conducted the première of Stravinsky's *"Dumbarton Oaks"* Concerto in Washington, D.C. (1938) and was invited to conduct some concerts of the Boston Symphony and the New York Philharmonic. She was the first woman to conduct a major symphony orchestra in the United States.

During World War II, Boulanger lectured and taught at several colleges and universities in the United States. In 1946 she returned to Paris and resumed teaching responsibilities at the American Conservatory; four years later, she became director of the Conservatory. She continued private teaching until she was well into her eighties and had a reputation for being a strict taskmaster.

Nadia Boulanger. *(Wide World Photos, Inc.)*

Nadia Boulanger was the most influential woman in the history of music pedagogy. Her masterly teaching was a shaping force in the lives of many twentieth-century composers. Among the numerous Americans who studied with her in Paris were Aaron Copland, Virgil Thomson, Walter Piston, Roy Harris, and Elliott Carter. With regard to contemporary music, Boulanger had definite preferences. She admired the work of Stravinsky, Debussy, and Ravel; she did not like Schoenberg's music. Not all of Boulanger's students agreed with her musical tastes; Philip Glass was one who, after studying with her, followed his own dictates into Eastern music and minimalism (pp. 888–89).

Boulanger was much interested in early music—that of Bach and those who preceded him. During the 1920s and 1930s, she was influential in promoting performances of Monteverdi madrigals in Paris and frequently conducted or performed works by French composers of the Renaissance and Baroque eras.

United States

During the years between the two World Wars significant changes occurred in the United States relative to music. There was an appreciable increase in the number of American composers creating works of high quality—major works comparable with those of European composers. Gradually, there dawned an awareness of the excellent training available in American colleges, conservatories, and universities in composition, performance, education, musicology—in fact, in all areas of music. From time to time, the quality teaching done by Americans was supplemented by guest lecturers from Europe. Moreover, a number of European composers emigrated to America to escape impending or actual persecution, and, at one time or another, taught in American schools. Among those composers were the cream of Europe's crop—Rachmaninov, Prokofiev, Schoenberg, Bartók, Stravinsky, Milhaud, Hindemith, and others. Some became naturalized United States citizens. Perhaps the most outstanding native American composer during this era was Aaron Copland.

Copland

Copland was born in Brooklyn, New York, in 1900. As a child, he was strongly attracted to music and learned to play piano at home by gleaning information from his older sister. When he had exhausted that resource, he went, of his own free will, to a professional piano teacher. By 1917 Copland had decided he wanted to be a composer. He began to study harmony and counterpoint with Rubin Goldmark (1872–1936) and wrote a few pieces, most of them for solo piano. In 1920 Copland went to Paris for further study. Shortly before he left Brooklyn, he composed a short piano piece entitled *Humoristic scherzo: The Cat and the Mouse* (1920), based on La Fontaine's poem *La chat et la souris* (The cat and the mouse). Because he felt certain Goldmark would not approve of the piece's "modern" harmonies and unconventional rhythms, Copland did not show it to his teacher. However, it was to be Copland's first published work—in Paris he sold the composition outright to M. Durand for 500 francs.

In Paris Copland attended many concerts and thus observed the styles of many different composers, past and contemporary. He enrolled at the American school

Aaron Copland. *(American Symphony Orchestra League.)*

at Fontainebleau and was urged by another student, harpist Djina Ostrowska, to visit Boulanger's harmony class. Once Copland visited Boulanger's class, he, too, became excited about her teaching. Copland studied with Boulanger for four years, and a lifelong friendship developed between the two. While studying in Paris, Copland wrote a few songs, a choral work, some piano pieces, and music for a ballet named *Grohg* (1922–25). That ballet was never performed or published, but later Copland extracted from it portions that he arranged as the *Dance Symphony* (1930).

When Copland returned to United States in 1924, he earned his living by teaching piano privately, but he continued to compose. Then, Damrosch invited Boulanger to concertize in America, and Serge Koussevitzky (1874–1951) gave Copland's career as composer a strong boost by commissioning him to write a work for her to perform, as organ soloist with the Boston Symphony Orchestra. The *Symphony for Organ and Orchestra* (1924) resulted. Boulanger performed it at least twice—with Boston and New York orchestras. In 1928 Copland arranged the work without organ; it became his Symphony No. 1.

Soon the quality of Copland's compositions attracted attention. He wanted his music to be as clearly American as that of Musorgsky and Stravinsky was Russian. For that reason, he began to incorporate some

Developments between the World Wars

Example 25.18 Copland's *Short Symphony*, mvt. 1, mm. 1–2: oboe, heckelphone, and flute present the nine-note germinal sequence. *(SHORT SYMPHONY © Copyright 1955 by Aaron Copland; Copyright Renewed. Reprinted by permission of Aaron Copland, Copyright Owner, and Boosey & Hawkes, Inc., Sole Licensee.)*

Figure 25.4 Scene from Copland's ballet *Appalachian Spring*.

ragtime, blues, and jazz elements in his works, e.g., in the suite *Music for the Theatre* (1925) and the Piano Concerto (1926). Copland was quite concerned that new music by American composers be heard. To promote the performance of such music, he and Roger Sessions (1896–1985) founded the Copland-Sessions Concerts in New York (1928), a series that continued for three years. Also, in 1927–37, at the New School for Social Research, Copland lectured to laypersons on various aspects of music. Those lectures provided the material for his books *What to Listen for in Music* (publ. 1939) and *Our New Music* (publ. 1941). The latter, revised and enlarged, was published in 1968 under the title *The New Music, 1900–1968*.

In 1932, at the invitation of composer Carlos Chávez, Copland visited Mexico. There, he composed his *Short Symphony* (Symphony No. 2) for the Orquesta Sinfónica de México. The symphony, whose performance lasts about 15 minutes, is in three movements (fast, slow, fast) played without a pause. It is a rhythmically intricate, rather dissonant tonal work, but in the first movement all of the melodic figures are derived from a nine-note sequence—a kind of row—presented at the outset (ex. 25.18). Because it is so difficult to perform, the *Short Symphony* has been unduly neglected. Copland returned to Mexico many times during the ensuing decades and found inspiration there for several orchestral works, including *El Salón México* (1933–36), a depiction of a dance hall by that name that he had visited with Chávez. That work and several others contain Mexican folk material.

Memories of a visit to Havana, where Copland heard a *danzón* sextet playing in a nightclub, inspired *Danzón cubana* (2 pianos, 1942; orch., 1944). The *danzón* is a stately dance, usually performed in alternation with more animated Latin American dances such as the rhumba and tango. Other visits to Latin America are reflected in the three orchestral *Latin American Sketches* (1972).

On two occasions Copland taught at Harvard University as sabbatical replacement for Sessions; in 1952 Copland was appointed Norton Professor of Poetics at Harvard. From those lectures came the book *Music and Imagination* (1952). In 1940, when Koussevitzky founded a summer music school at Berkshire Music Center, Copland began to teach there. Soon he became chairman of the faculty and held that position until he retired in 1965.

Commencing in 1938, Copland received commissions for several ballets, including *Billy the Kid* (1938), *Rodeo* (1942), written for Agnes de Mille (b. 1905), and *Appalachian Spring* (1943–44; fig. 25.4), written for Martha Graham (b. 1894). In addition, the *Clarinet Concerto* (1947–48; cl. solo, strings, harp, piano) that Copland wrote for Benny Goodman (1909–86) provided the music for the ballet *Pied Piper*. Orchestral suites were derived from all of the ballets.

The *Appalachian Spring Suite* has been Copland's most popular orchestral work; for it he received the Pulitzer Prize in 1945. Originally, i.e., for the ballet, the music was scored for a 13-piece chamber

Example 25.19 The Shaker song *Simple gifts.*

ensemble: flute, clarinet, bassoon, 9 strings, and piano. *Appalachian Spring* depicts the celebration of spring and the wedding of a young couple, with all of the attendant elation and spiritual feelings, in a rural community in Pennsylvania in the early nineteenth century. The ballet comprises eight scenes. The seventh scene (DWMA227), portraying daily activities of the young married couple, consists of theme and variations on the Shaker song *Simple Gifts,* which originated c. 1837–47 (ex. 25.19). The section culminates in a mighty hymn. Other scenes in the ballet sound particularly "American country," e.g., the fourth, which is quite fast, includes music suggestive of square dancing and fiddling. In all of Copland's ballets, the music is vibrant and appealing, not without technical sophistication, frequently sounding much simpler than it really is.

Copland wrote for all musical media and in all genres. His full-length opera *The Tender Land* (1952–54; rev. 1955) met with severe criticism by the concert-going public as well as reviewers. Between 1938 and 1961 Copland wrote eight film scores, the most important being for *Of Mice and Men* (1939; Steinbeck), *Our Town* (1940; Wilder), and *The Red Pony* (1948; Steinbeck). Occupying a unique position among Copland's works is *Lincoln Portrait* (1942), for speaker and orchestra. Written as part of a series of musical portraits of American heroes, and commissioned by André Kostelanetz, the music includes

tunes from Lincoln's time, and the text (prepared by Copland) presents excerpts from Lincoln's letters and addresses. *Lincoln Portrait* has been performed frequently; poet Carl Sandburg (1878–1967) and Illinois statesman Adlai Stevenson are among those who have effectively read the text.

During World War II, conductor-composer Eugene Goossens (1893–1962) decided to open each of the Cincinnati Symphony Orchestra concerts in the 1942–43 season with a different fanfare by an American composer. He asked Copland to write one for brass and percussion. Copland's response, *Fanfare for the Common Man* (1942), has been performed many times at all kinds of public events and has been subjected to numerous and varied arrangements for ensembles both large and small, including "popular" performing ensembles such as Mick Jagger and the Rolling Stones. Copland reused the fanfare in the introduction to the Finale of his Symphony No. 3 (1944–46). That symphony, a four-movement cyclical work, does not follow Classical form. Its first movement opens and closes in E major and formally is an arch with an animated central section. The second movement is a Scherzo in duple meter, with a lyrical Trio in triple time; return of the Scherzo is not literal repetition. The Andantino third movement is constructed sectionally, each section flowing smoothly into the next. As introduction, unaccompanied first violins state the first movement's third theme. Then solo flute presents a new melody whose subsequent metamorphoses form the succeeding section. Near the end of the movement, the single melodic line of the introduction recurs, played by solo violin in harmonics and by piccolo, accompanied by celesta and harps. A sustained chord links third and fourth movements. The animated principal theme of the sonata-form Finale is announced by oboe; the broad, lyrical second theme is placed within the development section and is stated by clarinets. Recapitulation is unusual: themes of the Finale are polyphonically combined with the symphony's introductory melody. Copland concluded the symphony with a massive orchestral restatement of the phrase that began it. This symphony provides excellent examples of Copland's ability to use instrumental colors to obtain unusual sonorities. When the Third Symphony was first performed, Copland wrote the program notes, and, in addition to analyzing the composition, pointed out that it is absolute music and contains no folk or popular material. The Third Symphony was awarded the New York Music Critics Circle Prize as the best orchestral work by an American composer performed during the 1946–47 season.

From time to time Copland experimented with serial techniques. The first of his works in which serialism was used to any extent is the Piano Quartet (1950). Some features of dodecaphony appear in other works: *Twelve Poems of Emily Dickinson* (1950; vc., pno.), *Piano Fantasy* (1952–57), *Inscape* (1957; orch.), and *Connotations* (1962; orch.), written for the opening of Philharmonic Hall at Lincoln Center in New York City. In general, however, a strong sense of tonality is always present in Copland's music. At times, he wrote on two tonal levels or strata, combining major and minor or tonic and dominant. Such writing occurs in several sections of *Appalachian Spring*. He writes simple chords with variable spacings and is adept at writing syncopations, polyrhythms, and, on occasion, devising rhythmic intricacies. Copland has been an important influence in the lives and careers of many American composers, and many persons consider him the "dean of American composers."

Gershwin

George Gershwin (1898–1937) began his career in music in 1914 by playing piano for a New York publishing house to demonstrate new popular songs to prospective buyers. He had relatively little technical training for composition but possessed a gift for melodic and rhythmic invention, and within two years he was writing popular songs for publication as sheet music and for inclusion in Broadway shows. As a song writer, his first big success came with *Swanee* (1919), popularized by singer Al Jolson.

In 1919 Gershwin wrote a musical of his own; by 1933 he had composed 28 of them. Most were highly successful. The Broadway musical (sometimes called musical comedy) is an important genre of twentieth-century American music. Recognition of that fact came when Gershwin's *Of Thee I Sing* (1931), a political satire, was awarded the Pulitzer Prize—the first musical to be accorded that honor. Gershwin was composing music for films, also. But he had not been content with writing only popular music. In 1924,

George Gershwin. *(The Bettmann Archive.)*

he composed *Rhapsody in Blue,* a combination of jazz elements and Romantic music for solo piano and orchestra, and performed the work with Paul Whiteman's (1890–1967) jazz ensemble at a special concert on 12 February 1924 in New York's Aeolian Hall. Thus, blues entered the concert hall in America. Pianist-composer Ferde Grofé (1892–1972), arranger for Whiteman's band, orchestrated the Rhapsody. (Grofé composed a piano concerto and a number of suites, e.g., *Grand Canyon Suite,* in which he combined jazz rhythms and ballad-like melodies.) Gershwin determined that he would orchestrate any future works himself and demonstrated his ability to do so in his Piano Concerto (F major; 1925) and symphonic poem *An American in Paris* (1928). Both were commissioned by Walter Damrosch and were first performed by the New York Philharmonic, Damrosch conducting.

Gershwin's ambition to compose a full-length opera was realized in 1935 with *Porgy and Bess,* written for black singers. It is generally referred to as a "folk opera," but it contains no actual folk music. At first, reviews of *Porgy and Bess* were mixed—some praising, some condemning the work. For a time, the opera was seldom performed, but several songs from it became popular: "Summertime," "I Got Plenty o' Nuttin'," "It Ain't Necessarily So," and "Bess, You Is My Woman Now." When the opera was revived in the United States in the 1950s, and was performed by an American opera company on tour in Europe and South America as well, it was acclaimed internationally.

Ruth Crawford Seeger

Ruth Crawford (1901–53) began teaching piano at the School of Musical Arts in Jacksonville, Florida, as soon as she graduated from high school. In 1920 she entered the American Conservatory of Music in Chicago to prepare further for a career as pianist. When problems with muscular tension in her arms made piano playing increasingly more difficult, she concentrated on composition but did not give up piano playing. After receiving her baccalaureate degree from the Conservatory (1924), she began work on her master's and at the same time taught piano at the Conservatory and at Elmhurst College of Music. During those years she composed, among other things, *Five Preludes for Piano* (1924–25), the Sonata for violin and piano (1926), several chamber music suites, and *The Adventures of Tom Thumb* (1925) for piano and narrator. The latter was, of course, for children's entertainment.

Among Crawford's friends in Chicago were clarinetist (later, music critic) Alfred Frankenstein and his family. At their home, she heard recordings of music by contemporary European composers, and, through Frankenstein, met poet Carl Sandburg. A close friendship developed between Crawford and the Sandburg family. Sandburg stimulated Crawford's interest in folk song and in preparing books for children. Almost all of her songs are settings of Sandburg's poems.

Crawford spent the summer of 1929 at The MacDowell Colony, where she met many composers and writers. She seems to have written only three pieces that summer, the songs *Joy, Sunsets,* and *Loam* (Sandburg poems). In the vocal lines declamation and lyricism alternate; there is some use of tone clusters and whole-tone scales. At the end of the summer, she decided to move to New York. Henry Cowell, cognizant of her talent, persuaded composer Charles Seeger (1886–1979) to accept her as a student. The

Ruth Crawford Seeger. *(Courtesy Michael Crawford.)*

first fruits of that study were Crawford's *Diaphonic Suites Nos. 1–4,* dissonant chamber music. In 1930 Crawford was awarded a Guggenheim Foundation Fellowship to study composition in Europe for a year; she was the first woman to receive such a grant. During that year she created her most important compositions: *Three Chants for Women's Chorus* and the String Quartet. Also, she had opportunities to discuss music with Bartók, Berg, Ravel, and other noted composers.

The *Three Chants,* settings of meaningless phonemes, are filled with dissonant counterpoint and, in the third chant, intricate polyrhythms. The String Quartet (1931), a four-movement work, placed Crawford firmly among the avant-garde composers of the time. In the third movement, constant legato and continually changing dynamic patterns, different in each part, produce a kind of "dynamic counterpoint." The fourth movement closely approaches total serialism, for all of the musical elements are organized according to preset patterns. The second half of the movement is a transposed retrograde of the first half. Such use of retrograde motion is found in many of Crawford's compositions, as are also strong dissonance and ostinato patterns.

When Crawford returned to the United States, her marriage to Seeger altered her priorities, pushing composition into the background of her life. She and Seeger decided to collect and study American folk music. Soon they joined John and Alan Lomax in their similar endeavors and made translations of field recordings for their publications. While the Seegers lived in Washington, D.C., in the 1940s, Ruth became interested in teaching young children. For them she compiled and published several books of folk songs, arranged for voice and piano: *American Folk Songs for Children* (1948), *Animal Folk Songs for Children* (1950), and *Christmas Folk Songs for Children* (1953). In this she was a pioneer, and music educators duly appreciated her work.

Crawford completed only a few original compositions after her marriage, the most important being *Rissolty, Rossolty* (1939; orch.), based on three folk songs, and the *Suite for Wind Quintet* (1952), which is in the abstract, dissonant, contrapuntal style of her early works.

Other American Composers

A number of American-born composers were active during the decades between the two World Wars. Several included folk music or specifically American idioms such as blues and jazz elements in their works; others set texts relating to American topics or wrote program music on American subjects. The works of some composers were not at all nationalistic.

Virgil Thomson (b. 1896) is best known for his opera *Four Saints in Three Acts* (1927–28), on a libretto by Gertrude Stein (1874–1946). The work is a series of tableaux and processions without a central plot. His opera *The Mother of us all* (1947; Stein libretto) concerns Susan B. Anthony and the woman's suffrage movement and includes some nineteenth-century American music. Thomson provided nationalistic music for the documentary films *The Plow that Broke the Plains* (1936), *The River* (1937), and *Louisiana Story* (1948). Most of Thomson's music is characterized by basically diatonic harmonies, though some bitonality is present, and by quotations from folk tunes, hymns, patriotic songs, and dances. His operas are witty and entertaining, but most of them are not deeply emotional. Thomson has written several books on contemporary music, including *The State of Music* (1939), *The Musical Scene* (1945), and *American Music since 1910* (1971).

Roy Harris (1898–1979) wrote mainly choral music and orchestral works. He composed a few works specifically for band, e.g., *Cimarron* (1941) and *West Point Symphony* (1952). Harris particularly liked the poetry of Walt Whitman (1819–92) and set many of his works. The finest of his 14 symphonies, and probably his best-known work, is the Third Symphony (1937). It contains many elements that became characteristic of his style: a broad opening motive; melody in long lines, and, frequently, modal melody; emphasis on harmonic counterpoint; contrapuntal devices favored over motivic development; diverse rhythmic patterns. Harris did not use key signatures, but his music conveys a strong sense of tonality. The first of his works to include folk music was *When Johnny Comes Marching Home* (1935; chorus); he used a lot of it in his fourth symphony, the *Folksong Symphony* (1940), for chorus and orchestra.

William Grant Still (1895–1978) began his studies in composition at Oberlin Conservatory, Ohio, then served in the U.S. Navy during World War I. After the war, he resumed studies in composition with Edgard Varèse and George W. Chadwick (1854–1931). Following Chadwick's advice to write specifically American music, Still began to compose large-scale works in the 1920s. His early works include the symphonic poem *Darker America* (1924), the suite *From the Black Belt* (1926), and *Afro-American Symphony* (1930), the first of his five symphonies. In some of his works he used jazz and blues idioms. Occasionally, he included authentic Negro folk melodies, but usually he fabricated themes that simulated them. Still's *Pastorela* (1946), a sonata for violin and piano, is excellent.

In the output of most American composers, non-nationalistic works far outnumber those that are decidedly nationalistic. Roger Sessions (b. 1896) first attracted attention with his orchestral suite *The Black Masters* (1923). His music is filled with dense counterpoint and his harmonies are quite dissonant. One of his finest works is his cantata setting Walt Whitman's *When Lilacs Last in the Door-Yard Bloomed*. Whitman wrote the poem as an elegy for Abraham Lincoln; Sessions's work (for S,A,Bar. soloists, chor., orch.) was written in 1970 as a memorial to Martin Luther King, Jr. and Robert Kennedy.

Many of Walter Piston's (1894–1976) works are Neo-Classical. Piston came to the attention of the musical world with the ballet suite *The Incredible Flutist;* his reputation spread after the première of his Symphony No. 2 (1944). Piston preferred to write in the large forms that were favored during the late eighteenth and nineteenth centuries—concerto, sonata, string quartet, and symphony—but his complex harmonies are not from those eras.

Howard Hanson's (1896–1981) opera *The Maypole of Merry Mount* (1933), based on Nathaniel Hawthorne's *The Lovers of Merry Mount,* is one of his few compositions on American subjects. Another is *A Sea Symphony* (Sym. No. 7; 1977; orch., chor.), based on Walt Whitman's poem. Hanson's music is basically Romantic in style, e.g., *Symphony No. 2: Romantic.* Many of his compositions, e.g., his *Symphony No. 1: Nordic,* reflect the influence of Sibelius, whom he greatly admired. Hanson's work in the field of education was admirable. As director of the Eastman School of Music, he was largely responsible for the elevation of that school to its present prestigious status.

Latin and South American Composers

Most important among the Latin and South American composers during this era were Heitor Villa-Lobos (1887–1959) of Brazil, Alberto Ginastera (1916–83) of Argentina, and Carlos Chávez (1899–1978) of Mexico. All used traditional forms to some extent, and all were nationalistic to some degree.

Villa-Lobos was a master of both 'cello and guitar but did not confine his writing to works for those instruments. Though he incorporated authentic Brazilian rhythms and melodic types in many of his works, he refrained from actually quoting Brazilian songs. As a youth, he spent a considerable time playing popular music, particularly the dance form called *chôros,* with the musicians of Rio de Janiero. Between 1920 and 1928 he composed a series of 15 *Chôros* for various instruments, ensemble and solo. To improve his compositional techniques, Villa-Lobos seriously studied the works of the great masters. Bach's music interested him greatly, and he transcribed several pieces from *Das wohltemperirte Klavier* for chorus and for 'cello ensemble. Later, he composed nine suites entitled *Bachianas Brasileiras* (1932–44) in which he combined Bach-style counterpoint with melodies resembling those of Brazilian folk and popular music. To each piece he gave two titles, one typical of the Baroque, the other referring to Brazilian popular music. Especially lovely is *Bachianas Brasileiras No. 5,* for soprano soloist accompanied by 'cello soloist and an ensemble of seven 'celli. The work has two movements, the first being an *Aria* in ternary form

(DWMA228). The expressive melody of the A sections is vocalized or hummed by the soloist. The middle section, syncopated and with frequent tempo changes, is texted and resembles a Brazilian popular song. *Bachianas Brasileiras No. 9* is textless, intended for vocalization by *a cappella* mixed chorus, which Villa-Lobos called "an orchestra of voices." There is also a version of No. 9 for string orchestra.

In Ginastera's music, nationalism (both objective and subjective), Neo-Classicism, Expressionism, and serialism mingle. His twelve-tone writing is not always strict serialism, and frequently, for his instrumental pieces, he used sonata form and theme and variations. Argentinian folk melodies and rhythms appear in his early works, e.g., the ballets *Panambi* (1936) and *Estancia* (1941) and the piano pieces *Danzas Argentinas* (Argentinian dances; 1937). The excellent quality of Ginastera's work was recognized internationally after the première of his String Quartet No. 2 (1958), his first entirely serial composition. From that time on, dodecaphony became a feature of his works, along with polytonality, and some use of microintervals. His Piano Concerto No. 2 (1972) uses a tone-row derived from the opening of the Finale of Beethoven's Symphony No. 9. The concerto's second movement is for left hand alone. Serial techniques and unusual sound effects, as well as traditional forms, are found in all three of Ginastera's operas: *Don Rodrigo* (1964), *Bomarzo* (1967), and *Beatrix Cenci* (1971). At the conclusion of *Don Rodrigo* some unusual polyphony is achieved by three groups of bells playing from different places in the theater, and in *Beatrix Cenci* instruments eerily mimic the palace mastiffs' baying. In accord with the historical subject matter of *Bomarzo* and *Beatrix Cenci,* Ginastera used some Renaissance musical forms. *Bomarzo,* dealing with events in the life of Pier Francesco Orsini, Duke of Bomarzo, was banned for a time in some countries because of its portrayal of sexual violence.

Carlos Chávez played a decisive role in the development of music in Mexico during the second quarter of the twentieth century. He was a fine conductor, an excellent composer, and a remarkable educator. After the Mexican revolution (1910–21), the government assumed patronage of the arts and stressed the importance of native Indian cultures. Chávez's first important nationalistic work was *El fuego nuevo* (The new fire; 1921), written in response to a commission from the Mexican minister of education for a ballet on an Aztec subject. During 1922–28, Chávez spent much time in the United States. When the first permanent symphony orchestra was formed in Mexico in 1928, he became its conductor and served in that capacity for 20 years. During the 6 years that Chávez was director of the National Conservatory of Music, he reformed the curriculum, instigated series of concerts with students as soloists, established committees to research folk and popular music, and constantly encouraged talented Mexicans to compose. One whom he aided was Silvestre Rivueltas (1898–1940). Chávez was one of the founders of the Colegio de México and the Mexican Academy of the Arts. One of his best-known works is his second symphony, *Sinfonia India* (1936), one of the few pieces in which he incorporated authentic Aztec themes. Many of Chávez's works convey the character of native Indian music without actually using indigenous materials. In part, he achieved that effect by including folk instruments (percussion and ocarinas) in the scores. Rhythm is an important factor in his music. His skill at handling irregular meters, cross-rhythms and syncopation, and polyrhythm is apparent in *Sinfonia India*. Of Chávez's five ballets, the most remarkable is *La hija de Côlquide* (Côlquide's daughter; 1943) written for Martha Graham, with music scored for string quartet and wind quartet. Later that year, Chávez fully orchestrated the music, as a symphonic suite.

Summary

In the years between the World Wars, nationalism continued to be expressed musically, and folk music was an important aspect of that expression. As scientific investigation of folk music increased, more and more composers incorporated the peculiar attributes of regional folk musics into their works. Scholarly research on central European folk music was carried out by Janáček, Kodály, and Bartók; scientific investigations by others ensued. The most complete synthesis of folk idioms and art music was achieved by Bartók.

Primarily a virtuoso pianist, Bartók also composed and taught. His *Mikrokosmos,* a six-volume progressive course in piano technique, is a compendium of his style and of many of the compositional devices used during the first half of the twentieth century. His six string quartets present a comparable summary of his style. After Bartók emigrated to America, Kodály worked alone collecting, scientifically studying, and codifying the folk music of central European peoples. In addition, he made significant contributions in the field of vocal music education, particularly, the "Kodály method" of sight-singing. Kodály's music, more narrowly nationalistic than Bartók's, is an amalgamation of many influences— Bach-style counterpoint, the choral writing of Palestrina, Gregorian chant, and Hungarian folk music, including *verbunkos*.

Orff was also greatly interested in the music education of elementary school children, especially with regard to rhythmic proficiency and fluidity of movement. The *Orff-Schulwerk* graded music exercises and the "Orff instruments" are well known. Orff's principal interest was complete or "total" theater, in which all aspects of words, music, and movement formed a cohesive whole.

Until the advent of Vaughan Williams and Britten, England had no native-born composer of the stature of Henry Purcell. In the twentieth century, there was a revival of interest in Purcell's music, and several of Britten's compositions reflect his knowledge of and appreciation for Purcell's works. Vaughan Williams's style is nationalistic in character, without being tied to folk song, yet is highly personal. He blended archaic procedures from the Tudor era with techniques of his own time, and he handled counterpoint and homophony and modes and keys with equal skill. Vaughan Williams's nine symphonies did a great deal to establish the symphony as an important form in English music. England had no tradition of native opera. The operas of Vaughan Williams and Britten provided a firm foundation for the future of English opera. Britten's principal contributions lie in the area of vocal music, specifically, solo songs, choral works, and operas. He wrote a large amount of challenging music for amateurs and children.

Cultural conditions in Russia differed vastly from those in western Europe. All of the arts were placed under state supervision in 1921, and in 1932 the Union of Soviet Composers formally resolved that all music should be socialistic and should be easily understood by the masses. Use of folk material and expression of "national feelings" were advocated. Western modern music was banned, and performance of individualistic works with a semblance of modern techniques was prohibited. Among composers whose works were severely criticized and censored were Shostakovich, Prokofiev, Khachaturian, and Kabalevsky, who were the most significant of the composers living in Russia in 1917–45. Many of Khachaturian's compositions reenforce Soviet ideology and exemplify the ideals of the Soviet school of composition: diatonic melodies, basically tonal harmonies that include dissonance, energetic rhythms, traditional forms. Prokofiev is probably best known for his symphonies. In his Haydnesque *Classical Symphony* (1917), he unconsciously anticipated the Neo-Classical trend that emerged a few years later. To avoid unsatisfactory conditions in Russia during 1918–32, Prokofiev concertized and composed in western Europe and America. In 1936, when conditions had ameliorated somewhat and he believed he could comply with Soviet regulations, he returned to Russia, but often his works were severely criticized or rejected. Shostakovich's most significant contributions to repertoire are his symphonies. Many persons consider him the greatest symphonist of the mid-twentieth century.

The name "Second Viennese School" has been applied to Schoenberg and his few private pupils, especially Berg and Webern. From that group there emerged a new style of music called dodecaphony, an atonal/pantonal style in which all 12 chromatic pitches in the octave were considered equal and none had any special function. Among the factors generating the new style were the increased use of linear counterpoint with motives and melodies that dictated harmonies, and the abundant use of unresolved dissonances (nonfunctional harmonies) in post-Romantic music. Largely due to Schoenberg's efforts, an organizational system called serialism was developed, in whih a composer prearranged the order in which the 12 chromatic pitches were to be used, thus establishing a Series or Row. Schoenberg, in his last style period, tried to reconcile the principles of tonality and atonality but always slipped into atonality. His orchestral *Variations,* Op. 31 could serve as a textbook on serial techniques. Berg and Webern adopted Schoenberg's principles but modified them. Berg never completely relinquished Romanticism and tonality. He did not adhere to a single row for an entire composition, and he often combined tonal and nontonal elements in a work. His treatment of twelve-tone music

may be seen in his Violin Concerto and the Expressionist opera *Wozzeck*. Webern strictly adhered to serial principles, used one row per movement, and wrote highly ordered counterpoint, concentrated in extremely compressed forms. Characterized by economy of means, his compositions are extremely compressed, and some of his pieces are pointillistic (athematic music seemingly constructed of isolated notes). Not until after Webern's death was the significance of his work realized. Then, his work was emulated by avant-garde composers internationally.

Neo-Classicism, a movement against late Romanticism, began near the end of World War I, gathered momentum in the early 1920s, and remained strong until after 1945. It is characterized by a preference for the objectivity of absolute music, greater emphasis on counterpoint, economy of performing resources, and a revival of eighteenth-century traditional forms, with thematic material subject to techniques and compositional processes then favored. Many composers turned to Neo-Classicism after having explored other styles. One such was Hindemith; he and Stravinsky are considered the chief exponents of Neo-Classicism. Twentieth-century composers' historical awareness of early music led to a revival of forms and characteristic styles of previous eras. Also, an unwillingness to accept twentieth-century musical styles as suitable for church music caused composers to use as models sixteenth- and seventeenth-century styles and techniques. In addition to the general back-to-Bach-and-Handel movement, composers in each country were motivated by nationalism to turn to the musical styles of their respective countries' historical past.

In France, each of The Six took a separate path. Durey joined the French Communist Party and his views and works became politically oriented. Auric's most important contributions were his stage and theater music; he did much to revitalize opera in France. Tailleferre's music followed the traditional lines established by Fauré and continued by Ravel. Honegger wrote mainly stage and dramatic works, often with demanding speaking and singing parts that included *Sprechstimme* and other unusual vocal techniques. Poulenc was master of the *mélodie* and wrote religious choral music. Milhaud composed with rapidity and facility that rivaled Telemann and Mozart. His works, which are in all genres, are characterized by lyrical melodies, formal clarity, skillful use of counterpoint, and bitonality or polytonality.

Hindemith made significant contributions as performer, composer, theorist, teacher, and author. He believed that music must be understood as a means of communication between composer and consumer. By writing some music specifically for amateurs, he hoped to narrow the gap between composer and amateur performer. Music performed purely for enjoyment was important. The term *Gebrauchsmusik* (music for use) became associated with that kind of music; it was a term Hindemith disliked. Hindemith was convinced a composer must be a performing musician, familiar with instruments through participation in ensembles. He considered key tonality unavoidable. He wholeheartedly endorsed the theory expressed in the writings of the ancient Greek philosophers that the principles of order governing the acoustical ratios of musical intervals and the order within a musical composition symbolize and reflect, as microcosm to macrocosm, the principles that govern the orderly behavior of the universe. These beliefs—Hindemith's philosophy—influenced his compositions.

Stravinsky was one of the twentieth century's most outstanding composers. From Rimsky-Korsakov, his teacher and mentor, Stravinsky learned how to use timbres effectively and to express psychological states and physical movements through music; he adeptly applied all that he learned. Undoubtedly, his most famous composition is *Le sacre du printemps,* a work filled with polytonality, polyrhythms, *ostinati,* contrasting instrumental timbres, and the frenetic rhythms of primitivism. Stravinsky was a versatile composer with mastery of all compositional techniques available to him. Though he moved from one genre to another, from one style to another, keeping in touch with contemporary trends, some things remained constant. He never completely abandoned tonality, though he composed some atonal pieces. Many times, he worked with opposing tonal poles; he used modality, bitonality, polytonality, and dodecaphonic techniques. Rhythm is probably the most significant feature of his works. He based his rhythms on the constancy of a minimum value and used multiples of that; the barline became subservient to his purposes.

Just as the teaching of Rimsky-Korsakov provided an excellent foundation for the work of his students, so the teaching of Nadia Boulanger was a shaping force in the careers of many composers. Boulanger was the most influential woman in the history of music pedagogy. Copland was one of many Americans who studied with her. Copland wanted his music to be as clearly American as Musorgsky's was Russian. In the 1920s he incorporated some ragtime, blues, and jazz elements into his works. He did much to promote the performance of new music by American composers. To help provide greater understanding of music among the general public, he lectured to laypersons on various aspects of music. Copland wrote for all musical media and in all genres. Occasionally, he experimented with serial techniques, but, for the most part, his music has a strong sense of tonality. He has written a number of works on American subjects, e.g., *Appalachian Spring* and *Lincoln Portrait.* Many persons consider Copland the "dean of American composers."

Gershwin's first successful compositions were popular songs. His Broadway musical, *Of Thee I Sing,* a political satire, was the first musical to be awarded the Pulitzer Prize. With the performance of his *Rhapsody in Blue,* jazz and blues elements entered the concert hall in America.

A number of American-born composers were active during the decades between the two wars. Several included folk music or specifically American idioms such as blues and jazz elements in their works; others set texts relating to American topics or wrote program music on American subjects, but the works of some composers were not at all nationalistic. In fact, in the output of most American composers, nonnationalistic works far outnumber those that are decidedly nationalistic. W. G. Still wrote large-scale works representative of black Americans, though he usually did not include authentic Negro melodies in them.

Most important among Latin and South American composers were Villa-Lobos of Brazil, Ginastera of Argentina, and Chávez of Mexico. All used traditional forms to some extent, and all were nationalistic to some degree. Chávez played a decisive role in the development of music in Mexico. He served as conductor of Mexico's first permanent symphony orchestra, was director of the National Conservatory of Music, and constantly encouraged talented Mexicans to compose.

26

Music Since 1945

After World War II ended (1945), restoration was needed on many fronts—political, physical, psychological, and cultural. Nazi Germany had suffered defeat and the suicide of its leader, Hitler; the devastation of Hiroshima and Nagasaki by nuclear bombing had shocked Japan and horrified other countries. Disputes over territory and distrust of one another's intentions caused communist-capitalist national alliances to degenerate and resulted in a "cold" war. British and French colonies in Asia and Africa sought and obtained independence or commitments granting independence at specified later dates. Then, in 1962, the United States became involved in the internal warfare in Vietnam and for more than a decade experienced a conflict that brought true victory to no one. At the same time, within the United States there was domestic agitation for economic, political, and social justice and equality for minorities—women, blacks, and various ethnic groups. Tremendous technological achievements were realized, including the exploration of outer space, with men landing on the moon and walking in space, and the development of computers and robots for industrial use.

Where music was concerned, there were many World War II casualties, some more severe than others. Webern had been killed; some musicians and composers had experienced capture and imprison-ment behind enemy lines, and some had suffered indignities and horrors in concentration camps. When the Nazi and Fascist parties rose to power, many prominent European composers and performers had taken refuge in the United States; Bartók, Schoenberg, Hindemith, and Milhaud are a few who fled their native lands and whose talents considerably enriched American music. The works of some composers who remained at home had been subjected to their government's censorship; other composers had had royalties cut off, bank accounts frozen, other assets seized, and family members mistreated. The war had disrupted concert life, and music publishing had virtually ceased. Moreover, because of difficulties in or lack of communication during the war years, many composers were out of touch with what others were doing. That was both bad and good, for it encouraged independent initiative, and new styles and techniques came into being.

After World War II, there was an extensive search for true values. In the arts, this brought innovation and experimentation, particularly on the part of young artists and composers. As might be expected, considerable diversity resulted. Not all the music that was created was good; in fact, some of it was quite bad, and a lot of it was mediocre, as is the case in every era.

Figure 26.1 Europe in 1978.

Technology

1877 Phonograph invented; wax cylinders
1885 Wax-covered cardboard cylinders
1896 Flat disc recordings 78 rpm
c. 1924 Microphones; electrical amplifiers
1948 Nonbreakable discs LP (33⅓ rpm)
1957 Stereophonic recordings
c. 1960 Quadraphonic sound
c. 1980
Compact discs

1898 Recording on steel piano wire
c. 1925 Recording on steel bands
1935 Flexible coated tape
Plastic film tapes
1947 Tape recordings used in radio broadcasting
c. 1958 Tape cartridges/cassettes
1965 8-track cassette tapes

1923 "Talking pictures"
1928 *The Jazz Singer*—talking picture with music

1960s Video tape recorder
1980s Video disc
systems
(1500 rpm)

c. 1920 AM radio   1950 FM radio   1970 VHF
1930s BBC television service
1951 Color television in USA

1964–65 Moog synthesizer
1966 *Silver Apples of the Moon*

1957 Computer-generated musical score
Computer-generated sounds
Computer playing in 1980s

c. 1920 Theremin invented

c. 1924 Ondes Martenot invented

Though the time was ripe for striking out in new directions, some composers sought restoration and continued along old paths. In communist countries of Eastern Europe, composers found the symphony a safe and suitable vehicle. That form was cultivated in Britain and America, also. Some excellent symphonies were written. In California, Stravinsky was writing in Neo-Classical style, and Schoenberg, in the last years of his life, continued to write Expressionistic twelve-tone music. In dealing with serialism, Schoenberg, Berg, and Webern used fascinating, in-depth technical procedures but did not live long enough to develop serialism to its fullest potential. Their work was continued by young avant-garde composers in France and America, who, independently of each other, worked toward and eventually achieved total serialism and created new styles—*musique concrète,* electronic music, indeterminacy (aleatory, chance, or choice music), and others. Several of the European leaders of the avant-garde music acknowledged their indebtedness to the music of Webern and to the teaching and guidance of Messiaen.

Technology

The twentieth century has witnessed tremendous technological advances that have affected the development of music. When the first recording devices were invented, in the late nineteenth century, they were valued for their ability to store materials and were of particular assistance to persons gathering folk songs. With each improvement in the recording

Music Since World War II

Messiaen:
Quartet pour le fin de temps
    1944 *Vingt-regards* . . .
        1949 *Mode de valeurs et d'intensités*
            1956 *Oiseaux exotiques*   1969 *Méditations sur . . . la Sainte Trinité*
                                                 Saint François d'Assise 1983 (opera)
                                         Livre du saint sacrement 1985 (organ)

PARIS: Musique concrète
        1948 Schaeffer; Henry
        1948 Boulez, leader of young serialists in Paris
            1952 *Le marteau san maître*
              1957 *Piano Sonata No. 3* (chord multiplication)
                              Founded, c. 1975, Institute de Recherche et
                                    Coordination de Acoustique/Musique

GERMANY: 1951 Eimert founded Studio für Elektronische Musik

        Stockhausen: 1953 *Kontra-Punkte*
                    1956 *Gesang der Jünglinge*

            1952–1985 *Klavierstücke I–XIV* -

                                    Series of *Licht* operas 1980, 1983, 1984 - - - - - -

ITALY: Berio: 1958–1985 *Sequenza* series; *Chemins* series -

AMERICA:
          Varèse: 1950–54 *Déserts* (tape, instrs.)
                1957 *Poème electronique* (tape)

      Babbitt: Combinatoriality; total serialization
          1947 *Three Compositions for Piano*
                1961 *Composition for Synthesizer*
                                   1981 *Ars combinatoria*

                Wuorinen: 1969 *Time's Encomium* (tape)

Cage: Prepared piano, after Cowell
      1946–48 *Sonatas and Interludes*
         1951 *Music of Changes* (aleatory)
        1953–58 *Music for Piano*

New Movements: - - "Happenings" - - - - "Fluxus" - -

            Oliveros: 1961–67 electronic works
                            Ivey: 1976–86 Tape + live performance

                   Crumb: 1970 *Ancient Voices of Children*
                     1972–79 *Makrokosmos*, Vols. I–IV

              Musgrave: *Harriet, the Woman called "Moses"* 1984 (opera)

      Ligeti: 1955 *Éjszaka; Reggel*
                  1965 *Requiem Mass*

        Penderecki: 1960 *Threnody* . . .   1978 *Paradise Lost* (opera)

           Riley: c. 1964 *In C;* Minimalism

                          Glass: 1974 *Music with Changing Parts*

          Reich: 1967 *Violin Phase* (phase shifting)
                          The Desert Music 1984
                     Music for Percussion and Keyboard 1984

        Del Tredici: 1968–1981 the series of *Alice* pieces

mechanisms, the possibilities for their use loomed larger. By 1896 Edison's method of recording sounds on a wax cylinder had been supplanted by Émile Berliner's method using a flat disc. In addition to storing material, the disc could serve as a master from which multiple copies could be reproduced—a commercial advantage. Performances by outstanding musicians could be recorded and marketed, thus providing to both composers and performers a wide dissemination of their artistic talents. The early standard speed for playing such discs with reasonable fidelity was 78 rpm. By the early 1920s, Berliner's gramophone was in many homes. Microphones and electrical amplifiers were available c. 1924 and were another aid in the recording industry. Columbia Records made one of the earliest recordings with these devices in March 1925 in Metropolitan Opera House. World War II interrupted research, but in 1948 Columbia Records produced recordings on nonbreakable microgroove discs playable at 33⅓ rpm—the long-playing record, capable of storing much more material on a 12-inch disc than was possible with 78 rpm speed. By 1957 stereophonic recording and reproduction were possible. The next development was quadraphonic (four-channel) sound. By 1980 there were available digital players with laser beams scanning metal-coated discs.

Before World War II, some composers had begun to experiment with disc recordings as a compositional tool. By recording sounds and then manipulating or altering the recording, new sounds could be created. However, when magnetic tape became readily available, it proved to be a much more workable tool.

As early as 1898, Vladimir Poulsen had invented a means of recording sounds as patterns of magnetized domains on steel piano wire that was wound around a cylinder. The prime purpose for his research was to find a way to record telephone conversations, and he called his invention the telegraphone. Because round wire twisted easily, flat steel bands came into use. These could be edited, and by c. 1927–29 methods had been devised for high-frequency erasing and substitution of sounds.

Real progress in magnetic tape recording came when flexible coated tapes became available around 1935. At first these were made of coated paper, then plastic film was used for the tape base. With this, editing was easier, for the tape could be cut and spliced; also, several tracks could be recorded simultaneously, and more material could be stored on a single tape than on a single disc. This opened up countless opportunities for composers. Not only could they record resource materials, they could—and eventually did—work directly with source materials to create entire compositions on tape and thus avoid the difficult task of trying to notate their works precisely so that performers would interpret them correctly and recreate them with reasonable accuracy. Rhythm and slow glissandos were especially difficult to notate. Taped compositions could be marketed, just as discs were, but not until after 1955 was there any real endeavor to do so. Of course, World War II caused delays, but by 1947 tape recording was used in radio broadcasting studios. The manufacture of stereo disc records led to similar developments with stereophonic tapes. Then, in the late 1950s and early 1960s, tape cartridges and cassettes were designed, and in 1965 the eight-track cassette was developed, primarily for use in automobiles. In such a cassette, the tape is a continuous loop, wound to provide the listener with uninterrupted sound. Composers used the tape loop as a compositional tool for creating ostinato passages in their tape compositions. Pierre Schaeffer, Karlheinz Stockhausen, and Steve Reich are some who did.

Recording sounds on film became a reality in 1923 when Lee de Forest (1863–1961) developed the photoelectric cell that enabled motion pictures to become "talking" pictures. The earliest successful one with music was *The Jazz Singer* (1928). At first, a sound track was put on a film through variable density optical recording to achieve reliable synchronization of sound and action. Then, magnetic recording techniques were applied to "movie" film. This opened another vista—composing for cinema. Composer-conductor John Williams (b. 1932) began his career writing background music for films and won Academy Awards for his music for *Jaws* (1975) and *Star Wars* (1977). Later developments include videotape recorders (introduced by Ampex in the 1960s), electronic video recording (1968), and video disc systems operating at 1500 rpm (in the 1980s).

Radio was another realm that opened to composers c. 1920. It has progressed from amplitude modification (AM) to frequency modulation (FM; in the 1950s), with use of very high frequency (VHF) transmission that reduces interference noise and achieves a quiet background, hence greater fidelity of the music (or other sounds) transmitted for reception in the home. Many composers, including Aaron Copland, have written music for radio. And, since the advent of television, composers have written theme, background, and incidental music for telecasts, e.g., John Williams's theme music composed in 1986 for NBC's "TODAY" and "Nightly News" shows.

Electronic Instruments

Composers sought new sounds and new means of generating them electronically and encouraged electrical engineers to invent new instruments. In 1964–65, at the instigation of composer Herbert A. Deutsch, Robert Moog (b. 1934) built a voltage-controlled synthesizer for composing music. Organist-composer Wendy Carlos (née Walter Carlos; b. 1939) popularized the sounds of the Moog Synthesizer by recording several of J. S. Bach's compositions as *Switched-On Bach*. At about the same time that Deutsch contacted Moog, composer Morton Subotnik (b. 1933), in California, requested electrical engineer Donald Buchla to construct some electronic music equipment for him. Subotnik installed one of Buchla's voltage-controlled Electronic Music Systems in his New York studio and used it to create *Silver Apples of the Moon* (1966), the first electronic music composition composed specifically (i.e., commissioned) for a record (Nonesuch 71174). For this piece, Subotnik used the sequencer module, a control voltage source in the Buchla System, to perform the same functions as a tape loop more rapidly and more efficiently.

The first instance of a computer being programmed to produce the score of a musical composition occurred in 1957, at the University of Illinois, when Lejaren Hiller (b. 1924) and Leonard Isaacson (b. 1925) wrote *Illiac Suite for String Quartet*. Only the score was computer generated; the music was performed by a string quartet. Between 1959 and 1962 Iannis Xenakis (b. 1922), working in Paris, used computer calculations to produce the scores of seven compositions, e.g., *Stratégie, Jeu pour deux orchestres* (Strategy, Game for two [small] orchestras). In other words, the computer was employed as a kind of composing machine to produce scores for performance on conventional instruments.

In 1957, at Bell Telephone Laboratories in New Jersey, under direction of Max Mathews, computer-generated sounds were produced through use of a digital-to-analog converter (DAC). This means that numbers, in a specific order, are input to the computer either by typing or by punched cards. (cf., Ada Lovelace's ideas in 1843 for musical composition on Babbage's analytical engine; p. 623.) The numbers represent various elements of the music each of which the computer translates into either 0 or 1 and transmits to magnetic digital tape or disk. The disk or tape is sent through the DAC, the digital information is converted to voltages (the analog), the voltages are recorded on tape (on a conventional tape recorder), and the tape recorder head translates the voltages to sounds. Further research at Bell Laboratories produced a light pencil whose graphic representations replaced the punched cards, and in 1968 Mathews and Frederick Moore used a computer to control a synthesizer. Advanced technology has produced home computers, such as the Apple IIgs (gs, graphic-sound) available in October 1986, capable of "playing" as many as 15 lines of music sounded simultaneously and printing out the notated score via Imagewriter II printer.

The original intent of recording technology—to provide a means for storing, transmitting, and faithfully reproducing live sounds—has been extended considerably. Technology has made available to composers every sound in the universe as source material. Not only the proportions of the macrocosm, but the *musica mundana* (or inaudible cosmic music) about which Pythagoras, Plato, and Boethius wrote, and everything within it—even its silence—has been placed within reach of those creating the microcosm, audible *musica instrumentalis*.

Serialism

Schoenberg began to use serialism consistently in the 1920s and continued to do so for the remainder of his life, without exploring its possibilities beyond the element of pitch. He taught serial principles to his pupils, especially Berg and Webern, each of whom applied them in his own way and relayed the technique to his pupils. Outside that circle of pupils, serialism had little use until after 1945. Then, in Paris, René Leibowitz (1913–72) taught Schoenberg's technique for a few years, and Pierre Boulez attended some of his classes. In the opinion of Boulez and other European avant-garde composers, the late works of Webern provided the best models for serial composition. Because of Webern's economy, it was easy to follow his procedures. Moreover, his use of counterpoint was intriguing.

For a time, Messiaen decried serialism, then began to use it with discrimination. After he applied serial principles to rhythm in *Quatre études de rhythme* and composed some of those pieces while teaching in the summer courses at Darmstadt, other young composers became interested in the procedures he was using, particularly those in *Mode de valeurs et d'intensités*. (However, *Mode de valeurs . . .* is not a serial piece; see pp. 864, 866.) Among those composers were Boulez, Karel Goeyvaerts (b. 1923), Karlheinz Stockhausen (b. 1928), and Luigi Nono (b. 1924). All wrote compositions directly influenced by *Mode de valeurs et d'intensités*. Through continued interest and experimentation with multiple serialism, the scope of that technique was extended until eventually total serialism was attained. Boulez, Stockhausen, and Goeyvaerts explored use of serial principles in *musique concrète* and electronic music. Meantime, in the United States, Milton Babbitt had analyzed and studied the late works of Schoenberg and Webern and in 1947 had arrived at serialization of rhythm and dynamics, as well as pitch. None of the composers used precisely the same procedures, yet each, working individually, achieved results comparable with those of the others. One of the features of serialism—perhaps its most exciting facet—is the fact that no two composers used precisely the same procedures or produced music that sounds the same.

Messiaen

French composer Olivier Messiaen (b. 1908) is one of the twentieth century's most individualistic composers. Though he has adhered to no single style, his personal techniques of composition have remained more or less constant. Since the mid-1940s, Messiaen

Olivier Messiaen. *(© François Lochon/Gamma-Liaison.)*

has been highly influential as teacher and composer, but his teaching and his works have affected his students and other young composers differently.

Messiaen's parents were not musicians—his mother was poet Cécile Sauvage (1883–1927); his father, a professor of English, translated Shakespeare's works into French. The Messiaens encouraged Olivier but did not consider him a prodigy, even when, at age 9, he began to compose piano pieces. When Olivier was 11, he entered Paris Conservatoire. He was a brilliant student, winning first prizes in several subjects in successive years. His earliest published compositions, *Le banquet céleste* (The heavenly banquet; organ; 1928) and eight *Préludes* (pno.; 1929) were products of his student years but exhibit some features of his mature style.

In 1931 Messiaen was appointed organist at L'Église de la Sainte Trinité, Paris, and also began teaching at L'École Normale de Musique and the Schola Cantorum. During 1932–36, he and three other young composers formed *La Jeune France* (Young France), a group that aimed to promote modern French music. Among the significant works Messiaen created in the 1930s are *La nativité du Seigneur* (The Nativity of the Lord; organ; 1935) and two song cycles written for his wife, violinist Claire Delbos (1910–1959), *Poèmes pour Mi* (Poems for "Mi"; vc., pno.; 1936) and *Chants de terre et de ciel* (Songs of earth and sky; 1938).

During World War II, Messiaen was captured and held prisoner at Görlitz, Silesia. There he composed *Quatuor pour le fin du temps* (Quartet for the end of time; vln., vcl., cl., pno.; 1940), which he and three other prisoners performed at Stalag VIIIA in January 1941. Later that year Messiaen was repatriated and resumed his position at Trinité. In 1942 he was appointed professor of harmony at Paris Conservatoire; the following year he began teaching semiprivate classes in analysis at the home of Guy-Bernard Delapierre, whom he had met at prison camp. Pierre Boulez (b. 1925), Yvette Grimaud (b. 1920), and Yvonne Loriod (b. 1924) were among the young composers attending those seminars. Messiaen was not teaching serial techniques, so some of his pupils went to Leibowitz for private lessons in serial music. Leibowitz, who had studied with Schoenberg and Webern, was the chief exponent of twelve-tone music in France in the 1940s.

Messiaen's semiprivate teaching ceased when he was appointed professor of analysis and rhythm at Paris Conservatoire in 1947. Though the Conservatoire was aware that Messiaen was becoming an important influence in avant-garde music after 1945 and recognized his compositional talents, not until 1966 was he named professor of composition there. He was an excellent teacher, thorough in analyzing works from all historical periods. He did not found a school of composition, for he encouraged his students to be individualistic in their writing, and they heeded his advice. None of them copied his style. Commencing in 1947, Messiaen began to teach outside France for short periods and to lecture as a composer—in Darmstadt, Budapešt, America, and elsewhere.

Messiaen's religious philosophies and the Roman Catholic faith have always been extremely important to him and have colored many of his compositions. He has set some Biblical texts and has sought to express musically the meaning of others. He has written vocal lines in the style of psalm tones, combined melodic motives in the manner of centonization, followed the formal patterns of chants in some of his works, and used phrases of music and texts of liturgical chants as basis for or within compositions. His eight-movement *Quatuor pour le fin du temps* depicts events of the Apocalypse, and in the two very slow movements (fifth and eighth) praises the eternity and immortality of Jesus. The two excellent piano works that followed the quartet are also deeply religious. *Visions de l'amen* (Amen visions; 2 pnos.; 1943) has seven sections, all concerning "amen." The composition thoroughly explores all registers of the keyboard. *Vingt regards sur l'enfant Jésus* (Twenty contemplations of the infant Jesus; 1944) comprises, as the title indicates, 20 movements that express contemplations of the infant Jesus by various spiritual and human beings and symbolic or immaterial entities: God, Holy Spirit, angels, Mary, Wise Men, the Star, the Cross, Time, and others.

In 1942 Messiaen explained the characteristics of his musical style up to that point in *Technique de mon langage musical* (Technique of my musical language), which he illustrated with examples from his compositions. Perhaps the most unusual characteristic of his music is his treatment of rhythm. Frequently, he has referred to himself as composer and rhythmician. While a student, he became interested in the rhythms of ancient Greek poetry, then studied the thirteenth-century treatise *Saṅgīta-Ratnākara* (Ocean of Music) in which theorist Sārṅgadeva listed and discussed the 120 *desī-tālas* (provincial rhythms) used in Hindu music. Both kinds of rhythms found permanent places in Messiaen's compositional style. In some works, he identified the unusual rhythms he used, e.g., the Greek Cretic pattern ♩ ♪ ♩ and the Hindu *râgavardhana* pattern ♫♩♫ ♩. in *Couleurs de la cité céleste* (Colors of the heavenly city; pno., winds, perc.; 1963). For Messiaen, much of the time, rhythm amounted to an accumulation of durations rather than a division of time into equal parts. Many of his works are ametrical, with barlines placed only to indicate phrasing; probably, this is another influence of plainchant. Sometimes he used barlines as in measures but without meter signatures. In those instances, the performer relies on a basic unit of beat, comparable with the idea of the *chronos protos* (single beat) of the ancient Greeks.

(a)   (b)   (c)

Example 26.1 Examples of rhythmic patterns altered by means of added values at the place in the measure marked with +: (*a*) short note added; (*b*) short rest inserted; (*c*) note lengthened in value.

(a)   (b)

(c)   (d)

(e)

Example 26.2 Some types of augmentation and diminution used by Messiaen: (*a*) inexact or uneven augmentation; (*b*) cumulative augmentation; (*c*) augmentation by one-fourth of original note value; (*d*) augmentation by one-half of original note value; (*e*) diminution by three-fourths of original value.

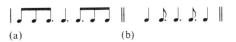

(a)   (b)

Example 26.3 Rhythmic palindromes.

Messiaen altered rhythmic patterns by means of added values, i.e., by adding a short note, inserting a short rest, or lengthening the value of one of the notes (ex. 26.1). Augmentation or diminution of rhythms was effected by means other than doubling or halving values. The augmentation or diminution might be uneven or cumulative (ex. 26.2a, b), or it might be brought about by increasing or diminishing all notes proportionately, e.g., by adding or subtracting a quarter, or a half, or three-fourths of a note's value (ex. 26.2c, d, e).

Messiaen used nonretrogradable rhythms, or rhythmic palindromes, also (ex. 26.3). These are rhythmic patterns designed so that they read the same backward and forward. They are comparable with word or phrase palindromes, such as "kayak"; "Madam, I'm Adam"; or, "able was I ere I saw Elba."

Another contrivance Messiaen used is rhythmic ostinato, which he termed "rhythmic pedal." This is identical with the device of isorhythm used by Machaut and other late Medieval and early Renaissance composers. In *"Liturgie de cristal,"* the first movement of *Quatuor pour le fin du temps,* Messiaen used a combination of melodic and rhythmic ostinati that do not coincide, a procedure similar to Machaut's use of *color* and *talea* in isorhythm (see Ch. 8). There is isorhythm in the first movement of Messiaen's *Turangalîla-symphonie* (1946–48), also. Of course, the combination of different rhythmic pedals in several voices creates polyrhythm, as does also the rhythmic canon that Messiaen sometimes uses.

Still another device used by Messiaen is rhythmic interversion. He arranged note values "chromatically" in order of duration and numbered them, as though forming a row. Then, commencing at the center of that arrangement, he took numbers in order from each side to form the first interverted row (table 26.1). Succeeding interversions were formed in the

Table 26.1 Interversion Permutation Process

Original Series:	12	11	10	9	8	7	6	5	4	3	2	1
Interversion I:	6	7	5	8	4	9	3	10	2	11	1	12
Interversion II:	3	9	10	4	2	8	11	5	1	7	12	6
Interversion III:	11	8	5	2	1	4	7	10	12	9	6	3
Interversion IV:	7	4	10	1	12	2	9	5	6	8	3	11

Note: This is only the first part of the matrix that can be constructed. It can be carried through ten interversions, and the tenth one produces a duplicate of the Original Series. Messiaen applied this process to a Series of duration in *Île de feu II*.

same manner. Such interversion is limited, for the tenth permutation (interversion) reproduces the original rhythmic row. Also, in the third and eighth columns of the rhythm grid two rhythmic values alternate.

Messiaen's melodies were strongly influenced by plainchant and folk song, particularly Russian folk song, which are modal and evidence use of centonization technique. Instead of relying on Greek or ecclesiastical modes, or on pentatonic and whole-tone scales, Messiaen invented his own modal scale patterns, containing six, eight, nine, or ten pitches per

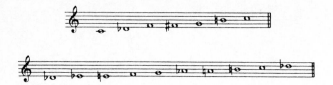

Example 26.4 Two of the modal scale patterns Messiaen invented for use in his music. (© *by Alphonse Leduc Paris, France, owners and publishers for all countries.*)

Example 26.5 Resonance chords of the sort Messiaen used.

Example 26.6 Three rhythmic neumes, one neume per "measure," used by Messiaen in *Neumes rhythmiques*. (*Source: Olivier Messiaen,* Neumes rhythmiques, *Durand Publishers, Paris, France.*)

octave, with tones and semitones arranged in various combinations (ex. 26.4). He called these "modes of limited transposition" for the obvious reason that after a few transpositions pitches recur. Messiaen did not limit himself to his modes but used major and minor scales, too. Messiaen's modes of limited transposition are counterparts to his palindromic (nonretrogradable) rhythms. The rhythms present horizontally what transposition of the modes realizes vertically. Messiaen stated that another complementary relationship exists between his rhythms with added values and chords with added notes. For him, these complementary relationships possessed "the charm of impossibilities."

Where harmonies are concerned, Messiaen stated that he envisions colors as he writes or hears harmonies. This accounts for some of the complex chords that he has written. Certain aggregations of pitches, designed as "resonance chords," include several overtones of a fundamental pitch—the overtones Messaien said he hears as "natural resonance of a sounding body." He uses these prisms in sound to produce what he terms "rainbows," or "stained-glass window" effects (ex. 26.5). Messiaen makes considerable use of the added sixth and the augmented fourth (the tritone). He stated that this was influenced by some music of Debussy and Musorgsky.

Timbres were varied by using many different percussion instruments, or new instruments such as ondes Martenot (see Insight, "Theremin and Ondes Martenot"), or by including transcribed birdsongs. Later, in some vocal music, the text contains phonemes or vocalized sounds instead of actual words, e.g., in *Cinq rechants* (Five songs reset; chorus; 1949).

During 1949–52 Messiaen ventured into serialism and wrote some experimental music that proved to be influential: *Cantéyodjayâ* (Song with *djayâ* refrains; pno.; 1948) and *Quatre études de rythme* (Four rhythmic studies; pno.; 1949–50). A passage in *Cantéyodjayâ* is three-voice polyphony with each voice in its own mode and each pitch in each mode assigned a specific duration and dynamic level. This was a move toward **total serialism,** along lines explored by Milton Babbitt in America two years earlier. (Total serialism is the application of the rules of serial composition to all possible musical parameters.)

Messiaen carried the principle of serialization further in *Quatre études de rythme*. In one of the études, *Neumes rythmiques* (Rhythmic neumes; 1949), strophes constructed of rhythmic neumes alternate with two refrains. The neumes (name derived from plainchant neumes) are short rhythmic groups with structured pitches and intensities (ex. 26.6). Another of the études, *Mode de valeurs et d'intensités* (Mode of values and intensities; 1949), is a three-voice piece in which the mode in each voice contains all 12 pitches of the chromatic scale, and each pitch has an assigned constant duration, register, and articulation.

Theremin and Ondes Martenot

The theremin and ondes Martenot are purely electronic monophonic instruments—electronic oscillators generate the tones. An **oscillator** is a device (or circuit) capable of producing an alternating current or wave form. An oscillator may have a fixed frequency, or variable frequency, producing different pitches in response to a keyboard or other pitch-designating device. Both theremin and ondes Martenot use two supersonic oscillators, one fixed and one variable, and a tone is produced by the heterodyne action of the two oscillators. (To **heterodyne** is to combine radio oscillations in a manner that results in the production of beats whose frequency is the difference, or the sum, of the frequencies of the oscillators. In other words, pitches are produced as either difference tones or summation tones, not directly generated.) The resulting pitch is amplified and emitted from the instrument's loudspeaker. However, the manner of activating tone production differs in the two instruments.

The theremin, originally called "aetherophone," was invented c. 1920 by Léon Thérémin (b. 1896), a Franco-Russian physicist working in Petrograd, and was first used in an orchestral work by Russian composer Andrei Pashchenko in 1924. The theremin is unique in that the performer does not actually touch any part of it to produce tones. The instrument's variable frequency oscillator is connected to an antenna (a metal rod) that projects vertically from the instrument. The frequency of the pitch produced and emitted from the instrument's speaker depends on the proximity of the player's hand to that antenna. Pitch changes are caused by moving the hand back and forth and varying its distance from the antenna. The player controls volume by moving the left hand in relation to a metal loop on the instrument. Different timbres are available, selected by manipulating controls governing a system of filters that vary the harmonics (fig. 26.3).

The ondes Martenot (also called *ondes musicales,* musical waves) was invented in Paris c. 1928 by Maurice Martenot (1898–1980). The instrument is equipped with a seven-octave keyboard—a separate unit from the speaker cabinet—that controls the frequency of the variable oscillator. The player's right hand operates the keyboard but can produce only one pitch at a time; if the player depresses more than one key, as in a dyad or chord, only the lowest pitch sounds. Each key can be slightly moved laterally to create a vibrato (cf., clavichord *Bebung*). A wide glissando sweep is produced by an alternative method of tone production—the player moves a finger ring that is attached to a metal ribbon, and the sliding ribbon controls the frequency. The player's left hand varies the dynamics and timbres by manipulating switches that control filters (fig. 26.4).

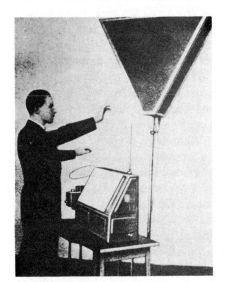

Figure 26.3 L. Theremin with a theremin.

Figure 26.4 John Morton with his ondes Martenot.

But *Mode de valeurs . . .* is *not* a serial piece. The preface to the work explains its structure. The other rhythmic études, *Île de feu I* and *Île de feu II* (Isle of fire I, II; 1950), have rhythmic interversion and rhythm-pitch associations but incorporate only a few assigned intensities and kinds of attack.

In only one piece did Messiaen use the conventional matrix (or grid) pattern of twelve-tone serialism, *Pièce en trio I* (Trio piece I) in *Livre d'Orgue* (Organ Book; 1951). Like Bach's trio sonatas for organ, the trio consists of the two manuals and the pedalboard of the organ. The principal melody is in the pedals. A unique quality in Messiaen's serial music is its ability to retain a sense of modality, even when all 12 pitches of the chromatic scale are present. This is particularly apparent in *Pièce en trio I* and may be due to Messiaen's emphasis on the tritone. Some aspects of serial technique appear in *Messe de la Pentecôte* (Pentecost Mass; 1950), an organ Mass intended for his use at church. Actually, that Mass is a summation of all of Messiaen's compositional techniques up to 1950. Though Messiaen did not pursue serialism in his own music beyond a few years of experimentation, his nonserial *Mode de valeurs . . .* greatly influenced the work of some of his pupils and young colleagues. Karlheinz Stockhausen, Karel Goeyvaerts, Michel Fano, and Pierre Boulez all wrote piano pieces incorporating procedures directly related to Messiaen's works.

Near the end of those years of experimentation, Messiaen collaborated with Pierre Henry in creating a piece of electronic music: *Timbres-durées* (Timbres-durations; tape; 1952). Messiaen has not composed another. The association between sound and duration in *Timbres-durées* is presented through percussion and water sounds.

From his youth, Messiaen has been interested in birdsong. He is a member of several ornithological societies and has collected and transcribed hundreds of birdsongs. (Ornithology is the branch of zoology dealing with birds.) He first included birdsongs in his music in *Quatuor pour le fin du temps*. Since 1950, they have become an integral part of many of his compositions. His principal works based chiefly on birdsongs are *Réveil des oiseaux* (Awakening of birds; pno., orch.; 1953), *Oiseaux exotiques* (Exotic birds; pno., winds, perc.; 1955–56), *Catalogue d'oiseaux* (Catalog of birds; pno.; 1959), and *La fauvette des jardins* (The garden warbler; pno.; 1970). Yvonne Loriod, who became Messiaen's second wife, was piano soloist in the première of all of those works. *Oiseaux exotiques* is a collage or counterpoint of approximately 40 birdsongs (all identified) from India, China, Malaysia, and North and South America with which Messiaen at times combined authentic Greek and Hindu rhythms. Harmony was added principally to simulate original timbres; in some sections, however, the Greek and Hindu rhythms superimposed on the birdsongs are assigned to nonpitched percussion instruments (side drum, wood block, gong and tamtam, temple blocks). *Oiseaux exotiques* strongly resembles a piano concerto whose form is an overall arch with two main sections. Each main section commences with a *tutti* and continues with subsections that alternately feature soloist and ensemble. The last two subsections are, respectively, a piano cadenza and a coda that is an abridged version of the introduction.

Color figures prominently in many of Messiaen's compositions. The large orchestra for *Chronochromie* (The color of time; 1960), one of his few works without piano, uses a gamelan-type pitched percussion section. Pitches are less important to the composition than durations and colors. Formally, the work follows the strophe-antistrophe-epode structure of Greek poetry and is in seven parts, not clearly separated. With the exception of *Chronochromie* and *Sept Haïkaï* (Seven Haiku poems; small orch.; 1962), Messiaen's works of the 1960s have religious connotations. In addition to Christian symbolism and actual Gregorian chant melodies, the compositions contain birdsongs, color-chords, and Hindu and Greek rhythmic patterns. In *Couleurs de la cité céleste* (Colors of the celestial city; 1963), for chamber ensemble comprising piano, 13 winds, and 7 percussion, Messiaen wrote in the score the colors he associated with the chords. For *Méditations sur le mystère de la Sainte Trinité* (Meditations on the mystery of the Holy Trinity; organ; 1969; DWMA229), Messiaen created a communicable musical language based on an alphabet of pitches. He began with the German pitch associations A through H (B = B♭; H = B♮), then gave letter names to pitches in other registers and assigned a fixed duration to each pitch used in forming words (ex. 26.7).

His message is conveyed through musical nouns, adjectives, and verbs only; special motivic formulas connote "God," "to be," and "to have." Though Messiaen supplies all the information for deciphering the musical language, the true message is still concealed, as is the mystery of the Holy Trinity.

In the 1970s, Messiaen produced two major works: *Des canyons aux étoiles* (From the canyons to the stars; pno., orch.; 1971–74), a 12-movement suite that commences in a desert in Utah and concludes with a combination of Zion Park and the Celestial City; and the opera *Saint François d'Assise* (Saint Francis of Assisi; 1975–83; perf. November 1983). Actually, Messiaen wrote all of the music for the opera in 1975–79 and orchestrated it in 1979–83. The opera is in eight Franciscan scenes presented in three Acts. It requires nine soloists (all male except the angel, a soprano), a ten-part chorus of 150, and an orchestra of 120 players, with very large wind and percussion sections and three ondes Martenots. Each major character has a special theme, and often the vocal solo lines resemble modal chant. Color is important—Messiaen specified the colors for costumes, and colored lighting plays a significant part in the production, especially in the last Act, which concerns the transplanting of Christ's wounds to Francis and the latter's death and resurrection. In the final scene, after Francis's body is carried off the stage, intense and dazzling light fills the place where it had lain, and the orchestra and chorus present a resurrection chorale that ends in C major. The powerful C-major conclusion of the opera reminds one of Haydn's great C-major chord on the word "light" in the *The Creation.*

Almut Rössler performed Messiaen's *Livre du saint sacrement* (Book of the blessed sacrament; organ; 1984–85) in its world première on 1 July 1986 in Detroit, Michigan, in Messiaen's presence (fig. 26.2). *Livre du saint sacrement* comprises 18 movements of various lengths. The first 4 movements represent acts of adoration before the hidden God, the unseen Christ; movement 5 concerns the Nativity, and movements 6–11 deal with events in Jesus's life and with his words. In movements 12 ("The Transubstantiation") through 16 ("Prayer after Communion") Messiaen refers to the Communion sacrament. Movement 17 ("The Presence multipled") portrays Christ's eternal presence in all consecrated hosts on earth. *Livre du saint sacrement* concludes with *Offrande et Alleluia final* (Offering and final Alleluia), an offering to God of the prayers of all the saints, presented on the Cornet of the Positif of the organ, and a brilliant, joyous toccata that includes passages of alleluias. For each movement Messiaen provided a quotation that is the key to what he said musically— quotations from *The Bible* (Jerusalem Bible version), the Roman liturgy, prayers of St. Thomas Aquinas and St. Bonaventure, Kempis's *Imitation of Christ,* and Marmion's *Christ in His Mysteries.* In addition,

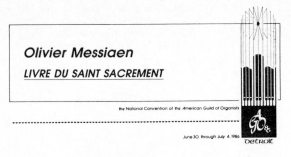

Olivier Messiaen
LIVRE DU SAINT SACREMENT

the National Convention of the American Guild of Organists

June 30 through July 4, 1986

DETROIT

For Organ

World Premier Performance
by
Almut Rössler

in the presence of the composer

The Merton S. Rice Memorial Organ
Metropolitan Methodist Church
July 1, 1986 — 8:30 p.m.
July 3, 1986 — 8:00 p.m.

the National Convention of the American Guild of Organists
Detroit, Michigan

Figure 26.2 Cover of program from world première of Messiaen's *Livre du saint sacrement. (Copyright 1986 by the American Guild of Organists. Reprinted by permission of the American Organist magazine.)*

Messiaen wrote lengthy program notes for the work. All characteristic features of Messiaen's music are present in *Livre du saint sacrement,* including plainsong and liturgical references, birdsongs, color chords (rainbow-hued, stained-glass window), and rhythmic precision. The birds whose songs appear in this composition are found in Israel; Messiaen notated the birdsongs there.

According to Messiaen, all of his music is an expression of his faith, just as J. S. Bach's music was, and he stated that he rejoiced whenever, during the homily of a Mass, the celebrant priest at Trinité referred to his works as interpreting the message of the Service. Messiaen divides music into three basic categories. From the lowest level to the highest, these are: (1) liturgical music, which consists solely of plainsong (e.g., Gregorian chant); (2) religious music, which comprises all sacred music other than chant; and (3) "Sound-color and dazzlement" music—music

whose colors merge into dazzling light like that mentioned in Revelation and carry a person to unprecedented heights in an approach to true Faith. Messiaen's music is an individually conceived composite of many styles and many cultures. The full impact of his influence may not be realized for another half century. Certainly he is one of the twentieth century's greatest composers.

France — *Musique concrète*

Musique concrète (concrete music) was the term Pierre Schaeffer (b. 1910) used to describe music he composed directly on disc or tape by recording natural sounds that he manipulated by means of reversal, changes of speed, or other editing. The term was intended to denote that the sounds were from natural (concrete) sources and that the compositions were created directly on tape (concretely) rather than through notation that had to be interpreted by performers. Schaeffer, who invented the technique in 1948, was a telecommunications engineer. He had worked at Radiodiffusion Française and in 1942 helped found the Studio d'Essai, which became the center for the Resistance movement in French radio during World War II.

At first Schaeffer experimented by manipulating disc recordings (varying speeds, altering the grooves, playing sections backward) but when the tape recorder became readily available, he worked with magnetic tape. In 1948 he created the first *musique concrète* compositions: *Étude violette* (Violet study), *Étude au piano* (Study with piano), *Étude aux chemins de fer* (Study with railroads), and others with similar titles. Then Schaeffer began to share his techniques and to collaborate with others, notably, Pierre Henry (b. 1927). Together, Schaeffer and Henry prepared *musique concrète* for ballet, radio, pantomime, and for the opera *Orphée 53* (Orpheus 1953). One of their collaborations is *Symphonie pour un homme seul* (Symphony for one man; 1950, rev. 1953), whose 12 short movements were created from sounds made by the human body. In the 1960s, Schaeffer devoted his time to teaching electronic techniques and to writing about them rather than to composing; in 1968 he was appointed professor of electronic composition at Paris Conservatoire.

Pierre Henry joined the Groupe de Recherche de Musique Concrète (Group for research in *musique concrète*) in 1951 and headed the Groupe in 1952–58. Some of Henry's early *musique concrète* pieces consisted mainly of sounds from percussion instruments and prepared piano. While working with the Groupe, he formulated an index of sounds of all kinds that could be used in creating music on tape. In 1952 he prepared *musique concrète* for the film *Astrologie* (Astrology), the first electronic music compositions used in commercial cinema in France.

When Henry left the Groupe in 1958, he and Jean Baronnet established the Apsone-Cabasse Studio, the first private electronic music studio in France. Then Henry no longer restricted his compositions to natural sounds but began to combine *concrète* and purely electronic techniques. The first of his works to explore such a synthesis were aptly titled *Coexistence* (1959) and *Investigations* (1959). Henry has prepared electronic music for several Béjart ballets, and since 1964 he has composed several religious works, including Masses. *La messe de Liverpool* (Mass for Liverpool; 1967–68), commissioned for the consecration of the Cathedral of Christ the King, was created from sounds produced by a voice, a 'cello, a flute, and synthesized sounds. Though much of the music is complex, the text is intelligible. *L'apocalypse de Jean* (The apocalypse of John; 1968) is a dense polyphony of electronic sounds, but the voice of the narrator reading the Biblical text comes through clearly.

In the 1970s, Henry tried a variety of approaches to recorded composition. For *Gymkhana* (1970), he reverted to use of sounds produced by conventional instruments. Then he experimented with lighting effects and created audiovisual works, e.g., *Mise en musique du corticolart* (Cortex art set to music; 1971), which attempts to depict brain waves as electronic sound and light. Another of Henry's large-scale works is *La dixième* (The tenth; 1973), based on electronic reproduction and manipulation of material borrowed from Beethoven's nine symphonies.

Boulez

Pierre Boulez, a pianist, enrolled in Messiaen's harmony class at Paris Conservatoire in 1942. At the same time, he arranged for private lessons in counterpoint from Andrée Vaurabourg (1894–1980),

Pierre Boulez. *(Wide World Photos.)*

Arthur Honegger's wife. Boulez became a superb analyst and a fine composer. He regarded music from a scientific viewpoint and was firmly convinced of the necessity for atonality. Consequently, when Leibowitz offered instruction in Schoenberg's serial techniques, Boulez eagerly joined the class. After the death of Schoenberg, Boulez publicly decried Schoenberg's failure to develop serialism to its fullest and affirmed that Webern was the serialist composer to emulate.

Boulez has withdrawn all of his earliest works except Piano Sonata No. 1 (1946) and *Sonatine* (fl., pno.; 1946). *Sonatine,* a single movement more than 500 measures long, is divided into sections comparable with those of a four-movement sonata. The row, characterized by tritones, is presented in its entirety by flute. The arrangement of pitches in the row gave rise to melodic motives or cells that Boulez treated as thematic material; such motivic treatment is a feature of many of his works. The piano part seems to go its own way rather than support the flute or provide counterpoint related to it, though there are some instances of intervallic and rhythmic imitation.

By 1948 Boulez was recognized as the leader of the young serialist composers working in Paris. That year he wrote Piano Sonata No. 2 and provided the music for a radio broadcast of René Char's (1907–88) play *Le soleil des eaux* (The sunlight of the waters). In 1950 Boulez transformed the play music into a cantata for three soloists, chorus, and chamber orchestra. Piano Sonata No. 2, modeled on Beethoven's Classical four-movement sonatas, comprises a sonata-form first movement, a slow two-part second movement, a scherzo with three trios, and finale. Two different pitch series were used, one row for movements 1 and 3, another for movements 2 and 4. In addition, the finale concludes with a section based on the pitches H-C-A-B, in homage to Bach. Though serial, the rows are broken into segments and the music relies heavily on motivic cells. Basically, the texture is three- and four-voice. The piano is treated percussively, and the mood of much of the sonata is violent.

For *Structures, livre 1* (Structures, book 1; 2 pnos.; 1952), Boulez borrowed the pitch series from Messiaen's *Mode de valeurs et d'intensités,* constructed a matrix denoting the various transpositions of the row, and serialized attacks and dynamics. Then he assigned registers to the pitches and arranged tempo changes as palindromes. Though the musical elements are well organized, Boulez carefully mixed them so that his scheme is not easily recognized. Of the three pieces in the volume (labeled *Ia, Ib,* and *Ic*), *Ib* was composed last and is extremely complex.

Boulez's best-known composition, and one that is probably his most expressive musically, is *Le marteau sans maître* (The hammer without a master; 1952–54, rev. 1957). The work is in nine short movements, for alto voice and a chamber ensemble composed of alto flute, viola, guitar, vibraphone, xylorimba, and unpitched percussion. Boulez's choice of instrumentation was prompted by some relationships between them: Voice and flute are in alto range and produce sounds by means of breath; alto flute and viola can sustain tones; viola played *pizzicato* has affinity with guitar; and so on. The settings of three verses by Char that lie at the heart of the work (mvts. 3, 5, 6) generated the other movements that complement them. The ninth movement is essentially a variation of the fifth but recalls short passages from the other two vocal movements. The remaining movements are instrumental: first and seventh serve as prelude and

postlude to the third (DWMA230); second, fourth, and eighth are commentaries on the sixth. With the exception of movements 6 and 9, which use all performing resources, no two movements are scored the same. The vocal line contains wide intervals, grace notes, melismas, glissandos, and sometimes is *Sprechstimme.* The flute part becomes virtuosic at times, and includes harmonics and fluttertonguing.

It is important to realize, when analyzing Boulez's compositions, that he did not regard a series as an order of succession but considered it source material capable of providing small motivic cells and countless possiblities for treatment of a basic idea. He stated that a series could be handled strictly, or it might be carefully contrived so that it actually allowed the composer considerable freedom. Most often, he chose to do the latter.

Boulez's aim was to expand musical composition perpetually. With this in mind, he created some works that allow the performer(s) a degree of choice in what is played. Piano Sonata No. 3 (1955–57) has five movements, to be played in any order. There are choices to be made within the movements, too. For example, the movement named *Trope* is supplied with interpolations (tropes) that, at the discretion of the performer, may be performed or omitted. (Cf., Ch. 4, tropes.)

Boulez's next contribution to serialism was the idea of chord multiplication. For example, a chord can be squared (multiplied by itself) by transposing it to the level of each of its pitches and then combining all of the small chords to form one large new one (ex. 26.8). The same procedure is used to multiply one chord by another chord. Multiplied chords appear in the *Constellation-Miroir* movement of Piano Sonata No. 3.

Several of Boulez's works were influenced by poetry or philosophies of poets. Among these are *Pli selon pli* (Fold by fold; sop., orch; 1957–62), an unfolding of Mallarmé's esthetic philosophies, and *e. e. cummings ist der Dichter* (e. e. cummings is the poet; 1970–76), a chamber cantata for 16 voices and 24 instruments. *Messagesquisse* (1977), for 'cello solo and an ensemble of six 'cellos, is based on pitches derived from the name Sacher (Paul Sacher, Swiss conductor, b. 1906). *Rituel* (Ritual; orch; 1974–75) was written

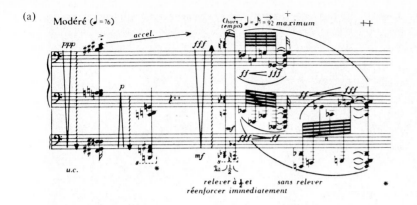

(a) Modéré (♩=76)

(b)

Example 26.8 (*a*) Chord multiplication as used by Boulez in *Blocs I* of *Constellation-Miroir:* The four pitches of the row between the small arrows form the chord + and that chord squared forms the chord + +. (*b*) The process of chord multiplication: To determine the square of a chord, transpose the chord to the tonal level of each of its component pitches, and form a chord by combining the pitches of all transpositions. *(From Paul Griffiths,* Boulez. *Copyright © 1978 Oxford University Press, Oxford, England. Reprinted by permission.)*

as an epitaph for Italian conductor Bruno Maderna (1920–73). The orchestra is divided into eight ensembles, each accompanied by unpitched percussion: solo oboe; clarinet duo; flute trio; violin quartet; woodwind quintet; string sextet; woodwind septet; 14 brass players. The piece commences with oboe and tabla, and gradually adds ensembles until, in the coda, the entire orchestra is involved. The tritone figures prominently in the pitch series on which *Rituel* is based.

Around 1975 Boulez founded the Institut de Recherche et de Coordination Acoustique/Musique, located in the center of Paris, "next door and underground" from the Pompidou museum for contemporary art. As director of the Institut, which the French government generously subsidizes, Boulez has at his disposal the most advanced and extensive studios for electronic computer-generated music in the world.

Germany — Electronic Music

In Germany, developments in electronic music were taking place independently of and almost simultaneously with those in France. Herbert Eimert (1897–1972), composer and theorist, led the German movement. While studying at Cologne Conservatory (1919–24), Eimert became interested in atonal music. Working independently—having no contact with Schoenberg and Webern—Eimert wrote *Atonale Musiklehre* (Atonal music textbook; 1923) in which

he systematically described dodecaphonic technique and supplied music examples illustrating his principles. He then composed five twelve-tone pieces for string quartet (*Five Pieces;* 1923–25). Eimert continued to work with serial techniques, using them in his ballet *Der weisse Schwan* (The white swan; 1926) for flute, saxophone, and mechanical instruments.

From 1927 until the war, Eimert worked in radio broadcasting at Cologne; in 1945 he resumed that work at Westdeutscher Rundfunk (West German Radio). There, in 1951, he founded the Studio für Elektronische Musik and served as its director until 1962. His *Vier Stücke* (Four pieces; tape; 1952–53) are among the earliest compositions created from purely synthetic sounds. Eimert continued to compose electronic works on tape and directly influenced the career of Stockhausen and stimulated the work of other young avant-garde composers. From 1965 to 1971 Eimert taught electronic music at Cologne Hochschule für Musik. He published several texts on twelve-tone music, and, with Stockhausen, edited the journal *Die Riehe* (The Row).

Stockhausen

While a student at University of Cologne, Stockhausen became interested in contemporary music and, encouraged by Eimert, attended Messiaen's summer class at Darmstadt in 1951. There he met Karel

Karlheinz Stockhausen. *(Wide World Photos.)*

Goeyvaerts and Luigi Nono, and, like them, was influenced by Messiaen's *Quatre études de rythme,* especially *Mode de valeurs et d'intensités.* When Stockhausen returned to Cologne, he composed *Kreuzspiel* (Crossplay; 1951), for piano, with oboe, bass clarinet, and three percussion instruments. In this piece, pitch, duration, and intensity are serialized; timbre is not. The title is derived from Stockhausen's treatment of register—he began at opposite ends of the instruments' available range, moved to the center, then crossed over, with crossplay of pitch register between instruments. An important feature of *Kreuzspiel* is Stockhausen's pointillistic treatment of the pitches—each note is an important point individually and is not related to a motive or a melody.

For a little over a year, Stockhausen studied with Messiaen in Paris. He became acquainted with Boulez and Schaeffer and worked in the *musique concrète*

studio. Stockhausen applied the same technique used in *Kreuzspiel* to groups or units of pitches, but at first he was disappointed in the results because the pieces seemed too thematic. One of those pieces was *Punkte* (Points; orch; 1952), which underwent three revisions before being performed in 1962. However, *Kontra-Punkte* (Counter-points; 1952, rev. 1953), for piano and nine conventional orchestral instruments, was performed successfully at Cologne in 1953 and was Stockhausen's first published composition. In this one-movement work, the antitheses of individual notes, temporal relationships, and timbres are resolved into homogeneity. "Counter-points" occur in this manner: (1) Stockhausen first presents single pitches (points) sounded by various individual instruments, and ultimately combines the first six pitches to form a chord (a counter-point) sounded by one instrument, the piano (ex. 26.9 a, c). (2) There is a counter-point of

Example 26.9 Stockhausen, *Kontra-Punkte*: (*a*) mm. 1–5, showing presentation of the Row in pointillistic style; (*b*) mm. 341–44, counterpoint of groups; (*c*) homogeneous resolution in the concluding measures of the piece. *(Copyright 1953 by Universal Edition (London) Ltd., London. Copyright renewed. All Rights Reserved. Used by permission of European American Music Distributors Corporation, sole U.S. and Canadian agent for Universal Edition London.)*

timbres. The instruments are arranged in six groups or families of related instruments; gradually, instruments drop out, until only the piano remains. (3) The pointillistic style found at the beginning of the piece gradually changes to a counterpoint of groups (ex. 26.9 b). After the successful performance of *Kontra-Punkte,* Stockhausen was recognized as the leader of the young avant-garde composers.

In 1953, Eimert invited Stockhausen to become codirector of the electronic music studio at Cologne. There, Stockhausen composed two *Elektronische Studien* (Electronic Studies) on single-track tape. The first of these, *Studie I* (1953; unpubl.), is built entirely from sine-wave sounds (pure frequency tones) organized serially. *Studie II* (1954) commences with **white noise** (all possible frequencies sounding simultaneously), then some of the sounds are gradually filtered out, until Stockhausen has isolated those he wants to use for structuring his composition. *Studie II* was the first electronic music composition to be published in score. Preparing scores for electronic music compositions gave rise to new kinds of musical notation involving graphic symbols (ex. 26.10).

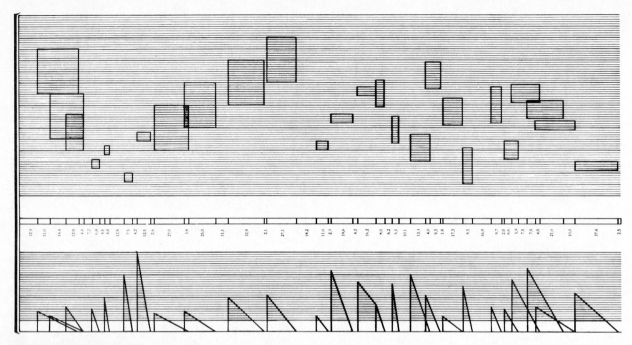

Example 26.10 Stockhausen: *Studie II*, page 14 of score.
(Copyright 1956 by Universal Edition (London) Ltd., London. Copyright renewed. All Rights Reserved. Used by permission of European American Music Distributors Corporation, sole U.S. and Canadian agent for Universal Edition London.)

Stockhausen composed music for conventional instruments even while experimenting with electronic music. In 1956 he wrote major works in both areas: *Zeitmasze* (Measures of time) for woodwind quintet and *Gesang der Jünglinge* (Song of the youths) on tape. *Zeitmasze* is concerned with tempos and durations and calls for the simultaneous performance of music written in different tempi. Stockhausen used this technique on a larger scale in *Gruppen* (Groups; 1955–57), written for three orchestras, each with its own conductor. With the score of that work he published a seating chart, detailing the arrangement of instruments in each of the orchestras and the placement of the orchestras on three sides of the audience in the performance hall.

From 1953 to 1956 Stockhausen studied phonetics, acoustics, and communications theory with Werner Meyer-Eppler at University of Bonn and became interested in using the sound of the human voice in electronic compositions. For *Gesang der Jünglinge,* he recorded a boy's treble voice reciting Bible verses from the apocrypha to the Book of Daniel, then manipulated the recorded words by splitting them into vowels and phonemes and duplicating them synthetically. Next, he rearranged the component parts of the words, forming synthetic words and literally garbling the text. The resultant word-sounds were mingled with and completely imbedded in purely electronic sounds. Stockhausen treated spoken words as pure sound and electronic sounds as speech in order to make them interchangeable. Finally, a mixture of electronic sounds, intelligible text excerpts, and manipulated text was recorded on five single-track tapes. (Later, Stockhausen rerecorded the composition on a single four-track tape.) The work was intended for performance in Cologne Cathedral, with the music to issue forth antiphonally from five groups of loudspeakers that were spatially separated. As Gabrieli had used *cori spezzati* in St. Mark's during the late Renaissance, so Stockhausen employed physical space as a component part of *Gesang der Jünglinge*. For the first time, space became an important element in electronic composition. In combining the human voice and electronic sounds, Stockhausen merged the techniques of the Parisian *musique concrète* and the Cologne electronic music studios. An additional factor in the merger was his belief that, in order to be truly expressive, music needed more than precisely regulated serialism.

In the sixth issue of *Die Riehe,* Stockhausen analyzed three compositions that combined the human voice with serialism and electronic or *musique concrète* techniques: *Gesang der Jünglinge,* Boulez's *Le marteau sans maître,* and Luigi Nono's *Il canto sospeso* (The suspended song). All were written in 1955–56, and each composer treated the voice differently. Nono's text is derived from letters of Resistance fighters.

Over the years, Stockhausen composed a series of *Klavierstücke* (Piano Pieces). *Klavierstücke* I–IV (1952–53) are complex and are extremely difficult rhythmically, especially because of the composer's insistence on rhythmic precision. Stockhausen recognized the problem, and *Klavierstücke* V–X (1954–55) are a little less demanding of the pianist. Stockhausen's use of the Fibonacci numbers series (1, 2, 3, 5, 8, 13, 21, 34, 55, etc.) is apparent in several of the *Klavierstücke;* he used that series in other compositions, too. *Klavierstück III* is an example—it contains 55 notes, uses 34 different pitches, and covers a range of 50 semitones ($3 + 5 + 8 + 13 + 21 = 50$). In *Klavierstück XI* (1956) the performer's choices determine the form of the piece. Stockhausen notated 19 musical "groups" and instructed the pianist to play them in random order, making spontaneous choices as the performance proceeds.

In 1957 Stockhausen began to teach composition at Darmstadt, and in 1963 he founded the Cologne Courses for New Music, the nucleus of the Cologne Institute for New Music. He was recognized internationally not only for his compositions but for his teaching, and he traveled widely in response to invitations to lecture or to teach. Trips to Japan influenced several of his works. *Telemusik* (1966), prepared on four-track tape in Tokyo's NHK radio studios, combines folk music of various countries with electronically produced sounds. The composition is designed in 32 sections, each announced by the sounding of an Oriental temple instrument, as is customary in the Japanese Noh drama. The number of sections associated with each of the Oriental instruments corresponds with the Fibonacci numbers series: 13, 8, 5, 3, 2, 1. *Mantra* (1969–70; 2 pianos, woodblock, crotales, and 2 ring modulators for sine tones) is also concerned with a ritual of the Japanese Noh drama. A **mantra** is a special melodic formula associated with ritual. *Mantra* is Stockhausen's first composition to be based on a specific melodic formula.

In the 1970s, Stockhausen began writing a cycle of seven operas, under the common title *Licht* (Light), and has completed *Donnerstag aus Licht* (Thursday from Light; 1977–80), *Samstag aus Licht* (Saturday from Light; 1981–83), and *Montag aus Licht* (Monday from Light; 1984–86). The cycle is intended to contain borrowings from various cultures, especially exotic ones, and to be representative of the entire world. In its wideness of scope, the cycle has been likened to Wagner's *Der Ring . . .,* but in sound and techniques Stockhausen's operas are quite different from Wagnerian music drama. Those that have been completed resemble some of the religious theatrical works of Japan and Indonesia.

Stockhausen wants to write music that is representative of the entire universe—the cosmos and all of life within it. One of his endeavors to depict activity outside the plant Earth is *Sterrnklang* (Starsounds; 1971), which is park music designed for five groups of performers. As names of stars or constellations are called out by the director, a group looks at the night sky and is supposed to read and realize (i.e., perform) the music of that star or constellation. Thus, in **aleatory** (chance) music, a connection may be made, through meditation and inspiration, with the music of the spheres about which Boethius and Plato wrote.

Music in America

Varèse

Though Edgard Varèse (1883–1965) was born in France, he spent most of his life in the United States and is usually regarded as an American composer. He was educated in science and technology in Turin and in music in Paris at the Schola Cantorum and Conservatoire. For several years he lived in Berlin, where, in 1912, he heard Schoenberg's *Pierrot Lunaire* and became interested in nonserial twelve-tone music. In

1913 Varèse moved back to Paris but left the majority of his manuscripts in storage in Berlin, and they were destroyed by fire. Reportedly, those early works, e.g., the symphonic poem *Bourgogne* (Burgundy; c. 1907), were Romantic in style. Around 1913–14, the musical styles of Debussy and Stravinsky interested him; Debussy's influence, particularly, is evident in Varèse's works written in the 1920s and 1930s.

When, by 1915, Varèse had not found a permanent position in Paris, he came to America. He was dissatisfied with the sounds produced by conventional means, sought new resources, and wanted new musical instruments. He seldom wrote for strings because he disliked vibrato. He never liked the term "music" and preferred to call his work "organized sound." His earliest published composition was *Amériques* (Americas; c. 1918–21). The work requires a huge orchestra with harp, two sets of timpani, and a siren, the latter replaced in 1929 by ondes Martenot. Varèse used sirens in his works to produce long, slow glissandos and could not achieve the precise effect he wanted by other means.

In the 1920s Varèse began writing for groups of percussion instruments and was especially interested in the effects he could obtain from nonpitched percussion. Representative of his pieces for winds and percussion are *Hyperprism* (1922–23; 9 winds, 7 percussionists) and *Integrales* (1924–25; 11 winds, 4 percussionists). Most of *Ionisation* (1929–31; 13 percussionists, pno.) is for unpitched instruments; only in the last several measures are definite pitches sounded.

For some time, Varèse had been wanting electronic instruments. He knew about Thérémin's invention of an electronic instrument variously called "aetherophone" and "theremin" (Insight, "Theremin and Ondes Martenot") and c. 1932 requested him to make two of them for use in a new composition, *Ecuatorial* (1932–34), setting a prayer from Popol Voh of Maya Quiché. However, when the composition was performed, two ondes Martenot were substituted for theremin. With electronic instruments Varèse was able to extend the range to e'''''.

After writing *Density 21.5* (1936) for Georges Barrère to play on his platinum flute, Varèse did not compose for a decade. During that time, he taught composition and orchestration in several schools and promoted performances of Renaissance and Baroque choral music in the United States. In 1947 his *Étude pour Espace* (Étude for space; chor., 2 pnos., perc.) appeared, then he lapsed into a compositional silence that lasted several years.

Around 1950 Varèse commenced another orchestral work but wanted to mingle new sonorities with those of conventional instruments. In 1953 an anonymous donor sent him an Ampex tape recorder, and with it he began to collect the sounds that he used in the tape portions of *Déserts* (c. 1950–54). He completed the tape portions of the piece in Pierre Schaeffer's studio at RTF in 1954, and the finished composition was broadcast via French radio later that year. It was the earliest major composition created on tape. According to Varèse, the title refers to all deserts—on earth, in space, in city streets, and in the minds of humans. The composition contrasts sounds of conventional instruments with tapes of real (i.e., not electronically generated or otherwise artificially produced) sounds that cannot be obtained from conventional musical instruments. The sounds on magnetic tape are on two channels, transmitted stereophonically, to convey to the listener a sense of spatial distribution. The contrast of timbres makes the piece a kind of alternating form: ABABABA, the A sections being performed on conventional instruments, and the B sections being taped organized sounds transmitted stereophonically. The first and last tape interpolations are organized sounds gathered from industrial sources (in factories) and electronically manipulated in various ways—filtered, transposed, mixed, transmuted, etc. Sounds for the second B section were produced by percussion ensemble. The sections become shorter, higher pitched, and more intense, until a climax is attained in the last two sections; then the music fades to a *pianissimo* conclusion. The piece is atonal but not serial. Despite the lack of recognizable thematic material, there is unity and continuity in the work, and the contrast of timbres is less stark than one would expect.

Working at Philips Research Laboratories in Eindhoven in 1957, Varèse created *Poème électronique* on three-track tape. The work was designed for performance in the Philips pavilion at the 1958 World Exhibition in Brussels. Spatial effects were obtained

Milton Babbitt. *(Courtesy of Milton Babbitt.)*

by transmitting the tape through many strategically placed loudspeakers, so that the listener was surrounded by sound. A control tape regulated special lighting effects that came from a variety of sources in the pavilion. *Poème électronique* was the last composition Varèse completed. Over the years since 1925, he began at least a half dozen other pieces, using conventional means of tone production, but never finished them. Among those works are *Nocturnal* (1961; completed by one of his students in 1973) and *Nocturnal II* (1961–65), both based on Anaïs Nin's *The House of Incest*. Of Varèse's output, only 14 complete pieces survive. He was highly respected by avant-garde composers and was influential through his desire for new sound sources and his writing for unpitched percussion instruments. He composed two of the earliest major compositions created on tape.

Babbitt

The interests of Milton Babbitt (b. 1916) lie in mathematics as well as in music; he has served on the music and mathematics faculties at Princeton University and has taught music at many schools. For Babbitt, arithmetic served as a compositional tool in structuring his works. At first, he was interested in the music of Stravinsky and Varèse, then was attracted by the serialism of Schoenberg and Webern.

Example 26.11 Combinatoriality in the Row Schoenberg used in *Variations* for orchestra: (*a*) Original Row; (*b*) Inversion, transposed down a minor third; (*c*) Retrograde Inversion of the transposition.

In studying their construction of tone rows, Babbitt found that in some of them the unordered six-note set in the first hexachord (the first six pitches) of the row could be inverted and transposed, or used retrograde and transposed, and still not duplicate any of the pitches in the original hexachord. Obviously, the same would be true of the unordered six-note set in the second hexachord of the original row (ex. 26.11). The hexachords from such rows could be combined in a variety of ways and still produce a complete dodecaphonic row. Not all rows have this special property, which Babbitt termed **combinatoriality.** Schoenberg used rows of this kind in *Klavierstück*, the *Violin Concerto*, and *Variations* for orchestra. Babbitt used the principle of combinatoriality and developed it extensively.

Babbitt's *Three Compositions for Piano,* No. 1 (1947; DWMA231) uses a row constructed so that it is **all-combinatorial,** i.e., a hexachord of the original row may be combined with its transposed inversion, retrograde, or retrograde-inversion to form a complete dodecaphonic series. In this piece, Babbitt serialized rhythm and dynamics independently of the pitch series. The serialization of rhythm was based on constancy of the 16th note, and he established a rhythmic row with the arrangement of 16th-note values in groups of 5, 1, 4, 2, thus forming a 5 1 4 2 series that could be manipulated (ex. 26.12). He devised a method of inverting the rhythm series by subtraction, in this case, by subtracting the numbers from 6. Thus, the inversion of his 5 1 4 2 series is 1 5 2 4, and a retrograde inversion is 4 2 5 1. *Three Compositions for Piano* provides the first real example of rhythmic serialization. Babbitt "transposed" rhythms by delaying them. *Three Compositions for Piano,* No. 1 contains six sections (marked off musically by rests or sustained pitches), the last of which is symmetrical with the first.

For his *Composition for Twelve Instruments* (1948), Babbitt devised a system of rhythm serialization closely related to the 12-note pitch series. He constructed a rhythmic counterpart to the chromatic scale of pitches—a chromatic scale of durations commencing with a small durational value and increasing each succeeding duration by that same amount, until 12 durations or time points were created. In other words, the rhythm series and pitch series are isomorphic—a set of 12 durations is operational, as well as 12-note pitch rows. Moreover, in this work, each of the 12 instruments has its own pitch series. In *All Set* (1957), for an eight-piece jazz ensemble, Babbitt combined an all-combinatorial set with jazzlike solos.

For some time, Babbitt had been interested in the possibilities of synthesizer as an aid to musical composition, primarily because it offered absolute control of all musical events—the kind of control he, as composer, wanted. The fact that the synthesizer could produce new sounds was of lesser importance. When, in the 1950s, he joined RCA as composer-consultant, he became the first composer to work with the Mark II synthesizer. With it he created *Composition for Synthesizer* (1961), his first totally synthesized composition. Next came *Vision and Prayer* (1961), a set-

Example 26.12 Babbitt's rhythmic row established for *Three Compositions for Piano,* No. 1.

ting of stanzas by Dylan Thomas, for soprano and synthesizer (tape). Other compositions using tape followed, including *Ensembles for Synthesizer* (1962–64); *Concerti* (1974; vln., small orch., tape); and *Ars combinatoria* (Combinatorial art; 1981).

Babbitt has not used any aspects of chance in composition or performance. His music is precise and should be performed with precision. He has indicated that he wants each of his compositions to be as much as it possibly can be; this accounts for the complexity of many of his works. He has become involved with synthesizer but has not limited his compositions to works on or including tape. In *Relata I* (1965), he wrote for a large orchestra, treating it as groups or families of timbres: four trios of woodwinds, three quartets of brass instruments, and two string sextets, one of them bowed, the other plucked. The polyphony of timbres richly enhances the serialism of that orchestral work. Another example of Babbitt's work with conventional sources is *A Solo Requiem* (1976–77; soprano, 2 pnos.), a setting of poetry by several authors, including Shakespeare and Dryden.

Among those who have been influenced by Babbitt are Peter Westergaard (b. 1931) and Charles Wuorinen (b. 1938). Some of Westergaard's pieces are quite economical, e.g., the *Quartet* (1960; vln., vibraphone, A cl., vcl.), in which the twelve-tone row governs the succession of pitches through all four lines of the polyphony. In *Variations for Six Players* (1963), he directs the performers to match sonorities through the method of attack used (e.g., violin harmonic matches glockenspiel tone). His other works include a cycle of cantatas and the chamber opera *Mr. and Mrs. Discobbolos* (1965).

Wuorinen, a virtuoso pianist and brilliant composer, has written well over 100 works, including *Symphony III* (1959) for orchestra and tape; *Concerto* (1972) for amplified violin and orchestra; a percussion symphony (1976); and numerous chamber music works. *Time's Encomium,* (1969) for tape, is probably his best-known work. In it, he took full advantage of electronic means to control all musical

John Cage. *(© Dorothy Norman.)*

happenings. The Mark II synthesizer at RCA was used in preparing the work, which combines pure synthesized sounds with electronically processed synthesized material supplemented by reverberation. Wuorinen ventured into theater music with the masque *The Politics of Harmony* (1966–67), for ATB soloists and a 12-piece chamber orchestra. The plot is based on a Chinese fable warning against bizarre music's power to corrupt; the rhyming of the poetry is emphasized by the music, with definite pitches being assigned to certain vocal sounds. Wuorinen attempts to differentiate clearly between taped music and music for live performance. His works for conventional instruments have more grandeur and stronger rhythms than his electronic pieces.

Cage

John Cage (b. 1912) studied music with Schoenberg in California and with Cowell in New York. The influence of both teachers is apparent in the pieces Cage wrote in the 1930s. His early compositions are based on organized arrangements of the pitches in the chromatic scale. After he observed Cowell introducing foreign objects among the strings of a piano to produce unusual timbres, Cage became interested in **prepared piano.** For dancer Syvilla Fort (c. 1917–1975) in Seattle, he composed *Bacchanale* (1938), using the percussive sounds of a single prepared piano as substitute for percussion ensemble. Essentially, "preparing" a piano transforms the instrument into a kind of one-person percussion ensemble. Cage wrote a second piece for prepared piano in 1938, *Metamorphosis,* then turned to works for percussion ensemble and, in 1939–42, created nine of them. In 1942 Cage moved to New York. By 1948, he had written, among other things, almost three dozen works for prepared piano and had become well known for that kind of writing. His *Sonatas and Interludes* (16 sonatas, 4 interludes; 1946–48), performed in Carnegie Hall in January 1949, brought him several awards. The score of that work gives instructions for altering 45 of the piano's pitches to produce new, percussive sounds. In *Sonatas and Interludes,* Cage used a number sequence to determine rhythm in the various pieces. The idea of fixed rhythm was an Oriental influence. All of the *Sonatas and Interludes* are intended to portray traditional Indian ideas of "permanent emotions"— pain, mirth, heroism, tranquillity, and others. To plan the durations in the works, Cage prepared grids (matrices). Such durational plans were a means of unifying a piece and served as an aid in avoiding metric regulation and the so-called tyranny of the barline.

Cage used number sequences to determine the structure of rhythm in several other works, including *String Quartet in Four Parts* (1950) and *Concerto* for prepared piano and chamber orchestra of 22 soloists (1951). In the quartet, the "parts" are the four movements, which express the American Indians' connotations of the four seasons: summer as preservation; autumn, destruction; winter, peace; and spring, creation. Much of the quartet sounds polyphonic, but Cage considered the music an unaccompanied melodic line, even though it contains triads and other aggregates of pitches produced by more than one instrument. The harmonies are not functional but are unrelated sonorities designed as elements of color. *Concerto* harmonies follow the same principle.

Meantime, Cage had studied Zen, a Buddhist philosophy, and he determined to express musically the idea of zero thought. Endeavoring to create purposeless music, he composed *Imaginary Landscape no. 4* (1951) for 12 radio receivers. So that none of his personal preferences would enter into the composition, he used the element of chance to determine the choices of wavelengths, duration, and volume (numbers on the radio dial). These choices were determined by procedures comparable with those outlined in the ancient Chinese *I Ching: The Book of Change,* for divining answers to problems. Cage used charts based on *I Ching* and tossed three coins. Though he precisely notated the choices chance determined, he stated that his work was indeterminate of composition and indeterminate of performance, meaning that (1) chance operations produced the score, and (2) the performers' choices (in this case, the radio receivers) produced the sounds. To this type of composition Cage applied the term **indeterminacy.** Other composers who used the element of chance or choice in their works referred to the music as **aleatory** (from Latin *alea,* dice). Another aleatory work that Cage created through *I Ching* charts and coin-tossing is *Music of Changes* (1951), four volumes of piano music.

Cage wanted to produce some music in which he said nothing—music that would let silence itself speak. Eventually he did so, with *4'33"* (1952), a piece entirely *tacet,* to be performed by one or more instrumentalists who sit in silence on the stage for 4 minutes and 33 seconds. Cage's aim was, in his words, "to let sounds be themselves in a space of time." The audience is expected to listen attentively to all sounds that occur during the allotted time span.

In 1951, Vladimir Ussachevsky (b. 1911) began to experiment with electronic music at Columbia University. Cage, too, became interested in creating pieces on magnetic tape, and, working in a private recording studio, applied his aleatory methods in preparing the tape compositions *Imaginary Landscape no. 5* (1952) and *Williams Mix* (1952). For *Imaginary Landscape no. 5* the source material consists of any 42 recordings. *Williams Mix* is a mixture of sounds gathered from six broad categories, such as "city sounds," "country sounds," and "wind-produced sounds." Cage used tape primarily as a means of assembling a musical collage; Ussachevsky used tape to manipulate and alter sounds, as well as to record them.

Cage's next innovation was music created from "happenings"—actions and presentations, musical and nonmusical, that are simultaneous but uncoordinated. He also created "theater music," such as *Water Music* (1952), whose performance requires of a pianist actions not related to the piano, e.g., pouring water and blowing whistles that are under water. The visual events are an important part of the composition. Cage's music from events, or "happenings," was a forerunner of the **Fluxus** movement in New York in 1960–65, which presented concerts of "music" created from unusual sources and often humorous happenings. One of the leaders of the Fluxus group was George Brecht (b. 1924), who created *Drip Music,* a live presentation consisting entirely of water dripping from a source into a container. Action/happening composition drew a satirical response from Ligeti in works such as *Poème symphonique* (1962) for 100 metronomes (see p. 886).

The idea of indeterminacy led Cage to write pieces with open form—works that allowed the performer(s) to choose the order in which movements or portions of movements were played. He wrote several groups of numbered pieces that might be performed individually or combined, by one or more pianists: *Music for Piano* 4–19 (1953), *Music for Piano* 21–36 (1955), *Music for Piano* 37–52 (1955), *Music for Piano* 53–68 (1956), and *Music for Piano* 69–84 (1956). Perhaps the ultimate in work with open form is Cage's *Concert for Piano and Orchestra* (1957–58), in which: (1) the music for each of the orchestral parts was determined by chance operations; (2) each instrumentalist chooses the pages he or she will play, and the sequence in which those pages will be played; and (3) the conductor has no score, but uses his arms as the hands of a clock to indicate elapsed time.

Cage's work has been highly influential, especially with regard to chance operations and indeterminacy. He has continued to write experimental music of all kinds—chance music involving the audience; action pieces for any number of people performing any kind of actions (*Variations III;* 1963); music indeterminate as to number of performers and instrumentation, as in the *Variations* numbered II and IV;

sounds derived from plants, animals, various inanimate sources, electronic means, and music of the cosmos (*Études astrales,* Star studies; 32 pieces for piano; 1974–75). Cage worked with computers in the production of highly integrated compositions. He collaborated with Lejaren Hiller in preparing *HPSCHD* (1967–69), to be performed on one to seven amplified harpsichords and using 1 to 51 electronic tapes each played through its own amplifier. The tapes contain computer-generated sounds and may be combined in various ways to produce different arrangements. As prepared, *HPSCHD* consists of seven harpsichord solos created from computer-generated sounds. Only the first solo is completely original music. The second solo uses material from Mozart's musical dice game K.294d; the third and fourth contain material from Mozart piano sonatas; the next two superimpose material taken from piano works by Beethoven, Chopin, Schumann, Gottschalk, Busoni, Schoenberg, Cage, and Hiller; and the last solo mixes Mozart's music, as the performer chooses. Not only does *HPSCHD* combine techniques of quotation, collage, and indeterminacy, its performance becomes a multimedia event, for the music is enhanced by colored lights, films, and slides.

Why does Cage create such unusual works? Judging from remarks he has made in lectures, his response to that question might be: To affirm the reality of life and living in our world, to break down the distinctions and barriers between art and living, to make persons realize that we are surrounded by sounds and that everything we do is music.

Oliveros

Pauline Oliveros (b. 1932) is a talented performer on many conventional instruments. From childhood, she has been intrigued by all kinds of sounds and, in her compositions, has sought new sonorities, even subliminal ones. Her earliest works were for conventional instruments, but even then she wrote unconventional harmonies. Soon, she became interested in electronic music. The San Francisco Tape Music Center was established in 1959, and in 1961 Oliveros joined Ramon Sender, Morton Subotnik, and others in musical experiments there. In 1966–67 Oliveros was director of the Center.

Pauline Oliveros.

Between 1961 and 1967, Oliveros created a great deal of electronic music, and on 22 July 1967, in San Francisco, she presented a 12-hour program of her recorded electronic works. Not all of her electronic pieces have been produced through studio techniques—several of her works have involved live electronics. *I of IV* (1966) could be performed live, for it was created on tape in "real" time, i.e., without tape editing or splicing. To compose that work she connected 12 oscillators to a keyboard, amplified and reverberated the sounds, and used two tape recorders to produce double feedback loops and time delays.

In *Sound Patterns* (1961), a textless choral work, Oliveros explored various vocal techniques in the production of sound masses. Some of her works, written with the intent of inducing sonic meditation, are filled with vocalizations that vary from quiet murmuring to exuberant ululation. In her search for the unusual, she ventured into action (happening) music and theatrical scenes, requiring musicians to assume all kinds of nonmusical roles, from being page turners and piano movers to barking like dogs. Most of Oliveros's works are in mixed media, combining theater, art, and music to create unusual scenic events. For a short time during the 1960s, her mixed media works seemed to be carrying activities to extremes, bordering on the ridiculous. In the early 1970s, she introduced a psychic element into her works. Since 1975 most of her writing has been for voices and instruments without electronics, but she has not abandoned electronic music composition.

Ivey

Jean Eichelberger Ivey (b. 1923), founder and director of the electronic music studio at Peabody Conservatory, has concertized internationally as pianist. She has composed works in various styles—tonal, Neo-Classical, dodecaphonic, and electronic—and in most media, vocal and instrumental, solo and ensemble, including music for films and television. Influences of the music of Ravel and Bartók are visible in several of her works, electronic as well as conventional. Some of Ivey's electronic pieces are for tape alone, e.g., *Continuous Form* (1969), a work of indeterminate length, and *Pinball*, whose musical material was derived entirely from pinball machine sounds. In other works Ivey combined tape and live performance, including *Testament of Eve* (1976; Mezzo, orch., tape); *Sea-Change* (1982; orch., tape); and *Terminus* (1986; voice, tape). Both *Testament of Eve* and *Sea-Change* have been performed several times by major symphony orchestras.

Testament of Eve, which is in part a tribute to Ivey's mother, is based on the Biblical story of Eve and the Tree of Knowledge. Ivey said she depicted Eve as a heroic woman who chose "knowledge and growth for herself and her children instead of remaining a pampered pet in the Garden of Eden." The (taped) voice of Lucifer, disembodied and coming out of turbulent winds, represents also Eve's awareness of her self and her awakened desire for personal growth. The words Eve sings were written by Ivey.

Sea-Change, a work filled with Ivey's memories of her father, was based on several lines from one of Ariel's songs in Act I of Shakespeare's *The Tempest*:

> Full fathom five thy father lies;
>   Of his bones are coral made;
> Those are pearls that were his eyes;
>   Nothing of him that doth fade
> But doth suffer a sea-change
> Into something rich and strange.

Taped electronic sounds enter the piece four times; sometimes mingling with the orchestral playing, sometimes sounding alone. The taped music is transmitted through four loudspeakers placed in the four corners of the hall, so that the audience is surrounded by music. None of the sounds are bizarre. Rather, they resemble water, sea birds, bells tolling under water, and fairy voices and are intended to represent some of the rich changes wrought by the sea. Some of the electronic sounds in *Sea-Change* resemble textless choral singing, but the piece contains no actual singing. The music, which is a changing kaleidoscope of delicate colors, is basically quiet and contemplative but does work up to one major climax. In this composition, too, some passages reflect the influence of Debussy and Ravel.

Terminus, which concerns an individual's realization that time is running out, is for solo voice accompanied by taped electronic sounds and has some solo tape interpolations. In many places, the taped music resembles passages in *Sea-Change.*

Italy — Berio

The works of Italian composer-conductor Luciano Berio (b. 1925) exhibit a variety of musical styles including (among others) twelve-tone serialism, electronic music, multimedia, and eclecticism. In his early works, e.g., *Due pezzi* (Two pieces; 1951; vln., pno.), he followed standard 12-note serial procedures. Then he began to treat serialism freely; his String Quartet (1956) is an example of this.

In 1955, Berio joined Bruno Maderna at Studio di Fonologia, Milan, and experimented with electronic music techniques. From 1956 to 1960 Berio edited the publication *Incontri musicali* and, with Maderna, managed the *Incontri musicali* concert series, in which internationally known artists and composers participated. At Studio di Fonologia Berio created *Thema: Omaggio a Joyce* (Theme: Homage to Joyce; 1958; 2-track tape), based on a portion of Joyce's *Ulysses*. *Thema* commences with an exposition of the basic material, a spoken recitation of the complete text, unaltered, lasting approximately two minutes. The remainder of the work (six minutes) is a development of that material through tape manipulations of the words out of context and filtering to suppress overtones and change timbres. At the conclusion of the section a cadential effect is achieved through soft hissing sounds. Except for the fact that there is no recapitulation, the structural pattern resembles sonata form. In *Circles* (1960; voice, harp, 2 percussionists), there is a mixture of spoken and sung text, of meaningful words and phonetic sounds, and of physical gestures. The piece was written for American vocalist Cathy Berberian (1928–83), whom Berio considered the best interpreter of his vocal music. (From 1950 to 1966 Berberian and Berio were married.)

Berio resigned as director of Studio di Fonologia in 1961 and moved to the United States, where he taught and worked with synthesizers and computers in the studios at Columbia University and Bell Telephone Company Laboratories. In 1972 he returned to Italy, where he has participated in research, composed for television, and served as artistic director of Accademia Filarmonica Romana.

In 1958 Berio began a series of virtuosic solo works entitled *Sequenza* (Sequence) for conventional instruments. The first of these was for flute. The series continued with pieces for harp (1963), female voice (1966), piano (1966), trombone (1966), viola (1967), oboe (1969), violin (1975–77), clarinet (1980; arr. for sax. 1981), and trumpet (1985). The solos for violin and clarinet present a melodic theme and variations. As counterparts of the *Sequenza* pieces, Berio has begun a series entitled *Chemins* (Paths) for solo instrument and small orchestra, each *Chemins* based on a *Sequenza*. *Chemins V* (1980) is for clarinet and electronics.

Labyrintus II (Labyrinth II; 1965), which Berio regards as a theatrical speech on Dante, contains a series of quotations from various poets (Dante, Ezra Pound, T. S. Eliot, Sanguineti), with Dante's *Inferno* considered as a foreshadowing of twentieth-century capitalist society.

Sinfonia (1968; mvt. 5 added 1969), for eight solo voices and orchestra, contains a variety of textual quotations and numerous recognizable musical ones, sometimes mingled. In the middle movement of *Sinfonia,* Berio quotes the entire Scherzo from Mahler's Symphony No. 2 as basic material, but, with it, uses material from many other composers' works, including Debussy, Wagner, and Richard Strauss. The movement is, in a way, a kind of historical résumé—a presentation of excerpts from compositions written during the previous two and a half centuries—woven into the fabric of Mahler's Scherzo according to Berio's plan. By comparison, Berio's treatment of voices and instruments in the first and last movements of *Sinfonia* seem to be references to music's primitive stages.

Berio's later works confirm that he is still writing in several styles and for different media. Among these works are a concerto for piano and orchestra (1977), *Coro* for 40-voice chorus and 40-piece orchestra (1975–76), *Duo* (1977; violin/'cello), *Chants parallèle* (1974–75; tape), and two operas (*La vera storia,* 1972; *Un re in ascolto,* 1984) in which he explores ways in which stories can be told musically. *La vera storia* (The true story) includes acrobats and features textless music for soprano soloist.

Composers Working Outside Electronics

Not all composers were intrigued by electronic music. Some, e.g., Britten and Copland, did not subscribe to any of the avant-garde techniques. Other persons, like George Crumb, obtained new sounds by ingenious choices of sound sources and unusual combinations of instruments: mingling Occidental and Oriental instruments from various cultures (Japanese, Chinese, Tibetan, Balinese, African), adapting conventional instruments (prepared piano), including toys (toy piano), instruments sometimes thought of as "primitive rural" or "backwoods" (harmonica), and adaptations of household tools (musical saw) and other objects usually considered nonmusical. György Ligeti created unusual sound masses with voices. Still other composers, e.g., Thea Musgrave, have written a few electronic pieces but have relied basically on conventional means of sound production for most of their works.

Crumb

George Crumb (b. 1929) received much of his musical training at home, began composing while still in school, and heard some of his earliest works performed by the Charleston, West Virginia, Symphony. He continued his music study in college, then began teaching piano and composition. Crumb cites Debussy, Bartók, and Mahler as major influences in his music.

In his vocal works, Crumb has set mainly verses by Frederico García Lorca (1899–1936) and regards these settings as an extended cycle. Crumb's vocal music is exceptionally demanding, requiring the vocalist to sing microintervals as well as very wide leaps, to produce special sound effects (by tongue clicking, singing through a tube or into the piano, shrieking, hissing, etc.) and unusual timbres (imitate various muted trumpet sounds), and to sing and shout phonemes and nonsense syllables. An example is *Ancient Voices of Children* (1970; DWMA232), a song cycle for soprano, boy soprano, oboe, mandolin, harp, electric piano, and toy piano.

Performers are spatially separated for some of Crumb's pieces. *Star-Child* (1977), for soprano, two antiphonal choirs of children, male speaking choir, bell ringers, and huge orchestra, requires coordination of four conductors. At its première, the piece was under general direction of Pierre Boulez.

In some pieces, Crumb included quotations from well-known works by other composers. There are such quotations in *Ancient Voices of Children*. *Black Angels,* subtitled *13 Images from the Dark Land* (1970; amplified string quartet) is a kind of parable, with God and the devil in polarity, and incorporates such musical associations as *diabolus in musica* (the tritone), the *Dies irae* Sequence in plainchant, Tartini's *Trillo di diavolo* (Devil's Trill, vln./pno. sonata), and, from numerology, the numbers 7 and 13, accorded diabolic significance.

Crumb has written four volumes entitled *Makrokosmos* (cf., Bartók, *Mikrokosmos*). Volumes I and II are each subtitled *12 Fantasy-Pieces after the Zodiac,* the first volume for piano (1972), the second for amplified piano (1973). Volume III, *Music for a Summer Evening* (1974), is for two amplified pianos and percussion; Volume IV, *Celestial Mechanics* (1979), for amplified piano, four hands, constitutes cosmic dances. Among his later works are *Processional for Piano* (1983) and *A Haunted Landscape* (orch; 1984).

Crumb designed several works for virtuoso mezzo soprano Jan DeGaetani (b. 1933), who is internationally acclaimed for her ability to sing unusual intervals accurately, to produce the finest gradations of dynamic nuances, and to interpret texts with keen insight. DeGaetani's performances of ultramodern vocal works and traditional Lieder are equally superlative. She has recorded several of Crumb's compositions, including *Ancient Voices of Children.*

Musgrave

Thea Musgrave (b. 1928), who studied with Boulanger in 1950–54, wrote her earliest compositions in predominantly diatonic harmonies. After filling some commissions for vocal works for performance in Scotland in 1953–54, she became interested in opera. Her first, a chamber opera, *The Abbott of Drimock* (1955), based on a Scottish story, is in conventional nineteenth-century lyrical style. Gradually, Musgrave's music became more chromatic and more abstract, and by 1960 she was writing serial music. Many of her works in the 1960s were instrumental—solos, accompanied solos, chamber music, orchestral pieces. Opera still interested her greatly, and during 1964–65 she composed *The Decision* (perf. 1967). Since then, most of her compositions have been commissioned instrumental works. Perhaps the most significant of these are the Horn Concerto (1971) and the Viola Concerto (1973), the latter first performed by her husband, Peter Mark. Only occasionally has Musgrave included tape in her works: *Soliloquy* (1969; guitar, tape); *From One to Another* (1970, vla., tape; 2d version, vla., stgs., 1979–80); and the ballet *Orfeo* (1975; dancer, flute, tape).

The three-act opera *Mary, Queen of Scots* (Musgrave libretto) was commissioned by the Scottish Opera for the 1977 Edinburgh Festival. In 1978–79, Musgrave wrote the two-act opera *A Christmas Carol* (her own libretto), based on Dickens. Her finest opera is *Harriet, The Woman Called 'Moses'* (1984), the story of Harriet Tubman (1820–1913), "conductor" of the Underground Railroad network used by slaves seeking transportation into free territory. Musgrave had heard a group of black singers perform in New York in 1980 and wanted to write an opera for them. The opportunity came when she received a joint commission from London Royal Opera and Virginia Opera Association. She incorporated well-known black songs, such as *Go down, Moses,* into the opera. The work is remarkable for Musgrave's ability to set the black speech-patterns correctly. At times, the slave chorus participates in the action; at other times, it stands to the side and offers comment, as did the citizens' chorus in ancient Greek plays. The opera contains some dancing and requires a large orchestra.

Ligeti

From 1945–49 Hungarian composer György Ligeti (b. 1929) was a student at Budapešt Academy of Music. For the next year, he did field research in Romanian folk music, then returned to the Academy as professor of harmony, counterpoint, and analysis. He became interested in serialism as practiced by Schoenberg and Webern and began to develop an individualistic style of composition. However, until the death of Stalin, political conditions in Hungary prevented publication or performance of some of his most adventuresome works. Only the pieces he based on folk or peasant songs were acceptable. Most of the music Ligeti composed in 1945–56 is tonal, at least nominally, though he seldom used key signatures. Typical of his writing in the 1950s are the choruses *Éjszaka* (Night; SSAATTBB; 1955; DWMA233) and *Reggel* (Morning; S, Mez., ATB; 1955). Poems by Sandor Weöres form the texts. *Éjszaka* uses a theme that commences as a C-major scale and is treated as canon at the unison at the distance of one measure, a procedure that produces a long procession of cluster chords through most of the piece. In the final portion of the work, the chorus sings a series of sustained chords formed from broad clusters of pitches located on the black keys of a piano. The composition closes with a C-major chord sung *ppp* by tenors and basses (ex. 26.13). Three things present in *Éjszaka* became characteristic of Ligeti's compositional style: clusters, extremely soft sustained chords, and canon.

After the Russian invasion of Hungary in 1956, Ligeti went to Vienna, then moved to Cologne, where, at Eimert's invitation, he worked in the Westdeutscher Rundfunk electronic music studios. Ligeti composed very few pieces on tape, however; he was more interested in the avant-garde extensions of serialism. Eventually, he concluded that serial principles were self-defeating, and he concentrated on the development of musical textures, to the extent that the importance of other elements of music was pushed into the background in several of his works. In the orchestral pieces *Apparitions* (1959) and *Atmosphères* (1961), he concentrated on chromatic complexes, with pitches in sustained clusters, and avoided any feeling of harmony, rhythmic pulse, or definite durations. However, he wrote the scores for these works in precise conventional notation.

The most characteristic features of Ligeti's works are the clusters and the "clouds"—the whisperlike *ppp* and *pppp* sustained chords and passages marked *pppppp*. His use of clusters was highly influential in the work of other composers during the 1960s and 1970s, e.g., Krzystof Penderecki's use of "sound masses."

Ligeti uses canon often. It is an important structural factor in some sections of his Requiem Mass (1963–65), and his choral *Lux aeterna* (1966) is constructed entirely as strict canon. There are clusters in the Requiem, and there is evidence that harmony was a definite consideration, but for the most part it is well concealed and surfaces only momentarily. Some text painting occurs in the *Dies irae* section of the Mass. For composition of the Requiem, first performed in Stockholm in 1965, Ligeti was awarded the Bonn Beethoven prize in 1967.

Harmonies are evident in *Lontano* (Distant; orch.; 1967), too. *Mélodien* (Melodies; small orch.; 1971) contains many small melodies that appear fleetingly. In several works Ligeti used microtones: *Ramifications* (1968–69) for two groups of string instruments tuned a quarter tone apart; String Quartet No. 2 (1968); and the Double Concerto for flute and oboe with orchestra (1972).

Ligeti was well aware of new developments in other composers' music. Those with which he disagreed or of which he disapproved he sometimes satirized, as in *Poème symphonique* (1962) written for 100 metronomes. Those 100 different metrical tickings become quite complex layers at times. Ligeti recognized some new techniques, such as **minimalism,** by incorporating them in one or more of his works. Minimal works are based on short figures that are repeated many times; the technique is particularly associated with works written in the mid-1960s by Steve Reich (b. 1936), Terry Riley (b. 1935), and Philip

Glass (b. 1937). Though Ligeti had arrived at the technique of frequent repetition independently, he paid tribute to the work of the young Americans in the central piece of the triptych *Monument–Selbstporträt mit Reich und Riley (und Chopin ist auch dabei)–Bewegung* (Monument–Self-portrait with Reich and Riley, and Chopin is also near–Movement; 2 pnos.; 1976), in which small bits of music are repeated incessantly and blur the harmonies. The numerous repeated figurations in the first part of *Bewegung* conceal some canon, and the movement concludes with a chorale that is an eight-voice mirror canon.

Though Ligeti stated that he would not write a traditional opera because he considered that form incompatible with late twentieth-century music, he did write a work for performance in an opera house (*"Opernhaus Stück"*). Several analysts consider that opera house piece, *Le grand macabre* (The great gruesome [one]; 1974–77), quite close to a traditional opera. Evidently Ligeti's distaste for twentieth-century opera has diminished somewhat, for he has been working on a second operatic piece, *The Tempest.*

Ligeti's significance lies in the fact that he has moved away from the areas that attracted the attention of many avant-garde composers—serialism and expansions thereof, and electronic music—into other technical developments that have influenced a younger generation of composers.

Penderecki

Krzystof Penderecki (b. 1933), of Poland, suddenly attracted attention in 1958 with *Psalmy Dawida* (Psalms of David; chorus, perc.) and *Strophe* (Strophes; reciter, sop., 10 instrs.), a multilingual work with texts taken from the Bible's Old Testament prophets, Omar Khayyam, Sophocles, and Menander. International recognition came in 1960 after performances of *Anaklasis* for 42 strings and percussion and *Tren pamieci ofiarom Hiroszimy* (Threnody in memory of victims of Hiroshima; DWMA234) for 52 string instruments. *Threnody . . . ,* Penderecki's most frequently performed work, is filled with sound masses (mainly clusters and glissandos) and concludes on a massive two-octave tone cluster. The focus of the music is on textures and timbres, and many of the

Krzystof Penderecki. *(Courtesy of Chicago Lyric Opera.)*

sonorities are expressively agonizing. Most of the time the performers are asked to produce sounds by unconventional means, e.g., using the wood of the bow on the strings or on the instrument itself, rubbing the body of the instrument, tapping or snapping fingertips against the body of the instrument, or obtaining extremely high pitches by stopping a string in the area between fingerboard and bridge. Sometimes the tones sound as though they had been produced electronically. Penderecki uses such devices to help produce the dramatic effects that are characteristic of all of his music.

Many of Penderecki's compositions are large works for vocal soloists, chorus, and orchestra and are liturgical or on religious subjects. He seems to favor topics with dramatic situations characterized by mourning, conflict, or victory. Among his liturgical text settings are *Stabat mater* (1962; 3 choruses), *Dies irae* (1967; solo vcs., chor., orch.), *De profundis* (1977; chor., orch.), *Te Deum* (1979; solo vcs., chor., orch.), and a Magnificat (1973–74; bass solo, boys' chor., chor., orch.). The *Dies irae* concerns the Auschwitz killings during World War II. Penderecki's music is more traditional and restrained in *Passio et mors domini nostri Jesu Christi secundum Lucam* (Passion and death of our Lord Jesus Christ according to Luke; 1963–65). As a kind of sequel to the Passion,

Penderecki composed *Utrenja* (Morning prayer; 1970–71), a two-part work: (1) *Zlozeni* (The laying in the tomb) and (2) *Zmartwychwstanie* (The Resurrection). *Utrenja* is based on Orthodox liturgy and contains some quotations of Orthodox chant; its text is in old Slavonic. In several of his large-scale vocal works, Penderecki effectively mingled materials from Roman and Orthodox liturgies, texts in various ancient and modern languages and from sources as diverse as ancient Greek plays, prisoners' letters, and astronauts' comments. His music, whether vehement or delicate, is designed to be dramatic; to that end, he exploits all available sonic resources.

In the early 1960s, and again in the early 1970s, Penderecki prepared a few pieces on tape, then abandoned that kind of composition. *Concerto for Violino Grande and Orchestra* (1967) requires a specially constructed five-string violin, but his other concerti are for conventional instruments: a violin concerto (1976), two 'cello concerti (1972, 1981–82), a viola concerto (1982–83). *Partita* (1971) features solo harpsichord and four electrically amplified solo instruments, with chamber orchestra. In 1973 he wrote his first symphony; his second, *Christmas Symphony* (1979–80), was first performed in New York on 1 May 1980.

Penderecki has completed two stage works: the opera *Diably z Loudon* (The devils of Loudon; 1968) and *Paradise Lost* (1975–78), a *sacra rappresentazione* after John Milton's (1608–74) epic poem. An opera, *Ubu roi* (King Ubu), is in preparation.

Paradise Lost was written for performance by the Chicago Lyric Opera Company and was given its world première on 27 November 1978. The fact that Penderecki labeled the work *sacra rappresentazione* links it with Cavalieri's theatrically oriented allegorical *Rappresentazione di anima et di corpo* (Rome, 1600). In *Paradise Lost,* Sin and Death are personified, as offspring of Satan. *Paradise Lost* is as much oratorio as opera. Though staged as an opera, with scenery, costumes, acting, and ballet, some scenes resemble tableaux, and the role of John Milton, designed to be spoken rather than sung, is that of a narrator explaining the circumstances for and events in his poem. The man portraying Milton also proclaims the words of God who, unseen, speaks through dazzling light to create, and admonishes, commands,

Music Since 1945

(a)

(b)

Figure 26.5 Two scenes from Penderecki's opera *Paradise Lost*: (*a*) Adam and Eve, double roles, with both pairs on stage at the same time; (*b*) stage setting using the huge glass dome. 1978 performance, Chicago Lyric Opera. *(Courtesy of Chicago Lyric Opera.)*

and condemns. The two roles of Adam and Eve are double, each requiring a dancer and a singer; both pairs may be on stage at the same time (fig. 26.5a). The chorus is an integral part of the work, participating in the drama as unseen voices, a celestial chorus, Satan's fallen angels, an angelic guard moving through Eden, and also singing from two scaffolding towers positioned at the sides of the stage. In fact, the choral portions are the finest music in the composition. Performing forces for the work are colossal: a chorus of 100, childrens' choir of 35, 90-piece or-

chestra, 45 dancers, 20 soloists. The music is a mixture of tonality and atonality, with some borrowings from chant (e.g., *Dies irae* used in the visions of war and pestilence), from Bach ("Oh, wondrous Love" from *St. John Passion,* used when Messias offers to sacrifice himself for mankind's sins), and from Wagner (e.g., a quotation from *Lohengrin* used when the swan appears). The scenery is minimal—a huge glass dome (resembling a gigantic Tiffany lampshade; fig. 26.5b) rises and falls as needed, and the action occurs either on a bare dark stage or in clouds of smoke from hell.

Paradise Lost is in two Acts, comprising, respectively, 20 and 22 Scenes. Except for the very beginning and the conclusion, the plot is a flashback. The story begins with John Milton announcing his intention of writing an epic poem justifying God's treatment of mankind. As Milton declaims the first line of the poem *Paradise Lost,* the setting becomes the Garden of Eden, with Adam berating Eve for causing him to break God's only command. Then Milton begins to explain Satan's reasons for leading the first humans into disobedience, and the scene flashes back to Lucifer's rebellion and the fallen angels' banishment from Heaven to Hell. Next comes the creation of the world, of Adam and the creatures in the Garden of Eden, and then the creation of Eve, depicted in a ballet. Another ballet depicts the courtship and marriage of Adam and Eve. The plot presents the treachery of Satan, the disobedience of Adam and Eve, God's condemnation of them, the rise in status of Sin and Death, Messias's offer to die for mankind's sins, and His request that God hear and answer mortals' prayers. The last few scenes depict Adam's visions of future murder, pestilence, war, and flood, and the presentation concludes with celestial voices proclaiming that humans shall wander until they learn the secret power of harmony.

Minimalism

Minimalism is the name given to the style of music that is based on the repetition of short figures. A minimal amount of musical material is used, but the composition may be quite long. La Monte Young (b. 1935) was one of the first to write music of this type. Since c. 1964, his music has been characterized by repetitive figures, static harmonies, and just intonation. Some minimal works consist entirely of prolonged chanting on one note, e.g., Philip Corner's (b. 1933) *Om Breath* and *Om Entrance.*

In other pieces, a single figure or a single measure is reiterated numerous times. One of the best-known minimal works is Terry Riley's (b. 1935) *In C* (1964; DWMA235), for an ensemble of an unspecified number of musicians, including piano. The work is both minimal and aleatoric. The notated score comprises 53 small figures (ex. 26.14); the piano part, not notated, consists entirely of the pulsation of eighth-note octaves drummed out on the top two C's of the keyboard. Against this background, each member of the ensemble plays the 53 minimal motives "in sync with the pulse," moving consecutively from 1 through 53. Each ensemble player decides for himself when to move from figure to figure, where to place the primary accent (or "downbeat"), and how often to repeat each figure. Performance of the piece can last from 45 to 90 minutes. Another of Riley's works is *Poppy Nogood's Phantom Band* (1966), in which short fragments played on soprano saxophone are repeated via tape loops. A single saxophonist's playing forms the "band."

Philip Glass (b. 1937), in his harmonically static works, not only reiterates motives, but, after several repetitions of a figure, lengthens or shortens it by the addition or deletion of a rhythmic unit. Such is the case in *Music in Similar Motion* (1969) (ex. 26.15). Glass's early minimal works are characterized by

parallel motion—chord streams, and passages in octaves or fifths that resemble ninth-century organum, e.g., *Music in Fifths* (1970). Later works, such as *Music with Changing Parts* (1974), exhibit greater harmonic variety.

The extensive repetition of small figures in ostinato fashion can be found in nonminimal works, also. John Williams's *Scherzo for TODAY,* commissioned by NBC for use as theme music for the "TODAY" television program, provides an example. The reiterated motives serve at times as vamp preceding a melody, at other times as background for a melody.

Reich

Steve Reich (b. 1936) is one of the principal exponents of minimalism. At the beginning of his career, he was interested in jazz and drumming and studied African music and Balinese gamelan music. Then he began to work with tape loops and became fascinated with possibilities involved in repetition, especially **phase shifting,** which places parts out of synchronization. For example, Tape 1 and Tape 2, containing the same material, are lined up to commence in unison; then Tape 2 is gradually moved out of phase (out of synchronization) with Tape 1, so that Tape 2 lags farther and farther behind. Reich used phase shifting with tape loops containing a few spoken words in *It's Gonna Rain* (1965). Through such shifting, the continuity of the individual line disappears; what remains audible are isolated elements being repeated. After working with phase shifting of tapes, in 1967 Reich transferred the idea to music performed on conventional instruments, in *Piano Phase* and *Violin Phase* (ex. 26.16). Reich next carried out his phase shifting idea via the technique of canon, treating the

Example 26.14 First six figures (the first line of the score) of Riley's *In C. (Copyright 1964 by Terry Riley.)*

Example 26.15 Four excerpts from Glass: *Music in Similar Motion.* In performance, each motivic unit is repeated until the composer signals his ensemble to proceed to the next unit. The first three units presented here are cumulative; each unit contains all notes of the previous unit and adds several notes. *("Music in Similar Motion,"* © *1973 Philip Glass. ALL RIGHTS RESERVED. REPRINTED BY PERMISSION.)*

Example 26.16 Excerpt from Reich: *Violin Phase,* showing the effect of phase shifting. (© *1979 by Universal Edition (London) Ltd., London. All Rights Reserved. Used by permission of European American Music Distributors Corporation, sole U.S. and Canadian agent for Universal Edition, London.)*

melodic lines as though they were tapes moving out of phase with one another. An example occurs in *Tehillim* (Psalms; 3 sopranos, 1 alto, orch.; 1981), a setting of four passages from Psalms, in Hebrew. The composition is in four sections, the first and last of which contain canonic vocal passages that simulate phasing (DWMA236).

Reich's interest in repetitive figures and patterns led him to minimalism and a considerably reduced harmonic vocabulary in a work. He has created compositions from a single chord (*Four Organs;* 1970) or from a few words (*Come Out;* 1966). Reich has referred to some of his music as being related to that of Pérotin and the *ars antiqua* of the Notre Dame school. Indeed, some of Reich's parallelisms sound like Pérotin's organum. Often, Reich entitles his music by the kind or number of instruments involved.

During the 1970s, Reich turned to writing more melodic music, including submelodies within his repetitive patterns. His music has evidenced a greater interest in tonality of a new, nonfunctional kind. For a time during the 1970s he abandoned electronic music in favor of writing for conventional instruments, e.g., *Variations for Winds, Strings, and Keyboards* (1979; small orch.; 1980, full orch.) and *Octet* (1979; string quartet, 2 pnos., 2 cls. doubling on bass cl. and fl.). He did not completely forgo composition on tape, however; *Vermont Counterpoint* (1982) is for 11 flutes, 10 of them recorded on tape. Reich's compositions of the mid-1980s include *The Desert Music* (1984; chor., orch.) and *Music for Percussion and Keyboards* (1984). Audiences, particularly young people, have greatly admired Reich's work.

After 1970

During the 1970s, changes took place in composers' attitudes toward music. There was still a search for the new and different, and experimentation never ceased. Serial music was still being written, but it was no longer a dominant force, and in 1977 Messiaen stated that it was "over and done with." For a time, it seemed that serialism would be replaced by minimalism, and that may eventually be the case, for minimalism has continued to gain adherents. Moreover, its influence can be seen in the use of repetitive material by composers whose work cannot be specifically classed as minimalism. The compositions of John Adams (b. 1947) provide several examples of various uses of minimalist features: the lyric *Phrygian Gates* (1977; pno.), whose repeated figures continually modulate to different modes; *Shaker Loops* (1978; str. septet); and *Harmonielehre* (1985; orch.), a three-movement work that, in addition to the repetitive figures of minimalism, evidences the influence of Schoenberg's *Gurre-Lieder* and Sibelius's symphonies. A number of composers were eclectic, choosing not only from styles prevalent in the twentieth century but from styles of all centuries and even mingling characteristic traits from different stylistic movements and eras. Philip Glass's combination of minimalism with the parallelism of medieval organum is one example; others are Penderecki's and Musgrave's treatment of opera chorus in the manner of the citizens' chorus in ancient Greek drama. Frequently, composers quoted from the works of others, as Ives had done earlier in the century. Both Crumb and Berio are eclectic composers and have used quotation extensively in major works.

Gradually, more emphasis has been placed on melody and on tonality, but it is a different kind of tonality from that of the nineteenth century. The first and fifth scale degrees no longer possess the tonal pull, the functional direction they held in traditional key tonality. Instead, chordlike aggregations of pitches form harmonies that succeed one another without the feeling that functional relationships exist between them. Pieces are written without designation of a "key tonality," but tonal centers appear within the work, and movement from one tonal center to another is achieved without the traditional processes of modulation. However, some composers still write diatonic harmonies and use tonality as they were used traditionally.

The term "Neo-Romanticism" has been used to describe many composers' return to the forms and genres used during the Romantic period, to a greater emphasis on melody, and to the appearance of tonal centers within the music. Among the Americans writing Neo-Romantic music is David Del Tredici (b. 1937). He was trained as a concert pianist, and his early compositions are for keyboard. During 1959–66 he wrote mainly settings of James Joyce's poetry, with music that is Expressionistic, highly dissonant, and using canon and palindromes. In 1968, when he was inspired by Lewis Carroll's (1832–98) *Alice's Adventures in Wonderland* (1865) and *Through the Looking-Glass . . .* (1871), Del Tredici's style changed, due primarily to the nineteenth-century style of Carroll's writing. To balance that writing style, Del Tredici wrote Neo-Romantic music that has some resemblance to R. Strauss's orchestral style but with strong dissonances. Del Tredici has been criticized for the "Straussian" sound of that music. In the "Alice" compositions written between 1968 and 1976, to reflect Carroll's puns and word play, Del Tredici juxtaposed soprano soloist and full orchestra against a small instrumental ensemble, either a folk group or a rock group. The vocal line, which is amplified, often contains highly virtuosic passages. Included in the musical "Alice" series are *Pop-Pourri* (1968), *An Alice Symphony* (1969), *Adventures Underground* (1971), *Vintage Alice* (1972), *Final Alice* (1976), and *Child Alice* (1977–81). *Final Alice,* originally intended to be the last composition in the series, deals with events in the concluding chapters of *Alice in Wonderland,* presented as a narrative with orchestral music, recitatives, and arias. Thematic transformation (Liszt's influence) and *Leitmotifs* are used. *Child Alice* presents Del Tredici's unrealistic view of Carroll's memories of hours he spent with the child Alice Liddell. Near the end of most of the "Alice" pieces, Del Tredici's musical signature appears: some players count from 1 to 13 in Italian (*uno to tredici*), with special emphasis on *tredici.*

The last quarter of the twentieth century has been characterized by diversity. Some composers have found a certain style that expresses what they have to say and have worked almost exclusively in that style. Other composers have been eclectic, choosing the styles in which they wish to write, moving from one style to another, and freely mingling elements of several styles, if that pleases them. The diversity of this era is comparable with that prevalent during the middle third of the eighteenth century. Late twentieth-century historians can speak of the present era only as an Age of Diversity; they are too close to the period to be objective in assigning it a definitive name.

Summary

The twentieth century witnessed tremendous technological advances that affected the development of music: devices for recording on discs and magnetic tape, putting sound tracks on movie film, radio, television, computer, synthesizer, and other electronic instruments. The original intent of recording technology—to provide a means for storing, transmitting, and faithfully reproducing live sounds—has been extended considerably. Technology has made available to composers every sound in the universe as source material.

The principles of serialism, applied to pitch by Schoenberg and his pupils, were extended to other elements of music, and ultimately total serialization was attained. By 1947, Babbitt had arrived at serialization of rhythm and dynamics, as well as pitch. Messiaen used serial techniques only briefly. He has been one of the twentieth century's greatest and most influential composers and teachers, though his style—an individually conceived composite of many styles and many cultures—has not been copied by any of his pupils. One of them, Boulez, became leader of the young serialist composers working in Paris in 1948. Working independently of Babbitt, Boulez also serialized musical elements other than pitch.

Musique concrète was the term Schaeffer used to describe music composed directly on disc or tape by recording natural sounds that are manipulated by various means. In Germany, developments in electronic music took place independently and almost simultaneously with those in France. The German movement was led by Eimert, who was joined by Stockhausen, one of Messiaen's pupils. Stockhausen composed music for conventional instruments even while experimenting with electronic music, and he wrote major works in both areas. In some works, he mingled manipulated word sounds with electronic sounds. As Gabrieli had used *cori spezzati,* so Stockhausen employed physical space in some of his works.

Varèse, working in America, began writing for groups of wind and percussion instruments in the 1920s and wanted electronic instruments. When theremin and ondes Martenot became available, he included them in ensembles. Around 1950 Varèse began writing compositions that mingled taped sounds with the sonorities of conventional instruments. He composed two of the earliest major works created on tape.

Babbitt used arithmetic as a compositional tool in structuring his works. Intrigued by the manner in which Schoenberg and Webern constructed tone rows, particularly those in which unordered hexachords formed combinatorial sets, Babbitt developed the principle of combinatoriality further in his own works. He was interested also in the possibilities of synthesizer as an aid to musical composition, primarily because it offered absolute control of all musical events. He was the first composer to work with RCA's Mark II synthesizer.

Cage is usually associated with prepared piano, a technique he learned from Cowell. Cage was primarily an experimentalist, seeking new sounds, new media, and has been influential with regard to chance operations and indeterminacy in music. Among his works are theater music, happenings, aleatory music, and computer-generated pieces.

Berio first worked with electronics in Italy, then came to the United States where he worked with synthesizers and computers, as well as composing for conventional instruments. American women composing music by electronic means include Ivey and Oliveros.

Not all composers were intrigued by electronic music. Some, like Britten and Copland, did not subscribe to any avant-garde techniques. Others, like Crumb, obtained new sounds by ingenious choices of sound sources and unusual combinations of instruments, including those from Africa and the Orient, and even toys. Scottish composer Thea Musgrave is well known for her operas.

Ligeti's works are characterized by large tone clusters and whisperlike sustained "clouds." He was well aware of new developments in other composers'

music and incorporated some of them in a few of his works. But he moved away from areas that interested many composers—serialism and expansions thereof and electronic music—into other technical developments, such as the frequent repetition of figures or short passages, that attracted younger composers.

In a number of his works, Penderecki asks performers to produce sounds from conventional instruments by unusual means. Many of his compositions are large works for vocal soloists, chorus, and orchestra and are liturgical or on religious subjects. His *Paradise Lost,* though staged as an opera, with scenery, costumes, acting, and ballet, contains tableaux and a major role for narrator.

Minimalism is the name given to the style of music that is based on the repetition of short figures and uses a minimal amount of musical material. Among its principal exponents are Young, Riley, Glass, and Reich.

During the 1970s, experimentation and diversity continued. Serial music was still being written but was no longer a dominant force. Minimalism gained adherents and influenced composers writing in other styles to include repetitive figures in works. A number of composers have been eclectic, choosing not only from styles prevalent in the twentieth century but from styles of all centuries and even mingling characteristic traits from different movements. Gradually, more emphasis has been placed on melody and on tonality, but it is a different kind of tonality from that of the nineteenth century—a tonality in which there is no tonal pull by tonic or dominant, and functional relationships between chords seem to be lacking. The term "Neo-Romanticism" has been used to describe many composers' return to the forms and genres used during the Romantic period, to a greater emphasis on melody, and to the appearance of some tonal centers within the music.

Throughout the twentieth century, as in the nineteenth, composers have created works of varying degrees of quality. A great deal of bad music has been written, and a lot that is mediocre, as well as excellent compositions written by fine composers. The last quarter of the twentieth century has been characterized by diversity. Contemporary historians can speak of the present era only as an Age of Diversity; they are too close to the period to be objective in assigning it a definitive name.

Appendix

Guide to Pronunciation of Liturgical Latin According to Roman Use

Syllables

There are as many syllables in Latin words as there are vowels or diphthongs. In the division of words into syllables:

1. A single consonant goes with the following vowel.
2. Division is made between double consonants, and each of the consonants must be sounded clearly, e.g., bello = behl-loh, *not* as in English word bellow.
3. If two or more consonants are between two vowels, the division is *generally* made before the last consonant, e.g., ma-gis-ter. Exceptions are: (a) If the last consonant of the group is h, l, or r, the last two consonants go with the following vowel, e.g., pa-tria. (b) Compound words are divided into their original parts, e.g., de-scen-do. (c) x goes with the preceding vowel, e.g. dux-i.

Vowels

1. a as in father: Ma-ri-a = Mah-ree-ah.
2. e as in met: Chris-te = Krees-teh (generally sung Kree-steh).
   Avoid the diphthong sound ay-ee as in stay.
3. i as in marine: Fi-li-i = fee-lee-ee.
4. y is the same as i: Ky-ri-e = Kee-ree-eh.
5. o as in for: cor-po = kawr-poh; no-mi-ne = naw-mee-neh.
6. u as in moon: lu-na = loo-nah.
   Avoid the diphthong sound ee-oo.
   When u is preceded by q, the combination qu is pronounced kw as in square: qui = kwee.
7. When two vowels come together each vowel is pronounced, except in diphthongs ae and oe. In singing, the first vowel is sustained and the second vowel is sounded on passing to the next syllable: a-it = ah-eet.

Diphthongs

1. ae and oe are pronounced like e: sae-cu-lum = seh-koo-loom.
2. au and eu are pronounced as a single syllable, but each vowel must be distinctly heard. In singing, the first vowel is sustained as in other combinations of two vowels: la-u-da = lah-oo-dah.

Consonants

1. b, d, f, l, m, n, p, and v are pronounced the same as in English.
2. c before e, i, y, ae, oe is pronounced ch as in church: coe-lum = cheh-loom; otherwise, c is pronounced k as in can: sa-crum = sah-kroom.
3. cc before e, i, y, ae, ce is pronounced t-ch: ec-ce = et-cheh.
4. ch is pronounced as k: che-ru-bim = keh-roo-beem.
5. g is soft before e, i, ae, oe, y, as in generous: ge-mi-nus = jeh-mee-noos; otherwise, g is hard, as in get: ga-rum = gah-room. The word gigas contains both sounds: jee-gahs.
6. gn is pronounced as ny in canyon: a-gnus = ah-nyoos.
7. h is mute, except in mi-hi = mee-kee, and in ni-hil = nee-keel.
8. j is pronounced as i or y: e-jus = eh-yoos, or ju-bi-lus = yoo-bee-loos.
9. q is always followed by u and another vowel and is pronounced as in square: quam = kwahm; qua-lis = kwah-lees.
10. r is slightly rolled on the tongue and is never given a hard sound such as ar.
11. sc before e, i, ae, oe, y, is pronounced sh as in shed: de-scen-dit = deh-shehn-deet.
12. th is pronounced t: ther-ma = tehr-mah.
13. ti is pronounced tzee when followed by another vowel and not following s, x, t: gra-ti-a = grah-tzee-ah.
14. x is pronounced ks as in vex: ex-cla-mat = eks-klah-maht.
15. xc before e, ae, oe, i, y is pronounced ksh: ex-cel-sis = ek-shel-sees; xc before other vowels has the hard sound of ksk: ex-cus-so-rum = eks-koos-saw-room.
16. z is pronounced dz: za-mi-a = dzah-mee-ah.

Select Bibliography
for Further Reading

General

Detailed bibliography of collected works and editions: (a) "Editions, Historical," *The New Harvard Dictionary of Music,* ed. Don M. Randel (Cambridge, MA: Harvard U. Press, 1986), pp. 264–76. (b) "Editions, Historical," *The New Grove Dictionary of Music and Musicians,* 20 vols., ed. Stanley Sadie (London: Macmillan, 1980–81), Vol. 5, pp. 848–69.

Detailed bibliography of primary source materials: "Sources," *The New Grove Dictionary of Music and Musicians,* 20 vols., ed. Stanley Sadie (London: Macmillan, 1980–81), Vol. 17, pp. 590–753.

Biblia sacra, Vulgate edition (Paris: Librairie Garnier Frères, 1868).

Austin, William W. *Music in the Twentieth Century: From Debussy through Stravinsky* (New York: Norton, 1966).

——, ed. *New Looks at Italian Opera* (Westport, CT: Greenwood Press, 1976).

Béhague, Gerard. *Music in Latin America: An Introduction* (Englewood Cliffs, NJ: Prentice-Hall, 1979).

Bowers, Jane, and Judith Tick. *Women Making Music: The Western Art Tradition, 1150–1950* (Urbana, IL: U. of Illinois Press, 1986).

Bukofzer, Manfred. *Music in the Baroque Era: From Monteverdi to Bach* (New York: Norton, 1947).

Bulfinch, Thomas. *Bulfinch's Mythology* (New York: Crowell, n.d.).

Claudon, Francis, J. Mongrédien, C. de Nys, and K. Roschitz. *Histoire de L'Opéra en France* (Paris: Nathan, 1986).

Clough, Shepard B., et al. *European History in a World Perspective,* 2 vols., 3d ed. (Lexington, MA: Heath, 1975).

Egan, Edward W., C. B. Hintz, and L. F. Wise, comp. and eds. *Kings, Rulers, and Statesmen,* rev. ed. (New York: Sterling Publishing, 1976).

Farmer, Henry G. *A History of Music in Scotland* (London: Hinrichsen, 1947; repr. New York: Da Capo Press, 1970).

Ferguson, Donald N. *Image and Structure in Chamber Music* (Minneapolis: U. of Minnesota Press, 1964).

Gardner, Helen. *Gardner's Art Through the Ages,* 6th ed., rev. by H. de la Croix and R. G. Tansey (New York: Harcourt Brace Jovanovich, 1975).

Gies, Frances, and Joseph Gies. *Women in the Middle Ages* (New York: Crowell, 1978).

Gillespie, John. *Five Centuries of Keyboard Music: An Historical Survey of Music for Harpsichord and Piano* (Belmont, CA: Wadsworth, 1965).

Grout, Donald J. *A Short History of Opera,* 2d ed. (New York: Columbia U. Press, 1965).

Grun, Bernard. *The Timetables of History,* new updated ed. (New York: Simon & Schuster, 1979).

Harrison, Frank Ll., *Music in Medieval Britain,* 2d ed., ed. Egon Wellesz (London: Routledge and Kegan Paul, 1963).

Hitchcock, H. Wiley. *Music in the United States: A Historical Introduction,* 3d ed. (Englewood Cliffs, NJ: Prentice-Hall, 1988).

Hope-Wallace, Philip. *A Picture History of Opera* (London: Hulton, 1959).

Hoppin, Richard H. *Medieval Music* (New York: Norton, 1978).

Hughes, Andrew. *Medieval Music: The Sixth Liberal Art* (Toronto: U. of Toronto Press, 1980).

Kirby, Frank E. *A Short History of Keyboard Music* (New York: Free Press, 1966).

Kralik, Heinrich. *The Vienna Opera,* trans. Richard Rickett. (London: Methuen, 1963).

Leonard, Richard A. *A History of Russian Music* (New York: Macmillan, 1956; repr. New York: Minerva Press, 1968; repr. Westport, CT: Greenwood Press, 1977).

MacKerness, Eric D. *A Social History of English Music* (Westport, CT: Greenwood Press, 1976).

Marcuse, Sibyl. *Musical Instruments: A Comprehensive Dictionary* (New York: Doubleday, 1964).

McGee, Timothy J. *The Music of Canada* (New York: Norton, 1985).

Meggett, Joan M. *Keyboard Music by Women Composers: A Catalog and Bibliography* (Westport, CT: Greenwood Press, 1981).

Longyear, Rey M. *Nineteenth-Century Romanticism in Music,* 3d ed. (Englewood Cliffs, NJ: Prentice-Hall, 1988).

Neuls-Bates, Carol, ed. *Women in Music: An Anthology of Source Readings from the Middle Ages to the Present* (New York: Harper & Row, 1982).

The New Grove Dictionary of Music and Musicians, 20 vols., ed. Stanley Sadie (New York: Macmillan, 1980–81).

The New Oxford History of Music, 10 vols., ed. Jack A. Westrup, Gerald Abraham, et al. (London: Oxford U. Press, 1954–).

Newmarch, Rosa. *The Music of Czechoslovakia* (London: Oxford U. Press, 1972; repr. New York: Da Capo Press, 1978).

Plantinga, Leon. *Romantic Music* (New York: Norton, 1984).

Raynor, Henry. *A Social History of Music: From the Middle Ages to Beethoven* (New York: Schocken, 1972).

——. *Music & Society Since 1815* (New York: Schocken, 1976).

Reese, Gustave. *Music in the Middle Ages* (New York: Norton, 1940).

——. *Music in the Renaissance,* rev. ed. (New York: Norton, 1959).

Roberts, Alexander, and James Donaldson, eds. *The Ante-Nicene Fathers,* Vol. VIII [Apocryphal Books of *The Bible*] (Buffalo, New York: The Christian Literature Co., 1886).

Salzman, Eric. *Twentieth-Century Music,* 3d ed. (Englewood Cliffs, NJ: Prentice-Hall, 1988).

Simms, Bryan. *Music of the Twentieth Century: Style and Structure* (New York: Schirmer Books, 1986).

Strunk, Oliver. *Source Readings in Music History* (New York: Norton, 1950).

Subira, José. *Historia de la Música española e Hispano Americana* (Barcelona and Madrid: Salvat Editoreo, 1953).

Sumner, William L. *The Organ: Its Evolution, Principles of Construction and Use,* 3d ed. (London: Macdonald, 1962).

Trevelyan, Janet P. *A Short History of the Italian People,* 3d ed. (New York: Pitman, 1956).

Ulrich, Homer. *Symphonic Music: Its Evolution Since the Renaissance* (New York: Columbia U. Press, 1952).

———. *Chamber Music,* 2d ed. (New York: Columbia U. Press, 1966).

Walker, Ernest. *A History of Music in England,* 3d ed., rev. by J. A. Westrup (Oxford: Clarendon, 1952).

Chapter 1. Heritage from Antiquity

General

Quasten, Johannes. *Music & Worship in Pagan & Christian Antiquity* (Munster: Aschendorff, 1973), Eng. trans. Boniface Ramsey, O. P. (trans. 1973; publ. Washington, D.C.: National Association of Pastoral Musicians, 1983).

Sachs, Curt. *The Rise of Music in the Ancient World* (New York: Norton, 1943).

Wellesz, Egon, ed. *Ancient and Oriental Music,* Vol. I of *The New Oxford History of Music,* 10 vols., ed. J. A. Westrup, et al. (London: Oxford U. Press, 1957).

Greek Music

Anderson, Warren D. *Ethos and Education in Greek Music* (Cambridge, MA: Harvard U. Press, 1966).

Aristotle. *The Works of Aristotle,* ed. W. D. Ross, trans. J. J. Beare et al. (Oxford: Oxford U. Press, 1908–52), especially *Politics,* Book VIII. See also Aristotle, *Politics,* bilingual edition in *The Loeb Classics Library* (Cambridge, MA: Harvard U. Press, 1932).

Aristoxenus. *Harmonics,* ed. and trans. Henry S. Macran, publ. as *The Harmonics of Aristoxenus* (Oxford: Clarendon Press, 1902).

Barker, Andrew, ed. *Greek Musical Writings,* Vol. I, *The Musician and His Art* (Cambridge, Eng.: Cambridge U. Press, 1984).

Crocker, Richard. "Pythagorean Mathematics and Music," *Journal of Aesthetics and Art Criticism* 22 (1963–64), pp. 189–98, 325–35.

Lippmann, Edward. *Musical Thought in Ancient Greece* (New York: Columbia U. Press, 1964).

Mountford, James Frederick. "The Harmonics of Ptolemy and the Lacuna in II,14" *Transactions and Proceedings of the American Philological Association,* ed. Joseph W. Hewett, lvii (1926) (Middletown, CT: American Philological Association), pp. 71–95.

Plato. *Republic,* trans. Desmond Lee (Harmondsworth, Eng. and Baltimore, MD: Penguin, 1974), esp. Book III.

———. *Timaeus,* trans. Robert G. Bury, bilingual ed., *The Loeb Classics Library* (Cambridge, MA: Harvard U. Press, 1929; repr. 1981).

Hebrew

Vantoura, Suzanne Haïk. *La Musique de la Bible Révélée* [book and cassette tape] (Paris: Dessin et Tolra, 1978).

India

Kaufmann, Walter. *The Rāgas of North India* (Bloomington, IN: Indiana U. Press, 1968).

Wade, Bonnie C. *Music in India: The Classical Traditions* (Englewood Cliffs, NJ: Prentice-Hall, 1979).

Near and Middle East

Bibikov, Sergey N. *The Oldest Musical Complex, Made of Mammoth Bones* (Kiev: Iadatelstvo "Naukova Dumka," 1981).

Kilmer, Anne Draffkorn, Richard L. Crocker, and Robert R. Brown. *Sounds from Silence* (Berkeley, CA: Bit Enki Publications, 1976).

Chapter 2. The Early Christian Era

General

Cattin, Giulio. *Music of the Middle Ages I,* trans. Steven Botterill (Cambridge, Eng.: Cambridge U. Press, 1984).

Levi, Peter. *The Frontiers of Paradise: A Study of Monks and Monasteries* (New York: Weidenfeld & Nicolson, 1988).

Boethius, Cassiodorus

Boethius, A. M. S. *Consolation of Philosophy,* trans. H. F. Stewart and E. K. Rand, bilingual ed., in *The Loeb Classics Library* (Cambridge, MA: Harvard U. Press, 1946; repr. 1953).

———. *De institutione musica,* trans. Calvin M. Bower, publ. as *Fundamentals of Music* (New Haven, CT: Yale U. Press, 1989).

Carpenter, N. C. *Music in the Medieval and Renaissance Universities* (Norman, OK: U. of Oklahoma Press, 1958).

Rand, Edward K. *Founders of the Middle Ages* (Cambridge: Harvard U. Press, 1929; repr. New York: Dover, 1957), Chapter 5.

Schrade, Leo. "Music in the Philosophy of Boethius," *The Musical Quarterly* xxiii (1947), pp. 188–200.

Byzantine

Strunk, Oliver. *Essays on Music in the Byzantine World* (New York: Norton, 1977).

Wellesz, Egon. *A History of Byzantine Music and Hymnody,* 2d ed. (Oxford: Clarendon, 1961; repr. 1971).

———. *Eastern Elements in Western Chant* (Oxford: Byzantine Institute, 1947).

———. "Music of the Eastern Churches," in *The New Oxford History of Music,* Vol. II, ed. Anselm Hughes, 2d ed., rev. (London: Oxford U. Press, 1955), pp. 14–51.

Christian Church

Augustinus, Aurelius [Saint Augustine]. *Confessions,* trans. Edward B. Pusey, Vol. 7 in *The Harvard Classics* (New York: Collier, 1909). Also, *Confessions of St. Augustine,* trans. E. M. Blaiklock (Nashville: T. Nelson, 1983).

Backhouse, Janet. *The Lindisfarne Gospels* (Oxford: Phaidon Press, 1981).

Chabannes, Jacques. *St. Augustine* (Paris: Empire, 1961), trans. Julie Kernan (Garden City, NY: Doubleday, 1962).

Jungmann, Josef A. *The Early Liturgy to the Time of Gregory the Great* (Notre Dame, IN: U. of Notre Dame Press, 1959).

McCann, Justin, ed. and trans. *The Rule of St. Benedict in Latin and English* (London: Burns, Oates, 1952).

Migne, Jacques Paul, ed. *Patrologiae cursus completus . . . Series latina,* 221 vols. (Paris: J. P. Migne, 1841–79), re: writings of specific church fathers.

———. *Patrologiae cursus completus . . . Series Graeca,* 161 vols. (Paris: J. P. Migne, 1857–87), re: writings of St. John Chrysostomus and other church fathers.

Oates, Whitney J. *Basic Writings of Saint Augustine* (New York: Random House, 1948).

Roberts, Alexander, and James Donaldson, eds. *The Ante-Nicene Fathers: Translations of the Writings of the Fathers down to A.D. 325,* 10 vols. (New York: Scribner's, 1899–1900).

Treitler, Leo. "Homer and Gregory: The Transmission of Epic Poetry and Plainchant," *The Musical Quarterly,* lv (1974), pp. 333–74.

Gregory the Great

Dudden, Frederick H. *Gregory the Great: His Place in History and Thought,* 2 vols. (London: Longmans, Green, 1905; repr. New York: Russell & Russell, 1967).

Richards, Jeffrey. *Consul of God: The Life and Times of Gregory the Great* (London: Routledge & Kegan Paul, 1980).

Hebrew

Idelsohn, A. Z. *Jewish Music in Its Historical Development* (New York: Schocken Books, 1967).

Rothmuller, Aron M. *The Music of the Jews,* new, rev. ed. (Cranbury, NJ: A. S. Barnes, 1975).

Werner, Eric. *The Sacred Bridge,* Vol. I: *Liturgical Parallels in Synagogue and Early Church* (New York: Columbia U. Press, 1959; Schocken Books, 1970; repr. Da Capo Press, 1979); Vol. II: *The Interdependence of Liturgy and Music in Synagogue and Church during the First Millennium* (New York: KTAV Publishing House, 1984).

Chapter 3. Ecclesiastical Chant

Music

Benedictines of Solesmes, eds. *The Liber Usualis with Introduction and Rubrics in English* (Tournai, Belgium: Desclée & Co., 1960).

Frere, Walter H., ed. *Antiphonale Sarisburiense,* 17 vols. (London: The Plainsong & Mediaeval Music Society, 1901–26; repr. 1966).

———. *Graduale Sarisburiense* (London: The Plainsong & Mediaeval Music Society, 1894; repr. Farnborough, Eng.: Gregg, 1966).

———. *The Use of Sarum* (Cambridge, Eng.: Cambridge U. Press, 1898, 1900).

Legg, J. W., ed. *The Sarum Missal* (Oxford: Clarendon, 1916; repr. 1969).

Paléographie musicale: Les principaux manuscrits de chant Grégorien, Ambrosien, Mozarabe, Gallican [Facsimiles of The principal manuscripts of chant: Gregorian, Ambrosian, Mozarabian, Gallican] (Solesmes, France: Imprimerie St.-Pierre, and Tournai, Belgium: Desclée, Lefebure, 1889–), 2 series.

Suñol, G. M., ed. *Antiphonale missarum juxta ritum Sanctae Ecclesiae Mediolanensis* [Ambrosian Antiphonale] (Rome, 1935).

———. *Canti ambrosiani per il popolo* (Milan, 1936).

For Further Reading

Anglès, H. "Latin Chant before St. Gregory," *New Oxford History of Music,* Vol. II (1954), pp. 58–91.

Apel, Willi. *Gregorian Chant* (Bloomington, IN: Indiana U. Press, 1958; 3d ed., 1966).

Backhouse, Janet. *The Lindisfarne Gospels* (Oxford: Phaidon Press, 1981).

Cattin, Giulio. *Music of the Middle Ages I,* trans. Steven Botterill (Cambridge, Eng.: Cambridge U. Press, 1984).

Harrison, Frank L. *Music in Medieval Britain* (London: Routledge & Kegan Paul, 1958; 2d ed., 1963).

Hughes, David. "Evidence for the Traditional View of the Transmission of Gregorian Chant," *Journal of the American Musicological Society,* xl (1987), pp. 377–404.

Jesson, R. "Ambrosian Chant," in W. Apel: *Gregorian Chant* (Bloomington, IN: Indiana U. Press, 1958; 3d ed., 1966).

Jungmann, Josef A. *The Early Liturgy to the Time of Gregory the Great* (Notre Dame, IN: U. of Notre Dame Press, 1959).

Lechner, R. F. "Mozarabic Rite," and Wortman, I., "Mozarabic Rite, Chants of," in *New Catholic Encyclopedia,* x (New York: McGraw-Hill, 1967), pp. 58–60.

Levy, Kenneth. "Charlemagne's Archetype of Gregorian Chant," *Journal of the American Musicological Society,* xl (1987), pp. 1–30.

Porter, William S. *The Gallican Rite, Studies in Eucharistic Faith and Practice,* Vol. IV (London: Mowbray, and New York: Morehouse-Gorham, 1958).

Chapter 4. The Roman Liturgy

Liturgical Books

Abbatiae Sancti Petri de Solesmis and Consociatio Internationalis Musicae Sacrae. *Liber cantualis* (Solesmes, France: Abbaye Saint-Pierre, and Tournai, Belgium: Desclée, 1978).

Abbaye Saint-Pierre de Solesmes. *Graduale Sacrosanctae Romanae Ecclesiae de tempore & de sanctis* (Solesmes, France: Abbaye Saint-Pierre, and Tournai, Belgium: Desclée, 1979).

———. *Graduale Triplex* (Solesmes, France: Abbaye Saint-Pierre, and Tournai, Belgium: Desclée, 1979).

Benedictines of Solesmes, eds. *The Liber Usualis with Introduction and Rubrics in English* (Tournai, Belgium: Desclée & Co., 1960).

Lectionary for Mass, Eng. trans., American version, being *The Roman Missal* revised by decree of The Second Vatican Council and published by authority of Pope Paul VI (New York: Catholic Book Publishing Co., 1970).

The Rites of the Catholic Church as Revised by The Second Vatican Council and published by Authority of Pope Paul VI, Eng. trans., The International Commission on English in the Liturgy (New York: Pueblo Publishing Co., 1976).

The Sacramentary, Eng. trans. by The International Commission on English in the Liturgy, revised by decree of The Second Vatican Council and published by authority of Pope Paul VI (New York: Catholic Book Publishing Co., 1974).

For Further Reading

Abbott, Walter M., S. J., gen. ed. *The Documents of Vatican II*, trans. Msgr. Joseph Gallagher (The America Press, 1967).

Cattin, Giulio. *Music of the Middle Ages I*, trans. Steven Botterill (Cambridge, Eng.: Cambridge U. Press, 1984).

Handschin, Jacques. "Trope, Sequence, and Conductus," *Early Medieval Music up to 1300*, ed. Dom Anselm Hughes, Vol. II of *New Oxford History of Music*, rev. ed. (London: Oxford U. Press, 1955), pp. 128–74.

Jungmann, Josef A. *The Mass of the Roman Rite: Its Origins and Development*, 2 vols., trans. Francis A. Brunner (New York: Benziger, 1951–55; repr. 1986).

———. *The Mass: An Historical, Theological, and Pastoral Survey*, trans. Julian Fernandes, ed. Mary E. Evans (Collegeville, MN: Liturgical Press, 1976).

Marty, Martin E. *A Short History of Christianity* (New York: Meridian, 1959).

McKinnon, J. W., ed. *Music in Early Christian Literature* (Cambridge, Eng.: Cambridge U. Press, 1987).

Richstatter, Thomas, O. F. M. *Liturgical Law: New Style, New Spirit* (Chicago: Franciscan Herald Press, 1977).

Liturgical Drama

Music

Coussemaker, Edmond de. *Drames liturgique du moyen-âge* [Liturgical dramas of the Middle Ages], an anthology (New York: Broude, 1964).

Greenberg, Noah, ed. *The Play of Daniel* (New York: Oxford U. Press, 1959).

———. *The Play of Herod* (New York: Oxford U. Press, 1965).

Texts, and For Further Reading

Bevington, David. *Medieval Drama* (Boston: Houghton Mifflin, 1975).

Lipphardt, Walther. *Lateinische Osterfeiern und Osterspiele* [Latin Easter plays] (Berlin: DeGruyter, 1975–).

Young, Karl. *The Drama of the Medieval Church* (Oxford: Clarendon, 1933).

Notker

Crocker, Richard L. *The Early Medieval Sequence* (Berkeley, CA: U. of California Press, 1977).

Steinen, Wolfrem von den. *Notker der Dichter und seine geistige Welt*, 2 vols., bilingual (Bern, Switz.: A. Francke, 1948).

———, ed. *Notkeri Poetae Liber Ymnorum* [Book of Hymns of Notker, Poet] (Bern, Switz.: Francke, 1960).

Chapter 5. Early Middle Ages

General

Barraclough, Geoffrey. *The Crucible of Europe* (Berkeley, CA: U. of California Press, 1976).

Caldwell, John. *Medieval Music* (Bloomington, IN: Indiana U. Press, 1978), pp. 114–30.

Coussemaker, C. Edmond de. *Scriptorum de musica medii aevi nova series* (Paris: A. Durand, 1864–76; repr. Hildesheim: G. Olms, 1963).

Gerbert, Martin. *Scriptores ecclesiatici de musica sacra*, 3 vols. (St. Blasien, 1784; repr. Hildesheim: Olms, 1963).

Henderson, Ernest F., ed. and trans. *Select Historical Documents of the Middle Ages* (London: George Bell and Sons, 1892; repr. New York: AMS Press, 1968).

Hoppin, Richard. *Medieval Music* (New York: Norton, 1978), pp. 187–214.

Hughes, Andrew. *Medieval Music: The Sixth Liberal Art* (Toronto: U. of Toronto Press, 1974; repr. 1980).

Hughes, Dom Anselm. "The Birth of Polyphony," and "Music in the Twelfth Century," *Early Medieval Music up to 1300*, vol. II of *The New Oxford History of Music* (London: Oxford U. Press, 1954; rev. 1955).

Munrow, David. *Instruments of the Middle Ages and Renaissance* (London: Oxford U. Press and EMI Records, 1976).

Ogg, Frederic A., ed. *A Source Book of Mediaeval History: Documents illustrative of European Life and Institutions from the German Invasions to the Renaissance* (New York: American Book Co., 1907).

Palisca, Claude, ed. *Hucbald, Guido and John on Music* (New Haven, CT: Yale U. Press, 1978).

Reese, Gustave. *Music in the Middle Ages* (New York: Norton, 1940), pp. 249–71, 387ff.

Stoddard, Whitney S. *Monastery and Cathedral in France* (Middletown, CT: Wesleyan U. Press, 1966).

Guido

Chailley, Jacques. "*Ut queant laxis* et les Origines de la Gamme," [*Ut queant laxis* and the origins of the scale], *Acta Musicologica*, lvi (1984), pp. 48–58.

Waesberghe, Joseph Smits van. "Guido of Arezzo and Musical Improvisation," *Musica Disciplina*, v (1951), pp. 55–63.

———. "The Musical Notation of Guido of Arezzo," *Musica Disciplina*, v (1951), pp. 15–53.

Organum

Anonymous. *Ad Organum faciendum & Item de Organo*, ed. and trans. Jay A. Huff (Brooklyn, NY: The Institute of Mediaeval Music, 1969).

Anonymous. *Musica enchiriadis*, trans. Leonie Rosenstiel (Colorado Springs, CO: Colorado College, 1976).

Anonymous. *Scolica enchiriadis*, trans. Nancy C. Phillips (Diss., Ann Arbor, MI: University Microfilms, 1985).

Frere, W. H. *The Winchester Troper* (London: Henry Bradshaw Society, 1894).

Britain

Baxter, J. H., ed. *An Old St. Andrews Music Book*, facsimile ed. (London: St. Andrews U. Publications, 1931).

Galpin, Francis W. *Old English Instruments of Music* (London: Methuen, 1910; repr. 1978).

Harrison, Frank L. *Music in Medieval Britain* (London: Routledge & Kegan Paul, 1958; 2d ed., 1963), Chapter 3.

Planchart, Alejandro. *The Repertory of Tropes at Winchester*, 2 vols. [music] (Princeton, NJ: Princeton U. Press, 1977).

Santiago de Compostela

Wagner, Peter, ed. *Die Gesänge der Jakobusliturgie zu Santiago de Compostela aus dem Sog. Codex Calixtinus* [The songs of the Jacobus liturgy at Santiago de Compostela in the so-called Codex Calixtinus] (Freiburg, Switz.: Universitaets-Buchhandlung, 1931).

Whitehill, Walter M., and G. Prado. *Liber Sancti Jacobi, Codex Calixtinus,* 3 vols. [facsimile, transcriptions, commentary] (Santiago de Compostela, 1944).

St. Martial

Treitler, Leo. "The Polyphony of St. Martial," *Journal of the American Musicological Society,* xvii (1963), pp. 29–42.

Chapter 6. The Middle Ages — *Ars Antiqua*

General

Barraclough, Geoffrey. *The Crucible of Europe* (Berkeley, CA: U. of California Press, 1976).

Caldwell, John. *Medieval Music* (Bloomington, IN: Indiana U. Press, 1978), pp. 131–58.

Henderson, Ernest F., ed. and trans. *Select Historical Documents of the Middle Ages* (London: George Bell & Sons, 1892; repr. AMS Press, 1968).

Kubach, Hans Erich. *Romanesque Architecture* (New York: Harry N. Abrams, 1975).

Ogg, Frederick A., ed. *A Source Book of Mediaeval History* (New York: American Book Co., 1907).

Reese, Gustave. *Music in the Middle Ages* (New York: Norton, 1940), pp. 272–330.

Temko, Allan. *Notre-Dame of Paris* (New York: Viking Press, 1955).

Notation, Theory

Apel, Willi. *The Notation of Polyphonic Music, 900–1600,* 5th ed. (Cambridge, MA: Medieval Academy of America, 1961), pp. 282–324.

Parrish, Carl. *The Notation of Medieval Music* (New York: Norton, 1957, 1959), pp. 60–140.

Franco of Cologne

Franco of Cologne. *Ars cantus mensurabilis,* trans. and annotated, in Oliver Strunk: *Source Readings in Music History* (New York: Norton, 1950), pp. 139–59.

Hocket

Grocheo, Johannes de. *De musica,* trans. A. Seay, publ. as *Johannes de Grocheo: Concerning Music* (Colorado Springs, CO: Colorado College, 1967; 2d ed., 1973).

Sanders, Ernest H. "The Medieval Hocket in Practice and Theory," *The Musical Quarterly,* lx (1974), pp. 246–56.

Notre Dame School

Music

Manuscript: Wolfenbüttel Helmstedt 628 (formerly 677), [W₁]. Facsimile: *An Old St. Andrews Music Book,* ed. J. H. Baxter (London: St. Andrews U. Publications, 1931).

Manuscript: Wolfenbüttel Helmstedt 1099 (formerly 1206), [W₂]. Facsimile: *Wolfenbüttel 1099,* ed. Luther Dittmer (Brooklyn, NY: Institute of Medieval Music, 1960).

Manuscript: Pluteus 29.1, Biblioteca Medicea-Laurenziana, Florence. Facsimile: *Firenze, Biblioteca Medicea-Laurenziana, pluteo 29.1 [sic],* 2 vols., ed. L. Dittmer, publ. as Vols. 10–11 of *Publications of Medieval Music Manuscripts* (Brooklyn, NY: Institute of Mediaeval Music, 1966–67).

Husmann, Heinrich, ed. *Die drei- und vierstimmige Notre-Dame Organa* [The three- and four-voice Notre Dame organa] (Leipzig: Breitkopf & Härtel, 1940; repr. Hildesheim: G. Olms, 1967).

Thurston, Ethel, ed. *The Works of Perotin* (New York: Kalmus, 1970).

———. *The Conductus Collection of MS Wolfenbüttel 1099,* 3 vols. (Madison, WI: A-R Editions, 1980).

For Further Reading

Anonymous IV, trans. and ed. Luther Dittmer, Vol. I of *Musical Theorists in Translation* (Brooklyn, NY: Institute of Mediaeval Music, 1959).

Guérard, Paul. *Collection des Cartulaires de France,* Vol. IV, *Cartulaire de l'Église Notre-Dame de Paris,* Tome I [Documents of the Church of Notre Dame of Paris, unedited] (Paris: Crapelet, 1850).

Hoppin, Richard. *Medieval Music* (New York: Norton, 1978), pp. 215–55.

Husmann, H. "The Origin and Destination of the *Magnus liber organi,*" *The Musical Quarterly,* xlix (1963), pp. 311–30.

Roesner, Edward H. "The Origins of W₁," *Journal of the American Musicological Society,* xxix (1976), pp. 337–80.

Sanders, E. H. "The Question of Perotin's Oeuvre and Dates," *Festschrift für Walter Wiora,* ed. L. Finscher and C.-H. Mahling (Kassel: Bärenreiter, 1967), pp. 241–49.

Tischler, Hans. "The Dates of Perotin," *Journal of the American Musicological Society,* xvi (1963), pp. 240ff.

———. "The Evolution of the *Magnus liber organi,*" *The Musical Quarterly,* lxx (1984), pp. 163–74.

———. "The Structure of Notre Dame Organa," *Acta Musicologica,* xlix (1977), pp. 193ff.

Waite, William G. *The Rhythm of Twelfth-Century Polyphony* (New Haven, CT: Yale U. Press, 1954).

Wright, Craig. "Leoninus, Poet and Musician," *Journal of the American Musicological Society,* xlix (1986), pp. 21–52.

Motet

Music

Bamberg Codex. (a) Manuscript: Lit.115 (formerly Ed.IV.6), Staatliche Bibliothek, Bamberg, West Germany (Federal Republic of Germany). (b) Editions: Aubrey, Pierre. *Cent motets du XIIIe siècle: publiés d'après le manusrit Ed.IV.6 de Bamberg* (Paris: A. Rouart, Lerolle & Cie, P. Guethner, 1908), 3 vols. (1, facsimile; 2, transcription; 3, commentary). Anderson, G., ed. *Compositions of the Bamberg Manuscript,* Vol. 75 of *Corpus mensurabilis musicae,* American Institute of Musicology (Neuhausen-Stuttgart: Hänssler, 1977).

Las Huelgas Codex. (a) Manuscript at Monasterio de Las Huelgas, Burgos, Spain. (b) Edition: Anglès, Higini. *El codex musical de Las Huelgas* (Barcelona: Institut d'estudis Catalans, Biblioteca de Catalunya, 1931), 3 vols. (1, commentary; 2, facsimile; 3, transcription).

Montepellier Codex. (a) Manuscript: H 196, Faculté de médecine, Montpellier, France. (b) Editions: Rokseth, Yvonne. *Polyphonies du XIIIe siècle: Le manuṣrit H 196 de la Faculté de Medicine de Montpellier* (Paris: Éditions de l'Oiseau Lyre, 1935–39), 4 vols. (1, facsimile; 2, 3, transcription; 4, commentary). Tischler, Hans, ed. *The Montpellier Codex,* 3 vols. (Madison, WI: A-R Editions, 1978).

Comparative edition of early motets from various manuscripts: Tischler, Hans. *The Earliest Motets (to circa 1270): A Complete Comparative Edition* (New Haven, CT: Yale U. Press, 1982), 3 vols. (1, 2, music; 3, notes).

Britain

Harrison, Frank L. *Music in Medieval Britain,* 2d ed. (London: Routledge & Kegan Paul, 1963), pp. 115–49.

Wooldridge, H. E., and H. V. Hughes, eds. *Early English Harmony from the 10th to the 15th Century,* 2 vols., Plainsong and Mediaeval Music Society (London: Quaritch, 1897–1913).

Chapter 7. Medieval Monophony

Latin Songs

Bingen, Hildegard von. *Lieder,* ed. Prudentiana Barth, M. Immaculata Ritscher, and Joseph Schmidt-Görg (Salzburg: Otto Müller Verlag, 1969).

Bruel, Karl, ed. *The Cambridge Songs: A Goliard's Song Book of the XIth Century* (Cambridge, Eng.: Cambridge U. Press, 1915; repr. AMS, 1973, 1978).

Raby, F. J. E. *A History of Secular Latin Poetry in the Middle Ages,* 2 vols. (Oxford: Clarendon, 1934; repr. 1957).

Waddell, Helen. *Songs of the Wandering Scholars,* ed. Felicitas Corrigan (London: The Folio Society, 1982).

England

Armstrong, Robert B. *The Irish and the Highland Harps,* Vol. I of *English and Irish Instruments,* 2 vols. (Edinburgh: D. Douglas, 1904–8; repr. Shannon, Ireland: Irish U. Press, 1969, and New York: Praeger, 1970).

Galpin, Francis W. *Old English Instruments of Music: Their History and Character* (London: Methuen, 1910).

Trend, J. B. "The First English Songs," *Music and Letters,* ix (1928), pp. 111–27.

France

Adam de la Halle

Manuscript: MS 657 (formerly 139), Bibliothèque municipale, Arras. Facsimile: *Le Chansonnier d'Arras,* ed. Alfred Jeanroy (Paris, 1925; repr. New York: Johnson, 1968).

Adam de la Halle. *Works,* Vol. xliv, *Corpus mensurabilis musicae,* ed. A. Carapetyan (Rome: American Institute of Musicology, 1947–).

Coussemaker, E. de, ed. *Oeuvres complètes de Adam de la Halle: poésies et musique* (Paris, 1871); repr. as *Complete Works of the Troubadour Adam de la Halle* (New York: Broude, 1964).

Gennrich, F., ed. *Adam de la Halle: Le jeu de Robin et de Marion; Li Rondel Adam* (Frankfurt am Main: Langen, 1962).

Ruelle, Pierre. *Les Congés d'Arras: Jean Bodel, Baude Fastoul, Adam de la Halle* (Liège: Presses Universitaires de Bruxelles; Paris: Presses Universitaires de France, 1965).

Troubadours, Trouvères

Manuscript: MS 5198 (formerly B.L.F. 63), Bibliothèque de l'Arsenal, Paris. Facsimile, with some transcriptions: *Le Chansonnier de l'Arsenal,* ed. Pierre Aubry (Paris: P. Guethner, 1909–10).

Manuscript: MS *fr.*844, Bibliothèque nationale, Paris. Facsimile: *Le Manuscrit du Roi,* 2 vols., ed. Jean Beck and L. Beck (Philadelphia: U. of Pennsylvania Press, 1938).

Manuscript: *fr.*846 (Cangé 66), Bibliothèque nationale, Paris. Facsimile: *Le Chansonnier Cangé,* 2 vols. (1, facsimile; 2 transcriptions), ed. Jean Beck (Philadelphia: U. of Pennsylvania Press, 1927).

Briffault, R. *The Troubadours* (Bloomington, IN: Indiana U. Press, 1965).

Gennrich, F., ed. *Troubadours, Trouvères, Minne- und Meistergesang,* Vol. II of *Das Musikwerk,* ed. K. G. Fellerer (Cologne: Arno Volk, and London: Leeds Music, 1951); Eng. trans. publ. as *Anthology of Music* (1960).

Page, Christopher. *Voices and Instruments of the Middle Ages: Instrumental practice and songs in France 1100–1300* (Berkeley, CA: U. of California Press, 1986).

Van der Werf, Hendrik. *The Chansons of the Troubadours and Trouvères* (Utrecht: A. Ousthoek, 1972).

Trobairitz

Bogin, Meg [Magda]. *The Women Troubadours* (London: Paddington Press, 1976).

Coldwell, Maria V. "Jougleresses and Trobairitz: Secular Musicians in Medieval France," *Women Making Music: The Western Art Tradition, 1150–1950,* ed. Jane Bowers and Judith Tick (Urbana, IL: U. of Illinois Press, 1986).

Gies, Frances, and Joseph Gies. *Women in the Middle Ages* (New York: Crowell, 1978; repr. Barnes & Noble, 1980).

Neuls-Bates, Carol, ed. *Women in Music: An Anthology of Source Readings from the Middle Ages to the Present* (New York: Harper & Row, 1982), pp. 11–36.

Germanic Lands

Moser, H., and J. Müller-Blattau, eds. *Deutsche Lieder des Mittelalters* [German Songs of the Middle Ages] (Stuttgart: Klett, 1968).

Taylor, R. J., ed. *The Art of the Minnesinger,* 2 vols. (Cardiff: U. of Wales Press, 1968).

(Also see Gennrich, above.)

Iberia

Manuscripts: (1) MS b.I.2 (also known as j.b.2), Real Monasterio de El Escorial; (2) MS T.j.I, Real Monasterio de El Escorial; (3) MS 10069, Biblioteca national, Madrid.

Anglés, Higinio. *La Música de las cantigas de Santa María del rey Alfonso el Sabio* [The music of *Las cantigas de Santa Maria* of King Alfonso the Wise], 3 vols. (1, MS b.I.2 facsimile; 2, MS b.I.2 transcription; 3, other cantigas) (Barcelona: Biblioteca Central, Sección de Música, 1943–64).

———. "Hispanic Musical Culture from the Sixth to the Fourteenth Century," *The Musical Quarterly,* xxvi (1940), pp. 494–528.

Stevenson, Robert. *Spanish Music in the Age of Columbus* (The Hague: M. Nijhoff, 1960).

Italy

Liuzzi, Fernando, ed. *La Lauda e i primordi della melodia italiana,* 2 vols. (Rome: Libreria dello Stato, 1935).

Chapter 8. Late Medieval Music

General

For Further Reading

Boorman, Stanley, ed. *Studies in the Performance of Late Mediaeval Music* (Cambridge, Eng.: Cambridge U. Press, 1983).

Carli, Enzo. *Giotto and His Contemporaries,* trans. Susan Bellamy (New York: Crown Publishers, 1958).

Günther, Ursula. "The Fourteenth-Century Motet and Its Development," *Musica Disciplina,* xii (1958), pp. 27ff.

Harman, Alec. *Man & His Music,* 3 vols., *Part One: Mediaeval and Early Renaissance Music* (New York: Schocken Books, 1969).

Lecaldano, Paolo, ed. *The Complete Paintings of the Van Eycks* (New York: Abrams, 1968).

Prato, Giovanni Gherardi da. *Il Paradiso degli Alberti* (1389), (repr. Rome: Salerno, 1975).

Swann, Win. *The Late Middle Ages: Art and Architecture from 1350 to the Advent of the Renaissance* (Ithaca, NY: Cornell U. Press, 1977).

Van Puyvelde, Leo. *L'Agneau mystique d'Hubert et Jean van Eyck* [The mystic lamb, i.e., the Ghent Altarpiece] (Brussels: Meddens, 1964).

Music

Manuscript: MS Pal. 87 (Squarcialupi Codex), Biblioteca Medicea Laurenziana, Florence. Facsimile: *Der Squarcialupi Codex Pa. 87 der Biblioteca Medicea Laurenziana zu Florenz,* ed. Johannes Wolf (Lippstadt: Fr. Kistner & C. F. W. Siegel & Co., 1955).

Manuscript: *fr.*146 (*Roman de Fauvel*), Bibliothèque nationale, Paris. Text: Gervais du Bus, *Le Roman de Fauvel,* ed. Arthur Langfors (Paris: Didot et Cie., 1914). Transcription: *Polyphonic Music of the Fourteenth Century,* Vol. 1, ed. L. Schrade (Monaco: L'Oiseau-Lyre, 1956).

Corpus mensurabilis musicae, ed. A. Carapetyan (Rome: American Institute of Musicology, 1947–), Vols. 2, 13, 29, 36, 37, 39, 53.

French Secular Compositions of the Fourteenth Century, ed. Willi Apel (Cambridge, MA: Mediaeval Academy of America, 1950); also, as Vol. liii of *Corpus mensurabilis musicae* (Rome: American Institute of Musicology, 1970).

Les monuments de l'Ars nova: la musique polyphonique de 1320 à 1400 environ, ed. G. de Van (Paris: L'Oiseau-Lyre, 1938). [Only 1 volume published; series continued in *Polyphonic Music of the Fourteenth Century.*]

Polyphonic Music of the Fourteenth Century, 24 vols. to date. (Monaco: Éditions de L'Oiseau-Lyre, 1956–). [Vol. 1, *Roman de Fauvel;* 2, 3, Machaut; 4, Landini; 5, Ivrea MS; 6–14, Italian music; 15–17, English music; 18, 19, MSS of Chantilly, Musée Condé.]

Machaut

Music

Guillaume de Machaut: Musikalische Werke, ed. Friedrich Ludwig, 4 vols.; Vol. 4 rev. by H. Besseler (Leipzig: Breitkopf & Härtel, 1926–54; repr. 1954–62; repr. 1968).

Machaut, Guillaume de. *Works,* Vols. 2, 3, of *Polyphonic Music of the Fourteenth Century,* ed. Leo Schrade (Monaco: Éditions de L'Oiseau-Lyre, 1956).

For Further Reading

Gombosi, Otto. "Machaut's *Messe Notre-Dame,*" *The Musical Quarterly,* xxxvi (1950), pp. 204–24.

Levarie, Siegmund. *Guillaume de Machaut,* ed. John J. Becker (New York: Sheed and Ward, 1954; repr. New York: Da Capo Press, 1969).

Macabey, A. *Guillaume de Machaut: la vie et l'oeuvre musicale* [Guillaume de Machaut: Life and musical works] (Paris, 1955).

Perle, George. "Integrative Devices in the Music of Machaut," *The Musical Quarterly* xxxiv (1948), pp. 169–76.

Reaney, Gilbert. *Guillaume de Machaut* (London: Oxford U. Press, 1971).

Theorists

Schrade, Leo, ed. *The Works of Philippe de Vitry,* Vol. I of *Polyphonic Music of the Fourteenth Century* (Monaco: L'Oiseau-Lyre, 1956).

Strunk, Oliver, ed. *Source Readings in Music History* (New York: Norton, 1950), pp. 160–92: excerpts from: (a) Marchetto da Padua, *Pomerium;* (b) Jean de Muris, *Ars novae musicae;* (c) Jacob of Liège, *Speculum musicae.*

Vitry, Philippe de. *Ars nova,* trans. Leon Plantinga, *Journal of Music Theory,* v (1961), pp. 204–23.

England

Greene, R. L. *The Early English Carols* (Oxford: Clarendon, 1935; repr. 1977).

Hughes, Andrew, and M. Bent. "The Old Hall Manuscript," *Musica Disciplina,* xxi (1967), pp. 97–147.

Kenney, S. W. " 'English Discant' and Discant in England," *The Musical Quarterly,* xlv (1959), p. 26ff.

McPeek, Gwynn S., ed. *The British Museum Manuscript Egerton 3307* (London: Oxford U. Press, and Chapel Hill, NC: U. of North Carolina Press, 1963).

The Old Hall Manuscript, ed. Andrew Hughes and Margaret Bent, Vol. 46 of *Corpus mensurabilis musicae,* ed. A. Carapetyan (Rome: American Institute of Musicology, 1969).

Ramsbotham, A., H. B. Collins, and Anselm Hughes, eds. *The Old Hall Manuscript,* 3 vols. (London: The Plainsong and Mediaeval Music Society, 1933–38).

Stevens, John, ed. *Medieval Carols,* Vol. iv of *Musica Britannica* (London: Stainer & Bell, 1952).

Dunstable

J. Dunstable: Complete Works, ed. Manfred Bukofzer, Vol. viii, *Musica Britannica* (London: Stainer & Bell, 1953; 2d ed., rev. by M. Bent, I. Bent, and B. Trowell, 1970).

Italy

L'Ars nova italiana del trecento, 3 vols. (Certaldo, 1959–60).

Landini, Francesco. *Complete Works,* 2 vols., ed. Leo Schrade (Monaco: L'Oiseau-Lyre, 1958; repr. 1982).

———. *Works,* ed. L. Ellinwood (Cambridge, MA: Mediaeval Academy of America, 1939; repr. New York: Kraus, 1970).

Marrocco, Thomas, ed. *Fourteenth-Century Italian Cacce* (Cambridge, MA: Mediaeval Academy of America, 1942; 2d ed., 1961).

———. *The Music of Jacopo da Bologna* (Berkeley, CA: U. of California Press, 1954).

Chapter 9. Transition to Renaissance

General

Codex Tridentinus 87–93 [Trent Codices], facsimile ed. (Rome: Bibliopola, 1969–70).

Fenlon, Iain, ed. *Music in Medieval and Early Modern Europe: Patronage, Sources, and Texts* (Cambridge, Eng.: Cambridge U. Press, 1981).

Hamm, Charles, and A. B. Scott. "A Study and Inventory of the Manuscript Modena, Biblioteca Estense, α.X.1.11," *Musica disciplina,* xxvi (1972), pp. 101–43.

Hanen, Martha. *The Chansonnier El Escorial, IV.a.24,* 3 vols., Vol. 1, commentary; Vols. 2–3, transcriptions (Henryville, PA: Institute of Medieval Music, 1983).

Kottick, Edward. "The Chansonnier Cordiforme," *Journal of the American Musicological Society,* xx (1967), pp. 10–27.

Lane, Frederic C. *Venice: A Maritime Republic* (Baltimore: The Johns Hopkins U. Press, 1973).

Marix, Jeanne. *Histoire de la musique et des musiciens de la cour de Bourgogne sous le règne de Philippe le Bon (1420–1467)* [History of the music and musicians at the Burgundian court during the reign of Philippe the Good (1420–1467)] (Strasbourg: Heitz, 1939).

———, ed. *Les musiciens de la cour de Bourgogne au XV* siècle [The musicians at the Burgundian court in the Fifteenth Century] (Paris: L'Oiseau-Lyre, 1937).

Sparks, Edgar H. *Cantus Firmus in Mass and Motet 1420–1520* (Berkeley, CA: U. of California Press, 1963; repr. New York: Da Capo Press, 1975).

Strohm, Reinhard. *Music in Late Medieval Bruges* (Oxford: Clarendon Press, 1985).

Binche (Binchois)

Die Chansons von Gilles Binchois (1400–1460), ed. W. Rehm, *Musikalisches Denkmäler,* Vol. ii (Mainz: Schott, 1957).

Parris, A. *The Sacred Works of Gilles Binchois* (Diss., Bryn Mawr College, 1965).

Busne (Busnois)

Brooks, C. "Antoine Busnois, Chanson Composer," *Journal of the American Musicological Society,* vi (1953), p. 111ff.

Guillaume Du Fay (Dufay)

Music

G. Dufay: Opera omnia, ed. Guglielmus de Van and Heinrich Besseler, *Corpus mensurabilis musicae,* i (Rome: American Institute of Musicology, 1947).

Dufay, Guillaume. *Zwölf Geistliche und Weltliche Werke,* Vol. 19 in *Das Chorwerk* (Wolfenbüttel: Moseler Verlag, 1932).

———. *Samtliche Hymnen,* Vol. 49 in *Das Chorwerk* (Wolfenbüttel: Moseler Verlag, 1937).

Stainer, J. F. R., and C. Stainer. *Dufay and His Contemporaries* (Amsterdam: Frits A. M. Knuf, 1966).

For Further Reading

Fallows, David. *Dufay* (London: Dent, 1982).

Hamm, Charles. *A Chronology of the Works of Guillaume Dufay* (Princeton, NJ: Princeton U. Press, 1964).

Houdoy, Jules. *Histoire artistique de la cathêdrale de Cambrai, ancienne église métropolitaine de Notre-Dame: comptes, inventaires et documents inédits* [Artistic history of Cambrai Cathedral, ancient metropolitan church of Notre-Dame: accounts, inventories and unedited documents] (Lille: Mémoires de la Société des Sciences, de l'Agriculture et des Arts de Lille, 4th series, Vol. VII, 1880).

Millon, Henry A., ed. *Key Monuments of the History of Architecture* (New York: Henry N. Abrams, 1965).

Papers of the Dufay Quincentenary Conference: Brooklyn College, Brooklyn, NY, 1974, ed. Allan W. Atlas (Brooklyn: Music Dept., Brooklyn College of the City University of New York, 1976).

Planchart, Alejandro E. "Guillaume Dufay's Masses: Notes and Revisions," *The Musical Quarterly,* lviii (1972), pp. 1–23.

Warren, Charles W. "Brunelleschi's Dome and Dufay's Motet," *The Musical Quarterly,* lix (1973), pp. 92–105.

Wright, Craig. "Dufay at Cambrai: Discoveries and Revisions," *Journal of the American Musicological Society,* xxviii (1975), pp. 175–229.

England

The Eton Choirbook, transcribed by F. Ll. Harrison, *Musica Brittanica,* x-xii, Royal Music Association (London: Stainer & Bell, 1951).

Frye

Kenney, Sylvia W. *Walter Frye and the Contenance Angloise* (New Haven, CT: Yale U. Press, 1964).

Tinctoris

Tinctoris, Johannes. *Dictionary of Musical Terms* and *Terminorum Musicae Diffinitorium,* Latin and English edition, trans., annotated, Carl Parrish (London and New York: The Free Press of Glencoe, 1963).

Printing

Barksdale, A. Beverly. *The Printed Note: 500 Years of Music Printing and Engraving* [Toledo Museum of Art exhibition catalog] (Toledo, OH: Toledo Museum of Art, 1957; repr. New York: Da Capo Press, 1981).

Hind, Arthur M. *An Introduction to the History of Woodcut,* 2 vols. (Boston: Houghton Mifflin Co., 1935; repr. New York: Dover, 1963).

King, A. Hyatt. *Four Hundred Years of Music Printing* (London: Trustees of the British Museum, 1964; 3d ed., London: British Library, 1977).

Chapter 10. The Renaissance: Franco-Netherlands Composers

General

Music

Corpus mensurabilis musicae, ed. A. Carapetyan (Rome: American Institute of Musicology, 1947–). Each volume is devoted to works of an individual composer, a number of whom are discussed in this chapter, including Clement (Clemens non papa), vol. iv; Gombert, vi; Isaac, lxv; Mouton, xliii; Pipelare, xxxiv; Willaert, iii.

The Chanson Albums of Marguerite of Austria, ed. Martin Picker (Berkeley, CA: U. of California Press, 1965).

The Medici Codex of 1518, ed. Edward E. Lowinsky, Vols. 3–5 in *Monuments of Renaissance Music* (Chicago: U. of Chicago Press, 1968).

The Mellon Chansonnier, facsimile and modern edition, ed. Leeman Perkins and Howard Garey (New Haven, CT: Yale U. Press, 1979).

Slim, H. Colin, ed. *A Gift of Madrigals and Motets* (Chicago: U. of Chicago Press, 1972).

For Further Reading

Blume, Friedrich. *Renaissance and Baroque Music: A Comprehensive Survey,* trans. M. D. Herter Norton (New York: Norton, 1967), pp. 3–82.

Brown, Howard M. *Music in the Renaissance* (Englewood Cliffs, NJ: Prentice-Hall, 1976).

Bukofzer, Manfred. *Studies in Medieval and Renaissance Music* (New York: Norton, 1950), Chapters 5, 6, and 7.

Burckhardt, Jacob. *The Civilization of the Renaissance in Italy* (1860), 2 vols. (New York: Harper & Brothers, 1958).

Glareanus, Henricus [Henrici Loriti Glareani; Henrich Loris]. *Dodecachordon* (Basle, 1547), facsimile ed. (New York: Broude, 1967).

Lesser, George. *Gothic Cathedrals and Sacred Geometry,* 2 vols. (London: Alec Tiranti, 1957).

Lowinsky, Edward E. *Secret Chromatic Art in the Netherlands Motet* (New York: Columbia U. Press, 1946).

Reese, Gustave. *Music in the Renaissance* (New York: Norton, 1954; 2d rev. ed. 1959), esp. Part I.

Sparks, E. H. *Cantus Firmus in Mass and Motet, 1420–1520* (Berkeley, CA: U. of California Press, 1963).

Stevenson, R. *Spanish Cathedral Music in the Golden Age* (Berkeley and Los Angeles: U. of California Press, 1961).

Clement (Clemens; Clemens non papa)

Clemens non Papa. *Souterliedekens,* Bks. I-III (Antwerp, 1556–57), facsimile ed., Vols. xvi-xviii in Corpus of Early Music in Facsimile (Brussels: Éditions Culture et Civilisation, 1972).

Isaac

H. Isaac: Choralis Constantinus, 3 vols., I, ed. E. Bezecny and W. Rabl, *Denkmäler der Tonkunst in Österreich,* x (Vienna: Artaria, 1898); II, ed. A. von Webern, *Denkmäler der Tonkunst in Österreich,* xxxii (Leipzig: Breitkopf & Härtel, 1909); III, ed. Louise Cuyler (Ann Arbor, MI: U. of Michigan Press, 1956).

H. Isaac: Messen, ed. M. Staehelin, *Musikalische Denkmäler,* vii, viii (Mainz: B. Schott, 1970–73).

H. Isaac: Opera omnia, ed. E. R. Learner, 7 vols., *Corpus mensurabilis musicae* 65 (Rome: American Institute of Musicology, 1974–84).

Josquin Desprez

Josquin Desprez: Werken, ed. A. Smijers, et al. (Amsterdam: Uitgaven der Vereniging voor nederlanse muziekgeschiedenis, 1921–69).

Lowinsky, Edward E., with Bonnie J. Blackburn, eds. *Josquin des Prez* [sic]: *Proceedings of the International Josquin Festival-Conference, New York, 1971* (London: Oxford U. Press, 1976).

La Rue

P. de La Rue: Liber missarum, ed. A. Tirabassi (Malines: Maison Dessain, 1941).

Morales

C. de Morales: Opera omnia, 8 vols., ed. H. Anglés, *Monumentos de la música española* (Rome: Escuela Española de Historia y Arquelogia, 1952–).

Stevenson, R. "Cristóbal de Morales: A Fourth-centenary Biography," *Journal of the American Musicological Society,* vi (1953), pp. 3–42.

Obrecht

Werken von Jacob Obrecht, 8 vols., ed. J. Wolf (Amsterdam: Alsbach, and Leipzig: Breitkopf & Härtel, 1912–21; repr. Gregg International, 1968).

Jacob Obrecht: Opera omnia, 5 vols., ed. A. Smijers and M. van Crevel (Amsterdam: Alsbach, 1953–).

New Obrecht Edition, gen. ed. C. Maas (Amsterdam: Uitgaven der Vereniging voor nederlanse muziekgeschiedenis, 1983–).

Murray, Bain. "Jacob Obrecht's Connection with the Church of Our Lady in Antwerp," *Revue belge de musicologie,* xi (1957), p. 329ff.

———. "New Light on Jacob Obrecht's Development—A Biographical Study," *The Musical Quarterly,* xliii (1957), p. 500ff.

Ockeghem

J. Ockeghem: Sämtliche Werke (Messen I-VIII), ed. Dragan Plamenac, *Publikationen älterer Musik* (Leipzig, 1927), rev. as *J. Ockeghem: Collected Works: I, Masses I-VIII; II, Masses and Mass Sections IX-XVI,* ed. D. Plamenac (New York: American Musicological Society, 1947; 2d, corrected ed. 1959, 1966).

Plamenac, Dragan. "A Postscript to Volume ii of the Collected Works of Johannes Ockeghem," *Journal of the American Musicological Society,* iii (1950), p. 33ff.

Van Ockeghem tot Sweelinck, ed. A. Smijers. Amsterdam: Uitgaven der Vereniging voor nederlanse muziekgeschiedenis (1949–56).

Willaert

Willaert, Adrian. *Musica nova* (Venice: A. Gardano, 1559), ed. H. Colin Slim, *Monuments of Renaissance Music,* i (Chicago and London: U. of Chicago Press, 1964).

Petrucci

Harmonice Musices Odhecaton A (Venice: Petrucci, 1504; repr. New York: Broude, 1973). Also, edition by Helen Hewitt (Cambridge, MA: Medieval Academy of America, 1946).

Canti B (Venice: Petrucci, 1502; repr. New York: Broude, 1975). Also, *O. Petrucci: Canti B numero cinquante (Venice, 1502),* ed. Helen Hewitt, *Monuments of Renaissance Music,* ii (Chicago: U. of Chicago Press, 1967).

Canti C (Venice: Petrucci, 1504; repr. New York: Broude, 1978).

Boorman, S. "The 'First' Edition of the *Odhecaton A,*" *Journal of the American Musicological Society,* xxx (1977), p. 183ff.

Norton, Frederick J. *Italian Printers 1501–1520* (London: Bowes & Bowes, 1958).

Reese, Gustave. "The First Printed Collection of Part-music (the *Odhecaton*), *The Musical Quarterly,* xx (1934), pp. 39–76.

Chapter 11. The Rise of Regional Styles

General

Music

Corpus mensurabilis musicae, ed. A. Carapetyan (Rome: American Institute of Musicology, 1947–). Most volumes are devoted to works of an individual composer, a number of whom are discussed in this chapter, including Arcadelt, xxxi; Crequillon, lxiii; Festa, xxv; Marenzio, lxxii; Rore, xiv; Sermisy, lii; Verdelot, xxviii; Vicentino, xxvi; Wert, xxiv; Willaert, iii.

Italy

Music

D'Accone, Frank, ed. *Music of the Florentine Renaissance,* Vols. xi and xxxii in *Corpus mensurabilis musicae,* ed. A. Carapetyan (Rome: American Institute of Musicology, 1966–69).

Cardamone, Donna, ed. *Canzone villanesche alla Napolitana and Villotte: Adrian Willaert and His Circle,* Vol. xxx, *Recent Researches in Music of the Renaissance* (Madison, WI: A-R Editions, 1978).

Slim, H. Colin, ed. *A Gift of Madrigals and Motets* (Chicago: U. of Chicago Press, 1972).

For Further Reading

D'Accone, Frank. "The Musical Chapels at the Florentine Cathedrals and Baptistry during the First Half of the Sixteenth Century," *Journal of the American Musicological Society,* xxiv (1971), pp. 1–50.

Anglès, H. "The Musical Notation and Rhythm of the Italian Laude," *Essays in Musicology: A Birthday Offering for Willi Apel* (Bloomington, IN: Indiana U. Press, 1968), p. 51ff.

Einstein, Alfred. *The Italian Madrigal* (Princeton, NJ: Princeton U. Press, 1949; repr. 1971).

Fenlon, Iain. *Music and Patronage in Sixteenth-century Mantua,* 2 vols. (Cambridge, Eng.: Cambridge U. Press, I, 1980; II, 1982).

Haar, James, ed. *Chanson and Madrigal, 1480–1530* (Cambridge, MA: Harvard U. Press, 1981).

———. *Essays on Italian Poetry and Music in the Renaissance, 1350–1600* (Berkeley, CA: U. of California Press, 1986).

———. "Isabella d'Este and Lucretia Borgia as Patrons of Music: The Frottola at Mantua and Ferrara," *Journal of the American Musicological Society,* xxxviii (1985), pp. 1–33.

Lockwood, Lewis. *Music in Renaissance Ferrara 1400–1505* (Cambridge, MA: Harvard U. Press, 1984).

Newcomb, Anthony. *The Madrigal at Ferrara 1579–1597,* 2 vols. (Princeton, NJ: Princeton U. Press, 1980).

Prizer, William. *Courtly Pastimes: The Frottole of Marchetto Cara* (Ann Arbor, MI: UMI Research Press, 1981).

Roche, Jerome. *The Madrigal* (New York: Scribner's, 1972).

Canti Carnascialeschi

Music

Gallucci, Joseph G., Jr., ed. *Florentine Festival Music 1480–1520* [Canti Carnascialeschi, Trionfi, and Related Forms] (Madison, WI: A-R Editions, 1981).

Ghisi, Federico. *I canti carnascialeschi nelle fonti musicali del xv e xvi secolo* (Florence: Olschki, 1937).

———. *Feste musicali della Firenze medicea 1480–1589* (Florence: Vallecchi, 1939; repr. 1969).

Italian Madrigalists

Marenzio

Marenzio, Luca. *Sämtliche Werke,* ed. A. Einstein (Leipzig: Breitkopf & Härtel, 1929–31; repr. Hildesheim: Olms, 1967).

Arnold, Denis. *Marenzio* (London: Oxford U. Press, 1965).

Chater, J. *Luca Marenzio and the Italian Madrigal, 1577–1593* (Ann Arbor, MI: UMI Research Press, 1981).

Monte

Monte, Philippe de. *Opera, New Complete Edition,* ed. R. B. Lenaerts (Louvin: Leuven U. Press, 1975–81).

Mann, Brian. *The Secular Madrigals of Filippo di Monte, 1521–1603* (Ann Arbor, MI: UMI Research Press, 1983).

France

Music

Janequin, C. *Chansons polyphoniques: Oeuvres complètes,* ed. A. T. Merritt and François Lesure (Monaco: Éditions de L'Oiseau-Lyre, 1965–71).

Lesure, François. *Anthologie de la chanson parisienne au XVIe siècle* (Monaco: Éditions de L'Oiseau-Lyre, 1953).

Picker, Martin. *Chanson Albums of Marguerite of Austria* (Berkeley, CA: U. of California Press, 1965).

For Further Reading

Brown, Howard M. *Music in the French Secular Theater, 1400–1550* (Cambridge, MA: Harvard U. Press, 1963).

Heartz, Daniel. *Pierre Attaingnant, Royal Printer of Music: A Historical Study and Bibliographical Catalogue* (Berkeley, CA: U. of California Press, 1969).

———. "A New Attaingnant Book and the Beginnings of French Music Printing," *Journal of the American Musicological Society,* xiv (1961), p. 9ff.

Walker, D. P. "The Aims of Baïf's *Academie de poésie et de musique,*" *Journal of Renaissance and Baroque Musique,* i (1946–47), p. 91ff.

England

Music

The Collected Lute Music of John Dowland, ed. Diana Poulton
  and B. Lam (London: Faber, 1974; repr. New York: Dover).
The English Madrigal School, ed. E. H. Fellowes, 36 vols.
  (London: Stainer & Bell, 1913–24); rev. ed. published as *The
  English Madrigalists,* ed. Thurston Dart (1956–).
The English School of Lutenist Song Writers, ed. E. H.
  Fellowes, 32 vols. (London: Stainer & Bell, 1920–32); rev. ed.
  publ. as *The English Lute-songs,* ed. T. Dart (London:
  Stainer & Bell, 1956–66).
Ledger, Philip, ed. *The Oxford Book of English Madrigals*
  (London: Oxford U. Press, 1979).
Musica Britannica, Vols. vi [Dowland]; ix, xxii, xl [Consort
  music]; xxiii [Weelkes]; xviii [Court music, Henry VIII];
  xxxvi [Early Tudor Music, ed. J. Stevens], Royal Music
  Association (London: Stainer & Bell, 1951–).

For Further Reading

Fellowes, E. H. *The English Madrigalist Composers,* 2d ed.
  (London and New York: Oxford U. Press, 1948).
———. *The English Madrigal* (Oxford: Oxford U. Press, 1925;
  2d ed. 1948; repr. Salem, NH: Ayer, 1984).
Kerman, Joseph. *The Elizabethan Madrigal* (New York:
  American Musicological Society, 1962).
Poulton, Diana. *John Dowland* (London: Faber & Faber, 1972).

Iberia

J. del Encina: L'opera musicale, ed. Clemente Terni (Florence:
  Casa Editrice d'Anna, 1974).
Chase, Gilbert. *The Music of Spain* (New York: Norton, 1941;
  repr. New York: Dover, 1959).
Stevenson, Robert. *Spanish Music in the Age of Columbus* (The
  Hague: Nijhoff, 1960; repr. 1987).

Chapter 12. Reformation and Counter-Reformation

General

For Further Reading

Reese, Gustave. *Music in the Renaissance* (New York: Norton,
  1954; 2d rev. ed. 1959), esp. Chapters 8, 9, 11, 13, and 15.

Reformation

Anderson, Charles S. *Augsburg Historical Atlas of Christianity
  in the Middle Ages and Reformation* (Minneapolis, MN:
  Augsburg Publishing House, 1967).
Appel, Richard. *Music of the Bay Psalm Book, 9th ed.*
  (Brooklyn, NY: Institute for Studies in American Music,
  1975).
The Bay Psalm Book [*The Whole Book of Psalmes Faithfully
  Translated into English Metre*], facsimile ed. (Chicago: U. of
  Chicago Press, 1956).
Blume, Friedrich. *Protestant Church Music* (New York: Norton,
  1974).
Pidoux, Pierre, comp. *Le Psautier Huguenot du XVIᵉ siècle,
  mélodies et documents* (Basle: Bärenreiter, 1962).

Pratt, Waldo S. *The Music of the French Psalter of 1562* (New
  York: Columbia U. Press, 1939).
Riedel, J. *The Lutheran Chorale: Its Basic Traditions*
  (Minneapolis: Augsburg, 1967).

Luther

Music

Das Acht Lieder Buch (1524), facsimile ed., ed. Konrad Ameln
  (Kassel & Basel: Bärenreiter, 1957).
Luther, Martin. *Deudsche Messe* (1526), facsimile ed. (Kassel:
  Bärenreiter, 1934).
Luther's Works, 55 vols., gen. eds. Jaroslav Pelikan (Vols. 1–30)
  and Helmut T. Lehmann (Vols. 31–55), Vol. 53, *Liturgy and
  Hymns,* ed. Ulrich S. Leupold (Philadelphia: Fortress Press,
  1965).

For Further Reading

Bainton, Roland H. *Here I Stand: A Life of Martin Luther*
  (New York: Abingdon-Cokesbury Press, 1950).

Rhau (Rhaw)

Music

*G. Rhau: Musikdrucke aus den Jahren 1538 bis 1545 in
  praktischer Neuausgabe* (Kassel: Bärenreiter, 1955–).
Rhau, Georg. *Musikdrucke VI: Bicinia gallica, latina,
  germanica,* Tomus I, II (1545), ed. Bruce Bellingham
  (Kassel: Bärenreiter, and St. Louis, MO: Concordia
  Publishing House, 1980).

For Further Reading

Schrade, Leo. "The Editorial Practice of Georg Rhaw," *The
  Musical Heritage of the Church,* iv (1954), p. 31ff.

Walter (Walther)

Music

J. Walter: Sämtliche Werke, ed. O. Schröder (Kassel:
  Bärenreiter, 1953–73).
Walter, Johann. *Geystliches gesangk Buchleyn* (Wittenberg,
  1524), in Vol. vii (Jg. vi), *Publikationen älterer praktischer
  und theoretischer Musikwerke, vorzugsweise des XV. und
  XVI. Jahrhunderts,* 29 vols. in 33 Jg., ed. R. Eitner (Berlin:
  Bahn & Liepmannssohn, 1873–1905; repr. 1967).

For Further Reading

Buszin, W. E. "Johann Walther, Composer, Pioneer, and Luther's
  Musical Consultant," *The Musical Heritage of the Church,*
  Valparaiso [IN] University Pamphlet Series, ed. Hoelty-
  Nickel (St. Louis, MO: Concordia Publishing House, 1954).

Counter-Reformation

Barthel, Manfred. *The Jesuits: History and Legend of the
  Society of Jesus,* trans. and adapted by Mark Howson (New
  York: William Morrow, 1984).
Culley, T. *Jesuits and Music: A Study of the Musicians
  connected with the German College in Rome durng the 17th
  Century and of Their Activities in Northern Europe* (Rome:
  Jesuit Historical Institute Press, 1970).
Stevenson, Robert. *Spanish Cathedral Music in the Golden Age*
  (Berkeley and Los Angeles, CA: U. of California Press,
  1961).

Lassus

Music

O. de Lassus: Sämtliche Werke, ed. F. X. Haberl and A.
Sandberger (Leipzig: Breitkopf & Härtel, 1894–1927; repr.
Broude, 1974).
O. de Lassus: Sämtliche Werke, neue Reihe, ed. S. Hermelink,
W. Boetticher, et al. (Kassel: Bärenreiter, 1956–).

For Further Reading

Roche, Jerome. *Lassus* (London: Oxford U. Press, 1982).

Palestrina

Music

G. P. da Palestrina: Werke, ed. F. X. Haberl, T. de Witt, et al.
(Leipzig: Breitkopf & Härtel, 1862–1903; repr. Farnborough,
Eng.: Gregg International, 1968).
G. P. da Palestrina: Le opere complete, ed. R. Casimiri and L.
Virgili (Rome: Fratelli Scalera, 1939–).

For Further Reading

Jeppesen, Knud. *Palestrinastil med saerligt henblik paa
dissonansbehandlingen* (Copenhagen, 1923); Eng. trans.
Edward J. Dent, as *The Style of Palestrina and the
Dissonance* (London: Oxford U. Press, 1927, 2d ed., 1946).

Victoria

Music

T. L. de Victoria: Opera omnia, ed. F. Pedrell (Leipzig:
Breitkopf & Härtel, 1902–13; repr. Farnborough, Eng.:
Gregg Press, 1968).
T. L. de Victoria: Opera omnia, corrected, augmented, ed. H.
Anglès, *Monumentos de la Música Española,* Vols. 25, 26,
30, and 31 (Rome: Escuela Española de Historia y
Arquelogia, Consejo Superior de Investigaciones Científicas,
Delegacíon de Rome, 1965–68).

England: Reformation and Counter-Reformation

Music

Early English Church Music, ed. F. Ll. Harrison, British
Academy (London: Stainer & Bell, 1972–).
Tudor Church Music, ed. P. C. Buck, E. H. Fellowes, et al., 10
vols. (London and elsewhere: Oxford U. Press, 1922–29;
appendix 1948; repr. New York: Broude, 1963). [Music of
Byrd, Gibbons, Tallis, Taverner, Tomkins, and White.]

For Further Reading

Fellowes, E. H. *English Cathedral Music,* 5th ed., rev. Jack A.
Westrup (London: Methuen, 1969).
Le Huray, Peter. *Music and the Reformation in England, 1549–
1600* (London and New York: Oxford U. Press, 1967).
Stevens, Denis. *Tudor Church Music* (New York: Merlin, 1955;
repr. New York: Da Capo, 1973; 2d ed., London: Faber &
Faber, and New York: Norton, 1966).

Byrd

Music

The Collected Works of William Byrd, ed. E. H. Fellowes
(London: Stainer & Bell, 1937–50); rev. T. Dart, et al.
(London: Stainer & Bell, 1962–).
(See also *Tudor Church Music,* Vols. 2, 7, and 9.)

For Further Reading

Fellowes, E. H. *William Byrd* (London: H. Milford and Oxford
U. Press, 1936; 2d ed., Oxford U. Press, 1948).
Kerman, Joseph. *The Music of William Byrd,* Vol. 1, *The
Masses and Motets of William Byrd* (Berkeley, CA: U. of
California Press, 1980).
Neighbour, Oliver W. *The Music of William Byrd,* Vol. 3, *The
Consort and Keyboard Music of William Byrd* (London:
Faber, 1978).
Brett, Philip. *The Music of William Byrd,* Vol. 2, *The Songs,
Services, and Anthems of William Byrd* (in preparation).

Tallis, Taverner, Tye

Music

(See *Tudor Church Music,* above.)
T. Tallis: English Sacred Music, I: Anthems, ed. L. Ellinwood,
rev. P. Doe, *Early English Church Music,* xii, 2d ed.
(London: Stainer & Bell, 1974).
T. Tallis: English Sacred Music, II: Service Music, ed. L.
Ellinwood, rev. P. Doe, *Early English Church Music,* xiii, 2d
ed. (London: Stainer & Bell, 1974).
J. Taverner: I. The Six-part Masses, ed. H. J. Benham, *Early
English Church Music,* xx (London: Stainer & Bell, 1978).
J. Taverner: II. The Votive Antiphons, ed. H. J. Benham, *Early
English Church Music,* xxv, (London: Stainer & Bell, 1981).
C. Tye: The Latin Church Music, ed. J. Satterfield (Madison,
WI: A-R Editions, 1977).
C. Tye: The English Sacred Music, ed. J. Morehen, *Early
English Church Music,* xix (London: Stainer & Bell, 1977).

For Further Reading

Davison, N. "The Western Wind Masses," *The Musical
Quarterly,* lvii (1971), p. 427ff.
Doe, Paul. *Tallis* (London: Oxford U. Press, 1968).
Donington, Robert, and Thurston Dart. "The Origin of the *In
Nomine,*" *Music and Letters,* xxx (1949), p. 101ff.
Hand, Colin. *John Taverner: His Life and Music* (London:
Eulenberg, 1978).
Josephson, D. S. *John Taverner, Tudor Composer* (Ann Arbor,
MI: UMI Research Press, 1979).
Reese, Gustave. "The Origins of the *In Nomine,*" *Journal of the
American Musicological Society,* ii (1949), p. 7ff.
Stevens, D. "The Background of the English *In Nomine,*" *The
Monthly Musical Record,* lxxxiv (1954), p. 199ff.

Chapter 13. Renaissance Instrumental Music

General

Apel, Willi. *The History of Keyboard Music to 1700,* trans. and
rev. Hans Tischler (Bloomington, IN: Indiana U. Press,
1972).
Arnold, Denis. *Giovanni Gabrieli and the Music of the Venetian
High Renaissance* (London: Oxford U. Press, 1979).
Baines, Anthony. *Brass Instruments: Their History and
Development* (London: Faber, 1976).
———. *European and American Musical Instruments* (London:
Batsford, 1966).
———, ed. *Musical Instruments through the Ages*
(Harmondsworth, Eng.: Penguin Books, 1961).

————. *Woodwind Instruments and Their History* (London: Faber, 1957; 3d ed. 1967).

Blades, James. *Percussion Instruments and Their History* (New York: Praeger, 1970).

Boyden, David D. *The History of Violin Playing from Its Origins to 1761* (London: Oxford U. Press, 1965).

Dart, Thurston. "The Fretted Instruments, III: The Viols," *Musical Instruments through the Ages,* ed. A. Baines (Harmondsworth, Eng.: Penguin Books, 1961; 2d ed., rev. 1966), p. 184ff.

Gillespie, John. *Five Centuries of Keyboard Music: An Historical Survey of Music for Harpsichord and Piano* (Belmont, CA: Wadsworth, 1965).

Kirby, Frank E. *A Short History of Keyboard Music* (New York: Free Press, 1966), pp. 1–62.

Marcuse, Sybil. *A Survey of Musical Instruments* (London: David & Charles, and New York: Harper & Row, 1975).

————. *Musical Instruments: A Comprehensive Dictionary* (Garden City, NY: Doubleday, 1964).

Munrow, David. *Instruments of the Middle Ages and Renaissance* (London: Oxford U. Press, 1976).

Praetorius, Michael. *Syntagma musicum,* Vol. II (*De Organographia*) (Wolfenbüttel, 1618); reprint of Parts I and II, plus *Theatrum organorum,* trans. Harold Blumenfeld (New York: Da Capo Press, 1980).

Russell, R. *The Harpsichord and Clavichord* (London: Faber, 1959; 2d ed., rev. 1973).

Selfridge-Field, Eleanor. *Venetian Instrumental Music from Gabrieli to Vivaldi* (Oxford: Blackford, 1975).

Sumner, William L. *The Organ: Its Evolution, Principles of Construction and Use* (London: Macdonald, 1952; 3d ed., rev. and enlarged, 1962).

Virdung, Sebastian. *Musica getutscht und aussgezogē* (Basle, 1511), facsimile ed. (New York: Broude, 1966).

Gabrieli

Music

A. and G. Gabrieli: *La musica striamentale in San Marco,* 2 vols., ed. G. Benvenuti, Istituzioni e monumenti dell'arte musicale italiana (Milan: Ricordi, 1931–41).

G. Gabrieli: *Opera omnia,* ed. Denis Arnold, [10 volumes planned], Vol. xii in *Corpus mensurabilis musicae,* ed. A. Carapetyan (Rome: American Institute of Musicology, 1956–).

G. Gabrieli: *Opera omnia,* ed. Fondazione Giorgio Cini, Venice (Mainz: Universal, 1969–).

G. Gabrieli: *Canzoni e sonate,* ed. M. Sanvoisin, *Le Pupitre,* Vol. xxvii (Paris: Heugel, 1971).

For Further Reading

Arnold, Denis. *Giovanni Gabrieli and the Music of the Venetian High Renaissance* (London: Oxford U. Press, 1979).

Kenton, Egon. *The Life and Works of Giovanni Gabrieli, Musicological Studies and Documents,* Vol. xvi, ed. A. Carapetyan (Rome: American Institute of Musicology, 1967).

Chapter 14. The Baroque Era

For Further Reading

Arnold, Frank. *The Art of Accompaniment from a Thorough-Bass as Practiced in the XVIIth and XVIIIth Centuries,* 2 vols. (New York: Dover, 1965).

Blume, Friedrich. *Renaissance and Baroque Music: A Comprehensive Survey,* trans. M. D. Herter Norton (New York: Norton, 1967), pp. 83–167.

Bukofzer, Manfred F. *Music in the Baroque Era* (New York: Norton, 1947).

Palisca, Claude V. *Baroque Music,* 2d ed. (Englewood Cliffs, NJ: Prentice-Hall, 1981).

Chapter 15. Baroque Vocal Music

Early Opera

Series of facsimile editions: *Italian Opera, 1640–1770,* gen. ed. Howard M. Brown (New York: Garland, 1978–).

Donington, Robert. *The Rise of Opera* (London: Faber & Faber, 1981).

Grout, Donald J. *A Short History of Opera,* 2d ed. (New York: Columbia U. Press, 1965).

Marco, Guy A. *Opera: A Research and Information Guide* (New York: Garland, 1984).

Murata, Margaret. *Operas for the Papal Court, 1631–1668* (Ann Arbor, MI: UMI Research Press, 1981).

Pirrotta, Nino. "Early Italian Opera and Aria," *Music and Theatre from Poliziano to Monteverdi,* trans. K. Eales (Cambridge: Cambridge U. Press, 1982).

Porter, William. "Peri and Corsi's *Dafne*: Some New Discoveries and Observations," *Journal of the American Musicological Society* xviii (1965), pp. 170–96.

Walker, D. P., ed. *Les fêtes du mariage de Ferdinand de Médicis et de Christine de Lorraine, Florence, 1589* [The festivities for the marriage of Ferdinande de Medici and Christine of Lorraine] (Paris: Éditions du Centre national de la recherche scientifique, 1963).

Worsthorne, Simon T. *Venetian Opera in the Seventeenth Century* (Oxford: Clarendon Press, 1954).

Florence: The Camerata

Galilei, Vincenzo. *Dialogo della musica antica, et della moderna* (Florence: Giorgio Marescotti, 1581), facsimile ed. (New York: Broude Brothers, 1967).

Palisca, Claude V. *Girolamo Mei: Letters on Ancient and Modern Music to Vincenzo Galilei and Giovanni Bardi* (Neuhausen-Stuttgart: American Institute of Musicology, 1960; 2d ed., 1977).

Caccini

Music

Caccini, Giulio. *Le nuove musiche* (Florence: 1600/1601), facsimile ed. (New York: Broude Bros., 1973). Modern transcription, ed. H. Wiley Hitchcock (Madison, WI: A-R Editions, 1970).

————. *Nuove musiche e nuova maniera di scriverle* (Florence, 1614), ed. H Wiley Hitchcock (Madison, WI: A-R Editions, 1978).

Cavalieri

Music

Cavalliere [sic], Emilio del. *Rappresentatione di Anima, et di Corpo* (Rome: Nicolò Mutij, 1600), facsimile ed. (Farnborough, Eng.: Gregg International, 1967).

Peri

Peri, Jacopo. *Euridice,* ed. Howard M. Brown (Madison, WI: A-R Editions, 1981).

Monteverdi

Music

C. Monteverdi: Tutte le opere, ed. G. F. Malipiero (Asolo: Malipiero, 1926–42; rev. 1954; suppl. 1966).
C. Monteverdi: Opera Omnia, ed. R. Monterosso, Fondazione Claudio Monteverdi (Cremona: Athenaeum cremonense, 1970–).

For Further Reading

Arnold, Denis. *Monteverdi* (London: Dent, 1963; rev. 1975).
Arnold, Denis, and Nigel Fortune, eds. *The Monteverdi Companion* (New York: Norton, 1968, 1972).
———. *The New Monteverdi Companion* (London: Faber, 1985).
Redlich, Hans F. *Claudio Monteverdi and His Works,* trans. Kathleen Dale (London: Oxford U. Press, 1952; repr. Westport, CT: Greenwood Press, 1970).
Schrade, Leo. *Monteverdi: Creator of Modern Music* (New York: Norton, 1950; repr. 1964, 1969; repr. New York: Da Capo Press, 1979).
Whenham, John, ed. *Claudio Monteverdi: Orfeo* (New York: Cambridge U. Press, 1986).

Cavalli

Glover, Jane. *Cavalli* (London: Batsford, 1978).

Scarlatti, A.

Music

The Operas of Alessandro Scarlatti, 8 vols., gen. ed. Donald J. Grout (Cambridge, MA: Harvard U. Press, 1974–83).

For Further Reading

Dent, Edward J. *Alessandro Scarlatti: His Life and Work* (London, 1905); rev. with additions by Frank Walker (London: Edward Arnold, 1960; repr. 1962).
Grout, Donald J. *Alessandro Scarlatti: An Introduction to His Operas* (Berkeley: U. of California Press, 1979).

France

Music

Les chefs d'oeuvres classiques de l'opéra français, 40 vols., ed. J. B. Weckerlin, et al. (Paris: T. Michaelis, 1878–83; repr. New York: Broude, 1972).

For Further Reading

Anthony, James R. *French Baroque Music from Beaujoyeulx to Rameau,* rev. ed. (New York: Norton, 1978).
Isherwood, Robert M. *Music in the Service of the King: France in the Seventeenth Century* (Ithaca, NY: Cornell U. Press, 1973).

Lully

Music

J.-B. Lully: Oeuvres complètes, ed. Henri Prunières, 10 vols. (Paris: Éditions de La Revue Musicale, 1930–39; rev. M. Sanvoisin New York: Broude Brothers, 1935–1966; repr. 1972).

For Further Reading

La Laurencie, Lionel de. *Lully* (Paris: Alcan, 1911; repr. New York: Da Capo, 1977).
Newman, J. E. W. *Jean-Baptiste de Lully and His Tragedies lyriques* (Ann Arbor, MI: UMI Research Press 1979).

England

Music

Blow, John. *Venus and Adonis,* ed. A. Lewis (Monaco: Éditions de l'Oiseau-Lyre, 1949).
Shirley, Davenant, and Lawes. *Trois masques à la cour de Charles Ier d'Angleterre,* ed. M. Lefkowitz (Paris: Éditions de Centre National de la Recherche Scientifique, 1970).
The Works of Henry Purcell, ed. The Purcell Society (London: Novello, 1878–1965; rev. 1961–).

For Further Reading

Fellowes, Edmund. *English Cathedral Music* (London: Methuen, 1941; rev. by Jack A. Westrup, 1969).
Moore, Robert E. *Henry Purcell & the Restoration Theatre* (London: Heinemann, 1961; repr. Westport, CT: Greenwood Press, 1974, 1976).
Westrup, Jack A. *Purcell* (New York: Collier, 1962).
Zimmerman, F. B. *Henry Purcell: His Life and Times* (London: Macmillan, 1967; 2d rev. ed., Philadelphia: U. of Pennsylvania Press, 1983).

Spanish Operas

Calderón de la Barca, Pedro. *Celos aun del aire matan,* ed., with intro., trans. and notes by Matthew D. Stroud (San Antonio, TX: Trinity U. Press, 1981).
Torrejón y Velasco, Tomás. *La Púrpura de la Rosa,* trans. Robert Stevenson (Lima, Peru: Organización de los Estados Americanos, 1976).

Oratorio

Smither, Howard E. *A History of the Oratorio,* 3 vols. (Chapel Hill, NC: U. of North Carolina Press, 1977–87); Vol. 1: *The Oratorio in the Baroque Era: Italy, Vienna, Paris.*

Carissimi

Music

G. Carissimi: Le opere complete, ed. L. Bianchi, et al. (Rome: Pubblicazioni dell'Istituto italiano per la storia della musica, Monumenti, iii, 1951–73).

For Further Reading

Rose, Gloria. "The Cantatas of Carissimi," *The Musical Quarterly,* xlviii (1962), p. 204ff.
Smither, H. E. "Carissimi's Latin Oratorios: Their Terminology, Functions, and Position in Oratorio History," *Analecta Musicologica,* 17 (1976), p. 54ff.

Schütz

Music

H. Schütz: Sämtliche Werke, 18 vols., ed. P. Spitta, et al. (Leipzig: Breitkopf & Härtel, 1885–1927; repr. 1968–73).
H. Schütz: Sämtliche Werke, ed. G. Graulich et al. (Kassel: Bärenreiter, 1955–).
H. Schütz: Sämtliche Werke, ed. G. Graulich et al. (Stuttgart: 1971–).

For Further Reading

Moser, Hans Joachim. *Heinrich Schütz*, trans. C. F. Pfatteicher (St. Louis: Concordia Publishing House, 1959).

Skei, Allen. *Heinrich Schütz: A Guide to Research* (New York: Garland, 1981).

Smither, H. E. *A History of the Oratorio*, vol. 2, *The Oratorio in the Baroque Era: Protestant Germany and England* (Chapel Hill, NC: U. of North Carolina Press, 1977).

Cantata

Music

The Italian Cantata in the Seventeenth Century [facsimiles of cantatas], gen. ed. Carolyn Gianturco (New York: Garland, 1986–).

Fibonacci

Pascoe, Clive B. *Golden Proportion in Musical Design* (Diss., 1973; Ann Arbor, MI: University Microfilms, 1981).

Vorob'ev, N. N. *The Fibonacci Numbers* (New York: D.C. Heath, 1963).

Chapter 16. Baroque Instrumental Music

General

Anthony, James R. *French Baroque Music from Beaujoyeulx to Rameau*, rev. ed. (New York: Norton, 1978).

Apel, Willi. *The History of Keyboard Music to 1700*, trans. and rev. Hans Tischler (Bloomington, IN: Indiana U. Press, 1972).

Boyden, David D. *The History of Violin Playing from Its Origins to 1761* (London: Oxford U. Press, 1965).

Engel, Hans. *The Concerto Grosso*, trans. R. Kolben, Vol. 23 in *Anthology of Music*, ed. K. G. Fellerer (Cologne: Arno Volk, 1964).

———. *The Solo Concerto*, trans. R. Kolben, Vol. 25 in *Anthology of Music*, ed. K. G. Fellerer (Cologne: Arno Volk, 1964).

Farga, Franz. *Violins and Violinists*, trans. Egon Larsen (London: Rockliff, 1950; repr. 1955).

Fux, J. J. *Gradus ad Parnassum* (Vienna, 1725), facsimile ed. *Monuments of Music and Music Literature in Facsimile*, Series 2, Vol. xxiv (New York: Broude, 1966). English translation, published as *Steps to Parnassus: The Study of Counterpoint from Johann Joseph Fux's Gradus ad Parnassum*, trans. and ed. by Alfred Mann and J. Edmunds, rev. ed. (New York: Norton, 1965).

Giegling, F. *The Solo Sonata*, Vol. 15 in *Anthology of Music*, ed. K. G. Fellerer (Cologne: Arno Volk, 1960).

Gillespie, John. *Five Centuries of Keyboard Music: An Historical Survey of Music for Harpsichord and Piano* (Belmont, CA: Wadsworth, 1965).

Horsley, Imogene. *Fugue: History and Practice* (New York: Free Press, 1966).

Hutchings, Arthur J. B. *The Baroque Concerto* (London: Faber & Faber, 1961).

Kirby, Frank E. *A Short History of Keyboard Music* (New York: Free Press, 1966).

Mishkin, Henry G. "The Solo Violin Sonata of the Bologna School," *The Musical Quarterly*, xxix (1943), pp. 92–112.

Newman, William S. *The Sonata in the Baroque Era* (Chapel Hill, NC: U. of North Carolina Press, 1959; 3d ed. New York: Norton, 1972).

Schenk, E. *The Italian Trio Sonata*, trans. F. Giegling, Vol. 7 in *Anthology of Music*, ed. K. G. Fellerer (Cologne: Arno Volk, 1953).

Selfridge-Field, Eleanor. *Venetian Instrumental Music from Gabrieli to Vivaldi* (Oxford: Blackford, 1975).

Smithers, Don L. *The Music and History of the Baroque Trumpet before 1721* (London: Aldine Press, Letchworth & Herts, 1973; Syracuse, NY: Syracuse U. Press, 1973).

Sumner, William L. *The Organ*, 3d ed., rev. and enlarged (London: Macdonald, 1962).

Valentin, Erich. *The Toccata*, Vol. 17 in *Anthology of Music*, ed. K. G. Fellerer (Cologne: Arno Volk, 1958).

Wasielewski, Jos. Wilh. von, ed. *Anthology of Instrumental Music from the End of the Sixteenth to the End of the Seventeenth Century* (Berlin: Liepmannssohn, n.d.; repr. New York: Da Capo Press, 1974).

(See also *Das Musikwerk*, ed. K. G. Fellerer (Cologne: Arno Volk-Verlag, 1951–); Eng. trans. published as *Anthology of Music* (Cologne: Arno Volk, 1959–75); anthologies organized by genre in individual vols.)

Buxtehude

Music

D. Buxtehude: Klaverwaerker, ed. E. Bangert (Copenhagen: W. Hansen, 1942).

D. Buxtehude: Orgelwerke, ed. J. Hedar (Copenhagen: W. Hansen, 1952).

D. Buxtehude: Sämtliche Orgelwerke, ed. K. Beckmann (Wiesbaden: Breitkopf & Härtel, 1971–72).

For Further Reading

Hutchins, F. K. *Dietrich Buxtehude: The Man, His Music, His Era* (Paterson, NJ: Music Textbook Co., 1955).

Snyder, Kerala J. *Dietrich Buxtehude: Organist in Lübeck* (New York: Schirmer Books, 1987).

Bononcini

Klenz, William. *Giovanni Maria Bononcini of Modena: A Chapter in Baroque Instrumental Music* (Durham, NC: Duke U. Press, 1962).

Cabanilles

J. B. Cabanilles: Opera omnia, Vols. I-IV, ed. H. Angles, in Biblioteca Central Sección de Musica *Publicaciones*, Vols. iv, viii, xiii, xvii (Barcelona: Biblioteca de Catalunya, 1927–56).

Corelli

Music

A. Corelli: Historisch-kritische Gesamtausgabe der musikalischen Werke, 5 vols., gen. ed. Hans Oesch (Cologne: Arno Volk, 1976–); supplement, ed. Hans J. Marx (Cologne: Arno Volk, 1980).

A. Corelli: Les oeuvres de Arcangelo Corelli, ed. J. Joachim and F. Chrysander (London: Augener, 1888–91; repr. 1952).

For Further Reading

Pincherle, Marc. *Corelli: His Life, His Music*, trans. Hubert E. M. Russell (New York: Norton, 1956; repr. 1968).

Select Bibliography

Couperin, F.

Music

F. Couperin: Oeuvres complètes, ed. M. Cauchie, P. Brunold, et al. (Paris: Éditions de l'Oiseau-Lyre, 1932–33). New critical edition, ed. K. Gilbert, et al. (Monaco: Éditions de l'Oiseau-Lyre, 1980–).

F. Couperin: Pièces de clavecin, ed K. Gilbert, in Le Pupitre: Collection de musique ancienne, xxi-xxiv (Paris: Heugel, 1969–72).

F. Couperin: Pièces de violes (1728), ed. L. Robinson, in Le Pupitre, li, (Paris: Heugel, 1974).

Couperin, F. L'Art de toucher le clavecin (Paris, 1716); ed., trans. A. Linde and M. Roberts (Leipzig: Breitkopf & Härtel, 1933).

———. L'Art de toucher le clavecin (Paris, 1716); ed., trans. Margery Halford (Sherman Oaks, CA: Alfred Publishing, 1974).

For Further Reading

Mellers, Wilfred. François Couperin and the French Classical Tradition (London: Denis Dobson, 1950; New York: Dover, 1968).

Tunley, David. Couperin (London: British Broadcasting Corporation, 1982).

Frescobaldi

Music

G. Frescobaldi: Opere Complete, ed. O. Mischiati and L. F. Tagliavini, Monumenti musicali italiani (Milan: Edizioni Suvini Zerboni, 1975–).

G. Frescobaldi: Orgel- und Klavierwerke, ed. P. Pidoux (Kassel: Bärenreiter, 1949–54).

For Further Reading

Hammond, Frederick. Girolamo Frescobaldi (Cambridge, MA: Harvard U. Press, 1983).

Froberger

Music

J. J. Froberger: Orgel- und Klavierwerke (Organ and Keyboard Works), ed. G. Adler, in Denkmäler der Tonkunst in Österreich, Vols. 8 [Jg. iv/1], 13 [Jg. 6/2], and 21 [Jg. x/2] (Vienna: Artaria, 1897–1903).

J. J. Froberger: Oeuvres complètes (Complete Works), ed. H. M. Schott, Le Pupitre (Paris: Heugel, 1979–).

Gaultier

Gaultier, Denis. La Rhétorique des Dieux et aultres Pieces de Luth de Denis Gaultier, transcr. by André Tessier, Vol. vi in Series I of Publications de la Société Française de Musicologie (Paris: Droz, 1932).

Jacquet de La Guerre

Jacquet de La Guerre, Elisabeth. Pièces de clavecin, ed. Thurston Dart (Monaco: Éditions de L'Oiseau-Lyre, n.d.).

Bates, Carol H. The Instrumental Music of Elisabeth-Claude Jacquet de la Guerre (Diss., Indiana U., Bloomington, IN, 1978).

Borroff, Edith. An Introduction to Elisabeth-Claude Jacquet de La Guerre (Brooklyn, NY: Institute of Mediaeval Music, 1966).

Kuhnau

Kuhnau, J. Klavierwerke, ed. K. Päsler, Vol. iv in Denkmäler deutscher Tonkunst (Leipzig: Breitkopf & Härtel, 1958).

———. Six Biblical Sonatas for Keyboard (1700), ed., trans., and annotated by Kurt Stone (New York: Broude, 1953).

Muffat

Muffat, Georg. Florilegium . . . . (1695), ed. Heinrich Rietsch, Vols. 2 (Jg. i/2) and 4 (Jg. ii/2) in Denkmäler der Tonkunst in Österreich, ed. Guido Adler (Graz: Akademische Druck- und Verlagsanstalt, 1959).

Purcell

Music

The Works of Henry Purcell, ed. The Purcell Society (London: Novello, 1878–1965; rev. 1961–).

For Further Reading

Westrup, Jack A. Purcell (New York: Collier, 1962).

Zimmerman, F. B. Henry Purcell: His Life and Times (London: Macmillan, 1967; 2d rev. ed., Philadelphia: U. of Pennsylvania Press, 1983).

Sweelinck

J. P. Sweelinck: Opera omnia, editio altera, ed. R. Lagas, G. Leonhardt, et al., Vol. I: The Instrumental Works, Uitgaven der Vereeniging voor Nederlandse Muziekgeschiedenis (Amsterdam: Alsbach, 1968; 2d rev. ed., 1974).

J. P. Sweelinck: Werken, ed. M. Seiffert, et al. (The Hague: Nijhof; Leipzig: Breitkopf & Härtel, 1894–1901; repr. 1968); rev., enlarged (Amsterdam: Alsbach, 1943).

Chapter 17. Eminent Composers of the Early Eighteenth Century

J. S. Bach

Music

J. S. Bach: Werke, ed. Bach-Gesellschaft, 61 vols. [in 47 Jahrgänge] (Leipzig: Bach Gesellschaft, 1851–99; repr. [except Jg. 47] Ann Arbor: J. W. Edwards, 1947). Neue Bach-Ausgabe sämtliche Werke, ed. Johann-Sebastian-Bach-Institut, Göttingen, and Bach-Archiv, Leipzig (Kassel: Bärenreiter, 1954–). Faksimile-Reihe Bachser Werke und Schriftstücke (Leipzig: Verlag für Musik, 1955–). J. S. Bach, Organ Chorales from the Neumeister Collection [MS LM4708, at Yale U.] (Kassel: Bärenreiter, and New York: Yale U. Press, 1985).

For Further Reading

Boyd, Malcolm. Bach (London: J. M. Dent, 1983).

David, Hans, and Arthur Mendel. The Bach Reader (New York: Norton, 1966).

Dickinson, A. E. F. Bach's Fugal Works, with an Account of Fugue before and after Bach (London: Pitman & Sons, 1956; repr. Westport, CT: Greenwood Press, 1979).

Emery, Walter. Bach's Ornaments (London: Novello, 1953).

Geiringer, Karl. Johann Sebastian Bach: The Culmination of an Era (New York: Oxford U. Press, 1966).

———. The Bach Family: Seven Generations of Creative Genius (London: G. Allen Unwin, 1954; repr. New York, 1971).

Leaver, Robin A., ed. *J. S. Bach and Scripture,* with intro. and notes by Leaver (St. Louis: Concordia, 1985).

Marshall, Robert. *The Compositional Process of J. S. Bach: A Study of the Autograph Scores of the Vocal Works* (Princeton, NJ: Princeton U. Press, 1978).

Schwendowius, Barbara, and Wolfgang Dömling, eds. *J. S. Bach: Life, Times, Influence* (Kassel: Bärenreiter, 1976).

Stauffer, George, and Ernest May, eds. *J. S. Bach as Organist* (Bloomington, IN: Indiana U. Press, 1986).

Stiller, Günther. *Johann Sebastian Bach and Liturgical Life in Leipzig,* trans. H. J. A. Buman, et al., ed. Robin A. Leaver (St. Louis: Concordia Publishing House, 1984).

Terry, C. S. *Bach's Chorales,* 3 vols. (Cambridge, Eng.: Cambridge U. Press, 1917–21).

Wesley, Samuel. *The Bach Letters of Samuel Wesley,* ed. Elisha Wesley (London, 1878; repr. New York: Da Capo, 1981).

Williams, Peter, ed. *Bach, Handel, Scarlatti: Tercentenary Essays* (Cambridge, Eng.: Cambridge U. Press, 1985).

———. *The Organ Music of J. S. Bach,* 2 vols. (Cambridge, Eng.: Cambridge U. Press, 1980–84).

Handel

Music

G. F. Handels Werke: Ausgabe der Deutschen Handelgesellschaft, ed. F. W. Chrysander, vols. 1–48, 50–94, with 6 suppl. vols. (Leipzig: Breitkopf & Härtel, 1858–1903; repr. Ridgewood, NJ: Gregg International, 1965–66). *Hallische Händel-Ausgabe,* ed. M. Schneider, R. Steglich, et al. (Kassel: Bärenreiter, 1955–).

For Further Reading

Deutsch, Otto E. *Handel: A Documentary Biography* (New York and London: Adam and Charles Black, 1955).

Landon, H. C. Robbins. *Handel and His World* (London: Weidenfeld & Nicolson, 1984).

Lang, Paul H. *George Frideric Handel* (New York: Norton, 1966).

Dean, Winton. *Handel and the Opera Seria* (Berkeley: U. of California Press, 1969).

———. *Handel's Dramatic Oratorios and Masques* (London: Oxford U. Press, 1959).

Dean, Winton, and J. Merrill Knapp. *Handel's Operas, 1724–1726* (Oxford and New York: Clarendon Press, 1987).

Williams, Peter, ed. *Bach, Handel, Scarlatti: Tercentenary Essays* (Cambridge, Eng.: Cambridge U. Press, 1985).

Rameau

Music

J.-P. Rameau: Oeuvres complètes, ed. C. Saint-Saëns, C. Malherbe, et al. (Paris: A. Durand et fils, 1895–1924; repr. New York, 1968).

Writings

Jean-Philippe Rameau: Complete Theoretical Writings, ed. E. Jacobi, 6 vols. (Rome: American Institute of Musicology, Series Misc. 3, 1967–72).

Rameau, J. P. *Traité de l'harmonie reduite à ses principes naturels* (Paris, 1722), trans., with introduction and notes, Philip Gossett (New York: Dover, 1971).

For Further Reading

Anthony, James R. *French Baroque Music from Beaujoyeulx to Rameau* (New York: Norton, 1974).

Claudon, Francis, Jean Mongrédien, Carl de Nuys, and Karlheinz Roschitz. *L'Histoire de l'Opéra en France* (Paris: Fernand Nathan, 1984).

Delmuth, N. *French Opera: Its Development to the Revolution* (Sussex: Artemis Press, 1963).

Girdlestone, Cuthbert. *Jean-Philippe Rameau: His Life and Work* (London: Cassell & Co., 1957; repr. New York: Dover, 1969).

Launay, D., ed. *La Querelle des Bouffons,* repr. of pamphlets publ. Paris and The Hague, 1752–54 (Geneva: 1974).

Telemann

Music

G. P. Telemann: Musikalische Werke (Kassel & Basel: Bärenreiter, 1950–).

G. P. Telemann: Orgelwerke, ed. T. Fedtke (Kassel, 1964).

For Further Reading

Petzoldt, Richard. *Georg Philip Telemann,* trans. H. T. Fitzpatrick (New York: Oxford U. Press, 1974).

Vivaldi

Music

(Note: Only about half of Vivaldi's music is available in modern editions, and very little of that is vocal music.)

Scholarly edition of Vivaldi's works, in preparation, by Istituto Italiano Antonio Vivaldi (Milan: Ricordi, 1982–). Collected practical edition of Vivaldi's works, ed. A. Fanna (Rome: Edizioni Ricordi, 1947–), with thematic catalog of the instrumental works by A. Fanna (Milan: Ricordi, 1968). *A. Vivaldi: Motetti a canto solo con stromenti,* ed. R. Blanchard, *Le pupitre,* vii (Paris: Heugel, 1968). Thematic catalog: Ryom, P. *Verzeichnis der Werke Antonio Vivaldis,* 2d ed. (Leipzig: VEB Deutscher Verlag für Musik, 1977).

For Further Reading

Collins, M., and E. Kirk, eds. *Opera and Vivaldi* (Austin: U. of Texas Press, 1984, 1971).

Kolneder, Walter. *Vivaldi,* trans. B. Hopkins (Berkeley: U. of California Press, 1971).

Pincherle, Marc. *Vivaldi, Genius of the Baroque,* 2 vols. (Paris: Floury, 1948), trans. Christopher Hatch (New York: Norton, 1957). Vol. 2 is a thematic catalog.

Talbot, Michael. *Vivaldi* (London: J. M. Dent, 1978).

Fischer

Johann Kaspar Ferdinand Fischer: Sämtliche Werke für Klavier und Orgel, ed. Ernest V. Werra (New York: Broude, 1965), esp. *Ariadne Musica.*

Chapter 18. Eighteenth-Century Pre-Classical Music

General

Burney, Charles. *The Present State of Music in Germany, the Netherlands, and United Provinces* (London: T. Becket, 1773; 2d ed. 1775), and *The Present State of Music in France and Italy* (London: T. Becket, 1771); ed. Percy Scholes as *Dr. Burney's Musical Tours* (London and New York: Oxford U. Press, 1959; repr. Westport, CT: Greenwood Press, 1979).

Duckles, Vincent, and Minnie Elmer. *Thematic Catalog of a Manuscript Collection of Eighteenth-Century Italian Instrumental Music in the University of California, Berkeley, Music Library* (Berkeley, CA: U. of California Press, 1963).

Helm, E. Eugene. *Music at the Court of Frederick the Great* (Norman, OK: U. of Oklahoma Press, 1960).

Lang, Paul H. "Rococo—Style galant—Empfindsamkeit," *Music in Western Civilization* (New York: Norton, 1941), pp. 530–617.

Newman, William. *The Sonata in the Classic Era* (Chapel Hill, NC: U. of North Carolina Press, 1983).

Salerno, Henry F., trans. *Scenarios of the Commedia dell'arte: Flaminio Scala's "Il Teatro delle favole rappresentatione"* (New York: New York U. Press, 1967).

Sheldon, D. A. "The Galant Style Revisited and Re-evaluated," *Acta Musicologica,* xlvii (1975), pp. 240–69.

Performance Practice

Treatises

Bach, C. P. E. *Versuch über die wahre Art das Clavier zu spielen, mit Exempeln. . . .* (Berlin: Winter, 1753), trans., ed. William J. Mitchell, as *Essay on the True Art of Playing Keyboard Instruments* (New York: Norton, 1949).

Mozart, Leopold. *Versuch einer gründlichen Violinschule* (Augsburg: Lotter, 1756), facsimile ed. (Leipzig: H. L. Grahl, 1956), trans. Editha Knocker as *A Treatise on the Fundamental Principles of Violin Playing,* 2d ed. (London and New York: Oxford U. Press, 1951).

Quantz, Johann Joachim. *Versuch einer Anweisung die Flöte traversière zu spielen* (Essay on Playing the Transverse Flute; Berlin: C. F. Voss, 1752); facsimile of 3d ed., Breslau, 1789 (Kassel: Bärenreiter, 1953); trans. Edward R. Reilly, *On Playing the Flute* (New York: Schirmer Books, 1966; rev. ed. 1985).

Tartini, Giuseppe. *Traité des Agréments de la Musique* (Treatise on Ornaments in Music), trans. Pierre Denis (Paris: Denis, 1771), and *Regole per arrivare a saper ben suonar il violino* (MS compiled by G. F. Nicolai, in Conservatorio di Musica "Benedetto Marcello," Venice), ed. Erwin R. Jacobi and publ. in multilingual edition (Celle and New York: Moeck, 1961). Also, *Libro de regole, ed Esempi necessari per ben Suonare,* MS It. 00987, Music Library, U. of California, Berkeley.

Other Writings

Boyden, David D. "Dynamics in Seventeenth- and Eighteenth-Century Music," *Essays on Music in Honor of Archibald Thompson Davison* (Cambridge, MA: Harvard U. Press, 1957), p. 185ff.

Williams, P. "The Harpsichord Acciaccatura: Theory and Practice in Harmony, 1650–1750," *The Musical Quarterly,* liv (1968), p. 503ff.

J. S. Bach's Sons

Barford, Philip. *The Keyboard Music of C. P. E. Bach* (London: Barrie & Rockliff, 1965; repr. New York: October House, 1966).

Geiringer, Karl. *The Bach Family: Seven Generations of Creative Genius* (London: G. Allen Unwin, 1954; repr. New York, 1971).

Newman, William S. "Emanuel Bach's Autobiography," *The Musical Quarterly,* li (1965), pp. 363–73, includes translation of the Autobiography (1773).

Schulenberg, David. *The Instrumental Music of C. P. E. Bach* (Ann Arbor, MI: UMI Research Press, 1984).

Terry, Charles S. *John Christian Bach* (London: Oxford U. Press, 1929); 2d rev. ed., by H. C. R. Landon, 1967 (Westport, CT: Greenwood Press, 1980).

Warburton, E. "J. C. Bach's Operas," *Proceedings of the Royal Musical Association,* xcii (1965–66), p. 95ff.

Young, Percy M. *The Bachs, 1500–1850* (New York: Crowell, 1970).

D. Scarlatti

Music

Opere complete per clavicembalo di Domenico Scarlatti, 10 vols. and suppl., ed. A. Longo (Milan: 1906–08; New York: Ricordi, 1947–51). *D. Scarlatti: Sixty Sonatas,* 2 vols., ed. R. Kirkpatrick (New York: G. Schirmer, 1953). *D. Scarlatti: Complete Keyboard Works in Facsimile,* 18 vols., ed. R. Kirkpatrick (New York: Johnson Reprint, 1971–72). *Domenico Scarlatti: 100 Sonatas,* 3 vols., ed. Eiji Hashimoto (New York: G. Schirmer, 1975).

For Further Reading

Boyd, Malcolm. *Domenico Scarlatti—Master of Music* (New York: Schirmer Books, 1987, cpr. 1986).

Kirkpatrick, Ralph. *Domenico Scarlatti* (New York: Crowell, 1968; new ed. Princeton: Princeton U. Press, 1953; rev. 1968; new ed., 1983).

Opera

Anonymous. [Benedetto Marcello]. *Il Teatro alla Moda* (Venice, c. 1720; repr. Milan: Ricordi, 1956). Translation by R. G. Pauly, in *The Musical Quarterly,* xxxiv (1948), pp. 371–403; xxxv (1949), pp. 85–105.

Charlton, David. *Grétry and the Growth of Opéra-comique* (Cambridge, Eng.: Cambridge U. Press, 1986).

Dent, E. J. "Italian Opera in the Eighteenth Century and its Influence on the Music of the Classic Period," *Sammelbände der Internationalen Musik-Gesellschaft,* xiv (1912–13), p. 500ff.

Gagey, E. M. *Ballad Opera* (New York: Columbia U. Press, 1937).

Pitou, Spire. *The Paris Opera,* Vol. 2, *Rococo and Romantic, 1715–1815* (Westport, CT: Greenwood Press, 1985).

Paris

Brook, Barry S. *La Symphonie française dans la seconde moitié du XVIIIe siècle,* 3 vols. (Paris: Institut de musicologie de l'Université de Paris, 1962).

Launay, D., ed. *La Querelle des Bouffons,* repr. of pamphlets publ. Paris and The Hague, 1752–54 (Geneva, 1974).

Macdonald, R. J. *François-Joseph Gossec and French Instrumental Music in the Second Half of the Eighteenth Century* (Diss., U. of Michigan, 1968).

Pergolesi

Opera omnia di Giovanni Battista Pergolesi, 26 vols., ed. F. Caffarelli (Rome: Gli Amici della Musica da Camera, 1939–42; repr. in 5 vols., 1953). [New edition in progress, Pergolesi Research Center, City U. of New York.]

Chapter 19. The Classic Era

General

Blume, Friedrich. *Classic and Romantic Music: A Comprehensive Survey,* trans. M. D. Herter Norton (New York: Norton, 1970), pp. 3–94.

Landon, H. C. Robbins. *Essays on the Viennese Classical Style: Gluck, Haydn, Mozart, Beethoven* (New York: Macmillan, 1970).

Pauly, Reinhard. *Music in the Classic Period,* 2d ed. (Englewood Cliffs, NJ: Prentice-Hall, 1973).

Rosen, Charles. *The Classical Style: Haydn, Mozart, Beethoven* (New York: Viking Press, 1971; New York: Norton, 1972).

———. *Sonata Forms* (New York: Norton, 1980).

Ratner, Leonard. *Classic Music: Expression, Form, and Style* (New York: Schirmer Books, 1980).

Stolba, K Marie. *A History of the Violin Étude to about 1800* (repr. New York: Da Capo Press, 1979).

Webster, James. "Towards a History of Viennese Chamber Music in the Early Classical Period," *Journal of the American Musicological Society,* xxvii (1974), pp. 212–47.

Gluck

Music

C. W. Gluck: *Sämtliche Werke,* ed. R. Gerber, G. Croll, et al. (Kassel & Basel: Bärenreiter, 1951–). Edition of operas, commencing with *Orfeo ed Euridice,* publ. in 7 vols., by J. Pelletan, et al. (Leipzig, 1873–96).

For Further Reading

Cooper, Martin. *Gluck* (New York: Oxford U. Press, 1935).

Einstein, Alfred. *Gluck* (London: J. M. Dent, 1936; repr. New York: Collier, 1962).

Newman, Ernest. *Gluck and the Opera* (London: 1895; repr. 1964).

Haydn

Music

J. Haydn: *Werke,* ed. J. Haydn-Institut, Cologne, directed by J. P. Larsen (1958–61) and G. Feder (1962–), 59 vols. (Munich and Duisberg: G. Henle, 1958–). J. Haydn: *Kritische sämtliche Symphonien,* 12 vols., ed. H. C. R. Landon, Philharmonia series (Vienna, 1965–68).

For Further Reading

Barrett-Ayres, Reginald. *Joseph Haydn and the String Quartet* (New York: Schirmer Books, 1974).

Brown, A. Peter. *Joseph Haydn's Keyboard Music: Sources and Style* (Bloomington, IN: Indiana U. Press, 1986).

Geiringer, Karl. *Haydn: A Creative Life in Music* (Berkeley: U. of California Press, 1968; 3d rev. ed., 1982).

Hokky-Sallay, Marianne. *The Esterházy Palace at Fertöd,* trans. Judith Szöllösy and Zsuzsa Béres (Budapest: Petöfi, 1979).

Hughes, Rosemary. *Haydn,* rev. ed. (London: J. M. Dent, 1974).

———. *Haydn String Quartets* (Seattle: U. of Washington Press, 1969; rev. 5th ed., 1975).

Keller, Hans. *The Great Haydn String Quartets: Their Interpretation* (London: J. M. Dent, 1986).

Landon, H. C. Robbins. *Haydn: Chronicle and Works,* 5 vols. (Bloomington, IN: Indiana U. Press, 1976–80).

———. *Haydn: A Documentary Study* (New York: Rizzoli, 1981).

———. *The Symphonies of Joseph Haydn* (London: Universal Edition, 1955; supplement, Barrie & Rockliff, 1961).

W. A. Mozart

Music

W. A. *Mozarts Werke,* ed. L. von Köchel, et al., 14 series incl. supplements (Leipzig: Breitkopf & Härtel, 1877–1910; repr. Ann Arbor: Edwards, 1951–56; repr. in miniature, New York: Kalmus, 1969). W. A. *Mozart: Neue Ausgabe sämtlicher Werke,* ed. E. P. Schmid, et al. (Kassel: Bärenreiter, 1955–).

For Further Reading

Abert, Hermann. W. A. *Mozart,* 2 vols. (Leipzig: Breitkopf & Härtel, 1956; rev. 1975).

Badura-Skoda, Eva, and Paul Badura-Skoda. *Interpreting Mozart on the Keyboard,* trans. Leo Black (London: Barrie & Rockliff, 1962).

Dearling, Robert. *The Music of W. A. Mozart: The Symphonies* (Rutherford, NJ: Fairleigh Dickinson U. Press, 1982).

Dent, E. J. *Mozart's Operas,* 2d ed. (London: Oxford U. Press, 1960).

Deutsch, Otto E. *Mozart: A Documentary Biography,* 2d ed., trans. E. Blom, et al. (London: Adam & Charles Black, 1965).

Einstein, Alfred. *Mozart: His Character, His Work,* trans. Arthur Mendel and N. Broder (New York: Oxford U. Press, 1945; 4th ed., 1961).

Girdlestone, Cuthbert M. *Mozart's Piano Concertos* (London: Cassell, 1958; 3d ed., 1978).

Godwin, Joscelyn. "Layers of Meaning in *The Magic Flute.*" *The Musical Quarterly* lxv (1979), pp. 471–92.

Hutchings, Arthur. *Mozart: The Man, the Musician* (London: Thames & Hudson, 1976).

King, A. Hyatt. *Mozart* (London: Bingley, 1970).

———. *Mozart Chamber Music* (London: British Broadcasting Corporation, 1968; Seattle, WA: U. of Washington Press, 1969).

Landon, H. C. Robbins. *Mozart and the Masons: New Light on the Lodge "Crowned Hope"* (New York: Thames & Hudson, 1983).

Levey, Michael. *The Life & Death of Mozart* (New York: Stein & Day, 1971).

Liebner, János. *Mozart on the Stage* (New York: Praeger, 1972).

Mann, William. *The Operas of Mozart* (London: Oxford U. Press, 1960).

Nettl, Paul. *Mozart and Masonry* (New York: Philosophical Society, 1957; repr. New York: Da Capo, 1970; repr. New York: Dorset, 1987).

Rothschild, Fritz. *Musical Performance in the Times of Mozart & Beethoven* (London: Adam & Charles Black, 1961).

Saint-Foix, Georges de. *The Symphonies of Mozart,* trans. Leslie Orrey (London: Dennis Dobson, 1947; repr. New York: Dover, 1968).

American Music

Antes

Kroeger, Karl. "John Antes at Fulneck," *Moravian Music Journal,* xxx/1 (1985), p. 12ff.

McCorkle, Donald M. *John Antes, American Dilettante* (Winston-Salem, NC: Moravian Music Foundation, 1956; rev. 1980).

Stolba, K M. "Evidence for Quartets by John Antes, American-born Moravian Composer," *Journal of the American Musicological Society,* xxxiii (1980), p. 565ff.

———. "From John Antes to Benjamin Franklin: A Musical Connection," *Moravian Music Foundation Bulletin,* xxv/2 (1980), p. 5ff.

Billings

W. Billings: Complete Works, 4 vols.; Vols. 1, 3, 4, ed. Karl Kroeger, Vol. 2, ed. H. Nathan (Charlottesville, VA: American Musicological Society and University Press of Virginia, 1977–81).

Nathan, Hans. *William Billings: Data and Documents* (Detroit: 1976).

Hopkinson, Lyon

Sonneck, Oscar G. T. *Francis Hopkinson and James Lyon* (Washington, D.C., 1905; repr. New York: Da Capo Press, 1967).

Chapter 20. From Classicism to Romanticism

The London School

Music

J. L. Dussek: Sämtliche Werke für Klavier [Oeuvres de J. L. Dussek] (Leipzig: Breitkopf & Härtel, 1813–17; repr. New York: Da Capo Press, 1978).

The London Pianoforte School: 1766–1860, 20 vols., Nicholas Temperley, gen. ed. (New York: Garland, 1985).

Muzio Clementi: Complete Works (Leipzig: Breitkopf & Härtel, 1803–19; repr. New York: Da Capo Press, 1973).

For Further Reading

Clementi

Plantinga, Leon. *Muzio Clementi: His Life and Music* (London: Oxford U. Press, 1977).

Dussek

Klima, S. V. "Dussek in England," *Music and Letters,* xli (1960), p. 146ff.

Kraw, H. A. *A Biography and Thematic Catalog of the Works of J. L. Dussek (1760–1812)* (Diss., U. of Southern California, 1964).

Field

Piggott, Patrick. *The Life and Music of John Field* (London: Faber, 1973).

———. "John Field and the Nocturne," *Proceedings of the Royal Musical Association,* xcv (1968–69), p. 55ff.

Southall, Geneva. *John Field's Piano Concertos: an Analytical and Historical Study* (Diss., U. of Iowa, 1966).

Temperley, Nicholas. "John Field's Life and Music," *The Musical Times,* cxv (1974), p. 386ff.

———. "John Field and the First Nocturne," *Music and Letters,* lvi (1975), p. 335ff.

Bohemian Pianists

Music

Sachs, J. "A Checklist of the Works of Johann Nepomuk Hummel," *Notes,* xxx (1973–74), p. 732ff.

Tomášek: Principal MS collection of works is in Prague: Národni Muzeum, Music Division.

For Further Reading

Hummel

Davis, R. "The Music of J. N. Hummel, its Derivation and Development," *The Music Review,* xxvi (1965), p. 169ff.

Sachs, J. *Hummel in England and France: A Study in the International Musical Life of the Early Nineteenth Century* (Diss., Columbia U., 1968).

Voříšek

DeLong, K. G. *The Music of Jan Hugo Voříšek: A Stylistic Study* (Diss., Stanford U.).

Simpson, Adrienne. "A Profile of Jan Václav Voříšek," *Proceedings of the Royal Musical Association,* xcvii (1970–71), p. 125ff.

Beethoven

Music

Ludwig van Beethovens Werke, 24 series and suppl. (Leipzig: Breitkopf & Härtel, 1864–90; repr. Ann Arbor: J. W. Edwards, 1949; repr. in miniature, New York: Kalmus, 1971). *Supplement zur Gesamtausgabe,* ed. W. Hess (Wiesbaden: Breitkopf & Härtel, 1959–71). *Neue Ausgabe sämtliche Werke,* ed. J. Schmidt-Görg (Munich & Duisburg: Henle, 1961–).

For Further Reading

Abraham, G., ed. *The Age of Beethoven, 1790–1830* (New York: Oxford U. Press, 1982).

Anderson, Emily, ed., trans. *The Letters of Beethoven,* 3 vols. (New York: St. Martin's Press, 1961).

[A. W.] Thayer's Life of Beethoven, rev. and ed. Elliot Forbes, 2 vols. (Princeton: Princeton U. Press, 1969; 1-vol. paperbd. ed., 1970).

Cooper, Martin. *Beethoven: The Last Decade, 1817–1827* (London: Oxford U. Press, 1970).

Grove, Sir George. *Beethoven and His Nine Symphonies* (London: Novello, 1884; repr. New York: Dover, 1962).

Landon, H. C. Robbins. *Beethoven: A Documentary Study* (London: Macmillan, 1970).

Lang, Paul H., ed. *The Musical Quarterly Special Issue Celebrating the Bicentennial of the Birth of Beethoven,* Vol. lvi, No. 4 (New York: G. Schirmer, October 1970).

Newman, William S. *Performance Practices in Beethoven's Piano Sonatas: An Introduction* (New York: Norton, 1971).

Schindler, Anton. *Beethoven as I Knew Him* (Münster, 1840), ed. D. W. McArdle, trans. C. S. Jolly (Chapel Hill: U. of North Carolina Press, 1966; repr. New York: Norton, 1972).

Solomon, Maynard. *Beethoven* (New York: Schirmer Books, 1977).

Szigeti, Joseph. *The Ten Beethoven Sonatas for Piano & Violin,* ed. Paul Rolland (Urbana, IL: American String Teachers Association, 1965).

Tovey, Donald F. *A Companion to Beethoven's Pianoforte Sonatas* (London: The Associated Board of the Royal Schools of Music, 1931; repr. New York: AMS Press, 1976).
———. *Beethoven* (London: Oxford U. Press, 1945).

Chapter 21. Beethoven's Contemporaries

General

Abraham, Gerald. *A Hundred Years of Music* (London: Duckworth, 1964; 4th ed., Duckworth, 1974).

Abrams, Meyer H. *The Mirror and the Lamp: Romantic Theory and the Critical Tradition* (New York: Oxford U. Press, 1953).

Blume, Friedrich. *Classic and Romantic Music: A Comprehensive Survey,* trans. M. D. Herter Norton (New York: Norton, 1970), pp. 95–194.

Durant, Will, and Ariel Durant. *The Age of Napoleon* (New York: Simon & Schuster, 1975).

Einstein, Alfred. *Music in the Romantic Era* (New York: Norton, 1947).

Longyear, Rey M. *Nineteenth-Century Romanticism in Music* (Englewood Cliffs, NJ: Prentice-Hall, 1969; 2d ed., 1973).

Newman, William S. *The Sonata Since Beethoven* (Chapel Hill, NC: U. of North Carolina Press, 1970; 3d ed., New York: Norton, 1983).

Plantinga, Leon. *Romantic Music* (New York: Norton, 1984).

Tischler, Hans. "Classicism, Romanticism and Music," *The Music Review,* xiv (1953), pp. 108–205.

Opera

Claudon, Francis, Jean Mongrédien, Carl de Nuys, and Karlheinz Roschitz. *L'Histoire de l'Opéra en France* (Paris: Fernand Nathan, 1984).

Crosten, William L. *French Grand Opera: An Art and a Business* (New York: King's Crown Press, 1948; repr. New York: Da Capo Press, 1972).

Dent, Edward J. *The Rise of Romantic Opera,* ed. Winton Dean (Cambridge, Eng.: Cambridge U. Press, 1976).

Grout, Donald J. *A Short History of Opera,* 2d ed. (New York: Columbia U. Press, 1965).

Pitou, Spire. *The Paris Opera,* Vol. 2, *Rococo and Romantic, 1715–1815* (Westport, CT: Greenwood Press, 1985).

Garcías

Levien, John J. N. *The García Family* (London: Novello, 1932; 2d rev. ed., publ. as *Six Sovereigns of Song,* 1948).

Mattfeld, Julius. *A Hundred Years of Grand Opera in New York, 1825–1925* (New York: New York Public Library, 1937; repr. New York: AMS Press, 1976).

Sterling-Mackinlay, M. *Garcia the Centenarian and his Times* (Edinburgh: W. Blanchard, 1908; repr. New York: Da Capo Press, 1976).

Subíra, José. *Historia de la música española e hispano-americana* (Barcelona: Salvat, 1953; repr. Salvat, 1987, p. 628ff).

Loewe

Carl Loewes Werke: Gesamtausgabe der Balladen, Legenden, Lieder und Gesänge, ed. M. Runze (Leipzig: Breitkopf & Härtel, 1899–1904; repr. 1970).

Loewe, Carl. *Selbstbiographie,* ed. Karl H. Ritter (Berlin: W. Müller, 1870; repr. Hildesheim: Olms, 1976).

For Further Reading

Brown, Maurice J. E. "Carl Loewe, 1796–1869," *The Musical Times,* cx (1969), p. 357ff.

Rossini

Stendhal, Mme [Marie Henri Beyle]. *Vie de Rossini* (Life of Rossini; Paris: 1824); trans. R. N. Coe (New York: Orion Press, 1970; repr. Seattle, WA: U. of Washington Press, 1972).

Weinstock, Herbert. *Rossini: A Biography* (New York: Knopf, 1968).

Schubert

Music

F. Schuberts Werke: Kritisch durchgeschene Gesamtausgabe, ed. J. Brahms, E. Mandyczewski, et al. (Leipzig: Breitkopf & Härtel, 1884–97; repr. New York: Dover, 1964–69; repr. in miniature, New York: Kalmus, 1971).

F. Schubert: Neue Ausgabe sämtlicher Werke, ed. W. Dürr, C. Landon, et al. (Kassel and New York: Bärenreiter, 1964–).

F. Schubert: Lieder, 7 vols. (Frankfurt and New York: C.F. Peters, 1985–88).

For Further Reading

Abraham, Gerald, ed. *The Music of Schubert* (Washington, DC and New York: Kennikat Press, 1969).

Brown, Maurice J. E. *Schubert: A Critical Biography* (London: Macmillan, 1958; repr. New York: Da Capo Press, 1977).

———. "Schubert: Discoveries of the Last Decade," *The Musical Quarterly,* xlvii (1961), p. 293ff.

———. "Schubert: Discoveries of the Last Decade," *The Musical Quarterly,* lvii (1971), p. 351ff.

Capell, Richard. *Schubert's Songs,* 3d ed. (London: Duckworth, 1973).

Deutsch, Otto E. *Schubert: A Documentary Biography,* trans. E. Blom (London: Dent, 1946; repr. New York: Da Capo Press, 1977).

———. *The Schubert Reader: A Life of Franz Schubert in Letters and Documents,* trans. E. Blom (New York: Norton, 1947).

Marek, George R. *Schubert* (New York: Viking, 1985).

Spohr

Spohr, Louis. *Selbstbiographie,* 2 vols. (Kassel: City of Kassel, 1860–61), Eng. trans. (London: Longmans, Green, 1865; repr. New York: Da Capo Press, 1969).

Weber

Warrack, John H. *Carl Maria von Weber* (London: Hamilton, 1968; New York: Macmillan, 1968; 2d ed., Cambridge, Eng.: Cambridge U. Press, 1976).

Weber, Max Maria von. *Carl Maria von Weber: ein Lebensbild,* 2 vols. (Leipzig: E. Keil, 1864–65; Eng. trans. London: Chapman & Hall, 1865; repr. Westport, CT: Greenwood Press, 1969).

Chapter 22. Musical Expansion in Mid-Nineteenth Century

General

Claudon, Francis, Jean Mongrédien, Carl de Nuys, and Karlheinz Roschitz. *L'Histoire de l'Opéra en France* (Paris: Fernand Nathan, 1984).

Crosten, William L. *French Grand Opera: An Art and a Business* (New York: King's Crown Press, 1948; repr. New York: Da Capo Press, 1972).

Lovelace, Ada. *Notes upon the Memoire, Sketch of the Analytical Engine invented by Charles Babbage* (Geneva, 1842) reprinted in *Charles Babbage and His Calculating Engines,* ed. Philip Morrison and Emily Morrison (New York: Dover, 1961).

Pitou, Spire. *The Paris Opera,* Vol. 2, *Rococo and Romantic, 1715–1815* (Westport, CT: Greenwood Press, 1985).

Bellini

Orrey, Leslie. *Bellini* (London: J. M. Dent & Sons; New York: Farrar, Straus & Giroux, 1969).

Weinstock, Herbert. *Vincenzo Bellini: His Life and His Operas* (New York: Knopf, 1971).

Berlioz

Music

H. Berlioz: Werke, 20 vols., ed. C. Malherbe and F. Weingartner (Leipzig: Breitkopf & Härtel, 1900–10). *New Berlioz Edition,* ed. H. Macdonald, et al. (Kassel: Bärenreiter, 1967–).

Writings

Grand traité d'instrumentation et d'orchestration modernes (Treatise on Instrumentation and Orchestration), Op. 10 (Paris, 1843; 2d ed. 1855; rev. and enl. by Richard Strauss, 1905; trans. Theodore Front, New York: Kalmus, 1948, and Melville, NY: Belwin Mills, 1948).

Memoires de Hector Berlioz from 1803 to 1865 (Paris, 1870); Eng. trans. by Holmes rev. by Ernest Newman (New York: Knopf, 1932; repr. New York: Dover, 1966).

For Further Reading

Barzun, Jacques. *Berlioz and His Century* (Boston: Little, Brown & Co., 1969).

———. "Berlioz a Hundred Years After," *The Musical Quarterly,* lvi (1970), p. 1ff.

Cairns, D. "Spontini's Influence on Berlioz," *From Parnassus: Essays in Honor of Jacques Barzun,* ed. Dora B. Weines and Wm. R. Keylor (New York: Harper & Row, 1976).

Comboroure, C. "Harriet Smithson, 1828–37," *Berlioz Society Bulletin,* No. 86 (1975), p. 15ff.

Dickinson, Alan E. F. *The Music of Berlioz* (London: Faber, 1972).

Macdonald, Hugh. *Berlioz* (London: Dent, 1982).

Primmer, Brian. *The Berlioz Style* (London: Oxford U. Press, 1973).

Rushton, Julian. *The Musical Language of Berlioz* (Cambridge: Cambridge U. Press, 1973).

Bizet

Curtiss, Mina. *Bizet and His World* (New York: Knopf, 1958).

Dean, Winton. *Georges Bizet: His Life and His Work* (London: Dent, 1948; 3d ed. [enlarged], 1975).

Chopin

Music

F. F. Chopin: Dziela wszytkie (Complete Works), ed. I. J. Paderewski, et al. (Warsaw: Institut Fryderyka Chopina, 1949–61).

For Further Reading

Abraham, Gerald. *Chopin's Musical Style* (London: Oxford U. Press, 1939).

Hedley, A. *Chopin* (London: Dent, 1947); rev. by Maurice J. E. Brown (London: Dent, 1974).

Kelley, Edgar S. *Chopin, the Composer* (New York: Cooper Square Publishers, 1969).

Melville, Derek. *Chopin* (London: Clive Bingley, 1977; Hamden, CT: Linnet Books, 1977).

Walker, Alan, ed. *The Chopin Companion* (New York: Norton, 1973).

Weinstock, Herbert. *Chopin: The Man and His Music* (New York: Knopf, 1949; 4th repr. 1969).

Donizetti

Ashbrook, William. *Donizetti* (London: Cassell, 1965).

———. *Donizetti and His Operas* (Cambridge: Cambridge U. Press, 1982).

Weinstock, Herbert. *Donizetti and the World of Opera in Italy, Paris, and Vienna in the First Half of the Nineteenth Century* (New York: Pantheon Books, 1963; repr. Octagon, 1979).

Farrenc

Friedland, Bea. *Louise Farrenc, 1804–1875: Composer, Performer, Scholar* (Ann Arbor, MI: UMI Research Press, 1980).

Hensel

Citron, Marcia J. "The Lieder of Fanny Mendelssohn Hensel," *The Musical Quarterly,* lxix (1983), pp. 570–93.

———. *The Letters of Fanny Hensel to Felix Mendelssohn* (New York: Pendragon Press, 1987).

Hensel, Sebastian. *Die Familie Mendelssohn 1729–1847, nach Briefen und Tagebüchern* [The Mendelssohn Family, 1729–1847, according to Letters and Diaries] (Berlin, 1879; 18th repr. 1959; Eng. trans., 1882, repr. New York: Haskell House, 1969).

Sirota, Victoria R. *The Life and Works of Fanny Mendelssohn Hensel* (Ann Arbor, MI: University Microfilms, 1981).

Mendelssohn

Music

F. Mendelssohn-Bartholdy: Werke: kritisch durchgesehene Ausgabe, 35 vols., ed. J. Rietz (Leipzig: Breitkopf & Härtel, 1874–77; repr. Farnborough, Eng.: Gregg International, 1967; repr. in miniature, New York: Kalmus, 1971). *Leipziger Ausgabe der Werke Felix Mendelssohn Bartholdys,* ed. Internationale Felix-Mendelssohn-Gesellschaft (Leipzig: Deutscher Verlag für Musik, 1960–).

Paintings

Mendelssohn Bartholdy, Felix. *Aquarellenalbum* [Album of Watercolor Paintings] (Berlin: Staatsbibliothek Preussischer Kuklturbesitz, 1968).

Writings

Elvers, R., ed. *Felix Mendelssohn Bartholdy Briefe* (Frankfurt am Main, 1984), trans. C. Tomlinson and publ. as *Felix Mendelssohn: A Life in Letters* (New York: Fromm International, 1986).
Mendelssohn, Felix. *Reisebriefe aus den Jahren 1830 bis 1832* (Letters from the years 1830 to 1832), ed. P. Mendelssohn Bartholdy (Leipzig, 1871). Also, *Briefe aus den Jahren 1830 bis 1847* (Letters from the years 1830 to 1847), comp. J. Rietz (Leipzig, 1861–63).

For Further Reading

Blunt, Wilfred. *On Wings of Song: A Biography of Felix Mendelssohn* (New York: Scribner's Sons, 1974).
Jacob, Heinrich E. *Mendelssohn and His Times,* trans. Richard and Clara Winston (Englewood Cliffs, NJ: Prentice-Hall, 1963).
Radcliffe, Philip. *Mendelssohn* (London: J. M. Dent & Sons; New York: Farrar, Strauss & Giroux, 1967; rev. ed. 1976).

Paganini

Courcy, Geraldine I. C. de. *Paganini, the Genoese,* 2 vols. (Norman, OK: U. of Oklahoma Press, 1957; repr. 1977).
———. *Chronology of Nicolò Paganini's Life* (Wiesbaden: Erdmann Musik Verlag, 1961).
Kendall, Alan. *Paganini: A Biography* (London: Chappell, 1982).

Schumann, Clara Wieck

Litzmann, B. *Clara Schumann: Ein Künstlerleben* [Clara Schumann: An Artist's Life] (Leipzig: Breitkopf & Härtel, 1902–08; repr. 1971; Eng. trans. 1913, repr. New York: Da Capo, 1979).
May, Florence. *The Girlhood of Clara Schumann* (London: Longmans, 1912).
Meichsner, A. *Friedrich Wieck und seine beiden Töchter Clara Schumann, geb. Wieck, und Marie Wieck* [Friedrich Wieck and his two Daughters, Clara Wieck Schumann and Marie Wieck] (Leipzig: 1875).
Reich, Nancy B. *Clara Schumann: The Artist and the Woman* (Ithaca, NY: Cornell U. Press, 1985).

Schumann, Robert

Music

R. Schumann: Werke, ed. Clara Schumann, Johannes Brahms, et al. (Leipzig: Breitkopf & Härtel, 1881–93; repr. in miniature, New York: Kalmus, 1971).

Writings

Schumann, Robert. *Gesammelte Schriften über Musik und Musiker* [Collected Writings on Music and Musicians] (Leipzig: G. Wiegand, 1854; repr. 1968; Eng. trans. 1877; new Eng. trans. [selections], 1947).
———. *Tagenbücher, 1827–38* [Diaries] (Leipzig: Deutscher Verlag für Musik, 1971).

For Further Reading

Abraham, Gerald, ed. *Schumann: A Symposium* (London: Oxford U. Press, 1952).
Brion, Marcel. *Schumann and the Romantic Age,* trans. Geoffrey Sainsbury (New York: Macmillan, 1956).
Chissell, Joan. *Schumann* (New York: Collier Books, 1962; rev. ed., London: Dent, 1977).
Ostwald, Peter. *Schumann: Music and Madness* (London: Victor Gollancz, 1985).
Plantinga, Leon. *Schumann as Critic* (New Haven, CT: Yale U. Press, 1967; repr. 1977).
Sams, Eric. "Schumann's Hand Injury," *The Musical Times,* cxii (1971), pp. 1156–59.
———. *The Songs of Robert Schumann,* 2d ed. (London: Methuen, 1975).
Walker, A., ed. *Robert Schumann: The Man and His Music* (London: Barrie & Jenkins, 1972; 2d ed., 1976).

American Composers

Foster

Howard, John T. *Stephen Foster: America's Troubadour* (New York: Crowell, 1934; rev. 3d ed., 1962).
Smith, S. B. *A Tribute to Stephen Collins Foster* (Bardstown, KY: Smith, 1976). [Includes facsimiles.]

Gottschalk

Music

The Piano Works of Louis Moreau Gottschalk, ed. Vera B. Lawrence (New York: Arno Press, 1969).

Writings

Gottschalk, L. M. *Notes of a Pianist,* ed. Clara Gottschalk Peterson (Philadelphia: Lippincott, 1881), ed. J. Behrend (New York: Knopf, 1964; repr. New York: Da Capo, 1979).

For Further Reading

Lowens, Irving. "The First Matinée Idol: Louis Moreau Gottschalk," *Musicology,* ii (1948); repr. in *Music and Musicians in Early America* (New York: Norton, 1964), p. 223ff.
Marrocco, W. T. "America's First Nationalist Composer: Louis Moreau Gottschalk (1829–1869," *Scritti in onore di Luigi Ronga* (Milan and Naples: R. Ricciardi, 1973), p. 293ff.

Mason

Pemberton, C. A. *Lowell Mason: His Life and Work* (Diss., U. of Minnesota, 1971).
Rich, A. L. *Lowell Mason* (Chapel Hill, NC: U. of North Carolina Press, 1946).
Thayer, A. W. "Lowell Mason," *Dwight's Journal of Music,* xxxix (1879), pp. 186, 195.

Chapter 23: Master Composers of the Late Nineteenth Century

Brahms

Music

Johannes Brahms sämtliche Werke, 26 vols. (Leipzig: Breitkopf & Härtel, 1926–27; repr. Ann Arbor, MI: J. W. Edwards, 1949; repr. in miniature, New York: Kalmus, 1970).

For Further Reading

Burnett, James. *Brahms: A Critical Study* (New York: Praeger, 1972).

Frisch, Walter. *Brahms and the Principle of Developing Variation* (Berkeley: U. of California Press, 1984).

Gal, Hans. *Johannes Brahms: His Work and Personality,* trans. Joseph Stein. (New York: Alfred A. Knopf, 1963).

Geiringer, Karl. *Brahms: His Life and Work,* 2d ed., rev. (Garden City, NY: Doubleday & Co., Inc., 1961).

Harrison, Max. *The Lieder of Brahms* (New York: Praeger, 1972).

Horton, John. *Brahms Orchestral Music* (Seattle: U. of Washington Press, 1969).

Mason, Daniel G. *The Chamber Music of Brahms,* 2d ed. (New York: Macmillan, 1950).

Musgrave, Michael. *The Music of Brahms* (Boston: Routledge & Kegan Paul, 1985).

Bruckner

Music

Anton Bruckner: Sämtliche Werke, kritische Gesamtausgabe, ed. L. Nowak, et al. (Vienna: Musikwissenschaftlicher Verlag, 1951–).

For Further Reading

Doernberg, Erwin. *The Life and Symphonies of Anton Bruckner* (London: Barrie & Rockliff, 1960; repr. New York: Dover Publications, 1968).

Redlich, H. F. *Bruckner and Mahler,* rev. ed. (London: J. M. Dent & Sons, 1963).

Schönzeler, Hans-Hubert. *Bruckner* (New York: Grossman, 1970).

Simpson, Robert. *The Essence of Bruckner* (New York: Crescendo Publishing, 1967).

Watson, Derek. *Bruckner* (London: J. M. Dent & Sons, 1975).

Liszt

Music

F. Liszt: Musikalische Werke, ed. F. Busoni, P. Raabe, et al., 34 vols. [but incomplete] (Leipzig: Breitkopf & Härtel, 1907–36; repr. 1967).

F. Liszt: Neue Ausgabe sämtliche Werke, ed. Z. Gárdonyi, I. Sulyok, et al. (Kassel and Budapest: Bärenreiter, 1970–).

For Further Reading

Beckett, Walter. *Liszt,* rev. ed. (London: J. M. Dent & Sons, 1963).

Perényi, E. *Liszt: The Artist as Romantic Hero* (Boston: Little, Brown & Co., 1974).

Searle, Humphrey. *The Music of Liszt,* 2d rev. ed. (New York: Dover, 1966).

Walker, Alan, comp. *Franz Liszt: The Man and His Music,* 2d ed. (London: Barrie & Jenkins, 1976).

———. *Franz Liszt: The Virtuoso Years, 1811–1847* (New York: Knopf, 1983).

Verdi

Music

"Complete Works" not published. "Study scores" of *Rigoletto, La traviata, Un ballo in maschera, Aïda, Otello,* and *Falstaff* published by Ricordi, in 1930s; repr. in miniature by Kalmus, New York. Full score of *Otello* and *Falstaff* repr. by Dover, New York, 1988.

For Further Reading

Budden, Julian. *The Operas of Verdi,* 3 vols. (New York: Praeger, 1973–82).

Godefroy, Vincent. *The Dramatic Genius of Verdi: Studies of Selected Operas,* 2 vols. (New York: St. Martin's Press; I, 1975; II, 1977).

Hussey, Dyneley. *Verdi* (London: J. M. Dent & Sons, 1963).

Martin, George. *Verdi: His Music, Life and Times* (New York: Dodd, Mead & Co., 1963).

Toye, Francis. *Giuseppe Verdi: His Life and Works* (London: Heinemann, 1931; repr. New York: Vienna House, 1972).

Walker, Frank. *The Man Verdi* (New York: Knopf, 1962).

Weaver, William, comp., ed., trans. *Verdi, a Documentary Study* (London: Thames & Hudson, 1977).

Weaver, William, and Martin Chusid, eds. *The Verdi Companion* (New York: W. W. Norton, 1981).

Wagner

Music

Richard Wagners Werke [incomplete edition], ed. M. Balling (Leipzig: Breitkopf & Härtel, 1912–29). *R. Wagner: Sämtliche Werke,* ed. C. Dahlhaus (Mainz: B. Schott's Söhne, 1970–). Full scores of *Der Ring des Nibelungen, Die Meistersinger, Lohengrin, Parsifal, Tannhäuser,* and *Tristan und Isolde,* publ. by Dover, New York.

For Further Reading

Barth, Herbert, Dietrich Mack, and Egon Voss, eds. *Wagner: A Documentary Study,* trans. P. R. J. Ford and M. Whittall (New York: Oxford U. Press, 1975).

Burbridge, Peter, and Richard Sutton, eds. *The Wagner Companion* (Cambridge, Eng. and New York: Cambridge U. Press, 1979).

Dalhaus, Carl. *Richard Wagner's Music Dramas,* tr. Mary Whittall (Cambridge, Eng. and New York: Cambridge U. Press, 1979).

Jacobs, Robert L. *Wagner,* rev. ed. (London: J. M. Dent & Sons, 1965).

Mander, Raymond, and Joe Mitchenson. *The Wagner Companion* (New York: Hawthorn Books, 1978).

Newman, Ernest. *Life of Richard Wagner,* 4 vols. (London: Cassell, 1933–47; repr. 1976).

Westernhagen, C. von. *Wagner: A Biography,* 2 vols., tr. Mary Whittall (Cambridge, Eng.: Cambridge U. Press, 1979).

Chapter 24. Late Nineteenth-Century — Early Twentieth-Century Music

Russia

General

Abraham, Gerald. *Studies in Russian Music* (London: W. Reeves, 1935; rev. 1969).

Leonard, Richard A. *A History of Russian Music* (New York: Macmillan, 1956; repr. London: Minerva Press, 1968; repr. Westport, CT: Greenwood Press, 1977).

Seaman, Gerald. *History of Russian Music:* Vol. 1, *From Its Origins to Dargomïzhsky* (New York: Praeger, 1967).

Balakirev

Garden, Edward. *Balakirev: A Critical Study of His Life and Music* (London: Faber & Faber, and New York: St. Martin's Press, 1967).

Borodin

Calvocoressi, Michel D. "Alexander Borodin," in M. D. Calvocoressi and Gerald Abraham, *Masters of Russian Music* (London: Duckworth, 1936), p. 155ff.

Cui

Cui, César. *La musique en Russie* [Music in Russia] (Paris: Fischbacher, 1880; trans. and repr. 1974).

Dargomïzhsky

Baker, J. "Dargomïzhsky, Realism and *The Stone Guest*," *The Music Review*, xxxvii (1976), p. 193ff.

Taruskin, Richard. *Opera and Drama in Russia as Preached and Practiced in the 1860s* (Ann Arbor, MI: UMI Research Press, 1981).

Glinka

Brown, David. *Mikhail Glinka: A Biographical and Critical Study* (London and New York: Oxford U. Press, 1974).

Musorgsky

Calvocoressi, M. D. *Mussorgsky* [sic] (1946), rev. G. Abraham (London: Dent, 1946; rev. London: Dent, 1974, 1977).

———. *Modest Mussorgsky: His Life and Works* (London: Rockliff, 1956; repr. Boston: Crescendo, 1967).

Leyda, Jay, and S. Bertensson, eds. *The Musorgsky Reader: A Life of M. P. Musorgsky in Letters and Documents* (New York: Norton, 1947; repr. 1970).

Lloyd-Jones, David. *Boris Godunov: Critical Commentary* (London: Oxford U. Press, 1975).

Orlova, A. *Musorgsky's Days and Works: A Biography in Documents* (Moscow, 1963), trans. and ed. R. J. Guenther (Ann Arbor, MI: UMI Research Press, 1983).

Serov, Victor I. *Modest Musorgsky* (New York: Funk & Wagnalls, 1968).

Rimsky-Korsakov

Writings

Rimsky-Korsakov, N. *Chronicle of My Musical Life* (St. Petersburg, 1909); Eng. translation by J. Joffe publ. as *My Musical Life* (New York: Knopf, 1923; repr. 1974).

———. *Principles of Orchestration* (St. Petersburg, 1913); Eng. trans. Edward Agate, ed. Maximilian Steinberg (New York: Dover, 1964).

For Further Reading

Abraham, Gerald. *Rimsky-Korsakov: A Short Biography* (London: Duckworth, 1945).

Scriabin

Baker, James M. *The Music of Alexander Scriabin* (New Haven, CT: Yale U. Press, 1986).

Bowers, Faubion. *Scriabin: A Biography of the Russian Composer, 1871–1915,* 2 vols. (Tokyo and Palo Alto, CA: Kodansha International, 1969).

———. *The New Scriabin: Enigma and Answers* (New York: St. Martin's Press, 1973).

Hull, Arthur Eaglefield. *A Great Russian Tone-Poet: Scriabin* (London: Kegan Paul, Trench, Trubner & Co., 1918; repr. New York: AMS Press, Inc., 1970).

Macdonald, Hugh. *Skryabin* [sic] (London: Oxford U. Press, 1978).

Schloezer, Boris de. *Scriabin: Artist and Mystic,* trans. N. Slonimsky (Berkeley, CA: U. of California Press, 1982).

Swan, Alfred J. *Scriabin* (London: John Lane, 1923; repr. New York: Da Capo Press, 1969).

Tchaikovsky

Brown, David. *Tchaikovsky: A Biographical and Critical Study,* Vol. I, *The Early Years, 1840–1874* (New York: Norton, 1978); Vol. II, *The Crisis Years, 1874–1878* (New York: Norton, 1982); Vol. III, *The Years of Wandering, 1878–1885* (London: Gollancz, 1986).

Garden, Edward. *Tchaikovsky* (London: Dent, 1973).

Czechoslovakia

Abraham, Gerald. *Slavonic and Romantic Music* (New York: St. Martin's Press, 1968).

Eckstein, Pavel. *Czechoslovak Opera: A Brief Outline* (Prague: Theatre Institute, 1964).

Newmarch, Rosa. *The Music of Czechoslovakia* (London and New York: Oxford U. Press, 1942; repr. New York: Da Capo, 1978).

Dvořák

Writings

Dvořák, Antonín. *Letters and Reminiscences,* ed. Otakar Sourek, trans. Roberta Samsour (Prague: Artia, 1958; repr. New York: Da Capo Press, 1983).

For Further Reading

Clapham, John. *Antonín Dvořák* (London: Faber, and New York: St. Martin's Press, 1966; rev. ed. New York: Norton, 1979).

Layton, Robert. *Dvořák's Symphonies and Concertos* (London: British Broadcasting Corporation, 1978).

Robertson, Alec. *Dvořák* (London: Dent, 1943; repr. New York: Collier, 1962; rev. London: Dent, 1974).

Janáček

Ewans, Michael. *Janáček's Tragic Operas* (Bloomington, IN and London: Indiana U. Press, 1977).

Vogel, J. *Leoš Janáček: His Life and Works* (Kassel, 1958); trans. Geraldine Thomsen-Munchova (London: P. Hamlyn, 1962); rev. and ed. by K. Janovický (New York: Norton, 1981).

Smetana

Clapham, John. *Smetana* (London: Dent, 1972).
Karásek, Bohumil. *Bedřich Smetana* (Prague: Státni hudební vydavatelstuí, 1966), trans. (Prague: Editio Supraphon, 1967).
Large, Brian. *Smetana* (London: Duckworth, and New York: Praeger, 1970; repr. New York: Da Capo Press, 1985).
Malý, Miloslav. *Bedřich Smetana* (Prague: Orbis, 1954), trans. (Orbis, 1956; 1976).

Scandinavia

General

Hodgson, A. *Scandinavian Music: Finland and Sweden* (Rutherford, NJ: Fairleigh Dickinson Press, and London: Associated University Presses, 1984).

Grieg

Abraham, Gerald, ed. *Grieg: A Symposium* (London: Lindsay Drummond, 1948; repr. Westport, CT: Greenwood Press, 1972).
Horton, J. *Grieg* (London: Dent, 1974).
Johansen, David M. *Edvard Grieg*, trans. Madge Robertson (Princeton, NJ: Princeton U. Press, 1938; repr. 1967; repr. New York: Kraus Reprint, 1972).

Nielsen

Simpson, Robert. *Carl Nielsen, Symphonist* (London: Dent, 1964).

Sibelius

Burnett, James. *The Music of Sibelius* (Rutherford, NJ: Fairleigh Dickinson Press, 1983).
Layton, Robert. *Sibelius* (London: Dent, 1965; 2d ed., 1978).
Tawaststjerna, Erik. *Sibelius* (Helsingfors: Söderstroms, 1976); trans. Robert Layton (London: Faber & Faber, 1976).

Germany, Austria

Mahler, G.

Blaukopf, Kurt. *Mahler: A Documentary Study* (New York: Oxford U. Press, 1976).
Cooke, Deryck. *Gustav Mahler: An Introduction to His Music* (London: Faber & Faber, 1980).
Greenberg, Egon. *Mahler: The Man and His Music* (New York: Schirmer Books, 1978).
Kennedy, Michael. *Mahler* (London: Dent, 1974).
La Grange, Henri-Louis de. *Mahler* (Garden City, NY: Doubleday, 1973).
Lea, Henry A. *Gustav Mahler: Man on the Margin* (Bonn: Bouvier, 1985).
Mitchell, Donald. *Gustav Mahler: The Early Years* (London: Rockliff, 1958), rev. ed. P. Banks and D. Mathews (Berkeley, CA: U. of California Press, 1980).
———. *Gustav Mahler: The Wunderhorn Years* (Boulder, CO: Westview Press, 1976).
Werfel, Alma Mahler. *Mahler: Memories and Letters*, 3d ed., rev., ed. D. Mitchell and K. Martner, trans. B. Creighton (Seattle: U. of Washington Press, 1975).

Mahler, A.

Monson, Karen. *Alma Mahler: Muse to Genius* (Boston: Houghton Mifflin, 1983).

Strauss, R.

Armstrong, T. *Strauss's Tone Poems* (London: Oxford U. Press, 1931).
Del Mar, Norman. *Richard Strauss: A Critical Commentary on His Life and Work*, 3 vols. (Philadelphia: Chilton Books, 1969–73; repr., corrected, 1978).
Jefferson, Alan. *The Lieder of Richard Strauss* (New York: Praeger, 1972).
Krause, Ernst. *Richard Strauss: The Man and His Work*, trans. J. Coombs (London: Collett's, 1964).
Mann, William. *Richard Strauss: A Critical Study of His Operas* (London: Cassell, 1964).

Wolf

Sams, Eric. *The Songs of Hugo Wolf* (London: Methuen, 1961; 2d ed., 1981).
Walker, Frank. *Hugo Wolf, A Biography* (London: Dent, 1951; 2d ed., enlarged, 1968).

Verismo

Dahlhaus, Carl. *Realism in Nineteenth-Century Music*, trans. Mary Whittall (Cambridge, Eng. and New York: Cambridge U. Press, 1985).

Puccini

Ashbrook, William. *The Operas of Puccini* (New York: Oxford U. Press, 1968).
Carner, Mosco. *Puccini: A Critical Biography* (London: Duckworth, 1958; 2d ed., 1974).
Kaye, Michael. *The Unknown Puccini: A Historical Perspective on the Songs* (London: Oxford U. Press, 1987).

France

Cooper, Martin. *French Music from the Death of Berlioz to the Death of Fauré* (London: Oxford U. Press, 1951).
Shattuck, Roger. *The Banquet Years: The Arts in France, 1885–1918* (London: Flammarion, 1959; rev. 1968).

L. Boulanger

Rosenstiel, Leonie. *The Life and Works of Lili Boulanger* (Rutherford, NJ: Farleigh Dickinson U. Press, 1978).

Debussy

Writings

Debussy, Claude. *Monsieur Croche, anti-dilettante* (Paris, 1923), collected by François Lesure, trans. and ed. R. L. Smith, and publ. as *Debussy on Music* (New York: Knopf, 1977).
Lockspeiser, Edward, comp. *Debussy et Edgar Poe: Manuscrits et Documents ineditées* [Manuscripts and unedited documents] (Monaco: Éditions Rocher, 1962).

For Further Reading

Lockspeiser, Edward. *Debussy* (London: Dent, 1936; rev. ed., 1963).
———. *Debussy: His Life and Mind*, 2 vols., 2d ed. (London: Cassell, 1965–66).
Vallas, Léon. *Claude Debussy: His Life and Works*, trans. M. and G. O'Brian (London: Oxford U. Press, 1933).
Wenk, Arthur B. *Debussy and the Poets* (Berkeley and Los Angeles: U. of California Press, 1976).
———. *Claude Debussy and Twentieth-Century Music* (Boston: Twayner, 1983).

Fauré

Koechlin, Charles. *Gabriel Fauré* (London: Dobson, 1945; repr. New York: AMS Press, 1976).

Orledge, Robert. *Gabriel Fauré* (London: Eulenberg, 1979).

Suckling, Norman. *Fauré* (London: Dent, and New York: Dutton, 1946).

Vuillermoz, Émile. *Gabriel Fauré* (Paris: Flammarion, 1960), trans. Kenneth Schapin (Philadelphia: Chilton Book Co., 1969; repr. New York: Da Capo Press, 1983).

Franck

Davies, Laurence. *César Franck and His Circle* (London: Barrie & Jenkins, 1970).

————. *Franck* (London: Dent, 1973).

Demuth, Norman. *César Franck* (London: Dobson, and New York: Philosophical Library, 1949).

d'Indy

Davies, Laurence. *César Franck and His Circle* (London: Barrie & Jenkins, 1970).

Demuth, Norman. *Vincent d'Indy* (London: Rockliff, 1951).

Paul, G. B. "Rameau, d'Indy, and French Nationalism," *The Musical Quarterly,* lviii (1972), p. 46ff.

Ravel

Demuth, Norman. *Ravel* (London: Dent, 1947; repr. New York: Collier Books, 1962).

Myers, Rollo H. *Ravel: His Life and Works* (London: Duckworth, 1960; repr. Westport, CT: Greenwood Press, 1973).

Orenstein, A. *Ravel, Man and Musician* (New York: Columbia U. Press, 1975).

Saint-Saëns

Harding, James. *Saint-Saëns and His Circle* (London: Chapman & Hall, 1965).

Rolland, Romain. *Camille Saint-Saëns,* in *Musiciens français d'aujourd'hui* series (Paris, 1908; repr. 1946, trans. 1915, repr. 1969).

Britain

Elgar

Burley, Rosa, and Frank C. Carruthers. *Edward Elgar: The Record of a Friendship* (London: Barrie & Jenkins, 1972).

McVeagh, Diana. *Edward Elgar: His Life and Music* (London: Dent, 1955; repr. Westport, CT: Hyperion Press, 1979).

Parrott, Ian. *Elgar* (London: Dart, 1971; repr. 1977).

Young, Percy. *Elgar O. M.: A Study of a Musician* (London: Collins, 1955; rev. ed., Westport, CT: Greenwood Press, 1973).

Holst

Holst, Imogen. *Gustav Holst: A Biography* (London: Oxford U. Press, 1938; 2d ed. 1969).

————. *The Music of Gustav Holst* (London: Oxford U. Press, 1951; 3d ed., rev., 1975).

————. *Holst's Music Remembered* [book written 1984] (New York: Oxford U. Press, 1986).

America

Chase, Gilbert. *America's Music,* 2d ed. (New York: McGraw-Hill, 1966).

Hamm, Charles. *Music in the New World* (New York: Norton, 1983).

Hitchcock, H. Wiley. *Music in the United States: A Historical Introduction* (Englewood Cliffs, NJ: Prentice-Hall, 1969, 1974; 3d ed., 1988).

Ives

Writings

Ives, Charles. *Essays Before a Sonata and Other Writings,* ed. H. Boatwright (New York: Norton, 1961).

For Further Reading

Burkholder, J. P. *Charles Ives: The Ideas Behind the Music* (New Haven, CT: Yale U. Press, 1985).

Cowell, Henry, and Sidney Cowell. *Charles Ives and His Music* (New York: Oxford U. Press, 1955).

Hitchcock, H. Wiley. *Ives* (London and New York: Oxford U. Press, 1955; repr. 1974).

Hitchcock, H. Wiley, and Vivian Perlis, eds. *An Ives Celebration: Papers and Panels of the Charles Ives Centennial Festival Conference* (Urbana, IL: U. of Illinois, 1977).

Kirkpatrick, John, ed. *Charles E. Ives, Memoirs* (New York: Norton, 1972).

Perlis, Vivian. *Charles Ives Remembered* (New Haven, CT: Yale U. Press, 1976).

Rossiter, Frank. *Charles Ives and His America* (New York: Liveright, 1975).

Wooldridge, David. *From the Steeples and Mountains: A Study of Charles Ives* (New York: Knopf, 1974).

MacDowell

Gilman, Lawrence. *Edward MacDowell: A Study* (New York and London: J. Lane, 1908; repr. New York: Da Capo Press, 1969).

Jazz

Gridley, Mark C. *Jazz Styles: History and Analysis,* 3d ed. (Englewood Cliffs, NJ: Prentice-Hall, 1988).

Taylor, Billy. *Jazz Piano: A Jazz History* (Dubuque, IA: Wm. C. Brown Publishers, 1983).

Tirro, Frank. *Jazz: A History* (New York: Norton, 1977).

Chapter 25. Developments between the World Wars

General

Austin, William W. *Music in the Twentieth Century from Debussy through Stravinsky* (New York: Norton, 1966).

Collaer, Paul. *A History of Modern Music* (Brussels: Elsevier, 1955), trans. Sally Abeles (Cleveland and New York: The World Publishing Co., 1961).

Simms, Bryan. *Music of the 20th Century: Style and Structure* (New York: Schirmer Books, 1986).

Whittall, Arnold. *Music Since the First World War* (London: St. Martin's Press, 1977).

England

Britten

Evans, Peter. *The Music of Benjamin Britten* (Minneapolis, MN: U. of Minnesota Press, 1979).

Herbert, David, ed. *The Operas of Benjamin Britten* (London: H. Hamilton, 1979).

Howard, P. *The Operas of Benjamin Britten* (London: Barrie & Rockliff, 1969; New York: Praeger, 1969).

Kennedy, Michael. *Britten* (London: J. M. Dent & Sons, 1981).

Palmer, Christopher, ed. *The Britten Companion* (London: Faber & Faber, 1984).

White, Eric W. *Benjamin Britten: His Life and Operas,* 2d ed. (Berkeley, CA: U. of California Press, 1981).

Young, Percy M. *Benjamin Britten* (London: E. Benn, 1966).

Vaughan Williams

Writings

Vaughan Williams, Ralph. *National Music and Other Essays* (London: Oxford U. Press, 1963; repr. 1972, 1987).

For Further Reading

Howes, Frank. *The Music of Ralph Vaughan Williams* (London and New York: Oxford U. Press, 1954; repr. Westport, CT: Greenwood Press, 1975, 1977).

Kennedy, Michael. *The Works of Ralph Vaughan Williams* (London: Oxford U. Press, 1964; rev. ed. 1982).

Ottaway, H. *Vaughan Williams* (London: Novello, 1966).

———. *Vaughan Williams Symphonies* (London: British Broadcasting Corp., 1972; repr. Seattle, WA: U. of Washington Press, 1973).

Schwartz, Elliott S. *The Symphonies of Ralph Vaughan Williams* (Amherst: U. of Massachusetts Press, 1964; repr. New York: Da Capo Press, 1982).

France

N. Boulanger

Campbell, Don G. *Master Teacher Nadia Boulanger* (Washington, DC: The Pastoral Press, 1984).

Kendall, Alan. *The Tender Tyrant: Nadia Boulanger* (London: Macdonald and Jane's, 1976; repr. Wilton, CT: Lyceum Books, 1977).

Rosensteil, Leonie. *Nadia Boulanger: A Life in Music* (New York: Norton, 1982).

Les Six

Writings

Honegger, Arthur. *Je suis compositeur* [I am a composer] (Paris: Éditions du Conquistador, 1951), trans. O. Clough (London: Faber & Faber, 1966).

Milhaud, Darius. *Notes Without Music* (Paris: Julliard, 1949), trans. Donald Evans, ed. Rollo H. Myers (London: Dobson, 1952; New York: Knopf, 1953; repr. New York: Da Capo, 1970).

For Further Reading

Bernac, Pierre. *Francis Poulenc: The Man and His Songs* (London: V. Gollancz, 1977), trans. Winifred Radford (New York: Norton, 1977).

Collaer, Paul. "Eric Satie and the Six," and "Milhaud, Honegger, Auric, Poulenc: After the Six," *A History of Modern Music* (Brussels: Elsevier, 1955), trans. Sally Abeles (Cleveland and New York: The World Publishing Co., 1961), pp. 201–73.

Daniel, Keith W. *Francis Poulenc: His Artistic Development and His Musical Style* (Ann Arbor, MI: UMI Research Press, 1982).

Palmer, Christopher. *Milhaud* (London, 1976).

Robert, F. *Louis Durey: l'ainé des Six* [Louis Durey: Oldest of The Six] (Paris: L'Editeurs français réunis, 1968).

Werner, W. Kent. *The Harmonic Style of Francis Poulenc* (Diss., Ann Arbor, MI: University Microfilms, 1966).

Germany

Orff

Liess, Andreas. *Carl Orff: Idee und Werk* (Zurich: Atlantis Verlag, 1955), trans. Adelheid and Herbert (New York: St. Martin's Press, 1966; 2d ed. 1971).

Hindemith

Writings

Hindemith, Paul. *A Composer's World: Horizons and Limitations* (Cambridge, MA: Harvard U. Press, 1952; repr. Garden City, NY: Anchor Books, Doubleday & Co., 1961).

———. *The Craft of Musical Composition* (New York: Associated Music Publishers, 1954).

For Further Reading

Neumeyer, David. *The Music of Paul Hindemith* (New Haven, CT: Yale U. Press, 1986).

Skelton, Geoffrey. *Paul Hindemith: The Man Behind the Music* (London: Gollancz, 1975; New York: Crescendo, 1975).

Hungary

Bartók

Antokoletz, Elliott. *The Music of Béla Bartók: A Study of Tonality and Progression in 20th-Century Music* (Berkeley, CA: U. of California Press, 1984).

Crow, Todd, ed. *Bartók Studies* (Detroit, MI: Information Coordinators, 1976).

Griffiths, Paul. *Bartók* (London: J. M. Dent & Sons, 1984).

Lendvai, Erno. *Béla Bartók: An Analysis of His Music* (London: Kahn & Averill, 1971).

———. *The Workshop of Bartók and Kodály* (Budapešt: Editio Musica, 1983).

Stevens, Halsey. *The Life and Music of Béla Bartók* (New York: Oxford U. Press, 1953; rev. ed., 1964; rev. 1968).

Kodály

Writings

Kodály, Zoltán. *Folk Music of Hungary,* trans. R. Tempest and C. Jolly (London: Barrie & Jenkins, 1971).

For Further Reading

Eösze, L. *Zoltán Kodály: His Life and Work* (London: Collet's, 1962; New York: Crescendo, 1962).

———. *Zoltán Kodály: His Life in Pictures* (Budapešt: Corvina Kiadó, 1971; repr. 1982).

———. *Zoltán Kodály: Chronicle of His Life* (Budapešt: Corvina Kiadó, 1977).

Lendvai, Erno. *The Workshop of Bartók and Kodály* (Budapešt: Editio Musica, 1983).

Szabó, Helga. *The Kodály Concept of Music Education* (London and New York: Boosey & Hawkes, 1969).

Stevens, Halsey. "The Choral Music of Zoltán Kodály," *The Musical Quarterly,* liv (1968), p. 147ff.

Russia

General

Abraham, Gerald. *Eight Soviet Composers* (New York: Oxford U. Press, 1943).

Brown, Malcolm H., ed. *Russian and Soviet Music: Essays for Boris Schwarz* (Ann Arbor, MI: UMI Research Press, 1984).

Krebs, Stanley D. *Soviet Composers and the Development of Soviet Music* (London and New York: Allen & Unwin, 1970).

Schwarz, Boris. *Music and Musical Life in Soviet Russia, Enlarged Edition, 1917–1981* (Bloomington, IN: Indiana U. Press, 1983).

Prokofiev

Nest'yev, Izrael V. *Prokofiev: His Musical Life* (Moscow: Gos. muz, 1957), enlarged, trans. F. Jonas (Stanford, CA: Stanford U. Press, 1960; repr. 1971).

Robinson, Harlow. *Prokofiev: A Biography* (New York: Viking, 1987).

Shostakovich

Blokker, Roy, with Robert Dearling. *The Music of Dmitri Shostakowich: The Symphonies* (London: Tantivy Press, 1979; Rutherford, NJ: Fairleigh Dickinson U. Press, 1979).

Norris, Christopher, ed. *Shostakovich: The Man and His Music* (London: Lawrence & Wishart, 1982; Boston and London: Marion Boyars, 1982).

Seroff, Victor. *Dmitri Shostakovich: The Life and Background of a Soviet Composer* (New York: Knopf, 1943; repr. 1947; repr. Freeport, NY: Books for Libraries Press, 1970).

Second Viennese School

Berg

Carner, Mosco. *Alban Berg: The Man and the Work* (London: Duckworth, 1975); 2d ed. (London: Duckworth, and New York: Holmes & Meier, 1983).

Jarman, Douglas. *The Music of Alban Berg* (Berkeley, CA: U. of California Press, 1979).

Perle, George. *The Operas of Alban Berg: Wozzeck* (Berkeley, CA: U. of California Press, 1980).

Redlich, Hans. *Alban Berg: The Man and His Music* (Vienna: Universal Edition, and New York: Abelard-Schuman, and London: Calder, 1957).

Reich, Willi. *Alban Berg* (Zurich: Atlantis Verlag, 1965), trans. Cornelius Cardew (New York: Harcourt, Brace & World, 1965; repr. New York: Da Capo Press, 1981).

Schmalfeldt, Janet. *Berg's Wozzeck: Harmonic Language and Dramatic Design* (New Haven, CT: Yale U. Press, 1983).

Schoenberg

Berg, Alban, et al. *Arnold Schönberg* (München: R. Piper & Co., 1912).

Leibowitz, René. *Schoenberg and His School: The Contemporary Stage of the Language of Music* (Paris: Éditions du Seuil, 1947), trans. Dika Newlin (New York: Philosophical Library, 1949).

Newlin, Dika. *Schoenberg Remembered: Diaries and Recollections (1938–76)* (New York: Pendragon Press, 1980).

Payne, Anthony. *Schoenberg* (London: Oxford U. Press, 1968; repr. 1974).

Reich, Willi. *Schoenberg: A Critical Biography,* trans. Leo Black (London: Longman, and New York: Praeger, 1971; repr. New York: Da Capo Press, 1981).

Rosen, Charles. *Arnold Schoenberg* (New York: Viking Press, 1975).

Smith, Joan. *Schoenberg and His Circle: A Viennese Portrait* (New York: Schirmer Books, 1986).

Wellesz, Egon. *Arnold Schönberg,* trans. W. H. Kerridge (London: J. M. Dent & Sons, 1925; repr. New York: Da Capo Press, 1969).

Webern

Kolneder, Walter. *Anton Webern: An Introduction to His Works* (Rodenkirchen: P. J. Tonger, 1961), trans. Humphrey Searle (London: Faber & Faber, 1968; repr. Westport, CT: Greenwood Press, 1982).

Moldenhauer, Hans. *Anton von Webern: Chronicle of His Life and Works* (New York: Knopf, 1979).

———. *The Death of Anton Webern: A Drama in Documents* (London: Vision, and New York: Philosophical Library, 1961; repr. New York: Da Capo Press, 1989).

Stravinsky

Writings

Stravinsky, Igor. *An Autobiography,* Eng. trans. (New York: Simon & Schuster, 1936; repr. New York: Norton, 1962; repr. Calder & Boyars, 1975).

———. *Poétique musicale,* Eng. trans. (Cambridge, MA: Harvard U. Press, 1947; 3d ed. 1966).

For Further Reading

Craft, Robert. *A Stravinsky Scrapbook 1940–1971* (New York: Thames & Hudson, 1983).

———. *Stravinsky: Chronicle of a Friendship 1948–1971* (London: Gollancz, 1972; New York: Knopf, 1973).

Druskin, Mikhail S. *Igor Stravinsky: His Life, Works, and Views* (Leningrad: "Sov. kompozitor," 1974; rev. 1979), trans. Martin Cooper (Cambridge, Eng. and New York: Cambridge U. Press, 1983).

Griffiths, Paul. *Igor Stravinsky, The Rake's Progress* (Cambridge, Eng. and New York: Cambridge U. Press, 1982).

Tansman, Alexandre. *Igor Stravinsky: The Man and His Music,* trans. Therese and Charles Bleefield (New York: G. P. Putnam's Sons, 1949).

Van den Toorn, Peter C. *The Music of Igor Stravinsky* (New Haven, CT: Yale U. Press, 1983).

Vlad, Roman. *Stravinsky,* 2d ed., trans. Frederick and Ann Fuller (London: Oxford U. Press, 1967).

White, Eric W. *Stravinsky: The Composer and His Works* (London: Faber, 1966); rev., enlarged (London: Faber, and Berkeley, CA: U. of California Press, 1979).

United States

Copland

Writings

Copland, Aaron. *Music and Imagination* (Cambridge, MA: Harvard U. Press, 1952).

———. *Copland on Music* (Garden City, NY: Doubleday, 1960).

———. *Our New Music* (New York: McGraw-Hill, 1941); rev. ed. publ. as *The New Music 1900–1960* (New York: Norton, 1968).

———. "The Role of the Composer," *Canadian Composer,* No. 63 (1971), p. 24ff.

———, with Vivian Perlis. *Copland: 1900–1942* (New York: St. Martin's Press, 1984).

For Further Reading

Berger, Arthur. *Aaron Copland* (New York: Oxford U. Press, 1953).

Butterworth, Neil. *The Music of Aaron Copland* (London: Toccata Press, 1985, and New York: Universe Books, 1986).

Oja, Carol J. "The Copland-Sessions Concerts and Their Reception in the Contemporary Press," *The Musical Quarterly,* lxv (1979), p. 212ff.

Skrowronsky, J. *Aaron Copland: A Biobibliography* (Westport, CT: Greenwood Press, 1985).

Gershwin

Goldberg, I. *George Gershwin: A Study in American Music* (New York: Simon & Schuster, 1931); rev., enlarged ed. (New York: Simon & Schuster, 1958).

Jablonski, Edward. *Gershwin* (New York: Doubleday, 1987).

Schwartz, Charles. *Gershwin: His Life and Music* (Indianapolis: Bobbs & Merrill, 1973; repr. New York: Da Capo Press, 1979).

Ruth Crawford Seeger

Gaume, Matilda. *Ruth Crawford Seeger: Her Life and Works* (Diss., Ann Arbor, MI: University Microfilms, 1973).

Sessions

Sessions, Roger. *The Musical Experience of Composer, Performer, Listener* (Princeton, NJ: Princeton U. Press, 1950).

Daniel, Oliver, et al. *Roger Sessions* (New York: Broadcast Music, Inc., 1965).

Olmstead, Andrea. *Roger Sessions and His Music* (Ann Arbor, MI: UMI Research Press, 1985).

Still

Haas, R., ed. *William Grant Still and the Fusion of Cultures in American Music* (Los Angeles: Black Sparrow Press, 1972; repr. 1975).

Southern, Eileen. *The Music of Black Americans: A History* (New York: Norton, 1971; 2d ed., 1983), p. 422ff.

Thomson

Writings

Thomson, Virgil. *American Music Since 1910* (London: Weidenfeld & Nicolson, 1967).

———. *The Art of Judging Music* (New York: Knopf, 1948).

———. *A Virgil Thomson Reader* (Boston: Houghton-Mifflin, 1981; repr. New York: E. P. Dutton, 1984).

———. *Virgil Thomson* (New York: Knopf, 1966; repr. 1977).

For Further Reading

Hoover, Kathleen, and John Cage. *Virgil Thomson: His Life and Music* (New York: T. Yoseloff, 1959).

Meckna, Michael. *Virgil Thomson: A Biobibliography* (New York: Greenwood Press, 1986).

Jazz

Gridley, Mark C. *Jazz Styles: History and Analysis,* 3d ed. (Englewood Cliffs, NJ: Prentice-Hall, 1988).

Tirro, Frank. *Jazz: A History* (New York: Norton, 1977).

Latin and South America

Chávez

Writings

Chávez, Carlos. *Toward a New Music: Music and Electricity,* trans. H. Weinstock (New York: Norton, 1937; repr. New York: Da Capo Press, 1975).

———. *Musical Thought* (Cambridge, MA: Harvard U. Press, 1961).

———. "The Music of Mexico," (1933), in *American Composers on American Music,* ed. Henry Cowell, 2d ed. (New York: F. Ungar, 1962).

For Further Reading

Copland, Aaron. "Composer from Mexico," in *The New Music: 1900–1960* (New York: Norton, 1968).

Cowell, Henry. "Chávez," in *The Book of Modern Composers,* ed. David Ewen, 2d ed. (New York: Knopf, 1942); 3d ed., rev., enlarged, publ. as *The New Book of Modern Composers* (New York: Knopf, 1967).

Villa-Lobos

Mariz, Vasco. *Heitor Villa-Lobos* (Rio de Janiero: Serviço de Publicações, 1949); Eng. trans. (Gainesville: U. of Florida Press, 1963; repr. 1970).

Romero, M. "Heitor Villa-Lobos," *Inter-American Music Bulletin,* 15 (1960), p. 4ff.

Sprague-Smith, C. "H. Villa-Lobos (1889–1959)," *Inter-American Music Bulletin,* 15 (1960), p. 1ff.

Wright, S. "Villa-Lobos: The Formation of His Style," *Soundings,* ix (1979–80), p. 55ff.

Chapter 26. Music Since 1945

General

Brindle, Reginald S. *The New Music: The Avant-Garde Since 1945* (London: Oxford U. Press, 1975; repr. 1987).

Cope, David. *New Directions in Music,* 4th ed. (Dubuque, IA: Wm. C. Brown Publishers, 1984).

Griffiths, Paul. *Modern Music: The avant garde since 1945* (New York: George Braziller, 1981).

———. *Modern Music: A Concise History from Debussy to Boulez* (New York: Thames & Hudson, 1978).

———. *The Thames and Hudson Encyclopaedia of 20th-Century Music* (New York: Thames & Hudson, 1986).

Lang, Paul Henry, ed. *Problems of Modern Music,* a reprint of *The Musical Quarterly* April 1960 issue (New York: Norton, 1962).

Martin, William R., and Julius Drossin. *Music of the Twentieth Century* (Englewood Cliffs, NJ: Prentice-Hall, 1980).

Rockwell, John. *All American Music: Composition in the Late Twentieth Century* (New York: Knopf, 1983).

Ruhe, Harry, ed. *Fluxus, the Most Radical and Experimental Art Movement of the Sixties* (Amsterdam: "A," 1979).

Salzman, Eric. *Twentieth-Century Music: An Introduction,* 3d ed. (Englewood Cliffs, NJ: Prentice-Hall, 1988).

Simms, Bryan R. *Music of the Twentieth Century: Style and Structure* (New York: Schirmer Books, 1986).

Vinton, John, ed. *Dictionary of Contemporary Music* (New York: Dutton, 1974).

Electronic Music

Ernst, David. *The Evolution of Electronic Music* (New York: Schirmer Books, 1977).

Griffiths, Paul. *A Guide to Electronic Music* (London and New York: Thames & Hudson, 1979).

Minimalism

Mertens, Wim. *American Minimal Music: La Monte Young, Terry Riley, Steve Reich, Philip Glass,* trans. J. Hautekiet (London and New York: Kahn & Averill, 1983).

Nyman, Michael. *Experimental Music: Cage and Beyond* (New York: Schirmer Books, 1974).

Reich, Steve. *Writings about Music* (Halifax, Nova Scotia: Press of Nova Scotia Art and Design, 1974).

Schwarz, K. Robert. "Steve Reich: Music as a Gradual Process," *Perspectives of New Music,* Fall/Winter 1980 and Spring/Summer 1981, pp. 373–92; Fall/Winter 1981 and Spring/Summer 1982, pp. 225–86.

Boulez

Writings

Boulez, Pierre. *Boulez on Music Today,* trans. Susan Bradshaw and Richard R. Bennett (Cambridge, MA: Harvard U. Press, 1971).

———. *Notes of an Apprenticeship,* compiled by Paula Thévenin, trans. Herbert Weinstock (New York: Knopf, 1968).

For Further Reading

Glock, William, ed. *Pierre Boulez: A Symposium* (London: Eulenberg, 1986).

Griffiths, Paul. *Boulez* (Oxford and New York: Oxford U. Press, 1978).

Peyser, Joan. *Boulez: Composer, Conductor, Enigma* (New York: Schirmer Books, 1976).

Cage

Writings

Cage, John. *Notations* (West Glover, VT: Something Else Press, 1969).

———. *Silence* (Middletown, CT: Wesleyan U. Press, 1961).

———. *A Year from Monday: New Lectures and Writings* (Middletown, CT: Wesleyan U. Press, 1967).

For Further Reading

Gena, Peter, and Jonathan Brent, eds. *A John Cage Reader: In Celebration of his 70th Birthday* (New York: Peters, 1983).

Griffiths, Paul. *Cage* (London: Oxford U. Press, 1981).

Kostelanetz, Richard, ed. *John Cage* (New York: Praeger, 1970).

Ligeti

Griffiths, Paul. *György Ligeti* (London: Robson Books, 1983).

Messiaen

Writings

Messiaen, Olivier. *The Technique of My Musical Language,* 2 vols., trans. John Satterfield (Paris: Leduc, 1944; repr. 1966).

For Further Reading

Bell, Carla Huston. *Olivier Messiaen* (Boston: Twayne, 1984).

Griffiths, Paul. *Olivier Messiaen and the Music of Time* (Ithaca, NY: Cornell U. Press, 1985).

Johnson, Robert Sherlaw. *Messiaen* (Berkeley, CA: U. of California Press, 1975; repr. 1980).

Kaufmann, Walter. *The Rāgas of North India* (Bloomington, IN: Indiana U. Press, 1968).

Nichols, R. *Messiaen* (Oxford: Oxford U. Press, 1985).

Rössler, Almut. *Contributions to the Spiritual World of Olivier Messiaen,* "with original texts by the composer" (Duisberg, W. Ger.: Gilles & Francke Verlag, 1986).

Wade, Bonnie C. *Music in India: The Classical Traditions* (Englewood Cliffs, NJ: Prentice-Hall, 1979).

Stockhausen

Harvey, Jonathan. *The Music of Stockhausen* (Berkeley, CA: U. of California Press, 1975).

Maconie, Robin. *The Works of Karlheinz Stockhausen* (London and New York: Oxford U. Press, 1976).

Wörner, Karl H. *Stockhausen: Life and Work,* trans. and ed. Bill Hopkins (Berkeley, CA: U. of California Press, 1973).

Varèse

Bernard, Jonathan. *The Music of Edgard Varèse* (New Haven, CT: Yale U. Press, 1987).

Van Solkema, Sherman, ed. *The New Worlds of Edgard Varèse* (Brooklyn, NY: Institute for Studies in American Music, 1979).

Varèse, Louise. *Varèse: A Looking-Glass Diary* (New York: Norton, 1972).

Index

Ave nobilissima creatura, 202
Ave Redemptoris mater-Ave Regina coelorum, 200
Ave Regina (Frye), 176
Ave Regina celorm (Binchot), 170
Ave vera virginitas, 201
Ave verum corpus, 512
Avidius, 195–96
Avignon Grand Chapelle, 124, colorplate 7
A vous, douce debonaire, 130
Ayre, **234**

b

Baba Yaga, 729
Babbage, Charles, 623
Babbitt, Milton, 861, 877–79
Bacchanale, 879
Bach, Anna Magdalena, 412
Bach, Carl Philipp Emanuel, 359, 398, 401, 403, 434, 435, 438, 439, 442, 443–48, 449, 454, 471, 497, 545, 563, 572, 580
  keyboard works, 446–47
  orchestral and chamber music, 447
  portrait, *444*
  vocal music, 448
Bach, Johann Ambrosius, 400
Bach, Johann Bernhard, 471
Bach, Johann Christian, 404, 432, 443, 463–64, 478, 479, *480*, 485, 517
  concertos, 479, 480
  galante-style operas, 463–64
Bach, Johann Christoph, 353, 354, 400, 404, 443
Bach, Johann Ernst, 471
Bach, Johann Ludwig, 402
Bach, Johann Michael, 400
Bach, Johann Sebastian, 188, 203, 244, 287, 291, 335, 339, 353, 354, 355, 358, 359, 360, 373, 378, 384, 385, 389, 390, 393, 399–418, 422, 442, 472, 518, 538, 553, 575, 582, 636, 642, 644, 716, 752, *825*, 829, 860, 868, 888
  chamber music, 416–18
  influences on, 404
  keyboard music, 411–16
  life, 399–404
  portrait, *400*
  travels, *418*
  vocal music, 405–10
Bach, Johann Sebastian (artist), 444, 445
Bach, Wilhelm Friedemann, 401, 404, 406, 413, 443
Bachinas Brasileiras, 851
Bagatelles (Bartók), 803
Bagatelles (Beethoven), 548
Bagpipe (instrument), 69
Baïf, Jean-Antoine de, 231
Baiser de fée, Le, 842
Baisez moy, 197
Baker, Theodore, 787
Balada dance song, 110–11
Balakirev, Alexander, 740
Balakirev, Mily, 729, *730*, 731
Balázs, Béla, 803
Balducci, Francesco, 332
Balfe, Michael, 676
Ballad (Foote), 788
Ballade equivocée, 158

Ballade form, 111, 112–13
  Guillaume de Machaut, 134–35
  late medieval Italian, 145
Ballade in Form von Variationen . . . (Grieg), 751
Ballades (Brahms), 707
Ballad opera, **468**–69, 811
Ballarino, Il, 276
Ballet, 322, 323, 734. *See also* Dance music
  Copland, A., 845, 846
  Monteverdi, C., 310
  Strauss, R., 765
  Stravinsky, I., 838–41
  Tchaikovsky, P., 740, 741
Ballet d'action, 486
Ballet de Casandre, 322
Ballet de cour (dance), 276, 322, 324, 341
Ballet de la nuit, 322
Balletti, gighe, correnti, alemande, e sarabande (D. Gabrielli), 373
Balletti a cinque voci . . . (Gastoldi), 225
Balletto, Italian Renaissance, 225
Ballets to Five Voyces (Morley), 225
Ballo delle ingrate, Il, 303, 304, 306, 310
Ballo in maschera, Un, 694, 696, 697
Bamberg Codex, 95
Bambini, Eustache, 467
Banchetto musicale, 349, 385
Banchieri, Adriano, 296
Banister, John, 432
Banjo, Le, 679
Banquet Céleste, Le, 861
Banshee, The, 794
Barbapiccola, Nicolo, 319
Barbe-bleu, 662
Barber, Samuel, 755
Barberini, Cardinal Antonio, 314
Barberini family, 313, 316
Barbier de Seville, Le (Beaumarchais), 615
Barbiere di Siviglia, Il (Rossini), 615, *616*, 620
Barbiere di Siviglia ovvero La precauzione inutile, Il (Paisiello), 467
Barcarolle, 632, 642
Bardi, Giovanni de', 295, 296, 297
Bar form, 117, **118**
Baronnet, Jean, 869
Baroque era, 283–91, 387
  affections, 285–86
  basso continuo texture, 286–87
  idiomatic instrumental composition, 285
  key tonality, 288
  notation, 288–89
  printed music, 289–91
  rhythm, 288
  styles and practices, 283–85
  violin making, 368
Baroque era composers, 387–428
  Bach, J. S., 399–418
  Handel, G., 418–27
  Rameau, J.-P., 395–99
  Telemann, G., 390–95
  Vivaldi, A., 387–90
Baroque instrumental music, 345–86
  Bach, J. S., 411–18
  clavier keyboard instruments, 358–66
  ensemble music, 366–86
  French lute music, 351–52
  Handel, G., 426–27
  organ music, 352–59
  Rameau, J.-P., 398

Telemann, G., 394
  types of, 345–51
  Vivaldi, A., 389–90
Baroque vocal music, 293–343
  Bach, J. S., 405–10
  cantata, 340–42
  Handel, G., 424–26
  monody, 293–95
  opera, 295–34 (*see also* Opera)
  oratorio, 331–34
  passion, 334–39
  Rameau, J.-P., 397
  Teleman, G., 394
Barrère, Georges, 876
Bartered Bride, The, 746
Bartók, Béla, 802–6, 845, 855
Bartolino da Padova, 144
Bartoš, František, 744, 749
Barzelletta, 215
Basile, Adriana, 303
Basile, Margherita, 311
Basil of Caesarea, Saint, 23, 24
Bass (voice), 172
Basse danse (dance), 168, 275, 277, 348, colorplate 12
Basso continuo, 286–87
Basso ostinato, 329
Basso seguente, 286, 287
Bastien und Bastienne, 507, 513
Bataille de Marignan, La, 229
Battle Symphony (Beethoven), 544
Baudelaire, Pierre, 773
Bay Song Book, 177
Beach, Amy M. Cheney (Mrs. H. H. A.), 788
Beata es, Maria, 310
Béatitudes, Les, 626
Béatrice et Benedict, 668
Beatritz, Countess of Dia, 115
Beatrix Cenci, 851
Beatus vir, 310
Beaujoyleux, Baltasar de, 276, 322
Beaulieu, Lambert de, 276
Beaumarchais, P. A., 467, 514, 615
Beccaria, Cesare, 432
Becker, Cornelius, 336
Bedford, Duke of, England, 141
Beecham, Thomas, 784
Beethoven, Johann van, 539
Beethoven, Kaspar Anton Karl, 539, 543
Beethoven, Ludwig van, 468, 475, 477, 494, 521, 528, *537*, 538, 539–75, 580, 584, 627, 636, 665, 703, 713, 718, 725, 851
  life, 539–43
  music, 544–45
    chamber music, 554–62
    piano sonatas, 548–53
    piano variations, 553
    for solo instruments and orchestra, 571–72
    style periods, 545–48
    symphonies, 562–71
    vocal works with orchestra, 572–75
  personal characteristics, 543–44
  portrait, *542*
Beethoven, Nikolaus Johann, 539
Beggar's Opera, The, 421, 468, 469
Beglückte Florindo, Der, 419
Beiden Grenadiere, Die, 650, 653
Beiden Pâdagogen, Die, 642

Romantic (see Romantic music)
    term, 3
    theory (see Theory of music)
    treatise (see Treatise(s), musical)
    20th-century (see Twentieth-century music,
        early years of; Twentieth-century
        music after 1945; Twentieth-century
        music between the World Wars)
    vocal (see Vocal music)
*Musica de meser Bernardo Pisano sopra la
    canzone del Petrarcha,* 218
Musica enchiriadis, 71
Musica ficta, 104
    chromatic alterations and, 104, 146–48, 205
    late medieval, 146–48
    Renaissance, 182, 185, 186
Musica getutscht, 177, *269*
Musical Antiquarian Society, 781
Musical drama, Puccini's view of, **768**
Musicalische Exequien, 338
Musicalische Quack-Salber, Der, 361
Musicalisches Gesang-Buch, 403
*Musicalische Vorstellung einiger Biblischer
    Historien,* 360
Musical Scene, The, 850
Music and Imagination, 846
Musica nova, 208, 274, 283
Musica reservata, 227, colorplate 16
Musica secreta, 227, colorplate 16
Musica sopra Il pastor fido . . . libro secondo,
    220
Musica transalpina, 232, 255
Music for a Summer Evening, 884
Music for Percussion and Keyboards (Reich),
    890
Music for Piano (Cage), 880
Music for Strings, Percussion, and Celesta
    (Bartók), 804, 805, 806, *807*
Music for the Royal Fireworks, 423, 426
Music for the Theatre (Copland), 846
Music in Fifths (Glass), 889
Music in Similar Motion (Glass), *889*
Music of Changes (Cage), 880
Music of the spheres, 13
Musicology, **705**
Musico prattico, 370
Music with Changing Parts (Glass), 889
Musikalisches Opfer, 373, *403*, 415
Musikalisches Vierley, 446
Musikalisches Wochenblatt, 471
Musik für Kinder, 808
Musique concrète, 868–71, 872, 875
Musique d'ameublement, 780
Musique de table partagée en Trio Production,
    393
Musique en Russie, 732
Musique mesurée, 231–32
Musorgsky, Modest, 729, *730,* 733–36, 737, 766,
    774, 779, 864
Musque de Biscaye, Un, 197
Mussolini, Benito, 799
Mustel, Auguste, 740
Mutation, **65**
Myaskovsky, Nikolay, 815
My days have been so wondrous free, 530, 531
My Lady Carey's Dompe, 276
My Old Kentucky Home, 678
Myrick, Julian, 790
Mystery Sonatas (Biber), *384*

n

Nabucodonosor, 693
Nacht (Schoenberg), 822
Nachtgesang, 528
Nachtstücke, 650
Nähe des Geliebten, 538
Nänie, 716
Nanino, Giovanni Maria, *290*
Naples, Kingdom of, 154
    opera in, 318–21
Napoleon, Louis, France, 623, 660
Napoleon Buonaparte, 564, 577
N'aray je jamais mieulx que j'ay, 175
Nardini, Pietro, 454, 455
Narváez, Luys de, 276
National Eisteddfod, Wales, 785
Nationalism in Europe
    late 19th/early 20th-century, 725–26
    mid-19th-century, 623–25
    in Russia, 727–39
*Nations: sonades et suites de simphonies en trio,
    Les,* 382
Nativitas gloriosae virginis, 134
Nativité du Seigneur, La, 862
Naufrageurs, Les, 784
Navarro, Juan, 209
Nazi party, 799
Neale, John M., 28, 245
Neefe, Christian G., 446, 470, 539
Neo-Classicism, 831–37
Neo-Romanticism, 891
Neri, Filippo, 213, 259, 331
Nero (Handel), 329, 419
Nero, Emperor, 19
Nesciens mater virgo virum, 204
Nessun visse giamai, 264
Netherlands
    Reformation in, 245–46
    Renaissance composers (see Franco-
        Netherlands composers, Renaissance)
Neue Arien, 342
Neue Bahnen, 649, 705
Neue Clavier-Übung, 360
Neue Kraft fühlend, 557
Neue Leipsiger Zeitschrift für Musik, 647
Neue Liebeslieder, 714
Neues vom Tage, 835
Neue teutsche Gesäng nach Art . . . , 236
Neumatic Biblical text settings, **34,** *35*
Neumeister, Erdmann, 392
Neumes, **32**–33, 627
    accent, 63, 74
    heighted, 72
    ligatures, 87, *88*
    point, 63, 74, *75*
    staffless, 106
Neumes rhythmiques, 864
*Newe auserlesene Paduanen, Galliarden,
    Canzonen . . . ,* 349
*Newe deudsche geistliche Gesenge CXXIII . . . .
    244–45*
New England Idyls, 787
New-England Psalm-Singer, The, 529, *530*
Newe Padouan, Intrada, Däntz . . . , 349
Newman, Cardinal John, 783
New Music: 1900–1968, The, 846
New Music Quarterly, 791
New School for Social Research, 846

Newton, Isaac, 431
Niagara Symphony, 679
Niccolò da Perugia, 144
Nicene Creed, 23, 49
Nicholas I, Russia, 728, 729
Nicholas II, Pope, 60
Nicholas V, Pope, 156, 370
Nicolai, Giovanni Francesco, 454
Nicolai, Otto, 595
Nicolai, Philipp, 406
Niedhardt von Reuenthal, 117, 118
Nielsen, Carl, 752–53
Nietzsche, Friedrich Wilhelm, 742, 763, 799
Night Has a Thousand Eyes, The, 788
Nightmare, The, 435
Nijevelt, Willem van Zuylen van, 205
Nijinsky, Vaclav, 839
Nin, Anaïs, 877
Nine enchanted stags, The, 805
Nineteenth-century music, 623–82
    in Austria and Germanic lands, 628–56,
        755–68
    classical era in early, 475–77 (see also
        Classical music)
    in Czechoslovakia, 744–50
    in Denmark, 656–57
    in England, 675–76, 781–85
    in France, 657–70, 768–81
    Impressionism, 772–79
    instrumental music, 627–28
    in Italy, 670–75
    master composers of mid-, 683–724
    nationalism, 725–26
    in North America, 676–80, 785–96
    romanticism (see Romantic music)
    in Russia, 727–44
    summary, 680–82, 796–98
    transition from classical to romantic, 535–39
    verismo (realism) in late, 766–68
    vocal music, 625–27
    in Wales, Ireland and Scotland, 785
Nisi Dominus, 419
Nobilissima visione, 837
Noces, Les (Stravinsky), 808, 831, 840
Nocturnal (Varèse), 877
Nocturne, 437, 634
Nocturne (L. Boulanger), 779
Nocturne (Williams), 811
Nocturne in A flat major (Chopin), 634
Nocturne in A major (Field), 634
Nocturne in E flat (Chopin), 631, 634
Nocturnes (Debussy), 774, 838
Noe, 211
Non al suo amante, 144
Nonet Op. 38, 670
Non moriar, sed vivam, 241
Nonne, Die, 645
Nono, Luigi, 861, 872, 875
Non schivar, non parar, 305
Nordlandske bondestand, Den, 751
Nordraak, Richard, 751
Norges fjelde, 751
Norma, 506, 674–75
Norway, 751–53
Notation. See also Tablature
    agréments, 352
    ancient Greek instrumental, 7
    baroque, 288–89
    bass clef sign, 183

Reflets dans l'eau, 777
Reformation, 151, 239–51. See also Counter-
    Reformation
  in England, 246–51
  in France, Switzerland, and Holland, 245–46
  in Germanic countries
        chorale music, 242–44
        Luther, M., 240–42
        Rhau, G., 244–45
        Walter, J., 244
  in Scandinavia, 245
Reformation Symphony (Mendelssohn), 638, 639
Reform operas, 487–90
Refrain, **142**
Regal, **272**
Regensburg Edition, 627
Reger, Max, 766
Reggel, 885
Regina caeli laetare, 41
Regle pour l'accompagnement, 364
Regnat, 98
Regole per arrivare a saper ben suonar il
    Violino, 454
Rehearsal, The, 483
Reich, Steve, 859, 886, 889–90
Reichardt, J. F., 470, 471, 611
Reichardt, Juliane Benda, 611
Reichardt, Luise, 611
Reims Cathedral, France, 131
Re in ascolto, Un, 883
Reinhardt, Siegfried, 483
Reinken, Johann Adam, 347, 400
Reis glorios, 110
Rejoice unto the Lord, 250
Relâche, 780
Relata I, 878
Remède de Fortune, 131
Reményi, Eduard, 704
Reminiscence, **585**
Renaissance, 179–82. See also Counter-
    Reformation; Reformation
  composers (see Franco-Netherlands
        composers, Renaissance)
  music printing, 177, 210–11, 276
Renaissance instrumental music, 267–82
  dance music, 275–76
  improvisory works, 277–79
  instrument collections, 273
  instruments, 267–73
  variations, 276–77
  Venetian school, 279–82
  from vocal models, 273–75
Renaissance music, transition from Middle Ages
        to, 151–78
  in Britain, 175–76
  in Burgundy, 164–73
  du Fay, G., 155–64
  in Germany, 176–77
  music printing, 177
  political history, 151–55
  in Spain, 175
Renaissance regional music, 213–38
  in England, 232–35
  in France, 228–32
  in Germanic lands, 235–37
  in Italy, 213–28
  in Spain, 237–38
Rencontre imprévue, La, 487
Reniement de St-Pierre, Le, 333
Renoir, Pierre Auguste, 725, 772

Renzi, Anna, 312
Rè pastore, Il, 513
Republic, The, 12, 13, 285
Requiem (Mozart), 495, 512, 513
Requiem aeternam, 46
Requiem Canticles (Stravinsky), 843
Requiem for Fanny (Mendelssohn), 637
Requiem für Mignon (Schumann), 649, 653
Requiem in C minor (Cherubini), 584
Requiem in D minor (Cherubini), 584
Requiem mass, 44, 46, 51, 52
Requiem Mass (Bomtempo), 618, 619
Requiem Mass (Bruckner), 718
Requiem Mass (Donizetti), 673
Requiem Mass (Fauré), 771
Requiem Mass (Liszt), 704
Requiem Mass (Mozart), 495, 512, 513
Requiem Mass (Nunes García), 620
Requiem Mass (Ockeghem), 188
Requiem Mass (Schumann), 649
Requiem Mass (Verdi), 626
Rerum conditor respice, 170
Rescue opera, **468**
Resinarius, Balthasar, 245
Reson and Sensuallyte, 148
Respighi, Ottorino, 738, 779
Responsorial passion, **334**
Responsorial psalmody, **29,** 35
Resta di darmi noia, 224
Resurrection Symphony (Beethoven), 553
Resurrexi, 46
Resveillez vous, 206
Retour à la vie, Le, 664
Retrograde composition, **136**
Return of the Native, The, 782
Revecy venir du printans, 232
Rève d'amour, 660
Réveil des oiseaux, 866
Rêverie, 742
Reverie et caprice (Berlioz), 665
Revue de Paris, 657
Rex seculorum, 140
Rhapsody (Brahms), 708
Rhapsody in Blue, 848
Rhapsody No. 1 (Bartók), 803, 804
Rhapsody No. 2 (Bartók), 804
Rhau, Georg, 244–45
Rheingold, Das, 685, 689
Rhetorique des dieux, La, 351, 352
Rhyme, musical, 135
Rhythm. See also Cadence(s)
  ancient Greece, 13–14
  baroque, 288
  Gregorian chant, 31–32
  isorhythm, **128–29**
  Landini cadence, 135
  Messiaen, O., 862–63
  modes in Parisian school of polyphony, 87–88
  rhythmic palindrome, **132**
  syncopation, 135, 138
  Vitry, P. de, codification of, 125–26
Ricercar, 206, 207, 273, 274, 345
Ricercare del 12 tono, 274
Ricercare dopo il Credo, 353
Richard III (Smetana), 704, 745
Richard Coeur-de-Lion, 113, 114, 119
Richard Coeur-de-lion (Grétry), 468
Richardson, Samuel, 466
Richelieu, Armand Jean de, 322
Richter, Franz X., 481, 482

Richter, Jean Paul, 650
Riders to the Sea, 811
Riehe, Die, 871, 875
Rienzi, der Letzte der Tribunen, 685, 687
Ries, Franz, 540
Righini, 540
Rigoletto (Verdi), 693, 694, 696, 697
Rig Veda, 782
Riley, Terry, 886, 889
Rimsky-Korsakov, Andrey, 737
Rimsky-Korsakov, Nikolai, 729, 730, 733,
        736–39, 742, 775, 777, 837, 843
Rinaldo (Handel), 327, 420, 716
Ring des Nibelungen, Der (Wagner), 588, 685,
        686, 689, 690, 691, 817, 875
Rinuccini, Ottavio, 296, 297, 298, 299–301, 303,
        317, 328, 464
Ripresa, 117
Rip van Winkle, 679
Rissolty, Rossolty (Crawford), 850
Ritornello, 302, 311, 313, 314, 315, 316
Ritorno di Tobia, Il, 496
Ritorno d'Ulisse in patria, Il, 307, 312, 314
Ritterballett, 540
Ritter Toggenburg, 528
Rituel, 870, 871
River, The, 850
Rivueltas, Silvestre, 852
Robert le diable, 587, 658, 659, 732
Robertsbridge Codex, 120
Rococo style, 387
Rode, Pierre, 561
Rodelinda, 421, 424
Rodeo, 846
Rodil, Antonio, 456
Rodin, Auguste, 725
Roerich, Nicholai, 839
Roger, Estienne, 291, 375, 389
Roger-Ducasse, J.-J., 771
Roh, Jan, 239
Roi David, Le, 832
Roi Lear, Le, 665
Roi s'amuse, Le, 698
Roland (Lully), 323, 325, 489
Rolling Stones, 847
Roma gaudens iubila, 94
Romana, Caterina, 228
Roman Catholic Church. See also Counter-
        Reformation; Reformation
  chant (see Ecclesiastical chant)
  early (see Christian era, music of early)
  liturgy, 39–55 (see also Liturgy)
        books, 39–40
        liturgical year, 39
        mass, 41–51 (see also Mass)
        offices, 40–41
        requiem mass, 51
  services, 39, 40
  tropes, 52–53
Romance (song)
  in France, 470, 663
  in Spain, 237
Romance (Balakirev), 731
Romance in D flat major (Williams), 812
Romances (Beethoven), 571
Romances sans paroles (Verlaine), 773
Roman de Fauvel, Le, 124, 127–30
Roman du Mont-Saint-Michel, 109

Schaeffer, Pierre, 859, 868, 876
Schauspieldirektor, Der, 510
Schedula diversarum artium, 66
Scheherazade, 738
Scheibe, Johann A., 486, 488
Scheidler, Dorette, 588
Scheidt, Samuel, 347, 353, 354, 384
Schein, Johann Hermann, 349, 385
Schemelli, G. C., 403
Schenk, Johann, 540
Scherzi, Gli (Haydn), 499
Scherzi da violino solo (Walther), 384
Scherzi musicali (Monteverdi), 307
Scherzo (Bartók), 803
Scherzo (Schumann), 648
Scherzo for TODAY (Williams), 889–90
Scherzo in C minor (Brahms), 708
Scherzo in E flat minor (Brahms), 707
Schiavo di sua moglie, Il, 318
Schicksalslied, 716
Schiebe, Johann, 359
Schiffende, Die, 645
Schikaneder, Emanuel, 572
Schiller, Johann, 538, 544, 570, 696, 739, 745
Schindler, Alma, 758, 759
Schlaflos! Frage und Antwort, 702
Schlick, Arnolt, 272, 273, 275
Schloss Liebeneck, 645
Schmeider, Wolfgang, 402
Schmelker, J. A., 108
Schmetzl, Walter, 237
Schmitt, Florent, 771, 779
Schnitger, Arp, 358
Schnitger, Caspar, 358
Schnitger, Johann Georg, 358
Schober, Franz von, 598
Schobert, Johann, 447, 507
Schöne Müllerin, Die (Schöne), 600
Schoenberg, Arnold, 763, 778, 801, 818, 819, 820–23, 827, 843, 845, 855, 860, 875, 877, 879, 890
Schola Cantorum, Paris, 768, 769
Scholica enchiriadis, 71, 72
Scholze, Johann S., 471
Schöne Melusine, Die (Schöpfungs), 638
School for the Left Hand, 778
School of Athens (Raphael), 194, colorplate 15
School of Extemporaneous Performance, 572
Schöpfung, Die (Haydn), 494, 496, 497
Schöpfungs-Messe (Haydn), 496
Schubart, J. M., 400
Schubert, Ferdinand, 597, 648
Schubert, Franz Peter, 477, 528, 596–611, 636, 653, 702
  life and work, 596–602
  music, 602–4
    chamber music, 608–10
    contributions, 610–11
    orchestral music, 610
    piano works, 606–8
    vocal music, 604–6
  portrait, *597*
Schubert Abend bei Jovon Spaun, 601
Schübler Chorales, 415
Schultz, Johann A. P., 471
Schumann, August, 646
Schumann, Clara Wieck, 628, 647–48, 650, 654–56, 704, 706, 745
  music, 655–56
  portrait, *654*

Schumann, Robert, 590, 626, 629, 646–54, 704, 708, 745, 756, 771
  critical writings, 647, 654
  life and work, 646–49
  music
    chamber music, 651
    contributions and style, 649–50
    opera, 648–49
    piano music, 650–51
    symphonies, 651–52
    vocal music, 652–53
  portrait, *647*
Schuppanzigh, Ignaz, 555
Schütz, Heinrich, 316, 317, 328, 335–39
Schütz-Werke-Verzeichnis, 336
Schwanengesang, 602
Schwind, Moritz von, *601*
Scielta della Suonate, 373
Scop, 118
Scordatura, 369, 370, 384, 416, 760
Scotland, 785
Scott, Sir Robert, 812
Scott, Sir Walter, 579, 594
Scottish Concerto (Mackenzie), 785
Scottish Rhapsody No. 1 (Mackenzie), 785
Scottish symphony (Mendelssohn), 638, 640
Scott of the Antarctic (film), 812
Scriabin, Alexander, 739, 741–44
Scribe, Eugène, 586, 587, 658, 696
Scuola degli Amanti, La, 515
Scythian Suite, 815
Sea-Change (Ivey), 882
Sea Drift (Delius), 784
Sea Pieces (MacDowell), 787
Seasons, The (Haydn), 394, 496–97
Seasons, The (Vivaldi), 389, 390
Sea Symphony, A (Williams), 808, 851
Se cerca, se dice, 460, *461*
Sechs Gedichte nach Heinrich Heine, 787
Sechs Lieder für eine Frauenstimme, 755
Sechs Orchesterlieder, 821
Sechter, Simon, 718
Seconda prattica, 284–85, 304, 306–8
Secondary sources, **8**
Second Booke of Songs or Ayres . . . (Dowland), *234*
Seconde année: Italie, 701
Second livre de guiterre . . . (Le Roy), 231
Second livre de sonates (Leclair), 383
Second livre de symphonies . . . en trio (Gillemain), 452–53
Second Mephisto Waltz (Liszt), 702
Secondo libro delle laudi, Il (Animuccia), 331
Secondo libro di toccata (Frescobaldi), 351, 356
Second Overture on Russian Themes (Balakirev), 731
Second Piano Sonata: "Concord, Mass. 1840–60" (Ives), 790
Second Viennese School, 818–30
Sederunt, 86, *91, 92,* 94
Seductor arrepentido, El, 617
Seeger, Charles, 849
Seeger, Ruth Crawford, 849–50
Sehnsucht, 645
Sei Concerti Grossi (Handel), 426
Sei concerti per il cembalo o piano e forte (J. C. Bach), 443, 479
Sei Solo à violino senza Basso accompagnato, 401

Seixas, Carlos de, 365
Séjour de l'éternelle paix, 397
Se la face ay pale, 158, 162–63
Selle, Thomas, 335
Selva sin amor, La, 329
Semele, 327
Seminarist, 734
Semiramide, 485, 616
Sender, Ramon, 881
Senfl, Ludwig, 172, 202, 236, 237, 245, 264
Senleches, Jacob, 138
Sept Haïkaï, 866
Septième livre de danceries, 348, *349*
Septiesme livre des chansons, 196
Sequences, 53–54
Sequenza, 883
Serenade. *See* Divertimento
Serenade (Beethoven), 545, 555
Serenade (Schoenberg), 822
Serenade (Stenhammar), 751
Serenade (Stravinsky), 841
Serenade (Tchaikovsky), 740
Serenade No. 1 in D major Op. 11 (Brahms), 705, 710
Serenade No. 2 in A major (Brahms), 705, 710
Sergius I, Pope, 50
Serialism, **819**–20, 860–61. *See also* Babbitt, Milton; Boulez, Pierre; Messiaen, Olivier; Schoenberg, Arnold
  all-combinatorial, 878
  combinatoriality, 877
  total, 864
Series (Tone Row), **819**
Serly, Tibor, 806
Sermisy, Claudin de, 229, *230*
Serpent (instrument), 711
Serse, 422, 425
Serva padrona, La (Pergolesi), 393, 460, 461, 463, 465, 467
Service, Anglican, **247**
Service sacrê (Milhaud), 834
Services of the Church, 39, 40, 42. *See also* Mass
Sessions, Roger, 846, 850
Settimo libro de madrigali, Il, 222
Seven Last Words, The, 500
Seven Songs, 531
Seven Sonnets of Michelangelo, 813
Séverac, Déodat de, 779
Se vous n'estes, 136
Seys libros del delphin, Los, 276
Sfogava con le stelle, 294
Sforza, Ascanio, 331
Sforza family, 153, 195, 270
S. Geminiano vescovo e protettore di Modena, 333
Shaker Loops, 890
Shakespeare, William, 275, 663, 668, 694, 696, 745, 766, 811, 812, 882
Shanewis or The Robin Woman, 788
Shawm (instrument), 69, 270
Shelley, Percy Bysshe, 579
Shema Yisroel, 823
Sheppard, John, 248
Shining Shore, The, 790
Shirley, James, 326
Shofar (instrument), 69, *70*
Short Service, Anglican, **247**
Short Symphony (Copland), *846*
Shostakovich, Dmitry, 814, 815, 816–18

Symphony in C (Stravinsky), 842
Symphony in C major (Balakirev), 731
Symphony in C major (Wagner), 686
Symphony in D for 'Cello and Orchestra (Britten), 813
Symphony in D minor (Balakirev), 731
Symphony in D minor (Strauss), 762
Symphony in F major (Mozart), 517
Symphony in F minor (Bruckner), 718
Symphony in F minor (Strauss), 762
Symphony in Three Movements (Stravinsky), 842
Symphony K. 183 (Mozart), 509
Symphony K. 201 (Mozart), 509
Symphony No. 1 (Balakirev), 731
Symphony No. 1 (Barber), 755
Symphony No. 1 (Beethoven), *562, 573,* 627
Symphony No. 1 (Borodin), 732
Symphony No. 1 (Brahms), 705, *712, 713*
Symphony No. 1 (Bruckner), 721
Symphony No. 1 (Gade), 656
Symphony No. 1 (Gottschalk), 679
Symphony No. 1 "Nordic" (Hanson), 851
Symphony No. 1 (Ives), 790
Symphony No. 1 "Titan" (Mahler), 760
Symphony No. 1 (Mendelssohn), 636, 638
Symphony No. 1 (Mozart), *517*
Symphony No. 1 (Nielsen), 752
Symphony No. 1 (Schubert), 597
Symphony No. 1 "Spring" (Schumann), 651, *652*
Symphony No. 1 (Shostakovich), 816
Symphony No. 1 (Stravinsky), 837
Symphony No. 2 (Beethoven), 563, *564*
Symphony No. 2 (Borodin), 732, *733*
Symphony No. 2 (Brahms), 706, 713
Symphony No. 2 (Copland), *846*
Symphony No. 2 (D'Indy), 770
Symphony No. 2 (Gottschalk), 679
Symphony No. 2 "Romantic" (Hanson), 851
Symphony No. 2 (Mahler), 883
Symphony No. 2 "Lobgesang" (Mendelssohn), 639
Symphony No. 2 (Piston), 850
Symphony No. 2 (Prokofiev), 816
Symphony No. 2 (Schubert), 597
Symphony No. 2 (Schumann), 648, 652
Symphony No. 2 "To October" (Shostakovich), 816
Symphony No. 2 (Söderman), 751
Symphony No. 3 (C. P. E. Bach), 447, 563
Symphony No. 3 "Eroica" (Beethoven), 544, 547, 553, 564, *565, 566*
Symphony No. 3 (Brahms), 713, *714*
Symphony No. 3 (Bruckner), 718, 721
Symphony No. 3 (Copland), 847, 848–49
Symphony No. 3 (Harris), 850
Symphony No. 3 "Liturgique" (Honegger), 832
Symphony No. 3 "Scottish" (Mendelssohn), 638, 640
Symphony No. 3 (Roussel), 779
Symphony No. 3 "Organ Symphony" (Saint-Saëns), 770
Symphony No. 3 (Schubert), 597
Symphony No. 3 (Schumann), 652
Symphony No. 3 (Scriabin), 742
Symphony No. 3 "May First" (Shostakovich), 816
Symphony No. 3 "Irish" (Stanford), 785
Symphony No. 4 (Beethoven), 566
Symphony No. 4 (Brahms), 713

Symphony No. 4 "Romantic" (Bruckner), 721
Symphony No. 4 "Deliciae Basilienses" (Honegger), 832
Symphony No. 4 (Mahler), 760
Symphony No. 4 "Italian" (Mendelssohn), 638, 639
Symphony No. 4 (Nielsen), 752
Symphony No. 4 (Roussel), 779
Symphony No. 4 "Tragic" (Schubert), 598, 602
Symphony No. 4 (Schumann), 648, 652
Symphony No. 4 (Shostakovich), 817
Symphony No. 4 (Tchaikovsky), 740, 741
Symphony No. 4 (Williams), 812
Symphony No. 5 (Beethoven), 544, 547, 551, 553, *567,* 627, 713
Symphony No. 5 "Di tre re" (Honegger), 832
Symphony No. 5 "Reformation" (Mendelssohn), 638, *639*
Symphony No. 5 (Nielsen), 752, 753
Symphony No. 5 (Prokofiev), 816
Symphony No. 5 (Schubert), 598
Symphony No. 5 (Shostakovich), 817, *818*
Symphony No. 5 (Söderman), 751
Symphony No. 5 (Tchaikovsky), 740, *741*
Symphony No. 5 (Williams), 812
Symphony No. 6 "Pastoral" (Beethoven), 544, 567–68
Symphony No. 6 (Haydn), 492, 568
Symphony No. 6 in C major (Schubert), 598
Symphony No. 6 (Sibelius), 754
Symphony No. 6 "Pathétique" (Tchaikovsky), 740, *741*
Symphony No. 6 (Williams), 812
Symphony No. 7 (Beethoven), 568, *569*
Symphony No. 7 (Bruckner), 719, 721
Symphony No. 7 (Dvořák), 748
Symphony No. 7 (Haydn), 492, *502*
Symphony No. 7 in E major (Schubert), 599
Symphony No. 7 "Leningrad" (Shostakovich), 816, 817
Symphony No. 7 (Sibelius), 754
Symphony No. 8 (Beethoven), 568–70
Symphony No. 8 (Bruckner), 721
Symphony No. 8 (Haydn), 492
Symphony No. 8 "Symphony of a Thousand" (Mahler), 760
Symphony No. 8 "Unfinished" (Schubert), 599, 600, 610
Symphony No. 8 (Williams), 811, 812
Symphony No. 9 "Choral" (Beethoven), 543, 544, 553, 570–71, 574, 851
Symphony No. 9 "Unfinished" (Bruckner), 719, 721, 722, 743
Symphony No. 9 (Dvořák), *748*
Symphony No. 9 (Schubert), 600, 610
Symphony No. 9 (Williams), 811, 812
Symphony No. 10 (Shostakovich), 814, 817, *818*
Symphony No. 13 (Shostakovich), 817
Symphony No. 14 (Shostakovich), 817, 818
Symphony No. 15 (Shostakovich), 817, 818
Symphony No. 20 in D major (Mozart), 517
Symphony No. 25 (Mozart), 509, 517
Symphony No. 29 (Mozart), 517
Symphony No. 31 in D major (Haydn), 502
Symphony No. 31 (Mozart), 518
Symphony No. 35 (Mozart), 511, 518
Symphony No. 36 (Mozart), 511, 518
Symphony No. 38 (Mozart), 511, 518
Symphony No. 39 (Mozart), 518

Symphony No. 40 (Mozart), 518, *519, 520,* 562, *567*
Symphony No. 41 (Mozart), 518
Symphony No. 45 (Haydn), 492
Symphony No. 82 "Ours, L' " (Haydn), 503
Symphony No. 85 "*La Reine*" (Haydn), 504
Symphony No. 92 (Haydn), 494, 504
Symphony No. 94 (Haydn), 505
Symphony No. 100 (Haydn), 505
Symphony No. 102 (Haydn), 505
Symphony No. 104 (Haydn), *505*
Symphony of a Thousand (Mahler), 760
Symphony of Psalms (Stravinsky), 842
Symphony Op. 21 (Webern), 829, *830*
Syncopation, 135
  displacement, 138
Synge, 811
Syntagma musicum, 269
Syrinx, 10, 18
Syrinx (Debussy), 776
Székely, Zoltán, 804, 806
Szenen aus Goethes "Faust," 648, 653
Szigeti, Joseph, 804, 806
Szymanowska, Maria, 631, 655

t

Ta'amim markings, *5*
Tabarro, Il, 767
Tabasco, 789
Tablatura de Vihuela, 365, 455
Tablature, 210, **267**
  Italian and French lute, *268*
Tablature de mandure, 351
Tableaux of Pagan Russia, 838
Tábor, 746
Tabulatura nova, 347, 353, 354
Tabulaturen etlicher lobgesang . . . , 272, 275
Tagelied song, 117
Tageszeiten, Die, 394
Tailleferre, Germaine, 780, *781,* 832
Tajemství, 747
Taktus, 194
Talea (rhythmic pattern), 128, 129, 132, 133
Tales of Hoffman, 590, 662
Tallis, Thomas, 247, 249
Tambourin, 398
Tamerlano, 421, 424
Tam o'Shanter, Scottish Rhapsody No. 3 (Mackenzie), 785, 789
Tancredi, 614
Tannhäuser (Wagner), 685, 687, 718
Tannhäuser, Der, 117, 118
Tansillo, Luigi, 264
Tant que vivray, 229, *230*
Tanz dance, 119
Tapiola, 754, 755
Tapissier, Jean, 166
Tarantelle (Chopin), 632
Tartini, Giuseppe, 380, 434, 438, 454–55
Tasso, 221, 296, 309
Tasso (Liszt), 703
Tate, Nahum, 327
Taubenpost, Der, 602
Taverner, John, 248–49, 275, 381
Taylor, John, 404
Tchaikovsky, Pyotr I., 590, *739*–41, 774, 842
Teatro alla moda, Il, 459
Teatro armonico, 331